ENVIRONMENTAL MANAGEMENT IN SOUTH AFRICA

ENVIRONMENTAL MANAGEMENT IN SOUTH AFRICA

Edited by

R F FUGGLE

M A RABIE

Juta & Co, Ltd

CAPE TOWN　　WETTON　　JOHANNESBURG

This book is the successor to *Environmental Concerns in South Africa* which was first published in 1983.

PO Box 14373, Kenwyn 7790

Cover design by GERHARD SCHWEKENDIEK

ISBN 0 7021 2847 3

SET, PRINTED AND BOUND IN THE REPUBLIC OF SOUTH AFRICA BY
THE RUSTICA PRESS (PTY) LTD, NDABENI, CAPE
D677

PREFACE

Almost a decade has elapsed since the publication of *Environmental Concerns in South Africa*. Developments during this period have been so substantial that we have compiled a new book rather than a second edition of its predecessor. Most of the subjects that were addressed in *Environmental concerns* again feature in this book, but 13 new chapters have been introduced. Whereas 22 authors contributed to *Environmental concerns*, 52 authors have participated in the new venture.

The scope of this book is such that experts from some 15 major different disciplines are represented in the research team. This has contributed greatly to the variety, scope and depth of the book. The amalgamation of different disciplines, mostly within individual chapters, has nevertheless again proved to be a formidable challenge, with respect to both substance and form. We trust that the compromise which we have sought to reach as regards style, based upon that of *Environmental concerns*, will be acceptable to both legal and technical disciplines. References correspond to legal usage. Footnotes now appear at the bottom of the relevant pages, rather than at the end of the chapters to which they relate. We hope this will overcome a difficulty experienced by users of *Environmental concerns*.

Most chapters are again composite efforts consisting of a discussion of the nature and extent of the relevant issue in South Africa, an exposition of the legal position, followed by an analysis of the degree to which existing provisions meet South African requirements. Although distinct subjects are addressed in the individual chapters, the inter-relatedness of environmental concerns serves to underscore the fact that water-tight distinctions between the various chapters—and even parts—do not exist. This is clearly demonstrated by the three chapters dealing respectively with fresh-water systems, rivers and water pollution, the two chapters related to mining and the three chapters encompassing respectively marine systems, offshore mining and the coastal zone. While part two is specifically devoted to environmental law, legal aspects of topics are discussed in almost all chapters. As in *Environmental concerns* this book does not specifically address urban problems or problems of cultural resource management nor does it address population growth, environmental education, ecotourism or energy consumption as independent issues. This is not because these matters are considered unimportant; their inclusion would simply have extended the compass of this book beyond that which could be contained in a single volume. We trust that material relevant to these resource problems will nevertheless be found in various chapters.

The fact that contributions to the book have been received over a time span of almost two years has necessitated several adjustments and up-dating as developments have occurred and new legislation has been promulgated. Also, the on-going rationalization of the civil service has resulted in regular changes in the titles and composition of government departments and other public bodies. Moreover, the continuing devolution of functions from central to provincial and local government has sometimes rendered it difficult to accurately identify the authority currently responsible for a particular environmental matter.

We wish to acknowledge the invaluable and kind assistance we received from Vernon de Vries, Madeline Lass, William Rabie and Richard Cooke of Juta & Co Ltd, the superb editorial support rendered by John Linnegar and the highly professional performance by Rod Prodgers and the staff of Rustica Press. Our sincere thanks are also due to Helen King for her secretarial support and to Grant Wroe-Street for compiling the Index to Legal Materials. Above all, we express our most sincere gratitude to all the individual authors who have made this book possible. In rendering their respective contributions they have been motivated by idealism to serve the cause of environmental conservation, without gaining financial benefit from the venture.

Finally, the supreme motivation which dominates our involvement in this book is our Christian commitment and understanding of man as a steward of God's creation.

To God be the glory.

Richard Fuggle
André Rabie

CONTRIBUTORS

Pam Baskind BComm (Natal) BComm (Hons) MComm (Unisa)
Environmental Specialist
Centre for Technical & Environmental Specialists
Development Bank of Southern Africa, Midrand

Peter Blignaut BSc (Cape Town) PrL (SA) MIPLS TRP (SA)
Land Surveyor, Town and Regional Planner
Blignaut, Rommelaere, Lewis and Chapman, Cape Town

Llewellyn Botha Dip Law (Rhodes) BA (Hons) (Unisa) MA (Cape Town)
Environmental Law Consultant
The Environmental Law Consultancy, Cape Town

Koos Bothma BSc MSc (Pretoria) PhD (Texas A & M)
Professor: Eugéne Marais Chair of Wildlife Management
Head: Centre for Wildlife Research
University of Pretoria

Elmene Bray BIuris LLB LLM (Unisa)
Senior Lecturer
Department of Constitutional and Public International Law
University of South Africa

Michael Bruton BSc (Hons) MSc PhD (Rhodes)
Professor of Ichthyology and Director
JLB Smith Institute of Ichthyology
Rhodes University

Yvonne Burns BIuris LLB LLM LLD (Unisa)
Associate Professor
Department of Constitutional and Public International Law
University of South Africa

Piet Claassen TRP (SA) PrEng BSc BSc (Eng) M(TRP) DPhil (Stellenbosch)
Senior Lecturer
Department of Town and Regional Planning
University of Stellenbosch

Richard Cowling BSc (Hons) PhD (Cape Town) MSAIE
Professor
Plant Conservation Unit
Department of Botany
University of Cape Town

Jenny Day BSc (Hons) PhD (Cape Town)
Senior Lecturer
Department of Zoology
Deputy Director
Freshwater Research Unit
University of Cape Town

Gert De Beer BSc MSc DSc (Potchefstroom)
Senior Consulting Scientist
Atomic Energy Corporation of South Africa Ltd, Pelindaba

Dermott Devine BA LLB (NUI) LLB (Unisa) LLD (Cape Town)
Professor and Director
Institute of Marine Law
University of Cape Town

Willemien Du Plessis BIuris LLB LLD (Potchefstroom)
Professor
Department of Roman Law and Legal Pluralism
Potchefstroom University for CHE

Gerhard Erasmus BIuris LLB (Orange Free State) MA (Fletcher) LLD (Leyden)
Professor
Department of Public Law
University of Stellenbosch

Paul Fatti BSc (Hons) (Witwatersrand) MSc DIC (London) PhD (Witwatersrand)
Professor
Department of Statistics and Actuarial Science
University of the Witwatersrand
President: Mountain Club of South Africa

John Field BSc (Hons) PhD (Cape Town)
Professor
Department of Zoology
University of Cape Town

Richard Fuggle BSc (Hons) (Natal) MSc (Louisiana) PhD (McGill) MSAIE
Professor
Department of Environmental and Geographical Science
Director: Environmental Evaluation Unit
University of Cape Town

Jan Giliomee BA (Unisa) BSc(Agric) MSc(Agric) M(TRP) (Stellenbosch) PhD (London)
Professor
Department of Entomology and Nematology
University of Stellenbosch

Bruce Glavovic BSc(Agric) (Natal) MSc (Cape Town)
Senior Environmental Officer
Coastal Management Office
Department of Environment Affairs

Peter Glavovic BA LLB (Rhodes)
Associate Professor and Director
Institute of Environmental Law
University of Natal, Durban

Jan Glazewski BComm LLB MA (Cape Town) LLM (London)
Senior Research Officer
Institute of Marine Law
University of Cape Town

John Gurney BSc (Hons) PhD (Cape Town)
Professor
Department of Geochemistry
University of Cape Town

John Hanks BA MA PhD (Cantab)
Chief Executive
Southern African Nature Foundation, Stellenbosch

Tim Hart BA MA (Witwatersrand) TTHD (JCE)
Senior Manager: Urban Policy
Urbanization Unit
Urban Foundation, Johannesburg

Allan Heydorn BSc (Stellenbosch) BSc (Hons) MSc PhD (Cape Town)
Specialist Consultant
Southern African Nature Foundation, Stellenbosch

Clif Johnston BSc (Eng) PhD (Eng) (Natal) FSAAI
Director: Electronic Engineering and Physics Department
South African Bureau of Standards, Pretoria

Melissa Kirkley BSc MSc (Colorado State) PhD (Cape Town)
Research Officer
Department of Geochemistry
University of Cape Town

Reynecke Le Roux BSc MSc (Stellenbosch) PhD (Cape Town)
Director: Radiation Control
Department of National Health and Population Development

Ray Lombard BSc (Natal) MIWM (SA)
Executive member
Lombard, De Mattos & Assoc, Durban
President: Institute of Waste Management (Southern Africa)

Cheryl Loots BA LLB (Witwatersrand)
Senior Lecturer
School of Law
University of the Witwatersrand

John Lusher BSc ARCS (London) PhD (Witwatersrand) CChem MRCS FIWEM
Deputy Regional Director: Quality
Department of Water Affairs and Forestry (Western Cape Region)

Rosemary Lyster BA LLB LLM (Natal)
Lecturer
School of Law
University of the Witwatersrand

Ian McLachlan BSc (Hons) (Witwatersrand)
Geological Consultant
Soekor, Cape Town

John Milton BA LLB LLM PhD (Natal)
Professor
School of Law
University of Natal, Pietermaritzburg

Kobus Muller BSc (Hons) (Agric) B (Hons) (Publ Admin) MPA PhD (Stellenbosch)
Senior Lecturer
School of Public Management
University of Stellenbosch

Jay O'Keeffe BSc (Hons) (East Anglia), PhD (London)
Senior Research Officer
Institute for Water Research
Rhodes University

Nic Olivier BA BA (Hons) MA LLB LLD (Pretoria) BA (Hons) B Phil (Potchefstroom) DrsIuris LLD (Leyden)
Professor
Department of Roman Law and Legal Pluralism
Potchefstroom University for CHE

James Petrie BSc Chem Eng (Cape Town) MS Chem Eng (Houston) PhD (Cape Town)
Senior Lecturer
Department of Chemical Engineering
University of Cape Town

Guy Preston BA HED (Unisa) MSc PhD (Cape Town)
Principal Scientific Officer
Environmental Evaluation Unit
University of Cape Town

André Rabie BA LLB (Pretoria) LLD (Unisa)
Professor and chairman
Department of Public Law
University of Stellenbosch

Tom Ramsden BA LLB PhD (Witwatersrand)
General Manager
Corporate Services
Rand Water Board, Johannesburg

Nicola Robins BSc (Hons) (Cape Town)
Research Assistant
Environmental Evaluation Unit
University of Cape Town

Bennie Schloms BSc(Agric) BSc (Hons) (Agric) MSc (Stellenbosch)
Lecturer
Department of Geography
University of Stellenbosch

Erwin Schwella BA BA (Hons) B (Hons) (Publ Admin) MPA PhD (Stellenbosch)
Professor
School of Public Management
University of Stellenbosch

Roy Stauth BA (Colorado State) MA PhD (Cape Town)
Peace Corps: Senior Environmental Officer
Corporación Nacional de Forestal, Chile
Consultant
National Commission on the Environment, Chile

Maritza Uys BA LLB LLM (Stellenbosch)
Legal Research Consultant
Water Research Commission, Pretoria

Dannie Van As BSc MSc PhD (Stellenbosch)
General Manager
Business Development (Science and Technology)
Atomic Energy Corporation of South Africa Ltd, Pelindaba

Mynhardt Van der Merwe BSc MSc PhD (Stellenbosch)
Senior Radiation Scientist
Directorate: Radiation Control
Department of National Health and Population Development

Louwine Van Meurs BA LLB LLM PhD (Witwatersrand)
Consultant
Mining Rights Department
General Mining, Metals and Minerals Ltd, Johannesburg

Eben Verster BSc (Stellenbosch) MSc Agric (Natal) DSc (Orange Free State)
Professor
Department of Geography
University of South Africa

Yasmin Von Schirnding BSc (Hons) (Cape Town) BSc (Hons) (Stellenbosch), MSc PhD (Cape Town)
Director of Environmental Health
Directorate of Health and Housing
Johannesburg City Council

Digby Wells BSc (Agric) (Natal)
Manager
Environmental Protection Department
Rand Mines (Mining and Services) Ltd, Johannesburg

CONTENTS

Page

Preface v
Contributors vii

PART ONE: ELEMENTS OF ENVIRONMENTAL MANAGEMENT

Chapter One *ENVIRONMENTAL MANAGEMENT: AN INTRODUCTION*

1.1 Present-Day Relationships between Human Beings and Environment 1
1.1.1 Caring for the earth 2
1.1.2 Environmental management 3
1.2 The Term 'Environment'? 4
1.3 A Classification of Environmental Problems 4
1.3.1 Degradable wastes 5
1.3.2 Persistent wastes 5
1.3.3 Reversible biological and geophysical impacts 5
1.3.4 Irreversible biological and geophysical impacts 5
1.3.5 Legal implications of different classes of environmental problems. 6
1.4 Reasons for Environmental Deterioration 6
1.5 Ethics of Environmental Conservation 7
1.5.1 Utilitarianism 8
1.5.2 Judeo-Christian ethics 8
1.5.3 Other religions 10

Chapter Two *THE RISE OF ENVIRONMENTAL CONCERN*

2.1 Introduction 11
2.2 Indicators 13
2.2.1 Unofficial indicators 13
2.2.2 Official indicators 13
2.3 Early Settlement in the 17th Century: Environmental Conservation Commences 13
2.4 The 18th Century: Stagnation on the Environmental Front 14
2.5 Environmental Conservation gains Momentum: The Period from 1800 until Union 14
2.6 First Environmental Control at National Level: The Three Decades from Union to the Second World War 15
2.7 Three Decades of Intensified Environmental Concern: 1940–1969 16
2.7.1 Marine resources 16
2.7.2 Advertising along roads 16
2.7.3 Soil conservation 16
2.7.4 Nature conservation 17
2.7.5 Water pollution 17
2.7.6 Air pollution 17
2.7.7 Noise 17

Page

2.7.8 Pesticides 18
2.7.9 Ionizing radiation 18
2.7.10 Non-renewable resources 18
2.7.11 Land-use planning 18
2.8 The Dawn of an Environmental Era 18
2.8.1 Governmental concern 19
2.8.2 Legislation 20
2.8.2.1 Mountain environments 20
2.8.2.2 Nature conservation 20
2.8.2.3 Protected areas 20
2.8.2.4 Soil conservation 21
2.8.2.5 Coastal and marine environments 21
2.8.2.6 Noise 21
2.8.2.7 Solid waste 22
2.8.2.8 Ionizing radiation 22
2.8.2.9 Water pollution 22
2.8.2.10 Air pollution 22
2.8.2.11 Non-renewable resources 23
2.8.2.12 Environment Conservation Act of 1989 23
2.8.3 Voluntary bodies 23
2.8.4 Conferences 23
2.8.5 Official publications 23
2.8.6 Popular publications 24
2.8.7 Black involvement in environmental conservation 24
2.9 Conclusion 25

Chapter Three *RESOURCE ECONOMICS*

3.1 Introduction 26
3.1.1 The purpose of this chapter 26
3.1.2 The challenge of resource management in South Africa 26
3.2 Developing a Philosophy of Resource Management 27
3.2.1 What is environmental economics? 27
3.2.2 The nature of our environmental and economic problems 28
3.2.3 New environmental dimensions in economic thinking 29
3.2.4 Selecting evaluation criteria 29
3.2.4.1 Premises 31
3.2.4.2 Policy goal 31
3.2.4.3 Criteria 32
3.3 Practical Methods for Evaluating Proposed Resource Uses 32
3.3.1 The concept of costs and benefits 32
3.3.2 The need for a measuring rod 33
3.3.3 Cost-benefit analysis 35
3.3.4 The problem of valuing common property resources 36
3.3.5 Shadow-pricing techniques 37
3.3.5.1 Input valuation 37
3.3.5.2 Output valuation 38
3.3.5.3 Travel-cost valuation 38
3.3.5.4 Contingent valuation 38
3.3.5.5 Threshold valuation 38
3.3.5.6 Dynamic opportunity cost valuation 38
3.3.5.7 Panel valuation 38

Page

3.4 Methods for Implementing a Sound Resource Policy 39
3.4.1 Direct controls.. 39
3.4.2 Economic incentives.. 40
3.4.2.1 Pollution charges 42
3.4.2.2 Subsidies... 43
3.4.2.3 Marketable permits 43
3.4.2.4 Environmental bonds....................................... 44
3.4.2.5 Compensation.. 45
3.4.2.6 Benefits.. 46
3.4.3 Making the 'big trade-off' 47
3.5 Summary and Discussion 49
3.5.1 Adopting a rational approach to meeting economic and environmental needs 49
3.5.2 The situation in the 'New South Africa'......................... 50
3.5.3 Conclusion.. 51

Chapter Four *SOCIO-POLITICAL FACTORS*

4.1 Introduction.. 53
4.2 Environmental Management as a Socio-political Issue 53
4.3 Division and Reconciliation 54
4.4 Key Issues for the 1990s.. 55
4.5 Population and Resources 55
4.6 Land Distribution and Management 57
4.7 Urbanization and Cities 58
4.8 Management Institutions 60
4.9 Environmental Management under a Post-apartheid Government 62

Chapter Five *ENVIRONMENTAL ADMINISTRATION*

5.1 Introduction.. 64
5.2 Theoretical Considerations.. 64
5.2.1 Theoretical orientation.. 65
5.2.2 Conditioning factors... 65
5.2.3 Strategic options for service-provision systems 66
5.2.3.1 Sectoral placement.. 66
5.2.3.2 Political approach.. 68
5.2.3.3 Institutional types and arrangements...................... 68
5.2.3.4 Constitutional and hierarchical placement................. 69
5.2.3.5 General organizational considerations..................... 70
5.2.4 Concluding guidelines: summary................................... 71
5.3 The Administration of Environmental Affairs in South Africa 71
5.3.1 Conditioning fators of environmental management.................. 71
5.3.2 Historical perspective... 72
5.3.2.1 Preservation of species through legislation (1655–1875) 72
5.3.2.2 Institutionalization of the conversation function (1875–1960) 72
5.3.2.3 Need for a comprehensive approach (1960–80) 73
5.3.2.4 The quest for a national environmental policy and conservation strategy (1980–90) 73
5.3.2.5 Integrated environmental management (1990–) 74
5.3.3 Environmental policy and conservation strategy 75

Page

5.3.4 Legislative framework ... 76
5.3.5 Macro-organizational arrangements ... 76
5.3.5.1 International level ... 76
5.3.5.2 National level ... 76
5.3.5.3 Regional level ... 78
5.3.5.4 Local level ... 78
5.4 Evaluation and Recommendations ... 78
5.5 Summary ... 81

PART TWO: ENVIRONMENTAL LAW

Chapter Six *NATURE AND SCOPE OF ENVIRONMENTAL LAW*

6.1 Introduction ... 83
6.2 The Concept 'Environment' ... 83
6.2.1 Extensive approach ... 84
6.2.2 Limited approach ... 86
6.2.3 Avoidance of the term 'environment' ... 88
6.2.4 Towards a realistic demarcation of 'environment' ... 89
6.3 Scope of Environmental Law ... 92
6.3.1 Environmental conservation/environmental management ... 92
6.3.2 Degree of relevance ... 92
6.3.2.1 Exclusive environmental legislation ... 93
6.3.2.2 Legislation predominantly containing environmentally specific norms ... 93
6.3.2.3 Legislation incidentally containing environmentally specific norms ... 93
6.3.2.4 Legislation with direct environmental relevance ... 94
6.3.2.5 Legislation with potential environmental relevance ... 94
6.3.2.6 Legislation regulating environmental exploitation ... 94
6.3.2.7 Legislation with no environmental relevance ... 94
6.3.2.8 Common law norms ... 95
6.3.3 Towards an identification of environmental law ... 95
6.4 Nature of Environmental Law ... 96

Chapter Seven *ENVIRONMENT CONSERVATION ACT*

7.1 Title, Scope and Purpose ... 99
7.2 The Term 'Environment' ... 99
7.3 Public Participation in Environmental Affairs ... 99
7.3.1 Public participation in parliamentary legislation ... 99
7.3.2 Public participation in subordinate legislation and other administrative decision-making ... 100
7.4 Multiple Administrative Jurisdiction in respect of Environmental Affairs ... 101
7.4.1 The problem ... 101
7.4.2 The challenge ... 101
7.4.3 Co-ordination of environmental administration ... 101
7.4.4 Co-operative governmental decision-making ... 102
7.4.5 Environmental policy ... 102
7.4.5.1 Policy in White Paper ... 103
7.4.5.2 Administrative policy without statutory basis ... 103

Page

7.4.5.3 Administrative policy as subordinate legislation 103
7.4.5.4 Policy determined by legislature 106
7.5 Statutory Bodies 107
7.6 Controlled Activities 108
7.6.1 Identified activities 108
7.6.1.1 Area 108
7.6.1.2 Type of activity 108
7.6.1.3 Procedure 108
7.6.1.4 Effect 108
7.6.1.5 Environmental impact reports 109
7.6.1.6 Conditions 109
7.6.2 Limited development areas 109
7.6.2.1 Area 109
7.6.2.2 Type of activity 109
7.6.2.3 Procedure 109
7.6.2.4 Effect 109
7.6.2.5 Environmental impact report 110
7.6.2.6 Conditions 110
7.6.3 Analysis 110
7.7 Protected Areas 112
7.8 Principal Control through Regulations 112
7.9 Consent Requirement 113
7.10 Remedies and Sanctions 113
7.10.1 Appeals 113
7.10.2 Board of Investigation 114
7.10.3 Review and the giving of reasons 114
7.10.4 Criminal penalties 116
7.10.5 Civil remedies 116
7.10.6 Financial redress 117
7.11 Conclusion 118

Chapter Eight *IMPLEMENTATION OF ENVIRONMENTAL LAW*

8.1 Introduction 120
8.2 Implementation of Environmental Law by Administrative Bodies 120
8.2.1 Direct environmental functions 121
8.2.2 Establishment of control provisions 121
8.2.2.1 General provisions 121
8.2.2.2 Individual provisions 122
8.2.3 Activation of control provisions 122
8.2.4 Authorization of actions by individuals 123
8.2.5 Granting of rights 124
8.2.6 Exemptions 124
8.2.7 Rendering of financial aid 124
8.2.8 Acquisition of land 124
8.2.9 Performance of judicial functions 125
8.2.10 Appointment of staff, establishment of administrative bodies and appointment of their numbers 125
8.3 Securing Compliance by Individuals through the Use of Control Provisions 126
8.3.1 Direct administrative enforcement powers 126
8.3.1.1 Informing and assisting individuals. 126
8.3.1.2 Administrative sanctions 126

Page

8.3.2 Enforcement through the judiciary and other state organs 128
8.3.2.1 Employment of civil process 128
8.3.2.2 Application of criminal sanctions 128
8.4 Implementation of Environmental Law by Individuals 132
8.4.1 The problem of standing 132
8.4.1.1 Personal interest 132
8.4.1.2 Environmental interests 133
8.4.1.3 Types of adverse effects 133
8.4.1.4 Rights and interests 134
8.4.1.5 Citizen suit clauses 135
8.4.1.6 Group interests 135
8.4.1.7 Interests of natural objects 136
8.4.2 Private-law remedies 137
8.4.3 Public-law remedies 138
8.4.3.1 Judicial review 138
8.4.3.2 Administrative appeals 138
8.4.3.3 Environmental ombudsman 140
8.4.3.4 Constitutional remedies 142
8.4.4 Environmental dispute resolution 146
8.4.4.1 Introduction 146
8.4.4.2 Negotiated rule-making 147
8.4.4.3 Liability for clean-up costs 148
8.4.4.4 Environmental enforcement 149
8.4.4.5 Land use and resource problems 151
8.4.4.6 Looking ahead 153

Chapter Nine *INTERNATIONAL ENVIRONMENTAL LAW*
9.1 Introduction 155
9.1.1 The nature of international law 155
9.1.2 Sources of international law 155
9.1.3 Binding nature of international law 156
9.1.4 The limits of traditional international law 157
9.1.5 International environmental law 158
9.1.6 Economic factors 158
9.2 Customary International Law 160
9.2.1 Relevant fundamental principles 160
9.2.1.1 The principles of sovereignty, freedom of the high seas and state responsibility 160
9.2.1.2 Self-defence 160
9.2.1.3 Good neighbourliness 161
9.2.2 Decisions applicable to environmental conservation 161
9.2.2.1 The Trail Smelter arbitration (United States v Canada 1941) 161
9.2.2.2 The Corfu Channel case (United Kingdom v Albania 1949) 162
9.2.2.3 The Lac Lanoux arbitration (France v Spain 1957) 162
9.2.2.4 The nuclear test cases (Australia v France, New Zealand v France 1974) 162
9.3 Conventional International Environmental Law 163
9.3.1 Pollution 163
9.3.1.1 Marine pollution 163

Page

9.3.1.2 Atmospheric pollution 168
9.3.1.3 Harmful products 170
9.3.1.4 Hazardous waste 171
9.3.1.5 Nuclear pollution 171
9.3.1.6 Pollution of Antarctica 172
9.3.1.7 Pollution of space and from space 172
9.3.2 Conservation of natural resources 173
9.3.2.1 Marine living resources 173
9.3.2.2 Marine non-living resources 175
9.3.2.3 Antarctic mineral resources 175
9.3.2.4 Wild fauna and flora 175
9.3.2.5 Destruction of cultural heritage 175
9.4 Regional Conventions 176
9.4.1 The environment of a region in general 176
9.4.2 The marine environment of the region in general 176
9.4.3 Oil pollution 176
9.4.4 Nuclear pollution 177
9.4.5 Dumping 177
9.4.6 Pollution from land-based sources 177
9.4.7 Specially protected areas 177
9.4.8 Rivers 177
9.4.9 Conservation of culture 177
9.4.10 Fisheries conservation 177
9.4.11 Particular provisions 177
9.5 General Approaches to the Environment 177
9.5.1 The declaration of principles 178
9.5.2 The Nairobi Declaration 1982 178
9.5.3 The World Charter for Nature 178
9.5.4 OECD approaches 179
9.6 Conclusion 179

PART THREE: RENEWABLE RESOURCES

Chapter Ten *SOIL*

10.1 Introduction 181
10.2 What is Soil 181
10.2.1 Components of soil 182
10.2.1.1 The mineral fraction 182
10.2.1.2 The organic fraction 183
10.2.1.3 Size and organization of particles 183
10.2.1.4 Soil pores, liquids and gases 183
10.2.2 The soil profile 184
10.2.3 Soil horizons 184
10.3 Soil Properties 185
10.3.1 Morphological or physical soil properties 185
10.3.1.1 Soil depth 185
10.3.1.2 Soil colour 185
10.3.1.3 Soil texture 186
10.3.1.4 Soil structure 187
10.3.1.5 Water in the soil 187

Page

10.3.1.6 Soil consistence 188
10.3.2 Chemical properties 188
10.3.2.1 Exchange properties of soils 188
10.3.2.2 Soil reaction 189
10.4 The Basis of Soil Classification in South Africa 190
10.5 Soil Degradation 190
10.5.1 Physical degradation 191
10.5.1.1 Soil erosion 191
10.5.1.2 Soil compaction and crusting 191
10.5.2 Chemical deterioration 192
10.5.2.1 Loss of fertility 192
10.5.2.2 Acidification 192
10.5.2.3 Salinization 192
10.5.2.4 Soil pollution 192
10.5.3 Biological degradation 192
10.5.3.1 Invasive biota 192
10.5.3.2 Eelworms and plant pathogens 193
10.6 Soil Conservation Legislation 193
10.6.1 Introduction 193
10.6.2 Forest and Veld Conservation Act 194
10.6.3 Soil Conservation Act of 1946 194
10.6.4 Soil Conservation Act of 1969 195
10.6.5 Conservation of Agricultural Resources Act 197
10.6.5.1 Background 197
10.6.5.2 Application of the Act 198
10.6.5.3 Conservation structure 198
10.6.5.4 Duties of land user 202
10.6.5.5 Miscellaneous measures 203
10.6.5.6 Practical problems and recommendations 203
10.6.6 Other related legislation 206
10.6.6.1 Water Act 206
10.6.6.2 Forest Act 206
10.6.6.3 Mountain Catchment Areas Act 207
10.6.6.4 Common Pasture Management Act 208
10.6.6.5 Settlement Acts 208
10.6.6.6 Unbeneficial Occupation of Farms Act 208
10.6.6.7 Subdivision of Agricultural Land Act 209
10.6.6.8 Nature conservation legislation 209
10.6.6.9 Soil conservation and the construction of roads and railways 209
10.6.6.10 Land-use planning and control 210
10.6.6.11 Soil conservation in black areas 210
10.6.6.12 Mining legislation 210
10.7 Conclusion 210

Chapter Eleven *PLANTS*

11.1 Introduction 212
11.2 Ecological Driving Variables 213
11.2.1 Geomorphology and soils 213
11.2.2 Climate 213
11.2.3 Grazing 214

Page

11.2.4 Fire 214
11.3 Biodiversity 215
11.3.1 Fynbos biome 215
11.3.2 Savanna biome 217
11.3.3 Grassland biome 218
11.3.4 Nama-karoo biome 218
11.3.5 Succulent-karoo biome 219
11.3.6 Desert biome 219
11.3.7 Forest biome 220
11.4 Resource Degradation 220
11.4.1 Agriculture 220
11.4.2 Urbanization 221
11.4.3 Alien plants and afforestation 221
11.4.4 Other transformations 222
11.5 Conservation 222
11.5.1 Conservation inside nature reserves 222
11.5.2 Conservation outside nature reserves 223
11.5.3 Justifying conservation 223
11.6 Summary 224
11.7 Legislation for the Conservation of Plants 224
11.7.1 Introduction 224
11.7.2 Conservation of plants within protected areas 225
11.7.3 Conservation of plants outside protected areas 225
11.7.3.1 Introduction 225
11.7.3.2 Protected plants 225
11.7.3.3 Picking protected and other indigenous plants 227
11.7.3.4 Purchase and sale of protected plants 228
11.7.3.5 Exportation and importation of protected plants 228
11.7.3.6 Conveyance of protected plants 228
11.7.3.7 Possession of protected plants 228
11.7.3.8 Forests 228
11.7.3.9 Natural vegetation in mountain catchment areas 234
11.7.3.10 Vegetation in lake areas 234
11.7.3.11 Plants as national monuments 234
11.7.3.12 Vegetation and soil conservation 234
11.7.3.13 Aquatic plants 235
11.7.4 Control of noxious plants 236
11.7.4.1 Weeds 236
11.7.4.2 Intruding vegetation 237
11.7.4.3 Agricultural pests 237
11.7.4.4 Other legislation 238
11.7.4.5 Noxious aquatic growths 239
11.8 Sufficiency of Legislation for Plant Conversation 239
11.8.1 Conservation methods and available legislation 239
11.8.1.1 Introduction 239
11.8.1.2 Discovery, identification and listing of protected sites 240
11.8.1.3 Prevention of damage outside protected areas 240
11.8.1.4 Creation of various types of protected areas 241
11.8.1.5 Establishment of botanic gardens 241
11.8.1.6 Environmental interpretation programmes 241
11.8.1.7 Maintenance and control of threats in protected areas 241

Page

11.8.1.8 Legal measures for critically rare and threatened plants 241
11.8.1.9 Provision for scientific collection and study of plants... 242
11.8.2 Administration of legislation ... 242
11.8.2.1 Problems concerning the general plant control framework 243
11.8.2.2 Environmental protection ... 245
11.8.2.3 Protected areas ... 246
11.8.2.4 Forest Act ... 246
11.8.2.5 Plants and veld ... 247
11.8.2.6 Conservation of agricultural resources ... 248
11.8.2.7 President's Council ... 248
11.8.2.8 Final recommendations ... 248

Chapter Twelve *WILD ANIMALS*

12.1 Introduction ... 250
12.2 The African Framework ... 250
12.3 The Development of Wildlife Conservation in South Africa ... 251
12.4 The Current Conservation Status of Wild Animals in South Africa ... 251
12.4.1 Definition of categories ... 252
12.4.2 Invertebrates ... 252
12.4.3 Vertebrates: fishes ... 253
12.4.4 Vertebrates: amphibians and reptiles ... 254
12.4.5 Vertebrates: birds ... 255
12.4.6 Vertebrates: terrestrial mammals ... 256
12.4.7 Factors affecting the conservation status of vertebrates ... 256
12.5 Wildlife Law ... 257
12.5.1 Introduction ... 257
12.5.2 Philosophical and socio-economic perspectives ... 257
12.5.3 International wildlife law ... 258
12.5.4 Private law ... 259
12.5.5 Game farming and game ranching ... 259
12.5.6 Public law ... 260
12.5.7 Provincial ordinances ... 260
12.5.8 Natal Nature Conservation Ordinance ... 261
12.5.8.1 Natal Parks Board ... 261
12.5.8.2 Game ... 262
12.5.8.3 Private reserves ... 266
12.5.8.4 Mammals ... 266
12.5.8.5 Professional hunters and hunting-outfitters ... 267
12.5.8.6 Amphibians, invertebrates and reptiles ... 267
12.5.8.7 Wild birds ... 268
12.5.8.8 The need for law reform ... 268
12.6 Review and Suggestions ... 270
12.6.1 Ecosystem-based conservation ... 270
12.6.2 Rarity ... 271
12.6.3 Size and number of nature reserves ... 271
12.6.4 Human beings and conservation ... 273

Chapter Thirteen *FRESHWATER SYSTEMS*

13.1 Characteristics of Southern African Freshwater Ecosystems ... 277
13.2 Availability and Use of Freshwater in South Africa ... 278

Page

13.3 Environmental Problems Associated with Freshwater Resources 283
13.3.1 Catchment changes 283
13.3.2 River regulation 284
13.3.3 Pollution and eutrophication 285
13.3.4 Water abstraction 288
13.3.5 Barriers to migration 291
13.3.6 Alien biotas 291
13.3.6.1 Alien animals 292
13.3.6.2 Aquaculture 292
13.3.6.3 Alien plants 292
13.4 Conservation of Water Resources 293
13.5 Legal Provisions 295
13.5.1 Introduction 295
13.5.2 Running water 295
13.5.2.1 Water Act 295
13.5.2.2 Mountain Catchment Areas Act 302
13.5.2.3 River conservancy districts in terms of the Natal Nature Conservation Ordinance 303
13.5.2.4 Electricity Act 303
13.5.3 Ground water 304
13.5.4 Wetlands 305
13.5.4.1 Water Act 305
13.5.4.2 Conservation of Agriculture Resources Act 306
13.5.4.3 Mountain Catchment Areas Act 307
13.5.4.4 Forest Act 307
13.5.4.5 Lake Areas Development Act 307
13.5.5 Impoundments 307
13.5.5.1 Water Act 308
13.5.6 Precipitation 309
13.5.6.1 Water Act 309
13.5.7 Living freshwater resources 309
13.5.7.1 Fish 309
13.5.7.2 Other living freshwater resources 312
13.5.8 Environmental policy 312
13.6 Review of Legislation for the Control of Freshwater Systems 314

Chapter Fourteen *MARINE SYSTEMS*

14.1 The South African Coastline 316
14.2 The West Coast and Benguela Current 316
14.3 The East Coast and Agulhas Current 317
14.4 Fisheries 318
14.4.1 The bottom trawl fishery 319
14.4.2 The purse seine fishery 321
14.4.3 Rock lobster fishery 322
14.4.4 Squid fishery 323
14.4.5 Line fishery 324
14.4.6 Abalone fishery 325
14.5 Marine Law 325
14.5.1 International Law of the sea 325
14.5.1.1 Introduction 325
14.5.1.2 Maritime zones 326

Page

14.5.2 Fisheries 329
14.5.2.1 Introduction 329
14.5.2.2 International law aspects 330
14.5.2.3 Control under the Sea Fishery Act 331
14.5.3 Marine Pollution 335
14.6 Conclusion 335

PART FOUR: NON-RENEWABLE RESOURCES

Chapter Fifteen *TERRESTRIAL MINERALS*

15.1 Introduction 337
15.2 Industry Guidelines 338
15.2.1 Introduction 338
15.2.2 Guidelines 339
15.2.3 Environmental management programme 339
15.3 Mining Methods 340
15.3.1 Surface mining 340
15.3.1.1 Introduction 340
15.3.1.2 Strip mining 341
15.3.1.3 Open-pit mining 342
15.3.1.4 Dredge mining 343
15.3.1.5 Dump reclamation 344
15.3.2 Shallow underground mining 346
15.3.2.1 Old bord-and-pillar mining 346
15.3.2.2 Other shallow underground mining 348
15.3.3 Deep underground mining 348
15.3.3.1 Introduction 348
15.3.3.2 Increased extraction coal mining 348
15.3.3.3 Surface subsidence as a result of dewatering 349
15.3.3.4 Disposal of water pumped from underground 350
15.4 The Nature of the Minerals 351
15.4.1 Introduction 351
15.4.2 Coal 351
15.4.3 Gold 352
15.4.4 Platinum group metals and chrome in the Bushveld Igneous Complex 354
15.4.5 Asbestos 354
15.4.6 Heavy minerals 355
15.4.7 Other minerals 355
15.5 Mine Residue Deposits 355
15.5.1 Introduction 355
15.5.2 Water pollution 356
15.5.2.1 The role of iron pyrites 356
15.5.2.2 Prevention or treatment of acid rock damage (ARD) 356
15.5.3 Air pollution 357
15.5.3.1 Smoke and gases 357
15.5.3.2 Dust 359
15.5.3.3 Aesthetic aspects 359
15.5.4 Principles of residue deposit rehabilitation 360

Page

15.5.4.1 Plan for closure 360
15.5.4.2 Water control 360
15.5.4.3 Minimize and isolate area of influence 360
15.5.4.4 Revegetation 360
15.5.4.5 Minimize maintenance 361
15.6 Research 361
15.6.1 Aspects currently being researched 361
15.6.2 Aspects to be investigated in the future 361
15.7 The Law Relating to Terrestrial Mining 362
15.7.1 Importance of mining in South Africa 362
15.7.2 Mineral policy 362
15.7.3 Sources of mining law 362
15.7.4 State control of mining 363
15.7.5 Common law 363
15.7.5.1 Rights of mineral holder 363
15.7.5.2 Liability for environmental degradation 364
15.7.5.3 Duty of lateral and subsurface support 365
15.7.6 Legislative development 366
15.7.7 Minerals Act 366
15.7.8 Minerals and mineral rights 367
15.7.9 Mining and prospecting 367
15.7.10 Rehabilitation of mining surfaces 368
15.7.10.1 Particulars concerning manner of rehabilitation as a prerequisite to issuance of a prospecting permit or mining authorization 369
15.7.10.2 Approval of rehabilitation programme prior to commencement of prospecting or mining operations... 370
15.7.10.3 Rehabilitation during prospecting or mining operations 371
15.7.10.4 Rehabilitation as condition for removal or disposal of minerals 371
15.7.10.5 Rehabilitation after prospecting or mining operations cease 371
15.7.10.6 Certificate of completed rehabilitation 372
15.7.10.7 Pecuniary provision for rehabilitation 372
15.7.10.8 Sanctions 372
15.7.11 Environmental impact assessment of mining 373
15.7.12 Restriction of environmental encroachment, disturbance and damage 373
15.7.13 Mining and soil conservation 373
15.7.14 Mining and water pollution 374
15.7.15 Mining and air pollution 375
15.7.16 Mining and waste 376
15.7.17 Mining and ionizing radiation 377
15.7.18 Mining in protected areas 377
15.8 Conclusion 377

Chapter Sixteen *OFFSHORE MINERALS*

16.1 Introduction 380
16.2 Diamonds 381
16.2.1 Introduction 381
16.2.2 Nature of resource 381

Page

16.2.3 Location and size of resource 382
16.2.4 Development of interest in exploitation 383
16.2.5 Namibian lease areas 383
16.2.6 Current diamond mining activities in Namibia 386
16.2.7 Republic of South Africa lease areas 386
16.2.8 Current prospecting and mining activities in South African diamond lease areas 388
16.2.9 Technology used to exploit diamonds 389
16.2.10 Value of resource 390
16.3 Oil and Gas 390
16.3.1 Nature of resource 390
16.3.2 Location and size of resource 391
16.3.3 Development of interest in exploration 394
16.3.4 Mineral rights 395
16.3.5 Technology required to exploit 396
16.3.6 Value of resources 396
16.3.7 Short- or long-term exploitation 396
16.4 Heavy Minerals 396
16.4.1 Nature of resource 396
16.4.2 Location and size of resource 396
16.4.3 Exploration and mining activities 397
16.5 Phosphorite 397
16.5.1 Nature of the resource 397
16.5.2 Size and location 398
16.5.3 Current interest in exploitation 399
16.5.4 Technology required to exploit 400
16.6 Glauconite 400
16.6.1 Nature of resource 400
16.6.2 Size and location 400
16.6.3 Current interest in exploitation 400
16.7 Manganese Nodules 402
16.7.1 Nature of resource 402
16.7.2 Size and location of resource 402
16.7.3 Technology required to exploit 402
16.7.4 Current interest in exploitation 403
16.8 Environmental Concerns of Offshore Mining 404
16.8.1 Diamonds 404
16.8.1.1 Deep-sea areas 404
16.8.1.2 Near-shore areas 404
16.8.2 Oil and gas 405
16.8.2.1 Environmental concerns during routine exploration 405
16.8.2.2 Environmental concerns during production 405
16.8.2.3 Will exploration destroy other resources? 405
16.9 The Legal Regime 406
16.9.1 Introduction 406
16.9.2 The legal approach of defining 'offshore' 406
16.9.3 The international-law basis for South African offshore mining rights 406
16.9.3.1 The continental shelf doctrine and exclusive economic zone (EEZ) 406
16.9.3.2 The area beyond national jurisdiction 407

Page

16.9.3.3 Territorial extent of South African law 408
16.9.4 Common-law principles 408
16.9.5 Statute law 409
16.9.5.1 Introduction 409
16.9.5.2 Oil and gas 410
16.9.5.3 Diamonds 412
16.9.5.4 Concession areas 412
16.9.5.5 Boundary demarcation 413
16.9.5.6 Mining leases 414
16.9.5.7 The marketing of diamonds 414
16.9.6 Minerals found landward of high-water mark 415
16.10 Conclusion 415

PART FIVE: CONTROL OF ENVIRONMENTAL QUALITY

Chapter Seventeen *AIR POLLUTION*

17.1 Introduction 417
17.1.1 Areas of environmental concern in air pollution 418
17.1.1.1 Acidic deposition 418
17.1.1.2 Smog formation and visibility reduction 418
17.1.1.3 Hazardous air pollutants 418
17.1.1.4 Stratospheric ozone depletion 419
17.1.1.5 Global climate change—greenhouse effect 419
17.1.2 Relationship between energy and environment 419
17.2 Fossil Fuels in South Africa 420
17.2.1 Coal 420
17.2.2 Oil 421
17.3 Atmospheric Pollutant Formation and Dispersion Mechanisms 423
17.3.1 Atmospheric dispersion 423
17.3.1.1 Atmospheric stability 423
17.3.1.2 Plume rise and effective stack height 423
17.3.1.3 Wind speed and direction 424
17.3.2 Consideration of meteorological factors: case study—the meteorology of the eastern Transvaal highveld (ETH) 424
17.4 Air Quality Measurements in South Africa 425
17.4.1 Total national pollutant quantities 425
17.4.2 Pollutant concentrations in the ETH 426
17.4.2.1 Ambient sulphur dioxide concentration 426
17.4.2.2 Ambient nitrogen oxides concentration 426
17.4.2.3 Aerosol measurements 427
17.4.2.4 Visibility 427
17.4.2.5 Acidic deposition 427
17.4.2.6 Pollution above surface inversion layer 428
17.4.3 Comparison with emissions elsewhere 428
17.4.4 Comparison with emissions in residential areas in South Africa .. 429
17.4.5 Regional and national significance 430
17.5 Air Pollution Control Technologies 430
17.5.1 Particulate removal equipment 430
17.5.2 Sulphur dioxide controls 431
17.5.3 Nitrogen oxides control 432

Page

17.5.4 Advanced energy technologies 433
17.5.5 Costs of control technologies........................ 433
17.6 Analysis of Air Pollution in South Africa........................ 435
17.7 Air Pollution Control Legislation 435
17.7.1 Introduction........................ 435
17.7.2 Establishment of committee, boards and officials 437
17.7.3 Control of noxious or offensive gases........................ 438
17.7.3.1 Objectives and policy........................ 438
17.7.3.2 Scheduled processes........................ 438
17.7.3.3 'Best practicable means' 439
17.7.3.4 Registration certificates 440
17.7.3.5 Penalty 441
17.7.4 Smoke control........................ 442
17.7.4.1 Applicability 442
17.7.4.2 Objectives........................ 442
17.7.4.3 Smoke control levels 442
17.7.4.4 Control authorities........................ 442
17.7.4.5 Regulations........................ 443
17.7.4.6 Manufacture and importation of fuel-burning appliances 444
17.7.4.7 Installation of fuel-burning appliances........................ 444
17.7.4.8 Siting of fuel-burning appliances and construction of chimneys 444
17.7.4.9 Smoke constituting a nuisance 444
17.7.4.10 Offences........................ 445
17.7.4.11 Appeals........................ 445
17.7.4.12 State not bound 446
17.7.5 Dust control........................ 446
17.7.5.1 Sources of dust........................ 446
17.7.5.2 Control provisions 446
17.7.5.3 Appeals........................ 448
17.7.5.4 Penalties 448
17.7.6 Control of vehicle emissions 448
17.7.6.1 Applicable areas and authorities 448
17.7.6.2 Objectives........................ 448
17.7.6.3 Control procedure 448
17.7.6.4 Appeals........................ 449
17.7.6.5 Regulations........................ 449
17.7.6.6 Road traffic legislation........................ 449
17.7.7 Emissions in mines and workplaces 450
17.7.8 Secrecy........................ 450
17.7.9 Administrative structure........................ 450
17.7.10 Enforcement of legislation........................ 451
17.7.10.1 Fragmented administration 451
17.7.10.2 Monitoring stations 451
17.7.10.3 Smoke and dust 452
17.7.10.4 Vehicle emissions........................ 452
17.7.11 Appeals 452
17.8 Concluding Remarks........................ 453

Chapter Eighteen *WATER POLLUTION*

18.1 The Nature and Extent of the Water Pollution Problem 456

Page

18.1.1 Introduction 456
18.1.2 Public attitudes to water 456
18.1.2.1 Availability of water 457
18.1.2.2 Price of water 457
18.1.3 Ineffective or plural legislation 459
18.1.4 Inconsistencies in secondary and tertiary government structure .. 459
18.2 Policy Regarding Freshwater Pollution 460
18.3 Policy Regarding Marine Discharges 462
18.4 Approaches to Water Pollution control 463
18.4.1 Uniform Effluent Standards approach 463
18.4.1.1 Advantages of the UES approach 463
18.4.1.2 Drawbacks of the UES approach 464
18.4.2 Receiving Water Quality Objectives approach 464
18.4.1.1 Advantages of the RWQO approach 464
18.4.2.2 Drawbacks of the RWQO approach 464
18.4.3 Pollution prevention approach 464
18.5 Compliance Monitoring 465
18.5.1 Statistical methodology and hypothesis 465
18.5.2 Sampling techniques 465
18.5.3 Network design 466
18.5.4 Sampling frequencies 466
18.6 The National Water Quality Monitoring System 466
18.6.1 A South African water quality index 466
18.6.2 Objectives and information reporting 467
16.6.3 The monitoring system 467
18.6.4 Constraints on NWQMS 468
18.6.4.1 The Act as an 'administration generator' 468
18.6.4.2 Public service employment conditions 469
18.6.4.3 Training 469
18.6.4.4 Divided interests 469
18.7 The Way Ahead 469
18.8 Water Pollution Control Legislation 470
18.8.1 Introduction 470
18.8.2 Legislation primarily affecting the source of pollution or dealing with activities which cause pollution 470
18.8.2.1 Pollution resulting from the use of water for industrial purposes 470
18.8.2.2 Pollution associated with mining operations 473
18.8.2.3 General pollution 473
18.8.2.4 Pollution associated with waterborne transportation ... 473
18.8.2.5 Pollution caused by wrecks 474
18.8.2.6 Pollution through dumping of substances at sea 474
18.8.2.7 Marine oil pollution 476
18.8.2.8 Pollution from certain farming operations 477
18.8.3 Legislation dealing primarily with the effects of pollution 477
18.8.3.1 Pollution detrimental to the marine habitat and its resources 477
18.8.3.2 Pollution detrimental to other aquatic environments ... 479
18.8.3.3 Pollution detrimental to public health 479
18.8.4 Legislation relating primarily to pollution in geographical areas .. 480
18.8.4.1 Pollution of harbours 480

Page

18.8.4.2 Pollution of protected water areas 482
18.9 An Analysis of Existing Water Pollution Legislation and its Administration 482
18.9.1 Water management.................................. 482
18.9.1.1 Surface water 482
18.9.1.2 Subterranean water 483
18.9.1.3 Marine matters................................... 484
18.9.1.4 Research 484
18.9.1.5 Conclusion 484
18.9.2 Legislation.. 485
18.9.2.1 The control of consumption 485
18.9.2.2 The discharge of effluents 485
18.9.2.3 General pollution 487
18.9.2.4 Definition of 'pollution'......................... 488
18.9.2.5 Some marine pollution problems 488
18.9.3 Divided administrative control 489
18.9.4 Future trends....................................... 489
18.9.4.1 Suggested improvements to the Water Act 490
18.9.4.2 Subsequent legislative amendments 490
18.9.5 Conclusion... 491

Chapter Nineteen *SOLID WASTE*

19.1 Introduction.. 493
19.2 Waste Management Strategy for South Africa........................ 493
19.3 Waste Generation and Classification............................. 495
19.4 Waste Storage 496
19.5 Waste Collection.. 497
19.6 Waste Transfer/Transportation 497
19.7 Reduction Potential and Disposal Options.......................... 498
19.7.1 Goals 498
19.7.2 Waste disposal options................................. 498
19.7.2.1 Thermal treatment............................... 498
19.7.2.2 Isolation from the environment 499
19.7.2.3 Recycling/resource recovery 500
19.7.2.4 Physico-chemical treatment...................... 500
19.7.2.5 Biological treatment/bioremediation 500
19.7.2.6 Landfill and co-disposal........................... 500
19.8 Landfill Site Classification, Selection and Design 501
19.8.1 Site classification..................................... 501
19.8.1.1 Class I sites....................................... 501
19.8.1.2 Class II sites...................................... 502
19.8.1.3 Class III sites & Class IV sites 502
19.8.2 Site selection.. 502
19.8.2.1 Legal requirements 502
19.8.2.2 Environmental impact assessment 503
19.8.2.3 Site selection criteria 503
19.8.2.4 Site design....................................... 504
19.8.2.5 Operational guidelines............................ 504
19.8.2.6 Site closure 508
19.8.2.7 Monitoring and control 508
19.9 Formal and Informal Waste Streams.............................. 509
19.9.1 The problem of litter 509

Page

19.9.2 Informal urbanization . . . 509
19.9.3 Clean Community System (CCS) . . . 510
19.10 Summary . . . 510
19.11 Waste Control Legislation . . . 510
19.11.1 Introduction . . . 510
19.11.2 Definition of waste . . . 512
19.11.3 National waste management policy . . . 513
19.11.4 National legislation . . . 514
19.11.4.1 Wastes on roads . . . 514
19.11.4.2 Wastes in protected areas . . . 515
19.11.4.3 Mine waste . . . 515
19.11.4.4 Health-related wastes . . . 515
19.11.4.5 Littering . . . 515
19.11.4.6 Waste-disposal sites . . . 515
19.11.4.7 Waste management regulations . . . 516
19.11.4.8 Hazardous waste . . . 516
19.11.4.9 Pesticides . . . 517
19.11.4.10 Radioactive waste . . . 517
19.11.4.11 Tax deductions for recycling plant . . . 518
19.11.5 Provincial legislation . . . 518
19.11.6 Local legislation . . . 519
19.11.7 Shortcomings in solid waste legislation and its application . . . 521
19.11.8 Towards comprehensive waste management legislation . . . 521

Chapter Twenty *PESTICIDES*

20.1 Definition . . . 523
20.2 Historical Background . . . 523
20.3 Environmental Impact . . . 524
20.3.1 Impact on the individual level . . . 524
20.3.2 Impact on the population level . . . 528
20.3.3 Impact on the community level . . . 528
20.3.4 Impact on the ecosystem level . . . 529
20.4 Reducing Impacts through Pest Management . . . 530
20.5 Control Legislation . . . 531
20.5.1 Private-law controls . . . 531
20.5.1 Fertilizers, Farm Feeds, Agricultural Remedies and Stock Remedies Act . . . 532
20.5.2.1 Legislative history . . . 532
20.5.2.2 Comparative perspectives . . . 533
20.5.2.3 The concepts 'agricultural remedy' and 'stock remedy' 535
20.5.2.4 Administration . . . 535
20.5.2.5 Registration . . . 535
20.5.2.6 Cancellation of registration . . . 536
20.5.2.7 Appeals against decisions of the registrar . . . 537
20.5.2.8 Manufacture and related actions . . . 537
20.5.2.9 Importation . . . 538
20.5.2.10 Sale, disposal or use . . . 538
20.5.2.11 Offences and penalties . . . 539
20.5.3 Other relevant legislation . . . 539
20.6 Conclusion . . . 541

Page

20.6.1 Public interest ... 541
20.6.2 International implications ... 541
20.6.3 Criminal sanction ... 541
20.6.4 Health risk to end-users ... 542
20.6.5 State liability ... 542
20.6.6 Law reform ... 542
20.6.7 Final considerations ... 543

Chapter Twenty-one *RADIATION*

21.1 Introduction ... 544
21.2 Ionizing Radiation ... 545
21.2.1 Sources of ionizing radiation ... 545
21.2.2 Radiation effects ... 547
21.2.3 Principles of radiation protection ... 548
21.2.4 Environmental control ... 549
21.3 Non-ionizing Radiation ... 550
21.3.1 Introduction ... 550
21.3.2 Sources of non-ionizing radiation ... 550
21.3.2.1 Electro-optical devices ... 550
21.3.2.2 Radio-frequency and microwave devices ... 551
21.3.2.3 Ultrasound devices ... 551
21.3.3 Biological effects of non-ionizing radiation ... 552
21.3.3.1 Ultraviolet radiation ... 552
21.3.3.2 Lasers ... 552
21.3.3.3 Radio-frequency and microwave devices ... 553
21.3.3.4 Ultrasound ... 554
21.4 Radiation Control Legislation ... 555
21.4.1 Ionizing radiation ... 555
21.4.1.1 Introduction ... 555
21.4.1.2 Nuclear Energy Act ... 556
21.4.1.3 Hazardous Substances Act ... 563
21.4.2 Non-ionizing radiation control legislation ... 567
21.5 Administration of Legislation ... 568

Chapter Twenty-two *NOISE*

22.1 Introduction ... 569
22.1.1 Sound ... 569
22.1.1.1 Amplitude and frequency ... 569
22.1.1.2 Sound propagation ... 569
22.1.1.3 Human perception of sound ... 570
22.1.2 Noise ... 571
22.1.2.1 Physical effects ... 571
22.1.2.2 Physiological effects ... 571
22.1.2.3 Effects on communication and productivity ... 571
22.1.2.4 Psychological effects ... 571
22.1.2.5 Summary of environmental effects of noise ... 572
22.1.3 Measurement of noise ... 572
22.1.3.1 Frequency weighting ... 572
22.1.3.2 Time weighting ... 572

Page

22.1.3.3 Long-term noise descriptors ... 573
22.1.3.4 Additional correction factors ... 574
22.1.4 Assessment of noise ... 574
22.2 Noise Control ... 575
22.2.1 Control at source ... 575
22.2.2 Control in transmission path ... 577
22.2.3 Control at receiver ... 578
22.3 Legislation ... 578
22.3.1 National legislation ... 578
22.3.1.1 Standards Act ... 578
22.3.1.2 Environment Conservation Act ... 579
22.3.1.3 Road Traffic Act ... 579
22.3.1.4 Aviation Act ... 580
22.3.1.5 Occupational exposure ... 580
22.3.2 Provincial legislation ... 581
22.3.3 Local authority legislation ... 581
22.3.3.1 By-laws ... 581
22.3.3.2 Local authority implementation of national noise regulations ... 582
22.4 Noise Control in Developing Communities ... 585

Chapter Twenty-three *ENVIRONMENTAL HEALTH*

23.1 Introduction ... 590
23.1.1 Scope of environmental health ... 590
23.1.1.1 Definition ... 590
23.1.1.2 Environmental health concerns ... 590
23.2 State of Knowledge ... 591
23.2.1 Uncertain hazards ... 591
23.2.2 Databases ... 592
23.2.3 The nature of ill-health effects ... 592
23.2.4 The nature of exposures ... 593
23.2.5 Health risk assessment ... 594
23.3 Health Aspects of Air Pollution ... 596
23.3.1 Introduction ... 596
23.3.1.1 Deposition of pollutants in respiratory tract ... 597
23.3.1.2 Air pollution episodes ... 597
23.3.1.3 General nature of health effects ... 597
23.3.2 Ambient air pollutants ... 598
23.3.2.1 Ozone ... 598
23.3.2.2 Carbon monoxide ... 598
23.3.2.3 Nitrogen dioxide ... 598
23.3.2.4 Sulphur dioxide and particulate matter ... 598
23.3.3 Other air pollutants ... 599
23.3.3.1 Cigarette smoke ... 599
23.3.3.2 Indoor air pollution ... 599
23.3.3.3 Global air pollution ... 600
23.3.4 South African situation ... 600
23.3.4.1 Domestic air pollution ... 601
23.3.4.2 Acute respiratory infections ... 601
23.3.4.3 Industrial air pollution ... 601
23.3.5 Environmental lead exposure ... 602

Page
23.3.5.1 Low-level health effects 602
23.3.5.2 Multifactorial nature of exposure 602
23.3.5.3 Blood lead levels in South African children 603
23.3.6 Exposure to environmental asbestos from mine dumps 604
23.3.6.1 Mortality rates 604
23.3.6.2 Morbidity rates 604
23.4 Health Aspects of Water 604
23.4.1 Introduction 604
23.4.2 Water and sanitation 605
23.4.2.1 Access to basic facilities 605
23.4.2.2 Water-related diseases 605
23.4.2.3 South African situation 605
23.4.3 Tropical diseases 606
23.4.3.1 Malaria 606
23.4.3.2 Schistosomiasis (bilharzia) 607
23.4.3.3 Polio 607
23.4.3.4 Hepatitis A 607
23.4.3.5 Cholera 608
23.4.3.6 Typhoid 608
23.4.4 Chemical contamination of water 608
23.4.4.1 Drinking water standards 608
23.4.5 Recreational water quality 610
23.4.5.1 Bathing-related health aspects 610
23.4.5.2 South African situation 610
23.5 Health Aspects of Hazardous Waste 611
23.5.1 Introduction 611
23.5.1.1 Pathways of environmental exposure 611
23.5.2 Epidemiological studies 612
23.5.2.1 Self-reported symptoms: recall bias 612
23.5.2.2 Documented ill-health effects 612
23.5.3 Need for epidemiological surveillance and monitoring 613
23.6 Health Aspects of Pesticides 613
23.6.1 Introduction 613
23.6.2 Ill-health effects 613
23.6.2.1 Accidental exposures 614
23.6.2.2 Airborne exposure 614
23.6.2.3 Uptake by crops 614
23.6.2.4 Drinking water contamination 614
23.6.2.5 Mortality and morbidity statistics 614
23.7 Microbiological and Chemical Safety of Food 615
23.8 Health Implications of Noise 615
23.9 Accidents 615
23.9.1 Common cause of death 615
23.9.2 Work-related accidents 615
23.9.3 Accidents in and around the home 616
23.9.4 Industrial accidents 616
23.10 Occupational Health 616
23.10.1 Health services 616
23.11 General Management Considerations 617
23.11.1 Acceptable risk 617
23.11.1.1 Public perception of risk 617

Page

23.11.1.2 Ready access to information 617
23.11.2 Training needs 618
23.11.2.1 Shortage of environmental health professionals 618
23.11.2.2 Multi-disciplinary approach 618
23.11.2.3 Technikon courses 618
23.11.2.4 University courses 618
23.11.3 Research 619
23.11.3.1 Medical Research Council 619
23.11.3.2 Other related research activities 619
23.11.4 Environmental health legislation 619
23.11.4.1 Introduction 619
23.11.4.2 Health Act 619
23.11.4.3 Atmospheric Pollution Prevention Act 620
23.11.4.4 Hazardous Substances Act 620
23.11.4.5 Other relevant legislation 620
23.11.4.6 Regulation in the workplace 620
23.11.5 Environmental health administration 620
23.11.5.1 Intersectoral responsibility 621
23.11.5.2 Rationalization of environmental health services 621
23.11.5.3 Health inspectorate 622
23.11.5.4 Need for national environmental health objectives 622

PART SIX: FEATURES OF PARTICULAR CONCERN

Chapter Twenty-four *MOUNTAINS*

24.1 Definition of Mountain 624
24.1.1 Topographical features 624
24.1.2 Ecological features 624
24.1.3 Mountain catchments 624
24.2 The Extent and Ownership of Mountains in South Africa 625
24.3 The Value of Mountains and the Need for their Conservation 626
24.4 The Conservation Status of Mountains 628
24.5 Man's Impact on Mountain Environments 628
24.5.1 Agriculture 628
24.5.2 Afforestation 628
24.5.3 Infrastructure services 629
24.5.4 Mining 629
24.5.5 Recreation 629
24.6 South African Legislation: General Remarks 630
24.7 Individual Control Provisions 631
24.7.1 Conservation of soil, vegetation and water 631
24.7.2 Control of afforestation 632
24.7.3 Control of invader plants 633
24.7.4 Fire control 633
24.7.5 Control of flower harvesting 635
24.7.6 Mountains in protected areas 635
24.7.7 Mountains in defence areas 635
24.7.8 Control of recreation 635
24.7.9 Control of mining 636
24.7.10 Control over the provision of infrastructure services 636

Page

24.8 Administrative Functions Related to Conservation Management 636
24.8.1 State conservation management 636
24.8.1.1 State-owned mountains 636
24.8.1.2 Private mountains 637
24.8.2 State control of management by individuals 637
24.8.3 Formulation of policy 638
24.8.4 Mountain zoning 638
24.8.4.1 Zoning as a holistic concept 638
24.8.4.2 Some uses and advantages of zoning over natural resource lands 639
24.8.4.3 Proposed categories of zoning for South African mountains 641
24.9 Mountain Club of South Africa and Other Voluntary Conservation Organizations 641
24.10 Conclusion: Towards Uniform Administration of Mountain Catchments .. 642
24.10.1 The interrelationship between the MCAA and the CARA 642
24.10.2 Revocation of the MCAA not desirable 643
24.10.3 Extended implementation of the MCAA 644
24.10.4 Continued role of the CARA 645
24.10.5 Integrated catchment management 645
24.10.6 Final remarks 646

Chapter Twenty-five *RIVERS*

25.1 Water Availability in South Africa 647
25.2 Some Aspects of South African Rivers 648
25.2.1 Freshwater systems 648
25.2.2 Classification of rivers 648
25.2.3 River zones 648
25.2.4 Constituent parts of rivers 649
25.2.5 The need for river conservation 649
25.2.6 The conservation status of South African rivers 649
25.3 Human Use of and Impact on Rivers 649
25.3.1 Agriculture 649
25.3.1.1 Excessive abstraction 649
25.3.1.2 Destruction of riparian vegetation 650
25.3.1.3 Weed infestation 650
25.3.1.4 Catchment mismanagement 650
25.3.1.5 Deterioration in water quality 650
25.3.1.6 Impoundments 650
25.3.1.7 Salinization 651
25.3.1.8 Indirect demands 651
25.3.2 Urbanization 651
25.3.2.1 Impoundments 651
25.3.2.2 Sewage effluent 651
25.3.2.3 Urban refuse 651
25.3.2.4 Stormwater drainage 651
25.3.2.5 Interbasin transfers 651
25.3.3 Human population concentrations in rural areas 652
25.3.4 Industrial use of water 652
25.3.4.1 Mining 652
25.3.4.2 Manufacturing industries 652

Page

25.3.4.3 Power generation 652
25.3.5 Aquaculture 652
25.3.6 Road-building 653
25.3.7 Recreation 653
25.3.8 Environmental conservation 653
25.4 South African Water Law 653
25.5 Legal Categories of Rivers 654
25.5.1 Public and private rivers 654
25.5.2 Tidal rivers and tidal lagoons 657
25.6 Public Rivers as Res Publicae 657
25.7 Navigability of Public Rivers 658
25.8 Ownership of Public Rivers 658
25.9 State Control of Public Rivers 659
25.9.1 The principle 659
25.9.2 Administrative bodies involved 660
25.10 Legal Categories of Water 660
25.11 Rights in Respect of Water in Rivers 660
25.11.1 Private water 660
25.11.2 Public water 660
25.11.2.1 Rights of riparian owners 660
25.11.2.2 Other individual rights granted in terms of the Water Act 660
25.11.2.3 Public rights 661
25.12 Statutory Control Measures 661
25.12.1 Declared water-related areas 661
25.12.2 Control of water use 662
25.12.3 Control of water quality 662
25.12.4 Control of course and flow of rivers 662
25.12.4.1 Alteration in the course of rivers 662
25.12.4.2 Interference with river flow 662
25.12.5 Conservation of aquatic fauna and flora in rivers 662
25.12.6 Control of land use 663
25.12.6.1 Land-use planning 663
25.12.6.2 Expropriation of land or rights 663
25.12.6.3 Conservation of soil and vegetation in river catchments. 663
25.12.6.4 Control of afforestation in river catchments 664
25.12.7 Control over the impoundment of water 664
25.12.8 Assessment of potential environmental impact of proposed water projects 664
25.13 Conclusion 665
25.13.1 Uniform and comprehensive management of water sources 665
25.13.2 Water management strategy and river conservation 666
25.13.3 River conservation options 667
25.13.3.1 Total conservation of rivers 667
25.13.3.2 The conservation of rivers as a compromise with development 667
25.13.4 River conservation authority 668

Chapter Twenty-six *THE COASTAL ZONE*

26.1 Introduction 669
26.2 Coastal Zone Management in South Africa 672
26.2.1 Definition of coastal zone 672

Page

26.2.2 Objectives of CZM 674
26.2.3 Principles for undertaking activities in high-risk areas of the coastal zone 674
26.3 The Legal Regime 675
26.3.1 Juridical nature of the sea, sea-shore and marine resources 675
26.3.1.1 The sea and sea-shore 675
26.3.1.2 Marine resources 677
26.3.2 Definition of coastal zone and coastal zone regulations 677
26.3.3 Admiralty reserve 678
26.3.4 Territorial extent of South African law 678
26.3.5 Moving or ambulatory boundaries 680
26.3.6 Planning and development control 682
26.3.7 Natural resources 683
26.3.8 Protected areas 683
26.3.9 Pollution control laws 683
26.4 Current Problems with the Implementation of CZM 683
26.4.1 Current legal and administrative problems 684
26.4.1.1 Plethora of legislation and fragmented, unco-ordinated administration 684
26.4.1.2 Staff shortages and limited environmental expertise 684
26.4.1.3 Inadequate control over administrative actions 685
26.4.1.4 Legislation not specifically aimed at promoting effective CZM 685
26.4.1.5 Limitations of criminal sanctions 686
26.4.1.6 Dominance of private rights over public interest 686
26.4.1.7 Narrow definition of locus standi 686
26.4.1.8 Alienation of state land in the coastal zone 686
26.4.2 Limitations inherent in the Environment Conservation Act 687
26.4.2.1 No legally entrenched national environmental policy, including a CZM policy 687
26.4.2.2 Compensation for loss of development opportunity 687
26.4.2.3 No legal requirements for the application of environmental impact assessment procedures 687
26.5 The Challenge for CZM 688

Chapter Twenty-seven *PROTECTED AREAS*

27.1 Modern International Concepts of Protected Areas 690
27.1.1 Introduction 690
27.1.2 Primary conservation objectives for protected areas 690
27.1.3 IUCN's revised criteria for classifying protected areas 691
27.1.3.1 IUCN Category I: scientific reserves and wilderness areas 691
27.1.3.2 IUCN Category II: national parks and equivalent reserves 693
27.1.3.3 IUCN Category III: natural monuments 694
27.1.3.4 IUCN Category IV: habitat and wildlife management areas 694
27.1.3.5 IUCN Category V: protected land-/seascapes (ecosystem conservation areas) 695
27.1.4 Transfrontier protected areas 696
27.2 Protected Areas Recognized under International Instruments 697

Page

27.2.1 Introduction 697
27.2.2 World heritage sites 697
27.2.3 Biosphere reserves 697
27.2.4 Ramsar sites 697
27.3 Protected Areas: Legislation 698
27.3.1 Introduction: historical background 698
27.3.2 National Parks Act 698
27.3.2.1 National parks 698
27.3.3 Mountain Catchment Areas Act 700
27.3.3.1 Mountain catchment areas 700
27.3.4 Lake Areas Development Act 700
27.3.4.1 Lake areas 700
27.3.5 Environment Conservation Act 701
27.3.5.1 Protected natural environments 701
27.3.5.2 Special nature reserves 702
27.3.5.3 Limited development areas 703
27.3.5.4 Protected areas recognized under international instruments 703
27.3.5.5 Penalty 703
27.3.6 Forest Act 704
27.3.6.1 State forests 704
27.3.6.2 Nature reserves and wilderness areas 704
27.3.6.3 National botanic gardens 706
27.3.7 National Monuments Act 706
27.3.7.1 National monuments 706
27.3.7.2 Conservation areas 707
27.3.8 Defence Act 708
27.3.8.1 Defence areas 708
27.3.9 Sea Fishery Act 708
27.3.9.1 Marine reserves 708
27.3.10 Sea-Shore Act 708
27.3.10.1 Sea-shore 708
27.3.11 Sea Birds and Seals Protection Act 709
27.3.12 Provincial Nature Conservation Ordinances 709
27.3.12.1 Cape Province 709
27.3.12.2 Natal 710
27.3.12.3 Orange Free State 710
27.3.12.4 Transvaal 711
27.3.13 Other protected areas 711
27.3.13.1 Conservancies 711
27.3.13.2 Biosphere reserves 711
27.3.13.3 Natural heritage sites 712
27.3.13.4 Public resorts 712
27.3.14 The need for national policy and for uniform legislation 712

Chapter Twenty-eight *LAND-USE PLANNING*

28.1 Introduction 715
28.2 The Scope of Town and Regional Planning 715
28.2.1 Origins of modern town and regional planning 715
28.2.2 Nature of town and regional planning in South Africa 716
28.3 Scale and Nature of Environmental Problems 717

Page

28.4 Town-planning System in South Africa 718
28.4.1 Development control mechanisms 718
28.4.2 Subdivision of land and establishment of towns 720
28.4.3 Development policy and long-range planning 721
28.4.4 Strategic planning 722
28.5 Regional Planning 722
28.5.1 Metropolitan regions 722
28.5.2 Rural regions 724
28.6 National Planning 725
28.7 Summary 725
28.8 Land-use Planning Legislation 726
28.8.1 The objects of land-use planning legislation 726
28.8.1.1 Introduction 726
28.8.1.2 Cadastral controls 726
28.8.1.3 Zoning 727
28.8.1.4 Nuisance 727
28.8.1.5 Agricultural and industrial development 728
28.8.1.6 Environmental protection 733
28.8.2 Land-use control mechanisms of planning law 733
28.8.2.1 Introduction 733
28.8.2.2 Expropriation 733
28.8.2.3 Prohibitions and restrictions 734
28.8.2.4 Licensing of land-use practices 734
28.8.2.5 Purchase and sale of land 735
28.8.2.6 Administrative directives 735
28.8.3 Land-use limitations and private property 735
28.8.3.1 Compensation 736
28.8.3.2 Uncompensated limitations upon land-use 737

Chapter Twenty-nine *AGRICULTURE*

29.1 Introduction 739
29.2 Characteristics and Environmental Impacts of Modern Agro-ecosystems 739
29.2.1 Diversity changed to uniformity 739
29.2.2 High nutrient inputs 741
29.2.3 The addition of water through irrigation 742
29.2.4 Regular cultivation 743
29.2.5 Application of chemicals for pest control 744
29.3 Towards Sustainable Agriculture 744
29.3.1 Past failure 744
29.3.2 The challenge: agro-ecology 745
29.3.3 Future prospects 746
29.4 Legal Aspects 746
29.5 Conclusion 746

PART SEVEN: ENVIRONMENTAL EVALUATION

Chapter Thirty *INTEGRATED ENVIRONMENTAL MANAGEMENT*

30.1 Introduction 748
30.1.1 The emergence of environmental impact assessment 748

Page

30.1.2 Environmental evaluation requirements in South Africa 748
30.2 Rationale for IEM 749
30.2.1 Purpose 749
30.2.2 Principles of IEM 749
30.3 The IEM Procedure 750
30.3.1 Stage 1: Develop and assess proposal 751
30.3.1.1 Develop proposal 751
30.3.1.2 Classification of proposal 751
30.3.2 Stage 2: Decision 751
30.3.2.1 Authority review 751
30.3.2.2 Record of decision 752
30.3.2.3 Appeal 752
30.3.3 Stage 3: Implementation 752
30.3.3.1 Implementation of proposal 752
30.3.3.2 Environmental management plan 752
30.3.3.3 Environmental contract 752
30.3.3.4 Monitoring 753
30.3.3.5 Audits 753
30.4 Requirements of the Assessment Routes 753
30.4.1 No formal assessment 753
30.4.2 The initial assessment 753
30.4.3 The impact assessment 754
30.5 Implementing IEM 754
30.5.1 Listed environments, listed activities and checklist of environmental characteristics 754
30.5.2 Scoping 755
30.5.2.1 Identification and notification of interested and affected parties 755
30.5.2.2 Participation of disadvantaged communities 755
30.5.2.3 Identification and selection of alternatives 756
30.5.3 Report requirements 757
30.5.4 Review 757
30.5.4.1 Department of Environment Affairs' review guidelines 757
30.5.4.2 Common inadequacies in assessment 759
30.6 Problem Areas 759
30.6.1 Defining 'significance' 759
30.6.2 Cumulative impacts 760
30.6.3 Bias 760
30.6.4 Confidentiality 761
30.6.5 Legal status 761

Chapter Thirty-one *ENVIRONMENTAL EVALUATION*

31.1 Environmental Evaluations: Purpose and Definitions 762
31.1.1 Purpose 762
31.1.2 Definitions 763
31.1.2.1 Environmental impact assessment and related terms ... 763
31.1.2.2 Types of impacts 764
31.1.3 What environmental evaluation methods cannot do 766
31.1.4 What environmental evaluation methods should do 766
31.2 A Short Survey of Methods of Evaluation 767
31.2.1 Checklist and matrix methods 767

Page

31.2.1.1 Checklists 768
31.2.1.2 The Leopold matrix 768
31.2.2 Overlays and mapping methods 769
31.2.3 Panel evaluation techniques 770
31.3 Methods Suitable for Use in South Africa 771
31.3.1 Introduction 771
31.3.2 The cross-tabulation or matrix approach 772
31.3.2.1 General features and formats 772
31.3.2.2 Identifying environmental elements 773
31.3.2.3 Identifying specific actions 774
31.3.2.4 Assessment 774
31.3.2.5 Entries in matrix cells 774
31.3.2.6 Review of completed matrix 775
31.3.2.7 Presentation 775
31.3.3 The environmental mapping or overlay approach 776
31.3.3.1 General feature 776
31.3.3.2 Selecting data for mapping 777
31.3.3.3 Evaluation 777
31.3.3.4 Presentation 779
31.4 Conclusion 779

Index to Legal Materials 781
Subject Index 803

CHAPTER 1

ENVIRONMENTAL MANAGEMENT: AN INTRODUCTION

R F FUGGLE

1.1 PRESENT-DAY RELATIONSHIPS BETWEEN HUMAN BEINGS AND ENVIRONMENT

In the second half of the 20th century the relationship between human beings and their environment has become a topic of widespread concern. Scientific and popular books have been published, governments have issued policy statements, and all the world's major religions have made declarations formally stating the moral responsibilities that their adherents have towards the earth.[1] It is now universally accepted that, according to present trends, we must expect the world, and South Africa, to become more crowded, more polluted, less ecologically stable and more vulnerable to natural hazards in the years ahead[2]. These trends are leading to a reduction in the quality of life for all people. There are two components to environmental deterioration. One is the depletion of essential resources for the maintenance of present-day life styles. The other is the deterioration and destruction of natural processes which ultimately sustain life on earth. Both are aggravated by an increasing human population. Our time is different from any other in history because of the rates at which we are using resources, modifying natural systems and increasing our numbers.[3]

Some of the changes are direct and obvious and have been known for a long time, such as soil erosion and a deterioration of fertility as a result of poor agricultural practices. Others have been the product of industrialization and urban growth; air and water pollution and alienation from nature. In the past three decades more subtle changes, often affecting the entire planet, have been discovered: the protective ozone layer some 20 km above the earth's surface is less concentrated than it was; average global temperatures are increasing; rainfall is becoming more acidic; agricultural practices are eliminating genetic diversity, and both harvests from ecosystems and animal populations have exceeded sustainable yields.[4]

---

[1] *The Assisi Declaration, messages on man and nature from Buddhism, Christianity, Hinduism, Islam and Judaism* World Wildlife Fund (1986).

[2] For example, First Report of the Club of Rome *Limits to growth* (1972); Second Report of the Club of Rome *Mankind at the turning point* (1974); United Nations Report *The future of the world economy* (1976); US Council on Environmental Quality *The global 2000 report to the President* (1980); International Union for the Conservation of Nature and Natural Resources *World conservation strategy* (1980); World Commission on Environment and Development *Our common future* (1987); United Nations Environment Programme *Environmental perspective to the year 2000 and beyond* (1988); The World Conservation Union *Caring for the earth* (1991); United Nations Environment Programme *Environmental data report* (3 ed, 1991); South African studies include *Proceedings of the international symposium 'Planning for environmental conservation'* (Pretoria, 1973); *Proceedings of the agricultural congress 'Production for a growing population'* (Pretoria, 1977); President's Council *Report on a national environmental management system* (1991).

[3] Both the UN Report *The future of the world economy* (1976) and *The global 2000 report* indicate that in the last quarter of the 20th century the world will consume at least three times as many minerals as have been consumed through the entire previous history of civilization.

[4] A convenient compendium of facts and figures on the state of the South African environment appears in the report of the President's Council, above n 2.

1.1.1 Caring for the earth

A significant contribution to fostering human responsibility for the earth is the worldwide initiative *Caring for the earth, A strategy for sustainable living* launched in partnership by the World Conservation Union, the United Nations Environment Programme, and the World Wide Fund for Nature. *Caring for the earth*[5] puts the case succinctly:

'Because of the way we live today our civilization is at risk. The 5.3 billion people alive now, especially the 1 billion in the best-off countries, are mis-using natural resources and seriously overstressing the Earth's ecosystems. World population may double in 60 years, but the Earth will be unable to support everyone unless there is less waste and extravagance, and a more open and equitable alliance between rich and poor. Even then the likelihood of a satisfactory life for all is remote unless present rates of population increase are drastically reduced.'

There are no easy solutions to this situation and action will have to proceed simultaneously on several fronts. The two fundamental requirements stressed in *Caring for the earth* are to secure a widespread and deeply held commitment to an ethic for sustainable living, and to integrate conservation and development—'. . . conservation to keep our actions within the Earth's capacity, and development to enable people everywhere to enjoy long, healthy and fulfilling lives'. *Caring for the earth* continues:

'. . . living sustainably depends on accepting a duty to seek harmony with other people and with nature. The guiding rules are that people must share with each other and care for the Earth. Humanity must take no more from nature than nature can replenish. This in turn means adopting life-styles and development paths that respect and work within nature's limits. It can be done without rejecting the many benefits that modern technology has brought, provided that technology also works within those limits. This . . . is a new approach to the future, not a return to the past.'

Nine principles for building a sustainable society have been proposed:

Respect and care for the community of life

This ethical principle requires that human actions should not be at the expense of other human groups or later generations nor threaten the survival of other species. It recognizes that our survival depends on the use of other species, but that we need not and should not use them cruelly or wastefully.

Improve the quality of human life

The underlying aim of all development is to improve the quality of human life. It is a process that enables people to lead lives of dignity and fulfilment and to realize their potential. People everywhere want to lead long and healthy lives, to have access to education and the resources needed for a decent standard of living, to attain political freedom and freedom from violence. Development must address all these factors and not only economic growth.

Conserve the earth's vitality and diversity

The human species is utterly dependent upon the earth's natural systems. There must be deliberate action to protect the structure, functions and diversity of the world's ecosystems. The ecological processes that govern climate, recycle essential elements, form soil, disperse wastes, and keep the planet fit for life, must be conserved. The variety of plants and animals and other organisms as well as the different ways these are assembled in communities must be preserved, and human use of living resources must be within the resource's capacity for renewal.

---

[5] Above n 2.

Minimize the depletion of non-renewable resources

Minerals and fossil fuels are non-renewable, so they cannot be used sustainably. Nevertheless, their usefulness to human beings can be extended by avoiding over-use or wasteful use, through recycling and by using renewable substitutes where possible.

Keep within the earth's carrying capacity

Policies that bring human numbers and life styles into balance with nature's capacity must be developed together with technologies and management practices that enhance that capacity.

Change personal attitudes and practices

Through educational programmes and the dissemination of information individuals must be encouraged to re-examine their values and to alter their behaviour to accord with the ethic of living sustainably.

Enable communities to care for their own environments

Authorities and governments are too far removed from the everyday activities of communities for them to constantly intervene to protect the environment from human actions. Communities must themselves be empowered to contribute to and enforce decisions that affect their environment. Care for the environment is the responsibility of all communities; it must not be made to appear the predominant responsibility of government or conservation agencies.

Provide a national framework for integrating development and conservation

To ensure action to harmonize conservation and development, all countries need an acceptable framework of law and institutions consistent with their social and economic norms. Such programmes must be adaptive and responsive to changing national circumstances. What will work in one country will be different from what will work in another; each country must therefore assume responsibility for a framework that will ensure a movement towards sustainability within its own domain.

Create a global alliance

All nations of the world are interdependent. No nation is economically self-sufficient and the life-supporting systems of the planet do not respect political boundaries. For sustainable living, all nations of the world must act in accord. It is fallacious to think that either the developed or the developing countries will be able to proceed towards sustainability without the co-operation of the other.

1.1.2 Environmental management

The need for human beings to be conscious of the effects of their actions and to conduct their activities so as to optimize benefits and minimize costs has become widely accepted. Management is the execution of planned controls so as to achieve a desired outcome. And when management skills and techniques are applied to care for the earth so as to achieve the goals inherent in the nine principles outlined in the previous section, we are dealing with environmental management.

The compass of environmental management is vast. General goals and specific objectives must be formulated and this must be undertaken with due regard to ethical, social and political norms. The goals and objectives must be given operational form, hence legislation and associated regulations come into being. Economic and technical decisions must be made and alternative courses of potential action assessed. These activities span a spectrum from central government to personal decisions; they require moral, social, political, legal, scientific, technological and economic expertise and, consequently, the inputs from many disciplines. The chapters which follow are intended to assist those persons charged with any aspect of environmental management in gaining a South African overview of the topic they must address. This is a book of first reference intended to indicate the scope and nature of environmental concerns in South Africa as well as the legal instruments that are in place to regulate human interaction with the environment.

1.2 THE TERM 'ENVIRONMENT'

The term 'environment' is widely used, but it means various things to different people. It is particularly important for an environmental manager to recognize that different professions attach specific connotations to the term. By way of example: what is understood by 'environment' as applied to a city? The urban designer will understand the term to apply to the spatial structure of the city; the architect will envisage the fabric of buildings; the municipal engineer will relate it to essential services; the medical officer of health will think of living conditions; the horticulturist thinks of parks and gardens, and tour organizers will understand the physical landscape within which the city is set. There are also other nuances of meaning.

In everyday usage it has thus become common to speak of a natural environment, a built environment, a social or cultural environment, and even an economic environment. This qualification of the term has become necessary to give precision to communication by focusing attention on a subset of what is encompassed by the noun 'environment'. When applied to human beings the single term relates to the totality of objects and their interrelationships which surround and routinely influence the lives of human beings. When used in this broad context the term 'human environment' might be appropriate; it has a vast compass, possibly too vast to be useful. It has thus become common for problems from Architecture to Zoology to be labelled 'environmental'. The use of the adjective is not wrong if its purpose is to indicate that a direct interrelationship between human beings and their physical habitat is the topic of concern. But it should not be used when the concern or problem relates only to habitat, or when the interrelationship is between animals other than human beings and their physical surroundings. It is also wrong to use the term 'environment' in place of the words 'circumstances', 'situation' or 'milieu' when the user's intention is to indicate context or circumambiance rather than interrelationship.

Similarly, the terms 'ecology' and 'environment' are not interchangeable and neither are 'ecological' and 'environmental'. Ecology is the scientific study of the interrelationships between living organisms and their habitat. Common scientific usage restricts the term to living organisms other than human and the term 'human ecology' is usually used if people are the subject of ecological enquiry. To speak or write of 'the ecology of the mountain' is also incorrect, unless a particular type of scientific study of the mountain is meant. But uninformed everyday use has led to a situation in which, for most people, 'the ecology of the mountain' means 'the natural habitat of the mountain'. Unfortunately such incorrect use of the terms 'environment' and 'environmental', as well as 'ecology' and 'ecological', has led to confusion. Strictly speaking, reference to 'environmental problems' should indicate that impaired interrelationships between human beings and their physical surroundings are the central concern. In everyday usage the words 'environmental problems' almost always relate to an unfavourable relationship between human beings and their natural environment. The concept 'environment' is discussed more fully in chapter 6.

1.3 A CLASSIFICATION OF ENVIRONMENTAL PROBLEMS

There are various ways in which human actions damage the interrelationships between people and nature. Some of the types of damage are more serious than other forms of impact, because the effects cannot be reversed—either by human beings or by nature. It is therefore necessary to consider four classes of environmental problems as each class requires a different approach for its effective solution. It is not possible to adopt any one hard-and-fast rule for solving different types of environmental problems.

1.3.1 Degradable wastes

These are among the earliest environmental problems which were formally recognized and comprise the pollution of water by organic wastes, pollution of air by products of combustion, thermal pollution, and noise disturbance. This class of problems is largely understood, while the difficulties are essentially technical and can frequently be solved by adequate dilution or dispersion. This does not imply that these problems are not to be taken seriously; rather that, given the will, we could act successfully against this class of problem within existing legal, economic and societal frameworks.

1.3.2 Persistent wastes

Substances that are removed from the biosphere very slowly by natural processes fall into this class. They include heavy metals (lead, cadmium and mercury), certain human-produced chemical compounds (notably DDT and plastics), and nuclear wastes with a long half-life. These problems require a different treatment to those first considered. Dilution and dispersion of these products is not an answer because in the long-term cumulative effects may pose serious threats; there is also the problem of biological accumulation in successive levels of a food chain, which produces toxic levels relatively quickly. For this class of problem technological answers are not yet generally available and solutions call for rigorous administrative control. This is feasible, as is illustrated by the strict regulation of nuclear wastes, but some restrictions on everyday freedoms currently enjoyed would be required and this is a real difficulty. The problem of persistent wastes therefore requires a different and more radical approach than that of degradable wastes.

The most important single factor to be borne in mind is possibly that of time. Scales of hundreds or even thousands of years are appropriate to persistent wastes and we find it most difficult, if not impossible, to think in such terms. We should therefore regard persistent wastes in a serious light.

1.3.3 Reversible biological and geophysical impacts

Owing to poor knowledge of the interacting web of habitat and life, drawing a distinction between reversible and irreversible impacts is not clear-cut. The examples listed are therefore open to criticism and correction. Reversible impacts might include agriculture, road-building, or opencast mining operations in large stable ecosystems. An effect of such activities is that they are likely to deprive communities of environmental amenity services and consequently lead to an insidious reduction in the quality of living. With the adequate passage of time, or given adequate and timely planning and expenditure, such impacts on the environment can be minimized and brought to acceptable levels.

The problem is serious, because social and political inertia are allowing vast areas of the earth to be degraded to such an extent that the damage is no longer taking place in large stable ecosystems but in unstable fragmented areas which do not allow for the reversal of actions. Failure to recognize the need to bring human actions into harmony with natural processes at a level acceptable to ourselves must ultimately lead to natural processes setting limits on human actions—at a level which may not be acceptable.

1.3.4 Irreversible biological and geophysical impacts

The most obvious of such problems is the extinction of animals, plants and fragile ecosystems. Another much-discussed problem in this class relates to possible changes in world climate and weather resulting from certain actions, while the final insult is total exploitation of an earth resource to the point of extinction.

There are distinct problems associated with this class of impact. First, we have little or no feeling or understanding for the seriousness of the threat. A far deeper knowledge of the interaction of biological and geophysical processes so as to identify particularly sensitive areas is required. Secondly, we must recognize that it is distinctly possible that we may trigger off large-scale environmental changes through such actions. Consequently, international rather than local or national control is required. Finally, it is within this class that major social and political adjustments are likely once the prospect of final depletion of an earth resource arises or widespread change occurs. Irrespective of whether technology provides answers to global warming, ozone depletion, alternative energy sources, minerals substitution and population problems, the social, administrative and political arrangements that will be required to order life once a definite limit is accepted will tax mankind's ingenuity to the limit.

1.3.5 Legal implications of different classes of environmental problems

Consideration of environmental problems under these four categories indicates that we should adopt different strategies in dealing with different types of problem. For degradable wastes the application of penalties after the pollutant has been emitted is tolerable, because cosmetic action is possible. This allows sanctions to be applied in one or more of the following forms: criminal prosecution, civil remedies such as actions for damages, seizure and forfeiture, or effluent taxes.[6] Such penalties could also be applied to persistent wastes, but it is clearly desirable that emission of these pollutants should rather be subject to total prohibition with heavy penalties for violations, as the environmental problems arising from these actions will be long-term and cumulative. Legislation should draw a clear distinction between these two forms of pollution.

In both cases the crucial test for any legal sanctions imposed on pollution emission is effective prevention. If detection is unlikely, or effective enforcement is not applied, laws dealing with pollutants may have negative results, as people tend to feel that the problem is solved once a law is passed; on the other hand, positive results can be expected only if there is a high probability of prevention of the unacceptable conduct.

In the case of actions leading to biological or geophysical impact the physical scale of the offence is usually much larger than the waste problems so that detection is seldom a problem. But, unfortunately, each action of this type is likely to be unique and no blanket provision can be laid down to cover all cases. The state of our knowledge about many such problems is also in most instances too meagre to allow for codification. In such instances it is impossible to invoke legal sanctions to ensure that individuals and society conform to acceptable practices. Effective legislation to deal with these problems must therefore ensure that major developments which are likely to have significant biological or geophysical impacts do receive careful scrutiny before development takes place. Provision must also be made for the complete prohibition of developments which are then found to be irreversible. Allowance must also be made for conditions—enforceable by sanctions—to be imposed on reversible impacts so as to ensure that a return to a condition close to that originally existing does, in fact, take place.

1.4 REASONS FOR ENVIRONMENTAL DETERIORATION

The aforegoing classification of environmental problems aids an understanding of the types of problems demanding attention but does little to elucidate why they have arisen.

Over most of history humankind has been nomadic. There was always somewhere

[6] A discussion of the merits and defects of each procedure has been given by Rosenthal in Grad, Rathjens & Rosenthal *Environmental control, priorities, policies and the law* (1971).

else to go when things became problematic either by reason of depletion of natural resources or because of changes in the social structure in the place where one was living. This has been termed a frontier attitude. When soil fertility declined, streams dried up or someone took a dislike to his neighbour's smoke or flag, it was possible to trek on a few more miles and to have available more natural resources and fewer constraints from society. Changing one's own lifestyle to accommodate changing circumstances was not necessary.

The growth of human numbers and our occupation of the entire planet make movement to new frontiers no longer possible. One reason, then, for 20th-century environmental deterioration is the fact that the earth's resources are not limitless and neither is nature's ability to cleanse itself of waste products arising from closely spaced human activities.

Since the advent of space exploration, it has become commonplace to talk of a spaceship mentality being required to replace the frontier attitude. This metaphor has considerable merit in that it calls to mind the need to match consumption to resources, and also how essential correct waste-disposal procedures are. What is not often appreciated is how well planned, restrictive, and filled with mutual responsibility life on a spacecraft is. The metaphor is nevertheless misleading as the human occupants of a spaceship are perceived to be separate from the inanimate craft they occupy. Human beings are an integral part of the earth and should not be perceived as being separate from it.[7] Much environmental deterioration results because we ignore the intimacy of human dependence on the earth and the need for adequate planning, restraint and responsibility towards others, in our private, corporate and state actions. Damage to the environment is seldom the deliberate act of evil men, nor is it the inevitable by-product of advancing technology; it is very much due to a human lack of restraint and demand for resources far in excess of our biological needs, omitting to plan for the side-effects of our actions, and placing our own short-term interests far ahead of our broader responsibilities.

A further reason for the occurrence of environmental problems is their often insidious nature. A problem arises from the collective impact of many small actions—discarding a beer can, a smoking chimney, picking wild flowers, catching under-sized fish, damming a river, the loss of one or two hectares of farm land—in themselves these may be insignificant, but they become serious if multiplied several thousand times.

Another reason for many environmental problems is, paradoxically, the present-day emphasis on specialization. In professional and technical training we are schooled in dissecting problems to study detail and we are taught reductionist methods of approaching specific problems. As specialists we are often ignorant of, or insensitive to, elements of the total problem outside our sphere of expertise. We are actually trained to have a biased view of real-world problems. But human–land relationships require a holistic perspective, an ability to appreciate the many aspects that make up the real problem—economic, technical, biological, social, legal and moral. An ability to understand relationships between the specific elements is central to the dealing with human-environment problems. It is for this reason that most responsible attempts to analyse environmental problems in recent years have been undertaken by multidisciplinary teams. Technical excellence in a specific field must not be mistaken for good judgment.

1.5 ETHICS OF ENVIRONMENTAL CONSERVATION

Thus far we have classified environmental problems and sought to understand why they have come about; we now ask 'Why conserve the environment?' This is not a

---

[7] A holistic and provocative view of life on earth is provided by Lovelock in his books *Gaia, a new look at life on earth* (1979) and *The ages of Gaia, a biography of our living earth* (1989).

descriptive empirical enquiry but a question based on what is good, right, or obligatory. It is an ethical question which attempts to provide a normative basis for environmental conservation. It is a philosophical question rather than one of a scientific nature; there is thus no single answer to be found by observation, but several possible answers, each based on an established moral philosophy.

Although several ethical bases for conservation can be put forward, they all seek to provide a basis by which an individual can decide whether a course of action which requires human beings to modify their environment is acceptable. All ethical systems recognize that individual desires must be regulated and limited, and that expediency is not an appropriate basis for judging human actions. Established moral philosophies deal with relationships between individuals and relationships between societies; the ethics of environmental conservation seek to provide a basis for the relationship between human beings and their world.

1.5.1 Utilitarianism

Both the world and South African conservation strategies[8] which were developed in the late 1970s are based on the credo 'Conservation is for man', and they provide a rationale for conservation based on the environment's utility to humans.[9] Their link to utilitarian ethics is not based primarily on nature's usefulness to human beings but on the ground that environmental conservation will produce the greatest amount of good for humankind.

A utilitarian ethic presumes a common currency with which to judge whether actions are advancing the greatest good; it does not allow for incommensurable values. Utilitarian ethics have general appeal in a society in which economic values are dominant and in which no appeal is made to religious considerations. Another attraction to many is that moral issues are, in principle, determined by empirical calculation of consequences with grey areas being due to technical limitations in assessing what constitutes 'good'.

Conservation ethics based on utilitarianism evoke consideration of the well-being of future generations and thus introduce the notion of time into the assessment of greatest good. So today a widely accepted reason advanced for environmental conservation is that such action will produce the greatest good for the greatest number of people for the greatest period of time. This accords with the old adage 'cum igitur hominum causa omne ius constitutum sit', which implies that law is created to serve humans. Environmental law, consequently, is often aimed at pollution control and the conservation of natural resources in order to ensure that the environment remains useful to human beings rather than because it is seen as having value in its own right.

There are other bases for environmental ethics which are not dependent upon an anthropocentric view and which accord to nature a right to existence for its own sake. These arguments have mainly been advanced by those who set human beings in a transcendental framework and who believe that humankind and the universe were created by God.

1.5.2 Judeo-Christian ethics

The books of the Old Testament are regarded as sacred writings by the world's three major monotheistic religions—Christianity, Judaism and Islam. The ethical teachings

---

[8] *The world conservation strategy* was compiled jointly by the International Union for the Conservation of Nature, the United Nations Environment Programme and the World Wildlife Fund and was published in 1980. *A policy and strategy for environmental conservation in South Africa* was compiled by the Wildlife Society of Southern Africa during 1978 and revised in 1980.

[9] See, for full discussion: Schaeffer *Pollution and the death of man: the christian view of ecology* (1970); World Council of Churches *Faith and science in an unjust world* vol 1 secs 5 and 12; vol 2 part 1 secs 2 and 5. See also WCC *Faith science and the future* part 1 chs 2 and 5, part 3 chs 11–13 (1979); Moss *The earth in our hands* (1982).

of these books are thus familiar to most of the world's peoples, though interpretation may differ slightly due to the influence of other writings associated with each of these religions. Judaism, Christianity and Islam all hold that a human being is not the Ultimate Being but is a product of God's creation, as is the earth and all plants and animals. All of creation—plant and animal species, the land, the sea and its resources—is seen as being as much a part of God's creation as human beings, and also subject to God's love and concern. Human beings reside in a cosmos created by and belonging to God. They are an integral part of nature.[10] God, not human beings, is Lord of all;[11] all creation glorifies God, not human beings.[12] Ethical systems based on these religions thus clearly differ from utilitarian theories of ethics which are based on the notion that the environment exists solely for humankind's support and pleasure.

Although the Bible does not contain detailed instructions regarding environmental conservation, human beings are given some injunction concerning their relationship with nature. They are to be fruitful and increase in number; they are to fill the earth and subdue it. They are to rule over the fish of the sea and the birds of the air and over every living creature that moves on the ground.[13] These commands may at first glance seem to be rather sweeping. However, the instruction to 'fill the earth' does not give human beings carte blanche to expand their numbers indefinitely. A limit seems to be implied; once the earth is full, population growth should cease. It must be conceded, however, that the question of when the earth is 'full' is a relative one. Moreover, God's placing of nature under human charge and control is not equivalent to His giving humankind the right to unlimited or indiscriminate exploitation or destruction of living things or natural resources. Human beings exercise their control under delegated responsibility from God; they are not the owner and are accountable for their actions. They are to act as stewards and should regard the earth and its resources as things held in trust. God has made provision within nature for essential human needs, not for our greed.[14]

There are clear indications in the Bible that other creatures and the environment have an intrinsic value to God, apart from being useful to humankind. In the first place, God, after creating them, blessed the living creatures of the air, sea and land and was pleased with them.[15] It is significant that God viewed the earth and its resources as good—even before humans were created—according to the first account of the Creation[16] and that the fish and birds are specifically directed to multiply as human beings were.[17] Moreover, the Fourth Commandment relating to Sabbath observance also includes animals,[18] and a sabbatical year is awarded even to the land.[19] Another indication of God's concern for His creatures is the fact that Noah had to take with him in the Ark pairs of every kind of animal and bird, and this irrespective of whether the animals were ritually clean or unclean, ie irrespective of their utility to humankind.[20] And after the Flood, God made His covenant not only with Noah and his progeny but also with the birds and animals.[21] Jesus also said that although human beings are of more value, our heavenly Father also cares for birds and flowers.[22] The point is that birds and flowers have a value as such and are important to God not only because they

[10] Gen 3: 19; Ps 90: 3; Eccl 3: 20.
[11] Job 38; Ps 24: 1.
[12] Ps 150: 6; Rev 4: 11.
[13] Gen 1: 28. See also Gen 1: 26; 9: 2–3; Ps 8: 6–8.
[14] Gen 1: 29.
[15] Gen 1: 21–22, 25, 31.
[16] Gen 1: 3–25.
[17] Gen 1: 22.
[18] Exod 20: 10; 23: 12.
[19] Exod 23: 11.
[20] Gen 7: 2–3.
[21] Gen 9: 10, 15, 16, 17.
[22] Matt 6: 26–28.

serve humankind. They are of value because God created them and cares for their existence.[23]

Judeo-Christian ethical norms require human beings to recognize that nature has a right to exist over and above its utility to them. They hold that humankind has been given control and management of the environment only to meet its needs and that it is our responsibility to ensure that natural processes are sustained and that natural phenomena are not destroyed. Judeo-Christian belief is that, although both human beings and nature are created by God, the relationship between them is no longer perfect because of human sin.[24] Christian belief is that it is through Jesus Christ that human beings will be reconciled with nature, their fellows and God.[25] This echoes a commonly occurring theme in modern studies of environmental problems, namely that their solution lies not so much in technological or scientific advance but in awakening an awareness of the non-material dimension in human-environment relationships.

1.5.3 Other religions

The last decade has seen a marked convergence between the world's major religious faiths and the world's leading conservation organizations. The most notable event was the interfaith ceremony[26] which took place in the Franciscan basilica at Assisi, Italy on 29 September 1986 to mark the 25th anniversary of the World Wildlife Fund.[27] At this ceremony religious leaders from the Buddhist, Christian, Hindu, Jewish and Moslem traditions celebrated the association between faith and responsibility for the earth. Each leader made a formal declaration of their faith's stance on human ethical responsibility for nature.[28] Subsequently many other faiths have associated themselves with the Assisi declarations and have contributed their own.

A direct consequence of the recognition that religion has an important role to play in caring for the earth has been the change in rationale for conservation between the *World conservation strategy* and its successor *Caring for the earth*. In 1980 the ethical basis for conservation was entirely utilitarian, whereas in 1991 it is recognized and stated that the world's major religions have a key role to play.[29]

[23] Psalm 104 provides a beautiful picture of God's loving care for His creation. Cf also Jon 4: 11, which indicates that one important consideration why God decided not to destroy Nineveh was the presence there of many animals.

[24] Gen 3: 17.

[25] Rom 8: 19–22; Col 1: 15–20; Eph 1: 9–12.

[26] Published by the Word Wildlife Fund as *Religion and nature interfaith ceremony* (1986).

[27] The name of this organization has subsequently been changed to World Wide Fund for Nature.

[28] World Wildlife Fund *The Assisi declarations, messages on man and nature from Buddhism, Christianity, Hinduism, Islam and Judaism* (1986).

[29] *Caring for the earth* above n 2, chapter 2.

CHAPTER 2

THE RISE OF ENVIRONMENTAL CONCERN

M A RABIE
R F FUGGLE

2.1 INTRODUCTION

It is common cause that concern for the environment is a modern-day social phenomenon. Throughout the world governments, international organizations, major corporations as well as ordinary citizens are insisting that planning and decisions must take cognizance of the impact of human actions on the environment. The rise of this concern has not been without setbacks or variation in opinion, nor has it been a steady linear process. Environmental concerns have swelled up in much the same way as water moves up a beach on a rising tide. The level of the waters of environmental concern at any one time is different at different points as waves push up further in one spot and retreat in another. When the wind is onshore the level of the water is higher than when it is offshore; when swells are big water levels are higher than when swells are small, but irrespective of waves and wind the water level rises during a rising tide. On occasion and at particular locations environmental concerns have not been high and may have decreased in significance, but overall there has been an undoubted rise in environmental awareness throughout the world and in South Africa.

It is sometimes thought that concern for the environment is a product of the 1970s. Although significant events certainly took place between 1970 and 1980, environmental matters had received much attention before this decade. A historical perspective on the rise of environmental concerns is essential.

For millennia moral philosophies have informed relationships between individuals and between social groups, but both ethical norms and legislation regulating human use of the environment have been slow to develop. While isolated injunctions and attempts to control misuse of the environment can be traced from biblical times, laws specifically designed to regulate environmental deterioration have been a product of the last 300 years. But, until the late 19th century, environmental laws were directed at specific forms of pollution, particularly air and water pollution after the Industrial Revolution, and at protecting occasional natural areas, usually privately owned, as hunting preserves for privileged groups. Public responsibility for the conservation of natural areas was established only implicitly with the first proclamation of national parks and nature reserves by governments in the late 19th and early 20th centuries. The first nature reserve to be proclaimed by a national government was probably the Yosemite Valley in California as the United States' Congress passed a Bill preserving Yosemite Valley 'for public use, resort and recreation' in 1864.[1] This was followed in 1872, when America's—and the world's—first national park was proclaimed in the Yellowstone region of north-west Wyoming.

In South Africa President Paul Kruger established a game reserve in the Pongola area in 1894. In 1897 four game reserves were proclaimed in Zululand; three of them, Umfolozi, Hluhluwe and St Lucia, still exist today. The Sabie Game Reserve was

[1] Dassman *Environmental conservation* (3 ed, 1982).

opened in 1898 and this led in due course to the formation of the Kruger National Park in 1926. Most of South Africa's other national parks were proclaimed in the 1930s. It is salutary to discover that South Africa's recognition of nature conservation as a public responsibility dates from the National Parks Act 56 of 1926, and that the first comprehensive provincial nature conservation ordinances are as recent as 1965 for the Cape, 1967 for the Transvaal, 1969 for the Orange Free State and 1974 for Natal.[2] Legislation relating holistically to environmental matters first came into being in the 1960s.

The notion that there should be public control over the use of private land and that developments on private land should be controlled for the common good finds its first legislative expression in town and country planning legislation adopted by Western countries during the first decades of the 20th century. (The history of South African planning legislation is discussed in chapter 28.) It was only by the mid-20th century that it was generally accepted that governments could and should regulate the use of the environment for conservation as well as for social purposes. Mechanisms for the protection of the environment are therefore still in their infancy and during the 1950s and 1960s several shortcomings in the machinery for regulating development so as to safeguard the environment for the common good and for future generations became apparent.

Problems arose because institutional arrangements were better suited to regulating exploitation of the environment than to its protection. Public authorities interpreted their role as that of umpire between competing and conflicting resource interests rather than as conservators of the environment. The prevailing concept related to discrete resources and not to holistic environments. Thus, despite co-ordinating mechanisms, public authorities were committed to a problem-by-problem approach to environmental policy; the relationships between particular environmental problems were ignored and no national facilities were created to concern themselves centrally with policy questions relating to the management of the environment.

A turning point in human–environment relationships was reached on 1 January 1970. On this day the United States' National Environmental Policy Act (NEPA) was made law—the culmination of many years of debate in committees of the United States Congress. This legislation recognized that human–environment relationships cannot be adequately addressed through piecemeal legislation which tackles problems on an ad hoc basis.

Throughout the world the 1970s became a decade of environmental concern and the passage of legislation for the protection of the environment. In the United States over 20 separate pieces of legislation either expanded Federal control or introduced it into new areas of environmental concern,[3] approximately half the nations of the world enacted some form of legislation for environmental protection, and numerous international agreements on environmental matters were signed.[4] Although the legislation passed by different countries is highly varied, consideration of the procedure adopted by many Western nations reveals the undoubted influence of NEPA. Procedures for the assessment and evaluation of plans and projects likely to have environmental consequences have been introduced and administrative arrangements have been altered to ensure that decision-makers are informed of the environmental consequences of schemes which they approve.

Two other emerging social issues that have influenced the growth of environmental awareness have been the move throughout the world towards participatory democracy

---

[2] Hey 'The history and status of nature conservation in South Africa' in Brown (ed) *Scientific endeavour in South Africa* (1977); Rabie *South African environmental legislation* (1976) 54–5.

[3] *12th Annual report of the Council on Environmental Quality* (1981).

[4] Chapters on 'Global environment' in annual reports of the Council on Environmental Quality.

and demands for less official secrecy and the greater disclosure of information related to individuals and to state affairs.

In the text that follows various indicators that can be used to gauge changing environmental concerns will be discussed, followed by an analysis of changing South African environmental concerns based on formal law-based indicators.

2.2 INDICATORS

2.2.1 Unofficial indicators

Informal barometers indicating the rise of environmental concern are constituted by the activities of concerned individuals and especially by those of environmental groups and organizations. Such growth is also mirrored in news media activities such as newspaper reports, articles and campaigns, and radio and television programmes. Other measures might be the number of conferences or the publication of books and articles on the environment.

2.2.2 Official indicators

Environmental concern at official level is manifested through a variety of indicators such as departmental and other official reports, governmental White Papers, the reports of commissions of inquiry and parliamentary debates. It is also demonstrated regularly through the administrative actions of governmental bodies at national, regional and local level. Perhaps the most important reflection of official environmental concern is the law. The promotion of the public interest in environmental conservation is rendered possible through the law, which authorizes or obliges public bodies to undertake appropriate actions. The source of such authorization is almost exclusively legislation, common-law provisions playing only a very limited role. Case law also plays a negligible role: South Africa does not have a tradition of public-interest litigation. The most important available remedy, that of judicial review, is severely restricted in that it enables the review only of the legality of the administrative action in question. Furthermore, litigation in the public interest is positively discouraged through the courts' requirement of locus standi in which a direct, personal interest on the part of the applicant is required before the courts will entertain litigation against public bodies. We shall accordingly concentrate mainly on environmental legislation as an indicator through which to demonstrate the rise of environmental concern in South Africa.

2.3 EARLY SETTLEMENT IN THE 17TH CENTURY: ENVIRONMENTAL CONSERVATION COMMENCES

During the first half-century of settlement at the Cape the small white community was understandably preoccupied with survival and the fulfilment of its task of providing food and supplies to the ships of the Dutch East India Company. But from the start of European settlement concern for the protection of the environment is discernible. Five placaats[5] were promulgated within 5 years of Van Riebeeck's arrival to protect gardens, lands and trees from destruction.[6] The often-repeated prohibition on starting grass fires[7] served the same purpose. A related issue was control over the felling of trees for firewood and for timber.[8] The two most prominent environmental issues which were the subject of legislative regulation were the protection of drinking-water from contami-

---

[5] The Cape placaaten represented legislative measures and, although they were, strictly speaking, ultra vires, were nevertheless de facto enforced. Cf Visagie *Regspleging en die reg aan die Kaap van 1652 tot 1806* (1969) 63.

[6] Placaaten of 14 October 1652, 21 December 1653, 22 August 1654, 10/12 April 1655 and 20 July 1657.

[7] Placaaten of 19 November 1658, 16 December 1661, 8 April/11 June 1680 and 19/20 February 1687.

[8] Placaaten of 1 October 1659, 26 September 1660, 3/6 December 1670, 1/4 July 1671, 10 July 1676 and 17 February 1683.

nation[9] and the protection of wild animals. No less than eight placaaten addressed the steadily growing problem of diminishing wildlife as a consequence of illegal and excessive hunting during the first 40 years of white settlement at the Cape.[10] During the same time a beginning was made with the attempted extermination of problem animals, particularly lions and leopards, as is evident from resolutions providing for increased bounties for the killing of these animals.[11]

2.4 THE 18TH CENTURY: STAGNATION ON THE ENVIRONMENTAL FRONT

The 18th century saw very little manifestation of environmental awareness or concern on the part of the authorities. If anything, the slight momentum which had been generated during the latter part of the previous century seems to have been lost, the only exception being the conservation of wild animals. Repeated placaats, promulgated by successive Governors, reflected growing official distress over illegal hunting. These laws contained harsh sanctions in an effort to eradicate the problem 'met allen ernst en vigeur'.[12] It is also noteworthy that during this century a start was made with the official control of living marine resources. This was done through the prohibition of seal hunting on Dassen Island[13] and the control of whaling in Table Bay and False Bay.[14] A promising development, at the turn of that century, was the legislative provision for control of state forests.[15]

2.5 ENVIRONMENTAL CONSERVATION GAINS MOMENTUM: THE PERIOD FROM 1800 UNTIL UNION

The latter part of the 19th century and the first decade of the 20th century witnessed a substantial growth in legislation aimed at wildlife conservation. The newly established legislatures of Transvaal, the Orange Free State and Natal, following the Cape example, continued to pass game laws at regular intervals.[16] Fish were also included in conservation legislation,[17] although, ironically enough, legislative provision was made at the same time to encourage the introduction of exotic fish species into rivers.[18] Other provisions related to problem animals[19] and noxious weeds. A particular problem was caused by the weed *Xanthium spinosium*, known as burrweed or Scotch thistle: several colonial statutes provided solely for its control,[20] while more generally oriented noxious weed legislation was passed in the Orange Free State just before the formation of Union.[21]

---

[9] Placaaten of 10/12 April 1655, 26 August 1656, 6 February 1661, 16 December 1661, 22 December 1676, 5 January 1677 and 10/11 February 1687.

[10] Placaaten of 1 January 1657, 23 July 1665, 3 October 1667, 25 October 1667, 3/11 September 1668, 8/9 April 1680, 20 January 1688 and 20 July/23 August 1690.

[11] Placaat of 31 August 1682.

[12] Placaaten of 27 April 1751, 3/9 September 1771 and 18 September/1 October 1792.

[13] Placaat of 20 October 1709.

[14] Placaat of 29 September/1 October 1792.

[15] Laws of 20 October 1795 and 26 January 1801.

[16] Cape Game Proclamation of 21 March 1822, amended by Game Preservation Acts 36 of 1886, 38 of 1891, 33 of 1899 and 11 of 1908, consolidated in Act 11 of 1909; Natal Game Laws 10 of 1866, 23 of 1884, 24 of 1885, 28 of 1890, 16 of 1891 and Game Acts 24 of 1894, 4 of 1904, 8 of 1906 and 18 of 1910.

[17] Cape Acts 7 of 1883, 29 of 1890 and 43 of 1899; Natal Laws 8 of 1868, 13 of 1880 and 21 of 1884.

[18] Cape Act 10 of 1867.

[19] Natal Law 8 of 1866 and OFS Act 7 of 1909.

[20] Cape Acts 27 of 1864 and 22 of 1905; Natal Acts 20 of 1861 and 38 of 1874. Transvaal Act 4 of 1897; OFS Ordinances 2 of 1874, 10 of 1880, 11 of 1895 and OFS Law Book 1891 (chapter 126).

[21] Act 23 of 1909.

Extensive legislative provision continued to be made for the control of grass-burning and the protection of trees.[22] The first major forest legislation nevertheless dates back only to a Cape statute of 1888.[23] This enabled state forests to be demarcated as the first formal protected areas in South Africa. This was followed, as was mentioned earlier in the chapter, by the establishment of the Pongola Game Reserve in 1894, with the Hluhluwe, Umfolozi and St Lucia game reserves being established in 1897, the Sabie Game Reserve (later to become part of the Kruger National Park) in 1898, and Giant's Castle in the Drakensberg during 1903. Related to this development was the establishment towards the end of the 19th century of the first conservation societies, known initially as Game Protection Associations. The Natal association was the first, being established in 1883. The Transvaal Game Protection Association (1902) was the forerunner of the Wildlife Society of Southern Africa, while the South African Ornithological Union, forerunner of the Southern African Ornithological Society, was founded in 1904.

Finally, colonial legislation related to the protection of public health provided for the control of nuisances, which concept encompassed several aspects of environmental pollution.

2.6 FIRST ENVIRONMENTAL CONTROL AT NATIONAL LEVEL: THE THREE DECADES FROM UNION TO THE SECOND WORLD WAR

The first statute related to environmental conservation (as opposed to wildlife protection) passed by Parliament was the Irrigation and Conservation of Waters Act 8 of 1912. This followed various pre-Union irrigation statutes. In spite of its name, the Act—as with the other irrigation legislation—had little positive environmental significance.

Another early conservation-oriented statute was the Forest Act 16 of 1913. This also does not qualify as wholly conservation legislation, although some 11 forest nature reserves were to be established before 1940 by virtue of this legislation. The Public Health Act 36 of 1919—in force for more than half a century—also contained incidental environmental provisions, in that it provided for control over nuisances, which included instances of environmental pollution. A beginning was made with the protection of cultural resources through the National and Historical Monuments, Relics and Antiques Act 4 of 1934. This Act and its successors, although primarily concerned with the built environment, also provided for the protection of certain natural resources. The only pre-1940 environmentally relevant legislation which still applies more than 50 years later is the Sea-Shore Act 21 of 1935.

Provision for the eradication of weeds was made by the Jointed Cactus Eradication Act 52 of 1934 and the Weeds Act 42 of 1937. Further agricultural legislation with environmental relevance was the Fertilisers, Farm Foods, Seeds and Pest Remedies Act 21 of 1917, which followed a similar Cape statute of 1907. The main concern of this legislation was, however, the economic welfare of farmers, protecting them against the sale of undergrade farming remedies rather than ensuring control over the environmental hazards associated with the use of biocides.

While nature conservation legislation continued to be passed at provincial level after the formation of Union, the first national legislation of an exclusively environmental nature concerned the establishment of protected areas in the form of national parks, through the National Parks Act 56 of 1926.[24] Natal is the only province in which

[22] Cape Laws 5 of 1836, 28 of 1846, 18 of 1859, 28 of 1888, 20 of 1902 and 20 of 1908; Natal Laws 21 of 1865, 31 of 1895 and 18 of 1902; OFS Law Book of 1891 and Act 32 of 1908; Transvaal Laws 2 of 1870, 8 of 1870 and 15 of 1880.

[23] Act 28 of 1888.

[24] Unless one wishes to accord this honour to the short Wild Birds Export Prohibition Act 6 of 1925.

provincial nature reserves were established during the relevant period—some five in total—while a like number of national parks were declared, commencing with the Kruger National Park, in 1926.

Three societies devoted to aspects of environmental conservation were established during the decades under review. Shortly after Union, during 1913, the Botanical Society was established simultaneously with the foundation of the National Botanic Gardens at Kirstenbosch. The Wildlife Society of Southern Africa was established during 1926, while the Southern African Ornithological Society was founded in 1930.

The most important environmental function that was exercised at provincial level was that of fish and game preservation (nature conservation), which function was specifically entrusted to the various provincial councils by the South Africa Act of 1909. Environmental control at local level related mainly to the control of environmental nuisances.

Together with the conservation of wild animals, the environmental issue which drew most official attention during the early period of Union was that of soil conservation. The problem of soil erosion gained attention on account of the economic losses being sustained by farmers as a result of periodic droughts. This led to the submission of two now famous reports, that of the select committee on droughts, rainfall and soil erosion (1914) and that of the drought investigation commission (1923). These reports were followed by numerous further official efforts aimed at the control of soil erosion.

2.7 THREE DECADES OF INTENSIFIED ENVIRONMENTAL CONCERN: 1940–1969

2.7.1 Marine resources

This period was heralded by the Sea Fisheries Act 10 of 1940, which, for the first time, regulated sea fisheries on a comprehensive and national basis. However, being aimed principally at marketing, the Act had little conservation emphasis, although some five marine sanctuaries of limited area and scope were established in the year following the Act's promulgation. Thirty years were to pass before the Act was again used for the establishment of marine sanctuaries.

2.7.2 Advertising along roads

A remarkably far-sighted piece of legislation was the Advertising on Roads and Ribbon Development Act 21 of 1940, in terms of which control could be exercised over the display of advertisements along roads. It is one of the most far-sighted but—due probably to its effective prevention of a potential problem—least known environmental statutes. Its aim was the prevention of visual disturbance of the roadside environment. It is remarkable that almost all the emphasis in this Act was on the need for environmental conservation; road safety was hardly mentioned during the second-reading debate in Parliament, while it would probably today be regarded as a consideration of at least equal importance.

2.7.3 Soil conservation

During the Second World War, the battle against soil erosion, which had commenced in 1914, culminated in the first substantial control legislation, i e the Forest and Veld Conservation Act 13 of 1941. This Act was soon followed by a landmark statute, the Soil Conservation Act 45 of 1946, which was eventually replaced by the Soil Conservation Act 76 of 1969. The struggle against soil erosion during this period is also reflected in the reports of several committees and commissions of inquiry, conferences, and a White Paper on agricultural policy, besides the launching of schemes aimed at veld reclamation and stock reduction. A once prominent national conservation organization, the National Veld Trust, was established in 1943 and did much to further the cause of soil conservation. Another relevant organization is the Tree Society, which was established during 1948.

2.7.4 Nature conservation

Nature conservation, at both provincial and national level, continued to grow. Most of the provincial legislation was consolidated in single nature conservation ordinances during the 1960s, the exception being Natal, where nature conservation was regulated not by a comprehensive ordinance but by a variety of ordinances which addressed different aspects of nature conservation separately.

The National Parks Act of 1926 was replaced by the National Parks Act 42 of 1962. A further five new national parks were created in the interim years and many new provincial nature reserves were proclaimed: 17 in Natal, while provincial nature reserves were established for the first time in the Cape (10) and in the Transvaal (13). The Southern African Nature Foundation, the southern African representative of the World Wildlife Fund,[25] was established in 1968.

A new Forest Act 72 of 1968 replaced the old Act of 1941, while the National Monuments Act 28 of 1969 replaced the Act of 1934.

A pioneering event in the conservation of mountains was the investigation which culminated in the 1961 *Report of the interdepartmental committee on the conservation of mountain catchments in South Africa*.

2.7.5 Water pollution

The extensive development of industry after the Second World War gave rise to concern over different forms of chemical pollution affecting water bodies. This was demonstrated by the introduction of the Water Act 54 of 1956. This Act was not primarily concerned—as was its predecessor, the Irrigation and Conservation of Waters Act of 1912—with water for agricultural use. On the contrary, it was the first national legislation under which industrial water pollution was extensively controlled. This Act came into being as a direct result of the *Report of the commission of enquiry concerning the water laws of the Union* which was published in 1952.

2.7.6 Air pollution

Industrial development also required more effective control of air pollution. A National Committee on Air Pollution was established by the Department of Health in 1955. A Bill for air pollution control was produced by this committee during 1957–58 and it received a first hearing in Parliament during 1961. The Bill was subsequently modified and eventually was passed as the Atmospheric Pollution Prevention Act 45 of 1965.

2.7.7 Noise

Although comprehensive noise control legislation has yet to be passed, official interest in this subject dates back to more or less the same time as the commencement of air pollution control. The South African Bureau of Standards (SABS) became involved in 1959 on the initiative of the South African National Council for the Deaf, which was concerned about hearing damage in the industrial environment. The Johannesburg City Council was the first local authority (in 1964) to request the SABS to suggest methods for the reduction of noise in cities. Four years later the SABS, for co-ordination purposes, formed a steering committee for acoustics and noise abatement. This was followed in 1969 by the publication of a comprehensive report on

[25] Now known as the World Wide Fund for Nature.

a large variety of noise sources prepared by the Advisory Council of the Department of Planning.

2.7.8 Pesticides

The control of pesticides started with the promulgation of the Fertilizers, Farm Feeds, Agricultural Remedies and Stock Remedies Act 36 of 1947, which, even today, after several amendments, is still the operative legislation.

2.7.9 Ionizing radiation

Authorization for control over radioactive material was initiated through the Atomic Energy Act 35 of 1948, which was replaced by the Atomic Energy Act 90 of 1967. The Atomic Energy Board was established by virtue of this legislation. Provision was also made for control over nuclear installations by the Nuclear Installations (Licensing and Security) Act 43 of 1963.

2.7.10 Non-renewable resources

During 1964 and 1967 four statutes consolidating most pre-Union mining legislation were passed which, together with subsequent amendments, formed the legislative basis for almost all mining for precious stones, precious metals, base minerals, natural oil and source material: the Precious Stones Act 73 of 1964, the Mining Rights Act 20 of 1967, the Mining Titles Registration Act 16 of 1967 and the Atomic Energy Act 90 of 1967.

2.7.11 Land-use planning

During the three decades under review the first steps were taken to centralize land-use planning, something which had been left to provincial and local authorities. This was done through the institution in 1942 of the Social and Economic Planning Council, a non-statutory body. Next followed the Natural Resources Development Act 51 of 1947, which provided for the establishment of the Natural Resources Development Council, whose broad objective was to plan and promote better and more effectively co-ordinated exploitation, development and use of natural resources. After some 20 years and after the establishment in 1964 of the Department of Planning—the forerunner of the present Department of Environment Affairs—the Act was replaced by the Physical Planning and Utilization of Resources Act 88 of 1967.

2.8 THE DAWN OF AN ENVIRONMENTAL ERA

With respect to environmental matters, 1970 must be regarded as a watershed year, both nationally and internationally. Public concern was particularly evident in the United States of America where, significantly, the National Environmental Policy Act was signed on the first day of the decade. (South Africa had to wait another two decades for similar legislation.) The first 'Earth Day' was held at Woodstock in Vermont on 22 April 1970. International concern was reflected in the United Nations' Conference on the Human Environment, held in Stockholm in 1972, and in the publication, in the same year, of the Club of Rome's *Limits to growth—a project on the predicament of mankind* and The Ecologists' *Blueprint for survival*.

In South Africa this era, fittingly enough, was ushered in by the declaration of 1970 as 'The Water Year', followed by 'Our Green Heritage' in 1973. Chairs of Nature Conservation were established at the University of Pretoria (the Eugene Marais Chair) and the University of Stellenbosch in 1970; the Shell Chair of Environmental Studies was endowed at the University of Cape Town in 1972; in 1973 an Institute of Fresh Water Studies was established at Rhodes University, an Ecological Institute at the

University of Bloemfontein, and the Percy Fitzpatrick Institute for African Ornithology was attached to the Zoology Department of the University of Cape Town. A national conference on 'Man and his environment' was held in Stellenbosch in 1972 and this led directly to the formation of the Habitat Council as well as the Environmental Planning Professions Interdisciplinary Committee (EPPIC) in 1974. Both of these bodies seek to co-ordinate and propagate responsible private-sector environmental concerns: EPPIC being the body representing the planning professions and the Habitat Council various non-government conservation organizations.

2.8.1 Governmental concern

Serious national environmental concern on the part of the government was demonstrated in January 1971, when a cabinet committee was appointed to investigate environmental pollution. Pollution and environmental conservation were discussed in the Senate on 12 March 1971 and in the House of Assembly on 26 March of that year. Subsequently, in April 1971, a pollution subsidiary committee of the Prime Minister's Planning Advisory Council was appointed to investigate and report on the matter. This committee produced a comprehensive report, entitled *Besoedeling* 1971, which was published at the beginning of 1972. (The English edition was published in 1974.) A summarized version of this report was published in March 1972 under the title *Pollution in South Africa: a report on pollution by the Planning Advisory Council of the Prime Minister*. In May 1972 a permanent cabinet committee on environmental conservation was established.

A non-statutory South African Committee on Environmental Conservation was in turn established to advise the cabinet committee. This non-statutory committee, which was renamed the Council for the Environment in 1975, consisted of representatives from government departments and other administrative bodies concerned with environmental affairs. The council, which functioned until the early 1980s, was given broad terms of reference in respect of environmental conservation generally.

Prior to 1973 priority and policy determination had been done through the Planning Advisory Council, while the important function of co-ordinating legislation relating to the control of pollution and the conservation of natural resources had been entrusted to the Department of Planning, which in 1973 became the Department of Planning and the Environment to meet this need. Thereafter, in 1975, the Physical Planning Act 88 of 1967, which was administered by this department, was amended and renamed the Environment Planning Act 88 of 1967, to make provision for the consideration of environmental factors during land-use planning. In 1979 this department became the Department of Environmental Planning and Energy. As a result of a process of rationalization in the Civil Service that commenced in 1980, the omnibus Department of Water Affairs, Forestry and Environmental Conservation was formed. This Department's name was subsequently changed to the Department of Environment Affairs, water affairs having been excised from its jurisdiction. The Department of Environment Affairs acquired jurisdiction over a number of environmental statutes which previously had been administered by other departments. It therefore no longer only co-ordinates the environmentally relevant actions of other administrative bodies, as did its predecessor, the Department of Planning, but now itself administers some environmental statutes or, with the process of devolution of powers, provides the policy guidelines for their administration.

Another important development at national governmental level was the publication, during 1980, of the *White paper on a national policy regarding environmental conservation*. This document sought to formulate the government's policy on a variety of environmental aspects. (A little earlier, in 1978, the Wildlife Society of Southern Africa had compiled a document entitled *A policy and strategy for environmental conservation in South Africa*.) A direct outcome of the White Paper was the

Environment Conservation Act 100 of 1982 and the establishment, in 1983, of the Council for the Environment—differently constituted—as a statutory advisory body to the Minister of Environment Affairs.

A further significant contribution was rendered by the Planning Committee of the President's Council through the publication, in 1984, of two reports on *Nature conservation in South Africa* and on *Priorities between conservation and development*.

A more recent manifestation of governmental concern for the environment was the State President's directive to the President's Council to investigate and report on a policy for a national environmental management system. The *Report of the three committees of the President's Council on a national environmental management system* was published in October 1991. In April 1992 a draft White Paper relating to a policy on a national environmental management system for South Africa was compiled by the Department of Environment Affairs in response to this report.

2.8.2 Legislation

With the advent of the environmental era a variety of new legislation provided for control of environmental matters that had either not previously been subject to control or that had not been treated satisfactorily. These are briefly discussed below.

2.8.2.1 *Mountain environments*

The promulgation of the Mountain Catchment Areas Act 63 of 1970, the first substantial legislation aimed specifically at the conservation of mountains, heralded the environmental era, as far as environmental legislation was concerned. This subject received further attention during a conference on mountain environments, organized by the Habitat Council (1976) and at a workshop on a national policy and strategy for the conservation and utilization of mountain areas in South Africa, held under the auspices of the Council for the Environment (1989). Some 17 mountain catchment areas have been declared by virtue of this Act.

2.8.2.2 *Nature conservation*

Both the Cape and the Transvaal nature conservation ordinances were substituted by new ordinances during 1974 and 1983 respectively, while in Natal a first comprehensive nature conservation ordinance was promulgated during 1974.

2.8.2.3 *Protected areas*

The National Parks Act of 1962 was replaced by the National Parks Act 57 of 1976. Protected areas were established on a remarkably increased scale after 1970.

All nine provincial nature reserves in the Orange Free State were proclaimed after 1970, while the Cape and Natal each added more than 10 nature reserves to their existing lists. Although only three new provincial nature reserves were proclaimed in the Transvaal, 22 new unproclaimed areas are for all practical purposes managed as reserves. The growth in private nature reserves, established in terms of provincial nature conservation ordinances, has been phenomenal: the Transvaal heading the list with some 500. Another new development was the establishment of game farms, the Cape and the Transvaal having some 1 200 apiece. Although only four new national parks were added to the list, an important principle was implemented for the first time in that privately owned land was included within the boundaries of proclaimed national parks. Barring a few forest areas in Ciskei and Transkei that had been established before 1930, all protected areas in the black states of South Africa—almost 30 such areas in total—have been proclaimed since 1970.

A 1971 amendment to the Forest Act of 1968, which has since been replaced by the Forest Act 122 of 1984, provided for the establishment of a new type of protected area, i e a wilderness area. Some nine such areas have been established since 1973. A further 11 forest nature reserves have also been established since 1970.

Yet another new type of protected area which has been conceived is the 'lake area'.

Only one such area has been established by virtue of the Lake Areas Development Act 39 of 1975. Lake areas have subsequently been taken over by the National Parks Board and are now administered as national parks.

A novel form of protected area has been that of 'nature area'. Such areas were established in terms of the Physical Planning Act 88 of 1967, which has now been substituted by the Physical Planning Act 125 of 1991. Only two such areas have been proclaimed, one in 1977 and in 1984. This concept has now been substituted by that of 'protected natural environment', declared by virtue of the Environment Conservation Act 73 of 1989.

At least six national monuments comprising natural areas, and established through the National Monuments Act 28 of 1969, came into being after 1970.

Some nine marine sanctuaries have been established since 1970, by virtue of the Sea Fisheries Act 58 of 1973. This Act replaced the Sea Fisheries Act of 1940 and has itself been replaced by the Sea Fishery Act 12 of 1988.

2.8.2.4 *Soil conservation*

The control of soil erosion and of noxious weeds has been consolidated and improved by the Conservation of Agricultural Resources Act 43 of 1983, which replaced the Soil Conservation Act of 1969 and the Weeds Act of 1937. The malpractice of the creation of uneconomic farming units with its concomitant adverse effects on soil conservation was at last comprehensively eliminated by the Subdivision of Agricultural Land Act 70 of 1970.

2.8.2.5 *Coastal and marine environments*

The coastal zone and the sea have become the focus of special attention from an environmental perspective. Apart from traditional legislation pertaining to living marine resources, i e the Sea Fishery Act, additional legislation has been enacted in the form of the Sea Birds and Seals Protection Act 46 of 1973. Moreover, comprehensive provision for marine oil pollution control was made for the first time in the Prevention and Combating of Pollution of the Sea by Oil Act 67 of 1971, which has since been substituted by Act 6 of 1981. Further control over marine pollution was authorized by the Dumping at Sea Control Act 73 of 1980. The first significant legislation since the Sea-Shore Act of 1935 to deal with the coastal zone was enacted during 1986 in the form of regulations by virtue of the Environment Conservation Act of 1982.[26] One of the main reasons for the renewed momentum as regards the conservation of coastal and marine systems and resources is the fact that the jurisdiction of the Department of Environment Affairs has been extended since the early 1980s to include all of the above legislation. The renewed interest in marine resources is also reflected in the reports of four commissions of inquiry into the fishing industry: *The fishing industry, the utilization of fish and other living marine resources of South Africa and South West Africa* (1972), *The conservation and utilization of the living marine resources of the RSA* (1980), *The exploitation of pelagic fish resources of South Africa and South West Africa* (1983) and *The allocation of quotas for the exploitation of living marine resources* (1986).

2.8.2.6 *Noise*

The provisions of the Factories, Machinery and Building Work Act 22 of 1941 (which has been substituted by the Machinery and Occupational Safety Act 6 of 1983) in respect of the protection of employees in factories and similar situations, were formally implemented for the first time, as far as noise control is concerned, during 1974. Extensive noise control by-laws were promulgated by the local authorities of

[26] GN 2587 of 12 December 1986.

Johannesburg and Pretoria during 1978. The South African Acoustics Institute, founded in 1975, singled out noise control as an urgent priority and arranged several conferences and seminars on this subject. The statutory Council for the Environment, likewise, devoted much attention to the problem, which effort eventually led to the publication of the first comprehensive set of noise control regulations, in terms of the Environment Conservation Act of 1989.[27]

2.8.2.7 *Solid waste*

Efforts have been intensified to control solid waste more effectively. During 1973 the legislative powers of provincial councils were extended to include control over litter, resulting in the proclamation of the Prohibition of the Dumping of Rubbish Ordinance 8 of 1976 (OFS) and the Prevention of Environmental Pollution Ordinance 21 of 1981 (Natal). At national level a draft bill on the disposal of containers was published in 1977, but was not proceeded with. Likewise, comprehensive draft regulations on solid waste control, published by virtue of the Environment Conservation Acts of 1982 and 1989[28] have so far failed to come to fruition. Littering and waste management are issues which have been addressed extensively in the Environment Conservation Act of 1989.

The Health Act 63 of 1977 substituted the veteran legislation of 1919, and deals with various types of pollution from a variety of sources.

2.8.2.8 *Ionizing radiation*

Ionizing radiation control gained new significance with the establishment of South Africa's first nuclear power station at Koeberg. As a result of the Roux Committee's recommendations a new Nuclear Energy Act 92 of 1982 was enacted, providing for the Atomic Energy Board's re-establishment as a public corporation, the Nuclear Development Corporation of South Africa (Pty) Ltd, while control functions were entrusted to the Atomic Energy Corporation of South Africa Ltd and the Council for Nuclear Safety. Control over the exposure of persons to ionizing radiation from electronic products was provided for the first time during 1971, with an amendment to the Public Health Act of 1919. Control is now exercised in terms of the Hazardous Substances Act 15 of 1973.

Apart from being relevant to radioactive material, the Hazardous Substances Act provides for control over a wide variety of declared hazardous substances belonging to any of certain defined groups, including biocides and solid wastes.

2.8.2.9 *Water pollution*

The Water Act of 1956 remains the most important legislation for the control of freshwater pollution and of marine pollution from land-based sources. A number of amendments, especially those during 1972, 1975, 1984 and 1987, nevertheless served to strengthen the operation of the Act. Moreover, water pollution associated with mining operations was subjected to control in terms of regulations issued under the Act in 1976.[29]

2.8.2.10 *Air pollution*

The Atmospheric Pollution Prevention Act of 1965 remains the principal legislation upon which air pollution control is based. However, the scope of its implementation has increased significantly since the early 1970s, particularly in respect of smoke and vehicle emission control and its application to scheduled processes (industrial pollution).

[27] GN R2544 of 2 November 1990.
[28] GN 1549 of 12 July 1985; GN 591 of 26 August 1988 and GN R1481 of 28 June 1991.
[29] GN R287 of 20 February 1976.

2.8.2.11 *Non-renewable resources*

Apart from the Nuclear Energy Act referred to above, new legislation included the Tiger's-Eye Control Act 77 of 1977, the Coal Act 32 of 1983, the Coal Resources Act 60 of 1985, the Diamonds Act 56 of 1986 and the Energy Act 42 of 1987. Recently most minerals legislation has been consolidated in the Minerals Act 50 of 1991.

2.8.2.12 *Environment Conservation Act of 1989*

To date, the most significant legislative development related to holistic environmental concerns has been the promulgation of the Environment Conservation Act 73 of 1989, which replaced the Act of 1982, the ambit of which it extended considerably. In fact, it may now arguably be regarded as the single most important South African environmental statute, constituting a major milestone in the development of South African environmental law, although not amounting to a codification of it. Of particular significance is the fact that it enables the authoritative determination of an environmental policy with which all administrative bodies should comply. The Council for the Environment advises the Minister of Environment Affairs on policy and other matters, while a new body created by the Act—the Committee for Environmental Management—advises the Director General: Environment Affairs on matters affecting activities which may influence the protection and utilization of the environment. This committee is also responsible for co-ordinating and promoting the implementation of the Act's provisions.

2.8.3 Voluntary bodies

The heightened public concern for the environment was reflected in the establishment of more than 20 new conservation organizations between 1970 and 1975 alone. Since then, the number has been growing steadily, confirming the need for co-ordinating bodies such as the Co-ordinating Council for Nature Conservation in the Cape (1970), a similar body in the Eastern Cape (1973) and the Habitat Council (1974).

2.8.4 Conferences

The environmental era has also been characterized by numerous conferences, symposia and workshops on a great variety of environmentally relevant subjects. Among the most important such conferences at the beginning of the era were a National conference on the protection of the environment (Stellenbosch, October 1971); Natural resources in southern Africa: scientific and policy aspects (Johannesburg, December 1971); Air pollution control in the southern hemisphere (Pretoria, March 1973); Wildlife conservation and utilization in Africa (Pretoria, June 1973), and Planning for Environmental conservation (Pretoria, September 1973).

2.8.5 Official publications

The development of public environmental concern is reflected mainly in publications of an official nature, although such concern is also evinced through the numerous other environmental publications which have appeared since 1970. Among some of the more important official publications to appear during this period are the 1980 *White paper on a national policy regarding environmental conservation*, referred to above, and the 1989 *White paper on environmental education*; the 1984 reports of the President's Council on *Nature conservation in South Africa* and on *Priorities between conservation and development* and the 1991 *Report on a national environmental management system*; the reports by commissions of inquiry on the Bill relating to the disposal of containers (1978) and into environmental legislation (1982) and the reports of the above-mentioned four commissions of inquiry into aspects of South Africa's marine resources. Reference has already been made to the Department of Planning and the Environment's report entitled *Pollution* 1971 and the subsequent summary of it by the

Planning Advisory Council. Numerous environmental reports have been published by the Council for Scientific and Industrial Research (CSIR) as part of its South African National Scientific Programmes report series. A major comprehensive publication by the Department of Water Affairs was entitled *Management of the water resources of the Republic of South Africa* (1986). Among the more important publications by the Council for the Environment have been its *Integrated environmental management in South Africa* (1989), *An approach to a national environmental policy and strategy for South Africa* (1989) and *A policy for coastal zone management in the Republic of South Africa* Part 1 *Principles and objectives* (1989) and Part 2 *Guidelines for coastal land-use* (1991). The CSIR, commissioned by the Department of Environment Affairs, recently prepared three important reports: a comprehensive report on waste management and pollution control in South Africa (1991), a report comprising five volumes on hazardous waste in South Africa (1992), and *Building the foundation for sustainable development in South Africa* (1992), the national report to the United Nations Conference on Environment and Development, held in Rio de Janeiro during June 1992.

2.8.6 Popular publications

South Africa has a good tradition of publishing in the field of natural history. Our bookshops abound with books on South African plants, animals, trees, birds, landscapes and nature reserves. In recent years a new genre of books on the environment has been published to challenge a South African tendency to regard the environment only in terms nature conservation. In this respect, books such as *South African environments into the 21st century,*[30] *Guide to green living in South Africa*[31] and *Going green*[32] come to mind.

There are many well produced magazines devoted to nature and environmental conservation, including the Wildlife Society's *African Wildlife* and the Botanical Society's *Veld and Flora* which both enjoy wide circulation. The Ornothological Society's *Bokmakierie* and the National Parks Board's *Custos* are also widely read and circulated. The Department of Environment Affairs produces *Conserva* as well as *Skipper*, a magazine for children. *Toktokkie* is another publication for children produced by the Wildlife Society. Many newsletters and occasional publications emanate from groups and organizations that promote environmental conservation as well as from the provincial Directorates of Nature Conservation.

Environmental Action is a new (1990) privately published bi-monthly report for leaders in government, business and education that has broken away from the traditional South African perception of what constitutes environmental issues; it includes material on economic, political and technological relationships to the environment.

2.8.7 Black involvement in environmental conservation

The perception that concern over environmental matters in south Africa is entirely based in the white community must be examined. In the first decades of this century several black organizations came into being to promote aspects of environmental conservation. These included the African National Soil Conservation Association, the Indian National Soil Conservation Association, the Native Farmers Association, and the African Wildlife Society. Subsequent to 1970 the Soweto-based National Environmental Awareness Campaign (NEAC) has been the most prominent environmental organization with its base in the black community. The African Conservation

---

[30] Huntley, Siegfried & Sunter *South African environments into the 21st century* (1989).
[31] McLintock *Guide to green living in South Africa* (1990).
[32] Cock & Koch *Going green* (1991).

Education (ACE) programme of the Wildlife Society as well as various initiatives of Keep South Africa Beautiful have also been rooted in black communities.

In recent research and publications Farieda Khan[33] has examined in detail the factors that have acted to shape black attitudes towards the environment. Her work demonstrates clearly that the injustices perpetrated on South African blacks during the apartheid era, particularly those related to dispossession of land, have had a significant impact on the perceptions that they hold towards the environment. Since blacks view environmental concerns and issues pertaining to land ownership as two sides of the same coin, it should be expected that the negative attitudes generated by unfair land practices have spilled over to environmental matters. It should also be anticipated that with the resolution of land issues during the constitutional negotiations that are currently underway, considerable interest in and demands for a better environment will be generated from within the black community. A challenge facing environmental managers will be to accommodate this demand without causing further environmental deterioration.

2.9 CONCLUSION

In this chapter an attempt has been made to illustrate how concern for the South African environment has developed over the past three centuries. Various indicators have been used but the focus has been mainly on trends that are appear from an analysis of the legislation that has been enacted.

The impression that is gained is that protection and conservation of the country's wildlife heritage has been the overwhelming environmental concern in South Africa until quite recently. Although attention was also given to water, air, soil and human artefacts, this was often piecemeal and reactive. From 1970 onwards South African perspectives on what elements should be encompassed by environmental legislation have broadened considerably. The inclusion of economic, political and social perspectives as an integral part of environmental planning and protection is to be welcomed, as are the efforts that are being made to have the right to a wholesome environment written into a new constitution for the country. Most of the subjects addressed in this chapter are discussed in detail in subsequent chapters.

---

[33] *Contemporary South African environmental response: an historical and socio-political evaluation, with particular reference to blacks* (unpublished MA thesis, University of Cape Town, 1990); 'Mass environmental politics: responding to the environmental crisis' 1990 (2) *Southern African Discourse*; 'Beyond the white rhino: confronting the South African land question' 1990 (44) *African Wildlife* 321; 'Post-apartheid South Africa and the environment' 1991 (2) *Earthyear*.

CHAPTER 3

RESOURCE ECONOMICS

R B STAUTH
P H BASKIND

3.1 INTRODUCTION

3.1.1 The purpose of this chapter

While this chapter is intended for the general reader, who is assumed to have no special knowledge of environmental or economic science, it is principally directed at two audiences: people who have decision-making responsibilities for managing resources ('resource manager') and people who are in the habit of criticizing resource managers.

Resource managers have an unenviable task. Some groups want more conservation, others more development. Since individuals have conflicting interests and different value systems, it is often hard to determine what the best way is to use our limited environmental and economic resources.

If you are one of those who have resource management responsibilities, environmental economics offers a way to help you evaluate alternatives and make sound decisions. Specifically, the principles and concepts presented in this chapter should help you to reconcile competing demands and find an acceptable balance between conservation and development interests.

If, however, you are a conservationist or developer who tends to be critical of resource managers, try to imagine what it would be like if you were given sole responsibility for determining how South Africa should use all its resources both now and in the future. How would you start to think about the problem? What steps would you take to ensure that your decisions would be rational? This chapter is intended to help you think about this daunting challenge, and to suggest a logical and practical way of proceeding.

3.1.2 The challenge of resource management in South Africa

Many people think South Africa is a rich country, but in fact this is not so. Although some resources are in abundance, including many kinds of minerals, the supply of other important resources, such as water, soil and forests, is quite limited. In addition, most of the people in this country still have a very low standard of living and, to make matters worse, our population is growing rapidly.[1] There is thus a great need to increase the pace of development and some people say that we cannot afford to spend much on conservation—or 'lock up' many resources—at a time when so many people are still living in poverty.

On the other hand, there is growing evidence that resource destruction from pollution and over-exploitation is now occurring on a scale that could endanger the process of development.[2] There is thus a great need to expand conservation efforts, and some say that even in developing countries such as South Africa more resources should

---

[1] Fuggle 'Population growth and resource demands' in Fuggle & Rabie (eds) *Environmental concerns in South Africa* (1983); Huntley, Siegfried & Sunter *South African environments into the 21st century* (1989).

[2] Ibid.

be conserved in order to protect society from suffering even greater poverty in the future.

Yet the real issue is not whether South Africa needs development *or* conservation—it needs both. True *economic development* is the process of using resources to improve human well-being for this and succeeding generations through a careful *balance* of development and conservation. The question that must be addressed, therefore, is *how much* conservation is needed to make economic development more effective and more sustainable. The supreme challenge of resource management is to make the right trade-offs between conservation needs and development needs.

Just as development efforts cannot succeed without some conservation, so conservation cannot succeed if the economy is not able to satisfy the basic desires and aspirations of the great majority of the population. Where there is great want, there is always the danger of over-exploitation, three major causes of which are: poverty, ignorance and greed. To some extent, ignorance and greed can be handled through education and regulation, but only economic development can alleviate poverty.

Economic development is generally understood to entail some degree of economic growth, which is the process of increasing the output of goods and services produced by an economy. In a developing country such as South Africa, with a rapidly growing population and large numbers of poor, *rapid* economic growth is wanted. But economic growth can cause great environmental problems, which can in turn *impede* economic development. So one of the principal tasks in formulating a policy of economic development is to find ways to foster strong economic growth without causing significant environmental damage from pollution, waste and lost options.

South Africa should, therefore, strive for economic growth *and* environmental protection. The question is how to pursue—and satisfactorily accomplish—both these objectives simultaneously. This question is addressed by environmental economics.

3.2 DEVELOPING A PHILOSOPHY OF RESOURCE MANAGEMENT

3.2.1 What is environmental economics?

Environmental economics is a philosophy of resource management.[3] A 'philosophy' is both a way of thinking and a guide to action. Environmental economics offers a carefully reasoned way of thinking about resource alternatives and provides a practical guide to making sound, defensible decisions.

The central concern of this relatively new discipline is the problem of how to manage *all* of our resources wisely, including unpriced environmental resources such as scenic landscapes, the ozone layer and well-functioning natural ecosystems. Specifically, environmental economics addresses the problem of 'choice', and is directed at answering the question:

'What is a sensible way to think about the possible uses of our resources, to compare the pros and cons of the choices we have, and to make the *best* choice—the choice that is in the best interests of society?'

How we answer this question will depend on our perception of the problems and opportunities facing us. More and more observers agree that the situation confronting humankind has changed dramatically in recent years. Within the last three decades it has become apparent that regional and even global ecosystems are now being

---

[3] See, generally, Kneese 'Environmental economics' in *The science of the total environment* (1986) 155–69; Pearce 'Economists befriend the earth' 1988 (19) *New Scientist* 34–9; Pearce & Turner *Economics of natural resources and the environment* (1990); Seneca & Taussig *Environmental economics* (1979); Stauth 'Environmental economics' in Fuggle & Rabie above n 1.

adversely affected by economic activity.[4] Growing out of this awareness, environmental economics provides a rational approach to resource decision-making that is appropriate to our new environmental and economic circumstances.

More specifically, environmental economics explicitly links environmental concerns and economic concerns. On the one hand, there is the danger of *overstressing the environment*. If we destroy too many natural and cultural resources, our quality of life could decline; and if we significantly damage certain natural ecosystems, our very survival could be seriously threatened. On the other hand, there is the danger of *underutilizing our resources*. If we fail to develop our resources sufficiently, we may not be able to provide an acceptable standard of living for all members of our society and this in turn could result in great social unrest, economic collapse and political upheaval.

Many people think that 'environmentalists' and 'economists' are natural enemies and that the two camps have irreconcilable philosophies. But, in fact, environmentalists and economists share fundamental insights into the nature of our resource management problems, and theorists and practitioners of the two disciplines are in basic agreement as to how these problems should be analysed and evaluated.

3.2.2 The nature of our environmental and economic problems

Environmentalists and economists of all hues agree 'there is no such thing as a free lunch': if we want more of something, we have to give up all or part of something else. This is because we live in a world of scarcity—almost all resources are scarce relative to wants.[5] That is, nature does not provide enough of anything (with a few exceptions, like the oxygen we breathe) to satisfy everyone's desire for all that is wanted. For example, even though we may all have enough oxygen to breathe, clean air is still scarce in many places.

And this means that to meet a particular demand—such as an increase in the availability of electric power or an improvement in air quality—some sacrifices are going to be required. For example, if we want to increase the supply of electricity by building more coal-fired power-generating plants, we will either have to (1) give up some of our air quality or (2) spend some of our other resources (eg, labour and capital) to prevent more pollutants from entering the atmosphere.

So the problem is that we must choose how much we want to give up of one thing in order to have more of something else. And the kernel of the long-standing argument between environmentalists and economists has been about the seriousness of the environmental costs that have to be paid to get more economic growth.[6]

---

[4] See, generally, Allen 'How to save the world' 1980 (10 (6/7)) *Ecologist* 190–4; Boulding 'The economics of the coming spaceship earth' in Jarret (ed) *Environmental quality in a growing economy* (1966); Clark 'Managing planet earth' 1989 (261 (3)) *Scientific American* 18–26; Daly 'The economic growth debate: What some economists have learned but many have not' 1987 (14) *J of Environmental Economics and Management* 323–36; Dohan 'Economic values and natural ecosystems' in Hall & Day (eds) *Ecosystem modelling in theory and practice* (1977); *The global 2000 report to the President* vols 1 & 2 (US 1980); Hollick 'The role of quantitative decision making methods in environmental impact assessment' 1981 (12) *J of Environmental Management* 65–78; *World conservation strategy* International Union for the Conservation of Nature (1980); Page *Conservation and economic efficiency: an approach to materials policy* (1977); Price 'To the future: with indifference or concern?—The social discount rate and its implications in land use' 1973 (24) *J of Agricultural Economics* 393–7; *Our common future* World Commission on Environment and Development (1987).

[5] Lipsey *An introduction to positive economics* (1979); Samuelson *Economics* (10 ed, 1973).

[6] See, generally, Baumol & Oates *The theory of environmental policy* (1975), *Economics, environmental policy and the quality of life* (1979); Beckerman 'Economic development and the environment: a false dilemma' 1972 (586) *International Conciliation* 57–71, *In defense of economic growth* (1974); Common *Environmental and resource economics: An introduction* (1988); Fisher & Krutilla 'Economics of nature preservation' in Kneese & Sweeney (eds) *Handbook of natural resource and energy economics* vols 1 & 2 (1985); Mishan *The costs of economic growth* (1969), *The economic growth debate: an assessment* (1977); Seneca & Taussig above n 3.

3.2.3 New environmental dimensions in economic thinking

In the past, many economists were simply concerned with increasing economic productivity or growth and they gave little thought to what was happening to the resources that are valued by environmentalists, such as wildlife, natural scenery, cultural heritage, clean rivers and indigenous plant communities. In addition, these economists tended to regard certain resources—such as soil, marine fisheries, and atmospheric conditions—as being so abundant or resilient that they could be treated as if they were inexhaustible or indestructible.

Only recently has it become clear that many highly valued renewable resources are being lost or badly damaged by economic activity and that environmental costs are now a major consideration in determining whether a proposed resource use is worthwhile. As a result, the concept of 'economic resources' has been broadened to encompass things that used to be considered 'free resources'. These resources include ecological processes and natural amenities which cannot be owned, or traded in the market, but which are nevertheless economic goods and services because

- their supply is limited,
- their availability and condition are affected by economic activity, and
- they confer real benefits to members of society.

So economists have started listening to ecologists and other environmental scientists about the nature and potential seriousness of environmental impacts resulting from economic activity, and these impacts are now being incorporated into economic analysis. In addition, there is growing agreement that mankind's new environmental predicament dictates that new economic criteria or tests should be applied to any proposed resource use before a decision is taken.[7] Economists and environmentalists are finally starting to speak the same language,[8] think the same way and accept the same guidelines for judging the merit of proposed uses of resources.

3.2.4 Selecting evaluation criteria

Before one can design tests that can be used to evaluate proposed uses of resources, it is necessary to define clearly what it is that resource managers are (or should be) trying to accomplish. In other words, we need to specify a policy goal for resource management which is sufficiently broad to encompass all forms of resource use, yet which is also sufficiently precise to indicate what specific criteria should be applied to any proposed resource use. Another important consideration is that, in order to get most people's support, the policy goal needs to be based on assumptions which would be acceptable to most people, whether they think of themselves as conservationists or developers, or as capitalists or socialists.

The underlying assumption on which environmental economics is based is that the object of resource use is to improve human fulfilment or satisfaction. This means that human beings are managing the world for the sake of human beings and that impacts on other species and on natural systems are relevant only because people care about these things.[9]

Not everyone agrees with this view, but without this assumption there would be no meaningful frame of reference for a system of valuation. For example, how would one measure the net effect an action has on other species from the point of view of the affected species, and then weigh that against the net effect on human beings?

Aldo Leopold once suggested that our system of ethics should be extended to

[7] Boulding above n 4; Daly above n 4; Page above n 4.

[8] One of the problems in communicating between (and even within) different disciplines is that people often define words in different ways.

[9] Dohan above n 4.

embrace all living things and ecosystems in what he called a 'land ethic'. His idea was to manage the land in accordance with an ethical system (ie, judgments about what is right and what is wrong) rather than an economic system (ie, judgments based on what brings utility). Leopold[10] eloquently expressed the essence of this land ethic, and the implicit decision rule that should be adopted for implementing it, in this memorable passage:

'A thing is right when it tends to preserve the integrity, stability and beauty of the biotic community. It is wrong when it tends otherwise.'

Leopold's land ethic is an appealing concept, but unfortunately there is an insurmountable difficulty in putting it into practice. The problem is that virtually every resource management decision involves some adverse impacts to some part of the natural environment; the question is to what extent should man's activities be constrained by the decision rule (ie, not to harm nature) implicit in the land ethic? If nature is to be managed for nature's sake rather than man's sake, then there is very little that man can do to further his own interests.

To be of use, a resource management philosophy must provide a practical guide to action. While Leopold's dictum constitutes a valuable reminder that resource management has an ethical dimension, it cannot provide the basis for developing practical decision rules to guide choice in specific instances when there is a trade-off between man's interests and nature's interests. It is, therefore, a matter of practical necessity to develop evaluation criteria that are restricted to the effects of actions on human welfare.

Nevertheless, conservationists can still advance strong arguments for protecting nature within an economic (or utilitarian) framework because man's survival and well-being depend, in a very fundamental way, on maintaining the integrity, stability and beauty of the biotic community. The land ethic is relevant to resource decisions because what happens to the land affects people and therefore matters to people. Leopold's ethical considerations can thus be framed in a human context as one of the benefits of preservation which must be properly evaluated when comparing different resource options.

In addition, conservationists can argue that human fulfilment or satisfaction should not be interpreted in terms of 'wants' alone, as is done in conventional economic theory and practice, but rather in terms of 'needs'. One can make an important distinction between wants and needs. For example, there is a psychological theory which suggests that gratifying wants does not always result in a sense of fulfilment or constitute an improvement in well-being; but all individuals have certain basic needs the satisfaction of which advances human well-being through a developmental process which allows individuals to realize more of their life potential.[11]

We may wish to consider, therefore, that a resource use improves human well-being if it allows more individuals to satisfy biologically determined needs rather than culturally induced wants.[12] Surely any enlightened system of resource management requires that this subjective condition be evaluated in some way and not be based solely on expressed preferences.

While there will never be complete agreement on such matters, the literature on environmental economics suggests that resource managers could expect broad support if they were to adopt a management policy which is based on the following premises and goal statement and which involves application of the following criteria for evaluating proposed uses of resources.

---

[10] *A sand county almanac* (1966).

[11] Maslow 'Toward a humanistic biology' 1969 (24) *American Psychologist* 724–35, *Motivation and personality* (2 ed, 1970).

[12] Herfindahl & Kneese *Economic theory of natural resources* (1974); Maslow above n 11.

3.2.4.1 *Premises*

(a) If a resource can be made to yield more benefits without imposing extra costs on anyone, then society as a whole can be made better off.[13] Even if some members of society were to bear costs from an action, society as a whole could still be made better off if the people who bore the costs could be adequately compensated without imposing a net cost on those who stand to gain from the resource use. Therefore *it is necessary to consider whether and to what extent the total benefits of a proposed use of resources would exceed the total costs.*

(b) Each possible resource use promises different potential satisfactions (benefits) and dissatisfactions (costs) for different people. it is not always practicable to compensate adequately those who would bear a net cost, yet the well-being of each individual in society is inherently as important as that of any other individual.[14] Therefore *it is necessary to consider the extent to which different individuals or groups comprising society would be made better or worse off by a proposed use of resources.*

(c) The composition of society is constantly changing as some people die and others are born, and today's resource management decisions could affect the well-being of present and future individuals in very different ways. We can expect (and hope) that many human generations will succeed us, and the well-being of future generations is inherently as important as that of present generations.[15] *Therefore it is necessary to consider the extent to which future generations would be made better or worse off by a proposed use of resources.*

3.2.4.2 *Policy goal*

If these premises are accepted, then they can be used to derive the following policy goal:

'The goal of resource management is to achieve the highest possible level of human well-being over a time period spanning multiple generations.'[16]

A policy designed to advance this goal could be termed a 'sustainable development policy'. It would be concerned with obtaining the most rapid rate of economic development that can be safely sustained and would be based on the assumption that both economic progress and environmental quality are needed to improve human well-being. There are thus two major components to the policy: the pursuit of 'economic development', and the pursuit of 'sustainability':

(a) *Economic development* is concerned with the management of man-made and environmental capital to better *satisfy human needs and aspirations.*

(b) *Sustainability* is concerned with the management of man-made and environmental capital to *maintain the capability* of satisfying the needs and aspirations of both present and future generations.

To determine whether a proposed resource use would advance these objectives, clear evaluation criteria need to be specified. One suggestion is to adopt a cost-benefit framework for formulating and applying evaluation criteria.[17] In such a framework, a

---

[13] Lipsey above n 5; Samuelson above n 5.

[14] Lutz & Lux *The challenge of humanistic economics* (1979); Okun *Equality and efficiency: the big tradeoff* (1975).

[15] Daly above n 4; Hardin *The limits of altruism: an ecologist's view of survival* (1977); Page above n 4.

[16] Stauth *An environmental evaluation methodology for improving resource allocation decisions: a treatise with selected South African case studies* (unpublished PhD thesis, University of Cape Town, 1989).

[17] Stauth above n 3.

cost or benefit is anything which is perceived as affecting human well-being, whether or not it can be priced or objectively measured.

3.2.4.3 *Criteria*

When evaluating and comparing different proposed uses of resources in terms of the goal of resource management, it is necessary to apply three tests or criteria (which are related to the three premises from which the policy goal has been derived):

(a) The **'efficiency criterion'**: Would the proposed action be *efficient*? (ie, would the benefits exceed the costs?)

(b) The **'equity criterion'**: Would the proposed action be *equitable*? (ie, would the benefits and costs be distributed fairly among the individuals constituting present-day society?)

(c) The **'sustainability criterion'**: Would the action be *sustainable*? (ie, would benefits continue to exceed costs over intergenerational time periods?)

Although people may disagree as to how much weight should be given to each of these tests, everyone should be able to agree that it would always be desirable for a proposed resource use to 'pass' all three tests. For example, a free-market capitalist would probably be inclined to give considerable weight to efficiency, whereas a socialist might give relatively more weight to equity and a conservationist more weight to sustainability. But the important point is that no one should object to the tests themselves; an individual who feels that a test is not very important can always argue that the results of that test should be given a very low weighting.

In order for a proposed resource use to be unambiguously acceptable, it would have to satisfy all three tests. But resource managers have found that this seldom happens. For example, when comparing a development proposal with a conservation proposal, the former might be judged more efficient (or more equitable), while the latter might be judged more sustainable. This means that it is necessary to 'weigh up' the forecast outcomes for each of the proposed resource uses and then make some kind of trade-off between them to determine which proposed use is in the best overall interests of society.

Having defined a policy goal and identified the evaluation criteria which should be applied to any proposed resource use, the next question is: What approach should we take to gathering and weighing value information so that we can judge the relative desirability of competing uses of resources? The environmental economist suggests that we devise methods of evaluation which utilize a cost-benefit framework.

3.3 PRACTICAL METHODS FOR EVALUATING PROPOSED RESOURCE USES

3.3.1 The concept of costs and benefits

Anything that happens to any individual or group can be regarded as either a cost or a benefit.[18] Therefore, all of the potential outcomes of any proposed resource use—including outcomes affecting efficiency, equity or sustainability—can be expressed in terms of 'benefits' and 'costs', depending on how they are perceived to affect human fulfilment or satisfaction. For example, a great risk of incurring some adverse outcome (or cost) is itself a cost, the significance of which will depend on such considerations as the probability of occurrence, the magnitude of the cost if it occurs and one's attitude towards risk.[19]

Labelling all potential outcomes as costs or benefits makes it possible to evaluate a proposed resource use in terms of the stated goal. In other words, attaching these labels

---

[18] Dohan above n 4; Pearce *Cost-benefit analysis* (2 ed, 1983).

[19] Barbour *Technology, environment and human values* (1980).

is a necessary first step in determining whether the proposed resource use will serve to move society towards or away from our goal of achieving the highest possible level of human well-being over multiple generations.

The concept of costs and benefits thus makes it theoretically possible to apply the same 'measuring rod' in all three tests:

- if benefits exceed costs, the proposed resource use is efficient;
- if benefits and costs are distributed fairly, the proposed resource use is equitable; and
- if benefits continue to exceed costs over multiple generations, the proposed resource use is sustainable.

3.3.2 The need for a measuring rod

A major challenge is to find an acceptable measuring rod for evaluating costs and benefits in terms of the three tests. Money is the most obvious and widely used measuring rod, and many people naturally equate economic measures of value with monetary measures. But the eminent economist Samuelson[20] has pointed out that it is not necessary to measure value in terms of money:

'. . . economics is the study of how men and society end up choosing, with or without the use of money, to employ scarce productive resources that could have alternative uses, to produce various commodities and distribute them for consumption, now or in the future, among various people and groups in society. It analyses the costs and benefits of improving patterns of resource allocation.'

Although we could use other means of measurement to guide resource allocation, money has proved an extremely useful way to measure the value of unlike goods and services. This is particularly true in free-market economies, where great numbers of transactions involving willing sellers and buyers result in the emergence of 'market prices'. These prices provide low-cost information as to the value people attach to the many goods and services which are traded in the market.[21]

But price signals indicate the value of only those goods and services which can be owned and consciously traded for something else. This is a serious limitation because many resources, such as ecological processes and certain natural amenities, are not owned by anyone and it is not possible to effect a trade contract in the market. The value of these resources is, therefore, not recorded in the market.

Even for those goods and services which are valued by the interaction of supply and demand in the market, the prices which emerge often do not reflect all the costs associated with the production of some good or service. For example, environmental costs are often not expressed in the accounting information used by the producer to set prices; this happens when environmental costs are not charged to the person or firm whose activity is causing the environmental damage.[22] In addition, people often do not perceive the links between their consumption of some commodity and the damage that is inflicted on the environment (or themselves) through the production or consumption of that commodity. The market therefore often fails to capture environmental information needed to make accurate value judgements.

According to environmental economists, the most fundamental reason for market failure is that many environmental costs and benefits simply cannot be 'captured' by the market because property rights are inadequately specified and it is not practical to assign property rights. In these cases, the resource is so large, or diffuse, or

---

[20] Above n 5.

[21] Lipsey above n 5; Samuelson above n 5.

[22] In the economics literature these costs are called 'spillover' or 'external' costs, because they spill over on to other members of society and are external to the accounting processes of the individual or firm creating the 'externality'.

unmanageable for some reason, that no one can exercise the rights of ownership completely enough to appropriate the full benefits from it.[23]

Another problem with using prices as indicators of value is that, contrary to a widely held tenet of economic theory, the consumer is not always rational. For example, misleading advertising can distort value judgements. In addition to creating 'wants' of dubious value, advertising is effective at exaggerating the benefits and hiding or discrediting the costs of consuming some good or service.

Still another shortcoming of market valuation is particularly relevant to the management of those environmental goods and services which may be approaching critical thresholds in their levels of availability or functioning: the price system works well only when consumption is not dramatically affecting the exchange opportunity available, but it begins breaking down when extreme disruptions in the supply of valued goods and services are imminent.

In all these cases prices do not constitute an accurate measure of value.[24] And in addition to these problems there are other difficulties in using money as a measuring rod of value. For example, we can expect demand and supply conditions to vary greatly over time, but it is impossible to forecast the conditions that will obtain for future generations. Therefore, while current price information (which is based on prevailing conditions and expectations) and present value calculations of the net benefit of a proposed resource use may be very useful in applying the efficiency test, these measures are not very helpful in applying the sustainability test. In fact, while free market forces do bring about more efficient use of privately owned resources, price information generated by the market does not serve to bring about a more equitable or sustainable use of these resources.

Economists are not completely happy with monetary measures of costs and benefits, but money has proved to be an extremely useful measuring rod for value of utility, and no other measuring rod has been found to be more acceptable. In fact, the classical theory of demand in economics was modified because it was determined that utility is essentially a psychological concept which is incapable of direct measurement in absolute units.[25]

While we may never have a fully satisfactory theoretical explanation of how utility might be measured, we should at least try to develop more practical and acceptable methods and techniques to improve on the way utility is now being measured. All too often in resource management, no formal or overt approach is taken to measuring the utility of unpriced costs and benefits, and what evaluations are done are purely subjective and not liable to public scrutiny. Because of this, the evaluation process tends to rely too heavily on what are considered 'objective measures' of value (eg, prices which emerge in the market) and outputs which cannot easily be measured in these terms are given little consideration.

So it is important to recognize that, while money has proved a useful measuring rod of value, it also has serious limitations; in addition, money need not be the only measuring rod for judging the utility of alternative uses of resources. Finally, the lack of a precise measuring rod is not essential to accomplishing a satisfactory evaluation. What *is* important is that:

- all costs and benefits are identified and explicit judgements made as to their relative value;
- all three evaluation criteria are systematically applied; and
- all concerned parties find the method of evaluation acceptable.

---

[23] In the economics literature this problem is due to what are called excessive 'transaction costs', because the costs of effecting transactions in order to appropriate the benefits of the resource are exorbitant.

[24] Common above n 6; Rees *Natural resources: allocation, economics and policy* (1985).

[25] Bannock, Baxter & Rees *The penguin dictionary of economics* (1978).

Thus, whatever measuring rod(s) and trade-off techniques are used, an evaluation method should be comprehensive in scope, systematic in approach and explicit in its appraisal of all the outcomes associated with alternative uses of resources.

3.3.3 Cost-benefit analysis

One of the most accepted and widely practised methods of resource evaluation is cost-benefit analysis.[26] Cost-benefit analysis is concerned with:

- identifying all the costs and all the benefits of a proposed resource use;
- measuring the value of each cost and benefit (and adjusting the value of future costs and benefits to reflect their present value); and
- adding the measured values to see whether the benefits outweigh the costs or vice versa.

If a proposed resource use has a net benefit, it is efficient; if it has a higher net benefit than an alternative resource use, it is more efficient than the alternative.

Cost-benefit analysis is conceptually simple and appealing, but in practice there are complications and difficulties. In particular, there have been two major criticisms of it:

First, *it is difficult to measure costs and benefits which are not normally expressed in monetary terms*. The result of this shortcoming is that resource managers have tended to be inordinately influenced by conventional monetary measures of the net benefit of a proposed resource use (i e, present discounted values[27] of those goods and services which can be priced by the market), while unpriced costs and benefits have been given relatively little weight.[28]

Secondly, although there have been a number of attempts to incorporate equity concerns into cost-benefit analysis (such as 'extended cost-benefit analysis'), no *truly satisfactory way has been found to compare and trade off distributional effects (either intragenerational or intergenerational) with efficiency effects*.[29] The result of this shortcoming is that resource managers seldom conduct a systematic or explicit trade-off between the efficiency, equity and sustainability effects when comparing alternative uses for resources, and there has been a tendency to approve a proposed resource use simply because it passes the efficiency test, even though it may fail either the equity or the sustainability test.

Environmental economics differs from other branches of economics primarily in that it focuses on finding acceptable ways (both in theoretical and in practical terms) to resolve these two problems.[30] As indicated earlier, there have been two challenges in extending the horizons of economics to make it more relevant to our new environmental circumstances:

The first challenge has been to develop techniques for measuring and comparing *all*

---

[26] Dohan above n 4; Gregory 'Economic analysis of environmental issues' in Lenihan & Fletcher *Environment and man* vol 10 *Economics of the environment* (1979); Pearce above n 18.

[27] In the economics literature 'discounting the future' refers to the fact that people tend to give a lower value to costs and benefits occurring in the future than to those occurring today. While conservationists have correctly pointed out that this practice generally discriminates against the interests of future generations, it is still rational and correct to employ discounting procedures in cost-benefit analysis. Conservationists are thus advised to treat resource allocation conflicts between generations as a *distributional* problem and not as an efficiency problem.

[28] Daly above n 4; Dohan above n 4; McAllister *Evaluation in environmental planning* (1980); Mishan above n 6; Page above n 4; Stauth above n 3.

[29] Biswas & Geping *Environmental impact assessment in developing countries* (1987); Goodin 'Discounting discounting' 1982 (2) *J of Public Policy* 53–71; Hardwick, Khan & Longmead *An introduction to modern economics* (2 ed, 1986); McAllister above n 28; Page above n 4; Pearce above n 18; Rees above n 24; Sharp *The economics of time* (1981).

[30] Herfindahl & Kneese above n 12; Stauth above nn 3, 16.

costs and benefits—priced and unpriced—which could result from a proposed resource use.

The second challenge has been to redefine the objectives of resource allocation to take explicit cognizance of the well-being of future generations and to develop techniques for applying and trading off the three evaluation criteria.

Unfortunately, little progress has yet been made with resolving the second problem—apart from pointing out the importance of tackling the trade-off problem in a systematic way that makes subjective value judgements explicit. To date more attention has been given to the first problem, at the heart of which lies the question: 'How can we measure the value of resources for which no reliable pricing mechanisms exist because they are common property?'

3.3.4 The problem of valuing common property resources

A major criticism of cost-benefit analysis has been the failure to give adequate consideration to evaluating environmental goods and services which cannot be traded in the market. For example, how does one place a value on things which are not held in exclusive ownership or exchanged between individuals, such as the waste-assimilation capacity of the atmosphere, radiation protection from the ozone layer, pleasure taken in the sight and sounds of wild birds, or the aesthetic and spiritual satisfactions provided by a wilderness area? Certain resources are owned in common, either because it is impractical to assign property rights to them or because we think it only right that they should belong to everyone. These resources are sometimes called 'common property resources'.[31]

The problem with common property resources is that, since no one 'owns' them, people tend to abuse them.[32] For example, the atmosphere and the ocean have become dumping grounds because individuals are not sufficiently motivated to protect them. This problem is sometimes referred to as 'the tragedy of the commons', after a paper which described the choices faced by a group of hypothetical herdsmen pasturing their cows in a common pasture. Hardin's thesis was that any time one of the herdsmen had the opportunity to put another cow onto the common, it would always be to his advantage to do so, even though it reduced the quality of the pasture for himself and the rest of the herdsmen.

The reason is that the individual herdsman would receive all the benefits from pasturing the extra cow (because it belonged exclusively to him) whereas he would bear only a fraction of the costs from the action (because the effects of the extra overgrazing would be spread over all the herdsmen). Hardin further pointed out that if all the herdsmen were to do this, then it would do no good for this herdsman to refrain from pasturing the extra cow: he would receive only a fraction of the benefits of this action but suffer the full cost of lost grazing to the extra cow, as well as 'his share' of the costs of overgrazing by cows owned by other herdsmen.

Many environmental 'goods' and 'services' have this 'common property' nature. Examples include whales, fisheries, rainforests, clean air, and atmospheric processes affecting rainfall, sea level and radiation levels. Environmental economists suggest that resources which have this common property characteristic are not used efficiently, and this is what gives rise to our environmental problems.

---

[31] In the economics literature a distinction is sometimes made between resources which are open to *all* groups (ie, there is 'open-access' to the resource), and those which are open only to a *single* group (ie, the group holds 'common property' rights to the resource). In this chapter the term 'common property resources' is used to refer to both categories since many resources which are under common ownership are also exploited by individuals as if there were open access.

[32] Coase 'The problem of social cost' 1960 *J of Law and Economics*; Hardin 'The tragedy of the commons' 1968 (162) *Science* 1243–8, 'Living on a lifeboat' in Hardin & Baden (eds) *Managing the commons* (1977).

Some economists feel that the solution to make more efficient use of common property resources is to grant individuals and groups property rights in these resources. The idea is that private and communal ownership would serve to reduce the external costs which result when individuals treat environmental resources as free goods. If transaction costs are not excessive, then legal ownership will result in more efficient utilization of resources and thus reduce pollution and over-exploitation to more acceptable levels.

While there appears to be some scope for the 'private property solution', in many cases there would be objections to assigning to a specific individual or group the right to use a resource which is now regarded as common property. In addition, transaction costs would often be excessive, so that this solution would not always be practicable. Finally, even if specifying property rights were to make resource use more efficient, it would not necessarily bring about a more equitable or sustainable use of the resource.

Because in many cases market mechanisms alone cannot ensure that common property resources will be used efficiently (much less in an equitable or sustainable way), it is necessary to establish other mechanisms for making people accountable for how they use them. One way to do this is to give the government authority for regulating these resources.

Just as the high transaction costs of the market bargain approach can result in 'market failure', the information and management costs of government intervention may sometimes exceed the benefits and result in 'government failure'. But in many cases, some form of government intervention is both possible and desirable to prevent dangerous levels of pollution or gross levels of over-exploitation.

To do a good job of managing common property resources, the government still needs to obtain value information in some way, and since market prices are either non-existent or unreliable for these resources, some other valuing mechanism must be employed. Environmental economists have developed a number of ways to estimate the value of costs and benefits for which no market values are available, and this has helped overcome some of the objections which environmentalists have had to cost-benefit analysis. The general approach to valuing unpriced goods is sometimes called 'shadow pricing'.

3.3.5 Shadow-pricing techniques

A 'shadow price' is an estimate of the value that a good or service would have if a market could be established for it. Several shadow-pricing techniques are discussed in the literature. *Indirect procedures* involve the calculation of 'dose-response' relationships between an environmental loss and the subsequent effect on human well-being. *Direct procedures* involve the search for preferences between competing environmental conditions, and the strength of those preferences, as revealed by surrogate markets or hypothetical markets.[33]

Different names are sometimes used for techniques which employ direct procedures. The four techniques discussed below have been called input valuation, output valuation, travel-cost valuation and contingent valuation.

3.3.5.1 *Input valuation*

This technique measures the value of some unpriced input to a system by calculating the changes to outputs of the system which are priced by the market.[34] For example, filling in a salt marsh would reduce inputs to an estuarine or marine fishery, which could reduce fish stocks. The market value of commercial fish can then be used to estimate at least part of the value of the salt marsh.

---

[33] Pearce & Turner above n 3.

[34] Dohan above n 4.

3.3.5.2 *Output valuation*

This measures the value of some unpriced output of a system by comparing market-based values of close substitutes.[35] For example, the costs of noise pollution from a proposed airport can be estimated by comparing the difference in market prices of homes in two communities which are similar in all meaningful respects except that one community is subjected to airport noise while the other is not.

3.3.5.3 *Travel-cost valuation*

This technique measures the value of an amenity by calculating the costs of travel and time to utilize that amenity.[36] For example, the recreation value of a dam can be estimated by surveying visitors to the dam and calculating the value of the time and other resources expended to enjoy that dam.

3.3.5.4 *Contingent valuation*

This measures the value of an unpriced good or service by asking people about their willingness to pay for the good or service.[37] For example, the value of a fynbos reserve can be estimated by using questionnaires or bidding games to establish a hypothetical market in which people can indicate their maximum willingness to pay for protection of the plant communities and other environmental goods and services associated with the reserve.

It is not always necessary to estimate the monetary value of specific resources to accomplish a satisfactory evaluation of alternative resource uses. Sometimes other techniques—which are not, strictly speaking, shadow-pricing techniques—can be used to obtain sufficient value information for making resource allocation decisions.

3.3.5.5 *Threshold valuation*

This is concerned with estimating what the value of specific goods or services would have to be to alter a resource management decision.[38] For example, if a proposed agricultural development would destroy a wetland and a cost-benefit analysis has indicated that the net value of the development is R50 m, then the question is whether the wetland values associated with the site exceed R50 m or not.

3.3.5.6 *Dynamic opportunity cost valuation*

This technique projects how conservation values might be expected to change over time relative to development values.[39] For example, if it is proposed to dam a wild and scenic river for hydroelectric power, it might be acceptable to forecast that the scarcity value of recreation, scenic and other conservation-related values associated with the river will increase over time relative to the scarcity value of hydroelectric power. This could happen if demand for wild and scenic rivers goes up as population increases and the number of unspoiled rivers decreases, while demand for hydroelectric power goes down as technological advances are made for other types of power generation.

3.3.5.7 *Panel valuation*

This involves having a group of respected persons undertake several iterations of an explicit weighting procedure for judging the relative significance of all the priced and

---

[35] Flowerdew 'Choosing a site for the third London airport: the Roshill Commission's approach' in Layard *Cost-benefit analysis* (1972).

[36] Farber 'The value of coastal wetlands for recreation: an application of travel cost and contingent valuation methodologies' 1988 (26) *J of Environmental Management* 299–312.

[37] Sinden & Worrell *Unpriced values: decision without market prices* (1979).

[38] Ibid.

[39] Krutilla, Cicchetti, Freeman & Russell 'Observations on the economics of irreplaceable assets' in Kneese & Bower (eds) *Environmental quality analysis* (1972).

unpriced costs and benefits of a proposed resource use.[40] For example, if it is proposed to allow mining in a national park, an unbiased panel (the composition of which has been approved by the principal interested parties) might be asked to rank, in order of significance, the costs and benefits of the proposed mine and then estimate how significant the lowest ranked cost/benefit is in comparison with every other cost and benefit.

3.4 METHODS FOR IMPLEMENTING A SOUND RESOURCE POLICY

A major responsibility of any national government is to formulate policies which are in the national interest and then to devise methods for implementing these policies effectively. When developing a resource policy, environmental and economic interests are intertwined. If the goal and evaluation criteria presented in this chapter were to be adopted in South Africa, then policy would be concerned with promoting the efficient, equitable and sustainable use of the nation's resources. This would benefit both the environment and the economy.

A particular policy challenge is the task of managing common property resources. One major problem is that private producers and consumers have historically had free and ready access to many common property resources and therefore people are reluctant to pay for or accept restricted access to these resources. For example, individuals and firms have long enjoyed the privilege of dumping pollutants into the atmosphere and no one wants to be prohibited from exercising this privilege or to have to pay for it.

Another problem is that common property resources are not always concentrated in easy-to-manage blocks; in addition, they are often found on private property or are adversely affected by lawful activities. For example, important waterfowl habitat is scattered over large areas and much of it occurs on private farms, where farmers have had the right to destroy wildlife habitat to raise crops or pasture livestock.

There are two general approaches to regulating economic and environmental behaviour in the use of resources: direct controls, and economic incentives.[41]

3.4.1 Direct controls

One approach to controlling environmental pollution and over-exploitation of resources is to set standards or prescribe certain actions. To control pollution, for example, the government can either set a permissible level of emissions (eg, *x* units per hour), or require certain devices to be used to minimize emissions (eg, install precipitators of *y* size). Or to control over-exploitation the government might regulate the mesh size of fishing nets or proclaim quotas for catches. While direct controls can be effective in implementing policy, there are several difficulties with this approach.

The government usually has inadequate information to establish cost-effective controls (the polluter or resource user is likely to have better information but is unlikely to provide accurate data). In addition, blanket regulations mandating specific control measures are inefficient as each case is different, and the most efficient action would vary from case to case; yet tailoring regulations to fit each case could be prohibitively costly. A related problem is that some individuals or firms may bear inordinate costs in complying with the regulations without any significant improvement to the environment; this could be judged to be both inefficient and inequitable.

Another major difficulty is that monitoring and enforcement of regulations can be expensive and unpopular tax increases may be necessary to fund adequate enforcement measures. Finally, if individuals or firms have to meet only certain standards or take

[40] Stauth above n 16.

[41] Dohan above n 4; Page above n 4; Pearce above n 3; Pearce & Turner above n 4; Stauth above n 3.

certain actions, they will not be motivated to conceive or initiate even more effective measures for reducing pollution or over-exploitation.

3.4.2 Economic incentives

Another approach to influencing environmental behaviour and promoting the economically efficient and equitable use of natural resources is the application of economic incentives.

Economic incentives attempt to correct market signals which lead to environmentally damaging activities, and have a number of advantages over the regulatory or command and control approaches referred to in the previous section.

Environmental degradation occurs because the private, rational use of natural resources by individuals is inconsistent with society's goals. This results because the 'systems guiding individual choices are distorted by informational, institutional or temporal parameters of the decision-making process'.[42] This means that socially non-optimal outcomes may arise because individuals lack information or knowledge as to the effects of their individual actions on the resource base now and in the future, and as to the spatial effects of their actions.

The rate-of-time preference guiding an individual's decisions is another issue affecting the use of natural resources. For example, a poor subsistence dweller will tend to exploit resources beyond their regenerative capacity to provide life support, because it is not rational to delay consumption. This problem is evidenced by the extent of deforestation, cultivation of steep slopes, overstocking of rangelands and the eradication of numerous species in South Africa's rural areas. As population pressures increase and rural poverty deepens, the rate-of-time preference narrows and environmental abuse is reinforced. In contrast, a successful commercial farmer has the capacity to conserve today in order to ensure continued production benefits in the future.

The institutional parameters which distort individual decisions include those relating to weaknesses of the market mechanism. Where access to natural resources is not circumscribed, where they are collectively consumed and where externalities occur, degradation of the resource will result unless there is some form of intervention to correct the market deficiency. The most efficient and equitable form of intervention in instances of market failure such as these is the application of economic incentives.

The advantages and disadvantages of using economic incentives in the pursuit of socially optimal environmental quality are best illustrated with an example of degradation resulting from a negative externality—an economic cost arising from one person's consumption or production activity and accruing to another party, without this cost being reflected in prices.

Take, for instance, a paper mill discharging its effluent into a stream at no cost to itself, but its activities imposing costs on downstream users. These external costs may relate to a fall in yields of an irrigation farmer; increased health costs of communities drinking the polluted water; or the degradation of a pristine environment that carries a cost in terms of future use.

The downstream costs may be many, varied and diffuse, and may often become evident only after a considerable time delay. They are therefore difficult to assess or calculate in monetary terms.

If the mill is not obliged to compensate the downstream users, it will not include these costs in its production calculations. If it is operating in a perfectly competitive environment, it will produce at the point where the selling price of its product equals the incremental cost of production—its marginal cost. But the costs it includes in its

[42] Costanza & Perrings 'A flexible assurance bonding system for improved environmental management' 1990 (2) *Ecological Economics* 57–75.

production calculations are those calculated entirely by the entrepreneur (ie his private costs) and include only those which accrue directly to him and within a limited time frame—ie the cost of labour, materials and capital within a particular financial year.

Costs that accrue to downstream users as a result of the mill's production and polluting activities are not reflected in its cost calculations. If the external costs could be returned to the mill, ie in terms of the polluter pays principle, its cost curve would reflect the full social costs of its actions, and its production and polluting activities would adjust to what is socially optimal.

In a very simple setting, with only the mill (the acting party) and the irrigation farmer (the affected party) involved, the costs associated with the farmer's lower yields can be shifted back to the polluter without the need for public sector involvement, if the farmer has the right to water of a specified quality. Once he has accurately assessed the damage, the farmer can then institute legal proceedings against, or negotiate with, the mill for compensation. This will act as an incentive for the mill to implement pollution control measures up to the point at which the cost of control equals the cost of the farmer's damages. Over and above this amount, it will pay the mill to compensate the farmer.

Though this appears to be a simple solution, certain complexities arise. If the farmer moved into the area knowing of the water-pollution problems, but taking advantage of the resultant lower property prices, his entitlement to compensation would be questionable. Secondly, not only the farmer but other downstream users also would suffer damage. The damage may be insufficient to warrant the institution of legal action by individuals—despite the extent of aggregate damages—and the transaction costs, relating to the organization of all affected parties, prohibitively high to file a class action suit.

In addition, the effects of environmentally damaging activity are often subtle and uncertain, yet the long-term or cumulative effects are notable. Not only is it difficult to assess the extent of the damages or external costs, but the information necessary to do this may not be available to the affected parties. Where unsophisticated communities are affected, the lack of resources and necessary information and high transaction costs associated with enforcing their rights, relative to those available to the mill, may lead to an inequitable outcome.[43]

Because of the numerous difficulties arising from individual attempts to apply and enforce the polluter pays principle, environmental protection agencies in many countries have sought alternative mechanisms to force producers and consumers to assume the full social costs of their actions and alter their polluting behaviour accordingly. Economic incentives, which lead to a convergence of private and social costs and therefore to socially optimal production decisions, appear to be the direction in which many countries are moving today. In many instances they operate in tandem with command-and-control approaches.

Economic incentives attach a cost—determined by the authorities or in the market—to polluting activity. This cost is related to damages suffered as a consequence of the externalities resulting from the acting party's activities and should result in environmental quality meeting the goals set by the environmental authorities.[44]

There are a number of different and innovative economic incentives suited to various situations, some of which will be discussed individually below.

---

[43] Portney (ed) *Public policies for environmental protection* (1990).

[44] Baskind *A reconciliation of conservation and development objectives in South Africa* (unpublished MComm thesis, Unisa, 1989).

3.4.2.1 *Pollution charges*

A pollution charge serves to attach a price to the previously free use of the natural resource as a sink for wastes, or to use of the resource in excess of regenerative capacity.

In the example outlined above, the environmental authority, acting as the agent for downstream users, would force the mill to take all costs associated with its production process into account by imposing a charge equal to the difference between the mill's marginal private costs (as calculated by the entrepreneur) and the marginal social costs of its production process (as calculated by the environmental authority). The intention is to internalize the negative externalities currently being borne by society. The mill will then consider the charge as a regular cost of production and will limit its discharges up to the point at which the cost of control equals the charge. Beyond this point, where the cost of control exceeds the charge, it is rational for the polluter to pay the charge.

Charges therefore have the advantage of being both equitable—the polluter pays—and economically efficient: control is achieved at the lowest cost to society, so freeing resources for other productive uses.

In contrast to regulation, where a certain amount of pollution is allowed and is 'free' up to the point at which the standard applies, a charge ensures that all pollution carries a price—the polluter pays for all damage that occurs. This is considered to be equitable.

Charges also lead to an economically more efficient outcome than do command-and-control approaches. Those polluters for whom the cost of control is lowest will be the first to limit their discharges, while those for whom the costs are greater—more than the charge—will elect to pay the charge. This ensures that a certain amount of control will be achieved at least cost to society, so freeing resources to satisfy other pressing needs in the country. Conversely, regulations interfere directly in the internal operations of the acting party. Control becomes mandatory and in some instances the necessary equipment is specified—there is no distinction in terms of the relative costs of control. The envisaged amount of control will therefore not be achieved at minimum cost to the society.

Charges allow the entrepreneur greater flexibility in his response than do regulations, and they provide a continuing incentive for control: all polluters, even those with minimal discharges, will continually attempt to limit the external damage they cause in order to reduce their cost burden. Regulations provide no incentive to reduce pollution beyond the legally required level.

The desire to minimize additional costs will also provide an incentive for technological advance. Regulations, and particularly those which specify control equipment, tend to lock the polluters into technologies which may not be the most effective or cost efficient, and the burden for technical advance reverts to the environmental authority, leading to an expansion of the environmental bureaucracy.

Once responses to the levying of the charge have been assessed, and if the required environmental quality goal is not being met, it is relatively routine and simple to raise the charge and allow polluters to make the appropriate adjustments. The payment of taxes is part of any economic unit's normal routine, and, since compliance is voluntary and needs only to be reinforced by random audits, administrative and monitoring costs are theoretically lower than where the regulatory approach is used.

The imposition of a charge may meet with political opposition from acting parties, since a previously 'free' activity now carries a cost. But, it may be welcomed by the affected parties and favoured by a financially constrained environmental control agency—the polluter pays for costs currently being borne by society and income is generated for, rather than expended by, the environmental authority.

In the United States, environmental policy and law continue to favour command-and-control approaches over incentive-based approaches. A number of European countries—France, the Netherlands, Sweden, Norway, Denmark, Italy and Germany—have adopted air and water pollution charges, but they act primarily as revenue-raising tools, and do not recover the full social cost as theoretically envisaged.[45]

3.4.2.2 *Subsidies*

Though the payment of a per unit subsidy by the environmental authority to the polluter for abatement theoretically leads to the same outcome as the imposition of a charge, it has certain disadvantages.

If the mill receives a subsidy for unit reductions in discharges, it will decrease pollution to the point where the cost of abatement equals the subsidy. After this point, it will prefer to pollute because the subsidy will be less than the cost of abatement.

But, where a subsidy is applied, it is necessary to establish a benchmark from which a reduction in damages can be estimated in order for payment to be made. In addition to administrative problems, this will discriminate against parties who have taken abatement action prior to the imposition of the subsidy, relative to those who have not. It may also provide an incentive to increase pollution levels prior to the subsidy's institution.

Secondly, a charge increases the acting parties' costs of production and influences the polluting industry's profitability. This will discourage entrepreneurs from entering into the environmentally damaging activity. Conversely, polluters will attempt to use the subsidy to maximize profits, so increasing the industry's profitability and attracting others into the polluting activity.

Finally, subsidies are generally financed from general taxation. This spreads the costs of abatement across all taxpayers, rather than returning it to the polluter, and utilizes scarce government funds for pollution control.[46]

3.4.2.3 *Marketable permits*

Another economic incentive available to circumvent problems relating to market and institutional failure is the marketable permit. The environmental authority determines the quality goal it wishes to achieve in terms of the assimilative capacity of the resource. This will be equivalent to that desired under a regulatory or charge system. It then makes permits available for the damage allowed in terms of its environmental goal. Because permits set a limit to allowable aggregate discharges, they are preferable to charges where the outcome is uncertain.

The initial allocation of permits to polluters is a thorny problem—equity and political issues need to be taken into consideration. The permits can be auctioned off, distributed according to existing regulatory permits—free or at some cost—or decided on some other basis. Each has its advantages and drawbacks. But, once the permits have been allocated, it is essential that they be fully tradeable and transferable so that an efficient market in the particular pollutant can be established.

The effects of marketable permits on the actions of the acting party, and hence on environmental quality, will be similar to that of an effluent charge. Those who can reduce their discharges cheaply—where the cost is less than the market price of the permit—will do so, and the environmental goal will be met at minimum cost to society. Marketable permits are therefore economically efficient, and they are equitable because the polluter pays for the damage he causes. In addition, permits offer a continuing incentive for abatement, while monitoring is relatively routine and automatic. Their effectiveness is not vulnerable to erosion through inflation—the market price will adjust accordingly—and they generate revenue for, rather than deplete the resources of, the environmental authority.

---

[45] *Project 88—Round II incentives for action: designing market-based environmetal strategies. A public policy study sponsored by senator Wirth and senator Heinz* (May 1991) Washington DC.

[46] Baskind above n 44.

Another advantage of the permit system is that it more closely mirrors the existing system than does a system of charges. But there may be serious political difficulties in establishing the market initially. Not only will a previously 'free' activity have a price attached, but the initial allocation of permits could prove controversial and meet with strong opposition from existing sources of pollution and potential new sources.

There is a danger that powerful individual polluters will buy up permits to capture and control the pollution market and limit competitive entrants into its product field. Innovative conditions may need to be attached to the permits to prevent this and to make provision for spatial and locational problems.[47]

Environmental policy in the United States has evolved, particularly in its approach to air pollution, away from the standard-and-permit approach towards a system of marketable permits.[48]

The emissions trading programme evolved from internal trading in terms of the netting programme (new sources of emissions within a plant can be offset by reducing emissions from another source within the plant) to an offset policy (whereby new sources of the pollutant are allowed in areas where the determined ambient standards have not been met. This is only if existing sources are reduced by even larger amounts). Offsets can be obtained from both internal and external trading. The so-called 'bubble' policy now allows sources within a designated area to aggregate emissions of a specific pollutant, so that the sum of the emissions does not exceed the legal limit. This policy also provides scope for internal and external trades. 'Banking' is another aspect of the emissions' trading programme. It allows polluters to bank emission reductions over and above what they currently require, for future use.[49]

The emissions trading approach is also being applied in the United States for automotive fuel, chlorofluorocarbon and sulphur dioxide control.[50]

Operational experience in the United States has highlighted limitations to the use of marketable permits as an efficient and equitable means of control. Cost savings relative to command-and-control approaches have been less than expected and trades, particularly external trades, have been limited.[51] This is both a function of the high transaction costs of external trades, the limited number of potential participants in some cases, and strategic behaviour to restrain competitors in others.

Though a system of marketable permits offers a possible solution to trade-offs between economic growth and the maintenance of environmental quality (once the limits of the environmental quality goal have been reached), its applicability for use in South Africa may be limited. The development of an efficient market—a function of the number of potential participants and trades occurring—is unlikely because of the relatively small size of the country's industrial and commercial sectors.

3.4.2.4 *Environmental bonds*

Environmental bonds as an instrument of control derive from the traditional refundable deposit or 'materials use fee'. These fees act as an incentive for individuals to dispose of environmentally damaging resources in a socially desirable way. For example, in South Africa, refunds available on some glass bottles attempt to encourage recycling rather than littering. The fee should be set at a level at which the bottle's return is profitable to the individual and the percentage rate of return is high. In

---

[47] Tietenberg *Emissions trading—an exercise in reforming pollution policy* (1985).
[48] Portney above n 43.
[49] Hahn 'Economic prescriptions for environmental problems: how the patient followed the doctor's orders' 1989 (3(2)) *J of Economic Perspectives* 95–114.
[50] *Project 88* above n 45.
[51] Hahn above n 49.

countries where there is widespread poverty, the necessary fee is likely to be lower than in First World countries.

It is important to note that the envisaged social costs of disposing of the bottle in a socially unacceptable way are paid for in advance by the consumer. The application of the 'materials use fee' could be expanded to encourage the socially optimal disposal of many other recyclable and hazardous containers in the hands of consumers, eg insecticide and pesticide containers, lead-acid batteries, motor-vehicle oil etc.

A number of states in the United States, provinces in Canada and European countries have enacted 'bottle bills' to control the littering that arises from beverage containers.[52]

In Sweden, a successful deposit-refund system operates for beer and soft drink cans. A company, Svenska Returpack AB, is responsible for developing, co-ordinating and administering the collection and deposit system. The value of the deposit has been adjusted to influence return rates, and in 1990 83,3 per cent of cans were returned. The aim is to reach a return rate of 90 per cent by 1993. The success of the system is ascribed, in part, to the smooth collection procedure.[53]

An environmental bond is a sophisticated version of the 'materials use fee'. Its use is recommended where the environmental effects of production or consumption activities are unknown or uncertain in advance and where environmental damage is extremely difficult to ascertain—where rational decisions are misguided by informational deficiencies. Where the effects are known and the risks can be calculated, commercial insurance against future environmental damage could be sought. Examples of potential use include the disposal of hazardous waste and the rehabilitation of opencast mines.

A bond, equal in value to the best estimate of potential environmental damage in the future, is posted by the acting party (the mine or the waste disposal company) with the authorities in an account ideally bearing a market-related interest rate.[54] The bond, plus interest, will be repayable if the acting party provides proof that the potential environmental damage has not occurred. In the event of damage occurring, the bond would provide the finance for restoration and possible compensation of affected parties—the polluter pays principle will apply.

The bond also provides an incentive for the private sector to develop innovative and cost-effective technologies, and to discover the true social costs applicable to their various operational options (thus influencing the potential value of the bond).[55]

The desirability of using this approach for the rehabilitation of mining sites is currently being debated in South Africa. The new Minerals Act 50 of 1991 makes provision for the submission of rehabilitation programmes and the rehabilitation of all mines. The posting of environmental bonds is to be negotiated between the Chamber of Mines and the office of the Mining Engineer (Department of Mineral and Energy Affairs) in 1992.

If this approach had been adopted in the past, it is likely that the cost of controlling pollution from abandoned coal mines in the eastern Transvaal highveld could have been recovered from the polluters via bonds posted by them prior to potentially polluting activities taking place, rather than at the taxpayers' expense.

3.4.2.5 *Compensation*

Although economic incentives have been shown, in terms of equity and efficiency and in other respects, to be preferable to regulation and public sector provision, they are

[52] Portney above n 43.

[53] Andersson Paper presented to the ad hoc review meeting on bauxite UNCTAD 13–17 May 1990 (1991).

[54] Perring 'Environmental bonds and environmental research in innovative activities' 1989 (1) *Ecological Economics* 95–110.

[55] Costanza & Perrings above n 42.

often perceived to place an unfair burden on poor communities. The imposition of a charge or other form of economic incentive will increase the cost of production of the economic unit for any quantity of product produced and consequently narrow the available profit margin. Depending on market circumstances, this profit decline will either be absorbed by the entrepreneurs or shareholders or will be recouped via a price increase to consumers, some of whom are poor. (The cost of installing and operating equipment to meet regulatory requirements will similarly be passed on to consumers, but because the effects are piecemeal they are not perceived to be as onerous.) This is not seen as undesirable from an allocative perspective, since the higher price should cause consumption of the environmentally damaging product to decline to a level that would benefit the environmental health of the society as a whole.

In addition to equity considerations relating to the poor, a move towards economic incentives may also generate another set of losers: eg if a charge on sulphur dioxide emissions leads to a fall in the demand for high-sulphur coal, affected miners will lose their jobs.

In both instances, where cost-effective economic incentives are implemented which adversely affect some members of society, the payment of compensation may be advisable for reasons of social equity and political expediency. But the amount of compensation and the manner in which it is paid can be complex. First, a baseline is needed against which damage inflicted—ie the amount of harm occurring as a result of a change from no policy, or regulation, to the alternative approach—can be assessed. The loss as a result of the policy change then needs to be quantified.

Monetary compensation is thought to be the best option in terms of economic efficiency, but it is usually extremely difficult to place an accurate monetary value on damage suffered. This means also provides individuals with a profit-maximizing opportunity to misrepresent their claims and discourages them from taking appropriate evasive action.[56]

An alternative to monetary compensation is 'linked compensation', where the form of compensation relates directly to the type of damage suffered. For example, if the price of electricity rises due to the imposition of an effluent charge, compensation could be provided to poor communities via a deduction on their electricity bills. This should not entail a substantial financial burden in South Africa, since poor communities use less than 5 per cent of electricity consumed.

3.4.2.6 *Benefits*

The use of economic incentives to redirect individual choices distorted by institutional, informational or temporal deficiencies appears, in theory, to be superior to control by regulation. Such incentives act as an encouragement for point-source polluters to move towards a more equitable allocation of the costs of environmental damage, in that the polluter pays for not only his private costs but also the social costs of damage caused as a result of his actions. They also result in an economically efficient outcome: the predetermined environmental goal is achieved at the least cost to society, so freeing resources for other productive uses in the economy.

The efficiency aspect is of particular importance in South Africa, where socio-political priorities will increasingly be directed towards visible public-sector goods, such as health and basic infrastructure.[57] Environmental control should not be seen as a trade-off against the achievement of these goals. Nor should social equity be compromised by the poor bearing the financial burden of control.

---

[56] Burtraw 'Compensating losers when cost-effective environmental policies are adopted' 1991 (104) *Resources* 1–5.

[57] Mckenzie *Policy, politics and soil conservation in the agricultural sector* Paper presented at EPPIC World Environment Day Symposium, June 1991.

Where society perceives that the poor will be unfairly affected, the payment of compensation is possible. But because, on the whole, the poor account for a relatively small proportion of the consumption of polluting goods, this should not place an undue burden on the fiscus, nor should it exceed the benefits of control. Compensation can be offset against income generated through the imposition of the economic incentive.

Economic incentives also tend to be less demanding in terms of the need for monitoring and enforcement mechanisms. This is an important advantage, since institutional problems severely limit the effectiveness of existing policy, and it is desirable to prevent an explosion of administrators in the future. But lean and mean monitoring and enforcement systems are essential for the success of any policy.

It is important to note that most areas in which economic incentives are applicable are limited to those areas where the sources of pollution or degradation are easily identifiable and where monitoring and control are practical and financially feasible.[58] In addition, there must be a tax base or financial resources available in the community to which the legislation applies.

This limits the application of economic incentives to point sources of pollution or utilization in the industrial and commercial sector. Charges, marketable permits or environmental bonds therefore cannot be used to control problems of over-exploitation of natural resources in poor rural areas. Despite their many drawbacks, subsidies could be applied in specific instances where monitoring is possible and materials use fees may be effective for waste.

The political will to implement a specific policy, in the face of strong opposition from well-organized lobby groups and apathy on the part of the general public, is also crucial to its success.[59]

In addition to policy, government and non-government organizations can, through a process of education, influence citizens to consider the long-term health of the environment in their decision-making processes. The objective should be to replace apathy with a heightened awareness of the natural resource base and the development of an environmental ethic in terms of which the current decisions of producers and consumers do not preclude the options of future generations to meet their needs and improve the quality of their lives.

3.4.3 Making the 'big trade-off'

As mentioned earlier, no generally accepted formal procedure has yet been found for making trade-offs between the often conflicting objectives of efficiency, equity and sustainability. But this should not discourage decision-makers from adopting some systematic approach to accomplishing this trade-off in a way that ensures that all judgements will be made clear and explicit. For example, one possible approach is simply to:

- list the efficiency gains of alternative uses of resources against their distributional consequences and their perceived potential for sustained utilization of resources;
- scrutinize the specific trade-offs involved (preferably using some formal procedure designed to make the process comprehensive, systematic and explicit); and
- produce a clear statement of specific arguments justifying selection of the preferred alternative in terms of the evaluation criteria.

The lack of an objective, universally acclaimed procedure for making this important trade-off has made it difficult to persuade decision-makers to give adequate attention to

---

[58] Xapapadeas 'Environmental policy under imperfect information: incentives and moral hazard' *J of Environmental Economics and Management* 113–26.

[59] Cumberland 'Public choices and the improvement of policy instruments for environmental management' 1990 (2) *Ecological Economics* 142–62.

this task.[60] Historically, managers of resources have been primarily concerned with making the use of resources more efficient and most economists have tended to agree that efficiency should be given the highest priority. The result has been that decision-makers have tended to turn a deaf ear to concern that resources are being used in a way that is either inequitable or unsustainable.

For example, if a sociologist complained about the inequitable distribution of a project's costs and benefits, the decision-maker was likely to say that this was a political problem which could be taken care of by tax and transfer. It was also usually argued that the extra benefits from more efficient uses of resources would eventually 'trickle down' to the disadvantaged and that this would preclude the need to take extreme (and possibly inefficient) redistribution measures to redress any inequities.

If an ecologist complained that a particular use of a resource might not be sustainable, the decision-maker was likely to say that if a resource was lost some substitute would eventually be found or created, and in any case we have to be more concerned about solving today's pressing problems, so that to some extent we must let future generations look after themselves. It was also generally argued that just by looking after ourselves we would be looking after future generations too, because progress for us would surely be progress for them.

All these arguments seemed particularly appropriate for addressing the situation in developing countries such as South Africa. The desperate poverty and underdevelopment in the Third World seemed to call for radical new approaches to resource management, relying on highly sophisticated, imported technology to increase the efficiency of production.[61] The thinking was that only rapid improvements in efficiency could bring Third World countries to the 'take-off' stage of development, and that by increasing the pie you would be able to give every individual a larger piece. As for future generations, it seemed axiomatic that stronger economies would always make it easier to provide for future needs.

In recent years, however, it has been recognized that technology can fail and that, when environmental costs are taken into account, seemingly efficient projects often turn out to be grossly inefficient. But in addition there has been a growing realization that the warnings about inequitable and unsustainable development are more serious than many people used to think.

In many countries in the world, particularly in Africa, the poor are getting poorer—either in relative or absolute terms (or both)—and despite considerable development aid, there has been increasing suffering and instability.[62] More recently still (and more ominously), regional and even global ecosystems have begun showing signs of serious damage, bringing into question the efficacy of technological and market solutions in solving environmental problems.[63]

In these new environmental circumstances—in which the magnitude and speed of biophysical and socio-economic change are unprecedented and still accelerating—market and political mechanisms may prove incapable of coping with the complexities of environmental realities. It is also possible that technological solutions may be developed too late to maintain environmental quality at a reasonable cost, or even to prevent catastrophic consequences.

These considerations have put the 'economic problem'—the problem of scarcity—in a new light: it has become a 'moral problem'. In the present situation, the most significant thing about the concept of scarcity is not that an individual must choose to

---

[60] Herfindahl & Kneese above n 12; Page above n 4; Stauth above n 3.

[61] Rostow *The stages of economic growth* (2 ed, 1971).

[62] *The global 2000 report to the President* above n 4.

[63] Clark above n 4; Fisher & Krutilla above n 6; *The global 2000 report to the President* above n 4; *Our common future* above n 4.

have less of one thing in order to have more of another, but that he must also choose how much he is to have relative to what others have, both now and in the future.

There has always been a moral dimension to the economic problem, but for a long time economists avoided subjectivity and claimed to have developed an objective, 'value-free' science. And so early economists insisted that efficiency was the only test that was relevant to economic analysis.

Now most economists agree that true economic development (and therefore economic analysis) must be guided by subjectively determined guidelines and that we have now entered an era in which efficiency considerations should not dominate the management of resources as they did in the past.[64] First, welfare economists suggested that in addition to being efficient, true economic development must also be broad-based—i e, must serve to reduce the dangerous maldistribution of wealth and income.[65] Then environmental economists suggested that true economic development must also be stable and continuous over very long time horizons—i e, must increase the prospect that social progress will be sustainable and that future generations will be left with the means to enjoy a secure and satisfying existence.[66]

Yet because individuals have different values and different visions of the future, there is still no universally acceptable way to make the big trade-off between efficiency, equity and sustainability. The weight given to equity, for example, depends partly on perceptions of the extent of relative deprivation and partly on how much compassion is felt by those who are now better off for those who are now worse off. The weight given to sustainability depends on our concern for future generations, which in turn depends largely on highly problematic estimates of the circumstances attending future conditions, such as judgements concerning the efficacy of technology, the resilience of the biosphere, the tastes and preferences of the unborn, and the degree of risk associated with present development activities.

But while there will always be disagreement about these things, in recent years mankind's growing environmental predicament (which encompasses a plethora of social, economic and ecological problems) has led many observers to conclude that it is now time to give greater attention to the pursuit of equity and sustainability. For example, observers such as Wilson[67] and Kane-Berman[68] have suggested that historically recent developments in the economic, social and political circumstances of many countries now dictate that it is in the self-interest of the dominant groups in every society to give more attention to the needs of the less dominant or disadvantaged groups. Equitable development is thus becoming more important relative to efficient development.

At the same time other observers have pointed to the growing evidence of damage to regional and global ecosystems, as well as extensive losses to stocks of renewable resources, which has persuaded many managers of resources around the world to give more attention to the problem of meeting the needs of future generations.[69] Sustainable development is therefore also becoming more important relative to efficient development.

3.5 SUMMARY AND DISCUSSION

3.5.1 Adopting a rational approach to meeting economic and environmental needs

Environmental economics offers a way of thinking about environmental and

[64] Daly above n 4; Rees above n 24.

[65] Lutz & Lux above n 14; Page above n 4.

[66] Herfindahl & Kneese above n 12; Mishan *An introduction to normative economics* (1981); Page above n 4; Stauth above n 3, n 16.

[67] *On human nature* (1978).

[68] *South Africa's silent revolution* (1990).

[69] Allen above n 4; Clark above n 4; *World conservation strategy* above n 4; *Our common future* above n 4.

economic problems that is more appropriate to the realities of the late 20th century than was the thinking which gave rise to neo-classical economics in the late 19th century. This new discipline is also concerned with developing a more practical guide to action which has been a great strength of economic philosophy. In particular, techniques have been developed for (1) estimating the value of unpriced goods and services, and (2) systematically and explicitly addressing the distributional implications of economic activity over time horizons spanning many generations. This way of thinking and guide to action is based on the formulation of clearly stated premises, a carefully defined goal and a comprehensive set of evaluation criteria all of which are in themselves relatively non-contentious.

There are still formidable difficulties in applying evaluation criteria. While more reliable and cost-effective procedures are needed for judging the relative value of unlike goods and services, the major challenge in environmental economics is to develop more acceptable ways of analysing and evaluating the trade-offs between three important criteria for determining whether a proposed use of resources should be adopted. It no longer seems reasonable to pursue efficiency slavishly while ignoring considerations of equity and sustainability; yet many decision-makers have not yet changed their approach and, very often, not enough thought is given to the degree of deprivation and risk imposed on disadvantaged groups and future generations.

Although economic activity has, since the Industrial Revolution, given rise to great prosperity in many parts of the world, it has in more recent times also given rise to environmental damage and risks of great regional and global significance. Examples are acid rain, the destruction of the ozone layer, the widespread loss of species and major ecosystems, and changes in weather patterns and possible rises in sea-level due to the 'greenhouse effect'.[70] It is conceivable that, for the first time in the history of humankind, economic activity could now have environmental impacts which pass critical thresholds necessary to the continued provision of certain ecological processes and natural amenities needed to attain a satisfactory quality of life for the present generation, and to maintain that quality of life for future generations.

3.5.2 The situation in the 'New South Africa'

With apartheid behind us in South Africa, it is to be hoped that racial and cultural differences will no longer constitute such a formidable barrier to economic development. Nevertheless, there are still great structural impediments to progress which are linked to disparities in the socio-economic circumstances of different groups in society. These disparities—in education, skills, health, housing and a host of other factors—are in turn linked to poverty.

With the battle against apartheid won, the next must be against poverty. This battle will be won only if we are successful on two fronts: there must be political stability and economic development. These are of equal importance and must be pursued simultaneously because they are interlinked: political stability will be maintained only if there is economic development, and economic development can occur only if there is political stability.

Historically, most conservationists have been more concerned with curbing the excessive consumption which has been associated with affluence than with promoting economic development to alleviate the pressure on resources which has been associated with poverty. Conservationists have therefore been inclined to promote their objectives with tools such as education and regulation. But the excesses of the relatively affluent are more amenable to these treatments, and in the long run this sector of society

[70] Clark above n 4.

presents fewer risks to sustainable development since wealth creation provides the means (as well as the motivation) for environmental protection.[71]

The situation is different with the excesses of the relatively impoverished sector of society. With this group conservationists have tended to stress population control as the way to alleviate poverty, and thereby reduce environmental degradation, rather than economic growth or redistribution. But while efforts to reduce population growth (of all socio-economic groups) can certainly help reduce environmental deterioration, the alleviation of poverty is perhaps even more important: it can reduce environmental deterioration directly, by reducing pressure on critical resources exploited by the poor, as well as indirectly by reducing the high population growth rate which is correlated with poverty. It is often stated that people are a resource, and this is true; but people can be either an asset or a liability, depending on whether or not they are properly prepared to play a productive role in society. The elimination of poverty is at least as important as population control in solving our environmental and economic problems.

3.5.3 Conclusion

The great environmental and economic tasks facing South African policy-makers in the nineties and beyond are to:

- control the exploitation of common property resources,
- adopt an effective population policy,
- develop instruments for accomplishing an equitable distribution of income and wealth,
- identify levels of maximum sustained yield for renewable resources, and
- calculate optimum depletion rates over time for non-renewable resources.

The situation now facing 'Spaceship Earth'[72] should give resource managers cause to consider whether there should not now be much greater weight given to the equity and sustainability tests. The new environmental and moral dimensions of resource management have led some to suggest that the conventional ordering of the three tests should now be reversed.[73]

First and foremost, since social progress can and should be sustainable, *one should always require that a proposed action does not violate the sustainability test*.[74] One potentially valuable approach would be to adopt a 'shadow project policy' under which projects which could reduce renewable resources below some minimum level must be accompanied by a shadow project which either restores the resources to their original condition or else recreates them (or suitable substitutes) elsewhere.[75]

Secondly, since poverty and injustice are morally offensive and politically dangerous, *the next consideration should be to ensure that the proposed action serves to close (or at least that it does not widen) the 'income gap'*.[76] Some economists have suggested that, rather than trying to 'maximize welfare', economic development should be directed at 'minimizing illfare'—the idea being to improve human welfare in ways that maintain environmental capital, and achieve an acceptable state of social well-being with a sustainable flow of resources.[77]

Finally, since ultimately the only way that a growing and substantially impoverished world population can ever attain a reasonable standard of living for all is by increasing

---

[71] Beckerman above n 6; Seneca & Taussig above n 6.
[72] Boulding above n 4.
[73] Herfindahl & Kneese above n 12; Stauth above n 16.
[74] Allen above n 4; Hardin above n 15; *World conservation strategy* above n 4; Mishan above n 66.
[75] Page above n 4; Pearce above n 3.
[76] Daly above n 4; Lutz & Lux above n 14.
[77] Boulding above n 4; Herfindahl & Kneese above n 12; Juster 'Alternatives to GNP as a measure of economic progress' in *US economic growth from 1976 to 1986* (1977).

the benefits that can be obtained from our limited resources, *no proposed resource use should be accepted which cannot pass the efficiency test* and every effort should be made to maximize the net benefits from resource use. But what is of most importance here is to encourage the efficient production of goods and services which meet real, biologically determined needs.[78]

Not all environmental economists would agree with this ordering and there is still considerable debate about the relative importance of efficiency, equity and sustainability. But there *is* widespread agreement that humankind is entering a new era characterized by unprecedented dangers as well as opportunities. When decision-makers evaluate proposed uses of resources and consider the overall effect in terms of the three tests, they must take adequate cognizance of the rapidly changing environmental circumstances.

[78] Maslow above n 11; Mishan above n 6.

CHAPTER 4

SOCIO-POLITICAL FACTORS

T HART

4.1 INTRODUCTION

It is clear that environmental management is gaining importance on socio-political agendas all over the world. A powerful demonstration of this is the United Nations Conference on Environment and Development (UNCED) held in Rio de Janeiro in June 1992 which drew representatives from governments worldwide, together with an unprecedented array of non-government organizations (NGOs) and interest groups.[1] Despite the growing recognition of a broad environmental management imperative, however, it is incorrect to imagine that countries and groups within countries necessarily agree on environmental priorities, let alone the nature and implementation of systems of environmental management. Indeed, since management of the environment has to do with relationships, resources and power, it is likely to be highly contested in specific contexts.[2]

The issues that are contested will vary in place and time, but environmental management priorities will sometimes be weighted differently across one or several of the following social, economic and political divides: rich vs poor; urban vs rural; market vs central regulation; government vs business; power elites vs the masses; centre vs regions and local areas; men vs women.[3] Reflecting this, it is inevitable that institutions for environmental management will have divergent and sometimes contradictory agendas. They will draw upon a range of support bases and will enjoy varying levels of legitimacy in their spheres of influence. They will also differ according to their broader affiliations (if any), among which may be political movements, conservation bodies and business alliances.

Against this background, it is essential to make two key points. The first is that the environment and environmental management are not neutral. The second is that environmental management is bound to have to engage the many social and political issues that are salient globally, across regions, within individual countries and among national sub-populations.

4.2 ENVIRONMENTAL MANAGEMENT AS A SOCIO-POLITICAL ISSUE

In line with other parts of the world, the environment is moving closer to the centre of the socio-political stage in South Africa. Evidence of this is the recently released *Report of the three committees of the President's Council on a national environmental*

* Much of the Third World environmental literature used in this chapter was assembled by professor Chris Rogerson as part of a broader Urban Foundation monitoring project.

[1] *Earth summit in focus* United Nations (1991).

[2] Recent publications on Amazonia illustrate the diversity of struggles over the control of environmental resources. These range from local confrontations between rubber tappers and lumberjacks to tension between international environmental interests and governments with Amazonian jurisdiction. See Allen 'Amazonia 1990: the burning question' 1990 (12) *Third World Quarterly* 229–35.

[3] Examples of some of these divisions are to be found in the Amazonia debate. See n 2 above. Many of the satellite meetings timed to coincide with UNCED demonstrate the nature and diversity of special environmental interest groups. Topics include women and the environment, indigenous people and the environment, north–south policy dialogue, and industry and the environment. See *The '92 global forum* International Facilitating Committee (1991).

management system,[4] and the publication of environmental policy statements by major extra-parliamentary political actors such as the African National Congress (ANC), the Pan Africanist Congress (PAC) and the Inkatha Freedom Party (IFP).[5] In addition, popular organization around issues of the environment is becoming more frequent and activist NGOs and issue-based lobby groups are joining the already varied but more conservative ranks of South African non-government environmental organizations.[6]

But as environmental management becomes the focus of increased social and political mobilization, divergent positions become more apparent. For example, the President's Council was given the brief of developing a policy for a national environmental management system. In practice, there is a striking absence of black viewpoints in the oral and written evidence collected in support of the report. This is not to imply that such viewpoints were not welcome, but it does suggest that the council or its environmental brief were evaluated differently by different sections of South African society.

As they stand, the council's policy report and the environmental policy positions of the ANC, the PAC and NEAC[7] (an NGO with ANC connections) show key differences of emphasis, some of which presage important areas of national environmental debate. For example, in contrast to the President's Council, the ANC, PAC and NEAC place considerable emphasis on the political and environmental legacy of apartheid, with the PAC going as far as to claim that a precondition for environmental management is the abolition of the structures that supported apartheid, and the 'democratization' of South African society.[8] Other differences relate to the treatment of population–resources relationships, the interpretation of environmental issues related to land, and the relative importance accorded urban environments. Each of these is discussed in greater detail later in this chapter.

4.3 DIVISION AND RECONCILIATION

South Africa is similar to many other countries in terms of the growing social and political importance of environmental matters. However, it is different in the sense that heightened environmental concern coincides with a period of social and political transition. This process of transition has a number of consequences for environmental management.

First, it is now difficult for the government to introduce new policy unilaterally. The recent decision to postpone proposed rural development legislation in the face of a broad front of opposition suggests that the State is unwilling to risk major confrontation while constitutional negotiations are in progress. The implementation of the President's Council's recommendations has been delayed subject to public input, and it is likely that the government will be sensitive to the weight of opinion before taking action.

Secondly, the broad political debate engendered by the transition process has served to draw divergent environmental viewpoints into the open. Further, key environmental issues have been raised in the context of broader constitutional deliberations—for

---

[4] PC 1/1991.

[5] See Sisulu & Sangweni 'Future environmental policy for a changing South Africa: ANC discussion paper' in *History in the making* (1991) 37–45. Desai 'An environmental policy for the Pan Africanist Congress of Azania' in *History in the making* (1991) 46–9; Inkatha Freedom Party 'Environmental policy of the Inkatha Freedom Party' in *History in the making* (1991) 50–2.

[6] For example, Earthlife Africa, the Society Against Nuclear Energy and the Dolphin Action and Protection Group.

[7] National Environmental Awareness Campaign (NEAC) 'Position Paper 1990' *History in the making* (1991) 33–7.

[8] Desai above n 5.

example, as diverse interests examine and discuss the notion of third-generation human rights and an environmental code of ethics.[9]

A third feature of transition and more particularly of the period leading up to political negotiation is the erosion of management systems, some of which have important environmental responsibilities. An environmental setback that is not widely recognized is the collapse of local government in many parts of the country. This collapse has roots in apartheid urban policy, but in many areas an outcome has been the disruption of essential services, the breakdown of the provision of housing, and a serious decline in the quality of urban environments.[10]

Against this background, the current period of socio-political transformation signals uncertainty for environmental management, but it also offers a unique opportunity to address divergent environmental agendas and to develop management systems that enjoy the broadest possible support and legitimacy. In this sense, the environment has the potential to act as a force for conciliation.[11] However, given the historic race and class biases that have divided environmental opinion in the past, the environment also has the potential to be the last frontier of the old order.

4.4 KEY ISSUES FOR THE 1990s

Through the transitionary period and beyond, several challenging and durable themes are likely to remain at the focus of environmental management in South Africa. Some of these are:

1. Population and resources.
2. Land distribution and management.
3. Urbanization and cities.
4. Management institutions.

Of course, these challenges are not uniquely South African,[12] but the sections that follow will seek to illustrate their particular salience in the contemporary social and political milieu.

4.5 POPULATION AND RESOURCES

Human population growth and absolute numbers are often seen to be the most fundamental threat to sustained development and the environment. This view is expressed by the President's Council, which holds that 'the rapid increase in population in South Africa is indisputably the biggest threat to the environment'.[13] Several other influential commentators on the South African environment concur.[14] The relationship between population and resources in the environment is complex, however, and statements implying overpopulation have to be very carefully considered.

Internationally, the population issue became highly contentious in the 1960s and 1970s, following population programmes initiated by the World Health Organization and other major agencies. In essence, the charge was that such programmes displayed a fundamental class bias, in terms of which rich, developed countries sought to solve

---

[9] Glazewski 'The environment, human rights and a new South African constitution' 1991 *SAJHR* 167–84.

[10] Lawson 'The ghetto and the greenbelt: the environmental crisis in the urban areas' in Cock & Koch *Going green* (1991) 46–63.

[11] Several authors discuss aspects of conciliation and the environment. See Khan 'Beyond the white rhino: confronting the South African land question' 1990 (44) *African Wildlife* 321–4; Koch 'Rainbow alliances: community struggles around ecological problems' in Cock & Koch above n 10, 20–32.

[12] The well-known World Commission on Environment and Development report *Our common future* (1987) lists similar areas of environmental challenge.

[13] Report of the President's Council above n 4, para 2.1.1.

[14] For example, Huntley, Siegfried & Sunter *South African environments into the 21st century* (1989).

population–resource issues elsewhere, whilst failing to address their own excessive resource consumption and waste production.[15]

In South Africa, similar criticisms have been directed at population programmes.[16] It is beyond the ambit of this chapter to discuss the merits and demerits of so-called 'population development'. However, it is important that environmental managers should recognize the extent to which population matters are emotionally and politically charged. Suspicion of the motives of population 'management' protagonists should come as no surprise, given South Africa's recent history of social engineering on a massive scale and its manipulation of access to basic environmental resources such as land.

Many countries like South Africa have strategies to deal with population growth.[17] It is now fairly widely accepted that economic upliftment, access to economic opportunity, and improvement of the quality of life are a route to population stabilization. However, South Africa will probably have to go further if a nationally accepted population programme is envisaged. If a well-meaning programme to reduce population growth is seen to divert attention from the highly skewed distribution of resources such as land, it will fail to win broad political support.

It may well be that political and social consensus is possible on the question of population management. However, it is critical to recognize the divergent priorities and the circumstances that underpin them. From a conservative environmental position, the management of resource use and environmental impact are central. However, from the perspective of material and political disadvantage, improved living and working conditions and access to resources and the systems that mediate their distribution are often the environmental priorities.

An international literature on 'environments of poverty' has begun stressing that poverty often determines the manner in which people relate to and experience the environment.[18] It is argued that the poor often feel the effects of resource depletion and environmental degradation more acutely than others, but that they have no political and economic power to change this situation. In many cities, for example, the poor are forced to seek shelter on marginal, unsafe and environmentally vulnerable land, with limited or no access to waste disposal systems and purified piped water. In addition, the poor often pay more for fuel and water, often despite the fact that the latter has been drawn from a contaminated source.

Urban and rural environments of poverty have been documented in South Africa,[19] but their implications have yet to be seriously considered in mainstream environmental management literature. The point is that these are the 'real' environments for a significant number of South Africans. Population and other broad environmentally motivated progammes must seem remote and other-worldly, and will remain so while the poor have little power to deal with their immediate environmental circumstances. Of course, the poor are powerless in many parts of the world, but Third World research suggests that their local socio-environmental interests are best served when government is accountable to them.[20] Hence it can be argued that representative democracy is a

---

[15] The political dimension of the population–resources debate is discussed by Harvey in his paper 'Population, resources and the ideology of science' 1974 (50) *Economic Geography* 256–77.

[16] Klugman 'Victims or villains: overpopulation and environmental degradation' in Cock & Koch above n 10, 66–77.

[17] The World Bank *World development report* (1984) focuses on population issues and programmes.

[18] See the work of Hardoy & Satterthwaite *Squatter citizen: life in the urban Third World* (1989) and 'Third World cities and the environment of poverty' 1984 (15) *Geoforum* 307–33.

[19] Most notably in the context of the second Carnegie enquiry into poverty and development in southern Africa. See Wilson & Ramphele *Uprooting poverty: the South African challenge* (1989).

[20] Handelman 'The role of the State in sheltering the urban poor' in Patten *Spontaneous shelter: international perspectives and prospects* (1988) 326–47.

foundation for sound environmental management, a point which has been made with reference to South Africa.[21]

It is possible to draw a broad spectrum of South Africans into serious discussion around a national population strategy. However, such a discussion will have to deal with underlying questions of socio-economic and political disadvantage and the manner in which these remain entrenched. It will also have to deal with historically etched perceptions of past population-related policies and the motives of those who designed them.

4.6 LAND DISTRIBUTION AND MANAGEMENT

Of the many resource issues that confront environmental managers in South Africa, land is probably the most emotionally and politically charged. While recent environmental policy statements show a strong and shared concern for the non-sustainable utilization of land and the degradation of the soil, they differ widely in the prominence and centrality they ascribe to historic conflicts over land.

On the one hand, the President's Council deals with the diverse facets of land management in some detail, but it gives proportionately little attention to the legislation that has imposed racial criteria on land-use, or to the political, social and environmental consequences of such fundamental resource manipulation. In fairness, the President's Council does call for broad participation in future land-use planning, and it endorses the principle that 'land as a basic resource will be available to all South Africa's inhabitants'.[22]

By contrast, statements by some extra-parliamentary groups place the resolution of historic land conflicts at the hub of environmental management policy. Expressing this, NEAC asserts:

> 'We question those whose concern for the environment focuses on saving various species of animals from extinction or preserving small areas of land for game parks patronized mainly by whites whose financial status enables them to enjoy nature in its natural state. None of these groups has seen fit to question the government's land policies which have impoverished land and forced people of colour to live in degrading living conditions'.[23]

In similar vein, the PAC evokes some of the deep political and cultural symbolism of land when they speak of the 'spiritual and physical alienation of blacks from the environment' as a consequence of land policy and dispossession.[24] In the opinion of a commentator on politics and the environment, this alienation is a fundamental determinant of contemporary black attitudes to the environment.[25]

Hence, against the background of a widely held concern with the deterioration of land-linked resources in South Africa, managers seeking to broaden consensus around management issues will have to contribute constructively to the swelling land redistribution and land reform debate. But this must be done recognizing that land is a grassroots issue which offers considerable potential for political mobilization. The politicization of land is a reality in South Africa, with black pressure for redistribution matched by pockets of white resistance.

The statistics illustrating the stark racial imbalance in South African land distribution are familiar, and need not be repeated here. There is a growing acknowledgement in the broader society that this imbalance is both politically volatile and socially and

---

[21] Huntley, Siegfried & Sunter above n 14.
[22] Report of the President's Council above n 4, para 2.2.4.1.
[23] NEAC position paper above n 7.
[24] Desai above n 5.
[25] Khan 'Involvement of the masses in environmental politics' 1990 (June) *Veld and Flora* 36–8.

economically dysfunctional,[26] but as yet there have been few serious proposals to deal with it. The Development Bank of Southern Africa and the Urban Foundation have offered suggestions,[27] but most environmental interests have yet to take a position. Environmental managers must realize that land reform will almost certainly be demanded of a broadly representative government, and that there is considerable advantage to be gained from entering creative debate and negotiation as soon as possible.

Beyond the pivotal issue of land *distribution*, there are many complex areas of land *management* policy and practice that remain to be argued openly and in detail.[28] Among these are:

1. State, private-sector, community and individual roles in land management.
2. The extent and nature of rural development and the case for affirmative action.
3. Socio-politically and environmentally appropriate systems of land tenure and the manner in which to implement tenure reform.
4. Short- and long-term mechanisms for the resolution of conflict over rural and urban land.

A realm of potential conflict that will be familiar to many environmental managers is that which lies at the interface between the imperatives of conservation and those of resource-poor communities. Conservation-led land dispossession has long been a focus of rural political mobilization, and the human violation of areas set aside for conservation has on occasion spurred the responsible managers to strong and sometimes controversial action.[29]

An emerging orthodoxy stresses the need to link conservation with socio-economic development, by allowing proximate communities to have sustainable access to the life-supporting and income-earning potential of nature reserves and other protected areas.[30] But while conservative conservationists might see the establishment of community-permeable protected areas to be a way in which to buy insurance for such areas, it is likely that a government accountable to the rural poor will see such initiatives through the lens of employment and local wealth creation.

The potential tension between these positions rests in the possibility that some natural area managers will seek to maintain the minimum necessary interaction with communities, while the State seeks to extend and expand the social and economic opportunities that many protected areas offer to impoverished neighbours. Against this background, the new challenge to environmental managers is to explore the potential of a broad front of co-operation with communities, not as a form of appeasement, but with the objective of tangible and sustainable rural development.

There is little doubt that rural poverty will be one of the most difficult yet insistent issues facing a newly elected democratic government. If conservation/rural development ventures are demonstrated to be effective, political support will probably follow.

4.7 URBANIZATION AND CITIES

Cities and urbanization are issues somewhat neglected by environmental interests worldwide. This is probably a consequence of the many and complex ways in which the urban–environment interface can be viewed, but it may also be the legacy of a Eurocentric bias toward the management of resources in the natural environment. The

[26] Cooper 'From soil erosion to sustainability' in Cock & Koch above n 10, 176–92; *Agriculture and redistribution: a growth with equity approach* Development Bank of Southern Africa (1991); 'Rural development: towards a new framework' *Urban debate 2010* Urban Foundation (1990). See also Huntley, Siegfried & Sunter above n 14; Khan above n 11 and Wilson & Ramphele above n 19.

[27] See above n 26.

[28] See sources listed in n 26 above.

[29] Khan above n 11.

[30] Report of the President's Council above n 4, para 2.5.3.17.

relative lack of concern with the environmental problems of urban areas has been highlighted particularly by commentators on Third World urbanization, and it has also been noted in the context of southern Africa.[31]

In South Africa itself, there is parallel evidence that cities have not gained the position they merit on the agendas of mainstream institutions and organizations involved with environmental management. For example, the Department of Environment Affairs has only a sub-directorate concerned with the built environment. The President's Council report recognizes the challenges that face this unit (rapid urbanization, informal settlement), but in its recommendations the built environment remains a sub-directorate, albeit in a newly created directorate concerned with environmental planning.[32] However, the under-representation of urban environmental concerns extends beyond the formal structures of the State. South Africa has an impressive array of established environment-oriented NGOs but very few of these have missions and objectives that are explicitly or even predominantly urban.

This curious imbalance persists against the background of a society which is becoming increasingly urban.[33] It is inevitable that urban environmental questions will become more pressing, and that this will be reflected more strongly across the spectrum of bodies involved in environmental management. However, it is likely that urban environmental imperatives will be seen in diverse and often divergent ways by interests with particular socio-economic characteristics and political objectives. Perspectives on the urban environment forged in crowded and poorly serviced shack towns are certain to be different to those nurtured in the more affluent suburbs.

There are two fundamental ways of looking at cities and environment. The first is to consider the roles and impacts of urban areas *in* environments, and the second is to see cities *as* environments. With reference to the former, the policy documents of both the President's Council and the ANC devote attention to the environmental impacts of urban/industrial activity, and to matters of management and regulation. However, while the President's Council deals comprehensively but somewhat blandly with air and water pollution and urban and industrial waste, the ANC chooses to focus on two issues that have impacted on black communities in recent years. The first is air pollution, which is recognized as a major problem in the townships, and the second is toxic waste, around which there have been notable cases of local mobilization.[34]

In the broad framework of urban impacts *in* the environment, a politically charged issue which has yet to emerge strongly in management policy and practice is that of the identification, assembly and development of land for low-income urban residential development. Heated debates around the permanent settlement of 'squatters' in Hout Bay and Randburg have demonstrated something of the social and political complexity of the urban land issue. The essence of the conflict lies in the opposing forces of massive and growing homelessness[35] and the 'not in my backyard' resistance of settled communities. In this context, bland master plans will not ensure the management of urban settlement. This can be achieved only by engaging the social and political

[31] Hardoy & Satterthwaite above n 18; *Urban policy and economic development: an agenda for the 1990s* World Bank (1991); Potts 'Urban environmental control in southern Africa with special reference to Lilongwe' 1989 (6) *Resource Management and Optimisation* 321–34.

[32] Report of the President's Council above n 4, para 6.4.7.22.

[33] The majority of South Africans already live in urban areas (approximately 57 per cent in 1985) and the proportion will increase rapidly in the two decades to 2010. Urbanization will be particularly striking among the black population, which is expected to move from 53 per cent urban in 1985 to 69 per cent in 2010. In absolute terms, this means that the black population of urban areas in South Africa will increase by around 20 million between 1985 and 2010. 'Population trends' *Urban Debate 2010* Urban Foundation (1990).

[34] Sisulu & Sangweni above n 5.

[35] 'Informal housing: part 1' *Urban Debate 2010* Urban Foundation (1991).

obstacles: land-use management in the cities (as elsewhere) will have an inevitable political dimension, and environmental managers will have to look beyond plans to processes which expose and resolve the tensions between entrenched positions.

Built environments are extremely varied. In some cases, it has been noted, the living environments endured by poor people in cities are among the most life-threatening and unhealthy anywhere.[36] Against the backdrop of growing international environmental awareness, the relative lack of attention accorded urban environments of poverty is striking. With notable exceptions,[37] the same research and policy vacuum is evident in South Africa. However, it is probable that facets of cities *as* environments will move closer to the centre of political/environmental debate, as organizations with a significant support base among the urban poor seek to address the immediate environmental concerns of their constituents.

Among the environmental policy documents that have emerged from the major extra-parliamentary political groups and their affiliates, overcrowding, inadequate housing, poor working conditions and problems with urban services are significant themes. All stress the role of racial settlement policy in perpetuating these conditions. In addition, an emergent 'green' or 'progressive' environmental literature has begun presenting case studies of the relationship between apartheid and environments of poverty, with examples ranging from the planned establishment of a toxic waste dump close to Azaadville in Krugersdorp to the collapse of waste disposal services in Alexandra. Other issues include the failure of some employers to ensure the safety of workers handling toxic substances, the siting of black townships close to heavy industry, and township overcrowding and the spread of infectious diseases.[38]

In responding to evidence gleaned mainly from organizations and individuals based in middle- and upper-class communities, the President's Council has relatively little to say about urban environments of poverty, or about the role of apartheid. This is not to suggest that there is some correct balance: it is simply to underline the point that sections of our society accord very different levels of environmental and political priority to the environments occupied by poor and disadvantaged people.

The demand for the transformation of environments of poverty (linked to the agenda of redressing manifestations of racial inequality) is an issue that will increasingly confront environmental managers as South Africa moves through its political transition. However, the need to address the acute problems of cities *as* environments is not simply a populist position. Influential development agencies such as the World Bank are emphasizing that urban productivity is critical to national economic development and wellbeing, and that environments of poverty are a central impediment to such productivity.[39]

4.8 MANAGEMENT INSTITUTIONS

It has been argued that one of the key threats to environmental management in the countries of the developing world is the lack of institutional capacity to undertake this complex task.[40] In this regard it has been noted that many Third World governments do not have the organizational machinery to enforce environmental regulations, or in some cases the political will to oppose powerful vested interests. Against this background, there is strong international support for the principle of spreading the institutional load of environmental management as widely as possible. In this vein, it is significant to note

[36] Hardoy & Satterthwaite above n 18.

[37] For example, the urban-oriented papers collected under the banner of the second Carnegie enquiry above n 19.

[38] See various articles in Cock & Koch above n 10.

[39] *Urban policy and economic development: an agenda for the 1990s* above n 31.

[40] Hardoy & Satterthwaite above n 18.

the importance UNCED organizers have attached to NGO and citizen participation in the Rio de Janiero 'earth summit'.[41]

However, it is all too easy to be lured into a vision of the State, civil society and the private sector co-operating harmoniously in the management of the environment. This is a particularly troublesome view in South Africa, where the legitimacy of the State is questioned by a significant proportion of the population and where a variety of political and non-government organizations have until recently been repressed under apartheid. In fact, one of the less recognized environmental impacts of apartheid is the extent to which it has polarized institutions and stunted institution-building outside government,[42] and has supported top-down and fragmented management systems within it.[43]

With constitutional negotiations focused on matters of broad principle, there is at present little political debate around the fine detail of state environmental management structures and responsibilities. The President's Council has made recommendations in terms of its brief, but it acknowledges that its proposals have to accommodate the possibility of a new constitution.[44] An important and emerging area of discussion has to do with the establishment and extension of institutional capacity in the non-government sector. For the purposes of this chapter, it is pertinent to expand on three themes: the re-orientation of 'traditional' environmental NGOs; the 'greening' of development-oriented, labour and civic organizations; and the collective mobilization of NGOs active in the realm of environmental management.

Some of the traditional environmental NGOs have been criticized for their apparent insensitivity to the social and political forces shaping environmental perceptions and priorities among blacks. Hence it has been observed that black membership of the well-established formal NGOs is low.[45] In their response to changing socio-political circumstances in South Africa, two fundamental options are open to the traditional NGOs. The first is a conservative route, in which such organizations entrench their role as protectors of habitats and species and continue to draw on a largely middle-class support base. The second option is that of re-orientation, in which the big environmental NGOs seek aggressively to expand their base of support. It has been argued that such a re-orientation will require traditional NGOs to address political issues, and to shift their focus to the needs of resource-poor people in urban and rural environments.[46] The extent to which such re-orientation is possible will depend in part on the willingness of sponsors and members to enter new socio-political terrain, and on the receptiveness of the new target communities, who may be constrained by negative conservation stereotypes, or simply by lack of interest in organizations that appear to belong in another world.

As many traditional environmental NGOs show a growing determination to extend their influence beyond entrenched nature-oriented briefs, there is a matching trend in which a wide range of non-environmental groups and organizations are becoming increasingly vocal on 'green' issues. In many respects, this movement is filling the 'environments of poverty' environmental management vacuum by exposing threats to vulnerable communities to wider scrutiny. So, for example, civic associations have taken action on pollution and inadequate waste disposal; the labour movement has drawn public attention to hazardous working environments; and service organizations

---

[41] Above n 1.

[42] Khan above, n 25.

[43] The Report of the President's Council (above n 4, para 6.1.1) refers to such fragmentation without linking it explicitly to apartheid policy.

[44] Report of the President's Council above n 4, para 6.7.5.

[45] Khan above n 25.

[46] Khan above n 25.

have offered specialized legal and technical assistance to communities contesting access to environmental resources such as land.[47]

While traditional NGOs may be cautious about entering the realm of environmental politics (itself a political position), a significant portion of the 'green mobilization' of popular organizations is explicitly political. Green politics merges demands for improved urban and rural living and working environments with the struggle for political participation at diverse levels of the State. Given the widespread existence of environments of poverty, this is doubtless a potential growth area for environmental involvement.

Even a crude overview of the activities of NGOs involved in the environment will demonstrate a diversity of points of departure, and a range of social, political and environmental objectives. In the context of maximizing institutional capacity for environmental management, a key question has to do with the extent to which NGOs can and should work collectively. The emergence of 'rainbow alliances' in the face of specific socio-environmental threats has been noted, but these coalitions are often ephemeral.[48] The idea of an independent environmental monitoring agency capable of serving NGOs with research and information has been mooted in 'green' circles, and the President's Council has proposed an umbrella forum for both traditional NGOs and diverse green groups.[49]

While such a forum would have been politically impractical under rigid apartheid, the notion may well be worthy of consideration in the present climate of negotiation and transition. In this regard it is worth noting that the elements of the green movement have called for unity among environmental groups,[50] and that an embryonic trend towards convergence is evident as traditional NGOs become more involved in grassroots environmental problems and other organizations and groups take up environmental issues in their areas of activity. Naturally, the nature and objectives of the forum will be argued, and some NGOs may see little advantage in participation. The strongest argument in favour of a forum is not the expectation of consensus on all environmental management questions. Much more importantly, in the words of the President's Council, a broad NGO-based forum will 'promote the broadest possible involvement of the organized public in environmental issues'.[51] Seen from most political and environmental vantage points, this would constitute a significant advance over the existing environmental management system.

4.9 ENVIRONMENTAL MANAGEMENT UNDER A POST-APARTHEID GOVERNMENT

Population and resources, land distribution and management, urbanization and cities, and management institutions will remain areas of challenge and opportunity through the current period of socio-political change. They will also test the environmental management system under any future government. While it is not possible to foresee the details of environmental policy and practice in a new post-apartheid democracy, various pointers can be identified:[52]

1. A new representative government will be under immediate pressure to deal with the material and perceived legacy of apartheid. In environmental management terms

[47] Many examples are documented in Cock & Koch above n 10.
[48] Koch above n 11.
[49] Report of the President's Council above n 4, para 3.2.2.2.
[50] Koch above n 11.
[51] Report of the President's Council above n 4, para 3.2.2.5.
[52] See Hart 'Socio-political change and the effectiveness of the existing environmental management system' in *Environmental management in a new democracy* Human Sciences Research Council (1990) 17–21.

this might mean a shift in focus to living and working environments, and to land reform.

2. Relationships between NGOs and the government will change in various ways. For example, development-oriented NGOs may get increased support. It is premature to speculate on interactions between a new government and the big environmental NGOs. However, it is clearly in the interests of these organizations to give strategic thought to this matter.
3. The state environmental management system will be subject to various sources of change. At the centre, new priorities and portfolios may lead to restructured departments, and new arrangements for the devolution of power may influence environmental management structures at regional and local level.

Present and future environmental managers face substantial social and political obstacles. For the most part, these are common to many countries in the developing world. Past discriminatory policy has added a layer of complexity in South Africa, but there are also several factors that give this country a potential environmental management edge on a number of Third World nations. These include an economy with considerable promise; a depth of skills, management ability and achievement in environmental and related fields; growing environmental mobilization; and a socio-political 'window of opportunity' as structures and relationships are changed and remoulded. History will reflect on the will of South African environmentalists to build on the advantages available.

CHAPTER 5

ENVIRONMENTAL ADMINISTRATION

E SCHWELLA
J J MULLER

5.1 INTRODUCTION

The administration of service-provision systems in any particular society should be subjected to an analytical approach in terms of which strategic decisions can be reached about various available options with regard to conditioning factors such as the political, economic, social and technological situation. This analytical approach is useful for evaluating present service-provision systems as well as for recommending possible adaptations to these systems to improve their compatibility to prevailing conditions and their effective performance.

In this chapter an effort is made to address the question of an administrative model for the environmental management service-provision system in South Africa. This is approached in the following way:

- The theoretical considerations such as the basic theoretical model, conditioning factors and the strategic options are first identified and then used to generate guidelines for the evaluation of the present position and to make proposals about the future design of an administrative model.
- A historical and institutional description of the present administrative model for the environmental management function in the South African society is provided.
- This present approach is then evaluated against the guidelines, and proposals are made for an appropriate administrative model.

When we consider these matters, a number of terms are used that have ambiguous and confusing meanings. These include terms such as 'administration', 'management' and 'environment'. As a general rule, the meaning of these terms should be considered and derived from the context in which they are employed. In most cases, however, 'administration' is used to convey the meaning of the execution of government policies. Thus an administrative model, e g, refers to a model for the execution of government policies.

'Management' will be used as a comprehensive term that includes administration as explained above as well as scientific and technical aspects pertaining to the natural environment—as in the phrase 'environmental management'.

The term 'environment' is used in organizational theory to indicate the external context of an organizational system. To avoid confusion, the term as used in organizational theory will be avoided as far as possible and is substituted by terms such as 'context' and 'conditioning factors'. 'Environment' as used in this analysis therefore generally refers to the natural/physical environment. See chapters 1 and 6.

5.2 THEORETICAL CONSIDERATIONS

When evaluating present models or recommending new models for the administration of societal functions and the provision of services, a number of theoretical considerations have to be taken into account. These provide insight into conditioning factors, the nature of the problems that have to be addressed, possible alternative strategic options for service provision and a basis for the evaluation and choice of the applicable options. It is generally accepted that there is no 'one best way' of deciding administrative questions and that the approach should rather be to select the most appropriate administrative strategies in the prevailing conditions. This approach necessitates an investigation into the nature of important conditioning factors, the bases of administrative strategies, and strategic choices in accordance with these findings.

It has to be accepted that such a contingency approach does not result in final, rigid and unchangeable administrative models. The approach necessitates a constant re-evaluation of conditions and regular adaptation of administrative structures and functions to changing conditions. As such, it represents a dynamic, organic, rather than a static, bureaucratic—approach to administrative decisions.

5.2.1 Theoretical orientation

The most recent approaches to administrative phenomena are the open-systems and contingency approaches. These are based upon common fundamental premises—indeed, the contingency approach may actually be viewed as open-systems theory applied to administrative problems.

The open-systems approach regards administrative systems as complex sets of interrelated variables and parts collaborating to reach objectives by using inputs from outside the system. The approach rejects the notion of so-called 'principles of administration' and any search for the 'one best way' of administration which is supposedly applicable to all situations. Moreover, it provides a macro perspective for the analysis and study of administrative phenomena by furnishing a framework for analysis. This framework enables decision-makers to consider contextual conditioning factors and to select the most appropriate strategies in the circumstances. The importance thus granted to context in analysis and decision-making is the critical aspect distinguishing the open-systems approach from others. Such an orientation provides the capacity to keep the administrative structures and functions in a state of dynamic equilibrium with their circumstances. This is regarded as essential for the continued effective functioning of an administrative system.[1]

The contingency approach shares the fundamental premises of the open-systems approach and elaborates upon its implications for administrative decision-makers. These implications are that decision-makers should be analytical, flexible and ingenious. Administrative models should be selected and adapted with the particular contextual conditioning factors in mind. It can be accepted that this approach facilitates strategic decision-making practices by which strategic decisions are made in terms of contextual analysis and situation assessments.[2]

In terms of the open-systems and contingency approaches, conditioning factors have to be considered from the administrative context. A selection of the kinds of factors to be taken into account will be now considered.

5.2.2 Conditioning factors

Factors from the organizational context which may influence administrative decision-making are numerous. A selection of these conditioning factors will be considered here in a theoretical and general sense only.

Political factors that have a bearing upon strategic administrative decisions include, inter alia, political ideology, political institutions such as political power groupings including political parties, pressure and interest groups, political policy, legislation and political and executive authorities. These factors can be analysed in terms of their

[1] Schwella *'n Organisasie-omgewingsontledingsmodel vir Suid-Afrikaanse owerheidsinstellings* (unpublished MPA thesis, University of Stellenbosch, 1983) 15–19.

[2] Hodge & Anthony *Organization theory* (1984); McCurdy *Public administration* (1977).

nature, power positions, legitimacy and stability. The results of this analysis should be considered when making strategic administrative choices.

Economic factors that have to be taken into account include the structural configuration of the national economy, patterns of economic growth, inflation, rate of exchange and savings and investment trends. Also of importance are the availability and levels of natural resources such as land, water, mineral and energy resources as well as the international economic position of the country.

Social factors to be considered include trends regarding demography, urbanization, employment, housing, education and training, human development and societal values. The value component of the social environment could also be viewed as part of a distinct cultural component. These social factors have to be accounted for in evaluating or devising administrative models for the provision of services.

The technological factors focus on aspects such as the nature of technology, trends in technological development and the natural and social impact of technology.[3]

All the relevant conditioning factors, therefore, are of importance in the evaluation of, and decision-making about, administrative models for the provision of services. Strategic choices have to be made, based upon the assessment of these factors.

5.2.3 Strategic options for service-provision systems

Once the relevant conditioning factors have been identified, considered and evaluated, decisions have to be made about a number of strategic options for a service-provision system. We now turn to a discussion of some of these options.

5.2.3.1 *Sectoral placement*

A basic strategic decision has to be made about whether the service-provision system should be placed in the public or the private sector of a national economy. This decision will be influenced by factors such as the prevailing economic ideology, the nature of the service and the need for governmental authority to enforce certain decisions made within the service-provision system.

The prevailing national economic ideology of a country could be more socialistic or capitalistic. Where a socialist ideology is accepted by the populace and the government, the role of the public sector in the economy will be larger and will tend to increase. Where a capitalist ideology is accepted, the role of the public sector in the economy will be less significant and will tend to decrease. In more socialist-oriented economies, a greater number of service-provision systems will be government controlled and included into the public sector of the economy than in more capitalist-oriented economies; and strategies such as nationalization and regulation are used in the former to incorporate a larger number of services into the public sector of the economy, whereas, in the latter, strategies such as privatization and deregulation are used to incorporate a larger number of services into the private sector of the economy. The decision about the sectoral placement of a service-provision system will therefore be determined by the prevailing economic ideology.

The nature of the service to be provided has a bearing on the sectoral placement of the service-provision system and should also be considered. According to Gildenhuys,[4] services can be classified in terms of their nature, being collective, particular or quasi-collective.

Collective services are usually provided by the government and are therefore part of the public sector of the economy. They are *non-divisible*, owing to the following characteristics:

---

[3] Spies *Business futures* (1985).

[4] *Owerheidsfinansies* (1989) 35–9.

- They are *non-appropriable*, since the price per unit of service consumed related to the cost per unit of service delivered cannot be established. They cannot be divided into units to be sold on demand to a consumer.
- They are also *non-excludable* as people cannot be excluded from the benefits of the service, irrespective of whether they have paid for it or not.
- A third characteristic is that they are *non-exhaustible*, because they cannot be exhausted by use and remain available as long as they are maintained. It is also not possible to calculate a direct quid pro quo as a price for the service.
- They are also of a *monopolistic* nature, owing to the absence of competition.

From the above it is evident that services of a collective nature will probably be provided by the government as part of the public sector of the economy and will be financed from some form of taxation.

Particular services bear opposite characteristics to those of collective services and are therefore *appropriable*, *divisible*, *excludable* and *exhaustible*. It is also possible to calculate a price per unit of service consumed as a quid pro quo for the service provided. Particular services are also not naturally monopolistic and unless governments place restrictions on them, there will be competition for their delivery. Usually these services will be delivered by government institutions only if the private sector omits to deliver them or where there are economies of scale benefits which may be gained from collective action. Particular services will usually be financed by means of a price or levy arrived at within the market and paid directly by the consumer.

Quasi-collective services are subsidized particular services which are rendered by the public sector to subsidize their costs to the consumer public. These services may have positive spill-over effects which benefit not only those using them directly but also a larger section of the community. There is also the possibility that some services which are consumed on a particular basis may have negative spill-over effects for the community; they are, therefore, either provided or controlled by the government. In this way such services are brought into the domain of the public sector.

The placement of a service-provision system in the public or private sector will, therefore, have to consider the nature of the service concerned. If the service is collective or tends in that direction, it should be provided by the government, placed in the public sector of the economy and financed by taxes.

Finally, the sectoral placement will be influenced by the need for government authority involved in the provision of the service. Because governments have unique sanctions and coercive powers derived from their positions of authority in societies, they can use coercive powers to enforce certain policies and programmes. If commitment to particular societal objectives cannot be expected to be voluntary, and if such commitment is of sufficient importance to society, the service-provision systems striving to attain these objectives have to be vested with government authority, coercive powers and sanctions.

If the prevailing economic ideology is socialist-oriented, the services provided are of a collective nature, and there is a need for the service-provision system to be vested with government authority and coercive powers, the service provision should be placed in the public sector. If, however, the prevailing economic ideology is capitalist-oriented, the services provided are of a particular nature, and there is no need for the system to be vested with government authority and coercive powers, the service-provision system should be placed in the private sector.

It can also be expected that, even if there is a capitalist-oriented economic ideology or trend in that direction, the collective nature of the service and/or the need for governmental authority and coercive powers will result in the placement of the service-provision system in the public sector of the economy.

5.2.3.2 *Political approach*

The provision of services requires basic decisions to be made about the political approach to be selected for decision-making regarding the scope, nature and actions of the service-provision system in question. Two basic approaches are possible here, ie either a democratic or a technocratic approach.

The *democratic approach* emphasizes the principle of maximum participation in decision-making regarding the service-provision system, by everyone with an interest in or influenced by the service. As such, it institutionalizes possibilities for participation on an informed basis by all those stakeholders who are involved in or influenced by the service-provision system.

Such an approach is usually associated with the devolution of decision-making and decentralized execution of decisions. The purpose is to provide for maximum involvement and responsibility in the service-provision system at a point as close to the users of the service as possible. Through this involvement an attempt is made to increase the legitimacy and acceptability of decisions and actions and to make a maximum number of people accept mutual responsibility for the execution of action by virtue of their intimate involvement with the service. A possible problem with this approach is that scientific and technical considerations may be made subject to political and popular influences.

The *technocratic approach* emphasizes the need for incorporating scientific and technical considerations into decision-making regarding the nature, scope and function of the service-provision system in question. This approach reasons that service-provision systems are constantly increasing in complexity and that they therefore demand decisions based on scientific and technical rationality and rational scientific information. Such decisions require expertise and should be taken by knowledgeable and skilled scientific experts rather than be left to the whims and fancies of uninformed lay persons, even if they are the democratic representatives of those involved with or influenced by the decisions. Public participation is often viewed as dilettante meddling that leads to irrational and technically inferior decisions and actions.

Depending on their nature, services may require a more democratic or technocratic-oriented approach or even some sort of combination between the two extremes—the equilibrium point has to be decided strategically by taking into account the nature of the service and the relevant conditioning factors.

If the service requires decisions of a highly technical nature, the equilibrium point will tend towards the technocratic orientation. If the service requires responsibility and commitment from those involved with or influenced by it, a more democratic and participative approach is indicated.

5.2.3.3 *Institutional types and arrangements*

Strategic decisions have to be made about the type of institution to be utilized for a service-provision system.

Public sector service-provision systems usually have to consider aspects related to their needs for governmental authority, participative decision-making structures and collective financing through taxes or similar means, on the one hand, while calculating the effects of political control and a possible loss of autonomy, on the other.

Within the public sector different institutional options for service provision may be considered. They can be classified on a continuum in terms of their relative autonomy. The traditional government department as institutional arrangement is most subject to political control and therefore the least autonomous of the available institutional types. Next in line are state commercial enterprises which usually function like a government department under the supervision of a Minister of State but with more autonomy in terms of their functions, financial and personnel matters than the normal government department. (Examples of these that existed in South Africa before the government's privatization attempts include the South African Transport Services and the Department of Posts and Telecommunications.) Other institutional types positioned towards the more autonomous side of the continuum are collectively known as fringe organizations, parastatals or quasi non-governmental organizations (quangos). These institutional types are usually created for specified purposes and are vested with certain authoritative governmental powers. Although they are to a certain extent financed from public or collective funds they enjoy a greater autonomy from political control than government departments or state commercial enterprises. They may be entrepreneurial bodies (for instance, Sasol and Overvaal Public Resorts), regulatory bodies (for instance, agricultural control boards and the Medical and Dental Council) and benefactory agencies for functions such as economic development and social and welfare assistance.[5]

When selecting the institutional type, it can therefore be accepted that a quest for greater autonomy will result in selecting from the parastatal type of options. This will also result in less direct political control and political influence over the institution. It has to be realized, however, that the greater the need for governmental authority and especially the greater the dependence upon financing from public funds, the less acceptable this option will be to the political rulers of the day and to the general public. It can be expected that the people subject to the authority of the institution or contributing to its financing have a right to and will demand participation in its functioning as well as proper political control over its activities. The degree of freedom from control and autonomy granted to a service-provision system should therefore be decided with reference to the scope of governmental authority vested in it and the extent of public funds used to finance it.

If the service-provision system requires more autonomy and less political control due to limited needs for governmental authority and public funding, an institutional type or arrangement approximating a parastatal approach is indicated. If, on the other hand, political authority is necessary due to a need for governmental authority and total or substantial public funding, an institutional type of arrangement approximating that of a traditional government department is indicated.

5.2.3.4 *Constitutional and hierarchical placement*

Public service-provision systems have to be placed within the constitutional framework of a country. In most constitutional frameworks provision is made for different levels of government. These levels may include a central, regional or local level. In some cases provision is made only for a central and a local level, without a regional level. The levels of authority and autonomy granted to the tiers of government are also influenced by the constitutional arrangements of the particular country. Broadly speaking, a federal type of constitutional arrangement will allow more scope and autonomy to the lower tiers of government than would be allowed under a unitary constitutional arrangement.

The placing of a service-provision system within the pattern of constitutional arrangements of a particular country should consider factors such as the nature of the service in terms of its impact, its divisibility, its status and its political needs. Generally, it can be accepted that if a service-provision system has a national impact, the nature of the services provided is indivisible and the services need status and political power, then the service-provision system will be placed at the central government level. If the impact of the service provision is regional or local, the nature of the services are divisible and the services are not in need of high status and substantial political power, then they could be placed at lower levels.

---

[5] For a more detailed discussion, see Baxter *Administrative law* (1984) ch 8.

It must also be accepted that a service-provision system may exercise diverse functions ranging from the actual rendering of products or services to the regulating of activities related to the service. It is therefore possible that the service system may be organized and divided in such a way that various aspects may be placed at different levels or within different departments or other institutional types of governmental arrangement. These divisions could, however, create serious problems of fragmentation, disintegrated policy-making and planning as well as poor control and co-ordination. Generally, service-provision systems that have a national impact should at least provide for a central national policy-making, planning and co-ordination body. This need for a central link will be strengthened if the nature of the service is such that it comes into strong competition with powerful interest groups and therefore needs a higher status and substantial political backing to reach its objectives.

The above approach may create a centralizing tendency for a particular service-provision system with the attendant dangers of overcentralization such as a lack of local participation and an absence of sensitivity for local needs and conditions. This may be alleviated by centralizing broad aspects of policy-making and co-ordination, while at the same time creating complementary units at the other tiers on a regional basis. Such units could be given the opportunity to be fairly autonomous within the parameters of general policy and under the control of governing bodies elected by local citizens. In this way, opportunities are created to incorporate scientific and technical expertise in the broad policy, while allowing for democratic participation and community commitment at the local level.

5.2.3.5 *General organizational considerations*

After having evaluated the conditioning factors, strategic decisions have to be made regarding the following macro-organizational aspects:

- the sectoral placement of the service-provision system;
- the selection of an applicable political approach for the service-provision system;
- the institutional types of and arrangements for the service-provision system; and
- the constitutional and hierarchical placement of the service-provision system.

These macro-organizational aspects should, however, also take into account a number of general organizational requirements which affect the service-provision system. When organizing the service-provision system, *objectives* have to be established for the organization as a whole and for all its sub-units. Organizational activities have to be arranged in such a way that they facilitate the effective attainment of these objectives, with the most efficient utilization of scarce resources.

To attain these objectives, it is usually necessary to introduce a process of *division of labour*, taking into account the advantages and disadvantages of specialization, the capacity of organizational units and workers and the sensible combination of tasks. The division of labour is the basis for the creation of individual jobs, sections and departments. The division of labour creates specified tasks for specific individuals or groups. To enable these functionaries to fulfil their tasks, *delegation of authority* is necessary. The concerned organizational units or functionaries have to be vested with the applicable authority for proper performance.

The division of labour and delegation of authority tend to create differentiation and fragmentation. Such differentiation and fragmentation have to be checked by the balancing processes of *co-ordination* and *control* to gain integrated and purposeful action. Co-ordination is aimed at bringing together the magnitude of diverse specialized activities and to concentrate them on the achievement of objectives; control also functions to concentrate action on the achievement of objectives. It provides the parameters for action and must be aimed at detecting possible deviations from standards timeously.

The organization of functions may be done on the basis of supervisor/subordinate ratios, the nature of functions performed, the product or service produced, the client group served, the geographical area served, the process used in service provision or a combination of these.[6]

5.2.4 Concluding Guidelines

With regard to the *sectoral placement* of the service-provision system, the guidelines are the following: If the prevailing economic ideology is socialist-oriented, the services provided are of a collective nature and there is a need for the service-provision system to be vested with governmental authority and coercive powers, the service-provision system should be placed in the public sector. If the prevailing economic ideology is capitalist-oriented, the services provided are of a particular nature and there is no need for the service-provision system to be vested with governmental authority and coercive powers, the service-provision system should be placed in the private sector. It can also be expected that the collective nature of the service and/or the need for governmental authority and coercive powers will result in the placement of the service-provision system in the public sector of the economy, even if there is a capitalist-oriented economic ideology or a trend in that direction.

When selecting the *political approach* for the service-provision system, the guidelines are that, if the service requires decisions of a highly technical nature, the equilibrium point will tend towards the technocratic orientation; if, however, the service requires responsibility and commitment from those involved with or influenced by the service, a more democratic and participative approach is indicated.

When deciding about the *institutional types and arrangements* for the service-provision system, the guidelines are that, if the system requires more autonomy and less political control is necessary due to limited needs for governmental authority and public funding, an institutional type or arrangement approximating a parastatal approach is indicated. If political authority is necessary due to a need for governmental authority and total or substantial public funding, an institutional type of arrangement approximating that of a traditional government department is indicated.

With regard to the *constitutional and hierarchical placement* of the service-provision system, the guidelines are that if a system has a national impact, the nature of the services provided is indivisible and the services need status and political power, then the service-provision system should be placed at the central government level. If the impact of the system is regional or local, the nature of the services is divisible and the services are not in need of high status and political power, then placement at lower levels may be indicated.

All these guidelines should also bear *general organizational considerations* in mind. These include matters regarding objective-setting, the division of labour, the delegation of authority, the processes of co-ordination and control and the bases for organization.

It has to be realized that various guidelines considered in relation to the nature, characteristics and needs may possibly indicate ostensibly different strategic options. These have to be reconciled through flexibility, adaptability and ingenuity.

The sensible administration of a public-service system demands that strategic decisions will be taken with a proper regard for the conditioning factors and by selecting the optimal macro- and micro- organizational options. These theoretical guidelines may then be used to evaluate present service-provision systems and to recommend possible changes and adaptations of such systems.

5.3 THE ADMINISTRATION OF ENVIRONMENTAL AFFAIRS IN SOUTH AFRICA

5.3.1 Conditioning Factors of Environmental Management

Conditioning factors which influence and determine the government's choice of an

[6] Robbins *The administrative process* (1980) 196–207.

environmental management system for South Africa are of crucial importance for the design and evaluation of appropriate administrative structures. South Africa, in common with other countries, must develop its own dynamic model and make its own trade-offs between economic growth, the state of the environment and the quality of life, because there are no readily transferable models which have proved successful elsewhere in the world.[7] This view does not play down global trends such as world population growth, global warming or the so-called 'greenhouse effect', the depletion of the ozone layer or the omnipresent threat of nuclear war as being of lesser or limited importance in our context. It rather implies that a shifting balance between the economy, the environment and the quality of life must be found that will satisfy the needs and aspirations of the majority of South Africans.

Such an integrated environmental management system will have to exploit the opportunities and overcome the constraints which constitute the environmental 'rules of the game' for South Africa.[8] Any solution to environmental problems demands a comprehensive perspective, taking account of factors such as the need for economic growth, changing consumer patterns, the distribution of wealth and land and equal access to resources. See, generally, chapters 1–4.

5.3.2 Historical Perspective

The present administrative system for environmental management in South Africa is the product of an evolutionary process. The advantages and disadvantages associated with the present system should therefore be considered within the context of its historical perspective. The historical development of environmental conservation in South Africa followed a similar path to that in other countries where the conservation focus changed from species preservation to a more comprehensive approach of habitat and ecosystem conservation. For the purposes of this historical perspective the time period since the arrival of Van Riebeeck in 1652 is classified into five distinct developmental phases. This classification is somewhat arbitrary, but may serve to guide the analysis and to highlight some of the milestones. The development of environmental management is more fully discussed in chapter 2.

5.3.2.1 *Preservation of species through legislation (1655–1875)*

The accepted principle was that the State had the right and the duty to control the exploitation of wild animals and plants on behalf of the people as a whole. Although early legislation to protect wild animals as a useful natural resource was introduced by the Dutch settlers shortly after their arrival at the Cape and restrictions were placed on the cutting of trees, control measures were seldom applied effectively.

5.3.2.2 *Institutionalization of the conservation function (1875–1960)*

The governmental conservation function was formally institutionalized for the first time with the establishment of the Cape Forest Department in 1875 and the first formal conservation areas in South Africa were demarcated forest reserves established in terms of the Cape Forest Act 28 of 1888. The Transvaal and Orange Free State established forestry sections in their respective Agricultural Departments in 1903, whereas Natal integrated the forestry function with the other activities of its Agricultural Department. The forestry and agricultural services of the four provinces were amalgamated in 1910 into the central Department of Forestry and Department of Agriculture.

A number of other protected areas were also established at an early stage, principally for the protection of wild animals in the Transvaal and Natal. The respective provincial authorities took over control of these areas after unification in 1910. The rest of this

---

[7] Huntley, Siegfried & Sunter *South African environments into the 21st century* (1989) 123.

[8] Huntley, Siegfried & Sunter above n 7, 43–75.

developmental phase was dominated by the activities of the four provincial administrations in providing for nature conservation. See, generally, chapter 27.

The history of the conservation of living marine resources can be traced back to 1895, when the government of the Cape Colony appointed a biologist to undertake fishery surveys. The surveys were terminated with the start of the South African War in 1899, and were resumed on a part-time basis in 1918 until 1928, when a Division of Sea Fisheries was formally established in the former Department of Mines and Industry. The legal responsibility for the rational exploitation of marine resources was eventually vested in the Division of Sea Fisheries, then part of the Department of Commerce and Industry, in 1940. See, generally, chapter 14.

5.3.2.3 *Need for a comprehensive approach (1960–80)*

The first deliberate step at national level in administering man-environment interactions in a more comprehensive sense was the establishment of a Social and Economic Planning Council in 1942 to assist the government with the formulation of an integrated economic and social policy. The Natural Resources Development Act 51 of 1947 followed which established the Natural Resources Development Council to assist the government to regulate the exploitation of natural resources. The 1960s saw a major step in South African natural resource management with the establishment in 1964 of a Department of Planning and the promulgation of the Physical Planning and Utilization of Resources Act 88 of 1967, which in part recognized the multidisciplinary nature of physical planning.

The 1970s were characterized by a growing demonstration of serious national environmental concern on the part of government. A cabinet committee was appointed in 1971 to investigate environmental pollution. A pollution subsidiary committee of the Prime Minister's Planning Advisory Council was subsequently appointed to investigate and report on the matter. This committee produced a comprehensive report on pollution which was published in 1972. A permanent Cabinet Committee on Environmental Conservation, chaired by the Minister of Planning, was established in the same year. A non-statutory South African Committee on Environmental Conservation was in turn established to advise this cabinet committee. This non-statutory committee, which was renamed the Council for the Environment in 1975, consisted of representatives from government departments and other administrative bodies concerned with environmental affairs. In 1973 the Department of Planning became the Department of Planning and the Environment to address the important function of co-ordinating legislation relating to the control of pollution and the conservation of natural resources. The Physical Planning Act was amended to make provision for the consideration of environmental factors during land-use planning. This department was reorganized again in 1979 to become the Department of Environmental Planning and Energy.

5.3.2.4 *The quest for a national environmental policy and conservation strategy (1980–90)*

The beginning of the 1980s saw the publication of the government's *White Paper on a national policy regarding environmental conservation*. This *White Paper* was at the time regarded as a major commitment on the part of the government to attempt to recognize and resolve some of the more serious environmental issues that faced and were to face South Africa. The specific problems which were identified as requiring attention were inter alia soil conservation, noise pollution, marine pollution, radiation pollution and solid waste management. The promotion of environmental education and the institutionalization of environmental impact studies were the two approaches that were singled out in the *White Paper* as possible solutions to these problems. The Department of Water Affairs, Forestry and Environmental Conservation was formed in

1980 as a result of the process of rationalization of the public service. This move was, in part, a manifestation of certain provisions of the *White Paper* that outlined the government's intention to amalgamate certain state responsibilities that had a direct bearing on the administration of natural-resource conservation. The department's name was subsequently changed to the Department of Environment Affairs in 1981. The Sea Fisheries Branch was transferred from the Department of Commerce and Industry in the rationalization programme and united with other agricultural services in a new Department of Agriculture and Fisheries. Sea Fisheries, now known as Marine Development, was again transferred in 1982 to the new Department of Environment Affairs.

The promulgation of the Environment Conservation Act 100 of 1982 was one of the first steps in the implementation of the government's policy as outlined in the *White Paper*. The Planning Committee of the President's Council also investigated and reported on *Nature conservation in South Africa*[9] and on *Priorities between conservation and development*.[10] The Council for the Environment became a statutory body in 1982 in terms of the Environment Conservation Act, with the stated aim of advising the Minister of Environment Affairs on all matters pertaining to the environment. A number of important policy proposals and management guidelines relating to various components of the environment, from environmental education to an integrated environmental management system, were produced by the council. The conservation function was also affected by the constitutional changes during this period when certain executive functions pertaining mainly to the management of specific categories of protected areas and the enforcement of protective measures with regard to marine resources were transferred in 1986 by the State President in terms of the Provincial Government Act 69 of 1986 from central government level to the respective provincial authorities.

5.3.2.5 *Unified environmental management (1990–)*

The President's Council was requested by the State President in December 1989 to investigate and make recommendations on a policy for a national environmental management system, with specific reference to the ecological, economic, social, and legal implications of such a policy. In the *Report of the three committees of the President's Council on a national environmental management system*,[11] submitted during October 1991, the President's Council endorsed the view that environmental management is, and should remain, the responsibility of central government.[12] This view is justified on account of the factors that the environmental threats facing South Africa are so serious and demand such urgent action, and that central government is the most appropriate institution to manage the environment. The capacity of central government to fulfil its primary responsibility to determine policy on the environment is seriously hampered because control over the environment is fragmented and compartmentalised and the policy-making process is constrained by legal obligations regarding the process of consultation. The recommendations of the President's Council focus primarily on streamlining the policy-making function and the organizational strengthening of central government's ability to monitor the application of the policy, although it was not believed that the Department of Environment Affairs should be converted into a 'super department' vested with executive responsibility for all aspects of environmental management.[13] Moreover, while some changes and restructuring of

---

[9] PC 2/1984.
[10] PC 5/1984.
[11] PC 1/1991.
[12] Para 6.2.2.
[13] Para 6.1.11.

the Department of Environment Affairs and of other departments that are concerned with environmental administration have been recommended, as will be shown, a large-scale rearrangement of administrative and executive functions was not considered to be a solution at this stage. This makes sense because the administration of environmental affairs in South Africa and the design of the appropriate administrative models will to a large extent depend on the outcome of constitutional negotiations. The future constitutional arrangements will affect the final allocation of responsibilities and could involve a possible further restructuring of government institutions at all levels.

5.3.3 Environmental Policy and Conservation Strategy

The need for a national environmental policy and conservation strategy arises from a growing awareness of the urgent need to manage wisely the finite natural resources on which mankind depends. The publication in 1980 of the *World conservation strategy* by the International Union for the Conservation of Nature (IUCN), now called the World Conservation Union, with the support of the World Wide Fund for Nature (WWF) and the United Nations Environment Programme (UNEP) set off a chain reaction throughout the environmental movement. *The World conservation strategy* addressed a far wider spectrum of land-use options and issues than merely the protection of nature and sought to provide a practical outline to nations throughout the world on problems and principles relating to the sustained use of natural resources. The South African Government's *White Paper* of 1980 at the same time gave notice of the changing attitude of government to the impact of human actions on the environment. The aim as stated in the *White Paper* was to seek a golden mean between dynamic development and the vital demands of environmental conservation. Although the *White Paper* could be considered a major commitment by government, the first attempt to develop a national environmental conservation policy and strategy in South Africa was that of the Wildlife Society of Southern Africa, which published its document in 1981. The document set broad environmental goals and the principles and policies to achieve them and also provided outlines of the approaches and actions required to realize policy objectives as an environmental strategy. The development of environmental policy gained momentum when the statutory Council for the Environment was established in 1982 and various policy proposals and strategic guidelines for the administration of components of the environment were formulated since its inception. The above-mentioned reports of the Planning Committee of the President's Council were also notable developments in this regard. The broad environmental goals which a national policy on environmental conservation must address are enumerated in the Environment Conservation Act 73 of 1989. See chapter 7.

The publication of the Council for the Environment's document entitled *An approach to a national environmental policy and strategy for South Africa* in October 1989 can be regarded as a major step in this ongoing process. The document comprises two parts. The first part outlines an approach to a policy and gives the conceptual framework on which the stated goals and policy are based. The second describes individual environmental components and resources, conservation objectives relevant to their wise management and strategies to meet these objectives. This preliminary document was published to obtain further comment and evaluation before the final recommendations on national environmental policy and strategy are to be submitted to the Minister of Environment Affairs. The *Report of the President's Council on a national environmental management system* conceded that, although the primary responsibility of the Department of Environment Affairs is to determine policy on the environment, it is, in fact, regarded as powerless to do so.[14] However, the recommendations aim to

---

[14] Para 6.1.12.3.

ensure that the central government authority for environmental affairs and its responsible political office-bearers are, after the institution of the management system, in a position to

- determine policy on the best possible advice and to promulgate such policy;
- ensure that cognizance is taken of the fragility of ecosystems in the management system, and that usage of resources is permitted only within the limits of the natural reproductive capacities of such ecosystems;
- translate such policy into concrete action by public bodies;
- monitor the extent to which such policy has been applied and with what success, and to ensure that laws relating to the environment are enforced; and
- adapt policies where necessary and, by access to an appropriate forum, ensure the co-operation of departments and officials.[15]

5.3.4 Legislative Framework

The ultimate success of environmental administration in South Africa is dependent, to a very substantial degree, upon the legislative framework within which the policy goals are transformed to legal mandates to be implemented by the different executive authorities. Environmental legislation is discussed in most chapters. See particularly chapters 2 and 6.

5.3.5 Macro-organizational Arrangements

The present unitary constitutional system in South Africa provides for a three-tier system consisting of the central or national level with Parliament as the supreme legislature and the central executive governmental institutions; the regional level consisting of the four provincial administrations as well as the self-governing national states with their own legislative assemblies and administrations; and the local level consisting of the numerous local or municipal councils with their own executive institutions, as well as the recently established system of regional services councils. The different tiers of government have their own fields of jurisdiction and executive institutions to implement legislation. The distinct hierarchy of status and power dictates that Parliament, which enjoys the supreme authority, has the power to make use of both the regional and local executive institutions to attain its objectives. This brief outline of the scope and nature of the different tiers of government serves as the basis for an analysis of the macro-organizational arrangements for environmental administration.

5.3.5.1 *International level*

The existence of a number of international treaties on the conservation and utilization of natural resources signals the need to recognize an international dimension as an additional level that should be included in the analysis of the macro-organizational arrangements of environmental administration. South Africa is a party to a number of such treaties and a member of various international conservation organizations. The above-mentioned treaties and the resolutions of international organizations could have a direct impact on the administration of environmental affairs at national level. See, generally, on international environmental law, chapter 9.

5.3.5.2 *National level*

The central government plays the major role in the administration of environmental affairs at a national level in South Africa and, if the abovementioned recommendation of the President's Council is accepted, will continue to do so. The government

[15] Ibid.

institution which occupies the pivotal position is the Department of Environment Affairs. The major function of this central government department is, first, the formulation of environmental policy; secondly, the co-ordination of environmental administration and thirdly, the monitoring of the actions of the different executive institutions applying the policy. The department's jurisdiction has been steadily extended as more environmental legislation was entrusted to its care, although the policy of devolution has served to deflect the administration of much of this legislation to other bodies. The *Report of the President's Council on a national environmental management system* contains a number of recommendations directed at streamlining the policy-making function as well as the organizational strengthening of the department's ability to monitor the application of policy. In an effort to rationalize the fragmented control over pollution which currently vests in no less than five state departments, besides every local authority, the establishment of a single organizational unit for this function (a branch: pollution control) within the Department of Environment Affairs is recommended in the President's Council's report.[16] In line with this recommendation the directorates of water pollution control (currently located in the Department of Water Affairs) and of air pollution control (at present with the Department of National Health and Population Development), besides two new directorates dealing with noise control and with control over solid and hazardous waste, respectively, should be located within this proposed branch.[17] Further efforts aimed at rationalization include recommendations for the establishment of three further branches: The branch: environmental conservation,[18] to deal with environmental education, the management of natural resources, environmental research and regional and international liaison; the branch: marine resources,[19] comprising living marine resources and the coastal zone and the branch: planning and management,[20] comprising, inter alia, environmental planning, which includes integrated environmental management and environmental impact assessment.

A number of statutory bodies are also answerable to the Minister of Environment Affairs ie the Council for the Environment which advises the Minister on national environmental policy and strategy, the Committee for Environmental Management which promotes effective co-ordination between the different State departments and other executive institutions involved in environmental management and the National Parks Board, which is responsible for the establishment and management of national parks. Other bodies include the National Botanical Institute, the National Hiking Way Board and the Sea Fisheries Advisory Council.

Several other central government departments are also involved in the administration of some or other aspect of the environment. The land-use planning function is the responsibility of the Department of Regional and Land Affairs, while the conservation of soil and generally of agricultural resources falls under the jurisdiction of the Department of Agriculture. The Department of Water Affairs is responsible for the management of water sources, while certain health aspects of water quality, radiation and air pollution fall under the jurisdiction of the Department of National Health and Population Development. The responsibility for oil pollution control at sea is shared by the Departments of Transport and of Environment Affairs, while the Department of National Education and the National Monuments Council are responsible for the preservation of certain cultural and historical assets. The Department of Mineral and Energy Affairs is concerned with exercising control over energy matters and the

[16] Para 6.4.4.
[17] Para 6.4.4.9.
[18] Para 6.4.5.
[19] Para 6.4.6.
[20] Para 6.4.7.

exploitation of minerals. The President's Council, in its *Report on a national environmental management system*, made recommendations concerning the structure and function of several government departments which administer aspects of the environment.[21]

5.3.5.3 *Regional level*

The most important environmental function at regional level traditionally entails the conservation of wild animals, indigenous plants and freshwater fish. The nature conservation function at provincial level was strengthened in 1986 with the devolution of certain executive functions from central to provincial level. The provincial nature conservation authorities are now inter alia also responsible for the management of the sea-shore, mountain catchment areas and certain categories of protected forestry areas and for the enforcement of protective measures with regard to marine resources. The provincial councils were abolished and replaced by nominated executive committees which are now directly accountable to Parliament for their province's nature conservation responsibilities. The KwaZulu Bureau for Natural Resources, the Kangwane Parks Corporation and the QwaQwa Tourism and Nature Conservation Corporation of the self-governing national states can also be classified as regional nature conservation authorities. The national states now all have nature conservation legislation which has replaced the provincial nature conservation ordinances previously applicable in these areas. The administration of the various land-use and town-planning ordinances has also become a significant environmental function of the provinces, while aspects of waste disposal are directly or indirectly controlled by provincial ordinances.

Finally, the President's Council, in its *Report on a national environmental management system*, while accepting that the ultimate and final authority should lie with central government for all aspects of environmental management, recommended that certain defined functions can be delegated to institutions of second- and third-tier government where this is scientifically desirable, and where the institution concerned commands the required resources to undertake the responsibility adequately.[22] Moreover, it was recommended that the Department of Environment Affairs establish regional offices.[23]

5.3.5.4 *Local level*

The different general purpose (municipal and city councils as well as regional services councils) and special purpose (e g the Natal Sharks Board and the Rand Water Board) local authorities exercise a variety of environmental functions mainly concerning town-planning, air pollution, noise control, waste and water management, the sea-shore, outdoor recreation and the management of local nature reserves.

5.4 EVALUATION AND RECOMMENDATIONS

The present administrative system for environmental management in South Africa is the product of a historical developmental process. As such, it came about in an evolutionary way. This evolutionary process brings about advantages and disadvantages associated with the present administrative system for environmental management. As a product of socio-economic and political change, the system incrementally adapted to needs emanating from its context. This incremental adaptation, however, also led to problems manifesting themselves when the system as an integrated whole was considered. These problems include the following:

- A lack of a central mission, goals and objectives at which the system is directed as

---

[21] Para 6.6.
[22] Para 6.5.1.7.
[23] Paras 6.5.2–6.5.5.

illustrated by the quest for a national environmental policy and conservation strategy during the 1980s.

- Owing to the present constitutional arrangements, a multiplicity of institutions have been created to deal with various aspects of environmental management. This results in fragmentation of the service-provision system and creates serious problems of co-ordination.
- Because environmental management was until recently not considered as a high national priority, the institutions involved with it were not vested with high political status and the administrative system was not given sufficient official authority to handle possible conflicts of interest in respect of environmental management.
- Owing to the fragmented and unco-ordinated functioning of the administrative system, dualistic conservation/exploitation assignments were conferred upon particular institutions. This inevitably led to conflicts of interest within these institutions.

The present position with regard to the sectoral placement of the service-provision system is that the vast majority of environmental management services are placed within the public sector of the economy. This placement seems correct, given the generally collective nature of the services. Environmental protection services are by definition collective and therefore have to be placed in the public sector of the economy where they are at present. The utilization of natural resources is of a more particular nature and should ideally be placed in the private sector of the economy. The State's role in the utilization of natural resources could—depending on the economic ideology and reasons linked to positive and negative spillover effects—be considered for privatization and deregulation. The protection service, consisting mainly of regulatory activities, also needs to be vested with political and administrative authority which strengthens the need for placement in the public sector of the economy. Where the State is directly involved in the utilization of natural resources—e g when managing a natural resource owned by itself—it does not require the same extent of political and administrative authority. After all, the State, as owner of the resource, may exercise its common-law authority in a similar fashion as any other resource owner.

When assessing the present political approach to the administration of environmental management, it has to be realized that the assessment is value-laden and could therefore not be fully objective. With this caveat in mind, it is submitted that the present approach approximates a more technocratic thrust. The reasons for this view are:

- South Africa under the present constitutional and administrative arrangements is by definition undemocratic, since the majority of its citizens do not have democratic rights.
- Except for the appointed councils of some statutory boards, there are very few formal institutionalised opportunities for real participation by the majority of citizens in environmental management decisions.
- If the seemingly minor effect of the actions of interest and pressure groups is considered in terms of the reactions elicited from responsible official authorities, it seems to indicate a bias towards the more technocratic approach. Any other explanation would imply that the responsible official authorities regard neither democratic nor technocratic influences on their decision-making.

The service-provision system for environmental management in South Africa is currently characterised by numerous and diverse institutions. The institutional types include conventional government departments at central and regional levels as well as more autonomous parastatal bodies functioning at national and provincial level. This institutional diversity and diffusion is probably the result of the evolutionary development of the environmental management function. On balance, the situation can be viewed as functional. It is difficult to assess the effectiveness of present institutional arrangements because no objective empirical evidence is available. If, however, there is a move towards decreasing political control and more autonomy—that is, towards a parastatal institutional type—it will have to be accompanied by a decrease in governmental authority and a decrease in state funding.

When the present constitutional and hierarchical placement of the environmental management system is considered, it is evident that aspects of the system are situated at all three tiers of government. This factor, viewed in conjunction with the multi-institutional approach discussed in the previous paragraph, has dysfunctional effects in terms of general organizational considerations. These effects include fragmentation, poor co-ordination, a lack of control, jurisdictional conflicts, an overlap of functions, a disunity of purpose among institutions, and clashes of interest.

Taking the theoretical considerations as point of departure and relating these considerations to the present situation, it is possible to make recommendations regarding strategic options in respect of an administrative model for environmental management in South Africa. The application of the guidelines, once again, may result in seemingly conflicting prescriptions. This is normal and compatible with the emphasis of the contingency approach, which holds that prescriptions are not static and bureaucratic but should remain dynamic and flexible in terms of an organic model.

The collective and regulatory environmental protective services in an environmental management service-provision system should be placed in the public sector of the economy. The systems delivering these services should also be vested with governmental authority. Where there is a possibility of the economic utilization of the products or services associated with environmental management, such as protected areas, tourism, forestry or fisheries, these services may be quasi-collective or even particular and could therefore be placed in the private sector of the economy. This should, however, be considered only if such utilization will not in any way conflict with overall collective conservation goals and objectives.

The decisions regarding a national policy and conservation strategy require a scientific and technical input. These policy decisions, which will provide the general scientific and technical frameworks, should incorporate, as an overall approach, a substantial technocratic input. This technocratic bias, however, will have to be checked to a certain extent through the normal political process involved in enacting parliamentary legislation. The gist of the policy framework has to be based primarily on technocratic inputs taking scientific, objective and technical criteria into consideration.

After the general policy framework has been set, taking scientific and technical considerations into account, the remaining actions and decisions regarding environmental management should be more democratic. This implies the institutionalization of opportunities for public participation in environmental decision-making. It also implies a devolution of decision-making and a decentralization of executive actions to public bodies which function at regional and local levels. These decisions may be autonomous and democratic within the general policy framework. Such an approach, rather than a highly centralized one, will better reflect the different value systems pertaining to the cultural and traditional utilization of the natural environment in a heterogeneous society. Since environmental concerns probably do not feature as a priority for a majority of South Africans, even strict and sophisticated legislation will not necessarily induce favourable attitudes to environmental concerns. Democratic involvement and participation in decision-making and executive actions on the other hand, may well result in an improvement of the legitimacy of environmental policies, objectives and actions.

With regard to institutional types and arrangements, it seems that institutional diversity may be necessary and functional, due to the diverse nature of the environmental services performed. It is, however, necessary to establish a central government institution with high political status and sufficient governmental authority, funded by public money, to render the required environmental protection service. Such an institution must provide the general policy framework mentioned above and should be able to act decisively when conflicts arise between powerful interest groups. Such an approach is also compatible with the currrent evolution of the environmental management systems. Such a body may seek advice in the form of technical expertise from advisory bodies. The democratic input at this level has to be provided by the central legislative authority which could be a fully representative and democratic Parliament.

The remaining environmental management functions, except for the broad aspects allocated to the central government institution, may then be institutionalized through diverse and applicable institutional types, depending on the nature of the services, the scope of governmental authority and the extent of the need for public funding. These institutions functioning with devoluted decision-making and decentralized executive powers have to provide for maximum democratic participation at the regional and local levels. Institutional types used here may include regional parks boards, special multi- or single-purpose authorities (e g, catchment and river management authorities, harbour management authorities and water boards) and entrepreneurial bodies (e g, public resorts authorities).

The policy-making, co-ordinating and monitoring functions concerning the environment have to be provided for at the level of central government. These functions should be allocated to the central government institution mentioned above. Any centralising tendency created by this approach should be counterbalanced through maximum devolution and decentralization of the remaining functions to institutions at regional and local levels where provision should also be made for democratic participation in decision-making.

The approaches suggested above constantly have to take account of general organizational considerations, which should be integrated into the final administrative model for providing environmental management services.

In summary, the proposals for a system for the administration of environmental management can be illustrated by means of the diagram in Figure 5.1.

5.5 SUMMARY

Decisions about administrative models for service-provision systems should seek to maximize the benefits to be gained from available strategic options. The most recent theoretical approach to strategic decision-making is the contingency approach. This approach is based upon open-systems assumptions and it accepts that strategic decisions have to be made in accordance with the results of environmental analyses and situation assessments.

The possible strategic options for an administrative model for a service-provision system have to consider the sectoral placement of the system, the political approach to the system, the institutional types most applicable to the system, the constitutional and hierarchical placement of the service-provision system and general organizational aspects.

The decisions regarding the sectoral placement have to indicate whether this placement should be within the public or private sector of the economy. The available political approaches may range from a more democratic to a more technocratic inclination. The institutional type which is selected could tend towards either a parastatal or a traditional government department type of arrangement. The constitutional and hierarchical placement may range from a more central to a more local option. The relative position in terms of these dimensions has to be decided in accordance with the conditioning factors influencing the particular service-provision system.

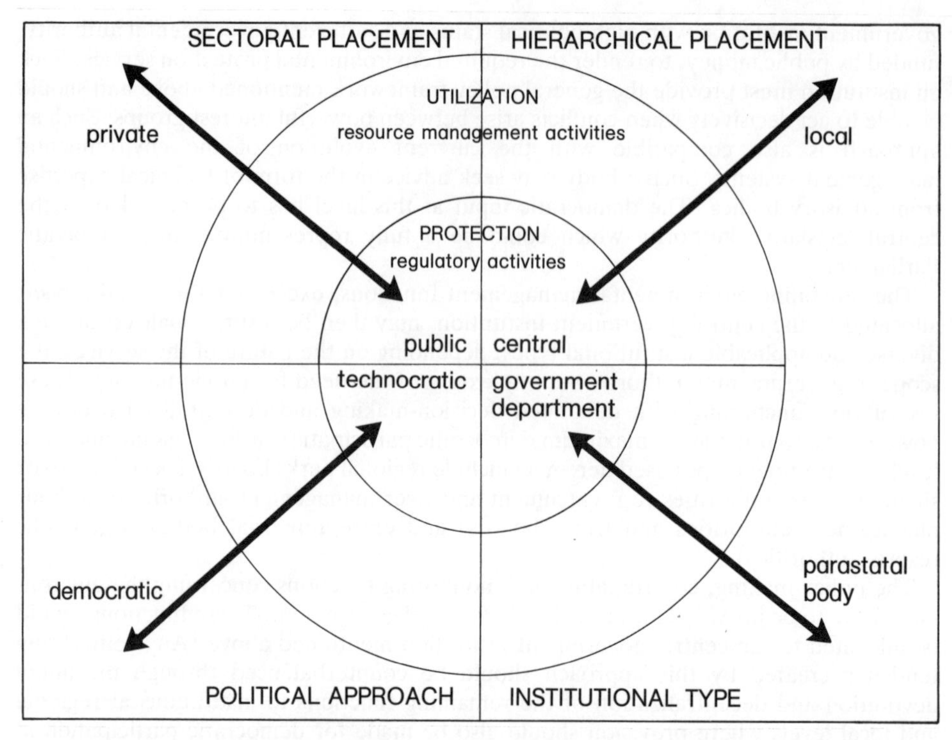

Figure 5.1 A proposed system for the administration of environmental management.

The administration of environmental management in South Africa is linked to the process of constitutional development and has a long history. When the present position is considered and analysed in terms of the above factors, it indicates that the protection and regulatory activities should preferably be part of the public sector, have a technocratic inclination and be organized along the lines of a government department with strong central powers. The utilization and management activities, on the other hand, should:

- be placed in the private sector;
- be democratically inclined;
- be organized along parastatal lines; and
- be devolved and decentralized to local levels.

This approach, as a contingency approach, does not presuppose final, rigid and unchangeable administrative models. On the contrary, it necessitates a constant re-evaluation of conditions and a regular adaptation of administrative structures and functions to changing conditions. As such, it represents a dynamic organic approach to administrative modelling rather than a static bureaucratic approach.

CHAPTER 6

NATURE AND SCOPE OF ENVIRONMENTAL LAW

M A RABIE

6.1 INTRODUCTION

The concept 'environment' was virtually unknown in legal language before 1970 and was introduced in the natural sciences only during this century. However, during the past two decades much attention has been focused on environmental law and many legislative provisions have been passed to deal with environmental problems. Moreover, the label 'environmental' was retrospectively attached to a great number of pre-1970 legal provisions—dating back even to the 17th century—as the realization dawned that those provisions, in fact, dealt with problems which today are identified as 'environmental'. On the historical development of environmental law in South Africa see, generally, chapter 2. There is nevertheless a considerable degree of uncertainty as to what exactly constitutes environmental law. This uncertainty is due mainly to a lack of clarity over two fundamental issues, i e

(a) what is understood by the term 'environment' and
(b) which legal rules pertaining to the environment constitute environmental law?

Public concern over the deteriorating state of our environment has become increasingly manifest during the past two decades. This has led to intensified efforts directed towards combating the problem. Environmental conservation, during this period, has become official government policy, mirrored also in the publication of a *White Paper on a national policy regarding environmental conservation*[1] and the establishment of a Department of Environment Affairs, assisted by an advisory Council for the Environment.

6.2 THE CONCEPT 'ENVIRONMENT'

There is no general agreement on exactly what the concept 'environment' encompasses. Curiously enough, its meaning is often simply taken for granted and many commentators and even official publications discuss environmental problems without attempting to define 'environment'. It is obvious, nevertheless, that any meaningful classification and discussion of environmental problems, as well as any advocacy of the cause of environmental conservation, presuppose clarity over the pivotal concept of environment. Such clarity is required also for the demarcation and analysis of the field of environmental law, if environmental law is understood to be the law relating to the environment.

Until recently, practical environmental conservation was not unduly hampered by this uncertainty concerning the concept environment. Traditionally, individual components of the environment were identified and treated separately. However, as the need for a comprehensive approach to environmental problems becomes manifest, concern should centre on the concept of environment as a whole and not only on its individual components. It is especially the declaration of an environmental policy and the processes of integrated environmental management and of environmental impact

[1] WPO—1980.

assessment which highlight the need for agreement on what is to be understood by 'environment.'

Although the concept of environment featured in the titles of a few statutes, notably the Cape Nature and Environmental Conservation Ordinance 19 of 1974, the Natal Prevention of Environmental Pollution Ordinance 21 of 1981 and the Environment Conservation Act 100 of 1982, it was nowhere defined. Nor was environment circumscribed in official documents such as the *White Paper on a national policy regarding environmental conservation* or the *Report by the commission of inquiry into environmental legislation*.[2] It was only during 1989, with the promulgation of the Environment Conservation Act 73 of 1989, that a first legislative attempt was made to define the concept.

Relatively few attempts have been made to define environment in law. This may be explained partly by the fact that such definition, if required at all, was regarded as being necessary mainly for the purpose of identifying and systematizing environmental law as an emerging field of law. This, it may have been argued, was primarily of academic concern. Nevertheless, the need to define environment was clearly underscored by the use of that concept in legislation, especially by provisions governing the declaration of an environmental policy and the submission of environmental impact reports.

It should be recognized that environment is a relational concept; it denotes an interrelationship between man and his surroundings. Depending upon how extensively the latter is conceived, different approaches may be identified:

6.2.1 Extensive approach

According to this approach 'environment' is a concept which embraces a multitude of ingredients, including the following:

(a) **Natural environment**, i e in a strict sense the natural world in its pure state, but more generally regarded as referring to renewable and non-renewable natural resources such as air, water, soil, plants, animals, etc.
(b) **Spatial environment**, i e man-made and natural areas such as a suburb, town, city, region, province, country, as well as certain specific landscapes, for instance mountains, wetlands, rivers, sea-shore, forests, etc.
(c) **Sociological or social environment**, i e other people such as the family, group, society, etc.

Other components of the environment that have been identified, include the following:

(d) **Economic environment;**
(e) **Cultural-historic environment;**
(f) **Built environment;**
(g) **Political environment;**
(h) **Labour or work environment.**

From a purely semantic perspective, an extensive approach is evident. Environment is defined comprehensively in *The Oxford English Dictionary*[3] as 'the conditions under which any person or thing lives or is developed; the sum-total of influences which modify and determine the development of life or character'. *Webster's Dictionary*[4] also relates the concept of environment to both natural and socio-cultural conditions, while Brockhaus,[5] similarly, defines environment as the entire surroundings of an organism, for man also the totality of his natural and culturally altered living space.

[2] RP 10/1982.
[3] 2nd ed 1989.
[4] *Webster's third new international dictionary of the English language* (1961).
[5] *Deutsches Wörterbuch* (1984).

This extensive definition is indeed the one which has been proposed by some commentators. Swaigen & Woods,[6] for instance, submit that environment should not be defined narrowly as the physical environment alone; account should be taken also of the ineffable: the inter-dependency of man and his social, cultural and physical life-support systems. The extensive concept may be referred to as the *human* environment, which 'embraces everything in man's living space that may possibly have an effect on man or that may be affected by man',[7] or simply includes all factors that determine human existence.

Such an extensive approach would, of course, also affect one's perception of the ambit of environmental law. Rodgers,[8] supporting this approach, thus contends that environmental law is not concerned solely with the natural environment: 'It embraces also the human environment—the health, social and other man-made conditions affecting a human being's place on earth.'

The extensive concept was first employed in legislation in the United States' National Environmental Policy Act of 1970, which referred to the human environment. Interpretations by the courts of this concept (which is not defined in the Act), confirm that it has a vast compass. For instance, it has been held that urban environmental ills should be subsumed under the human environment and that they include 'noise, traffic, overburdened mass transportation systems, crime, congestion and even availability of drugs'.[9] This legislation requires the submission of environmental impact statements in respect of certain proposed governmental actions. Similar legislation in Canada, i e the Ontario Environmental Assessment Act[10] went further and set out to define environment as

'(i) air, land or water,
(ii) plant and animal life, including man,
(iii) social, economic and cultural conditions that influence the life of man or a community,
(iv) any building, structure, machine or other device or thing made by man,
(v) any solid, liquid, gas, odour, heat, sound, vibration or radiation resulting directly or indirectly from the activities of man, or
(vi) any part or combination of the foregoing and the interrelationships between any two or more of them'.

Certain Australian legislation also employs extensive definitions of environment. For example, according to the Commonwealth Environment Protection (Impact of Proposals) Act of 1974[11] environment 'includes all aspects of the surroundings of man, whether affecting him as an individual or in his social groupings', while the Queensland State and Regional Planning and Development, Public Works Organization and Environmental Control Act of 1971[12] refers to 'the conditions and influences to which living matter is sensitive and is capable of reacting'.

More recently, the South African legislature for the first time sought to define environment, in the Environment Conservation Act 73 of 1989.[13] In terms of the Act, it means 'the aggregate of surrounding objects, conditions and influences that influence the life and habits of man or any other organism or collection of organisms'. The human

---

[6] 'A substantive right to environmental quality' in Swaigen (ed) *Environmental rights in Canada* (1981).

[7] *Report of the Planning Committee of the President's Council on priorities between conservation and development* PC 5/1984 para 3.1.

[8] *Handbook on environmental law* (1977) 1.

[9] *Hanly v Mitchell* (I) 460 F 2d 640, 647, 2 ELR 20216, 20220 (2d Cir 1972).

[10] Section 1*(c)*.

[11] Section 3.

[12] Section 5.

[13] Section 1*(x)*.

environment, thus defined in its broadest sense, 'would comprise the external circumstances, conditions, and things that affect the existence and development of an individual or group'.[14] In the context of development and conservation, this 'would consist of both a source of materials for creating things that will improve the human condition, and a source of natural amenities and life-support systems which directly contribute to human well-being and survival'.[15] This more or less corresponds to the dictionary meaning of the concept and is about as all-embracing as may be imagined. That a comprehensive definition was intended may be inferred from the qualification of the concept in certain provisions, namely natural environment,[16] man-made environment[17] and physical environment.[18]

Viewed in such a wide context, environment would include almost everything which somehow—either positively or negatively—may influence human existence or even the quality of life. Such a wide concept of environment would defeat entirely any effort at distinguishing environmental conservation as a separate branch of knowledge. Almost anything could then be subsumed under the term environment. For instance, a programme aimed at the prevention and combating of crime or at the provision of housing would be very much part of efforts at conserving the social environment, while attempts to combat inflation or to alleviate unemployment would rank as conservation of the economic environment.

Since the entire body of law regulates man's relationship to the above extensive environment, all law would be considered as environmental law, thus effectively ruling out any place for environmental law as a distinct field of law.[19]

6.2.2 Limited approach

Under the limited approach environment is more narrowly construed, as pertaining to only certain components of a comprehensively defined concept of environment. In fact, any view which restricts the wide ambit of the extensive approach may be generally regarded as constituting a limited concept. According to one such view it would thus relate only to the *natural* environment[20] or simply to nature.[21] Natural would seem a satisfactory adjective to exclude social, cultural, economic and most instances of spatial environment—in short, the anthropogenic environment. Natural thus stands in contrast to anthropogenic.

This approach probably has been influenced by ecological studies which basically have been aimed at researching the natural environment with its natural ecosystems.[22] It may also have been derived from the concept of nature conservation. Nature, although part of the concept of environment, is usually viewed as being more limited in extent. In its narrowest sense, it refers to indigenous wild animals and plants as well as freshwater fish. This is the tenor and content of the respective provincial ordinances on nature conservation, although nature is not therein specifically defined. In a somewhat

---

[14] *Integrated environmental management in South Africa* Council for the Environment (1989) 6.

[15] Ibid.

[16] Sections 2(1)*(a)* and 26*(a)*(iii). *Cf* also s 16.

[17] Section 26*(a)*(iii).

[18] Section 26*(a)*(ii).

[19] Steiger 'Begriff und Geltungsebenen des Umweltrechts' in Salzewedel (ed) *Grundzüge des Umweltrechts* (1982) 4; Huber 'Umwelt und Umweltschutz als Rechtsbegriffe' in *Festschrift für Hans R Klecatsky* 1 (1980) 355–6.

[20] Loretan *Die Umweltverträglichkeitsprüfung. Ihre Ausgestaltung im Bundesgesetz über den Umweltschutz, mit Hinweisen auf das amerikanische und deutsche Recht* (1986) 35; Prümm *Umweltschutzrecht* (1989) 4; Erbguth *Rechtssystematische Grundfragen des Umweltrechts* (1987) 48.

[21] Winter 'Perspectives for environmental law—entering the fourth phase' 1989 *J of Environmental Law* 38.

[22] *Umweltgutachten 1987*. Der Rat von Sachverständigen für Umweltfragen (1988) 38.

broader sense, it refers to 'all living and therefore renewable natural resources',[23] while in a still broader sense, it would, in addition, make provision for 'non-renewable natural resources, such as landscapes, natural phenomena such as habitats, as well as biological organisms and communities'.[24] In its broadest, albeit unusual, sense, it would, according to the President's Council include 'the works of man that are of lasting cultural value and that serve to enhance the quality of the environment.'[25] In its most recent environmental report the President's Council defines the environment as 'the aggregate of physical, biological and cultural conditions affecting the life of an individual human being or the community'.[26] Usually, though, nature is taken to refer to *natural* resources and this, as has been remarked, may have influenced the view that the concept environment should be restricted to the *natural* environment.

Human beings are part of the natural environment; in fact, their existence depends on it entirely. Initially, primitive humans, like any animal, managed to fulfil all their needs by direct reliance upon the natural environment. Gradually, however, human needs, following upon development, increased to the extent that they began transforming their environment to meet those needs. Although this anthropogenic environment consists of components of the natural environment (and despite the continued functioning of natural processes), the natural environment has been modified to the extent that one can no longer speak of a natural environment in the strict sense. Various agricultural practices have transformed large tracts of natural landscape into human-induced environments such as orchards, vineyards and wheatlands, while afforestation has led to the establishment of plantations. Humans have created infrastructure such as powerlines, roads, railroads and dams. They have built houses and have established towns and cities, besides industrial and mining complexes. Such anthropogenic environments intermingle with the original, natural environment, from which they cannot be separated. This transformation of natural environments has occurred gradually over a considerable period. The era of industrialization and of technological development has now brought about such a drastic acceleration of the process that very little remains of truly natural environments—at least as far as land areas (with the exception of certain polar regions) are concerned. In fact, desperate efforts are undertaken to protect remnants of such natural environments. Even such 'island' environments often can no longer subsist independently, but must now be managed by man. Perhaps the closest semblance of natural environments in today's developed countries are wilderness areas. A wilderness, in contrast to those areas where humans and their works dominate the landscape, is an area where the earth and its community of life are untrammelled, where the primeval character and influence are retained, without permanent improvements or human habitation.[27]

It would thus appear that we have, to a greater or lesser extent, transformed almost our entire natural inhabited terrestrial environment. Natural environment, accordingly, is too limited a concept and it would be unrealistic to restrict our conservation efforts only to the strictly natural environment.[28] Moreover, it has been stated that conservation of only the natural environment would presuppose a reliance upon the

---

[23] *Report of the Planning Committee of the President's Council on priorities between conservation and development*, above n 7, para 3.1.1.

[24] Barkhuizen *Koördinasie van openbare natuurbewaring in Suid-Afrika* (1979) referred to in the *Report of the Planning Committee of the President's Council on nature conservation in South Africa* PC 2/1984 par 2.1.

[25] *Report of the Planning Committee of the President's Council on nature conservation in South Africa*, above n 24, para 4.1.1.1.

[26] *Report of the three committees of the President's Council on a national environmental management system* PC 1/1991 para 1.3.2.

[27] Cf 43 USC para 1131*(c)*.

[28] Huber above n 19, 360.

philosophy that nature should be protected for its own sake.[29] However, this is not necessarily the case, as is evident from the establishment of protected areas, where the natural environment is conserved for human benefit. The prevailing philosophy, in any case, is that conservation is not an end in itself but is aimed at fulfilling human needs.[30]

A related, but different approach would restrict the term environment to the natural environmental elements[31] such as air, water and soil, which have not been created by humans, but which they may modify either through exploitation or the introduction of foreign matter. This view seems more realistic in that account is taken not only of the natural environment in its pure state, but also of modifications imposed on it by humans.

A further view which may be said to involve a limited concept of environment is that of the President's Council, according to which environment refers to 'man's physical and cultural environment'.[32]

Finally, what may be classed as a narrower approach would relate environment to certain basic components of the biosphere, i e to air, water, soil, plants and animals. For instance, environment, according to the 1976 US Toxic Substances Control Act[33] includes water, air and land and the interrelationship which exists among and between water, air, and land and all living beings.[34] While this definition is not exhaustive, Storm,[35] in fact, restricts the concept environment to the elements of soil, water, air, animals and plants and their interrelationship with each other and with humans. A similar definition is contained in the Tasmanian Environment Protection Act of 1973,[36] according to which environment means the land, water and atmosphere of the earth. The definition in the State of Victoria's Environment Protection Act of 1970[37] has a wider ambit and relates to the physical factors of the surroundings of human beings and includes the biological factors of animals and plants and the social factor of aesthetics.

6.2.3 Avoidance of the term environment

Although the concept environment is essential to demarcate the scope and content of environmental management and of environmental law, the sectoral approach to environmental problems in the past did not require of legislatures to define environment. In fact, the concept did not feature in the individual legislative provisions relating to the control of specific types of pollution or to the conservation of specific natural resources. Dempfle & Müggenborg[38] contend that this is preferable to the prevailing position in German legislation, where the concepts 'environment' and 'harmful environmental impact' have widely differing meanings, depending upon the particular legislation in question.

More recently, deliberate efforts have been made to avoid the term of environment and instead to refer to life-support systems or to foundations for life ('Lebensgrundlagen'). However, this does not avoid the difficulty of qualifying such systems or foundations. Here again, an extensive and a restrictive approach may be identified. According to the former such foundations would encompass all circumstances—

---

[29] Steiger above n 19, 6.

[30] *Report of the Planning Committee of the President's Council on priorities between conservation and development*, above n 7, para 6.3.

[31] Von Wallenberg *Umweltschutz und Wettbewerb* (1980) 6.

[32] *Report of the Planning Committee of the President's Council on priorities between conservation and development*, above n 7, para 6.1.

[33] 15 USC 1601, s 3(5).

[34] A similar definition is contained in s 2*(j)* of the 1972 Federal Insecticide, Fungicide, and Rodenticide Act (PL92–516).

[35] *Umweltrecht. Einführung in ein neues Rechtsgebiet* (3 ed 1988) 17.

[36] Section 2(1).

[37] Section 4(1).

[38] 'Die "Umwelt", ein Rechtsbegriff?' 1987 *Natur und Recht* 301.

including those brought about by humans—which influence their life,[39] while a more limited approach would be restricted to the *natural* foundations of life ('die natürliche Lebensgrundlagen').[40] The latter approach is also evident in definitions of the environment which relate to 'the interlocking web of plants, animals and resources, and the associated flow of energy from the sun and from one form to another, that make up our life-support system.'[41]

Instead of environment, reference is sometimes made to the biosphere.[42] Nevertheless, although the biosphere is normally taken to refer to the thin film close to the earth's surface where all life exists, even this concept is sometimes extended to include the environment in its totality, consisting of both natural and cultural elements.[43] On the other hand, if the environment should be restricted to the biosphere, certain generally acknowledged environmental problems, such as the depletion of the stratospheric ozone layer by chlorofluorocarbons, would fall outside its realm.

It has been shown, nevertheless, that the concept environment cannot be avoided if clarity is sought as to the nature and scope of environmental management and of environmental law. Moreover, recent environmental legislation, evidencing a more comprehensive approach, depends upon a definition of the concept for the application of a number of provisions.

6.2.4 Towards a realistic demarcation of environment

It seems obvious that an all-embracing concept of environment, although probably satisfactory from a linguistic perspective, is unacceptable as a workable basis for determining the scope and content of environmental law. It would defeat the aim of identifying environmental law as a separate branch of law, because the all-encompassing nature of environment would tend to make all law environmental law. Many commentators accordingly acknowledge the necessity of modifying the extensive definition of environment.[44]

At the one end of the spectrum, it is submitted that use of the concept environment to indicate man's relationship with other human beings or with human institutions—as is reflected in phrases such as the social and political environment—is therefore inappropriate. The same should apply to human resources such as labour or the economy. In fact, there is even some doubt whether occupational exposure to unhealthy or unsafe environmental conditions, for instance, noise in the workplace, qualifies as an environmental problem. See chapters 22 and 23. Much the same applies to radiation from electronic products, which involves only operators and patients. The above submission seems to be implicitly endorsed by the government's *White Paper on a national policy regarding environmental conservation*,[45] since environmental factors are therein contrasted with financial, social, technological and economic considerations.

At the other end of the spectrum, it would be unrealistic to restrict environment to the purely natural environment, because most of the erstwhile natural environment is

---

[39] Von Wallenberg above n 31, 4–5.

[40] Kimminich, von Lersner & Storm *Handwörterbuch des Umweltrechts* vol 2 (1988) s v 'Umwelt'; Triffterer 'Die Rolle des Strafrechts beim Umweltschutz in der Bundesrepublik Deutschland' 1979 *Zeitschrift für die gesamte Strafrechtswissenschaft* 309, 310–11; Kloepfer *Umweltrecht* (1989) 13.

[41] Franson & Lucas *Environmental law commentary* (1978) 201.

[42] Bender & Sparwasser *Umweltrecht. Grundzüge des öffentlichen Umweltschutzrechts* (2 ed 1990) 1.

[43] Cf the *World conservation strategy*, referred to in the *Report of the Planning Committee of the President's Council on priorities between conservation and development*, above n 7, para 2.1.

[44] Kloepfer above n 40, 13; Hoppe & Beckman *Umweltrecht* (1989) 3–4; Prümm above n 20, 3–4; Erbguth above n 20, 46–7. The President's Council in its *Report on a national environmental management system* above n 26, para 5.1.4, acknowledges that an all-embracing concept of 'environment' is unacceptable as a workable basis for determining the scope and content of environmental law.

[45] Above n 1, para 3.1.

no longer in that state but has, to a greater or lesser degree, been modified by humans. Environment, accordingly, should not be defined only in terms of human impact thereon. The concept does, of course, include the natural environment, as is evident, for instance, in the establishment of protected areas. The point is that it should not be limited to the natural environment. Moreover, environmental conservation does not imply the protection of the entire remaining natural environment. For instance, even if a virus or bacteria is considered part of the natural environment, it for this reason only, should not therefore be subject to protective measures. The same applies to other components of the natural environment which are considered as harmful, eg certain insects.

There probably would be general agreement that the term environment, at its core, refers to the earth's natural resources, both renewable and non-renewable. It is those resources which are the object of prevailing conservation and pollution-control endeavours and it is principally with regard to them that development is sought to be reconciled with conservation. The *White Paper*[46] referred to above thus identifies the following aspects that should be the subject of an environmental policy: air pollution, marine pollution, noise pollution, radiation pollution, water polution, solid waste and littering, soil conservation and nature conservation. As far as environmental pollution is concerned, much the same aspects were identified in the first comprehensive governmental report on pollution.[47] All the above aspects relate to potentially detrimental consequences for man through his impact upon natural resources.

However, the *White Paper* also includes cultural-historical aspects and motivates their inclusion in the following manner: 'The physical environment does not consist only of natural elements but also has cultural components in regard to which a rural environment, natural as well as man-made, and an urban environment can be distinguished. In modern society most people already live in urban environments and it is important to enhance the quality of life in towns and cities. The preservation of the prehistoric, historic and contemporary cultural components contributes to the quality of life created in the urban and rural environment'.[48] The President's Council, likewise, includes 'the works of man that are of lasting cultural value and that serve to enhance the quality of the environment'[49] in the definition of nature conservation. A tendency may thus be discerned to extend the concept environment beyond natural resources, but only to a limited extent, ie to cultural-historical aspects.

On the other hand, although all natural resources may conceptually be subsumed under the environment, such resources are not in fact conserved comprehensively. For instance, little thought has traditionally been given to the conservation of some non-renewable resources, as is evidenced in the exploitation of certain minerals, while renewable resources are usually conserved on a sustained-yield basis, although certain such resources, for instance many plant and animal species, enjoy no protection at all. Moreover, mention has been made above to harmful components of the natural environment which do not qualify for protection.

Although natural means 'existing in, or formed by nature; not artificially made, formed, or constructed'[50] and natural resources usually means 'materials (as mineral deposits and waterpower) supplied by nature,'[51] the words may be given an extended

---

[46] Para 4.

[47] *Pollution 1971* Report by the Pollution Subsidiary Committee of the Prime Minister's Planning Advisory Council (1974).

[48] Para 4.3.

[49] *Report of the Planning Committee of the President's Council on nature conservation in South Africa*, above n 24, para 4.1.1.1. *Cf* also the committee's *Report on priorities between conservation and development*, above n 7, para 3.1.2.

[50] *Oxford English dictionary* (2 ed 1989) s v natural.

[51] *Webster's third new international dictionary of the English language* (1961) s v natural resources.

meaning in legislation. According to the Natural Resources Development Act 51 of 1947[52] natural resources thus include 'land, minerals, water, the means of generating power, labour and the means of transport.'

Attention has been drawn to the fact that humans have transformed large parts of the natural environment, to the extent that not much remains of a purely natural environment. Nevertheless, it does seem possible to draw a distinction in principle between God's created physical environment—even though modified by humans—and the physical creations with which they surround themselves. It is submitted that, from a conservation perspective, such a differentiation is valid, in spite of the fact that both the created and the anthropogenic environments exist side by side and that both serve human needs. It is not contended that the created environment exists as a sphere separate from human actions, ambitions and needs and that it is to be defended in isolation from human concerns. This approach therefore is not in conflict with the view that 'our physical nature, our mental health, our culture and institutions, our opportunities for challenge and fulfillment, our very survival—all of these are directly related and affected by the environment in which we live'.[53] But the physical object of environmental conservation should not be confused with its importance and with its purpose. Although it may be designed to serve human needs, this does not necessarily mean that environmental conservation must therefore also be taken to pertain to the anthropogenic environment, nor that the latter cannot in principle be distinguished from the created environment. Nor does the approach adopted here militate against the view that 'our interaction with the natural environment can only be understood with reference to our perception of it and behavioural response to it, both of which are conditioned by our complex cultural environment'.[54] Although our cultural environment may determine our perception of, and response to, the created environment, it does not mean that the God-created environment cannot in principle be distinguished from human creations.

As far as the modified natural environment is concerned, the point is that environmental conservation does not imply the protection of human achievement in effecting modifications to the natural environment. In fact, the very opposite is implied, i e that humans seek to protect natural resources against their own exploitation thereof, to the extent that a satisfactory compromise should be reached between such exploitation (development) and the protection of the natural environmental elements involved.

As regards the protection of humans' own physical creations, it is submitted that the concept environment will be over-extended if it should relate to every anthropogenic object, structure, installation, etc which surrounds human life. Probably the most controversial issue is whether at least a part of the anthropogenic environment, i e the so-called cultural-historical environment, or, to use the phrase of the President's Council, 'the works of man that are of lasting cultural value and that serve to enhance the quality of the environment', should be subsumed under the term environment. This phrase is intended, presumably, to correspond with that of 'national monument' in the National Monuments Act 28 of 1969,[55] i e 'any immovable or movable property of aesthetic, historical or scientific interest'. National monument, nevertheless, seems to have a wider compass, since it includes components of both the anthropogenic and the created environment. Most declared national monuments, such as huts, houses, forts, churches, pulpits, chairs, railway stations, locomotives, passes, roads, bridges, irrigation tunnels, water wheels and wells involve anthropogenic objects and structures.

---

[52] Section 1.
[53] *Environmental quality* First annual report of the Council on Environmental Quality (1970) vi.
[54] White, Mottershead & Harrison *Environmental systems. An introductory text* (1984) 8.
[55] Section 10(1).

A number of national monuments, nevertheless, relate to the created environment, e g caves, koppies, trees, gardens, waterfalls and even nature reserves. This may be explained by the fact that the created environment can, of course, also be of aesthetic, scientific or cultural importance. This, none the less, does not obliterate the distinction between the created and the anthropogenic environment. Traditionally, the conservation of the cultural environment does not seem to have been regarded as forming part of environmental conservation in the narrower sense of the word. This approach is underscored by the National Monuments Council's being subject to the jurisdiction of the Department of National Education, rather than of the Department of Environment Affairs. Nevertheless, reference has been made to the more recent tendency—displayed, inter alia, in the *White Paper* of 1980—to subsume the cultural-historical environment under the concept environment. It is noteworthy that among commentators who support a limited definition of environment there is a difference of opinion as to whether or not the cultural-historical environment should be included in the definition.[56]

What is to be regarded as the environment seems, in the final analysis, to be a policy question upon which opinions may differ. This implies that what is regarded as environmental conservation and as environmental law may even differ from one country to another and from one time period to another. The underlying issue may also exert an influence; e g environmental impact assessment may well demand an extensive approach. The parameters of the concept environment are obviously still evolving and it would be unwise to attempt to formulate a fixed definition of the concept. In other words, it must to some extent be regarded as open-ended. Sufficient clarity nevertheless exists with regard to its hard core, as has been indicated.

6.3 SCOPE OF ENVIRONMENTAL LAW

Once the meaning of environment has been determined, the broad scope of environmental law is established: an environmental law norm is one which relates to the environment.

6.3.1 Environmental conservation/environmental management

Not every legal norm relating to the environment is regarded as constituting environmental law. Environmental law presupposes that the norm in question is aimed at or is used for environmental conservation. Environmental conservation is concerned with the conservation of natural resources and with the control of environmental pollution. The modern phrase, which comprises both the above actions, but which more adequately reflects a necessary compromise with development, is that of environmental management. Environmental-law norms thus relate ultimately to the management of the environment.

6.3.2 Degree of relevance

An important question which arises is whether a legal norm should qualify as constituting environmental law merely on account of its relevance or even potential relevance for environmental management or whether there should be a more direct, specific connection. In other words, what should be the degree of environmental relevance before a provision will qualify as constituting environmental law?

At this juncture, it may be helpful to consider the spectrum of legislation which regulates environmental management. According to the general aim of the legislation and the degree of environmental relevance of the norms in question, the following gradations may be identified:

---

[56] While Kloepfer above n 40, 13, supports its inclusion, Hoppe & Beckmann above n 44, 4, and Prümm above n 20, 4, reject the contention that monuments and buildings should be subsumed under the concept 'environment'.

6.3.2.1 *Exclusive environmental legislation*

This category refers to legislation (phrase used to cover parliamentary acts, provincial ordinances, local by-laws and ministerial regulations) which aims exclusively at environmental management and which contain only environmentally specific norms. Strictly speaking, such legislation is rare, since almost no legislation is so single-minded in its scope. Purely administrative and related provisions not having a bearing specifically on the subject in question are encountered almost universally, even in legislation directed at a specific aim. Discounting such provisions, we may regard the following legislation as examples of statutes which are exclusively environmental in nature.

***(a)* Conservation of natural resources**

National Parks Act 57 of 1976
Conservation of Agricultural Resources Act 43 of 1983;
Provincial Nature Conservation Ordinances.

***(b)* Pollution Control**

Atmospheric Pollution Prevention Act 45 of 1965;
Hazardous Substances Act 15 of 1973;
Dumping at Sea Control Act 73 of 1980;
Prevention and Combating of Pollution of the Sea by Oil Act 6 of 1981;
International Convention for the Prevention of Pollution from Ships Act 2 of 1986;
International Convention Relating to Intervention on the High Seas in Cases of Oil Pollution Casualties Act 64 of 1987;
OFS Prohibition of the Dumping of Rubbish Ordinance 8 of 1976;
Natal Prevention of Environmental Pollution Ordinance 21 of 1981.

***(c)* General**

Environment Conservation Act 73 of 1989.

6.3.2.2 *Legislation predominantly containing environmentally specific norms*

In this category is included legislation which is calculated to promote an environmental object and which contains, predominantly, environmentally specific norms, but which also has other provisions. Examples are the following:

Mountain Catchment Areas Act 63 of 1970;
Lake Areas Development Act 39 of 1975;
Forest Act 122 of 1984.

6.3.2.3 *Legislation incidentally containing environmentally specific norms*

A further class which may be distinguished consists of legislation of which the general purpose is not environmental conservation or management, but which includes individual provisions with that aim, for instance

Sea-Shore Act 21 of 1935 (eg regulations concerning the use of the sea-shore, the removal of material from the sea-shore and the sea and the control over nuisances in respect of the sea-shore);
Water Act 54 of 1956 (eg provisions relating to water pollution control);
Income Tax Act 58 of 1962 (eg allowance of deductions for expenditure incurred in respect of the eradication of noxious plants and the prevention of soil erosion);
National Roads Act 54 of 1971 (eg control of wastes on or near roads);
Health Act 63 of 1977 (eg regulations controlling environmental nuisances);
Nuclear Energy Act 92 of 1982 (eg the Council for Nuclear Safety's power in respect of the granting of nuclear licences); and
Sea Fishery Act 12 of 1988 (eg provisions governing the protection of fish and the establishment of marine reserves).

6.3.2.4 *Legislation with direct environmental relevance*

This category of legislation is not calculated to further environmental management, but comprises provisions that are of direct environmental relevance.

Perhaps the best example of such legislation is that governing land-use planning, such as the Physical Planning Act 125 of 1991 and the Cape Land Use Planning Ordinance 15 of 1985. It has been recognized that neither pollution-control measures nor the conservation of natural resources can succeed by themselves, unless they are co-ordinated and directed by means of adequate provisions relating to rational land use. Legislative provisions, however, are broadly based and are not aimed specifically at environmental conservation. This is reflected in the title of the Physical Planning Act, which during 1975 was amended to read the Environment Planning Act, only to be renamed, in 1981, the Physical Planning Act.

Another example of legislation with direct environmental relevance is the Subdivision of Agricultural Land Act 70 of 1970, which serves to combat the creation of uneconomic farming units, which, in their turn, may give rise to over-utilization of the land, resulting in soil erosion.

6.3.2.5 *Legislation with potential environmental relevance*

Yet a further category that may be differentiated—varying only slightly from the latter—consists of legislation which, although not aimed at environmental management, includes provisions that are potentially of environmental significance. Examples include the following:

Income Tax Act 58 of 1962 (eg deductions allowable on new or unused machinery such as a machine designed to process scrap metal, thus stimulating recycling);
Customs and Excise Act 91 of 1964 (eg control of the importation or manufacture of environmentally harmful goods);
Foodstuffs, Cosmetics and Disinfectants Act 54 of 1972 (eg prohibition of the sale, manufacture or importation of any foodstuffs which contain or have been treated with a prohibited substance (such as a pesticide);
Expropriation Act 63 of 1975 (eg expropriation of land for conservation); and
Patents Act 57 of 1978 (eg registration of inventions that may serve environmental conservation).

6.3.2.6 *Legislation regulating environmental exploitation*

In the past, legislation could have been distinguished which was aimed not at environmental conservation or management, but at the very opposite, ie the exploitation of the environment, and which made no provision for countering the environmentally detrimental consequences of such exploitation. The early mining legislation probably belonged in this category. But even if environmentally exploitive legislation does make provision for ameliorating its potentially harmful impact upon the environment, it may be argued that such provisions basically should be subsumed under this category, since they still relate to the exploitation of the environment. Examples of such provisions include legislation designed to promote agricultural production, afforestation, fishing, mining, the establishment of townships, the generation of electricity, the construction of roads and the establishment of waste disposal sites.

6.3.2.7 *Legislation with no environmental relevance*

Relatively few statutes have absolutely no relevance for the environment. Among such legislation, the following may perhaps be reckoned:

Dental Technicians Act 19 of 1979;
Mediation in Certain Divorce Matters Act 24 of 1987;
Children's Status Act 82 of 1987.

The above gradation of legislation is not intended to reflect a watertight demarcation but merely constitutes different degrees of intensity, illustrating the wide spectrum of legislation with environmental significance. Moreover, it may sometimes be possible to classify a particular statute in either of two or even more categories, while individual provisions of a given statute may be classified in different categories.

6.3.2.8 *Common-law norms*

In addition to legislation, account must be taken also of common-law norms that may be applied to effect environmental conservation. There seems to be no common-law norm designed specifically to serve this purpose.

It has been recognized, nevertheless, that common-law provisions such as an interdict, the actio legis Aquiliae, a public servitude, a trust and judicial review of administrative actions, although not designed specifically for environmental conservation, may be employed for this purpose.[57] Such common-law provisions should probably be classified in categories 6.3.2.4 and 6.3.2.5.

6.3.3 Towards an identification of environmental law

We now need to ascertain which of the above provisions should qualify as environmental law norms. To commence with the obvious, the environmentally specific norms of categories 6.3.2.1 and 6.3.2.2 undoubtedly constitute environmental law, while the last category would clearly fall outside the purview of environmental law. As far as category 6.3.2.3 is concerned, it is submitted that an environmentally specific norm retains its nature, even though it is encountered in legislation which generally seeks to further some other cause. Purely exploitive legislation (category 6.3.2.6) would obviously not constitute environmental law, but if legislation governing environmental exploitation contains provisions which seek to minimize the harmful impact upon the environment, such provisions should be regarded as establishing environmental law. The minimization of such impact is, after all, the tenor of all pollution-control provisions even if they are contained not in exploitive legislation, but in a separate statute aimed specifically at controlling pollution, e g the Hazardous Substances Act 15 of 1973.

The most controversial question would probably be whether the provisions included in categories 6.3.2.4 and 6.3.2.5 should be regarded as environmental law norms. Their environmental significance is established only when they are actually employed to serve the cause of environmental conservation. In and of themselves they constitute neutral provisions. In fact, they may even be utilized for environmentally harmful purposes. The question nevertheless remains whether such norms may be viewed as amounting to environmental law if they are applied to serve the cause of environmental conservation. Conflicting views have been expressed on this issue. Kloepfer[58] contends that only legislation which would fall into categories 6.3.2.1 and 6.3.2.2 should be regarded as constituting environmental law, while Steiger[59] is of the opinion that norms which may merely be relevant, even though not designed for environmental conservation, should yet be reckoned to belong to the field of environmental law.

If the question is approached in a purely dogmatic fashion, one would be inclined to rule out the label of environmental law for categories 6.3.2.4 and 6.3.2.5. On the other hand, it may be argued that as environmental law constitutes cross-divisional law, implying that it contains norms belonging also to other (traditional) fields of law (par 6.4), these categories could fall within the purview of environmental law. After all, a case in which, say, an interdict is obtained to restrain threatening environmentally harmful conduct would generally be viewed as an environmental case, even if it

[57] Fuggle & Rabie *Environmental concerns in South Africa* (1983) 38ff.
[58] *Systematisierung des Umweltrechts* (1978) 75–7.
[59] Above n 19, 11. Cf also Hoppe & Beckmann above n 44, 24; Erbguth above n 20, 56–7.

simultaneously involves a private-law remedy. In fact, as will become apparent in the next paragraph, the label of environmental law is commonly attached to provisions belonging to conventional branches of law, which have potential significance for environmental conservation even though in the abstract they are environmentally neutral.

Perhaps one should refer to environmental law in a narrow and a wide sense. It is significant that while most commentators agree on the central core of environmental law, there is some difference of opinion as to peripheral areas, displaying a degree of arbitrariness in the treatment of the subject matter.[60]

6.4 NATURE OF ENVIRONMENTAL LAW

Among the best-known legislative provisions governing environmental conservation are those relating to the declaration of environmental policy, the establishment of protected areas and the obligation to assess the potential environmental impact of proposed actions. Perhaps the commonest provisions consist of regulations and directives issued by administrative bodies to landowners and other persons in terms of empowering legislation, as well as of control through administrative authorization, registration or licensing. In addition, many provisions establish and empower administrative bodies themselves to manage various aspects of the environment.

Control through the issuing of regulations or directives or through a licence system is, of course, not unique to environmental law. The declaration of policy, previously regarded as belonging in a white paper or being expressed through some other political medium, has lately become an increasingly popular legislative technique, as is evident, for instance, in the National Policy for General Education Affairs Act 76 of 1984, the National Policy for General Housing Matters Act 102 of 1984 and the National Policy for Health Act 116 of 1990. Likewise, provision for the establishment of particular areas is not restricted to environmental law. A notorious example is that of the repealed Group Areas Act 36 of 1966. Moreover, the requirement governing the submission of an environmental impact report may be likened to an environmental audi alteram partem. In essence it is an administrative procedural provision, which, like audi alteram partem, is designed to influence administrative decision-making through an increased awareness of its potential consequences. The increasing insistence by environmentalists on public participation in such decision-making is shared by many others.

Thus far, it appears that the greater proportion of environmental law falls squarely within the domain of administrative law, most of it being special administrative law.[61] This characteristic is shared by a number of other fields of law, such as those relating to housing, public health, food and drugs, agriculture and aviation. It seems that in none of these fields have any distinctive principles yet evolved. This has not, however, prevented their recognition as separate areas of law. Nor should it imply that the search for such principles should be abandoned. Few distinctive principles have emerged to identify even some traditional fields of law. Thus it may be argued that much commercial law is simply applied private law.

What distinguishes environmental law further is that its norms are encountered in several other conventional branches of law. Mention has already been made of its important administrative-law component. Criminal law is almost invariably involved in environmental provisions, because most of these provisions are buttressed by criminal sanctions. Moreover, because land-use practices and planning are fundamental to

---

[60] Cf Prümm above n 20, 6; Kloepfer above n 40, 26–36.

[61] It is significant that environmental law lately is included in treatises on particular administrative law. Cf Breuer 'Umweltrecht' in Von Münch (ed) *Besonderes Verwaltungsrecht* (8 ed 1988) 607.

environmental conservation, property law is relevant, besides private-law remedies generally, especially to combat environmental nuisances and to obtain compensation for environmental damage. The unsuitability and failure of claims for compensation, moreover, have led to the involvement of insurance law, through efforts to establish compulsory insurance in respect of certain types of environmental damage. Constitutional law has become relevant particularly through suggestions for the recognition of a fundamental right to environmental integrity. Finally, the global nature and scale of some environmental problems underscore the involvement of international law. In German law, indeed, reference is regularly made to 'Umweltstrafrecht' (environmental criminal law), 'Umweltverwaltungsrecht' (environmental administrative law), 'Umweltsteuerrecht' (environmental tax law), 'Umweltprivatrecht' (environmental private law), 'Umweltschadensrecht' (environmental liability law), 'Umweltverfassungsrecht' (environmental constitutional law) and 'Umweltvölkerrecht' (environmental international law).

Environmental law thus consists of a potpourri of legal norms encountered in a number of conventional fields of law, a feature it shares with other recognized areas of legal regulation, such as medical law, labour law, press law, social welfare law and the law relating to consumer protection. This factor, accordingly, does not disqualify the recognition of environmental law as a separate area of law.

Environmental law thus practically serves a type of omnibus function, accommodating principles of traditional fields of law, which are united only by their common object in serving environmental conservation. In spite of the fact that it lacks systematic unity and may be referred to as cross-divisional law ('Querschnittsrecht'),[62] it is submitted that environmental law has gradually, over the past 20 years, established itself as an identifiable branch of law.

It has been stated that unless distinctive legal criteria can be established to characterize environmental law, the subject will continue to lack coherence and logical structure.[63] Although this view commends itself, all attempts to identify such distinctive principles seem to have been unsuccessful. In German law, for instance, a number of principles have been identified which are said to characterize environmental law. Three such principles, the precautionary principle, the originator principle and the principle of co-operation, are usually distinguished,[64] while some identify a few more.[65] The precautionary principle ('Vorsorgeprinzip')—in contradistinction to the reparation of damage which has already occurred or the protection against threatened damage—implies the application of preventive measures whereby the potential impairment of the environment may be entirely precluded. The originator principle ('Verursacherprinzip') is viewed as the cornerstone for liability in respect of environmental harm: costs incurred in the avoidance or removal of environmental harm or in the compensation for environmental damage should be borne by the person who was causally responsible for them. The principle of co-operation presupposes collaboration between the public and the private sector in attaining environmental goals.

These principles frequently amount to no more than political ideals or principles of legal policy and may be regarded as constituting binding legal norms only when they are

---

[62] Cf Bender & Sparwasser above n 42, 3; Kloepfer above n 40, 26.

[63] Cowen 'Toward distinctive principles of South African environmental law: some jurisprudential perspectives and a role for legislation' 1989 *THRHR* 3, 11.

[64] Cf Breuer above n 61, 610–14; Ketteler & Kippels *Umweltrecht* (1988) 79–83; Schmidt & Müller *Einführung in das Umweltrecht* (1989) 7–11.

[65] Cf Rehbinder 'Allgemeines Umweltrecht' in Salzwedel (ed) *Grundzüge des Umweltrechts* (1982) 87–9.

enshrined in legislation. None of them applies consistently in environmental law and many instances may be found where they have no application. Moreover, those same principles often find application in other fields of law. They do not, therefore, constitute exclusive environmental law principles and, as has been pointed out, frequently do not even amount to legally enforceable principles.[66]

---

[66] Sendler 'Grundprobleme des Umweltrechts' 1983 *Juristische Schulung* 256–7; Kloepfer above n 40, 72–4; Erbguth above n 20, 143–4.

CHAPTER 7

ENVIRONMENT CONSERVATION ACT

M A RABIE

7.1 TITLE, SCOPE AND PURPOSE

A prominent feature of South African environmental legislation is its diffuse nature, with provisions being contained in an extremely wide variety of parliamentary Acts, provincial ordinances, local by-laws and ministerial regulations. There never has been, nor is there likely to be, a single statutory instrument which comprehensively codifies environmental law. It is doubtful whether such an instrument is even feasible. The Environment Conservation Act 100 of 1982, in spite of is all-embracing title, in fact regulated only a few environmental aspects. The Environment Conservation Act 73 of 1989 considerably extends the scope of the 1982 Act, but in no way constitutes a codification; the title accordingly remains misleading.

Whereas the primary purpose of the 1982 Act was merely to make provision for the co-ordination of all actions directed at or liable to have an influence on the environment, the preamble to the 1989 Act (hereafter referred to as 'the Act') evidences a much wider intent by now providing for the effective protection and controlled utilization of the environment. 'Effective protection' indicates a non-utilitarian, ecocentric perspective, while 'controlled utilization' indicates a utilitarian, anthropocentric emphasis.[1]

7.2 THE TERM 'ENVIRONMENT'

The meaning of the word environment has been discussed in chapters 1 and 6 and it was shown there that the Act contains the first legislative attempt to define the term environment.

7.3 PUBLIC PARTICIPATION IN ENVIRONMENTAL AFFAIRS

Environmental affairs, par excellence, concern issues in which the broad public as well as informed individuals often display a particular interest. This is due, in large measure, to the fact that the state of the environment, to a greater or lesser degree, affects everyone.

7.3.1 Public participation in parliamentary legislation

The Act and its predecessor were preceded by extensive deliberations. The 1982 Act followed on the publication during 1980 of a *White Paper on a national policy regarding environmental conservation*.[2] Subsequently, also during 1980, an Environmental Conservation Bill was published for general information and comment.[3] The Environment Conservation Bill 39 of 1981 was thereafter read a first time in Parliament, but was not further proceeded with. Instead, a select committee of the House of Assembly was appointed early in 1981 to inquire into and report on the Bill. The

---

[1] Glavovic 'Some thoughts of an environmental lawyer on the implications of the environment Conservation Act 73 of 1989: a case of missed opportunities' 1990 *SALJ* 107, 108.

[2] WPO—1980.

[3] GN 521 of 25 July 1980.

committee was later reconstituted as a commission of inquiry into environmental legislation. In spite of the wide scope of its assignment, the commission dealt only with the 1981 Bill, and, in its turn, during 1982, submitted its own Environmental Conservation Bill, incorporating its recommendations.[4] Subsequently the Environment Conservation Bill 100 of 1982 was submitted to Parliament and eventually the Environment Conservation Act 100 of 1982 was promulgated.

The new Act, likewise, resulted from a process of intense analysis and discussion. This is reflected in the three official Bills and the one unofficial Bill that preceded the Act. The first draft Bill was published for general information and comment in May 1987[5], while the second Bill followed in October of that year.[6] A third draft Bill was prepared early in 1988, but was not published. Eventually, the Environment Conservation Bill of 1989 was published in final version.[7] After some amendments, initiated by the Joint Committee on Environment Affairs, the Environment Conservation Act 73 of 1989 was finally promulgated. This extensive effort in the drafting and redrafting of draft parliamentary legislation, accompanied by ample opportunities for public comment, is quite remarkable. The two Acts were preceded by a total of eight Bills, of which three were published to elicit public comment. Moreover, a White Paper provided the initial basis for the first Act, while a commission of inquiry also offered an opportunity for public contributions. This effort sets a commendable example of inviting public participation in parliamentary legislation—something which is not at all familiar in South Africa, and, it need hardly be noted, is not obligatory. The benefits of such public participation are obvious.[8] In keeping with the democratic spirit which accompanied the establishment of the Act, provision is made in the Act for public participation in several respects.

7.3.2 Public participation in subordinate legislation and other administrative decision-making

The Act provides ample opportunities for the articulation of the public's interest in a variety of actions of several bodies. In the first place, a draft notice, published in the *Government Gazette* or the *Official Gazette*, is required if the Minister of Environment Affairs, the Minister of Water Affairs, an Administrator or any local authority intends to issue a regulation or a direction in terms of the Act, or to declare an area as a protected natural environment, a special nature reserve or a limited development area, or to identify certain activities or to determine an environmental policy.[9] The publication of the draft notice is aimed at eliciting public comment on the proposed administrative action in question.[10] Although it is obvious that this should be the case, the Act nevertheless does not expressly oblige the administrative body concerned to consider the comments that have been received. Without such consideration, the whole exercise will, of course, be meaningless. It would probably be preferable, ex abundanti cautela, explicitly to provide, as has been done in the Act with regard to comments on the proposed declaration of an area as a limited development area,[11] that the comments and representations in question must be considered by the decision-making body

---

[4] RP 10/1982.

[5] GN 353 of 29 May 1987.

[6] GN 798 of 30 October 1987.

[7] B 60–89 (GA).

[8] Cf Fuggle & Rabie (eds) *Environmental concerns in South Africa* (1983), 52–4 in respect of public participation in administrative decision-making. It is submitted that the motivation for such participation in legislation is even stronger since legislative precepts are of general application and endure over a long time-period.

[9] Sections 32(1).

[10] Section 32(2).

[11] Section 23(4)*(c)*.

concerned. Failure by such body duly to apply its mind to such comments and representations may conceivably result in its decision being set aside on review.

The above provision is to be heartily welcomed in principle as a most refreshing innovation. It is doubtful whether any other South African legislation provides more extensive opportunities for public comment and representations in respect of administrative decision-making.

There can be hardly any contention as to the many advantages associated with opportunities for public participation in administrative decision-making.[12] Such advantages include potentially improved decision-making due to broadened environmental perspectives as well as improved public compliance with such decisions.

7.4 MULTIPLE ADMINISTRATIVE JURISDICTION IN RESPECT OF ENVIRONMENTAL AFFAIRS

7.4.1 The problem

Most government departments, at all levels, as well as other administrative bodies, are in some way or another involved in the administration of environmental affairs. Nevertheless, the Minister and the Department of Environment Affairs have been specially commissioned to administer environmental affairs. A potential overlap or conflict of jurisdiction accordingly arises.

Moreover, policies made and executed by development-oriented administrative bodies often lie at the root of environmental pollution and the degradation and depletion of natural resources, problems which have to be addressed by conservation-oriented administrative bodies. However, the latter bodies usually are not involved in the formulation of policy and the decision-making by the former bodies. The autonomy of government departments has served further to exacerbate the problem, bringing about a situation in which administrative bodies responsible for the making of policy decisions have become institutionally separated from those having to attend to the effects of such decisions.[13] Furthermore, this eventually has led to a most unfortunate separation between economics and ecology ensuing to the detriment of both economic development and environmental conservation.

7.4.2 The challenge

It has been shown that development cannot subsist upon a deteriorating environmental resource base and that the environment cannot be conserved when economic growth leaves out of account the costs of environmental degradation and destruction.[14] The ideal therefore is to achieve economic growth upon an environmental foundation which can sustain such growth, in short, to strive towards sustainable development. The institutional strategy to achieve this aim, simultaneously constituting what has been referred to as 'the chief institutional challenge of the 1990s',[15] requires that 'the ecological dimensions of policy be considered at the same time as the economic, trade, energy, agricultural, industrial, and other dimensions—on the same agendas and in the same institutions'.[16] Different responses to this challenge may be identified.

7.4.3 Co-ordination of environmental administration

The first solution to the problem, dating back to the early 1970s, was attempted through the function of co-ordination, which was entrusted to what has now become the

---

[12] Cf Fuggle & Rabie above n 8, 52–4.

[13] *Our common future* World Commission on Environment and Development (1987) 39, 310.

[14] *Our common future* above n 13, 37. See also in general the *Report of the Planning Committee of the President's Council on priorities between conservation and development PC 5/1984* and chapter 3.

[15] *Our common future* above n 13, 313.

[16] Ibid.

Minister and Department of Environment Affairs. This function was of an overarching nature and involved the integration and harmonization of the actions of the various public bodies that administered environmental affairs. However, the Minister's function of co-ordination did not entail the power to come to any binding decision in respect of the actions of administrative bodies, other than his own department, which were the subject of such co-ordination. This would seem to have been the position at least as far as administrative bodies at central government level were concerned. After all, the Minister of Environment Affairs holds a limited portfolio and thus cannot undertake actions that involve aspects relating to the portfolio of another Minister. The Minister does indeed now hold the most important portfolio as far as environmental affairs are concerned, but, as has been mentioned, almost all other government departments are to a greater or lesser extent involved in actions that have a bearing upon the environment. The Minister, in exercising his function of co-ordination, would at the most seem to have had advisory powers. This would seem to be an inevitable consequence of our constitutional dispensation, according to which one government department at national level cannot dictate to another such department. The memorandum accompanying the 1989 Bill also identified this deficiency, namely that there was no effective way in which co-ordinated action regarding environmental conservation of all governmental bodies concerned could be directed. Apart from this aspect, an environmental bias would be built into the system of government if the Minister of Environment Affairs should be granted overriding powers.

7.4.4 Co-operative governmental decision-making

Another way in which state action may be authoritatively harmonized, allowing for a homogeneous treatment of environmental problems, is through co-operative decision-making by the bodies involved. In this way some of the objections referred to in the previous paragraph may be met. The Act provides for such decision-making; in certain instances the concurrence of particular bodies is required before a particular environmental action, authorized by the Act, may be performed, while in other cases the Act merely requires that certain bodies be consulted. Such provisions concern the determination of policy,[17] the declaration of protected natural environments[18] and the issuing of related directions,[19] the declaration of special nature reserves,[20] the identification of certain activities,[21] the declaration of limited development areas[22] and the making of certain regulations.[23] Where consultation of concerned bodies is required, it may slow down the decision-making process, but holds the potential for improved decision-making as well as for improved co-operation between the bodies concerned. In the final analysis, however, it would still amount to one administrative body exercising overriding powers over others. Where concurrence is required, a potentially similar situation prevails, except for the important difference that, since the principle of departmental autonomy is recognized, the refusal of but one Minister to agree may entirely frustrate the intentions of the body seeking to achieve a conservation objective.

7.4.5 Environmental policy

Perhaps potentially the most promising strategy to ensure a sound environmental base upon which development may proceed is provided by the authoritative

[17] Section 2(2).
[18] Section 16(1)*(b)*.
[19] Section 16(2)*(b)*.
[20] Section 18(2)*(c)*. Cf also s 18(4)*(a)* and *(b)*.
[21] Section 21(3).
[22] Section 23(4)*(d)*.
[23] Section 28*(i)*.

determination of an environmental policy with which all administrative bodies should comply. The provision of a binding national environmental policy seems essential in view of the wide-ranging, fragmented and diffuse nature and treatment of environmental issues. Moreover, it is a prerequisite for effective environmental impact assessment, as will be shown. There are different methods by which the establishment and enforcement of an environmental policy may be accomplished.

7.4.5.1 *Policy in White Paper*

During 1980 the government published a *White Paper on a national policy regarding environmental conservation.*[24] This *White Paper* signalled an official commitment to recognize and resolve some of the more serious environmental problems that South Africa had to contend with. However, a White Paper represents merely a declaration of intention and has no legal force. It does not serve as an obligatory guideline for administrative actions that affect the environment. In fact, it cannot even be used in the interpretation of legislation in terms of which actions affecting the environment are undertaken.

7.4.5.2 *Administrative policy without statutory basis*

Environmental policy directives may be announced administratively, independent of statutory authorization, even at the highest level in the form of a cabinet resolution. Although such policy guidelines may be enforced internally as regards the administration through the remedies for administrative insubordination, they could not be enforced against the public, since they would lack the necessary legal foundation.[25] Moreover, there would be no remedy available to the public to ensure that the guidelines would in fact be complied with. Furthermore, they would normally come about through administrative announcement, allowing no scope for public participation in respect of their contents.

7.4.5.3 *Administrative policy as subordinate legislation*

(a) General

This is the approach adopted by the Act. The Minister of Environment Affairs is empowered by notice in the *Government Gazette* to determine (or to amend or withdraw[26]) the general policy to be applied with a view to

(a) the protection of ecological processes,[27] natural systems and the natural beauty as well as the preservation of biotic diversity in the natural environment;
(b) the promotion of sustained utilization of species and ecosystems[28] and the effective application and re-use of natural resources;
(c) the protection of the environment against disturbance, deterioration, defacement, poisoning or destruction as a result of man-made structures, installations, processes or products or human activities; and
(d) the establishment, maintenance and improvement of environments which contribute to a generally acceptable quality of life for the inhabitants of the RSA.[29]

The subjects in respect of which policy may be made are phrased in an extensive manner, allowing ample scope and flexibility for the formulation of a comprehensive environmental policy. Although it seems clear that the Act does not require a single

---

[24] Above n 2.
[25] Rabie & Van Zyl Smit 'The nature and effect of legislative and quasi-legislative administrative acts' 1988 *SA Public Law* 193; 1989 *SA Public Law* 74.
[26] Section 2(3).
[27] Defined in s 1(viii).
[28] Defined in s 1(ix).
[29] Section 2(1).

policy, but that various policies may be determined with regard to the various aspects enumerated, it does create the impression that such policies must apply to the entire country, being general policies. This may not always be practical, since different areas may require different policies.

(b) Determination of policy

The Minister does not determine such policy on his own. He may do so only after consultation with the Council for the Environment and the Administrator of each province; moreover, he must obtain the concurrence of each Minister charged with the administration of any law which in the opinion of the Minister, relates to a matter affecting the environment and of the Minister of Finance and of Economic Affairs and Technology.[30] Reference has been made to the fact that almost every ministry is involved in the administration of environmental legislation. With the addition of the two further ministries, it would, for all practical purposes, mean that the entire Cabinet's consent is required for the determination of policy.

The determination of policy may prove to be difficult to accomplish in practice. There is no compulsion on the Minister to determine environmental policy. Moreover, seeking to obtain the concurrence of the many bodies which the Act obliges the Minister to do, may lead to inordinate delays and at worst to positive obstruction, even on the part of a single body. On the other hand, however, it should be noted that the alternative, namely that the Minister may be empowered on his own to determine environmental policy which would nevertheless be binding on all other bodies seems to affect the principle of ministerial and departmental parity, besides introducing a potential environmental bias. But then development-oriented administrative bodies regularly perform actions which affect the environment, without consulting the Minister of Environment Affairs. A draft amendment to the Act is aimed at eliminating the consent requirement and substituting it with mere consultation.

(c) Contents of policy

The content of the policy is naturally of crucial importance. There is, however, no guarantee that the policy which is eventually formulated will indeed be satisfactory from an environmental perspective. It is true that ample opportunity is afforded for public representations in respect of draft policy and that the Council for the Environment and the various Administrators need to be consulted in the process. Such input, valuable though it undoubtedly may be, is nevertheless of a merely advisory nature. The problem is that the Minister, in seeking to obtain the required concurrence of the bodies mentioned in the Act, may be obliged to resort to environmentally unacceptable compromises. It is acknowledged that a compromise needs to be effected between development and environmental conservation, but there is little, if any, pressure on development-oriented ministries to concur with the Minister's framed policy.

Although no provision is made in the Act for control over the contents of a policy once it has been determined, a measure of such control may conceivably be effected through the common-law remedy of judicial review. The general policy would seem to amount to subordinate legislation. However, the grounds upon which such legislation may be invalidated on review, notably those of unreasonableness and vagueness, provide little scope for applicants who are dissatisfied with the policy from an environmental perspective. Besides, the requirement of locus standi will be difficult to satisfy. See chapter 8.

The first three draft Bills preceding the Act contained a provision setting out a list of principles, according to which the policy should be framed.[31] Perhaps these

---

[30] Section 2(2).

[31] Clause 2(2) of the Bill of May 1987, clause 2(1) of the Bill of October 1987 and clause 2 of the 1988 Bill.

principles may have served to improve the scope of control over the contents of the policy.[32]

(d) Enforcement of policy

The next issue relates to the mechanism whereby such policy, once determined, may be enforced. The Act provides that each Minister, administrator, local authority and government institution upon which any power has been conferred or to which any duty has been assigned in connection with the environment by or under any law, must exercise such power and perform such duty in accordance with the abovementioned policy.[33] The Act states explicitly that its provisions bind the State.[34] Although an obligation is thus introduced to comply with the policy, the Act itself does not buttress this provision with a sanction against those who should fail to act in accordance with the policy. Nor, it would seem, would such failure amount to misconduct in terms of the Public Service Act 111 of 1984,[35] which would have activated certain provisions governing action that may be taken in response to such misconduct.[36]

The above policy provision—if it in fact results in the determination by the Minister of a satisfactory general environmental policy—nevertheless may have far-reaching implications for administrative decision-making. Our law, by and large, has failed to oblige administrative bodies to consider the environmental implications of their actions; worse, it has in most cases failed even to authorize them to do so. The determination of an environmental policy in terms of the Act can eliminate these shortcomings, since a duty is thereby cast upon every Minister, administrator, local authority and government institution which exercises functions in connection with the environment to do so in accordance with that policy. This means that the various administrative-law remedies in principle are available to ensure that the policy is taken into consideration as far as administrative decision-making is concerned.

In this connection, it seems necessary to distinguish between two aspects, ie the administrative body's awareness and consideration of the policy and its action in accordance therewith. Should the body be unaware of the policy or fail to take it into account in the exercise of its powers or the performance of its duties, its action may be set aside on review for its failure duly to apply its mind to a relevant matter. Likewise, an interdict may be obtained to restrain actions in violence of the above provision, or a mandamus may be granted whereby an administrative body is required to comply with its abovementioned statutory duty. Judicial redress, however, may be sought only by a person who has the necessary locus standi and it seems unlikely that conservationists will meet this requirement merely on account of their concern for the potential environmental effect of the administrative action in question.

As far as the second aspect is concerned, it is uncertain whether judicial review would be available as a remedy to determine whether the relevant administrative act was in fact performed in accordance with the policy. Normally the court on review would refuse to become involved in ruling on the merits. The proper remedy in such an instance is an appeal, either to a court of law or to an administrative tribunal, for which, however, no provision is made in the Environment Conservation Act. On the other hand, the relevant enforcement provisions of the second[37] and third[38] draft Bills provided that administrative bodies must properly *consider* the policy in the execution of their official powers. This would have corresponded to the above interpretation that

[32] Cf Bray 'The new Environment Conservation Act versus the demands of environmental realities' 1990 *SA Public Law* 101, 102.

[33] Section 3.

[34] Section 40.

[35] Cf s 19.

[36] Section 20.

[37] GN 798 of 30 October 1987, clause 3(1).

[38] Unpublished Bill, clause 4(1).

judicial review would be restricted to controlling only the awareness or consideration of the policy in question. Since the 1989 Bill[39] and the Act[40] now provide that powers should be exercised and duties performed *in accordance with* the policy, a change in meaning seems to have been intended, ie that the actual performance of the administrative body concerned should match the policy. The obvious intention of the legislature is that the determined environmental policy must in fact influence administrative actions affected by that policy. If this provision is to constitute more than a mere guideline, the court's review power should extend also to measuring administrative performance against the environmental policy.

While dealing with the enforcement of policy, it should be noted that the first three draft Bills contained further enforcement devices, which devices have been excised by the 1989 draft Bill and the Act. All the above-mentioned Bills, with slight variations, provided for consultation between the Minister and the authority responsible for the preparation of draft legislation on any matter in respect of which an environmental policy has been determined.[41] Moreover, they provided that all laws should be interpreted and administered in accordance with the policy in question.[42] It seems unfortunate that these draft provisions failed to find their way into the Act, since they would undoubtedly have strengthened the enforcement of the policy provision.

The duty to act in accordance with the environmental policy extends much further than administrative bodies. It may, in fact, be imposed upon any body: 'government institution' is defined in the Act as any body, company or close corporation established by or under any law or any other institution or body recognized by the Minister by notice in the *Government Gazette*.[43]

The extension to the private sector of the duty to comply with the policy where functions are exercised in terms of law is to be welcomed. Obviously, compliance with the policy should be universal, otherwise such policy cannot be expected to achieve the desired results. It is nevertheless strange, at least semantically, that private bodies should be labelled 'government institutions' in order to be bound by the Act. It is uncertain how the policy provision would be enforced against such bodies, since failure to comply with the policy, as has been mentioned, carries no penalty in terms of the Act. Presumably such failure may be taken into account as a factor in determining the lawfulness of the body's conduct in a private-law context. Where the body concerned is not an administrative body, the above administrative-law remedies would not, of course, be applicable.

7.4.5.4 *Policy determined by legislature*

The United States of America, through its National Environmental Policy Act of 1970, opted for the determination of environmental policy not by the executive, as in South Africa, but by the national legislature.[44] In other words, the national environmental policy has been laid down in the Act itself. This has the advantage that the establishment of a satisfactory policy cannot be frustrated by executive failure. Moreover, objections of inflexibility have been forestalled by the formulation of a broad general policy, leaving room for administrative discretion in balancing environmental interests against the need to be served by the proposed action. The Act contains a number of so-called 'action-forcing' procedures designed to ensure that the

---

[39] B 60–89 (GA), clause 3.
[40] Section 3.
[41] Clause 3(2) of the first two drafts and clause 4(2) of the third draft.
[42] Clause 3(3) of the first two drafts and clause 4(3) of the third draft. The latter draft refers only to principles contained in the Act and omits the reference to policy.
[43] Section 1(xii).
[44] Cf generally Rabie 'Disclosure and evaluation of potential environmental impact of proposed governmental action' 1976 *THRHR* 40.

policy is implemented.[45] It has been suggested that national environmental policy should be determined legislatively, not administratively, because legislative determination is more effective and more enduring.[46]

It seems that the South African legislature is bent upon consistently providing for policy to be determined by the administration and not by the legislature. This is reflected in the following empowering provisions: the National Education Policy Act 39 of 1967,[47] the National Policy for General Education Affairs 76 of 1984,[48] the National Policy for General Housing Matters Act 102 of 1984,[49] the Sea Fishery Act 12 of 1988[50] and the National Policy for Health Act 116 of 1990.[51] A similar provision was contained in the Physical Planning Bill of 1990,[52] but has not been included in the Physical Planning Act 125 of 1991.

7.5 STATUTORY BODIES

The Act establishes two bodies, ie the Council for the Environment and the Committee for Environmental Management. The Council for the Environment has its origins in a non-statutory advisory committee, established in the early 1970s, known as the South African Committee on Environmental Conservation, and renamed the Council for the Environment in 1975. The council was reconstituted as a statutory body by the Environment Conservation Act of 1982 and has now been reconstituted by the new Act.[53] The council is, in essence, an advisory body which advises the Minister on any matter relating to policy and generally on any matter which the Minister refers to it or which the council itself deems necessary.[54] On account of its close connection with the Minister and Department of Environment affairs, the council may, unfortunately, tend to be regarded as an extension of the Department of Environment Affairs and even as a mouthpiece for government policy.[55]

The Committee for Environmental Management[56] is a continuation and extension of the National Committee for Nature Conservation (Nakor) which, on its own initiative, played an important role in the co-ordination of nature conservation during the past 15 years.[57] The dual function of the committee is, on the one hand, to advise the Director-General: Environment Affairs on any matter affecting activities which may influence the protection and utilization of the environment and on the other, to co-ordinate and promote the implementation of the Act's provisions.[58] The establishment of this committee has been welcomed because it creates a forum for the resolution of potential conflict between government departments behind closed doors. For that reason its success or failure is unlikely to be gauged by the public.[59]

There is a clear difference between the constitution of the council and that of the committee. While the former is to consist of persons who are appointed on account of

---

45 Ibid.

46 Glavovic above n 1, 108–9. Cf also Glazewski 'A new Environment Conservation Act: an awakening of environmental law?' 1989 *De Rebus Procuratoriis* 872, 873.

47 Section 1B(1).

48 Section 2(1).

49 Section 6.

50 Section 2.

51 Section 2(1).

52 Clause 2(1) of GN 77 of 9 February 1990.

53 Section 4.

54 Section 5(1)*(a)* and *(b)*.

55 Hoogervorst 'A personal perspective on the Environment Conservation Act 73 of 1989' 1989 (15(2)) *Southern African J of Aquatic Sciences* 250, 253–4.

56 Section 12.

57 Cf the memorandum accompanying the 1989 Bill, para 7.

58 Section 13*(a)* and *(b)*.

59 Hoogervorst above n 55, 254.

their environmental expertise,[60] the latter consists of representatives from government and semi-government institutions.[61] However, while only the council's advice relates to policy, the line of demarcation between these bodies' general advisory functions is not entirely certain. Moreover, it is not clear how the committee's function of co-ordination and promotion of the Act's provisions is to be distinguished from that of the Minister and Department of Environment Affairs.

The establishment of two further bodies is envisaged by the Act. The Minister is obliged from time to time to appoint a Board of Investigation[62] (which body is discussed below), while an Administrator may in respect of a protected natural environment establish a management advisory committee to advise him with regard to the control and management of such area.[63]

7.6 CONTROLLED ACTIVITIES

Two sets of similar provisions govern the control of activities which may have a detrimental effect upon the environment. In both instances primary control is exercised by the Minister of Environment Affairs.

7.6.1 Identified activities

7.6.1.1 *Area*

The area in which activities may be controlled may be unrestricted, i e everywhere, or it may be restricted to certain areas.[64]

7.6.1.2 *Type of activity*

Only activities that have been identified in accordance with the Act are subject to control. The Act lists broad categories, all having environmental significance, to which identified activities should belong, but does not limit identification to these categories.[65] In other words, in principle, any activity may be identified. There is no indication of what criteria the Minister will apply in deciding when an activity should be identified.[66]

7.6.1.3 *Procedure*

An activity may be identified by the Minister (by notice in the *Government Gazette*) only after consultation with the Council for the Environment and each Administrator, and with the concurrence of the Minister of each government department responsible for the execution, approval or control of such activity, the Minister of Finance and the Minister of Economic Affairs and Technology.[67]

In addition, the general procedure relating to publication for comment applies to the above identification.[68]

7.6.1.4 *Effect*

Undertaking an identified activity (or causing it to be done) amounts to an offence, unless it is effected by virtue of a written authorization issued by the Minister or a local authority or an officer designated by the Minister.[69]

---

[60] Section 6(1).
[61] Section 14(1).
[62] Section 15(1).
[63] Section 17(1).
[64] Section 21(1).
[65] Section 21(2).
[66] Cf Hoogervorst above n 55, 255.
[67] Section 21(3).
[68] Section 32(1)*(b)*
[69] Section 22(1) read with s 29(4).

7.6.1.5 *Environmental impact reports*

The authorization referred to above must be preceded by a consideration of reports concerning the impact of the identified activity and of alternative activities on the environment; such reports must be compiled and submitted by such persons and in such manner as may be prescribed.[70] The Minister may make regulations concerning several details of such reports.[71]

7.6.1.6 *Conditions*

The authorization may be granted subject to conditions determined by the Minister or other relevant body.[72] Failure to comply with a condition, besides amounting to an offence,[73] entitles the Minister or body to withdraw the authorization.[74]

7.6.2 Limited development areas

7.6.2.1 *Area*

Activities or development may be controlled only in an area which has been defined by the Minister (by notice in the *Government Gazette*) as a limited development area.[75] Any area may be thus defined.

7.6.2.2 *Type of activity*

Only activities or development that have been prohibited by the Minister (by notice in the *Government Gazette*) are subject to control.[76] There is no definition of, nor restriction on the type of development or activity which may be prohibited. In fact, there is no indication that the development or activity must have any environmental relevance. However, it may be assumed, with reference to the provision relating to an environmental impact report, that this is the implied intention. But if the comprehensive nature of the concept environment is taken into account, it would seem that the Minister is in fact empowered to prohibit almost anything.

7.6.2.3 *Procedure*

A limited development area may be declared only after the Minister has followed a prescribed procedure aimed at eliciting public comment on the proposed declaration and has considered all the representations that have been received.[77] Moreover, he must consult with each Minister charged with the administration of any law which in the Minister's opinion relates to a matter affecting the environment in the limited development area in question, as well as with the Administrator concerned.[78] In addition, somewhat tautologically, the general procedure relating to publication for comment applies also to the above declaration.[79]

7.6.2.4 *Effect*

Undertaking any prohibited development or activity in a limited development area (or causing it to be done) amounts to an offence, unless it is effected by virtue of an authorization by the Minister or a local authority designated by the Minister.[80]

---

[70] Section 22(2).
[71] Section 26.
[72] Section 22(3).
[73] Section 29(4).
[74] Section 22(4).
[75] Section 23(1).
[76] Section 23(2).
[77] Section 23(4)*(a)*–*(c)*.
[78] Section 23(4)*(d)*.
[79] Section 32(1)*(b)* and 32(2). Cf para 3.2.
[80] Section 23(2) read with s 29(4).

7.6.2.5 *Environmental impact report*

In considering an application for authorization, the Minister or the designated local authority may request the applicant to submit a report as presented, concerning the influence of the proposed activity on the environment in the limited development area.[81]

7.6.2.6 *Conditions*

The authorization may be subjected to conditions.[82] Failure to comply with any condition amounts to an offence.[83]

7.6.3 Analysis

The most significant improvement brought about by the above provisions is the power they confer upon the Minister timeously to identify and to subject to control actions that may have a detrimental effect on the environment. One of the main shortcomings in the past often has been the government's inability or unwillingness to act in a preventive capacity where actions that threaten the environment were concerned. It may be thought that where the valid performance of such actions was dependent upon official permission, such permission could simply have been withheld, or granted subject to conditions which sought to guarantee development that was in harmony with the environment. A similar contention may be put forward regarding entrepreneurial actions by the State itself, e g the building of dams or roads. However, given even the willingness on their part, many administrative control bodies had no legislative mandate to take account of environmental factors in their decision-making. This implied that, should they in the above manner have sought to support a conservation objective, their actions may have been set aside on review, either for taking irrelevant factors into consideration or for pursuing an unauthorized purpose.[84]

At the most, certain conservation-oriented bodies entrusted with the administration of conservation legislation may validly have taken environmental factors into consideration. But the worst problems, as far as detrimental environmental impact was concerned, obviously related to the administration of development-oriented legislation, in respect of which there almost invariably was no obligation or even authorization to consider the potential environmental impact of proposed actions.[85]

To return to the Act: its intention seems to be not to prohibit absolutely actions that may have a detrimental effect on the environment but to ensure that their performance will be accompanied by the necessary respect for the environment. The way in which this is to be accomplished is through the determination of an enforceable environmental policy, which authorizes and obliges administrative bodies to consider environmental factors, coupled with the submission by the applicant for authorization of an environmental impact report, i e a report which should address the potential impact on the environment of the proposed action.[86]

---

[81] Section 23(3).

[82] Section 23(2).

[83] Section 29(4).

[84] *Administrator, Cape v Associated Buildings Ltd* 1957 (2) SA 317 (A) 329A–B.

[85] Cf generally on the legal problems which prevailed before the introduction of the Act, Rabie 'Strategies for the implementation of environmental impact assessment in South Africa' 1986 *SA Public Law* 18, 21–5.

[86] The scope and content of environmental impact reports may include the following:

(i) a description of the activity in question and of alternative activities;

(ii) the identification of the physical environment which may be affected by the activity in question and by the alternative activities;

(iii) an estimation of the nature and extent of the effect of the activity in question and of the alternative activities on the land, air, water, biota and other elements or features of the natural and man-made environments;

The ultimate aim of environmental impact assessment is that the environmental risks of a proposed action must be considered in a manner that allows the existence of such risks to influence the decision whether or not the proposed action should be proceeded with and, if so, how it should be executed. The idea is to place before the decision-making body the environmental implications of the proposed action, so that these potential effects can be weighed against other relevant considerations, thus stimulating informed decision-making.[87]

The need for obligatory environmental impact assessment by governmental bodies, preceded by and based upon environmental impact reports, has been recognised world-wide, with the introduction since 1970 of some form of such assessment in many countries. Two decades after the United States' National Environmental Policy Act of 1970, South Africa has now followed suit in enacting legislation which provides for environmental impact assessment to be built into the decision-making process and for the determination of an authoritative environmental policy to guide administrative decision-making.

It should be noted, nevertheless, that it is only in respect of identified activities that the submission of environmental impact reports is obligatory and where regulations may augment extensively the provisions of the Act. As far as actions within limited development areas are concerned, the request for submission of such reports depends upon the discretion of the administrative body concerned.

A further observation relates to making an authorization subject to conditions. It may be assumed that the assessment by the Minister or other relevant body of the potential environmental impact of the proposed action, as revealed in the environmental impact report, will find expression in the laying down of conditions. Failure by the holder of an authorization to abide by such conditions amounts to an offence both in respect of identified activities and of activities within limited development areas. But it is only with regard to the former that the Minister or other responsible body is also empowered to withdraw the authorization. This latter sanction, obviously, is potentially more effective.

Finally, whereas both the identification of activities as well as the declaration of limited development areas must be preceded by a process whereby allowance is made for public comments, the former is dependent on the concurrence of certain bodies, while the latter requires that certain bodies merely be consulted. Reference has already been made to the potential difficulty of obtaining the required concurrence of ministries, the portfolios of which are development-oriented. A draft amendment seeks to abolish this restrictive requirement.

Perhaps it is unnecessary to have two sets of provisions both providing for substantially the same subject matter, ie the control of activities which may have a detrimental environmental effect. The provisions governing limited development areas apparently are aimed principally at control over development in the coastal zone.[88] It would seem that this object may be realized equally through the provisions relating to identified activities. The former provisions, however, would prove more readily applicable, since their implementation does not depend on the concurrence of other bodies.

(iv) the identification of the economic and social interests which may be affected by the activity in question and by the alternative activities;

(v) an estimation of the nature and extent of the effect of the activity in question and the alternative activities on the social and economic interests;

(vi) a description of the design or management principles proposed for the reduction of adverse environmental effects; and

(vii) a concise summary of the finding of the report: s 26*(a)*. Cf generally Glazewski above n 46, 873–4.

[87] Rabie above n 85, 26.

[88] Memorandum accompanying the 1989 Bill, par 13.

In conclusion, it should be noted that the South African legislature, unlike its American counterpart,[89] has opted for a system whereby ultimate control is left entirely in the hands of the Minister or other relevant body. It is he who decides, at least in respect of limited development areas, whether or not an environmental impact report should be submitted, he decides whether it is satisfactory, it is at his discretion that the authorization in question is refused, granted or withdrawn and he decides upon the conditions, if any, subject to which the authorization may be granted.[90]

7.7 PROTECTED AREAS

The Act creates two further categories of protected areas, ie protected natural environments[91] and special nature reserves.[92] The former category is supposed to substitute that of nature area[93] which could have been declared by virtue of the Physical Planning Act 88 of 1967.[94] An improvement is that establishment and control of such areas, which formerly were regulated by virtue of different Acts and administered by different bodies, are now effected in terms of the same Act. However, the provision of the Physical Planning Act which sought to freeze land use in such areas to the existing use, was not re-enacted. A special nature reserve constitutes a new category of protected area, providing for maximum protection in extreme circumstances, such as in the case of the Prince Edward Islands.[95] These provisions confirm the submission that the time is ripe for a reconsideration of all legislation dealing with protected areas, with a view to rationalizing the situation by establishing an Act dealing comprehensively with all such areas. See chapter 27.

7.8 PRINCIPAL CONTROL THROUGH REGULATIONS

There seems to be a tendency, evidenced in the Environment Conservation Act of 1982,[96] and proceeded with in the 1987 amendment to the Act[97] and further extended in the new Act, to relegate the treatment of almost entire fields of environmental control to an administrative level, ie through the issuing of ministerial regulations. Extensive coastal zone regulations[98] have been promulgated in terms of the 1982 Act, while comprehensive sets of noise control[99] and waste control regulations[100] have been published, the former in final and the latter in draft form. The new Act, while rendering littering[101] and waste disposal[102] criminal offences and providing for control over disposal sites,[103] leaves all other control over waste management to the Minister to be exercised through regulations.[104] Moreover, the making of regulations for the control of the entire field of noise, vibration and shock is left to the Minister's discretion.[105] In

[89] Cf Rabie above n 44, 40.
[90] For alternative strategies see Rabie above n 85.
[91] Section 16.
[92] Section 18.
[93] Memorandum accompanying the 1989 Bill, para 9.
[94] See generally Visser 'Nature area legislation in South Africa' 1988 *SALJ* 249.
[95] Memorandum accompanying the 1989 Bill, para 10.
[96] Section 12(2)*(a)*–*(c)* before its amendment.
[97] Act 61 of 1987 considerably extended the scope of ministerial regulations by adding further matters in respect of which regulations may be made. Cf s 12(2)*(a)*–*(e)* of the 1982 Act after its amendment.
[98] GN 2587 of 12 December 1986.
[99] GN 2407 of 21 November 1986, GN 547 of 5 August 1988 (drafts) and GN R2544 of 2 November 1990 (final).
[100] GN 1549 of 12 July 1985 and GN 591 of 26 August 1988.
[101] Section 19(1) read with s 29(3).
[102] Section 20(6) read with s 29(4).
[103] Section 20(1)–(5).
[104] Section 24.
[105] Section 25.

fact, he may even define the field which he is to regulate.[106]

While provision for effective overall control at national level over noise and waste is to be welcomed, it may be questioned whether such control should, in principle, be exercised administratively through regulations, rather than through Parliament itself.

Administrative legislation, of which regulations are a manifestation, is normally viewed as a technique through which the practical and technical detail of principal legislation is supplied. Regulations provide a flexible tool since they can readily and easily be promulgated and amended to adapt to new situations; their promulgation is much easier than the promulgation of an Act of Parliament. But there is a good reason for this difference. Matters of principle and basic control provisions should be exposed to debate in Parliament. Moreover, while regulations, as subordinate legislation, may be declared void by the courts if they are ultra vires, vague or unreasonable, no such unstable and subordinate status is attached to parliamentary legislation. The main reason for this difference is that whereas parliamentary legislation is enacted by elected representatives, regulations are made by an executive body.

It is accordingly submitted that it is undesirable to relegate almost the entire fields of noise and of waste to the realm of control through regulations, just as it would have been equally undesirable, for instance, to effect air-pollution control through regulations instead of through the Atmospheric Pollution Prevention Act 45 of 1965. In short, what is required is a separate Noise Control Act and a separate Waste Control Act, much along the lines, for instance, of the Atmospheric Pollution Prevention Act, or, for that matter, the many other Acts that provide for specific forms of pollution control. See chapters 19 and 22. Similar considerations apply to the coastal zone. See chapter 26.

7.9 CONSENT REQUIREMENT

The promulgation of regulations in terms of the Act is inhibited by the requirement that the Minister must first obtain the concurrence of a number of bodies. If the proposed regulation will entail the expenditure of state funds, the concurrence of the Minister of Finance is required,[107] while a regulation which may affect economic development or the creation of job opportunities requires the concurrence of the Minister of Economic Affairs and Technology.[108] The most severe restriction is that a regulation which may affect the activities of any local authority or government institution (which includes any body, company or close corporation established by or under any law[109]) may be promulgated only with the concurrence of such bodies.[110] If one bears in mind the extremely wide ambit of phrases such as 'economic development or the creation of job opportunities' and the fact that almost every conceivable regulation may affect the activities of local authorities or of companies, the Minister's power is effectively neutralized. A draft amendment to the Act, prepared by the Department of Environment Affairs, seeks to repeal this restrictive requirement.

7.10 REMEDIES AND SANCTIONS

7.10.1 Appeals

Provision is made for appeals to the Minister of Environment Affairs, the Minister of Water Affairs and the various Administrators. These appeals have very little significance from a conservation perspective. They concern only certain limited aspects and then, as far as the Ministers are concerned, only when delegated powers (which

[106] Section 25*(a)*.
[107] Section 28*(i)*(i).
[108] Section 28*(i)*(ii).
[109] Section 1(xii).
[110] Section 28*(i)*(iii).

may be conferred only as regards certain provisions[111]) have been exercised.[112] Moreover, their institution is dependent upon the payment of a prescribed fee,[113] which may, depending upon the amount involved, serve to deter prospective appellants, even if the fee or part thereof may, at the discretion of the Minister or Administrator concerned, be refunded.[114] Furthermore, the appeals amount to forms of internal control, which drastically reduces their value as control mechanisms. Only forms of external control enjoy true credibility. Finally, and this is the most fundamental objection, potential appellants would probably mostly be persons whose interests have been affected by an administrative body which, through the exercise of its powers, has sought to further a conservation objective; in other words, their interests would be the very ones that have come into conflict with the public's interest in conservation.

7.10.2 Board of Investigation

In order to assist him in the evaluation of any appeal, or of any other matter, the Minister of Environment Affairs must appoint a board of investigation.[115] This board, which seems to be a type of ad hoc body,[116] obviously fulfils a merely advisory function, to be distinguished from the advisory function of the Council for the Environment on account thereof that while the council should concentrate more on broad policy, the board will deal with specific matters[117]—a rather tenuous distinction. Moreover, no individual or body, other than the Minister, has any right to approach the board. It therefore does not at all qualify as an administrative tribunal, which can review the administrative action in question on its merits and come to a binding and final decision. It is submitted that in view of the severe limitations of judicial review,[118] the lack of effective parliamentary control over administrative actions[119] and the non-existence of any external appeal, consideration should be given to transforming the board of investigation into a true environmental tribunal, with the power to review administrative actions affecting the environment, on their merits.[120] See chapter 8.

7.10.3 Review and the giving of reasons

The Act has adopted a model provision which had been proposed by the South African Law Commission in its draft Bill on the extension of the courts' review power.[121] It determines that any person whose interests are affected by a decision of an administrative body under the Act may, within 30 days after having become aware of such decision, request such body in writing to furnish reasons for the decision within 30 days after receiving the request.[122] It is further provided that within 30 days after having been furnished with such reasons, or after expiry of the period within which reasons had

---

[111] Cf s 33.
[112] Section 35.
[113] Section 35(1), (2) and (3).
[114] Section 35(4).
[115] Section 15(1). Although its appointment is obligatory, this seems to be dependent upon the lodging of an appeal or the emergence of a matter calling for the Minister's evaluation.
[116] It must be appointed from time to time: s 15(1). A board with some degree of permanence would obviously be more satisfactory.
[117] Cf para 8 of the memorandum accompanying the 1989 Bill.
[118] Cf Fuggle & Rabie above n 8, 48.
[119] Baxter *Administrative law* (1984) 211–15, 272–9.
[120] Cf generally on administrative appeals Baxter above n 119, 255–72; Rabie 'Administratiefregtelike appèlle' 1979 *De Jure* 128.
[121] Cf its *Investigation into the courts' review power in respect of administrative acts* Project 24 Working Paper 34 (1992).
[122] Section 36(1).

to be so furnished, the person in question may apply to the Supreme Court to review the decision.[123]

The introduction of an obligation upon administrative bodies to give reasons for their decisions is a most welcome innovation. Unless this has been specifically provided for in legislation (which very seldom is the case), administrative bodies are not obliged to furnish reasons for their decisions, although a negative inference may under certain circumstances be drawn from a failure to supply reasons.[124] Among the many potential benefits associated with the giving of reasons are improved decision-making, the provision of a democratic safeguard against arbitrariness, and a greater readiness on the part of the public to accept administrative decisions.

However, the obligation to furnish reasons is imposed in favour only of a person whose interests are affected by an administrative body's decision. In other words, locus standi to apply for reasons is restricted to a limited class of persons. Those affected would almost invariably be developers and others whose individual interests have been affected by an administrative body's decision to act in the public interest in conservation or pollution control. Conservationists concerned about administrative decisions, however, are not likely to fulfil the above strict locus standi requirement. For instance, if a decision is taken to grant an authorization in respect of an identified activity or a limited development area, or a permit in respect of a waste disposal site, those concerned about the decision would probably fail to qualify as persons whose interests are affected. The same would apply to instances where the administrative body in question should fail to exercise its power in making a decision, eg to determine policy, to declare protected natural environments or to identify a particular activity, while conservationists may feel that such a decision is urgently required. The reason why conservationists would probably fail to establish locus standi is that the courts are likely to superimpose their own requirements for locus standi in respect of judicial review, which requirements are rather narrowly interpreted as amounting to a direct personal interest.[125] See chapter 8. This inference is strengthened by the provision which determines that a person who has applied for reasons may apply to a court for review. It seems unlikely that the courts will be inclined to extend their review jurisdiction to a person who does not satisfy their requirements for locus standi, unless the Act clearly determines otherwise. It has been claimed that since South Africa's environmental resources are the heritage of the entire nation, the public disclosure of reasons should have been available on application to any concerned citizen or organization.[126]

While dealing with the courts' review function, it should be noted that the concept of 'review' is capable of at least three distinct and separate meanings.[127] If regard is had to the Law Commission's model provision, referred to above, it would appear, nevertheless, that the legislature's intention probably is to provide for the traditional common-law remedy of judicial review. As such it would have been a mere restatement of the common law, but for the fact that a failure to furnish reasons where they are required constitutes an additional ground for review. Another deviation from the common-law remedy of review is that review in terms of the Act is possible only in respect of a *decision* of an administrative body, whereas common-law review is aimed

[123] Section 36(2).

[124] Baxter above n 119, 746–8. See generally on the requirement of reasons Stander *Die verskaffing van redes as geldigheidsvereiste vir administratiewe handelinge* (unpublished LLM thesis University of Stellenbosch 1990).

[125] Cf Rabie & Eckard 'Locus standi: the administration's shield and the environmentalist's shackle' 1976 *CILSA* 141; Loots 'Locus standi to claim relief in the public interest in matters involving the enforcement of legislation' 1987 *SALJ* 131; Bray 'Locus standi in environmental law' 1989 *CILSA* 872–5.

[126] Glavovic above n 1, 113.

[127] *Johannesburg Consolidated Investment v Johannesburg Town Council* 1903 TS 111.

more generally at administrative *actions*. It may be questioned whether every act necessarily implies a decision and whether these concepts accordingly may for this purpose be treated as synonymous.

The scope of the court's review power is not altogether clear. While it seems certain that an administrative decision may be set aside if the body in question failed altogether to furnish reasons, it is less certain whether such a decision can be impugned if the reasons given were unsatisfactory. It seems, nevertheless, that the legislature did in fact intend the court to exercise control over the quality of the reasons furnished. After all, the provision governing review includes instances both where reasons were furnished and where there was a failure to supply them. It would seem to make no sense for the legislature to provide for the review of reasons that were in fact given, if such review did not relate to the content of those reasons. If this is indeed the case, there is some uncertainty as to the standard or criterion against which the reasons are to be evaluated. The general environmental policy—if in fact established by the Minister—would probably serve this purpose.

7.10.4 Criminal penalties

In order to secure compliance with its precepts the Act relies mostly upon the criminal sanction.[128] What is noteworthy is the substantial maximum punishment of R100 000 or 10 years' imprisonment prescribed for some contraventions, combined with a maximum fine of three times the commercial value of any thing in respect of which the offence was committed.[129] (Even a magistrate's court may impose this penalty.[130]) Moreover, in the event of a conviction the court is empowered to impose further penalties: in addition to the customary forfeiture clause,[131] the court may order that any damage to the environment resulting from the offence in question be repaired by the offender, to the satisfaction of the Minister or local authority concerned.[132] Failure to comply with such order entitles the Minister or local authority itself to take the necessary steps to repair the damage and to recover the cost from the offender.[133] Where the damage is not irreparable—as, unfortunately, it often is—this provision is potentially a very effective weapon, even if it is employed ex post facto. See also chapter 8. A draft amendment to the Act, circulated by the Department of Environment Affairs for comment, seeks to confer power upon certain bodies to issue abatement notices, unrelated to the commission of a criminal offence.

7.10.5 Civil remedies

Certain civil remedies, such as an interdict, may serve as an effective tool to prevent environmental harm.[134] Although an interdict is principally a private-law remedy, it is often used also by administrative bodies. Such bodies, however, are not automatically entitled to seek interdicts for securing compliance with legal or administrative precepts; they should be authorized thereto, either expressly or impliedly.[135] It may, for instance, be argued that the availability of other remedies, notably the criminal sanction, rules out the inference that the Act by implication authorizes administrative bodies to obtain interdicts. In any case, the matter would have been put beyond doubt had the Act expressly authorized the use of interdicts by the State.

---

[128] Section 29.
[129] Section 29(4).
[130] Section 29(9).
[131] Section 30.
[132] Section 29(7).
[133] Section 29(8).
[134] Cf Fuggle & Rabie above n 8, 39–40.
[135] Baxter above n 119, 696.

7.10.6 Financial redress

Landowners and holders of real rights in land are afforded some degree of reimbursement in respect of expenses and losses incurred by them on account of restrictions or obligations imposed upon them by the Act.

Although there is no right to financial aid, such aid may be rendered by an Administrator to the owner of, or the holder of a real right in land situated in a protected natural environment, in respect of expenses incurred by such persons in compliance with directions issued in terms of the Act.[136] This is a re-enactment of the provision of the 1982 Act relating to nature areas.[137] It has been argued that where restrictions upon private land are imposed in the public interest, the expenses thus incurred should be borne by the State.[138] If this contention is to be accepted, provision should have been made for a right to compensation in the above circumstances. However, such a contention cannot be accepted without qualification. Other legal systems, such as those of the USA and of Germany, acknowledge that, to a certain degree, it may be required of an individual landowner to render some sacrifice to serve the public interest in environmental conservation. Both these systems distinguish between two categories of land-use control measures at the disposal of the State, ie regulation of land use and expropriation, or expropriation-like drastic curtailment of land use. The importance of the distinction is reflected in the fact that while the latter involves a right to compensation, the former in principle does not. However, no clearly evident principle has emerged consistently to demarcate the dividing line between a compensable expropriation and a non-compensable regulation. It seems doubtful whether a uniformly applicable formula will ever be devised satisfactorily to distinguish between these categories. Ultimately, the decision as to the circumstances in which compensation is payable is governed by public policy.[139]

The Act does indeed grant landowners and holders of real rights in land a right to recover compensation from the Minister or Administrator concerned, but only in respect of *actual loss* suffered by them consequent upon the application of limitations on the purposes for which land may be used or on activities which may be undertaken on the land.[140] This is an extension of the 1982 Act's provision governing compensation payable to owners and occupiers of land situated in a nature area.[141] The new provision covers limitations imposed by virtue of the Act upon *any* land and includes holders of real rights in land, although occupiers are now excluded. The new provision, furthermore, extends the right to compensation to include not only limitations on the purposes of land use but also limitations on activities which may be undertaken on the land. It is not clear whether the omission in the new Act of the adjective 'patrimonial' from the phrase 'actual patrimonial loss' of the 1982 Act is designed to broaden the base for claims to compensation. Nor is it certain what is meant by 'actual loss suffered by him consequent upon the application of such limitations'. For instance, can a reduction in the market value of the land be considered as actual loss? This subject is also addressed in chapters 8 and 28.

---

[136] Section 16(5).

[137] Section 10(6).

[138] Cf Rabie 'The impact of environmental conservation on land ownership' 1985 *Acta Juridica* 289, 305–7.

[139] Cf Glazewski *Conservation of private land by means of compensatory mechanisms and incentives* (unpublished MA thesis, University of Cape Town, 1986) 47, 58; Rabie 'The influence of environmental legislation on private landownership' in Van der Walt (ed) *Land reform and the future of landownership in South Africa* (1991) 81.

[140] Section 34(1). Cf also s 34(2) and (3) in respect of the determination of the recoverable amount.

[141] Section 10(5)*(a)*. Cf also s 10(5)*(b)* and *(c)*.

7.11 CONCLUSION

On the whole, the Environment Conservation Act should be welcomed as an important legislative milestone in the development of South African environmental law. In spite of its title, however, it cannot be regarded as a codification of South African environmental legislation, although it might now—as opposed to its predecessor—arguably be regarded as our single most important environmental statute. Nor does the Act establish legal principles—if ever they can be devised—which seek to identify environmental law as a separate branch of law in the sense of containing rules with their own identity, distinct from the rules of other traditional branches of law. Cowen[142] has stated that unless distinctive legal criteria can be established which characterize environmental law, the subject will continue to lack coherence and logical structure. In any case, the definition of environment in the Act is much too sweeping to hold out any prospect of the recognition of environmental law as a distinct branch of law. The democratic spirit in which the Act came into being, as well as the extensive opportunities for public participation in administrative decision-making provided for in the Act itself, are to be highly commended. This is one of the important features of the Act and augurs well for improved governmental decision-making and for public co-operation.

Parliament has, for the first time, set out rather courageously to define the key concept of environment. However, it is likely that this definition will give rise to difficulties, on account of its breadth.

Another important issue addressed for the first time through legislation is the difficulty of orchestrating the administration of environmental affairs by the multitude of government departments and other administrative bodies. The tool that has been devised, i e the determination by the Minister of Environment Affairs of environmental policy, theoretically holds much promise. However, it is foreseeable that its practical implementation, which involves seeking the concurrence of other ministries, will meet with formidable obstacles. The draft amendment to the Act, which has been referred to above, aims to eliminate the consent requirement—also in respect of identified activities.

Yet a further welcome innovation is the control that may now be exercised by the Minister of Environment Affairs over activities which may have a detrimental effect upon the environment. The provision in this regard for environmental impact reports fulfils a long-felt need.

In certain respects, unfortunately, the Act gives the impression of serving as a catchment, to deal more effectively—mostly through subordinate legislation—with matters that are simultaneously controlled in terms of other legislation. Consideration should be given to rationalizing the position by treating matters such as noise, waste, protected areas and the coastal zone in separate Acts of Parliament. See chapters 19, 22, 26 and 27.

Another improvement in principle is the Act's adoption of the Law Commission's model provision relating to the giving of reasons for administrative decisions. Unfortunately, however, the Act's restrictive locus standi requirement will serve to disqualify conservationists from requesting reasons.

Yet a further novel provision which holds much potential is the power conferred upon a court, in the event of a conviction, to order that any damage to the environment resulting from the offence in question be repaired by the offender to the satisfaction of the relevant administrative body.

The extension of the provision governing compensation payable to private landowners on account of restrictions imposed in the public interest, however, is cause

---

[142] 'Toward distinctive principles for South African environmental law: some jurisprudential perspectives and a role for legislation' 1989 *THRHR* 3, 11.

for concern. This is an ad hoc regulation of a controversial issue, which will serve to inhibit the imposition of limitations upon land ownership. The whole issue of compensation in such circumstances needs to be resolved by Parliament in a uniform manner.

Perhaps the most outstanding feature of the Act is that it is primarily an enabling statute which leaves the ultimate control of environmental affairs in the hands of the executive and, in traditional fashion, makes no provision for any effective control over the merits or wisdom of administrative actions. In fact, almost all the provisions of the Act are of an empowering nature, which means that they will have effect only if the administrative body concerned utilizes the powers conferred upon it. The Act contains a number of potentially effective provisions and sanctions, but everything depends upon whether they will be used and if so, how? The state of our environment, in other words, will continue to be dependent, to a decisive degree, upon the willingness and ability of administrative bodies to fulfil their role as trustees of the public interest in environmental conservation. See chapter 8.

* Since going to press, the Environment Conservation Amendment Act 79 of 1992, containing the proposed amendments to which reference was made, as well as other important amendments, has been published. Further amendments, containing mainly transitional provisions, are contained in the Environment Conservation Second Amendment Act 115 of 1992. The most important amendments concern ss 2, 21, 22, 23 and 28 of the Environment Conservation Act, while ss 19A, 24A, 28A and 31A constitute significant new provisions.

CHAPTER 8

IMPLEMENTATION OF ENVIRONMENTAL LAW

M A RABIE
C LOOTS
R LYSTER
M G ERASMUS

8.1 INTRODUCTION

The mere existence of a body of environmental law, though essential in establishing a basis for action, does not in itself provide a solution to environmental problems. In fact, the mere promulgation of environmental legislation may lull the public into a false sense of security that the problems are being addressed, whereas there can be no realistic expectation of success without the adequate implementation of such legislation. To be sure, the establishment of legal provisions which are potentially effective to address environmental problems is indispensable. However, it is their satisfactory application that is decisive for ultimate success. In so far as conservation efforts have thus far failed, the failure, in general, may be ascribed not to insufficient or deficient legislation but primarily to the unsatisfactory application of existing legislation. And the reason for this is to be found not only in the lack of compliance by individuals with environmental-law precepts but especially in the lack of credibility of public bodies entrusted with the administration of environmental law: the political will to implement existing environmental controls is suspect.

This is reflected in the low political status and poor budgetary provision which have traditionally characterized such bodies. Although the position has improved during the past few years, and while several administrative bodies fulfil their environmental obligations with determination, it is submitted that the above generalization is still valid.

Moreover, environmental legislation is implemented not only by environmentally oriented public bodies such as the Department of Environment Affairs but also by bodies that have a primary mission which may even be in potential conflict with conservation, e g the Departments of Mineral and Energy Affairs, Agriculture and Water Affairs.

The emphasis in this chapter is on the role of administrative bodies in implementing environmental legislation rather than on an examination of the compliance by individuals with environmental-law precepts. Nevertheless, some attention is given to the use of remedies by individuals in the implementation of environmental law.

8.2 IMPLEMENTATION OF ENVIRONMENTAL LAW BY ADMINSTRATIVE BODIES

Environmental law consists mostly of provisions which either directly impose obligations or prohibitions upon individuals or which, more frequently, entrust the care of natural resources and the control of pollution to administrative bodies, i e central government departments, provincial administrations, local authorities, statutory and other public bodies. Such latter provisions comprise primarily discretionary powers which are conferred upon the administrative bodies concerned. The successful implementation depends upon whether the exercise of such powers in fact furthers the public interest in environmental conservation. The point is that the success of environmental law depends decisively upon administrative bodies.

8.2.1 Direct environmental functions

The most comprehensive powers that are conferred usually relate to those instances in which the administrative body in question performs its functions in respect of land held in ownership by the State—for instance, the powers conferred in terms of the National Parks Act 57 of 1976 as regards the management of national parks[1] and powers by virtue of the Forest Act 122 of 1984 relating to the management of state forests,[2] including forest nature reserves and wilderness areas.[3] In these instances the bodies in question themselves extensively regulate, in the public interest, the use of the natural resources that are entrusted to their care.

Other examples of where administrative bodies themselves undertake certain actions required to conserve a given resource, or to control pollution, even in respect of land or resources not belonging to the State, occur, for instance, in the Conservation of Agricultural Resources Act 43 of 1983. In terms of this Act the Minister of Agriculture may on his own perform or cause to be performed on or in respect of any land certain actions related to soil and water conservation, as well as the control of weeds and invader plants, and which he deems necessary in order to achieve the objects of the Act.[4] See chapter 10. A similar provision is contained in the Mountain Catchment Areas Act 63 of 1970.[5]

The own performance of environmental functions by administrative bodies often relates to activities which require communal involvement because they are beyond the capacities of private enterprise, e g the supply of water, the disposal of waste (especially hazardous waste) and the combating of marine oil pollution. The management of the country's water resources, for instance, is entrusted by the Water Act 54 of 1956 to the Minister of Water Affairs,[6] while preventing and combating marine oil pollution are the responsibilities of the Ministers of Transport and of Environment Affairs, in terms of the Prevention and Combating of Pollution of the Sea by Oil Act 6 of 1981.[7]

Another example of where the administrative body concerned may itself execute the provisions of the relevant legislation is to be found in the abatement notice procedure, which is discussed below.

Although the powers conferred upon administrative bodies are usually couched in the form of discretionary provisions, in certain instances duties are imposed upon the bodies concerned—for instance, the duties to prevent nuisances and pollution with which local authorities must comply in terms of the Health Act 63 of 1977.[8]

8.2.2 Establishment of control provisions

8.2.2.1 *General provisions*

In many instances the very establishment of control provisions is dependent upon administrative bodies. Most environmental statutes authorize administrative bodies (usually the Ministers concerned) to issue regulations in respect of the environmental

---

[1] Section 12.
[2] Part III.
[3] Section 15(3).
[4] Section 11(1). He may even recover the costs involved from the landowner concerned: s 11(2)*(a)* and *(b)*.
[5] Section 12.
[6] Section 2.
[7] Section 5(1) and (2).
[8] Section 20(1).

aspects subject to their control. For instance, smoke[9] or vehicle emission[10] control regulations in terms of the Atmospheric Pollution Prevention Act 45 of 1965 and sea-shore control regulations[11] by virtue of the Sea-Shore Act 21 of 1935 must be issued by the respective Ministers or local authorities before effective control can be exercised over the relevant matters provided for in these statutes. Perhaps the best example is provided by the Environment Conservation Act 73 of 1989, by virtue of which the entire field of noise control is subjected to ministerial discretion as regards the making of regulations.[12] In so far as potentially effective regulations are not promulgated, the purpose of the enabling legislation is frustrated.

8.2.2.2 *Individual provisions*

Other examples where administrative bodies are authorized to establish environmental control provisions themselves are statutes that enable such bodies to issue directives which are applicable to the individuals concerned, mostly landowners. For instance, both the Mountain Catchment Areas Act[13] and the Conservation of Agricultural Resources Act[14] authorize the respective Ministers to issue environment-related directions or to prescribe environmentally relevant control measures which must then be complied with by the individual landowners and others to whom they apply. Both these Acts will have little effect if directions and control measures are not administratively prescribed. Instances where a person other than a landowner is involved are the registrar's power in terms of the Fertilizers, Farm Feeds, Agricultural Remedies and Stock Remedies Act 36 of 1947 to order a pest control operator to discontinue the use of certain equipment[15] and the responsible Minister's powers by virtue of the Prevention and Combating of Pollution of the Sea by Oil Act to require certain actions of the master or owner of a ship or tanker, with a view to preventing marine oil pollution.[16]

In contrast to instances where environmentally harmful conduct is prohibited in the legislation concerned (eg the prohibition in the Atmospheric Pollution Prevention Act against the installation of fuel-burning appliances[17]), administrative bodies are often authorized themselves to impose such prohibitions. Examples are provided by the Sea Fishery Act 12 of 1988, which enables the Minister of Environment Affairs to prohibit a variety of actions in order to protect fish,[18] and by the Forest Act, which authorizes the Minister, with a view to protecting natural water sources, to prohibit the planting of trees within a defined area or the reafforestation of such an area.[19]

8.2.3 Activation of control provisions

Related to the previous category are provisions which are potentially effective in the sense that upon their activation certain other provisions become operative. In other words, the application of the latter provisions is dependent upon the activation of the former.

[9] Sections 18 and 19.
[10] Sections 37 and 39.
[11] Section 10.
[12] Section 25.
[13] Section 3(1).
[14] Section 6(1).
[15] Section 6A.
[16] Section 4(1).
[17] Section 15(1).
[18] Sections 33(1), 35(1), 36(1) and 37(1).
[19] Section 8(1).

For instance, the Atmospheric Pollution Prevention Act determines that its provisions relating to the control of noxious or offensive gases,[20] smoke,[21] dust[22] and vehicle emissions[23] apply only in areas which have been declared by the Minister of National Health and Population Development to be subject to control. All the former provisions thus take effect only if the latter provisions are activated. See chapter 17.

Other examples are provisions authorizing the establishment by various administrative bodies of a variety of protected areas, eg a national park in terms of the National Parks Act. The many provisions of the Act are applicable only in respect of an area declared to be a national park. See chapter 27.

The Environment Conservation Act stipulates that administrative bodies are obliged to exercise their functions in accordance with the declared environmental policy.[24] However, this provision can become operative only if the Minister of Environment Affairs does in fact declare an environmental policy, as he is authorized to do in terms of the Act.[25] Again, although provision is made in the Act for requiring environmental impact reports by developers and others,[26] this is dependent upon the Minister's identifying certain activities[27] or declaring limited development areas[28] by virtue of empowering provisions of the Act, since such reports are required only in respect of the above-mentioned activities or areas.

Finally, the provisions of the Hazardous Substances Act 15 of 1973 can take effect only after the Minister of National Health and Population Development has declared substances to be grouped hazardous substances.[29]

8.2.4 Authorization of actions by individuals

Common provisions encountered in almost all environmental legislation are those which enable administrative bodies to authorize individuals to perform actions that would otherwise be prohibited or restricted. Apart from the obvious importance to the individuals concerned, especially in cases of occupational or commercial licences, the exercise of such discretionary powers is of the utmost environmental importance. The permit or licence system constitutes the prime regulatory technique as far as environmental conservation and pollution control are concerned. For example, no person may carry on a scheduled process unless he is the holder of a registration certificate, issued by the chief officer in terms of the Atmospheric Pollution Prevention Act.[30] Likewise, a permit is required by the Environment Conservation Act for the lawful establishment, provision or operation of a waste disposal site;[31] nuclear licences are required by the Nuclear Energy Act 92 of 1982 in respect of a variety of activities related to nuclear installations, sites and nuclear-hazard material;[32] agricultural and stock remedies (pesticides) may not be sold unless they are registered under the Fertilizers, Farm Feeds, Agricultural Remedies and Stock Remedies Act,[33] and a permit is required by the Water Act before water exceeding a certain quantity may be

---

20 Section 8.
21 Section 14.
22 Section 27.
23 Section 36.
24 Section 3.
25 Section 2(1) and (2).
26 Sections 22(2) and 23(3).
27 Section 21.
28 Section 23(1).
29 Section 2.
30 Section 9(1)*(a)*.
31 Section 20(1).
32 Section 30(1).
33 Section 7(1).

used for industrial purposes.[34] In all these and similar instances an important discretion is conferred upon the administrative body in question whether or not to permit the potentially harmful conduct and, if it is authorized, to determine the conditions subject to which it may be performed.

8.2.5 Granting of rights

Environmentally relevant legislation sometimes enables administrative bodies to grant certain rights, the exercise of which is potentially harmful to the environment. Examples are the granting of rights of exploitation in terms of the Sea Fishery Act[35] and the granting of servitudes or other rights of any nature in respect of forest nature reserves or wilderness areas, by virtue of the Forest Act.[36] Rights in respect of mining also constitute a prominent example. It is obvious that the exercise of the above discretionary powers involves significant environmental issues.

8.2.6 Exemptions

Related to the authorization of actions by individuals are instances where the administrative body concerned is empowered to exempt persons from compliance with environmentally relevant legislative provisions. Exemptions impose an even greater responsibility upon administrative bodies, because they remove individuals from the range of application of the environmental provisions concerned. For instance, the Minister of Water Affairs may exempt any person or category of persons from the requirements of the Water Act relating to the purification and disposal of effluent.[37] Similarly, the Minister of Transport may exempt any ship, tanker or class of ships or tankers from any or all of the provisions of the Prevention and Combating of Pollution of the Sea by Oil Act[38] and the Minister of Environment Affairs may exempt certain persons from any or all of the provisions of the Sea Fishery Act.[39]

8.2.7 Rendering of financial aid

Certain statutes make provision for the discretionary dispensing of financial aid to persons, mostly landowners, to assist them to comply with administrative directives aimed at environmental conservation. The judicious exercise of this power can clearly operate to the benefit of conservation. Examples are the payment of subsidies in terms of the Conservation of Agricultural Resources Act to land-users for the performance of certain conservation-related acts[40] and the rendering of financial aid by virtue of the Mountain Catchment Areas Act to owners and occupiers of land for expenses incurred in compliance with a fire protection plan or a direction.[41] The Atmospheric Pollution Prevention Act authorizes discretionary contributions by the Minister of National Health and Population Development towards the expenditure incurred by any person in connection with research relating to the combating of air pollution.[42]

8.2.8 Acquisition of land

Administrative bodies are authorized to acquire private land for conservation purposes either by purchase or by expropriation. Such provisions are contained, inter

---

[34] Section 12(1).
[35] Section 25.
[36] Section 15(4)*(a)*.
[37] Section 21(4)*(a)*.
[38] Section 25(1).
[39] Section 41(1).
[40] Section 8(1).
[41] Section 10*(b)*.
[42] Section 45A*(a)*.

alia, in the National Parks Act,[43] the Conservation of Agricultural Resources Act,[44] the Lake Areas Development Act 39 of 1975[45] and the Forest Act.[46] The expropriation of land in the public interest entails drastic consequences for the individual landowner concerned and requires a correspondingly responsible exercise of discretion on the part of the administrative body involved. However, once land is held in state ownership, the State enjoys more comprehensive powers and the potential for effective conservation is accordingly increased.

8.2.9 Performance of judicial functions

Apart from the fact that mero motu internal administrative appeals are regularly lodged, certain statutes expressly provide for appeals against the decisions of administrative bodies to other administrative bodies. These latter bodies are then authorized to reconsider the decisions against which the appeal was brought and to confirm, set aside or vary the decisions concerned. An example of appeals to certain Ministers and Administrators is encountered in the Environment Conservation Act,[47] while both the Fertilizers, Farm Feeds, Agricultural Remedies and Stock Remedies Act[48] and the Atmospheric Pollution Prevention Act[49] provide for appeals to appeal boards. The performance of judicial functions involves the passing of judgment on contentious matters—something that is usually reserved for a court of law. Exceptional qualities are required of public bodies which are entrusted with such functions.

8.2.10 Appointment of staff, establishment of administrative bodies and appointment of their members

A significant discretionary power enjoyed by some administrative officials and bodies is the appointment of staff members to assist in implementing the environmental legislation concerned. For instance, the Minister of National Health and Population Development may appoint the chief officer and inspectors concerned with the administration of the Atmospheric Pollution Prevention Act.[50] Moreover, statutes such as the Environment Conservation Act,[51] the Atmospheric Pollution Prevention Act,[52] the Fertilizers, Farm Feeds, Agricultural Remedies and Stock Remedies Act[53] and the National Parks Act[54] enable the Ministers concerned (or the State President) to establish administrative bodies, such as boards, and to appoint their members. In instances where administrative bodies are established by virtue of the relevant statutes themselves—for instance, the Council for Nuclear Safety (Nuclear Energy Act[55]), the National Air Pollution Advisory Committee (Atmospheric Pollution Prevention Act[56]) and the Council for the Environment (Environment Conservation Act[57]), the responsible Ministers may none the less appoint the members of these bodies. It is obvious that the judicious exercise of discretion in the appointment of administrative

[43] Section 3(1).
[44] Section 14(1).
[45] Section 16(2).
[46] Section 14(2).
[47] Section 35.
[48] Section 6.
[49] Sections 13, 25, 35 and 38.
[50] Section 6(1).
[51] Section 15(1) and (2).
[52] Section 5.
[53] Section 6(2).
[54] Section 5(1) and (3)*(a)*.
[55] Section 24(2).
[56] Section 2(1).
[57] Section 6(1).

staff and members of public bodies is of decisive importance for the success of environmental conservation.

8.3 SECURING COMPLIANCE BY INDIVIDUALS THROUGH THE USE OF CONTROL PROVISIONS

It is a well-known fact that, for a variety of reasons, individuals are not always inclined to obey legal provisions and their implementation by administrative bodies. Mechanisms are therefore required to ensure compliance in such circumstances. A broad distinction may be drawn between instances in which the administration itself is authorized to secure such compliance and instances in which the involvement of the courts is required.

8.3.1 Direct administrative enforcement powers

8.3.1.1 *Informing and assisting individuals*

An important facet of the administration's task in implementing environmental legislation is its supervisory function as regards individuals upon whom the legislation concerned is applicable. The administration of legislative precepts which are applicable to individuals presupposes that the individuals concerned are familiar with such precepts. An important duty of the administration accordingly is that it should participate in the process of informing individuals of their obligations in terms of the relevant legislation. This is of particular importance in view of the relative inaccessibility of legislation, especially subordinate legislation. Regulations constitute a considerable proportion of environmental law and, although such regulations must be published in the *Government Gazette*, it is not always easy for those subject to the provisions of their own accord to be aware of the existence of such provisions or of amendments which are regularly promulgated. A special effort is accordingly required of administrative bodies to inform individuals of their legal obligations. Administrative bodies, furthermore, should try to assist persons to comply with the legislation in question. Some government departments have even established special divisions whose sole task it is to advise and assist individuals to comply with their legal obligations, e g the extension staff of the Department of Agriculture.

8.3.1.2 *Administrative sanctions*

Where an individual fails to comply with an administrative precept, the administrative body in question is normally not itself empowered to enforce compliance, but is obliged to rely upon the regular legal machinery of civil or criminal justice. None the less, in certain instances powers are conferred upon administrative bodies to act on their own in securing compliance by individuals with administrative obligations. Owing to the potential abuse of such far-reaching administrative powers, provision is sometimes made for an appeal to an administrative tribunal against the administrative action in question.

(a) Abatement notice procedure. Certain administrative bodies are authorized to serve a notice on a person causing environmental pollution or destruction, calling upon him to perform certain actions in order to control the pollution or to prevent its aggravation or recurrence. Failure to comply with this notice usually amounts to an offence. Moreover, the administrative body may, upon failure of the person subject to control, itself cause the required action to be performed and even to recover the costs involved. Such a procedure is prescribed, for example, in the Atmospheric Pollution Prevention Act.[58] See chapter 17. This power is not always predicated upon the failure

[58] Sections 17 and 19.

to perform by the person subject to the notice or order; it may also be activated by the administrative body's opinion that that person is incapable of compliance or that compliance cannot reasonably be expected of him, as is demonstrated by the Prevention and Combating of Pollution of the Sea by Oil Act.[59]

(b) Administrative suspension or cancellation of authorizations. A powerful sanction is sometimes made available to administrative bodies, ie the discretionary suspension or cancellation of authorizations in certain circumstances, usually of non-compliance by the holders of such authorizations or if it is demanded by the public interest. Examples of such powers are the following: the Sea Fishery Act provides for the suspension, cancellation or reduction of quotas[60] and the suspension or termination of rights of exploitation;[61] the Atmospheric Pollution Prevention Act authorizes the suspension or cancellation of registration certificates,[62] while the Fertilizers, Farm Feeds, Agricultural Remedies and Stock Remedies Act provides for the cancellation of certain registrations,[63] the Nuclear Energy Act authorizes the revocation of nuclear licences[64] and the Minerals Act 50 of 1991 makes provision for the suspension or cancellation of prospecting permits and mining authorizations.[65]

(c) Detention as security. Some administrative bodies are authorized to detain objects involved in incidents which are environmentally harmful, pending the payment of costs for which their owners are liable. For instance, the Prevention and Combating of Pollution of the Sea by Oil Act authorizes the Minister in question to detain a ship if the owner fails to pay the costs for which he is liable owing to damage caused by pollution resulting from the discharge of oil from the ship.[66]

(d) Powers of investigation and seizure. Administrative bodies are usually authorized to enter premises, vehicles etc and to conduct examinations in order to ascertain whether environmental precepts are being complied with. They are often also empowered to seize anything which may furnish proof of any contravention of the provisions concerned. Examples of such powers are encountered in the Fertilizers, Farm Feeds, Agricultural Remedies and Stock Remedies Act,[67] the Sea Fishery Act[68] and the Conservation of Agricultural Resources Act.[69] In these instances the administrative bodies involved do not themselves ultimately enforce the provisions concerned, but they do assist in bringing offenders to justice.

(e) Enforcement of court orders. Although again not, strictly speaking constituting an example of independent administrative action to secure compliance with environmental provisions, the administration is sometimes itself authorized to take action where a person who has been convicted of an environmental offence fails to comply with the relevant court order. The Environment Conservation Act, for instance, provides that in the case of conviction of an offence in terms of the Act, the court may order that any environmental damage resulting from the offence concerned be repaired by the person so convicted[70] and that, upon his failure to do so, the relevant

---

59 Section 4(2)*(a)*; cf s 22(1).
60 Section 20.
61 Section 25(3)*(c)*.
62 Section 12(4).
63 Section 4.
64 Section 40(1).
65 Section 14(1).
66 Section 19.
67 Section 15.
68 Section 53.
69 Sections 18 and 20.
70 Section 29(7).

administrative bodies may themselves take the necessary steps to repair the damage and recover the cost involved.[71]

8.3.2 Enforcement through the judiciary and other state organs

The enforcement of administrative acts by the administration itself, as has been mentioned, is traditionally regarded as an exceptional power.[72] Normally, administrative bodies are obliged to rely upon other state organs such as the police and the courts to enforce compliance with legislative provisions or with their own precepts.

8.3.2.1 *Employment of civil process*

Among the more familiar remedies available to the administration in order to secure compliance with the law or with directions issued by public bodies is the potentially effective remedy of an interdict. Administrative bodies are not automatically entitled to seek interdicts for such purposes; they must be authorized—either expressly or impliedly—to do so.[73]

8.3.2.2 *Application of criminal sanctions*

(a) Primary and subsidiary application. The criminal sanction has been employed extensively in South African environmental legislation and it is by far the most widely prescribed sanction for contraventions of legal and administrative provisions. As far as the statutory prescription of the criminal sanction to buttress environmental provisions is concerned, a distinction should be drawn between the application of the criminal penalty as a primary or independent sanction, and its application as a subsidiary or supporting sanction. In environmental legislation the criminal sanction has been prescribed mainly as a subsidiary or indirect sanction, but it has also been used as a primary or direct sanction. Its application as a direct sanction means that the environmentally harmful activity is outlawed directly. Reliance upon the criminal sanction is accompanied by several problems, which problems are intensified when it is used as a primary sanction.[74]

The criminal sanction is used as a secondary or subsidiary sanction in instances where reliance for compliance with legislative precepts is placed primarily upon administrative control, the criminal penalty being invoked only if and when such administrative control fails. Well-known examples of such application include use of administrative directives, the licensing system and the abatement notice procedure.

It is submitted that application of the criminal penalty as a subsidiary sanction is preferable to its application as a primary sanction. It will in many instances be far easier to prove the elements of the crime of engaging in an activity without a licence, or of disobeying an administrative direction, than to prove that the accused has committed a certain kind of environmentally detrimental activity. But, most important of all, by employing the criminal penalty as a subsidiary sanction it is not necessary to wait until the environmentally detrimental conduct has actually materialized before action can be taken. The advantages of a preventive approach to environmental damage can hardly be overemphasized.

Although the traditional approach of South African environmental criminal law is supported, some shortcomings should be attended to. First, use of the criminal sanction in a subsidiary manner means that the application of criminal law is thereby rendered

[71] Section 29(8).

[72] Wiechers *Administrative law* (1985) 161–3.

[73] Baxter *Administrative law* (1984) 696; cf 662 in respect of their standing to sue.

[74] The section on criminal sanctions is based upon Fuggle & Rabie *Environmental concerns in South Africa* (1983) 43–7 and para 5.15 of the *Report of the three committees of the President's Council on a national environmental management system* PC 1/1991.

accessary to the application of administrative controls.[75] Reference has been made to the deficient enforcement of environmental law by the administrative bodies concerned. This implies the automatic transfer of shortcomings in environmental administration to criminal-law enforcement. Apart from the fact that administrative bodies fail effectively to enforce environmental legislation—thereby effectively paralyzing the bodies concerned with criminal justice—there is a further difficulty, from a criminal-law perspective: once an administrative body has authorized certain environmentally harmful conduct, there is no scope for protection by the criminal law, even if such authorization may be highly questionable from an environmental point of view. The only way in which the administrative subordination of environmental criminal law can be eliminated is through the creation of definitions of criminal conduct which render such conduct absolutely forbidden, ie without any intervention or control by administrative-law precepts or by an administrative body. In effect, this means that reliance will have to be placed upon the criminal sanction as a primary sanction. However, it is inconceivable that there are many actions which threaten the environment to such a degree that they should be criminally forbidden under all circumstances. Moreover, it seems difficult to define such conduct satisfactorily. In order to do this, it would often be necessary to set standards in the legislation itself, which will bring about an undesirable element of rigidity.

While, therefore, we will have to continue relying to a large extent upon the subsidiary application of the criminal sanction, it is important that there should be close co-operation between the bodies responsible for the administration of environmental legislation and those concerned with criminal justice. Although perhaps desirable, it is not essential that the police establish specialized environmental units, but if a charge involving criminal pollution is laid, the police should at least be required to refer the case to the relevant specialized body, eg the Department of National Health and Population Development and local authorities in cases of air pollution or the Department of Agriculture in cases involving pesticides and soil erosion. In many cases these departments themselves lay the charges, but, where this is not the case, there should be some machinery for ensuring that their expertise will be used when a case of criminal pollution or environmental degradation is investigated. Another problem is that officials of these specialized departments investigating a case usually have no legal training. This can cause much of their valuable work to be rendered nugatory. To overcome this difficulty, these officials should receive some training in the law of criminal procedure and the law of evidence. A further suggestion is that these departments should have their own prosecutors, who could then specialize in the relevant field of criminal environmental law. Alternatively, the Department of Justice could be encouraged to include an environmental component in the training programmes for prosecutors and magistrates and could allocate selected prosecutors and magistrates to environment-related cases.

Another problem associated with the application of the criminal sanction as a subsidiary sanction is that some safeguard is required to ensure that effectiveness is not the sole criterion that underlies the administrative action in question, and that considerations of justice towards the 'offender' will be taken into account. This is best accomplished through the provision of an appeal to an administrative tribunal against the administrative action which is the subject of the complaint.

(b) Prosecutions. In general, the enforcement of environmental legislation has not relied strongly on criminal prosecutions. For instance, very few, if any, prosecutions have resulted in terms of legislation relating to air pollution, biocides and radiation, nor

---

[75] For problems resulting from such administrative accessoriness, see Rabie 'The principle of administrative accessoriness in German environmental criminal law' 1992 *SACJ* (in press).

have criminal sanctions been applied vigorously as regards solid waste and noise control. Prosecutions have featured more prominently as far as nature conservation, soil conservation and water pollution are concerned.

It is difficult, however, to assess the effectiveness of such prosecutions. For instance, of the 40 prosecutions initiated by the Department of Water Affairs between 1984 and 1990 30 accused (mainly companies and local authorities) admitted guilt. Among the different inferences that may be drawn from this statistic is the possibility that the accused are quite willing to pay the rather small fine and not incur legal costs as well as bad publicity. This would suggest that the criminal sanction operates merely as a kind of tax instead of as a deterrent measure.

It should also be borne in mind that statistics on criminal prosecutions reveal only the ultimate phase of control where all other strategies have failed and the sanction is engaged as a last resort. Such statistics tend to conceal the considerable persuasive force of the negotiation process which precedes—and in many instances obviates—criminal proceedings. For instance, during the past five years 91 criminal cases involving soil erosion were served in the courts. Of this number, 25 were withdrawn because of the accused's compliance, while 11 are still pending. In 38 of the remaining 55 cases, the outcome was successful. However, these statistics do not reveal that informal negotiation led to compliance by 52 per cent of the approximately 1 400 land-users who are annually identified as transgressors of soil conservation control measures. Moreover, 47 per cent of land-users comply with such measures after having been formally served with a direction in terms of the Conservation of Agricultural Resources Act. It is only in respect of 1 per cent of land-users that court proceedings are eventually initiated. It is important, nevertheless, to remember that the success of the above negotiation process is due, in large measure, to the threat of criminal proceedings which underpins the process. Furthermore, the 1 400 land-users who are reached annually through inspections represents only 1 per cent of the farming community, whereas it is generally acknowledged that a successful campaign requires that at least 7 per cent of land-users should be reached.

(c) Penalties. The typical criminal penalty which is normally imposed is a fine. A common complaint is that fines provided for and imposed in respect of environmental offences are generally far too low. This view is supported. A review of all criminal penalties is urgently required, with a view to bringing them into line with the seriousness of the offences in question. Moreover, a number of discrepancies regarding the magnitude of fines for polluting various environments exist. For example, the maximum fine for a first conviction under the Water Act is R50 000, while under the Atmospheric Pollution Prevention Act it is only R500. The maximum fine for contravening the provisions of the Environment Conservation Act relating to the operation of a disposal site is R100 000, while the maximum fine for contravening regulations passed under the Hazardous Substances Act on the disposal of empty containers is R500. However, since many polluters are typically affluent corporations, the threat and imposition of prison sentences may be of significantly greater deterrent value than the severity of a fine. Suspended sentences may be of considerable practical significance, since measures to control or prevent further pollution can be stipulated in the conditions of suspension—for example, the installation of adequate pollution control equipment.

In addition to the regular penalty, provision is sometimes made for the imposition of further sanctions. It is submitted that such sanctions should be investigated closely with a view to their more frequent prescription, since they may in many instances be more effective than the regular penalty of a fine or imprisonment. Such additional sanctions include the following: a provision that the court, in addition to the normal punishment, must summarily inquire into and determine the monetary advantage that the convicted person may have gained in consequence of the offence, and impose a fine equal to the amount so determined.[76] A further provision that has considerable deterrent effect is one which provides that, in addition to any other penalty that is imposed upon conviction, articles and objects which were used in connection with the commission of the offence may be declared by the court to be forfeit (this type of provision is, for instance, encountered in all provincial nature conservation ordinances). Forfeiture can also relate to the spoils of the crime and thus remove any advantage from the commission of the crime. An important remedial measure, already referred to above, has been introduced in the Environment Conservation Act. This is the authorization of a court, upon conviction and in addition to the customary forfeiture clause, to order that any damage to the environment resulting from the offence in question be repaired by the offender to the satisfaction of the authority concerned.[77] Moreover, failure by the offender to comply with such an order entitles the authority itself to take the necessary steps to repair the damage and to recover the cost from the offender.[78] See chapter 7. Another deterrent provision is that any licence or permit that the accused holds may be cancelled and he may be disqualified from obtaining another licence or permit for a prescribed period. Yet another deterrent provision is provided for in the Water Act; it empowers the Minister to order that upon the commission of certain offences the supply of water for industrial purposes be suspended or reduced.[79] Similar types of provisions should, whenever appropriate, be designed and prescribed in environmental legislation which relies upon the criminal sanction.

(d) Alternative remedies. A constant search should be conducted to find alternative environmental remedies which may be less cumbersome, expensive, oppressive and time-consuming and more effective than the criminal sanction. Regulatory controls, such as a licence system, supported by criminal sanctions, in practice often imply a type of one-off exercise, with licences being granted for a lengthy period, or even indefinitely, while environmental conditions and abatement technology are constantly changing. Although the conditions of licences may enable authorities to pressurize licensees into employing new pollution abatement or conservation technology, little, if any, incentive is offered to do so, other than the threat of criminal sanction. An additional or alternative reliance upon economic instruments, in a profit-motivated economy, provides economic solutions to what are often essentially economic problems. Examples of such economic instruments are charge systems, e g effluent, user and product charges, market instruments such as emissions trading, subsidies such as grants, tax allowances and tax exemptions and deposit-refund systems. The delivery of satisfactory financial guarantees prior to the undertaking of environmentally hazardous activities (for instance, mining) can eliminate problems that may arise when environmental repair is required. See chapter 3.

Another alternative or additional sanction is that of environmental audits. Environmental auditing, usually undertaken by professional consulting firms, and overseen by the administrative body involved, seeks to provide the firm in question with recommendations on how it can improve its environmental management practices, followed by a report from the firm setting forth its response to such recommendations. Besides emphasizing an entrepreneur's environmental responsibility, one of the aims of an environmental audit is to assist the realization that environmental compliance is good business practice which will probably save money in the long run. An environmental audit may be undertaken as a matter of routine, but may be required after a violation of an environmental provision has been revealed.

A further potentially effective deterrent is constituted by the strategy of listing those

---

[76] eg s 47(2)*(a)* of the Sea Fishery Act.
[77] Section 29(7).
[78] Section 29(8).
[79] Section 24(2).

firms which have violated environmental provisions and preventing them from obtaining government contracts, subsidies or loans. A similar strategy is that by which environmental qualifications are set before government contracts, subsidies or loans will be awarded—for instance, the condition that drought aid subsidies will be available only to farmers who have applied conservation farming practices.

8.4 IMPLEMENTATION OF ENVIRONMENTAL LAW BY INDIVIDUALS

Individuals can play an important role in assuring the implementation of environmental law. Such implementation is relevant where their own private interests have been affected and those interests display an environmental nature. For instance, the subjection of a person to a form of environmental nuisance such as noise or air pollution gives rise to the potential engagement of private-law remedies against the wrongdoer. The successful reliance upon such remedies could in effect support the conservation of the environment.

Nevertheless, most instances of pollution or environmental degradation primarily affect the public interest in the conservation of natural resources and pollution control. It has been shown that the advancement of this public interest is almost invariably entrusted to public bodies through their administration of the environmental legislation concerned. However, it is simplistic to assume that the public interest is automatically represented by the public authority in question merely because the latter has been established in order to further the public interest.[80] There have traditionally been few effective remedies by which individuals, particularly conservationists, can obtain an assurance that the public interest in conservation has indeed been furthered by the administrative body concerned.[81]

8.4.1 The problem of standing

8.4.1.1 *Personal interest*

One of the major problems with regard to the enforcement of environmental law through court proceedings initiated by individuals is that the courts will not allow a party to claim relief in the public interest.[82] A person who seeks to claim relief such as an interdict or a declaratory order or who requests the court to review an administrative decision must show that he personally has an interest in the relief claimed in that he is adversely affected by a wrongful act,[83] or an administrative act or decision,[84] or that his legal rights are in issue.[85] Relief may not be claimed merely on the basis that the defendant or respondent is doing something which is contrary to the law and that it is

[80] Baxter above n 73, 57.

[81] See, generally, Rabie 'Towards assuring administrative furtherance of the public interest in environmental conservation' 1990 *Stell LR* 219.

[82] *Bagnall v The Colonial Government* 1907 (24) SC 470; *Dalrymple v Colonial Treasurer* 1910 TS 372, 386; *Director of Education, Transvaal v McCagie* 1918 AD 616, 621, 627; *Roodepoort-Maraisburg Town Council v Eastern Properties (Prop) Ltd* 1933 AD 87, 101; *Wood v Ondangwa Tribal Authority* 1975 (2) SA 294 (A) 310F; *Cabinet for the Transitional Government for the Territory of South West Africa v Eins* 1988 (3) SA 369 (A) 387I–389A.

[83] *Patz v Greene & Co* 1907 TS 427, 433–5; *Natal Fresh Produce Growers' Association v Agroserve (Pty) Ltd* 1990 (4) SA 749 (N) 758G–759D.

[84] *Bagnall v The Colonial Government* above n 82; *Director of Education v McCagie* above n 82, 621–2, 631; *Cabinet for the Transitional Government for the Territory of South West Africa v Eins* above n 82, 389I; *Shifidi v Administrator-General for South West Africa* 1989 (4) SA 631 (SWA) 637D–F; *Milani v South African Medical and Dental Council* 1990 (1) SA 899 (T) 902D–903G; *Waks v Jacobs* 1990 (1) SA 913 (T) 917B–919C.

[85] *Dalrymple v Colonial Treasurer* above n 82, 380–1; *Bamford v Minister of Community Development and State Auxiliary Services* 1981 (3) SA 1054 (C) 1060A.

in the public interest that he should be stopped.[86] The person who approaches the court for relief must be able to show that he personally is affected by the breach of the law. A plaintiff or applicant who is not able to establish such an interest is said to lack 'standing' or 'locus standi'. He has no right to be before the court in respect of the relief being claimed.

8.4.1.2 *Environmental interests*

The state of the environment affects all persons who live in that environment. Problems relating to the macro-environment such as the diminishing ozone layer affect all mankind. Other environmental problems affect only those persons physically present in a particular area. The more widespread the problem, the more difficult it is likely to be for an individual to establish that he is affected. It may be relatively easy to establish locus standi in respect of a plaintiff who lives within close proximity of a factory which is polluting the atmosphere. It is likely to be much more difficult to establish locus standi in respect of something as pervasive as depletion of the ozone layer. This should not be so, for as long ago as 1910 our courts held that South African law did not require that the interest of the person suing should be greater or more special than that of other members of the public. Provided only that some right which he personally was required to exercise was interfered with, or that he was personally injured by the act complained of, it made no difference that his right or his injury was no greater than those of other members of the public.[87] In terms of this dictum every person could establish locus standi to claim relief in respect of harm to the environment which has an adverse effect on mankind generally. Other courts have, apparently, adopted a more restrictive approach, requiring the applicant for relief to have a greater interest than that which the public in general have.[88] It is difficult to reconcile the aforesaid dicta, but it seems that, provided the applicant can establish interference with a right which he enjoys, personal harm or some other personal interest, he should have locus standi, even though other members of the public may be in the same position that he is in.[89] What the courts are not prepared to countenance is the 'ideological plaintiff' who alleges no personal right or personal injury, but comes to court on the basis that he is claiming the relief in the public interest.

8.4.1.3 *Types of adverse effects*

What kind of adverse effect will give a person standing? It is quite clear from our case law that a plaintiff who can establish financial harm or physical damage which is quantifiable in financial terms will have no problem establishing locus standi, provided

[86] *Bagnall v The Colonial Government* above n 82; *Patz v Greene & Co* above n 83, 433; *Von Moltke v Costa Areosa (Pty) Ltd* 1975 (1) SA 255 (C) 259A–C.

[87] *Dalrymple v Colonial Treasurer* above n 82, 380 approved in *Director of Education, Transvaal v McCagie* above n 82, 629. See also *Bamford v Minister of Community Development and State Auxiliary Services* above n 85, 1060A.

[88] *Roodepoort-Maraisburg Town Council v Eastern Properties (Prop) Ltd* above n 82, 101; *Von Molkte v Costa Areosa (Pty) Ltd* above n 86, 258E.

[89] *Bamford v Minister of Community Development and State Auxiliary Services* above n 85, 1060A; *Roberts v Chairman, Local Road Transportation Board, Cape Town* 1979 (4) SA 604 (C) 605G–606A; *Aucamp v Nel NO* 1991 (1) SA 220 (O) 233B–234I. In *Shifidi v Administrator-General for South West Africa* above n 84, 637D–F the court, referring to review proceedings, said that the interest which an applicant must have cannot be defined with precision but that it would ultimately always be a question of fact whether sufficient interest exists to give the applicant locus standi. In England the test of 'sufficient interest' is used in respect of applications for review of administrative action: Lord Denning *The Discipline of Law* (1979) 118–32. The United States Supreme Court has been prepared to recognize a minimal interest no greater than that of any other member of the public as sufficient to found standing in an environmental suit: *United States v Students Challenging Regulatory Agency Procedures* 412 US 669 (1973).

that he has a legally enforceable right.[90] However, financial harm is not an essential requirement for locus standi.[91] A threat to the plaintiff's health was accepted early in South African law as a ground for claiming relief.[92] What is not clear is whether an interest in maintaining an aesthetically pleasing environment or preventing environmental degradation will give a person standing. This necessarily raises the question whether individuals have a right to environmental integrity.[93]

8.4.1.4 *Rights and interests*

The issues of 'right' and 'interest' are difficult to separate. Time and again the courts have held that in order to have standing a plaintiff or applicant must have a legally enforceable right.[94] His 'interest' in claiming relief in respect of that right arises when the right is infringed. Where a person claims enforcement of a statutory provision, a problem arises because provisions in statutes which create obligations do not necessarily create rights.[95] Perhaps for this reason the courts have found a way around the problem of identifying a legally enforceable right arising from statute by formulating a rule that determines the circumstances under which a party claiming enforcement of a statute will have standing.[96] The rule is that, where the statute was enacted in the public interest, the party claiming its enforcement must establish that he personally has been or will be adversely affected by the breach of the statute; where the statute was enacted in the interest of a particular group of persons a person belonging to that group automatically has standing.[97] Thus, where a litigant claims relief on the basis that a statutory provision should be enforced, one simply has to apply this rule to decide whether the party has locus standi.

Where the litigant does not seek to enforce a statutory provision, it seems that he must first establish that he has a legally enforceable right and then that he is adversely affected by the infringement of that right. The question whether it is essential to establish a legally enforceable right is very important when one is dealing with rights which have not been clearly defined and formulated in law, such as the right to environmental conservation. A number of the authorities which have dealt with the requirement that the applicant must have an interest in the relief which he claims have indicated that such an interest will exist either where the applicant has a right or where

---

[90] *Patz v Greene & Co* above n 83, 432–3; *Waks v Jacobs* above n 84, 918J–919A.

[91] *Director of Education, Transvaal v McCagie* above n 82, 629; *Shifidi v Administrator-General for South West Africa* above n 84, 637E–F; *Aucamp v Nel NO* above n 89, 233I.

[92] *Dell v Town Council of Cape Town* 1879 (9) Buch 2.

[93] The only South African case relevant to this question is *Von Moltke v Costa Areosa (Pty) Ltd* above n 86, in which the court found that the applicant did not have locus standi, but did not consider specifically whether he had a right to the enjoyment of the natural surroundings which he alleged were being destroyed.

[94] *Bagnall v The Colonial Government* above n 82, 692–3; *Dalrymple v Colonial Treasurer* above n 82, 380; *Roodepoort-Maraisburg Town Council v Eastern Properties (Prop) Ltd* above n 82, 101; *Aucamp v Nel NO* above n 89, 234D–H.

[95] Hahlo & Kahn *The South African legal system and its background* (1968) 76.

[96] The courts in the United States of America also developed a test for standing to enforce statutory provisions in order to avoid the necessity of establishing a 'legal right'. The American plaintiff must establish *(a)* that he has suffered or will suffer 'injury in fact' and *(b)* that the interest which he seeks to protect falls within the 'zone of interests' which the statute was intended to make provision for: Homburger 'Private suits in the public interest in the United States' 1974 (23) *Buffalo Law Rev* 343, 385–405. See also Rabie and Eckard 'Locus standi: the administration's shield and the environmentalist's shackle' 1976 *CILSA* 141, 149.

[97] This rule was adopted from English law in *Patz v Greene & Co* above n 83, 433 and approved by the Appellate Division in *Madrassa Anjuman Islamia v Johannesburg Municipality* 1917 AD 718 and *Roodepoort-Maraisburg Town Council v Eastern Properties (Prop) Ltd* above n 82, 96, 102. It has since been applied in a long line of cases.

he suffers harm.[98] This may support an argument that it is not necessary for the applicant to prove the existence of a legally enforceable right if he can establish that he is being adversely affected by the conduct complained of. On the other hand, there is a well-established line of cases in which it has been held that the mere fact that a party has suffered harm, even considerable financial harm, will not give him a right of action or entitle him to be a party to litigation if he does not have a legally enforceable right.[99]

8.4.1.5 *Citizen suit clauses*

The whole problem of standing to protect the environment can be resolved by legislation which has environmental conservation as its object and which specifically confers upon citizens and organizations the right to take action to enforce its provisions. In the United States of America many laws have been enacted along these lines since 1970.[100] The clauses granting a right of action are generally referred to as 'citizen suit clauses'. Some American statutes completely open the doors of standing in that they grant a right of action to any person irrespective of whether he has an interest,[101] while other citizen suit clauses give a right of action only to interested parties.[102] The only slight concession in this regard made by the legislature to date in South African law is the Environment Conservation Act,[103] which provides that any person whose interests are affected by a decision of an administrative body under the Act may request reasons for the decision and may apply to the Supreme Court for a review of the decision. In effect, this achieves nothing with regard to standing, since at common law a person whose interests are affected by an administrative decision has standing to take such decision on review.[104] See chapter 7.

8.4.1.6 *Group interests*

Some people are specially interested in promoting environmental quality. Will such an interest give a person locus standi to claim relief relating to the environment? Sadly,

[98] *Dalrymple v Colonial Treasurer* above n 82, 380; *Director of Education, Transvaal v McCagie* above n 82, 621. In *Bamford v Minister of Community Development and State Auxiliary Services* above n 85, the court found that the applicant had locus standi on the basis of a clear right without proof that he personally was adversely affected by the infringement of such right. This decision has been criticized: Beck 'Locus standi in judicio or ubi jus ibi remedium' 1983 *SALJ* 278, 286–7.

[99] *Brauer v Cape Liquor Licensing Board* 1953 (3) SA 752 (C) 759G–761H; *United Watch and Diamond Co (Pty) Ltd v Disa Hotels Ltd* 1972 (4) SA 409 (C) 405; *PE Bosman Transport Works Committee v Piet Bosman Transport (Pty) Ltd* 1980 (4) SA 801 (T), 803B–804E; *Milani v South African Medical and Dental Council* above n 84, 902D–903D. The case which most forcefully illustrates that an interest without a legally enforceable right does not give one a right of action is *Paton v British Pregnancy Advisory Service Trustees* (1979) 1 QB 276; (1978) 2 All ER 987, an English case in which the court held that the applicant had no legally enforceable right to prevent his wife from obtaining an abortion, even though he was admittedly the father of the foetus.

[100] Boyer & Meidinger 'Privatizing regulatory enforcement: a preliminary assessment of citizen suits under federal environmental laws' 1985 (34) *Buffalo L Rev* 833; Austin 'The rise of citizen suit enforcement in environmental law: reconciling private and public attorneys general' 1987 (81) *Northwestern Univ L Rev* 220.

[101] The Michigan Environmental Protection Act of 1970 (Mich Comp Laws Ann 691.1201–1207 (Weas Supp 1984) was the first statute expressly to authorize citizen-initiated environmental lawsuits. The Act provides that any person may maintain an action if he can make out a prima facie case, showing that the defendant's conduct has polluted, impaired or destroyed the air, water or other natural resources or the public trust therein or is likely to do so. The Clean Air Act (s 304*(a)* 42 USC 7604(a) (1976 & Supp IV 1981)) citizen suit provision authorizes 'any person' to bring a suit against 'any person', including the United States and other government agencies, alleged to be violating an emission standard, limit or order: Boyer & Meidinger above n 100, 847.

[102] The Clean Water Act (s 505, 33 USC 1365 (1982)) defines the citizen eligible to bring a suit as 'a person or persons having an interest which is or may be adversely affected'.

[103] Section 36.

[104] Eckard *Die locus standi van aansoekers by die geregtelike hersiening van administratiewe handelinge* (unpublished LL D thesis, Unisa, 1975) 181.

the answer seems to be 'no'. This is the crux of the problem of standing. Concerned individuals or groups of individuals will not be given a hearing by the court unless they can establish a right and interest as set out above. This is unfortunate because the people directly affected by a particular environmental problem may not be in a position to approach the court. Litigation is extremely expensive, time-consuming and emotionally traumatic. Most individuals are unable or unwilling to approach the court, even where they are adversely affected, yet a person who is in a position to represent their interests is not permitted to go to court on their behalf. Our courts have not allowed a concerned individual or organization to approach the court on behalf of others, except where the life or liberty of the individual is in danger.[105]

People tend to club together in groups to promote their interests. Thus, we have experienced the emergence of a large number of organizations formed for the purpose of promoting environmental interests. Such organizations are usually in a much better position to undertake litigation than are individuals, yet on a number of occasions it has been held that an organization may not come to court as the representative of the interests of its members, but is required to establish locus standi in its own right by showing that it, as distinct from its members, is adversely affected.[106] Some courts have recognized that this is impractical and unnecessary and have granted locus standi on the grounds that the interests of the organization are the same as the interests of its members.[107] Where the organization is able to prove that it is itself adversely affected, then there is no problem with regard to its standing, as long as it is an organization which has the capacity to litigate.[108]

8.4.1.7 *Interests of natural objects*

An even more difficult problem in environmental law is the question whether a person or organization can possibly have locus standi to represent the interests of animals and plants or aspects of the environment such as rivers or the sea-shore. Stone[109] has argued that animals, plants and even inanimate objects such as rivers and rocks should be regarded as having rights and should be capable of being cited as plaintiffs in order to claim protection of their rights. In the United States of America such plaintiffs have been cited in a number of cases, but always together with a recognized legal person.[110] In South Africa it is not likely that the courts would ever allow a plaintiff of this nature to be cited as a party and there is no reported case in which this has been tried. A representative action in which a person claimed relief in the interests of animals, plants or other aspects of the environment would also be fraught

[105] *Wood v Ondangwa Tribal Authority* above n 82, followed in *Deary NO v Acting President, Rhodesia* 1979 (4) SA 43 (R) and *Parents Committee of Namibia v Nujoma* 1990 (1) SA 873 (A) 880B–881F. *Wood's* case was restrictively interpreted in *Christian League of Southern Africa v Rall* 1981 (2) SA 821 (O) 826–7; *Admadiyya Anjuman Ihaati-Islam Lahore (South Africa) v Muslim Judicial Council (Cape)* 1983 (4) SA 855 (C) 864E–F and in *National Education Crisis Committee v State President of the Republic of South Africa* (WLD case no 16736/86, unreported), discussed by Loots 'Keeping locus standi in chains' 1987 *SAJHR* 66, 69.

[106] *Ahmadiyya Anjuman Ihaati-Islam Lahore (South Africa) v Muslim Judicial Council (Cape)* above n 105, 863H–864G; *South African Optometric Association v Frames Distributors (Pty) Ltd* 1985 (3) SA 100 (O) 103F–105C; *Natal Fresh Produce Growers Association v Agroserve (Pty) Ltd* 1990 (4) SA 749 (N) 758G–759D.

[107] *Transvaal Indian Congress v Land Tenure Advisory Board* 1955 (1) SA 85 (W) 89G–90B; *Ex parte Natal Bottle Store-Keeping and Off-Sales Licensees Association* 1962 (4) SA 273 (D). See also Loots 'Keeping locus standi in chains' above n105, 69–71. Cf *PE Bosman Transport Works Committee v Piet Bosman Transport (Pty) Ltd* above n 99, 805C–E.

[108] *Transvaal Canoe Union v Butgereit* 1986 (4) SA 207 (T) 209F–G; *Molotlegi v President of Bophuthatswana* 1989 (3) SA 119 (B) 127D.

[109] 'Should trees have standing?—toward legal rights for natural objects' 1972 (45) *Southern California Law Rev* 450.

[110] Stone 'Should trees have standing revisited' 1985 (58) *Southern California Law Rev* 1.

with difficulties because, in the first place, the existence of a right would have to be established and, secondly, the plaintiff's locus standi to represent the affected aspect of the environment would be in issue. The Appellate Division in *Wood v Ondangwa Tribal Authority*[111] displayed an enlightened approach to locus standi when it allowed church leaders to represent the interests of people who were, practically speaking, unable to come to court themselves and it is not impossible that the court might adopt a similar attitude with regard to animals and inanimate aspects of the environment, if one could overcome the first obstacle, which is establishing a right on the part of the represented subject.

A basis on which an organization might be afforded locus standi is that it is expressly or impliedly authorized by statute to take action with regard to the protection of animals or other aspects of the environment. This is the basis on which the SPCA has been held to have locus standi to claim interdicts for the purpose of protecting animals. In an unreported judgment[112] the court granted locus standi on the basis that, since the Animals Protection Act 71 of 1962 gives the society the authority to take action in the event of an offence being committed in terms of the Act,[113] the legislature must have intended that the society should also have a civil right of action to claim an interdict to prevent an offence from being committed or continued. In a subsequent reported decision[114] it was argued that the society's rights regarding animal welfare were narrowly circumscribed by the Act and that it had no locus standi to act beyond such powers. The court held that, in view of the vast powers granted to the society under the Act, it would be most surprising if it did not have the lesser powers to prevent the injury apprehended.

8.4.2 Private-law remedies

For many decades our courts have been confronted with disputes that today would be referred to as environmental cases. Even before environmental legislation had been passed, reliance was placed on traditional common-law remedies, viz the interdict and the actio legis Aquiliae, for protection against polluters. Even today, private remedies for the protection of the environment, apart from their value to individual plaintiffs, are of some public importance where the administrative enforcement of legislation remains ineffective.[115]

In spite of their value to individual plaintiffs, however, private-law remedies fulfil a very restricted role so far as environmental conservation is concerned. The fact of the matter is that by definition the plaintiff relying upon private-law remedies is not assumed to be serving the public interest and the court, in coming to its decision, will be concerned only with balancing the interests of the individual litigants—it will not take account of the public interest. Furthermore, many individuals feel threatened or harmed by actions that do not directly affect their individual subjective rights, but which are harmful to the environment.

The significance of private-law remedies even to individuals whose rights are affected by the environmentally detrimental activities of others may gradually diminish as

---

[111] Above n 82.

[112] *Society for the Prevention of Cruelty to Animals v The University of the Witwatersrand* (WLD case no 23288/87, unreported).

[113] Section 8 of the Act confers wide powers on the holder of a certificate issued in terms of that section, including the right to enter premises for the purposes of examining conditions under which any animal is kept, the arrest without warrant of any person who is suspected of having committed an offence under the Act, and the right to seize any animal in the possession or custody of that person for due treatment in terms of the Act. A certificate may be issued by a magistrate in favour of any officer of any society for the prevention of cruelty to animals.

[114] *Society for the Prevention of Cruelty to Animals, Standerton v Nel* 1988 (4) SA 42 (W) 47A–E.

[115] See generally Fuggle & Rabie above n 74, 39–43.

increasingly effective administrative controls are established. Such potential plaintiffs will in effect have their rights protected indirectly through the enforcement of environmental legislation by the administrative body concerned.

8.4.3 Public-law remedies

8.4.3.1 *Judicial review*

Judicial review is a remedy which is aimed at determining whether administrative bodies have acted within the scope of their powers, in other words, whether their actions have been valid. A valid administrative action is one that complies with the requirements of the law.

Although judicial review is regarded as the most important form of external control of administrative actions, it is a remedy that is subject to several crucial shortcomings.[116] The two most serious shortcomings from an environmental perspective are the locus standi requirement (which has already been discussed) and the limited scope of judicial review as a remedy to ensure administrative promotion of the public interest in conservation.

The court which reviews a particular administrative action can adjudicate only on the validity or legality of the action in question; it cannot rule on the merits of that action, that is, whether the administration's conduct was indeed in the public interest. And it is invariably the merits rather than the legality of administrative actions that is the environmentalist's concern. In any case, the extensive powers which are routinely conferred upon administrative bodies render it unlikely that contention would relate to such bodies' exceeding their already vast powers. Rather, the issue which environmentalists normally wish to contest is the environmental soundness of the administrative action concerned. The Environment Conservation Act has introduced provisions which may serve to broaden the ambit of control to some extent. See chapter 7.

8.4.3.2 *Administrative appeals*

The remedy by which the merits of a decision or action are controlled is that of appeal. Appeals can be lodged either to the judiciary or to the executive.

(a) Judicial control. An appeal against an administrative action to a court of law is an exceptional remedy because, unlike judicial review, it is not a common-law remedy which is generally available, but may be relied upon only if provision for it has been made in legislation. South African environmental legislation makes no provision for such appeals. Our courts are in any case reluctant to become involved in policy considerations affecting the merits of administrative actions, even in the case of existing appeals, mainly because they do not consider themselves competent to rule on such issues.[117]

(b) Internal administrative control. Control over administrative action can be exercised by the executive itself as internal control, usually an appeal to or a mero motu review by a higher body in the same administrative hierarchy. The Environment Conservation Act, for instance, makes provision for such appeals.[118] This is potentially the most comprehensive form of control since all aspects of an administrative action may be subjected to control, including the question whether or not the action is environmentally sound. However, since such control is not exercised by an independent body, its value to concerned citizens is restricted.

There is an even more fundamental objection: appeals are usually available only to persons aggrieved by a particular administrative decision. If the provision is interpreted

---

[116] Cf Fuggle & Rabie above n 74, 48.
[117] Cf *Publications Control Board v William Heineman Ltd* 1965 (4) SA 137 (A) 156–7.
[118] Section 35.

subjectively, conservationists may qualify as appellants. However, an objective interpretation, which seems more likely to be followed, may lead to the conclusion that only those who have locus standi in the traditional sense can be regarded as being aggrieved persons. It is only in instances where an individual has a special interest in the environment, such as ownership, that there would be no doubt as to his locus standi. Moreover, only where that interest is of a conservationist nature will his appeal (indirectly) serve the public interest in conservation. Such appeals, presumably, would mostly be brought against development-oriented administrative bodies, while appeals against conservation-oriented administrative bodies would usually be initiated by individuals concerned about their business enterprises rather than about conservation.

(c) Control by environmental tribunals[119]

(i) *Need for appeals to independent body.* From the above remarks it would appear that there is a need for an independent body to control administrative actions that affect the environment. A right of appeal is an invaluable safeguard as it provides aggrieved individuals with the assurance that the wisdom of the affected administrative action will be reconsidered by an independent body which can substitute its own decision for that of the administrative body in question. This body should be able to subject the deplored decision, and the facts on which it is based, to calm and careful scrutiny, detached from the immediacy of the initial decision.

(ii) *Existing environmental tribunals.* An appeal to an administrative tribunal, as has been mentioned, is available only if the legislature has established such a tribunal and has granted a right of appeal. Very few examples of such appeals are encountered in South African environmental law.

One such instance is the Air Pollution Appeal Board (and regional appeal boards), which may be appointed by the Minister of National Health and Population Development in terms of the Atmospheric Pollution Prevention Act. Provision is made for appeals by persons who are aggrieved by decisions or notices of certain administrative bodies.[120] The appeal board has extensive powers: when reviewing a decision of the chief officer, it may make such order as it may consider equitable[121] or may confirm, modify or set aside certain notices.[122] Moreover, its decision in all cases is final. See chapter 17. Although this is a fine example of an appeal to an administrative tribunal, it would not be available to environmentalists who seek to vindicate the public interest, if an objective interpretation is applied to the phrase 'aggrieved person', as explained above.

The Board of Investigation, the establishment of which is envisaged by the Environment Conservation Act,[123] does not constitute a true administrative appeal tribunal, because this board has no power to come to binding decisions in respect of disputes laid before it: it merely assists (advises) the Minister concerned. Moreover, there is no right of appeal to this board: appeals are to Ministers and Administrators.[124] See chapter 7.

The basic problem with an appeal to an environmental tribunal is that, whereas it provides an assurance to developers that the decision of the conservation-oriented public body to affect their interests will be reconsidered, it affords no opportunity to

[119] This section is based upon Rabie 'Towards assuring administrative furtherance of the public interest in environmental conservation' 1990 *Stell LR* 219 and the *Report of the President's Council on a national environmental management system* above n 74, paras 5.13.8–9.

[120] Sections 13, 25, 35 and 38.

[121] Section 13(2).

[122] Sections 25(1), 35(1) and 38(1).

[123] Section 15.

[124] Section 35.

members of the public who are opposed to or concerned about the particular development to articulate a conservation perspective; for this, reliance must be placed entirely upon the public body whose action is the subject of the appeal.

(iii) *Establishment of a general environmental tribunal.* It would appear that the establishment of administrative tribunals and the corresponding granting of rights of appeal is something which occurs on an ad hoc basis, dependent entirely upon the grace of the legislature. No coherent system is discernible. The desirability of the establishment of an environmental appeal tribunal in South Africa should be investigated. Issues that will have to be addressed include the following:

(a) Should the tribunal be a permanent body or should it be established only for specific disputes?

(b) Who should appoint the members of the tribunal and should only persons regarded as environmental experts serve on the tribunal or should provision also be made for others such as industrialists, economists, planners or agriculturists?

(c) Should there be a general right of appeal to the tribunal or should the right of appeal be specifically provided for in each statute?

(d) At whose instance should the appeal lie? Should locus standi be restricted to persons directly affected by the administrative action in question or should it be extended to include persons who are concerned that the public interest in environmental conservation has not been served, but who cannot prove that they have been personally aggrieved by the action in question?

(e) What should the jurisdiction of the tribunal be, that is, which actions and decisions should be subject to appeal?

(f) What should the scope of the appeal be, that is, to which aspects of the administrative act in question should the appeal relate?

(g) What criterion should the tribunal employ in coming to its conclusion?

(h) Should the tribunal be obliged to provide reasons for its decisions and should the decisions be published?

(i) What rules of procedure and of evidence should govern the proceedings?

(j) What orders may the tribunal make after handing down its decision?

When considering the introduction of an appeal to an environmental tribunal, two fundamentally different approaches or models may be identified. The appeal may, on the one hand, be viewed as a remedy aimed at ensuring that individuals affected by the administrative action in question have been treated justly and that their interests have been satisfactorily taken into account and balanced against the public interest. The existing appeals seem to belong to this class. Locus standi would typically be restricted to those personally aggrieved by the action or decision in question, because it is their interests which are at stake. This type of appeal obviously would not remedy the situation.

An opposite type of appeal would be that which would seek to ensure that the public interest in environmental conservation has been satisfactorily advanced. Locus standi should not be required for the lodging of such an appeal, because no individual interest would be at stake. Provision of such an appeal could in principle establish a mechanism through which an independent assessment may be made as to whether or not the public interest in conservation was indeed promoted satisfactorily or at least taken into account.

8.4.3.3 *Environmental ombudsman*

A form of parliamentary control over administrative actions which has been employed with considerable success in a number of countries is the institution of an ombudsman. An ombudsman is an office concerned with the in-depth and independent investigation of complaints against the administration. In modern society where the individual is increasingly overwhelmed by the impersonal machinery of public administration, the ombudsman is valuable, not only as regards individual cases for which his office is primarily designed but also because his investigation of cases may lead to significant legislative and administrative reforms.

The ombudsman is usually empowered to obtain all relevant information and thus to familiarize himself fully with all aspects of the investigation which he conducts. He is enabled to act swiftly with the minimum of formality and cost. After his investigation he makes recommendations to the administrative bodies concerned and eventually reports to Parliament. His role is especially significant in cases where judicial review of administrative decisions and other remedies are unavailable or insufficient. Since the ombudsman relies heavily on favourable public opinion to buttress his own persuasiveness, his influence, in view of the increased public response towards stricter environmental protection, could be considerable.

The establishment of a specialized ombudsman for environmental affairs could be valuable in augmenting other forms of control, and in rendering the government more responsive to the needs of the individuals whom it governs. An ombudsman may at least go some way towards lessening the frustrations of persons exposed to environmental deterioration where administrative and judicial controls are not effectively or adequately applied. Moreover, he may contribute towards improved relations between governmental bodies and concerned citizens and better environmental decision-making by those bodies.

The position in South Africa is that the advocate-general, appointed in terms of the Advocate-General Act 118 of 1979, did not constitute an ombudsman in the true sense of the word. His terms of reference were narrowly circumscribed, relating only to the investigation of the dishonest utilization of state moneys and the unlawful or improper enrichment of any person arising out of the affairs of the State. The advocate-general's investigative powers were extended by the Advocate-General Amendment Act 104 of 1991 to instances where the State or the public in general is being prejudiced by maladministration in connection with the affairs of the State.[125] His jurisdiction has thus been broadened to resemble more closely that of a true ombudsman. It is significant that his office has now been renamed 'ombudsman' and that the title of the Act has been changed to the Ombudsman Act of 1979.

Some relief is therefore available to individuals who can show that the public interest in environmental conservation is being prejudiced by maladministration. However, several shortcomings in the Act[126]—compared to ombudsman legislation in other countries—have not been attended to in the amendment Act. Moreover, the discretion conferred upon the ombudsman to insist upon the exhaustion of all available legal remedies prior to his investigation,[127] may serve to frustrate those seeking relief. In any case, no provision is made in the Act for the specialized treatment of environment-related complaints. The positive approach of the President's Council in its *Report on a national environmental management system*[128] towards the establishment of an environmental ombudsman is to be welcomed, although a lack of understanding of the true nature of the ombudsman's function is revealed in the report.[129]

---

[125] Section 4(1)(*a*A).

[126] Cf eg Kachelhoffer ' 'n Ombudsman vir Suid-Afrika binne die raamwerk van die nuwe konstitusionele bedeling' in Jacobs (ed) *'n Nuwe grondwetlike bedeling vir Suid-Afrika: enkele regsaspekte* (1981) 219; Rudolph 'The ombudsman and South Africa' 1983 *SALJ* 92.

[127] Section 4(3).

[128] Above n 74, para 5.13.5.

[129] For instance, the President's Council identifies the need for an appeal to the courts arising from decisions of the ombudsman as a disadvantage. Such an appeal, however, is completely foreign to the function of an ombudsman, which normally consists only in the making of recommendations.

8.4.3.4 *Constitutional remedies*

(a) The nature of constitutional protection. One of the most important characteristics of a new constitution for South Africa which is currently being negotiated, and one on which all parties already seem to agree, is that it will constitute supreme law. This is of far-reaching consequence and will fundamentally change the South African legal order. Hitherto the constitution has been just another Act of Parliament and the courts could not ascribe any special status to it. Parliamentary sovereignty implies that legislation cannot be tested by the courts, even if it were to be in conflict with the constitution. The constitution can also be amended by an ordinary subsequent Act of Parliament unless a provision is specially entrenched. Such an amendment can even be effected by implication.[130]

A new, supreme constitution will fundamentally change this position: subsequent legislation and executive acts will have to comply with the constitution in order to be valid. The courts will then also fulfil a new role. Full judicial review will become possible, which means that if legislation and executive actions are found to be in conflict with the constitution they will be declared invalid by the courts.

There are several reasons why such a new dispensation is called for in South Africa. Important political changes result in the need for truly democratic structures of government and the effective protection of individual rights. Therefore the new constitution will also contain a justiciable bill of rights which will, for the first time, allow for the effective implementation of human rights. That will bring this country in line with the accepted international tendency of securing the rule of law through appropriate constitutional arrangements.

Is it not also appropriate to protect the environment through such a supreme constitution? And if the answer is in the affirmative, how should it be done? One approach would be to include environmental protection in the bill of rights. A typical bill of rights deals with the civil and political rights and freedoms of the individual. The aim is to protect such rights and freedoms against infringement by the powerful organs of the State. The individual's personal freedom, physical integrity, property and participation, on the basis of equality, in political, cultural and societal activities are to be secured. In a technical sense this is done by recognizing the existence of such rights as residing in every individual. Infringements by the State entitle the individual to a judicial remedy. The nature of the remedy lies in the injunction to the State not to behave in a certain manner, ie not to infringe these rights. In this sense it has a 'negative' character. No positive action on the part of the State is required in order to secure these rights.

This is the classical approach to so-called first-generation human rights which aim at protecting the individual's 'natural' rights against the State. Historically it coincides with the liberal preference for limited government and a perception of the State as a 'night watch' whose only real function was to provide the legal and institutional framework permitting a laissez-faire political and economic order.

Is it possible to protect the environment in the same manner? Should the individual be entitled to a right to a clean environment? Should environmental protection therefore be contained in the bill of rights which will form part of the constitution? What will then be required of the State?

In order to answer these questions, other fundamental issues have to be addressed. What legal measures are required in order to protect the environment? What are the needs of the emerging South African society and what are the implications for the role of the State? The protection of the environment should not be discussed in abstract terms. It has to be dealt with in the context of the needs of the present South African

[130] See eg *Nasopie (Edms) Bpk v Minister van Justisie (2)* 1979 (4) SA 438 (NC).

society and the actual process of its constitutional reshaping, which has already started. Now is also an opportunity for innovation.

(b) The changing role of the State. The modern State is no longer considered a potential enemy of the individual against which the law should provide protection. It is now perceived also to be the necessary instrument to assist in the creation of the socio-economic conditions which determine the quality of life. The welfare State, for example, provides for basic needs through public financing, legislation and administration. Education, health services and unemployment benefits are the legitimate functions of the modern State from which all inhabitants benefit and on which they rely.

This development has had a worldwide impact on the concept of human rights. So-called second-generation rights deal with social, economic and cultural concerns. Their enjoyment depends on a *positive* involvement by the State. It has also resulted in a re-evaluation of the concept of individual freedom. An employer, for example, is not free to exploit workers. Welfare and labour legislation prescribes conditions of employment, safety, age, gender and minimum wages.

The same is true of the environment. For instance, a factory owner (or the State) should not be permitted to pollute a river and in so doing to destroy an asset in which society as a whole has an interest. Through legislation and administration the State has become involved in balancing opposing needs—aimed at furthering the public good.

These changes have coincided with important political changes within the State and in the international community. Democratization of government and concern for human rights and the environment have changed decision-making procedures, the content of policy and the function of state organs. South Africa belatedly faces the same challenges. The demise of apartheid and the creation of a democratic government will fundamentally change the nature of South African society. It has become accepted policy—and will indeed strengthen respect for human rights generally—to expand the function of the law not only to protect individual freedoms but also to determine the socio-economic quality of life.

(c) Constitutional mechanisms

(i) *A bill of rights.* The concept of human rights has been expanded in certain municipal systems and in international law to include the protection of the environment as a so-called third-generation right.[131] It has been contended that our law should likewise recognize such a right in a bill of rights.[132]

The generally accepted view is that rights to the environment should be treated as collective rather than as individual rights.[133]

The South African Law Commission has recently gone further and now proposes the following formulation in its *Interim report on group and human rights*:[134]

[131] Cf Glazewski 'The environment, human rights and a new South African constitution' 1991 *SAJHR* 167; *Interim report on group and human rights* South African Law Commission Project 58 (1991) para 8.211–229.

[132] Glavovic 'Human rights and environmental law; the case for a conservation bill of rights' 1988 *CILSA* 52. Cf also Cowen 'Toward distinctive principles of South African environmental law: some jurisprudential perspectives and a role for legislation' 1989 *THRHR* 3, 23–5; Bray 'The new Environment Conservation Act versus the demands of environmental realities' 1990 *SA Public Law* 101, 102; Rabie 'Towards assuring administrative furtherance of the public interest in environmental conservation' 1990 *Stell LR* 219, 240–2.

[133] Glazewski above n 131, 172, 176.

[134] Above n 131, para 8.264. This is art 30 of the Commission's proposed bill of rights.

'Everyone has the right not to be exposed to an environment which is dangerous to human health or well-being or which is seriously detrimental thereto and has the right to the conservation and protection of such[135] environment.'

The African National Congress, likewise, has proposed a draft bill encompassing environmental rights.[136]

Effective rights require judicial involvement. How can the State be obliged to create the conditions which permit the actual enjoyment of such rights?

What is to be recognized is the different role to be played by the courts in protecting such rights. First- and third-generation rights (to which environmental rights belong) are obviously enforced differently on account of the different roles which the State must fulfil. It is relatively easy to order the State to discontinue certain practices which infringe upon first-generation rights. However, if resources are to be used in order to provide for a clean environment, the issuing of a court order becomes a more complicated matter.

The normal formulation of some individual rights in a bill of rights authorizes positive action by the individual concerned. Freedom of speech, for instance, allows the individual to publish and to engage in communication. The right not to be exposed to an unhealthy environment, as formulated by the Law Commission, does not entitle the individual to act in a particular positive manner. Rather, it constitutes a protection against potentially detrimental environmental activities of others. This negative formulation amounts to a 'passive' entitlement.

The Commission makes a further important contribution by linking the enforcement of environmental rights to a limitation clause. Traditionally, limitation clauses have been applied only in respect of first-generation rights, which, as a rule, are not absolute. Freedom of speech, for example, does not permit defamation or contempt of court. It is the function of the limitation clause in the bill of rights to provide for limits to the exercise of individual rights. The actual limitation will be contained in the ordinary law of the land. For example, an Act of Parliament which provides for reasonable limits to what newspapers may publish with regard to highly sensitive matters of state security will therefore not necessarily be in conflict with the freedom of the press as stated in the bill of rights. In the final analysis, it will be for the courts to decide whether a particular limitation is compatible with the objectives of the limitation clause. A limitation clause lays down the grounds for and the scope of the limitation power. It therefore also contains the limits to the limitation power in order to prevent possible abuse of such power.

Limitation clauses are enforced by the courts. That is what makes the protection of human rights effective. The courts have also demonstrated that they are capable of interpreting limiting grounds such as 'the public interest' or 'necessary in a democratic society'.[137] The same approach is propagated with respect to third-generation rights. The Commission's proposal for such a clause suggests that a limitation shall be permissible only in so far as it is reasonably necessary for considerations of state security, the public order and interest, good morals, public health, the administration of justice, public administration, or the rights of others or for the prevention and combating of disorder and crime.[138]

The successful implementation of such a clause will depend on the approach adopted by the courts. It will call for a certain degree of innovation and for a sensitive balancing

---

[135] Obviously the reference here should relate to the conservation of a healthy environment, but a literal reading of the text implies the opposite.

[136] *Interim report on group and human rights* above n 131, para 8.267.

[137] This is a standard phrase in the European Convention for the Protection of Human Rights and Fundamental Freedoms of 1950 and the Namibian Constitution of 1990.

[138] Article 34.

of competing interests.[139] This is, however, typical of the judicial function. An important additional benefit of such an approach is that open government may be stimulated. If, for example, a state organ seeks to convince a court of law not to grant an application by an individual for enforcing an environmental right, persuasive factual evidence will have to be produced. Both the individual and public interest are entitled to judicial protection. The rights involved are not absolute and it is for the courts to balance the interests involved. The practice of courts elsewhere underscores the viability of such an approach.[140]

The theoretical opposition to the inclusion of environmental rights in a bill of rights flows from an unwillingness to recognize entitlements to the environment as rights. It is feared that acknowledgment of environmental rights may lead to exorbitant demands being made on the State. In any case, it has been claimed that the right cannot be formulated with sufficient clarity. This applies both to the concept 'environment' and to adjectives sought to qualify it. A further objection is the relativity of such a right. A constitutional right to a clean environment would often come into conflict with other constitutional rights, such as the right to property and the freedom to exercise one's occupation. Social priorities, it is claimed, need to be determined politically.[141] Many of these criticisms in any case also apply to the adjudication of conflicting first-generation rights. It is submitted that the Law Commission's negative formulation of the right and the proposed linking of environmental concerns to the limitation clause can provide a solution to some of the above problems.

(ii) *Other constitutional devices.* Less controversial are other mechanisms, such as the preamble to the constitution and principles of state policy which are written into the constitution. The latter identify the ideals to be pursued by the State and their achievement depends on the availability of resources. Such principles are not directly enforceable by the courts but guide the government in making and applying laws in order to give effect to the fundamental objectives of these principles. The courts are entitled to have regard to the principles in interpreting any laws based on them.[142] The Indian Supreme Court has employed this concept quite effectively in decisions on socio-economic and environmental matters.[143]

The concept of an ombudsman (see section 8.4.3.3) may also be dealt with in the constitution, as has been done in the Namibian Constitution.[144]

Another constitutional mechanism which is often overlooked is the application of international law by the municipal courts. International law deals with the rights and duties of states and now includes a well-developed body of rules on environmental matters. See chapter 9. If the constitution of a country provides for the incorporation of international law into the law of the land (as many constitutions do), it opens a further source to domestic institutions and permits the uniform application of legal norms to the environment. This recognizes the fact that the environment is indivisible. Pollution knows no respect for legal niceties such as state boundaries and lack of territorial jurisdiction. South Africa is already party to several international environmental agreements (see chapter 9) and there should therefore be sympathy for the expanded and uniform application of environmental protection.

---

[139] Cf Rabie above n 132, 242.

[140] Cf Glazewski above n 131.

[141] These and other objections to the acknowledgment of a constitutional right to a clean environment have been raised by German lawyers. This has led to the German legislature's refusal to include such a right in the constitution. See Rabie 'A constitutional right to environmental integrity: a German perspective' 1991 *SAJHR* 208.

[142] Cf art 101 of the Namibian Constitution.

[143] See Glazewski above n 131 for a discussion.

[144] Article 91*(c)*.

Theoretically, the domestic application of international law poses no insurmountable problems.[145] Provision can be made for the different modes of application of treaties and customary international law in the municipal legal sphere. The harmonization of international-law obligations with municipal law can also be dealt with in the constitution.

8.4.4 Environmental dispute resolution

8.4.4.1 *Introduction*

The phrase 'alternative dispute resolution' (ADR) encompasses a collectivity of processes to which disputing parties might have recourse as an alternative to litigation. Implicit in the notion of environmental dispute resolution (EDR) is the idea that ADR processes may be used, rather than litigation, to settle environmental disputes. However, while alternative processes are invaluable in an environmental framework, the courtroom remains a necessary and desirable forum both for the settlement of environmental disputes and for enforcement purposes. Reasons for this are that:

- Disputes may never reach negotiation unless litigation reveals that, without the resolution of the problem by negotiation, a disinterested third party will determine the outcome.
- The balance of power can be altered through litigation. Environmental disputes are often between established organizations with substantial resources and ad hoc organizations whose power arises from protest and confrontation. Ad hoc organizations can gain power and acquire the requisite status to warrant the attention of government and administrative agencies through litigation.
- Judicial resolution of a dispute may be desirable for its effect on the development of the law.
- Publicity surrounding criminal convictions and delictual claims is desirable as a disincentive to pollute.[146]

Moreover, there seems to be little empirical evidence to suggest that ADR is cheaper and faster than litigation in environmental disputes. Litigating an environmental dispute may be time-consuming, but settlement usually precedes the court process. It has been stated that ADR processes are not necessarily expeditious where the issues are complex. The costs of preparing for negotiation may equal those of preparation for litigation, while applicable procedural constraints are no less demanding in the negotiating context than in litigation. The average duration for resolution of an environmental dispute is between 5 and 6 months, while 10 per cent of cases endure for 18 months.[147]

Essentially, then, environmental disputes call for the most appropriate form of dispute resolution. However, to appreciate the nature and quality of a negotiated outcome, one has to rethink, fundamentally, one's traditional notions of efficiency. In appropriate cases a superior result emanates from alternative, as distinct from adversarial, processes. A successfully negotiated agreement, which satisfies the parties' interests, is more likely to endure and be successfully implemented. This is distinct from the adversarial process which leads to the classic 'win-loose' scenario in which the winner takes all and the adversary is alienated. Litigation may also result in irreparably damaged relationships.

Environmental dispute resolution has become a well-established discipline in the

---

[145] See Erasmus 'The Namibian Constitution and the application of international law' 1989–90 (15) *SAYIL* 81–110. Cf also art 144 of the Namibian Constitution.

[146] Riesel 'Negotiation and mediation of environmental disputes' 1985 *Ohio State J of Dispute Resolution* 99, 99–102.

[147] Bingham & Haygood 'Environmental dispute resolution: the first ten years' 1986 (41) *The Arbitration J* 1, 12–13.

United States, where the practice has become professionalized and institutionalized. In South Africa, environmental law has yet to develop into a discrete branch of law and environmental litigation is scarce. However, given the development and growth of the South African ADR movement, and the emergence of an environmental ethic, it would seem that EDR is a real possibility in the future.

Legislation in the United States, often incorporating citizen suit clauses,[148] the environmental lobby and administrative agencies committed to the use of ADR processes, has empowered the EDR movement. A variety of ADR processes have been used, e g negotiation, mediation, arbitration, mini-trials and non-binding fact-finding. The primary areas in which EDR has been used are:

- negotiated rule-making;
- clean-up obligations;
- environmental enforcement, and
- land-use and the allocation of natural resources.[149]

8.4.4.2 *Negotiated rule-making*

In order to understand the role of negotiated rule-making, one must recall that competition between interest groups, all attempting to persuade or pressurise elected representatives, is inherent in the legislative process. With environmental legislation the stakes are high, because the standards that are adopted in the new law establish the framework for subsequent bargaining over its application. Indeed, the legislative process can be seen as a process of general influence trading.[150] Even after the legislation has been enacted, however, the law-making process is not over, as most environmental legislation is of an enabling nature, i e the legislation endorses a fairly broad policy, then delegates to an administrative body the task of promulgating regulations.

Traditionally, administrative decision-making in South Africa has been solely in the hands of administrative officials, thus excluding the participation of interested parties. In the United States, however, the Administrative Procedure Act empowers administrative agencies to adopt rule-making procedures. This requires the agency to publish notice of an intended rule in the Federal Register and invite comment from interested parties before a decision is made. Such notice and comment procedures are desirable, since they enhance public participation in administrative decision-making.[151]

Since the Environment Conservation Act has provided that notice and comment procedures be adopted before regulations in respect of noise, environmental impact assessments and waste-disposal sites are made, it is interesting to note recent developments in the rule-making process in the United States.[152]

While during the New Deal agencies were granted wide discretionary powers to protect their expertise from political interference, the US courts and Congress began to expand administrative procedures in the 1960s. The courts required agencies to give

[148] Loots *Citizen suits—the American experience* Paper presented at the 1989 conference of the Society of University Teachers of Law. Such clauses allow private citizens a civil action for enforcement to complement the enforcement of environmental laws by the State. In the United States, citizen suit clauses have been incorporated in environmental statutes at both the federal and state level; see Hanks & Hanks 'An environmental bill of rights: the citizen suit and the National Environmental Policy Act of 1969' 1971 *Environment Law Rev* 147.

[149] Grad 'Alternative dispute resolution in environmental law' 1989 *Columbia J of Environmental Law* 157–85.

[150] Bacow & Wheeler *Environmental dispute resolution* (1984) 279.

[151] See Lyster 'Administrative rulemaking' 1990 *SA Public Law*; Loots & Lyster *Appropriate legislation for the protection of the environment* Paper presented at the southern African international conference on environmental management 28–29 October 1991.

[152] Harter 'Negotiating regulations' 1982 (71) *The Georgetown Law J* 1, 8–18.

reasons for their actions and substantiate decisions with adequate factual information.[153] Moreover, the standard of judicial review was expanded to scrutinize the data used by agencies to support a rule.[154] New statutes augmented the notice and comment procedures by requiring a rule to be supported by substantial evidence. Hence, agencies could no longer rely on their expertise to claim legitimacy. The rule-making process would be legitimate only if affected interests had the right to present facts and arguments to the agency.

A serious shortfall in the seemingly democratic rule-making process is that interested parties are not permitted to participate directly in the process. As a result, representations made to the agency by competing parties have become increasingly adversarial. To address this problem, the 1982 Administrative Conference of the United States recommended that guidelines be drawn up for negotiated rule-making procedures.[155] The Environmental Protection Agency (EPA) adopted such procedures in the belief that the costs of negotiated rule-making would be offset by long-range savings, ie a negotiated agreement develops better rules than the traditional process.

Now negotiated rule-making is used to develop a notice of proposed rule-making for publication in the Federal Register. After comments have been received from interested parties, the negotiations are resumed before publication of the final rule.

Harter[156] states that:

> '[t]he prime benefit of direct negotiations is that it enables the participants to focus squarely on their respective interests. They need not advocate and maintain extreme positions before a decision-maker. Therefore, the parties can develop a feel for the true issues that lie within the advocated extremes and attempt to accommodate fully the competing interests.'

It is obviously necessary for the administrative official to review the proposal for consistency with law and departmental policy. While final responsibility for the decision must always rest with the administrative agency, this must be reconciled with the need to accommodate the consensus reached during negotiations.

Importantly, negotiations may reduce the likelihood of judicial challenges to the decision. The reason is that those who formerly would have sought judicial review would now participate in the development of the rule. It is for this reason that negotiated rule-making is regarded as being more cost-effective than traditional notice and comment procedures.

8.4.4.3 *Liability for clean-up costs*

While there is no general statute in South Africa which establishes strict liability for clean-up costs,[157] it seems that there are moves in this direction. The Minister of Environment Affairs has indicated that manufacturers of litter-creating products may soon have to pay the cost of keeping South Africa clean. Strict liability clauses have been incorporated in some statutes. For example, the Nuclear Energy Act creates liability on the part of a licensee for any nuclear damage caused during his period of responsibility.[158] It is possible that, as strict liability clauses are incorporated in environment related legislation, EDR processes will become relevant for the assessment of liability.

---

[153] *Kennecott Copper Corp v EPA* 462 F 2d 846 (DC Cir 1972) ordering the EPA to supply a factual basis on which the agency promulgated a standard.

[154] *Citizens to Preserve Overton Park, Inc v Volpe* 401 US 402 (1971).

[155] Grad above n 149, 162.

[156] Harter above n 152, 29.

[157] The general principle underlying strict liability provisions is that fault in the sense of careless or intentional wrong-doing need not be established in order to create liability on the part of the polluter. Thus mere ownership or operation of a facility would result in liability if it were established that pollution emanated from that facility. Cf Loots & Lyster above n 151, 9.

[158] Section 41.

In the United States, strict liability for clean-up costs by the polluter is statutorily provided for by the Comprehensive Environmental Response, Compensation and Liability Act (CERCLA).[159] The settlement of clean-up obligations is only partially a matter for ADR, however, as liability must first be established by the court. Thereafter, the nature of the judgment may become a matter for negotiation and consensual arrangements. Alternatively, parties may concede liability in order to shorten the litigation process and then negotiate the terms of an agreement for clean-up costs.

In 1985 the United States' EPA declared a policy relating to the clean-up obligations of hazardous waste sites under CERCLA. The policy document provides guidelines to help determine whether to negotiate a settlement for the clean-up costs or to proceed with litigation. Criteria to be considered are the volume of waste contributed to the site by each potentially responsible party, the nature of the waste deposited and the strength of the evidence imputing the waste to the settling parties. Other factors for consideration are the ability of the settling parties to pay, public-interest considerations, the precedential value derived through litigation and the value of receiving a certain negotiated sum. This settlement policy may be used as the basis for ADR in computing the obligations of potentially responsible parties to the EPA.[160]

8.4.4.4 *Environmental enforcement*

Environmental dispute resolution is relevant to environmental enforcement in three respects, ie in the case of civil enforcement cases; where the pollution control officer negotiates with the polluter to secure compliance and where resort to criminal enforcement by the courts results in abject failure.

(a) Civil enforcement. Noting the established practice in South Africa of using ADR processes for the resolution of many disparate disputes, there is every reason to anticipate that EDR will be used in the settlement of civil claims against polluters.

In 1987 the EPA published an internal memorandum establishing a policy to apply in the use of ADR in the resolution of civil enforcement cases. A 95 per cent success rate has been recorded.[161] The memorandum describes some of the applicable types of ADR, including arbitration, mediation, mini-trial and non-binding fact-finding. It also establishes qualifications for third-party neutrals.

The types of cases identified as being suitable for ADR are those which have been pending in a court for a number of years, without any indication of resolution, those presenting impasses and those in which ADR presents a cheaper resolution option for the EPA.[162]

The memorandum notes that ADR may also be used where an interested party is not party to an enforcement action, eg where an interest group has or is likely to express an interest in the matter, or where the remedy will affect the community in which the polluter is located.[163] Here it is recommended that, early on in the enforcement process, the EPA establish communication with the interested parties, using a neutral third party. The reason for this is that their understanding and acceptance of the remedy is important to the effective resolution of the case. The fact that the EPA found it advisable or necessary to include and specify these remedies in a professional guidance document indicates the success of the movement to make ADR a significant part of the resolution of environmental problems.[164]

---

159 § 122, 42 USC § 9622(b) (3) (Supp IV 1986).
160 Grad above n 149, 170.
161 Grad above n 149, 173–4.
162 Grad above n 149, 174.
163 Ibid.
164 Grad above n 149, 177.

(b) Negotiating for compliance. In South Africa, pollution control and conservation measures are established in terms of statutes and attendant regulations, while enforcement is often the purview of departmental inspectors. The inspectorate will attempt to attain the ends of the legislation by whatever means appropriate. The fact that prosecution is a relative rarity indicates that enforcement officers use informal dispute resolution techniques to resolve disputes with offenders. The potential for conflict is inherent in the enforcement process, for industrialists and farmers tend to regard pollution control and conservation measures as an unnecessary and costly burden on their production processes. This perspective must be contrasted with that of the field inspector who tries to improve the quality of a polluting effluent or to install preventive conservation works.[165]

The field inspector's strategy to elicit compliance through negotiation has to be continuously maintained by means of routine monitoring. He is therefore involved in an endless series of negotiation with industry and agriculture. It takes months of bargaining and persuasion to secure the compliance of polluters, particularly in cases where, despite allegations that its intention to comply is honourable, the polluter continues to violate statutory provisions.

Negotiated compliance can be successful as there is an incentive for companies to avoid being tainted by the formal process of law, which could damage the reputation of the company. A recent case[166] in which a mining company was found criminally liable for the pollution of a public stream lends credence to this proposition. The court sentenced the accused to a R10 000 fine conditionally suspended for 5 years. Interestingly, prior to conviction, clean-up was voluntarily undertaken, costing in excess of R3 000 000. While the bona fides of the company are not in question, it can be assumed that the clean-up was undertaken with the environmental image of the company in mind. The fact that the company has declined to appeal gives rise to the inference that it wishes to avoid attracting the attention attendant upon further judicial proceedings.

Another incentive for compliance is that companies generally desire to maintain workable relationships with administrative departments. The polluter thus brings goodwill, co-operation and ultimate compliance to the negotiating table, while the enforcement officer offers free information and advice on pollution control measures, and a certain amount of tolerance.[167] Although negotiations do not always secure immediate compliance, the officer has an array of negotiating tactics at his disposal. For example, in the case of soil conservation, the farmer may be advised to construct certain soil conservation works. If this is not complied with, the farmer may be formally issued with a direction in terms of the relevant legislation demanding compliance, followed by the threat of prosecution. See chapter 10.

(c) Environmental dispute resolution where judicial enforcement has failed. There is a belief in society that the State is able to enforce the orders of the courts, the ultimate arbiters of civil disputes and criminal sanctions. *S v Nyele*[168] has shown that this is often more fantasy than fact. The case involved the environmental disaster which occurred in the Dukuduku state forest near Mtubatuba, where between 2 000 and 3 500 squatters had destroyed about 25 per cent of the forest to make way for their dwellings. The forest is particularly valuable as it represents the best remaining example of lowland coastal forest in South Africa. On 6 July 1990, seven men were convicted for contravening the Prevention of Illegal Squatting Act 52 of 1951, and given suspended

---

[165] Hawkins 'Issues in developing the practice of environmental mediation in Ohio: a mini-symposium' 1986 (1) *Ohio State J of Dispute Resolution* 308–19.

[166] *S v Anglo American Prospecting Services* (Nelspruit Magistrate's Court case no SH438/91, unreported).

[167] Hawkins above n 165, 315.

[168] (Mtubatuba Magistrate's Court case no 2288/89, unreported.)

fines of R1 000 each. One of the conditions of the suspension was that they leave the forest with their families by 6 August. None of the squatters has left the forest.

The background to this case is that during 1988 squatters began moving into the forest in large numbers. They were not detected until conservation organizations, undertaking aerial examinations of the area, revealed that large parts of the forest had been destroyed. The squatters contended that they had traditional rights to the forest, while others claimed that they had been forced into the area after being dispossesed of their traditional tribal lands adjoining the forest.

During the hearing of the *Nyele* case a representative of the Wildlife Society of Southern Africa, while giving evidence on the value of the forest, stated that the society would be prepared to act as a mediator in an effort to resolve the dispute. The mediation process began on 25 July 1990 when a meeting was held between the squatters, their legal representatives and members of the Natal Provincial Administration.[169] While the squatters indicated at the meeting that they would not leave and the officials declared that they would evict them if necessary, both sides were faced with a dilemma. The squatters faced criminal sanctions as well as the threat of violence if they disobeyed, while the authorities, in possession of a legally enforceable court order, were loath, primarily for political reasons, to create a climate of violence.

During the mediation process, the Wildlife Society indicated that alternative sites, suitable for occupation by squatters, had been considered. The squatters indicated a willingness to consider such alternatives and to participate in the negotiation process pending a continued suspension of their sentences. Although no alternative site has yet been identified, the squatters have shown an intention to abide by the spirit of the negotiations by not destroying any of the large trees in the forest.

8.4.4.5 *Land use and resource problems*

Bingham & Haygood,[170] reflecting on their environmental mediation experience between 1974 and 1984, identify six broad categories of environmental disputes handled. These are:

- Land use—involving neighbourhood and housing issues, commercial and urban development issues, parks and recreation, preservation of agricultural land and other regional planning issues, facility siting and transportation.
- Natural resource management and use of public lands—involving fisheries resources, mining, timber management, and wilderness areas,[171] among others.
- Water resources—involving water supply, water quality, flood protection and the thermal effects of power plants.
- Energy—involving such issues as siting small-scale hydro-electric plants, conversion of power-plant fuel from oil to coal, and geothermal development.
- Air quality—involving odour problems, national air-quality legislation, and acid rain.
- Toxins—involving national policy on the regulation of chemicals, plans for the removal of asbestos in schools, pesticides, and hazardous materials clean-up.[172]

The mediation experiences elucidated by Bingham & Haygood are pertinent to many unresolved environmental conflicts in South Africa. The following are offered as examples:

---

[169] Ridl *Peace in our time: conflict resolution in environmental law* Paper presented at the 1991 conference of the Society of University Teachers of Law.

[170] Bingham & Haygood, above n 147, 3.

[171] See also Rankin 'The wilderness advisory committee of British Columbia: new directions in environmental dispute resolution' 1989 *Environmental and Planning Law J* 5.

[172] Bingham & Haygood above n 147, 9.

(a) Land-use planning. The planning process has traditionally been regarded as a legislative activity related to the physical control of land-use development.[173] This comprehensive, rational model has attracted severe criticism for the way in which it artificially detaches planning from political and social conditions, and concerns itself with a single public interest. See chapter 28.

By the 1980s, the practice of environmental mediation had spread to the broader urban planning field in the United States. Similarly, South African planners have recently argued that a new planning approach should resolve the tension between static models of planning and the turbulent social context. Boden states: '[p]olitical changes will inevitably demand consequential, parallel modification in the planning approach.'[174] He proposes that planners engage in mediation to develop alternatives, identify the implications of particular actions and build an informed consensus. It is encouraging that a solution to the current housing crisis facing the Johannesburg City Council is likely to be negotiated. Planning authorities seem intent on accommodating millions of homeless people on the farm Rietfontein 35 km south of Johannesburg. This is in spite of the fact that inner-city options such as using mine land exist. The council's management council has, however, indicated that a 'think tank agency of all interested parties—including the communities involved—is being established to resolve such issues.'[175]

(b) Natural resource management

(i) *Allocation of natural resources.* No more cogent reason can be advanced for the peaceful allocation of natural resources than that wars have been waged to secure control. The conflict which developed between the erstwhile UDF and Inkatha in Ashdowne, near Pietermaritzburg, illustrates this phenomenon. Ashdowne, then sympathetic to the UDF, is a formal township in close proximity to Mpumuza, a rural settlement affiliated to Inkatha. In the mid-1980s, Ashdowne residents assumed control of all the water points in the area, effectively excluding Mpumuza from access to water. Access was gained by force. There is no doubt that the ADR structures, established in terms of the National Peace Accord, will have frequent reference to conflict which emanates inherently from competition for scarce natural resources.[176]

(ii) *Mining.* There are many natural resource management disputes in South Africa which have not yet been resolved. Controversy surrounds the mining of sand dunes on the Natal north coast, the Transkei coast and in the Noordhoek area near Cape Town. The St Lucia estuarine system, currently under threat, contains five distinct ecosystems and one of the most important wetland systems in the world. The area, being rich in mineral deposits, has been identified as a potential mining site by Richards Bay Minerals. The mining company holds a prospecting permit which can be converted to a mining lease. Owing to public pressure, the Cabinet has called for a comprehensive environmental impact assessment (EIA) to be completed prior to such conversion.

The procedure to be followed in conducting an EIA—although not yet legally enforceable—has been developed by the Council for the Environment, and essentially incorporates notice and comment procedures. An assessment management committee (consisting of representatives from the Department of Environment Affairs, principal consultants employed by the mining company, representatives of the mining company and such other members as are deemed necessary) must identify interested and affected

---

[173] Boden 'The potential of environmental mediation for planning in South Africa' 1987 *Town and Regional Planning* 18.

[174] Boden above n 173, 20.

[175] *The Star* 6 December 1991.

[176] See Stavrou & Shongwe 'Violence on the periphery: the greater Edendale complex' 1989 (7) *Indicator SA* 53.

groups. Thereafter it is required to generate alternatives for evaluation and specialist studies and to conduct an EIA. Prior to the production of a draft EIA report, public participation is obtained. Interested and affected parties may comment on the draft and such comment is included in a final draft presented to a review panel.[177]

It seems that the procedure recommended by the Council for the Environment could be substituted by EDR. The dispute surrounding the mining at St Lucia is perfectly suited to a mediated settlement. The reasons for this are twofold; first, experience in the United States has shown that direct negotiations between all interested and affected parties, facilitated by a third party, produce wise and legitimate solutions to environmental problems. Unless parties meet face-to-face to gain an understanding of each other's standpoint and bargain in good faith, suspicion will surround the decision-making process. If all interested parties feel that they have participated in and contributed to the negotiated settlement they will have a sense of ownership over the agreement. Secondly, given that the mining process is lengthy, such negotiations establish a hitherto non-existent relationship between the parties on which they can rely for the resolution of future disputes.

(c) Toxic waste. In 1990, considerable conflict surrounded the proposed building of a toxic waste-disposal site near Azaadville, a segregated township for Indians near Krugersdorp. Earthlife Africa began enlisting the co-operation of civic organizations and the community council of Azaadville to oppose the establishment of the site. Internal political tensions were mended in an effort to present a united front, while tentative approaches for support were made to the Conservative Party.[178] Susskind[179] has recommended the use of ADR to resolve waste-disposal facility disputes by involving the receiving community. Successful siting should begin with joint fact-finding, while fears of the adverse consequences of the siting could be innovatively allayed by an agreement that comprehensive insurance be obtained. Compensation for having a waste-disposal facility in close proximity could also be proposed to the community.

8.4.4.6 *Looking ahead*

Experience in the United States has shown that the use of EDR in South Africa will depend on its being professionalized and institutionalized. Even though the Ford Foundation and the William A and Flora Hewlett Foundation were instrumental in the establishment of independent, non-profit organizations in the United States, foundation funding has inherent drawbacks. The lack of institutional mechanisms means that individual mediators are engaged not only in the practice of mediation but also in its promotion, while referrals are made on an ad hoc basis devoid of any systematic identification and assessment of appropriate cases.

In recent years, however, the practice of environmental mediation has become institutionalized. Numerous states have enacted statutes which require applicants for solid or hazardous waste sites to negotiate with the host community. Other states have established mediation offices which offer, inter alia, training and outreach about dispute resolution processes and refer cases, including environmental disputes, to independent professionals and provide funding. As already mentioned, EDR processes have also been incorporated into administrative procedures. More recently, special masters have been appointed by the courts to help resolve environmental disputes that are in litigation.

With the successful resolution of environmental disputes and an increasing interest in

[177] Ridl above n 169, 39.

[178] Cock & Koch *Going green* (1991) 24.

[179] 'The siting puzzle—balancing environmental gains and losses' 1985 (5) *Environmental Impact Assessment Rev* 157–63.

environmental mediation, mediators have begun to define EDR as a profession.

Bingham & Haygood,[180] commenting on growth in the field of EDR, note:

'It will be important to identify and put into practice mechanisms that will encourage the use of environmental dispute resolution processes, increase the likelihood that disputes will be resolved successfully, and protect the parties from potential abuses of these processes. To accomplish this without losing the flexibility that is an inherent strength of voluntary dispute resolution will be a challenge.'

These considerations are equally relevant to the establishment of EDR as a distinct branch of ADR in South Africa.

[180] Above n 147, 14.

CHAPTER 9

INTERNATIONAL ENVIRONMENTAL LAW

D J DEVINE
M G ERASMUS

9.1 INTRODUCTION

9.1.1 The nature of international law

International law (the law of nations, public international law) governs relations between states and is primarily concerned with the rights and duties of states.[1] Basically, it is interstate law. Municipal (national) law, on the other hand, is the internal law of every state.

The modern state is equipped with powerful instruments to 'make' and 'enforce' its internal law: the legislature enacts the law; the judiciary tries violations of the law; and the executive enforces the decisions of the legislature and the judiciary.

International law, on the other hand, is made and enforced differently. In the absence of a world government, legislature, judiciary or executive, the basis of international society is that states are sovereign. This means that *within* the state there exists some entity with supreme legislative and political power, whereas on the *international* plane states are independent, i e not subject to the will of other states or international organizations.

Care should be taken, however, not to explain international law in terms of the municipal-law analogy only, tempting though this may be as a result of the familiarity of the latter. Because international law is created and enforced in a totally different manner, it is more realistic to consider it as law of a different type.

9.1.2 Sources of international law

The sources of international law are treaties (conventions), custom, general principles of law and, as subsidiary means, judicial decisions and the teachings of highly qualified publicists.[2] Treaties are written agreements between states. They are very important because they constitute a direct means of creating rights and duties for states and because of the increasing need for co-operation across national boundaries. Treaties can cover any conceivable topic—from the creation of an international organization, the setting up of trade, the granting of economic aid, and diplomatic relations to the conservation of the environment.

Treaties have different effects in international and municipal law. No state is bound by a treaty unless it has given its consent to it. But before a treaty can be said to contain binding rules of international law, it must first come into force. This depends on the will of the contracting states.[3] In the case of multilateral treaties, the normal requirement is ratification by a predetermined number of states.

The precise legal effect of such a treaty within a state will depend on that state's

---

[1] International orgnizations, corporations and even individuals are, however, increasingly recognized as also having certain rights and duties under modern international law.

[2] Article 38(1) of the Statute of the International Court of Justice.

[3] Article 24 of the Vienna Convention on the Law of Treaties 1969.

constitutional law. In the case of South Africa an Act of Parliament is required to give local effect to treaties,[4] and two distinct levels of legal application are therefore involved—the international and the municipal. South African courts cannot take the provision of international treaties directly into account; they must first be enacted in national legislation. This could be exactly the type of obligation that a state takes upon itself in terms of an international treaty and as long as the required domestic laws have not been passed, such a state could be in breach of its international-law obligations. Such defects have to be remedied on the interstate level.

Customary international law is a second important source of international law. It is to be found in the practice of states based on the conviction that such behaviour is required or permitted by international law. The bulk of traditional international law has been created this way. Long before there were any conventions on, for example, diplomatic immunity or the law of the sea, the rules governing these areas were clearly established and respected.

The remaining two sources of international law are not that important. General principles of law is a method for extending rules by inferring broad principles from more specific rules and by borrowing from municipal-law rules. Finally, judicial decisions and the works of academic writers tell us what the law is, but they do not really create the law.

9.1.3 Binding nature of international law

What needs to be considered next is the binding nature of international law. Why do states obey international law and how is it enforced? Since there is no international judiciary with automatic compulsory jurisdiction, there is a basic rule that states must give their consent before an international tribunal will have jurisdiction over them. It should, however, be stressed that international law is not devoid of sanctions. Some international organizations exercise direct control over their members,[5] or may provide the means for mobilizing international opinion against a wrong-doing state. The fear of sanctions is not however the main reason why states obey international law (this is probably also the case in municipal-law systems): because states create international law for themselves, it is unlikely that they will make rules which they will freely break. It is, moreover, impossible for states to exist and prosper in isolation. They need the advantages of international co-operation, which in turn, requires rules, and a state which shows no respect for the rules of the game will soon encounter negative reactions. Such reactions may not always take the form of direct punishment, but other states will, for instance, at least become reluctant to deal with the state. The reciprocal effects of breaches of international law should always be borne in mind. When it comes to the protection and preservation of a common resource such as the international environment, the existence of rules is to everyone's advantage.

To conclude: international law is neither perfect nor complete, but it is nevertheless indispensable. We should be careful not to infer from news coverage that international law is never obeyed. For one thing, it should be remembered that respect for the law hardly ever makes the headlines—that is considered too mundane to be newsworthy.

---

[4] Booysen *Volkereg—'n inleiding* (1980) 75. Similar positions prevail in the United Kingdom and many Commonwealth countries. In some other Western states ratification is also a legislative act and treaties become effective in international and municipal law simultaneously.

[5] The Security Council of the United Nations may impose sanctions on aggressor states; the funds of the International Monetary Fund will not be available to an excluded member-state experiencing balance of payments difficulties; and in the EEC the European Court of Justice has compulsory jurisdiction over member-states and the Council may adopt regulations that are directly applicable in member-states.

9.1.4 The limits of traditional international law

Until recently, international law did not really concern itself with the conservation of the environment.[6] But it has been realized that we must take account of the interdependence of global ecosystems, that the resources of the earth are finite and we all have to share them and that the conservation or exploitation of the environment cannot be left to one single state or even to a group of them. International co-operation and the creation of international rules have therefore become inevitable.

South Africa's oceans, rivers and wildlife resources, for example, cannot be effectively conserved through purely domestic measures. We are bound to co-operate with our neighbours and other states in order to achieve this objective and the only mechanism of which we can avail ourselves to do so is international law. The preservation of fishing stocks, for instance, cannot be achieved unless foreign fishermen, adhering to international-law rules, respect South African legislation. Similarly, South Africa would have had no basis for action against marine pollution by foreign ships operating beyond her rather narrow territorial waters, unless her action had been sanctioned by international law.

Traditional international law did not address itself to environmental conservation; instead it emphasized the sovereignty of states, which implied considerable freedom to act unilaterally, and few limits to what a state could do on its own territory existed. The environmentally detrimental results of national activities, although having effects well beyond national boundaries, had not become of concern to the international community. There was also a lack of awareness and knowledge. Traditional international law had no basis for the strict or absolute liability of states resulting from large-scale environmental pollution,[7] nor did it provide a basis for regulating barely measurable but continuous and cumulative forms of pollution. Traditional international law, furthermore, seemed 'either [to] permit or be uncertain about pre-emptive policies whereby the first comer is entitled to "shut-out" the other participants in any activity, or at least permanently reduce the utility of a resource to those others'.[8] Examples include the contamination of an international river by an upper riparian state, and overfishing.

Modern developments have highlighted the ambiguity in the traditional notion of state freedom. The freedom of the high seas may, for example, either mean (among the activities of navigation, overflight, fishing, laying cables etc) 'absence of constraint from discharging fuel oil' or the 'competence to traverse and use an unpolluted sea . . .'.[9]

Unilateral action by states provides no effective protection of the environment: environmental conservation under municipal law is unilateral conservation that is in principle restricted to the territory of the particular state; states cannot enforce their laws or court decisions beyond their own boundaries; with regard to the sea, full jurisdiction of coastal states is limited to territorial waters, the breadth of which is generally accepted to be 12 nautical miles (22 km), or to specially created zones. There is an obvious need for international law to provide for the conservation of those common areas which fall outside of state jurisdiction and where almost unrestricted freedom has been exercised.

---

[6] Note that even the Charter of the United Nations Organization (UNO), the only document purporting to form the basis of universal international co-operation, is silent on the problem of environmental pollution. So was the constitution of the International Maritime Organization (IMO) until 1975.

[7] Goldie 'A general view of international environmental law. A survey of capabilities, trends and limits' 1973 *Colloquium Hague Academy of International Law* 35. Contra see Brownlie *Principles of public international law* (1979) 436, 476. For a critique of this standpoint see Grad *Treatise on environmental law* vol 3 (1980) 13–30.

[8] Goldie above n 7, 35.

[9] O'Connell *International law* vol 2 (1965) 710.

9.1.5 International environmental law[10]

International environmental law is that part of international law which deals with the conservation of the environment and with the control of environmental pollution. Ecological factors demand the creation of such a branch of law. Because traditional international law is largely deficient, international environmental law has developed mainly through international conventions (treaties)—ie deliberate international standard-setting. This is a speedier process (provided the coming into force of the conventions encounters no problems) and has the advantage that it can be very explicit in laying down technical standards. The bulk of the discussion that follows will deal with a number of such treaties.[11] It will be clear that they have very much an ad hoc nature.

Two points should be mentioned about the treaties to be discussed: first, space does not permit an exhaustive treatment of each; secondly, only treaties primarily concerned with environmental conservation have been considered. Furthermore, in many instances (eg the banning of nuclear tests) the primary aim is something else and environmental conservation is of secondary importance.

No introduction to the problems of international law would be complete without mentioning another group of factors—the economic implications of uniform international rules and standards—and so it is to these that we first turn our attention.

9.1.6 Economic factors[12]

Measures to conserve the environment are costly in economic terms and may cause distortions of trade and investment. Pollution control measures for domestic products, for example, make them more expensive, while the absence of uniform international standards may diminish the competitiveness of such products. The imposition of differing standards for environmental protection thus creates non-tariff barriers and discrimination in international trade. It is therefore also in the economic interests of countries in which strict environmental protection measures apply to work towards international acceptance and enforcement of the same standards, to ensure that domestic and foreign products compete on an equal basis.

Secondly the existence of different environmental standards may also cause a re-routing of investments away from those states where higher standards apply to those

---

[10] In recent years South African literature on international environmental law has been fairly extensive and includes the following: Barrie 'Fisheries and the 1982 United Nations Law of the Sea Convention' 1986 *Acta Juridica* 43; 'South Africa and nuclear energy—national and international aspects' 1987 *TSAR* 153; 'International nuclear energy law—present and future' 1988 *TSAR* 201; De Quintal 'Sovereign disputes in the antarctic' 1984 *SAYIL* 161; Devine 'Sea passage in South African maritime zones: actualities and possibilities' 1986 *Acta Juridica* 203; 'Authorisation of foreign fishing in the South African fishing zone: some anomalies and uncertainties' 1988 (7) *Sea Changes* 79; 'Towards an effective implementation of the intervention convention in South Africa' 1988 *Sea Changes* 56; 'Statutory offences committed at sea' 1990 *De Rebus* 65; Gertenbach 'Fishery convention areas in the South East Atlantic and adjacent seas: overlapping issues' 1986 *Acta Juridica* 51; Glazewski 'Atmospheric pollution and the ozone layer: plugging holes in international law' 1989 (43) *African Wildlife* 174; Jackson *International marine pollution conventions and the independent states of southern Africa* Publication 8 (1989), Institute of Marine Law, University of Cape Town; Moll 'Antarctica: the Antarctic Treaty and the Antarctic Treaty system' 1985 (1) *Sea Changes* 96; Scheepers 'South African law of shipwrecks: contemporary and international law perspectives' 1989 (10) *Sea Changes* 41; Siegfried 'The legal system affecting exploitation of Antarctic natural resources' 1986 *Acta Juridica* 61; Soni '*Control of Marine Pollution in International Law*' (1985); Stewart 'Civil liability for pollution damage caused by the discharge of oil from vessels—some aspects of international and South African law' 1986 (4) *Sea Changes* 106; Van Rensburg & Bartlett 'Technical, economic and institutional constraints on the production of minerals from the deep sea-bed' 1986 *Acta Juridica* 69; Vrancken 'Sub-Saharan African regional marine and coastal environment conventions: analysis and possible implications for South Africa' 1988 (7) *Sea Changes* 62; Wolfrum 'Antarctic mineral resources regime' 1986 *Acta Juridica* 125.

[11] A list of conventions to which South Africa is a party is contained in table 9.1.

[12] Taken from Grad above n 7, 13–14ff.

with lower standards. This latter group normally consists of less industrialized countries, when they literally become havens for pollution as a result.

The same phenomenon occurs with shipping. Shipowners who have to obey regulations with regard to safety and construction are at a disadvantage when they have to compete with vessels registered in countries that have no comparable requirements. The disruptive effect of being subjected to different sets of regulations every time another port is visited is also obvious.[13] On the other hand, if shipping companies fail to meet the standards which apply to certain sea-routes or in coastal waters of other countries they will suffer a loss of business.

The division of the world into rich and poor nations has had profound effects on international, political and economic relations. It also affects the conservation of the environment.[14] In cases of hunger and overpopulation people will in desperation destroy much of the natural habitat in order to ensure a living, a phenomenon which can have any of the following environmental consequences: deforestation, overgrazing, the 'creeping-desert' phenomenon, salinity and so on. Then follow further repercussions in the form of remedies: international food aid, the development of applicable technology, agricultural assistance and population control are required. For many of the developing nations these are very expensive programmes which can be funded only through international organizations and by the developed countries.

Some developing countries see the answer to their problems in terms of greater industrialization and energy use. They view emphasis on environmental conservation as slowing their development.[15] They criticize the rich countries that have already achieved their development and which now want to impose controls on other nations.

The poor countries were also opposed to the 'polluter-pays' principle, according to which, industry in one state should not gain an economic advantage over competitors in other states as a result of pollution-control costs being subsidized.[16] Developing countries not only refrain from imposing pollution control measures (to attract investment or because enforcement machinery is too expensive) but also fear that they will end up paying more for imports to defray pollution control in developed countries. In other instances they fear that their export markets will be reduced as a result of stricter standards in rich importing countries. The developed countries face embarrassing problems in this regard. They cannot justify their consumption patterns to the poorer countries of the world when they are emphasizing the 'oneness' of the world and its resources. This is another telling reason why the gap between rich and poor countries should be bridged and why development aid is also to the advantage of the rich donors.

---

[13] See further Abecassis *The law and practice relating to oil pollution from ships* (1978) 24.

[14] The efforts by developing countries to change the international economic system in their favour culminated in the adoption of the Declaration and the Programme of Action on the Establishment of a New International Economic Order (A Res 3201 (S-VI) and 3202 (S-VI)) and the Charter of Economic Rights and Duties of States (A Res 3281 (XXIX)). Article 30 of this Charter determines that all states shall try to establish their own environmental developmental policies in conformity with their responsibility to protect the environment. (Cf n 15 below.) See, further, UNEP decisions of governing council of 1975 in 1975 *ILM* 1070.

[15] Article 30 of the Charter of the Economic Rights and Duties of States (for text, see n 14 above), for example, states inter alia that 'The environmental policies of all states should enhance and not adversely affect the present and future development potential of developing countries'.

A meeting of a number of development banks in 1980 adopted a 'declaration of environmental policies and procedures relating to economic development' in which it is stated that the environmental problems of developing countries are not necessarily the same as those of developed countries and that governments have the sovereign right to determine their own priorities and development patterns. On the other hand, it is also said that 'in the long run environmental protection and economic and social development are not only compatible but interdependent and mutually reinforcing'. For text see 1980 (19) *ILM* 524.

[16] See further the European Communities Council recommendation on the application of the 'polluter-pays principle' 1975 *ILM* 138.

9.2 CUSTOMARY INTERNATIONAL LAW

9.2.1 Relevant fundamental principles

9.2.1.1 *The principles of sovereignty, freedom of the high seas and state responsibility*

It has already been pointed out that the doctrines of sovereignty of states and freedom of the high seas have resulted in a laissez-faire approach. In the past, states enjoyed considerable freedom in their use of the high seas and their own territories. Today some of these earlier permitted uses are perceived as abuses of the environment. The reason for this is our changed awareness of the nature of ecosystems and therefore of the need for a different application of the law.

State sovereignty has a dual character. It is the basis both of a state's freedom to act without outside interference and of its responsibility in international law for acts that injure other states. Sovereignty does not permit uses of national territory that result in violations of another's sovereignty. On this basis all states may demand that their own environments should not be polluted from outside sources. One state may therefore be held liable for damages to the environment of another as a result of activities within the jurisdiction of the former. This was the basis of the *Trail Smelter* case, to be discussed below.

The principles of sovereignty and state responsibility have been applied directly to environmental conservation through the Declaration of Principles adopted by the Stockholm Conference on the Human Environment. Principle 21 reads:

> 'states have, in accordance with the Charter of the United Nations and the principles of international law, the sovereign right to exploit their own resources pursuant to their own environmental policies, and the responsibility to ensure that activities within their jurisdiction or control do not cause damage to the environment of other states or of areas beyond the limits of national jurisdiction'.

This purports to be a statement of customary international law. It extends state responsibility to areas outside any nation's jurisdiction, such as the high seas. This is a state responsibility erga omnes, ie towards the whole international community. The capacity of states to assert claims with regard to this type of responsibility is somewhat uncertain. It is recognized that states have enforceable interests in the protection of their own territorial integrity, environment and citizens, when endangered by pollution of common areas such as the high seas. It is not at all certain, though, whether there exists an actio popularis in customary international law which would entitle states to claim on behalf of the general interest all people have in the integrity of the global environment.[17]

9.2.1.2 *Self-defence*

Customary international law has always recognized states' rights of self-defence. The right to use force in self-defence has been circumscribed by Article 51 of the United Nations (UN) Charter, which limits the use of force to instances of self-defence against armed attacks. In certain other cases, however, states may also use force. Intervention on the high seas (or in space beyond national control) to prevent or mitigate the effects of pollution is an example,[18] and was illustrated in the *Torrey Canyon* disaster of 1967. There, an oil tanker ran aground on a reef in the English Channel, the United Kingdom bombed it in self-defence and the Liberian Government (the state of registration) did not protest at the action taken.

---

[17] For a thorough discussion of this aspect, see Goldie above n 7, 103ff. For a general discussion of the existence of the actio popularis in international law, see Silagi 'Die Popularklage als Fremdkörper im Völkerrecht' 1978 *SAYIL* 10.

[18] For further examples of the permitted use of force on the high seas, see Sorensen (ed) *Manual of public international law* (1968) 772ff.

Where pollution stems from the territory of another state, international-law scholars are divided on the permissibility of the use of force. Article 51 of the UN Charter reads:

'Nothing in the present Charter shall impair the inherent right of individual or collective self-defense if an armed attack occurs against a member of the United Nations, until the Security Council has taken measures to maintain international peace and security. . . .'

One school would permit force only against armed attacks. Others argue that self-defence is broader and includes the right to use force in other instances also.[19] In terms of this latter view, the right to self-defence will permit 'forcible response by a state to a major injury, actual or imminent, to its territory, resources or people'.[20] Such measures of force will be subject to the criteria of necessity and proportionality.[21]

9.2.1.3 *Good neighbourliness*

In the case of international rivers and lakes shared by more than one state, the principle of 'good neighbourliness' is sometimes involved. Its basis is the fact that, where two or more states share a natural system (usually water systems), it should be done in such a manner that the use by the other state or states ('neighbours') is respected; but although this principle may not be very well defined, it is said to be useful for the 'equitable adjustment of rights of states sharing a watercourse, river basin, an air mass, or ecosystem'.[22]

9.2.2 Decisions applicable to environmental conservation[23]

The following decisions are important because they deal with the application of principles of customary international law to environmental protection.

9.2.2.1 *The Trail Smelter arbitration* (United States v Canada 1941)

This arbitration arose out of damages caused in the United States to private crops, pasture lands, trees and livestock by fumes carried by winds from a privately owned Canadian smelting plant. The controversy was submitted to an arbitration tribunal.

The tribunal held that Canada was liable for past losses and ordered damages of $78 000 to be paid for a period up to 1937. Canada was under a further obligation to abate the damage. In a second award, after the necessary scientific data had been obtained, a detailed regime, prescribing the permissible levels of sulphur emission, was established by the tribunal:

'The doctrinal basis for the decision was the principle of state responsibility for acts violating another state's sovereignty. Under principles of international law as well as the law of the United States, no state *has the right to use or permit the use of its territory* in such a manner as to *cause injury* by fumes in or *to the territory of another* or the properties of persons therein, when the case is of serious consequences and the injury established' (italics added).

Note that in this case Canada was responsible for the conduct of a private enterprise on the basis that the enterprise had operated on Canadian soil. This decision is also important because it gives indications of what constitutes injury. The nature of the activity will determine what amounts to an impermissible degree of pollution.

---

[19] Sorensen above n 18, 765ff.

[20] Grad above n 7, 13–36.

[21] These criteria were enunciated by the American Secretary of State, Webster, in connection with the *Caroline* case.

[22] Grad above n 7, 13–38. Brownlie above n 7, 285 prefers the principle of state responsibility to those of good neighbourliness or abuse of right.

[23] Largely taken from Grad above n 7, 13, 38ff and Goldie above n 7, passim.

9.2.2.2 *The Corfu Channel case* (United Kingdom v Albania 1949)

While this decision did not deal with environmental conservation, it is nevertheless important because it sheds light on the principles of sovereignty, self-defence and state responsibility.

Relying on the right of innocent passage through straits, the United Kingdom sent a number of cruisers through the North Corfu Channel in May 1946. Albania denied the existence of such a right (it claimed prior request and permission) and fired on the ships. On a second passage through the strait two British destroyers were damaged by exploding mines. The United Kingdom therefore decided, after Albania had refused permission, to sweep the Corfu Channel—an operation that took place within Albania's territorial waters.

The Court made no finding that Albania itself had done the minelaying, but the laying could not have taken place without her knowledge. This resulted in an obligation to inform British ships entitled to innocent passage. The basis of the obligation was 'the principle of the freedom of maritime communication, and every state's obligation not to allow knowingly its territory to be used for acts contrary to the rights of other states'. On the other hand, the United Kingdom had violated Albanian sovereignty by its minesweeping operation. The Court rejected the British plea that the minesweeping had been a method of self-protection or self-help.

9.2.2.3 *The Lac Lanoux arbitration* (France vs Spain 1957)

France started to transform Lake Lanoux (also on French territory) into a reservoir, but undertook to return to Spain, through the Carol River, waters equivalent to the total diversion. Spain, however, complained that France had violated a treaty by diverting a river before it entered Spain.

The tribunal found that no violation of the treaty had occurred. The following dictum by the tribunal is, however, frequently cited as pertaining to the duty to protect the environment:

> 'It could have been argued that the works would bring about an ultimate pollution of the waters of the Carol or that the returned waters have a chemical composition or a temperature or some other characteristics which would injure Spanish interests. Spain could then have claimed that her right had been impaired in violation of the Additional Act.'

But Spain had made no such allegation.

The tribunal also referred to good faith, good neighbourliness and the duty of a state to take into account the rights and interests of a neighbouring state. This decision may therefore be regarded as relevant to the use of natural resources shared by more than one state.

9.2.2.4 *The nuclear tests cases* (Australia vs France, New Zealand vs France 1974)

France carried out several atmospheric nuclear tests during the 1960s and 1970s in French Polynesia in the Pacific and planned more tests. Australia and New Zealand instituted separate cases against France in the International Court of Justice. In its application to the court, Australia based its claims on the following:

(1) the right to be free from atmospheric nuclear weapon tests by any country;
(2) the deposit of radioactive fall-out on territory and its dispersion in airspace without consent
    (a) as a violation of sovereignty over territory and
    (b) as an impairment of Australia's independent right to determine what acts shall take place within its territory and, in particular, whether Australia and its people should be exposed to radiation from artificial sources;
(3) infringement of the freedom of the seas by way of interference with ships and aircraft and by pollution from radioactive fall-out.

New Zealand claimed violations of

(1) the right 'that no nuclear tests that give rise to radioactive fall-out be conducted'; and
(2) the right to 'preservation from unjustified contamination of the terrestrial, maritime and aerial environment . . .'.[24]

France did not appear before the Court and actually demanded the removal of the case from the list. The Court refused[25] and issued interim orders asking France not to continue with the planned tests. France refused, but subsequently issued statements that no more tests would be carried out.

These statements were not communicated to the Court or to the two applicants. The Court held that they were addressed to the international community as a whole and that they constituted a legal undertaking. It was therefore of the opinion that the dispute had disappeared and consequently declared the case moot.

The Court did not explain the exact nature of the rights and obligations with regard to the environment that were involved, but some commentators argue that the obligation not to conduct atmospheric nuclear tests has been recognized as a rule of customary international law. This is important since France is not party to the Test Ban Treaty.[26]

It is also argued that the existence of nuclear test zones over the high seas and the pollution caused by the nuclear fall-out violate states' common and special rights with regard to freedom of navigation, overflight and fishing in the high seas.

9.3 CONVENTIONAL INTERNATIONAL ENVIRONMENTAL LAW

International environmental law is a young branch of international law which deals with a vast subject and has to provide rather precise standards. It is largely 'treaty law'. The following sections contain a brief discussion of some of these agreements. In these sections the focus is on agreements that have a general application; a subsequent section will deal with agreements that apply only in respect of a particular region. The aim is to give a general overview and to focus on the more important aspects. A list of environmental conventions to which South Africa is a party, is contained in table 9.1.

9.3.1 Pollution control

9.3.1.1 *Marine pollution*

(a) Introduction. One of the earliest efforts to create international environmental law relates to marine pollution and dates back to the 1920s,[27] but the first true agreement was the International Convention for the Prevention of Pollution of the Sea by Oil in 1954. The nations attending that meeting were not all convinced of the desirability of a general prohibition.[28] The next important step was the adoption of the Geneva Conventions on the Law of the Sea in 1958, which are still the binding agreements on this subject. These conventions codified and developed international law with regard to the territorial sea and contiguous zone, the high seas, fishing and conservation, and the continental shelf.

---

[24] 1973 *ICJ Reports* 103, 139–140.

[25] The court based its jurisdiction on the General Act of 1928, read together with Articles 36 and 37 of the Statute of the Court.

[26] See Grad above n 7, 13–53.

[27] The first international conference took place in 1926—in response to American concern about operational discharges by non-tankers off its east coast: see M'Gonigle & Zacher *Pollution, politics and international law* (1979) 81. Before that, unilateral action was taken by Britain and the United States: see Mangone *Law for the world ocean* (1981) 261.

[28] M'Gonigle & Zacher above n 27, 81.

Articles 24 and 25 of the Convention on the High Seas (which purports to be a codification of international law) charge states with a duty to prevent the pollution of the seas from the discharge of oil or the dumping of radioactive waste. International organizations, and especially the International Maritime Organization (IMO), have played important roles in facilitating interstate co-operation in achieving this objective.

Another important milestone in the development of the law of the sea was reached with the adoption of the Law of the Sea Convention 1982 (hereinafter called LOSC) after protracted negotiations dating from 1973. This is not yet a binding treaty and will only become such one year after the deposit of the 60th ratification or accession—to date over 40 ratifications or accessions have been deposited. LOSC contains several important provisions on environmental protection and conservation, many of which are in all probability declaratory of customary law or in the process of becoming so.

LOSC emphasizes unilateral action with regard to pollution control but also that states shall 'endeavour to harmonize their policies in this connexion'.[29] On the other hand, it provides that 'states shall refrain from unjustifiable interference with activities in pursuance of the rights exercised and duties performed by other states in conformity with this Convention'.[30] It further refers to global and regional co-operation, the notification of imminent or actual damage, contingency plans against pollution, the promotion of research, and special assistance to developing countries.

The status of the Convention remains uncertain, however. Western countries such as the United States, Germany and the United Kingdom refused to sign it. Their opposition relates mainly to the provisions on exploitation of the deep sea-bed. The majority of states, however, support the Convention and this will strengthen the cause of protecting the marine environment.

(b) Pollution from ships

(i) *Operational discharges*. Marine pollution results from various sources such as land-based activities, the operation of sea-going vessels,[31] accidents, and the exploitation of resources. Deliberate pollution from ships is best controlled by discharge regulations, a field in which IMO has been active for a long time.

The International Convention for the Prevention of Pollution of the Sea by Oil of 1954 aimed at preventing 'pollution of the sea by oil discharged from ships'. It did not contain a total ban on the discharge of oil, however, this activity being prohibited in specified zones only. In 1962 these zones were extended to 100 nautical miles from land, thus still leaving vast areas of the seas unprotected. Furthermore, the prohibition did not apply to non-oil pollutants and the Convention sought to reduce the amount of permissible discharge, not to place a total ban on discharges of oil. It further covered all ships registered in the territory of a party to the Convention, but excluded naval auxiliaries, whaling ships, ships navigating in the Great Lakes, tankers under 150 tons gross tonnage and other ships of under 500 tons gross tonnage. States of registry had to enforce the 1954 Convention. This was not a very effective measure and was criticized for encouraging the further use of 'flags of convenience'.[32]

The 1969 amendments introduced the load-on-top (LOT) system.[33] By this method

[29] Article 194(1).

[30] Article 194(4).

[31] The operation of nuclear ships is regulated by the 1962 Brussels Convention on the Liability of the Operators of Nuclear Ships.

[32] Out of seven cases of violations of the 1954 Convention reported during 1969–72, modest penalties were imposed in two: see Grad above n 7, 13–57.

[33] After a tanker has discharged its cargo, a considerable proportion of oil remains. This has to be removed because of the risk of explosion, incompatibility with subsequent cargoes, impossibility of inspection etc. Before LOT this clingage had been removed by washing the tanks with sea water and

oil which would otherwise have been discharged into the sea could be saved—a potentially good anti-pollution device.[34]

The 1973 Convention for the Prevention of Pollution from Ships (MARPOL) expands the 1954 Convention. New tankers over 70 000 deadweight tons must have segregated ballast tanks so that water and oil will not be mixed.[35] The maximum discharge of oil by new tankers was also reduced.[36]

An important innovation was the creation of 'special areas' where only 'clean ballast' is permitted.[37] Of equal importance was the acceptance of the principle requiring the provision of waste-reception facilities at ports for oil residues.

MARPOL contains five Annexes dealing with the discharge of different substances: oil (Annex I); noxious liquid substances in bulk (Annex II); harmful substances carried by sea in packaged form (Annex III); sewage (Annex IV), and garbage (Annex V). By virtue of the 1978 Protocol to MARPOL Annexes III to V are optional in that parties to MARPOL need not accept them.

(ii) *Accidents*. The *Torrey Canyon* disaster of 1967 brought home the danger of pollution resulting from accidents. This gave rise to the 1971 amendment to the 1954 Convention aimed at setting limitations to oil cargo tank sizes and construction standards.[38] This was clearly a pollution prevention measure and not simply a matter of technical safety.

As a result of a series of tanker accidents in 1976, and because the USA threatened unilateral action, the International Conference on Tanker Safety and Pollution Prevention was convened in 1978.[39] The Conference adopted protocols to the 1974 Safety of Life at Sea Convention, and to MARPOL, on matters such as steering gear, radar, collision avoidance aids, and the construction and size of ballast tanks. Of great importance is the requirement that new tankers of 20 000 deadweight tons or more (rather than 70 000 deadweight tons) should be fitted with segregated ballast tanks. It was further agreed that this should apply to all vessels to be constructed after mid-1979, and that certain types of existing tankers and product carriers would have to be retrofitted.

In LOSC the importance of seaworthiness is recognized. In terms of Article 210, a state which has ascertained that a vessel within its ports or at its offshore terminals 'is in violation of applicable international rules and standards relating to seaworthiness and thereby threatens damage to the marine environment shall, as far as practicable, take administrative measures to prevent the vessel from sailing'. Such a vessel may leave only upon rectification of the deficiencies or in order to have repairs undertaken.

In certain circumstances states may also intervene on the high seas to combat pollution resulting from accidents. This represents an important departure from customary international law. The International Convention Relating to Intervention on the High Seas in Cases of Oil Pollution Casualties of 1969 provides that:

'[p]arties to the present Convention may take such measures on the high seas as may be necessary to prevent, mitigate or eliminate grave and imminent danger to their coastline or related interests

returning the oil–water mixture to the sea. Under the LOT system the oil and water are separated on board and only the water discharged into the sea. See further Abecassis above n 7, 9; M'Gonigle & Zacher above n 26, 96; Mangone above n 27, 266.

[34] See Abecassis above n 13, 12 et seq. Mangone above n 27, 267 is critical even of the merit of LOT.

[35] Regulation 13. See M'Gonigle & Zacher above n 27, 114.

[36] M'Gonigle & Zacher above n 27, 113.

[37] Such areas are the closed seas of the Mediterranean, Baltic and Red seas and the Persian (Arabian) Gulf. Note, however, that implementation requires provision of reception facilities by littoral states. For possible flaws in this Convention, see M'Gonigle & Zacher above n 27, 120.

[38] Abecassis above n 13, 65.

[39] Abecassis above n 13, 40; M'Gonigle & Zacher above n 27, 122ff.

from pollution or threat of pollution of the sea by oil, following upon a maritime casualty, which may reasonably be expected to result in major harmful consequences.'[40]

Warships or ships in government service are excluded. This Convention represented a major step forward in the sense that states other than the flag state are now permitted to adopt enforcement measures.

A Protocol was added to the Convention in 1973 relating to Intervention on the High Seas in Cases of Pollution by Substances other than Oil. The customary-law principles of self-help and necessity are also available to all states threatened with such pollution, while the above conventional provisions are declaratory of customary international law. The right of intervention is also recognized by Article 221 of LOSC, which provides that states may take and enforce measures beyond the territorial sea to protect their coastline or related interests from pollution or threat of pollution following upon a maritime casualty which may be reasonably expected to result in major harmful consquences. The measures must be proportionate to the actual or threatened damage.

(iii) *Dumping.* The practice of using the sea-bed and the ocean floor for the dumping of toxic, radioactive and other noxious materials such as nerve gas has caused grave concern. It is sometimes argued that article 25 of the High Seas Convention of 1958 and General Assembly Resolution 2340 (XXII) forbid this type of activity,[41] but international concern led nevertheless to the adoption of a number of multilateral treaties.[42] The most important of these is the 1972 London Convention on the Prevention of Marine Pollution by Dumping of Wastes and Other Matter, which aims at controlling 'all sources of pollution of the marine environment'.[43] The London Convention defines dumping as 'any deliberate disposal at sea of wastes or other matter from vessels, aircraft, platforms or other man-made structures at sea'.[44]

Three categories of wastes were recognized. Dumping of wastes mentioned in Annexure I to the Convention is strictly prohibited. These include radioactive wastes, biological and chemical warfare materials, persistent plastics and synthetic materials, oils (taken on board for the purpose of dumping), cadmium, mercury and organohalogen compounds. The second category of wastes may be dumped only after a special permit has been issued. The third group requires a general permit.

Parties to this Convention are under an obligation to control the transportation from their territory, or transportation from other countries by ships flying their flag, of materials due for dumping at sea.[45] But if dumping 'appears to be the only way of averting' danger to human life or to vessels, aircraft or installations, it is permissible.[46]

LOSC Article 210 contains general provisions on dumping. Under it states are obliged to adopt laws to prevent, reduce and control pollution by dumping which shall not be carried out without the permission of the competent authorities of a state. The national laws adopted shall be no less effective than global rules and standards. States must also try to establish global and regional standards.

(iv) *Civil liability and compensation.* In terms of the International Convention on Civil Liability for Oil Pollution Damage 1969 a shipowner is liable for oil-pollution damage caused by oil from his tanker. This is strict liability and is subject only to limited

---

[40] Article I(1).
[41] Harris *Cases and materials on international law* (1979) 362.
[42] Examples are the Oslo Convention for the Prevention of Marine Pollution by Dumping from Ships and Aircraft of 1972 (which applies to the North Sea and the North East Atlantic), the London Convention on the Prevention of Marine Pollution by Dumping of Wastes and other Matter of 1972 (which applies to the seas everywhere) and the Convention of the Mediterranean Sea against Pollution of 1976.
[43] Article I.
[44] Articles III(1)*(a)*(i).
[45] Articles IV, VI, VII.
[46] Article V.

exceptions such as acts of war and third-party or government acts. Owners of ships of more than 2 000 tons carrying oil as cargo must take out insurance against oil-pollution damage. In the case of oil pollution by two or more ships, the owners of all of them will be jointly and severally liable for damage which is not reasonably separable. The damage must have occurred on the territory, including the territorial sea, of a contracting state, though offshore installations, dry cargo ships and river and lake vessels are excluded.

The decision to have the shipowner and not the cargo-owner bear the pollution damage cost was a controversial one. It was therefore decided to set up an International Oil Pollution Compensation Fund to supplement the International Convention on Civil Liability for Oil Pollution Damage, which was established in terms of the Convention on the Establishment of an International Fund for Compensation for Oil Pollution Damage 1971. Its basic objectives are twofold: first, to compensate plaintiffs (subject to a maximum limit) for pollution damage which they were unable to recover (and to some extent to reimburse shipowners for voluntary clean-up expenses); and, secondly, to give relief to shipowners.[47] Contributions come from oil companies in proportion to their share of the world transport of oil.

The major oil companies have entered into a private agreement, too: The Tanker Owners Voluntary Agreement on Liability for Oil Pollution 1969 provides for reimbursement to national governments for preventive or clean-up expenses. The major oil companies also created their own fund in 1971, and together these two private agreements are valuable supplementary provisions to the Conventions.

(c) Pollution from sea-bed exploitation. The 1958 Geneva Convention on the Continental Shelf authorizes states to exploit the natural resources on the continental shelf adjacent to their coasts. But coastal states have to adopt measures to protect 'the living resources of the sea from harmful agents'.[48] LOSC lays down that coastal states must adopt laws against marine pollution resulting from sea-bed activities in the exclusive economic zone (EEZ) and on the continental shelf.[49] These laws must not be inferior to international standards and must be co-ordinated.

Exploitation of the sea-bed of the deep sea is foreseen to take place under the authority of a new international organization, the International Sea-Bed Authority. This location falls outside the jurisdiction of individual states, and separate rules against pollution are to be adopted.[50]

(d) Pollution from land-based sources. Land-based activities result in several forms of marine pollution. Rivers, pipelines and outfall structures carry pollutants such as urban sewage, wastes discharged by factories, pesticides and chemical fertilizers into the oceans.

A Convention for the Prevention of Marine Pollution from Land-Based Sources was adopted in 1974,[51] while a Protocol amending the Convention was concluded in 1986.[52] The latter extends the scope of the Convention to include marine pollution through the atmosphere.[53] It may also be mentioned that LOSC advocates the adoption of national laws and measures, harmonization of policies at regional level and the establishment of global and regional measures for combating this kind of pollution.[54] A number of

---

47 See Articles 4 and 5.
48 Article 5(7).
49 Articles 208 and 214.
50 Article 209.
51 Text at 1974 (12) *ILM* 352.
52 Text at 1988 (27) *ILM* 625.
53 Articles I, II.
54 Article 207.

regional agreements (eg by Baltic and Mediterranean states) have been concluded in this respect.

(e) Enforcement. LOSC expands the scope of enforcement measures that coastal states may take. The basic approach is to require coastal states to adopt national legislation with extraterritorial effect, even though in terms of traditional views this is contrary to the sovereign equality of states. For centuries only flag states could legislate and enforce standards applying to their ships on the high seas; coastal states had very little power and their jurisdiction was limited to their territorial waters, a narrow zone of 3 nautical miles (now 12 nautical miles).

These were the rules of international law. For a state to apply its own laws beyond its territorial waters[55] international-law authorization is needed. This can be achieved either through the gradual and rather slow process of the formation of new customary law or through treaties, of which LOSC is an example.

With the affirmation of the EEZ regime (which has a breadth of 200 nautical miles),[56] the coastal states were given jurisdiction over this area with respect to the protection and preservation of the marine environment.[57] This was clearly an important departure from the traditional view in terms of which that part of the sea was regarded as high seas. Flag states, of course, also retain responsibility for their ships.[58]

It is not possible to discuss the details of LOSC here. Suffice it to state that an effort is made to strike a balance between the need of the coastal state for protection against pollution by ships passing through its EEZ and the need of maritime states for expeditious passage through the EEZ. The coastal state is now permitted to take enforcement measures with regard to dumping,[59] seaworthiness[60] and maritime casualties[61] and to inspect, obtain information, detain and undertake legal proceedings.

9.3.1.2 *Atmospheric pollution*

(a) Air pollution. Since the 1950s so-called acid rain and snow have been detected in the Scandinavian countries and North America. It occurs when sulphur and nitrogen oxides, emitted primarily by power plants and factories, combine with moisture in the air to form weak acids which then precipitate in rain or snow. The resulting damage occurs mostly in lakes and streams where fish stocks and other forms of aquatic life are affected. Acid rain may also damage crops, forests and buildings and may even contaminate drinking water.

In November 1979 the first international agreement covering acid rain and snow, the Convention on Long Range Transboundary Air Pollution,[62] was signed by 34 members of the United Nations Economic Commission for Europe. The driving forces behind the adoption of this agreement were the Scandinavian countries and the signatories include all of the eastern and western European nations (with the exception of Albania), Canada and the USA. This Convention provides for notification and consultation between the countries planning to increase their sulphur pollution levels and those countries likely to be affected. This is required when 'significant' changes in discharges are likely.

---

[55] Since the adoption of the 1958 Geneva Convention on the Territorial Sea and the Contiguous Zone, a state may also exercise control in the contiguous zone to prevent infringement of its customs, fiscal, immigration or sanitary regulations (article 24). See, too, LOSC article 33, which extends the contiguous zone to 24 nautical miles.

[56] Article 57.

[57] Article 56(1)*(b)*(iii).

[58] Article 217.

[59] Article 216.

[60] Article 219.

[61] Article 221.

[62] Articles 218 and 220.

Western European countries[63] and Canada followed this up with a Declaration on Acid Rain issued in Ottawa in 1984.[64] The signatories undertook a 30 per cent reduction of national annual sulphur emissions by 1993 and also promised measures to decrease emissions of nitrogen oxides.

Monitoring of air pollution under this Convention is foreseen as taking place through an existing programme which is funded and co-ordinated by the United Nations Environmental Programme (UNEP) and the World Meteorological Organization (WMO).

In 1984 European countries (both eastern and western) together with the United States and Canada adopted a Protocol to the 1979 Convention on Financing the Monitoring and Evaluation of Air Pollutants in Europe.[65] In 1985 a further Protocol was concluded on a 30 per cent reduction of sulphur emissions from transboundary flukes.[66] Eastern European participation in the Protocols was limited to Byelorussia, Hungary, Ukraine and USSR. Finally in 1988 a Protocol to the 1979 Convention was concluded concerning the control of emissions of nitrogen oxides or their transboundary flukes.[67] The Protocol implements the Convention and sets standards for emissions which cover both plants[68] and motor vehicles.[69] Six eastern European states participated in the Protocol.

(b) Ozone-layer depletion. International society became very conscious of the fact that human activities could have an effect in modifying the ozone layer and that this could produce adverse effects on the physical environment, including climatic change that results in harmful impacts on human health and the environment. The Vienna Convention for the Protection of the Ozone Layer was adopted in 1985.[70] The Convention provides general obligations for the parties to take appropriate measures to protect the layer from harmful modification;[71] includes general duties of co-operation, research, observation and information;[72] establishes a Conference of the Parties and a Secretariat,[73] and makes provision for dispute settlement.[74]

The Montreal Protocol on Substances that Deplete the Ozone Layer was adopted in 1987 as a follow-up to the 1985 Convention.[75] The Protocol contains a list of chlorofluorocarbons (CFCs).[76] Parties undertake to control and limit the consumption of CFCs[77] and not to import CFCs from states which are not parties to the Protocol.[78] There are also assessment, review, data reporting, research and information provisions.[79]

In the Helsinki Declaration on the Protection of the Ozone Layer 1989, the governments of the European Communities agreed to phase out CFCs not later than the year 2000, to phase out halons and other ozone-depleting substances, to develop

[63] Austria, Denmark, Finland, France, the Federal Republic of Germany, Netherlands, Norway, Sweden and Switzerland.

[64] Text at 1984 (23) *ILM* 662.

[65] Text at 1985 (24) *ILM* 484; 1988 (27) *ILM* 701.

[66] Text at 1988 (27) *ILM* 707.

[67] Text at 1989 (28) *ILM* 214.

[68] Technical Annex articles 3–15 (control technologies for NO_x emissions from stationary sources).

[69] Technical Annex articles 16–22 (control technologies for NO_x emissions from motor vehicles).

[70] Text at 1987 (26) *ILM* 1529.

[71] Article 2.

[72] Articles 2–5.

[73] Articles 6, 7.

[74] Article 11.

[75] Text at 1987 (26) *ILM* 1550.

[76] Annex A—controlled substances.

[77] Article 2.

[78] Article 4.

[79] Articles 6, 7, 9.

acceptable substitute technologies and to transfer technology and replacement equipment to developing countries at minimum cost.[80]

In 1989 an arbitration procedure was created under the Vienna Convention and environmental scientific, economic and technical assessment panels were established under the Montreal Protocol.[81]

(c) Climatic change ('greenhouse effect'). There has been increasing concern in recent years about the level of carbon dioxide emissions into the atmosphere. This has a 'greenhouse effect' in enclosing the atmosphere in a blanket of carbon dioxide, resulting in a rise in overall temperatures, melting polar ice, sea-level rise and general climatic change. The problem has been addressed in different forums. The UN General Assembly recognized the problem of climatic change in 1987.[82] Two years later, the Assembly recognized it as a common concern of mankind and considered the World Climate Programme to be of the highest priority. In this respect it endorsed the joint actions of UNEP and WMO, urged governments to treat the issue as a priority and called for support for the Intergovernmental Panel on Climatic Change.[83]

UNEP also addressed the issue in 1987 and 1989.[84] The Intergovernmental Panel on Climate Change was created within the framework of WMO,[85] one of its tasks being to prepare a convention on climatic change.[86] A World Climate Conference was held in 1990.[87]

The Council of the European Communities adopted a resolution in 1989 aimed at reducing the production and consumption of CFCs by 85 per cent as soon as possible and stressing that afforestation efforts should be intensified.[88]

Twenty-four states attended a conference at The Hague in 1989 at the end of which the Declaration of the Hague was issued. This declaration points out that most of the deleterious emissions originate in industrialized countries, which therefore have special obligations in this respect. It recommends the creation of a new institutional authority within the framework of the UN which will be responsible for combating any further global warming of the atmosphere.[89]

The above provisions create a number of important institutional mechanisms, though treaty obligations in relation to climatic change will be imposed only on states which become parties to an international convention still to be adopted. It may, however, be asked whether the principle established in the *Trail Smelter* arbitration[90] (previously discussed) could not also be applicable to damage caused by emissions which produce climatic change (or, for that matter, ozone-layer depletion) as a matter of international customary law.

9.3.1.3 *Harmful products*

As pointed out, specific legal measures on harmful products causing ozone-layer depletion have already been adopted and such measures are in the process of being formulated for harmful products which induce climatic change. The general problem of

[80] Text at 1989 (28) *ILM* 1335.
[81] See 1990 (29) *ILM* 217.
[82] A Res 42/184.
[83] A Res 43/53. Text at 1989 (28) *ILM* 1326.
[84] Governing council decisions 14/20; 15/36. Text at 1989 (28) *ILM* 1330.
[85] Ibid.
[86] Ibid.
[87] Op cit 1327.
[88] 89/C183/03. Text at 1989 (28) *ILM* 1306.
[89] Text at 1989 (28) *ILM* 1308.
[90] United States v Canada 1941.

products harmful to health and the environment has also been the subject of attention by the UN General Assembly. A resolution was adopted that products banned for domestic consumption or sale should not be sold abroad unless a request is received from the importing country or the latter officially permits the consumption of the product.[91] Two of the sectors principally envisaged here are pesticides and pharmaceutical products.

9.3.1.4 *Hazardous waste*

The problem of transboundary movement of hazardous waste has been addressed both by the Organization for Economic Co-operation and Development (OECD) and by UNEP. The OECD Council adopted a Recommendation on Principles concerning Transfrontier Pollution in 1974,[92] a Recommendation on certain Rights of Persons affected by it in 1976[93] and a Decision and Recommendation on Transfrontier Movements of Hazardous Waste in 1984.[94] The last-mentioned provides for proper management of hazardous waste, authorization of its transportation, respect for the laws of countries through which it is conveyed or in which it is situated, co-operation between countries and the supply of information. In 1986 the Council adopted a further Decision–Recommendation on Exports of Hazardous Wastes from the OECD area.[95] This provides for the monitoring of such exports, for the same control measures on exports to non-OECD members as to OECD member countries and for the prohibition of exports to non-members unless there is an adequate disposal facility in the country of destination.

Within the framework of the UNEP Programme the Basel Convention on the Control of Transboundary Movements of Hazardous Wastes and their Disposal was adopted in 1989.[96] The Convention includes obligations with respect to the production, management and movement of hazardous waste. It will provide a comprehensive regime when it comes into force, especially if the majority of industrialized countries are party to it.

9.3.1.5 *Nuclear pollution*

(a) Accidents. The risk of nuclear accident, with consequent damage through fall-out, has led to the adoption of the Convention on Assistance in case of Nuclear Accident or Radiological Emergency 1986 and the Convention on the Early Notification of a Nuclear Accident 1986. The Chernobyl accident, which also occurred in 1986, prompted the Board of Governors of the International Atomic Energy Agency to make certain decisions relevant to such cases.[97]

(b) Nuclear weapons and weapons testing. The development of nuclear weapons, the arms race, and the resulting 'overkill' capacity have brought home the devastating potential of modern weaponry. Not only human life but also the quality of life and the environment are directly endangered. Various efforts have been made to curtail the effects of weapons testing and to control the increase and proliferation of these weapons. The following discussion deals with some agreements in this field (some of them are not primarily concerned with environmental protection).

(i) *Nuclear weapons tests.* The Treaty Banning Nuclear Weapon Tests in the

---

[91] A Res 37/137. Text at 1983 (22) *ILM* 683.
[92] Text at 1975 (14) *ILM* 242.
[93] Text at 1976 (15) *ILM* 1218.
[94] Text at 1984 (23) *ILM* 214.
[95] Text at 1986 (25) *ILM* 1010.
[96] Text at 1989 (28) *ILM* 657.
[97] IAEA. Statement summarizing decisions taken at the special session of the board of governors concerning the Chernobyl nuclear accident. Text at 1986 (25) *ILM* 1009.

Atmosphere, in Outer Space and Under Water was originally concluded between the USA, USSR and UK in 1963. France and China, also nuclear powers, did not become parties to the Treaty. The agreement bans the testing of nuclear weapons in the atmosphere, outer space, under water or 'in any other environment' if such explosion causes radioactive debris to be present outside the territory of the testing state.[98] Other nuclear tests such as underground testing are, however, not banned. So-called 'peaceful' nuclear tests also fall within the ambit of the agreement.

(ii) *Other arms control.* The Treaty on the Prohibition of the Emplacement of Nuclear Weapons and other Weapons of Mass Destruction on the Sea-bed and the Ocean Floor and the Subsoil Thereof 1971, the Treaty on Non-Proliferation of Nuclear Weapons 1968 and the Convention on the Prohibition of the Development, Production and Stockpiling of Bacteriological and Toxic Weapons and on their Destruction 1972 are all indirectly relevant, as environmental hazards will result from accidents involving these weapons.

(iii) *Nuclear-free zones.* Attempts have been made to declare certain regions of the world to be nuclear-free zones, eg the South Pacific Nuclear Free Zone Agreement 1985.

(iv) *Outer space.* The Treaty on Principles Governing the Activities of States in the Exploration and Use of Outer Space, Including the Moon and Other Celestial Bodies of 1967 provides that spacecraft in orbit may not carry, or place in orbit, nuclear weapons or other weapons of mass destruction.[99] The Agreement Governing the Activities of States on the Moon and Other Celestial Bodies 1979[100] prohibits weapons testing, military installations and the placing of nuclear and other weapons of mass destruction on the moon.

9.3.1.6 *Pollution of Antarctica*

The Antarctic Treaty of 1959 lays down that this region shall be used only for peaceful purposes (meteorological and other scientific research is an important activity) and prohibits nuclear explosions and the disposal of radioactive waste. Several countries have been showing intense interest in this area. The Basel Convention on the Control of Transboundary Movements of Hazardous Wastes and their Disposal 1989 (previously discussed) prohibits the export of such wastes to Antarctica.

Antarctica has also been described as a region of untapped wealth. Vast reserves of coal have been detected, as well as iron ore, and it is believed that platinum, nickel, copper, chromium, cobalt and gold may be found there too.[101] It is also thought to have large reserves of oil and gas. Activities aimed at exploiting these natural resources could conceivably pose pollution problems for the unique Antarctic environment. The Convention on the Regulation of Antarctic Mineral Resource Activities 1988[102] contains detailed provisions aimed at protecting that environment,[103] but it has not yet come into force and is unlikely to do so in the near future as it is to be re-opened for discussion at the request of two of the negotiating states.

9.3.1.7 *Pollution of space and from space*

Under the Treaty Governing the Activities of States in the Exploration and Use of Outer Space, Including the Moon and Other Celestial Bodies 1967 activities in outer space must not contaminate the environment of the earth or of celestial bodies.

Under the Agreement Governing the Activities of States on the Moon and Other

---

[98] Article I.

[99] Akehurst *A modern introduction to international law* (1982) 288 is of the opinion that spacecraft in orbit may be used for other military purposes.

[100] Text at 1979 (6) *ILM* 1434.

[101] *South* April 1982 12.

[102] Text at 1988 (27) *ILM* 868.

[103] See, eg, arts 10, 13, 15, 34, 39(2)*(c)*, 41(1), 44(2)*(b)*(iii)(iv), 47*(b)(c)*, 51(1), 52(2), 53(3)*(b)*.

Celestial Bodies 1979 the moon's environment should not be disrupted or contaminated. States should also take measures to avoid harming the earth's environment as a result of the introduction of extraterrestial matter.[104]

9.3.2 Conservation of natural resources

9.3.2.1 *Marine living resources*

Environmental conservation entails the prevention and combating of pollution and the conservation of resources and species. There are minimum reproductive levels below which living resources should not be permitted to drop. Conservation agreements therefore frequently aim at the objective of 'optimum sustainable yield' which is determined by biological and other scientific criteria.[105] Here the emphasis is in the first instance on conservation, as is the case with most agreements dealing with the conservation of marine resources. There are, however, also endangered species to which different considerations apply.

International agreements on the conservation of the seas date back to the 1940s. In 1946 the Convention for the Regulation of the Meshes of Fishing Nets and the Size Limits of Fish was adopted. Several states began to proclaim fishery conservation zones unilaterally, a controversial measure. These were broad zones covering areas of the high seas and the aim was to prevent other nations from fishing in them. In terms of the freedom of the seas, however, all states are entitled to its use (which includes fishing) and such unilateral conservation measures have therefore met with resistance. On the other hand, treaty arrangement may provide a reasonably stable level of exploitation due to a negotiated distribution of marine resources. A great number of regional conservation agreements have been concluded and provide for some of the more successful arrangements of this kind (examples of which will be mentioned later when regional arrangements are discussed).

Today the concept of fishery conservation zones is clearly accepted as a principle of customary international law and the adoption of the EEZ concept, furthermore, has a direct bearing on conservation. In terms of this concept a coastal state obtains jurisdiction over a vast area formerly considered part of the high seas. Article 56 of LOSC speaks of 'sovereign rights for the purpose of exploring and exploiting, conserving and managing the natural resources' of this area. LOSC imposes a duty on coastal states to conserve the living resources of their EEZs, which means maintaining or restoring populations of harvested species at levels which can produce the maximum sustainable yield.[106] There are also detailed provisions on the utilization of living resources, stocks occurring in the EEZs of two states, highly migratory species, marine mammals, anadromous stocks, catadromous stocks and sedentary species.[107] LOSC goes on to impose conservation and management duties on states also on the high seas: they must take conservation measures for their own nationals on the high seas, co-operate with other states and take various criteria into account when establishing conservation measures.[108] There are also important provisions relating to particular species.

(a) Whales. The protection of Cetaceans has aroused much international attention. The International Convention for the Regulation of Whaling provides for the International Whaling Commission (IWC). This body comprises the states party to this Convention and adopts regulations which member countries have to implement with

---

[104] Article 7.

[105] Schneider *World of public order of the environment* (1979) 54. The objective of 'maximum sustainable yield' has often proved to be unrealistic and undesirable.

[106] Article 61.

[107] Articles 62–68.

[108] Articles 116–120.

respect to their nationals. These regulations deal with protected species, open and closed seasons and waters, sanctuary areas, size limits, methods and intensity of whaling, gear specifications and statistical and biological records.

The Commission cannot prescribe restrictions as to the number or nationality of factory ships, or land stations, and must take into account the interests of the whaling industry. Self-regulation is therefore the fact that determines the success or failure of this arrangement. The membership of the IWC traditionally consisted of states actively engaged in whaling; however, during the last decade this position changed, and the majority of IWC member states are now states that are not actively engaged in the activity. In view of the pressure exerted by conservationists a decision was taken at the IWC's annual meeting in 1982 to introduce a zero quota for all commercially exploitable whaling species as from 1985–86, but four member states objected to the IWC decision and consequently were not bound by it.

Pressure mounted, however, for the observance of the IWC Moratorium. The matter gave rise to litigation in United States' courts, which held that the US authorities were not obliged to sanction Japan for breaking the moratorium by halving its allotment of fish.[109] Later the US imposed sanctions on Norway and threatened to impose them on Iceland, Japan and Korea.[110] These actions had results—Norway agreed to stop commercial whaling in 1987;[111] Japan announced that it would observe the moratorium from the beginning of 1988;[112] Iceland concluded an agreement with the US on whaling for scientific purposes which came into effect in 1987;[113] Japan later commenced taking whales in Antarctic waters as part of a research expedition and the US sanctioned Japan by reducing its fishing allocation in the USA EEZ by one half.[114] At the meetings of the Scientific Committee of IWC in 1988 proposals by Iceland and Norway relating to research takes were rejected as not complying with IWC criteria. Japan proposed to the same committee that the introduction of a new category 'small-type whaling' should be examined which would apply to coastal whaling and would lie somewhere between the two other categories, aboriginal whaling (permitted) and commercial whaling (prohibited).[115]

The above events indicate that the ban on commercial whaling is now almost universally observed. Loopholes remain, however, in that research taking and aboriginal takes are still permissible.

South Africa's whaling industry ceased to function during 1975. It is an offence to catch, kill or disturb the breeding season of any whale within South Africa's 200 nautical miles fishing zone, which can, for all practical purposes, now be regarded as a whale reserve.

(b) Seals. The Interim Convention on Conservation of North Pacific Fur Seals brings sealing nations together in a North Pacific Fur Seal Commission which has the duty of preventing extensive killing, and of promoting research. Self-regulation dominates this mechanism, and its decisions and recommendations must be unanimous. There is also the Convention for the Conservation of Antarctic Seals.

(c) Antarctic krill. Krill is a protein-rich shrimp-like living resource found in Antarctic waters. It may become an important source of food.

Competition for influence in Antarctica has increased, with several countries claiming sovereign rights over certain sectors while others, especially the developing nations,

---

[109] 1986 (4) *Sea Changes* 21–2.
[110] 1987 (5) *Sea Changes* 24–5.
[111] Op cit 25.
[112] 1987 (6) *Sea Changes* 24–5.
[113] 1988 (7) *Sea Changes* 22.
[114] 1988 (8) *Sea Changes* 17.
[115] Op cit 13–14. See, generally, on the regulation of whaling Glazewski 'The regulation of whaling in international and South African law' 1990–1 *South African Yearbook of International Law* 61.

demand that Antarctica should be regarded as the 'common heritage of mankind' in the same manner as the deep sea-bed and ocean floor on the high seas. Partly as a result of all these developments the Convention on the Conservation of Antarctic Marine Living Resources was adopted in 1980.[116] This provides for the conservation of all living resources in the area. 'Rational use' is permitted[117] and a Commission has been established to frame conservation measures and facilitate research. These conservation measures must be implemented by the member states, although an escape clause does exist.[118] A system of observation and inspection is also envisaged.[119] Various other international agreements relating to Antarctica (eg the Convention for the Conservation of Antarctic Seals and Antarctic Fauna and Flora of 1972) will remain in force.

9.3.2.2 *Marine non-living resources*

Section 3 of Part XI of LOSC deals with the question of 'Development of Resources of the Area', the 'area' being the deep sea-bed. LOSC regulates the exploitation of deep sea-bed minerals by requiring authorization by the International Sea-bed Authority. Policies aimed at achieving rational production are laid down. As pointed out previously, LOSC is not yet in force and it is doubtful whether the relevant provisions of Part XI here are declaratory of international customary law.

9.3.2.3 *Antarctic mineral resources*

Detailed provisions aimed at the orderly and responsible exploitation of the resources in question are included in the Convention on the Regulation of Antarctic Mineral Resource Activities 1988. As pointed out, it is unlikely that the 1988 Convention will come into force in the near future as it is under reconsideration.

9.3.2.4 *Wild fauna and flora*

The Convention on International Trade in Endangered Species of Wild Fauna and Flora of 1973 (CITES) has as its objective the protection of all endangered animals and plants in the world. It seeks to do this by regulating the commercial exploitation of endangered species. Three categories of endangered species are recognized: those in present danger of extinction (Appendix 1 to the Convention); those species which, though not threatened with immediate extinction, may face this danger if trade in them is not controlled (Appendix II), and those endangered only in certain countries (Appendix III). Trade in the listed specimens is regulated through a system of export and import permits, certificates and reports.[120]

Among other relevant treaties are the Convention on Wetlands of International Importance Especially as Waterfowl Habitat of 1971 and the Convention on the Conservation of Migratory Species of Wild Animals of 1979.

9.3.2.5 *Destruction of cultural heritage*

The Convention Concerning the Protection of the World's Cultural and Natural Heritage was adopted by the General Conference of UNESCO in 1972 and deals with somewhat different subject-matter. It seeks to protect cultural and natural heritages of 'outstanding universal value'. In many countries, especially developing countries, the economic and scientific means necessary to undertake the required protective measures are lacking and an international arrangement has therefore become necessary.

The cultural heritage includes monuments, architectural works, archaeological structures and sites, inscriptions, buildings etc. The natural heritage includes physical,

---

[116] Article I.
[117] Article II.
[118] Article IX.
[119] Article VII.
[120] See arts 150, 151, 153.

geological and biological formations, habitats of threatened species of animals and plants, and other natural areas of outstanding universal value.

A World Heritage Committee has been established which has to consider requests for assistance. This committee also administers the World Heritage Fund.

Article 303 of LOSC imposes a duty on states to protect archaeological and historical objects found at sea. It provides that they shall co-operate in this respect. Coastal states are given the right to control traffic in such objects up to a distance of 24 nautical miles from their baselines.

9.4 REGIONAL CONVENTIONS

Many of the general principles of environmental law have been implemented by conventions concluded at the regional level. In addition, states in particular regions have also concluded conventions dealing with particular problems in the region. There is a vast number of such conventions and here it is proposed merely to give some examples.

LOSC envisages the implementation of provisions to protect the environment through regional co-operation.[121] It preserves the status of specific environmental conventions concluded before LOSC and it provides that those concluded afterwards should 'be carried out in a manner consistent with the general principles and objectives of this Convention'.[122] It should again be emphasized here that LOSC is not yet in force. Apart from general provisions on the marine environment,[123] LOSC also contains rules on particular geographical areas, namely 'Enclosed or semi-enclosed seas'[124] and 'ice-covered areas'.[125] Examples of specific regional conventions will now be given.

9.4.1 The environment of a region in general

The *Nordic* Convention on the Protection of the Environment 1974, the Convention for the Protection of the Natural Resources of the *South Pacific* Region 1986 with its Protocol concerning Co-operation in Combating Pollution Emergencies in the South Pacific Region and the *Latin American* Summit Declaration of Brazilia on the Environment 1990 are examples of conventions dealing with this.

9.4.2 The marine environment of the region in general

This is the subject-matter of the Convention on the Protection of the Marine Environment of the *Baltic Sea* area 1974, the Convention for the Protection of the *Mediterranean Sea* against Pollution 1976, the Convention for the Protection and Development of the Marine Environment of the *Wider Caribbean* Region 1983 (the Cartagena Convention), the Convention for Cooperation in the Protection and Development of the Marine and Coastal Environment of the *West and Central African* Region 1981, the Regional Convention for the Conservation of the *Red Sea and Gulf of Aden* Environment 1982, the Convention for the Protection and Management of the Marine Environment in the *Eastern African* Region 1985 and the Ministerial Declaration calling for a reduction of Pollution of the *North Sea* 1987.

9.4.3 Oil pollution

Examples of regional conventions here include the Agreement for Co-operation in Dealing with Pollution of the *North Sea* by Oil 1969, the *Nordic* Agreement concerning

---

[121] See Part XII Section 2.
[122] Article 237.
[123] Contained in Part XII.
[124] Part IX.
[125] Part XII Section 8.

Co-operation in Measures to deal with Pollution of the Sea by Oil 1971, the Protocol concerning Co-operation in Combating Pollution of the *Mediterranean Sea* by Oil and Other Harmful Substances in Cases of Emergency 1976, the Protocol concerning Regional Co-operation in Combating Pollution of the *Red Sea* and *Gulf of Aden* by Oil and Other Harmful Substances in Cases of Emergency 1982 and the Protocol concerning Co-operation in Combating Oil Spills in the *Wider Caribbean* Region 1983.

9.4.4 Nuclear pollution

The OAU Council of Ministers resolution on Dumping of Nuclear and Industrial Waste in *Africa* 1988 and the *South Pacific* Nuclear Free Zone Agreement 1985 are examples of instruments which deal with nuclear questions in particular regions.

9.4.5 Dumping

The Protocol for the Prevention of Pollution of the *Mediterranean Sea* by Dumping from Ships and Aircraft 1976 and the Protocol for the Prevention of Pollution of the *South Pacific* Region by Dumping 1986 are examples.

9.4.6 Pollution from land-based sources

The Protocol for the Protection of the *Mediterranean Sea* against Pollution from Land-based Sources 1980 is an example.

9.4.7 Specially protected areas

The Protocol on Protection concerning *Mediterranean* Specially Protected Areas in 1982 is an example.

9.4.8 Rivers

The Agreement on an Action Plan for the Environmentally Sound Management of the Common *Zambezi River* System 1987 concluded between Botswana, Mozambique, Tanzania, Zambia and Zimbabwe and the *Amazon* Declaration 1989 of Bolivia, Brazil, Columbia, Ecuador, Guyana, Peru, Surinam and Venezuela are examples.

9.4.9 Conservation of culture

The Council of *Europe* Convention for the Protection of the Architectural Heritage of Europe 1985 is an example.

9.4.10 Fisheries conservation

Examples of regional conservation conventions include the *North East Atlantic* Fisheries Convention 1959, the Fisheries Convention 1964 (*Europe*), the Convention for the Conservation of Salmon in the *North Atlantic Ocean* 1982, the Treaty on *South Pacific* Fisheries 1987 and the Convention on the Conservation of the Living Resources of the *Southeast Atlantic* 1969.

9.4.11 Particular provisions

States also regulate environmental matters of local concern by treaty. The following are a few examples: the Agreement (between *Denmark* and *Sweden*) concerning the Protection of the Sound from Pollution 1974; the Agreement (between the *United States* and *Mexico*) on Co-operation for the Protection and Improvement of the Border Area 1983; the Agreement on Co-operation regarding International Transport of Urban Pollution 1989 (Annex V to the previously mentioned Agreement); the Agreement (between the *United States* and *Mexico*) on Co-operation for the Protection and Improvement of the Environment in the Metropolitan Area of Mexico City 1989.

9.5 GENERAL APPROACHES TO THE ENVIRONMENT

The international legal response to environmental problems was initially an ad hoc and individualistic one, one that lacked a clear legal policy and an administrative framework. Traditional concepts have had to be applied in circumstances for which they were inadequate. Principles of customary international law (e g the freedom of the high seas) emphasized state freedom and illustrated the limitations inherent in such an approach.

The UN Conference on the Human Environment 1972,[126] which was convened in Stockholm, helped to change the rather vague and fragmentary approach by providing a framework of principles in terms of which the problem could be tackled in its totality and establishing a new international organization, the United Nations Environment Programme (UNEP), whose task it is to promote environmental conservation, research and co-operation.

The Conference adopted 26 principles and an Action Plan in the form of recommendations for action to be taken by governments and international organizations. The principles constitute a milestone in the development of international environmental law.

9.5.1 The declaration of principles

The Declaration cannot in itself be regarded as a binding document, for while some principles were couched in obligatory language, others dealt with aspirations or contained political guidelines. Most of them required national legislation and action in order to be fully implemented.

Principles 21 and 22 are generally considered to contain elements of contemporary international law.

Principle 21:

> 'States have, in accordance with the Charter of the United Nations and principles of international law, the sovereign right to exploit their own resources pursuant to their own environmental policies, and the responsibility to ensure that activities within their jurisdiction or control do not cause damage to the environment of other states or of areas beyond the limits of national jurisdiction.'

This principle touches upon the thorny issue of the relationship between development (sovereignty over national resources) and environmental protection.

Principle 22:

> 'States shall co-operate to develop further the international law regarding liability and compensation for the victims of pollution and other environmental damage caused by activities within the jurisdiction or control of such states to areas beyond their jurisdiction.'

9.5.2 The Nairobi Declaration 1982

On the tenth anniversary of the Stockholm Conference the members of UNEP convened in Nairobi and reviewed the progress made in implementing the Action Plan. Their findings were adopted in the Nairobi Declaration.[127]

By then the international community had become more aware of the interrelationship between the environment, development, population growth and urbanization, but management, assessment and co-operation were now required. In this respect the plight of the developing countries was central to the international environmental problem.

9.5.3 The World Charter for Nature

This is annexed to a resolution of the UN General Assembly adopted in 1982[128] and contains General Principles. For instance, nature is to be respected and protected against warfare and other hostile activities, conservation must be practised, the

---

[126] For background information to this conference, see, inter alia, Timagenis *International control of marine pollution* vol 1 (1980) 83 and Goldie above n 7, 110ff.

[127] Text at 1982 (21) *ILM* 676.

[128] A Res 37/7.

reproductive capacity of organisms and ecosystems must be respected and responsibilities in the use of resources and for the discharge of pollutants must be exercised. Implementation of the Charter had to take place through national legislation and action because being part of a resolution of the General Assembly, it is not in itself legally binding. However, state support for the norms in the Charter could transform them into customary international law.

9.5.4 OECD approaches

OECD has also adopted certain general approaches to environmental questions. One may refer to the following measures of a horizontal character: the Clarification of Environment Concerns in OECD-Guidelines for Multinational Enterprises 1985;[129] the Council Recommendation concerning an Environmental Checklist for Development Assistance 1989;[130] the Council Recommendation on the Application of the Polluter-pays Principle to Accidental Pollution 1989.[131]

9.6 CONCLUSION

For centuries 'pollution was inflicted on a generous but helpless environment'.[132] This was compatible with the laissez-faire character of traditional international law. But pollution came to bear a social cost—and therefore became a political issue. Many states threatened unilateral action and suddenly the law of nations was taken from the shelf, dusted, and looked to as part of the answer.

One of the most important changes has been a movement away from traditional views about the sovereignty of states and the lack of legal control over their activities both within their territory and in the commons, such as on the high seas. Suddenly states became aware of their interdependence and the commons were declared the common heritage of all mankind.

International environmental law is still in its formative period and leaves much to be desired. It abounds with escape clauses and exceptions, but this is no fault of the law. Sovereign states are the legislature; they make the law as they want it to be. Thus many international norms are either phrased as broad general principles or are devoted primarily to procedural matters.[133] It is not difficult to understand the frustration of those who want immediate and effective action on environmental conservation; in particular, they point out the neglect that has occurred for so long. The creation of legal norms is, however, a process that requires many inputs—both from citizens and business concerns who lobby and from diplomatic conferences. We should therefore focus not only on the outcome but also on the process and the inputs when we try to assess the impact of international law as a protector of the environment.

There are also many non-legal factors that affect the development of international environmental law. Pollution is only one element in economic and technological process; business interests are involved and business will endeavour to protect its interests, particularly since anti-pollution measures are expensive; states have competitive interests and will only compromise when forced to do so or when convinced that their best interests will be served. At a basic level, therefore, ecological and economic systems seem to be in conflict.[134]

The volume of environmental law is nevertheless steadily growing as conventions are adopted, eventually come into force and receive increasing numbers of ratifications.

---

[129] Text at 1986 (25) *ILM* 494.
[130] Text at 1989 (28) *ILM* 1314.
[131] Text op cit at 1320.
[132] M'Gonigle & Zacher above n 27, 255.
[133] Jackson *World trade and the law of GATT* (1969) 13.
[134] M'Gonigle & Zacher above n 27, 313.

Important milestones are the Intervention Conventions which allow states to intervene on the seas beyond their own zones when threatened by major pollution; the London Dumping Convention 1972 prohibiting with various degrees of severity the intentional dumping of certain substances; MARPOL 1973 with its provisions on different kinds of discharges; the Convention on Long Range Transboundary Air Pollution 1979; the Vienna Convention on the Ozone Layer 1985; the Montreal Protocol on Substances that Deplete the Ozone Layer 1987; LOSC 1982; the Basel Convention on the Transboundary Movements of Hazardous Wastes 1989. No doubt environmental law will continue to expand and new milestones will be created as new conventions are adopted—a convention on climatic change may, for instance, be the next important milestone.

The outstanding characteristic of international environmental law is that it restrains the permissive concepts of sovereignty and national autonomy in many respects. It increasingly limits the traditional freedoms of the State, including the 'freedom' to pollute.

TABLE 9.1

International environmental conventions to which South Africa is a party

Convention relative to the Preservation of Fauna and Flora in their Natural State, 8 November 1933 (London).

International Convention for the Regulation of Whaling, 2 December 1946 (Washington).

International Plant Protection Convention, 6 December 1951 (Rome).

Convention on the Territorial Sea and Contiguous Zone, 29 April 1958 (Geneva).

Convention on the Continental Shelf, 29 April 1958 (Geneva).

Convention on Fishing and Conservation of the Living Resources of the High Seas, 29 April 1958 (Geneva).

Convention on the High Seas, 29 April 1958 (Geneva).

The Antarctic Treaty, 1 December 1959 (Washington).

Treaty Banning Nuclear Weapon Tests in the Atmosphere, in Outer Space and Under Water, 5 August 1963 (Moscow).

International Convention for the Conservation of Atlantic Tunas, 14 May 1966 (Rio de Janeiro).

Convention on the Conservation of the Living Resources of the Southeast Atlantic, 23 October 1969 (Rome).

International Convention on Civil Liability for Oil Pollution Damage, 29 November 1969 (Brussels).

International Convention relating to Intervention on the High Seas in Cases of Oil Pollution Casualties, 29 November 1969 (Brussels).

Convention on Wetlands of International Importance Especially as Waterfowl Habitat, 2 February 1971 (Ramsar).

Convention on the Conservation of Antarctic Seals, 1 June 1972 (London).

Convention on the Prevention of Marine Pollution by Dumping of Wastes and Other Matter, 29 December 1972 (London, Mexico, Moscow, Washington).

Convention on International Trade in Endangered Species of Wild Fauna and Flora, 3 March 1973 (Washington).

International Convention for the Prevention of Pollution from Ships, 2 November 1973 (London).

Convention on the Conservation of Antarctic Marine Living Resources, 20 May 1980 (Canberra).

Convention for the Protection of the Ozone Layer, 22 March 1985 (Vienna).

Protocol on Substances that deplete the Ozone Layer, 16 September 1987 (Montreal).

CHAPTER 10

SOIL

E VERSTER
W DU PLESSIS
B H A SCHLOMS
R F FUGGLE

10.1 INTRODUCTION

Between 80 and 85 per cent of the surface area of South Africa is devoted to agriculture[1] and some 1,5 million households are directly dependent on agricultural production.[2] The country's soil supports this activity and is thus one of the most fundamental of the natural resources which sustain economic development and human wellbeing in South Africa. Unfortunately there is considerable evidence and general agreement that South African soils are deteriorating due to poor management practices.[3] The most serious threats to the resource are erosion, compaction, acidification, salinization, and infestation by weeds and pathogens. Before these problems are considered further, the nature and properties of soil will be considered, as well as the basis for the very useful South African soil classification system.

10.2 WHAT IS SOIL?[4]

When rocks are exposed to the atmosphere and living organisms, they undergo different kinds of weathering. The weathered debris accumulates on the earth's surface and in time organic materials become mixed with mineral matter. This is the way a true soil (a mixture of mineral and organic matter) is formed. A true soil is therefore a product of the living environment as opposed to mere weathered rock, a recent sand dune devoid of vegetation, or a recent deposit of river-borne sand. There is thus no true soil on the moon, because there is no life—although some people term the loose rock material on the moon's surface 'lunar soil'.

The term 'soil' can have different meanings to different people. For the farmer, rancher, forester, gardener and landscape architect, soil is the natural medium for plant growth. This meaning is probably the most common. The greatest interest in soil is probably because of its role as a growth medium for plants. Soil is also important as an engineering material to support buildings and roads, as landfill for waste disposal, as a dam-building material, as a medium to purify effluent, and so.

For the purposes of this chapter, soil is defined as a naturally occurring, terrestrial, three-dimensional body containing unconsolidated mineral and organic materials,

---

1 85 per cent as per Terblanche quoted by Du Plessis 'Grond as 'n natuurlike hulpbron in die RSA' 1987 (1) *Fert Soc S Afr J* 53–67; 83 per cent as per *Building the foundation for sustainable development in South Africa* National report to the United Nations Conference on Environment and Development (UNCED), prepared by the CSIR for the Department of Environment Affairs (1992).

2 UNCED report above n 1.

3 See Du Plessis 'Grondagteruitgang' 1986 (5) *SA Tydskrif vir Natuurwetenskap en Tegnologie* 126–38; UNCED report above n 1.

4 Detailed notes and references will not be provided for this basic material; the interested reader is referred to standard texts such as Buol et al *Soil genesis and classification* (2 ed, 1980) and Froth *Fundamentals of soil science* (7 ed, 1984).

supporting or capable of supporting land plants. Soils are modified by man and conditioned by relief over long periods of time, and have specific properties determined by the integrated effect of climate and living matter acting upon their parent materials.

In summary, soils are complex bio-geochemical materials on the land surface, with morphological, physical, chemical and biological properties that distinguish them from the materials from which they originate.

10.2.1 Components of soil

All soils consist of solid materials and pore space, both of which occur in different sizes and are organized in definite arrangements. As defined, soil is a mixture of rock debris and organic materials. Soil therefore has two kinds of solid components: inorganic minerals derived from weathered rocks and organic materials derived from plants, micro-organisms and animals. In addition, soil contains water and air which fill the pore spaces (the voids between the solid particles). Soil can thus be referred to as a three-phase medium, consisting of soil, liquid and gaseous fractions.

The relative proportions of the three phases vary considerably from one soil to another and even within a soil. In a loamy soil, for example, the solid phase makes up about 50 per cent of the total volume and air and water the remainder. Such soil would be called a mineral soil, because it consists predominantly of mineral matter. By definition, mineral or inorganic soils contain less than 15 per cent organic matter. Such soils comprise the majority of soils in southern Africa. On the other hand, organic soils, containing more than 15 per cent organic matter, are rare and cover less than 1 per cent of the earth's land surface.

10.2.1.1 *The mineral fraction*

Rocks decompose when exposed to water, air and organisms in the processes of weathering. Weathering causes the separation of the rocks' individual mineral particles and their alteration, destruction, or resynthesis to form new minerals. Sometimes water and wind transport the weathered material and deposit it in other localities. But whether it is removed or left in place (when it is called 'residual'), the weathered rock becomes the parent material in which mineral soils form.

A mineral is defined as a naturally occurring element or compound formed by inorganic processes and having a definite chemical composition and crystalline structure. Most of the earth's minerals are aggregated or clustered into types of rock. For example, granite is a common rock type that is composed predominantly of the minerals quartz, mica, and orthoclase and plagioclase feldspars. When affected by weathering, granite is broken down into smaller rock fragments and eventually into the individual minerals (eg quartz) that make up the mineral fraction of soils. These minerals can undergo further disintegration and decomposition (processes of weathering) to form weathering products. Clay minerals, compounds of iron and aluminium, and dissolved substances are the most important weathering products.

Clay minerals occur as small particles (smaller than 0,002 mm diameter) that stick to one another and also to other particles. Water, organic compounds and plant nutrients adhere to surfaces because they are surface active. This special property is ascribed to their colloidal nature, which, in turn, is the result of a large surface area per unit of mass. A soil's colloids are its active solid ingredients and in many soils, especially mineral soils, the dominant colloids are the clay minerals. The two most important types are the non-swelling clays (eg kaolinite) and the swelling clays (eg the smectitic group). Some important properties of soils, such as swell–shrink potential, cation exchange capacity and water-holding capacity, are consequently derived from the types of clay mineral present.

10.2.1.2 *The organic fraction*

Although the bulk of most soils consists of minerals, it is the presence of organisms and organic matter that makes soil essentially different from geological minerals. The organic matter is derived from plant and animal substances—which, apart from their small amounts of mineral matter, are made up largely of carbon, nitrogen and water. It is responsible for the brown or black colour of topsoils.

Living in the soil are organisms of many kinds: plants, bacteria, fungi, algae, small animals, worms and insects. Of these, plants, bacteria and fungi are especially important to soil formation. Plants, for example, in the process of photosynthesis, produce the organic compounds that feed the other organisms and man. The bacteria and fungi are the principal destroyers, decayers and decomposers of organic matter. During the decay process, relatively large and complex molecules are formed that remain in the soil as resistant by-products. These are called humus. Humus also has colloidal characteristics and consequently exhibits properties such as water-retention, nutrient-retention and cohesion that complement those of clay minerals.

The organic fraction thus plays an important role in soils. It furnishes essential plant nutrients such as nitrogen, phosphorus, potash and sulphur, while during the process of decomposition, organic acids (e g fulvic acid) are formed which aid in the solution of soil materials (all nutrients have to be in solution in order to be available to plants). Organic matter is essential to the existence of those micro-organisms in soil which decompose it. Soils containing appreciable quantities of organic matter have a greater water-holding capacity and cation exchange capacity. Owing to its cohesive property, the presence of organic material promotes a favourable structure in soils which, in turn, is favourable to cultivation and plant growth.

10.2.1.3 *Size and organization of particles*

Most soils are composed of mineral particles of different sizes: large particles called gravel or stones, smaller ones termed sand, still smaller ones called silt and finally submicroscopic clay (see Table 10.2 for size classes). The proportions of each size fraction determine the soil's texture: coarse (gravelly or sandy), medium (loamy) or fine (clayey). Soil texture therefore refers to particle size, whereas soil structure refers to particle arrangement.

In most soils (except very sandy soils) individual particles are grouped together into structural units or aggregates of varying size, form and strength. The adhesive agents are mainly clay and humus (e g humic gums such as polysaccharide). The presence of structure distinguishes most soils from weathered rock or other geological materials; the part it plays in soil behaviour can be ascribed to its influence on the spaces (pores or voids) within and between the aggregates.

10.2.1.4 *Soil pores, liquids and gases*

Picture the solid mineral particles with their organic coatings (known as peds) as the soil's skeleton. The openings (pores) between the particles control the soil's ventilation, water intake, water-storage and drainage. The sizes and shapes of pores and the total pore space are important soil properties. Small intra-aggregate pores hold water and make it available to plants, but large inter-aggregate pores allow water and air movement into and from the soil.

Because soil is a three-phase system, the solid, gas and liquid phases are in close contact. In general, the air within a soil is similar to that of the open atmosphere, but enriched with carbon dioxide and deficient in oxygen (Table 10.1), owing to the effects of plant respiration.

TABLE 10.1
Composition of soil air in relation to the open atmosphere.

	% by volume	
	Soil air	Open atmosphere
Nitrogen	79,0	79,01
Oxygen	18,0–20,8	20,96
Carbon dioxide	0,5–0,65	0,03

The liquid phase (soil water or soil solution) is the solvent in which many reactions occur: it supplies water and dissolved nutrients to plants and micro-organisms. Soil water differs from rainwater because it is richer in dissolved substances and is much less free to move, owing to the attraction forces exerted by soil particles. Water occurs in soil in various relationships. These will be discussed later.

The proportions of the air and liquid phases are not constant in a soil, but fluctuate continually as water is added to or lost from the soil. When a soil is slowly saturated with water, for example, the soil pores gradually fill with water until even the largest pores are filled. When this stage is reached, the soil is said to be waterlogged or anaerobic; that is, no free oxygen is available in the soil's pores. As the water drains out through the soil and more water is lost by plant uptake and evaporation, the soil once again becomes aerobic as some pores fill with air, and oxygen is again available to plant roots.

10.2.2 The soil profile

The first important step when studying soils is to dig a pit into the land surface. Its depth will be determined by the depth of the soil itself, and this will normally vary from a few centimetres to a metre or more. Below the soil layer one encounters the relatively unaltered geological material. When the pit is dug and a vertical face exposed, a characteristic layered pattern is revealed. Each individual layer is known as a horizon and the set of layers in a single pit is called a soil profile.

A profile description is a permanent record in which each soil horizon is described individually with regard to all its morphological properties, the depth limits of each horizon, and the nature of the transition between horizons. Normally a standardized recording form is used.

For the purpose of this study, the soil profile is regarded as the basic unit in the study of soils. The soil profile is to the soil scientist what a plant association is to the botanist, or a rock formation is to the geologist. If viewed as a system, the soil profile can be used to study soil processes. Three groups of processes are important: the inputs of raw materials to the profile, the loss of materials from the profile and the reorganization of these materials within the profile. Soil profiles are the individuals in the population of soils covering the land surface and are therefore used in soil classification.

10.2.3 Soil horizons

A soil consists of one or more dynamic soil layers or soil horizons. A horizon can be defined as a layer of soil material approximately parallel to the land surface and differing from adjacent layers in one or more properties, such as colour, texture and structure. The thickness of horizons varies from a few centimetres to 50 cm or more. The number and thickness of horizons have a direct bearing on soil depth.

Horizons are identified by letter and number codes, the master horizons being the A, E, B, C and R horizons. In addition, there may be an O horizon, which is dominated by organic matter. At the surface, we normally find an A horizon of high biological activity in which organic matter accumulates and darkens the topsoil. The A horizon is also a zone of leaching through which infiltrated rainwater moves. This water dissolves soluble components and picks up colloidal particles. The E horizon (E = eluvial) is one from which significant amounts of constituents such as clay, organic matter and iron have been removed. Under certain conditions this load of dissolved and suspended material moves downwards into the lower subsoil horizons.

What happens to the material that has left the A or E horizons? Some or all may accumulate in the B horizon, the zone of accumulation or illuvial horizon. Some may leave the profile entirely and find its way into groundwater or rivers. The C horizon is a layer that is hardly affected by the soil-forming processes and lacks the properties of the other overlying horizons. It commonly consists of weathered rock and unconsolidated sediments (eg alluvium). Consolidated hard rock is represented by R (regolith) in the horizon classification system.

10.3 SOIL PROPERTIES[5]

Soil properties reflect the environment of a soil and the parent material from which it was derived. It is possible to compare soils of different areas by focusing on their properties. Three broad groups of properties may be recognized. First, those that may be seen, felt or measured in the field are known as morphological or physical properties. Standardized terminology exists in order to describe morphological properties accurately and unambiguously. The properties that are normally recorded are colour, including a description of any mottling present, texture, structure, consistence, the presence of nodules and coarse materials, and the distribution of roots.

The second group of soil properties can be determined only by laboratory analysis. These may be simple or detailed analyses, depending on the nature of the soil and the information required. Chemical properties such as soil reaction (acidity or alkalinity) and exchangeable cations are examples of laboratory-determined soil properties.

The third group of soil properties are those that cannot be seen or felt, but can be inferred from the morphological and chemical properties on the basis of experience and an appreciation of soil formation. For example, the darkness of the topsoil colour may give a good indication of the amount of organic matter present, and the presence of mottling is usually indicative of a seasonally fluctuating water table.

10.3.1 Morphological or physical soil properties

10.3.1.1 *Soil depth*

Whereas the land surface is the soil's upper limit, the lower limit of a soil is defined by the depth to which weathering has been effective or by the depth of the root penetration, or both.

Decisions as to the depth of a soil are easy to make in some places and difficult in others. Obviously, solid rock is not soil, but in some places the boundary between rock and weathered material is irregular and not sharply defined. In other instances impermeable layers such as a dense claypan or hardpan restrict soil depth and hence root growth.

The depth of a soil is an important property. For plant growth, in agriculture for example, a reasonable depth is a prerequisite for optimum yields. The suitability of an area for the layout of a cemetery will depend on the depth of its soils.

10.3.1.2 *Soil colour*

A striking property of many soils is their colour. Soil colour often changes with depth. It also varies from place to place according to position in the landscape and parent material. Soil colour has little effect on soil behaviour, but it is particularly useful for making some qualitative predictions about a soil, such as its organic matter content,

[5] See above n 4.

drainage and aeration. Also, colour is an important aid in classifying soils. Soil colour is produced by:

- iron oxides weathered from the mineral fraction of the soil and occurring in appreciable quantities: they coat particles such as the clays and soil grains with a thin layer, causing reddish and yellowish colours in freely drained soils, and greyish and greenish stains in waterlogged soils;
- decayed organic matter (humus), which imparts a blackish or brownish layer;
- the neutral, usually pale or greyish, colours of the mineral fraction; and
- the whitish colours produced by calcium carbonate (lime).

Since organic matter content is usually very low in South African soils, colours depend mainly on the amount of iron oxides, the way these are distributed in the soil, and the drainage condition of the soil. Reddish colours usually occur in well-drained soils (aerobic conditions), because water content is not excessive and oxygen is available to oxidize the iron. In soils that are poorly drained (ie anaerobic conditions), such as swampy or valley bottom soils, excessive water is usually present. Under these conditions (normally in the subsoils) the iron cannot be oxidized because oxygen is unavailable; it is therefore in a reduced state and exhibits greyish or greenish colours. In soils with intermediate drainage conditions, colours may be yellowish owing to hydrated forms of iron oxides; they also may show mottling. Mottled soils have spots or streaks of different colours interspersed with the dominant soil colour. Reddish, brownish, yellowish or greyish mottles are sometimes present in the lower part of soil profiles because of alternating reduction and oxidation of the iron compounds caused by a fluctuating water table.

Soil identification by colour is done by comparing soil samples with colour charts designed specifically for the purpose of soil description. The charts are known as Munsell Soil Colour Charts.

10.3.1.3 *Soil texture*

Soil texture refers to the size distribution of its mineral particles. Particle sizes are classified into four general categories: gravel or stones, sand, silt, and clay (Table 10.2). Although the division of particle size into discrete size ranges is arbitrary, it is useful for the careful study of soils. Furthermore, particles so different in size obviously have different properties.

TABLE 10.2
Particle-size classification.

Particle class	Diameter (mm)
Gravel and stones	greater than 2,0
Very coarse sand	2,0–1,0
Coarse sand	1,0–0,5
Medium sand	0,5–0,25
Fine sand	0,25–0,10
Very fine sand	0,10–0,05
Silt	0,05–0,002
Clay	less than 0,002

The first important subdivision in the size of soil particles is made at 2 mm diameter to separate the coarse fraction (greater than 2 mm) from the so-called soil fraction (less than 2 mm). The coarser fraction influences some important soil properties. For example, stones of more than 10 mm in diameter occupy space but do not contribute space for air or water in the soil because they have no pores.

The volume of soil occupied by the coarser fraction therefore reduces the soil's capacity to hold water. The coarse fraction can also hinder cultivation and damage machinery.

Of the four size categories constituting soil, the clay fraction is the most important, because of its colloidal properties. Although clay minerals are the most abundant of the clay-sized minerals, this fraction can also contain some quartz and feldspars as well as oxides of iron and aluminium. The individual particles of the clay are too small to be seen under a normal microscope, so a high-power microscope (eg an electron microscope) must be used to detect them.

The silt fraction contains a wide range of minerals and may be examined (with some difficulty) under a normal microscope. The sand fractions may also contain a wide variety of minerals, but quartz is usually dominant. They may be examined with an ordinary hand lens or microscope.

Although, theoretically, soils may contain either 0 or 100 per cent of clay, silt or sand, such occurrences are extremely rare. Usually soils show a combination of particle sizes whose relative proportions determine the soil's texture. Since variations in texture occur continuously, soil particle size distributions have been conveniently classified into textural classes.

In the field a common method to determine soil texture is by means of 'feel', by which a moist sample of soil is rubbed between the fingers. The amount of sand, silt and clay is estimated by the sample's roughness, smoothness and stickiness respectively. In the laboratory, particle size distribution can be determined accurately in several ways, eg by the hydrometer or pipette methods.

Soil texture is an important soil property because several other soil properties are dependent on it. Sandy soils, for example, have large pores; consequently they are permeable and absorb water easily, but dry out rapidly. Their permeability also permits rapid leaching of soluble nutrients. Also, wind erosion can become a serious problem when sandy soils are bare. In contrast, clayey soils are very dense, making them difficult to cultivate. They absorb water slowly and then hold it with force. Medium-textured soils, such as loams, are of intermediate density (between sandy and clayey soils) and are usually best suited for crop growth.

10.3.1.4 *Soil structure*

'Structure' refers to the combination or arrangement of primary soil particles into compound units called aggregates or peds. Except in sand dunes, sand particles are usually attached to clay, silt and organic matter to form these peds. When most soil particles are aggregated, we say the soil has structure. Peds are described according to their shape, size, stability and the ease with which we can see them in the soil profile. Sometimes peds are strongly formed and very stable (ie have a strong structure); others fall apart when handled (ie have a weak structure). The smallest crumbs are roughly spherical, whereas the larger peds are more angular, being either blocky, elongated (prismatic) or flat (platy). The term apedal is used in the South African classification system to indicate materials that are well aggregated in a microstructure so that well-formed peds cannot be detected macroscopically.

Structure is an important morphological characteristic of soils, because it controls the size and number of pores associated with the aggregates. Structure therefore determines the rate of water infiltration, it facilitates air and water movement through the soil and controls the ease of root penetration.

10.3.1.5 *Water in the soil*

As we have seen, soil is a three-dimensional body with mineral and organic materials interspersed with pores. The total volume of pores is called porosity and is dependent on soil texture and structure. Although porosity is an important soil property, it is actually the relative size, shape and distribution of the pores that determine the movement and storage of water in a soil. Another important factor in soils is the presence of water itself. Because of the cohesion and adhesion forces of water, water molecules are attracted to one another and to solid surfaces respectively. All of these factors give rise to a complex soil–water system.

The maximum rate at which a soil can absorb water is called its infiltration capacity; this capacity depends on the soil's porosity, permeability, surface conditions and water content. However, if the rainfall intensity exceeds the infiltration capacity of the soil, overland flow will be effected. Infiltration is closely connected with the further downward movement of water in the soil, called percolation, and with the lateral movement of water known as throughflow. The rate of infiltration decreases with time, slowing to a rate equal to water flow through saturated soil.

As water percolates through the soil, molecular adhesion causes some water in the pores to cling to soil particles. Such water is held most effectively in small pores. In the large pores, adhesion is not strong enough to hold the greater masses of water against the pull of gravity, and consequently soil water drains away into groundwater. The maximum amount of water that can remain stored in a soil after gravitational water has drained away is known as the field capacity of a soil. Water held in pores in the root zone is used by plants for all growth and transpiration. For example, a plant may use more than two litres of water a day—a tremendous drain on soil water storage. After a time, the remaining soil water cannot be taken up by plant roots because it is held very tightly by the mineral and organic particles and the plant must exert considerable force through its roots to extract this water from the soil. Most plants begin to wilt when the soil water content is reduced to this level, which is called the wilting point. Field capacity and wilting point are the soil–water criteria for plant growth. They represent the upper and lower limits of soil water available for plants. The actual values differ from soil to soil, depending mainly on texture.

10.3.1.6 *Soil consistence*

Consistence refers to the degree of cohesion or adhesion within the soil mass. This is also related to its resistance to deformation or rupture. This property is important for traffic and tillage considerations. Dune sand, for example, exhibits minimal cohesion and adhesive properties. This, together with the fact that sand is easily deformed, results in vehicles getting stuck. Certain clay soils are very hard when dry and very sticky when wet, with the result that they are difficult to plough.

10.3.2 Chemical properties

The two essential things that plants absorb and remove from soil are water and nutrients. Plants will be deficient in an essential nutrient element not only when there is virtually none of the element in the soil, but also when there is a large quantity in the soil but too little of it is sufficiently soluble or available to supply plant needs. Both of these conditions have to do with the fertility or chemical behaviour of a soil, which in turn is closely related to colloidal properties and soil reaction.

10.3.2.1 *Exchange properties of soils*

Because of their colloidal properties, clay minerals (and humus to a lesser extent) are the most important constituents affecting the chemical characteristics of soils. The reason for this is their large surface area per unit mass and the fact that they are electrically charged. These properties make them highly chemically active in soils. For our purpose we can picture a clay particle as a platelike body. The molecular structure of clay minerals is such that they possess net negative charges; in other words, they have extra electrons in their atomic structure. This means that positive ions or cations will be drawn by means of electrostatic attraction to the clay particle surface (exchange complex). Because of the weak nature of this attraction, cations in solution can readily exchange places with those held on the exchange complex, in the process of cation exchange.

Ions of hydrogen (H^+), potassium (K^+), sodium (Na^+), calcium (Ca^{++}) and magnesium (Mg^{++}) are commonly found in the soil solution and are also present on clay particle surfaces. Cation exchange is regulated by a replacement order, that is, a general order of preference for replacing cations in exchange reactions. It is a kind of seniority system, in which an ion of a given rank can take over the position of ions of a lower rank. Several factors control this cation substitution order, such as charge and hydrated radius of the ion. In general, hydrogen ions can replace any of the other cations, the replacement order being H^+ Ca^{++} Mg^{++} K^+ Na^+. The significance of this principle is that, where organic acids are formed in a soil (with high rainfall and decay of organic matter), hydrogen ions will dominate the soil solution and will replace the other cations, enabling them to be leached from the soil, and acidification results.

Soils also have a cation exchange capacity (CEC), which is the total amount of exchangeable cations that can be held by a given mass of soil. Because electrical neutrality is a rule in nature, each positive charge is balanced by a negative charge. For example, Al^{+3} is missing three electrons, therefore it can balance three of the extra negative charges on the clay. CEC depends on the type and amount of clay in the soil and on the amount of organic matter present. The following sequence gives the relative magnitude of the exchange capacity of some soil colloids: organic colloids—200; montmorillonite—100; illite—30; kaolinite—8.

The significance of cation exchange is that a high value indicates that exchangeable ions are available as nutrients for plants, that they are retained in soils and not lost through leaching.

10.3.2.2 *Soil reaction*

Soil reaction refers to the acidity or alkalinity of the soil solution. Acidity is an expression of the hydrogen ion (H^+) concentration in the soil solution and is one of the most frequently measured and reported soil properties. The hydrogen ion concentration is measured in terms of the pH scale. Pure water has a pH of 7, which is regarded as neutral. Soils with concentrations below pH 7 are acid and those above 7 are basic or alkaline. Soils that are acid contain more H^+ than OH^- (hydroxyl) ions in the soil solution and the reverse applies to alkaline soils. Normally, the pH in soils ranges from about 3 to 10.

Perhaps the greatest general influence of pH on plant growth is its effect on the availability (or solubility) of nutrients. Phosphorus, for example, tends to be unavailable in alkaline soils, owing to a reaction with calcium. On the other hand, in very acid soils, phosphorus tends to be unavailable owing to the formation of insoluble complexes with aluminium. In general, the best agricultural yields are obtained from soils with pH values varying between slightly acid and neutral, because of the general solubility of most of the essential nutrients in this pH range. The pH also has an important influence on soil organisms, as some have a rather small tolerance to variations in pH. Organisms producing nitrogen, for example, become inhibited when the pH is less than 5,5. Finally, pH plays an important role in controlling the major soil processes. For example, podzolization (i e the process by which the upper layer of a soil becomes acidic through the leaching of bases which are deposited in the lower horizons) takes place in acid soils, and the intensity of weathering, especially hydration and hydrolysis, increases with more acid conditions.

Acidification (leaching of solutes) and salinization (accumulation of salts) are aspects of soil reaction that can cause major land-use problems. Acid soils occur most commonly where high rainfall and free drainage favour leaching and the biological production of acids. Saline soils with an alkaline soil reaction are most common where low rainfall, high evaporation and inadequate drainage inhibit leaching and promote the accumulation of salts.

10.4 THE BASIS OF SOIL CLASSIFICATION IN SOUTH AFRICA

Soil classification in South Africa originated in 1941, when Van der Merwe published the book *Soil groups and sub-groups of South Africa*.[6] This classification was based on the concept of zonality formulated by Russian pedologists and did not lend itself to application in the Natal Sugar Belt, where Beater[7] recognized an unmistakable relationship between soil and parent materials and consequently grouped the soils he was dealing with into *soil series* on the basis of the underlying rock types.

Soil surveys during the 1960s experimented with the United States Department of Agriculture 7th Approximation.[8] This intricate and elaborate system did not find favour in South Africa. Van der Eyk and co-workers[9] working in the Tugela Basin derived a classification system based on a combination of *soil form* and *soil series*. This classification gave planners, agronomists, soil scientists, farmers and engineers a good understanding of the properties of particular soils, it made identification easy and the terminology was rapidly taken into use in South Africa. This success led to the development and formalization of a form–series soil classification for South Africa as a whole. In 1977 the book *Soil classification—a binomial system for South Africa* was produced under the convenorship of Macvicar.[10] This classification, consisting of 41 soil forms made up of diagnostic horizons as well as 504 soil series, has become the widely used South African standard. A recent revision of the work was published in 1991.[11] It its latest form the South African soil classification systems recognizes 73 soil forms and the nomenclature of soil series has been changed to *soil family*. Soil forms provide a general level of classification and soil families provide more specific information. All soils having the same form have the same vertical sequence of diagnostic horizons[12] and materials. Forms are subdivided into families on the basis of other soil properties.[13] Each soil family has been given a geographical name and a code.

As the physical and chemical properties of each soil family are known, it follows that the soil characteristics important to agriculture and engineering will also be known if the soil family has been determined. Soil classification maps based on the South African soil classification system are therefore very useful aids. The availability of such maps for different parts of the country is steadily increasing.[14]

10.5 SOIL DEGRADATION[15]

Soil is susceptible to various types of degradation brought about by a variety of human actions. Physical, chemical and biological degradation will be considered below.

---

[6] *Science Bulletin* 231, Chemistry series no 165 Department of Agriculture and Forestry (1940).

[7] 'The soils of the sugar belt; a classification and a review' 1944 (18) *Proceedings of the SA Sugar Technology Association*.

[8] *Soil classification: a comprehensive system 7th Approximation* Soil Conservation Service, United States Department of Agriculture (1960).

[9] *Soil of the Tugela Basin*, Natal Town and Regional Planning Report vol 15 (1969).

[10] *Science Bulletin* 390, Department of Agricultural Technical Services (1977).

[11] Soil Classification Working Group *Soil classification: a taxonomic system for South Africa* Memoirs on the agricultural natural resources of South Africa no 15, Department of Agricultural Development (1991).

[12] See section 10.2.3.

[13] See sections 10.2.1 and 10.3.1.

[14] Enquiries may be made through the Soils and Irrigation Research Institute, CSIR, Private Bag X79, Pretoria.

[15] The factual material used in this section is taken largely from Du Plessis above n 3.

10.5.1 Physical degradation

10.5.1.1 *Soil erosion*

Loss of soil from a land surface is a natural process. It is only when the rate of soil loss exceeds the rate of soil formation at a given location that soil erosion is said to be occurring. In South Africa the rate of soil formation varies from 0,38 tons per hectare per year for light-textured soils to 0,25 tons per hectare per year for heavy-textured soils. For general purposes a figure of 0,31 tons per hectare per year (for medium-textured soils) is accepted. Expressed in a different way, South African soils form at an average rate of 1 mm every 40 years.[16]

Unfortunately, South African soils are susceptible to soil loss. This is due to a variety of physical factors (geology, climate, steep slopes) as well as to human use of the land. Determinations of soil loss have been attempted by several research workers using a variety of techniques.[17] There appears to be convergence close to a figure of 3 tons per hectare per year for average soil loss in South Africa. The significance of this figure is that it is ten times as great as the rate of soil formation! But the average figure is misleading. Over 30 per cent of South Africa suffers rates of soil loss in excess of 4 tons per hectare per year[18] and most cultivated soils experience losses of between 3 and 10 tons. An extreme case of soil loss of 120 tons per hectare per year has been quoted for land under pineapples.[19] Soil losses in the western Orange Free State exceeding 40 tons per hectare per year through wind erosion have been recorded[20] and over two million hectares are subject to serious wind erosion.[21] For the country as a whole, over three million hectares has been rendered unproductive as a consequence of severe soil erosion and over 60 per cent of the country's surface area is in poor condition with respect to soil erosion.[22]

Soil, one of South Africa's most basic resources, is being lost to erosion at a frightening rate: this may well be the greatest environmental problem facing South Africa, yet the South African population appears to be most complacent about it.

10.5.1.2 *Soil compaction and crusting*

Soils with a high percentage of fine sand have a tendency to compact when cultivated. It is estimated that there are over two million hectares under commercial maize production in which the formation of 'ploughpans' is reducing production by as much as 40 per cent.[23]

Crusting, or sealing of the soil surface, is a problem which occurs under conditions of inappropriate land-use, or incorrect land management. It is now recognized as a serious problem in South Africa, although its extent has not yet been fully established.[24]

An important consequence of crusting is that water-use efficiency decreases due to low infiltration rates and increased surface runoff. This is unacceptable in a country with limited water resources.

---

[16] Matthee & Van Schalkwyk *Inleiding tot gronderosie* Department of Agriculture Bulletin 339 (1984).

[17] Midgley *Preliminary survey of the surface water resources of South Africa* (unpublished PhD thesis, University of the Witwatersrand, 1952); Rooseboom 'Sedimentafvoer in Suid-Afrikaanse riviere' 1978 (4) *Water SA*; Schulze *The contribution of rainfall erosivity from thunderstorms in Natal* Proceedings of a CSIR symposium Pretoria, 1978; Biesenbach, *'n NPK-balansstaat vir die landbougrond van die RSA* Proceedings of the Nitrogen symposium, Technical Bulletin 187, Department of Agriculture (1982).

[18] Rooseboom above n 17.

[19] McPhee et al, quoted in Du Plessis above n 1.

[20] Schoeman & Scotney 'Agricultural potential as determined by soil, terrain and climate' 1987 (83) *S Afr J Sci.*

[21] Du Plessis above n 3.

[22] Bruwer, quoted by Du Plessis above n 3.

[23] Du Plessis above n 3.

[24] Du Plessis and UNCED report above n 1.

10.5.2 Chemical deterioration

10.5.2.1 *Loss of fertility*

One of the most insidious effects of soil erosion is the loss of plant nutrients that accompanies it. Du Plessis[25] has used findings of Biesenbach to calculate the value of the macro-nutrients, nitrogen, phosphate, and potash, that are lost from the South African land surface each year. He finds that in 1985 the loss amounted to R365 million: a loss of one million rands per day!

10.5.2.2 *Acidification*

Du Plessis reports that, although there is little reliable data on the extent of the problem of soil acidification in South Africa, some soil scientists regard it as one of the greatest threats facing South African commercial agriculture.[26] In 1980, over five million hectares were regarded as having a severe problem of acidification, over 10 million hectares were exhibiting tendencies towards moderate acidification, and over 10 per cent of areas under maize were experiencing acidification problems. In the South African National report to the United Nations Conference on Development and the Environment (UNCED)[27] it is estimated that some 10 per cent of the country's arable land is being negatively affected by acidification.

Acidification is caused mainly through injudicious use of nitrogen fertilizers. Excessive use decreases the soil pH (KCl) to below 5,5 (at which point moderate acidification occurs) and in extreme cases to below 4,5. At these pH levels plants are not able to take up the nutrients in the soil, and the application of fertilizers is therefore rendered ineffective. The problem must be corrected through the application of agricultural lime for cultivation potential to be restored. This is an expensive procedure when applied to large areas.

10.5.2.3 *Salinization*

Salinization occurs with overirrigation and poor drainage, especially if the quality of irrigation water has been reduced by mineralization as a consequence of industrial or sewage effluent. Alkali salts build up in the surface layers of the soil, reducing fertility and productivity. It is estimated that some 10 per cent of South Africa's irrigated lands is affected in this way.[28]

10.5.2.4 *Soil pollution*

In South Africa some 30 000 ha are being irrigated with polluted water and some 150 000 to 250 000 tons of dry sewage sludge is being disposed of per year—much of this on agricultural land.[29] A consequence of these practices is a build-up of heavy metals in affected soils. Research is being undertaken jointly by the Department of National Health and Population Development and the Council for Scientific and Industrial Research in an attempt to prevent serious problems arising in the future.

10.5.3 Biological degradation

10.5.3.1 *Invasive biota*[30]

In South Africa the introduction of alien organisms has in some cases led to the degradation of land by making it unsuitable for grazing or cultivation. The main

[25] Above n 3.
[26] Du Plessis above nn 1 and 3.
[27] Above n 1.
[28] Ibid.
[29] Ibid.
[30] See also ch 20 and Macdonald et al *The ecology and management of biological invasions in southern Africa* (1986).

organisms have proved to be jointed cactus (*Opuntia aurantiaca*), nasella tussock grass (*Stipa trichotoma*), Australian acacias (particularly *Acacia cyclops, A. longifolia* and *A. saligna*), hakeas (especially *Hakea sericia*), and pines (*Pinus halepensis, P. pinaster* and *P. radiata*). Almost one million hectares of land is infested by these species and millions of rands are spent each year in attempts to keep the problem under control.

10.5.3.2 *Eelworms and plant pathogens*

Although certain crops and areas are being severely affected by eelworm and other plant pathogens resident in soils, the full extent of the problem in South Africa has not been researched. The problems are nevertheless thought to be associated with poor agricultural practices and may thus respond to vigorous extension services.[31]

10.6 SOIL CONSERVATION LEGISLATION

10.6.1 Introduction

Legislation was introduced at an early stage in the Cape to protect cultivated gardens, lands and trees against damage and destruction.[32] Veld-burning was also prohibited.[33] These provisions, although related to soil conservation, were enacted to protect crops and trees. Possibly the first provision aimed directly at soil conservation—albeit of a very limited scope—was the obligation imposed upon landowners in 1681 to keep watercourses and furrows free from obstacles in order to prevent erosion of cultivated lands during the rainy season.[34]

It gradually became apparent that soil conservation could not be accomplished through reliance upon voluntary efforts by farmers. Conservationists began to question the validity of views which held property rights to be sacrosanct and immune to governmental interference, and which envisaged natural resources as being without limit to be used and abused by anyone for personal gain. It also became evident that since the individual landowner was not the only victim of this rape of the earth, effective legislation was necessary to restrain him.

Before 1941, however, there was no substantial legislation dealing with soil conservation. Only legislation which was indirectly related to soil conservation, such as provisions aimed at the control of grass-burning and at the conservation of trees, had been enacted.[35] Any conservation of the soil that may have resulted from this was coincidental.

---

[31] Du Plessis above n 3.

[32] See e g the Placaaten of 14 October 1652, 21 December 1653, 17 July 1657, 2/3 October 1658, 12–13 October 1658, 1/4 July 1671, 8 April/11 June 1680, and 18 October/17 November 1692. Rangers were eventually appointed to enforce the provisions (Resolution of 13 January 1693). The Cape Placaaten were, strictly speaking, ultra vires (see Visagie *Regspleging en reg aan die Kaap van 1652 tot 1806*. (1969) 63), but were de facto enforced. The section on soil conservation legislation is partly based on the chapter on soil in Fuggle & Rabie (eds) *Environmental concerns in South Africa* (1983).

[33] See e g the Placaaten of 19 November 1658, 16 December 1661, and 19/20 February 1687. A measure to prevent veld-burning which, incidentally, was recommended by the Drought Investigation Commission two-and-a-half centuries later (see the *Report of the Drought Investigation Commission* UG 49-23, 64), was already introduced in 1682 (Resolution of 23 February 1683). This was the prohibition of grazing stock in certain areas (veld-burning is practised in order to encourage the growth of a green veld). It was found that the enforcement of criminal sanctions in regard to the firing of the veld was extremely difficult, since it was almost impossible to detect and apprehend offenders. It was, however, relatively easy to enforce the prohibition of grazing stock in certain areas.

[34] Placaat of 13 May 1681.

[35] See e g Ord 5 of 1836, Ord 28 of 1846, Act 18 of 1859, Act 28 of 1888, Act 20 of 1902 and Act 20 of 1908 (Cape); Law 21 of 1865, Act 31 of 1895 and Act 18 of 1902 (Natal); Law 2 of 1870, Law 8 of 1870 and Law 15 of 1880 (Transvaal); Chapter 125 OFS Law Book of 1891 and Act 32 of 1908 (Free State). See also the Forest Act 16 of 1913 as amended by Acts 14 of 1917 and 28 of 1930.

10.6.2 Forest and Veld Conservation Act

The Forest and Veld Conservation Act 13 of 1941 was the first substantial legislation to provide for the control of soil erosion and related problems. The Act[36] provided that any land could be expropriated if, in the opinion of the Governor-General, this was required for the prevention of sand drift or soil erosion or for the protection of catchment areas or the conservation of water sources. In terms of the Act[37] any land which was considered, in the national interest, to warrant reclamation or conservation at public expense, together with such additional land as might be required for the proper conservation of the area, could be proclaimed as a conservation area. Several such areas were proclaimed before 1946.[38]

Although the Act gave the government wide powers to enforce conservation and the reclamation of land, these powers were exercised only in extreme cases.[39] The Act was, moreover, considered inadequate since it was aimed essentially at reclamation or correction rather than at soil conservation or the prevention of soil erosion.[40] Other shortcomings were the fact that the initiative for taking action rested solely with the State and that the farming community was not mobilized.[41]

10.6.3 Soil Conservation Act of 1946

The most important step in the struggle against soil erosion was the enactment of the Soil Conservation Act 45 of 1946. This Act replaced the Forest and Veld Conservation Act, in so far as the latter dealt with soil erosion control, and was designed both to remedy the shortcomings of that Act and to provide comprehensive control of action aimed at combating soil erosion. The Act, moreover, was not only intended to combat and prevent soil erosion but also provided for the conservation of vegetation and water supplies—which is logical in view of the close relationship between soil, water and vegetation.

Among the most important provisions of the Act were those dealing with the declaration of soil conservation districts upon application by landowners in a certain area,[42] and the establishment in such districts of soil conservation district committees.[43] The main task of the district committee was to prepare a soil conservation scheme[44] for land in its district[45] and to obtain each owner's consent or objections. After due notice by the Minister of Agriculture, a soil conservation scheme could be served on the landowners concerned and applied to their land.[46] The committee was required to take such steps as may have been necessary to ensure the proper implementation of the scheme.[47] The initiative for enforcement of the schemes was, in other words, left to the district committees.

The main feature of the Act was that it provided, in a democratic spirit, a basis for

---

36 Section 4.

37 Section 5.

38 *Annual report of the Secretary for Agriculture (year ended 31 August 1946)* 143ff.

39 Annual report above n 38, 142.

40 *Report of the Reconstruction Committee* GP-S-9278 (1943) 24.

41 *House of Assembly debates* 23 May 1946 8268.

42 Section 9.

43 Section 10.

44 A soil conservation scheme was a comprehensive plan designed for the reclamation of eroded land or for the prevention of soil erosion or, generally, for the conservation, protection and improvement of soil, veld and water supplies, and includes all necessary measures for the promotion of sound systems and methods of land-use. Such a scheme could include provisions relating to the temporary withdrawal from cultivation or grazing of land within a soil conservation district for specified periods, the restriction of the number or kinds of livestock which may for any specified period be grazed on such land and the regulation or prohibition of veld-burning: s 19.

45 Sections 13*(a)* and 16.

46 Section 16(5).

47 Section 13*(b)*.

co-operation between the State and the farming community in regard to soil conservation and the stimulation of conservation farming. The Act enabled farmers themselves to initiate action without waiting for the State to give the lead, and to play an active role in determining and carrying out appropriate soil conservation measures. In this respect the Act deviated completely from the Forest and Veld Conservation Act, which had been considered too authoritarian.

Sadly, the Act did not realize the high expectations that were cherished at its inception. One of the main reasons for this was the fact that it was promulgated at a stage when the great majority of South Africans were not aware of soil erosion. Although much publicity was given to the problems of soil erosion during the years immediately preceding and after the introduction of the Act, the general spirit which prevailed in South Africa until recently was one of ignorance or apathy towards environmental problems, of which soil erosion is one aspect. No law, however idealistically or strictly drawn up, can succeed against this background. In fact, it is surprising—and something to be greatly admired—that the Soil Conservation Act was placed on the statute book at all in 1946. This very spirit, however, necessitated that the Act be drawn up with democratic provisions, which hardly contributed to its enforcement against persons who were not yet ready for action on soil erosion control. Although the drastic measures provided for in the Forest and Veld Conservation Act of 1941 were taken over in the Soil Conservation Act of 1946, these were used only in very exceptional cases.

Implementation of the 1946 Act was left in the hands of the farmers themselves in that the declaration of soil conservation districts, as well as the preparation and enforcement of soil conservation schemes by district committees, were dependent upon the initiative of farmers. But experience proved that district committees composed mainly of farmer members were loath to take action against members of their own community, and a mere 21 prosecutions were instituted in terms of the Act of which 14 were successful.[48] Viewed against the background of a general lack of concern about soil erosion, it is not at all surprising that the Act failed to arrest soil erosion.[49]

10.6.4 Soil Conservation Act of 1969

In view of the failure of the Soil Conservation Act of 1946 it was decided to remedy the shortcomings by introducing new legislation. The Soil Conservation Act 76 of 1969 accordingly came into operation in 1970. One of the most important amendments was the replacement of the old soil conservation district committees by soil conservation committees (appointed by the Minister of Agriculture) which could be established for specific areas. Moreover, the new committees no longer enjoyed executive powers; their function was reduced to an advisory role and their former powers were transferred to the Division of Soil Protection of the Department of Agriculture.

Provision was no longer made for the compilation of soil conservation schemes with concomitant district and farm plans. The objects of the Act were to be realized in that the Minister[50] might by notice[51] to the owner or occupier of land[52] declare a direction to be applicable[53] to the land referred to in such notice, and take a wide

[48] *Annual report of the Soil Conservation Board* 1 July 1967–30 June 1968 20.

[49] On the reasons for the failure of the Act, see more fully Rabie *South African environmental legislation* (1976) 29–31.

[50] who was empowered to delegate his powers: s 23.

[51] Either by notice in the *Gazette* or by written notice: s 3(1).

[52] The directives were binding also upon successors in title: s 3(2).

[53] The notice could also be withdrawn, amended or suspended: s 3(3).

variety of actions connected with soil conservation.[54]

Apart from any personal direction declared to be applicable to an individual owner or occupier of land, guidelines of a general character were published for general information.[55]

A landowner could be ordered by the Minister by means of a direction[56] to construct soil conservation works if the Minister was of the opinion that the construction of such soil conservation works was necessary in order to achieve any object of the Act.[57]

An obligation was also placed upon the landowner who was ordered to construct soil conservation works to maintain these works.[58] Failure to construct or maintain soil conservation works entitled the Minister to cause such steps to be taken as he may have deemed necessary to construct or maintain the soil conservation works in question.[59] The costs involved could be recovered from such landowner.[60]

The Minister could make grants to any person in order to enable the latter to perform an act for the achievement of an object of the Act.[61] Land could be expropriated by the Minister if, in his opinion, such land was required for *(a)* the prevention of soil erosion or the stabilizing of land subject to it; *(b)* the prevention of drift sand or the stabilizing of land subject to it; or *(c)* the protection of catchment areas or the conservation of water sources.[62]

Soil conservation committees for determined areas were established by the Minister.[63] Such a committee consisted of as many members as the Minister determined and was appointed by him after consultation with the South African Agricultural Union.[64] The duties of a soil conservation committee were to advise the Minister, owner or occupier of land on all matters relating to soil conservation and to perform such other duties as the Minister assigned to it.[65]

A fire protection area[66] could be defined and declared by the Minister and a fire protection committee established for a certain area.[67] A fire protection committee had to prepare and submit to the Minister a fire protection scheme in respect of the area for which it had been established.[68]

Public attitudes towards the implementation of legislative measures aimed at soil conservation were far more favourable in 1969 than when the 1946 Act was introduced. Viewed against the background of a far greater awareness and concern over

---

[54] Section 3(1). There were, however, two provisos which limited the Minister's powers: The Minister of Mineral and Energy Affairs was to be consulted whenever a directive was to be applied to a person who carried on prospecting or mining activities on the land in question, and no directive might contain any provision which was in conflict with a provision of a fire protection scheme (in terms of s 13): s 3(1) provisos. Cf also s 3(1)*(a)*–*(m)*. Provision was made for a general clause including even directives not connected with any matter referred to in s 3(1) which the Minister considers necessary or expedient for achieving the objects of the Act in respect of the land in question: s 3(1)*(n)*.

[55] Annexure to GN R494 of 26 March 1970.

[56] Section 4(2)*(a)*(i)–(ii).

[57] Section 4(1). A subsidy could be paid to such landowner: s 6*(a)*. Cf *Minister van Landbou-Tegniese Dienste v Steyn* 1971 (2) SA 285 (O).

[58] Section 4(2A).

[59] Section 4(4). Cf also s 17.

[60] Section 4(4). Cf also s 16.

[61] Section 6*(b)*. Cf s 21(1)*(c*A*)*. Two important schemes aimed at soil conservation, the veld reclamation scheme and the stock reduction scheme, were launched in terms of the above-mentioned provision, and its predecessor in the 1946 Act. Cf also s 29*(c)*.

[62] Section 18(1)*(a)*–*(c)*.

[63] Section 9(1).

[64] Section 9(2).

[65] Section 10. Cf also ss 9(6) and 11.

[66] The boundaries of the area may be altered: s 12(5).

[67] Section 12(1)*(a)*. Cf also ss 12(1)*(b)*, 12(3) and 12(4).

[68] Section 13(1).

environmental issues, coupled with a relative weakening of the power of the rural vote, enforcement of the 1969 Act had at that time a better chance of success.

In addition, the removal of executive powers from the soil conservation committees and the vesting of these powers in the Division of Soil Protection greatly facilitated the enforcement of the Act. It was pointed out that effective enforcement of soil conservation legislation by district committees, consisting primarily of farmers, was not practicable. But the creation of the section Inspection Services, divorced from the Agricultural Extension Service, was considered to be conducive to the successful enforcement of the Act as the same people would not then be required to create a favourable climate for change and at the same time served as instruments for the prosecution of farmers.

Under the new Act soil conservation committees were no longer automatically established, but called into existence only at the request of a community, expressed through organized agriculture. Although these new arrangements meant that the farming community gained a greater share and say in the establishment of local organizations, however, the response was disappointing and requests for the establishment of only 91 committees were received by 1981. By March 1982 an additional 69 committees had been established—a total of 160 out of a possible total of about 300.

The proper enforcement of the Act depended upon co-operation by farmers primarily. However, where farmers refused to co-operate, recourse had to be had to the criminal sanctions provided by the Act. Although the 1969 Act was amended five times, it still did not solve all the problems that arose.[69]

10.6.5 Conservation of Agricultural Resources Act

10.6.5.1 *Background*

The Conservation of Agricultural Resources Act 43 of 1983 repealed the Soil Conservation Act 76 of 1969[70] and the Weeds Act 42 of 1937.

Various reasons were given for the enactment of the 1983 Act.[71] First, the State's programme of rationalizing legislation prompted a critical evaluation of the then existing soil conservation legislation; secondly, despite the above-mentioned Weeds and Soil Conservation Acts, South Africa's agricultural resources were deteriorating, which resulted in rising production costs. By 1983 R130-m had been spent by the State to improve land used for agriculture, but it was not enough. Dams silted up and veld used for grazing was changing into a desert (eg some parts of the Bushveld). A large proportion of South Africa, ie 65 per cent of the country, receives less than 500 mm of rain annually, which is barely half of the world average. Therefore legislation was necessary that could prevent rather than remedy future erosion. Thirdly, a major point of criticism against the 1969 Act was that it contained only preventive measures,[72] which were not always successfully applied. By 1983 1 672 land users who had contravened the Act had been identified, only 36 of whom were prosecuted. Moreover, 14-m ha of agricultural land were still unprotected as only 196 committees had been established in terms of the 1969 Act and there were obviously insufficient officials to enforce the Act.

The objects of the 1983 Act are 'to provide for the conservation of natural agricultural resources of the Republic by the maintenance of the production potential of land, by the combating and prevention of erosion and weakening or destruction of

[69] Cf Adler *Soil conservation in South Africa* (1985) 3–42.

[70] Except Part IV of the Act, subsequently repealed by the Forest Act 122 of 1984. Section 82 of the Expropriation Act 63 of 1975 was also repealed in 1983.

[71] *House of Assembly debates* 15 April 1984 4919–4922, 4926, 4943–4944.

[72] *House of Assembly debates* 15 April 1984 4934, 4936.

the water resources, and by the protection of the vegetation and the combating of weeds and invader plants.'[73]

In the light of these stated objectives, the principal purposes of the 1983 Act (as explained in Parliament) are to consolidate all measures concerning soil utilization and conservation and to transfer from the Minister to a functionary the power to make general day-to-day decisions. Government assistance is to be given only by way of schemes published in the *Government Gazette* in order to help the conservation-minded rather than wasteful, exploitive farmers.[74] Apart from the existing system of local committees being retained, regional conservation committees and a national committee may also be appointed. The participation of organized agriculture is still an important feature of the Act—the local community is also more involved than before.[75]

Although persuasion rather than coercion is one of the main goals of the Act, severe penalties are prescribed in the 1983 legislation.[76] It is also easier to institute prosecutions under the 1983 Act than under its 1969 predecessor.[77]

10.6.5.2 *Application of the Act*

The Act does not apply to *(a)* any land situated in urban areas (except in connection with weeds and invader plants); *(b)* South African Development Trust Land, and *(c)* land situated within a mountain catchment area, although the State President may extend the operation of the Act to the trust areas.[78]

10.6.5.3 *Conservation structure*

(a) Minister of Agriculture

Extensive powers are given to the Minister of Agriculture: he may appoint members of a conservation advisory board, establish regional and local conservation committees and designate an executive officer of the Department of Agriculture to perform certain duties and exercise functions in terms of the Act.

In order to achieve the objects of the Act, the Minister may prescribe control measures applying to certain land users or areas as determined by him.[79] These measures may, inter alia, relate to

- the cultivation of virgin soil;
- the utilization and protection of land which is cultivated;
- the prevention or control of waterlogging or salinization of land;
- the grazing capacity of veld, expressed as an area of veld per large stock unit;
- the prevention and control of veld fires and the utilization and protection of veld which has burned;
- the restoration or reclamation of eroded land or land which is otherwise disturbed or denuded, and

---

[73] Section 3.

[74] These farmers were always the first to apply for drought aid.schemes while the conservation-minded farmer was always last to hold out his hand for financial aid. The Minister is empowered to establish schemes that would, e g in times of drought, finance only conservation-minded farmers. *House of Assembly debates* 15 April 1984 4926–4928, 4950–4951.

[75] *House of Assembly debates* 15 April 1984 2921, 4944.

[76] Section 23. See below.

[77] *House of Assembly debates* 15 April 1984 4942–3. An official may be appointed to institute prosecution after consultation with the local committee concerned and the Department of Agriculture.

[78] Section 2 and s 41 of the Abolition of Racially Based Land Measures Act 108 of 1991.

[79] Sections 6(1) and 6(4).

- the construction, maintenance, alteration or removal of soil conservation works.[80]

These control measures may contain a prohibition or an obligation on the one hand or provide that the executive officer may exempt a person from such prohibition or obligation by means of written consent on the other.[81] Failure or refusal to comply with any control measure is an offence.[82]

A number of control measures have been prescribed by regulation.[83] These relate to the cultivation of virgin soil[84] and of land with a certain slope;[85] the protection of cultivated land against erosion through the action of water[86] and of wind;[87] the prevention of waterlogging and salinization of irrigated land;[88] the utilization and protection of vleis, marshes, water sponges and water courses;[89] regulating the flow pattern of run-off water;[90] the utilization and protection of veld;[91] the grazing capacity of veld,[92] the number of animals that may be kept on veld;[93] the prevention and control of veld fires,[94] and the restoration and reclamation of eroded,[95] disturbed or denuded land.[96]

The Minister, acting on the advice of the Conservation Advisory Board and with the concurrence of the Minister of Finance, has the power to establish a scheme in terms of which assistance may be granted to land users.[97] The scheme must be published in the *Government Gazette*[98] and subsidies can, for instance, be paid in respect of

- the construction of soil conservation works;
- the reparation of damage caused by flood or other disaster to natural agricultural resources or soil conservation works;
- the reduction of the number of animals being kept on land in order to restrict the detrimental effect of a drought;
- the restoration or reclamation of eroded, disturbed, denuded or damaged land, and
- the planting and cultivation of particular crops which improve soil fertility or counteract the vulnerability of soil to erosion.

In the notice by which a scheme is established the Minister may set out the objects of the scheme, mention the areas in which and the periods during which the scheme shall apply, mention the acts in respect of which assistance may be rendered, determine the requirements to be complied with and the procedure for application, mention the aims on which assistance may be rendered, and provide generally for any other matter which

---

[80] Section 6(2). A 'soil conservation work' means 'any work which is constructed on land for *(a)* the prevention of erosion or the conservation of land which is subject to erosion; *(b)* the conservation or improvement of the vegetation or the surface of the soil; *(c)* the drainage of superfluous surface or subterranean water; *(d)* the conservation or reclamation of any water resource; or *(e)* the prevention of the silting of dams and the pollution of water: s 1.

[81] Section 6(3).

[82] Section 6(5).

[83] Part I GN R1048 of 25 May 1984.

[84] Regulation 2.

[85] Regulation 3.

[86] Regulation 4.

[87] Regulation 5.

[88] Regulation 6.

[89] Regulation 7.

[90] Regulation 8.

[91] Regulation 9.

[92] Regulation 10.

[93] Regulation 11.

[94] Regulation 12.

[95] Regulation 13.

[96] Regulation 14.

[97] Section 8.

[98] Section 8(1).

in his opinion is necessary or expedient to achieve the objects of the Act.[99] A person who fails to comply with the conditions or terms of the scheme is guilty of an offence.[100]

The Minister may, out of money appropriated by Parliament, perform or cause any act (in relation to the control measures issued by him) to be performed on or in respect of any land. If such an act is performed, the costs may be reclaimed from any owner of land on whose land these acts may have a beneficial effect. The amount so due must be paid within 60 days in the absence of a written agreement in this regard.[101]

In concurrence with the owner of any land and subject to any conditions (as may be agreed upon between the Minister and that landowner) any act can be performed in respect of the land or the owner concerned for the purpose of public demonstration or research in any matter relating to veld, soil or water conservation or the combating of invader plants. Certain powers are conferred upon the Minister[102] and provision is made for compensation to the landowner.[103]

Moreover, the Minister may expropriate any land if he is of the opinion that the expropriation is necessary for the restoration or reclamation of the natural agricultural resources of that land.[104]

Some of the powers conferred upon the Minister in terms of the Act may be delegated in writing to one or more officers of the department. The Minister is, however, not divested of any power so delegated.[105] He is also empowered to make regulations concerning any matter he considers necessary or expedient to achieve or promote the aims of the Act.[106]

(b) Conservation Advisory Board

A conservation advisory board is established in terms of the Act[107] to advise the Minister on matters concerning:

- the desirability of specific control measures with regard to a particular area;
- the desirability of establishing a specified scheme, and the provisions thereof, and
- any other matter arising from the application of the Act or a scheme.

Members of the conservation advisory board are appointed by the Minister. The board consists of the executive officer and another official of the Department of Agriculture, one officer of the Department of Environment Affairs (nominated by the Minister of that department), one person from the members of each of the regional committees (appointed by them) and one person nominated by the South African Agricultural Union.[108]

(c) Regional conservation committees

A regional conservation committee can be established by the Minister in any region determined by him.[109] This committee must:

---

[99] Section 9.

[100] Section 9(2).

[101] Section 11(1)–(3).

[102] Section 11(4)–(5).

[103] Sections 11(4)*(b)* and 11(6). The compensation will be paid only if the act was performed on the owner's land or is likely to have a beneficial effect on such land.

[104] Section 14. The provisions of the Expropriation Act 63 of 1975 apply mutatis mutandis.

[105] Section 26; ss 2(3), 6, 8, 21 and 29 are excluded.

[106] Section 29. Proclamation R1048 of 25 May 1984 provides for control measures regarding soil and weeds (regs 2–16); directives (regs 17–18); conservation committees (regs 19–26); beacons and marks (regs 27–28); appeals (regs 29–31) and general matters (regs 32-33).

[107] Section 17.

[108] Section 17(3). The period of appointment, reappointment, vacancies and chairmanship are provided for in s 17(4)–(6).

[109] Section 16(1).

- advise every conservation committee in the region concerned on matters regarding the conservation of the natural agricultural resources;
- advise the department and the advisory board on any matter arising from the application of the Act or a scheme in the region concerned, and
- perform such other duties as may be imposed by the Minister.[110]

The committee is appointed by the Minister and consists of the regional director and an officer of the department in the region concerned, two representatives of each particular area in the region and one representative of each provincial agricultural union in that region.[111]

(d) Conservation committees

The Minister may establish a conservation committee for any area determined by him.[112] The committee has the following duties:

- to promote the conservation of natural agricultural resources in a specified area in order to achieve the objects of the Act;
- to advise the department on any matter as to the application of the Act or scheme in the area, and
- to exercise such other powers and perform such other duties as may be conferred or imposed upon it in terms of the Act or by the Minister.[113]

The members of a conservation committee are appointed by the Minister by virtue of their knowledge of and interest in the conservation of natural agricultural resources. The committee consists of two land users designated by the Minister and as many additional persons (not less than three) as may be determined by him. One of the additional members must be nominated by the farmers' association, farmers' union or district agricultural union.[114] Soil conservation committees established in terms of the 1969 Act are deemed to be established under the 1983 Act.[115]

(e) Executive officer and authorized person

An officer of the Department of Agriculture is designated by the Minister to exercise the powers and perform the duties conferred or imposed on him by the Act and to execute the instructions issued by the Minister.[116] The executive officer may delegate his powers and duties to another official (eg an inspector). Any decision or order of this official can be withdrawn or amended by the executive officer.[117] If the Minister deems it expedient, he may authorize a person who is not usually an official, to exercise any powers or perform any duties under the Act or a scheme.[118]

The executive officer may issue directives[119] and render advice to land users.[120] A directive is aimed at a land user to comply with particular control measures—issued by the Minister, as has been shown—which are binding on him or necessary to

---

[110] Section 16(2).
[111] Section 16(3). The Minister may appoint one additional representative of any particular region as a member of this committee from a list of names of at least four members of the conservation committee concerned (as recommended by the regional director after consultation with the provincial agricultural union): s 16(3)*(b)*–*(c)*. Further nominations, term of service and the expiration thereof, vacancies, meetings etc are described in s 16(3)*(e)*–16(9).
[112] Section 15(1).
[113] Section 15(2).
[114] Section 15(3).
[115] Section 15(3)*(f)*. Miscellaneous matters (eg relating to the chairman, secretary, subcommittees and remuneration) are set out in s 15(4)–(11).
[116] Section 4.
[117] Section 4(3).
[118] Section 4(5).
[119] Section 7.
[120] Section 10.

achieve the objects of the Act.[121] Such a directive must be published in the *Government Gazette* and, in addition, a written notice is served on the land user concerned; the land user and any successor in title are bound by it. On the other hand, a directive can be withdrawn in the *Government Gazette*, but a written notice must also be served on the land user.[122] A land user who refuses to receive a directive served on him or refuses or fails to comply with the directive is guilty of an offence.[123] Advice is given to land users by the executive officer or any other official relating to the utilization and conservation of natural agricultural resources or the control of weeds and invader plants.[124]

Considerable powers of investigation are conferred upon the executive officer,[125] including the power to order a land user to render reasonable assistance (for which no compensation is paid).[126] The executive officer may also consider any application or request made in terms of the Act or a scheme and is entitled to carry out any investigation he deems necessary.[127] He is empowered to alter fixed periods as set out in the Act or in a scheme. An approval, authorization or consent may be made subject to conditions, and may also be amended or withdrawn by the executive officer if he deems it expedient.[128] The officer must give written reasons if he refuses to approve an application or request or if he amends or withdraws an approval, authorization or a consent.[129]

10.6.5.4 *Duties of land user*

The term 'land user' includes the owner of the land, any person who has a personal or real right in respect of any land in his capacity as fiduciary, fideicommissary, servitude holder, possessor, lessee or occupier (irrespective of whether he resides thereon), and any person who has the right to cut trees or wood on land or to remove any other organic material from the ground. The term also relates to land under control of a local authority. A person who prospects or mines is not included.[130]

The land user and his successor in title are obliged to maintain soil conservation works at their own expense to ensure continued efficiency.[131] The executive officer may order a land user in writing or on application give written consent to the land user to alter, remove or destroy soil conservation work. If the land user (or his successor in title) refuses or fails to comply with these duties, the costs involved (less his own expenses) can be recovered from him.[132] If an executive officer becomes aware of any refusal or failure to comply with the above provisions, he may order a landowner to repair or reconstruct soil conservation work or to repeat an act in connection therewith. Although persuasion rather than compulsion is a feature of this provision, the land user

[121] Section 7(1).

[122] Section 7(3)–(4). A directive issued in terms of the 1969 Act is deemed to have been served under the 1983 Act—s 7(5).

[123] Section 7(6).

[124] Section 10(1).

[125] Section 18.

[126] Section 18(2)–(5). Cf also s 10(2). Any person who obstructs or hinders any officer, member of a conservation committee or any other authorized person in the exercise of his powers, furnishes a false statement or records or fails to render assistance is guilty of an offence: s 10(6).

[127] Section 20.

[128] Section 20(2)–(3).

[129] Section 20(4). A person who refuses or fails to comply with the conditions on which any approval, authorization or consent has been granted is guilty of an offence: s 20(5).

[130] Section 1. With regard to mining cf ss 38–42 of the Minerals Act 50 of 1991.

[131] Section 12(1).

[132] Section 12(2). The amount must be paid to the executive officer within 60 days after the written order has been received by the landowner: s 12(2)*(b)*.

is not discharged from prosecution on account of his payment of the costs concerning the construction or repair of soil conservation work.[133]

The Minister may order any landowner to compensate a land user in respect of the increase or likely increase in the value of land as a result of the beneficial effect of constructed soil conservation work. It is payable only if the work was required by a directive order or if the land user requested the Minister to order the landowner to construct soil conservation work (and the work was then done by the land user).[134] Any landowner may be ordered to pay an amount determined by the Minister to another landowner in respect of the decrease (or likely decrease) in the value of the latter's land as a result of soil conservation work, constructed by the first owner on his land.[135]

The land user (or his successor in title) is obliged, moreover, to maintain any beacon or mark that has been erected in terms of the Act. These beacons or marks may be destroyed, removed or altered only with the written consent of the executive officer.[136]

10.6.5.5 *Miscellaneous measures*

Any person who considers himself aggrieved by any decision or act of the executive officer in terms of the Act or a scheme may appeal to the Minister, whose decision is final.[137] He must give reasons for his decision; even if the answer is negative. The Act provides for secrecy,[138] presumptions and matters regarding evidence,[139] the liability of an employer or principal[140] and the limitation of the State's liability concerning acts done in good faith in terms of the Act or a scheme.[141]

10.6.5.6 *Practical problems and recommendations*

A number of practical problems ensue from the application of the Act.[142] A few minor interpretation problems concerning the Act and the regulations will most probably be remedied by amendments in 1992.[143]

A major practical problem is that the necessary manpower to enforce the Act is lacking. Only 14 inspectors serve the whole of South Africa. The need for agricultural technicians is an even more pressing problem, since they have to advise farmers on soil conservation and correct planning concerning productivity. As soon as an inspector has identified erosion on a farmer's land, the farmer should be able to ask for a technician's

---

[133] Section 12(4)–(5).

[134] Section 13(1). The amount due must be paid within 90 days, after which period a civil action may be instituted.

[135] Section 13(2). The period for payment is 90 days.

[136] Section 19(2). Any person who fails to comply with the provisions is guilty of an offence: s 19(3).

[137] Section 21. The appeal must be lodged with the Director-General within the prescribed time and manner. He then refers the appeal for inquiry and report to an official of the Department of Agriculture. An appellant may request or refuse to appear before this official and he may be assisted or represented. All the evidence is then submitted to the Minister, whose decision is given in writing. If a directive of the executive officer is set aside, all moneys already paid in this regard must be refunded. (This appeal is not an appeal in the normal sense of the word; provision is in fact made for administrative review by the Minister. An appeal to a court of law against the executive officer's decision seems to be excluded; only in cases where its inherent powers of review are concerned will the Supreme Court have jurisdiction.)

[138] Section 22.

[139] Section 24. A defect in a form does not render any administrative proceedings invalid: s 27.

[140] Section 25.

[141] Section 28.

[142] The advice of Mr PJ Theron, Head Resource Conservation Inspector, Directorate of Resource Conservation, western Transvaal and Vryburg in identifying the problems in the application of the Act as well as his recommendations for improvements are acknowledged.

[143] The following are instances of proposed amendments: *(a)* the control of weeds in urban areas (s 2 read with regs 6 and 29 of Proc R1048 of 25 May 1984); *(b)* the unification of Part II of the regulations (control measures regarding weeds) and Part I (Control measures); and *(c)* the rephrasing of s 29(3) concerning penalties as set out in Proc R1048.

support in reducing the erosion, but at the moment there are too few technicians by far to accomplish this important task.[144] Another problem is that the technicians and the inspectors are appointed by different departments; they therefore do not always have the same conservation priorities.

Part of the solution to this problem is to increase the number of technicians dramatically. This could, for instance, be done by means of privatization (partly or wholly). The State must, however, retain the initiative in this regard, as well as the control over the quality of the technicians' work and the amount of compensation payable for soil conservation works. Subsidies for soil conservation works should also be raised, but this is probably not practicable at present.

A further problem is caused by the fact that some of the conservation committees established in terms of the Act have not yet begun functioning, while in some parts of the country conservation committees have not even been established. In a number of cases conservation committees are being used primarily for purposes other than conservation (e g the discussion of farming and labour problems). If these conservation committees were to function properly (in that the members report on erosion in their district and refer cases on a frequent basis to the agricultural technician concerned), the compulsory measures of the Act would need to be applied only by exception. Legislation hardly ever succeeds in changing people's attitudes towards conservation, but a conservation committee (with the co-operation of the inspector, technician and regional director) could play an important role in creating a conservation attitude among the farmers concerned.

The regulation which prescribes the restoration and reclamation of land disturbed or denuded by mining or prospecting activities, can be applied only if there is sufficient co-operation between the mining executive and his agricultural colleagues (the mining industry is the principal functionary in this regard).[145]

During 1988–89 1 143 cases of contravention of the Act received attention. Of these, 419 directives were served of which only a further six resulted in prosecution; 711 malpractices were or are in the process of being rectified.[146] Furthermore, criminal prosecutions are instituted in the regional courts, where it seems that public prosecutors and magistrates are not always aware of the seriousness of soil erosion and its effect on the future of South Africa. It may be that the community does not regard a person who commits these offences as a criminal. On the other hand, the criminal sanction is used as a sanction of last resort, which means that causing soil erosion is not in itself a crime; only the failure to obey a directive of the executive officer constitutes an offence. Nevertheless, it is not always realized that soil erosion is, even in the short term, much more harmful than, for instance, illicit diamond dealing. Only the most serious cases of soil erosion come before the courts and therefore more attention should be given to them to raise public awareness. It is recommended that university courses and courses presented by the Department of Justice should give attention to the importance of

---

[144] There is supposed to be at least one technician in each town of South Africa: some larger agricultural areas need up to three. Most technicians cannot even cope with the requests of conservation-minded farmers. If erosion on an environmentally irresponsible farmer's land is therefore referred by the inspector to a technician, it is understandably not always seen as priority work. In some instances the private sector has tried to fill this gap, e g the Sugar Association supplies technicians in order to reduce the work of the State's officers. However, the farmers have to pay for this advice whereas the State's advice is free.

[145] Regulation 14 of Proc R1048 of 25 May 1984.

[146] In percentages: 62 per cent malpractices and 37 per cent directives. Only 1 per cent resulted in prosecutions. There have been only 49 prosecutions since the 1983 Act came into effect. Cf *Annual report of the Department of Agricultural Economics and Marketing* 1 April 1988 to 31 March 1989 (1990) 40.

conservation and the content of conservation measures.[147] See chapter 8.

Roads and railway lines should in principle be constructed as far as possible on land with a low rather than a high agricultural potential. However, because of the high cost of constructing roads and railways on low-potential soil, this often amounts to an ideal rather than a practical solution.

Too many government departments are currently partially involved in soil conservation. It has been recommended that all legislation concerning resource conservation be rationalized.[148] The number of state departments involved should be reduced and their control and administration should be vested in one department.

The present communication problem may be solved by the establishment of an information centre where all relevant soil conservation data (eg legislation and departmental notices) is stored. From this centre information can be disseminated to the various state departments, farmers, other authorities concerned with soil conservation as well as other interested parties.

Since the Act is at present not applicable to areas set aside for black occupation (South African Development Trust Land as well as land comprising the self-governing territories), it is recommended that it be made applicable to the whole of South Africa. Due consideration should also be given to applying state funds to reducing and preventing soil erosion in these areas.

The Act does not provide for an independent review tribunal—the Minister's decision is final. The potential underlying danger inherent in this can be minimized by the establishment of an independent appeal board, similar to the Air Pollution Appeal Board (established in terms of the Atmospheric Pollution Prevention Act 45 of 1965). The enactment of such a provision deserves the attention of the legislature, since the remedy of judicial review by the Supreme Court, which exists in so far as the Minister's action is administrative in nature, provides only very limited relief on limited grounds. See chapter 8.

The expropriation of land that is particularly vulnerable to soil erosion or that has been eroded to such an extent that it is beyond the power of an individual farmer effectively to reclaim it, is the only effective remedy available in such circumstances. This remedy has been provided for in soil conservation legislation since the Forest and Veld Conservation Act of 1941.

One way in which soil conservation can be stimulated is through offering financial rewards for actions directed at conservation. Under the 1946 Act, as well as the 1969 and 1983 Acts provision has been made for subsidies and grants that may be paid to owners or occupiers of land for works or measures undertaken with a view to soil conservation. These economic incentives have been used with some success, particularly by providing subsidies for soil conservation works, veld utilization works, drainage works and the stock-reduction scheme. Subsidies never cover all the costs, which means that farmers still have to contribute towards them; this has inhibited some farmers from spending money on such works, especially in view of the fact that the economic gains resulting from soil conservation works are of a relatively intangible nature that may only be realized 5 to 10 years after expenditure, or even later. Related to this is the fact that expenditure on soil conservation does not seem to increase the selling price of a farm by a corresponding amount, which must have a dampening influence on such expenditure, especially when regard is had only to the short term.

[147] The Department of Agriculture could for instance give a practical demonstration (or a tour of areas with serious erosion) during courses offered by the Department of Justice. Prosecutors should be encouraged to ask for an inspection in loco in serious cases of erosion and not only rely on aerial photography, as not everyone knows how to interpret these photographs. Heavy fines (even if a sentence is suspended in order to erect soil conservation works) to serve as a deterrent and compulsion to erect these works should be requested by the prosecutor.

[148] Anon 'Bewaring: soveel hoofde soveel sinne' 1990 *Agricultural News* (1 October 1990) 3.

Granting financial aid to stimulate soil conservation can at most be regarded as an exceptional relief measure where no other reasonable solution can be found. The intention of such aid should not be to raise the income of farmers but to enable them to raise their income through increased efficiency. Where increased production efficiency cannot be achieved, as in the case of uneconomic farming units, the State should rather expropriate the farm in question. It is of great importance that the granting of financial aid should always be made conditional upon the farmer's applying conservation farming. Financial relief is also to a limited extent provided by the Income Tax Act 58 of 1962.[149]

10.6.6 Other related legislation

Although the Conservation of Agricultural Resources Act constitutes by far the most important legislation regarding soil erosion control, provisions contained in other legislation are also relevant as far as soil conservation is concerned. These provisions are outlined below.

10.6.6.1 *Water Act*

In view of the close relationship between water conservation and soil conservation, provisions of the Water Act 54 of 1956 aimed at water conservation are of central importance to soil conservation.[150] Certain provisions even relate directly to soil conservation. Thus, catchment control areas may be declared if the State President is of the opinion that the flow of a public stream in a particular area should be controlled in the national interest for the prevention or control of silt, or for the purpose of limiting the possibility of damage to land which is riparian to such stream in the event of flood.[151] Moreover, some actions undertaken for the prevention of soil erosion are exempted from certain restrictive provisions of the Act.[152]

10.6.6.2 *Forest Act*

The Forest Act 122 of 1984 repealed the Forest Act 72 of 1968.[153] Apart from providing for the protection of land, vegetation and other forest produce[154] in state and other forests, the Forest Act contains provisions for setting aside state forests as protection forests for the prevention and combating of soil erosion and of veld, mountain and forest fires.[155] State forests may also be set aside as nature reserves[156] or as wilderness areas.[157] The protection of forests and forest produce should also be beneficial to soil conservation. Certain provisions, moreover, relate directly to the prevention of erosion and to the control of cultivation and grazing of land situated within forests. The Minister concerned may, for instance, by notice in the *Government Gazette* declare trees on any land that is not a state forest to be protected trees with a view to preventing soil erosion or sand drift, or reclaiming soil or drift sands.[158] Such a declaration means that no person may, without the written consent of the Minister, cut,

---

[149] Section 17A and sch 1 para 12(1)*(b)*.

[150] For the activities of the Department of Water Affairs relating to soil conservation, see generally the issues of the *Annual report of the Soil Conservation Board* until its dissolution in 1969.

[151] Section 59(2)*(a)*. Extensive provisions apply in respect of landowners in such areas: s 61.

[152] Sections 25(1)*(c)*, 25(2) and 52(5).

[153] Part IV of the Soil Conservation Act 76 of 1969 regarding the prevention and combating of veld, forest and mountain fires was also repealed. For activities of the then Department of Forestry in connection with soil conservation, see, generally, the issues of the *Annual report of the Soil Conservation Board* until its dissolution in 1969.

[154] See s 1 for the definition of 'forest produce'.

[155] Section 15(3)*(b)*(ii)–(iii).

[156] Section 15(1)*(a)*(i).

[157] Section 15(1)*(a)*(ii).

[158] Section 13*(b)*(i).

injure, destroy, disturb or remove any protected tree.[159] Another relevant provision is that regulations may under certain circumstances be made in respect of state forests, prohibiting the grazing of stock or the cutting of forest produce in order to prevent soil erosion or sand drift, or in order to reclaim soil or drift sands.[160] Moreover, regulations may generally be made regarding state forests as to the grazing of animals and the manner in which pasturage shall be used[161] and as to the clearing, breaking up or cultivation of land.[162] It is an offence to clear, break up or cultivate land without authority in or on a state or private forest.[163]

The 1968 Act did not deal with the protection and combating of fires. Part VI of the 1984 Act deals extensively with this matter. The Minister may (with the concurrence of the Minister of Agriculture) declare by notice in the *Government Gazette* certain areas as fire control areas[164] and fire protection committees may be established for each declared region.[165] These committees may prepare and submit to the Minister fire protection schemes.[166]

10.6.6.3 *Mountain Catchment Areas Act*

The close relationship between soil, vegetation and water conservation is again illustrated by the conservation of mountain catchment areas. Although provision for the protection of mountain catchment areas existed in other Acts—notably the Water Act 54 of 1956, the Forest Act 72 of 1968[167] and the Soil Conservation Act 76 of 1969—it was felt that those protection measures, as applied by the various government departments under whose control mountain catchment areas fell, did not always promote co-ordinated action.[168] For this reason, it was decided to centralize the task of the protection of mountain catchment areas and to entrust this matter to the then Department of Forestry.[169] The Mountain Catchment Areas Act 63 of 1970 was accordingly promulgated to provide for this centralized control.[170]

In terms of the Act, mountain catchment areas may be declared by the Minister of Environment Affairs, the power now having been devolved upon the provincial chief directorates of nature conservation.[171] Extensive powers allow the declaration of directives to be applicable to any owner or occupier of land situated in such areas.[172] These directives may relate to the conservation, use, management and control of such land, the prevention of soil erosion or the protection and treatment of natural vegetation.[173] The Act also makes provision for fire protection plans and the

---

159 Section 13(5). Contravention of this provision is an offence: s 13(6). Provision is made for certain exceptions: ss 13(5), 22 and 24.

160 Section 73(1)*(a)*(xiv)–(xv).

161 Section 73(1)*(a)*(v).

162 Section 73(1)*(a)*(vi).

163 Section 75(3)*(a)*(i).

164 Section 18.

165 Section 19. Regulations with regard to these committees may be issued—s 73(1)*(c)*.

166 Section 20. Offences are set out in s 75(2)*(b)*.

167 Now the Forest Act 122 of 1984.

168 See generally the *Report of the interdepartmental committee on the conservation of mountain catchments in South Africa* (1961) 30ff.

169 *House of Assembly debates* 9 September 1970 3708.

170 Cf Rabie 'The conservation of mountains in South African law' 1989 *SA Public Law* 213–31, 1990 *SA Public Law* 66–79.

171 Section 2.

172 Section 3.

173 Section 3(1)*(b)*(i) and (ii). The Minister may withdraw, amend or subject conditions or suspend a directive—cf s 3(3). Compensation is payable in respect of patrimonial loss caused by complying with these directives: s 4. The application of the Act has been further complicated by the repeal of para *(e)*

establishment of fire protection committees.[174] See, generally, chapter 24.

10.6.6.4 *Common Pasture Management Act*

In terms of the Common Pasture Management Act 82 of 1977 the Minister of Agriculture may, by notice in the *Government Gazette*, withdraw from the control of any committee of management[175] any State land which has been set apart as common pasture.[176] He may, moreover, reserve as common pasture any State land which in his opinion is suitable for such purpose.[177] The Minister may also designate one or more pieces of land as a particular agricultural unit[178] and may allot any particular common pasture to an agricultural unit.[179] Finally, the Act provides for the establishment by the Minister of a pasture management committee for any particular common pasture,[180] the object of such a committee being to control and manage, for the benefit and on behalf of the owners of the above-mentioned agricultural units, the common pasture for which it has been established.[181] Among the functions of the committee is the power to raise funds for the construction of soil conservation works.[182] The committee may, moreover, with the approval of the Minister, determine the kind and number of stock which the owner of any agricultural unit may graze on the common pasture concerned.[183] Regulations issued in terms of this Act deal with the conservation of vegetation and the prohibition of hunting.[184]

10.6.6.5 *Settlement Acts*

There are several other Acts concerning common pasture management in certain settlements. The Cannon Island Settlement Management Act 15 of 1939,[185] the Klipdrift Settlement Act 23 of 1947,[186] the Skanskop Settlement Act 24 of 1947,[187] the Mapochsgronden Water and Commonage Act 40 of 1916,[188] and the Settlement Committee and Management Act 21 of 1925[189] all provide for a settlement committee to make rules regarding the conservation of soil and vegetation in their specific areas.

10.6.6.6 *Unbeneficial Occupation of Farms Act*

The Unbeneficial Occupation of Farms Act 29 of 1937 provided for the appropriation and allotment of land which was not being beneficially occupied for farming purposes and from which (combined with any other source of income) the person or persons concerned did not derive a sufficient income to enable them to maintain a reasonable standard of living.

---

of the definition of 'owner' in s 1 by s 28*(b)* of the Abolition of Racially Based Land Measures Act 108 of 1991. It would seem that no directive may be declared concerning land belonging to the South African Development Trust (SADT); existing directives will probably not be binding on the SADT and its successor in title.

[174] Sections 7 and 8.

[175] Defined in s 1.

[176] Section 2(1)*(a)* and *(b)*.

[177] Section 2(1)*(c)*.

[178] Section 3(1)*(a)*.

[179] Section 3(1)*(c)*.

[180] Section 4(1).

[181] Section 4(2).

[182] The Act still refers to a performance of any act contemplated in the Soil Conservation Act 76 of 1969. The relevant section of the 1983 Act is s 5(1)*(d)*.

[183] Section 5(1)*(e)*.

[184] GN R1916 of 22 September 1978, regs 9 and 10.

[185] Cf s 16*(a)*, *(e)* and *(l)*.

[186] Cf s 6*(h)*–*(j)*.

[187] Cf s 6*(a)*, *(e)* and *(l)*.

[188] Cf s 5*(a)*, *(d)*–*(e)* and *(i)*.

[189] Cf s 6*(a)*, *(h)*–*(k)*.

In practice the Act was not implemented, due possibly to the fact that no machinery was created to enforce it.[190] The Act has been repealed by the Abolition of Racially Based Land Measures Act 108 of 1991.[191] No specific provision is now made for the control of unbeneficial occupation of agricultural land. Considering the fact that the Unbeneficial Occupation of Farms Act had been on the statute book since 1937, it is strange that this potentially useful statute had been ignored for so many years. Nevertheless, one of the main purposes of the 1937 Act is now being achieved through the Subdivision of Agricultural Land Act 70 of 1970.

10.6.6.7 *Subdivision of Agricultural Land Act*

Although some provisions for preventing the unnecessary subdivision of land did exist previously,[192] the malpractice which had been criticized so often, namely the creation of uneconomic farming units with concomitant adverse effects on soil conservation,[193] was comprehensively eliminated in 1970. The Subdivision of Agricultural Land Act 70 of 1970 stipulates that agricultural land[194] may not be subdivided unless the Minister of Agriculture[195] has consented to such subdivision. The belated promulgation of this important Act must be welcomed as a very effective instrument as far as soil conservation is concerned. It is a pity, however, that provision was not made at the same time for the consolidation of existing uneconomic farming units—for example, when one person farms land that is subject to more than one title deed.

10.6.6.8 *Nature conservation legislation*

Since nature conservation legislation is also aimed at the conservation of land and its vegetation, particularly in protected areas, such legislation plays an important role in effecting soil conservation in these areas. See chapters 11 and 27. Bennett[196] has made the following remarks regarding the intimate relationship between soil conservation and wildlife conservation:

> 'Soil conservation and wildlife conservation both depend fundamentally on the re-establishment and maintenance of vegetation. Each, therefore, may not only make important contributions to the other, but is actually essential to the other's highest expression. Without soil conservation, climax vegetation with its associated animal life must largely disappear; without wildlife conservation, the vegetation is deprived of important protection, and ultimately the soil itself must lose the benefit of a powerful factor in its upbuilding—the direct influence of animal life.'

10.6.6.9 *Soil conservation and the construction of roads and railways*

As road and railway surfaces are virtually impervious to water, some way must be found to dispose of the runoff water after rains. The methods employed to remove storm water from the immediate vicinity of roads and railways have led to extensive soil erosion alongside the roads and railways themselves and on adjoining farms.

The South African Roads Board has the power to plan, design or construct any national road, and to stimulate or protect vegetation with a view to preventing soil erosion on a national road or as a result of the construction of a national road.[197] It

---

[190] *Report of the Reconstruction Committee* GP-S 9278 (1943) 42.
[191] Section 13.
[192] Provision did exist to control the subdivision of agricultural land, but it was included in legislation aimed at the establishment of industries (cf s 2(1)*(b)* of the repealed Physical Planning Act 88 of 1967).
[193] Such small farms are usually overstocked and their owners usually do not have the capital to spend on implementing soil conservation measures.
[194] See s 1 for the definition of 'agricultural land'.
[195] The Minister may delegate his authority (see s 8).
[196] Quoted in March 1950 (11) *Veldtrust* 1.
[197] Section 5(1)*(c)* and *(e)* of the National Roads Act 54 of 1971. See also s 20(1)*(a)*.

seems strange to couch the prevention of soil erosion in the form of a power; it should preferably have been an obligation of the board, especially in view of the fact that land may be expropriated in order to take stone, clay, sand or any other material or substance for the construction of a national road.[198] As it is, the rehabilitation of a gravel-quarry (used for road construction) falls under the authority of the Inspector of Mines, and entails shifting top soil and re-using it to cover the quarry after completion of the work. Steps must be taken to ensure that no erosion takes place.[199]

There is nothing in the Road Traffic Act 29 of 1989 or in railway construction legislation comparable to the above-mentioned explicit reference to the prevention of soil erosion, although soil conservation is taken into account as a matter of policy.[200]

One way in which consideration of soil conservation measures relating to the construction of roads and railways could be made obligatory is through the introduction of a provision stipulating that, before any road or railway may be constructed, the plans must first be approved by the Directorate of Resource Conservation of the Department of Agriculture.

10.6.6.10 *Land-use planning and control*

Legislation relating to land-use planning and control may obviously be of great importance to soil conservation. Reference to this is made in chapter 28.

10.6.6.11 *Soil conservation in black areas*

There are a number of provisions aimed at soil conservation in areas previously reserved for occupation by black persons.[201] It is unnecessary to have different legislation pertaining to various areas based on race. One uniform system regarding soil conservation should as a matter of high priority be introduced for the whole of South Africa.

10.6.6.12 *Mining legislation*

Mining and agriculture both contend for the use of land. Moreover, once mining operations finally cease, the land often again becomes available for agriculture. However, it can be put to such use only if the surfaces concerned have been satisfactorily restored. Mining legislation since 1980 accordingly makes provision for such rehabilitation through regulations issued in terms of the Mines and Works Act 27 of 1956[202] and now applicable by virtue of the transitional clause of the Minerals Act 50 of 1991.[203] See chapter 15.

10.7 CONCLUSION

The state of a country's soil is a fair indication of the true state of the nation's culture: A nation writes its record on the land, and a civilization writes its record on the land—a record that is easy to read by those who understand the simple language of the land.

The record of South African land use is not something to be proud of. In fact, we have, through the injudicious use of our soil, threatened the quality of life of our people.

---

[198] Section 8.

[199] Powers provided for under the mining laws are excluded from the Road Acts: cf s 12 of the Advertising on Roads and Ribbon Development Act 21 of 1940.

[200] See the issues of the *Annual report of the Soil Conservation Board* until its dissolution in 1969.

[201] See Rabie above n 49, 43–7. The Black Land Act 27 of 1913 and the Development Trust and Land Act 18 of 1936 have been repealed by the Abolition of Racially Based Land Measures Act 108 of 1991. However, the regulations issued in terms of the 1936 Act (including soil conservation measures) remain in force: s 11(2) of the 1991 Act.

[202] GN R537 of 21 March 1980.

[203] Section 68(2).

Commenting on man's abuse of the soil in South Africa, the Drought Investigation Commission stated almost seven decades ago that it was unnecessary for it

'. . . to vie with the several writers who have, at various times, with facile pen depicted the gloomy and ghastly future which lies before our country, if we permit these processes to continue. The simple unadorned truth is sufficiently terrifying without the assistance of rhetoric. The logical outcome of it all is *"The Great South African Desert" uninhabitable by Man*.'[204]

Yet in the 1988–89 *Annual Report of the Department of Agricultural Economics and Marketing* the Director-General still admits:[205]

'There has not as yet been a turn-about in the condition of natural veld, with the result that the carrying capacity is still decreasing, excessive loss of soil is occurring on farmlands while farmers struggle to keep above the breadline. The influence of the drought is still more serious than it should be. The blame for this deterioration is wrongly put on the drought, instead of the farmers adapting the number of livestock and game to the available grazing.

The small percentage agricultural environment, consisting of high potential agricultural and horticultural soil, is treated too carelessly. Farmers cultivate crops on soil that is not conserved effectively. Too much top soil is being washed away by our rivers as sedimentation.'

Despite the fact that official and other action has been directed at soil erosion control in earnest since 1914; that numerous soil conservation campaigns have been launched over the years; that extensive soil conservation legislation was introduced in the 1940s; that the dangers of soil erosion have been repeated ad nauseam; and that the solutions to soil erosion problems have been repeatedly pointed out, soil erosion in South Africa has steadily increased. It should be clear, once again, that legislation, even of a very restrictive nature, is not per se sufficient to solve environmental—or other—problems. In the final analysis, legislative provisions and their enforcement can be effective only in a situation of general public consciousness and concern for the problem of soil erosion, coupled with an appreciation of efforts aimed at its solution. This state of mind, in turn, can be fostered only through the education of every citizen of our country, and of the farming community in particular, in the necessity for soil conservation.

---

204 *Final report of the Drought Investigation Commission* UG 49 (1923) 3.
205 *1988–89 Annual report of the Department of Agricultural Economics and Marketing* (1990) 2.

CHAPTER 11

INDIGENOUS PLANTS

R M COWLING
N J J OLIVIER

11.1 INTRODUCTION

Few South Africans realize that they live in a region which, in terms of plant life, is arguably the richest in the world[1] (Table 11.1). Even when the notable Cape Floristic Region is excluded, southern Africa (ie the area including South Africa, Botswana, Lesotho, Namibia, and Swaziland) still has the highest recorded plant species density in comparison with equivalent-sized areas.

TABLE 11.1

Number of plant species for regions of the world. Data from a compilation in Cowling et al above n 1.

Region	No of species	Area (10^6 km^2)	Species/ area*
Southern Africa	21 000	2,57	8,1
Southern Africa (excluding Capensis)	15 100	2,48	6,1
Brazil	40 000	8,6	4,7
India, Pakistan	20 000	4,89	4,1
Bangladesh, Burma, Australia	25 000	7,71	3,2
Europe	14 000	5,68	2,5
USA	20 000	9,36	2,1
West tropical Africa	7 300	4,50	1,6
Tropical Africa	30 000	20 00	1,5
Eastern North America	4 425	3,24	1,4
Sudan	3 200	2,51	1,3

* Species area ratios are calculated as 10^3 plants species per 10^6 km^2.

This extreme biodiversity places a burden of responsibility on all South Africans to conserve this resource. But why conserve plant species? What is the justification for the effort and expenditure by the State and private individuals for conservation of entities which not even biologists can adequately define nor comprehend?[2] In this chapter it will be argued that the maintenance of South Africa's plant diversity is compatible with the rational and sustained use of the country's plant resources which, in turn, are important for the maintainance of economic growth.

This chapter is divided into six parts. The first considers the ecological driving

[1] Cowling, Gibbs Russell, Hoffman & Hilton-Taylor 'Patterns of plant species diversity in southern Africa' in Huntley (ed) *Biotic diversity in southern Africa. Concepts and conservation* (1989) 19–50.

[2] Bond 'Describing and conserving biotic diversity' in Huntley (ed) above n 1, 2–18.

variables which have shaped South Africa's plant life. The second part documents patterns of plant diversity with southern Africa's seven biomes.[3] The third part summarizes degradation. The fourth discusses issues regarding plant resources conservation. The fifth deals with legislation for the conservation of plants, and the final section analyses the adequacy of South African legislation for the protection of plants.

11.2 ECOLOGICAL DRIVING VARIABLES

11.2.1 Geomorphology and soils

The South African landscape is characterized by great diversity and, relative to other parts of the world, great antiquity.[4] The geological history of the subcontinent extends back 3,8 billion years over which period the landscapes have evolved to their present state.[5] In simplest terms, the region is characterized by extensive plains and plateaux of the interior, spectacular mountain landscapes of the Great Escarpment and Cape regions, and a narrow undulating coastal plain. Thirty distinct terrain types are recognizable on the basis of relief and draïnage morphology.[6]

A consequence of this landscape antiquity is that most of the soils of the subcontinent are highly weathered and, especially in the wetter regions, relatively infertile.[7] Owing to the steeply dissected landscapes of the wetter eastern margin of the region and the duplex (sand on clay) structure of many of the soils, the potential for soil erosion is very high.[8] See chapter 10.

11.2.2 Climate

South Africa lies at the boundary between temperate and subtropical circulation features; climatic processes and patterns are therefore complex. Details on climatic determinants, rainfall-producing circulation types and climatic description can be found in several publications.[9] Only a short summary of some of the more important climatic features is given below.

South Africa, with a mean annual rainfall of 497 mm, is a semi-arid region. Only a comparatively narrow strip along the eastern and southern coastlines is moderately well watered. Summer rain, which influences all but the southwestern part of the subcontinent, is determined by a number of circulation patterns. These include the position of the centre of the Indian Ocean high-pressure cell which causes an onshore flow of moist air and high rainfall in the eastern parts; the presence of a heat-induced low in the arid interior which causes an inflow of moist air from the humid tropics; and the southward movement of the Inter-Tropical Convergence Zone, which also creates favourable conditions for rain over the eastern parts of the region.

The conditions favourable for adequate summer rainfall do not occur every year, and much of the subcontinent is subject to drought. A feature of the summer rainfall area is the apparent existence of eighteen-year cycles of approximately nine dry and nine wet

---

[3] Rutherford & Westfall 'The biomes of southern Africa—an objective characterization' 1986 (54) *Memoirs of the Botanical Survey of South Africa* 1–98.

[4] Wellington *Southern Africa* (1955); King *South African scenery* (1963).

[5] Truswell *The geological evolution of South Africa* (1977).

[6] Van Zyl ' 'n Kaart van die landvormstreke van Suid-Afrika' 1985 (13) *South African Geographer* 105–8.

[7] Von Harmse 'Schematic soil map of southern Africa' in Werger (ed) *Biogeography and ecology of southern Africa* (1978) 71–5.

[8] Schoeman & Scotney 'Agricultural potential as determined by soil terrain and climate' 1987 (83) *S Afr J Sci* 260–8.

[9] Schulze *Climate of South Africa Part 8 General survey* WB28 (1984); Tyson *Climatic change and variability in southern Africa* (1986); Van Heerden & Hurry *South Africa's weather patterns* (1989).

years.[10] These cycles have a profound impact on the region's plant ecological resources and processes.[11]

The southwestern part of the subcontinent is dry in summer because of the persistence of stable, dry anticyclonic conditions there. This region experiences relatively predictable winter rainfall associated with the passage of cold fronts which do not usually penetrate to the interior. Owing to the cooler conditions during the growing season, the southwest lacks extensive areas dominated by tropical, summer-growing grasses[12] which sustain high densities of indigenous ungulates in the summer rainfall areas.

Overall, the climate of southern Africa shows enormous spatial and temporal diversity. Conditions range from true desert to humid forest climates and from cool temperate to warm subtropical conditions. Crippling droughts are a common occurrence, particularly in the drier interior regions.

11.2.3 Grazing

Africa is exceptional amongst continents in that it has retained a diverse and dense large mammal fauna. The herbivore fauna has interacted with vegetation in a number of complex ways over evolutionary time.[13] These interactions regulate the balance of trees, bush and open grassland,[14] determine grassland species composition and growth form[15] and control ecosystem processes such as energy flow and nutrient cycling.[16]

Clearly, grazing by large mammals has been a major selective force in most South African ecosystems. Many of these ecosystems have shown surprising resilience to heavy, continuous grazing associated with pastoralism.[17] In most communities there is a suite of plant species which maintain high population density under conditions of heavy grazing.[18]

11.2.4 Fire

Fire has long been recognized as a natural phenomenon in African ecosystems and as an essential tool in man's management of those systems.[19] In southern Africa fire is an important ecological factor in the grasslands and savannas of the wetter summer rainfall regions and the fynbos of the southern and southwestern Cape.[20] In these areas fire has

---

[10] Tyson above n 9.

[11] For instance, Scotney 'The agricultural areas of southern Africa' in MacDonald & Crawford (eds) *Long term data series relating to southern Africa's renewable natural resources* South African National Scientific Programmes Report no 157 (1988) 316–36; Hoffman & Cowling 'Vegetation change in the semi-arid eastern Karoo over the last two hundred years: an expanding Karoo—fact or fiction? *S Afr J Sci* (in press); Huntley, Siegfried & Sunter *South African environments into the 21st century* (1989).

[12] Vogel, Fuls & Ellis 'The geographical distribution of Kranz grasses in South Africa' 1978 (74) *S Afr J Sci* 209–15.

[13] McNaughton, Ruess & Seagle 'Large mammals and process dynamics in African ecosystems' 1988 (38) *Bioscience* 794–800.

[14] For instance, Laws 'Elephants as agents of habitat and landscape change in East Africa' 1970 (21) *Oikos* 1–15.

[15] McNaughton 'Grazing lawns: animals in herds, plant form and coevolution' 1984 (124) *American Naturalist* 863–86.

[16] McNaughton 'The ecology of a grazing system: the Serengeti' 1985 (55) *Ecological Monographs* 259–94.

[17] Acocks 'Veld types of South Africa' 1975 (40) *Memoirs of the Botanical Survey of South Africa* (2 ed) 1–128; McKenzie *Ecological considerations of some past and present land-use practices in Transkei* (unpublished PhD thesis, University of Cape Town, 1984).

[18] See the references in Tainton (ed) *Veld and pasture management in South Africa* (1981).

[19] Phillips 'Fire: its influence on biotic communities and physical factors in South and East Africa' 1930 (27) *S Afr J Sci* 352–67.

[20] Edwards 'Fire regimes in the biome of South Africa' in Booysen & Tainton (eds) *Ecological effects of fire in South African ecosystems* (1984) 19–37.

been a major selective force in the evolution of plant and animal life histories.[21] Along with herbivorous mammals, fire plays a major role in determining the balance between trees and grass in southern African savannas[22] and grasslands.[23] The population sizes of many fynbos shrubs can undergo tremendous change (including local extinction) in response to different fires[24] and fire has been implicated as a determinant of speciation in the massively rich Cape flora.[25] One of the major strengths of southern African ecology has been the application, for judicious management, of knowledge relating to the effects of fire on ecosystem structure and functioning.[26]

11.3 BIODIVERSITY

As noted above, South Africa has one of the richest floras in the world. This is hardly surprising when one considers that the region contains one of the world's floral kingdoms (Cape flora), seven floristically distinct biomes[27] (Figure 11.1, Table 11.2) and 70 veld types.[28] The high level of species endemism (80 per cent) is another distinct feature of the southern African flora.[29] Below, the patterns of biodiversity within the biomes are briefly reviewed. Note that this analysis applies to southern Africa, as defined in section 11.1 above.

11.3.1 Fynbos biome

The fynbos biome includes three major vegetation formations: fynbos (evergreen; and largely small-leafed shrublands with an evergreen reed (Restionaceae) stratum), largely confined to the nutrient-poor soils of the Cape Folded Belt and the sandy coastal forelands; renoster shrublands (small-leafed, evergreen shrublands with a grassy understorey), confined to the base-rich, shale- and granite-derived soils of the coastal forelands and intermontane valleys; and subtropical thicket (large-leafed, evergreen shrublands), confined to calcareous coastal dunes and fire-protected valley and mountain sites.[30]

Despite its small size (2,7 per cent of southern Africa), the fynbos biome has the richest flora of southern African biomes (Table 11.2). The biome includes the Cape Floristic Kingdom, with exceptionally high levels of regional and local endemism.[31] The great richness of the biome is a function of the exceptionally high floristic turnover, or change, of moderately rich communities along environmental gradients (beta diversity) and high turnover within communities along geographical gradients (gamma diver-

---

[21] Frost 'The response and survival of organisms in fire-prone environments' in Booysen & Tainton (eds) above n 20, 273–309.

[22] Trollope 'Fire in savanna' in Booysen & Tainton (eds) above n 20, 149–75.

[23] Tainton & Mentis 'Fire in grassland' in Booysen & Mentis above n 20, 115–48.

[24] Kruger & Bigalke 'Fire in fynbos' in Booysen & Tainton (eds) above n 20, 67–113.

[25] Cowling 'Fire and its role in coexistence and speciation in Gondwanan shrublands' 1987 (83) *S Afr J Sci* 106–12.

[26] For instance, Edwards 'The use of fire as a management tool' in Booysen & Tainton (eds) above n 20, 349–62.

[27] Rutherford & Westfall above n 3.

[28] Acocks above n 17.

[29] Goldblatt 'An analysis of the flora of southern Africa: its characteristics, relationships and origins' 1978 (65) *Annals of the Missouri Botanical Garden* 369–436.

[30] Taylor 'Capensis' in Werger (ed) above n 7, 171–230; Kruger 'South African heathland' in Specht (ed) *Heathlands and related shrublands. Descriptive studies* (1979) 19–80; Moll, Campbell, Cowling, Bossie, Jarman & Boucher *A description of vegetation categories in and adjacent to the fynbos biome* South African National Scientific Programmes Report no 83 (1984); Campbell 'A classification of the mountain vegetation of the fynbos biome' 1985 (50) *Memoirs of the Botanical Survey of South Africa* 1–115.

[31] Bond & Goldblatt 'Plants of the Cape flora—a descriptive catalogue' 1984 (suppl vol 13) *J of South African Botany*; Cowling, Holmes & Rebelo 'Plant diversity and endemism' in Cowling (ed) *The ecology of fynbos. Nutrients, fire and diversity* (1991).

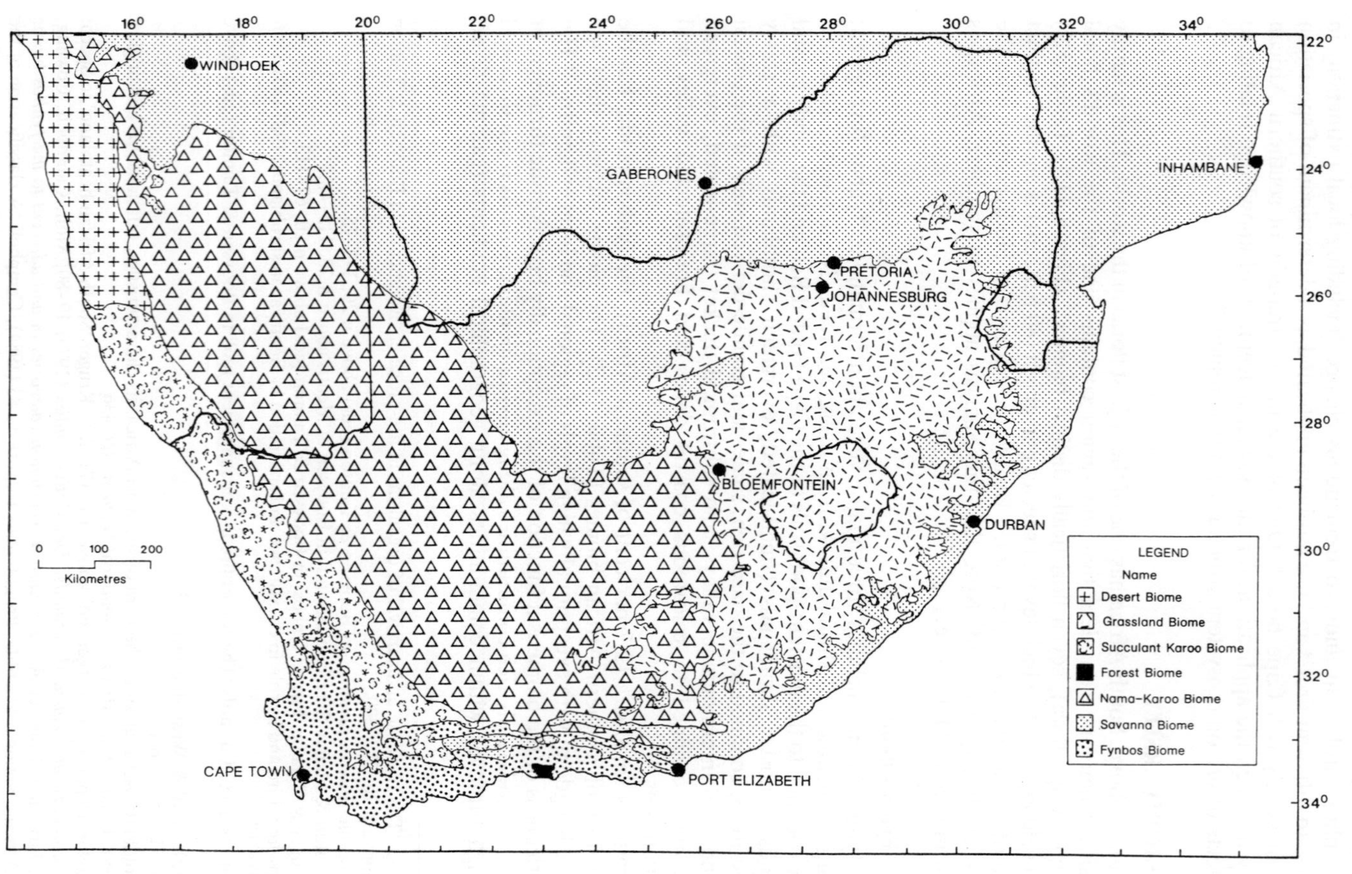

Figure 11.1 Biomes of southern Africa according to Rutherford and Westfall (n 3). Symbols indicate quarter-degree grids searched in PRECIS for each biome and comprise Gibbs Russel's (n 39) core biome regions.

sity).[32] This means that the floristic compositions show spectacular changes over very small distances. As a result, many species are rare. The fynbos biome has the highest number (1 326) of rare and endangered taxa for any biome in southern Africa.[33]

TABLE 11.2

Characteristics and plant species richness of southern African biomes. Data from a compilation in Cowling et al above n 1.

Biome	% of southern Africa	Rainfall (mm per annum)	Rainfall (season)	Vegetation	No of species in core biome* area	Core area as % of total biome
Fynbos	2,7	210–3 000	Winter (to all year)	Evergreen, sclerophyllous shrubland	73 156	52,4
Savanna	54,0	235–900	Summer	Wooded C_4grassland	5 788	45,3
Grassland	13,3	400–2 000	Summer	Grassland	3 788	32,6
Nama–Karoo	22,4	100–520	Summer	Dwarf and low open shrub-land	2 147	34,3
Succulent–Karoo	4,3	20–290	Winter (to all year)	Dwarf and low, open, succulent shrub-land	2 125	45,5
Desert	3,3	10–70	Summer	Open, ephem-eral herbland	497	48,8
Forest	<1	525–2 000	Winter to Summer	Closed, ever-green and semi-deciduous forest	No data	—

* For definition of core biome, see Cowling et al above n 1.

The maintenance of diversity in fynbos communities is poorly understood and apparently controlled by a wide array of factors.[34] In this respect, fire plays a major role[35] and is readily accessible as a tool for management.[36]

11.3.2 Savanna biome

The savanna biome includes the wooded grasslands of the subtropical summer rainfall regions of southern Africa (Figure 11.1). A distinction is normally made between arid (eutrophic or nutrient-rich) and moist (dystrophic or nutrient-poor) savanna.[37] Although this biome occupies 54 per cent of southern Africa, it has fewer species than the fynbos biome (Table 11.2). This is probably a function of lower beta

[32] Cowling, Holmes & Rebelo above n 31.
[33] Hilton-Taylor & Le Roux 'Conservation status of the fynbos and karoo biomes' in Huntley (ed) above n 1, 202–23.
[34] Cowling, Holmes & Rebelo above n 31.
[35] Kruger & Bigalke above n 24.
[36] Van Wilgen, Bond & Richardson 'The management of fynbos ecosystems. Current status and future scenarios' in Cowling (ed) above n 31.
[37] Huntley 'Characteristics of South African biomes' in Booysen & Tainton above n 20, 1–18.

and gamma diversity.[38] However, by African standards, the southern African savanna region is very species-rich and 43 per cent of the species are endemic to the subcontinent.[39]

The savanna biome is home to many large mammal species which, together with fire, play a decisive role in ecosystem processes and the maintenance of plant species diversity.[40]

11.3.3 Grassland biome

The grassland biome is centred on the high interior plateau of southern Africa (Figure 11.1) and occupies about 13 per cent of the subcontinent (Table 11.2). A distinction is usually made between 'sour' and 'sweet' grassveld.[41] The former implies a significant decrease in forage acceptability and nutritive value in winter; the latter implies that the acceptability and nutritive value of forage remain relatively unchanged from summer to winter. The distribution of these types is largely influenced by rainfall and the resultant extent to which soils are leached. Thus, in the grassland biome sweetveld and sourveld correspond broadly with arid savanna and moist savanna, respectively, in the savanna biome.

Grassland communities are as species-rich as those in the fynbos biome, but beta and gamma diversities are probably considerably lower.[42] The core region of the grassland biome includes 3 788 species (Table 11.2), a surprisingly high figure. The grassland biome flora is distinct and comprises a centre of diversity for many large genera.[43]

There are no data on the maintenance of species richness in southern Africa grasslands, despite many decades of intensive research in the biome.[44] However, fire and grazing have a major impact on the composition of grasslands and are almost certainly important determinants of species richness.[45] Manipulation of these factors for management is usually geared towards the maintenance of economically desirable species rather than species richness per se.[46]

11.3.4 Nama–karoo biome

The Nama–karoo biome covers the drier portion of the interior of southern Africa (Figure 11.1) and occupies 22,4 per cent of the subcontinent. The vegetation of the biome can best be described as grassy, dwarf shrubland.[47]

The Nama–karoo has a relatively depauperate flora for its size (2 147 species) (Table 11.2). Alpha richness is lower than the other biomes (excluding the desert biome, for which there are no data) and turnover is probably also low.[48] However, on a global scale, the Nama–karoo has rich flora for a semi-arid region, certainly as rich as the Sonoran Desert of North America—1,5 times its size.

There are almost no data on the maintenance of diversity in Nama–karoo communities. Ecosystems dynamics of semi-arid regions such as the Nama–karoo are non-equilibrial in that productivity is determined by stochastic rainfall events and is

---

[38] Cowling, Gibbs Russell, Hoffman & Hilton-Taylor above n 1.

[39] Gibbs Russell 'Preliminary floristic analysis of the major biomes in southern Africa' 1987 (17) *Bothalia* 213–27.

[40] For instance, McNaughton, Ruess & Seagle above n 13; Yeaton 'Porcupines, fire and the dynamics of the tree layer in the Burko African savanna' 1988 (76) *J of Ecology* 1017–29.

[41] Huntley above n 37.

[42] Cowling, Gibbs Russell, Hoffman & Hilton-Taylor above n 1.

[43] Gibbs Russell above n 39.

[44] Tainton above n 18.

[45] Tainton, Zacharias & Hardy 'The contribution of veld diversity to the agricultural economy' in Huntley (ed) above n 1, 107–20.

[46] Tainton above n 18.

[47] Rutherford & Westfall above n 3.

[48] Cowling, Gibbs Russell, Hoffman & Hilton-Taylor above n 1.

little affected by density-dependent feedback controls associated with herbivore numbers.[49] Thus, pulses of productivity, largely associated with the establishment and growth of grass from soil-stored seed banks, show enormous spatial and temporal variation over the Nama–karoo landscape. In pre-colonial times this productivity was exploited by migratory cells of indigenous ungulates.[50] Since colonial times, the trend has been towards the confinement of livestock to grazing camps. In many cases this has resulted in the spectacular destruction of Nama–karoo vegetation and an associated decline in species richness.[51]

11.3.5 Succulent–karoo biome

The succulent–karoo biome is largely confined to the arid coastal forelands of western southern Africa (Figure 11.1), a region which receives most of its rainfall in the winter months. The vegetation is overwhelmingly dominated by dwarf succulent shrubs; perennial grasses are rare but annuals (mainly dicots) are very prominent during the spring.[52] The succulent–karoo environment is relatively benign for a semi-arid region: temperature ranges are less extreme and rainfall less variable than the Nama–karoo.[53]

The succulent–karoo includes the world's richest succulent flora concentrated in families such as the Mesembryanthemaceae (southern Africa's largest family), Euphorbiaceae, Asclepidaceae and Crassulaceae.[54] Many species are regional and local endemics. A core region richness of 2 125 species (Table 11.2) is certainly an underestimate, owing to undercollecting. Le Roux[55] estimates that there are 3 500 taxa in Namaqualand alone.

The very high alpha richness in succulent–karoo communities (up to 113 species per 1 000 m^2) is unparalleled for semi-arid regions.[56] Nothing is known about how this diversity is maintained and, in particular, how coexistence of so many species belonging to the same growth form (succulent dwarf shrubs) is mediated.

11.3.6 Desert biome

The desert biome in southern Africa corresponds to what is known as the Namib Desert, which forms the broad coastal plain north of the Lüderitz area in Namibia. As such, no true desert occurs in South Africa.

The vegetation is characterized by the dominance of annuals (Table 11.1) but includes many dwarf shrubs, perennial grasses and trees which are largely confined to drainage lines.

The core region includes 497 species, by far the most species-poor of the southern African biomes (Table 11.2). Only 16 per cent of the species are endemic, but these include interesting and sometimes ancient taxa.[57] There are no data on community-level

---

[49] Roux & Vorster 'Vegetation change in the Karoo' 1983 (18) *Proceedings of the Grassland Society of Southern Africa* 25–9; Hoffman & Cowling 'Desertification in the lower Sundays River Valley' 1990 *J of Arid Environments* (in press).

[50] Hoffman 'The rationale for Karoo grazing systems: criticisms and research implications' 1988 (84) *S Afr J Sci* 556–9.

[51] Hoffman *Vegetation studies and the impact of grazing in the semi-arid eastern Cape* (unpublished PhD thesis, University of Cape Town, 1989).

[52] Rutherford & Westfall above n 3.

[53] Hoffman & Cowling 'Plant physiognomy, phenology and demography' in Cowling & Le Roux (eds) *The Karoo biome: a preliminary synthesis: part 2. Vegetation and history* South African National Scientific Programmes Report no 142 (1987).

[54] Hilton-Taylor 'Phytogeography and origins of the karoo flora' in Cowling & Le Roux (eds) above n 53; Van Jaarsveld 'The succulent riches of South Africa and Namibia' 1987 (24) *Aloe* 45–92.

[55] A Le Roux pers comm.

[56] Cowling, Gibbs Russell, Hoffman & Hilton-Taylor above n 1.

[57] Goldblatt above n 29.

richness; it is probably related directly to moisture levels.[58]

11.3.7 Forest biome

The forest biome includes the indigenous evergreen and semi-deciduous closed forests of the coastal lowlands and escarpment which occupy less than 1 per cent of southern Africa. The southern African forests are related to the upland Afromontane forests and lowland Guineo-Congolian forests of tropical Africa. Afromontane forest occurs in small patches along the eastern escarpment and along the coast from Humansdorp to the Cape Peninsula. Lowland forests occur on the coastal plain north of Algoa Bay.[59]

Geldenhuys & MacDevette[60] estimate a total forest biome flora of 1 285 species. This is about 5 per cent of southern Africa's species in an area occupying less than 1 per cent of the subcontinent. Forest communities are moderately rich in species and richness increases with decreasing latitude.[61] There are no data on turnover, although gamma diversity is probably low.

Very little is known regarding the maintenance of diversity in southern African forests. Geldenhuys & MacDevette[62] generalize, with reservation, that undisturbed forest is richer than disturbed forest, and that mature forest is richer than regrowth or seral forest.

11.4 RESOURCE DEGRADATION

Virtually every ecosystem in South Africa has been modified or transformed by human activities and this has led to extensive degradation of plant resources. The precise extent of these transformations and their impact on the structure and functioning of ecosystems is difficult to determine. MacDonald[63] has estimated that about 25 per cent of South Africa has been transformed largely by cultivation (55 per cent) and urban and peri-urban developments (26 per cent). The implications of these transformations for the degradation of plant resources are briefly discussed below.

11.4.1 Agriculture

In terms of agriculturally related transformations, cultivation has had the largest impact on South African plant resources. Schoeman & Scotney[64] estimate that about 12 per cent of the white-controlled portion of South Africa is under cultivation. MacDonald[65] cites unpublished data of the Department of Development Aid indicating that 13,5 per cent of the six 'national states' was estimated to be under cultivation in 1989.

Cultivation has been most severe on the shale-derived soils of the southern and southwestern Cape coastal forelands which once supported renoster shrublands.[66] McDowell[67] estimates that in 1979 73 per cent of the west coast renoster shrubland area had been cultivated. Much of the higher rainfall areas of the grassland biome have been

---

[58] Cf Yeaton 'The structure and function of Namib dune grasslands: characteristics of the environmental gradients and species distributions' 1988 (76) *J of Ecology* 744–58.

[59] Rutherford & Westfall above n 3.

[60] 'Conservation status of coastal montane evergreen forest' in Huntley (ed) above n 1, 224–38.

[61] Ibid.

[62] Ibid.

[63] 'Man's role in changing the face of South Africa' in Huntley (ed) above n 1.

[64] Above n 8.

[65] Above n 63.

[66] Cowling, Moll & Pierce 'Conservation and utilization of South Coast Renosterveld, an endangered South African vegetation type' 1986 (37) *Biological Conservation* 363–77.

[67] *Factors affecting the conservation of Renosterveld by private landowners* (unpublished PhD thesis, University of Cape Town, 1988).

cultivated.[68] These include the Transvaal Highveld and the mesic coastal lowlands and mistbelt region of Natal.[69]

About 70 per cent of South Africa is set aside as natural grazing.[70] Most of this natural grazing land is seriously overstocked and as much as 60 per cent of the veld is currently in poor condition.[71] MacDonald[72] documents grazing-induced vegetation changes in South Africa which have resulted in the partial destruction of indigenous plant resources. These include:

- encroachment of karoo shrubs into the drier portions of the grassland biome;[73]
- reduction of grass cover in the Nama–karoo biome;
- encroachment of shrubs, particularly *Acacia karoo*, into the eastern Cape grasslands;
- replacement of palatable grasses by unpalatable ones throughout the grassland biome;
- an increase in the density of trees and shrubs in the savanna biome.

Added to this list should be the elimination, as a result of overutilization by goats, of succulent thicket in the arid savanna biome of the southeastern Cape.[74]

11.4.2 Urbanization

MacDonald[75] estimates that by 1982 about 2,5 per cent of South Africa had been transformed by urbanization. Clearly, urbanization has an irreversibly destructive impact on plant resources. These impacts are most dramatic in urban areas which harbour rare species and communities. An example of such an area is the Cape Peninsula and Cape Flats where five species are extinct and a further 169 have an uncertain future.[76] The elimination of rare species and communities as a result of sprawling coastal development is a major threat to plant resources in the fynbos biome. A dramatic example exists in the southeastern Cape, where endemic-rich dune fynbos is threatened by coastal developments which have been proclaimed along the entire coast between Cape St Francis and the Gamtoos River Mouth.[77]

11.4.3 Alien plants and afforestation

Transformations associated with alien plants are most severe in the fynbos biome, where it is estimated that 14 321 km^2 (20,5 per cent of the biome) was invaded to some extent by species of *Acacia*, *Hakea* and *Pinus* in 1984.[78] Dense stands of aliens result in local extinctions of fynbos species and significantly reduce fynbos community-level richness.[79] These invasions currently pose the most serious threat to the survival of biomes both numerous and rare and of endangered plant species.[80]

---

[68] Rutherford & Westfall above n 3.
[69] MacDonald above n 63.
[70] Schoeman & Scotney above n 8.
[71] Scotney above n 11.
[72] Above n 63.
[73] But see Hoffman & Cowling above n 11.
[74] Hoffman & Cowling above n 49.
[75] Above n 63.
[76] Hall & Ashton *Threatened plants of the Cape Peninsula* Threatened Plants Research Group, University of Cape Town (1983).
[77] Cowling 'The coastal dune ecosystems of the Humansdorp district—a plea for their conservation' 1980 (70) *Eastern Cape Naturalist* 1–115.
[78] MacDonald, Jarman & Beeston (eds) *Management of invasive alien plants in the fynbos biome* South African National Scientific Programmes Report no 111 (1985).
[79] Richardson, MacDonald & Forsyth 'Reduction in plant species richness under stands of alien trees and shrubs in the fynbos biome' 1989 (149) *South African Forestry J* 1–8.
[80] Hall & Veldhuis *South African Red Data Book: plants—fynbos and karoo biomes* South African National Scientific Programmes Report no 117 (1985).

Other biomes are less severely invaded by aliens. Some 8 000 km^2 of the lowland forest biome of Natal is invaded by *Chromolaena odorata. Optuntia* spp have invaded extensive areas of arid savanna and dry grassland in the eastern Cape. Drainage lines in the arid savanna, Nama–karoo and desert biomes in the northern Cape and Namibia are invaded by *Prosopis* spp, *Nicotiana glauca* and *Datura* spp.[81] However, nowhere is the situation as serious in terms of resource degradation and species extinction as in the fynbos biome.

South Africa's demand for timber, currently produced entirely from plantations of exotic trees, is increasing at about 3 per cent per annum.[82] At present an area of 13 960 km^2 is afforested in southern Africa and more than half the area of plantation is located on the escarpment of the eastern Transvaal. That these plantations pose a threat to indigenous plant life is borne out by the fact that 30 per cent of the rare and endangered plants in the Transvaal occur in habitats subject to afforestation.[83]

11.4.4 Other transformations

Other transformations which pose a threat to indigenous plant life in South Africa include river impoundment, mining and transportation networks.[84]

11.5 CONSERVATION

11.5.1 Conservation inside nature reserves

Although 70 per cent of southern Africa's (here excluding Namibia and Botswana) publicly owned terrestrial nature reserves are relatively small,[85] Siegfried[86] has estimated that up to 74 per cent of the subcontinent's plant species is preserved in nature reserves. See chapter 27 for a full discussion of protected areas.

All of the biomes in southern Africa are represented in the reserve network (Table 11.3). Much of the fynbos biome is conserved but reserves are centred in the mountains: conservation status of the lowlands is critical where only 4,8 per cent of the fynbos and 2,2 per cent of renosterveld is conserved.[87]

The conservation status of the two karoo biomes is very poor. After the fynbos biome, the succulent–karoo has the highest concentration of rare and endangered species in South Africa.[88] The global significance of the succulent flora in this region demands that appropriate steps are taken to conserve it. Hilton-Taylor and Le Roux[89] list conservation priorities for both the succulent–karoo and Nama–karoo biomes.

With the exception of the grassland biome, the conservation status of the other biomes appears to be adequate. The savanna biomes include some very large reserves established for the conservation of large mammal species. Since almost 80 per cent of southern Africa's forest region is conserved, it is reasonable to assume that populations of most forest species are included in reserves. The conservation status of the desert biome in Namibia is exceptionally good as most of the area is conserved in the Namib–Naukluft Park, Skeleton Coast Park and unworked restricted diamond areas.[90]

Siegfried[91] draws attention to the woeful lack of a plant inventory data for southern

---

[81] See the references in MacDonald above n 63.
[82] Huntley, Siegfried & Sunter above n 11.
[83] Raal 'The Transvaal threatened plants programme' 1986 (44) *Fauna and Flora* 17–21.
[84] These are discussed by MacDonald above n 63.
[85] Siegfried 'Preservation of species in southern African nature reserves' in Huntley (ed) above n 1, 186–223.
[86] Ibid.
[87] Hilton-Taylor & Le Roux above n 33.
[88] Ibid.
[89] Ibid.
[90] Rutherford & Westfall above n 3.
[91] Above n 85.

Africa's reserves. There is also almost no information on the extent to which reserves conserve populations of indigenous plant species. In this respect a start has been made on understanding patterns and processes related to fragmentation of natural communities in the fynbos biome.[92] More research is required on the genetic and demographic impacts of fragmentation in order to predict the long-term sustainability of populations in reserves.[93]

TABLE 11.3

Conservation of plant species in southern African biomes. Southern Africa excludes Namibia and Botswana. Data from Siegfried above n 85.

	Percentage of southern African reserves	Biome area reserved (%)	No of plant species occurring in reserves (% of biome total)
Fynbos	22,9	26,3	2 540 (34,8)
Moist savanna	24,1	5,0	2 031 (53,4)
Arid savanna	17,4	12,01	1 673 (49,5)
Grassland	24,4	2,0	2 775 (82,1)
Nama–karoo	4,6	0,8	748 (34,8)
Succulent–karoo	1,9	0,8	843 (40,1)
Forest	4,8	88,4	no data

11.5.2 Conservation outside nature reserves

Most of South Africa's natural vegetation occurs on land which is privately or communally owned. Much of this land is managed for extensive pastoralism or, in parts of the fynbos biome, for the harvesting of wild flowers. It is generally accepted that management for sustained production from natural vegetation is usually compatible with the maintenance of species diversity.[94] The appropriate management of plant resources outside nature reserves will contribute massively to the overall conservation of plant biodiversity in South Africa. The establishment of nature conservancies in Natal and elsewhere is a positive step in this direction.

11.5.3 Justifying conservation

By global standards, southern Africa has an impressive network of protected areas which preserve enormous numbers of plant species in a great diversity of habitats. These reserves have been established and developed largely by private funds. The continued existence of protected areas may not be assured in a post-apartheid South Africa where racially based imbalances in access to land will need to be redressed. Is there any justification for the conservation of the subcontinent's plant diversity?

It is very difficult to place monetary value on plant diversity, whether as a commodity or an amenity.[95] Rural black South Africans, for example, are dependent on a wide

---

[92] Bond, Midgley & Vlok 'When is an island not an island? Insular effects and their causes in fynbos islands' 1988 (77) *Oecologia* 515–21; Cowling & Bond 'How small can reserves be? An empirical approach in Cape fynbos' 1990 *Biological Conservation*.

[93] Bond above n 2.

[94] Tainton, Zacharias & Hardy above n 45; Cowling 'Flames and flowers: challenges of the Cape flora' 1989 (85) *S Afr J Sci* 289–90.

[95] Huntley 'Introduction. The challenges of maintaining biotic diversity in a changing world' in Huntley (ed) above n 1, xiii–xix.

variety of indigenous plant resources for building materials, fuel wood and foodstuffs.[96] An important point is the potentially strong link between conservation and tourism. Thirty-six per cent of foreign tourists to South Africa, who in 1988 were the fifth largest earner of foreign exchange (R150 000 million), visited the country for its natural resources.[97] These resources include the spectacular plant life of South Africa, especially the flora of the fynbos and succulent–karoo biomes. It is expected that the foreign tourists will increase by as much as 15 per cent annually and this rate could well accelerate in a post-apartheid era. Researchers with the SA Tourism Board (Satour) believe that this country has enormous potential to attract 'natural resources-oriented visitors' who have money to spend and require less infrastructure than 'facility-oriented visitors'.[98] Clearly, the continued conservation of natural areas is a necessary requirement to attract these tourists.

A further point regarding protected areas relates to the benefits accrued by human populations surrounding them. Some of the most scenic and biologically interesting regions of South Africa occur in communally owned rural lands. It is believed now that wildlife conservation in these areas cannot be sustained without acceptance and support of the rural communities which surround them.[99] There is enormous potential to develop additional reserves and resorts, particularly in the coastal belt of Transkei and KwaZulu. However, such developments should not disrupt unduly traditional land-use and should provide direct benefits for local inhabitants (e g in the form of a levy) which could be used to provide community facilities and other needs.

11.6 SUMMARY

For areas of comparable size, southern Africa has the richest flora in the world. A combination of climatic, topographic and edaphic diversity has resulted in steep ecological gradients along which numerous species can be packed. Outstanding floristic features of the region include the exceptionally species-rich fynbos and succulent–karoo floras.

Nearly three-quarters of the subcontinent's plant species are preserved in a network of nature reserves located in all of the region's biomes and covering about six per cent of its area. The long-term conservation of these populations cannot be predicted, owing to a dearth of data on the demographic and genetic consequences of fragmentation.

Major challenges for the future include the consolidation of reserves in underrepresented regions, the improved management of natural plant resources outside reserves, and the need to justify protected areas within the framework of major and far-reaching socio-political change in South Africa.

The following sections of this chapter discuss the legal instruments available for the protection and conservation of plants.

11.7 LEGISLATION FOR THE CONSERVATION OF PLANTS

11.7.1 Introduction

There are a number of Acts and ordinances in terms of which plants, used in the wide sense denoting flora generally, are conserved. The principal legislation comprises the various provincial nature conservation ordinances and the Forest Act 122 of 1984. Some other important Acts include the National Parks Act 57 of 1976, the Mountain

---

[96] Cunningham 'Indigenous plant use: balancing human needs and resources' in Huntley (ed) above n 1, 93–106.

[97] Zevenbergen *Report on second survey of motivation for international tourism to RSA and evaluation of tourism facilities by foreign tourists* Satour Report no 15 (1989).

[98] C Fouche pers comm.

[99] Infield *Wildlife resources, utilization and attitudes towards conservation: a case study of the Hluhluwe and Umfolozi Game Reserves in Natal/KwaZulu* (unpublished MSc thesis, University of Natal–Pietermaritzburg, 1986); Cunningham above n 96.

Catchment Areas Act 63 of 1970, the Lake Areas Development Act 39 of 1975, the National Monuments Act 28 of 1969, the Conservation of Agricultural Resources Act 43 of 1983 and the Environment Conservation Act 73 of 1989. As in the case of wild animals and fish, it is necessary to draw a distinction between the conservation of plants within protected areas and conservation outside such areas.

11.7.2 Conservation of plants within protected areas

The various types of protected areas are dealt with in chapter 27. The general observation is made that, as is revealed in chapter 27, the conservation of plants within protected areas is much more substantial than is the case outside such areas. It is of decisive importance that the conservation of plants within protected areas relates to the entire habitat and not only to individual protected plant species.

11.7.3 Conservation of plants outside protected areas

11.7.3.1 *Introduction*

The most important legislation in terms of which indigenous plants outside protected areas are conserved is the various nature conservation ordinances, namely the Transvaal Nature Conservation Ordinance 12 of 1983, the Orange Free State Nature Conservation Ordinance 8 of 1969, the Natal Nature Conservation Ordinance 15 of 1974 and the Cape Nature and Environmental Conservation Ordinance 19 of 1974. The provisions of these ordinances will accordingly be set out in some detail. There is a variety of further legislation in terms of which plants (not necessarily indigenous) can be protected, namely the Forest Act, the National Monuments Act, the Conservation of Agricultural Resources Act, the Mountain Catchment Areas Act, the Sea Fishery Act 12 of 1988 and the Lake Areas Development Act.

11.7.3.2 *Protected plants*

Except for some endangered or rare species, only indigenous plants are protected in terms of the various provincial nature conservation ordinances. An indigenous plant is legally defined as being any species of plant, shrub or tree that is indigenous to South Africa (whether cultivated or not and whether it is no longer growing in the wild state or has for some time not been growing in the wild state) and includes the flower, seed, fruit, bulb, tuber, stem or root or any other part of such plant, shrub or tree; but not a plant, shrub or tree declared in terms of law to be a weed.[100]

Not all plants enjoy comprehensive protection in terms of the provincial nature conservation ordinances. A classification of plants into various categories has been made and the scope of a plant's protection depends to a large degree upon its status within this classification. The following categories are distinguished in schedules to the ordinances: unprotected, protected, and specially protected indigenous plants (Natal);[101] protected and specially protected plants,[102] as well as endangered and rare species (Transvaal);[103] protected plants as well as endangered and scarce species (OFS);[104] protected and endangered flora as well as indigenous unprotected flora

[100] Section 1(xxvi) of the Transvaal Ordinance; s 1 of the OFS Ordinance; s 1 of the Natal Ordinance and s 2(xxviii) and (xxxiii) of the Cape Ordinance.

[101] Section 1 ('protected indigenous plant'; 'specially protected indigenous plant'; 'unprotected indigenous plant'); Chapter II (ss 190–211) of the Natal Ordinance.

[102] Section 1(xlv)—('protected plant'); 1(liv)—('specially protected plant'); Chapter VII (ss 86–96) of the Transvaal Ordinance.

[103] Chapter VIII (ss 97–98) of the Transvaal Ordinance.

[104] Section 1 ('endangered species', 'scarce species'); chapter IV (ss 30–34) of the OFS Ordinance.

(Cape).[105] The Administrator may by notice in the *Official Gazette* include in or delete from some schedules the name of any indigenous plant.[106]

(a) Indigenous plants in general. Certain provisions of the various nature conservation ordinances apply to all indigenous plants. In Natal all plants indigenous to the Republic of South Africa or Namibia are in principle included in the schedule specifying protected indigenous plants.[107] Only a few plants are listed as unprotected indigenous plants,[108] while specially protected indigenous plants are listed separately[109] and further provisions apply specially to them. The Natal provisions for the conservation of plants thus apply in principle to all indigenous plants.

All indigenous plants on or along public roads are protected in all the provinces.[110] No indigenous plant may be picked without the permission of the landowner.[111] The Cape and Natal Ordinances also regulate the donation[112] and exportation[113] of all indigenous plants, while the Cape has separate provisions dealing with the possession of such plants[114] and with the sale of unprotected indigenous plants.[115] The Natal Ordinance also regulates the purchase,[116] sale,[117] donation and exchange[118] of indigenous plants.

It should be borne in mind that, since the above-mentioned provisions apply to all indigenous plants, they therefore also apply to the categories of plants which are discussed below.

(b) Protected indigenous plants. A category of protected plants (or flora) is distinguished in all the ordinances. A permit is required in Natal lawfully to sell protected indigenous plants.[119] As far as protected plants are concerned, the other provinces all have provisions dealing with the picking,[120] sale[121] and purchase[122] of such plants. In addition, the Transvaal and OFS have provisions regarding the donation,[123] conveyance,[124] exportation[125] and importation[126] of such plants.

(i) *Specially protected indigenous plants.* The Transvaal and Natal Ordinances identify a further category of protected plants, namely specially protected plants.[127] In

---

[105] Section 1(xxiv) ('endangered flora'); 1(liv) ('protected flora'); 1(xxxiv) ('indigenous unprotected flora'); Chapter VI (ss 62–72) of the Cape Ordinance.

[106] Section 86(2) of the Transvaal Ordinance (sch 7 and 7A) and s 30(2) of the OFS Ordinance (sch 6).

[107] Schedule 11.

[108] Schedule 10.

[109] Schedule 12.

[110] Section 89 of the Transvaal Ordinance; s 32 of the OFS Ordinance; s 63(1)*(b)*(ii) of the Cape Ordinance, and s 202 of the Natal Ordinance.

[111] Section 90 of the Transvaal Ordinance; s 31 of the OFS Ordinance; s 63(1)*(c)* of the Cape Ordinance. Cf also s 205 of the Natal Ordinance.

[112] Section 71 of the Cape Ordinance and s 197 of the Natal Ordinance.

[113] Section 70 of the Cape Ordinance and s 198 of the Natal Ordinance.

[114] Section 72.

[115] Sections 68 and 69.

[116] Section 194.

[117] Section 195.

[118] Section 197.

[119] Section 195.

[120] Section 87 of the Transvaal Ordinance; s 30(3) of the OFS Ordinance, and s 63(1)*(b)*(i) of the Cape Ordinance.

[121] Section 91 of the Transvaal Ordinance; s 33(1) of the OFS Ordinance, and ss 64, 66 and 67 of the Cape Ordinance.

[122] Section 92 of the Transvaal Ordinance; s 33(2) of the OFS Ordinance, and s 64 of the Cape Ordinance.

[123] Section 91 of the Transvaal Ordinance and s 33(1)–(2) of the OFS Ordinance.

[124] Section 93 of the Transvaal Ordinance and s 34 of the OFS Ordinance.

[125] Section 91 of the Transvaal Ordinance and s 33(1) of the OFS Ordinance.

[126] Section 93 of the Transvaal Ordinance and s 33(1) of the OFS Ordinance.

[127] Section 1(liv) of the Transvaal Ordinance and s 1 of the Natal Ordinance.

both of these ordinances the sale,[128] importation[129] and picking (or gathering)[130] of such plants are regulated, while the Transvaal Ordinance also regulates the possession, purchase, donation and receipt as well as the donation, conveyance and exportation[131] of such plants.

(ii) *Endangered and scarce plants.* A category of endangered and rare or scarce species of plants is distinguished in the Ordinances of the Transvaal and the OFS.[132] The Cape Ordinance lists endangered species as a special category.[133] In these ordinances the importation and exportation[134] of such plants are regulated, while the OFS and Cape Ordinances also deal with their sale or donation[135] as well as their purchase or receipt as a donation.[136] The Cape Ordinance regulates the picking[137] of endangered flora and also prescribes special measures to ensure the survival of such flora.[138]

11.7.3.3 *Picking protected and other indigenous plants*

It is an offence to pick a protected plant without a permit.[139] 'Pick' or 'gather' is defined in wide terms as including cut, chop off, take, pluck, uproot, break, damage or destroy.[140] Exemptions with respect to protected plants on his land are provided in favour of the owner of land and of some of his relatives.[141]

It is likewise an offence to pick protected and any other indigenous plants on land of which one is the occupier, without the written permission of the landowner.[142]

As set out above, the picking of any indigenous plant on a public road or within a certain area on both sides of a public road, without a permit, is also an offence.[143] Exceptions are provided in favour of the landowner and some of his relatives[144] and in respect of plants unavoidably destroyed in the course of lawful road development and maintenance[145] as well as any lawful agricultural or developmental activity.[146]

---

[128] Section 96 of the Transvaal Ordinance and s 196(1) of the Natal Ordinance.
[129] Section 96 of the Transvaal Ordinance and s 199 of the Natal Ordinance.
[130] Section 96 of the Transvaal Ordinance and s 200 of the Natal Ordinance.
[131] Section 96.
[132] Section 97 of the Transvaal Ordinance and s 1 of the OFS Ordinance.
[133] Section 2(xxvii) and (xxxii) of the Cape Ordinance.
[134] Section 98 of the Transvaal Ordinance; s 33(1) of the OFS Ordinance and s 62(1) of the Cape Ordinance.
[135] Section 33(1) of the OFS Ordinance and s 62(1) of the Cape Ordinance.
[136] Section 33(2) of the OFS Ordinance and s 62(1) of the Cape Ordinance.
[137] Section 63(1)*(b)*(i).
[138] Section 17.
[139] Sections 87 ('protected plants') and 96 ('specially protected plants') of the Transvaal Ordinance; ss 30(3) and 40(1)*(d)* ('all protected plants') of the OFS Ordinance; ss 200 and 208(1)*(a)*(ii) ('specially protected plants') of the Natal Ordinance, and ss 62(1) ('endangered'), 63(1)*(b)*(i) ('endangered or protected') and 85*(a)* of the Cape Ordinance. The Cape Ordinance also provides that it is an offence to uproot the plant in the process of (lawfully) picking any flora—s 63(1)*(a)*.
[140] Section 1(xxix) of the Transvaal Ordinance ('pick'); s 1 of the OFS Ordinance ('pick'); s 1 of Natal Ordinance ('gather'), and s 1(xlviii) of the Cape Ordinance ('pick').
[141] Section 87(1) of the Transvaal Ordinance; s 30(3) of the OFS Ordinance; s 200(2) of the Natal Ordinance, and s 63(3) of the Cape Ordinance.
[142] Section 90 of the Transvaal Ordinance; ss 31(1) and 40 of the OFS Ordinance; ss 200(1) and (3) and 208 of the Natal Ordinance, and ss 63(1)*(c)* and (2) and 85 of the Cape Ordinance.
[143] Section 89 of the Transvaal Ordinance; ss 32 and 40 of the OFS Ordinance; ss 202(1) and 208 of the Natal Ordinance, and ss 63(1)*(b)*(ii) and 85 of the Cape Ordinance.
[144] Section 89 of the Transvaal Ordinance; s 32 of the OFS Ordinance, and s 63(3) of the Cape Ordinance.
[145] Section 202(2) of the Natal Ordinance.
[146] Section 30(3)*(a)* of the OFS Ordinance.

11.7.3.4 *Purchase and sale of protected plants*

It is an offence to buy or receive consequent upon a donation a protected plant, except from a person lawfully selling or donating it.[147] It is likewise an offence, without a permit, to sell or donate a protected plant.[148] 'Sell' includes hawk, peddle, barter or exchange or offer, advertise, expose or have in possession for the purpose of sale, hawking, peddling, bartering or exchanging.[149]

In the Cape there are certain precepts relating to the place of sale or purchase of protected flora,[150] and even of unprotected flora.[151] Special provision is also made in the Cape for the registration and licensing of persons as flora growers and flora sellers, authorizing them to sell protected plants on the premises to which the certificate of registration relates.[152]

11.7.3.5 *Exportation and importation of protected plants*

It is an offence, without a permit, to export from or import into the province concerned any protected plant.[153] Following the precepts of the Convention on International Trade in Endangered Species of Wild Fauna and Flora (Washington, 1973), these provisions have been extended to include endangered and rare species of flora.[154]

11.7.3.6 *Conveyance of protected plants*

The conveyance of protected plants, without being the holder of a permit, constitutes an offence.[155]

11.7.3.7 *Possession of protected plants*

The possession of protected plants in certain circumstances constitutes an offence.[156]

11.7.3.8 *Forests*

(a) Background. The Forest Act provides for the protection, management and utilization of forests; the protection of certain animal and plant life; the regulation of

---

[147] Sections 92 and 96 of the Transvaal Ordinance, s 33(2) of the OFS Ordinance and s 194 of the Natal Ordinance. Cf s 62(1) of the Cape Ordinance which requires a permit for the sale or donation of endangered flora.

[148] Sections 91 ('protected') and 96 ('specially protected') of the Transvaal Ordinance; ss 33(1) and 40(1)*(b)* of the OFS Ordinance; ss 195(1) ('protected'), 196(1) ('specially protected') and 208 of the Natal Ordinance, and ss 62(1) ('endangered') and 85 of the Cape Ordinance. Certain exceptions are allowed: s 91(1)*(a)* and *(b)* of the Transvaal Ordinance; s 33(1)*(a)* and *(b)* of the OFS Ordinance, and s 195(2) of the Natal Ordinance. A protected plant may, however, be freely donated or exchanged in Natal: s 197(1), while in the Cape the provisions applicable to the donation of wild animals (ss 41 and 43) apply mutatis mutandis: s 71.

[149] Section 2(lxi) of the Cape Ordinance; s 1(lii) of the Transvaal Ordinance; s 1 of the OFS Ordinance, and s 1 of the Natal Ordinance.

[150] Sections 64 and 66.

[151] Sections 68 and 69.

[152] Section 65 and Part V PN 955 of 29 August 1975 (Cape). Cf also s 94 of the Transvaal Ordinance.

[153] Sections 91, 93 and 96 of the Transvaal Ordinance; ss 33(1)*(b)* and 40 of the OFS Ordinance; ss 198(1), 199(1) and 208 of the Natal Ordinance, and ss 62(1), 70 and 85 of the Cape Ordinance. Certain exceptions are allowed: s 91(1)*(a)* and *(b)* of the Transvaal Ordinance; s 33(3) of the OFS Ordinance, and ss 198(2) and 199(2) of the Natal Ordinance.

[154] Section 98 of the Transvaal Ordinance and s 33(1) of the OFS Ordinance. The OFS provision also covers the sale or donation of such species.

[155] Section 93 of the Transvaal Ordinance and ss 33(2) and 40 of the OFS Ordinance. Exceptions are allowed: s 93(1)*(b)* of the Transvaal Ordinance and s 34*(a)*–*(d)* of the OFS Ordinance.

[156] Sections 95 ('protected') and 96 ('specially protected') of the Transvaal Ordinance; ss 203 and 208(1)*(a)*(i) ('specially protected') of the Natal Ordinance, and ss 62(1) ('endangered'), 72 ('any flora') and 85 of the Cape Ordinance. Certain exceptions are allowed: s 96(1) of the Transvaal Ordinance; s 203 of the Natal Ordinance, and s 62(2) ('endangered') of the Cape Ordinance.

trade in forest produce;[157] the prevention and combating of veld, forest and mountain fires; the control and management of a national hiking way system, and national botanic gardens.[158] The Act is not applicable in respect of so-called black land (the self-governing territories and land controlled by the South African Development Trust).[159] The Forest Act was previously administered by the Minister of Environment Affairs, but is now administered by the Minister of Water Affairs and Forestry. However, the management of several state forests in the Cape, Natal and Transvaal has been assigned to the Administrators of the respective provinces.[160] The Minister may upon the written request of an owner of a private forest[161] declare any provision of the Act which applies only to state forests[162] to be applicable to such private forest if he is of the opinion that such declaration will contribute to the more effective conservation and protection of that forest or forest produce.[163] All or some of the powers conferred by the Act on forest officers may be granted to persons in control of private forests.[164] Provision is made for the designation of forest officers[165] and honorary forest officers.[166] The Minister may delegate all or some of his powers (excluding the power to make regulations),[167] and the Director-General may delegate all or some of the powers conferred on him by or in terms of the Act to any officer of the department.[168]

(b) Afforestation control. Part II of the Act contains afforestation control measures. Without the prior written approval of the Director-General no one may use land (including land in possession of the State) for commercial or industrial afforestation if such land has not been used previously for the establishment and management of a commercial timber plantation or has not been used as such for a period of more than five years.[169] Approval may be granted to applicants on conditions (binding on all successors in title)[170] imposed by the Director-General.[171] He may request the Registrar of Deeds to register such approval (or rejection) and conditions

---

[157] 'Forest produce' means anything which occurs, is grown or grows in a forest, timber plantation or state forest, including anything which is produced by any vertebrate or invertebrate member of the animal kingdom or any member of the plant kingdom in a forest, timber plantation or state forest: s 1.

[158] Cf the long title of the Act.

[159] Land as contemplated in s 25(1) of the Black Administration Act 38 of 1927 and s 21(1) of the Development Trust and Land Act 18 of 1936: s 2(1). However, s 2(1) is to be repealed by means of a proclamation of the State President in terms of s 43 of the Abolition of Racially Based Land Measures Act 108 of 1991. This will result in the Forest Act being applicable also in SADT areas; however, self-governing territories will still be excluded.

[160] State President's Minute 1109 of 18 November 1986.

[161] 'Private forest' means a forest or timber plantation on land not owned by the State excluding a forest or timber plantation on such land in respect of which the right to the trees thereon vests in the State: s 1.

[162] 'State forest' means state land which was acquired for the purposes of this Act or which was reserved for those purposes with the concurrence of the Minister of Public Works and Land Affairs, and includes a state plantation, state sawmill, state timber preservation plant, land controlled and managed by the department for research purposes as a tree nursery, or for the establishment of a commercial timber plantation, an area which has been set aside for the conservation of fauna and flora, for the management of a water catchment area, for the prevention of soil erosion or sand drift, or for the protection of indigenous forests, and all trees on (i) any other state land, excluding land purchased from the State but not yet transferred to the purchaser; and (ii) any other land if the right to those trees vests in the State: s 1.

[163] Section 2(2).

[164] Section 3.

[165] Section 5. See definition of 'forest officer': s 1.

[166] Section 6.

[167] Section 4(1).

[168] Section 4(2).

[169] Section 7(1).

[170] Section 7(4).

[171] Section 7(2); an appeal is available to the Minister: s 57(3).

against the title deed of the land concerned.[172] The Minister may protect natural water resources by prohibiting the planting of trees within the area defined in the notice or the reforestation of such an area.[173] The regeneration of a commercial timber plantation in such an area is also prohibited.[174] Loans for the planting (or replanting) of trees for commercial or industrial purposes may be granted by the Minister.[175]

(c) Control over state forests. The control over state forests is regulated by part III of the Act. 'Undemarcated forests' on state land may be converted to 'demarcated forests' by ministerial notice in the *Government Gazette*.[176] No demarcated forest or part of it may be deproclaimed except with the approval, by resolution, of Parliament.[177]

The Act contains important provisions concerning the limitations of rights in respect of state forests. No servitudes or any other rights can be obtained by prescription.[178] The Minister may, however, with the approval of Parliament, grant servitudal rights on such conditions as may be determined by Parliament.[179] The Director-General of Forestry may grant certain rights in the following instances:

- temporary or permanent rights for public purposes;[180]
- temporary rights to any person for the purpose of inter alia trading, grazing and cultivation of land, provided that the exercise of that right is not in any manner detrimental to the state forest in question or any forest produce occurring in it,[181] and
- prospecting and mining rights may be granted and such metals, minerals, stones, oil and source material may be disposed of; however, no forest produce shall be cut, damaged, taken or removed except on authority of a licence or permit issued by the Director-General.[182]

The Director-General must keep a register of all servitudes and rights of any nature in respect of state forests.[183]

(d) Protection of biota and ecosystems. The protection of biota and ecosystems is dealt with in part IV. The Minister is authorized to declare trees (a particular tree, a group of trees or a particular species) on private land to be protected.[184] Such notice may be published in the *Government Gazette* for the preservation of the scenic beauty or of some natural scenic attraction, the conservation of a distinctive specimen or specimens, the prevention of soil erosion or sand drift or the reclamation of land, the maintenance of the natural diversity of the species, the preservation of tree-dominated biotas and the conservation and development of natural resources.[185]

[172] Section 9.

[173] Section 8(1).

[174] Section 8(2).

[175] Section 9A.

[176] Section 10. Such notice may be published only after a notice of such intent has been published and a copy of it has been served on the body representing organized agriculture and the magistrate of that district, and written objections (if any) have been considered: s 10(2)*(b)–(c)*.

[177] Section 10(2).

[178] Section 11(1).

[179] Section 11(2).

[180] Section 11(2)*(a)*(i). He may grant such rights to a provincial administration, a local authority, Transnet Ltd, SA Post Office Ltd, Telcom SA, the National Roads Board or to any other state department or statutory body: s 11(2)*(a)*.

[181] Section 11(2)*(a)*(ii).

[182] Section 11(2)*(b)*.

[183] Section 11(4). Section 11(3) provides for the continuation of rights granted in terms of the Forest Act 13 of 1941. The use of roads in state forests may be restricted or prohibited: s 12.

[184] Section 13(1).

[185] Section 13(2)*(a)–(c)*.

The Minister may appoint a consultative committee to advise him[186] and local control committees to perform functions prescribed by regulation.[187] No protected tree may be cut, damaged, destroyed, disturbed or removed nor may any part or produce thereof be collected, removed, transported, exported, purchased, sold, donated or in any other way be acquired or disposed of except with the Minister's written consent, subject to conditions laid down by him.[188] Certain officials are empowered to enter upon private land and to search any vehicle or premises in order to investigate possible contraventions of this prohibition.[189] When patrimonial loss flows from the refusal to grant permission to cut a protected tree or the conditions imposed, compensation must be paid. Failing an agreement, the amount is to be determined by a competent court in terms of the Expropriation Act 63 of 1975.[190] If the protection notice substantially interferes with the beneficial occupation of land or if the land can no longer be used as it had been prior to such notice, the land must be expropriated as if it were for public purposes.[191]

State forests (or parts of them) may be set aside for certain purposes by ministerial notice in the *Government Gazette*. A nature reserve may be declared for the preservation of a particular natural forest or particular plants or animals or for some other conservation purpose,[192] and a wilderness area on the recommendation of the Council for the Environment[193] for the preservation of an ecosystem or the scenic beauty.[194] The Director-General is entrusted with their control and management.[195] Withdrawal of part or the whole of a declared nature reserve or wilderness area may take place only with the approval by resolution of Parliament subsequent to the publication of a prior notice of such intent in the *Government Gazette*.[196] No forest produce may be cut, disturbed, damaged, taken, collected, destroyed or removed.[197] However, the Director-General may perform acts or take measures not inconsistent with the following objectives: the restoration of ecologically disturbed habitats;[198] the prevention and combating of soil erosion[199] and of veld, forest and mountain fires;[200] the maintenance of the natural genetic and species diversity;[201] the exercise of control over undesirable plants and animals;[202] the removal and marketing of forest produce;[203] research;[204] education,[205] and, in the case of nature reserves, also the making available to the public of open-air recreation facilities.[206]

---

[186] Section 13(4)*(a)*(i).
[187] Section 13(4)*(a)*(ii).
[188] Section 13(5)*(a)*. Exemption may be granted by the Minister in respect of a cultivated tree belonging to a particular protected species: s 13(5)*(b)*.
[189] Section 13(6).
[190] Section 14(1).
[191] Section 14(2). An owner who claims in terms of s 14(2) must do so in the manner and time prescribed in reg 21(10) of the regulations in terms of the Act: GN R602 of 27 March 1986.
[192] Section 15(1)*(a)*(i).
[193] Established in terms of s 4 of the Environment Conservation Act.
[194] Section 15(1)*(a)*(ii).
[195] Section 15(1)*(c)*.
[196] Section 15(2).
[197] Section 15(3)*(a)*(i).
[198] Section 15(3)*(b)*(i).
[199] Section 15(3)*(b)*(ii).
[200] Section 15(3)*(b)*(iii).
[201] Section 15(3)*(b)*(iv).
[202] Section 15(3)*(b)*(v).
[203] Section 15(3)*(b)*(vi).
[204] Section 15(3)*(b)*(viii).
[205] Section 15(3)*(b)*(ix).
[206] Section 15(3)*(b)*(vii).

Servitudes and other rights may be granted by the Minister only with the approval of Parliament and on such conditions as Parliament may determine;[207] the Director-General may in the interests of national security grant temporary rights subject to subsequent approval by Parliament.[208] Servitudes and other permanent rights in force at the date of declaration as nature reserve or wilderness area remain in force.[209] Permanent or temporary rights for public purposes as well temporary rights granted in favour of the private sector may be renewed by the Director-General after declaration of the area in question as nature reserve or wilderness area if he is of the opinion that such renewal will not materially prejudice the aims of that particular area.[210] The same applies to the renewal of rights granted subsequent to the declaration as nature reserve or wilderness area.[211]

(e) Veld, forest and mountain fires. Part VI provides for the following measures in respect of the prevention and combating of veld, forest and mountain fires on state-owned and private land: the definition by notice in the *Government Gazette* (with the concurrence of the Minister of Agriculture) of fire control areas and fire control regions;[212] the establishment of fire control committees and regional fire control committees;[213] the preparation, submission, approval and publication of fire control schemes and their registration against the title deeds of the land concerned;[214] and the rendering of financial assistance to the various committees.[215]

The Act contains important provisions concerning the obligations of landowners such as the conclusion of agreements with adjacent owners to clear a fire belt on both sides or one side of boundaries;[216] the content of such agreements[217] and the jurisdiction of magistrate's courts (where agreement could not be reached or absentee owners be traced) to issue orders empowering a landowner to enter upon such land in order to clear and maintain a fire belt,[218] or to amending existing agreements.[219] Such agreements and court orders are binding on successors in title.[220] Exemption from the obligation to clear and maintain fire belts in fire control areas may be granted.[221]

On land outside fire control areas a landowner may request the adjacent owner to enter into an agreement, and failing such an agreement, obtain a court order.[222] The Director-General may, if he is of the opinion that an extraordinary fire hazard exists in respect of state or privately owned land, prohibit the lighting of fires in the open air.[223]

---

[207] Section 15(4)*(a)*.
[208] Section 15(4)*(b)*.
[209] Section 15(5).
[210] Section 15(5). Cf also s 11(2)*(a)*.
[211] Section 15(6).
[212] Section 18(1). Fire control regions comprise two or more fire control areas. Land under the jurisdiction of a local authority may be included only with its approval: s 18(2).
[213] Section 19.
[214] Section 20(1)–(7).
[215] Section 21.
[216] Section 22(1)*(a)*. A fire belt must be of such a nature and extent that it will, having regard to local circumstances, be reasonably sufficient to prevent a fire on land on one side of the belt from spreading to land on the other side of it: s 22(1)*(b)*. Owners whose land's boundaries coincide with South African borders (or with a fire control area boundary) are obliged to clear and maintain a fire belt: s 22(1)*(c)*.
[217] Section 22(2).
[218] Section 22(4)–(5): the magistrate's court may issue such order it may deem equitable.
[219] Section 22(6).
[220] Section 22(8). On disposal of such land present owners must notify new owners in writing of the content of such agreements or court orders: s 22(7).
[221] Section 23.
[222] Section 24. In terms of s 24A an owner of land outside a fire control area whose boundary coincides with the border of the Republic, must clear and maintain a fire belt on his land as close to that boundary as possible. Failure to comply with s 24A results in an offence: s 75(8)*(cA)*.
[223] Section 25(1).

If he is of the opinion that an increased fire hazard would ensue from the burning of any ground cover, including slash in timber plantations and harvest residue, he may prohibit such burning by notice.[224] He may likewise prohibit the clearing or maintenance of fire belts and the carrying out of blockburns.[225] Any person who has reasonable grounds to believe that a fire occurring on land may endanger life or property may enter upon such land (or adjacent land to which it may spread) for the purpose of preventing the spreading of that fire or of extinguishing it.[226] A forest officer may take control of the fighting and extinguishing of fires that occur within 10 km of the boundary of a state forest or of a mountain catchment area.[227] Compensation is payable where an agreement for the rendering of mutual assistance exists.[228]

(f) Forestry Council. Provision is made in part VIII for the establishment of the Forestry Council and its powers. Its objects are to promote and encourage the forest and timber industry.[229]

(g) National botanic gardens. Part IX provides for the establishment and control of national botanic gardens. The objects of the National Botanical Institute[230] are to promote the conservation and research in connection with southern African flora.[231] Its functions[232] include the establishment, management and maintenance of national botanic gardens[233] as well as the selling, exchange or donation of plant specimens or the acquisition of a plant for the purpose of establishing it in a national botanic garden.[234]

(h) Regulations, offences and related matters. The Minister may make regulations inter alia with regard to *(a)* state forests;[235] *(b)* the protection of trees;[236] *(c)* fire control committees and regional fire control committees;[237] *(d)* forest produce as well as the forest and timber industry;[238] *(e)* the combating of any fungus or bacterial disease or insect or parasitic pest which may affect state or private forests or any other land as well as their introduction and the prevention of their spread;[239] *(f)* national botanic gardens,[240] and *(g)* all other matters for the better carrying out of the provisions and objects of the Act.[241] A vast number of offences are created by the

---

[224] Section 25(2).

[225] Section 25(3). Section 25(1)–(3) also applies to state land in the area as defined in the notice: s 25(4).

[226] Section 26.

[227] Section 26(2). The powers of persons acting in terms of s 26(1) or (2) are set out in s 26(3). No compensation is payable for assistance rendered; however, an ex gratia amount may be paid: s 26(3).

[228] Section 27.

[229] Section 48.

[230] Established in terms of s 57.

[231] Section 58. The objects of the institute are to promote the utilization and conservation of, and knowledge and services in connection with, southern African flora, and to that end the institute may—

(a) by itself or in co-operation with any person assess the botanic research and conservation needs of the Republic and develop programmes to meet these needs;
(b) establish, develop and maintain collections of plants in national botanic gardens and herbaria;
(c) undertake and promote research in connection with indigenous plants and related matters;
(d) study and cultivate specimens of endangered plant species;
(e) investigate and utilize, and promote the utilization of, the economic potential of indigenous plants;
(f) promote an understanding and appreciation of the role of plants among the public.

[232] Section 61(1).

[233] Section 61(1)*(a)*.

[234] Section 61(1)*(k)*.

[235] Section 73(1)*(a)*.

[236] Section 73(1)*(b)*.

[237] Section 73(1)*(c)*.

[238] Section 73(1)*(e)*.

[239] Section 73(1)*(f)*.

[240] Section 73(1)*(g)*.

[241] Section 73(1)*(i)*.

Act.[242] Forest and police officers may arrest suspected persons without a warrant[243] and seize forest produce, weapons, vehicles, equipment or animals used in the commission of an offence in terms of the Act.[244] Forest officers are also empowered to enter upon land and to conduct an investigation or inspection, and have all the powers vested by law in police officers.[245] Illegal squatting, camping and cultivation in state forests are prohibited, and the removal of such trespassers and their structures or crops (or their destruction) may be ordered by the court concerned.[246]

11.7.3.9 *Natural vegetation in mountain catchment areas*

The Mountain Catchment Areas Act empowers the Minister of Environment Affairs to declare by notice in the *Government Gazette* or by written notice to the owner or occupier of land which is situated within a mountain catchment area, a direction to be applicable with reference to such land, relating to the protection and the treatment of the natural vegetation and the destruction of vegetation which is, in the opinion of the Minister, intruding vegetation.[247] Directions are binding on owners, occupiers and their successors in title.[248] The administration of the Act has been assigned to the respective provincial Administrators.

11.7.3.10 *Vegetation in lake areas*

In terms of the Lake Areas Development Act it is an offence, on state land placed at the disposal of the National Parks Board, to cut, take out, pick, damage, disturb or remove any trees, shrubs, plants, flowers or other vegetation,[249] or to remove any wood or firewood,[250] or to cause an unauthorized fire.[251]

11.7.3.11 *Plants as national monuments*

The National Monuments Act provides for any object of aesthetic, historical or scientific interest to be established as a national monument.[252] Damage to or destruction of such monuments without a permit is an offence.[253] Certain oak and baobab trees and modjadji palms have been declared national monuments, too, as have certain areas containing vegetation, such as Table Mountain and Paarl Mountain, certain urban parks, and a nature reserve (at the University of the Western Cape).

11.7.3.12 *Vegetation and soil conservation*

The Conservation of Agricultural Resources Act provides for control over the utilization of the natural agricultural resources of the Republic in order to promote inter alia the protection of vegetation and the combating of weeds and invader plants.[254]

---

[242] Section 75.
[243] Section 76.
[244] Section 77. Licences, permits or other authorization documents must be produced on demand: s 78.
[245] Section 79.
[246] Section 80.
[247] Section 3(1)*(a)*(i)*(bb)*. The destruction of intruding vegetation within a distance of 5 km of the boundary of a mountain catchment area may also be ordered by the Minister: s 3(1)*(b)*(ii). Failure to comply with the directions constitutes an offence: s 14*(b)*.
[248] Section 4(2)*(c)*.
[249] Regulations 6(1)*(e)* and 34 of the Regulations in regard to the Wilderness Lake Area, promulgated in terms of s 23 of the Lake Areas Development Act 39 of 1975: GN R311 of 22 February 1980.
[250] Regulations 6(1)*(f)* and 34.
[251] Regulations 6(1)*(g)* and 34.
[252] Section 10.
[253] Sections 12(2)*(a)* and 16.
[254] Section 3. One of the objects of the Soil Conservation Act of 1969 was to make provision for the conservation, protection and improvement of vegetation: s 2.

'Natural agricultural resources' include the vegetation but exclude weeds and invader plants.[255] The Minister of Agriculture[256] may prescribe control measures for the utilization and protection of the vegetation and the construction, maintenance, alteration or removal of soil conservation works:[257] (which include any work on land which is constructed on land for the conservation or improvement of the vegetation).[258] Control measures relating to the grazing capacity of veld (i e the production capacity of that veld to meet the feed requirements of animals in such a manner that the natural vegetation thereon does not deteriorate or is not destroyed):[259] may also be prescribed.[260]

Land users may be compelled to comply with such a control measure by means of a direction by the executive officer published in the *Government Gazette* or by written notice, which is binding both on the landowner in question and his successors in title.[261]

Schemes may be established for the reparation of damage to the natural agricultural resources or soil conservation works which has been caused by a flood, any other disaster or natural forces,[262] or for the planting and cultivation of particular crops which improve soil fertility or counteract the vulnerability of soil to erosion.[263] Monies may be granted to land users by means of the payment of subsidies.[264] Land may be expropriated for the restoration or reclamation of natural resources, including the protection of vegetation.[265] See generally on soil conservation, chapter 10.

11.7.3.13 *Aquatic plants*

The Sea Fishery Act provides for control over aquatic plants i e any kind of plant, alga or other plant organism found in the sea or in or on the sea-shore.[266] Subject to any regulation which the Minister of Environment Affairs may make,[267] no person may collect and remove or cause to be collected and removed any aquatic plants from the sea or the sea-shore, except for his own use and in prescribed quantities, without being the holder of a permit issued by the Minister and otherwise than in accordance with the conditions contained in the permit.[268] Contravention of this provision constitutes an offence.[269]

It is also an offence in terms of the Sea Fishery Act to pollute the sea with anything which is or may be injurious to aquatic plants or fish food (which may include plant material), or which may disturb or change the ecological balance in any area of the sea, or which may detrimentally affect the marketability of aquatic plants.[270] It is likewise an offence in terms of provincial nature conservation ordinances to pollute waters with anything which is or may be injurious to fish food.[271]

---

[255] Section 1.
[256] Section 6(1) and 6(2)*(g)*.
[257] Section 6(1) and 6(2)*(o)*.
[258] Section 1 ('soil conservation work').
[259] Section 1 ('grazing capacity').
[260] Section 6(2)*(h)*. Non-compliance amounts to an offence: ss 6(5) and 23.
[261] Section 7(1)–(4). Non-compliance amounts to an offence: ss 7(6) and 23.
[262] Section 8(1)*(a)*(ii).
[263] Section 8(1)*(a)*(v).
[264] Section 8(1).
[265] Section 14.
[266] Section 1 sv 'aquatic plant'.
[267] In terms of s 45.
[268] Section 38(1).
[269] Section 47(1)*(g)*.
[270] Section 47(1)(k).
[271] Section 84 of the Transvaal Nature Conservation Ordinance; s 48 of the Cape Nature and Environmental Conservation Ordinance and ss 152 and 183 of the Natal Nature Conservation Ordinance.

The National Parks Act provides that no marine plant in a national park may be cut, damaged, removed or destroyed.[272] A permit may, however, be obtained to gather and remove from a national park any quantity of any species of aquatic plant.[273]

11.7.4 Control of noxious plants

11.7.4.1 *Weeds*

With the exception of the Jointed Cactus Eradication Act 52 of 1934, all legislation before the Weeds Act 42 of 1937 dealing with noxious weeds was passed at provincial level.[274] During 1935 the Second Schedule to the then Financial Relations Act 10 of 1913 was amended by the removal of noxious weeds from provincial legislative competence.[275] The Jointed Cactus Eradication Act was repealed by the Weeds Amendment Act 32 of 1964. The Weeds Act was replaced by the Conservation of Agricultural Resources Act, which now deals with soil conservation and weeds.

Weeds and invader plants, which include their seeds and vegetative parts which reproduce themselves asexually, are thus controlled by virtue of the Conservation of Agricultural Resources Act. A plant is subject to control once the Minister of Agriculture has declared it to be a weed or an invader plant,[276] either throughout South Africa or in one or more areas of the country.[277] Principal control is effected through control measures which the Minister is authorized to prescribe in relation to the control of weeds and invader plants.[278] Such measures must be complied with by the land users to whom they apply and failure to do so constitutes an offence.[279] A further offence is committed if a land user should fail or refuse to comply with a direction by means of which he was ordered to comply with a particular control measure.[280] The Minister may establish a scheme in terms of which subsidies may be paid to land users in respect of the combating of weeds and invader plants.[281] Moreover, the Minister may perform or cause to be performed any act related to the control of weeds and invader plants[282] and may recover the relevant costs from the landowner concerned.[283]

It is an offence for anyone

(a) to sell, agree to sell or offer, advertise, keep, exhibit, transmit, send, convey or deliver for sale, or exchange for anything or dispose of to any person in any manner for a consideration, any weed; or
(b) in any other manner whatsoever to disperse or cause or permit the dispersal of any weed from any place in South Africa to any other place in the country.[284]

If seed, grain, hay or any other agricultural product contains any weed, the executive officer may issue an order that the seed, grain, hay or other agricultural product concerned

(a) be returned to its place of origin;
(b) be forwarded to a specified place in order to have the weed concerned removed from it; or

---

272 Section 21(1)*(i)*.
273 Section 21(2)*(f)*.
274 Cf the schedule to the Weeds Act.
275 Cf s 4*(a)* of the Financial Relations Amendment Act 50 of 1935.
276 Cf the definitions of 'invader plant' and 'weed' in s 1 of the Conservation of Agricultural Resources Act and GN R1048 of 25 May 1984 Part II.
277 Section 2(3).
278 Section 6(2)*(l)*.
279 Section 6(5).
280 Section 7(1) and (6).
281 Section 8(1)*(a)*(vi).
282 Section 11(1) and (4)*(a)*.
283 Section 11(2)*(a)*.
284 Section 5(1) and (6).

(c) be destroyed in such manner as he may determine.[285]

Finally, if any weed adheres to an animal which is driven on a public road, conveyed in a vehicle or offered for sale at a livestock auction, the executive officer may issue an order that the weed concerned be removed from that animal.[286]

In addition to the Conservation of Agricultural Resources Act, the Transvaal and OFS Nature Conservation Ordinances make provision for the eradication of plants which may be harmful to indigenous plants.[287] These ordinances, as well as the Cape Nature and Environmental Conservation Ordinance, empower the respective provincial departments of nature conservation to take such measures as may be necessary or desirable for the protection of plants.[288] Although rather vague, these provisions could be invoked in the battle against noxious plants.

11.7.4.2 *Intruding vegetation*

The Department of Environment Affairs is also involved to some extent in the eradication of noxious plants. The Mountain Catchment Areas Act empowers the Minister of Environment Affairs to require vegetation which is, in his opinion, intruding vegetation to be destroyed.[289] The direction may be applicable to a declared mountain catchment area[290] or to any area within 5 km of such an area.[291] Failure to comply with such a direction is an offence.[292] The administration of the Act has been assigned to the respective provincial Administrators.

11.7.4.3 *Agricultural pests*

The Agricultural Pests Act 36 of 1983 provides for control over plants[293] and plant diseases with a view to protecting plants that are agriculturally important. As such this Act is of some significance to nature conservation, particularly in respect of indigenous plants as it may indirectly or incidentally benefit such plants. Control is exercised over the importation of any plant,[294] pathogen,[295] insect,[296] growth medium,[297] exotic animal,[298] infectious thing,[299] honey, beeswax or used apiary equipment,[300] or other

[285] Section 5(2)*(a)*.
[286] Section 5(3)*(a)*.
[287] Sections 101*(g)*(iii) and 101*(h)*(iii) of the Transvaal Ordinance and s 38(1)*(o)* of the OFS Ordinance.
[288] Section 101*(g)*(ii) of the Transvaal Ordinance; s 38(1)*(h)* of the OFS Ordinance, and s 16(1)*(c)*(iii) of the Cape Ordinance.
[289] Section 3(1).
[290] Section 3(1)*(a)*(i)*(bb)*.
[291] Section 3(1)*(b)*(ii).
[292] Section 14*(b)*.
[293] Section 3.
[294] 'Plant' includes any live or dead part of a plant and any derivation of a plant: s 1.
[295] 'Pathogen', means any algae, fungus, bacterium, virus, mycoplasm, spiroplasm, viroid or rickettsia-like organism but does not include any such pathogen that can cause a disease in man or animal alone: s 1.
[296] 'Insect' means any invertebrate member of the animal kingdom (irrespective of the stage of its development) but not such a member as included in the definition of 'fish' in s 1 of the Sea Fishery Act, or that can only affect man or animal: s 1.
[297] 'Growth medium' means any solid or liquid substance in which or on which plants are or can be cultivated, including soil or structures used for the cultivation of plants: s 1.
[298] 'Exotic animal' means any vertebrate of the animal kingdom which is not indigenous to the Republic, and includes the eggs of such a member but does not include such a member which is an animal to which the Livestock Improvement Act 25 of 1977 applies or which is a fish as defined in s 1 of the Sea Fishery Act.
[299] 'Infectious thing' means anything, except a plant which may serve as a medium for the importation or spreading of a pathogen, insect or exotic animal: s 1.
[300] Section 3(1)*(a)*.

matters as determined by the Minister of Agriculture by notice in the *Government Gazette*[301] and the conveyance of any such imported items.[302]

If in the opinion of the Minister it is expedient that the destruction of plants,[303] the cleansing or destruction of any plant infected with any pathogen or insect,[304] the keeping, planting or cultivation of plants,[305] the removal of plants[306] and the notification of specified pathogens, insects or exotic animals on land[307] be made compulsory in any area, he may by notice in the *Government Gazette* prescribe control measures.[308] These control measures must be complied with or carried out by land users[309] in the particular area.[310] Exemption may be granted by means of a permit.[311] The executive officer (the officer designated as such by the Minister)[312] may by written notice order[313] any land user to observe or carry out the provisions of a particular control measure on or with regard to any quarantine area.[314] Compensation is payable if anything has been destroyed by notice of an order.[315]

The Minister may make regulations furthering the objects of the Act.[316] Failure to carry out the required steps to the satisfaction of the Minister, apart from constituting an offence,[317] entitles him, at the expense of the owner or occupier in question, to give effect to such steps.[318] Wide powers are granted to officials to enforce these and other provisions of the Act.[319] Contravention of any provision of the Act amounts to an offence.[320]

11.7.4.4 *Other legislation*

Other legislation that controls the importation of foreign plant material and the distribution of genetically engineered plant species includes the Plant Improvement Act 53 of 1976 and the Plant Breeders' Act 15 of 1976.

The Plant Breeders' Act provides for a system under which rights relating to new varieties of certain kinds of plants may be granted and registered as well as for the protection of such rights and the granting of licences in respect of their exercise. The Plant Improvement Act must be read in conjunction with the Plant Breeders' Act. It provides generally for the improvement of plants and propagating material inter alia through control over their sale, importation and exportation, the establishment of a system of certification of plants and propagating material and the recognition of certain varieties of plants. Although these Acts are of great importance to agriculture, they are

[301] Section 3(1)*(b)*.
[302] Section 3(2)*(c)*.
[303] Section 6(2)*(a)*.
[304] Section 6(2)*(b)*.
[305] Section 6(2)*(d)*.
[306] Section 6(2)*(f)*.
[307] Section 6(2)*(g)*.
[308] Section 6(1).
[309] 'User of land' is defined in s 1 and includes owners, possessors, occupiers (irrespective whether they reside there); a person who has the right to cut trees or wood on land or to remove trees, wood or organic material from land; a person who has the right to remove sand, soil, clay, stone or gravel from land; and a person who carries prospecting or mining activities on land.
[310] Section 6(4).
[311] Section 6(3)*(b)*.
[312] Sections 1 and 2*(a)*.
[313] Section 7(1).
[314] 'Quarantine area' is defined in s 1.
[315] Section 7(5).
[316] Section 16(1).
[317] Section 13.
[318] Sections 8(1)*(b)* and 10(1).
[319] Section 9.
[320] Section 13. Section 14 contains a number of presumptions. The liability of employers and principals for acts or omissions of managers, agents or employees is regulated by s 15.

not restricted to indigenous plants and, moreover, are not aimed at the conservation of indigenous plants as habitat or even as individual species.

11.7.4.5 *Noxious aquatic growths*

The Cape Nature and Environmental Conservation Ordinance provides that no person may cultivate, possess, transport, sell,[321] donate, buy[322] or otherwise acquire or import into the province any noxious aquatic growth.[323] There is a separate provision[324] which prohibits the release of any aquatic growth into inland waters.[325] The ordinance also provides that if the Chief Director of Nature and Environmental Conservation is of the opinion that any aquatic growth[326] found in any inland waters is injurious to any fish, other aquatic growth or the water in such inland waters, he may order the owner of such inland waters to take such measures as he may determine to destroy such growth, and he may render assistance to such owner if requested to do so.[327] If the owner refuses, or within a period of 12 months fails to comply with the order the chief director may cause the growth concerned to be destroyed and recover the costs from such owner.[328]

The Transvaal Nature Conservation Ordinance[329] provides that it is an offence for any person without a permit to possess, sell,[330] purchase, donate, receive as a donation, import, convey, cultivate or place in any waters[331] certain species of aquatic growth.[332] Moreover, the Administrator may take any measure which he deems necessary or expedient for the control of any weed, invader plant or aquatic growth.[333] The OFS Nature Conservation Ordinance contains a similar provision, although the placing of such aquatic growths[334] in waters is not covered by the prohibition.[335]

11.8 SUFFICIENCY OF LEGISLATION FOR PLANT CONSERVATION

11.8.1 Conservation methods and available legislation

11.8.1.1 *Introduction*

In the first section of this chapter, a broad review was given of the aims, objectives and methods of plant conservation. This review of first principles was necessary as plant conservation has often been neglected in favour of conserving animals (large mammals in particular), whereas in fact the upkeep of well-adapted and diverse natural plant life is of fundamental importance to entire ecosystems. In the present section various practical and legal problems are discussed and a wide range of possible methods of conservation is reviewed with a view to possible reform.

---

[321] 'Sell' includes hawk, peddle, barter or exchange or offer, advertise, expose or have in possession for the purpose of sale, hawking, peddling, bartering or exchanging: s 2(lxi).

[322] 'Buy' includes barter or exchange: s 2(xi).

[323] Section 60. Three species of such noxious aquatic growths are listed in sch 5: s 2(xlv).

[324] Section 50.

[325] 'Inland waters' means all waters which do not permanently or at any time during the year form part of the sea and includes any tidal river other than a tidal river in respect of which a notice issued under s 23(1)*(b)* of the Sea Fishery Act is in force: s 2(xxxv).

[326] 'Aquatic growth' means any vegetation which grows or is able to grow in inland waters: s 2(v).

[327] Section 19(1).

[328] Section 19(2).

[329] Section 85(1).

[330] 'Sell' means sell, barter, offer or expose for sale, display for sale or give or offer as a valuable consideration: s 1(lii).

[331] 'Waters' includes the waters in rivers, streams, creeks, lakes, pans, vleis, dams, reservoirs, furrows, canals and ponds: s 1(lx).

[332] ie those species referred to in sch 10 to the Ordinance. The Administrator may by notice in the *Provincial Gazette* include in or delete from this schedule the name of any species of aquatic growth: s 85(2).

[333] Section 101*(g)*(iii).

[334] ie those listed in sch 5 to the Ordinance: s 29.

[335] Section 29(1) read with s 40(1)*(c)*.

11.8.1.2 *Discovery, identification and listing of protected sites*

This operation is of fundamental importance to conservation at a time when increasing amounts of natural plant habitat are being converted to human uses.[336] Many sites that could have been of value for plant conservation have been lost, in some cases unnecessarily. An example is the lack of protected areas in the western Cape Lowlands, where 14 percent of the threatened plants of southern Africa occur.[337] On protected areas generally, see chapter 27.

The Council for the Environment and the Committee for Environmental Management, established in terms of the Environment Conservation Act may also play a meaningful role in initiating investigations to identify protected areas. All sites of potential value for the conservation of plants (indeed, perhaps of other elements of the heritage) in South Africa should be identified and listed. Such a study should cover the entire country, including the coasts and coastal waters (for potential marine reserves), estuaries, lakes and rivers. The results should be held in data banks that could be consulted by regional planning and development authorities.

11.8.1.3 *Prevention of damage outside protected areas*

Legislation is available to control damage to plants outside protected areas. This covers both direct damage by uncontrolled destruction and, in the case of cultivated plants and pastures, indirect damage by pathogens.

Legislation is also available for curbing invasions by noxious plants. Where a species infests state as well as private land, legislation cannot fairly be applied to private landowners until the state's property has had the noxious plants eradicated. As the noxious plants are often prolific seeders, it is often extremely difficult to eradicate them from state land when large stands occur on adjacent private land. A partial solution is the creation of co-operative programmes in water catchment areas, in which the provincial chief directorates of nature conservation are empowered to clear noxious plants within mountain catchment areas and even up to 5 km from their boundaries. In such co-operative programmes private landowners will see the results of their efforts firsthand through their membership of catchment boards.

This legislation for the prevention of direct damage to plant life is reasonably satisfactory. Damage can, however, also ensue from changes to ecosystems and habitats, and this can be of far greater significance than, for example, the destruction and extinction of a species. Immense changes have taken place with the increase in grazing pressures by domestic stock in natural pastures, to an extent that these have become critically sensitive to even quite small droughts.[338] Large-scale use of insecticides and fertilizers may have a severe effect on nearby natural insect populations, which have important functions in ecosystems as pollinators, and in other ways. Some insect species play a much more important role than others, in ecosystems, and their destruction may cause a collapse of entire ecosystem units. If their habitat is a rare or threatened element in the landscape, priority should be given to its conservation.

There is a need for the conservation of ecosystems and habitats to be made as much a subject of legislation as are species. At present this need is met only incidentally in areas outside protected areas as, for example, through the Conservation of Agricultural Resources Act and the Mountain Catchment Areas Act.

---

[336] Hall 'Endangered species in a rising tide of human population growth' 1978 (43) *Transactions of the Royal Society of South Africa*: 37–49.

[337] Hall 'Conservation status of the vegetation of the western Cape coastal lowlands'. In Moll (ed) *Proceedings of a symposium on the coastal lowlands of the western Cape:* (University of the Western Cape, 1982) 57–62.

[338] De Wet 'RSA se veld verswak steeds', *Landbounuus* 5 November 1982 8.

11.8.1.4 *Creation of various types of protected areas*

The purchase of land for protected areas has adequate legal support, as does leasing by the authorities of private land. A serious lack of funds for conservation, however, frequently frustrates such action. No such severe lack exists in the case of state land, or in respect of the establishment by the State of conservation status on land held in private ownership through the designation of limited development areas and mountain catchment areas. Extensive and effective use should be made of state land and of the above-mentioned mechanisms with regard to private land.

The establishment of private nature reserves for plant life and other natural heritages is recognized in the provincial nature conservation ordinances. It would be highly advisable to give material recognition to the landowners who are conserving natural elements that are of importance in the overall regional conservation plan. This could take the form of a grant-in-aid of maintenance.

The purchase of servitudes for access and conservation, although possible in terms of our law,[339] is, however, hardly ever resorted to. This must be seen as a major need, particularly for plants where there may often be an overlap of the conservator's and the landowner's potential uses of an area. Servitudes offer a much cheaper alternative to outright purchase and have proved valuable in conservation programmes elsewhere.

Management agreements are another method of conservation that is neglected in South Africa.

11.8.1.5 *Establishment of botanic gardens*

The National Botanic Board of South Africa (the predecessor of the National Botanical Institute) has established regional gardens near a number of the main population centres in South Africa. In view of their potential for acting as show places for local flora and for environmental interpretation, the extension of this programme to other areas should be investigated.

11.8.1.6 *Environmental interpretation programmes*

There are no legal requirements for environmental interpretation programmes in protected areas or botanic gardens. All state-funded protected areas and botanic gardens should at least have a map showing where to find the main natural features of the area that are accessible to the public. An exception would be sanctuaries set aside for special-purpose conservation aims from which the public must be excluded. Regulations should require interpretive standards in reserves appropriate to local needs and expectations.

11.8.1.7 *Maintenance and control of threats in protected areas*

Adequate legislation exists for most aspects of the maintenance and control of threats in protected areas. Once again there is inadequate treatment of the need to conserve ecosystems and habitats without which the conservation of species may ultimately fail. There is also a need for legal provisions to allow authorities in control of protected areas to remove noxious plants on private land up to 5 km away, as has been so successfully done in the case of mountain catchment areas. It would be helpful to establish statutory servitudes on private land bordering on protected areas, so as to be able to act on this kind of problem and prevent certain other impacts (such as the erection of unsightly buildings) from devaluating the natural quality of the reserved area.

11.8.1.8 *Legal measures for critically rare and threatened plants*

In general, there are adequate legal provisions for assisting in the conservation of critically rare and threatened plants. The lists of plants proclaimed as 'protected' should

[339] Cf Rabie 'South African law relating to conservation areas' 1985 *CILSA* 51, 76.

be revised more frequently. Once again, while the species are legally protected against destruction, their ecosystems and habitats are not.

South Africa is a signatory of the Convention on International Trade in Endangered Species of Wild Fauna and Flora. The South African regulations for the inspection of trade exports of plants should be strengthened with regard to expert official viewing of samples of the species being sent. At present this is at best carried out superficially, and in most cases is entirely absent, placing a question mark against the country's effective implementation of the Convention through national legislation. See chapter 9.

Another problem is that some important species are being threatened by factors that are driving them into extinction, yet there are not enough persons or funds to attend adequately to their rescue (as in the case of the several hundred proven threatened plants in the Cape Floristic Kingdom). It would be desirable to appoint rescue teams with legal powers and funding to establish emergency measures for their operations, such as imposing temporary servitudes to allow access, fencing off the population to prevent grazing or other damage, and research on pollinators, regeneration, and, if necessary, translocation tests to sites elsewhere with apparently similar ecosystems.

11.8.1.9 *Provision for scientific collection and study of plants*

At present a permit system exists that allows the bearer to approach a landowner for permission to collect plant specimens for scientific study. The relevant regulations allow a strictly limited number of plants to be collected, often no more than three per species. To an experienced field biologist with a good knowledge of the widespread destruction of the aerial parts of plants by planned veld-burning, by commercial wildflower picking and by grazing, agriculture and tree-planting, the restriction on the allowable number of specimens seems to be ill-founded. A select number of registered professional botanists should be exempt from this provision, and be given a long-term permit to allow entry and scientific study after the landowner has given permission for this, or after reasonable efforts have been made to obtain consent in the case of absent owners.

11.8.2 Administration of legislation

South African legislation for the conservation of plant-life is deficient in a number of instances, and in many cases the enforcement falls far short of what is desirable. This is a reflection not on the abilities of the actual law enforcers but on their small numbers and the vast size of areas subject to their control.

Part of the reason for the late recognition of the need to improve salaries and of the problems of effective law enforcement stems from an attitude (now disappearing) that conservation is unimportant and a marginal pursuit. The urgent need to implement an effective new approach to conservation is shown by the large concentrations of threatened plants in South Africa and the obvious degradation of the ecosystems upon which such vital elements as natural grazing depend.

Law-enforcement programmes are run by national, provincial and local authorities. They are aided by officially appointed honorary officers, inter alia, honorary forestry officers and honorary nature conservation officers. This system holds considerable potential for aiding the thinly spread inspectorates. However, their contribution should not be confused with the need for full-time inspectors, whose numbers should be increased in relation to the constantly rising pressures on the environment, and whose salary status should rise in keeping with the increasingly difficult tasks of law enforcement.

One of the most serious factors hampering the effective conservation of plants is the lack of co-ordination of the many activities carried out by various bodies that are involved in administering the legislation in question. As far as the conservation of plants is concerned, these bodies are: the Departments of Environment Affairs, Agriculture, Regional and Land Affairs, Water Affairs and Forestry as well as the National Parks

Board, the National Botanical Institute and the National Monuments Council. Moreover, the various provincial administrations are involved through their Chief Directorates of Nature Conservation, while local authorities and individual private landowners also play their respective roles.

Divided control and a lack of co-ordination are also evident as far as the control of noxious plants is concerned. The Department of Agriculture administers the Conservation of Agricultural Resources Act and the Agricultural Pests Act; the Department of Environment Affairs the Environment Conservation Act and the Mountain Catchment Areas Act, while provincial administrations enforce their respective nature conservation ordinances, besides also administering aspects of the Forest Act and the Mountain Catchment Areas Act which have been assigned to them. Moreover, the following bodies and groups, are also involved: the Weeds Research Unit of the Plant Protection Research Institute, the Working Group on Weeds and Poisonous Plants of the CSIR, the Flora Conservation Committee of the Botanical Society of South Africa, the Cape Research Group on Invasive Plants, as well as various other voluntary groups.

The conservation of plants should perhaps rather be undertaken by a single conservation-oriented body. At the very least, the efforts of all the above-mentioned bodies should be co-ordinated by a body whose main objective is environmental conservation. One of the main reasons why the control of noxious plants has not been effective is that the Department of Agriculture, which is mainly responsible for the task, is more concerned about plants that are noxious to agriculture than about plants that constitute a threat to our indigenous flora. It accordingly cannot be expected that areas that are not agriculturally significant, such as the Cape fynbos habitat, would receive the urgent attention of a department that is not responsible for nature conservation. A similar problem is encountered where the interests of conservation and those of agriculture clash. Even though a plant may be protected in terms of the various nature conservation ordinances, a landowner may with impunity destroy that plant if he wishes to cultivate the land on which the plant grows. Although the Minister of Agriculture may in terms of the Conservation of Agricultural Resources Act control such action, it is hardly likely that he will override agricultural interests in favour of conservation.

The Environment Conservation Act envisages the Council for the Environment as the body entrusted with the task of advising the Minister of Environment Affairs on the co-ordination of all actions directed at or liable to have an influence on any matter affecting the conservation and utilization of the environment. The effective functioning of the more representative Committee for Environmental Management which plays a co-ordinating role as well as the future implementation of an integrated environment policy should on the one hand lessen some of the above-mentioned problems and on the other promote the conservation of the natural habitat. See generally on the administration of legislation, chapter 8.

11.8.2.1 *Problems concerning the general plant control framework*

The absence of an all-encompassing environmental policy, the lack of central control (with its concomitant, the ever-increasing devolution of powers) as well as the existence of numerous legislative measures (each with its own aim, area of operation and functionary) form the cornerstone of a rather unsatisfactory system regulating the protection of plants.

(a) Environmental policy. No general environmental control policy has as yet been promulgated in terms of the Environment Conservation Act, although this Act is supposed to form the basis of environmental conservation in South Africa. If an environmental policy is eventually declared by the Minister of Environment Affairs,

this policy would have the status of subordinate legislation. It may have been more satisfactory had Parliament itself provided the policy in the Act. See chapter 7.

(b) Lack of central control and the devolution of powers. Owing to the fact that the Environment Conservation Act confers no effective co-ordinating functions upon the Department of Environment Affairs, the lack of central planning and control (and the concomitant countrywide execution of a national environmental policy) is simultaneously the central characteristic and the most important shortcoming of the set of measures currently in force, measures that cannot in any way be described as establishing an integrated system providing for plant conservation.

Subsequent to the devolution of certain powers from the Department of Environment Affairs to the various provincial administrations during 1987 (in terms of a cabinet decision of 1985), the absence of central control on the policy as well as at the administrative level has become one of the hallmarks of plant conservation. It is still uncertain which provisions of the Forest Act with respect to state forests that have been transferred to them, may be applied by the respective provincial administrations. This is exacerbated by the fact that transfer has not taken place where state forests and plantations are so closely entwined that division is impossible and where state forests consist of indigenous trees only. All of the forest nature reserves and all but one of the wilderness areas have been transferred to the provinces concerned. This has given rise to a number of problems:

- The management of these areas has not been uniform.
- The process of integration of forestry personnel in the various provincial administrations has not yet been completed.
- Some provincial administrations are loath to effect block fires for fear of civil claims. This applies especially to mountain catchment areas.

Some of the above-mentioned problems may be eliminated if senior officials of the various government bodies were to be transferred to the Department of Environment Affairs, thus providing for more effective centralized control.

(c) Conflicting aims. In the case of conservation the differing aims of different state departments are more often than not in conflict. Even within departments themselves this dichotomy manifests itself; in the case of the Department of Water Affairs and Forestry and the Department of Agriculture the aims of conservation and utilization are (in the absence of a central binding conservation policy) at odds with one another.

(d) The existence of numerous legislative measures. The existence of a large number of legislative measures operating at various levels and in different areas of jurisdiction is one of the most daunting problems facing conservation officials. In this context, officials are faced with a plethora of provincial ordinances, parliamentary legislation, ministerial regulations, the various conservation legislation of the self-governing territories (as well as subordinate legislation made in terms thereof) and by-laws made by local authorities.

Functionaries (each administering a particular legislative measure) include the Departments of Agriculture, Environment Affairs, Water Affairs and Forestry; the various provincial administrations; the governments of the self-governing territories; the South African Development Trust and the National Parks Board.

Even in the case of similar area-bound measures such as the provincial nature conservation ordinances and the relevant legislation of the self-governing territories, divergences in content, enforcement and prescribed penalties occur. Moreover, no provision is made for enforcement outside the area of application of the relevant legislation. Consequently, nature conservation officials and empowered officials have no jurisdiction over contraventions committed elsewhere. In the case of cycads, the ensuing lack of effective protection has led to the appointment of a commission of inquiry into the export of certain cycads.[340]

In many cases some areas are specifically excluded from the ambit of certain legislation—e g the Conservation of Agricultural Resources Act and the Forest Act do not apply in the self-governing territories and the South African Development Trust areas.

(e) Lack of public participation. A general characteristic of legislation pertaining to plants is the absence of compulsory measures providing for public participation in the formulation of policy, the administration of policy and the fulfilment of the public's role as watchdog. Although some Acts do involve interested parties such as farmers and public interest groups such as nature conservation bodies, they do not have a general statutory right to representation and participation. The Environment Conservation Act provides a welcome exception in this regard. See chapter 7.

(f) Developmental problems. The following developmental premises will, in the absence of a central co-ordinated policy, continue to pose an ever-increasing threat to the continued existence and protection of flora:

1. Agriculture
2. Afforestation for commercial purposes
3. Infrastructural needs
4. Rapid urbanization (especially in the absence of an urbanization strategy) in the urban and peri-urban areas, as well as in rural areas
5. The need for land for small-scale farming
6. Unrehabilitated mining land
7. The clearing of natural vegetation with a view to immediate short-term economic gain
8. The deterioration of the quality of the natural water supply as well as of the air (e g acid rain and chemical effluent in rivers)
9. The depletion by unscrupulous traders of indigenous trees and plants for medicinal purposes.

11.8.2.2 *Environmental protection*

Although certain species are protected by virtue of the provincial nature conservation Ordinances no effective provision for the conservation and protection of natural and indigenous communities exists. The Forest Act also provides for the protection of individual trees, species and forests (on state and private land), but no similar provision exists as to natural communities not covered by the Forest Act.

The lack of co-ordinated environmental protection has led to numerous instances of irreversible destruction of natural flora, e g the eradication of riparian growth on the banks of the Limpopo River and of natural vegetation in the Waterberg area. In some cases plants have been gathered to extinction.

No environmental policy has been framed under the Environment Conservation Act. This has resulted in the continuation of the legacy of fragmented and haphazard (also often conflicting) environmental conservation. In theory, the implementation of a policy of integrated environmental management (IEM) would harmonize developmental and conservation needs and also solve the majority of the above-mentioned problems. In practice, however, IEM does not operate effectively—mainly because it is not legally enforceable—and the institutions mentioned in the Environment Conservation Act do not function as umbrella bodies regulating all conservation matters. See chapters 7 and 30.

---

[340] GN R1257 of 9 June 1989. The Commissions Act 8 of 1947 was made applicable by Proc R98 of the same date.

11.8.2.3 *Protected areas*

The establishment of protected areas is not the prerogative of a particular body, but is undertaken by a multitude of bodies, in terms of a variety of legislative instruments. The lack of a co-ordinated conservation strategy in this regard is particularly unfortunate, since it is in protected areas where the conservation of plants as entire communities can achieve its maximum potential. See chapter 27.

11.8.2.4 *Forest Act*

(a) Parliamentary debate. A perusal of the 1984 parliamentary debate on the then Forest Bill demonstrates various policy problems:

- Two sets of conflicts are inherent to the Act:
  the conflict between the aims of conservation and providing for an economically sound timber industry meeting the needs of a developing South Africa;[341] and
  the conflict between the needs of the timber industry and the water needs of South Africa as a whole.[342]
- Public participation is provided for in the composition of the National Hiking Way Board, the Forestry Council and the National Botanical Institute; however, the interests of private conservation bodies are not adequately represented.[343]
- The granting of temporary rights in respect of state forests by the Minister for a period of 9 years and 11 months.[344]
- The provision of enough timber for South Africa's needs.[345]
- A decrease in the control by government of the timber industry.[346]

(b) Other problems. In addition to problems flowing from the devolution of powers to the various provincial administrations (discussed above), the application of the Forest Act has resulted in the following:

- The granting of afforestation permits without having regard to the opposition of provincial administrations and the IEM concept (e g on the eastern Transvaal escarpment where 64 per cent of the plant population is classified as rare). On the other hand, the views of the relevant provincial administration concerning any planned physical development must be taken into account. Regarding the impact of granting afforestation permits on the supply of water, the views of an interdepartmental committee (consisting of the Departments of Water Affairs and Forestry and of Agriculture) are deemed to be relevant. It would seem that the benefits of afforestation (e g stabilizing rural communities, the improvement of socio-economic conditions and employment creation) weigh heavily in favour of converting grassland to afforestation for commercial purposes.
- The list of protected trees was last published in 1976; the updated list has been referred to the provinces for comment. Even the existing listed protected trees are not adequately protected: in 1988–89 115 permits were issued to authorize the felling of protected trees.[347]
- The most important facets of conservation forestry are fire protection, control of invasive plants and patrolling by forest guards.[348] Indigenous timber is also harvested and sold.

---

[341] *House of Assembly debates* 12 July 1984 11042, 11049.
[342] *House of Assembly debates* 12 July 1984 11402.
[343] *House of Assembly debates* 12 July 1984 11400, 11409.
[344] *House of Assembly debates* 12 July 1984 11407.
[345] *House of Assembly debates* 12 July 1984 11405, 11410.
[346] *House of Assembly debates* 12 July 1984 11403–11404.
[347] *Department of Environment Affairs annual report* 1988/89 (RP 32/1990) 34.
[348] Ibid.

- There is increasing concern regarding the conservation of mountain areas.[349]
- A shortage in the number of law-enforcement officers.
- The validity of permits under the Forest Act, issued by the provincial administrations (since devolution), is open to question.
- The Forest Act applies only to trees, the provincial ordinances to trees and other plants.
- Wilderness areas as well as forest nature reserves have been transferred to the provincial administrations concerned. Central control has all but been lost.
- The majority of state forests have been demarcated in terms of the Forest Act (by which they enjoy statutory protection). On the other hand, a large number of areas are still to be declared nature reserves; it is unclear whether the devolution of powers under the Forest Act includes the power to establish nature reserves under that Act.
- It is uncertain whether a prohibition against the planting of trees with a view to the protection of natural water sources may be registered in the Deeds Office.[350] Consequently, successors in title without knowledge of the prohibition may impede the output of natural water resources.
- Likewise, fire-protection agreements and fire-protection orders cannot be registered;[351] subsequent owners are to be notified of them in writing.[352]
- Provision is made for the delegation of far-reaching powers from the Minister to the Director-General, who may further delegate those powers to other officials.[353] Such subdelegation may result in an official being made responsible for a task beyond his capacity.

11.8.2.5 *Plants and veld*

In addition to the discussion above of a number of problems concerning the statutory framework for the conservation and protection of plants and veld, various other problems need mentioning:

- The decimation of veld and indigenous communities of plant life as a result of increasing urbanization, industrialization and afforestation, as well as of the utilization of land for agricultural purposes, has reached alarming proportions. The protection of plant species as well as of natural and indigenous communities is not adequately provided for in existing legislation.
- Existing penalties are too low to have a deterrent effect. In many cases fines meted out by magistrate's courts are extremely low and bear no relation at all to the seriousness of the crime and its impact on the environment.
- Owners are generally exempted from the provisions of the provincial ordinances.
- The provisions of the Forest Act regarding the protection of trees do not apply to plants.
- The Cape Floristic Kingdom (one of the six major subdivisions of world flora) consisting of 2 373 species has only remnant patches of coastal fynbos; 1 621 species are in the endangered category, and 137 species face extinction.[354]
- Desertification and Karoo encroachment is increasing. Existing grassland (60 per cent of which is in a poor condition) is on the decrease on account of bush

---

[349] *Council for the Environment annual report* 1988 (RP 52/1989) 12.
[350] Section 9 (pertaining to registration) is not applicable in the case of s 8 prohibitions.
[351] Section 22.
[352] Section 22(8).
[353] Section 4(2).
[354] Huntley, Siegfried & Sunter *South African environments into the 21st Century* (1989) 41–2.

encroachment, and the stock-carrying capacity of land is generally overutilized.[355]

- Huntley, Siegfried & Sunter[356] emphasize the danger of the onward march of indigenous and alien invader plants: 800 000 ha are already infected by jointed cactus. The Department of Agriculture considers the speed at which exotic invader plants and weeds (eg *Acacia* species jointed cactus, nasella tussock grass, lantana and paraffin weed) are choking natural pasture and river systems to be a very serious problem.[357] Woody invasives (*Acacia* species, pines, and hakeas) have taken over one million ha of natural veld and are spreading through low land and mountain fynbos (this also poses insurmountable problems for the wildflower industry).[358] Woody indigenous invasive species are encroaching and multiplying at an increasing rate.[359] More than half the farms in the northern Transvaal suffer from bush encroachment.[360]

11.8.2.6 *Conservation of agricultural resources*

The main objective of the Department of Agriculture and the Conservation of Agricultural Resources Act is the maintenance and improvement of land in order to increase its agricultural potential. The existence and enforcement of conservation measures contained in the Act are thus not an end in itself, but serve to implement the primary aim of agricultural improvement.

In addition to the problems discussed above, the following difficulties need mentioning:

- The Act is not applicable in the self-governing territories or the South African Development Trust areas.[361]
- Not enough funds and personnel have been allocated for the control and eradication of weeds and invader plants.
- Although the Act excludes 'weeds' from the definition of 'agricultural resources',[362] the function of conservation committees is to promote the conservation of natural agricultural resources.[363] This should be extended to provide for compulsory reporting on and eradication of weeds.

11.8.2.7 *President's Council*

The *Report of the three committees of the President's Council on a national environmental management system*[364] contains recommendations with regard to the control of alien flora,[365] and the conservation of indigenous plants as natural resources.[366]

11.8.2.8 *Final recommendations*

In addition to the above remarks, the following final recommendations are made:

- Legislation at national level should be consolidated with the aim of protecting

[355] Huntley, Siegfried & Sunter above n 354, 40. The *Department of Agricultural Economics and Marketing annual report* 1988/89 (RP 67-1990) 39 states that '[p]asture condition is still poor in many parts of the country as a result of overgrazing. Some experts consider that only 60 per cent of the country's natural grazing is in reasonable condition.'

[356] Above n 354, 40.

[357] *Department of Agricultural Economics and Marketing annual report* 1988/89 (RP67-1990) 39–40.

[358] Huntley, Siegfried & Sunter above n 354, 40.

[359] *Department of Agricultural Economics and Marketing annual report* 1988/89 (RP67-1990) 39.

[360] Ibid.

[361] Section 2(1)*(b)*.

[362] Section 1.

[363] Section 15(1).

[364] PC 1/1991.

[365] Paras 2.5.2.13 and 2.5.5.

[366] Para 5.4.

indigenous vegetation, or at least harmonizing the various provincial nature conservation ordinances inter se as well as the ordinances with national legislation.

- The centralisation of environmental policy formulation and implementation by the Department of Environment Affairs with delegation to various conservation agencies (subject to control by and regular reporting to that department).
- The declaration of environmentally sensitive areas as limited development areas in terms of the Environment Conservation Act.
- Plants listed in the schedules to the provincial conservation ordinances should be protected nationwide.
- The jurisdiction of conservation and law-enforcement officers should be extended to the whole of South Africa.
- The issuing of permits should be thoroughly overhauled and consideration should be given to the introduction of a system by which permits are granted for specific individual plants (and not as is the case at present, for groups of plants).
- Blanket protection should be afforded to all endangered species that are commercially important, and in situ protection given to other scarce plants (e g by means of the declaration of protected areas and the certification of all plant growers).
- Afforestation permits should be granted only after consultation with all interested parties and within the ambit of integrated environmental management.
- The funds allocated and the number of officials appointed to enforce conservation legislation should be increased.
- A co-ordinated programme to contain the spread of invader plants and weeds, as well as for their eradication, should be introduced.
- Fines and other penalties should be substantially increased, and magistrates and prosecutors should receive in-service training in this regard. Provision should also be made for the compulsory confiscation of plant matter gathered in contravention of the relevant legislation. This should be accompanied by an order declaring such a convicted person unfit to register as a plant grower or to dispose of or acquire plants for commercial gain.

CHAPTER 12

WILD ANIMALS

J DU P BOTHMA
P D GLAVOVIC

12.1 INTRODUCTION

Legislation reflects human decision regarding what is acceptable for the society in which we live. Attitudes to wildlife also reflect the culture and society of which we are a product. Some people might view the death of the last disease-bearing tsetse fly with joy, while to others the same occurrence might evoke concern because it will pose a threat to wildlife from domestic stock colonizing new areas. Yet both groups will probably fail to mourn the loss of another species of animal (the tsetse fly) to the world.

The type of concern shown reflects our attitudes to the other animals living on earth with us, and the differences involved are often deeply rooted in instincts of survival and dominance. One of five basic sets of relationship between man and wildlife centres on man's competition with other animals for food and habitat.[1] It has also been suggested that human behaviour and attitudes reflect the relationship which humans have with others of their kind and the world about them, and that attitudes and relationships developed towards wildlife in the past still persist in the widely diverse cultures of today.[2] Such factors undoubtedly contribute to some wildlife species becoming threatened or even extinct.

It is also true that attitudes and perceptions change with time. The unknown or unacceptable a decade or two ago may now be a central issue of conservation. The current global threat to the environment, and hence the quality of life of most people, has already brought environmental conservation and management sharply into focus, and with it came the realization that all elements of the environment need protection. This holistic view is helping the rapid acceptance of the need for conserving biological diversity. As this requires protected areas of sufficient size to maintain genetic diversity, this approach will undoubtedly favour some wildlife species. However, other species, with less appeal to human beings, or with a more localized natural distribution, may still be under serious threat. Economic deprivation of landowners is one of the major factors which can lead to biological diversity being threatened. It has been shown that, although landowners may be well aware of the need for conservation, say, of wetlands and their associated biota, in times of economic need landowners will not hesitate to cultivate such wetlands for short-term economic survival.[3]

12.2 THE AFRICAN FRAMEWORK

No discussion of environmental management in South Africa is possible without recognizing that it is part of the African continent. Environmental and agrarian problems in Africa are being viewed seriously by the developed world. In the past, colonial conservation strategies set lofty goals but failed to address social and political reality. The approach to Africa was to adopt the false notion that Africa is an unspoiled Eden where the simple exclusion of rural people from 'wild areas' would lead to the

---

[1] Tochner & Milne 'A cross cultural comparison of attitudes towards wildlife' 1974 (39) *Transactions of the North American Wildlife and Natural Resources Conference* 145–70.

[2] Ibid.

[3] Botha *Die gedrag en persepsie van boere ten gunste van omgewingsbewaring* (unpublished Master of Agrarian Extension thesis, University of Pretoria, 1990).

ultimate protection of animals (mainly the large vertebrates) and their habitats. The reality of social and economic depression which is rife in Africa today have found most environmental programmes wanting.

There is a rapidly growing awareness[4] of the real need to bring the social context within which any conservation strategy in Africa must be implemented into much greater prominence. African governments now readily accept the value of conservation, but are unlikely to implement any environmental conservation programme unless they also gain the acceptance, active participation and the involvement and co-operation of the rural people whose lives will invariably be affected in the process.[5]

12.3 THE DEVELOPMENT OF WILDLIFE CONSERVATION IN SOUTH AFRICA

Victorian attitudes to conservation were decidedly predatory as the most ardent conservationists were travellers (explorers), settlers and officials who only a generation earlier had included the most bloodthirsty of hunters.[6] Nineteenth-century fears of an impending ecological disaster in South Africa stemmed from empirical observations, in the then Cape Colony, of the rapid deforestation and the increasing frequency of floods and soil erosion. This gradually led to the emergence of new thinking in which the Cape experience was pivotal.[7]

The first phase of the South African conservation debate focused on the use of the southern coastal forests. Haphazard exploitation of these forests and the destruction of pastures and scrubland around Cape Town evoked a sufficiently vocal public opinion that, in 1846, an Ordinance dedicated to the better preservation of the Cape Flats and Downs was passed. In 1854 the advent of the Cape Legislative Assembly transformed this embryonic nature preservation lobby into one backed by legislation. The Forest and Herbage Preservation Act 18 of 1859 was passed and, although slightly modified as the Forest Act 22 of 1888, this legislation remained the basis for Cape Colonial nature conservation until the establishment of the Union of South Africa in 1910.[8]

In 1858 the latent interest in the protection of land mammals was formalized when Government Notice 263 was issued to preserve the buffalo and elephant populations of the Cape. Also in 1858 the Knysna and Tsitsikamma forests became the first officially proclaimed game reserves in southern Africa. By 1880 a well-defined conservation structure deriving mainly from a mixture of Cape Colonial and Indian philosophies had been set up in South Africa. This structure was relatively holistic and predated formal conservation activities in the United States of America and in Europe.[9]

12.4 THE CURRENT CONSERVATION STATUS OF WILD ANIMALS IN SOUTH AFRICA

When discussing wild animals most people usually exclude invertebrates from their thinking. This is probably one of the reasons why the eradication (extinction) of an insect species harmful to agriculture may be met with jubilation by the same person who may react with anger and shock to the extinction of a species of large mammal. The simple fact is that most human beings have little or no concept of, or feeling for, the variety and abundance of invertebrate animals, and even less for the conservation status of these animals. The resulting ignorance is the reason why the discussion which follows focuses mainly on the vertebrates of South Africa.

---

[4] Anderson & Grove 'The scramble for Eden: past, present and future in African conservation' in Anderson & Grove (eds) *Conservation in Africa* (1989).

[5] Ibid.

[6] Beinart 'Introduction' in Anderson & Grove (eds) above n 4.

[7] Ibid.

[8] Ibid.

[9] Ibid.

12.4.1 Definition of categories

Wild populations of animals may be considered to be either threatened or safe.[10] A threatened taxon is one whose numbers have deteriorated through natural or unnatural causes to such an extent that it is considered to be rare, vulnerable or endangered in its natural habitat. Six other categories are recognized. They are: indeterminate, restricted, peripheral, extinct, out of danger, and safe. Briefly, the South African *Red Data Book* status categories are:

Endangered: Taxa in danger of extinction and whose survival is unlikely if the causal factors continue to operate.

Vulnerable: Taxa believed likely to move into the endangered category in the near future if the causal factors continue to operate.

Rare: Taxa with small populations that are not at present endangered or vulnerable, but are at risk.

Indeterminate: Taxa that are suspected of being endangered, vulnerable or rare but on whose status insufficient information is currently available.

Restricted: Taxa endemic to South Africa and localized within a limited geographical area, where they can easily be threatened and where their status should be closely monitored.

Peripheral: Taxa with a restricted distribution in South Africa but whose main distribution falls outside its political boundaries. The local populations could easily be threatened and their status should be monitored.

Extinct: Taxa which have definitely not been located in the wild during the last 50 years.

Out of danger: Taxa formerly included in one of the threatened categories (endangered, vulnerable or rare) but which are now considered as relatively secure, either because effective conservation measures have been taken or because the previous threat to their survival has been removed; or new information is available to show that the taxon is no longer threatened.

Safe: Taxa to which none of the above categories applies.

12.4.2 Invertebrates

It is strange that we know so little about invertebrates as they make up the majority of animal life on earth. This is no doubt due to ignorance as to their role, or existence, or even because some people may not regard invertebrates as animals. The only invertebrate group in South Africa which seems to have attracted conservation attention is the butterflies, which have more appeal than most other invertebrates. Currently some 632 species of butterfly are known to occur in South Africa.[11] Of these, 102 species are threatened, with two species being endangered, seven species and subspecies vulnerable and 91 species rare.

The most disturbing aspect of butterfly conservation is the rapid decline of butterfly populations in city areas due to habitat destruction. This mainly involves wetland destruction for housing developments and the frequent burning or clearing of vacant land. The relatively recent creation of the first butterfly reserve at Ruimsig by the Roodepoort City Council, and the declaration of a SA Defence Force property near Heidelberg as a natural heritage site—both intended specifically to protect butterflies—are significant occurrences which could have far-reaching consequences for butterfly conservation in South Africa. As some species are confined to a limited area, many butterfly taxa are extremely local in distribution and rare, and will never be safe or abundant. Such butterflies usually also have a severely limited resistance to changes

---

[10] Branch (ed) *South African Red Data Book—Reptiles and amphibians* South African National Scientific Programmes Report no 151 (1988).

[11] Henning & Henning *South African Red Data Book—Butterflies* South African National Scientific Programmes Report no 158 (1989).

in the floral, faunal or climatic conditions vital to their survival. The building of a single house, the construction of even a small road or the ploughing up of a small field can easily lead to the extinction of such a localized rare butterfly species.[12] It is clear that insect conservation, and hence probably all invertebrate conservation, requires a different strategy to that of conventional conservation. This should also be reflected in conservation legislation.

12.4.3 Vertebrates: fishes

The status of the fish species in South Africa has apparently deteriorated further from that reported earlier, when 28 species of fish in South Africa were reported as threatened.[13] According to the latest review, 50 fish species from South Africa and Namibia are threatened.[14] Of the 24 threatened endemic freshwater fish species of South Africa, seven are endangered, eight are vulnerable and nine are rare. The Namibian species include three threatened types of fish. In the endemic estuarine group there are three vulnerable and five rare species.

The most recent review represents a 79 per cent increase in the number of threatened fish species in 11 years. If the two species which have been removed from the 1977 list are taken into account, the percentage increase in the level of deterioration is even greater. The two species which have been removed are *Barbus afer* (the eastern Cape redfin) and *Barbus asper* (the small-scaled redfin). *Barbus afer* has been revised taxonomically and is now known to be more widespread than before. *Barbus asper* has also been revised taxonomically and, although now having a more restricted geographical range, it is still widespread as its habitat preference is now known to be less restricted as it is well adapted to a harsh environment.

The status of five fish species has improved since 1977 due to positive conservation programmes. Thus in the Kruger National Park the status of the two annual killifish *Nothobranchius orthonotus* and *Nothobranchius rachovii*, the lungfish *Protopterus annectens brieni*, the lowveld largemouth *Serranochromis meridianus* and the orange-fringed largemouth *Chetia brevis* has improved. New research has also resulted in a change of the status of *Barbus treurensis* from endangered to vulnerable. The status of *Barbus trevelyani* is now vulnerable and no longer endangered because of success with their artificial breeding.[15]

The status of two endemic freshwater fish species has deteriorated since 1977. These are *Barbus burgi*, which is now endangered instead of rare, and *Chiloglanis bifurcus*, which is now rare instead of vulnerable.

A dismaying 24 species have been added to the threatened list since 1977.[16] Of these, seven are endemic freshwater fishes, of which *Austroglanis barnardi* and a new and as yet unnamed *Nothobranchius* species are new to the known fish fauna since 1977. The latter two species both have extremely restricted distributions under threatened conditions. Four of the species, *Labeo seeberri*, *Barbus andrewi*, *Barbus serra* and *Sandelia bainsii*, are Cape Province endemics with restricted natural distributions that have shown a serious decline in recent years.

Five fish species have been added to the endemic estuarine threatened group. Especially the freshwater mullet *Myxus capensis*, which has a diadromous life cycle, has declined rapidly in the wild because of the increased construction of minor and major

---

[12] Ibid.
[13] Bothma & Rabie 'Wild animals' in Fuggle & Rabie (eds) *Environmental concerns in South Africa* (1983) ch 10.
[14] Skelton *South African Red Data Book—Terrestrial mammals* South African National Scientific Programmes Report no 125 (1987).
[15] Ibid.
[16] Skelton *South African Red Data Book—Fishes* South African National Scientific Programmes Report no 14 (1977); no 137 (1987).

weirs and dams on rivers. It is likely that more species will be added in future as our knowledge increases.

Of the 55 threatened fish taxa, 13 (24 per cent) occur in the south-western Cape Province (three endangered, three vulnerable and seven rare), four (7 per cent) in the southern Cape Province (all rare), four (7 per cent) in the eastern Cape Province (three vulnerable and one rare), two (4 per cent) in the northern Cape Province/Orange Free State contact zone (both rare), 21 (38 per cent) in Natal (two endangered, four vulnerable and 15 rare) and 11 (20 per cent) in the Transvaal (three vulnerable and eight rare). The rest occur in neighbouring territories. These include estuarine species.

Two geographical regions give rise to concern; the southern and south-western Cape Province for endemic freshwater fishes; and Natal and the eastern Transvaal for the majority of marginal freshwater and estuarine fish species.[17] Most species are rare because of a limited natural geographic range.

The nature of the threats involved vary from area to area but mostly involve one or more of the following: excessive tapping and hence restricted flow of stream systems; erection of barriers; sedimentation because of excessive soil erosion and unwise agricultural practices; chemical pollution; eutrophication and mineralization of water; acidification of water either from atmospheric or mining pollution; exotic biota, and the demand for aquarium specimens. The most effective conservation method is one directed at overall freshwater ecosystem conservation.[18]

12.4.4 Vertebrates: amphibians and reptiles

The most recent review of the conservation status of the amphibians and reptiles of South Africa has been done by Branch.[19] Data in the previous work by McLachlan[20] are not directly comparable to those of Branch mainly because of changes in the definitions of some of the classes. McLachlan[21] listed nine species of threatened amphibians for South Africa.

In South Africa alone there are currently some 233 endemic species of amphibians (60) and reptiles (173). Of the amphibians, six species are threatened, of which three are endangered, one is vulnerable and two are rare, while eight more are restricted, one is peripheral and one of indeterminate status. Of all these species, 12 are endemics.

The Cape platanna *Xenopus gilli*, a localized species with most specific habitat requirements, much of which has already been reduced by urban development, especially on the Cape Flats, is endangered. Also endangered is the micro frog *Microbatrachella capensis*, the smallest frog species in South Africa. The species is confined to the coastal lowlands in the Mediterranean region of the south-western Cape Province, where it is under severe threat from urban development and the invasion of its habitat by alien vegetation. The third endangered amphibian, Hewitt's ghost frog *Heleophryne hewitti*, occurs over a restricted range in the Elandsberg Mountains of the eastern Cape Province, where it is being threatened by over-utilization of its habitat for forestry. The Table Mountain ghost frog *Heleophryne rosei* is restricted to the mountain in the south-western Cape Province after which it has been named and where habitat destruction through the construction of reservoirs and the infestation of alien vegetation is placing it under pressure.[22]

Of the South African reptiles, Eastwood's longtailed seps is probably extinct, while a further three species are endangered, 13 vulnerable and 10 rare. In addition, 26 are

---

[17] Skelton above n 14.
[18] Ibid.
[19] Above n 10.
[20] *South African Red Data Book—Reptiles and amphibians* South African Natural Scientific Programmes Report no 23 (1978).
[21] Ibid.
[22] Branch above n 10.

restricted, 21 are peripheral and one is of indeterminate status. Of the reptiles under pressure, 40 species are endemic.[23].

Eastwood's longtailed seps *Tetradactylus eastwoodae* is a small lizard known only from two specimens collected at Woodbush in the Transvaal in 1913. It has not been found since and it is presumed to have become extinct when exotic plantations destroyed its probable mountain grassland habitat. The endangered reptiles include the geometric tortoise *Psammobates geometricus* from the low-lying parts of the Cape Province, and Smith's dwarf chameleon *Bradypodion taeniabronchum*, known only from a 20 km^2 area of fynbos on the eastern, upper slopes of Van Stadensberg near Port Elizabeth. Habitat destruction is threatening both species.[24] The leatherback sea turtle *Dermochelys coriacea*, previously thought by McLachlan[25] to be endangered, is now considered less threatened, and there is a likelihood of further improvement.[26]

Of all the vertebrate groups, the reptiles and amphibians have probably fared best at the hands of humans. Even when persecuted they have survived, probably because of their small size and their nocturnal and burrowing habits, all combined with long periods of hidden inactivity when they are not feeding. Thus the puffadder is still found in and around Cape Town and on Table Mountain despite more than 300 years of merciless persecution.[27]

Two areas of especial importance to threatened reptile species are the Woodbush–Soutpansberg area in the Transvaal, and the Lambert's Bay area in the Cape. Most of the reptile species, however, have restricted ranges, making their survival especially dependent on the continued protection of their habitat. The status of two reptile species is indeterminate. Poynton's caco *Cacosternum poyntoni* is known only from a single specimen collected in 1954 at Town Bush Valley in Pietermaritzburg, Natal, while Peringuey's leaftoed gecko *Phyllodactylus peringueyi* is known from two specimens only, the one probably from Little Namaqualand and the other probably from Port Elizabeth.

12.4.5 Vertebrates: birds

Bird species are numerous in South Africa. However, of the 102 species that breed on the South African mainland and the further six species found on the oceanic Prince Edward Islands, 72 are either threatened or extinct: two species are judged to be extinct, five are endangered, 21 vulnerable and 44 rare. The status of a further 35 species is vulnerable and one species formerly threatened, is now considered by Brooke[28] to be out of danger.

Two species of locally extinct birds, as listed by the above author, are the African skimmer *Rhynchops flavirostris* and the yellowbilled oxpecker *Buphagus africanus*, although the latter has been reintroduced successfully to limited areas in recent years. The five endangered species are: the Egyptian vulture *Neophron percnopterus*, the blackrumped buttonquail *Turnix hottentotta*, the wattled crane *Grus carunculata*, the roseate tern *Sternadougallii* and the blue swallow *Hirundo atrocaerulea*.[29]

The trend for the period 1976 to 1983 reveals that the conservation status of eight species has decreased and that of 11 has improved.[30] However, of all 108 species, the current population trend is up for only two species, stable for 52 and down for 54.[31]

---

[23] Ibid.
[24] Ibid.
[25] Above n 20.
[26] Branch above n 10.
[27] McLachlan above n 20.
[28] *South African Red Data Book—Birds* South African National Scientific Programmes Report no 97 (1984).
[29] Ibid.
[30] Cf Siegfried, Frost, Cooper & Kemp *South African Red Data Book—Aves* South African National Scientific Programmes Report no 7 (1976).
[31] Brooke above n 28.

12.4.6 Vertebrates: terrestrial mammals

Currently there are 243 species of terrestrial mammals known to occur in South Africa, of which 42 (17 per cent) are threatened with extinction.[32] These include three endangered species, 14 vulnerable species and 25 rare species. In addition, two species have become totally extinct and one has become locally extinct. The quagga *Equus quagga* and the blue antelope *Hippotragus leucophaeus* have long since become extinct in South Africa and Lichtenstein's hartebeest *Sigmoceros lichtensteini* has become locally extinct, according to Smithers—but has since been reintroduced to the Kruger National Park. Two formerly threatened species, the African elephant *Loxodonta africana* and the cheetah *Acinonyx jubatus*, are now considered out of danger.

The endangered species include the riverine rabbit *Bunolagus monticularis* from a limited area of the Karoo, the wild dog *Lycaon pictus*, which needs a large conservation area to survive in, and the roan antelope *Hippotragus equinus*, which seems to be increasing in numbers, especially on some game ranches.

The advent of commercial game ranching and of the conservancy movement has brought large, privately owned areas under conservation management,[33] a situation which has especially benefited the survival of terrestrial mammals. Yet agricultural practices and other developments continue to pose a serious threat, especially to the smaller terrestrial mammals, because of habitat destruction.

12.4.7 Factors affecting the conservation status of vertebrates

Human beings and their impact on the environment have clearly played a major role in the decline in numbers of many species of vertebrate animals in South Africa. Amongst the fish species, the introduction of exotic and predatory angling fishes, coupled with siltation due to poor agricultural practices, especially in catchment areas, are the major causes for decline. For the amphibians, habitat destruction due to urbanization is a particular threat, while over-exploitation by human beings and the destruction of habitat for agriculture pose the main threats to the survival of the reptiles. Birds suffer most from habitat destruction through agriculture and urbanization, and from human interference, especially at breeding areas.

For the smaller terrestrial mammals habitat destruction due to agricultural practices is a major reason for decline. An example is the effect of fire on rodents in savanna areas. Nel,[34] for example, maintains that rodents disappear immediately from burnt areas in the Kruger National Park, to recover only gradually. In his study, after burning, many rodents were caught by predators, especially raptors, while others moved to adjacent unburned areas. For the large terrestrial mammals human hunting pressure and incompatibility with agricultural practices are the main reasons for decline.

The picture that emerges points to humans as the proximate or ultimate cause of decline in the conservation status of the majority of threatened vertebrate species in South Africa. In this regard, South Africa follows the same trend as elsewhere in the world. However, professional game ranching, which has increased rapidly over the past decade or two[35] has led to the recovery and increased chance of survival of many large terrestrial mammals. The spin-off effect of the recovery of natural habitats in the process must also be beneficial to the survival of some of the smaller vertebrates and for many invertebrates and plants.

---

[32] Smithers *South African Red Data Book—Terrestrial mammals* South African National Scientific Programmes Report no 125 (1988).

[33] Bothma *Game ranching—an agricultural enterprise?* (1990) 9, 97.

[34] J A J Nel pers comm.

[35] Bothma *Professional game ranch management* (1989) 83–91; Bothma above n 33.

12.5 WILDLIFE LAW

12.5.1 Introduction

We live in an age of environmental alarm, an age in which the very survival of humankind appears to be threatened by systemic environmental damage. One of the major global threats facing our planet is the loss of genetic diversity. As wild areas have become reduced or modified to make way for agriculture and development, and as many wild species have become extinct or threatened with extinction, so have wildlife and the natural areas in which it occurs risen in society's hierarchy of values. A primary role of law is the regulation of human conduct in order to protect that which is perceived to be of value. Wildlife has acquired such scarcity value that it is now opportune, if not essential, for our legal system to provide a clearly defined body of law which will give effective protection to what remains of the wildlife resource. That body of law is best described as wildlife law,[36] having as its primary purpose the protection of wildlife and its habitat, thereby contributing to the maintenance of genetic diversity and healthy ecological systems.

12.5.2 Philosophical and socio-economic perspectives

The purpose of protection should determine the content of the law. What are the values which wildlife law should be designed to protect? A great deal has been written about the value of wildlife,[37] and it is generally accepted that it has instrumental value or value in terms of human utility. In recent years it has been argued that consideration should be given to extending not only moral rights but even legal rights to animals.[38] There is no valid reason, conceptually at least, why the circle of legal recognition of inherent worth should not expand to include wildlife. It is arguable that no theory of justice is truly complete unless in some way it accommodates the notion that rights are extended to animals, and that a modern legal order can contain such an accommodation within its framework. Inevitably, lawyers will have to face the logic of the pattern of extension of rights that has evolved, in terms of which legal rights have gradually been granted to children, slaves, women, blacks and fictitious persons. However, in the present context of South Africa's social, economic and political needs, it is perhaps too soon to expect general acceptance of an extension of rights to animals because of their intrinsic worth and not simply because they serve man's utilitarian needs. None the less, there are sound ethical reasons for recognizing that our fellow creatures have some rights, and all the ecological evidence and projections suggest that man's survival is dependent upon a reorientation of his conduct and policies from an anthropo-

---

[36] For a more comprehensive introduction to the topic of wildlife law, see Glavovic 'An introduction to wildlife law' 1988 *SALJ* 519.

[37] A useful summary of the reasons usually given for justifying wildlife conservation is given in the report of a working party which was set up by the United Kingdom Secretary of State for the Environment on the management of natural resources in preparation for the United Nations Conference on the Human Environment held in Stockholm in June 1972. They are that wildlife has value:

- as a contributory component of ecological stability and as a monitor of environmental pollution;
- for the maintenance of genetic variability and the provision of a source of renewable biological resources;
- for the needs of scientific research into the environment;
- for its cultural and recreational value and as a component of the aesthetic quality of the landscape;
- for environmental education;
- for the economic value of its resource, scientific and recreational components;
- to provide future generations with a wide choice of biological capital; and
- for moral and ethical reasons:

Sinews for survival Department of the Environment, London (1972) 50.

See further generally in regard to the values of wildlife Myers *The sinking ark* (1979); Myers *A wealth of wild species* (1983); Passmore *Man's responsibility for nature* (1980), and Ehrlich & Erlich *Extinction: the causes and consequences of the disappearance of species* (1982).

[38] See Stone 'Should trees have standing?' 1972 (45) *Southern California Law Review* 450.

centric to a biocentric perspective. Different philosophical commitments will produce different results. The controlled hunting of wild animals and the eating of their flesh may be acceptable from a biocentric perspective, provided that the integrity of the ecosystem is maintained. It may also be acceptable from the utilitarian viewpoint, which requires a sustained yield of natural resources. The animal rights view, however, eschews any acceptance of killing for sport.[39] From any perspective, however, control and protection are essential. In providing that control and protection, wildlife law must try to accommodate these different perspectives.

For any legal dispensation to be effective and enduring, it should be socially and economically relevant. South Africa is a developing country and its wildlife law must respond appropriately to its development needs and the apparent dilemma of conserving natural resources while at the same time recognizing the subsistence needs of indigenous people. It is essential that the last remnants of our wildlife and its habitat be legally protected, but the laws must be so formulated and applied as to permit of controlled taking on a sustained-yield basis, particularly in those areas where the traditional way of life is dependent upon access to flora and fauna for food, fuel, medicine and building materials. Local people should be permitted controlled access to natural resources within such areas, or defined buffer zones, consistent with their traditional harvesting practices. Irrespective of theoretical or philosophical commitments, the reality is that South African wildlife law must be human-oriented, otherwise it will not be effective.

For any conservation or development proposal to succeed, it needs popular support, which means that there should be consultation with and participation by recognized representatives of the people (that is, recognized by the people themselves) at every level of traditional authority. In any event, because of their close contact with, and cultural and subsistence dependence on their natural environment, indigenous people have over many years developed a rich traditional conservation wisdom and understanding of natural processes. They should therefore be involved in the control and planning of the use of those resources, including the wildlife resource. The harmonizing of local needs and local knowledge with conservation is sound environmental and socio-economic planning. There should be provision, as a matter of law and not of administrative policy, for local participation in the protection of wildlife and natural areas, the determination of reserve boundaries and preparation of management plans, and in the economic benefits derived from these resources.

12.5.3 International wildlife law

Wildlife issues often span geographical borders. The flyways of migratory species of birds, for example, traverse many national boundaries, and there is little point in one country imposing restrictions on shooting and trapping if neighbouring states do not do so too. Marine mammals do not recognize domestically defined territorial waters and land mammals, too, pay scant regard to the lines drawn on maps by man. The adverse impacts on wildlife of the transcontinental ivory and fur trades are well-known illustrations of the need for international co-operation. Bilateral or multilateral agreements with neighbouring states and legally effective participation in international treaties are an essential component of any national system of wildlife law. See chapter 9.

---

[39] A great deal has been written on the subject of animal rights. Reference may be made, for example, to Salt *Animals' rights* (1980 ed—originally published in 1892); Rollin *Animal rights and human morality* (1981), Regan & Singer *Animal rights and human obligations* (1976), and Regan *The case for animal rights* (1983).

12.5.4 Private law

Wild animals are classified in South African property law as res nullius and res intra commercium, that is as things which are unowned but capable of being owned. They are res nullius in their natural wild state, but become owned things as soon as they are 'occupied', that is, taken under effective control by occupatio, reverting to res nullius once that control is lost.[40] Their legal status is that of objects, not subjects of rights. Because of this status, there are no private-law remedies available to protect wild animals from being disturbed, captured, injured or killed, unless they are already the property of another.[41] The law does not permit intervention by concerned persons or organizations on their behalf. The rules relating to standing to sue (locus standi in judicio) are strict. See chapter 8. Nor do the common-law crimes of theft and malicious injury to property provide any legal protection to unowned wild animals. Without specific conservation legislation, wild animals would be without any effective legal protection.

12.5.5 Game farming[42] and game ranching[43]

The dedication of farms or portions of farms to game farming or game ranching will contribute to the prospects of survival of many endangered species. A recent survey suggests that game is utilized significantly on over 8 000 farms in South Africa.[44] Yet game farmers and ranchers remain largely unprotected by the common law. Farmers may pay large sums of money for game and incur substantial expenses in fencing off camps and providing fodder; but if the game escapes and regains its natural freedom, in common law the farmer loses his ownership of it as it reverts to the status of res nullius and ownership of it may be acquired by anyone who captures or kills it or otherwise exercises effective control over it.

Most wildlife now occurs in protected natural areas or on private property. The common law in this respect has become outmoded in present-day circumstances. Nor do the provincial ordinances offer adequate protection to game farmers and ranchers, notwithstanding the privileged position they occupy in relation to the game on their land in terms of the ordinances, which are aimed at nature conservation, not at protecting their interests. However, the common-law position has recently been amended by legislation, based upon research done by the South African Law Commission.[45]

The Game Theft Act 105 of 1991 provides that, notwithstanding the provisions of any other law or the common law: (1) a person who keeps or holds game[46] or on behalf of whom game is kept or held on land that is sufficiently enclosed, or who keeps game in a pen or kraal or in or on a vehicle, shall not lose ownership of that game if the game escapes from such enclosed land or from such pen, kraal or vehicle; (2) the ownership of game shall not vest in any person who, contrary to the provisions of any law or on the land of another person without the consent of the owner or lawful occupier of that

---

[40] On the subject of ownership of wild animals see, Van der Merwe & Rabie 'Eiendom van wilde diere' 1974 *THRHR* 38, and Rabie & Van der Merwe *Wildboerdery in regsperspektief* 1990 *Stell LR* 112.

[41] See, for example, *Richter v Du Plooy* 1921 OPD 117; *R v Mafohla* 1958 (2) SA 373 (SR).

[42] The phrase 'game farming' refers to the utilization of game in small enclosures or paddocks.

[43] The phrase 'game ranching' refers to the utilization of game which roams freely in large areas (albeit fenced).

[44] Mulder *Wildlife management and utilization—the economic imperative* Paper read at an international conference on wildlife management and utilization—the African experience, Pretoria 2–5 July 1990.

[45] *Acquisition and loss of ownership of game* South African Law Commission Working Paper 27 Project 69 (1989) 48.

[46] Section 1 defines 'game' as all game kept or held for commercial or hunting purposes and includes the meat, skin, carcass or any portion of the carcass of that game.

land, hunts, catches or takes possession of game, but it remains vested in the owner referred to in paragraph (1) or vests in the owner of the land on which it has been so hunted, caught or taken into possession, as the case may be.[47] Land is deemed to be sufficiently enclosed if, according to a certificate (which shall remain valid for three years) of the Administrator of the province in which the land is situated, or his assignee, it is sufficiently enclosed to confine to that land the species of game mentioned in the certificate.[48] The Act also makes it an offence for any person to enter another person's land with intent to steal game on it or to disperse game from that land or, without entering another person's land, intentionally to disperse or lure away game from another person's land.[49]

12.5.6 Public law

Van Riebeeck imposed restrictions on hunting in 1657 in the Cape.[50] Simon van der Stel introduced comprehensive controls over hunting in 1680.[51] Since then almost one hundred individual statutes and ordinances have been enacted for the conservation of wildlife. But the reduction of wildlife continues. The law has not been effective. There is an urgent need for an entirely new approach to nature conservation if the remnants of our wildlife and natural areas are to be preserved. Because of their legal status the extent to which wild animals are or should be protected, and their relationship to human beings, are at present matters of legislative and administrative policy, as there is nothing of any substance in private law on which the judiciary can operate in the interests of protection. There are various ways in which wildlife law may be expanded in public law, one of which is the development of the concept of a public trust doctrine and legislative assumption by the state of ownership of wildlife as a public trust on behalf of the nation.

Wildlife law at present is almost wholly contained in three categories of legislative enactment: laws which provide incidental protection of wildlife;[52] those which offer direct species protection, and those which protect wildlife habitat. The modern approach to nature conservation is to try to maintain biotic diversity by protecting entire ecosystems, biomes or landscapes. The protection of species cannot effectively be achieved without protecting their habitats. Habitat protection occurs primarily at national level, although protected areas are also established at provincial and municipal level. See chapter 27.

12.5.7 Provincial ordinances

In terms of the Financial Relations Act 65 of 1976, the responsibility for the preservation of flora and fauna and the regulation and control of hunting of game and other animals vests in the provincial administrations.[53] Each of the provinces has its own nature conservation ordinance containing extensive provisions relating to wildlife, ie the Orange Free State Nature Conservation Ordinance 8 of 1969, the Natal Nature Conservation Ordinance 15 of 1974, the Cape Nature and Environmental Conservation Ordinance 19 of 1974 and the Transvaal Nature Conservation Ordinance 12 of 1983. It is not possible within the confines of this chapter meaningfully to discuss the provisions of the different ordinances. An attempt will rather be made to discuss the Natal

---

[47] Section 2(1)*(a)* and *(b)*.
[48] Section 2(2)*(a)* and *(b)*.
[49] Section 3(1).
[50] Placaat of 1 January 1657.
[51] Placaat of 8 and 9 April 1680.
[52] These include laws relating to such matters as national monuments, integrated environmental management, soil conservation, acid rain and pollution control, all of which affect wildlife and its habitat to some extent, either directly or indirectly.
[53] Section 11(1)*(a)* as read with sch 2 paras 2 and 2A.

Ordinance as an example. It should be noted that the concept of 'nature conservation'—the object of the various ordinances—traditionally has come to be accepted as referring to the conservation of indigenous wild animals, plants and freshwater fish. This chapter is concerned only with wild animals, plants and freshwater systems being the subjects of other chapters. Moreover, the emphasis is on the conservation of wild animals outside protected areas. Conservation in protected areas is discussed in chapter 27. What follows then, is an overview of the relevant provisions of the Natal Ordinance. Although there are differences in the approaches of the different provinces, generally there are far more similarities in the ordinances than differences. Notwithstanding these similarities, a holistic, uniform approach to wildlife protection would be preferable and far more effective than the current fragmented state of wildlife law in South Africa. Although the topics of habitat protection, indigenous plants and freshwater resources are clearly relevant to wildlife conservation, passing reference only will be made to their treatment in the ordinances as they are dealt with more fully elsewhere in this book.

12.5.8 Natal Nature Conservation Ordinance

12.5.8.1 *Natal Parks Board*

The administrative agency charged with the control and management of national parks,[54] game reserves and nature reserves and with the enforcement of the provisions of the ordinance and other laws relating to game, fish and other fauna and flora generally in the province of Natal is the Natal Parks Board.[55] A primary function and duty of the board is to control, manage and maintain all such parks and reserves 'for the exhibition, propagation, protection and preservation therein of wild animal[56] life, wild vegetation and objects of geological, ethnological, historical or other scientific interest'.[57] Extensive powers are conferred upon the board to manage such protected areas,[58] including the power to make regulations generally for the effective control and management of parks and reserves.[59] Authorized officers or employees of the board have the power to arrest without warrant any persons suspected upon reasonable grounds of having contravened any of the provisions of the ordinance or of any other laws relating to game, fish and other fauna and flora, including any proclamations or regulations issued or made thereunder.[60]

Part I of chapter II deals primarily with the protection of wildlife within reserves. Protected areas are dealt with in chapter 27. Part II refers to the duties of the board with respect to game, fish and other fauna and flora in general. The board is required to take all such measures as it may deem necessary or proper for the enforcement of the provisions of the ordinance, as well as other laws relating to such wildlife.[61] The board or any officer or person authorized by it may enter any scheduled area or any released area for the purpose of ascertaining whether the provisions of such laws are being complied with therein, or for any other purpose connected with the administration of those laws.[62]

The board or any officer or other person authorized by it may, at any hour reasonable

---

[54] These are provincially established national parks as opposed to national parks established in terms of the National Parks Act 57 of 1976.

[55] Sections 4(1) and 24(1). Part I of chapter II deals with the establishment of such parks and reserves and the constitution of the Board.

[56] 'Animal' is defined in s 1 as any member of the animal kingdom other than man.

[57] Section 11(1)*(a)*.

[58] Sections 11, 15 and 16.

[59] Section 17.

[60] Sections 22(1) and 29.

[61] Section 24(1).

[62] Section 25.

for the performance of the duty, enter any private land or premises for the purpose of carrying out any investigation connected with the administration or enforcement of such laws.[63] Any person who fails to give or refuses access to such authorized person, or obstructs or hinders him in the course of any investigation, is guilty of an offence.[64] The board is also authorized to appoint officers, honorary officers and employees for the proper and efficient administration of laws relating to fauna and flora outside reserves.[65]

12.5.8.2 *Game*

Chapter III contains detailed provisions relating to game and the restrictions imposed on the hunting and other interference with game.[66] Schedules 1, 2, 3 and 4 create four classes or categories of game, namely ordinary game, protected game, specially protected game and open game. Cheetah, black rhinoceros and giraffe, for example, are deemed to be worthy of the special protection classification, while springbok and blesbok are listed as open game. The square-lipped rhinoceros, buffalo, eland and nyala, inter alia, are listed as protected game, while impala and grey duiker are ordinary game.

(a) Hunting, capture and keeping in captivity. The Administrator may from time to time by proclamation in the *Provincial Gazette* appoint an open season for the whole of the province of Natal, or for any defined area or areas of the province, during which ordinary game or protected game may be hunted.[67] He may proclaim different open seasons for different species of game. Unless otherwise permitted to do so in terms of the ordinance, no person may hunt game during the closed season.[68]

The ordinance makes provision for various classes of hunting licences and permits, including ordinary game licences, protected game permits, special game licences, commercial game-reserve licences and professional culling licences. All licences and permits are personal to the holder and are not transferable to any other person.[69] A licence or permit is required for the hunting of ordinary or protected game,[70] and no person may hunt open game except with the prior permission of the landowner or occupier concerned, or an authorized government officer in respect of state land occupied or reserved for a public purpose.[71] Licensing permits are issued subject to such conditions as may be prescribed by regulation.[72] The Administrator is authorized to make regulations in respect of a wide variety of matters relating to hunting, including the conditions subject to which licences and permits may be granted, the conditions

---

[63] Section 26(1).

[64] Section 26(2).

[65] Section 27.

[66] 'Game' is defined in s 1 as meaning any of the mammals or birds, alive or dead, mentioned in schs 1, 2, 3 or 4 of the ordinance, including any meat, fat or blood thereof, whether fresh, preserved, processed or manufactured in any manner, and also any tooth, tusk, bone, head, horn, shell, claw, hoof, hide, skin, hair, egg, feather, or other durable portion of any such mammal or bird, whether preserved, processed, manufactured or not, but not including any trophy.

[67] Hunting is widely defined. In terms of s 1, 'hunt', 'kill', 'catch' or 'capture' means to kill or capture by any means whatsoever and includes to search or lie in wait for, or wilfully disturb, drive, pursue, discharge any missile at or injure. Unlike the definitions in the other provinces, the words 'to search or lie in wait for' in this definition are not qualified by the addition of the words 'with intent to kill, shoot or capture', or similar words. The question whether searching for or lying in wait for an animal without the intention of killing or capturing it can amount to hunting was left open in the case of *R v Carter* 1954 (2) SA 317 (E). However, in the context of the definition, it is most unlikely that the courts will interpret the definition in such a way as to conclude that searching or lying in wait for an animal in order to photograph it, for example, amounts to hunting.

[68] Section 31.

[69] Section 33(2).

[70] Section 33(1)*(a)*.

[71] Section 33(1)*(b)* as read with s 42(1).

[72] Section 33(3).

subject to which any species of game may be hunted or captured, the regulation or prohibition of the use of any kind of calibre of firearm and ammunition for the purpose of hunting game, and generally any other matter which he may deem necessary or expedient for the effective and convenient administration of the provisions of chapter III of the ordinance.[73]

An ordinary game licence or a combined hunting and fishing licence entitles the holder to hunt ordinary game during the open season.[74] A special game licence entitles the holder to hunt ordinary game during the closed season upon land the owner or occupier of which consents to such hunting; but such owner or occupier must be in possession of a commercial game-reserve licence or ordinary game permit.[75] An ordinary game permit may be obtained by any owner or, with the owner's written consent, any occupier of land, which will then entitle him, his spouse and children, or any nominated full-time employee resident and actually working on the land, to hunt ordinary game as specified in the permit in the closed season. He may also allow the holder of a special game licence to hunt ordinary game on such land during the closed season.[76] The owner, or such an occupier, and his spouse and children, or such an employee, may hunt ordinary game on the land in the open season without being in possession of a licence.[77]

The holder of a protected game licence also requires the consent of the owner or occupier, but in this case the owner or occupier must be in possession of a commercial game-reserve licence or protected game permit.[78] An owner or occupier in possession of a protected game permit, and his spouse and children, are entitled to hunt on the land without a protected game licence, but only to the extent as far as number, sex and species are concerned as specified in the permit. He may also allow hunting on his land by the holder of a protected game licence.[79]

Without a written permit from the Administrator, no person may at any time hunt, capture or keep in captivity any specially protected game.[80] The significance of this provision is that the Administrator must grant a permit in relation to specially protected game, whereas the board issues permits in respect of other game. The capture or keeping in captivity of protected or ordinary game requires the permission of the board, which may be granted with the prior approval of the Administrator in respect of such game on land the owner or occupier of which has been granted an ordinary game permit or protected game permit.[81]

It is difficult to escape the conclusion that these provisions are unnecessarily complex and confusing. There are too many categories of wild animals, and too many different kinds of permits, licences and authorities. The ordinance is at present under review. It is to be hoped that these provisions will be simplified and the procedures streamlined.

(b) Hunter competence. In the past, one criticism of the licensing system has been that hunters were not required to pass examinations before being issued with a licence, so as to ensure that they could identify and distinguish between ordinary and protected game, that they had sufficient knowledge of sound hunting principles, and that they were familiar with the provisions of the ordinances. Enforcement of permit conditions and the control of the conduct of hunters in remote areas have also proved to be extremely difficult to realize in practice. To some extent, these concerns have been

---

[73] Section 58.
[74] Section 34(1)*(b)* and *(d)*.
[75] Section 34(1)*(c)*.
[76] Section 34(2).
[77] Section 34(3).
[78] Section 35(1).
[79] Section 35(2).
[80] Section 37.
[81] Section 38(1) and (2).

addressed in Natal. In a 1987 press release, for example, the board announced a new controlled hunting area, 4 200 ha in extent, adjoining the southern boundary of the Mkuzi Game Reserve, in which three initial hunts involving a limited number of animals were scheduled for the year. The announcement recorded that all hunts would be personally guided by experienced board staff, and that the hunter's marksmanship skills would be tested before each hunt.[82] In 1988 the board announced that it was offering ten hunts to local hunters from March to July 1988 in the area; that each hunting party might consist of only two hunters accompanied by two non-hunters; that the species to be hunted would be impala, nyala, warthog or duiker, which were excess animals which would normally have to be removed by board staff in routine management operations; and that the hunters would be required to pass a shooting test prior to hunting and would be accompanied at all times by trained board staff.[83]

As far as professional hunters were concerned, the board announced in 1988 that compulsory written examinations in theory and law would be held four times a year in the major centres of each province; that people intending to escort overseas hunters for reward were required to sit these examinations; that the theory paper was standard throughout the country; and that question papers on the hunting laws in all the other provinces would also be available at Natal examination venues should any of the candidates wish to write them. In addition to these written examinations, each candidate would be required to undertake a practical field test before being granted a professional hunting licence.[84]

In 1990 the board offered twelve hunts during April, May, July and September in the controlled hunting area adjacent to Mkuzi Game Reserve. Each hunt accommodated four hunters and four non-hunters and was subject to accompaniment by board staff of each group at all times and to the hunters, being required to pass a practical shooting test before being allowed to hunt.[85] The board also issued a news release of a joint announcement by the four provincial authorities for nature conservation to the effect that the testing of professional hunters and hunting-outfitters was to be undertaken by the hunters themselves. The past arrangement of testing by the four provincial departments would no longer be required during times of testing. Henceforth it would be necessary for prospective professional hunters or hunting-outfitters to be registered at professional hunting schools where the necessary testing and examinations would be undertaken. The newly formed national professional hunters committee would be the official body responsible for the registration of professional hunting schools, would serve as the appeal committee for applications for exemption from compulsory attendance at such schools, and would also function as the disciplinary committee to which the different nature conservation departments would refer instances of misconduct by professionals.[86]

In 1991 the board offered 14 hunts to South African hunters during April, May, July and September, and four overseas trophy hunts during June and August.[87]

(c) Other restrictions on hunting. It is an offence for any person to hunt or capture game on land on which he is trespassing, or to trespass upon any land on which game is or is likely to be found with any weapon or trap in his possession, or to be accompanied by any dog; provided that he will not be deemed to have trespassed if he satisfies the Court that his trespass was unintentional and that he was not aware that he

[82] Press release no 48 of 1 September 1987.
[83] Press release no 7/88 of 26 January 1988.
[84] Press release no 3/88 of 18 January 1988.
[85] News release no 53/89 of 12 December 1989.
[86] News release no 3/90 of 8 March 1990.
[87] News release no 32/90 of 3 November 1990.

was trespassing.[88] Unlicensed persons may be used to assist licensed persons, provided that they do not use any weapon to kill game.[89] The hunting, killing or capturing of game in any public road or in the road reserve of any public road is prohibited, as is the discharge of any weapon at any game which is off such road or reserve.[90] It is also an offence for any person to have any loaded firearm other than a revolver or pistol in his possession or in any vehicle in or upon which he is travelling, on any road, whether public or private, traversing land in any locality in which game is or is likely to be present; provided that this will not apply to the owner or occupier of any land, or his spouse or children, or to any person having shooting rights over any land, in relation to any private road situated on such land.[91]

Possession of a snare is an offence, unless the person in possession is able to prove that the snare is required for a lawful purpose.[92] Unless he is a holder of a permit issued by the board, and subject to such conditions as may be imposed in such permit, no person may hunt or capture game by means of any trap, snare or poison, or with the aid of any artificial light, or by means of veld fires or of a bow and arrow or crossbow and bolt, or from or within 200 m of any motor vehicle, aircraft, horse or other means of transport; provided that any person hunting birds listed in schs 1, 2, 3 or 4 may do so within 200 m of any horse. Prohibited times for hunting of game are between half-an-hour after sunset on any day and half-an-hour before sunrise on the following day.[93] The owner or occupier of any land shall not be convicted of an offence if he satisfies the Court that any trap or snare that he set was set or constructed by him, or poison was laid on such land by him, for the preservation of his livestock or crops or produce, or against the depredations of vermin or marauding dogs or the like, and that he took all reasonable precautions against game being caught or destroyed by it.[94]

(d) Sale and purchase of game. The board may purchase, sell or otherwise dispose of game, but no other person may sell game without a written permit from the board. However, no such permit is required by the owner or occupier of land who, subject to any municipal by-laws or veterinary or health regulations, sells game lawfully killed upon his land, or any person who is licensed or exempted under the Licences and Business Hours Ordinance 11 of 1973 and who resells game lawfully sold to him. No person may purchase game other than such game as may be sold in terms of these provisions.[95]

(e) Possession, sale and other disposal of trophies. Any person in possession of a trophy[96] derived from specially protected game is guilty of an offence unless it is proved that he is in lawful possession thereof or that he acquired it from an approved person. Without a written permit from the board, no person may sell or otherwise dispose of any trophy. Subject to any conditions which may be prescribed, an approved person may, however, sell or otherwise dispose of any lawfully acquired trophy.[97]

(f) Exportation of game. A permit is required from the board for the exportation of game from the province of Natal to any place in any other province of the Republic. For the exportation of game from Natal to any place outside the Republic, a permit issued

---

[88] Section 42(2).
[89] Section 44.
[90] Section 45(1).
[91] Section 46.
[92] Section 47.
[93] Section 48(1).
[94] Section 48(3).
[95] Section 49.
[96] 'Trophy' is defined in s 1 as meaning any mounted head or skin of any game used or intended for private display or museum purposes or any skin or portion of such skin used in a processed or manufactured article.
[97] Section 50.

by the board with the prior approval of the Administrator is required, and such exportation must not be contrary to any condition imposed by the Administrator and contained in such permit.[98]

(g) Destruction of crops by specially protected game. If it is alleged in writing by any owner or occupier of land that damage or destruction is being caused on his land by any species of specially protected game at any time, the Administrator is required to cause the matter to be investigated and, upon being satisfied that the complaint is well founded, to determine what measures, if any, should be taken in the circumstances.[99]

(h) Capture or destruction of game for special purposes. The Administrator may authorize, upon such terms and conditions as he may determine, the destruction, capture or removal of game or any species of game, if he deems that to be necessary or desirable for the prevention of human or animal diseases, or the preservation of fauna or flora, or for educational or scientific purposes, and he may also cause scientific and technical research to be undertaken in connection with any such matter. Any person authorized by him in writing, or any officer, may at any time reasonable for the purpose enter upon any land to carry out any such measures as the Administrator may direct in the exercise of this power, and any person who fails to give access to any officer, or obstructs or hinders him in the performance of his duties, shall be guilty of an offence. The Administrator may delegate his powers under these provisions to the board, subject to such conditions as he may impose.[100]

(i) Offences and presumptions. Any person who contravenes any of the provisions of chapter III or of the regulations made thereunder is guilty of an offence.[101] Several presumptions aid the prosecution of offenders.[102]

12.5.8.3 *Private reserves*

Chapter IV deals with private reserves. Upon the recommendation of the board, after written application to it by the owner, the Administrator may by notice in the *Provincial Gazette* proclaim an area of privately owned land to be either a private nature reserve or a private wildlife reserve.[103] On protected areas, see, generally, chapter 27.

12.5.8.4 *Mammals*

Chapter V deals with mammals but does not apply to any of the species listed in sch 5, namely chinchilla, mink and common hamster.[104] Without a permit issued by the director of the board, no person other than the board may at any time purchase, acquire by any means, possess, sell, exchange or otherwise dispose of, or keep in captivity any endangered mammal.[105] However, it is specifically provided that no such permit shall be granted in respect of any baboon or monkey which is an indigenous mammal, except in the case of research institutions, museums or circuses recognized as such by the board,

---

[98] Section 51.

[99] Section 40(1).

[100] Section 51.

[101] Section 55.

[102] Sections 39 and 57.

[103] Section 59. 'Private nature reserve' is defined in s 1 as meaning a privately owned area of land, enclosed by fence, in which rare or interesting indigenous plants or wild birds are protected and conserved, and which has been proclaimed as such. 'Private wildlife reserve' is defined as meaning a privately owned area of land, enclosed by a fence, in which rare or interesting indigenous plants, wild birds, ordinary game, protected game or specially protected game are protected and conserved, and which has been proclaimed as such.

[104] Section 78 and sch 5.

[105] Sections 79, 80, 81 and 84. 'Endangered mammal' is defined in s 1 as any indigenous or exotic mammal listed in sch 6.

or upon renewal of previously existing licences or permits. No permit is required in the case of stray baboons or monkeys acquired by any person and handed over to any officer within 30 days of acquisition, or in the case of registered zoos.[106]

There are detailed provisions relating to the establishment, conduct, maintenance and registration of zoos, and the issue of zoo licences.[107] There are also provisions relating to cruelty to indigenous mammals or exotic mammals,[108] and seizure and confiscation of them upon failure by any person to comply with the provisions of this chapter, the regulations, or the conditions attaching to any permit or licence.[109] Provision is also made for appeals to the Administrator,[110] and for criminal sanction by the creation of offences and penalties for contravention.[111]

12.5.8.5 *Professional hunters and hunting-outfitters*

Chapter VI deals with professional hunters and hunting-outfitters. No person may act as such unless he is the holder of a licence which authorizes him to do so. The requirements to be complied with in order to obtain a licence are determined by the board from time to time and it may appoint a testing team to ensure compliance. The testing team, upon payment by the applicant of the prescribed fee to the board, examines him and inspects his premises or facilities.[112]

A client may not hunt unless the hunt has been organized by a hunting-outfitter and he is escorted by a professional hunter, who is required to take all steps necessary to ensure that his client does not hunt contrary to the provisions of the ordinance. The holder of a professional hunting licence may kill ordinary, protected or specially protected game while accompanying a client, if such killing is in defence of life or property, or to prevent the suffering of any such game.[113] A hunting-outfitter may not present or organize the hunting of game for a client, and a professional hunter may not escort a client, on any land, unless the hunting-outfitter is the owner of the land or the holder of the written permission of the owner. The client must also be the holder of an appropriate licence or permit in terms of the ordinance.[114]

12.5.8.6 *Amphibians, invertebrates and reptiles*

By notice in the *Official Gazette*, the Administrator has the authority to suspend, for any stated period, the permits issuable in terms of chapter VII in respect of any family, genus or species of protected indigenous amphibian, invertebrate or reptile, whether generally or in any defined area or areas in the province. He may similarly declare that the provisions of this chapter shall not apply to any such family, genus or species, or shall apply only when such family, genus or species is found within any defined area or areas in the province. Any notice or proclamation so issued by him may be amended, varied or revoked by a like notice or proclamation.[115]

Without a permit, no person may kill or capture any protected indigenous amphibian invertebrate or reptile. However, such killing or capture without a permit is permitted

---

[106] Section 80(1).
[107] Sections 82, 83 and 85.
[108] Section 86.
[109] Section 88.
[110] Section 89.
[111] Section 90.
[112] Sections 93 and 94.
[113] Section 95.
[114] Section 96.
[115] Section 100. 'Indigenous amphibian, invertebrate or reptile' is defined in s 1 as meaning such as are indigenous to the RSA, or any part of or derivative from such amphibian, invertebrate or reptile, or the eggs or other immature stages thereof, but not including any marine invertebrates. 'Protected indigenous amphibian, invertebrate or reptile' is defined as meaning any species of amphibian, invertebrate or reptile included in sch 7, whether alive or dead, indigenous to the RSA.

if it is in defence of human life or property; but in such case any officer or honorary officer may require that it be surrendered to the board for disposal.[116] A permit is also required for keeping it in captivity or otherwise retaining it. If not protected, it may be kept without a permit; provided that if, on inspection by such an officer, it is his opinion that it is being kept in unsatisfactory conditions, the owner shall be required to improve the conditions to the satisfaction of the officer within 30 days.[117] A permit is required for the importation into the province of exotic amphibians, invertebrates and reptiles.[118]

Contravention of the provisions of chapter VII or the regulations made thereunder constitutes an offence.[119] Any permit or other authority granted to a person found guilty of an offence shall be cancelled by the Court and he may be declared to be ineligible for obtaining any such licence or permit or other authority under the ordinance for a period not exceeding three years.[120] Failure to comply may also result in seizure and confiscation of the relevant animal.[121]

12.5.8.7 *Wild birds*

Chapter VIII deals with wild birds.[122] Schedule 8 lists 'unprotected wild birds' and sch 9 'specially protected birds'. The Administrator may by notice in the *Official Gazette* declare that the relevant provisions of the chapter shall apply to any species of wild birds only when found in any defined area or areas of the province.[123] The chapter also makes provision for control measures relating to the following:

- the killing or capture of wild birds and the removal, destruction, injuring or disturbance of their nests or eggs;
- the sale, purchase and disposal of wild birds;
- the granting of permits to kill or capture wild birds;
- the registration and licensing of aviaries;
- the exhibition and display of wild birds;
- the importation and release from captivity of foreign birds;
- exportation of wild birds;
- prohibited methods of killing or capturing wild birds;
- control over trespassing in the exercise of permit rights;
- the prohibition of killing or capture in public roads or road reserves;
- offences and penalties, and presumptions of evidence.

12.5.9 The need for law·reform

The legal protection of species occurs at provincial level and is sought mainly through the control of hunting, capture and disturbance of wild animals. The ordinances all provide for different classes of wild animals and the measure of protection that is given to a species depends on how it has been classified. The Cape Province distinguishes between endangered wild animals and protected wild animals; the Transvaal between protected game, ordinary game and protected wild animals; and Orange Free State between protected game, ordinary game and specified wild animals. Natal has the most

---

[116] Section 101.
[117] Sections 102 and 103.
[118] Section 104A.
[119] Section 109.
[120] Sections 109A, 215B(1)*(c)* and 215B(2).
[121] Section 110.
[122] 'Wild bird' is defined in s 1 as any non-domestic bird of a species which inhabits either permanently or temporarily any part of the RSA, but does not include any such bird which is classified as game by virtue of its inclusion in schs 1, 2, 3 or 4 and shall include any skin or egg of any such bird which has not been completely processed.
[123] Section 112.

complicated legal machinery and prescription, with different schedules for ordinary game, protected game, specially protected game, open game, endangered mammals, protected amphibians, invertebrates and reptiles, unprotected wild birds and specially protected birds. Complexity and efficacy do not necessarily go hand in hand, however. A far simpler and more effective approach would be 'reverse' listing: instead of enumerating species that qualify for varying degrees of protection, and thereby running the risk of overlooking a species or migrant animals, all wild animals should be fully protected unless specifically excluded or afforded reduced protection. A holistic treatment and uniform approach would far better protect the wildlife resource. The listings in the class schedules differ from province to province, with the result that what may be an offence in regard to a particular species in one province will not necessarily be an offence in regard to that species in another province. Even recognizing that different regions may have different conservation needs, the current dispensation is clumsy and anomalous and clearly in need of reform.

Hunting requires a licence from the provincial agency and permission from the owner of the land upon which the animal is hunted. It is very difficult to control as it usually takes place in remote areas difficult to police; and the value of the licence system as a method of control is limited because most hunters do not depend on hunting for their livelihood and the sanction of losing a licence is therefore weak; furthermore, it is difficult to keep track of how many animals are killed by hunters and virtually impossible to do so in the case of those killed by poachers and owners who do not require licences. Owners of land are over-privileged in so far as the hunting of wildlife on their land and not owned by them is concerned. They do not require a licence to hunt ordinary game in the open season, and may be licensed to hunt in closed seasons. They enjoy further privileges in regard to the weapons and methods that may be employed in hunting, and may even hunt protected animals causing damage to property. Even though they do not own the wildlife on their property (that is, where they do not exercise the required control), they are masters of the destiny of wildlife because of their power to modify and destroy its habitat. Those animals which interfere with farming activities may qualify as 'problem' animals, previously referred to as 'vermin', for the purpose of their organized killing. The concept of vermin hunt clubs is not only offensive but also inconsistent with current conservation thinking: a farmer may kill in defence of person or property; but where is the line to be drawn? Should a leopard be shot merely because it appears to adopt a threatening attitude? Should a valuable animal be destroyed because of relatively small damage to crops? The privileged position of landowners and occupiers needs to be reassessed. Individual rights must be measured against public interest. There is a public dimension to wildlife that makes its legal classification as res publica more appropriate than as res nullius. These are particular issues which need to be addressed in modern wildlife law if the dwindling national heritage of wildlife is to be adequately protected.

There is an urgent need for reassessment of the adequacy of existing laws. Current conservation programmes are inadequate to meet the challenges confronting a developing South Africa. There are too many statutes and ordinances, and this plethora of laws represents a serious constraint on the effectiveness of wildlife law. The high prices paid at game auctions conducted by the Natal Parks Board—for instance, R2,2-m for five black rhinoceros and R38 000 for a roan antelope—suggest that current hunting fees and fines are disproportionately low. There is a severe shortage of nature conservation law-enforcement officers. Their salary benefits should be made more attractive.[124] Legally protected natural areas provide habitat protection for wildlife, and in effect constitute a national wildlife refuge system. What is required in South Africa

[124] Recently, salaries of conservation agency staff have in some instances been increased substantially.

is uniform and comprehensive species protection outside of protected areas. This would best be achieved through national prescription in the form of a Wildlife Protection Act, and regional administration by existing provincial conservation agencies. What is required, in other words, is the consolidation of the different provincial nature conservation ordinances in a national statute, comparable to the Road Traffic Act 29 of 1989, which effectively consolidates and co-ordinates the previous provincial road traffic ordinances. This suggestion is consistent with the recommendations of the *Report of the three committees of the President's Council on a national environmental management system*,[125] namely:

- That the four different provincial nature conservation ordinances be consolidated into one uniform Nature Conservation Act.
- That the diverse circumstances of individual provinces could be accommodated through regulations.
- That an issue which requires particular attention is that more emphasis should be placed on habitat and ecosystem protection rather than on the protection of individual plant and animal species.

12.6 REVIEW AND SUGGESTIONS

Effective conservation action must be based on a well-planned, holistic conservation strategy that encompasses and counters all deleterious effects which threaten the natural resource. This will, inter alia, require the growing shift from an overemphasis on large terrestrial mammal species towards a broader ecosystem-based approach to nature conservation. It will also mean that the needs of rural peoples must be established clearly and be incorporated into the conservation programmes of the future.

12.6.1 Ecosystem-based conservation

The key to understanding the current nature conservation problems in South Africa lies in the fact that while the African continent has the richest collection of fauna in the world, what remains today is but a meagre remnant of the immediate past.[126] One must view each animal species in relation to its ecological role, present and past. All animals ultimately depend on the vegetation of their habitat for survival. Yet few of the 70 veld types in South Africa are adequately provided with conserved areas and almost half have no properly constituted nature reserves.[127] This influences the long-term survival of many animal species that depend on one or more of these veld types as habitat.

Sound conservation approaches must increasingly regard nature reserves as dynamically integrated systems.[128] Yet the strategy for conserving the highest number of species in any available area cannot be generalized, as each situation requires independent examination and evaluation.[129]

One of the real problems of nature conservation today is the lack of a holistic approach which examines the impact of decisions on the entire spectrum of biota involved. For example, Van der Zel[130] discusses certain options for mountain catchment management in the southern Cape Province without reference to the impact of such practices on the animal life of the area; his concern was optimum water

---

[125] PC 1/1991 paras 5.4.3–4.

[126] De Graaff 'The Kruger National Park and wildlife conservation in Africa' 1971 (9) *Spectrum* 118–20.

[127] Codd 'The conservation status of ecosystems in South Africa' 1968 (64) *S Afr J Sci* 446–51.

[128] Miller 'Applying island biogeography to an East African reserve' 1978 (5) *Environmental Conservation* 191–6.

[129] Margules & Usher 'Criteria used in assessing wildlife conservation potential: a review' 1981 (21) *Biological Conservation* 79–80.

[130] 'Options for mountain catchment management in the southern Cape' 1980 (114) *South African Forestry J* 35–41.

production with a minimum of soil loss. In a subsequent paper,[131] he discusses the advantages of exotic timber plantations over natural vegetation. Again, no mention is made of the effect of such practices on the indigenous fauna of the area. Block-burning of veld is also recommended without reference to its effect on fauna. The conservation of rare animal species in such areas is neglected, despite evidence that animal species with specialized habitats, especially microhabitats, are particularly sensitive to climatic and vegetational changes[132] and to exotic afforestation.

In South Africa the focus of nature conservation activity and legislation has mainly been on animals, especially large terrestrial mammals. Relatively little attention has been given to protecting habitats and ecosystems: steps to remedy this deficiency are required urgently. The real need for halting the veld deterioration on agricultural land must also receive the attention necessary to reverse the steady degradation of much of the inherent diversity of South African vegetation.

12.6.2 Rarity

According to Margules & Usher,[133] rarity is one of five criteria that should be used to assess value and potential for wildlife conservation. The other criteria are diversity, naturalness, area, and threat of human interference. Rare species usually have peculiar ecological requirements. There are two types of rare species[134]—very localized and highly specialized—and three types of geographical distribution for them can be recognized:[135]

1. Species adapted to stressed sites; distributed as a few individuals wherever suitable habitat occurs, but at widely separated localities.
2. Widespread, but locally infrequent species; widely dispersed in the communities in which they occur, but nowhere common.
3. Species occurring in large numbers, but at few localities; for example, some African carnivores today.

A possible fourth type can be added,[136] namely species inhabiting environments which are rapidly changing. Some species may also appear to be rare because their populations fluctuate widely.[137] In whatever way rarity is defined it can be reasonably well quantified if knowledge of the distribution and abundance of species within a geographic area is adequate.[138] Therefore, many species of vertebrate animals currently considered rare in South Africa may move to the safe conservation category following more intensive collecting and surveys. Conversely, better data on the occurrence and number of species and population sizes, ecosystem by ecosystem, may show that more types of animal are threatened than may be expected. The absence of any centralized data bank on South Africa's biological resources makes countrywide enumeration of animals difficult, if not impossible. This is largely a reflection of the meagre resources of money and personnel available to nature conservation agencies in South Africa.

12.6.3 Size and number of nature reserves

There is a serious misconception even among many informed people that once an animal species is protected in a suitable reserve no more action is needed. Successful

---

[131] 'Optimum mountain catchment management in South Africa' 1981 (116) *South African Forestry J* 75–81.

[132] Soulé, Wilcox & Holtby 'Benign neglect: a model of faunal collapse in the game reserves of East Africa' 1979 (15) *Biological Conservation* 259–72.

[133] Above n 129.

[134] Mayr *Animal species and evolution* (1963).

[135] Drury 'Rare species' 1974 (6) *Biological Conservation* 162–9.

[136] Ibid.

[137] Margules & Usher above n 129.

[138] Ibid.

conservation depends on a diversity of protected areas. Some scientists question the biological validity of establishing nature reserves below certain sizes, stating that genetic stagnation will result in animals protected in small reserves. Whatever the viewpoint, there is general agreement that most conservation areas have to be managed scientifically if they are to continue operating dynamically.[139]

The argument against establishing small reserves often derives from the island biogeographic theory.[140] This theory holds that the faunal complement of an island increases with increasing island size and decreases with increasing distance from the colonizing source.[141]

Virtually all nature reserves in Africa are, or soon will be, islands of natural habitats in a sea of human modified inhospitable terrain.[142] The species most sensitive to insularity are those with relatively low population densities, i e the large herbivores such as the elephant, rhinoceros and hippopotamus; the top predators such as the lion, leopard, spotted hyaena and wild dog (hunting dog); and the top scavengers such as vultures, jackals and hyaenas.[143]

The island biogeographic theory implies, inter alia, that one large site generally contains more species than several small sites of equal total area.[144] This leads to the conclusion that unless a single large reserve can be established in an area for the protection of a number of animal taxa, threatened or not, it is useless to establish several smaller reserves for the same purpose. Economic realities often leave only the second alternative. It is of importance that the island biogeographic theory is increasingly being questioned as the basis for conservation planning.[145] Thus it is now being suggested that for a wide range of biota several small conserved sites may be better than one large site. Simberloff & Abele[146] further state that the ability of the island biogeographic theory to predict extinction rates and faunal equilibria, especially in savanna reserves which become isolated, is limited because political and economic policies instead of ecological principles are the most important influences on these reserves. Thus small and viable nature reserves designed to protect threatened vertebrates may well be realistic if they are properly managed.

Nature reserves are increasingly becoming surrounded by monocultures and areas of human development which cut the reserves off from adjacent natural systems.[147] Yet the dynamic interactions underlying the structure of the faunal communities in such nature reserves gradually adjust to this isolated condition and there is greater safety in diversity.[148] Several smaller reserves with the same conservation goals may therefore be as important for the conservation of threatened vertebrate species in the South Africa of the future as are the undoubtedly important large parks which exist: but only when the opportunity for establishing large, viable reserves no longer exists, and preferably when the smaller reserves are linked by conservation corridors.

In establishing a variety of small reserves it must be realized that diversity has an energy cost of its own, and thus there can be too much and too little diversity.[149] These

---

[139] Bothma above n 35.

[140] Diamond 'The island dilemma: lessons of modern biogeographic studies for the design of reserves' 1975 (7) *Biological Conservation* 129–45.

[141] Western & Ssemakula 'The future of the savannah ecosystems; ecological islands or faunal enclaves?' 1981 (19) *African J of Ecology* 7–19.

[142] Soulé, Wilcox & Holtby above n 132.

[143] Ibid.

[144] Simberloff & Abele 'Refuge design and island biogeography theory: effects of fragmentation' 1982 (120) *American Naturalist* 41–50.

[145] Ibid.

[146] Ibid.

[147] Miller above n 128.

[148] Odum 'Ecology—the commonsense approach' 1977 (7) *The Ecologist* 250–3.

[149] Ibid.

principles possibly already apply to the efforts aimed at conserving the bontebok and the Cape mountain zebra. Populations of these subspecies have therefore been established in a variety of reserves to promote genetic variation and to prevent a single catastrophe from eliminating the majority of the existing populations. Ultimately the availability of financial resources for nature conservation determines reserve establishment and design.[150]

For nature conservation, the role of the many game ranches which have been established in South Africa over recent years[151] and the conservancy concept now increasingly being established on what is largely agricultural land cannot be underestimated. Some movement of the smaller mammals especially occurs over game ranch boundaries, while conservancies and even natural heritage sites play a vital role in maintaining diverse gene pools in a variety of animal taxa. On protected areas generally, see chapter 27.

12.6.4 Human beings and conservation

In this day and age there are still people who ask: 'Why conserve threatened animal species, and is it not better to let those threatening to do so, die out?'

There are many known and unknown benefits to conserving organisms and ecosystems. Basically, all organisms should be allowed to exist, because there is an undefinable though recognizable benefit to be derived from their existence.[152] The danger of loss of species has often been one of the powerful rationales for nature conservation, because species represent a critical genetic resource. Conservationists must therefore be as much aware of the dangers of loss of unique gene pools and of genetic shifts in populations due to human influence as they are of losing whole taxa.[153] Threatened species, and the areas which contain them, must also be regarded as natural laboratories from which data and guidelines may flow for future conservation efforts. Even urban development can be geared to include the conservation of natural resources and thus prevent, rather than accelerate, the extinction of wildlife.[154] Industrial development, too, is not necessarily incompatible with environmental protection. In the future, conservation and development will have to be closely interlinked.[155] Experience gained, for example, from the damming of large African rivers, has shown that it is essential to anticipate environmental impacts and to take appropriate steps during the planning phases of all development projects. In this way deleterious effects can be avoided timeously.[156]

A mistake that we have made until recently is that we have left human beings out of the conservation picture. It is difficult to promote conservation amongst rural communities living a marginal or subsistence life.[157] Consequently, the social context must be incorporated into future conservation strategies.[158]

There is a current worldwide and growing awareness of the value of healthy ecological systems, and the consequences of human impact on them.[159] In many

---

150 Western & Ssemakula above n 141.

151 Bothma above n 35.

152 Margules & Usher above n 132.

153 White & Bratton 'After preservation: philosophical and practical problems of change' 1980 (18) *Biological Conservation* 241–55.

154 Crossen 'A new conception in park design and management' 1979 (15) *Biological Conservation* 105–25.

155 Talbot 'The world's conservation strategy' 1980 (7) *Environmental Conservation* 259–68.

156 Prelinès, Coke & Nicol *Some biological consequences of the damming of the Pongola River* International congress on large dams, Madrid (1973) Q40, R14, 175–90.

157 Anderson & Grove above n 4.

158 Ibid.

159 Tocher & Milne above n 1.

instances this awareness has led to careful ecological studies, balanced environmental and wildlife management procedures, and comprehensive legislation.

The recognition of the need for legal protection of natural resources goes back a long time. Thus Poland protected the European beaver in the sixteenth century and Switzerland has protected songbirds since 1535. What is new is the increasing attention to the survival of humankind as a fundamental benefit arising from the protection and sustained use of natural resources.[160] There is now general recognition that human influences, direct or indirect, remain the greatest threat to nature conservation goals. Conversely, controlled human use may be the key to the conservation of many areas. Yet, even after land is legally protected, ecological change continues to affect species and ecosystems. Biota in limited areas must therefore be continuously monitored and managed to offer long-term hopes for survival.[161] It must also be recognized that man-induced threats to nature include poor management and political decisions. Even though natural extinction may be inevitable in the long run, extinctions induced by human beings must be eliminated.[162]

While the official nature reserves in South Africa all have competent and appropriately trained biologists to study and manage these systems, vast areas of uncultivated land under private ownership are still subjected to haphazard and incompetent management based on inadequate knowledge. Some form of control must be established over such areas to ensure that the resources in question receive essential professional management.[163] This is of paramount importance where private land harbours the only remaining members of threatened species.

Human beings have established nature reserves to counteract their own actions, yet many reserves are established with an inherent contradiction—they are designed both to protect natural systems and to provide for public use of the area. Management thus seeks to maintain balance, with goals dependent upon the uniqueness of the biota of the area involved. The aim should be to keep the system dynamic, with natural processes continually operating, but not in the same direction over the whole area.[164]

The life and times of any organism are wedded to the life and times of the people of the country in which they all live together.[165] Local and international politics are often the ultimate factors responsible for producing negative or positive conservation results. Problems increase where movements across international borders are involved.[166] The historical, political, cultural and economic contexts in which foreign governments or even international conservation bodies involve themselves to protect threatened species are often so rigid that conservation actions can be little more than token efforts.[167] Yet the survival of most large organisms in the world may ultimately depend on the health and continuity of multinational conservation groups,[168] which should recognize that conservation principles are blind to political boundaries but not to the political needs and aspirations of the people involved. In South Africa the future comprehensive use of land will depend upon its productivity. Such productivity must be maintained and the

---

[160] Eidsvik 'National parks and other protected areas: some reflections on the past and prescriptions for the future' 1980 (7) *Environmental Conservation* 185–90.

[161] Bothma *Game ranch management* (2 ed, 1990); Eidsvik above n 160.

[162] White & Bratton above n 153.

[163] Bothma above n 35.

[164] White & Bratton above n 153.

[165] Teer & Swank 'International implications of designating species endangered or threatened' 1978 (43) *Transactions of the North American Wildlife and Natural Resources Conference* 33–41; Anderson & Grove above n 4; Siegfried, Frost, Cooper & Kemp above n 30.

[166] De Graaff 'The impact of development on wild areas (including national parks) and on such areas across international boundaries' *Proceedings of a SARCCUS symposium on nature conservation as a form of land use* Gorongosa, Mozambique (1971).

[167] Teer & Swank above n 165.

[168] Soulé, Wilcox & Holtby above n 132.

role of natural areas in this regard must be accepted. This must include the right of natural areas to exist for the benefit of their biota and for the benefit of human beings through optimal sustained use. Future land-use policies must also prevent human beings from plundering all natural areas without taking the ultimate consequences into consideration.[169] A poor environment can only produce low quality at all levels of life. This biological message must be recognized by all, especially by political policy-makers.

Furthermore, the recognition of wildlife conservation and management as a professional science is of paramount importance.[170] No person should be allowed to operate as a wildlife management specialist without proper knowledge of the philosophies, principles and techniques involved. Too many nature conservation decisions are still being made in South Africa without an adequate factual basis. Too often politics decide delicate conservation issues, without knowledge of or thought to the possible consequences to human beings or the greater environment.

The nature conservation officer is the image of nature conservation to most members of the public. These officers spend many hours working under difficult conditions and deserve proper recognition for their services. Their image, and that of nature conservation in general, could be improved by giving less emphasis to their law-enforcement activities and by focusing on their role as public advisers. With the increase in game ranching in South Africa,[171] each major environmental region in South Africa should have a well-trained nature conservation extension officer, operating on the same basis as the current agricultural extension officers. In such extension, however, verbal knowledge should be well supported by the practical demonstration of the techniques as well as the economic and ecological benefits involved.

A significant portion of South African society is still agriculture-bound and agricultural practices, and their competition with wildlife, have led to the demise of many species. Any animal species incompatible with specific agricultural activities is too easily condemned to the status of problem animal, while in reality the practice of improper agriculture is the greater ecological mistake[172] and should be subject to legal intervention. This attitude includes some veterinary actions which are often geared solely to achieving limited agricultural or veterinary goals while neglecting, or even ignoring, the broader ecological considerations involved. For example, the requirements of cattle dipping have led to the virtual elimination of yellowbilled oxpeckers. A holistic ecologically based land-use approach will eliminate most of these irritations and impediments to nature conservation. Only a concerted effort operating on all fronts can have any hope of real success. In all nature conservation ordinances there is a conspicuous absence of protection for most invertebrate species, while large terrestrial mammals figure prominently.

Ecological impact assessments done by registered ecologists (members of the South African Institute of Ecologists) should be part and parcel of any development scheme, irrespective of its size or its economic or political importance. Where any doubt exists, erring on the conservative side must be the rule. Such demands will present far-reaching practical and philosophical considerations to the wildlife biologist, the administrator and the developer, yet the ultimate result will be a new and vigorous thrust to protect threatened wildlife and restore them to safe or usable numbers.[173]

In all our actions we must remember that extinction is irreversible. What has been shaped by human hands can be shaped again, but what has been created by God can never be replaced by human beings once it has been destroyed. If human beings do not

---

[169] De Graaff above n 166.
[170] Bothma above n 35; Teer & Swank above n 165.
[171] Bothma above nn 33, 35, 161.
[172] Botha above n 3.
[173] Teer & Swank above n 165.

accept this responsibility voluntarily, then conservationists should help in the development of a legal system for the protection of nature in its own right. In that sense human beings will ultimately fulfil their proper biblical function as dependable custodians of the world in which they are merely temporary sojourners.

CHAPTER 13

FRESHWATER SYSTEMS

J H O'KEEFFE
M UYS
M N BRUTON

13.1 CHARACTERISTICS OF SOUTHERN AFRICAN FRESHWATER ECOSYSTEMS

The golden rule for the management of freshwater ecosystems is to remember that the conditions, water quality and biota of any body of freshwater are the product and reflection of events and conditions in its catchment or, to quote Hynes, the father of modern river ecology:[1]

'. . . in every respect the valley rules the stream. Its rock determines the availability of ions, its soil, its clay, even its slope. The soil and climate determine the vegetation, and the vegetation rules the supply of organic matter. The organic matter reacts with the soil to control the release of ions, and the ions, particularly nitrate and phosphate, control the decay of litter, and hence lie right at the root of the food cycle'.

Water that falls within a catchment may *(a)* evaporate, *(b)* run straight into a stream channel, *(c)* infiltrate into the soil, eventually to percolate into groundwater storage or into a stream channel, or *(d)* be lost by evapo-transpiration through plants. Land-use and the modification of natural vegetation therefore play a crucial role in determining the proportions of rainfall that reach each part of the system, and particularly the ratio of runoff to rainfall. About 40 per cent (26 000 km) of the total length of South Africa's 3 193 rivers and tributaries (65 000 km) is subject to seasonal flows.

Forests promote infiltration by intercepting raindrops, by improving soil structure through the production of a thick litter layer and by providing infiltration channels down deep roots.[2] Forests also stabilize soils, thereby reducing erosion, but they also reduce runoff, since evapo-transpiration is directly related to plant biomass.[3] Table 13.1 compares infiltration rates, runoff and soil loss for different rural land-uses in Zimbabwe. The clearance of natural vegetation obviously has profound effects on the hydrology of a catchment, as shown in Figure 13.1, which illustrates the difference in storm runoff when a catchment is cleared of its natural vegetation. The result is a larger flood of shorter duration, followed by lower base flows. In southern Africa the trend for constantly flowing (perennial) rivers to become seasonal, with no flow during the drier months, is a consequence of these land-use and vegetation changes in the catchment.

Southern Africa is generally an arid to semi-arid region, with an average rainfall of a little under 500 mm per annum. The distribution of rainfall (Figure 13.2) is very uneven, and some of the areas of highest demand, such as the Pretoria–Witwatersrand–Vereeniging (PWV) area, receive little rainfall. Because of high evaporation rates, the runoff to rainfall ratio is amongst the lowest for any populated region of the world (Figure 13.3). The result is that water is a very scarce resource in most of southern

[1] 'The stream and its valley' 1975 (19) *Verh Internat Verein Limnol* 1–15.

[2] Whitlow 'Hydrological implications of land use in Africa, with particular reference to Zimbabwe' 1983 (80) *Zimbabwe Agricultural J* 193–212.

[3] Alexander 'Hydrology of low latitude Southern Hemisphere land masses' 1985 (125) *Hydrobiologia* 75–83.

TABLE 13.1

Examples of the effects of different land-uses on A. Infiltration rates and B. Runoff and erosion, for Sandveld soils in Zimbabwe (modified from Whitlow above n 2).

A. Land-use		Infiltration Rates (mm h^{-1}) First Hour	Third hour
Cultivated		3,5 to 120,5	1,3 to 2,9
Newly cleared		13,8 to 20,4	5,5 to 9,2
Miambo woodlands		30,7	9,3
B. Land-use	Mean runoff (mm y^{-1})	Runoff as % MAP	Mean soil loss (kg ha^{-1} y^{-1})
Bare plots	206	30,3	4 320
Burned annually in mid-dry season	60	8,8	470
Burned every 4 years	33	4,8	280
Protected plots	26	3,8	200

Africa, which is otherwise blessed with an abundance of natural resources, and that water is often the limiting resource for development. Large-scale engineering techniques have therefore been used to store water (behind dam walls) and to distribute water from catchments with abundant supplies and low demand to those where demand is high but supplies are scarce (by means of inter-basin canals and pipelines).[4] By the time the massive Lesotho Highlands Water Scheme has been completed, more than 75 per cent of the flow in the Vaal River will have been imported from other catchments (the Usutu, Tugela and upper Orange rivers).

Superimposed on this scarcity and uneven distribution are regional and temporal variations in rainfall which further complicate the management of southern Africa's water resources. The broad regional climatological pattern shows an eastern area of summer rainfall, a southwestern winter rainfall belt, a southern belt of year-round rainfall and an arid western region. Long-term rainfall cycles of 18 to 20 years have been demonstrated for the summer rainfall region[5] (Figure 13.4).[6] It is therefore extremely important to avoid extrapolations of water supplies measured only during one part of this cycle.

13.2 AVAILABILITY AND USE OF FRESHWATER IN SOUTH AFRICA

There are practically no freshwater lakes in South Africa; exploitable water supplies are therefore confined to rivers, artificial lakes behind dams, and ground water. Total runoff from South Africa is estimated at 53 500 million m^3 per annum, of which about 33 000 million m^3 (62 per cent) could practically be exploited.[7] In addition, there are substantial groundwater reserves, but recharge estimates are uncertain, and so therefore is the renewable resource value. Recharge estimates of between 16 000 and 37 000 million m^3 per annum have been suggested,[8] but only a small part of this amount

[4] Noble & Hemens *Inland water ecosystems in South Africa—A review of research needs* South African National Scientific Programmes Report no 34 (1978).

[5] Dyer 'Expected future rainfall over selected parts of South Africa' 1976 (72) *S Afr J Sci* 237–9.

[6] Preston-Whyte & Tyson *The atmosphere and weather of southern Africa* (1988).

[7] *Management of the water resources of the Republic of South Africa* Department of Water Affairs (1986).

[8] Ibid.

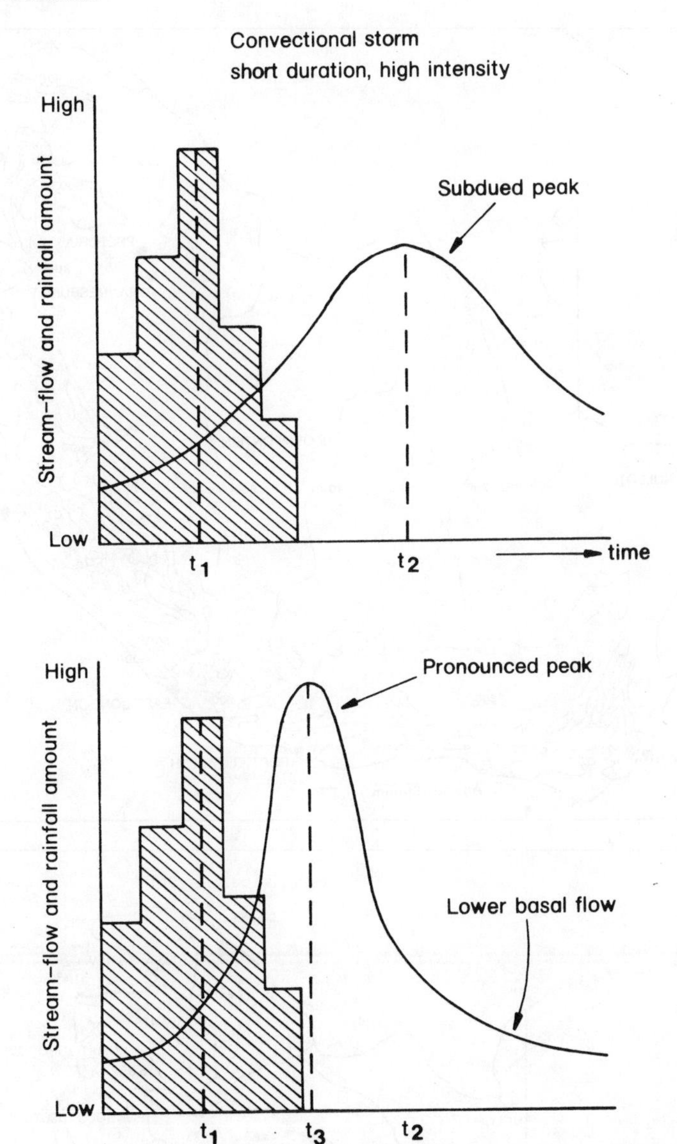

Figure 13.1 The effects of vegetation clearance in a catchment. For equal rainfall, there is greater infiltration in the naturally vegetated catchment (top) than in the cleared catchment (bottom). The result is a larger, shorter flood, followed by lower base flow in the cleared catchment (modified from Whitlow above n2).

can be recovered economically. Some 5 400 m^3 per annum might represent the realistic potential maximum ground water use, and this represents 16,4 per cent of the annual exploitable surface runoff from rivers. Table 13.2 lists the major types of water use in South Africa for 1990 (as estimated in 1986), and predicted changes by AD 2010. Present use amounts to nearly 50 per cent of available runoff and ground water and this is likely to rise to 67 per cent by 2010. This appears to be comfortably within the limits of available water, but has to be seen within the context of the spatial and temporal availability described above. The PWV area already uses far more than 100 per cent of

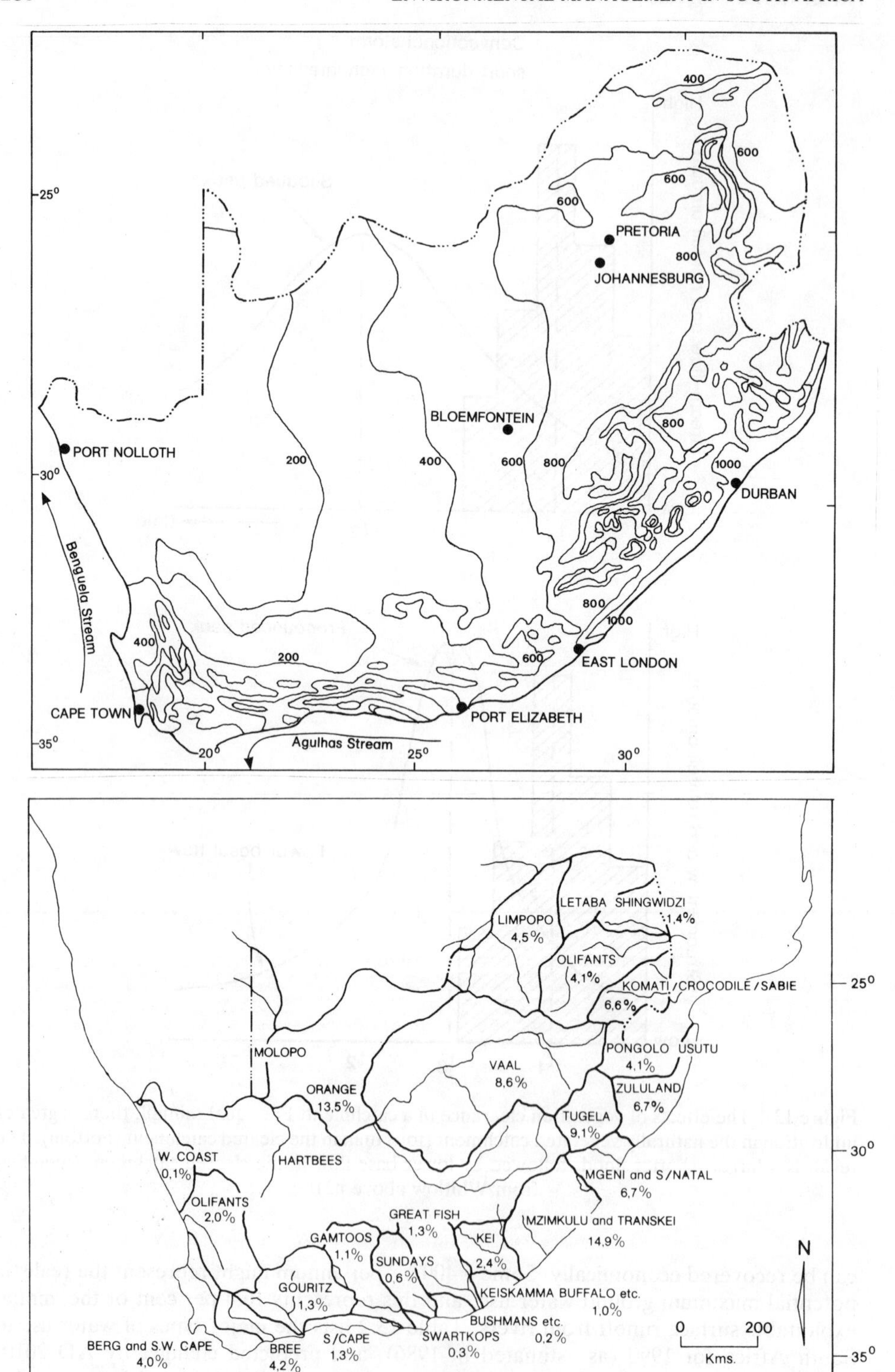

Figure 13.2 Top: Average annual rainfall isohyets (mm). Bottom: Principal drainage systems and their contribution to total mean annual runoff (from Noble & Hemens above n 4).

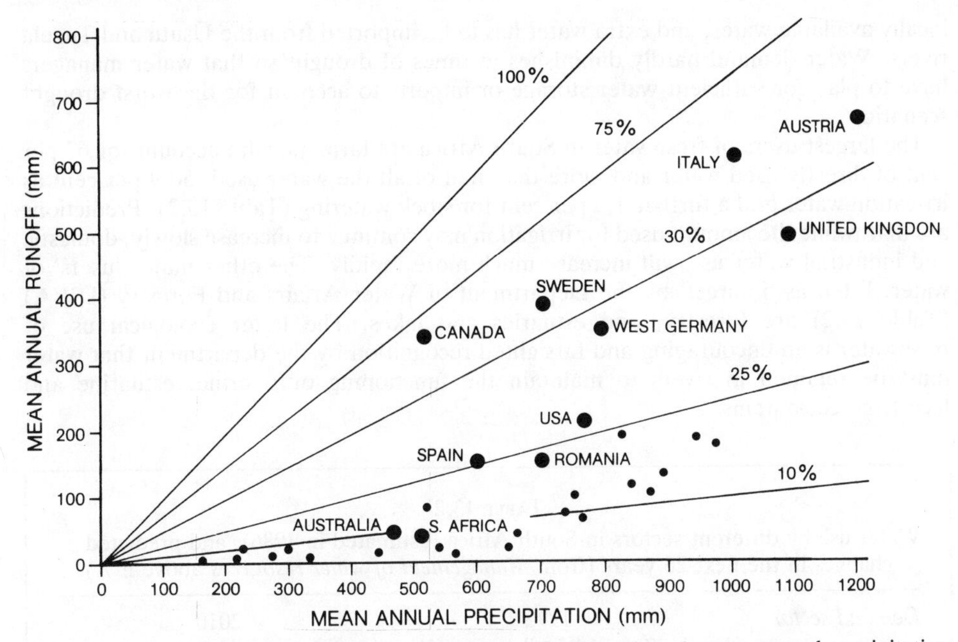

Figure 13.3 Relationship between mean annual runoff (MAR) and mean annual precipitation (MAP) for selected representative countries in the northern and southern hemispheres (named), as well as for major river basins in southern Africa (small circles) (adapted from Alexander above n 3).

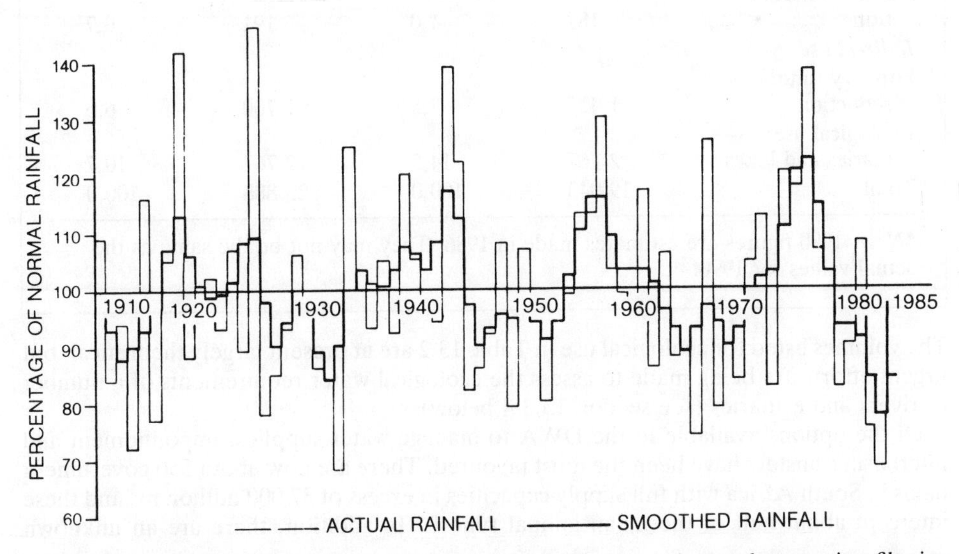

Figure 13.4 Rainfall patterns over southern Africa determined by various and appropriate filtering techniques. Rainfall zones averaged by area for the October to September year in the summer rainfall region (1910/11 to 1983/84) (from Preston-Whyte & Tyson above n 6).

locally available water, and extra water has to be imported from the Usutu and Tugela rivers. Water demand hardly diminishes in times of drought so that water managers have to plan for sufficient water storage or imports to account for the worst drought scenario.

The largest users of freshwater in South Africa are farmers, who account for 67 per cent of directly used water and more than half of all the water used, 50,9 per cent as irrigation water and a further 1,5 per cent for stock watering (Table 13.2). Predictions are that, while the amount used for irrigation may continue to increase slowly, domestic and industrial water use will increase much more rapidly. The other major 'users' of water, listed as 'indirect' by the Department of Water Affairs and Forestry (DWA) (Table 13.2) are forestry, and estuaries and lakes. The latter ecological use of freshwater is an encouraging and farsighted recognition by the department that water must be retained in rivers to maintain the functioning of riverine, estuarine and lacustrine ecosystems.

TABLE 13.2

Water-use by different sectors in South Africa (estimated in 1986), and predicted changes in the next 20 years (from *Management of water resources* above n 7.)

Demand sector	1990* (million m^3 y^{-1})	(%)	2010 (million m^3 y^{-1})	(%)
Direct use				
Municipal and domestic	2 281	12,0	4 477	17,3
Industrial	1 448	7,6	2 961	11,4
Mining	511	2,7	649	2,5
Power generation	444	2,3	900	3,5
Irrigation	9 695	50,9	11 885	45,9
Stock watering	288	1,5	358	1,4
Nature conservation	182	1,0	191	0,7
Indirect use				
Forestry runoff reduction	1 427	7,5	1 700	6,6
Ecological use, estuaries and lakes	2 767	14,5	2 767	10,7
Total	19 043	100,0	25 888	100,0

**Note*: 1990 figures are estimates made in 1986. They may not be the same as the actual values for 1990.

The volumes listed for ecological use in Table 13.2 are at present largely theoretical, but urgent efforts are being made to assess the ecological water requirements of a number of rivers and estuaries (see section 13.3.4 below).

Of the options available to the DWA to manage water supplies, impoundment and interbasin transfers have been the most favoured. There are now about 550 government dams in South Africa with full supply capacities in excess of 37 000 million m^3 and these intercept about half of the mean annual runoff.[9] In addition, there are an unknown

[9] Ibid. Cf also Rowlston 'Man-made barriers in South African rivers' in Cave, Klapwijk & Assoc (eds) *Fishways in South Africa* (1990).

number of privately owned farm dams built on and off rivers which impound a significant proportion of the remaining runoff. An idea of the number of these dams is given by recent surveys of the Nyls River catchment, on which 160 farm dams were found, and on the Palula River upstream of the Laphalala Wilderness, where there are an estimated 400 farm dams. Because of the variability of rainfall in South Africa, dams have to be larger, in relation to the discharge of the rivers, than in parts of the world that have steadier precipitation rates, in order to provide a reliable long-term yield. Because most South African rivers carry high sediment loads, dams also have to be larger than elsewhere in order to accommodate the sediment deposition in the reservoirs.

Interbasin water transfers are a means of increasing water supplies in catchments of low rainfall and high demand, by piping water from wetter areas with lower demand. As most suitable impoundment sites have been used, the DWA is increasingly using interbasin transfers as a method of augmenting local water supplies. There are currently seven interbasin transfer schemes in operation and a further eight are under construction or proposed. These currently divert 1 630 million m^3 of water per annum, but this figure will rise to 4 820 million m^3 (8,9 per cent of the mean annual runoff for South Africa) if all those planned are completed.[10]

The largest scheme currently under construction is the Lesotho Highlands Water Scheme, which will eventually divert 2 000 million m^3 of water from the headwaters of the Orange River system to the Vaal River annually. Tentative plans to divert water from the Zambezi River could eventually augment the Vaal River by 2 500–4 000 million m^3 a year.[11]

13.3 ENVIRONMENTAL PROBLEMS ASSOCIATED WITH FRESHWATER RESOURCES

13.3.1 Catchment changes

Reference has been made to the dependence of a river on its catchment and some examples have been provided of the consequences of land-use changes on water quality and flow patterns. One of the features of South African rivers is the very large sediment loads that they carry, especially during floods. This is partly a natural feature of semi-arid regions and the steep gradients of the rivers, and partly a consequence of poor land management. The latter causes heavy erosion, especially on the friable soils developed on the shales and mudstones that are characteristic of the sedimentary rocks of the Karoo System. For example, the Tarka River at Lake Arthur in the eastern Cape has an average sediment percentage (by volume) of 4,2, and the Stormberg River at Burgersdorp has 4,3 per cent. On the Mbashe River (Transkei) an 11 m weir at Collywobbles, built as a hydro-electric facility, has never been used, because floods during the first year after construction completely filled the impoundment with silt.[12] Estimates of erosion rates in parts of Natal indicate an increase of between 12 to 22 times the average geological rate of erosion.[13]

Vegetation clearance obviously increases erosion, but the replacement of natural vegetation by introduced species also causes unwelcome changes to rivers. The afforestation of upper catchments by alien species such as *Pinus radiata* may reduce

---

[10] Petitjean & Davies 'Ecological impacts of inter-basin water transfers: some case studies, research requirements and assessment procedures in southern Africa' 1988 (84) *S Afr J Sci* 819–28.

[11] *Report of the commission of enquiry into water matters* RP 34/1970 Table 4.

[12] O'Keeffe 'Conserving rivers in southern Africa' 1989 (49) *Biological Conservation* 255–74.

[13] Murgatroyd 'Geologically normal and accelerated rates of erosion in Natal' 1979 (75) *S Afr J Sci* 395–6; Martin 'Comparison of sedimentation rates in the Natal Valley, south-west Indian Ocean, with modern sediment yields in east coast rivers of southern Africa' 1987 (83) *S Afr J Sci* 716–24.

runoff by half,[14] and clear-felling causes periodic catastrophic changes in runoff and sediment loads. A recent hydrological simulation of the Sabie River (eastern Transvaal) estimates that the discharge has decreased by 27,5 per cent compared with natural conditions.[15] This is primarily due to the afforestation of 80 per cent of the upper catchment by pines and eucalypts.

13.3.2 River regulation

Few, if any, of the larger rivers of South Africa are still unimpounded or unaffected by interbasin transfers. South African rivers in their natural state tend to have variable flow regimes, to be governed by stochastic events such as floods and droughts and often to have a low seasonal predictability.[16] To supply water with a high degree of certainty therefore requires that this variability should be overcome. The consequences for the natural biota, which has co-evolved with variable and unpredictable events, can be severe. The Orange-Fish tunnel has changed the Great Fish River from a seasonal to a perennial system, with consequent advantages to farmers, who can now irrigate all year round. Although the diversity of the invertebrate fauna appears to be about the same, only 33 per cent of naturally occurring species are still found in the river.[17] The other two-thirds have recently colonized the river, which now has a more predictable flow following the introduction of Orange River water. One insect species whose lavae occurred in the river in low densities before the tunnel was opened, *Simulium chutteri*, now dominates the middle reaches of the river. *S chutteri* is a bloodsucking fly whose larvae live in flowing water, but whose adults emerge to feed on farm stock, causing severe distress and damage during high-density outbreaks in spring and early summer.[18]

Interbasin transfers have also been responsible for the breakdown of the natural biogeographical barriers between catchments. At least five fish species, not previously recorded from the Great Fish River, have successfully negotiated the Orange-Fish tunnel since it was opened in 1975.[19] Fish translocations have also taken place through interbasin connections between the Great Fish and the Sundays, the Vaal and Tugela, the Kavango and Kuiseb, and the Kunene and Cuvelai systems.[20]

Studies on the effects of impoundment in the Palmiet (southwestern Cape) and Buffalo (eastern Cape) rivers have demonstrated the effects of impoundment on water temperature,[21] suspended sediments,[22] and other physico-chemical variables.[23] Major changes were caused to water temperatures, nutrient status and

---

[14] Wicht 'The influence of vegetation in South African mountain catchments on water supplies' 1971 (67) *S Afr J Sci* 201–9.

[15] Chunnett, Fourie & Partners *Hydrology—Sabie river catchment* Report of a hydrological survey of the Sabie-sand catchment, Department of Water Affairs (1990).

[16] O'Keeffe *Ecological research on South African rivers—a preliminary synthesis* South African National Scientific Programmes Report no 121 (1986).

[17] O'Keeffe & De Moor 'Changes in the physico-chemistry and benthic invertebrates of the Great Fish River, following an interbasin transfer of water' 1988 (2) *Regulated Rivers: Research and Management* 37–55.

[18] Ibid.

[19] Laurenson & Hocutt 'Colonization theory and invasive biota—the Great Fish River, a case history' 1985 (6) *Environmental Monitoring and Assessment* 71–90.

[20] Hutchinson, Pickford & Schuurman 'A contribution to the hydrobiology of pans and other inland waters of South Africa' 1932 (24) *Archiv für Hydrobiologie* 1–154.

[21] Palmer & O'Keeffe 'Temperature effects of impoundments on the downstream reaches of a river in south eastern Africa' 1989 (116) *Archiv für Hydrobiologie* 471–85.

[22] Palmer & O'Keeffe 'Transported material in a small river with multiple impoundments' 1990 (24) *Freshwater Biology* 563–75.

[23] O'Keeffe, Byren, Davies & Palmer 'The effects of impoundments on the physico-chemistry of two contrasting southern African river systems' 1990 (5) *Regulated Rivers: Research and Management* 97–110.

suspended material, and the type and severity of these changes depended on the size of impoundment, its position along the river, and the pre-impoundment nutrient status of the river. Changes in the river below large impoundments persist for up to 30 km downstream.[24] These changes fundamentally altered the communities of plants and animals in the rivers downstream of the dams. In addition, dams act as barriers to the movement and migration of organisms (especially fish) along the river corridor. On rivers generally, see chapter 25.

13.3.3 Pollution and eutrophication

According to the DWA, the quality of many water sources in the Republic of South Africa is declining. This is primarily as a result of salinization and to a lesser extent because of eutrophication and pollution by trace metals and micro-pollutants.[25]

Many water bodies in South Africa are naturally high in dissolved salts, especially rivers flowing over old marine sediments such as the Karoo series. However, increasing industrialization, urbanization and irrigation have caused increases in salinity which threaten markedly to reduce the potential usefulness of many rivers. Figure 13.5 shows the increasing salinity of the water in the Vaal Barrage since 1934 and Table 13.3 gives the salinity status of a number of large dams. The maximum salinity of irrigation water

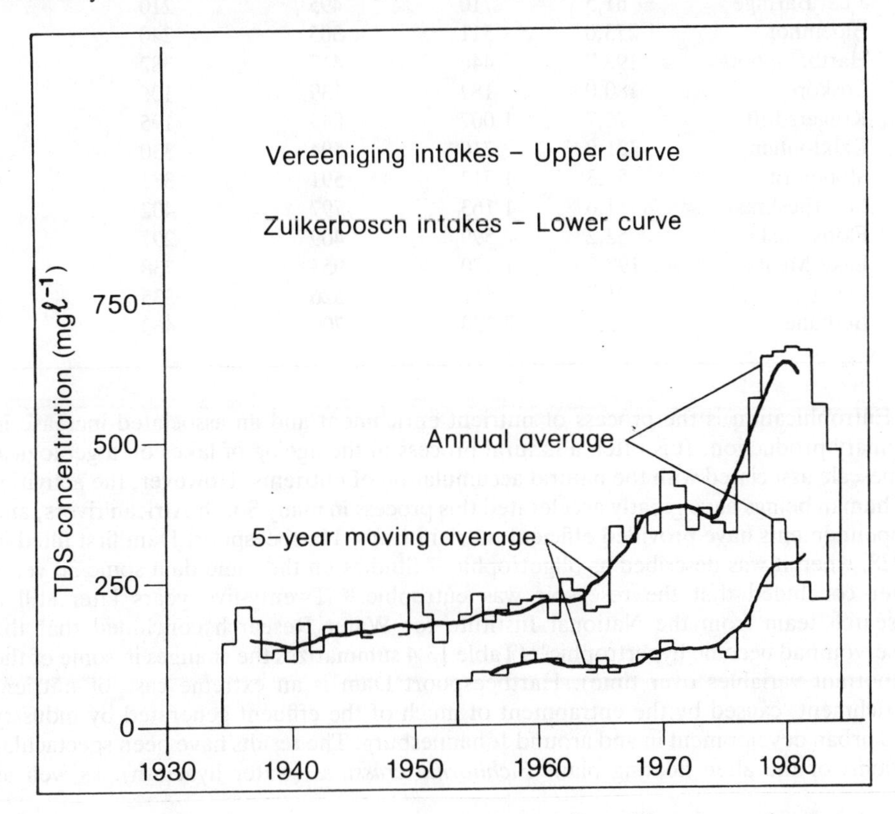

Figure 13.5 Annual TDS concentrations in the Vaal Barrage (from *Management of water resources* above n 7).

---

[24] Ibid.
[25] *Management of water resources* above n 7.

tolerated by many crops is 660 mg ℓ$^{-1}$ total dissolved salts (TDS).[26] These crops include maize, potatoes and many types of fruit. Vaal Barrage water, which was originally suitable for many of these crops, has generally had a higher TDS than this maximum since 1980, and many of the reservoirs listed in Table 13.3 are no longer suitable for irrigation for much of the time. Salinization is a particularly intractable problem, because the only known remedies are dilution with less saline water or very expensive reverse osmosis to remove dissolved salts.

TABLE 13.3

Salinity status of a number of dams in the RSA (from *Management of water resources* above n 7.)

Name of dam	*Capacity* (million m^3)	*TDS concentration, in mg ℓ$^{-1}$, equalled or exceeded for various percentages of time* 10 %	50 %	90 %
Vaal	2 190,6	177	137	99
Vaal Barrage	61,5	710	495	210
Bloemhof	1 273,0	511	305	240
Hartbeespoort	193,7	446	417	382
Loskop	180,0	182	139	106
Krugersdrift	76,7	1 007	849	195
Kalkfontein	321,8	710	594	330
Stompdrif	55,3	1 312	591	381
Miertjieskraal	1,6	1 163	797	402
Floriskraal	52,2	599	409	297
Lake Mentz	192,5	1 470	955	738
Laing	21,7	811	526	335
Bethulie	2,0	2 220	709	463

Eutrophication is the process of nutrient enrichment and an associated increase in primary production. It is often a natural process in the ageing of lakes on a geological timescale associated with the natural accumulation of nutrients. However, the activities of human beings have greatly accelerated this process in many South African rivers, and impoundments have provided efficient nutrient traps. Hartbeespoort Dam first filled in 1928, when it was described as oligotrophic.[27] Studies on the same dam some 30 years later concluded that the reservoir was eutrophic.[28] Twenty-five years later still a research team from the National Institute for Water Research concluded that the reservoir had become hypertrophic[29] (Table 13.4 summarizes the changes in some of the important variables over time). Hartbeespoort Dam is an extreme case of nutrient enrichment, caused by the entrapment of much of the effluent generated by industry and urban development in and around Johannesburg. The results have been spectacular blooms of the alien floating plant *Eichhornia crassipes* (water hyacinth), as well as

[26] Ibid.

[27] O'Keeffe, Byren, Davies & Palmer above n 23.

[28] Allanson & Gieskes 'Investigations into the ecology of polluted inland waters in the Transvaal. Part II. An introduction to the limnology of Hartebeespoort Dam, with special reference to the effect of industrial and domestic pollution' 1961 (18) *Hydrobiologia* 77–94.

[29] *The limnology of Hartebeespoort Dam* National Institute for Water Research, South African National Scientific Programmes Report no 110 (1985).

TABLE 13.4

Comparison of mean (range in brackets) surface water chemistry of Hartbeespoort Dam, 1928–84. Values in mg ℓ^{-1} unless otherwise stated (modified from *The limnology of Hartebeespoort Dam* above n 29.)

Parameter	1928	1958	1974	1981	1982	1983	1984
Nitrate-N	0,68	2,27	2,09	0,93	1,10	0,94	1,46
SRP (Phosphates)	0,005	0,05	0,64	0,30	0,39	0,42	0,52
pH	7,2	(7,8–9,1)	(8,5–10)	9,3	9,45	9,2	9,2
Silica	—	5,3	3,9	5,4	5,2	4,7	4,4
Magnesium	4	—	19	22	23	21	21
Chloride	7	—	42	43	48	65	58
Sulphate	10	—	64	—	100	113	114
Conductivity (mS m^{-1})	—	—	50	55	59	59	67
Alkalinity (as $CaCO3_3$)	127	—	130	142	160	135	138
Max SDT (m)	—	3,8	3,0	3,0	2,9	5,9	3,1

so-called 'hyperscums' of the blue-green alga *Microcystis* sp, which causes taste and odour problems in drinking water, may be toxic in some stages of its life cycle, and causes problems for water-related recreational activities on the reservoir.

Other catchments in South Africa are also subject to intense eutrophication as a result of the failure of water-quality conservation measures. The worst examples are associated with major urban developments and include the Buffalo River (downstream of Kingwilliamstown and Zwelitsha), the Black River, which flows through Cape Town, and the Msinduze River, which flows through Pietermaritzburg.

During the 1980s a special phosphate standard of 1 mg ℓ^{-1} was introduced in selected catchments to try to combat increasing nutrient enrichment in these important rivers. Phosphate was chosen because it is often the limiting nutrient for algal growth ie the nutrient that is required in greatest quantities relative to its availability. Phosphate is available in large quantities in urban effluent and it was felt that a reduction in phosphate concentration to below 1 mg ℓ^{-1} for all effluent in the selected catchments—the Jukskei/Crocodile and Vaal (Transvaal), the Mgeni and Mlaas (Natal), the Buffalo (eastern Cape) and the Great Berg (western Cape)—would reduce eutrophication to acceptable limits. Results to date have been mixed as a suitable length of time has yet to elapse before definite conclusions can be drawn. In the Buffalo River the standard has yet to be met; *median* available phosphate concentrations entering Laing Dam from 1986 to 1988 were approximately 4 mg ℓ^{-1}.[30]

This approach of setting uniform effluent standards is now being superseded by a new assessment methodology which combines receiving water quality objectives and the pollution-prevention approaches,[31] to produce a 'tailor-made' set of standards for defined portions of a river. Users are invited to state the maximum limits for all water quality variables which affect their operations, and the results are used to set the receiving water quality objectives. Present water quality in the receiving water is quantified, and the difference between the two is then defined as the assimilative

[30] Palmer & O'Keeffe 'Downstream effects of impoundments on the water chemistry of the Buffalo River (eastern Cape), South Africa' 1990 (202) *Hydrobiologia* 71–83.

[31] Van der Merwe & Grobler 'Water quality management in the RSA: preparing for the future' 1990 (16) *Water SA* 49–54.

capacity of the water, which can then be allocated to new or existing users. By using this approach, the DWA hopes to maintain water quality standards that are suitable to the users of water in any particular catchment. See chapter 18.

The Water Act 54 of 1956 controls the use of water in South Africa but contains no mention of environmental impacts resulting from water use. Consideration should therefore be given to the proposal that this Act should be amended to take into account the likely impacts of different water-uses and the measures that are necessary to ameliorate them.

13.3.4 Water abstraction

Salinization, increased sediment loads and eutrophication are typical problems associated with water supply from rivers. However, a more fundamental problem is becoming prevalent in South African rivers—a lack of water, caused either by direct abstraction or by changes in the hydrology due to urbanization and vegetation removal in the catchment. This problem has recently been reviewed and an attempt was made to quantify remedial measures.[32]

Reductions in the flow of South African rivers, due to river abstraction as well as impoundment, have compounded the effects of catchment degradation, and have converted a number of southern Africa's perennial rivers to seasonal rivers. Some of the most striking examples are the rivers that flow through the Kruger National Park (Figure 13.6). These rivers all rise to the west of the park boundary, and many have been heavily exploited before they flow into the park. Although there are no formal hydrological records, very reliable observations since the first half of the century are available from park rangers' notebooks. These indicate that all the main rivers (Luvuvhu, Great Letaba, Olifants, Sabie and Crocodile) were formerly perennial. In recent years the flow in the Letaba River has been so reduced that it flows for only a few months each year. The Luvuvhu River first stopped flowing in 1948, and again in 1964–65,[33] but it now stops flowing in most years. Even the large Olifants River has stopped flowing. Flow in the Crocodile River is maintained (and increased) due to the irrigation demands of sugar and citrus farmers on the south bank (outside the park). Only the Sabie River still has a natural perennial flow, but this may soon be threatened by proposed impoundments in the upper catchment. The conservation of one of the premier natural environments in southern Africa is, therefore, severely threatened by the over-exploitation of its rivers, which form almost the only water supply to the park.

Estuaries rank with tropical rainforests and coral reefs as some of the most productive ecosystems, yet 76 per cent of the estuaries in the Cape Province and 72 per cent in Natal are degraded to some extent.[34] At least 81 fish species are wholly or partially dependent on southern African estuaries for the completion of their life cycles, and of these at least 29 species are regularly taken by anglers and an additional 21 are suitable as human food.[35] Reduced water quantity and quality in estuaries has resulted in the impoverishment of these valuable systems and has reduced their ability to perform a variety of essential functions.[36]

In recent years the DWA has recognized the need to maintain a base flow in rivers.

---

[32] O'Keeffe 'The influence of man' in Allanson, Hart, O'Keeffe & Robarts (eds) *Inland waters of southern Africa* (1990).

[33] Joubert *Masterplan for the management of the Kruger National Park*. Unpublished report (6 vols) of the Kruger National Park (1986).

[34] Whitfield pers comm.

[35] Wallace, Kok, Beckley, Bennett, Blaber & Whitfield *South African estuaries and their importance to fishes* Port Elizabeth Museum (1984).

[36] Whitfield & Bruton 'Some biological implications of reduced fresh water inflow into eastern Cape estuaries: a preliminary assessment' 1989 (85) *S Afr J Sci* 691–4.

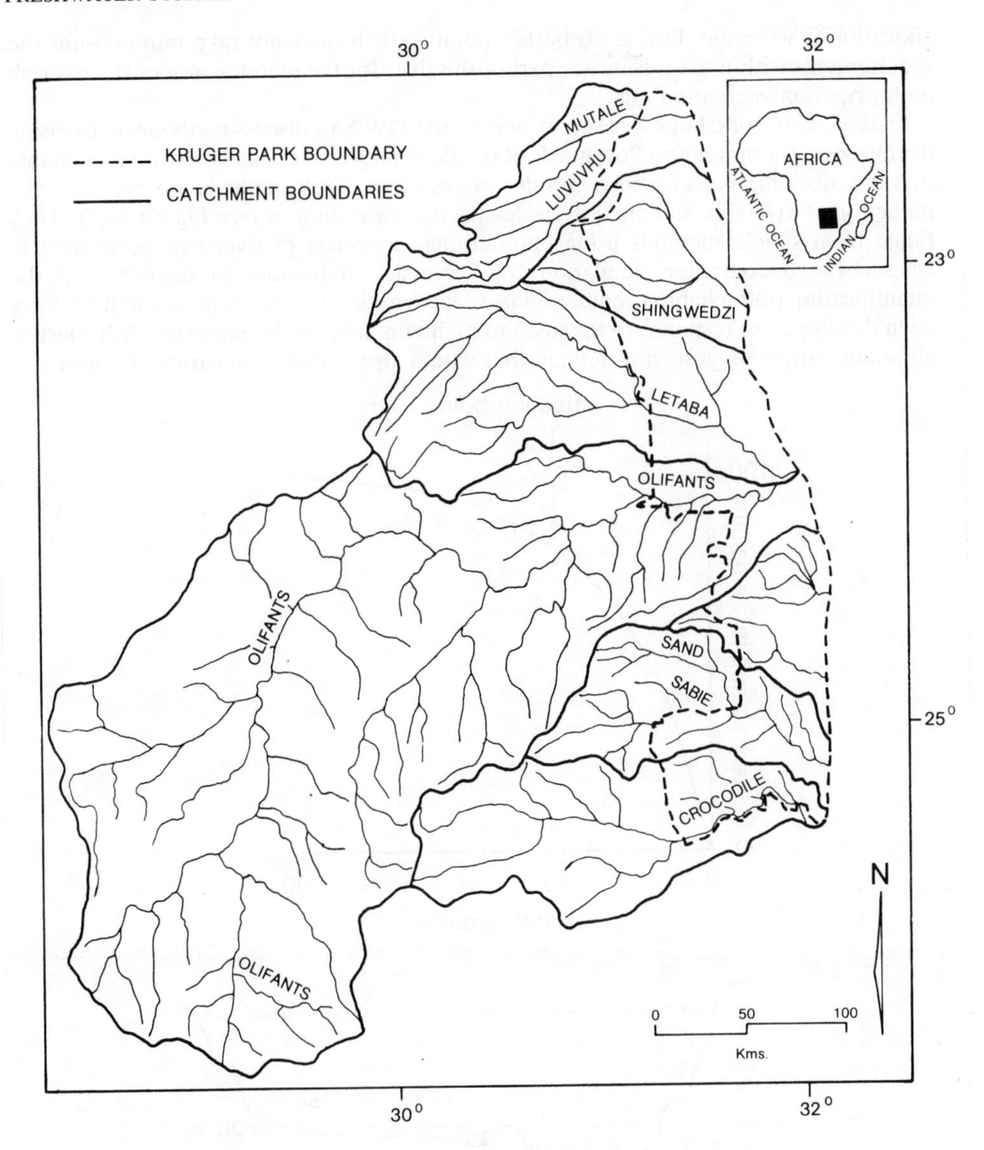

Figure 13.6 Upper catchment boundaries of the rivers draining through the Kruger National Park in relation to the park itself (from Allanson, Hart, O'Keeffe & Roberts above n 32).

Roberts[37] first attempted to quantify an environmental water allocation for South African rivers. His calculations were mostly based on the necessity to provide a freshwater input to estuaries, and amounted to 11 per cent of total water demand in AD 2000. More recently, this figure has been modified to 8 per cent of the total exploitable water resource.[38] This realization of the need for an environmental water

[37] Roberts 'Environmental considerations of water projects' in Hattingh (ed) *Water year + 10 and then?* Technical report no 10 (1981); Roberts 'Environmental constraints on water resources development' 1983 (1) *Proceedings of the South African Institution of Civil Engineers* 16–23.

[38] Jezewski & Roberts *Estuarine and lake freshwater requirements* DWA Technical report TR 12*a* (1986).

allocation is welcome, but, as Roberts[39] points out, it does not take into account the requirements within the freshwater part of the river for the maintenance of the riverine biota, riparian vegetation etc.

In 1987, two workshops were convened by the DWA to discuss methods of assessing the instream (or minimum) flow needs of rivers. A large American literature is available that describes methods for instream flow assessment. Most methods are based on the reduction of available habitat with successive decreases in flow (see Figure 13.7). They range from simple methods using photographic evidence of river-bed exposure[40] to transect-based computer simulations of successive reductions in habitat, and the quantification of the habitat requirements of key species.[41] Most of these methods have been developed in response to the need to maintain habitats for important fish species, although Gore[42] suggests a technique that would also conserve macroinvertebrates.

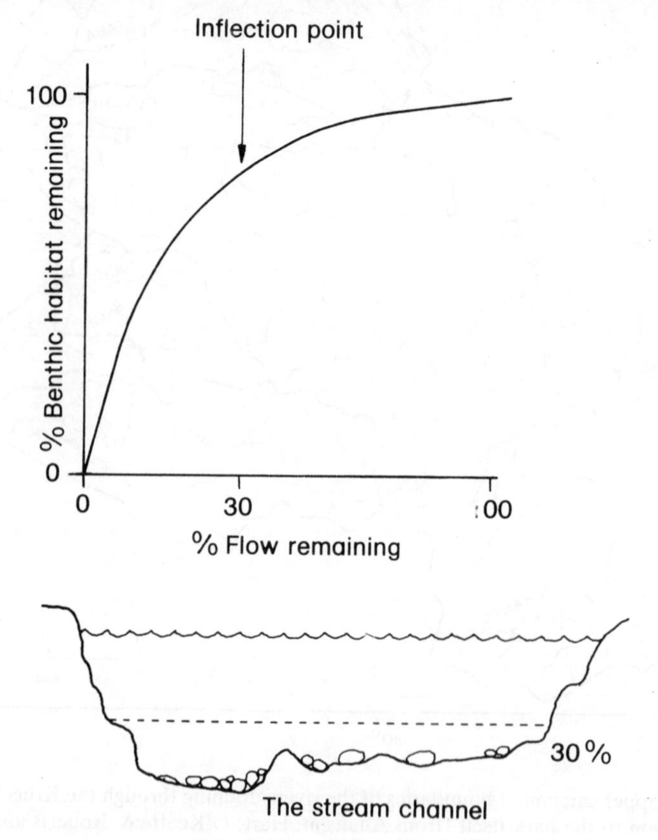

Figure 13.7 Reduction in benthic habitat at successively reduced flows. Initially, very little habitat is lost, until a hypothetical 'inflection point' is reached (30 per cent in this diagram). At flows less than 30 per cent, exposure of the stream bed increases rapidly (from Allanson, Hart, O'Keeffe & Robarts above n 32).

---

[39] Above n 37.

[40] Tennant *Instream flow regimes for fish, wildlife, recreation and related environmental resources* Report of the US Fish and Wildlife Service (1975).

[41] Cf Estes & Orsborn 'Review and analysis of methods for quantifying instream flow requirements' 1986 (22) *Water Resources Bulletin* 389–98.

[42] 'A technique for predicting in-stream flow requirements of benthic macroinvertebrates' 1978 (8) *Freshwater Biology* 141–51.

All these methods have been examined in the context of southern African rivers by O'Keeffe et al.[43] They conclude that existing methods do not tackle the difficult question of ecosystem water needs in rivers, but concentrate on the needs of one component of the biota (fishes). They may therefore be of limited use in the southern African context, where instream fisheries are not commercially important and where seasonal flow changes may be much more critical than the overall global amount of water allocated to a river. King at the University of Cape Town is currently engaged in a detailed assessment of American methods of quantifying instream flow needs.

O'Keeffe & Davies[44] describe new approaches to the quantification of instream flow needs for southern African rivers. Where little time and biological information are available, a method is suggested based on the hydrological record. This method relies on the mimicking of natural flow variation, sacrificing some high and medium flows, but maintaining a base flow that does not fall below a designated percentile of the recorded runoff average for any month. A more detailed approach, that requires biological data, relies on the calculation of the amount of water required for each component of the ecosystem. Some of these requirements (e g evapo-transpiration) are consumptive and must be accumulated. Others, for instance requirements to maintain fish habitats, are non-consumptive and only the largest need to be considered, since these will satisfy lesser requirements. The resulting total is a base flow requirement onto which must be added flooding and flushing requirements, for example, to cue fish spawning migrations and to flush out sediment.

These methods have yet to be applied, and considerable testing will be needed before they can be pronounced to be practicable, but the need for such techniques will become more urgent as water demands in the subcontinent increase.

13.3.5 Barriers to migration

Although South Africa has only four anadromous fish species that move between the sea and rivers, (ie three eels and a freshwater mullet),[45] there are large numbers of aquatic invertebrates and vertebrates that need to move up and down river courses in order to complete their life cycles. The movements of these species are severely affected by barriers to migration such as dams, causeways and other engineering works. The DWA has accepted the principle that fish passes need to be built whenever practical, but these structures are expensive and have to be carefully designed to cater for the swimming abilities and behaviour of all affected species.

13.3.6 Alien biotas

After habitat degradation, invasive animals and plants represent the greatest threat to the biotas of freshwaters in South Africa. An 'invasive' species in this context is defined as 'an alien species or a translocated indigenous species which, after introduction, has spread unaided into untransformed ecosystems and may be responsible for causing an imbalance there'.[46] At least 29 species of introduced alien animals and 23 species of translocated indigenous species are invasive and have established breeding populations in natural water bodies in southern Africa. Among the most harmful and widespread

---

[43] O'Keeffe, King, Day, Rossouw, Van der Zel & Skoroszewski 'General concepts and approaches to instream flow assessment' in Ferrar (ed) *Ecological flow requirements for South African rivers* South African National Scientific Programmes Report no 162 (1989).

[44] 'The conservation and management of the rivers of the Kruger National Park: suggested methods for calculating instream flow needs' in *Aquatic conservation, marine and freshwater ecosystems* (in press).

[45] Bruton, Boh & Davies 'Life history styles of diadromous fishes in inland waters of southern Africa' 1987 (1) *American Fisheries Society Symposium* 104–21.

[46] De Moor & Bruton *Atlas of alien and translocated indigenous aquatic animals in southern Africa* South African National Scientific Programmes Report no 144 (1988).

invasive alien animals are the ciliophoran *Ichthyophthirius multifilis*, a fish parasite; the cestode *Bothriocephalus acheilognathi*, another fish parasite; the free-living gastropod snail *Lymnaea columella*, an intermediate host of fascioliasis in cattle; and various fishes, including rainbow and brown trout, goldfish, common and grass carp, mosquito fish, guppies, swordtails, bluegill, three bass species, and various tilapia hybrids.

13.3.6.1 *Alien animals*

All major southern African river systems are inhabited by alien animals.[47] Invasive animals have been introduced or translocated for a variety of reasons, including sport fishing, aquaculture, biocontrol, for the aquarium trade, for enhancing fisheries, and by accident. Eighteen invasive animals are considered to have a major detrimental impact on indigenous species and communities through competition for food and space, predation, hybridization, the introduction of parasites and diseases, disruption of the breeding behaviour of other fishes, and habitat alteration.[48] Invasive fishes often distribute themselves as eggs and larvae and readily cross catchment boundaries through intercatchment connections. Invasive fishes may decrease water quality, as in the case of common carp which disturb bottom sediments while feeding and increase the turbidity, at the same time possibly releasing phosphates into the water.[49] Translocated *Tilapia rendalli* may decimate communities of submerged aquatic macrophytes. Invasive predatory fishes may cause the local extinction of rare species.[50]

13.3.6.2 *Aquaculture*

Aquaculture, which is one of the fastest-growing water-related industries in South Africa (yields increased from about 400 tons in 1984 to over 3 000 tons in 1988),[51] is one of the main sources of invasive crustacean parasites and fishes in southern African inland waters, and is likely to become an increased threat in the future.

13.3.6.3 *Alien plants*

Four species of alien aquatic plants have a marked impact on southern African freshwater ecosystems.[52] Three species are free-floating plants (*Eichhornia crassipes*, *Salvinia molesta* and *Azolla filiculoides*) and one is usually rooted in the river bank or in shallow water (*Myriophyllum aquaticum*). These invasive plants may have a marked impact on freshwater ecosystems by altering water-flow patterns, decreasing oxygenation from the atmosphere and reducing light intensities. The production and accumulation of large quantities of detritus promotes bacterial activity with the consequent transformation of food webs to a detritus base, a process that is accelerated by increased levels of eutrophication.

The major economic impacts of invasive aquatic plants arise from river blockages and interrupted water flows, evapotranspiration losses, difficulties in the treatment of water to attain potable standards, the development of increased breeding sites for vectors and intermediate hosts of human and stock diseases, and an inhibited use water bodies for recreational purposes.[53]

---

[47] De Moor & Bruton above n 46; Bruton & Van As 'Faunal invasions of aquatic ecosystems in southern Africa, with suggestions for their management' in Macdonald, Kruger & Ferrar (eds) *The ecology and management of biological invasions in southern Africa* (1986).

[48] Ibid.

[49] Bruton 'The effects of suspensoids on fish' 1985 (125) *Hydrobiologia* 221–41.

[50] Wager & Rowe-Rowe 'The effects of *Tilapia rendalli* and *T mossambica* on aquatic macrophytes and fauna in five ponds' 1972 (68) *S Afr J Sci* 257–60.

[51] Hecht *Aquaculture in South Africa* Aquaculture Association of South Africa (1990).

[52] Ashton, Appleton & Jackson 'Ecological impacts and economic consequences of alien invasive organisms in southern African aquatic ecosystems' in Macdonald, Kruger & Ferrar above n 47.

[53] Ibid.

Invasive aquatic plants and animals may therefore detrimentally affect both water quality and quantity as well as the usefulness of water to a variety of end users.

13.4 CONSERVATION OF WATER RESOURCES

In 1983, Allanson & Rabie[54] called for an overview of the influence of human beings upon the water resources of South Africa. In the intervening eight years much work has been done to produce such an overview. We are now in a better position to judge the trends in water supply and quality, and they are, on the whole, pessimistic. The demand for water is increasing, and will have to increase enormously to upgrade the basic requirements of the previously disadvantaged black population in the 'new South Africa'. Water quality is deteriorating in a number of ways, and will continue to deteriorate as more pressure is put on the scarce supplies. Rivers are literally running dry[55] as impoundment and abstraction increase, and as the buffering capacities of catchments are reduced by urbanization and devegetation.

There is, however, an optimistic note. The DWA, which is increasingly aware of the problems of supplying sufficient water of suitable quality, has been proactive in establishing research and management procedures to protect water resources. The recognition of the environmental requirements of rivers extends well beyond the requirements set by the Water Act, which governs the management of South Africa's water resources. The adoption of receiving water quality objectives to allocate waste loads on a catchment-by-catchment basis[56] is a far-sighted policy for the control of pollution in South African rivers. The main problem would appear to be the quantification of environmental freshwater requirements rather than the ability to implement the policy or to quantify the impacts of these requirements on the availability of water for conventional purposes. See chapter 18.

A further important conceptual advance by the DWA is the recognition of the need to manage catchments and river basins in an integrated way. Although water boards for the supply of bulk water were established 35 years ago in terms of the Water Act,[57] it is only in recent years that the ecological importance of integrated catchment management has been fully realized. The department has adopted a long-term strategy that is leading to the regional management of water services, particularly by water boards, and to the development of a total catchment management policy. According to the DWA,[58] as much autonomy as practicable is being devolved upon the non-central government sectors, particularly where regional rather than national interests are served. The Umgeni Water Board, for example, has adopted a policy of seeking to protect the quality of water in its rivers and dams by monitoring discharges and by actively preventing pollution and facilitating waste-water and sanitation treatment.[59] It is thought that regional water quality management is essential if an efficient and effective supply of water is to be realized for the particular needs of a given catchment. There is also an increasing realization that political-geographical units, such as regional service councils, should be delineated along catchment boundaries.[60]

The old Department of Forestry and the provincial nature conservation bodies have effectively conserved the upper catchments of many South African river systems, but too few protected areas have been established along the middle or lower reaches of

---

54 'Freshwater systems' in Fuggle & Rabie (eds) *Environmental concerns in South Africa* (1983) 237.

55 O'Keeffe above n 32; O'Keeffe & Davies above n 44.

56 Van der Merwe & Grobler above n 31.

57 Section 108.

58 *Management of water resources* above n 7.

59 Furness 'Water boards—their role in water management'. Oral contribution to the conference of the committee for terrestrial and freshwater systems, Wilderness (1984).

60 Bruton 'Report to the President's Council on behalf of Rhodes University on the investigation into a policy for a national environmental management system' (1990).

rivers. A further problem is that the good database on river ecology and conservation status has not always been converted into usable guidelines for management and, in particular, has not been effectively communicated to water users, especially farmers. Although there are large numbers of well-trained agricultural and land-use extension officers, there are few with the competence to advise on water-management procedures. The intricate laws relating to water use in South Africa, and the different legislation in the provinces and semi-independent states, also militate against effective water management. Many water-users still regard watercourses as means of waste disposal and do not recognize the intrinsic value of properly functioning aquatic ecosystems in the overall landscape. There is also a need for soil and water conservation to be considered together, preferably under the same ministry, and for more effective international cooperation in the long-term management of soil and water resources.

What are the management options for the future? There is existing technology to solve all our problems of water supply and quality: the importation of water from the Zambezi, recycling and re-use in centres of heavy demand, phosphate stripping (already in use in several sewage works), and desalination. These are some of the more realistic technical solutions, but all have one factor in common—they are expensive. Perhaps the real option is to start charging prices for water that reflect its real value as a scarce resource. This would have the added bonus of reducing demand in some sectors of the community which squander water at present price levels. The problem, however, is that the majority of the population has limited access to supplies of clean water, or to adequate waterborne waste removal, and the aim is to upgrade services to these sections of the community rather than to price them out of the market.

There is, however, an increasing realization that the resolution of aquatic management problems lies not only in technological or scientific advances as in an awakening of the ethical responsibility of water-users as custodians of aquatic resources for future generations. The conservation and rational use of water should therefore become a social attitude which does not need to be policed. Increasingly enlightened attitudes towards the conservation of the biotas of terrestrial environments now need to be extended towards the aquatic environment.

Water is a natural renewable resource. It can be exploited within sustainable limits—for water supply, for effluent removal, and for recreation and nature conservation. An analogy would be that our rivers are a capital asset from which we can draw interest. If we draw on the capital, the resource will ultimately cease to exist. Yet this is what we are doing with many of our rivers. We have limited the potential uses of several rivers through salinization and pollution—for example, the middle reaches of the Buffalo River have ceased to be a resource and have now become a problem and a potential health hazard. Other rivers now have restricted uses because too much water has been removed. Even the rivers flowing through the Kruger National Park, the premier nature conservation area of the country, are threatened by excessive abstraction and pollution.[61] If rivers are to continue to perform the services that we require of them, they will have to be maintained as functioning ecosystems.

Aquatic systems are too often regarded as common property resources that can be exploited for selfish short-term gains. Individuals maximize their own utilization of the system but society at large carries the cost. We also tend to ignore the value of public amenities associated with rivers, such as pristine scenery, wilderness areas and recreational opportunities, which have long-term benefits for society as a whole. Proper water management should maximize the welfare to the whole community and minimize the costs, whether they are financial, social or ecological. Agreement needs to be reached among different water-users on how to share water with a fair distribution of

---

[61] O'Keeffe above n 32; O'Keeffe & Davies above n 44.

benefits and costs. In doing so we need to make full use of recently developed technologies in the fields of engineering, information management, computer modelling and remote sensing, so that we can resolve the pressing problems of water supply and conservation using both reductionist and holistic methodologies.

In a country which is extraordinarily rich in natural resources, fresh water is perhaps the major exception. In South Africa, water is a vital but scarce resource that is distributed disproportionately in time and space relative to demand. Water is also one of the primary needs for the maintenance and improvement of the quality of life of all South Africans. Water consumption among black consumers has more than doubled over the past 20 years and is likely to increase further in future. In the nine years since the publication of *Environmental concerns in South Africa*,[62] the warning signs have become much clearer and they have been recognized, but the remedial measures are still in their infancy, and much remains to be done.

13.5 LEGAL PROVISIONS

13.5.1 Introduction

The law dealing with freshwater systems is scattered through our legislation. The Water Act 54 of 1956 constitutes the most important legislation in this respect in that it deals specifically with the control, conservation and use of water. Although this Act does not exclude wetlands, lakes and lagoons from its provisions, it is clear from the definitions of 'public water', 'public stream', 'natural channel', 'normal flow', 'riparian land' and 'surplus water', as well as from the provisions of the Act, that it is aimed mainly at inland running water.

13.5.2 Running water

13.5.2.1 *Water Act*

(a) Distinction between public and private water and streams. The Water Act draws a distinction between public and private water and streams. Private water is water which naturally rises, falls, drains or is led onto land but which is not capable of common use for irrigation purposes.[63] Although several provisions of the Act regulate the use of private water, in principle the owner on whose land it is found enjoys sole and exclusive use and enjoyment of it.[64] Public water is water flowing or found in or derived from the bed of a public stream.[65] A public stream is a natural stream of water which flows in a known and defined channel, if such water can be used for irrigation on two or more pieces of riparian land.[66] The control and use of this water is regulated by the Act and it cannot be privately owned.[67]

The distinction between public and private water and streams is not altogether clear: first, by takeover of previous legislative provisions,[68] the proviso to the definition of public stream determines that streams may be capable of being public only along certain parts. Secondly, the terms public water and private water are not defined as being the opposite of each other, which means that certain streams can be neither public nor private.[69] Thirdly, it is difficult to see why both the terms public stream and public water

---

[62] Above n 54.
[63] Section 1.
[64] Section 5.
[65] Section 1.
[66] Ibid.
[67] Section 6.
[68] The Irrigation and Conservation of Waters Act 8 of 1912.
[69] Rabie 'The conservation of rivers in South African law' 1989 *SA Public Law* 1, 11–12.

are defined while the terms are used interchangeably in the Act, both referring to running water regulated by the Act. Fourthly, the phrase 'capable of common use for irrigation on two or more pieces of land' is vague, as even the watering of a vegetable garden can be interpreted as irrigation.[70] Finally, the necessity of empowering the water court to determine the nature of a stream as being public or private indicates the lack of clarity regarding this distinction in the Act.[71] On public and private rivers, see also chapter 25 below.

With water being regarded as an increasingly scarce strategic resource in South Africa, requiring optimal management, development and allocation in the national interest,[72] it is no longer feasible to allow almost unlimited use and enjoyment of water to riparian owners.[73] Roman law, which is one of the main sources of South African law, considered all running waters to be common property and drew a distinction between public and private streams only for purposes of the application of certain interdicts.[74] This principle was abolished in Roman-Dutch law, partly by a misinterpretation of Roman law, and partly by the abundance of water in Holland, where the State needed to control only perennial or navigable streams. In South Africa the State should have the power, in the public interest,[75] to exercise control over any running water, irrespective of whether a stream can be used for common irrigation purposes.[76]

(b) Rights to public streams and water. The Water Act controls the use of public water as follows:

(i) *Riparian owners.* Subject to the provisions of the Act, every riparian owner is entitled to the reasonable use of the normal flow of a public stream for agricultural and urban purposes.[77] Although the term riparian ownership is often used to describe this principle in South African water law, the Act states clearly that ownership in public water does not vest in riparian landowners or anyone else.[78] It merely grants rights of 'reasonable use' of the water.[79] Riparian owners can, however, be owners of the banks and beds of such streams, depending on the provisions of their title deeds.[80]

This principle of common rights of use is essentially in accordance with Roman law,[81] although, according to Roman law, such rights could be exercised by all members of the

---

[70] See De Wet *Opuscula miscellanea* (1979) 27. Cf *Management of water resources* above n 7, 8.11.

[71] *Management of water resources* above n 7, 8.9. See, generally, De Wet 'Water' 1956 *THRHR* 28 30; De Wet *Opuscula miscellanea* above n 70, 23–33; Visser 'Water: Laws and management' 1989 *SA J of Aquatic Sciences* 159, 168ff.

[72] *Management of water resources* above n 7, 10.3.

[73] Rabie 'The conservation of rivers in the South African law' 1989 *SA Public Law* 186, 201; Visser above n 71, 159, 178.

[74] *D* 1.8.2..

[75] This undefined term should, inter alia, include the interest of environmental conservation. See below.

[76] Government control over private water already exists in current South African water law. (See ss 12, 22, 23(1), 28, 59(4) and (5) and 62A).

[77] Section 9(1).

[78] Section 6(1).

[79] Section 9.

[80] The border of ager limitatus is the line drawn on the diagram attached to the title deed, while that of ager non limitatus is presumed to be the middle of the stream. See, generally, Ramsden *Legal principles and wetland legislation in South Africa* (1987) 7 (unpublished paper read at a national symposium on the ecology and conservation of wetlands in South Africa 15 October 1987). The presumption of usque ad medium filum fluminis was incorporated in our water law by De Villiers CJ in *Municipality of Beaufort West v Wernich* 1882 (2) SC 36. It was confirmed as part of our law in *Struben v Colonial Government* 17 SC 249; *Van Niekerk & Union Government v Carter* 1917 AD 359; *Lange v Minister of Lands* 1957 (1) SA 297 (A).

[81] *D* 1.8.1pr; 1.8.2.1.

public and not only by riparian owners. In 1856 the Cape Supreme Court[82] vested the principle of riparian ownership in South African law with a single unsubstantiated interpretation of Roman water law:

'It is undoubtedly a rivulet or perennial stream, which, in the language of the Institutes, is said to be common, that is, *common to the different persons entitled to it, in respect of the land through which it runs.*'[83]

This opinion did not coincide with the Court's otherwise strong view of water being common to all who are in need of it, according to the principles of natural law.[84] However, it was halfheartedly accepted by the Court in *Hough v Van der Merwe*[85] and confirmed in *Van Heerden v Weise,*[86] where the Court used a paragraph from the Digest[87] as authority, which paragraph, in fact, did not support the principle of riparian ownership. Nevertheless, the principle of common rights faded in the course of time, until it was imported into 20th-century water legislation.

In spite of the acceptance of the riparian principle, the Roman rule of common use was not totally phased out. First, in terms of the Act[88] any person, while lawfully having access to public water, may use water from the stream for immediate purposes of watering stock, drinking, washing, cooking or using in a vehicle. Secondly, the water court may allocate rights of water utilization for any purposes.[89] Thirdly, a recent decision of the Appellate Division recognized the common use of rivers for recreational activities.[90] Fourthly, governmental policy often provides for the allocation of water rights for purposes other than riparian utilization.[91] Fifthly, statutory limitations in the form of state control, exercised by the Minister of Water Affairs, exist, and deserve discussion.

(ii) *State control.* The Minister is empowered, in specified instances, to restrict riparian owners' rights of water utilization. This is done mainly where the Minister, in his discretion, deems it necessary that certain public water should be controlled in the 'public or national interest'. Several mechanisms of state control exist:

Government control areas

Subterranean government control areas: Water which rises on or is led onto land[92] is private water whenever it is insufficient for common irrigation purposes.[93] In fact, as will be shown, it may be argued that all ground water qualifies as private water. However, if the Minister is of the opinion that it is desirable in the public interest that the abstraction, use, supply or distribution of subterranean water be controlled, he may

[82] In *Retief v Louw* 1874 (4) Buch 165, 175–6.

[83] Italics supplied.

[84] 'These things, by nature itself as it were, are attributed to, and may be occupied by, any one, provided the common and promiscuous use is not injured, for without the use of air and water no one could live or breathe' (at 176).

[85] 1874 (4) Buch 148, 153: 'Every individual of the nation, *those especially who have land adjoining*, are entitled to use the water for their private purposes' (italics supplied).

[86] 1880 (1) Buch AC 5, 9.

[87] *D* 8.3.6.

[88] Section 7(1). See also the other rights of water use granted by s 7.

[89] Section 11(1) and (2). This discretion of the Court is however, inter alia, restricted by the public interest, a term which is discussed below.

[90] *Butgereit v Transvaal Canoe Union* 1988 (1) SA 759 (A). In this case water rights were acknowledged for purposes of activities such as swimming, boating and fishing.

[91] eg interbasin water transfers.

[92] This term makes sense only if 'lead on to (sic)' can be interpreted as including water being pumped from underground.

[93] The question whether water is private when the amount led from a borehole is part of an otherwise public stream is contentious.

declare an area to be a subterranean government control area.[94] Thirteen such areas have already been declared.

Government water control areas: A government water control area is declared in respect of land which is likely to be affected by a government waterwork or in respect of an area within which the abstraction, utilization, supply or distribution of the water of any public stream should be controlled in the public interest. The declaration of such an area vests in the Minister almost complete control of water in any public stream or public water in any natural channel in the area. Control is exercised in that the Minister is empowered to authorize water utilization by specified riparian owners.[95] The Minister may declare a government water control area to be an irrigation district,[96] in respect of which an irrigation board is established,[97] exercising certain powers.[98] Some 176 government water control areas have already been declared, encompassing all significant rivers and government waterworks.

Government drainage control areas: If the Minister is of the opinion that the construction of a waterwork in such an area may reduce the availability of water in a public stream in that area, he may declare it to be a government drainage control area.[99] In such an area nobody may construct a waterwork for the storage of private water without the authorization of the Minister.[100]

Catchment control areas: A catchment control area is declared where land is required for the protection of any portion of the catchment of a public stream, or where the flow of a public stream should, in the national interest, be regulated or controlled by damming, cleaning, deepening, widening, straightening or altering the course of the channel, or by taking such other steps which might be necessary for the purpose of lessening the possibility of damage to riparian land in the event of a flood.[101] The declaration of such an area entitles the Minister to suspend landowners' rights, and to enter upon and take possession of the land concerned in order to carry out any work which he may deem necessary to fulfil the purposes of such a declaration.[102]

Only one such area has been declared. Because the motivation for the declaration of both areas might overlap, many catchment control areas are controlled as government water control areas.

Dam basin control areas: This type of area is declared whenever any particular area should, in the public interest, be reserved for a dam, being a government waterwork to be constructed at some future date.[103] Control over such areas is exercised by the Minister by means of issuing permits for certain activities and for water utilization.

Water sport control areas: When in the opinion of the Minister, an area is likely to become submerged by any water, and such water would be suitable for the practice of any water sport, he may declare it to be a water sport control area.[104] The right to use this water for any water sport vests in the Minister,[105] and he can make regulations for its control. No water sport control areas have yet been declared.

---

[94] Section 28.
[95] In terms of ss 62, 63.
[96] Sections 71, 73.
[97] Section 79.
[98] Sections 75 and 89.
[99] Section 59(5).
[100] Section 62A.
[101] Section 59(2).
[102] Section 61(1).
[103] Section 59(4)*(a)*.
[104] Section 164*bis*.
[105] Sections 164*bis*(2) and 164 *quat*.

Offences

Water pollution: The wilful or negligent pollution of any water is an offence.[106] Both the Water Act and other legislation contain extensive pollution control provisions, which are discussed in chapter 18.

Wastage: The Water Act[107] renders the wasteful use of public water an offence.[108] Furthermore, water used for industrial purposes should be purified and discharged into the source from where it was derived.[109]

Alteration in course: Nobody may alter the course of a public stream without a permit issued by the Minister.[110] Holders of water rights are protected by a number of provisions in the Act from losing their rights when the course of a stream is altered.[111]

Soil conservation works: Anybody storing water to use for soil conservation is restricted by specifications and conditions subject to which soil conservation works should be constructed. Non-compliance with these conditions constitutes an offence.[112]

Unauthorized use: It is an offence for anyone to take or store water in excess of the allowed quantity or at an unauthorized time or for a purpose contrary to the provisions of the Act.[113]

Other offences: Numerous activities relating to interference with state control measures are declared offences by the provisions of the Water Act.[114] This is to ensure that the government can effectively manage public water, it being a difficult commodity to control owing to its continuously moving nature.

Authorities

Water courts: Various provincial water courts have been established by the Act.[115] These courts inter alia resolve disputes relating to the use of public water, investigate, define and record rights to the use of public water, and grant permission for its use.

Water boards: Water boards may be established by the Minister whenever he deems it desirable that a combined scheme for supplying water for urban, industrial and agricultural purposes be established.[116] These boards are authorized to establish, construct, purchase or acquire, maintain and control any water provision scheme for such purposes.[117] The Rand Water Board is the longest-standing of these boards in South Africa, having been established in 1903. Its operations are governed by a private Act,[118] and the provisions of the Water Act do not derogate from the provisions of that Act.[119] In Natal, similar bodies known as regional water services corporations also exist in terms of the Water Services Ordinance 27 of 1963.[120]

---

[106] Section 23(1) read with s 170(2). Such intent or negligence is presumed until the contrary is proved.

[107] Sections 9(1)*(a)*, 19 and 52.

[108] Section 170(1)*(c)* and *(e)*.

[109] Section 21(1). A person who fails to comply with this preservation measure is guilty of an offence: s 21(5). See also ss 25(2) and 89(1)*(b)*.

[110] This is declared an offence in terms of s 20.

[111] Section 20(8) and (9).

[112] Section 25.

[113] Sections 170(1)*(b)*, 9B, 62 and 63.

[114] Sections 9A, 9B, 9C, 29, 62, 63, 166 and 170(1).

[115] Section 34.

[116] Section 108.

[117] Section 110.

[118] Rand Water Board Statutes (Private) Act 17 of 1950.

[119] Section 4(2) of the Water Act.

[120] Section 7.

Irrigation boards: The Minister may declare any area to be an irrigation district[121] for which an irrigation board is established.[122] Such a board is a body corporate, with functions assigned by the Minister, and is established generally to administer water utilization in the district on behalf of the Minister.

Advisory committees: The Minister may, for any control area, appoint an advisory committee to advise him on matters connected with the preservation, conservation, utilization, control, supply or distribution of water.[123] Representatives of interest groups in the control areas are nowadays being appointed as members of such committees, which is a meaningful development towards environmental conservation-oriented water control. Various other sections of the Act provide for the establishment of specified advisory committees, such as the advisory committee on the safety of dams,[124] technical review committees,[125] an advisory committee on the modification of precipitation,[126] and scheduling boards.[127]

Ministerial discretion

The Minister of Water Affairs is authorized to apply his discretion widely in order to control the use of public water effectively.

Discretionary provisions: In general, the Minister has the power to take the steps that he considers necessary for the development, control and utilization of water, and for giving effect to the provisions of the Act.[128] He is also vested with more specific powers, such as powers of construction, inspection and examination, development and maintenance of, inter alia, waterworks and other water utilization methods.[129] He is furthermore authorized to give advice,[130] gather and disclose information,[131] appoint employees,[132] declare and administer control areas,[133] issue permits for various water uses,[134] institute court proceedings,[135] generate and supply electricity,[136] enter into treaties with other states[137] and grant loans.[138]

The Minister may, notwithstanding any provisions to the contrary, whenever in his opinion a water shortage exists, control, regulate, limit or prohibit, as he in the public interest may deem expedient, the utilization of public water for agricultural, urban or industrial purposes.[139] This is the most comprehensive of his powers, giving him the right totally or partially to suspend the water rights of any person to any public water. The criteria are whether a water shortage exists (which, however, has to exist 'in his opinion', or 'is likely to arise'), and whether his decision is made in the public interest.[140]

---

[121] Section 73. In terms of s 71 this can also happen on the request of interested parties.
[122] Section 79.
[123] Section 68.
[124] Section 9C.
[125] Section 9C.
[126] Section 33F.
[127] Section 64.
[128] Section 2(1)*(m)*.
[129] Section 2.
[130] Section 2(1)*(i)*.
[131] Sections 2(1)*(f)*, *(g)* and *(h)* and 168A.
[132] Sections 3 and 68.
[133] Sections 59–61.
[134] Sections 9B, 11(1A)*(a)*, 12, 12A, 20, 33D, 62, 62A and 63.
[135] Section 42*ter*.
[136] Section 67.
[137] Section 138A.
[138] Section 157.
[139] Section 9A.
[140] See below for the meaning of this contentious term.

The Minister may exercise a similar discretion in respect of subterranean water in control areas.[141] He may grant permission to a local authority to use, for urban purposes, water to which a riparian owner is otherwise entitled subject, however, to compensation.[142]

The Minister has the sole and exclusive right[143] to use and control subterranean water in subterranean water control areas.[144] This right is limited thereby that the Minister must allocate to each piece of land in the control area a quota of subterranean water which the owner of the land may extract annually.[145] This quota is calculated in accordance with the estimated annual availability of subterranean water, and in accordance with each owner's water requirements for domestic and stock-watering purposes.[146]

Basically the same rights and limitations apply in government water control areas, although the Minister's decision is subject to even more extensive prescriptions on the procedure of quota allocations.[147]

In government drainage control areas the Minister may even control the construction of a waterwork for the storage of private water.[148]

The Minister has a supervising and controlling function as to the affairs of irrigation boards,[149] and may assume control of waterworks otherwise belonging to or controlled by irrigation boards.[150] The same wide discretionary controlling power does not apply to the functions of water boards, the Minister being involved only in their establishment and termination, and in the conclusion of certain contracts and inspections.[151]

In short, an all-embracing discretion to control all public water (and in some cases also private water) in the Republic is conferred upon the Minister. The Minister's discretion, however, is not absolute, since it is often limited first by statutory prescriptions[152] and secondly by the 'public interest'. This last-mentioned limitation deserves attention.

Public interest as a jurisdictional fact: The term 'public interest' or 'national interest' is frequently encountered in the Water Act, but is never defined. The public interest is a jurisdictional fact, in that it often serves as a prerequisite when the Minister exercises a statutory discretion.[153] Because the term public interest is nowhere defined in the Act, the Minister has a free and subjective discretion[154] to decide whether his administrative act is in the public interest. A court of law cannot therefore adjudicate the objective existence of the jurisdictional fact. The Court can, however, decide whether the Minister applied his mind to the matter, or whether he acted mala fide or with an ulterior motive.[155]

---

[141] Section 32F.
[142] Section 13.
[143] Subject to existing rights thereon: s 30.
[144] Section 28.
[145] Section 32B.
[146] Ibid.
[147] Sections 62 and 63.
[148] Section 62A.
[149] Section 95.
[150] Section 95A.
[151] Sections 107–138.
[152] eg those of ss 62 and 63.
[153] See Rabie 'Diskresies en jurisdiksionele feite in die administratiefreg' 1978 *THRHR* 419.
[154] Cf Rabie above n 153, 419–21, and Boulle, Harris & Hoexter *Constitutional and administrative law* (1989) 313–14. Where Rabie uses the terms 'vrye diskresie' and 'gebonde diskresie', Boulle, Harris & Hoexter use the terms 'subjective' and 'objective' discretion, to refer to discretions which respectively cannot and can be adjudicated by a court of law.
[155] Rabie above n 153, 420; Boulle, Harris & Hoexter above n 154, 313. See, in general, Baxter *Administrative law* (1984) 456–61.

It is submitted that if the Minister is empowered to subjectively determine what the public interest is, and whether the public interest requires certain administrative actions, and if the court is not empowered to adjudicate the existence of the jurisdictional fact, the use of the term public interest in the Act is hardly of any value.[156] Parties interested in water allocation and other administrative acts exercised in terms of the Act, should at least be entitled to submit an input to determine what the public interest requires and a court should be empowered to objectively test the discretion. It is therefore submitted that the term public interest should be defined in order to serve as an objective jurisdictional fact to which the Minister is bound whenever he exercises his allocation discretion.

The DWA—the custodian of water in the Republic—endeavours to promote the aims of a free enterprise economy in order to enhance the quality of life and to conserve the resource for present and future generations.[157]

In Roman law, running water qualified as common property in terms of natural law.[158] This implied that nobody could claim ownership or exclude anybody else from its reasonable use. Natural law was a dynamic system of legal rules based on man's natural sense of justice.[159] Although in South African law this principle made way for the allocation of streams to riparian owners, traces of it are still to be found in departmental policy and in the statutory limitation of the Minister's discretion.

Although the term national or public interest is nowhere defined, it refers to the principle that running water is a national asset which, in terms of man's sense of justice, should not be withheld from any party in need of it.

In Roman times environmental conservation played no significant role in the perception of a reasonable allocation of water rights. But in modern times environmental conservation should be considered in determining water rights. 'Public interest' should encompass not only immediate agricultural, urban or industrial use but also the interest of environmental conservation. This notion should be contained in a statutory definition of the 'public interest'. Only then will the Minister be obliged to give due consideration to the environmental impact which his decision might have. A decision totally or partly to suspend riparian rights in favour of the public interest will then not only involve the weighing of the interests of the riparian owners and the community at large, but also those of the environment.[160] Only such a decision will be in accordance with justice, as reflected in the old principle of natural justice.

13.5.2.2 *Mountain Catchment Areas Act*

Runoff from mountain catchments is the main source of most South African rivers.[161] To yield the maximum quantity of water of the highest possible quality on the most dependable basis, without reducing plant cover and the variety of species, optimal management of mountain catchment areas is necessary.[162]

The Mountain Catchment Areas Act 63 of 1970 was promulgated to provide for the conservation, use, management and control of land situated in declared mountain catchment areas.[163] In terms of the Act[164] any (private) area of which the water yield is

---

[156] Cf *Minister of the Interior v Bechler* 1948 (3) SA 409 (A) 442, where the Court held that subjective jurisdictional facts serve as guidelines for ministerial discretion.

[157] *Management of water resources* above n 7, 10.4.

[158] *D* 1.8.1.

[159] *I* 1. 2pr; *D* 1.1.1.3; Van Warmelo *Oorsprong en betekenis van die Romeinse reg* (1959) 218.

[160] Cf Hiddema 'The Water Act, 1956: water rights for the environment' 1989 (15) *Southern African J of Aquatic Sciences* 219.

[161] Rabie 'The conservation of mountains in South African law' 1989 *SA Public Law* 213, 214.

[162] See *Management of water resources* above n 7, 1.20–1.23 for the sensitivity of the balance between the soil, vegetation and water conservation in these areas.

[163] Long title of the Act. See in general, Rabie above n 73, 220ff, as well as Rabie 'The conservation of mountains in South African law' 1990 *SA Public Law* 66.

[164] Section 2.

of great importance may be declared to be a mountain catchment area. This declaration is initiated by regional action committees, who recommend it on behalf of all interested parties and who give consideration to the value of a certain area as a water source, the capacity of the area for yielding water and the degree of deterioration of vegetation and soil. The decision to proclaim the area is then taken by the Central Committee for the Delimitation of Mountain Catchment Areas.

Mountain catchment areas are managed by means of management guidelines relating to conservation, use and control of land, and vegetation within (and, in cases of invasive vegetation, even for 5 km outside) the area. Some 17 such areas have already been declared,[165] yielding 15 per cent of the mean annual runoff of the main river systems in the Republic. The process of proclamation is continuing, and 3,8 million ha[166] could eventually be so managed.[167]

Mountain catchment areas differ from catchment control areas[168] in two respects: first, catchment control areas can be declared in any area down the course of a stream and not only in mountain catchments and, secondly, they are usually declared for some project to be carried out by the State in the national interest,[169] whereas, in respect of mountain catchment areas, guidelines for ongoing management by owners are laid down.

Although it is realized that the circumstances and problems differ from catchment to catchment, consideration should be given to standardizing conservation directions to be implemented by all owners of land within river catchments, which will eliminate the necessity to declare mountain catchment areas. The Department of Environment Affairs has recently commenced the development of a catchment biosystem management model which aims at obtaining the maximum production per water unit, optimum preservation of the natural ecology and minimization of soil erosion. Such a model should contain the suggested standard directions applicable to all land concerned.

13.5.2.3 *River conservancy districts in terms of the Natal Nature Conservation Ordinance*

The Natal Nature Conservation Ordinance 15 of 1974 authorizes the Administrator to establish river conservancy districts.[170] The ordinance also provides for riparian owners to form themselves into voluntary associations, called river conservancies, for the purpose of advising the Natal Parks Board regarding matters pertaining to waters in such districts.[171] The concept of 'waters' includes rivers, streams and creeks.[172] Although the Administrator may regulate the functions of river conservancies, their success is dependent on voluntary compliance.

There are already some 78 such conservancies in Natal, covering an area of 6 547 km^2.

13.5.2.4 *Electricity Act*

Certain sellers of electricity are, in terms of the Electricity Act 41 of 1987, permitted to use defined quantities of public water for the generation of steam, electricity or energy. The Minister of Water Affairs is also authorized to use government waterworks

[165] Totalling an area of 600 000 ha.
[166] Yielding 8 100 million m^3 mean annual runoff.
[167] *Management of water resources* above n 7, 6.55–6.56. Cf Rabie above n 73, 74 ff for an evaluation of the value of the Act as compared with the Conservation of Agricultural Resources Act.
[168] In terms of s 59(5)–(6) of the Water Act.
[169] eg damming, cleaning, deepening, widening, straightening or altering the course of a channel.
[170] Section 136(1).
[171] Section 136(2).
[172] Section 1.

for generating and supplying electricity,[173] although this is subject to Eskom's preferential right to undertake the project. This power is confirmed by the Water Act,[174] vesting the control of the water in any government waterwork in the Minister and granting him, in the public interest, the discretion to use it for generating electricity.[175]

3.5.3 Ground water

The term 'ground water' refers to any water, whether running in a defined channel or not, found underground. The Water Act does not specifically regulate the use of ground water. However, in respect of ground water occurring in a subterranean government water control area, the Act contains specific provisions,[176] which vest the right to the use and the control of such water in the Minister.[177]

It may be argued that running ground water can be included in the definition of public water, in so far as it is found in a known and defined channel.[178] The definition of 'normal flow' would nevertheless exclude ground water from the provisions in the Act relating to its control.[179] Therefore ground water would be surplus water,[180] and every riparian owner entitled to so much of it as he can beneficially use for domestic purposes, watering stock and for agricultural and urban purposes.[181]

On the other hand, however, it may be argued that the Act's definition of public water[182] rules out any classification of ground water as public water, since that definition, read with the definition of public stream, presupposes a riparian landowner—something which does not seem possible in respect of ground water. It is submitted, however, that any soil surrounding such ground water forms part of the riparian land, due to the Roman law doctrine that an owner of land also owns everything below and above the surface.

No provision in the Act specifically regulates non-running ground water, such as underground lakes. Unless such water resources occur within subterranean government water control areas, it must be accepted that anyone can use this water as he pleases. The reason for this lack of control presumably lies in the limited possibilities of exploitation of such water.[183] Where substantial amounts of ground water occur and are easily exploitable, the government would probably declare a control area.

Although recognition is given to the limited knowledge on the development of ground-water resources,[184] it is suggested that the visibility of water should not be the criterion for control and that stagnant ground water should be included in the statutory control of freshwater resources.

It seems that the legislature did not contemplate the inclusion of ground water in these provisions and that any interpretative inclusion is strained. The Act should state clearly what the status of, and rights to ground water are.

---

173 Section 67 of the Water Act.
174 Section 56.
175 Section 56(3) and (4).
176 Chapter III.
177 Section 29. See also s 12B, where the removal of underground water from mines is regulated.
178 *Hiscock v De Wet* 1880 (1) Buch SC 58; *Southey v Schombie* 1881 (1) EDC 286; *Southey v Southey* 1905 (22) SC 650. Cf also Roos *Principles of Roman Dutch law* (1909) 48–50.
179 Section 1 defines normal flow to be public water actually and *visibly* flowing in a public stream.
180 Which is any water excluded from the definition of normal flow: s 1.
181 Section 10.
182 Section 1.
183 *Management of water resources* above n 7, 3.17; Rabie above n 69, 1.
184 *Management of water resources* above n 7, 3.22.

13.5.4 Wetlands

'Wetlands' is the common term for

'water dominated areas with impeded drainage where soils are saturated with water and where there is a characteristic fauna and flora'.[185]

The terms vleis, water sponges, marshes, bogs, swamps, pans, river meadows and river banks (up to 10 m outside the ten-year flood line) are often included in references to wetlands. Their ecological value is often emphasized, particularly by the DWA, which recognizes wetland water requirements as a legitimate user sector.[186] Various other potential benefits of wetlands have been identified, such as possibilities for agricultural and urban development, social activities, erosion and pollution control and natural hydrological uses, for example flood attenuation and water storage.[187] These potential values are currently being studied, inter alia to determine the need for legal protection.

Neither a national wetlands policy nor a uniform legislative system for wetland management exists in South Africa. The existing provisions in various Acts are enforced by a diversity of authorities, including the Departments of Water Affairs, Environment Affairs and Agriculture, as well as the different provincial nature conservation departments.

Although the ecological value of wetlands is recognized, very few legislative measures protect these areas from the deterioration of their plant and animal life. One of the reasons for poor legislative protection, besides a lack of knowledge, is the fact that these areas are often seen as being under private ownership. Therefore a policy similar to that applicable to private water under the Water Act is maintained. It is, however, submitted that such a view cannot be afforded in view of the increasing scarcity and value of these ecologically important habitats.

13.5.4.1 *Water Act*

The water of wetlands, being areas deriving their water from natural drainages, springs or rainfall, cannot contain public water, unless the water is derived from a public stream. On the other hand, private water is defined as all water which rises or falls naturally on any land or naturally drains or is led onto one or more pieces of land and which is not capable of common use for irrigation purposes.[188] This definition does not necessarily refer only to running water. Wetlands accordingly will normally contain only private water.[189] This means that the sole and exclusive rights of use and enjoyment of wetlands vest in the owner of the land where they occur.[190]

In terms of the definition of public water, and the proviso to it, the water of a public stream, when it loses one of its characteristics, also becomes private water. Therefore, when a public stream spreads out and for a distance stops flowing in a known and defined channel, becoming a wetland, it contains private water for that distance.[191] Although such water is 'derived from' a public stream and therefore qualifies as public water as far as this condition is concerned, it does not fulfil the above-mentioned

---

[185] Walmsley *A rationale for the development of a national wetland research programme* (1987) 3 (unpublished paper read at working group for wetland research 12 August 1987). See also Begg *The wetlands of Natal* (1986) 6–7.

[186] *Management of water resources* above n 7, 2.26.

[187] Walmsley above n 185, 3.

[188] Section 1.

[189] This, naturally, is subject to the requirement that private water is water which cannot be used for common irrigation purposes.

[190] Section 5.

[191] *Great Fish River Irrigation Board v Southey* 1928 Hall's Rep 237. Cf *Van der Merwe v McGregor* 1913 CPD 497; *Van der Westhuizen v Rabie* 1915 Krummeck's Rep 58. See, in general, Ramsden above n 80, 5 ff.

condition and the proviso would apply. It is submitted that the definitions of public water and public stream lack clarity and can even be contradictory.

A landowner's rights to private water are subject to the prohibition of using it for industrial purposes without a permit,[192] and to the strict pollution provisions of the Act.[193] They are also subject to existing rights and rights of long user. These restrictions on owners' rights relating to wetlands are, however, not sufficient to ensure the conservation of wetland ecosystems. The main threat to wetland survival comes from urban and agricultural development of these areas.

The only other provision in the Water Act, besides the above-mentioned, which can be interpreted as referring also to wetlands, and limiting an owner's exclusive use and enjoyment of land on which a wetland occurs, is that pertaining to catchment control areas.[194] In terms of this section[195] the Minister may declare land on either side of the channel of a public stream, or any other area situated within the catchment of such a stream, to be a catchment control area. As river banks and temporary dry beds can be regarded as wetlands, and as wetlands often form sources of public streams, this protection, in order to control silt or to lessen the possibility of flood damage, or merely to protect the catchment area, is valuable for the conservation of riverine habitat.

13.5.4.2 *Conservation of Agricultural Resources Act*

A few regulations issued by virture of the Conservation of Agricultural Resources Act 43 of 1983 represent the only legislation directly aimed at the conservation of wetlands.[196] The Act is administered by the Department of Agriculture, adding a further authority to wetland management.

First, the regulations forbid the use of the vegetation in wetlands that would cause deterioration or damage to agricultural resources.[197] Although this regulation is not specifically aimed at the conservation of wetland ecology, its protection is obtained simultaneously with the protection of agricultural resources, for example, through the prevention of overgrazing. Read with a further regulation[198] which prohibits the removal of an obstruction which could increase soil erosion during floods, more protection is provided for wetland ecosystems, since natural barriers often trigger wetlands to come into existence.[199]

Secondly, the regulations[200] instruct land users to remove vegetation in watercourses which could cause obstructions during floods, resulting in soil erosion. Although the value of interfering with natural floods is debatable and still to be ascertained,[201] this provision serves as protection for river banks and could save riverine habitat.[202]

Moreover, land users are forbidden (without written permission) to drain or cultivate any vlei, marsh or water sponge or portion thereof on their land, or to cultivate any land

---

[192] Section 12.
[193] Sections 21–24.
[194] Section 59.
[195] Section 59(2).
[196] GN R1048 of 25 May 1984.
[197] Regulation 7(1).
[198] Regulation 8(5).
[199] Begg above n 185, 77.
[200] Regulation 7(2).
[201] According to Begg (above n 185, 76), such activities would be environmentally damaging because of downstream consequences. He is further of the opinion that the passage of water through dense plant mass is crucial for the attenuation of flood and silt water and for the wetland to perform its natural hydrological functions.
[202] It seems as if reg 7(2) is in conflict with reg 8(5), since it is difficult to ascertain in advance whether the removal of vegetation will cause or prevent soil erosion during floods. The value of reg 7(2) is thus doubted.

within the flood area[203] of a watercourse.[204] 'Drainage' is not defined, but 'cultivation' is defined as 'mechanical disturbance'. Mechanical disturbance is a term which requires further definition, as it is not clear whether damage has to be proven and, if so, whether ecological detriment would be sufficient, or whether proof of economic loss is required. Furthermore, the permission required is obtainable from an executive officer, whose sole discretion decides the matter. The officer, an employee of the Own Affairs Department of Agriculture and Water Supply, is under no obligation to consider the environmental or ecological impact of his decision, and could make a decision on mere economic grounds. This can be prevented by the implementation of a uniform wetland management policy, to be applied by all authorities administering legislation relating to wetlands. Nevertheless, this regulation[205] represents a positive step in the direction of the protection of wetlands, and provides a mechanism to control ill-considered utilization and cultivation of these fragile areas.

The regulation which prohibits veld burning without written consent,[206] affords protection to wetlands, since it would cover the burning of vleis and reed beds.

13.5.4.3 *Mountain Catchment Areas Act*

Although the Act cannot be applied to catchments as a whole, where wetlands often occur on flats, it is often found that rivers originate from sponges on the slopes of mountains.[207] At least these areas can thus be included under the protecting provisions of the Act. So also are river banks, being important wetlands covered under the provisions of this Act, when they are included in declared areas.

13.5.4.4 *Forest Act*

The Minister of Environment Affairs may in terms of the Forest Act 122 of 1984 prohibit afforestation or reafforestation of certain land to protect any natural water source.[208] This prohibition is, in practice, dependent on the discretion of a forest officer, who will evaluate the status and hydrological value of a water source, and will determine how far from that water source the land may be afforested. This provision serves, inter alia, to protect riverine habitat from destruction and to prevent soil erosion.

13.5.4.5 *Lake Areas Development Act*

The Minister of Environment Affairs may in terms of the Lake Areas Development Act 39 of 1975 declare any land comprising or adjoining a tidal lagoon, a tidal river, or any other land comprising or adjoining a natural lake or river, which is in the immediate vicinity of a tidal lagoon or tidal river, to be a lake area. Such a declaration may serve to protect the natural habitats in and around lakes, while the protected areas can serve as natural breeding grounds for animal and bird species. No inland lake areas have yet been declared. Lake areas have been included in national parks. See chapter 27.

13.5.5 Impoundments

The Republic of South Africa has more than 500 government reservoirs and many more private dams. These areas are important sources of fresh water and could be regarded as man-made wetlands. Dams provide habitats for various forms of plant,

---

[203] This is including an area up to 10 m outside the ten-year flood line.
[204] Regulation 7(3). This provision is not applicable to wetlands where cultivation or drainage has already been commenced, unless signs of excessive soil erosion are visible: s 7(4).
[205] Regulation 7(3).
[206] Regulation 12(1).
[207] Ramsden above n 80, 9.
[208] Section 8(1).

animal and fish life and deserve consideration in a policy for conservation-oriented water management. Control over the construction of dams is vested in the Minister of Water Affairs and the Water Act regulates the control over impoundments.

3.5.5.1 *Water Act*

A riparian owner on whose land private water occurs, may impound such water at will, unless the land falls within a government drainage, subterranean or dam basin control area.[209] In such a case a permit issued by the Minister is necessary for the construction of a dam.[210]

Where public water occurs on a riparian owner's land, he may construct a dam to impound his reasonable share of this water.[211] Owners are, however, limited in the impoundment of public water: first, an owner of lower land feeling aggrieved by the storage or impoundment by upper owners who, to the detriment of the lower owner, store more than they are reasonably entitled to, may approach the water court.[212] Secondly, no waterworks storing more than 250 000 m^3 of public water may be constructed without a permit issued by the Minister.[213] Thirdly, strict directions apply to the construction or use of dams with a safety risk.[214]

The Minister may construct any waterwork which he may deem necessary for the conservation or utilization of any water or the drainage of land, or for the extraction or storage or supply of any water, or for the prevention of pollution or wastage of any water.[215] Ownership and control of the water in such waterworks vests in the State, and is exercised by the Minister. He may supply and distribute water from these waterworks as he may deem appropriate.[216] Furthermore, when he is of the opinion that an area should, in the public interest, be reserved for the construction of a waterwork, he may declare such an area to be a dam basin control area. In such an area no township, road, waterwork, building or permanent structure may be constructed without a permit. Activities connected to ordinary farming operations are also restricted in these control areas. The Minister may even expropriate land for the construction of government waterworks.[217]

Although very little control over the construction of dams is provided for in the Water Act, the *White Paper on a national policy regarding environmental conservation*[218] recommended environmental impact assessments (EIAs) to be a voluntary procedure. The DWA sets a precedent by undertaking EIAs for all its major water projects. The recommendations that arise from such assessments are implemented during the design, construction, operation and decommissioning phases of such projects. The department usually appoints landscape architects and horticultural technicians to assist with the planning and construction of waterworks. EIAs are often carried out through appointed environmental committees, which include representatives of numerous interest groups to accommodate public participation.[219]

---

[209] Sections 32C and 59(4).
[210] Section 62A.
[211] In terms of s 9.
[212] Section 19.
[213] Section 9B. But see s 9B(1)(C).
[214] Non-compliance with these directions is an offence: s 9C.
[215] Section 56.
[216] Section 56(3)–(5).
[217] Sections 59(4) and 60.
[218] WP O '80.
[219] *Management of water resources* above n 7, 6.43–6.46.

13.5.6 Precipitation

13.5.6.1 *Water Act*

In terms of the Water Act,[220] rain water is private water in so far as it falls on the land of an owner. No ownership in clouds is conferred by the Act; on the contrary, it is concluded that, like the air, clouds belong to no one and can be used by the whole community.[221] However, a chapter[222] was inserted into the Act in 1972,[223] to make provision for the control of activities which may alter the natural occurrence of atmospheric precipitation.

The State may carry out operations to effect any modification in precipitation, or cause it to be carried out by way of issuing permits to do so.[224] Such permits will be issued only after due opportunity was given to interested parties to object against such modification.[225] The issuing of permits is also subject to consultation with an advisory committee.[226] Besides the consideration given to public representations and the advice of the committee, the Minister should also be satisfied that the applicant is in possession of adequate knowledge and skill, as is recommended by the Minister of Transport.

It is clear that the State assumed the power to control the use of clouds, but not in total disregard of the Roman-law rule that the air is res omnium communis,[227] in that the public can, in certain instances, make representations in respect of the use of clouds.

The modifying of precipitation means a modification in the natural occurrence of atmospheric precipitation, which may have an effect on the runoff of water or on the quality of underground water. Two major rainfall augmentation experiments have been undertaken in the Republic, namely in Bethlehem and Nelspruit, where chemical seeding of clouds is effected to increase rainfall or suppress hail. The DWA realizes that the complexity and variability of clouds make it very difficult to understand and measure the effects of attempts at artificial modification. The results of intensive research in the USA and in Israel are being used for the South African projects, and if these experiments reveal promising results, the department intends to draw up a national weather modification policy to ensure the compatibility of further research with the national water management strategy,[228] and with issues such as cost considerations, environmental impact and public acceptability.

Since the effect of such a drastic interference with natural rainfall is not yet known, modification projects should, from an ecological point of view, be seen as potentially harmful. In-depth research concerning environmental impact should precede such projects.

13.5.7 Living freshwater resources

13.5.7.1 *Fish*

(a) Fishing. Roman law allowed every member of the community to fish in any running water, and even to conduct activities on river banks coupled with fishing, such

---

[220] Section 1.
[221] Rabie & Loubser 'Legal aspects of weather modification' 1990 *CILSA* 177.
[222] Chapter IIIA.
[223] By s 6 of the Water Amendment Act 45 of 1972. This chapter was substituted by s 7 of the Water Amendment Act 42 of 1975.
[224] Section 33B.
[225] Section 33D.
[226] Section 33D. This committee is established in terms of s 33F to advise the Minister on matters regarding the issuing of permits.
[227] ie common property (*D* 1.8.2pr).
[228] Which is to ensure the availability and supply of water on a national basis by promoting the aims of a free enterprise economy, enhancing the quality of life and conserving water resources for present and future generations. Cf *Management of water resources* above n 7, 10.4.

as tying boats to trees and drying fishing nets.[229] In Roman-Dutch law fishing was restricted in certain waters and streams by the application of a permit system.[230] This was, however, to protect private ownership of water and not to protect fish species. The South African principle of landowners being owners only of beds and banks, and not of the water within the channel of public streams, made room for the continuation of the rule of public use of running water. Although the Water Act confers rights of water use on non-riparian owners only for specific purposes, the Appellate Division has gone further by adapting principles of Roman-Dutch law, and allowing members of the public to use the water of public rivers for recreational activities, such as canoeing, and probably even fishing.[231] This does not, however, allow the public to trespass on private property. Fishing from a canoe, however, eliminates the problem of possible trespassing.

In government control areas, where rights to the utilization of public water vest in the State, any fishing rights are probably also suspended and will depend on the discretion of the Minister. However, fishing is usually allowed in government reservoirs—in fact, these are often popular fishing resorts.

The Forest Act forbids fishing in waters in state or private forests.[232] It is also an offence to injure, collect, take or remove any forest produce, which, in terms of the definition of forest produce, includes fish.[233]

The National Parks Act 57 of 1976 prohibits fishing in any water courses within the borders of national parks. This is done by declaring 'hunting' an offence,[234] where catching or any attempt to catch an animal is included in this term[235] and where fish is included in the definition of animals.[236] However, fishing is allowed in certain circumstances.[237] Similar measures apply in Natal parks.[238] In the Cape fishing in nature reserves is prohibited unless the Chief Directorate of Nature and Environmental Conservation sets aside areas where it is allowed.[239] In the Orange Free State and the Transvaal, nature conservation ordinances do not specifically prohibit fishing in nature reserves.[240] Outside nature reserves the different provincial nature conservation ordinances protect fish by limiting, inter alia, the size of fish being caught,[241] seasons in which angling is allowed[242] and the methods of fishing (eg prohibitions on types of fishing equipment and the obstructing,[243] snatching, spearing and trapping of fish and

---

[229] *D* 1.8.5pr.

[230] Grotius *Inl* 2.4.18, 19; Groenewegen *De Leg Abr* 2.1.2.3; Van Leeuwen *RHR* 2.1.12; Voet *Ad Pand* 41.1.6; Van der Keessel *Dict ad Just Inst* 2.1.1.

[231] *Butgereit v Transvaal Canoe Union* 1988 (1) SA 759 (A).

[232] Section 21(2)*(b)*.

[233] Sections 1, 21(1)*(a)*(i).

[234] Section 21(1)*(c)*.

[235] Section 1: 'hunt'.

[236] The definition of 'animal' in s 1 includes any member of the animal kingdom.

[237] Regulation 46(4) GN R2006 of 6 October 1978.

[238] Sections 1 ('animal') and 15(1)*(c)* of the Natal Ordinance 15 of 1974.

[239] Regulation 11*(h)* PN 955 of 29 August 1975.

[240] In fact, fish is excluded from the definition of game. Sections 1(lxii) ('wild animal'), 7 and 19 of the Transvaal Ordinance 12 of 1983; ss 1 ('wild animal'), 35(3), 36(3) of the OFS Ordinance 8 of 1969.

[241] Regulation 28 AN 2030 14 Dec 1983 (Transvaal); reg 11(1)*(b)* AN 184 of 12 August 1983 (OFS); s 55(1)*(b)* of the Cape Ordinance 19 of 1974; ss 61, 62 of Proc 357 of 1972 (Cape); reg 4 PN 141 of 1974 (Natal).

[242] Sections 68 and 69 of the Transvaal Ordinance; s 25(1) of the OFS Ordinance; s 52 of the Cape Ordinance; s 143(2)*(b)* of the Natal Ordinance; reg 2(4) PN 141 of 1974 (Natal).

[243] Sections 77 and 78 of the Transvaal Ordinance, s 49 of the Cape Ordinance; s 151(1)*(d)* of the Natal Ordinance; s 26(2)*(d)* of the OFS Ordinance.

the drainage of water, as well as using firearms, explosives or poisons).[244] Control is usually effected through licence systems,[245] the declaration of offences, as well as the encouraging of fishing clubs and the control of angling competitions.[246]

It is an offence wilfully to injure or disturb the spawn of any fish,[247] or the spawning bed, bank or shallow on or in which such spawn is deposited.[248] It is also an offence to place any obstruction in waters where it is calculated to prevent the free passage of fish.[249]

(b) Water pollution: In terms of the Water Act it is an offence to pollute any public or private water, including rain water, sea water and subterranean water in such a way as to render it less fit for the propagation of fish or other aquatic life.[250] The provincial nature conservation ordinances also render it an offence to deposit or discharge any solid, liquid or gaseous material into any waters, when such material could be injurious to any fish or fish food.[251] See chapter 18.

(c) Invasive plants and fish: It is an offence to cultivate, possess, convey, buy, sell, donate or import certain aquatic growths[252] or to place them into waters.[253] See chapter 11. It is also an offence to import or release live fish without a permit, except when they are released in the waters where they were caught, immediately after they were caught.[254] Special measures control the occurrence of fish in water when such fish could be noxious to other fish. When, for example, the Cape chief director of nature and environmental conservation is of the opinion that any fish found in any inland water is injurious to any other fish, aquatic growth or water, he may order and assist an owner to take specified measures to catch or kill such fish.[255] Similar measures exist in the Transvaal.[256]

(d) Interference with flow conditions: No legislation provides for the protection of fish when lawful interference with the course of streams is undertaken. Although an alteration in the course of a stream or the construction of waterworks may seriously

---

[244] Sections 71, 72, 73 and 76 of the Transvaal Ordinance; reg 40 AN 2030 of 14 December 1983 (Transvaal); ss 26 and 27 of the OFS Ordinance; reg 12 AN 184 of 12 August 1983 (OFS); ss 54 and 56 of the Cape Ordinance; ss 59(1), (2) and 60 of Proc 357 of 1972 (Cape); ss 151(1)*(d)*, *(e)* and 151(2) of the Natal Ordinance; regs 3 and 8 PN 141 of 1974 (Natal).

[245] Sections 74, 75, 80 and 82 of the Transvaal Ordinance; reg 37 AN 2030 of 14 December 1983 (Transvaal); s 23 of the OFS Ordinance; reg 10 AN 184 of 12 August 1983 (OFS); ss 143(2)*(a)* and *(d)* and 145(1) of the Natal Ordinance, reg 2(2) PN 141 of 1974 (Natal); ss 13, 50, 53, 57 and 59 of the Cape Ordinance.

[246] Section 142 of the Natal Ordinance; reg 40 AN 2030 of 14 December 1983 (Transvaal); reg 13 AN 184 of 12 August 1983 (OFS).

[247] Section 25(2)*(a)* of the OFS Ordinance; s 51 of the Cape Ordinance; s 143(3) of the Natal Ordinance. In the Transvaal and OFS this offence can be committed only in the closed season.

[248] Section 25(2)*(b)* of the OFS Ordinance; s 143(3) of the Natal Ordinance; s 51 of the Cape Ordinance.

[249] Sections 77 and 78 of the Transvaal Ordinance; s 49 of the Cape Ordinance; s 151(1)*(d)* of the Natal Ordinance.

[250] Sections 22 and 23(1)*(a)*(ii).

[251] Section 84 of the Transvaal Ordinance; s 48*(a)* of the Cape Ordinance and s 152 of the Natal Ordinance.

[252] Section 85 of the Transvaal Ordinance; s 29 of the OFS Ordinance; reg 14 AN 184 of 12 August 1983 (OFS); s 60 of the Cape Ordinance.

[253] Section 85 of the Transvaal Ordinance; s 50 of the Cape Ordinance. (The definition of 'aquatic growth' in s 2(v) of the Cape Ordinance refers to any vegetation which grows or is able to grow in inland waters.)

[254] Sections 79 and 81 of the Transvaal Ordinance; s 28 of the OFS Ordinance; s 50 of the Cape Ordinance; s 132 of the Natal Ordinance; reg 9 PN 141 of 1974. The last-mentioned ordinance does not make provision for the exception.

[255] Section 19(1) and (2) of the Cape Ordinance.

[256] Section 101*(h)*(iii) of the Transvaal Ordinance.

harm fish life, and especially that of migrating fish, the construction of fish ladders or ensuring a permanent water flow is not obligatory.

The impoundment of water could also be harmful to fish life in that certain species might need water in specific temperatures or volumes. Migratory fish species could be detrimentally affected where no fishways exist. Since very little is known about the habitat requirements of various fish species, an extensive research programme was launched in the Kruger National Park in 1987 to ascertain such needs. It is argued that only when this knowledge is at hand can claims as to legislative protection be made.

13.5.7.2 *Other living freshwater resources*

Aquatic life other than fish enjoys very little legislative protection. The Forest Act makes provision for the protection of forest produce in nature reserves and wilderness areas.[257] Forest produce includes anything which occurs, is grown or grows in a forest, as well as anything which is produced by any vertebrate or invertebrate member of the animal kingdom or any member of the plant kingdom.[258] In terms of the Act a nature reserve is any area declared as such for the preservation of a particular natural forest or particular plants or animals or for some other conservation purpose, while a wilderness area is declared for the preservation of ecosystems or the scenic beauty. Similar conservation measures exist in respect of national parks[259] and provincial nature reserves. The Conservation of Agricultural Resources Act stipulates that control measures may be prescribed relating to the cultivation of virgin soil and the utilization and protection of cultivated land, vleis, marshes, water sponges and vegetation, and the control of the grazing capacity of the veld, as well as control of veld fires, weeds and invader plants, the restoration of eroded land and protection against pollution.[260]

Although these measures protect aquatic resources against direct human disturbance, the conservation of such resources is greatly influenced by the quantity and quality of their water habitat. Unfortunately, no legislation exists to control water quality and quantity in order to protect such life. The river research programme mentioned earlier is, inter alia, also aimed at ascertaining the water needs of animal and plant life in and around water habitats, and at motivating statutory protection for these species and their habitats.

13.5.8 Environmental policy

Although no general underlying principle of environmental conservation exists in South African water legislation, there is an increasing tendency to afford legal protection to environmental interests, traces of which can also be found in the regulation of freshwater systems in the Republic. These traces are found not only in statutory provisions scattered through various acts, as discussed, but also in government policy.

In congruence with the increasing awakening of environmental conservation awareness during the last two decades, a need for a statutory policy of environmental conservation developed. In 1982 the first Environment Conservation Act was promulgated, which was substituted by the current Environment Conservation Act 73 of 1989. This Act was promulgated to provide for the effective protection and controlled utilization of the environment. 'Environment' is defined widely as the aggregate of surrounding objects, conditions and influences that affect the life and habitats of man or any other organism or collection of organisms. Provision is made for

[257] Section 15.
[258] Section 1.
[259] Section 21 of the National Parks Act.
[260] Sections 5–7.

the declaration of a policy for environmental conservation,[261] in accordance with which all authorities to which powers relating to the environment have been assigned should perform their duties.[262] No such policy has yet been declared. Moreover, upon the declaration of protected natural environments, the Administrator concerned may issue directions relating to the land or water in such an area.[263] Provision is also made for the declaration of special nature reserves on state-owned land.[264] In these areas a management plan will control the protection of the environment.[265] Water pollution is prohibited[266] and the Minister may identify activities which may have a substantial detrimental effect on the environment, relating to, inter alia, water use and disposal, resource removal and renewal, and agricultural processes.[267] Such activities will be prohibited unless ministerial authorization for their being undertaken is granted, which authorization is subject to the results of a report concerning the impact of such activities on the environment.

The object of this Act, namely to bind all authorities and to encourage the consideration of environmental impact in the undertaking of activities, is positive and potentially beneficial regarding a uniform environmental conservation effort. But since neither an environmental conservation policy nor protected areas or detrimental activities have yet been declared, the practical value of this legislation is yet to be demonstrated. See, generally, chapter 7.

Another positive indication of increasing environmental awareness in government was the *White Paper on a national policy regarding environmental conservation* issued in 1980,[268] which recommended that development projects should be undertaken with due regard to environmental considerations. The DWA is a leader in the application of these recommendations and various examples of its consideration of the environment are proof of its concern.

First, EIAs are voluntarily undertaken as part of the planning phase of all major water projects.[269] The recommendations of such assessments are implemented during the design, construction, operation and decommissioning phases of these projects.

Secondly, river basin studies are undertaken to promote the effective management of basins. These extensive, costly and time-consuming projects include reference to relevant environmental factors and initiate the compilation of balanced drainage basin development plans. Basin steering committees are appointed to oversee the work being done. Their members represent interest groups of all the facets of water utilization in the basin.

Thirdly, research is encouraged and carried out by the DWA to understand the influence of water management activities on the environment. The Water Research Commission was established by statute in 1971[270] to promote and finance water research. This body finances many research projects aimed at environmental considerations in water management.

Finally, provision is often made for consideration of the public interest in the exercising of ministerial discretion. This is done by inviting public input, as in the case of the establishment of advisory committees, as well as by imposing an obligation upon the Minister in the exercise of his discretion, to consider the public interest. Although

[261] Section 2.
[262] Section 3.
[263] Section 16(2).
[264] Section 18(1).
[265] Section 18(4)*(b)*.
[266] Section 19.
[267] Section 21.
[268] WP O '80.
[269] This issue has already been discussed in respect of impoundments.
[270] By s 2 of Act 34 of 1971.

this term lacks statutory definition, in terms of departmental policy and in the light of increasing environmental awareness, conservation considerations should play an important role when ministerial discretion is exercised in the public interest.

13.6 REVIEW OF LEGISLATION FOR THE CONTROL OF FRESHWATER SYSTEMS

The State acts as custodian in the national interest in respect of water.[271] Proper performance of this duty consists of effective management of the development, utilization and conservation of South African water resources. Such management is embodied in the policy of the DWA to promote the aims of a free enterprise economy, the enhancement of the quality of life and the conservation of the resource for present and future generations.[272]

Viewed from an environmental angle, some objections may be raised regarding current management of freshwater systems in South Africa:

First, the DWA is not the only authority concerned with the control of freshwater systems. Various other legislative instruments empower other national, provincial or local authorities to control water resources. These authorities' policies are not necessarily in unison with that of the DWA. The need for a uniform strategy exists, in accordance with which all legislative measures concerning water control should be streamlined. Provision for the realization of this ideal has been made by the Environment Conservation Act,[273] but since no environmental policy has yet been laid down by the Minister in accordance with the Act,[274] the process of conformation is still due.

Secondly, the Water Act deals with running water, which excludes wetlands from the responsibility of the DWA. Since the environmental importance of wetlands is now increasingly being realized, such systems ought to be specifically included under the protection of the Water Act. Currently the Conservation of Agricultural Resources Act is the only Act making explicit provision for wetland conservation. However, the emphasis is placed on conservation in the interest of agriculture and not necessarily in that of ecological survival, which deserves legal protection. It should be realized that, besides its role in basic human needs, water has intrinsic scientific, aesthetic and educational values which cannot readily be assessed in monetary terms.

Thirdly, the limited control over ground water means that a substantial source of water does not fall under the provisions of the Act. The Water Act should regard a freshwater system as an entity, irrespective of whether a part of it occurs under the surface.

Fourthly, South African water law draws a distinction between private and public water and places private water under the exclusive and unrestricted rights of use and enjoyment of owners of land where it occurs. It is submitted that this distinction is not only historically ill-founded but also undesirable in a country where water is an increasingly scarce strategic resource. State control should be possible over all water, whether it be surface or subterranean, running or not, capable of being used for irrigation or not, rising from, falling on or being led onto land.

Fifthly, it is acknowledged that EIAs are voluntarily undertaken by the DWA prior to the construction of major waterworks. However, although this is a positive step in the direction of environmental consideration, these assessments should be obligatory for all projects, undertaken by all authorities and individuals, which could have an influence on natural water systems.

---

[271] *Management of water resources* above n 7, 6.47.
[272] *Management of water resources* above n 7, 10.4.
[273] Section 3.
[274] Section 2.

Finally, no provision is made for the conservation of entire catchments. The Water Act makes provision for streams being public for certain parts only, while other parts may be private, as well as for a distinction between streams in or outside control areas, and under or above the surface. These segments are regulated by different legal principles and measures. Such a system makes no provision for the protection of catchment ecosystems, which do not lend themselves to fragmentation. What is necessary is a comprehensive approach in terms of which entire catchments are uniformly regulated. The DWA is realizing this requirement, and basin studies currently reflect a tendency to manage catchments as a whole.

The ideal, therefore, is to have a single authority in control of entire catchments, applying a uniform legislative management policy in order to achieve the conservation of freshwater systems in their entirety. The establishment of 'river reserves' as well as of 'river conservation authorities' has been suggested to achieve this goal.[275] This is attainable by subjecting all landowners and authorities to a national water management policy. The establishment of advisory committees is a positive development towards basin control, but the effectiveness of these bodies is still to be proved.

[275] Rabie above n 73, 203.

CHAPTER 14

MARINE SYSTEMS

J G FIELD
J I GLAZEWSKI

14.1 THE SOUTH AFRICAN COASTLINE

South Africa has a coastline some 3 000 km long, stretching from the Orange River where it borders with Namibia in the northwest to the Mozambique border in the east. The coastline is unusually straight, with few indentations or bays, making it inhospitable for yachtsmen and very exposed to swells and waves which have the full fetch of the South Atlantic and Southern oceans up to 10 000 km to the southwest. On the west coast, the only natural harbour is at Saldanha Bay, whereas on the south and east coasts there is a series of half-heart shaped bays, such as Algoa Bay at Port Elizabeth. The coastal zone extends beyond the land to include the continental shelf, a submarine extension of the continent of variable depth and width. Just as the form of mountains, valleys and plains affects local climate on land, with winds, temperatures and rainfall depending to varying degrees on the altitude and orientation of land forms, so also does the type of formation on the continental shelf affect marine conditions. Thus the shape of the continental shelf helps direct major ocean currents: a wide shelf tending to keep currents offshore, and a narrow shelf allowing the current close to the coast. For example, on the east coast the shelf widens off Durban, keeping the warm Agulhas Current offshore, whereas further south between Port St Johns and East London the shelf is narrow and the Agulhas Current flows strongly close inshore.

The occurrence of submarine valleys or canyons also influences marine matters, in that canyons may funnel cool, deep water inshore and towards the surface. For example the Cape Canyon, which cuts into the continental shelf off Saldanha Bay, occasionally brings water from the deep ocean inshore and with it midwater fish such as lantern fish, which get caught in purse-seine nets that are normally aimed at sardine and anchovy.

The continental shelf is often taken to extend out to a depth of 200 m, but this is a completely arbitrary definition—it usually extends out with a gentle slope seawards. The point at which this slope steepens—the shelf-break—is really the outer edge of the continental shelf, and this may occur at any depth from 50–500 m, but most often it occurs at a depth of between 100 and 300 m in South African waters. Again, the shelf may be only tens of kilometres wide, such as off the Cape Peninsula and Transkei, or it may be 200–300 km wide such as off the Orange River Mouth and the Agulhas Bank, south of Mossel Bay. From a biological and fisheries point of view, the shelf is very important because the sea water, at least for some of the year, is generally influenced by the sea floor over the shelf. Thus, decaying matter, whether from marine plankton or fish, or whether it orginates from land runoff, is mixed up into the surface sunlit layers allowing the 'garden' to be refertilized with natural compost. In the deep ocean, much of this material is lost for centuries or millennia. This is why continental shelves are much more productive than the deep ocean, and why nearly all the world's major fisheries are located over them. The South African shelf is no exception, as we shall see below.

14.2 THE WEST COAST AND BENGUELA SYSTEM

The Benguela current is a cool current which influences the continental shelf from somewhere east of Cape Agulhas to as far north as Cape Kunene on the

Namibia/Angolan border. Although formerly popularly believed to be an offshoot of the cool west-wind drift in the Southern Ocean, it is in fact separated from the Southern Ocean by a belt of warm surface water. There is also 'warm' oceanic water beyond the cool coastal Benguela water if one sails westwards from Cape Town. The oceanic boundary of the Benguela system is marked by a meandering front between cool water of various shades of green verging on brown (depending upon the stage of plankton growth) and warm blue water beyond. The main oceanic front is usually somewhere near the edge of the continental shelf, although it moves to and fro, depending upon the atmospheric conditions and the wind. The Benguela Current proper is a narrow jet current of largely upwelled water which flows swiftly northwards at 1–5 km per hour in the boundary region between cool coastal water and the warmer central Atlantic surface water beyond. The Benguela system consists of the northward flowing current itself, plus all the water on the continental shelf further inshore. This includes intermittent south-flowing counter-currents inshore and beneath the main Benguela Current, as well as cross-shelf upwelling water flowing towards the land, and gyres and eddies of water which vary in time and space.

The Benguela Current is characterized by regular and powerful upwelling. Wind from the south tends to push surface water northwards and, in the southern hemisphere, the rotation of the earth causes the moving water to veer to the left, offshore. The water blown offshore has to be replaced from somewhere, or else the sea level would drop dramatically, and in the process termed 'upwelling', it is replaced by cooler water (8–15 °C) from 100–300 m deep. This is below the depth to which light penetrates and the upwelled water is thus also rich in nitrogen, phosphorus, silicon and other plant nutrients. When these reach the sunlit surface layers of the sea, dense blooms of plantplankton or phytoplankton develop using up the nutrients over a period of 4–10 days after upwelling, discolouring the water various shades of green or brown, or even red. Simultaneously, the upwelled water tends to warm under the sun's rays.

In the south of the region, from Cape Agulhas to Saldanha Bay, the south-easter tends to be intermittent, blowing for several days at a time, mainly during the summer months from September to March or April. Upwelling here is also episodic, being driven by these southerly winds. The blooms of phytoplankton form the base of food chains leading to fish, particularly sardine (also known as pilchard) and anchovy. These tend to feed mainly on small animals in the plankton (or zooplankton), but the sporadic nature of the fast-growing phytoplankton blooms makes it difficult for longer-lived and slower-growing zooplankton to down them, and much of the phytoplankton therefore sinks to the bottom ungrazed.

Further up the west coast from St Helena Bay northwards, winds are steadier and less intermittent and denser populations of zooplankton have time to develop and form a more reliable food supply for fish schooling near the surface.

South of Cape Point and eastwards to Cape Agulhas and beyond lies the broad continental shelf known as the Agulhas Bank. The Agulhas Bank is influenced by warm surface water from the Agulhas Current overlying cool, dense water of temperature similar to that on the west coast. In summer the surface water is further warmed by the sun, making it so much less dense than the cool water below that they mix very little. The inshore part of the western Agulhas Bank, from Cape Hangklip at the mouth of False Bay to Cape Agulhas, is very much part of the Benguela system, and cool water upwells to the surface under the influence of longshore southeasterly winds. Just as further north along the west coast, the shallow rocky areas are populated by large kelps which are characteristic of the Benguela Current system.

14.3 THE EAST COAST AND AGULHAS CURRENT

The Agulhas Current is a warm current of 20–25 °C water at the surface which orginates in the Indian Ocean. It is formed partly from the Mozambique Current which flows southwards between Madagascar and Mocambique, partly from the South Equatorial Current which flows from east of Mozambique, and thirdly from recirculating gyres of water from the Agulhas Return Current to the south. The Agulhas Current tends to hug the edge of the continental shelf, occurring close inshore off Zululand where the shelf is narrow, further offshore near Durban, closer again off the Transkei coast and then further and further offshore as the shelf widens to form the Agulhas Bank south of Port Elizabeth. It is a swift, deep current, flowing at 5–10 km per hour at its core and reaching a depth of more than 1 000 m. Its swift passage gives rise to instabilities, causing it to meander and to shed eddies both clockwise onto the shelf and anti-clockwise offshore into the Indian Ocean. It also creates a dynamic upwelling of cool, deep water, which spins off to the right from under the Agulhas Current and onto the shelf, causing periods of cool water close inshore from the south coast of Natal southwards. Dynamic upwelling has the same end result as coastal upwelling such as occurs in the Benguela system, but it is caused by the dynamics of the fast current rather than by coastal winds.

South and west of Port Elizabeth the shelf is too wide for the Agulhas Current to cause dynamic upwelling at the coast, and the periodic cold water which may be so cold as to stun warm-water fish is here caused by longshore easterly winds, largely at capes and bays. The eastern Agulhas Bank, south of Mossel Bay, has recently been found to have a semi-permanent dome of cool water which normally stays beneath the surface. Its source and nature are not yet understood, but it may be related to the Agulhas Current offshore. It brings nutrient-rich cool water into the sunlit upper layers over the Agulhas Bank, and appears to promote plankton blooms below the surface; this may be the source of much nourishment for small fish, squid and the many types of line fish which utilize the Agulhas Current as a means of dispersal during their life histories (see para 14.4.5 below).

While the Agulhas Current flows rapidly south- and westward at the edge of the shelf, water over the main part of the shelf further inshore is subjected to pulsing counter-currents flowing in the opposite direction. This is utilized by shipping, with northward traffic lanes inshore of the south-bound ships. It is also utilized by fish and plankton in their migrations. Most linefish caught in the Cape Province tend to spawn off the Transkei coast. Their eggs and larval stages float in the plankton and get caught up in the Agulhas Current. Those that find themselves in gyres and eddies to the right of the Current end up on the Agulhas Bank where estuaries, domes of nutrient-rich water or coastal upwelling provide food for their development and growth and the completion of their life cycles. Adults presumably then stay inshore, taking advantage of the counter-currents to migrate back east and north to their spawning grounds off Transkei. The most well-known example of fish migrations taking advantage of the counter-currents is the annual 'sardine run' off Natal. The run is actually a migration of the Cape pilchard (or sardine) which commonly occur on the Agulhas Bank as adult fish. Some of these fish move eastwards to reach the Natal south coast in June or July each year. It is presumed that they stay inshore to feed on the plankton blooms caused by dynamic upwelling on the inner side of the Agulhas Current. This water tends to flow northwards as a counter-current, and carries the sardines with it.

14.4 FISHERIES

The extensive coastal waters of the Republic are rich in plankton; it is therefore not surprising that these waters support important fisheries. The South African fishing industry employs some 27 000 people, mostly in the western and southern Cape, and produces fish with a total wholesale value of over a R1 000 million.[1] The fisheries may be divided into a number of different types according to the method of fishing used and the type of fish caught. The fisheries may also be categorized into four main classes, in order of value: the demersal or bottom-trawl fishery (principally for hake); the purse-seine fishery for surface-schooling fish such as sardine and anchovy; the trap fishery for rock lobster, and the line fishery for fish caught from boats by hook and line, often over a rocky sea bottom. In addition, there is a fast-growing mariculture industry for shellfish such as mussels, oysters and soon possibly abalone for the luxury market, and a potential midwater trawling industry for horse mackerel (or maasbanker). The squid industry is also quite new.[2]

The total catch off South Africa and Namibia has fluctuated over the years from some 0,5 million metric tons after the Second World War, when the purse-seine fishery commenced, to approximately 2 million tons since 1980, with peaks in the late sixties (due to heavy exploitation of sardine), mid–seventies (due to heavy exploitation of hake), and late seventies (due to heavy exploitation of horse mackerel off Namibia).[3] In each case the peak was followed by a decline in the stocks of the heavily exploited fish, giving a strong suggestion of over-exploitation, probably coupled with environmentally induced changes in spawning or recruitment of young fish into the fishery.

14.4.1 The bottom trawl fishery

The bottom trawl fishery is the most important sector of the fishing industry in value, the catch being worth some R440 million per year. The total catch is of the order of 200 000 tons of 'white-fish'.[4] Some 140 000 tons of the catch is hake, which is not only sold locally fresh and frozen but also exported. Bottom trawlers range from 20 m long inshore vessels to large 80 m stern-trawler factory-freezer ships that can stay at sea for months. The deep-sea fishery is based in Cape Town, Saldanha Bay and Hout Bay, whilst Mossel Bay, Port Elizabeth and Hermanus are the main ports for small inshore trawlers. After hake, which is worth some 75 per cent of the value of the demersal (deepwater) catch, other important components are horse mackerel, chub mackerel, kingklip, soles, monkfish, snoek and squid.[5] The hake catch is gradually being allowed to increase as the stock picks up after the heavy international exploitation outside the 12 nautical mile limit in the sixties and early seventies, before the declaration of the 200 nautical mile exclusive fishery zone (see Figure 14.1). There are, however, year-to-year fluctuations in the recruitment of young fish into the fishery, presumably due to environmental variations. Environmental changes, such as the intrusion of warm water from the Agulhas Current onto the west coast, also affect the availability of fish to the fishing fleets, as hake appear to migrate out of reach of trawlers which operate on the mud banks on the edge of the continental shelf, when warm water intrusions occur. There are undoubtedly also other more subtle environmental effects on availability and recruitment.

Hake are caught mainly during daylight, when they are found near the bottom, by sock-shaped trawl nets which are dragged along the muddy sea floor. The fishery operates throughout the year, although there are seasonal fluctuations in the availability of fish. At night hake tend to rise off the bottom where they feed on smaller fish and crustaceans at mid-depths, and are not accessible to bottom trawlers. There have been some attempts at mid-water trawling, towing the net off the bottom to catch these fish

---

[1] *Composition and size of the South African fishing industry*, Economic Section, Chief Directorate of Sea Fisheries, Department of Environment Affairs (unpublished report, 1990).

[2] For more details, the reader is referred to a very readable account of South Africa's fisheries by Payne & Crawford *Oceans of life off southern Africa* (1989).

[3] Ibid.

[4] *Composition and size of the South African fishing industry* above n 1.

[5] Ibid.

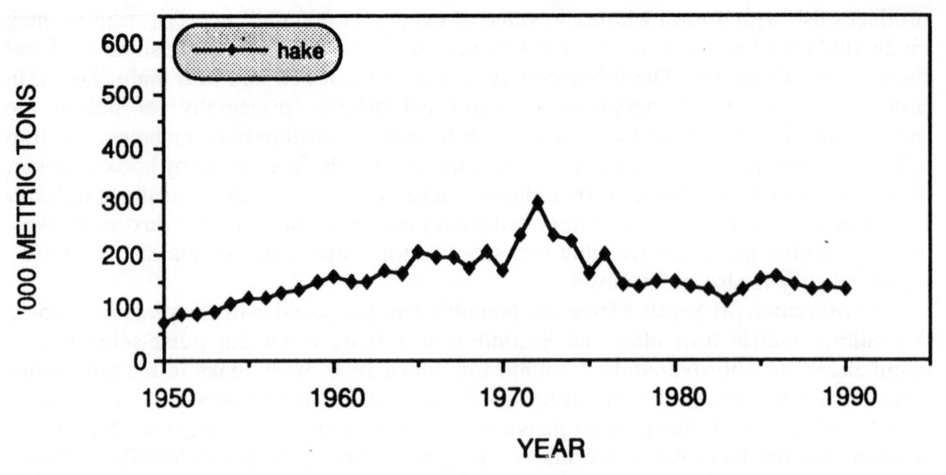

Figure 14.1 Graph depicting the total reported catch of hake in South African waters since 1950. Catches increased in the 1960s and early 1970s, when foreign fleets fished beyond the 12 nautical mile limit. Catches have been controlled more carefully since the introduction of the 200 nautical mile exclusive fishery zone in 1976, and the fishery is showing signs of recovery. Source: Official statistics of the Sea Fisheries Research Institute and the *South African fishing industry handbook and buyers guide* (1991).

at night and to catch other species such as horse mackerel. This method is more expensive in terms of fuel used, however, and recent trial fishing targetting at the large schools of horse mackerel on the Agulhas Bank have shown to be uneconomic unless other, more valuable fish are caught too. Kingklip are one of the most valuable fin fish per kilogram, but brief experimental fishing for kingklip using long lines in the late 1980s got out of hand very rapidly and did great damage to the old spawning stock on rocky grounds, which are inaccessible to the bottom trawlers. As these fish are slow growing, it may take decades for the kingklip stock to recover.

The demersal trawling fishery is regulated in a number of ways: a total allowable catch (TAC) for hake and sole, certain closed bays (e g False Bay, Plettenberg Bay, St Sebastian Bay, St Francis Bay) and other inshore areas, and minimum mesh size of the trawl net. No bottom trawling is allowed within five miles of the coast on the west coast north of Cape Point, except for research purposes by special permit. There is no closed season for the deep-sea trawl fishery, but certain inshore areas are closed during the squid spawning season to protect squid spawning grounds on the south coast, for example. Regulations are amended by the Minister of Environment Affairs from time to time, after consultation with the Sea Fishery Advisory Committee, and published in the *Government Gazette*. The TAC of hake is doubtless the most important method of regulation. This is split into quotas for individual registered fishing companies on the advice of the Quota Board. Enforcement is effected mainly by monitoring catches at the point of landing and through compulsory statistical returns rendered by fishing companies. It appears to be reasonably effective. One complaint is that some skippers may still use small mesh 'liners' inside the main net at the cod-end or toe of the sock, enabling larger catches of small fish, most of which should pass through the meshes to live longer and grow larger. Company managements claim that such practices are against their policies, but it is difficult to find the small liner nets among the spares and ropes carried on board.

Most trawled fish are gutted and beheaded at sea, and then either processed on board and frozen in factory ships or returned to port packed in ice in the ships' holds for skinning, filleting and further processing in factories ashore. There have been few complaints about pollution by 'white-fish' processing factories and these appear to operate to the highest standards. At sea, trawlers are followed by flocks of sea birds and herds of seals which feed on the discarded guts, heads, and trash-fish. Some ships are equipped to retain the heads and trash-fish for processing into fish meal ashore. Neverthless, a considerable amount of fish is discarded, and it remains controversial whether the bulk of hake earbones (otoliths) found in seal stomachs comes from discarded fish or whether there is serious competition between seals and the fishermen for hake.

14.4.2 The purse seine fishery

The purse-seine or pelagic fishery is based on small fish which school near the surface and are generally caught within sight of land. The main species caught are anchovy, sardine (or pilchard), round-herring (or redeye), chub mackerel, small horse mackerel, lantern fish and lightfish. Purse-seine nets are anything from 350–700 m long and hang down from floats at the surface to 60 or 90 metres depth. The fish are located by echo-sounder and caught by encircling the surface school with the purse-seine net, drawing the bottom of the net closed with a draw rope into a 'purse', and then pumping the fish into the ship's hold. Only the best quality fish, usually sardine or round-herring, are suitable for canning if returned to the shore factory in cool conditions or within a few hours. A large part of the catch is 'industrial' and used for making fish meal and fish oil. The main ports are along the west coast: Lamberts Bay, Laaiplek in St Helena Bay, Saldanha Bay, Hout Bay, and also Gansbaai beyond Hermanus. The main anchovy, sardine and chub mackerel tend to be caught as young fish. These spawn on the Agulhas Bank, most are transported as eggs and larvae in the plankton by the Benguela Current up the west coast and then recruit as juveniles inshore north of Lamberts Bay. They tend to move southwards close to land in the Benguela Counter-Current, and many get caught on the west coast as they migrate back towards the Agulhas Bank spawning grounds.

The fishery is very susceptible to fluctuations, because the fish are small and short-lived. Thus one or two years of poor spawning or poor recruitment, especially when coupled with heavy fishing, can reduce the anchovy stock to 50 per cent or less of its former size. The pelagic fishery is also subject to rapid changes in species composition, as evidenced by changes in the geological record of fish scales in the sediments off Walvis Bay in Namibia and in similar basins off California. The Cape fishery started as a sardine (pilchard) fishery in the late 1940s, using a 38 mm mesh net. It grew to a catch of some 400 000 tons in 1964, before declining dramatically, just as the California sardine fishery had declined in 1948. At this time a reduced mesh of 13 mm was introduced to enable the smaller anchovy to be caught. From then on anchovy became the mainstay of the industry, and canning declined in importance since anchovy are not a fish amenable to canning. In spite of the change from sardine-domination to anchovy-domination, the fishery remained remarkably stable by world standards for a pelagic fishery, the total catch of all species remaining about 350 000 tons from 1960–88 (See Figure 14.2). In 1989–90 the landed value of the catch was about R45-million, with a wholesale value of some R200-million.[6]

Pelagic fish are processed in factories at the main fishing ports mentioned above. Until the mid-1970s, fish were pumped ashore wet and the pumped water, together with its contents of blood, scales, oil and other organic matter, was simply allowed to run back into the harbour. This caused organic pollution at busy fishing ports such as Saldanha Bay, with the discharged organic matter decaying in the sediments where it settled, causing oxygen to be used up and black, sulphurous sediments smelling of

[6] Ibid.

rotten eggs resulted, killing almost all marine life in and on the muddy bottom. Regulations were introduced under the sea fisheries legislation and enforced by the authorities. These resulted in the 'wet-offloading' process being replaced and the cleaning up of the effluent returned to the sea. Surveys by the Sea Fisheries Research Institute and by the University of Cape Town have shown that marine invertebrates returned to the sediments in Saldanha harbour within a few years after the change of practice, and the mud has lost its black, smelly character. This demonstrates the principle that the effects of organic pollution on its own, without heavy metals or other industrial toxins, can be rapidly reversed by simply cleaning up the source of the organic matter.

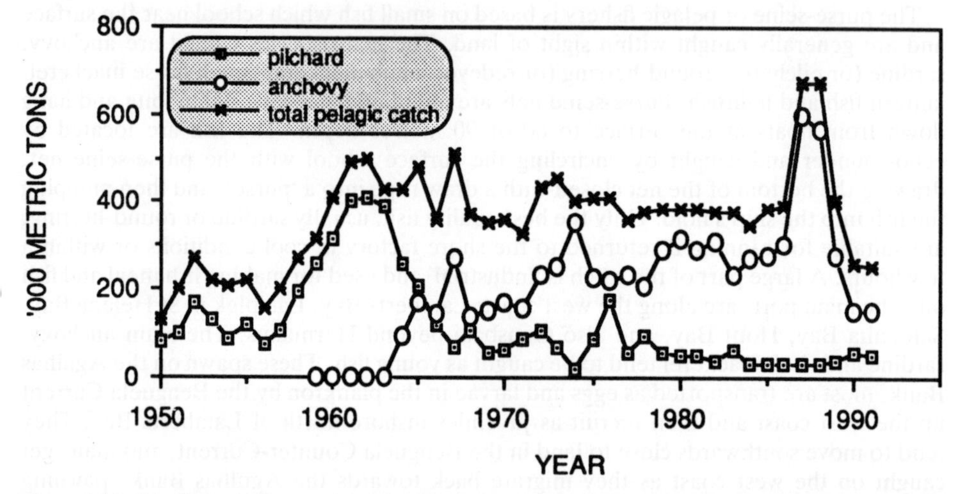

Figure 14.2 Graph depicting total South African catches of sardine (pilchard) and anchovy in the pelagic purse-seine fishery, illustrating the sardine boom and collapse in the early 1960s followed by anchovy which had bumper years in 1988–89. The total catch for all species of pelagic fish is also given and has been remarkably steady by world standards. Source: Official statistics of the Sea Fisheries Research Institute and the *South African fishing industry handbook and buyers guide* (1991).

14.4.3 Rock Lobster Fishery

The landed catch of spiny or rock lobsters is worth some R90-m, which is split between some 3 000–4 000 tons (whole) of west coast rock lobster (*Jasus lalandii*) (R66-m) and since the 1970s some 1 000 tons of deepwater south coast lobster (*Palinurus gilchristi*) (R26-m).[7] The west coast lobster is caught in shallow water in association with rocky bottoms and often kelp beds from the intertidal zone down to a depth of 80 m. Commercial fishermen may land lobsters only at registered fishing harbours such as Slangkop, Hout Bay, Cape Town, Saldanha Bay, St Helena Bay, Lamberts Bay and Port Nolloth. They are caught either by the traditional method of hoop nets, which are baited with fish and left on the bottom for 30–60 minutes at a time before being hauled up to small dinghies, or by means of larger baited rectangular traps which are left on the bottom for 6–24 hours, often in deeper water and using decked vessels with inboard motors. There is also an amateur recreational fishery for the west coast lobster. Amateurs need a licence and, at the time of writing, may catch up to four lobsters per person per day, with a maximum of 16 per boat or vehicle.[8]

The fishery is regulated by means of a TAC, a closed season, a minimum size, and

---

[7] Ibid.

[8] GN R1804 of 27 July 1990.

closed areas. In spite of all the regulatory measures, it remains a controversial fishery, because of the value of the luxury product, and its popularity as an amateur recreational activity. As regards the annual catch, there remains an unknown factor due to poaching activities, and the statistical returns of amateurs are not yet reliable, making analysis of the fishery difficult. During the 1980s, however, the commercial catch remained fairly steady at 4 000 tons, having previously plateaued at 10 000 tons in the period 1950–65, and at about 6 000 tons from 1967–80.[9] Catches decreased from the north southwards and, until the 1990s the Dassen Island area remained the most productive lobster ground. In 1990–91 catches declined to some 3 000 tons after a stable period.[10] The poor catches appear to be related to the slow growth and reduced availability of black and ribbed mussels, the main items in the lobster's diet. Certainly the problem is related to the lobster's rate of growth into the legal catchable size, as there is an abundance of small lobsters. There are different views among scientists as to whether the reduction in catches is attributable to natural environmental variations or whether it is part of a long-term trend allied to overfishing, or both.

The south coast rock lobster fishery uses larger vessels and round, baited plastic traps to fish over rocky bottoms in deeper water. The fishing grounds occur from south of Mossel Bay on the Agulhas Bank to the Ciskei coast in water 90–170 m deep. Lobsters are processed and the tails separated from the body and frozen at sea, unlike the west coast fishery. Vessels operate out of Port Elizabeth and Cape Town and tend to stay at sea for weeks on end.

Another deepwater spiny lobster is the basis of a small fishery out of Durban. This is the related *Palinurus delagoae* which is trawled at certain times of the year on soft sea bottoms from Maputo in Mozambique to Durban at the shelf edge in water 180–300 m deep. Inshore there is another fishery for the tropical shallow-water lobster *Panulirus homarus*, which inhabits rocky and coral reefs. This tends to be largely an artisanal[11] and recreational fishery from the rocks in shallow subtidal and intertidal warm water, and extends from Beira to Transkei coast.

14.4.4 Squid Fishery

Chokka squid (*Loligo vulgaris reynaudii*) are caught by three different fisheries: by the inshore and deep-sea trawl fisheries as a by-catch and, more recently, by a jigging fishery targetted at squid that has developed since 1983. In 1989 and 1990, a total of some 4 000–6 000 tons of squid was caught at a wholesale value of some R50-million.[12] Chokka spawn on the south coast in semi-protected bays between False Bay in the west and Port Alfred in the east.[13] The jig fishery is conducted when squid aggregate into schools and move inshore to spawn on sandy sea bottoms. Jigging involves attracting the squid using bait or lights at night to a ring of hooks or spikes which are periodically jerked to hook the squid, either manually on a handline or by machine. It is conducted from small vessels and ski-boats out of fishing harbours and launching ramps along the southeast coast. The spawning season is protracted, but the squid are believed to die soon after spawning. Most squid are fast-growing and believed to be short-lived, with a lifespan of 1–2 years. They are thus susceptible to rapid fluctuations in stock size due to changes in environmental conditions, and these fluctuations are likely to be aggravated by heavy exploitation. Soon after the jig fishery developed and expanded rapidly in 1983–85, regulations were introduced to limit the number of squid taken by unlicensed boats and the number of squid licenses issued to prevent the new industry

---

[9] Payne & Crawford above n 2.
[10] *Composition and size of the South African fishing industry* above n 1.
[11] ie traditional fishery using primitive apparatus and conducted by peasants.
[12] *Composition and size of the South African fishing industry* above n 1.
[13] Payne & Crawford above n 2.

over-investing. Catches started to fluctuate, and reduced catch rates by both jiggers and trawlers suggest that the squid fishery is unlikely to yield more than 3 000–5 000 tons per year on a sustainable basis. The jigging industry voluntarily closed the season for six weeks in November 1991 to prevent overfishing the spawning stock.

14.4.5 Line Fishery

The commercial line fishery is an industry whose origins can be traced back to before the arrival at the Cape of Jan van Riebeeck.[14] The fishery is a varied and complex one, being spread over so many species of fish right around the whole coast. Some 20 000 tons of fish are caught by line from small boats, ranging from open dinghies through ski boats to 20 m or longer decked vessels which can stay at sea for days and even weeks. The total wholesale value of the catch was some R100-million in 1989 and 1990. The most important components of the fishery are snoek (*Thyrsites atun*), tuna, kabeljou (kob) and yellowtail. Tuna are caught on long-lines—lengths of line which may reach several kilometres and carry hundreds or thousands of baited hooks—which are deployed by anchoring one or more buoys, paying out the line and then hauling it in by winch after 10 or more hours. This technique was also used to catch kingklip in a large-scale commercial experiment using long lines on the bottom in the late 1980s.

Catches of kingklip soared initially and large hake were also caught, but after about five years catch rates declined and it became apparent that the adult breeding stock, which tends to spawn over rocky grounds over the continental shelf, was being badly affected. Catch rates were also rapidly reduced to about one-fifth their previous level in the traditional deep-sea trawl fishery for kingklip.[15] It appears that at least part of the adult spawning stock was protected from the trawl fishery, which can only operate on soft sea bottoms, because they occurred over rock. With the advent of long-lining, these fish became available to the fishery and rapidly reduced both the size and the spawning potential of the stock. Permits for long-lining on the sea bottom for kingklip and hake were withdrawn in late 1990, but it is likely that the slow-growing kingklip will take decades to recover. At the time of writing there are persistent rumours that illegal long-lines are being directed at hake, because a legal loop-hole makes prosecution under the regulations difficult. There are fears that, if this is not rectified, hake, the traditional mainstay of the trawling industry, may eventually suffer a decline similar to the one the slower-growing and more valuable kingklip underwent.

Most of the traditional line fishery is based on hand lines, bearing one or two baited hooks and conducted from small fishing vessels on short trips lasting from hours to a few days. Many of the fish are migratory predators on smaller fish, such as anchovy and sardine, with life cycles that are attuned to the ocean currents and movements of their prey. Much of the fishery is located on the south coast, targeting the fish (e g steenbras, red stumpnose, kob) that spawn off the Transkei coast relying on the Agulhas Current to carry their eggs and larvae to the Agulhas Bank where they grow to adulthood before migrating inshore and eastwards to spawn. Similarly, the cool-water snoek frequent the west coast and probably exploit the Benguela Current and its inshore counter-current in the same way.[16]

Management of the multi-species line fishery is complex. Some of the more abundant fish are unrestricted as they are not considered to be vulnerable under strong fishing pressure. These include kob, chub mackerel, horse mackerel, snoek and carpenter. Others are 'restricted' and have bag and minimum size limits for all except commercial and semi-commercial fishermen (e g geelbek and hottentot). A third category consists of 'protected' species which are vulnerable and heavily exploited, including red

[14] Ibid.
[15] *Composition and size of the South African fishing industry* above n 1.
[16] For more details see Payne & Crawford above n 2.

stumpnose, red roman and other highly prized indigenous fish. Both recreational and semi-commercial fishermen are subject to bag and minimum-size limits. 'Critical' species are protected by enforcing control measures (closed seasons, bag and minimum-size limits) on all fishermen. These fish are: elf, galjoen, red steenbras and seventy-four.[17]

14.4.6 Abalone Fishery

Abalone or perlemoen (*Haliotis midae*) are caught by divers in shallow subtidal kelp beds, usually less than 10 m deep. Commercial divers operate from small dinghies or ski-boats wearing wet suits using hookah apparatus from an air compressor on the boat, but amateur divers may not use any breathing apparatus. Abalone are prised off the rock surface using a strong screwdriver or flattened rod. The geographic range of commercial stocks is very limited; effectively from Cape Hangklip at the eastern edge of False Bay, to Quoin Point near Cape Agulhas. Less dense populations extend as far east as Transkei and up the west coast past Saldanha Bay, but productivity is believed to be inhibited by warm temperatures in the east, and cool temperatures, which reduce the growth rate, in the west.[18]

The commercial fishery harvests some 600 tons annually, worth R24,8 million (wholesale value) in 1990.[19] The flesh is the most valuable South African seafood per kilogram, and most of the catch is exported either canned or frozen, to Japan and other countries in the east. The value of the product creates a potential for poaching which is a known problem of unknown magnitude in the fishery. The fishery has records going back to 1953, with peak catches of nearly 3 000 tons in 1965. This was undoubtedly beyond the maximum sustainable yield, but the commercial catch has been fairly stable at about 600 tons since 1971.[20] Management is based on a minimum size (11,43 cm breadth), a TAC, closed areas and a licensing system for both commercial and amateur fishermen. While commercial catches and catch rates in the main area have remained fairly constant, suggesting a stable resource, amateur catches have become increasingly difficult at the popular sites. Amateur fishermen have been controlled by licence and a bag limit of four abalone per person per day since 1988, but reliable statistics of how many abalone amateur divers really collect are not yet available. Thus the extent of the amateur harvest and poaching are not yet known, frustrating scientific managment of the resource. Recent studies at the University of Cape Town have shown that the stable isotopes of carbon and nitrogen in the flesh of abalone provide a 'signature' which is specific to particular parts of the coast. This information is likely to be of great value in prosecuting poachers who claim to have caught their abalone legally in different parts of the country.[21]

14.5 MARINE LAW

14.5.1 International Law of the Sea

14.5.1.1 *Introduction*

South African law relating to the marine environment has been shaped and influenced by the international law of the sea, which, in turn, is inseparable from international law generally. See chapter 9 for a full discussion of international law. International law of the sea historically dates back to virtually the dawn of civilization and was initially developed around the two traditional uses of the sea: fishing and

---

[17] The regulations current in 1989 are summarized by Penney et al in Payne & Crawford above n 2. Revisions are published annually in booklet form.

[18] Payne & Crawford above n 2.

[19] *Composition and size of the South African fishing industry* above n 1.

[20] Payne & Crawford above n 2.

[21] C Parkins, N Sweijd & P A Cook, Zoology Department, University of Cape Town, pers comm.

navigation. Major impetus for development of the subject occurred from the 16th century onwards, which saw the era of global exploration, the discovery of the New World and the colonization of new lands, all of which necessitated greater development of international law and relations.

Hugo Grotius (1583–1645), commonly regarded as the father of modern international law, had a profound influence on the development of the law of the sea. Interestingly, he is linked to the southern African subcontinent both because his great work, *Mare liberum*, published in 1609, was written in order to vindicate the claims of the Dutch East India Company to trade in the Far East and because he also shaped the private law of the then Province of Holland which was later to find its way into contemporary South African law.

The two chief sources of international law of the sea are international customary law and international conventions. See chapter 9. In customary international law are found fundamental norms such as the freedom of the high seas doctrine, applicable to areas beyond national jurisdiction. These comprise freedom of navigation, freedom of fishing, freedom to conduct scientific research, freedom of overflight and so on. These freedoms must, however, be exercised with due regard to the interests of other states.[22] There are also international customary norms dealing with pollution of the marine environment.

Customary international law of the sea has proved inadequate to deal with modern exigencies which have seen ever-increasing and sophisticated uses of the sea. These range from deep sea-bed mining, increased fishing effort and marine scientific research to energy utilization. Pollution of the marine environment, particularly of coastal waters, is also a relatively new and serious phenomenon. These developments have resulted in the negotiation and drafting of many international conventions dealing with the marine environment ranging from controlling the exploitation of marine resources to controlling various forms of pollution. In general, one can distinguish between general multilateral treaties, for example, the 1982 Law of the Sea Convention (LOSC), elaborated on below, regional treaties and bilateral agreements.

The most important general multilateral treaty is the 1982 LOSC which is discussed in chapter 9. In negotiating and drafting LOSC, the international community attempted to consolidate and develop the four 1958 Geneva Conventions dealing with the sea. As South Africa has not ratified LOSC, it continues to rely both on these conventions and customary international law as reflected in LOSC and other sources in its domestic legislation.

The international law of the sea sets out various rules in different maritime zones immediately off the shoreline of coastal states. We now outline these and examine the extent to which these have been incorporated into South African law.

14.5.1.2 *Maritime zones*

A number of maritime zones have been developed in the international law of the sea: internal waters, the territorial sea, the contiguous zone, the exclusive economic zone (exclusive fishing zone), continental shelf and a 'prohibited area'. Beyond these areas subject to national jurisdictions is the high seas which is also to some extent regulated by international law.

The baseline from which various maritime zones are measured is usually the low-water mark, but in certain cases international law permits straight baselines to be drawn from point to point along the coast.[23] The Territorial Waters Act 87 of 1963 calculates baselines from the low-water mark, which it defines as 'the lowest line to

[22] See, generally, Churchill & Lowe *The law of the sea* (2 ed, 1988).
[23] Article 7 of LOSC.

which the water of the sea recedes during periods of ordinary spring tides'.[24] We now discuss these maritime zones in turn.

(a) Internal waters. Internal waters are those which are landward of the baseline. These include estuaries, river mouths, points and bays where these have been closed off.[25]

Internal waters are assimilated to national territory and are subject to the control of the coastal state. The only exception is that foreign ships in distress have a right of entry and do not become subject to coastal state law or control. However, where such a vessel is posing a pollution threat to the coastline, the coastal state may have certain rights in international law to take appropriate action.[26]

The Marine Traffic Act 2 of 1981 defines 'internal waters' as the waters landward of the normal baseline as well as harbours, fishing harbours and seven named bays.[27] Although the Act lists seven bays, curiously no straight baselines have been drawn across them.[28] The Act also defines 'harbour' and 'fishing harbour' and according to international law, their outer perimeters may be used as baselines.[29] The Act also regulates entry and departure from internal waters and provides for regulations to be made in this regard.[30]

(b) Territorial waters. The most important maritime zone is the territorial sea. In it a coastal state may exercise complete sovereignty just as on its land territory. The implication is that everybody and everything in the territorial sea is subject to coastal state law and control. The exception to this rule is that foreign vessels have a right of innocent passage through the territorial sea.[31]

For centuries the legal nature and extent of coastal state's power over the territorial sea was disputed.[32] The physical extent of the territorial sea has also not been constant. Traditionally, it was 3 nautical miles, but today it is generally accepted that coastal states may claim 12 nautical miles from the baseline.[33] South Africa has claimed a territorial sea of 12 nautical miles under the Territorial Waters Act.[34]

What constitutes innocent passage is also a controversial question.[35] The Marine Traffic Act defines 'innocent passage' as 'passage which is not prejudicial to the peace, good order or security of the Republic' and provides that every ship (by implication also warships) shall enjoy the right of innocent passage through the territorial waters.[36] Innocent passage may be temporarily suspended provided that it does not discriminate between foreign ships.[37]

(c) The contiguous zone. International law grants coastal states enforcement but not legislative jurisdiction in a zone immediately seaward of the territorial sea.[38] This zone is known as the contiguous zone and may extend under international law to 24 nautical

---

[24] Section 1.

[25] International law permits bays whose mouths are not wider than 24 nautical miles wide to be closed off: art 8 of LOSC.

[26] Cf Devine 'The Cape's False Bay: a possible haven for ships in distress' 1990–91 *SAYIL* (in press).

[27] In terms of s 1 the seven named bays are Walvis Bay, Saldanha Bay, Hout Bay, False Bay, the Knysna Lagoon, the Bay of Natal and Richards Bay.

[28] See Devine, 'Bays, baselines, passage and pollution in South African waters' 1986 *CILSA* 85.

[29] Article 11 of LOSC.

[30] Section 4. Such regulations have been passed: GN R194 of 1 February 1985.

[31] This right is uncontroversial in the case of merchant ships but some doubt exists in the case of warships; it exists in the interests of freedom of navigation.

[32] See Churchill & Lowe, above n 22, ch 4.

[33] Article 3 of LOSC.

[34] Section 2.

[35] See Churchill & Lowe above n 22, 51.

[36] Section 2. This right extends to submarines provided that they navigate on the surface and show their flags: art 11 of LOSC and s 3 of the Act.

[37] Article 25(3) of LOSC and s 7 of the Act.

[38] Article 33 of LOSC.

miles from the baseline.[39] A coastal state cannot make laws in this zone but can enforce its customs, fiscal, immigration and health laws in it. Thus, if a foreign vessel commits an offence in respect of any of such subjects in the territorial sea, it may be possible to arrest it in the contiguous zone.

Neither the Marine Traffic Act nor the Territorial Waters Act defines the contiguous zone for purposes of South African law. The latter Act does, however, claim a 200 nautical mile contiguous zone[40] which is well beyond that allowed by international law.[41]

(d) The exclusive fishing zone. In the exclusive fishing zone a coastal state enjoys sovereignty over living marine resources. Historically, international law did not recognize such a zone, but since the middle of this century pressure for international-law recognition of such a zone—as well as for increasing its territorial extent—grew.[42] International law has extended the concept beyond an exclusive fishing zone and recognized a 200 nautical mile exclusive economic zone in which coastal states exercise sovereignty over all resources, ie including non-living natural resources found on or under the sea-bed.[43]

The South African legislature has confined itself to simply claiming a 200 nautical mile exclusive fishing zone[44] and has not claimed an exclusive economic zone. It is not prejudiced thereby, because it exercises jurisdiction over minerals under the sea-bed by virtue of the continental shelf doctrine. Foreigners exercise fishing rights in South Africa's exclusive fishing zone under the Sea Fishery Act 12 of 1988.[45] South Africa's fishing resources and the law governing their exploitation and conservation are described in para 14.5.2 below.

(e) The continental shelf. The continental margin physically comprises the continental shelf, slope and rise. The continental shelf is that section which slopes down gradually from the low-water mark to a depth of about 100–300 m (see para 14.1 above). It is essentially a shallow platform adjacent to the land mass. The section bordering the shelf and having a steeper slope and descending to up to 3 500 m is known as the continental slope. Beyond the slope is the continental rise which is a gentler falling away of the sea-bed resulting from sediments having been washed down from the continents. It is the legal continental shelf that is of concern here.

The continental shelf doctrine grants coastal states sovereignty over natural resources on or under the sea-bed. The legal continental shelf has not always coincided with the physical continental shelf.[46] It originated with the Truman proclamation of 1945, when the President of the United States proclaimed that the natural resources of the subsoil and sea-bed of the continental shelf beneath the high seas, but contiguous to the coasts of the United States, appertained to that country. Other countries followed suit and the adoption of the 1958 Geneva Convention on the Continental Shelf established that coastal states enjoyed sovereignty over the resources of the shelf, but preserved the status of the waters over it as high seas. The extent of coastal states' legal continental shelf was open-ended in that, although it referred to the 200 m isobath, it also referred

[39] Article 33.
[40] Section 4.
[41] It seems that this was done inadvertently, because the relevant section cross-refers to another section which deals with the fishing zone, which was previously 12 nautical miles and subsequently extended to 200 nautical miles. Section 4 claims the right to exercise any powers necessary for the contravention of any fiscal, customs, emigration or health laws in the fishing zone referred to in s 3. Prior to the 1977 amendment of the Territorial Waters Act the fishing zone was only 12 nautical miles.
[42] See Churchill & Lowe above n 22, chs 9 and 14.
[43] See part V of LOSC.
[44] Section 3 of the Territorial Waters Act.
[45] Section 52.
[46] See Churchill & Lowe above n 22, ch 8.

to an exploitability criterion which obviously increased with technological developments. The recognition subsequently of an exclusive economic zone (EEZ) granting sovereignty over all resources within 200 nautical miles has resulted in an overlap between these two legal regimes.

South Africa is accordingly not prejudiced by the fact that it has not declared an EEZ because it has an exclusive fishing zone and has ratified the Geneva Convention on the Continental Shelf. The Territorial Waters Act deems the continental shelf to be part of the Republic and provides that in so far as exploitation of natural resources is concerned, South African mining law, which applies to that part of the country immediately adjoining the continental shelf, will also apply to mining in this area[47]. It deems the continental shelf to be unalienated state land for this purpose.

(f) The prohibited zone. While all the zones dealt with above are part of international customary law, the prohibited zone emanates from an international marine pollution control treaty, the Convention on Prevention of Pollution from Ships, 1973, 1978. The convention provides for a 'prohibited area' of 50 nautical miles from the baseline and prohibits any operational discharge of oil in that zone. Whereas international law grants rights in other zones, here it curtails them.

The South African legislature has defined 'prohibited area' in the Prevention and Combating of Pollution of the Sea by Oil Act 6 of 1981[48] and has adopted the above-mentioned convention in the International Convention for the Prevention of Pollution from Ships Act 2 of 1986. See chapter 18.

It is evident from the above that adjoining or opposite coastal states may have to delimit their respective maritime zones. Thus, where opposite states are less than 400 nautical miles apart, they will have to locate the extent of their respective EEZs. The position can be complicated by the existence of islands belonging to one or other state. International law of the sea has developed a number of principles in this regard. These principles assumed practical importance with the independence of Namibia in 1990. The existence of twelve 'penguin' islands off the Namibian coast but which belong to South Africa complicated the matter.[49]

14.5.2 Fisheries

14.5.2.1 *Introduction*

In Roman and Roman-Dutch law fish (indeed, all wild animals) were classified as res nullius, ie objects which were not owned but were capable of private ownership. Ownership is acquired by occupatio, which entails taking physical control of the object together with having the intention of becoming owner.[50]

This common-law position has been fundamentally changed by statute. Historically, the main legislation governing fisheries has been the Sea Fisheries Acts 10 of 1940 and 58 of 1973. The exploitation and conservation of fisheries is currently regulated by the Sea Fishery Act 12 of 1988 and detailed regulations made under it.[51] The definition of 'fish' in this Act is very broad—wide enough to include whales and dolphins within its scope.[52] The exploitation and conservation of seals and sea birds is governed by separate legislation, ie the Sea Birds and Seals Protection Act 46 of 1973.

---

[47] Section 7.
[48] Section 1.
[49] See Devine 'Delimitation between the penguin islands and Namibia: some possible principles' 1989–90 *SAYIL* 122.
[50] See, generally, Van der Merwe *Sakereg* (2 ed, 1989) 217–22.
[51] The standing regulations are GN R1804 to R1811 of 27 July 1990.
[52] See Glazewski 'The regulation of whaling in international and South African law' 1990–91 *SAYIL* (in press).

While in the past these Acts were administered by non-conservation-oriented departments,[53] they are currently administered by the Chief Directorate: Sea Fisheries of the Department of Environment Affairs. The chief directorate comprises a research division, the Sea Fisheries Research Institute (SFRI) and an administrative and economic division. The enforcement of fisheries legislation is, however, carried out by the provincial authorities. Thus the law-enforcement section of the Cape Provincial Department of Nature and Environmental Conservation has a Marine Control Division.

South African legislation has to some extent been shaped by various commissions of inquiry which have investigated different aspects of the industry over the years. The most recent report was the *Report of the commission of inquiry into the allocation of quotas for the exploitation of living marine resources* (the Diemont Commission), which sat in 1986 and whose recommendations were to some extent incorporated into the 1988 Act.[54] Other relevant reports of commissions of inquiry have been the *Report of the commission of inquiry into the fishing industry, the utilization of fish and other living marine resources of South Africa and South West Africa* (the Du Plessis Commission of 1972),[55] the *Report of the commission of inquiry into certain aspects of the conservation and utilization of the living marine resources of the RSA* (the Treurnicht Commission of 1980),[56] and the *Final report of the scientific committee of enquiry into the exploitation of pelagic fish resources of South Africa and South West Africa* (the Alant Commission of 1983—not published).

Apart from national legislation, the respective provincial nature conservation ordinances also need to be considered, as will be shown below.

14.5.2.2 *International law aspects*

International law regulating marine fisheries falls into two distinct phases: prior to the mid-1970s it was characterized by the recognition of narrow fisheries zones (usually 12 nautical miles) in which coastal states enjoyed exclusive jurisdiction over fisheries in international law. At this time, international co-operation in fisheries management was effected through over 20 international fisheries commissions which had jurisdiction beyond the 12 nautical mile zones. These were established to regulate either particular species, for example ICCAT (the International Commission for the Conservation of Atlantic Tuna), or particular areas, for example NEAFC (North East Atlantic Fisheries Commission). South Africa was an active member of ICSEAF (International Commission for the South East Atlantic Fisheries), which comprised 18 member states active in fishing practices in a defined area off southern African waters. ICSEAF's area of jurisdiction covered the sea off Angola, Namibia (then South West Africa) and South Africa.[57] It was mainly concerned with the hake fishery.

After the mid-1970s, international law recognized that coastal states could claim 200 nautical mile EEZs and South Africa exercised its rights in this regard by declaring a 200 nautical mile exclusive fishing zone under the Territorial Waters Act in 1977. South Africa accordingly enjoys full sovereignty over the living resources of the sea up to an extent of 200 nautical miles. The advent of 200 nautical mile zones resulted in the international commissions referred to above becoming superfluous. In the southern African context ICSEAF has become redundant, as not only South Africa but also

---

[53] Cf Grindley, Glazewski & Rabie 'The control of South Africa's living marine resources' 1986 *Acta Juridica* 133, 150–1.
[54] RP 91/1986.
[55] RP 47/1972.
[56] RP 93/1980.
[57] See Gertenbach 'Fishery convention areas in the Southeast Atlantic and the adjacent seas: overlapping issues' 1986 *Acta Juridica* 51.

Angola and Namibia declared sovereignty over the living resources in their respective 200 nautical mile zones, in 1975 and 1990 respectively.

The Sea Fishery Act empowers the State President to enter into agreements with foreign countries to fish in South African waters.[58] South Africa has accordingly entered into a number of agreements with foreign governments permitting them and their nationals to fish in our waters. However, they have to comply with South African law and whatever other conditions the State President may impose when granting such permission.

At this point it would be as well to correct some popular misconceptions concerning the role of foreign fleets in the exploitation of South African fish resources. The purse-seine, rock lobster and line fisheries are all conducted by small fishing vessels, mostly less than 30 m long and generally fishing within sight of land and within the old 12 nautical mile (approx 24 km) limit. These are almost entirely South African vessels fishing quite close to port with almost no foreign involvement. These components of the industry catch about 75 per cent of the tonnage and some 50 per cent of the total South African catch by value.[59] The bottom trawling industry is split in two sectors, an inshore sector of smaller vessels trawling on the inner continental shelf in shallow water, generally less than 150 m depth on the south coast, and a deep-sea trawling sector which uses large vessels to drag the sea floor on the outer shelf and continental slope.[60] It is this deep-sea sector that suffered badly from foreign competition and overfishing in the 1970s before the introduction of the 200 nautical mile (some 400 km) exclusive fishing zone in South African waters in 1977. The hake fishery has been recovering steadily since the early 1980s, and only very limited quotas have been granted to a few foreign states (e g Japan, Israel, Republic of China, Portugal and Spain) for bottom trawling for hake, midwater trawling for horse mackerel on the south coast providing the only useful statistics for managing this new potential fishery, and long-line fishing for tuna. The foreign quotas amount to less than 1 per cent of the total South African catch, yet they bring in a substantial levy which is used for fisheries research and management of the South African fishery. The emotional and irrational public outcry against 'foreigners' pillaging our fisheries has had no basis in fact since the 1970s, apart from a small amount of illegal trespassing within the 200 nautical mile exclusive fishery zone by drift-net fishermen and the occasional bottom trawler. On the contrary, the small quotas allowed to foreign vessels have brought considerable foreign exchange into the country and the relatively heavy levy on foreign catches has provided up to 25 per cent of the Sea Fishery Fund. This fund (previously called the Sea Fisheries Research Fund), was re-established under the Sea Fishery Act of 1988 and is accumulated from levies on fisheries in South African waters. It is used for research into, and the management of, South Africa's fish resources.

14.5.2.3 *Control under the Sea Fishery Act*

Control under the Sea Fishery Act can be broadly divided into two aspects: *(a)* managerial aspects where the concern is those provisions which attempt to incorporate fisheries management principles into the statutory regime and *(b)* criminal aspects—being those provisions which invoke criminal liability if the respective control measures are not complied with. This is a distinction for convenience and obviously the two aspects overlap.

(a) Managerial aspects. A welcome feature of the Act, not contained in it predecessors, is the statutory provision for a general policy regarding the

[58] Section 52.

[59] *Composition and size of the South African fishing industry* above n 1.

[60] Payne & Crawford above n 2.

utilization of the Republic's fishery resources.[61] Provision is made for the statutory incorporation of fisheries management ideals such as the utilization of the resource on a sustainable basis.

The policy is unfortunately not entrenched in the statute but is left to the Minister to declare. To date he has not declared such a policy, but the Department of Environment Affairs takes cognizance of the need to protect and conserve marine ecosystems. It would have been preferable had a general policy have been incorporated into the Act and not left to ministerial discretion. It is particularly appropriate to reflect such a policy in the Act which is passed by Parliament, rather than being left to the discretion of the Minister who is responsible for the implementation of the policy and the day-to-day implementation of the Act.

(b) *Geographic extent.* The Act does not stipulate that it is to apply to a specific geographic area. Rather, it sets out areas where it is not applicable.[62] Thus it is inapplicable to fish found in waters which are not 'sea'.[63] 'Sea' is defined to include the sea-shore and the water and beds of tidal rivers and tidal lagoons.[64] Most South African rivers are not tidal, but some—for example, the Berg, Breede and Knysna rivers—are tidal for a substantial distance inland. The Act is accordingly applicable to fish found in parts of these rivers. However, the Act specifically stipulates that it is not applicable to tidal rivers, lagoons and estuaries in the province of Natal.[65] Here the Natal Nature Conservation Ordinance 15 of 1974, administered by the Natal Parks Board, is applicable.

The Act is also specifically rendered inapplicable to areas 'bordering on the sea' which have been declared to be national parks.[66] This presumably refers to the inter-tidal areas of national parks which straddle both the marine and the terrestrial environments—for example, the Tsitsikamma Forest and Coastal National Park and the West Coast National Park at Langebaan.

As far as the landward extent of application of the Act is concerned, therefore, it generally applies up to the high-water mark, as well as to tidal rivers and lagoons in the Cape Province but not in Natal. As regards its seaward extent, the Act is not specific. It implicitly applies to the sea,[67] but 'sea' is defined simply as the water and bed of the sea.[68] In the Sea-Shore Act 21 of 1935 'sea' is defined as the territorial sea, i e 12 nautical miles, but in the Sea Fishery Act it presumably refers to all waters up to 200 nautical miles, the extent of South Africa's exclusive fishing zone.[69]

(c) *The need for fisheries management.* Historically, the sea's resources were regarded as inexhaustible. Even Grotius, the father of international law, assumed this to be the case. However, in recent times the global fishing community has seen some spectacular collapses in different sectors of the industry. As regards southern African waters, the abundant pelagic resources located in the Benguela Upwelling System off the southern African west coast declined dramatically in the sixties and early seventies. For example, the South African annual pilchard catch peaked at 400 000 tons in 1963, having quadrupled average catches of previous years. But annual catches declined dramatically thereafter to reach an all-time low of 16 000 tons in 1974.[70] Similarly, in Namibian (then

[61] Section 2.
[62] Section 3.
[63] Section 3*(a)*.
[64] Section 1.
[65] Section 3*(b)*.
[66] Section 3*(c)*.
[67] Section 3.
[68] Section 1.
[69] See s 52(4).
[70] Branch & Branch *The living shores of southern Africa* (1983) 120.

South West African) waters the annual catch declined from 1 400 000 tons in 1968 to 500 000 tons in 1972 in the face of heavy international exploitation[71] (see para 14.4.1 above).

In the wake of the dramatic escalation in fishing effort which has occurred globally since the Second World War, there has been a general tendency to move away from allowing open access to fisheries resources and to imposing some form of control over exploitation by limiting access to the resource. Limited access can be achieved by market-based mechanisms or by reliance on state control, or by a combination of methods. Whatever the approach, the central authorities have to establish the TAC for a particular species, area and season.

In South Africa, as in most fishing nations, control has been achieved by extensive state intervention in controlling access to the resource or the quantity caught. This is reflected in the legislation elaborated on below.

(d) Managerial tools. Two key aspects of fisheries management are the need to limit the quantity of the resources being exploited at a particular time in a particular area and the allocation of the right to exploit the particular resource to a number of interested parties. The former entails establishing what the optimal catch tonnage should be (the TAC) and imposing a number of established managerial techniques to achieve this. For example, limitation of effort (eg the number of vessels allowed), imposing seasons, establishing closed areas, imposing gear specifications (eg mesh size) and size limitations, and laying down a TAC for individual species.

The last-mentioned decision entails allocating the right to exploit among a number of competing parties. This is normally done by the allocation of the quota (TAC) among interested persons. The setting of the TAC essentially involves determining the size of the allowable catch for a particular species in a particular area. The allocation of quotas entails deciding who will obtain what proportion of the TAC. The first decision entails determining the size of the cake, the second deciding who gets what size of slice.

Traditionally, the approach by the South African legislature has been to leave both these decisions, the determination of the TAC and its allocation, to the discretion of the Minister of Environment Affairs, assisted by the Sea Fishery Advisory Committee (SFAC) (previously the Sea Fisheries Advisory Council). Thus the Act provides that the Minister may, after consulting the advisory committee, prohibit the catching of fish in general or in a defined area and by specified persons or persons belonging to a particular class.[72] More pertinently, it also provides that the Minister may, after consulting the advisory committee, prohibit licensees from catching a greater quantity than a specified quantity of any fish or fish belonging to a particular species.[73] This in essence means that he can determine the TAC.

As regards the second aspect—the allocation of quotas—the current Act makes a marked departure from previous legislation by providing for a separate body, the Quota Board.[74] The advent of this board was a direct result of the investigations of the Diemont Commission, which recommended that the allocation function be placed in a separate body presided over by a person with a judicial background.

The advice given by the SFAC is accordingly crucial for determining the TAC, although legally the Minister is required only to consult it, not necessarily to implement its advice. The SFAC is established under of the Act[75] and has the potential to play an important role in fisheries management. The SFAC consists of the number of persons appointed by the Minister who, in his opinion, possess the necessary expertise in their

---

[71] Branch & Branch above n 70.
[72] Section 33(1).
[73] Section 35(1)*(a)*.
[74] Cf part V, ss 15–24.
[75] Sections 7–12.

relevant fields of study to make a substantial contribution towards the functions of the advisory committee.[76] Ideally, it should represent different interest groups such as the fishing industry, fisheries scientists and perhaps fisheries conservationists and those employed in the fishing industry. The Alant Commission critically analysed the composition of the old Sea Fisheries Advisory Council since its inception and made some positive recommendations in this regard.[77]

The SFAC receives scientific advice from the Director of the SFRI and his senior scientists responsible for research into the various fisheries. The SFRI convenes scientific working groups for each of the major fisheries with input from outside academic scientists. It also liaises with the appropriate sector of the industry concerning proposed TACs and other management measures. Ideally, industry, labour and scientists should be involved in a consensus management plan for each fishery, with revision at 4 or 5-year intervals. Once management plans are established, it should be a fairly technical matter to optimize the measures needed to implement the plans for each fishery, using a variety of mathematical models that are now available. Some progress has been made along this route, and basic management strategies have been formulated jointly by scientists and industry for the management of anchovy, for example.

Having heard the advice of the Director of the SFRI, his senior scientists and the appropriate working groups, the SFAC, which includes members of the fishing industry, makes recommendations to the Minister, who may take other factors into account in deciding whether or not to modify the advice given to him.

The Quota Board has been in operation only since 1991, having been preceded by an interim quota board. The Act implemented some but not all of the Diemont Commission's recommendations; it also modified them to some extent. For example, while placing the allocation function in the board, the Act provides for granting and termination of rights of exploitation. This empowers the Minister to determine who obtains a right of exploitation and to review and grant such rights to aspirant new applicants to the industry.[78]

(e) Licensing of fishing boats, factories and implements. The Act contains a number of provisions which in essence enable the Minister to limit fishing efforts. A fundamental control mechanism is the licensing requirement. No person may use any vessel as a fishing boat, or any premises, vehicle or vessel as a factory, unless it has been licensed under the Act.[79] The relevant provision also sets out in some detail circumstances under which the Director-General may refuse a licence, conditions which may be imposed and other details.[80] The standing regulations set out in more detail licensing requirements for fishing boats, factories and premises[81] as well as provisions regarding implements, mesh size, etc.[82]

This Minister is also empowered to impose gear specifications. He may therefore prohibit the use of any implement for the catching of fish or designated species of fish unless the implement is licensed in the prescribed manner.[83] Furthermore, he is

[76] Section 5*(x)*.
[77] Para 7.2.2 of its report.
[78] Section 25. See, generally, Cole 'Functions of the Quota Board established in terms of the Sea Fishery Act 1988' 1989 (9) *Sea Changes* 43.
[79] Section 30(1).
[80] Section 30(4)–(7). See also Cole 'A review of the provisions relating to licences and permits issued in terms of the Sea Fishery Act 1988' 1988 (8) *Sea Changes* 39.
[81] Parts II and III GN R1804 of 27 July 1990.
[82] Part VIII GN R1804 of 27 July 1990.
[83] Section 31.

empowered to pass regulations specifying the methods whereby fish belonging to a particular species may be caught.[84]

(f) Marine reserves. As regards area limitations, the Act empowers the Minister to set aside an area as a marine reserve for the protection within such reserve of fish in general or fish belonging to a particular species, or any aquatic plant.[85] In accordance with these powers, the following marine reserves have been declared: Walvis Bay, Rocher Pan, Millers Point, HF Verwoerd, De Hoop, Goukamma, Robberg, Sardinia Bay, Trafalgar, St Lucia and Maputaland.[86]

The positive contribution played by marine reserves in conserving marine resources is recognized among fisheries biologists, although their precise role is sometimes controversial among fishermen. A fundamental distinction can be made between a 'pure' marine reserve—in essence a sanctuary, where no exploitation, interference or disturbance of the marine ecology is permitted—and other 'limited' reserves where the exploitation of only certain species is prohibited. It has been demonstrated that the De Hoop Reserve near Cape Infanta has enabled the recovery of angling fish.[87] A mathematical model is being developed to calculate the optimal size and spacing of such reserves for angling fish. See, generally, as regards protected areas, chapter 27.

14.5.3 Marine Pollution

Virtually all forms of pollution and waste find their way to the sea.[88] The legal control of pollution of the marine environment is generally classified under the following distinct, but not logical heads: pollution from maritime activities (particularly shipping); the intentional dumping of matter at sea; pollution from land-based sources, and pollution from offshore mining activities. These issues are dealt with in chapter 18 and also to some extent in chapters 9 and 16.

14.6 CONCLUSION

South Africa's unique geographic proximity to three of the world's oceans, the Indian, Atlantic and Southern, presents great challenges and potentials. The country has access to vast living and non-living resources and the potential to conduct research of global significance, and responsibility to control pollution off the hazardous coastline. In general, the country has a well-developed legal and administrative infrastructure and succeeds in managing the area successfully. It has followed developments in international law of the sea and incorporated these into domestic legislation where appropriate. Increased momentum for international and regional co-operation will no doubt occur with political changes in South Africa. Thus it is conceivable that South Africa might become a key player in the development of a regional seas programme for southern Africa under the auspices of the United Nations Environment Programme. Regional seas conventions have been entered into in many other areas, as shown in chapter 9 above.

The optimal use of living marine resources requires constant interaction and liaison between those researching fisheries and those responsible for implementation of marine policy. For example, some research currently underway suggests that the traditional approach to managing the rock lobster resource may not be optimal. Historically, since the 1930s, the catch has been limited to taking lobster above a certain size (normally 89

[84] Section 45(1)*(c)*.

[85] Section 34(1)*(a)*.

[86] The location and extent of each of these reserves is set out in the standing regulations, which also set out specific prohibitions in each of them: regs 3–6 GN R1819 of 27 July 1990.

[87] See Bennett & Attwood 'Evidence for recovery of a surf-zone fish assemblage following the establishment of a marine reserve on the southern coast of South Africa' 1991 (75) *Mar Ecol Prog Ser* 173–81.

[88] Brown 'Marine pollution and health in South Africa' 1987 (71) *SAMJ* 244.

mm in length), but new research suggests that, in theory, it may be economically and ecologically better to take lobster from a broader size range. This raises additional problems of enforcement, since, if the fishery were opened to smaller size-classes of lobster, a much larger section of the lobster population would be vulnerable to legal exploitation and the adult spawning stock might become threatened. The new proposal hinges upon being able to enforce a strict TAC, in both the commercial and the amateur fisheries. If poaching were to become more difficult to curb because more of the stock became accessible, the whole proposal might result in disaster. This illustrates the need for research and implementation to proceed in close liaison, as indeed is the case with the SFRI being located in the Chief Directorate of Sea Fisheries.

It is clear that fisheries management in particular requires close co-operation between experts in fisheries management techniques, the industry and the Department of Environment Affairs, which is responsible for the implementation of fisheries management decisions. It has been seen that the Minister of Environment Affairs in particular has been granted wide discretionary powers under the Sea Fishery Act to carry out fishery management advice, which is increasingly based upon complex mathematical models. A heavy responsibility rests on his shoulders in this regard.

Fisheries management will no doubt come under the spotlight in the current climate of political change in South Africa. Traditional debates in the fisheries management community as to whether fisheries should be managed as open or closed-access resources will have to be examined against the background of broader policy decisions which will be made about the management of and access to, the country's resources generally. Under the present regime, scientific advice about management measures is subjected to close scrutiny, and quantitative justification is, for instance, required for the tonnages recommended for TACs. Fisheries science has become very quantitative. The same is not true of arguments made on socio-economic grounds, along the lines that people might be retrenched because of reduced TACs, for example. These arguments are generally presented in a broad, qualitative framework and, in the final analysis, the Minister has to make up his mind on the basis of conflicting evidence presented from different quarters. A greater involvement of sociologists, economists and hard socio-economic data will be required for rational decision-making in the future.

It is said that with the Voortrekker era last century, South Africans turned their backs to the sea and searched inland for new resources. With the advent of a 200 nautical mile EEZ towards the end of this century, it may be that in future years South Africa will have to look increasingly to the sea for the development of its economy and ultimately the welfare of all its people.

CHAPTER 15

TERRESTRIAL MINERALS

J D WELLS
L H VAN MEURS
M A RABIE

15.1 INTRODUCTION

Since they first started to use stone tools, humans have been dependent on minerals contained in or on the earth. This dependence has increased as we have evolved to our present industrialized status, to the point today where our livelihood is utterly dependent on mining.

Our dependence on modern mineral-derived artifacts and on energy is not going to decrease. Indeed, population growth and increasing standards of living will increase our dependence on both. Mining companies worldwide, and specially in mineral-blessed South Africa, are entrusted with the task of satisfying this demand, as are farmers entrusted with satisfying our food needs.

However, unlike farming where there is a choice of where and what to grow, mining can take place only where minerals occur. The choice between alternatives comes in the consideration of mining methods, location of mine infrastructure and waste deposit sites, and the sources of power, water and raw materials needed for mining. Mitigation of environmental impacts by moving a mine to a more environmentally suitable site cannot therefore be considered, as would be the case for most other development projects.

Another important aspect to consider is that mining is very often a temporary land-use. This is unlike almost all other developments which permanently alienate land from its original use. Being a true extractive industry, mining cannot be sustainable at one place because the deposit is finite and therefore is eventually exhausted.

Thus it is important to evaluate the residual biophysical environmental impacts of mining, after the operation has stopped, to arrive at a true measure of this impact. The residual impact results from a comparison of the 'before' and 'after' conditions rather than comparing the 'before' and 'during' situation. Evaluation of the residual impact must therefore take into account the mitigation measures that are implemented—for example, surface rehabilitation.

The overall environmental impact must also consider the economic and social impacts of a mining operation. Usually these impacts are positive (for instance, creating wealth and jobs; earning foreign exchange; providing housing, roads, power, water and other infrastructure in remote areas; providing training; a multiplier effect estimated at R4 injected into the economy for every R1 spent on the mine), but they can also be negative (such as adversely affecting local communities; being subject to global commodity failures and therefore premature closure with attendant job losses). This chapter does not, however, consider the socio-economic impacts of mining. These aspects are discussed in chapters 3 and 4.

Unfortunately, the argument of mining being a temporary land-use does not apply to some mining waste deposits. These usually permanently alienate land and, although they can be used for other purposes, their impact must be considered in the same light as other developments that alienate land.

An issue to bear in mind when considering the environmental impacts of mining is the total area of land that is affected and the water consumed. Only 1 per cent of the RSA is used for mining and in 1990 only 2,7 per cent of the country's water was used by the mining industry (which includes land and water used for processing the minerals).[1]

Although the magnitude of the impact on each hectare or cubic metre of water used may be higher than that of other sectors, the total impact of mining in the South African environment is small compared to other sectors.

Another issue to keep in mind is that optimum resource utilization is a philosophy which guides all responsible mining companies. In practice this means that as much as possible of a mineral deposit must be extracted but constrained by safety, environmental and economic considerations, because the deposits will one day run out.

How, then, do we mine with environmental sensitivity? The major environmental impacts associated with mining result from:

- The mining method used.
- The nature of the mineral itself.
- Mine residue deposits.

This chapter considers the biophysical environmental impacts of these three aspects and how they can be mitigated so as to minimize any residual negative impacts. The major mining methods are briefly described to indicate the principles involved rather than to give a detailed description, since no two mines, even when using the same method, are identical. Since each mine is site specific in its environmental impacts, only the type of residual impact is described in order to provide some insight into what to look for when considering mining proposals. The nature of the minerals and their occurrence are briefly described as these can have impacts of their own. Since mine residue deposits constitute one of the main environmental impacts of mining, they are discussed separately along with state-of-the-art mitigating measures.

The impacts associated with mine infrastructure such as the construction of headgears, reduction works, offices and mine housing are not discussed, since they are well understood and are not significantly different from those resulting from the construction of any other built environment.

Environmental management is fully integrated with mine management which plans, constructs, operates and finally closes down mining operations.

15.2 INDUSTRY GUIDELINES

15.2.1 *Introduction*

Parallel to the rapidly changing legal aspects covered in this chapter, the mining industry itself, through the leadership of the Chamber of Mines, has been pro-active in ensuring that mining activities do not unreasonably impact on the environment. Two examples of this are given below.

Research into using vegetation to prevent wind-blown dust coming from gold sand dumps and slimes dams was started by the Chamber in 1951. Ten years later, vegetation was successfully established for the first time on sand dumps and the flat tops of slimes dams.[2] It took another two years to successfully vegetate the very acidic sides of slimes dams. The practice was in common usage before the Atmospheric Pollution Prevention Act of 1965 came into force.

In 1976, soon after strip mining for coal started in South Africa, the collieries committee of the Chamber approved the code of practice for surface rehabilitation as

[1] Cf *Management of the water resources of the Republic of South Africa* Department of Water Affairs (1986) ch 2; *Report of the three committees of the President's Council on a national environmental management system* PC 1/1991 para 2.3.4.

[2] Marsden 'The vegetating of mine residue deposits on the Witwatersrand' 1987 (87) *J of the South African Institute of Mining and Metallurgy* 189–94.

a result of strip mining[3] which was circulated to coal mine managers. Legislation enforcing the rehabilitation of opencast mines came into force only in 1980, as will be shown.

These developments led to the realization that industry-wide environmental guidelines were needed and that these should be prepared if possible by acknowledged experts outside the industry.

15.2.2 *Guidelines*

A series entitled *Handbooks of guidelines for environmental protection* was then commissioned by the Chamber of Mines. These guidelines include:

Volume 1/1979: The design, operation and closure of residue deposits. This volume was revised and expanded to include coal residue and is now called Volume 1/1983: The design, operation and closure of metalliferous and coal residue deposits.

Volume 2/1979: The vegetation of residue deposits against water and wind erosion.

Volume 3/1981: The rehabilitation of land disturbed by surface coal mining in South Africa.

Volume 4/1982: The permeator—a device for obtaining liquid penetration into particulate material on flat and inclined surfaces. (Discontinued.)

Volume 5/1982: The Chamber of Mines erosion tester (comet) instrument (for determining the erodibility of slime).

Volume 6/1985: Pollution problems and hydrological disturbances resulting from increased underground extraction of coal.

Volume 7: Statutory requirements for environmental management. (In preparation.)

The guidelines are all in loose-leaf file form so that they can be readily updated as experience and technology change accepted operating practice.

The 'best practicable means' philosophy is used throughout the handbooks.

15.2.3 *Environmental management programme*[4]

The concept of rehabilitation following mining activities is well accepted and is entrenched in law. However, it does not cater for the modern trend towards a holistic consideration of the environment, nor does it stress the need for environmental management to be integrated into everyday mining management.

Recognizing these deficiencies and also the need for a wider involvement from other government departments and affected publics, the mining industry, in April 1991, accepted the concept of an environmental management programme (EMP) for prospecting and mining operations. An EMP includes the need for an environmental impact assessment (EIA) but takes this rather static concept further by fully integrating environmental management into the planning and day-to-day operations at a mine.

All new prospecting and mining projects will be required to submit an environmental management programme report (EMPR) before the operation commences, unless exemption is granted. An *aide-mémoire* for compiling an EMPR has been written and submitted to the Government Mining Engineer for consideration in conjunction with other departments concerned with approving mining applications. It contains the following elements:

- Brief project description.
- Detailed description of the pre-mining environment.

[3] Unpublished information was obtained from the deliberations of the following committees of the Chamber of Mines: the collieries committee; the high-level environmental working party and the environmental management subcommittee, which consolidated the restoration and reclamation of mining land subcommittee, the land management subcommittee, the pollution control subcommittee and the environmental protection subcommittee.

[4] Information in this section was obtained from unpublished sources referred to in n 3 above.

- Motivation for the proposed project, including a consideration of major alternatives.
- Detailed description of the proposed project.
- EMP, including how environmental impacts will be managed during the construction, operational, decommissioning and aftercare phases, the proposed programme of events (with dates) and the financial provision to implement the management measures described.
- Conclusion, describing the overall net environmental impact of the project.
- Statutory requirements.
- Amendments to the EMPR to accommodate changes that might occur so that the document remains dynamic and complete.
- References and supporting documentation.
- Confidential material to accommodate information of a business or financial nature that the proponent considers confidential but which may be required for a proper evaluation of the project.

The intention is that an EMPR will be the only document submitted for approval, that it should summarize issues of concern to all parties with a material interest and that it should present an overall picture so that responsible decision-makers can make their decisions without undue delay.

It will be necessary to change references to 'rehabilitation plans' in the Minerals Act to 'EMPRs' to give legal standing to the EMPR.

15.3 MINING METHODS

15.3.1 *Surface mining*

15.3.1.1 *Introduction*

When a mineral occurs fairly close to the surface in a massive or wide tabular body, or where the mineral is itself part of the surface soil or rock, it is generally more economical to mine it by surface-mining methods.

Complete disruption of the surface always occurs, which affects the soil, surface water and near-surface groundwater, fauna, flora and all types of land-use. Because of this, an understanding of the pre-mining environment is essential. So, too, is an understanding of the mining method employed so that surface rehabilitation, an essential component of this type of mining, can be designed and planned.

The most important aspect of this planning process is to set, and agree on, the overall objective for rehabilitation. Is the land to be returned to an agricultural land-use or converted to a nature reserve, a housing development, a lake or some other land-use? The post-mining land-use can be completely different from the pre-mining land-use. Therefore, in seeking agreement on what the land-use is to be, it is important to consider the macro-environment of the region or of the whole country if necessary. In the interest of creating wealth or jobs or in providing a strategic commodity, society, and ultimately the decision-makers, may accept a land-use with a lower capability than it had before. The assumption here is that high-capability land can be used for many purposes and lower-capability land for only a restricted number of uses—the less the potential uses, the lower the capability. However, even one or two potential uses could be very important. For example, a worked out surface mine could be used for waste disposal in an area with limited disposal sites. After waste disposal is completed, possibly only parkland could be created, which will be beneficial if there is a lack of urban open space.

Only after the rehabilitation objective has been established can rehabilitation be designed as part of the mine design. Once the design is done, the costs for rehabilitation can be determined and the overall project can then be tested for its economic feasibility.

If the cost of rehabilitation to the agreed standard for the land-use chosen makes the project uneconomic, mining should not take place.

15.3.1.2 *Strip mining*

Also frequently called opencast mining, strip mining is most frequently used when the deposit is horizontal or gently dipping and within about 60 m of the surface, such as shallow-lying South African coal seams.

The method, shown in Figure 15.1, involves removing and stockpiling the soil, drilling and blasting the rock (overburden) above the coal seam, removing the blasted overburden by draglines in long parallel strips (hence 'strip mining') to uncover the coal, then drilling, blasting and removing the coal. The removed overburden is placed in rows of spoil piles in the preceding strip from which the coal has been removed.

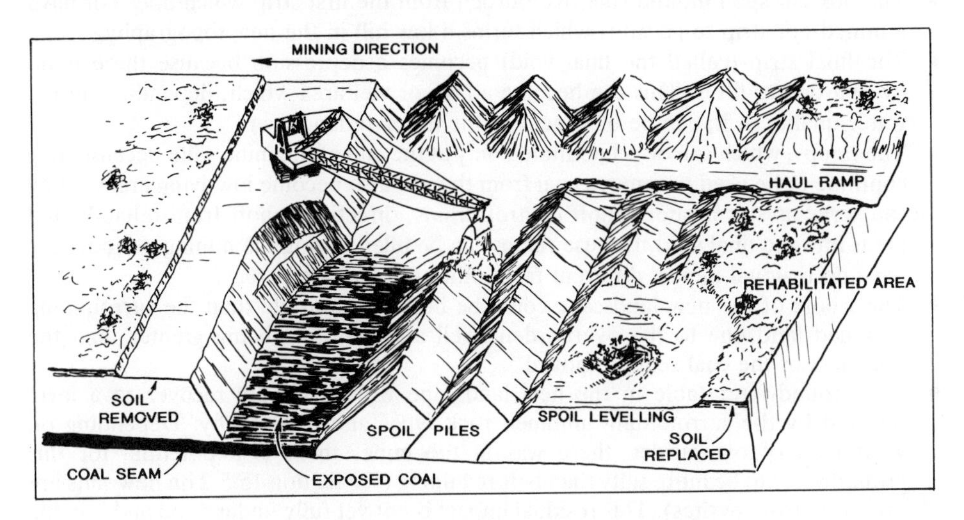

Figure 15.1 Strip mining with concurrent rehabilitation.

As soon as the mining strip (or pit) has been moved out of the way, the spoil piles can be landscaped—the start of the rehabilitation operation. Once the desired shape and slope have been achieved, soil previously stockpiled or sometimes brought directly from the unmined side is replaced. The new ground is then treated in a conventional agricultural way by fertilizing, liming and sowing to pastures. Sowing to pastures, as the first step in revegetating, is very important. It contributes significantly to erosion control and it allows the re-establishment of the soil's micro-organisms, which are required for nutrient cycling.

Because most of South Africa's coal suitable for strip mining occurs in the south-eastern Transvaal (Planning Regions 27 and 28 of Development Region F), about 50 per cent of which is high-potential farm land,[5] the main objective of rehabilitation is to return the land to productive agriculture.[6] The agricultural land capability is therefore determined before mining starts and rehabilitation is designed and planned to recreate the same proportion of land-capability classes after mining, wherever possible. The classes used are arable land, grazing land, wetland and wilderness land, which are

---

[5] *Report on the investigation into the long-term effects of high-recovery coal mining on agriculture in the eastern highveld of Transvaal* (1990) Report of the management committee (Van Niekerk Committee) at the request of the Ministers of Agriculture and of Mineral and Energy Affairs.

[6] Wells 'Long term rehabilitation planning for opencast mines' 1986 (86) *J of the South African Institute of Mining and Metallurgy* 89–93.

defined in the Chamber's guidelines. The creation of arable land requires flatter slopes and more soil than grazing land; wetland will develop in low-lying ground and wilderness land has minimal soil and is allowed to be steeply sloping.

During the mining operation, considerable volumes of groundwater may be encountered and rainwater also falls onto the pit and spoil piles; therefore there is considerable potential for water pollution. This potential is controlled by installing separate clean and dirty water collection circuits. Clean water running off unmined and rehabilitated land is channelled, where possible, into nearby streams. Dirty water from the pit, haul roads and plant areas is collected and re-used for activities that do not require good quality water such as dust control and coal washing.

The most important residual impacts remaining after rehabilitation are:

- The box-cut spoil mound (the overburden from the first strip which does not have a mined-out strip to go into) which forms a low hill in the new topography.
- The final strip (called the final void) becomes a depression because there is no overburden to fill it. This can become a lake or vlei area which, depending on the water quality in it, can be of benefit to the ultimate land-user.
- The ramps, which can be rehabilitated only at the end of the mine's life because they continue to be used to remove coal from the pit, also become low-lying areas. They can serve as stormwater runoff control drains, directing runoff from rehabilitated areas into the final void. If these ramps can be filled during the mining period, they have no residual impact different from other rehabilitated areas.
- The whole of the new landscape could be higher in altitude than the surrounding unmined land due to the overburden swell after blasting being greater than the thickness of the coal seam removed.
- The groundwater table in the new landscape will eventually recover to a level dictated by the surrounding unmined rock types and topography. Depending on what type of overburden there was in the mine, there is a potential for this groundwater to be more salty than before mining (see section 15.5.2 on how salts are produced from pyrites). This residual impact is not yet fully understood and is being researched.

If the shovel-and-truck method of strip mining is used, the box-cut spoil can sometimes be placed economically in the final void and the ramps can be progressively filled, obviating all residual topographic impacts. Unfortunately, this flexibility is not possible using a large dragline because of its mode of operation.

Considerable success has been achieved during the rehabilitation of strip mined land both overseas and in South Africa. High-yielding pastures are an immediate result and they can be used for hay production or grazing. After a number of years under pasture, those areas rehabilitated to an arable standard can be, and have been, returned to row crops.

15.3.1.3 *Open-pit mining*

This method of mining is used if the near-surface ore body is massive and it occurs in a steeply dipping seam or seams or a pipe or makes up the country rock. Here, the whole ore body is mined with no overburden to put back in the void. The Big Hole at Kimberley and a crusher stone quarry are good examples. A modern open-pit mine is shown in Figure 15.2.

The ore body is blasted and then loaded onto trucks which transport the ore out of the pit to the processing plant. The ore body is followed deeper and deeper into the ground in a series of benches. Sometimes rock surrounding the ore has to be removed also so that the sides of the pit do not become dangerously steep. This waste rock, and waste that is separated from the ore during processing, is dumped on the surface away from the pit.

The objectives for land-use following open-pit mining are more limited than for strip mining, because there is almost always insufficient waste or even tailings to fill the pit. The main objective is usually to make the pit walls safe and to landscape the waste rock dumps, but many innovative solutions have been used. These include using the pit as a waste disposal site, filling it with water with the intention of creating an ultimate recreation/water supply/nature conservation end-use or simply fencing it in and leaving it as a tourist attraction.

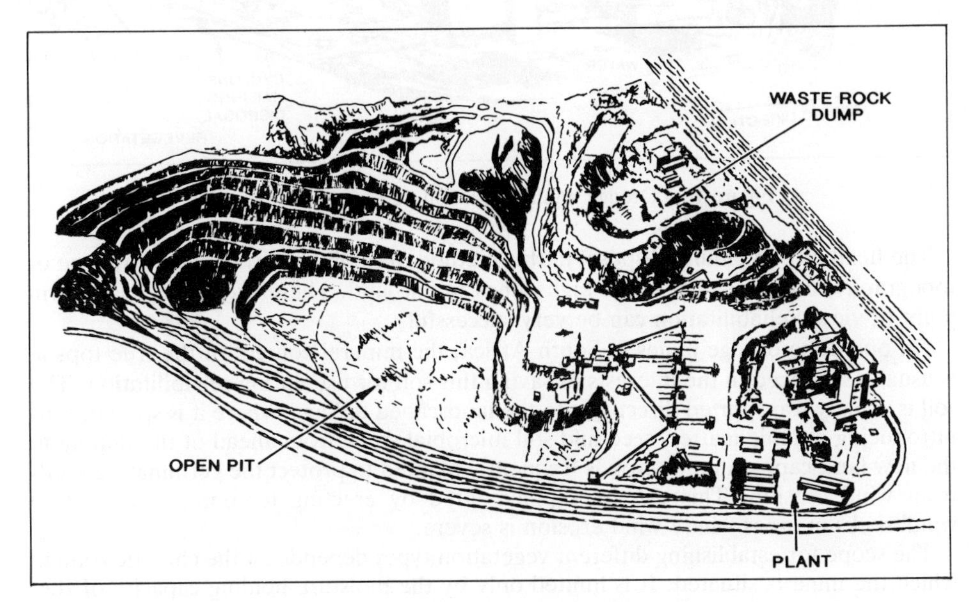

Figure 15.2 A modern open-pit mine with benches.

The residual impact of open-pit mining is usually a completely different land-use. With few exceptions (an open-pit coal mine could be one), ore bodies that lend themselves to open-pit mining are not prone to causing water pollution (although the tailings resulting from subsequent mineral processing may be—see section 15.5 for the management of residue deposits) and therefore water accumulating in the rehabilitated pit can usually be used for a number of purposes.

15.3.1.4 *Dredge mining*

Alluvial deposits and deposits of heavy minerals in dune sands lend themselves to this mining method. Essentially, the deposit must be soft, contain the mineral throughout its bulk (even if there are lenses of mineral concentration that are the main target) and be able to hold water.

A pit is excavated into the ore body and filled with water. On the pond formed, two items of equipment are usually floated—the dredge itself and a separation plant. The dredge excavates the deposit from underwater, sucks the material up and pumps it to the plant. In the plant, the heavy minerals are separated from the rest of the deposit material (gravel, soil, sand, silt and clay) and the concentrated minerals are either pumped ashore for further processing (typical of heavy minerals such as ilmenite) or collected and periodically removed (typical of a gold-dredging operation). The tailings from the separation plant are also pumped to shore, this time to the mined-out portion of the pond, and can be stacked in various ways as the first phase of rehabilitation. The dredge, separation plant and pond move in a snake-like way through the deposit, excavating at one end of the pond and depositing soil-like material at the other, until the deposit is worked out. Figure 15.3 shows a typical layout.

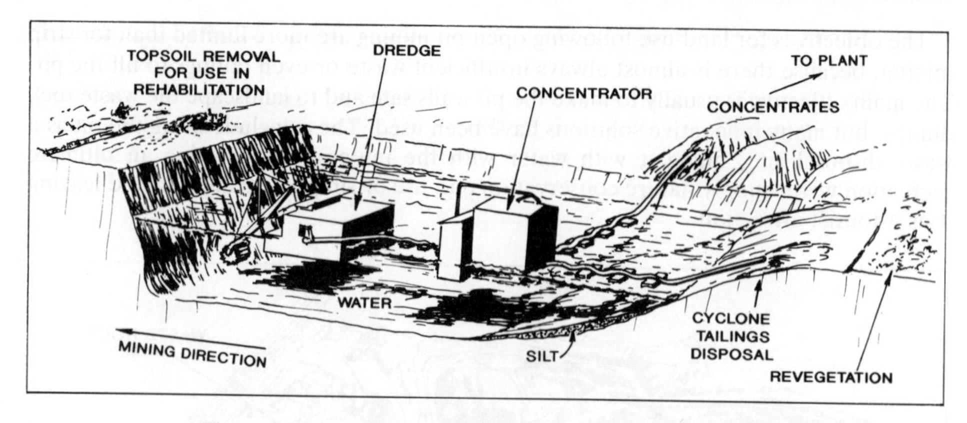

Figure 15.3 Dredge mining with concurrent rehabilitation.

The flexibility of tailings disposal in this method of mining allows almost any type of topography to be created—from high dunes to flat land. Therefore, from a landform point of view, rehabilitation can be very successful.

On operating dredge mines in South Africa, the mineral content of the true topsoil is usually sacrificed in the interests of saving this soil for use during rehabilitation. The soil is usually transported directly onto the landscaped tailings, where it is spread, thus introducing organic matter, seed and soil microbial stock from ahead of the mining to the new landscape. A nurse crop is frequently planted to protect the germinating seeds from wind erosion. This can be supplemented by erecting temporary shade-cloth windbreaks in areas where wind erosion is severe.

The scope for establishing different vegetation types depends on the climatic zone in which the mine is situated. It is limited only by the moisture-holding capacity of the, usually sandy, substrate, because rooting depth is frequently not a limiting factor and pyritic material is commonly absent from deposits of this nature, and there are therefore no toxic chemical effects.

From the above discussion it is obviously important to set an agreed goal for the land-use following rehabilitation. Furthermore, the timescale required to achieve the goal must be acceptable to society and decision-makers.

The major residual impacts of dredge mining, depending on circumstances and assuming that state-of-the-art mitigating measures are employed, could be among the following:

- Perched water tables due to the silt and clay fraction of the tailings being deposited first in the lower portion of the tailings deposit and then covered by the coarser fractions. This may occur when the cyclone method of tailings disposal is used.
- Consequential ecological changes induced by a higher water table should this occur.
- A temporal impact if indigenous forest is chosen as the rehabilitation goal since it will take time for this to grow.
- A possible depression remaining at the end of the dredge path (similar to the final void in strip mining).

15.3.1.5 *Dump reclamation*

The mineral extraction processes from past mining eras were not as efficient as those used today. Therefore the tailings generated at these old mines often still contain payable values of mineral, especially the sand and slime dumps at old gold mines.

'Dump reclamation' refers to the reprocessing of these dumps. Typically, the material in the old dump is monitored (squirted with a very high pressure jet of water which erodes the dump material away) into a sluice. The sluice gravitates the dump material to a low point where it is collected and pumped, via a pipeline, to the treatment plant which could be located some distance away. Figure 15.4 shows a typical monitoring operation. The main environmental protection activities during reclamation are to keep stormwater away from the working areas, to prevent rainwater that has fallen on the site from leaving it in an uncontrolled fashion and to prevent dust pollution during dry, windy conditions.

Figure 15.4 A typical slimes monitoring operation.

If the old dump material is coarser than slime, such as found on a sand or coal dump, it is often recovered by a front-end loader and transported to the plant by conveyor.

Once the whole dump has been reclaimed down to the original soil level under the dump, reclamation stops and rehabilitation of the site begins. The options available for different land-uses on these sites are varied. In an urban area they are usually earmarked for urban development—office and industrial parks, residential, and so on. In a rural area they can be returned to agriculture.

In many cases the top part of the soil profile at these sites has been contaminated with acid water seepage from the dump. This has to be ameliorated with agricultural lime. Radon seepage from the dump is found commonly in the soils but the concentration is usually below dangerous levels after rehabilitation. However, if buildings are constructed on these sites, special ventilated foundations may be required to prevent high levels of radon gas accumulating within the closed buildings. If this problem is suspected, a site-specific investigation is called for.

The main residual impact of reclaiming precious-metal dumps is not at the site of the reclaimed dump but rather the new slimes dam which has to be built to accommodate the same volume of material that was in the original dump. When coal dumps are reclaimed, a much smaller volume of material has to be redumped, but this waste may be more offensive due to an increased pyrite concentration. Extra precautions against acid seepage may have to be taken to minimize the residual impact from this type of dump.

15.3.2 Shallow underground mining

15.3.2.1 *Old bord-and-pillar mining*

Also sometimes called room-and-pillar mining, this mining method is mainly employed in coal mines. After sinking a shaft down to the coal seam, the seam is mined by extracting coal from the bords or rooms and leaving a regular pattern of pillars behind to support the overlying strata (the roof). Figure 15.5 shows a typical layout.

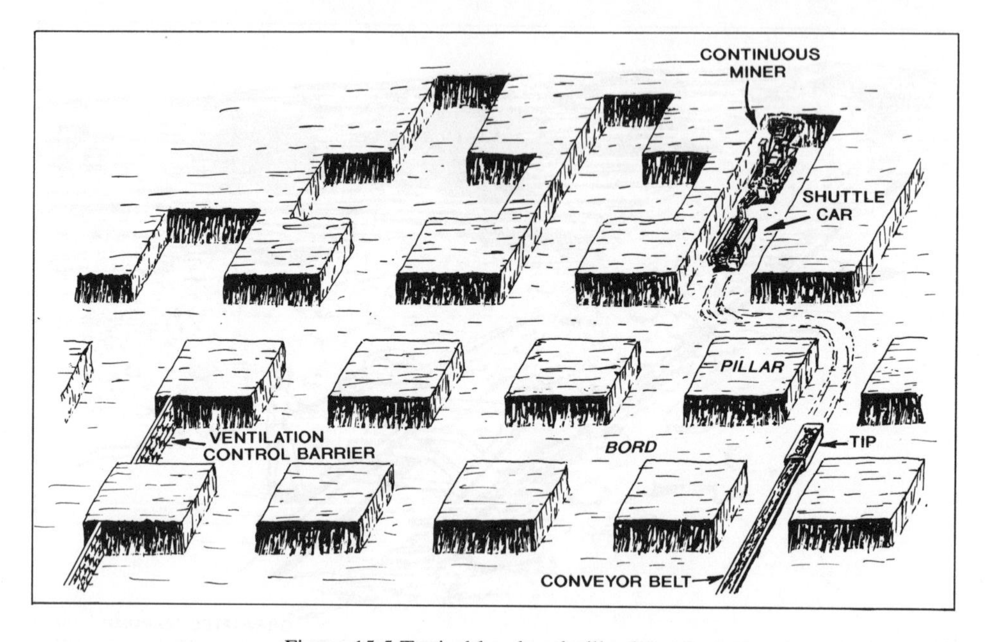

Figure 15.5 Typical bord and pillar layout.

Before the advent of modern pillar design in 1967,[7] or the adoption of special precautions when mining at depths shallower than about 40 m,[8] little was known about what size of pillars to leave behind. Sometimes, in their eagerness to extract the maximum amount of coal, the old miners left pillars too small to support the roof indefinitely. They sometimes 'robbed' the pillars on their retreat from the exhausted coalfaces.

The result of this was that, sometime after the mines were closed, certain areas of the roof collapsed into the bords and also into roadways and intersections underground.[9] In places, this collapse continued through to the surface. This allowed air to enter the old workings and to start spontaneous combustion in the residual coal (see Figure 15.6). Underground fires resulted which often further weakened the pillars, causing even more collapses to take place.

The environmental impacts at the time and the residual impacts are significant and numerous. For instance, in the Witbank area these fires are still burning. Random and unplanned surface subsidence occurs, rendering the land unsafe. Dangerous ground results where collapse has not yet taken place but may do at any time. Near-surface

---

[7] Salamon & Munro 'A study of the strength of coal pillars' 1967 (68) *J of the South African Institute of Mining and Metallurgy* 55–67.

[8] Madden 'Re-assessment of coal pillar design' in *The total utilization of coal resources* vol 1 South African Institute of Mining and Metallurgy, Coal School, 1989.

[9] Hardman 'The consequences of leaving vast mined-out areas standing on pillars' in *The total utilization of coal reserves* vol 2 South African Institute of Mining and Metallurgy, Coal School, 1989.

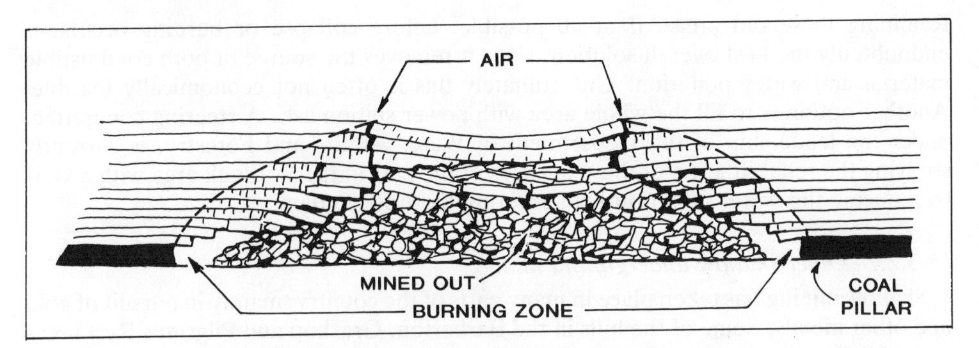

Figure 15.6 Collapse in old shallow bord and pillar workings.

aquifers may also break, draining water into the collapsed workings. Rain falling on these areas goes straight into the workings, adding to the water load. This water often becomes acidic and high in salt concentration. Because many of these workings occur in places where the coal seam outcrops on the surface, acidic seepage emerges along the outcrop or from adits, causing severe water pollution in streams draining the area. Also, significant air pollution occurs due to the sulphurous fumes.

Rehabilitation of these old workings is difficult (see Figure 15.7), because of the danger of collapse and because rehabilitation was not planned as part of the original mining operation. In some cases it is not possible until the fires have burned out. Many attempts have nevertheless been made: these include filling the collapsed areas with rubble, bulldozing the sides of the collapses to safe slopes, backfilling the workings with non-combustible material such as gravel, soil or ash and flooding the workings. None of these methods has yet solved the water pollution problem, although some have been partly effective in stopping the fires. Trenching around the burning areas and backfilling the trench has been attempted to stop the fires spreading with only limited success, since the fire often jumps to the other side of the trench. Forced collapsing of the roof of the old mine by blasting has also been attempted, but has proved unsuccessful due to the unpredictable outcome of the blast.

Figure 15.7 Collapsed old bord and pillar workings near Witbank—a legacy of the past.

Remining these old areas, if at all possible, before collapse or burning occurs, is undoubtedly the best overall solution, since it removes the source of both combustible material and water pollution. Unfortunately this is often not economically feasible. Another option is to fill the whole area with power station ash. A steering committee, under the leadership of the Department of Water Affairs and Forestry, is currently studying the rehabilitation of these legacies of the past in the Witbank area with a view to reducing the water pollution load entering the Loskop dam.

15.3.2.2 *Other shallow underground mining*

Shallow mining has taken place in many parts of the country, mainly in pursuit of gold and other metals. Some of the hills in the Barberton, Graskop and Pilgrim's Rest areas are riddled with tunnels and adits and sometimes minor collapsed areas.

Fortunately, the early miners who made these were in search of oxidized ore or visible gold, neither of which is usually associated with pyritic material. Therefore water pollution is not common in these old workings. The main residual impact is aesthetic and possibly the safety of persons exploring them; being situated mostly in remote areas, however, their impact is not considered significant.

This is not the case with the old adit type of coal mining in northern Natal. Here, numerous small flows of acidic or salty water from the adits have an impact on surface-water quality.

15.3.3 Deep underground mining

15.3.3.1 *Introduction*

In general, deep underground mining methods have little or no effect on the environment directly, the one exception being increased extraction coal mining. Indirectly, environmental impacts are associated with mine residue deposits (see section 15.5), surface subsidence as a result of dewatering and the disposal of water pumped from underground to enable mining to take place safely.

15.3.3.2 *Increased extraction coal mining*[10]

A limitation of bord and pillar coal mining is that a significant quantity (up to 40 per cent) of coal is left behind in the pillars which support the roof. Various methods of pillar extraction (called stooping in Natal) have been developed to remove these pillars so as to optimize coal recovery. Other mining methods, such as rib pillar extraction, shortwall mining and longwall mining, have been developed with the aim of recovering the maximum amount of coal directly. Collectively, these methods are referred to as increased extraction or high-recovery coal mining methods.

The main environmental concerns with all increased extraction methods relate to the lack of roof support following mining. The impacts include subsidence of the surface, the cracking of the strata between the coal seam and the surface and the subsequent dewatering of aquifers in this zone. However, the subsidence in this case is predictable both in time and extent. It is thus possible to design rehabilitation of the surface in advance, divert streams around areas that will subside, and provide surface landowners dependent on near-surface aquifers for their water supply with alternative supplies.

---

[10] See, generally, Van der Westhuizen, Kotze, Van der Merwe & Vergeer 'The influence of mining depth, seam thickness and face length on the success of longwall mining' in *The total utilization of coal resources* vol 1 (1989) above n 8; Plaistowe, Poultney, Van Schalkwyk, Hichens & Bradbury 'Decision-making considerations for pillar extraction' in *The total utilization of coal resources* vol 1 (1989) above n 8; Buddery & Oldroyd 'Rock engineering contributions to reducing cost, improving productivity and increasing extractable reserves on Trans-Natal collieries' *Proceedings of the symposium on the impact of rock engineering on mining and tunneling economics* (Welkom, 1991).

Roads, houses and, indeed, water reservoirs have been successfully undermined using these methods.[11]

The water from the overlying aquifers flows into the mine and, depending on its quality, can often be pumped out and discharged to surface streams. Where the water is naturally salty or becomes polluted in the mine, it can usually be used as mine service water, which may involve a certain amount of treatment.

The residual impacts may include all or some of the following:

- A change in agricultural cropping practice in subsided areas if they become waterlogged.
- An undulating topography, resulting from subsided land over the mining panels and non-subsided land over the barrier pillars and roadways which are left between panels as shown in Figure 15.8. Theoretically it is possible to mine out this coal to allow the whole surface to settle evenly. However, there are many practical difficulties which are being investigated by the industry to minimize this residual impact and increase coal recovery.

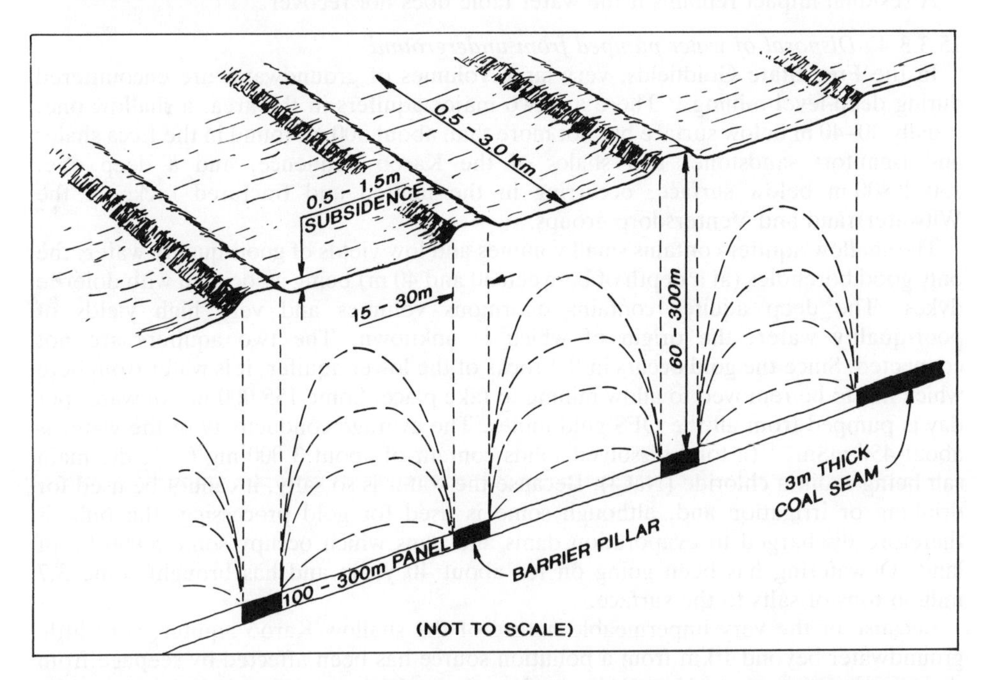

Figure 15.8 An example of undulating topography that could result following longwall mining.

- When this method is used to mine below a depth of about 60 m, the weight of the strata above the coal seam may be sufficient to close the cracks in the strata overlying the seam and thus allow recharge of near-surface aquifers, enabling them to be used again. This is dependent on the geology (presence of faults, dykes, sills etc) but if the cracks do not reseal, a residual impact would occur.

These residual impacts were of great concern to the Van Niekerk committee that enquired into the effects of increased extraction coal mining on agriculture.[12] A liaison committee has been established to investigate all aspects of such impacts and to steer research into finding ways to overcome them.

---

[11] J N van der Merwe, pers comm.
[12] Above n 5.

15.3.3.3 *Surface subsidence as a result of dewatering*

This occurs in dolomitic areas mainly in the western Transvaal gold mines. Natural voids in the dolomite are filled with water which imparts stability to the soft strata and soils overlying the voids. When gold mining takes place under these voids, they have to be dewatered to avoid flooding the mine and possibly causing loss of life.

The mine dewatering[13] can cause dewatering of previously water-filled caverns below the water table and erosion of fine soil material out of the overlying strata causing instability in the strata which in turn collapses, resulting in sinkholes. The collapse is sudden and it is difficult to predict when and where it will happen. The sinkholes allow surface water and rainfall to flow directly into the workings, which can significantly increase pumping costs.

Affected areas can be rehabilitated by pumping gold tailings (slime, which sometimes has to be stabilized with cement) into the sinkholes. The slime can then be covered with soil up to the level of the original surface and the area revegetated. If and when the water table is re-established, the danger of further sinkholes occurring is limited.

A residual impact remains if the water table does not recover.

15.3.3.4 *Disposal of water pumped from underground*

In the Free State Goldfields, very large volumes of groundwater are encountered during deep-level mining.[14] There are two major aquifers in the area: a shallow one, usually 30–40 m below surface but not more than about 300 m, found in the Ecca shales and Beaufort sandstones and shales of the Karoo Sequence, and a deep one, 150–1 800 m below surface, occurring in the faulted and fractured rocks of the Witwatersrand and Ventersdorp groups.

The shallow aquifer contains small volumes and low yields of good-quality water, the only good boreholes (at a depth of between 30 and 40 m) being associated with dolerite dykes. The deep aquifer contains enormous volumes and very high yields of poor-quality water, the origin of which is unknown. The two aquifers are not connected. Since the gold occurs in the rocks of the lower aquifer, it is water from here which has to be removed to allow mining to take place. Some 155 000 m^3 of water per day is pumped from all the OFS gold mines. The average conductivity of the water is about 450 mSm^{-1} (a total dissolved solids content of about 3 000 mg ℓ^{-1}), the main salt being sodium chloride (NaCl). Because the water is so salty, it cannot be used for drinking or irrigation and, although some is used for gold processing, the bulk is therefore discharged to evaporation dams and pans which occupy some 5 000 ha of land. Dewatering has been going on for about 40 years and has brought some 3,7 million tons of salts to the surface.

Because of the very impermeable nature of the shallow Karoo aquifer, very little groundwater beyond 1 km from a pollution source has been affected by seepage from these evaporation areas. However, overflows from the evaporation facilities caused by rainfall pose a pollution threat in the region, since these flows go directly into streams.

The residual impacts are those associated with land occupied by evaporation facilities, overflows from these and very local groundwater contamination. It is estimated that no new evaporation facilities will be required for new mines in the area because of a net loss of water due to evaporation. Therefore the impacts of dewatering new mines should be limited only to areas impacted already.

---

[13] Matthews & Wagener 'Some geological aspects affecting the site selection of tailings dams on dolomite' *Proceedings of the international conference on mining and industrial waste management* (Johannesburg, 1987).

[14] Cogho, Van Niekerk, Pretorius & Hodgson *The development of techniques for the evaluation and effective management of surface and groundwater contamination in the Orange Free State Goldfields.* Draft progress report to the Water Research Commission steering committee. (Institute for Groundwater Studies, University of the Orange Free State, 1990).

In the Witwatersrand gold-mining areas the situation is somewhat different. In the dolomitic areas to the west of Roodepoort, the water pumped from mines is generally of a good quality and can be discharged directly to streams. This water is often an essential source of water for downstream users.

However, east of Roodepoort through to Boksburg, there are kilometres of old worked-out mines which have filled with water.[15] Because of the pyrite in the workings, this water has become severely polluted mainly by calcium and magnesium sulphate, the result of sulphuric acid reacting with bases in the rocks underground. The water typically has a pH of 2–3 and a salt content of 3 000–5 000 mg ℓ^{-1} (conductivity 1 000–3 800 mSm^{-1}). It also contains high levels of iron and manganese.

To enable mining to continue on the eastern and western extremities of these old workings, the water in them has to be pumped out to maintain a level which will prevent it flooding the operating mines. The water is usually limed underground to correct the pH so as to prevent corrosion of the pumps and pipe columns. At East Rand Proprietary Mines in Boksburg it is also treated on the surface in a high-density sludge plant to precipitate most of the manganese and suspended solids. However, the total salt content is not significantly changed by the treatment. The water, in total about 20 000–30 000 m^3 per day (which varies seasonally), is then discharged into the Klip and Elsburg rivers, which flow into the Vaal barrage. This discharge adds some 60–150 t per day of salts to the barrage, a significant environmental and economic impact.

To date, society has accepted this impact due to the wealth created by mining the gold. However, as the demand for water in the PWV region increases, and the expense of meeting this demand from the Lesotho Highlands Water Scheme increases the cost of water, the situation will have to be re-evaluated. Innovative, new and cost-effective water-treatment techniques are being investigated at present to minimize the residual impact of this dewatering.

15.4 THE NATURE OF THE MINERALS

15.4.1 Introduction

Minerals occur in many locations, in many forms and in many types of host rock. Some have to be processed to extract their valuable content while others can be used directly. The inherent characteristics of the mineral should therefore be understood to appreciate the type of environmental impact that has to be managed. Accordingly, the nature of the major minerals mined in South Africa is briefly discussed.

15.4.2 Coal

South African coal is derived from plants which grew in swamps in a temperate climate some 250 million years ago, before Gondwanaland broke up and as that continent was emerging from an extensive ice age. Glacial meltwater carrying suspended rock flour poured into the peat swamps lying in the basin that we know today as the Karoo Basin. Iron and sulphur compounds were included in the detritus flowing into these swamps.

A depositional phase followed peat formation where the peat was buried by sediments, only to be followed by a further period of peat formation and another depositional phase. As the deposits accumulated in depth, the lower ones were subjected to elevated pressures and temperatures, bringing about the onset of coalification. Finally, only deposition occurred, covering the last peat layer and forming that, too, into coal.

---

[15] Unpublished records held by Rand Mines (Mining and Services) Ltd, Environmental Protection Department, Johannesburg.

Typical of peat swamps, the underwater environment was anaerobic. The iron and sulphur compounds therefore reacted to form iron sulphide (FeS_2), known also as pyrite, as well as sulphur compounds in the coal itself. Although less so than in the northern hemisphere, South African coal still contains this pyrite. The rock flour, in this case more so than in the northern coals, caused the high ash content of our coal.

These inherent characteristics give the coal two qualities that can have significant potential environmental impacts. First, on exposure to air and water the pyrites oxidize to form sulphuric acid which can lead to water pollution. Secondly, the high ash content has to be reduced so that our coal can be sold on the export market. This is done in a coal benefication plant, where two waste products are produced—slurry (fine-grained coal that is deposited with water) and coarse discard (low-grade coal and rock, which is dumped mechanically, has a high pyrite content and is susceptible to spontaneous combustion—see section 15.5.3).

The location of the major coal deposits[16] (Figure 15.9) is also of great importance for two reasons: the ease with which surface rehabilitation can be carried out and the potential to pollute water. Most of our coal lies in the large stable ecosystem of the highveld interior plateau. This rolling post-African surface changes little with time:[17]

'The topographic pattern is one of large scale features which carries over into all aspects of the natural environment. Climate, soil and vegetation types are wide-spread and boundaries are poorly defined; environmental diversity is low and extrapolation over hundreds of kilometres is possible.'

The highveld has also been extensively farmed and therefore little natural environment remains. For these reasons coal mining on the highveld has little residual impact on natural ecosystems and rehabilitation is a relatively simple, if expensive, matter. In areas less stable than the highveld and with a greater biological diversity, surface rehabilitation is often more difficult.

From a water quality perspective, South African coalfields occur in the worst possible location[18] since most occur in the vulnerable upper reaches of major river systems such as the Vaal, Olifants, Usutu, Komati, Pongola and Tugela rivers. Because of this, the impact of water pollution is more significant than if the coalfields were located elsewhere. Measures to control water pollution should therefore be uppermost in the minds of mining companies operating in these coalfields.

15.4.3 Gold

Unlike coal, gold in itself is the most stable of substances not capable of causing any environmental impacts, although it has impacted on the social order of the world perhaps more than any other single element.

However, it occurs in only minute quantities in its ore bodies and thus has to be extracted from them in sophisticated plants using complex metallurgical processes. Once the few grains from each ton mined have been extracted, the rest of the material is a waste product which creates the need to construct very large residue deposits on the surface. As with coal, pyrite is also associated with all but alluvial gold-bearing ores and, in the Barberton area, not only pyrite but also arsenic (in the form of arsenopyrite) actually contains the gold. The pyrite is not normally extracted with the gold and therefore ends up in the residue deposits where it constitutes a significant source of water pollution. In the case of arsenopyritic gold ore, the ore has to be oxidized to

---

[16] Erasmus, Hodgson, Kirsten, Roper, Smit, Steyn & Whittaker *Geological, hydrological and ecological factors affecting increased underground extraction of coal* (Vacation school, South African Institute of Mining and metallurgy, Johannesburg, 1981).

[17] Fuggle & Rabie (eds) *Environmental concerns in South Africa* (1983) ch 2.

[18] Van der Merwe *The significance of acid mine drainage in South Africa* AMD short course, Sandton, October 1990.

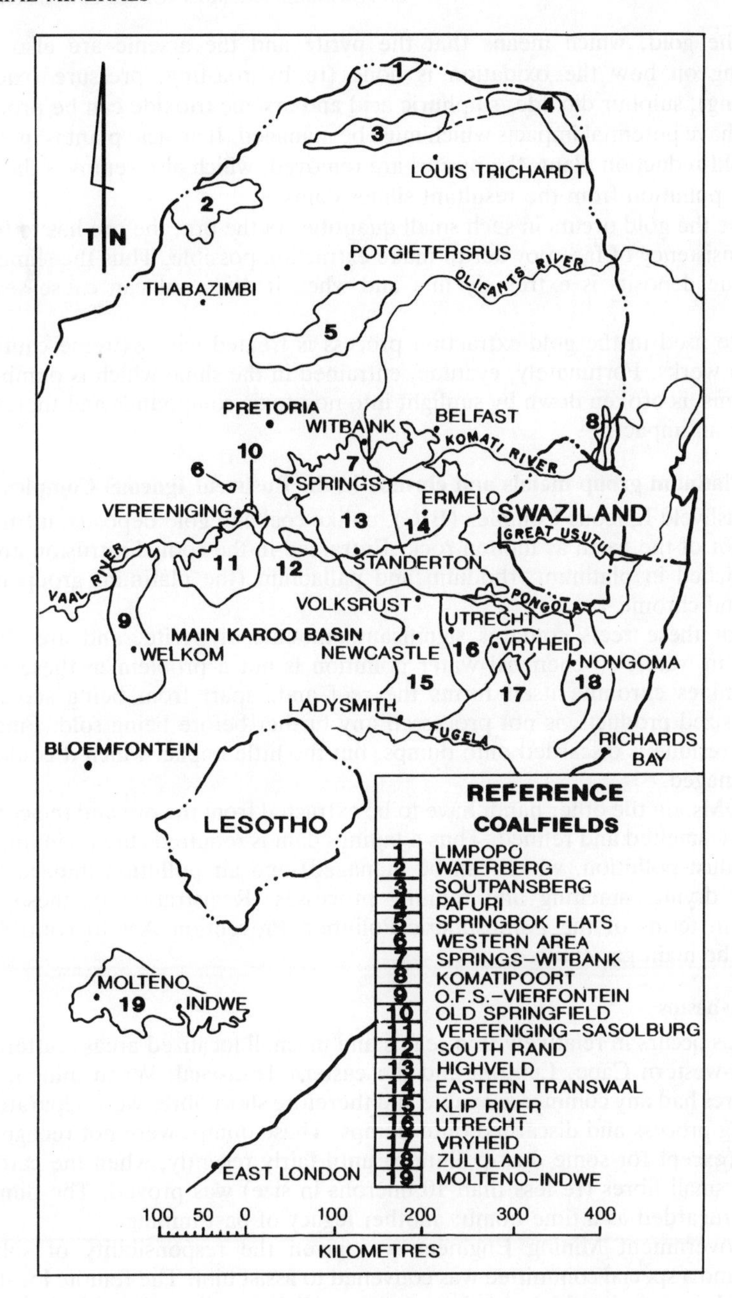

Figure 15.9 Distribution of the South African coalfields.

release the gold, which means that the pyrite and the arsenic are also oxidized. Depending on how the oxidation is done (ie by roasting, pressure oxidation or bioleaching), sulphur dioxide, sulphuric acid and arsenic trioxide can be produced, all of which have potential impacts which must be managed. If an acid plant is incorporated with a gold-reduction plant, the pyrites are removed, which also removes the potential for water pollution from the resultant slimes dams.

Because the gold occurs in such small quantities in the ore, the ore has to be ground to the consistency of face powder to make extraction possible. Thus the slime going to the residue deposits is extremely fine and when it dries out can cause severe dust pollution.

Cyanide used in the gold-extraction process is treated with extreme caution at all reduction works. Fortunately, cyanide, entrained in the slime which is pumped to the slimes dams, is broken down by sunlight into non-toxic compounds and therefore does not cause an impact.

15.4.4 Platinum group metals and chrome in the Bushveld Igneous Complex

The Bushveld Igneous Complex (BIC), unlike coal and gold deposits, intruded from the interior of the earth as molten rock. Entrained in the cooled intrusion are various reefs enriched in platinum, rhodium and palladium (the platinum group metals or PGMs) and chrome.

None of these reefs contains significant amounts of pyrite, and are themselves insoluble in water, so chemical water pollution is not a problem in these mines. In chrome mines chromite itself forms the reef and, apart from being screened into different-sized products, is not processed any further before being sold. Fine-grained chromite residue is discarded onto dumps, but the little impact which it could cause is easily managed.

The PGMs, on the other hand, have to be extracted from the ore and the concentrate then dried, smelted and refined. Thus a tailings dam is required (the main impact from which is dust pollution, which can be managed) and air pollution impacts from the coal-fired drying, smelting and refining processes. Registration of these plants is required in terms of the Atmospheric Pollution Prevention Act to control sulphur dioxide, the main gas emitted.

15.4.5 Asbestos

Asbestos occurs in relatively thin seams and in small localized areas scattered across the north-western Cape, Lebowa and the eastern Transvaal. When mined, only the longer fibres had any commercial value and therefore short fibres were separated during the milling process and discarded onto dumps. These dumps were not recognized as a problem (except for some dust pollution) until fairly recently, when the carcinogenic nature of small fibres (ie less than 10 microns in size) was proved. The dumps were suddenly regarded as a time bomb; another legacy of past mining.

The Government Mining Engineer was given the responsibility of solving the problem and a special committee was convened to assist him. The remote locations and inhospitable terrain in which the dumps occur called for all work to be done by hand. Experimentation by the Institute for Ecological Research[19] into the innovative use of non-palatable, poisonous and thorny plants to vegetate the dumps (to contain the dust and prevent people or animals getting onto them) began in 1986. At the same time, civil works were constructed to divert stormwater away from the dumps to prevent fibres eroding and being deposited downstream. Work on covering these dumps is still proceeding.

---

[19] 'Asbestos producers clean up Bewaarkloof' 1987 (September) *SA Mining World*.

15.4.6 Heavy minerals

Heavy minerals (ilmenite, magnetite, rutile, zircon and monazite) occur in economically extractable quantities in the coastal areas of South Africa, where they have been concentrated in ancient or younger dunes and beach sands by wind, wave and river action. It is this location alone which causes the controversy over their recovery, since the mining methods used can be mitigated to a very large extent by careful planning and rehabilitation. Unfortunately, coastal forest and wetlands often occur in the areas concerned. Although wetlands, grassland, arable land, *Acacia* forest, commercial forests and dunes, rolling hills or flatland can all be re-created successfully within a human time frame, it takes 100 years or more for coastal forests to regrow.

When considering such proposals, it is very important to realize that multiple land-use (mining being only one of them) is possible at the same time. If mining is allowed, it will take up only a small portion of land for a short time, unless mature indigenous forest is set as the rehabilitation goal.

15.4.7 Other minerals

Very briefly, the residual impacts associated with the nature of other minerals could be:

- Dimension stone—large qualities of off-cuts and unsuitable boulders discarded; open pit left.
- Iron ore—red dust; waste rock dumps; open pit left.
- Stone, gravel and sand—open pits left; soil erosion; dust.
- Diamonds—slimes deposits; possible open pit left.
- Andalusite, other felspathic minerals and fluorspar—slimes deposits; dust; possible open pit left.
- Other metals such as lead, copper, zinc, tin, manganese and vanadium—impacts from these are usually very variable, site specific and localized.

15.5 MINE RESIDUE DEPOSITS

15.5.1 Introduction

The mining sector is the largest single generator and accumulator of solid wastes in South Africa. Mine tailings and coal discard accounted for 74 per cent of the total waste stream in 1990.[20] The total area of land covered by mine residue was 10 700 ha in 1981,[21] most of which is in the Transvaal and OFS.

Historically, the planning of mine residue disposal sites was based on minimum cost, the availability of land and the safety of underground workings. Little or no regard was given to the environment.

Today the situation has changed dramatically. No fewer than six Acts and their attendant regulations govern the location of mine residue deposits. The President's Council has recommended that these be streamlined.[22] The mining industry has recognized the importance of its waste disposal as evidenced by the publication of its guidelines for this activity in 1979.

The main types of pollution resulting from residue deposits are water pollution and air pollution. Visual pollution and change of land-use can also be significant. All except change of land-use can be mitigated to some extent, if not fully. To do this it is important to understand the processes causing the pollution.

---

[20] *The situation of waste management and pollution control in South Africa* Report to the Department of Environment Affairs by the CSIR Programme for the Environment CPE 1/1991.

[21] Best 'Management and industrial waste management: state-of-the-art address' *Proceedings of the International conference on mining and industrial waste management* (Johannesburg, 1987).

[22] Above n 1, paras 5.5.6.13–17.

15.5.2 Water pollution

15.5.2.1 *The role of iron pyrites*

As mentioned in sections 15.4.2–3, iron pyrites, FeS_2, also called 'fool's gold', is the most important source of nearly all water pollution originating from mines themselves and from their residue deposits.[23]

When pyrite is exposed to air and water, it oxidizes to form sulphuric acid and iron oxides and hydroxides (yellow boy), which causes the pH to drop to about 4. The oxidation reaction is accelerated and extended by bacteria, the most important of which is *Thiobacillus ferrooxidans*, which causes the pH of the solution to drop to as low as 1.5.

The acid produced reacts with bases in the country rock or residue deposit to form salts and to mobilize heavy metals that may be contained in the rock or residue. During this reaction the acidity is often neutralized. The resultant drainage (referred to as acid mine drainage or, more recently, acid rock drainage (ARD) contains elevated levels of salts (primarily calcium and magnesium sulphates) and metals (mainly iron, manganese and aluminium).[24]

The longer water is in contact with the pyrite, the more chance the oxidation reaction has of proceeding and the more chance bacteria have of speeding it up and producing more acid. Wherever pyrite is exposed to air and water for a period of time the reactions can occur. However, coal discard and gold residue deposits (with high pyrite contents due to processing the minerals) and old workings (due to the long time exposure) produce the highest concentration of ARD.

15.5.2.2 *Prevention or treatment of acid rock drainage*

The impacts of ARD can be minimized by:

- Preventing water from getting to the pyrite by diverting rainwater away from workings or dumps.
- Preventing air from getting to the pyrite by compacting coal discard in thin layers—the same control measures employed to prevent spontaneous combustion.[25] This occurs naturally in a gold slimes dam where, because of the impermeable nature of the slime, air can penetrate only about 2 m into the dam[26] so after this outer layer has oxidized, acid production stops.
- Removing water entering pyritic mines as soon as possible to minimize residence time.
- If ARD cannot be prevented, treating it by neutralization with lime; in extreme cases, a biocide such as bromine can be added to kill the acidifying bacteria.
- Using passive treatment systems[27] where small seepage flows from abandoned workings, backfilled areas and dumps are acid and mineralized. These seeps often occur in remote locations, making it difficult to access and maintain or operate conventional treatment facilities. Passive treatment systems use natural geochemical

---

[23] Thompson 'Acid mine waters in South Africa and their amelioration' 1980 (6) *Water SA* 130–4; *Draft acid rock drainage: technical guide* vol II British Columbia acid drainage task force report no 66002/2 1990.

[24] Ibid.

[25] Cook 'Coal discard-rehabilitation of a burning dump' in Rainbow (ed) *Proceedings of the third international symposium on reclamation, treatment and utilization of coal mining wastes* (Glasgow, Scotland, 1990).

[26] Marsden 'The current limited impact of the Witwatersrand gold-mine residues on water pollution in the Vaal river system' 1986 (86) *J of the South African Institute of Mining and Metallurgy* 481–504.

[27] Holm, Bishop & Tempo 'Passive mine drainage treatment—promoting natural removal mechanisms for acidity and trace metals for mine drainage' in *Water management and treatment for mining and metallurgical operations* vol 3 (Division of Mineral Land Reclamation, Colorado Department of Natural Resources, USA, 1985).

and biological processes for acid neutralization and precipitation and absorption of metals. They can be natural or man-made and consist of wetlands or reedbeds densely planted with reeds (*Phragmites australis*) and bullrushes (*Typha* species). The plant roots, growing in a rich organic substrate containing millions of micro-organisms, provide sites for ion exchange, absorption, aeration (above water) and reduction (below water), precipitation, neutralization, filtration and plant uptake. Depending on the water quality and what has to be removed from the seepage, man-made reedbeds[28] can also incorporate crushed limestone zones (to neutralize acidity), cascades (to oxidize metallic ions), anaerobic zones (to reduce sulphates)and stilling ponds (to allow precipitation). The main advantages of constructed reedbeds are their relatively low construction costs and very low operating costs. Their main disadvantage is their inability to treat large volumes of water.

Bacterial activity in dumps has been inhibited in the USA using a detergent, sodium lauryl sulphate.[29] Tests done in South Africa on trial coal dumps with this compound have been unsuccessful, however.

15.5.3 Air pollution

15.5.3.1 *Smoke and gases*

Coal, coal discard and other carbonaceous material give out heat when exposed to air. If they are put in a heap which is porous enough to let air in but also large enough to prevent the heat escaping, the heat builds up. When the temperature gets to about 80 °C, the process becomes irreversible if let alone. The material then ignites on its own—a process called spontaneous combustion. This is very common on unconsolidated discard dumps and can also occur underground.

Smoke and gases (mainly sulphur dioxide, carbon monoxide and dioxide and the oxides of nitrogen)[30] are produced from these burning coal discard dumps, especially when more discard is end-tipped over the edge of the dump. Localized acid rain occurs as a result of rain washing these gases from the air.

This pollution can be greatly reduced simply by stopping the practice of end-tipping. It can be eliminated completely in time by encapsulating the dump with a skin of compacted discard as described by Cook.[31] Figure 15.10 shows this method. Unfortunately, it can be used only if there is a source of sufficient discard being produced from an operating coal-washing plant.

A cost-effective method has not yet been devised to rehabilitate burning dumps where there is no source of readily available discard. Covering them with soil is not recommended because the soil erodes, it is not thick enough to prevent oxygen getting to the burning zone and the heat in the dump drives out soil moisture, which prevents plant growth. Landscaping such dumps is also not recommended, because of the extreme danger of fire to the operators and their equipment and there is no guarantee that the fire will be extinguished. These dumps are therefore usually left to burn out and, once the ash is cool enough, can eventually be revegetated.

The modern practice of preventing this type of pollution is to prevent spontaneous combustion from occurring in the first place by compacting the discard from the start.

---

[28] Wood *Constructed wetlands for the treatment of acid mine drainage* (Unpublished report for Duvha Opencast Services (Pty) Ltd, 1988).

[29] Kleinman & Erickson 'Field evaluation of a bactericidal treatment to control acid drainage' *Proceedings of the symposium on surface hydrology, sedimentology and reclamation* (University of Kentucky, USA, 1981).

[30] Wells 'Coarse discard and slurry-safe storage' in *The total utilization of coal resources* vol 2 (1989) above n 9.

[31] Above n 25.

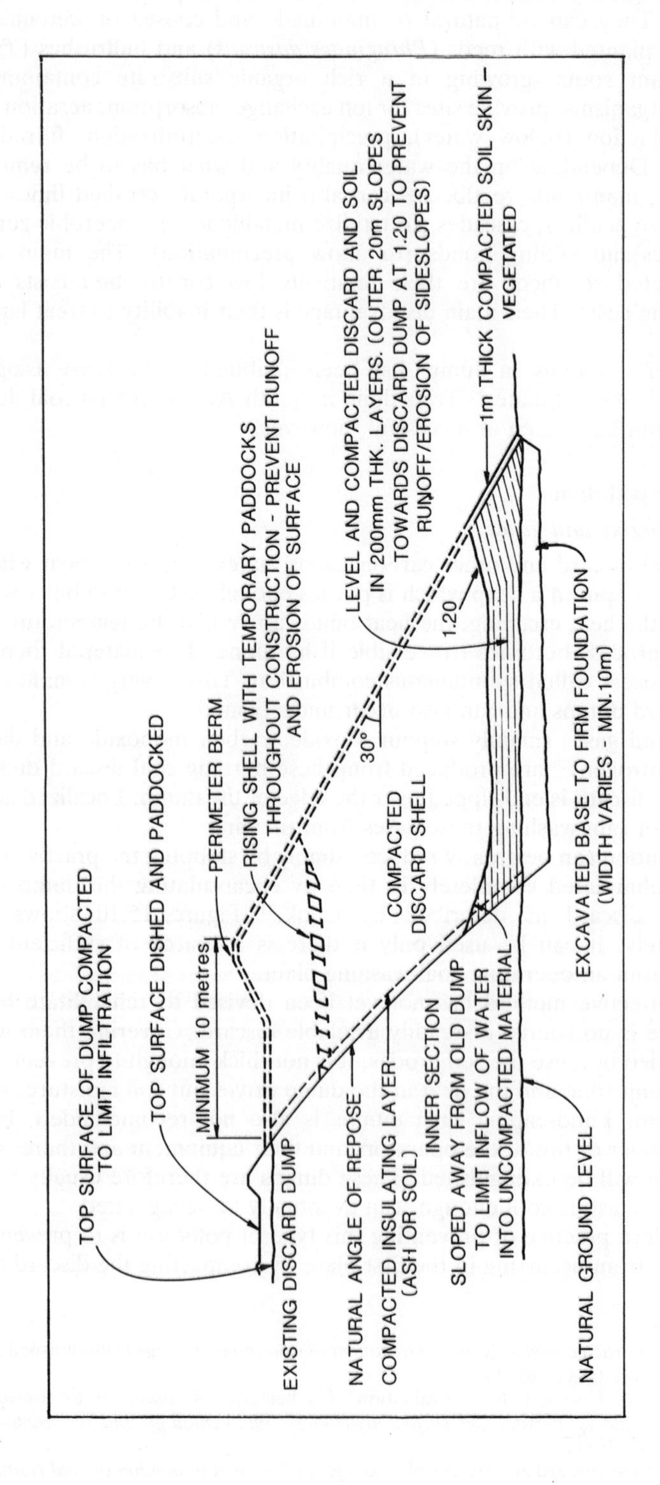

Figure 15.10 Typical cross-section through compacted shell around old burning discard dump

Compaction must reduce the air voids in the discard to less than about 15 per cent[32] and these voids must contain sufficient moisture to reduce the actual air content to less than about 10 per cent. To maintain this inert, moist environment in the dump and to obtain the compaction specification, it may be necessary to wet the discard during compaction. Also, rainwater falling on the dump should not be allowed to run off it.

15.5.3.2 *Dust*

Dust from most residue deposits is a significant nuisance and, in the case of asbestos, also a health hazard. Although many other methods have been tried, establishing a vegetation cover on the dump or slimes dam is the most practical and cost-effective long-term solution. Steep slopes, an acid and salty growing medium in gold dumps, a high phreatic water table emerging on the side, a low water holding capacity in coal discard dumps, a low nutrient content in almost all deposits and seasonal fires burning the established vegetation are the main challenges, all of which have been overcome to a greater or lesser extent in the mining industry's almost 40 years of experience.

A very effective temporary measure to control dust on fine-grained, flat surfaces, such as the top of a gold slimes dam, is to ridge plough them with a potato ridger.[33] The low-level wind turbulence induced by the ridges causes dust to be lifted from the crests of the ridges and to be deposited immediately in the adjacent valleys.

15.5.3.3 *Aesthetic aspects*

Much has been said recently about the aesthetic aspects of mine residue deposits. Suggestions have been made that they should be sloped to 18° or 22° or designed so that they form a mound that blends into the surrounding landscape. There are certain facts which must be considered before taking such decisions, namely:

- A steep slope (about 32° to 38° or 1:1,6 to 1:1,3, the natural angle of repose) erodes less than all other slopes until a slope of about 8° or 1:7 is reached. There are two reasons for this. First, the plan area of the slope (assuming the same height) increases as the slope becomes less steep. More rain therefore collects on it and more erosion occurs. Secondly, the control of this erosion requires the construction of contour banks and downdrains which are extremely difficult to construct on slopes steeper than about 1:7, because conventional earth-moving equipment struggles to operate on them. For this reason, slopes between these two limits should not be considered. Conversely, well-established vegetation is sufficient to control the erosion on the 1:1,6 to 1:1,3 slopes.
- To accommodate a certain volume of waste in a dump of the same height, more land is required for a gently sloping than a steeply sloping dump. Therefore more land is permanently alienated.
- The total area occupied for the same volume is larger for gentle slopes than steep slopes and therefore more vegetation has to be established. This is problematic on residues hostile to plant growth, because of the difficulty and cost of ameliorating the hostile conditions. On the other hand, gentle slopes could possibly be planted mechanically rather than by hand, the usual practice on steep slopes.
- Because more rain collects on the larger dump area, there is more chance for a larger volume of water being polluted, which compounds the problem of disposing of it.
- Although the observation is subjective, a well-vegetated, steep-sided dump can still have another landuse on top and need not be an eyesore.

[32] Cook above n 25; Wells above n 30.

[33] Cook 'The establishment and maintenance of vegetation on slimes dams' *Mine Metallurgical Managers' Association Circular* no 1 (1987).

15.5.4 Principles of residue deposit rehabilitation[34]

These principles apply to all mine residue deposits and also to municipal, industrial or any other waste deposits.

15.5.4.1 *Plan for closure*

It is essential that rehabilitation and closure are planned during the design and operating stages of a deposit. All attempts at rehabilitation during the life of a deposit must take cognizance of the conditions that must be met at closure. This includes items such as toe paddocks, pollution control dams, solution trenches and contour drains being sized for the conditions expected at closure as well as being able to perform their functions during the operating stages. In addition, funds to implement the closure plan must be generated during the operational phase.

15.5.4.2 *Water control*

This is a most important aspect of rehabilitation. Without it, erosion is inevitable and vegetation establishment and water pollution control are impossible. Four control areas are needed:

- *Top water control*—deposit tops should be shaped to force water away from the edges and to stop it spilling down the sides. Water must also be prevented from flowing from one side of the top to another. In short, rain falling onto the top of a dump should remain where it landed.
- *Side water control*—on steep-sided dumps, the small amount of rainfall that lands on the side is easily controlled by vegetation. On gently sloping dumps, contour berms, discharging at frequent intervals into downdrains, are required as well as vegetation. In both cases, toe paddocks are required to trap eroded material and polluted water at least until the sides are well vegetated.
- *Overland flow control*—stormwater flow must be diverted around the sides of deposits to stop it becoming contaminated or eroding the deposit's toe.
- *Seepage control*—most modern waste deposits are designed with underdrain systems to collect seepage and lead it to a collection point. On older dumps, a seepage interception trench excavated down to rock or an impermeable soil layer is required on the downslope side of the dump. This must also discharge safely to a collection point for recycling, evaporation or treatment.

15.5.4.3 *Minimize and isolate area of influence*

A waste deposit should be designed to use as little space as possible in order to save land and to reduce the volume of rainfall that could become polluted by falling on the dump. The water-control structures around the dump should be as close to it as possible and effectively isolate it from the outside water environment. Access to the dump by outsiders should be limited and controlled to prevent damage to vegetation and water-control structures.

15.5.4.4 *Revegetation*

As discussed in section 15.5.3.2, vegetation is the most cost-effective method of preventing wind erosion. It is also the best method to control water erosion. If the appropriate plants are chosen for a particular waste in a particular climate, vegetation can be self-sustaining and therefore reduce the need for maintenance.

---

[34] Wells 'The closure and rehabilitation of mining waste impoundments: state-of-the-art address' *Proceedings of the international conference on mining and industrial waste management* (Johannesburg, 1987).

15.5.4.5 *Minimize maintenance*

Although sometimes a Utopian dream, a maintenance-free end-product should be the target for deposit rehabilitation.

15.6 RESEARCH

15.6.1 Aspects currently being researched

Aspects of environmental concern that are currently being investigated by or with the co-operation of the mining industry include:

(a) A regional investigation into groundwater quality deterioration in the Olifants River catchment above Loskop Dam with specialized investigation in the Witbank Dam subcatchment. Water Research Commission (WRC) and Institute of Groundwater Studies, UOFS.
(b) Olifants River water quality management study. Department of Water Affairs and Forestry (DWA).
(c) The effect of air pollution and catchment development on the salinity regime of water resources of the Vaal Dam catchment. WRC.
(d) Modelling of tubular reverse osmosis systems. WRC and Natal University.
(e) A study on a mine-water reclamation test plant. Chamber of Mines Research Organisation (COMRO).
(f) An assessment of the feasibility and impact of alternative water pollution control options on TDS concentrations in the Vaal Barrage and Middle Vaal. WRC.
(g) Development of a strategic framework for water quality management regarding the mining industry. Steering Committee chaired by DWA.
(h) Minimum requirements for the monitoring of waste management facilities. WRC.
(i) Concentration ratios of selected radionuclides in aquatic ecosystems affected by mine drainage effluent. WRC and Rand Afrikaans University.
(j) Microbiological transformation of metal-contaminated effluents. WRC and University of Durban-Westville.
(k) The use of vegetation in the amelioration of the water quality impacts of mining—an assessment of species and water-use. WRC.
(l) Working party to consider regulations in terms of dam safety legislation. WRC.
(m) A land-soil classification system for rehabilitated land. National Energy Council.

15.6.2 Aspects to be investigated in the future

Research and investigations that will either start or be considered soon by or with the co-operation of the mining industry include:

(a) Establishing guidelines to assess and ameliorate the impact of gold mining operations on the water environment. COMRO.
(b) Interdepartmental working group to discuss guidelines for rehabilitation, amendment of regulations and mine closure. Department of Mineral and Energy Affairs.
(c) The Resource Liaison Committee, set up on the recommendation of the Van Niekerk committee of investigation into the effects on agriculture of increased extraction coal mining, through the Department of Agriculture, will consider the following:
  - The study of newly created soil profiles to determine various soil characteristics.
  - An investigation of methods of replacing soil, promoting soil stabilization and improving soil fertility.
  - An investigation to determine the most effective cultivation and tillage practices for rehabilitated land and the most suitable crops and crop patterns for such land.
  - The determination of the quality and quantity of water resources available for agriculture.

- An investigation into the effect of mining activities and into agricultural engineering matters.
- A determination of economic norms for farm size—to be done in conjunction with the Chamber of Mines' Mining Titles Department.
- An investigation into alternative farming enterprises.

(d) The National Energy Council is to consider the contribution of South Africa to global climatic changes and the impact on South Africa of the various international protocols that have been or are being proposed.

15.7 THE LAW RELATING TO TERRESTRIAL MINING

15.7.1 Importance of mining in South Africa

The highly mineralized nature of many parts of South Africa has led to the creation of a mining industry which is very important to the country's economy. A mineral deposit is only a potential source of wealth, and the significance of the deposit becomes evident only when a mineral is mined, resulting in disturbance of the natural environment. The mining industry, led by the Chamber of Mines,[35] has been practising environmental management for many years as a form of self-regulation. The Chamber, through its Environmental Management Services, provides a voluntary advisory service to its members and non-members and the operational guidelines drawn up by the Chamber are recognized by the State as authoritative. It is suggested that legal regulation ought to be on a level with these self-regulatory measures: legal measures ought not to represent only minimum standards.

Concern for the environment in the mining industry must be seen as being in line with the current worldwide trend to value the environment as an integral part of the economic process. Environmental issues and scientific studies almost always lead to higher costs; therefore a balance of interests has to be maintained for healthy production and sustainable development.

15.7.2 Mineral policy

The government in its *White Paper on the mineral policy of the Republic of South Africa*[36] accepted as the aim of its environmental strategy that due regard should be had to environmental considerations in all facets of the development and exploitation of the country's mineral resources. The ideal would be an acceptable balance between unrestricted mineral resource development, on the one hand, and a means to restore and conserve the environment, on the other. However, in view of the mineral industry's important contribution to the country's economic well-being, its continued growth is not at issue; accordingly, the imposition of excessively strict standards which could inhibit such continued growth is to be guarded against. Environmental issues that are highlighted in the White Paper are the rehabilitation of surface areas after mining has ceased and the control of water and air pollution associated with mining.

15.7.3 Sources of mining law

Mining law consists *(a)* of a body of common law derived mostly from English common law, and built up by our courts from the early mining times in the last century, and *(b)* for the greater part, of legislation, again commencing in the very early days of mining. Neither the common law nor earlier statute law specifically refers to the environment, but because of the nature of mining, words such as 'protection' and 'safety' have always featured in mining laws.

Remedies for environmental redress may be available under civil law by way of a court interdict or an Aquilian action for damages. However, mining legislation has led

[35] The Chamber of Mines is a service organization for South Africa's six major mining houses.

[36] WPJ—1986 para 4.6.

to mining law acquiring the nature of public law. The corresponding remedies of judicial review and of criminal sanctions accordingly have grown in importance.

15.7.4 State control of mining

A consequence of the national importance of the mining industry in any country that has great mineral wealth is that the State will seek to control the industry in some form or another.[37] In South Africa the basic policy regarding the exploitation of natural resources 'lies between the two absolutes of complete state monopoly and unfettered private enterprise'.[38] It has been state policy to encourage the exploration and exploitation of the country's mineral wealth by rewarding and protecting the interests of private enterprise while at the same time imposing a system of control by the State and securing for the State a substantial share in the profits derived from mining. This control relates to the exploitation of precious metals and precious stones and dates from the middle of the last century, when each of the four colonies, which in 1910 were to become the Union of South Africa, developed its own system of state control of precious metals and precious stones.[39]

However, the right to explore and exploit base minerals, such as coal, asbestos, chrome, manganese, copper and other minerals has at all times vested in the holder of the right to such base minerals.

15.7.5 Common law

15.7.5.1 *Rights of mineral holder*

The rights of the mineral holder have been established by case law in situations where the mineral rights have been separated from the surface and a potential conflict of interests arises.[40] As these rights relate to possible damage or other use or abuse of the surface, this issue has important environmental implications. It should, however, be noted that where the mineral holder and the surface owner are the same person or company, damage to the surface may equally well constitute an environmental issue even although no possible conflicting situation exists.

The mineral holder has certain ancillary rights which are important for the exercise of his rights as mineral holder in terms of the basic principle of law that whoever grants a thing is deemed also to grant that without which the grant itself would be of no effect.[41] The resulting problems over the years have given rise to a large number of cases.[42]

Hudson v Mann[43] is generally regarded as the leading case relating to the preference of mining use over surface use. In this case the holder of the mineral rights was granted an interdict restraining the surface owner from preventing him from having access to a shaft sunk on the property, and using it for prospecting and mining purposes. It was held that the mineral holder's preferential rights apply not only to his actual prospecting and mining operations but also to all such subsidiary or ancillary rights, without which he will not be able effectively to carry on his prospecting and/or mining operations, and that in the case of irreconcilable conflict, the use of the surface rights must be subordinated to mineral exploration. While he must act reasonably in the course of

---

[37] See Dale *An historical and comparative study of the concept and acquisition of mineral rights* (unpublished LLD thesis, Unisa, 1979).
[38] Franklin & Kaplan *The mineral laws of South Africa* (1982) 1.
[39] Dale above n 37, 172.
[40] See, generally, Norton *The conflict between the land owner, mineral right holder and the mining title holder in South African mining law* (unpublished LLM thesis, University of the Witwatersrand, 1985).
[41] *West Witwatersrand Areas Ltd v Roos* 1936 AD 62, 72.
[42] Cf Van der Walt 'Onteiening van die reg op laterale en onderstut' 1987 *THRHR* 462, 472.
[43] 1950 (4) SA 485 (T).

exercising his rights, he is not obliged to forgo their enjoyment merely because his operations are detrimental to the interests of the surface owner.[44]

The mineral holder's rights, however, exist only in so far as they are directly necessary for mining. The only limitation at common law is that the holder of the mineral rights must exercise them civiliter modo, that is, reasonably and in a manner least injurious to the property of the surface owner.[45]

It is suggested that opencast mining cannot be described as a method under which the mineral rights holder can exercise his rights civiliter modo as the surface owner is totally unable to use the affected area for any purpose while opencast mining is being conducted. Opencast mining is used quite extensively in South Africa for exploiting certain minerals, the most important of which in terms of value and surface area affected is coal. Surface mining necessitates a drastic disturbance of land including changes in topsoil characteristics with the potential for increased acidity, the development of nutrient deficiencies or imbalances, surface crustiness or desiccation; and changes in vegetation cover and land use with the potential for atmospheric dust and other pollution.[46]

Therefore, until the affected area has been completely rehabilitated, the surface owner is seriously inconvenienced. In many cases of intended opencast mining, negotiations are entered into between the surface owner and the party conducting mining operations for the purchase of the affected area or a larger area. However, at common law the holder of the mineral rights is not obliged to pay compensation to the surface owner for damage caused in the course of prospecting or mining operations, in the absence of anything in the relevant contract or grant obliging him to do so, provided he exercised his rights civiliter modo.[47] Nevertheless, if an action for damages based on delict were brought in respect of an alleged breach of the mineral holder's common-law rights, the measure of damages would be the amount by which the surface owner's patrimony has been diminished by the mineral holder's conduct, and the latter would have to establish that he had indeed exercised his rights civiliter modo for the case to be decided in his favour.

15.7.5.2 *Liability for environmental degradation*

Delictual actions for damages in environmental matters are not generally distinguishable from other actions for damages. The principle of no liability without fault is still of fundamental importance in South African law. However, rules of strict liability, excluding proof of fault, have been applied in environmental cases even although these cases are basically considered to be exceptions to the fault principle. The underlying principle of strict liability is that the party who acts or controls an activity, and not the injured party, should bear the burden of proof, and should demonstrate the harmless effect of the activity.[48] In environmental cases, consideration could be given to placing the burden of proof on the defendant to establish absence of negligence.

An important issue in environmental cases is the basis upon which compensation is assessed in civil proceedings, and specifically whether clean-up costs may be demanded or whether the sole head of damage must be confined to the specific amount of damage which the plaintiff can show to have suffered. It is suggested that assessed clean-up costs might constitute part of the actual damages which can be claimed.

---

[44] See Dale above n 37, 297.

[45] See Franklin & Kaplan above n 38, 132.

[46] Brink et al 'The changing impact of urbanization and mining on the geological environment' 1990 (86) *S Afr J Sci* 434, 437.

[47] Franklin & Kaplan above n 38, 135.

[48] Kasoulides 'State responsibility and assessment of liability for damage resulting from dumping operations' 1989 *San Diego Law Rev* 497, 514.

The second important common-law remedy, namely, an interdict, does not require proof of fault by the respondent in the form of either intent or negligence. A final interdict will be granted if the applicant can prove on a balance of probabilities that the respondent's conduct infringes a legally recognized right or threatens to infringe such a right. An interdict is therefore a very suitable form of remedy for environmental disturbances.

In general, where mining is concerned, note should be taken of the knowledge a mining company has that it is conducting an activity which is potentially a cause of pollution.

15.7.5.3 *Duty of lateral and subsurface support*

Although the holder of the mineral or mining rights is entitled to exercise such rights as are necessary for effectively carrying out his mining operations, the grant to a mineral holder of a right to mine does not deprive the surface owner of his right to have the surface supported in its natural state.[49] This is in accordance with the principle that the integrity or inviolateness of the object of a right is fundamental to its exercise.[50] Such right, however, does not entitle the surface owner to more support than is naturally required. It would follow from this that any structure erected—for example, buildings or railway lines—which would necessarily require additional support, would impose a greater obligation on the party conducting mining operations and would entitle such party to relief.[51] This would apply to structures erected subsequent to mining taking place; existing structures are usually dealt with under an agreement between the parties. In the case of mining at great depth such as gold mining, undermining of structures does not normally present a hazard due to mining operations, but cracking of the surface, subsidence or sinkholes can occur later if, for example, the water table has been affected.

The right of the surface owner to have the benefit of support is enforceable by an action for damages where withdrawal of support has resulted in damage, whether this constitutes actual caving in of land or any movement of or disturbance in the plaintiff's soil from its natural position (eg that caused by gradual erosion by rainwater); or by an interdict if there is imminent danger of a substantial kind.[52]

Regarding liability in respect of the duty not to interfere with lateral and subsurface support, the better view is that this is a strict duty which does not depend upon proof of culpa or dolus.[53] The Court in *Elektrisiteitsvoorsieningskommissie v Fourie*[54] held that the right of the owner of land to lateral support is an incident of the relationship between the owner and the mineral rights holder, and does not have an independent existence. In this case the notarial prospecting contract between the parties and the subsequent mineral cession expressly stipulated that mining operations would leave the surface intact and also made provision for pillars and props to prevent caving in. It has been submitted that the right to cause subsidence by means of high-extraction underground mining may be implied from the instrument granting the right to exploit a coal deposit, but this would depend in the first instance on a construction of the contract as a whole.[55]

---

[49] See Franklin & Kaplan above n 38, 114.

[50] Van der Vyver 'Expropriation, rights, entitlements and surface support of land' 1988 *SALJ* 1, 11.

[51] Franklin & Kaplan above n 38, 114.

[52] Franklin & Kaplan above n 38, 114–15.

[53] *Foentjies v Beukes* 1977 (4) SA 964 (C) 966–7; Franklin & Kaplan above n 38, 188; Dale above n 37, 303.

[54] 1988 (2) SA 627 (T).

[55] Shipman 'Subjacent and lateral support' in *Surface use in mining law* Symposium organized by the School of Law and the Department of Engineering, University of the Witwatersrand (1983) 36.

15.7.6 Legislative development

Pre-Union mining legislation revealed little concern for environmental conservation. In fact, an opposite intention was evident in that the legislation regulated the exploitation of minerals. The environment was only indirectly relevant, if at all, the primary concern having been the damage suffered by the landowner concerned. For instance, Transvaal Law 2 of 1872, relating to the issuing of prospecting licences on private and state land, provided that no prospector would have the right in his prospecting operations to prejudice houses, lands, gardens, roads, kraals, dams, water furrows and plantations.[56] Under an addendum to Law 1 of 1883, diggers were indemnified for polluting and muddying river waters, but the government was authorized to withdraw grants and rights in the public interest on payment of compensation to be decided, in the absence of agreement, by arbitration. Early Orange Free State legislation contained basically similar provisions to those in the Transvaal, but Cape legislation and particularly Natal legislation varied in some respects. Post-Union legislation generally carried on along the same lines.

The first serious environmental concern reflected in mining legislation was evidenced only in 1977, when the Mines and Works Act 27 of 1956 was amended to enable the Minister of Mineral and Energy Affairs to make regulations regarding the conservation of the environment at or near mines or works, including the restoration of land on which activities in connection with mines or works are performed or have been performed.[57] Subsequent regulations, issued in 1980 by virtue of this provision,[58] constituted the first substantial mining legislation aimed at environmental conservation.

15.7.7 Minerals Act

A new Minerals Bill was first published for general comment on 15 December 1988 and the private sector has had the opportunity to comment on it on two occasions. After some amendments by the Joint Committee on Environment, Mineral and Energy Affairs, the Minerals Act 50 of 1991 was passed by Parliament during April 1991 and signed by the State President in May 1991; it came into operation in January 1992.

Its objects are stated to be, *first*, the consolidation and rationalization of nine different mineral laws, namely:

- the Precious Stones (Alluvial) Amendment Act 15 of 1919;
- the Deep Level Mining Research Institute Act 27 of 1946;
- the Mines and Works Act 27 of 1956;
- the Precious Stones Act 73 of 1964;
- the Strategic Mineral Resources Development Act 88 of 1964;
- the Mineral Laws Supplementary Act 10 of 1975; and
- the Tiger's Eye Control Act 77 of 1988,

all of which have been repealed in toto, and the repeal of:

- the whole Mining Rights Act 20 of 1967 except Chapter XVI relating to dealing in unwrought precious metal; and
- section 47 of the Nuclear Energy Act 92 of 1982, which provides that no prospecting and mining for source material, or recovery of source material from residues, can be conducted without state permission.

The *second* object is the application of government policy in respect of privatization and deregulation, by the reduction of state involvement, and the introduction of a simplified system of granting permits or licences for prospecting and mining to the holder of the

---

[56] Cf, generally, Dale above n 37, 308–14.
[57] Section 12(1)*(h*A), inserted by s 3*(b)* of Act 83 of 1977.
[58] GN R537 of 21 March 1980.

right to any mineral, with no differentiation between precious metals, precious stones, natural oil and source material, on the one hand and all other minerals, on the other. *Thirdly*, and most importantly from the viewpoint of environmental conservation, is the object of ensuring that minerals are optimally and safely mined and that the surface damaged by mining operations is properly rehabilitated both during and after mining operations.

15.7.8 Minerals and mineral rights

The Mines and Works Act[59] defined a mineral as any substance, whether in solid, liquid or gaseous form, occurring naturally in or on the earth and having been formed by or subjected to a geological process, but which does not include water and soil unless they are taken from the earth for the production, or extraction, from them of a product of commercial value. The Minerals Act[60] defines 'mineral' even more comprehensively as meaning any substance, whether in solid, liquid or gaseous form, occurring naturally in or on the earth, in or under water or in tailings and having been formed by or subjected to a geological process, excluding water, but including sand, stone, rock, gravel and clay, as well as soil, other than topsoil. Both definitions are very wide, the main difference being the inclusion in the Minerals Act, besides substances occurring naturally in or on the earth, of substances in tailings, 'tailings' being defined as any waste rock, slimes or residue derived from any mining operation or processing of any mineral.[61] These definitions of minerals indicate the total range of substances likely to cause environmental hazards when mining takes place.[62] Regarding the specific inclusion of sand as a mineral, it was held in *Roets v Secundior Sand BK*[63] that sand is a mineral and accordingly that registration in the Deeds Office of a contract regarding the right to prospect for and remove sand is required.

The common-law principle relating to the ownership of land was stated in *Union Government v Marais*[64] as follows: 'The principle is fundamental that the owner of land is owner not only of the surface but of everything legally adherent thereto, and also of everything contained in the soil below the surface.' The rights to minerals are therefore automatically included in the right of ownership in the owner's title deed, except where the mineral rights or some specific mineral right or rights have been subtracted from the full ownership. The two main instances of severance of the mineral rights are *(a)* where the owner has sold the land but reserves to himself the right to minerals, which will then be registered under a certificate of mineral rights simultaneously with transfer of the land, or *(b)* where the owner has sold all or specific mineral rights and these rights are then registered under a title of cession of the mineral rights. It has been held that ownership of the minerals remains with the owner of the land, even where the mineral rights belong to another party, until such time as the minerals have been physically separated from the land.[65]

15.7.9 Mining and prospecting

The Mining Rights Act[66] described mine or mining as including any excavation work, together with boring and other operations necessary for or incidental to the exploitation of precious metals, base minerals or natural oil. The Precious Stones Act contained definitions relevant only to mining precious stones in an area within a pipe or similar

---

[59] Section 1(xi).
[60] Section 1(xiv).
[61] Section 1(xxxviii).
[62] See also Badenhorst 'Towards a theory on mineral rights' 1990 *TSAR* 243–6.
[63] 1989 (1) SA 902 (T).
[64] 1920 AD 240, 246.
[65] *Gluckman v Solomon* 1921 TPD 335; Franklin & Kaplan above n 38, 4–7.
[66] Section 1(xviii).

formation, or to an 'alluvial digging' which was an area proclaimed as such. The Mines and Works Act[67] provided an all-embracing definition of 'mine', which included both exploration and exploitation, in respect of any excavation whether abandoned or being worked, at or near a mine including crushing, reducing, concentrating, smelting or refining a mineral or producing a commercial product from a mineral.

All these statutes have been replaced by the Minerals Act, but only the Mines and Works Act definition resembled the definition in the Minerals Act. Under the Minerals Act[68] 'mine' is described as any excavation in the earth or in any tailings as well as any borehole, whether any of the above are being worked or not, for the purpose of prospecting or mining, or any other place where a mineral deposit is being exploited, and includes the whole mining area together with all buildings, structures, machinery, mine dumps and access roads.

The Minerals Act defines 'process' as meaning in relation to any mineral, the recovering, extracting, concentrating, refining, calcining, classifying, crushing, screening, washing, reduction, smelting or gasification of the mineral.[69]

In the original Minerals Bill prior to amendment 'the processing of any mineral in its ore where such processing comprises the main operation or where the main operation flows therefrom' was included with two other categories, namely, *(a)* transmitting and distributing to any other consumer of any form of power from a mine, or *(b)* training at any central rescue station, under the designation of 'works' which means 'any place, excluding a mine . . .'. The amendment, however, omits the 'processing' category from the designation of 'works'. The effect of the continued inclusion of the original definition of 'process' and the exclusion of 'processing' from the definition of 'works' is that the definition of 'works' becomes limited to the two categories as stated in *(a)* and *(b)* above, and that any form of processing will presumably be included under 'mine' if the particular process takes place within the 'mining area', such as a gold-reduction works or a coal-washing plant. A process such as refining, which is normally conducted away from the mine, would then be classified as a separate industry.

The above definitions indicate the limits of what comprises 'mining'. From the viewpoint of environmental control it is important to note that the inclusion in the Mines and Works Act's definition of mine of the words 'whether abandoned or being worked' and in the Minerals Act, of whether the excavations or tailings or boreholes 'are being worked or not', will necessitate detailed regulation to control a significant environmental hazard created by an abandoned or worked-out mine.

The concept of 'prospecting', earlier defined along similar lines in the Mining Rights Act, is now defined in the Minerals Act as intentionally searching for any mineral by means which disturb the surface of the earth, including the portion under the sea or under other water or of any tailings, by means of excavation or drilling necessary for that purpose, but does not include 'mine' when used as a verb.[70]

15.7.10 Rehabilitation of mining surfaces

Even where mining operations have been discontinued, environmental problems associated with mining frequently continue. Water emanating from an abandoned mine may, by reason of its acidity, continue to cause the pollution of both surface and ground water. Dust from abandoned mine dumps, soil erosion, especially in the case of abandoned opencast mines, and the dumping or impounding of solid or liquid waste, constitute further environmental problems which continue after mining operations have ceased. Furthermore, abandoned shafts, pits and other excavations, as well as

---

[67] Section 1(x).
[68] Section 1(xiii).
[69] Section 1(xxviii).
[70] Section 1(xxix).

subsidences or cavities, hold considerable danger to public safety. In order to combat these problems effectively—especially in the long term—provision should be made for the rehabilitation of the affected surfaces, once mining operations finally cease.

The Mines and Works Act never contained any provisions directly regulating the rehabilitation of mining surfaces. However, the Act was amended in 1977 to enable the Minister of Mineral and Energy Affairs to make regulations regarding the conservation of the environment at or near mines or works, including the restoration of land on which activities in connection with mines or works are performed or have been performed.[71] Legal requirements providing for the rehabilitation of mining areas were subsequently introduced for the first time in 1980, when the standing regulations, made in terms of the Mines and Works Act,[72] were amended.[73]

The concept of 'rehabilitation' is defined in the Minerals Act as meaning, in relation to the surface of land and the environment, the execution by the holder of a prospecting permit or a mining authorization of the rehabilitation programme referred to in the Act[74] to the satisfaction of the regional director.[75] This same definition is encountered in new draft regulations issued in March 1991 by virtue of the Mines and Works Act[76] and which will finally be promulgated in terms of the Minerals Act.[77] This definition gives little content to the concept of 'rehabilitation', other than describing it in terms of the regional director's discretion. Moreover, it is related only to the requirement of a rehabilitation programme, whereas rehabilitation is a relevant requirement also independently of a rehabilitation programme.[78]

15.7.10.1 *Particulars concerning manner of rehabilitation as a prerequisite to issuance of a prospecting permit or mining authorization*

The Minerals Act for the first time determines that considerations relating to surface rehabilitation may operate as a prerequisite to the granting of a prospecting permit or a mining authorization. It is an offence to prospect or mine without such permit or authorization.[79]

(a) Prospecting permit. Any application for a prospecting permit must be accompanied by particulars about the manner in which the applicant intends to prospect and rehabilitate disturbances of the surface which may be caused by his intended prospecting operations, which particulars must be acceptable to the regional director.[80] Although no direct discretion is conferred upon the regional director regarding the issuance of a prospecting permit,[81] a discretion is indirectly built into the process through the above requirement concerning particulars about surface rehabilitation. There are no provisions, comparable to those applicable to mining authorizations, relating to an applicant's ability to make the necessary provision for rehabilitation.

(b) Mining authorization. Whereas the rehabilitation requirement regarding prospecting permits is applied indirectly via the requirement relating to particulars which

---

[71] Section 12(1)*(h*A), inserted by s 3*(b)* of Act 83 of 1977.
[72] GN R992 of 26 June 1970.
[73] GN R537 of 21 March 1980.
[74] Section 39.
[75] Section 1(xxxv). The Minister of Mineral and Energy Affairs appoints an officer in the service of the department—in respect of each region (s 3)—as regional director: s 4. Such regional director may delegate any power conferred upon him by the Act to any officer in the service of the department: s 62(3).
[76] GN 275 of 22 March 1991.
[77] Cf s 68(2) for the transitional provision.
[78] Cf ss 6(2)*(b)*, 8(1), 9(3)*(b)* and *(c)*, 14(1), 38*(b)* and 40.
[79] Section 5(2) read with ss 60*(a)*(i) and 61(1)*(a)*.
[80] Section 6(2)*(b)*.
[81] Section 6(1).

are to accompany applications, the Minerals Act determines that no mining authorization may be issued, unless the regional director is satisfied with the manner in which the applicant intends to rehabilitate disturbances of the surface which may be caused by his mining operations.[82] Moreover, the regional director must also be satisfied that the applicant has the ability and can make the necessary provision to rehabilitate such disturbances of the surface.[83] For this purpose, an application for a mining authorization must be accompanied by particulars about the applicant's ability to make the necessary provision to rehabilitate surface disturbances that are acceptable to the regional director.[84]

15.7.10.2 *Approval of rehabilitation programme prior to commencement of prospecting or mining operations*

A layout plan and rehabilitation programme in respect of the surface of land concerned in any prospecting or mining operations or such intended operations must be submitted by the holder of the prospecting permit or mining authorization concerned to the regional director for his approval before any such operations are commenced with.[85] Before such approval, the regional director must consult with the officers designated for that purpose by the Minister of Agriculture and the Minister of Environment Affairs, respectively.[86] As far as the contents of such rehabilitation programmes are concerned, no specific aspects are prescribed in the Act, although draft regulations require information aimed at the prevention of soil erosion and water pollution,[87] while existing regulations relate to the re-establishment of disturbed vegetation[88] and both sets of regulations imply the replacement of topsoil[89] and subsoil.[90]

Although the Minerals Act requires a rehabilitation programme before *any* prospecting or mining operations may commence, it authorizes the regional director, subject to such conditions as he may determine, to exempt the holder of any prospecting permit or mining authorization from the above requirement or to approve of an amended programme.[91] The only restriction is that prior to his exemption or amendment, the director must consult with the above-mentioned officers of the Departments of Agriculture and of Environment Affairs.[92] The current regulations require merely the submission of a rehabilitation programme (no approval of it is prescribed) and then only in the case of a new opencast mine[93] which is planned to remove annually more than 12 000 tons of mineral, including overburden, before the commencement of the opencast mining operations or any activity incidental to them.[94] No specific mention is made of prospecting. As far as other opencast mines are concerned, a rehabilitation programme is required only when it is specifically requested, and then not even necessarily before operations commence.[95] The new draft

[82] Section 9(3)*(b)*.
[83] Section 9(3)*(c)*.
[84] Section 9(5)*(e)*.
[85] Section 39(1).
[86] Section 39(3).
[87] Draft regs 5.7.5–6 GN 275 of 22 March 1991.
[88] Regulation 5.13.2 GN R537 of 21 March 1980.
[89] Regulation 5.12.3 GN R537 and draft reg 5.7.3*(a)* GN 275. Cf n 102 below for the definition of 'topsoil'.
[90] Draft reg 5.7.3*(b)* GN 275. Cf n 104 below for the definition of 'subsoil'.
[91] Section 39(2).
[92] Section 39(3).
[93] An 'opencast mine' is defined as a mine, including prospecting operations and any hole, trench or other excavation made in the course of prospecting operations, where a mineral deposit is or has been worked at from the surface of the earth after removal of the overburden: reg 5.11*(c)* GN R537.
[94] Proviso to reg 5.12.1 GN R537.
[95] Regulation 5.12.1 GN R537.

regulations are not restricted to opencast mines and generally require the submission of a rehabilitation programme before the commencement of operations, but only in respect of new mines.[96] As far as the other mines are concerned, such a programme is required (not necessarily before operations commence) only at official request[97] or when the operations at an existing mine disturb or are likely to disturb the surface.[98]

15.7.10.3 *Rehabilitation during prospecting or mining operations*

According to the Minerals Act, the rehabilitation of the surface of land concerned in any prospecting or mining must be carried out by the holder of the prospecting permit or mining authorization concerned in accordance with the approved rehabilitation programme (if any), as an integral part of the prospecting or mining operations concerned and simultaneously with such operations (unless determined otherwise by the regional director) to the satisfaction of the regional director.[99] The new draft regulations,[100] as well as the current regulations[101] have similar provisions, although the latter relate only to opencast mines and, while both sets of regulations require, where applicable, rehabilitation in accordance with a programme approved by the Government Mining Engineer, the draft regulations provide that such approval must be given in consultation with the Director-General of Water Affairs. Moreover, both sets of regulations provide that, unless exemption is granted, all topsoil[102] removed at any opencast mine must be deposited at a specially selected site for replacement as topsoil during rehabilitation of the surface.[103] (The draft regulations have a similar provision regarding subsoil.[104]) However, where rehabilitation is carried out simultaneously with the mining operations, such topsoil (and subsoil) may be replaced directly in accordance with the rehabilitation programme.[105]

15.7.10.4 *Rehabilitation as condition for removal or disposal of minerals*

The Minerals Act prohibits the removal or disposal by the holder of any prospecting permit of any mineral found in the course of prospecting operations, except with the permission of the regional director, subject to such conditions in respect of rehabilitation as may be determined by him.[106]

15.7.10.5 *Rehabilitation after prospecting or mining operations cease*

The Minerals Act[107] as well as the current[108] and draft[109] regulations contain provisions prescribing that when prospecting for or the mining of a mineral finally ceases, the holder of the permit or authorization concerned must remove all debris and, as far as is practicable, restore the surface in question to its natural state to the

---

[96] Draft reg 5.7.1*(a)* GN 275.
[97] Draft reg 5.7.1*(c)* GN 275.
[98] Draft reg 5.7.1*(b)* GN 275.
[99] Section 38.
[100] Draft reg 5.7.2 GN 275.
[101] Regulation 5.12.2 GN R537.
[102] According to the current regulations (reg 5.11*(e)*, GN R537) 'topsoil' means all cultivable soil material that can be removed mechanically to a depth of one metre without blasting. The draft regulations (reg 5.6*(g)* GN 275) define 'topsoil' as that layer of soil which provides a suitable environment for the germination of seed, allows the penetration of moisture and is a source of micro-organisms, plant nutrients and, in some cases, seed.
[103] Regulation 5.12.3 GN R537 and draft reg 5.7.3*(a)* GN 275.
[104] Draft reg 5.7.3*(b)* GN 275. 'Subsoil' is defined as soil underlying topsoil and which is suitable for the sustenance of plant life (draft reg 5.6*(f)* GN 275).
[105] Proviso to reg 5.12.3 GN R537 and to draft reg 5.7.3 GN 275.
[106] Section 8(1).
[107] Section 40.
[108] Regulation 5.13.3 GN R537.
[109] Draft reg 5.8.2 GN 275.

satisfaction of the regional director. (Only the draft regulations refer to restoration in accordance with the rehabilitation programme.)

15.7.10.6 *Certificate of completed rehabilitation*

When the rehabilitation of the surface of a mine has been completed to the satisfaction of the Inspector of Mines, he may, in consultation with the Director-General of Water Affairs and with the approval of the Government Mining Engineer, issue a certificate to the effect that the provisions of the regulations, in so far as the rehabilitation of the surface is concerned, have been complied with.[110]

15.7.10.7 *Pecuniary provision for rehabilitation*

Regulations issued in terms of the Mines and Works Act[111] address the question of pecuniary provisions to ensure the rehabilitation of the surface of a mine (or the prevention of air and water pollution). The Government Mining Engineer may order the owner or manager of a mine to make such provision[112] and such owner or manager must determine annually the pecuniary provision which is necessary in order to comply with the above order, in consultation with an expert, to the satisfaction of the Government Mining Engineer.[113] It may be argued, however, that these regulations are ultra vires, because the Mines and Works Act does not authorize a requirement of pecuniary provision in the event of rehabilitation, or even for any other cause. However, the Minerals Act, which authorizes the Minister of Mineral and Energy Affairs to make regulations as to the rehabilitation of disturbed surfaces, also enables him to impose levies and to establish accounts in that regard.[114]

Although the empowering provision of the Minerals Act may cover the above regulations, it may still be argued that they are void for vagueness. There is no indication as to what type of pecuniary provision may be required of the owner or manager of a mine. For instance, there seems to be nothing which prevents the Government Mining Engineer from requiring the owner or manager to deposit the full amount of potential liability for rehabilitation in trust. Other more reasonable possibilities are the requirement of compulsory private insurance or the establishment of a state-operated rehabilitation fund. See also chapter 3.

15.7.10.8 *Sanctions*

Failure to comply with or contravention of the above-mentioned provisions is enforced through the criminal sanction.[115] Moreover, the Minerals Act authorizes the Minister of Mineral and Energy Affairs to suspend or cancel any prospecting permit or mining authorization if the holder of it contravenes or fails to comply with any relevant provision of the Act.[116] (No specific mention is made of a failure to comply with or a contravention of the conditions of a permit or authorization.[117]) Such suspension or cancellation is obligatory if the holder fails to rehabilitate the surface concerned in accordance with the provisions of the Act.[118] Furthermore, the regulations provide that,

---

[110] Regulation 5.12.5 inserted by GN R1339 of 22 June 1990 and draft reg 5.8.4 GN 275.

[111] Regulation 5.16 inserted by GN R398 of 1 March 1991. The draft regulations contain identical provisions: draft reg 5.11 GN 275.

[112] Regulation 5.16.1 GN R537 (draft reg 5.11.1 GN 275).

[113] Regulation 5.16.2 GN R537 (draft reg 5.11.2 GN 275).

[114] Section 63(1)*(d)*. Cf also s 63(1)*(c)*.

[115] Sections 5(2), 8(1), 38, 39(1), 40 and 60*(a)* of the Minerals Act and draft reg 5.7.8 GN 275 read with s 63(5) of the Act.

[116] Section 14(1).

[117] Cf s 63(1)*(p)*.

[118] Sections 14(1) and 38.

on failure to comply with the rehabilitation requirement,[119] the Inspector of Mines may, in addition to a prosecution for such failure, have the surface of the land concerned rehabilitated to his satisfaction at the expense of the owner or manager of the mine concerned.[120] Although this is potentially a very effective sanction, it would seem that neither the Mines and Works Act nor the Minerals Act authorizes such a provision: both Acts[121, 122] provide only for the prescription of criminal sanctions.

Finally, the Minerals Act confers a power of expropriation upon the Minister: if at any time he deems it necessary in the public interest to expropriate any right (including ownership) in respect of land, the surface or any portion under the surface of land or to a mineral in respect of land, he may expropriate any such right.[123] Provision is also made for the expropriation of land where the use of land for mining purposes prevents or hinders the proper use of such land for farming purposes.[124]

15.7.11 Environmental impact assessment of mining

Since mining operations have the potential to exert a negative impact on the environment, any mining development should be preceded by an environmental impact analysis. See chapter 30. The statutory strategies which have been designed to provide for the submission of environmental impact reports are identified activities and limited development areas in terms of the Environment Conservation Act 73 of 1989. Both are discussed in chapter 7. No mining-related activity or mining area has yet been subjected to the above-mentioned provisions. In other words, there is at present no general legal obligation upon owners or managers of mines to submit environmental impact statements prior to the commencement of mining operations.

The only indirect manner in which a type of environmental impact analysis may be required is through the procedure prescribed for applications for a prospecting permit or mining authorization. The regional director may require any information and documents to accompany such applications.[125]

15.7.12 Restriction of environmental encroachment, disturbance and damage

Both the current[126] and the draft[127] regulations in terms of the Mines and Works Act determine that no encroachment on the environment and no disturbance of the surface may take place or be allowed to take place outside the area which, in the opinion of the Government Mining Engineer, is actually required for prospecting, mining or works and such area must at all times be confined to the minimum compatible with the efficient functioning of such operations.

The Minerals Act authorizes the regional director to issue directives and determine conditions in relation to the use of the surface of land comprising the subject of any prospecting permit or mining authorization or upon which a works is situated in order to limit any damage to or the disturbance of the surface, vegetation, environment or water sources to the minimum necessary for any prospecting or mining operations.[128]

15.7.13 Mining and soil conservation

The provisions of the Minerals Act and of regulations made in terms of the Mines and Works Act relating to the rehabilitation of mining surfaces that have been discussed are

[119] In terms of reg 5.12.2 GN R537.
[120] Regulation 5.12.2.1 inserted by GN R398 of 1 March 1991 (draft reg 5.7.9 GN 275).
[121] Section 12(4).
[122] Section 63(5).
[123] Section 24(1).
[124] Sections 42(1)*(a)* and 42(2). For a critical assessment of the above provisions relating to rehabilitation, see Rabie 'Legislation for the rehabilitation of mining surfaces' 1991 *THRHR* 774, 780–2.
[125] Sections 6(2) and 9(5) of the Minerals Act.
[126] Regulation 5.13 GN R537.
[127] Draft reg 5.8 GN 275.
[128] Sections 41(1) and 60*(a)*.

aimed, to a large measure, at soil conservation. Certain regulations concerning the re-establishment of vegetation[129] and the restoration of river banks,[130] which are not specifically tied up with the rehabilitation process, also concern soil conservation.

15.7.14 Mining and water pollution

It has been shown that water pollution is the most serious environmental problem associated with mining. Mining is specifically listed as an activity included under 'use for industrial purposes' in terms of the Water Act 54 of 1956, thus rendering applicable the Act's provisions governing industrial water pollution. See chapter 18. The Act also deals with the use of water removed from a mine.

The necessity of pumping subterranean water from a mine was first dealt with under the Irrigation and Conservation of Waters Act 8 of 1912, which was the forerunner of the Water Act 54 of 1956, and which confined the removal of water from mines only to areas where dolomitic formations occur.[131] The Water Act now provides that a mine owner may remove from a mining area any water found underground if he is of the opinion that it is necessary for the efficient continuation of mining operations or for the safety of mine employees. The water so removed may be used for the operations of that mine or for domestic purposes connected with it, or for any other purpose provided a permit has been issued for such purpose.[132]

Moreover, water pollution control associated with mining is provided for in different sets of regulations, promulgated by virtue of the Water Act[133] and the Mines and Works Act.[134]. The regulations issued in terms of the Water Act[135] prescribe that the person who is in control of a mine or works and the person who intends to establish a mine or works must furnish the Director-General of Water Affairs with certain information relating to that mine or works.[136] A number of important obligations are laid upon the manager of a mine or works: he is responsible for the compilation of a plan which must depict all works constructed for the control of water on the surface of a mine or works and contain a list of prescribed details.[137] He must, moreover, cause effective measures to be taken to prevent effluent, including water pumped from underground or which flows naturally from a mine or works, flowing or seeping beyond the boundaries of the property on which the mine or works is situated.[138] The manager also has a number of specific duties to perform with respect to mineral tailings and waste rock dumps, slimes dams and other sources of pollution,[139] in respect of waterways, stormwater drains and dams,[140] and with regard to domestic effluent.[141] Contravention of any regulation is an

---

[129] Regulation 5.13.2 GN R537.

[130] Regulations 5.14, 5.14.1*(a)* and *(b)* and 5.14.2 GN R537.

[131] In terms of s 26(3) of the 1912 Act the owner of any mine which was being lawfully worked within a dolomitic geological area proclaimed under s 25 of the Act was empowered to take steps for removing any subterranean water from the mine if this was necessary for the efficient carrying out of mining operations or the safety of persons employed thereat. Under s 25, the expression 'subterranean water' meant such water naturally existing underground as is contained within the dolomitic geological areas of South Africa as defined from time to time by proclamation.

[132] Section 12B.

[133] Section 26.

[134] Section 12(1).

[135] GN R287 of 20 February 1976.

[136] Regulation 2.

[137] Regulation 5.

[138] Regulation 6.1.

[139] Regulations 7, 8, 11.1, 12, 14, 16 and 21.

[140] Regulations 9, 13 and 19.

[141] Regulation 18.

offence.[142] However, the Minister may grant exemption from compliance with the provisions of any of these regulations.[143]

Regulations made in terms of the Mines and Works Act[144] and applicable by virtue of the transitional clause of the Minerals Act[145] provide that water which contains poisonous or injurious matter in suspension or solution must be fenced off and may not be permitted to escape without previously having been rendered innocuous.[146] Moreover, sand may be extracted from the channel of a stream or river as well as from a dam, pan or lake only on condition that effluent produced from such operations may not be returned to any stream, river, dam, pan or lake unless such effluent conforms to the purity standards laid down by the Department of Water Affairs.[147] No sand dump or slimes dam may be established on the bank of any stream, river, dam, pan or lake without the permission of the Inspector of Mines.[148] Finally, during prospecting for or recovery of oil, all reasonable measures must be taken, to the satisfaction of the Government Mining Engineer, to prevent the escape of oil to the surroundings, either on land or in the sea.[149] It is advisable that the two sets of regulations should be consolidated in order to provide for uniform control over water pollution associated with mining.

15.7.15 Mining and air pollution

The Atmospheric Pollution Prevention Act 45 of 1965 provides for the performance by the Government Mining Engineer of the functions of the chief air pollution control officer of the Department of National Health and Population Development in respect of matters relating to mines, ie asbestos (as a scheduled process) and dust from mine-dumps.[150]

Dust control is particularly important to the mining industry, and areas which have been declared dust control areas include a number of districts in which mines are situated. The Act provides for the taking of prescribed steps or adopting the best practicable means to prevent dust pollution from industrial processes, which include any mining activities, by the person who carries on the activity.[151] Where such person has ceased to exist, the State, local authority or the owner concerned will bear the cost involved in taking the necessary steps. Regulations may be made prescribing the steps to be taken to prevent the creation of a nuisance by dust becoming dispersed.[152] A Dust Control Levy Account is established into which contributions, either as a single payment or as periodic payments, must be made which vary according to the nature and magnitude of the operation.[153] See, generally, chapter 17.

The above measures are of great significance with regard to mine-dumps which include all dumps permitted in terms of provisions of the Mining Rights Act, comprising tailings, slimes, waste rock, sand or other residues produced in the course of mining operations and deposited on land in respect of which mining operations are being or have been conducted. The surface owner is not necessarily the holder of the mineral rights or mining title, and in such cases the surface owner cannot prevent the mineral

---

[142] Regulation 24 read with s 170(3).
[143] Section 26.
[144] GN R537 of 21 March 1980.
[145] Section 68(2).
[146] Regulations 5.9.1 and 5.9.2.
[147] Regulation 5.14.1*(c)*.
[148] Regulation 5.14.3.
[149] Regulation 5.15.
[150] Section 6.
[151] Sections 28 and 30.
[152] Section 33.
[153] Section 31.

right or mining title holder from creating mine-dumps and, equally, there seems nothing at common law or statute to suggest that the surface owner can require the removal of such dumps unless their removal is part of an obligatory rehabilitation programme.[154]

An interesting question is whether claims for damages can succeed where pollution results from mine-dumps authorized by statute. Dale,[155] after a thorough examination of the vexed question of whether mine dumps constitute movables or immovables, concludes that mine-dumps are regarded as artificial and, in the event of claims for damages, defences by the polluter of statutory authority and normal and natural user are, in fact, unlikely to succeed in the case of pollution arising from mine-dumps. It is suggested that it is doubtful whether in the present era 'normal and natural user' could still serve as a defence in any case of pollution caused by mining.

The recovery of residues from mine tailings currently conducted under permit granted in terms of the Mining Rights Act[156] would be classified as 'mining' under the Minerals Act. Permission for conducting such mining would necessitate the furnishing of a rehabilitation programme which should include provision for compensation for pollution damage.

The practice of grassing dumps as a means of curbing pollution in terms of the Atmospheric Pollution Prevention Act has been in operation for many years: indeed, this procedure was introduced by the Chamber of Mines long before the Act came into force. This method entails the removal of excess water, contouring the slopes, and liming and fertilizing prior to planting a suitable grass.

Regulations issued by virtue of the Mines and Works Act[157] and applicable in terms of the Minerals Act, provide their own version of covering dumps in that to prevent the dissemination of any form of pollution such as dust, sand, smoke or fumes from any dump, the manager must cover the dump with soil or sludge or otherwise deal with it in a manner satisfactory to the Inspector of Mines.[158] The regulations furthermore provide detailed measures for ventilation, gases and dust. Where rock, ore, coal or other mineral compound is reduced in size, screened, moved, handled or otherwise subjected to any process which may produce dust, the liberation of dust into the atmosphere must be effectively controlled by the use of water or another dust allaying agent or by a dust-extraction system.[159] It is also determined that no dust, fumes or smoke from any extracting system may be discharged into the atmosphere unless adequate provision has been made to ensure that such discharge is harmless and inoffensive.[160] See also chapter 17.

15.7.16 Mining and waste

Solid waste control associated with mining is effected in terms of regulations issued by virtue of the Mines and Works Act[161] which are to be applicable in terms of the transitional clause of the Minerals Act.[162] The regulations provide that no dumping or impounding of rubble, litter, garbage, rubbish or discards of any description, whether liquid or solid, may take place elsewhere than at the demarcated sites. Every such site must be limited to a minimum and every dump must be so controlled as to ensure that the environment is, as far as is practicable, not polluted.[163] Whenever practicable, waste

---

[154] Dale above n 37, 48.
[155] Above n 37, 37–52.
[156] Section 161.
[157] GN R992 of 26 June 1970.
[158] Regulation 5.10.
[159] Regulation 10.2.1.
[160] Regulation 10.4.
[161] GN R537 of 21 March 1980.
[162] Section 68(2).
[163] Regulation 5.13.1.

material from certain plants and works must be disposed of in the workings of the mine.[164] During prospecting for or recovery of oil, all reasonable measures must be taken, to the satisfaction of the Government Mining Engineer, to prevent the escape of oil to the surroundings, either on land or in the sea.[165] Provision is, finally, made for the demolition of buildings and other structures or installations and the disposal of resultant rubble, once prospecting or mining has ceased.[166]

15.7.17 Mining and ionizing radiation

The prospecting for or mining of nuclear source material and the recovery of such material from tailings, slimes or other residues, have traditionally been controlled in terms of the Nuclear Energy Act 92 of 1982[167] and its predecessors. The relevant provisions of this Act,[168] however, have been repealed by the Minerals Act. The position is set out in chapter 21. The Minerals Act, through its transitional provisions, makes allowance for the continuation of prospecting and mining rights,[169] although the ultimate aim is that all prospecting and mining are to be brought within the purview of the Minerals Act.

15.7.18 Mining in protected areas

Mining is usually not expressly regulated in legislation relating to protected areas, but there are two exceptions: the National Parks Act 57 of 1976 and the Forest Act 122 of 1984. The former Act renders it an offence to conduct any prospecting or mining on land included in a sch 1 national park.[170] On the other hand, the Forest Act expressly provides for the granting of rights in connection with prospecting or mining in state forests.[171] As far as other legislation is concerned, it would depend upon the wording of the individual provisions whether or not prospecting or mining is included in the prohibitions. Even if either is included—as probably would be the case in most instances—few prohibitions are as absolute as that of the National Parks Act. Provision is mostly made for authorization of the prohibited activity concerned. For instance, although the National Monuments Act 28 of 1969 prohibits the destruction, damage, excavation, alteration or removal of a national monument, such actions may be authorized by a permit.[172] The Minerals Act, likewise, generally prohibits the prospecting on any land which has been reserved or is being used for government or public purposes (which would presumably include state protected areas), or which may be defined and so determined by the Minister of Mineral and Energy Affairs.[173] However, such prospecting may be authorized by the Minister.[174]

15.8 CONCLUSION

South Africa is blessed with the occurrence of many minerals, often in large quantities and of strategic importance to it and to other nations. The country also has one of the most sophisticated and developed mining industries in the world. Together they can provide a significant contribution to primary wealth creation which the country needs to meet the demands of a New South Africa.

---

[164] Regulation 5.13.4.
[165] Regulation 5.15.
[166] Regulation 5.13.3.
[167] Section 47.
[168] *Ibid.*
[169] Sections 44 and 47.
[170] Sections 20 and 24(8).
[171] Section 11(2)*(b)*.
[172] Section 12(2).
[173] Section 7(1)*(c)* and *(d)*.
[174] Section 7(1).

At present, a spirit of co-operation exists between the mining houses (both individually and through the Chamber of Mines) and the authorities with respect to the environmental management of mines. The co-operation extends from joint efforts to draft legislation through to improved implementation of the most up-to-date, cost-effective techniques.

The guiding principle in drafting the legislation is to entrench *what* should be achieved rather than *how* it should be achieved. This approach allows for the site specific nature of mining projects where it is not possible to stipulate detailed methods, techniques or standards for the whole country. The approach is embodied in the environmental management programme report (EMPR) concept and therefore, if the relevant provisions of the Minerals Act[175] are amended to incorporate an EMPR (instead of merely a rehabilitation plan), no further legislation need be promulgated with respect to managing the biophysical impacts of mining. As far as standards are concerned, the industry has well accepted guidelines which perhaps need updating and the compilation of additional volumes, particularly concerning water management.

The overall goal of managing these impacts should be to design and implement mitigating measures that minimize the residual impact of mining. Therefore, every mine should be planned for closure and a walk-away solution. This was not the case in the past, where there are many examples of significant residual adverse environmental impacts which have caused a widely-held belief that mining results in environmental disaster. In fact, with good management, it should not.

Part of good management is to manage project finances, which obviously include the finances to manage the environment. These usually fall into three areas—project capital (which provides for pre-mining environmental studies and the planning activities involved in compiling an EMPR), working costs (which cater for the implementation of the EMPR) and a provision for closure (which must be deducted from profit over the productive years of the mine's life). Responsible management usually establishes some sort of trust fund for this closure provision.

Provision for closure is the most controversial from three main points of view. First, the environmental objectives to be achieved at closure must be set. It is a fact that no development project has zero environmental impact. Therefore the closure objectives must allow for some residual impacts. Agreeing on what these are is a real challenge because:

- Our prediction capability is not yet developed to a point where the impacts can be quantified accurately.
- Setting objectives that aim at zero residual impact are uneconomic and could be ruinous for the mines.
- Setting objectives that are too low could leave residual impacts that will not be tolerated by society.

Secondly, in South Africa, the State assumes environmental responsibility for mines after a closure certificate has been issued. At present, this leaves the State in an unenviable position which has resulted in recent thoughts about legislating for a state administered fund (to be contributed to by existing and new mines) for post-closure pollution prevention. It has also resulted in a reluctance to issue closure certificates. However, if an approved EMPR is implemented (with the usual monitoring and auditing to ensure that the implementation is done according to plan) the risk of adverse residual environmental impacts is small. Since the State, and the country as a whole, benefit from mining projects, this small residual risk should be accepted as a state and

[175] Sections 38 and 39.

therefore a tax-payers liability. Bear in mind that the mining company has taken all the entrepreneurial and environmental risk up to the time closure activities stop.

Thirdly, the question of poor management or inadequate resources to provide for closure and ongoing rehabilitation strengthens the argument in favour of legislating for pecuniary provision, instead of self-regulation which is supported by the large mining companies.

The *aide-mémoire* for EMPRs states that particulars should be given about the developer's ability to make the necessary (financial) provision to implement the measures described in section 5 of the EMPR which, once agreed to, is the legally binding section. This leaves the door open for innovative financial management and should satisfy the need for legislative control of this issue.

The EMPR concept, which follows fully the class 1 route in the general procedure for integrated environmental management as recommended by the Council for the Environment, should be adopted by all mining projects and the authorities who must approve them. Coupled with the proposed changes to legislation already being processed, the concept should ensure that the wealth creation potential from mining can go hand in hand with enhancing environmental quality. All other development sectors which can cause significant impacts would do well to adapt the EMPR concept to their particular needs so that they too can demonstrate their commitment to the future environment.

*The artwork for this chapter was prepared by L E Waugh of Rand Mines (Mining and Services) Ltd. The figures were adapted from the following sources:
Figure 15.1: Doyle *Strip mining of coal, environmental solutions* (1976).
Figure 15.2: Wood & Young 'Coedmore quarry: a case study in cost-effective reclamation' 1987 (1) *Landscape southern Africa*.
Figure 15.3: PR brochures, Richards Bay Minerals Corporation.
Figure 15.4: *The Gold Fields Review* 1990–91.
Figure 15.5, 15.7, 15.8: Rand Mines (Mining and Services) Ltd. In-house.
Figure 15.6: Thomas *An introduction to mining* (1979).
Figure 15.9: Erasmus et al above n 16.
Figure 15.10: Cook above n 25.

CHAPTER 16

OFFSHORE MINERALS

J J GURNEY
I R McLACHLAN
M B KIRKLEY
J I GLAZEWSKI

16.1 INTRODUCTION

The coast of South Africa is naturally subdivided into three regions: a wide western margin which continues northward from Cape Columbine to the Kunene River in Namibia; the narrow eastern margin east of Algoa Bay, and the Agulhas Bank, off the south coast (Figure 16.1). Each of these regions has its own sedimentological and physical characteristics.[1] The wide western margin is dominated by sediments rich in organic debris as a result of upwelling of nutrient-rich waters. In contrast, the narrow eastern margin is characterized by land-derived sediments that are redistributed by the powerful Agulhas Current. The Agulhas Bank reflects characteristics of both the east and west coasts in that it is wide and contains sediments similar to those of the west coast, while being strongly affected by the Agulhas Current as is the east coast.

Geological surveys of the coastal areas of South Africa have explored the form of the coastal margin and the extent of offshore mineral resources occurring on the margin.[2] In general, the coastal region can be divided into three zones from the shoreline seaward (Figure 16.2): a narrow near-shore platform, a gently sloping shelf, and a steeper slope. 'Basement' rocks of the continental landmass form the continuous, upstanding near-shore platform which is usually not more than 5 nautical miles wide. This platform is covered by lime- and quartz-rich sands and gravels which locally include diamondiferous and heavy mineral sands. The platform is bounded by a steep cliff which drops to the shelf composed of limestones, clays and phosphorites. At the base of this cliff a layer of mud up to 10 m thick covers the shelf rocks, whereas seaward the mud content of the shelf sediments decreases and sands appear. The outer shelf is covered by a very thin veneer of sands. These outer shelf sands are rich in phosphate and glauconite and the shelf itself is littered with slabs of phosphorite. Beyond the edge of the shelf is the slope which is mantled by muds and muddy sands. Further seaward, on the deep sea floor (>4 000 m), manganese (Mn) nodules occur in large quantities. Oil and gas deposits occur deep beneath the continental shelf and slope as they require considerable overburden thickness to provide the right conditions for their generation and entrapment.

Diamonds, oil and gas are currently being extracted from offshore occurrences. The offshore equivalents of heavy mineral beach sands, along with phosphate and glauconite deposits on the shelf and deep-sea deposits of Mn-nodules could represent

* Sincere thanks are extended to Theo de Jager of Soekor, and to John Rogers of the Marine Geoscience Unit, University of Cape Town, for providing information on technical aspects of this chapter.

[1] Birch, Rogers, Bremner & Moir *Sedimentation controls on the continental margin of southern Africa* Poster session presented at the first interdisciplinary conference on marine and freshwater research in southern Africa, Port Elizabeth, July 1976. See also chapter 14.

[2] Summarized by Rogers, Summerhayes, Dingle, Birch, Bremner & Simpson *Distribution of minerals on the seabed around South Africa and problems in their exploration and eventual exploitation* ECOR symposium on the ocean's challenge to South African engineers, CSIR Stellenbosch, 1972.

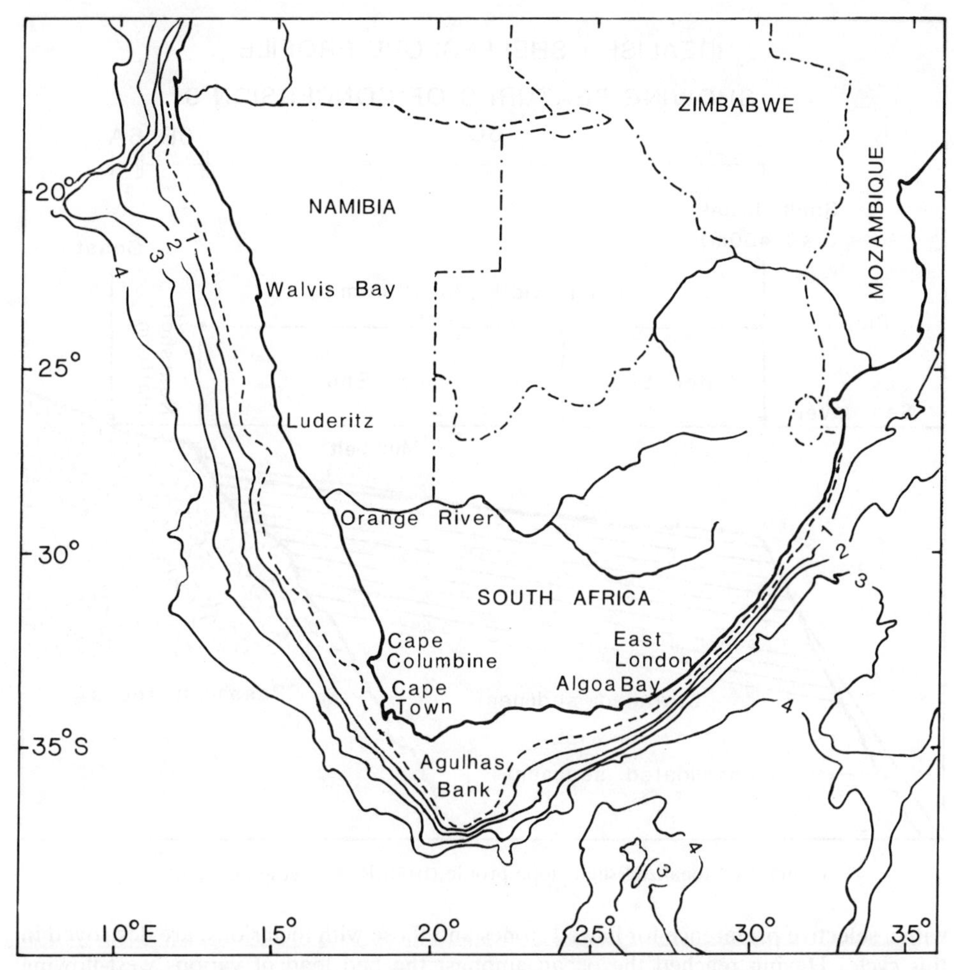

Figure 16.1 The coastal regions of southern Africa. The shelf break is shown by the dashed line; numbered contours represent depth in kilometres (from Seisser, Scrutton & Simpson 'Atlantic and Indian ocean margins of southern Africa' in Burk & Drake (eds) *The geology of continental margins* (1974)).

important mineral reserves. At present, however, the technology required to exploit such deposits on a large scale is not readily available, and their development is generally not considered to be economically viable when compared with land-based operations.

16.2 DIAMONDS

16.2.1 Introduction

Diamond is the only mineral mined from the near-shore platform of southern Africa at present—i e in both South Africa and Namibia. Namibia probably has the richer and larger deposits, but both are significant. The deposits in the territorial waters of the two countries are similar, namely, in the very high quality of diamond they produce and their manner of formation.

16.2.2 Nature of resource

The bulk of marine diamonds are derived from distant central continental (cratonic) locations and have been transported to the sea by erosional processes. Many diamonds,

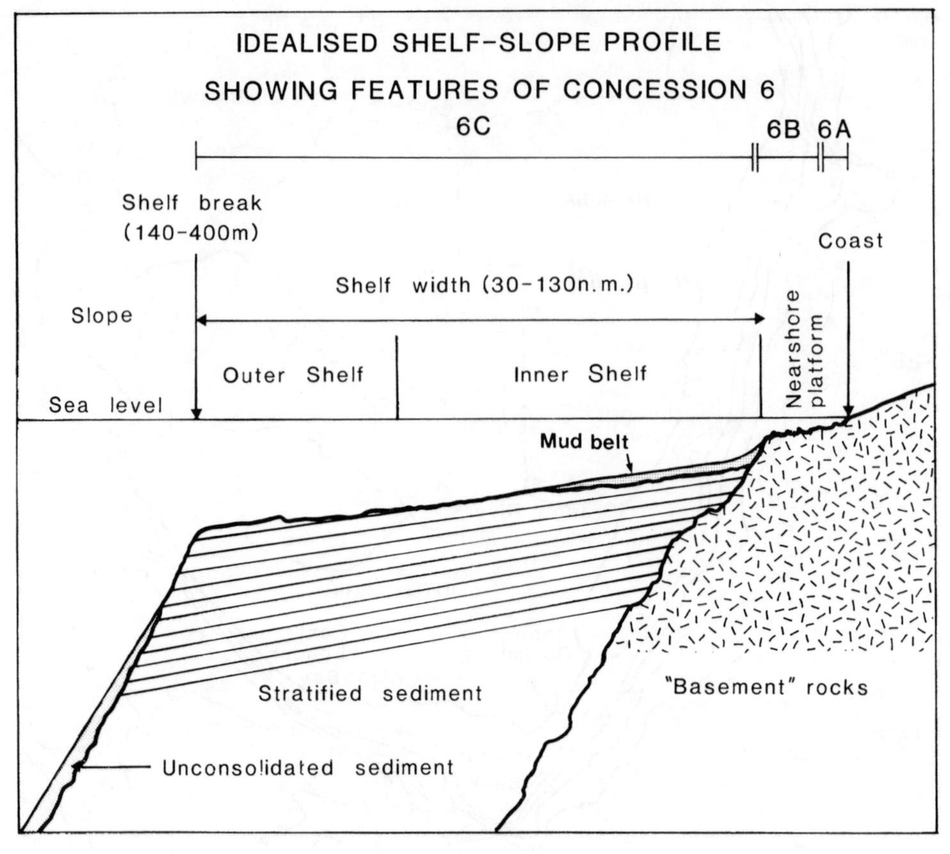

Figure 16.2 Idealized shelf-slope profile (from Rogers et al above n 2).

with a selective preference for flawed stones and those with inclusions, are destroyed in this cycle. Having reached the ocean amongst the bed load of various west-flowing rivers, the diamonds are dumped as a trace constituent offshore from river mouths. More than 90 per cent of the diamonds which survive are flawless crystals and frequently of gem quality. The river gravels deposited in the near-shore shallow-water environment are subsequently sorted, sized and subjected to attrition from the long-amplitude South Atlantic Ocean swells prevalent along the west coast of southern Africa. These waves approach the SSE-NNW trending coastline from a predominantly southwesterly direction, consequently creating a strong southerly long-shore drift that further sorts the sedimentary material as it transports it towards the equator.

16.2.3 Location and size of resource

Diamonds are found all along the west coast from Donkin's Bay south of the Olifants River to the Orange River mouth more than 400 km to the north, and on into Namibia. They have been mined from Doring Bay in the south to Hottentot Bay in the north. Favoured primary sources for these gemstones are Cretaceous kimberlites in the central Karoo which fall within the drainage basin of the Orange/Vaal River complex and from which it has been calculated more than 3 billion carats of diamonds have been eroded.[3] These were transported westwards during the last 80–100 million years. While the bulk

[3] Wilson 'The mission 3 billion carats of diamonds' 1971 (2) *International Diamonds Annual* 57–8.

of the diamonds were probably discharged into the ocean by the Orange River drainage system, that system has migrated during the relevant time period as far south as the current Olifants River mouth, where it entered the sea during a substantial period of time, perhaps 45 million years.[4] Pan remnants of ancient river channels are today found beneath Brandvlei and Van Wyksvlei; basal gravels in these channels contain diamonds, as they do at Bitterputs, Galputs and Bosluis Pan in the ancient Koa River valley in Bushmanland. These are remnants of the palaeo-drainages along which diamonds were transported to the ocean in earlier, wetter climates. Any of the larger west coast river channels which cut back to the old African land surface of King[5] can be diamondiferous. As a result, any beaches or near-shore surf zones from south of the Olifants River northwards far into Namibia may contain diamonds. However, the sea level fluctuated greatly in the past, with the result that there are both palaeo-beaches above sea level and even more submerged strand lines in the ocean. The raised beach deposits onshore were deposited in a small number of interglacial periods of short duration yet have yielded close to 100 million carats of diamonds to date in mining operations in Namibia and Namaqualand combined. Important deposits can also be predicted in the submerged strand lines by which the greater quantity of diamonds were probably delivered. Tertiary strand lines can be expected to be the most productive, but substantial deposits can also be forecast in other submerged beaches.

Increases in the average size of diamonds recovered at or near the mouths of the Olifants, Groen and Buffels rivers, in addition to the Orange, indicate that these rivers at least have carried diamonds to the ocean. Other channels such as the Somnaas, Hol, and the Spoeg have disrupted pre-existing diamondiferous beach horizons and redeposited portions of them back into the sea. Submerged river palaeo-channels can be followed into deep water, even in some cases right across the shelf deposits, by geophysical means. Storm beaches, cliff lines, wedge sediment and deltaic material are all known to be present, and are potentially diamond-bearing.

16.2.4 Development of interest in exploitation

Exploration of these potential resources was started in a small way by two small companies in 1954. Their efforts were greatly expanded by a Texan, the legendary Sam Collins, during the period 1961 to 1965 through the Marine Diamond Corporation (MDC). MDC was subsequently acquired by De Beers and is essentially the forerunner of the currently strongly active De Beers Marine (Pty) Ltd. This company operates prospecting and trial mining vessels in Namibian and South African waters. In South Africa its activity is confined to water essentially deeper than 100 m and there is no published information about the results of exploration in De Beers' prospecting leases. No other mining company approaches the size and scope of De Beers Marine in this field, which either holds or has joint venture agreements that dominate the available lease areas (see Figures 16.3 and 16.4). In South Africa there are three other groups that between them recovered more than 70 per cent of the diamonds produced annually from the Namaqualand sea diamond operations in 1989 and 1990. These are Alexcor, Benguela Concessions and Buffelsbank Diamante. Other minor contractors provide for the balance of production. Most of the diamonds (>70 per cent in 1990) are won from gravel recoveries in close proximity to the mouths of the Orange, Buffels and Olifants rivers.

16.2.5 Namibian lease areas

In Namibia, offshore diamond mining is dominated by Consolidated Diamond Mining (Pty) Ltd (CDM), which controls the offshore mining areas from the mouth of

[4] Dingle & Hendy 'Late mesozoic and tertiary sediment supply to the eastern Cape basin (SE Atlantic) and paleodrainage systems in southern Africa' 1984 (56) *Marine Geology* 13–26.
[5] *South African scenery* (3 ed, 1963).

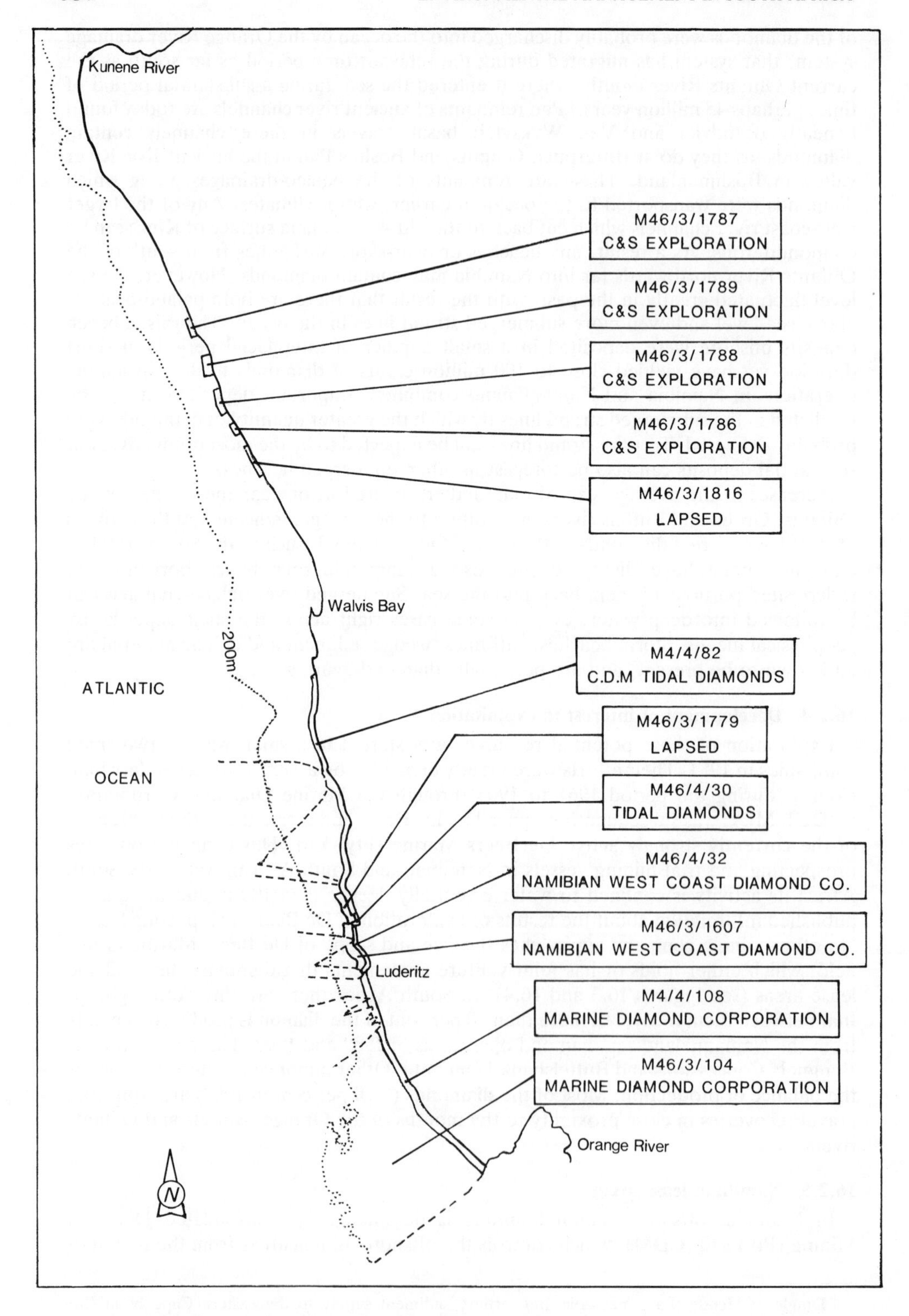

Figure 16.3 Namibian offshore diamond prospecting/mining lease areas.

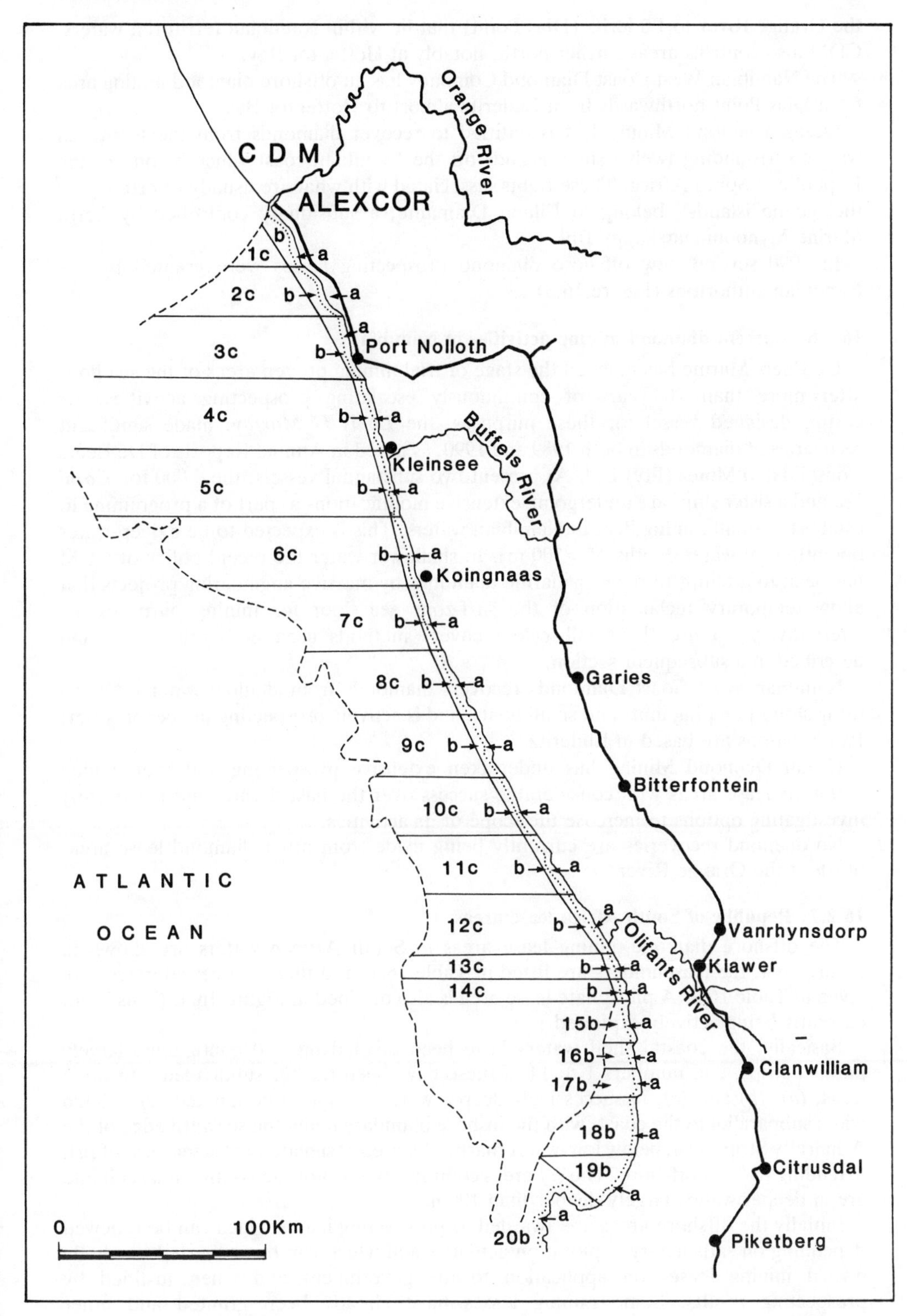

Figure 16.4 South African offshore diamond prospecting/mining lease areas. (See Table 16.1).

the Orange River to Lüderitz (Dias Point) that lie within Namibian territorial waters. CDM also controls areas further north, notably at Hottentot Bay.

The Namibian West Coast Diamond Company has an offshore diamond mining area from Dias Point northwards from Lüderitz almost to Hottentot Bay.

Ocean Diamond Mining Ltd is entitled to recover diamonds from the territorial waters surrounding twelve small islands off the Namibian coast which belong to the Republic of South Africa. These rights, associated with what are usually referred to as the 'guano islands', belong to Eiland Diamante, a subsiduary controlled by Terra Marine Mynboumaatskappy Bpk.

In 1990 several new offshore diamond prospecting leases were granted by the Namibian authorities (Figure 16.3).

16.2.6 Current diamond mining activities in Namibia

De Beers Marine has reached the stage of trial-mining proven areas of the sea floor after more than 20 years of continuously escalating prospecting activities. Its custom-designed vessel for these purposes, the *Louis G Murray*, made significant recoveries of diamonds in both 1989 and 1990, as noted in Annual Reports of De Beers Consolidated Mines (Pty) Ltd. At present two substantial vessels, the 6 000 ton *Coral Sea* and a sister ship, are undergoing extensive modifications as part of a programme to establish a small mining fleet in Namibian waters. This is expected to be a deep-water operation (at water depths of >100 m). In shallower water the recent policy of CDM has been to attempt to recover marine diamonds by massive engineering projects that allow temporary reclamation of the surf-zone sea floor for mining purposes or, alternatively, to use the small-scale recovery methods used in South Africa and described in a subsequent section.

Namibian West Coast Diamonds recovers diamonds from shallow water (<20 m) using shore-pumping units and small boats, and is actively prospecting in deeper water. Its operations are based in Lüderitz.

Ocean Diamond Mining has undertaken extensive prospecting and trial mining within its lease areas with considerable success over the past decade and is currently investigating options to increase the scope of its activities.

No diamond recoveries are currently being made from other diamond lease areas north of the Orange River.

16.2.7 Republic of South Africa lease areas

The offshore diamond-mining lease areas in South African waters are shown in Figure 16.4, the leaseholders are listed in Table 16.1, and their contact addresses are given in Table 16.2. A phosphate lease area is also outlined in Figure 16.4. (This is not currently being actively exploited.)

Basically, the coastal shelf waters have been divided into 20 contiguous, largely parallel strips, and numbers 1 to 14 of these have been further subdivided into three units, *(a)*, *(b)* and *(c)*, in successively deeper waters. An area designated *(a)* is 1 km wide, subparallel to the coast, with the inshore boundary being the seaward edge of the Admiralty Strip (30 m below low-water mark). An area designated *(b)* is seaward of *(a)*, extending to 5 km offshore. The *(c)* areas comprise the rest of the continental shelf and are in deeper water, largely deeper than 100 m.

Initially the offshore areas are awarded as prospecting leases which can be renewed depending on satisfactory exploration activities and which can be converted to wholly owned mining leases on application to the government and when justified by prospecting results. Some mining leases have already been granted and other applications are pending. Concession areas and boundary demarcation are also discussed in sections 16.9.5.4–5.

TABLE 16.1
Holders of marine diamond concessions as at December 1989.

Concessions No.	Name
1A	Alexcor
1B	Alexcor
1C	Alexcor
2A	Cliffs Diamond Ventures (Pty) Ltd
2B	Seediamantkonsessie 2B (Edms) Bpk
2C	Tinto Africa Exploration (Pty) Ltd
3A	Alexcor
3B	Marine West Diamond Concession Holders (Pty) Ltd
3C	Three Sea (Pty) Ltd
4A	Robbaai Beleggings (Edms) Bpk
4B	Aquamarine Diamonds (Pty) Ltd
4C	De Beers Consolidated Mines Ltd
5A	Terra Marine Mynboumaatskappy Bpk
5B	Benguela Concessions (Pty) Ltd
5C	De Beers Consolidated Mines Ltd
6A	Benguela Concessions (Pty) Ltd
6B	Benguela Concessions (Pty) Ltd
6C	Ocean Diamond Mining Ltd
7A	Terra Marine Mynboumaatskappy Bpk
7B	Oceaneering International Inc & Harry Winston Inc
7C	De Beers Consolidated Mines Ltd
8A	Namagroen Prospecting & Investments CC
8B	Bamagroen Prospecting & Investments CC
8C	Namagroen Eight Sea (Pty) Ltd
9A	Namagroen Prospecting & Investments CC
9B	Tenmohs Diamonds (Pty) Ltd
9C	De Beers Consolidated Mines Ltd
10A	Baggers (Edms) Bpk
10B	Baggers (Edms) Bpk
10C	De Beers Consolidated Mines Ltd
11A	Terra Marina Mynboumaatskappy Bpk
11B	Terra Marina Mynboumaatskappy Bpk
11C	Terra Marina Mynboumaatskappy Bpk
12A	Terra Marina Mynboumaatskappy Bpk
12B	Tinto Africa Exploration (Pty) Ltd
12C	Tinto Africa Exploration (Pty) Ltd
13A	North Bay Canning Co Ltd
13B	North Bay Canning Co Ltd
13C	Rand Mines (Mining Services) Ltd
14A	Sandveld Minerale (Edms) Bpk
14B	Seetek (Edms) Bpk
14C	Ocean Diamond Mining Ltd

TABLE 16.2
Names, addresses and telephone numbers of marine diamond concession holders.

Baggers (Edms) Bpk, 1 End Street, Bellville 7530. (021) 97-9635
Benguela Concessions Ltd, PO Box 527, Howard Place 7450. (021) 531-3170
Cliffs Diamond Ventures (Pty) Ltd, c/o Benguela Concessions Ltd, PO Box 14025, Green Point 8051. (021) 49-7403, (0255) 8597
De Beers Consolidated Mines Ltd, PO Box 616, Kimberley 8300. (0531) 2-2171
Namagroen Eight Sea (Pty) Ltd; Namagroen Prospecting & Inv CC, PO Box 493, Kempton Park 1620. (011) 974-3001
North Bay Canning Co Ltd, PO Box 2, Doringbaai 8157. (02723) 5-1002
Oceaneering International Inc & Harry Winston Inc, c/o Moodie & Robertson, PO Box 4685, Johannesburg 2000. (011) 28-2636
Rand Mines (M & S) Ltd, PO Box 62370, Marshalltown 2107. (011) 491-2911
Robbaai Beleggings (Edms) Bpk, PO Box 97, Port Nolloth 8280. (0255) 8822, (0251) 2-2607
Sandveld Minerale (Edms) Bpk, 1 End Street, Bellville 7530. (021) 949-9635
Seediamantkonsessie 2B (Edms) Bpk, PO Box 14025, Green Point 8051. (021) 49-7403, (0255) 8597
Seetek (Edms) Bpk, PO Box 6461, Parow East 7501. (021) 49-6100
Ocean Diamond Mining Ltd, PO Box 2688, Cape Town 8000. (021) 49-6100
Tenmohs Diamonds (Pty) Ltd, PO Box 264, Vredenburg 7380. (02281) 3-1539
Terra Marina Mynboumaatskappy Bpk, PO Box 723, Parow 7500. (021) 92-1105
Three Sea (Pty) Ltd, De Beers Marine (Pty) Ltd, PO Box 2605, Cape Town 8000. (021) 21-2376
Tinto Africa Exploration (Pty) Ltd, PO Box 784467, Sandton 2146. (011) 883-3860

16.2.8 Current prospecting and mining activities in South African diamond lease areas

The interests of De Beers Marine in South African deep-water lease areas is considerably larger than shown in Figure 16.4 and Table 16.1, since the company has aquired further involvement through various agreements with other leaseholders, notably Tinto Africa Exploration, Three Sea (Pty) Ltd, and Namagroen Eight Sea (Pty) Ltd. The company has an extremely active prospecting programme based in Cape Town and involving geophysical mapping and sediment sampling. The remaining deep-water concession-holders have their own prospecting programmes but are currently less active. There is no regular diamond production yet from any deep-water areas, but that is expected to change if De Beers Marine is successful in Namibia, where they have been active for longer and their programme is believed to be further advanced than any other prospector.

In a similar way, there are prospecting programmes in the midwater *(b)* areas, where Benguela Concessions is currently the most active company. Once again, mining operations cannot commence until the technical problems of mining diamonds underwater by mechanical means such as robotics, air lifts or other devices permit larger-scale recoveries than are currently being made. Consequently, there is also no regular diamond production from midwater areas at present, although areas 2*(b)*, 3*(b)*, 4*(b)* and 5*(b)* have been worked in the past.

In contrast, diamonds are actively recovered from all the shallow-water *(a)* concessions numbered from 1*(a)* to 13*(a)*. Detailed records are not available, but annual diamond production from the sea for the past 20 years is presented in Figure 16.5. This is made up largely of shallow-water recoveries. Some areas have been more rewarding than others, notably 1*(a)*, 2*(a)*, 5*(a)*, 6*(a)* and 12*(a)*, while no significant quantities of diamonds were recovered south of area 13 in this period. In 1990 a record production of approximately 128 000 carats was achieved. The average price of smaller diamonds such as those found in area 6*(a)* was approximately US $180 per carat, which would be below the industry average. Conservatively estimated, therefore, this production would exceed US $25 million in value.

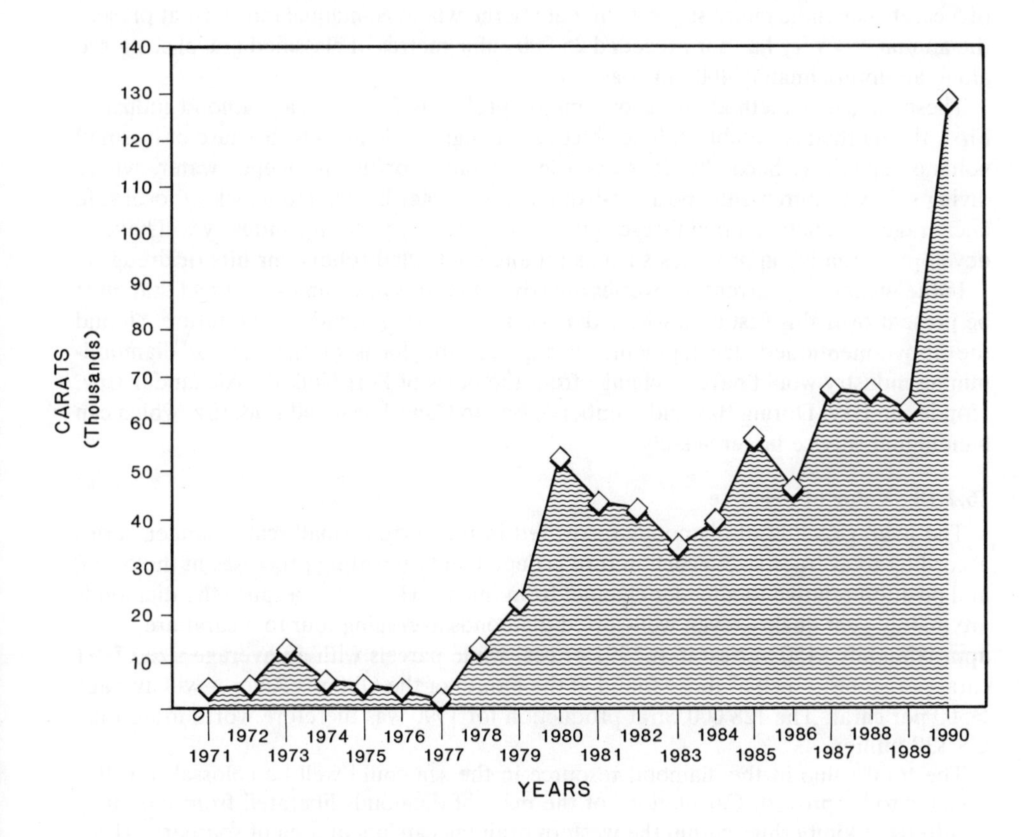

Figure 16.5 Annual marine diamond production for the last 20 years.

16.2.9 Technology used to exploit diamonds

Gravel recovery in the shallow water-operations is effected by boat or occasionally by shore-mounted gravel pumps which are used to deliver gravel to containers for subsequent sorting. The boats used are generally <30 m in length, of <100 tons displacement, and carry <50 tons of gravel at one time. Gravel is delivered to the pumps from the sea bottom through 100 mm, 150 mm or 200 mm steel-reinforced flexible pipes which have a suitable suction nozzle and clutch device to permit the unblocking of the nozzle mouth by boulders and are manipulated by divers. Operating water depths are always less than 35 m and usually less than 12 m. Boulders too large to fit through the nozzle are hand-stacked by the diver underwater. Gravel delivered by the pump is immediately classified mechanically and all sand and oversize cobbles are returned to the sea. Retained gravel is usually within the size 1,5–16 mm; from it the diamonds are extracted by various procedures in a shore-based plant.

Heavy mineral trap sites where diamonds may be found in viable concentrations are sought. These may be potholes, gullies, poorly sorted boulder beds or, occasionally, loose gravels and, very rarely, cemented gravels. Recovery methods will not cope with a sand or silt overburden thicker than 2 m and, in general, exposed gravel sites are sought and worked. Gravel recoveries are small in volume due to the equipment used and the difficult pumping characteristics of the boulder beds where the diamonds occur, in particular their poorly sorted nature. For instance, over a period of 14 years, classified gravel recovered from concession *6(a)* yielded a grade of 8,9 carats per cubic metre. This is a little higher than the industry average, but using a conservative grade of 5 carats per cubic metre suggests that along the whole Namaqualand coast at present the annual recovery has not exceeded 25 000 cubic metres of classified gravel scattered along an approximately 400 km coastline.

These recovery methods pose two major problems for the sea diamond industry. First, the method is suitable only for recovering high-grade gravels, because of its small volume capability. Secondly, it is even less suitable for use in deeper water, where diving safety requirements, position-fixing needs, larger boats, and a lack of local safe anchorages and habours rapidly escalate costs. In deeper water the industry will have to develop alternative approaches such as remote-controlled robots, air lifts or dredges.

In the meantime, current recoveries are trivial in terms of volumes of gravel that must be present over this vast area where diamonds have been found. In the future, should the above-mentioned developments take place, the focus of the marine diamond-mining industry would have to change from the ports of Port Nolloth, Alexander Bay, Hondeklip Bay, Doring Bay and Lambert's Bay to Cape Town and Lüderitz, which can handle and service larger vessels.

16.2.10 Value of resource

The average value of diamonds recovered in the current small-scale manner varies according to average size, which in turn is dependent on sorting processes in the ocean and position relative to a feeder channel from inland. However, because the diamonds are mainly gem quality, even well-sorted diamonds averaging four to a carat are worth approximately $180 per carat at 1991 prices, while parcels with an average size of >1 carat per stone—such as those found at the mouth of the Olifants River—will average >500 per carat. The 128 000 carat production for 1990 was therefore worth more than US $30 million.

The total value of the diamond resource in the sea could well be colossal, but this remains to be proved. Calculations of the mass of diamonds liberated from the many hundreds of kimberlites within the western draining catchment area of southern Africa are not reliable owing to uncertainties regarding the amount of erosion, the ore grade and the size of ore bodies at various erosional levels. Furthermore, the proportion of gemstones broken in transport is an unknown and therefore speculative figure. What can be said is that onshore palaeo-marine terraces have yielded >100 million carats of diamonds on this coast and it is plausible to expect submerged terraces off Namibia and South Africa to contain at least as many diamonds. If this is the case, the total value of the resource is of the order of billions of dollars, and it may represent the largest exploration target of gem diamonds in the world.

16.3 OIL AND GAS

16.3.1 Nature of resource

Petroleum differs from other mineral resources of the offshore area in being composed of complex mixtures of organic compounds, predominantly hydrocarbons. It can occur (1) as a solid in the case of gas hydrants (crystalline compounds in which the ice lattice of water expands to form cages that contain gas molecules),[6] (2) as liquids of various viscosities in the case of oil or tar, and (3) as gas or vapour, depending on the composition, ambient temperature and confining pressure.

Petroleum is generated from organic material, principally of plant origin, which has accumulated in sedimentary basins. Whereas gas can be generated from almost any organic material, the generation of oil requires a relatively high concentration of hydrogen-rich material. This is typically provided by lipid-rich remains of algae, bacteria and the waxy cuticle of land plants. With increasing burial beneath the surface, the organic material is subjected to increasing temperatures and becomes thermally unstable. Over the temperature range of about 60 to 120 °C, oil and gas are generated. At higher temperatures, gas continues to be generated, but oil already generated becomes unstable and is cracked to gas and progressively lighter liquid hydrocarbons. The temperature range over which oil is generated and preserved is known as the 'oil window' and is an important concept in oil exploration. The depth at which these critical temperatures are reached depends on the local thermal gradient.

For the development of economic accumulations of petroleum, certain conditions must be met:

- There must be source rocks with sufficient organic material of the right type to generate large quantities of oil and gas. In the South African offshore area, these are typically shales with an organic carbon content in excess of 1,5 per cent.
- The source rocks must be subject to sufficient temperatures to generate oil and gas.
- The hydrocarbons must have migrated from the source rock to reservoir rocks.
- Porous rocks must be present to act as reservoirs. In the South African offshore area, reservoirs are typically sandstones with porosities in the range of 8–30 per cent.
- Traps must be present to prevent the escape of reservoired hydrocarbons.

Gas or methane hydrates represent a potential resource of which little is known at present.[7] They are generally found on continental margins where water depths exceed 300–500 m and are inferred to occur as a unit of variable thickness just below the sea floor. Globally, these beds of ice–methane represent an enormous potential resource, but their direct exploitation is not currently feasible. A more practical possibility is that, where the methane hydrate bed caps a sea-floor topographic feature of some size, it could act as a seal to hydrocarbons trapped beneath it, as gas hydrates are impermeable to gas and oil. No direct evidence has yet been reported of the presence of methane hydrates in the South African offshore area.

16.3.2 Location and size of resource

The conditions set out above are met in the South African continental shelf only in sedimentary rocks of the Late Jurassic and a younger age which accumulated in sedimentary basins that developed from the early stages of the break-up of the ancient super-continent of Gondwanaland and the separation of South America from Africa, through to the present day. From Figure 16.6 it can be seen that the continental shelf out to the 500 m depth contour (isobath) is broadest off the west and south coasts and that it is generally narrow off the east coast, except for a small area north of Durban. It is in these areas that the greatest thickness of sediments exists and in which there is the best potential for discovering commercial petroleum accumulations. Figure 16.7 shows schematic sections through the continental shelf on the west, south and east coasts.

---

[6] Hunt *Petroleum geochemistry and geology* (1979).

[7] Kevenvolden 'Methane hydrate—a major reservoir of carbon in the shallow geosphere?' 1988 (71) *Chemical Geology* 41–51.

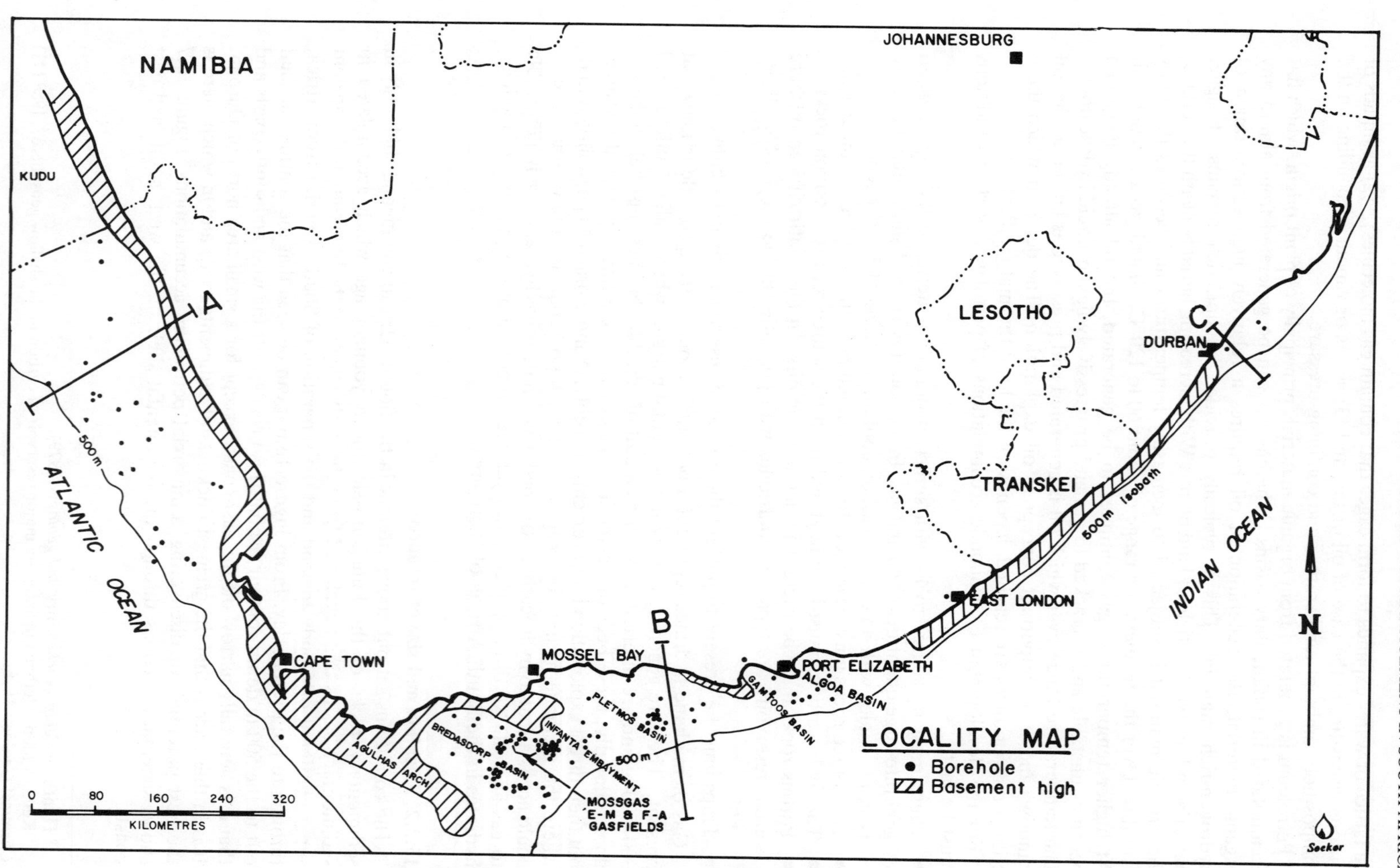

Figure 16.6 Locality map of geological sections. See Figure 16.7.

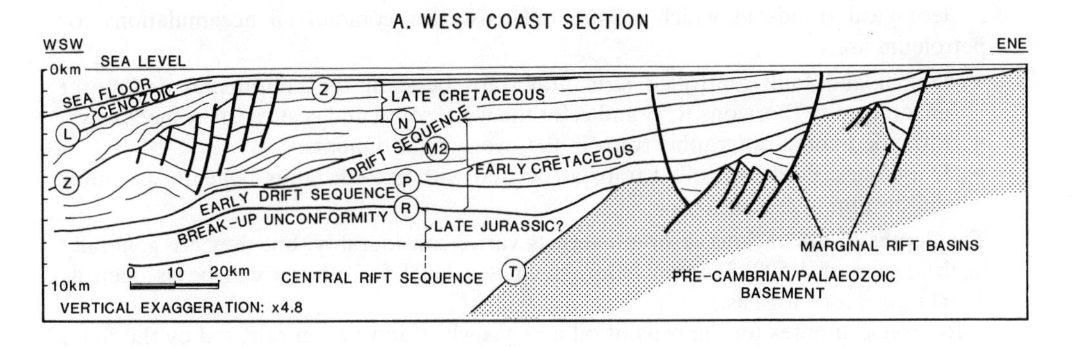

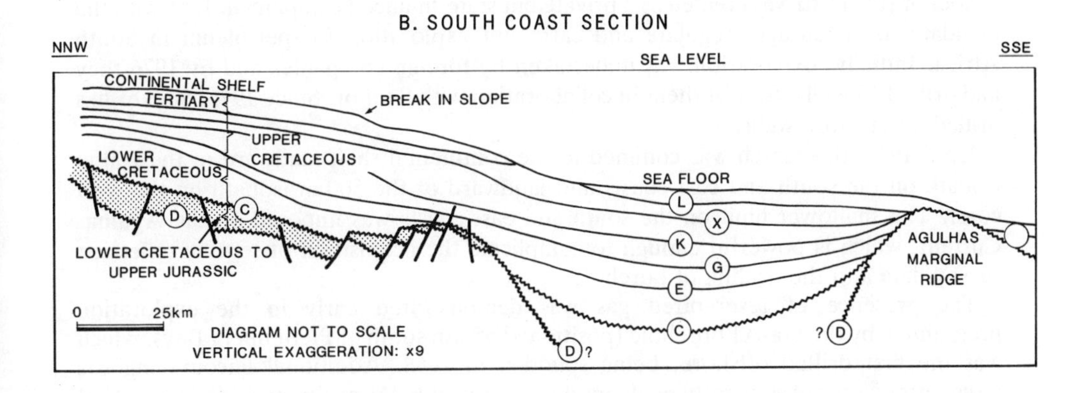

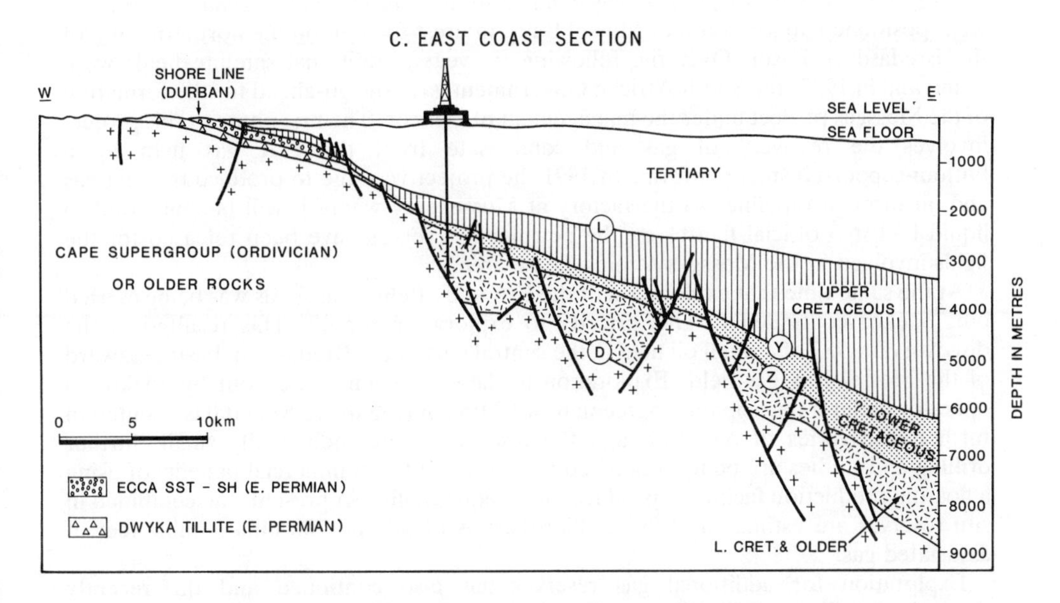

Figure 16.7 Geological sections through the South African continental shelf. For locations see Figure 16.6. The circled letters represent mapped marker seismic reflection horizons.

Geological trends in which a potential exists for commercial accumulations for petroleum are:

- Domal and fault-controlled structural traps beneath the continental drift-onset unconformity (horizons R, C and Z for the west, south and east coasts respectively).
- Mounded and stratigraphic traps in the overlying sediments.
- Domal and fault-controlled traps associated with growth faults beneath the outer shelf on the west coast.

The depths of the various reservoir targets varies considerably, but they are generally in the range of 1 500–3 700 m below mean sea level for oil and can be as deep as 4 500 m or more for gas.

Reserve estimates for deposits of oil and gas which have been released by the State for publication are set out in the next paragraph.

16.3.3 Development of interest in exploration

Soekor (Pty) Ltd was created as a private but state-financed company in 1965 with the mandate to encourage, regulate and carry out exploration for petroleum in South Africa. Initially, exploration was undertaken by foreign companies and by 1976 they had drilled 13 wells, four of them in collaboration with Soekor. Since 1976, Soekor has drilled all offshore wells.

Until 1991, the search was confined to the continental shelf landward of the 200 m isobath on the south and east coasts and landward of the 500 m isobath on the west coast. The shallower limit on the south and east coasts was imposed on the Agulhas Current, which is powerful enough to complicate the acquisition of seismic reflection survey data and the drilling of boreholes.

The presence of reservoired gas was demonstrated early in the exploration programme by the Ga-A1 borehole (positioned 65 km south of Plettenberg Bay), which was the first drilled offshore, being spudded in 1968. Additional encouraging gas discoveries were subsequently made until in 1978 well E-D1 positioned 145 km SSW of Mossel Bay proved the presence of oil.

With the discovery of the F-A gas condensate field in December 1980 by the F-A2 well (positioned 90 km south of Mossel Bay), interest focused on the northern flank of the Bredasdorp basin. Over the following six years, additional satellite fields were found and in 1987, the South African Government gave the go-ahead for the formation of the Mossgas project under the management of Gencor. The first phase of this project involves the recovery of gas and condensate from the F-A gas field by a bottom-supported steel platform. In 1991 the project was due to produce the first gas and oil through pipelines to the factory at Mossel Bay where it will be converted to liquid fuel. No official figures on the petroleum reserves have been released for the fields involved in the Mossgas Mining Lease area.

At the same time that exploration of the F-A and satellite gas fields was being carried out, Soekor continued to give priority to exploration for oil. This resulted in the discovery in 1987 of a small oil field in the central part of the Bredasdorp basin, seaward of the Mossel Bay gas field. Exploration to date has been carried out by Soekor as operator under a participation agreement with Engen (Figure 16.8) and has resulted in further discoveries of oil. Although the discoveries are individually small, further drilling and studies are being conducted to determine the commercial benefits of using a floating production facility to produce them sequentially. At present, the combined in situ reserves are estimated at 200 million barrels of oil and 700 billion cubic feet of associated gas.

Exploration for additional gas reserves has also continued and the recently discovered F-O gas field 115 km south-east of Mossel Bay contains a provisionally estimated 500 billion cubic feet of associated gas.

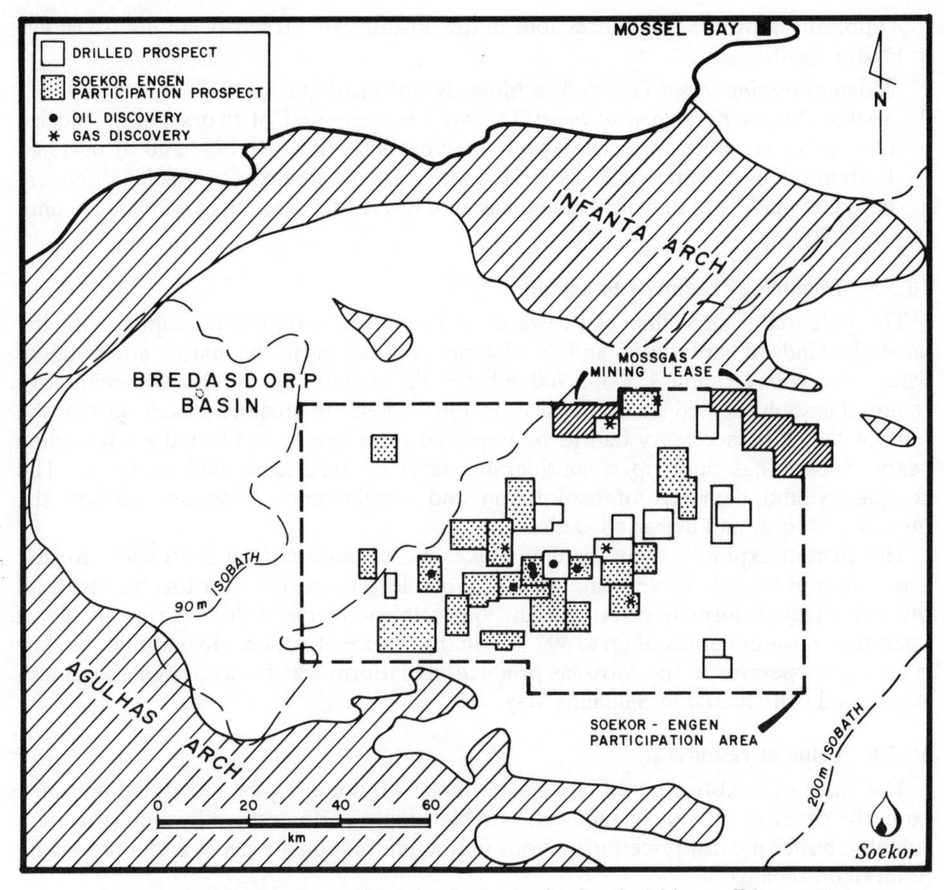

Figure 16.8 Exploration and mining leases in the South African offshore area.

In recent years, technology has advanced dramatically and has opened up the deeper water areas to exploration. Industry leaders elsewhere in the world are now drilling exploration wells in water depths of up to 2 300 m and producing oil from 800 to 1 100 m. These developments have opened up to exploration the deeper water areas around the South African continental shelf and Soekor is acquiring and evaluating data beyond the previously set 500 m and 200 m water depth limits for the west and the south-east coasts respectively.

16.3.4 Mineral rights

Under the Mining Rights Act 20 of 1967 all rights to natural oil (which term includes oil and gas) vested in the State. The rights for the continental shelf and territorial waters of South Africa were ceded to Soekor (Pty) Ltd under a prospecting lease (OP 26) dated 23 June 1967, which endures until 20 June 2007. This lease does not include the offshore areas of Transkei or Ciskei.

Soekor in turn is empowered to sublease areas, subject to the approval of the responsible Minister, to financially and technically competent oil-exploration companies. In the event of a discovery of a minimum defined size being made, Soekor must apply to the Minister for a mining lease for itself or on behalf of a sublessee. The mining lease, if granted, will endure until the deposit can no longer be commercially exploited.

At present there are two concessions in the offshore area (their positions are shown in Figure 16.8):

1. *Mossgas mining lease*: Granted to Mossgas (Pty) Ltd during 1991.
2. *Soekor–Engen participation area*: The area is composed of two separate blocks, covered by separate agreements with effective dates of 01-01-1987 and 01-09-1988. Both are due to expire on 31-09-1992. In the case of prospects in which a discovery has been made and in which Engen has an interest, the agreement will endure until 31-02-2003.

16.3.5 Technology required to exploit

The potentially large financial rewards of petroleum production coupled with the harsh demands of exploration and development operations in the marine environment where reservoirs lie some 1 500–3 700 m below the sea floor dictate that the technology required is sophisticated and expensive. In 1967, when the offshore search started, the bulk of the skills necessary had to be imported from overseas. Over the intervening years, Soekor has built up a considerable level of experience and expertise. The complexity and demands of exploration and development, however, require the blending of local and imported skills.

The current exploration programme makes use of international contractors for the acquisition of seismic survey data and of borehole geophysical data together with all other available information. At present, one semi-submersible drilling rig capable of operating in water depths of up to 497 m is in the service of Soekor. In addition, Soekor is acting as operator of the Mossgas production platform which was designed in South Africa and constructed in Saldanha Bay.

16.3.6 Value of resources

The value of the offshore oil and gas resources cannot easily be quantified but must be in the order of billions of rands. A reliable supply of domestic oil would provide a valuable buffer against price fluctuations on the international market and a big saving in foreign exchange.

16.3.7 Short- or long-term exploitation

In the case of oil, the technology exists for exploiting small deposits in the short term by using movable production facilities. In the case of gas or large accumulations of oil where a permanent bottom-supported structure is still needed, the life of a field is of the order of 25 to 50 years. Future trends in energy demand are difficult to predict, but in the developed world gas is currently receiving increasing attention as a relatively clean and cheap source of energy. Considerable scope exists in the South African context for developing a large gas market and specifically for extending the life of the Mossgas project from its currently planned 25-year term by discovering additional reserves which can be committed to it.

16.4 HEAVY MINERALS

16.4.1 Nature of resource

Heavy mineral sands represent the more resilient components of rocks being weathered further inland. Transportation of these minerals to the sea is similar to that described above for diamonds. The dominant constituent of the sands is quartz, with heavy minerals comprising from 2 to 25 per cent.

16.4.2 Location and size of resource

Heavy mineral-bearing beach sands occur intermittently along the east coast from East London to the Mozambique border and along the west coast in the Vredendal and

Namaqualand districts. The deposits between Richards Bay and St Lucia estuary have the most favourable location with respect to the harbour at Richards Bay, the large reserves available and ideal conditions for low-cost mining by dredging.

Along the Natal coast, from Cape Vidal in the north to south of Richards Bay, localized beach sand deposits contain ilmenite with an average of 36,8 per cent iron and 31,6 per cent titanium. In this area older dunes 150–180 m high rest on a raised fossil beach sand which contains a high concentration of heavy minerals. Heavy minerals are also found throughout the overlying dune sand, but because of cross-bedding, their distribution is erratic. The available sand is estimated to be of the order of 750 to 1 000 million tons, and the quantities of heavy minerals in a concentrate are usually as follows: ilmenite, 70–80 %; leucoxene, 2–5 %; rutile, 2–5 %; zircon, 8–10 %; magnetite, 2–8 %; monazite, trace to 0,3 %; garnet, pyroxene, etc, 1–5 %.[8] The source of these heavy minerals is assumed to be basement granites, Karoo dolerite and Stormberg basalts. Some Archaean schists and black sand concentrations in the Table Mountain Series and in the Karoo System also contain relatively abundant ilmenite.

Ilmenite-bearing black sand deposits have been found during prospecting for diamonds in the raised beach deposits along the west coast as far south as Tent Klip. Further south, black sand is present in small quantities on the present beach, in old dunes near the sea and in marine deposits as much as 180 m above sea level. In contrast to those on the east coast, heavy mineral concentrates from the west coast sands typically contain 28 % ilmenite, 58 % garnet and pyroxene, 10 % zircon, and 2 % each of rutile and magnetite.[9] These minerals are considered to be derived from the pre-Cape rocks towards the north, especially certain quartzose Malmesbury rocks that contain a high proportion in dark coloured layers.[10]

16.4.3 Exploration and mining activities

Richards Bay Iron and Titanium (Pty) Ltd produces both low manganese pig iron and titanium slag containing about 85 per cent TiO_2 from concentrates derived from the ilmenite-bearing beach sands north of Richards Bay.

The presence of heavy mineral deposits has been established offshore near Richards Bay. Sampling indicates an area carrying more than 5 per cent heavy minerals and a central zone with more than 10 per cent. The composition of the heavy mineral fraction is very similar to that of the adjoining onshore deposit, and similar offshore occurrences may be expected elsewhere in the vicinity of deposits on the coast.

Anglo American Corporation is studying the development of the onshore mineral sand deposits in Namaqualand, but so far there has been little interest in marine deposits of heavy minerals in this area.

16.5 PHOSPHORITE[11]

16.5.1 Nature of the resource

A wide variety of phosphatic material litters the southern African shelves, from large angular slabs up to 1 m across and weighing up to 100 kg, to nodular masses, to unconsolidated phosphatic sediments (sand and gravel-sized grains). This phosphatic

---

[8] Hammerbeck 'Titanium' *Mineral resources of the Republic of South Africa* Department of Mines geological survey handbook 7 (1976) 221–6.

[9] Lurie *South African geology for mining, metallurgical, hydrological and civil engineering* (1977).

[10] Visser & Toerien *Die geologie van die gebied tussen Vredendal en Elandsbaai* Departement van Mynwese geologiese opname, toeligting van blaaie 3118C (Doringbaai) en 3218A (Lambertsbaai) (1971).

[11] Any marine sediment containing over 18 per cent P_2O_5, the equivalent of 50 per cent apatite: $Ca_5(PO_4)_3(OH,F,Cl)$: Birch 'Phosphorite pellets and rock from the western continental margin and adjacent coastal terrace of South Africa' 1979 (33) *Marine Geology* 91–113.

material is considered to have been formed by the action of phosphate-rich ocean water circulating through pre-existing limestones and calcareous sediments which results in the replacement of calcium carbonate by the phosphate phase, carbonate-fluorapatite. The 'nodules' (a general term referring to fragments of lithified phosphatic sediments) and sediments have been eroded from outcrops of phosphorite which were exposed to weathering during periods of marine regression. Hence, the extent of the phosphate materials distributed on the sea floor generally reflects the extent of the original rock outcrops.[12] Chemical analyses of several types of nodules from the Agulhas Bank (Table 16.3) reflect the dominant mineral species which comprise phosphorite: collophane, calcite, quartz and glauconite.[13]

TABLE 16.3
Analyses of Mn-nodules from the Agulhas Bank*

C2	Fe-poor	NC1-3	Fe-rich	Cl
SiO_2	6,20	3,45	15,30	13,79
TiO_2	0,06	0,04	0,10	0,11
Al_2O_3	1,13	0,92	2,14	2,12
Fe_2O_3	1,40	25,80	5,58	7,34
MnO	0,01	0,06	0,01	0,02
MgO	0,97	1,49	1,34	1,45
CaO	47,02	33,42	37,04	36,54
Na_2O	0,62	0,34	0,78	0,73
K_2O	0,43	0,39	1,57	1,51
P_2O_5	14,82	10,26	17,89	16,82
S	0,31	0,21	0,46	0,45
F	2,12	1,42	2,21	2,04
LOF	25,52	23,24	16,15	16,89
TOTAL	100,61	101,04	100,56	99,81
LESS O	0,96	0,60	0,93	0,86
	99,72	100,44	99,63	98,95
No. of analyses:	(3)	(3)	(8)	(4)

* Fuller above n 13.

16.5.2 Size and location (Figure 16.6)

On the west coast, phosphate is concentrated in the coarser sand and gravel fractions of the middle and outer shelf at depths of 150–500 m. Between Lüderitz and Walvis Bay, at a depth of 160–360 m, is a very high-grade deposit of phosphatic sand containing as much as 22 % P_2O_5 and generally more than 5 % P_2O_5. Sands containing >20 % P_2O_5 cover at least 7 000 km² in a layer <0,5 m thick, which suggests the reserve may be as much as 2×10^9 metric tons.[14]

Concentrations of phospate 'nodules' occur on the outer shelf off the Cape Peninsula at depths of 200–500 m and between Cape Agulhas and Port Elizabeth at depths of

[12] Summerhayes 'Distribution, origin, and economic potential of phosphatic sediments from the Agulhas Bank, South Africa' 1973 (76) *Transactions of the Geological Society of South Africa* 271–8.

[13] Fuller 'Phosphate occurrences on the western and southern coastal areas and continental shelves of southern Africa' 1979 (74) *Economic Geology* 221–31.

[14] Rogers et al above n 2.

100–200 m. The average P_2O_5 content is 16 per cent, in common with similar deposits off California and Morocco.[15]

Phosphatic fragments and sediments containing up to 10 per cent P_2O_5 but generally less than 6 per cent P_2O_5 cover large parts of the Agulhas Bank at depths of 100–500 m.[16] Reserves are estimated at about 1.4×10^8 metric tons P_2O_5.[17]

16.5.3 Current interest in exploitation

The typically intimate mixture of glauconite (potash) with the phosphorite in these deposits, both of which are essential ingredients of fertilizers, suggests that the agricultural potential of these deposits could be significant. The Phosphate Development Corporation (Foskor) has conducted pot-plant experiments on nodular material

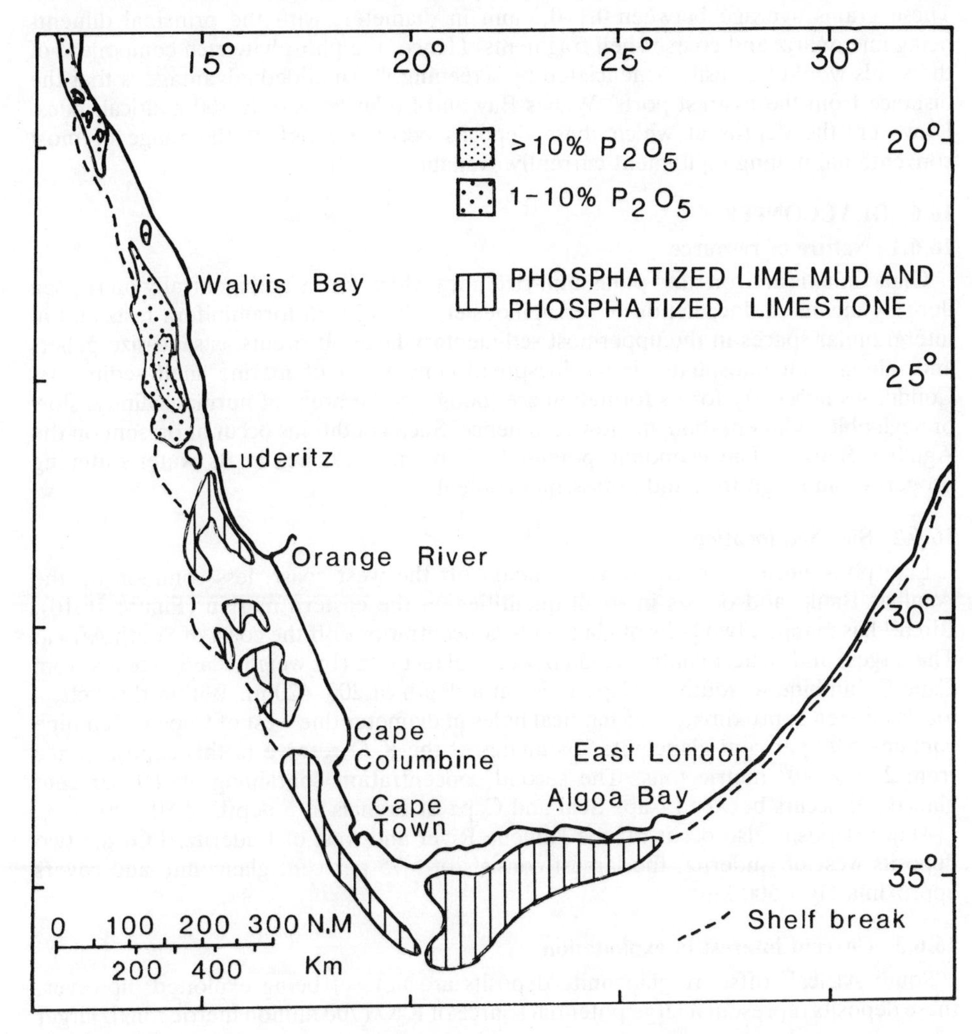

Figure 16.9 Distribution of phosphorite deposits on the continental margin of southern Africa (from Birch above n 11).

[15] Ibid.
[16] Summerhayes above n 12; Rogers et al above n 2.
[17] Summerhayes above n 12.

from Agulhas Bank and determined that the powdered but otherwise unrefined phosphorite has a phosphate availability comparable with commercial superphosphate.[18] Foskor holds a mining lease for the offshore area outlined in Figure 16.9; however, no plans to exploit the marine deposits have been mentioned. An on-land deposit of phosphorite is being worked at Saldanha Bay.

At present, most of South Africa's superphosphate requirement is obtained from apatite associated with the Phalaborwa carbonatite complex in the northeastern Transvaal. Grades are generally from 5 to 8 per cent P_2O_5 in these rocks.

16.5.4 Technology required to exploit

In the high-grade deposit between Lüderitz and Walvis Bay, the phosphatic components are grains of virtually pure phosphorite containing about 32 per cent P_2O_5. These grains average between 0,1–0,5 mm in diameter, with the principal diluents being fine quartz and coarse shell fragments. Hence, the phosphate-rich component of the sands would be easily beneficiated by screening.[19] An added advantage is that the distance from the nearest ports, Walvis Bay and Lüderitz, is only 100 nautical miles. However, the depths at which these deposits occur are out of the range of most conventional mining equipment currently available.

16.6 GLAUCONITE

16.6.1 Nature of resource

Glauconite is an iron- and potassium-rich mica which forms authigenically on the sea floor by means of flocculation of ferruginous clay colloids in foraminifera tests and in intergranular spaces in the uppermost sedimentary layer. It occurs as sand-size pellets and, along with phosphate, is a widespread constituent of marine shelf sediments. Conditions necessary for its formation are thought to be areas of normal salinity, slow or negligible sedimentation and low turbulence. Such conditions occur at present on the Agulhas Bank.[20] The economic potential of this mineral lies in its water-softening properties and high iron and potasssium content.

16.6.2 Size and location

Like phosphorite, glauconite is abundant off the west coast, less common on the Agulhas Bank, and occurs in small quantities on the eastern margin (Figure 16.10). Birch[21] has mapped two belts of glauconite concentrations off the coast of South Africa. The largest and richest contains >30 per cent glauconite (by weight) and extends from Cape Columbine to south of Cape Point at a depth of 200–420 m. Within this belt, a localized area approximately 25 nautical miles in diameter due west of Cape Columbine contains >90 per cent glauconite. Estimates of the K_2O reserve in this deposit range from 2–7 $\times$ 10^8 metric tons. The second concentration containing 30–60 per cent glauconite occurs between Cape Seal and Cape St Francis at a depth of 80–140 m.

Major deposits also occur off the Kunene River and west of Lüderitz.[22] Of the two deposits west of Lüderitz, the largest consists of >75 per cent glauconite and covers approximately 1 500 km^2.

16.6.3 Current interest in exploitation

South Africa's offshore glauconite deposits are not yet being exploited; however, these deposits represent a large potential source of K_2O (700 million metric tons), larger

[18] Ibid.

[19] Rogers et al above n 2.

[20] Birch *The glauconite deposits on the Agulhas Bank, South Africa* South African National Committee for Oceanographic Research Bulletin no 4 (1971).

[21] Ibid.

[22] Birch et al above n 1.

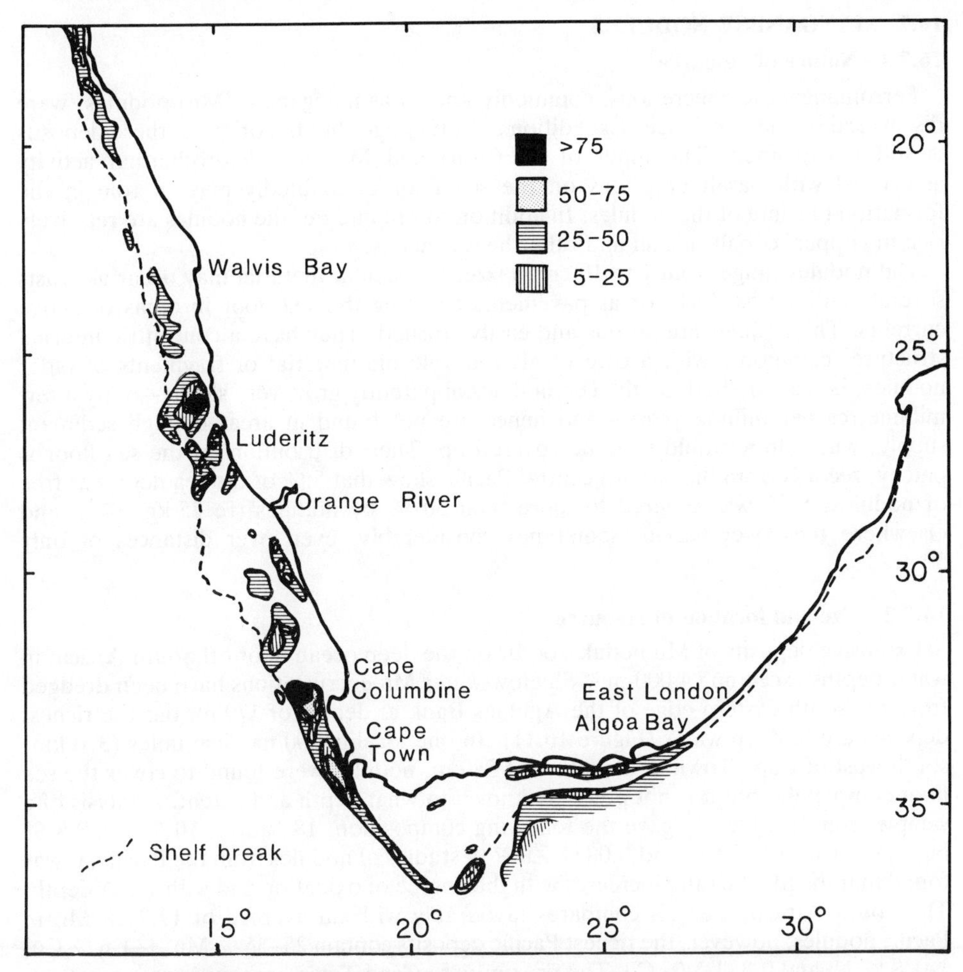

Figure 16.10 Distribution of glauconite on the continental margin of southern Africa (as weight per cent in total unconsolidated sediment; from Birch et al above n 1).

than that represented by phlogopite in the Phalaborwa complex, which has been considered the most promising potential source of K_2O (200 million metric tons) in South Africa.[23] World supply has been restricted over the past few years, largely due to a strong demand by China, Brazil and India, and to the closure of some mines in Canada (containing the world's largest reserves) and the erstwhile USSR. However, in general, the world industry's overall capacity is comfortably in excess of that required to satisfy demand.

South Africa imports most of its K_2O requirements, although the price of material landed at South African harbours (around $90 per metric ton in 1989) is considered to be below levels at which the exploitation of local resources would be economically attractive.[24] The technology being developed for the mining of diamonds offshore could have important ramifications for the exploitation of offshore glauconite deposits.

[23] Botha 'Potash' *South Africa's mineral industry* Minerals Bureau of South Africa (1987) 175–8.
[24] Ibid.

16.7 MANGANESE NODULES

16.7.1 Nature of resource

Ferromanganese concretions, commonly known as manganese (Mn) nodules, were discovered by the Challenger Expedition a century ago, but the origin of these deposits is still unexplained. The input of Fe (iron) and Mn from hydrothermal activity associated with basalt eruptions on the sea floor undoubtedly plays a role in the formation of some of the nodules. In addition to Mn and Fe, the nodules are relatively rich in copper, cobalt, nickel and other heavy metals.

The nodules range from 1 to 10 cm in size, but similar material may occur as crusts several centimetres thick, or as pavements covering the sea floor in areas of active currents. The nodules are porous and easily crushed. They have a concentric internal structure, commonly with a core of altered volcanic material or fragments of older nodules, bones, or shark teeth. The nodules apparently grow very slowly—only a few millimetres per million years—and hence are not found in areas of high sediment supply, where they would soon be covered up. Their distribution on the sea floor is patchy; records from the eastern central Pacific show that 5 % of the sea floor was free of nodules, 5 % was covered to more than 50 % by nodules (ie 25 kg m^{-2}), and elsewhere the cover varied, sometimes considerably, even over distances of only 50 m.[25]

16.7.2 Size and location of resource

Extensive deposits of Mn nodules occur on the deep ocean floor off South Africa, in water depths exceeding 4 000 m.[26] Shallow-water Mn encrustations have been dredged from the south-eastern edge of the Agulhas Bank at depths of 170 m, but the richest deposits are in deep water (Figure 16.11). In one locality 200 nautical miles (370 km) south-west of Cape Town at a depth of 4 580 m, nodules were found to cover the sea floor completely, but it is not precisely known to what depth and extent. Analysis of a sample from this locality gave the following composition: 18 % Mn, 10 % Fe, 0,8 % Ni, 0,3 % Cu, 0,1 % Co, and 0,08 % Zn.[27] In studies of nodules from the Pacific, it was found that the Mn:Fe ratio increases with the degree of oxidation and with water depth. The South African analysis compares favourably with an average of 17,2 % Mn in Pacific nodules; however, the richest Pacific deposits contain 25–35 % Mn, 1–1,6 % Cu, 1–1,8 % Ni and 0,3–1,5 % Co. The proximity to Cape Town harbour is an advantage, as the Pacific nodule occurrences are over 1 000 nautical miles (1 850 km) from the nearest port.

16.7.3 Technology required to exploit

Trial mining operations by Kennecott Exploration (Virginia, USA)[28] and Deepsea Ventures (California, USA)[29] involve pumping nodules as a slurry from the sea floor through a lift pipe similar in design to a large-diameter drill pipe and delivery to the surface vessel or 'mining platform', which serves as the support, control, and collection centre for the collector and pipe. The collector, which sweeps the nodules, has a self-steering capability run by electric and hydraulic motors. It also has instrumentation to measure flow conditions, status of actuators as well as acoustic and video instrumentation for determining the condition of the sea floor in the vicinity of the

---

[25] Seibold & Berger *The sea floor* (1982).

[26] Rogers et al above n 2.

[27] Ibid.

[28] Halkyard 'Ore handling and transfer at sea' *Marine Technology* Marine Technology Society, Washington DC (1980) 303–7.

[29] Dettweiler & Zahn 'Navigation and positioning for an ocean mining system' *Marine Technology* Marine Technology Society, Washington DC (1980) 358–61.

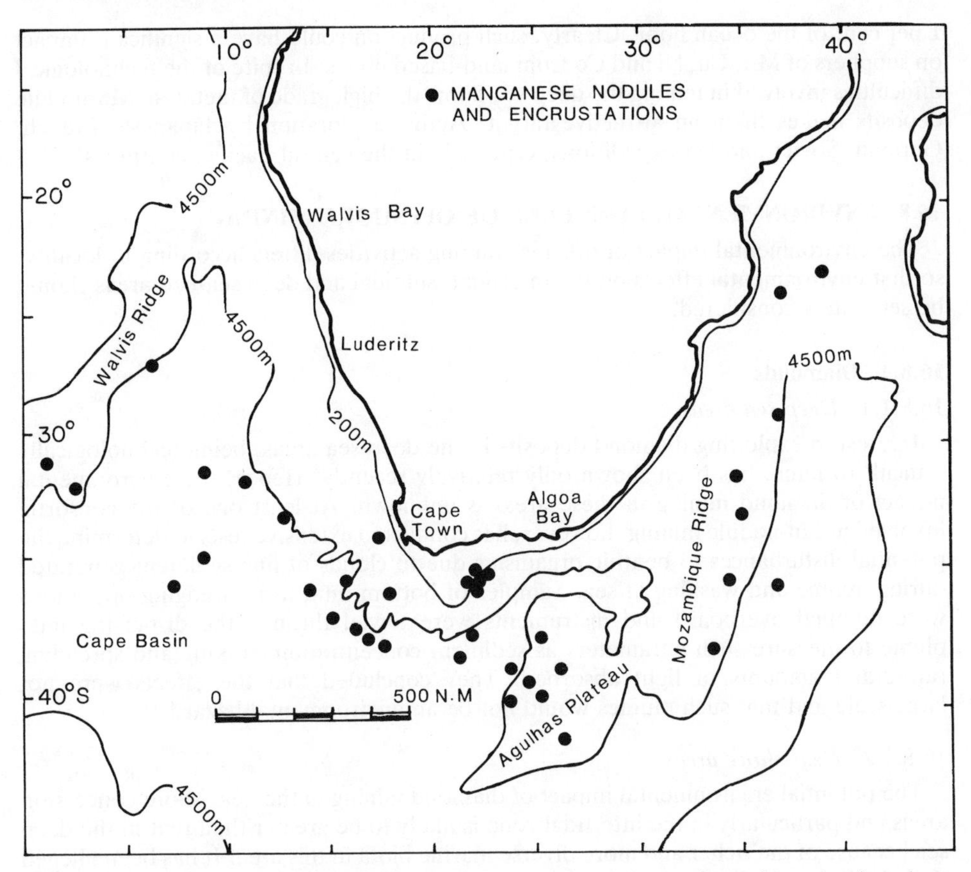

Figure 16.11 Occurrences of Mn-nodules and encrustations on the continental margin of southern Africa (from Rogers et al above no 2).

collector and to avoid collisions with obstacles that could cause damage to the collector and cause operations to cease. In order to collect nodules at a commercially viable rate, the collector sweeps the sea floor at a speed of from one to three knots in a path about 150 m wide. The collector also screens the nodules to remove unwanted sediment and other foreign particles. The lift pipe carries the nodules some 5 km vertically to the mining ship.

Once the slurry arrives at the surface, the nodule material must be concentrated, most simply by gravity settling and decanting, to reduce the volume of water that would have to be transported to shore. As the nodules cannot be beneficiated mechanically at sea, the transportation system carrying them to shore is a major component of the overall mining costs. Transfer of the concentrate is a unique problem in that the vessels involved must maintain a connection in all headings under a variety of sea conditions. The close proximity of the ships presents a potentially dangerous situation, whereas maintaining a safer (ie ship's length) distance between vessels complicates the mechanics of the transfer mechanism.

16.7.4 Current interest in exploitation

Assuming a relatively level deposit of nodules over an area of approximately 2 500 km^2, roughly 450 000 kg of nodules per year could supply a mine with a life of 20 years. The total amount of Mn in one such a deposit is approximately equivalent to the world's annual production, yet it would amount to almost an insignificant fraction of

1 per cent of the ocean floor. Clearly, such production could have a significant impact on suppliers of Mn, Cu, Ni and Co from land-based mines. In spite of the technological difficulties involved in mining the deep sea floor, the high grade of metals in Mn-nodule deposits makes them an attractive target. Active exploration by Japanese, French, German, Soviet and US expeditions, especially in the central Pacific, continues.

16.8 ENVIRONMENTAL CONCERNS OF OFFSHORE MINING

The environmental impact of offshore mining activities differs according to locality, so that environmental effects on the intertidal, subtidal and deep sea-bed areas should be separately considered.

16.8.1 Diamonds

16.8.1.1 *Deep-sea areas*

Interest in exploiting diamond deposits in the deep-sea areas, being technologically difficult to mine, has been shown only relatively recently. Hence, the environmental impact of diamond mining in these areas is unknown. At least one of the consortia involved in Mn-nodule mining, however, has conducted extensive tests to determine the potential disturbances to benthic organisms due to clouds of fine sediment generated during mining and washing at sea. Samples of bottom mud from dredging operations were dumped overboard and instruments were towed through the dispersing mud plume to measure such parameters as sediment concentration, sinking and spreading rates, and amounts of light absorbed. They concluded that the effects were not large-scale and that such plumes would not be an environmental hazard.[30]

16.8.1.2 *Near-shore areas*

The potential environmental impact of diamond mining in the near-shore concession areas and particularly in the intertidal zone is likely to be greater than that in the deep sea because of the richer and more diverse marine biota in this area. It has been alleged that, for instance, diamond exploitation activities in these shallow areas have adversely affected the rock lobster population resulting in past quotas not being maintained.[31] However, the decline of rock lobster populations was apparent prior to the establishment of the diamond mining industry and is a complex issue. Not the least significant of the factors involved is overfishing. Even the current (1991–92) quota (2 750 tons), which is substantially less than that in the past, amounts to over 8 million crayfish. Increasing seal populations in the present situation of public revulsion at the methods used to cull seals means that more crayfish are consumed by seals each year. Since some estimates put the protein requirements for a full-grown seal as high as 8 kg per day, this is a major consideration. It has also been suggested that other factors such as changes in patterns of sedimentation and devastation of the ribbed mussel population by algae have led to a decline in the food supply for crayfish. Low-water temperatures and poor oxygen availability along the west coast are further influences inhibiting crayfish growth.[32]

In March 1988 the Orange River discharged 64 million tons of sediment into the sea as the result of a single record flood. Littoral drift at the mouth of the river has been calculated at about 1 million tons per annum.

Compared to these figures, the marine diamond gravel recovery is trivial: less than 50 000 tons in 1990. Furthermore, those recoveries are scattered along 13 concessions

---

[30] Kent *Minerals from the marine environment* (1980).

[31] *Sunday Times* 13 October 1991 (Metro section).

[32] See Pollack & Shannon 'Response of rock lobster populations in the Benguela ecosystem to environmental change—a hypothesis' 1987 (5) *South African J of Marine Science* 887–99.

and approximately 40 km of coastline. The only relevant question would seem to be whether or not this limited mining activity is in some significant way upsetting the food chain of the near-shore ecosystem. The intertidal zone is the most important. A survey dealing with this issue has been commissioned by the marine diamond industry and is currently in progress.

One thing is certain. The number of mature crayfish in the South Atlantic Ocean off southern Africa has declined tremendously in recent years. The vast majority of those remaining are too small to be eligible for consumption by human beings according to current regulations. Since crayfish grow between 1 mm to 3 mm per year on average, it will be a long-term issue to restore the missing segment of the crayfish population. Short-term palliatives cannot succeed.

16.8.2 Oil and gas

16.8.2.1 *Environmental concerns during routine exploration*

In order to minimize negative environmental impact, it is Soekor's practice that:

(a) All contracted vessels are obliged to observe good anti-pollution practices.
Rubbish is incinerated.
Fuel and other storage tanks are not washed out at sea.

(b) Seismic acquisition is carried out using modern air or water guns to generate a sonic pulse which is not destructive to marine life.

(c) Drilling operations are conducted under strict procedures governing the release of material that could be damaging to the marine environment.
Rubbish is incinerated.
Drilling mud is retained in a closed circulation system.
Petroleum produced during testing is burned to prevent pollution.
Before leaving the drill site, cement plugs are set in the hole at several levels in accordance with international procedures to prevent the entry of fluids from the rock formation into the hole or from the hole to the sea floor.
All equipment is removed from the sea floor and the well-head is sealed.
Modern drilling rigs make use of sophisticated equipment and procedures to detect, monitor and control the drilling operation. In the event of severe bad weather, it is possible to shut the well and uncouple the drilling rig to avoid damaging the well-head.

16.8.2.2 *Environmental concerns during production*

In addition to the potential hazards outlined above, during production large volumes of oil and gas flow to surface, are separated and transferred directly to shuttle and storage tankers or piped to shore.

The approach taken by the State and by Soekor to the obvious environmental concerns has been to evaluate international procedures and to adopt strict regulations and design specifications for controlling all offshore operations. Ongoing training of staff instills an awareness of the value of safety consciousness. The various state departments have established good working relationships that involve close liaison and collaboration for routine and emergency operations.

16.8.2.3 *Will exploration destroy other resources?*

The State believes that by following, and even improving upon, good international practice, South Africa's offshore petroleum resources can be exploited without detriment to other marine resources.

On the basis of environmental risk, it is clear that the enormous volumes of oil transported around the Cape from the Middle East and Far East to the markets of North America and Western Europe represent a much greater hazard than the relatively small volumes of oil that will result from domestic production. It is beyond the scope of this chapter to discuss this issue beyond noting that shipping control is of considerable importance in preventing accidents. See, also, chapter 18.

16.9 THE LEGAL REGIME

16.9.1 Introduction

Legal control of the exploitation of offshore minerals is considered in the context of international law of the sea rules relevant to the exploitation of minerals occurring off the South African coastline; of relevant common-law principles, and of the applicable statutory regime.

16.9.2 The legal approach to defining 'Offshore'

A preliminary question to be considered is what area constitutes 'offshore'?

In chapter 26 the point is made that, from an ecological perspective, there is no distinct boundary between land and sea, the two being in a constant state of interaction. In general, the legal approach has been to choose an arbitrary line, usually the high-water mark, as a boundary between the terrestrial environment and offshore areas. However, in chapter 26 the recommendation is made that the legislature should not be rigid in this approach and attempts to depart from it are described. In this chapter we regard 'offshore' as the marine environment as well as the immediate coastal environment adjoining the high-water mark. The legal regime applicable to minerals occurring landward of the high-water mark—such as those occurring in the coastal dunes and dune-sands immediately landward of the high-water mark— is accordingly referred to.

16.9.3 The international-law basis for South African offshore mining rights

16.9.3.1 *The continental shelf doctrine and exclusive economic zone (EEZ)*

The international-law basis for South Africa's offshore mining rights lies in the international-law doctrine of the continental shelf. See, generally, chapter 9. This doctrine has its origins in the 1945 Truman Proclamation, when the President of the USA declared that the natural resources of the subsoil and seabed of the continental shelf beneath the high seas but contiguous to the coasts of the United States as appertaining to the United States, are subject to its jurisdiction and control.[33] Implicit in this statement was the right to mine the continental shelf.

The doctrine found more formal acceptance in the 1958 Geneva Convention on the Continental Shelf to which South Africa is a party. The convention recognizes the right of coastal states to exercise sovereignty over the continental shelf for purposes of exploring and exploiting its natural resources, the sea-bed and subsoil. The convention adopts a rather open-ended definition of the shelf, relying on a combination of both a bathymetric line and an 'exploitability criterion'. The continental shelf is defined as

> 'the seabed and subsoil of the submarine area adjacent to the coast but outside the area of the territorial sea, to a depth of 200 metres or, beyond that limit, to where the depth of the superadjacent waters admits of the exploitation of the natural resources of the said areas.'[34]

Apart from granting coastal states rights of exploitation of their respective continental shelves, the relevant international conventions impose certain duties on states in this regard. For example, under the Geneva Convention, exploration and exploitation of the continental shelf must not cause unjustifiable interference with the

---

[33] Harris *Cases and materials on international law* (1983) 354.
[34] Article 1.

navigation and fishing rights of other states nor with their conservation or scientific research programmes.[35]

In the two decades that followed the 1958 Geneva Convention, the international community saw increasing pressure from coastal states for greater jurisdiction over resources (both living and non-living) off their coasts. This eventually resulted in the acceptance by the international community and in the international law of the sea of a 200 nautical mile exclusive economic zone (EEZ). Under this doctrine, a coastal state has sovereignty over all resources (both living and non-living) occurring in this zone. The zone has been incorporated into the 1982 Law of the Sea Convention (LOSC), which sets out the legal rules applicable to the area. The LOSC is not yet in force as the requisite number of ratifications have not yet been received. However, these rules are by and large reflective of customary law in this regard. Under the EEZ doctrine, a state may claim sovereignty over offshore mineral resources up to 200 nautical miles, notwithstanding the physical extent of its continental shelf. A state may even claim a continental shelf beyond 200 nautical miles if it meets certain physical criteria set out in the LOSC.[36] The LOSC EEZ regime does not, however, supersede the continental shelf doctrine—it merely compliments it. The LOSC has also included the continental shelf doctrine amongst its provisions.[37]

South Africa signed but has not ratified LOSC and thus is not a party to it. However, it could do so in the future. It continues accordingly to rely on the Geneva Convention to substantiate its rights to mine offshore. This is reflected in the Territorial Waters Act 87 of 1963.[38]

Ownership of the sea-shore and the sea, including the sea-bed, vests in the State President and the area may not be alienated in terms of the Sea-Shore Act 21 of 1935. See chapter 26. The general purpose of this Act is to ensure the controlled utilization of the area and to maintain its public character. However, as regards mineral exploitation, the Act specifically provides:

> 'For the purposes of any law which is, or at any time has been in force in any part of the Republic relating to the exploitation of metals, minerals, precious stones, coal or oil, the land of the sea-shore and bed of the sea of which the State President is . . . declared to be the owner, shall be deemed to be State owned land.'[39]

The question of the territorial extent of South African law beyond territorial waters is discussed below as well as in chapters 9 and 26.

16.9.3.2 *The area beyond national jurisdiction*

From the above it is evident that in international law all states which have declared an EEZ, or which adhere to the continental shelf doctrine, have the right to mine the sea-bed up to an extent of 200 nautical miles, and even beyond that if certain conditions are met. Technological developments have been such that it has become realistic to assume that the sea-bed beyond national jurisdiction (the so-called deep sea-bed) will be subject to mineral exploration and exploitation in the future. Pressure from less-developed countries of the world has resulted in the incorporation in the LOSC of the notion that the deep sea-bed is the 'common heritage of mankind' and that its fruits should be distributed amongst all, including the less-developed countries. This fact was the main impetus for negotiating the LOSC. Ironically, it is also the main reason why many leading mining countries, including the USA, Germany, France and South Africa, have not ratified it.

---

[35] Article 5.
[36] Article 6.
[37] Part X of LOSC.
[38] Section 7.
[39] Section 7.

From a South African viewpoint the exploitation of the area beyond 200 nautical miles (370 km) is still largely theoretical, because currently all commercial exploitation takes place within 200 nautical miles. There has, however, been some exploration of Mn-nodules found roundabout 200 nautical miles offshore.[40]

16.9.3.3 *Territorial extent of South African law*

South Africa enjoys full territorial sovereignty up to the extent of its territorial sea (12 nautical miles) and beyond that (up to 200 nautical miles) as regards the exploitation of natural resources. The question, which South African laws apply to operations beyond 12 nautical miles (22 km), needs elaboration.

As seen above, the Territorial Waters Act deems the continental shelf to be part of the Republic of South Africa in so far as laws relating to mining, precious stones, metals, minerals and natural oil are concerned. But does this include related laws, for example laws dealing with employment conditions on mines beyond the territorial sea? In *Chemical and Industrial Workers' Union v Sopelog CC*,[41] the Industrial Court held, relying on the presumption against the extra-territorial application of domestic statutes, that the Labour Relations Act 28 of 1956 does not apply beyond the territorial sea in the absence of a statutory provision indicating the contrary.

From this it appears that only those statutory provisions which apply directly to mining apply to offshore operations—for example, mining rights. Ancillary laws—for example, those governing employment conditions on an offshore mine—will be applicable only if the statute specifies this to be the case. Naturally, conditions incorporated in the prospecting or mining lease will be of application notwithstanding where the mining activity may be taking place. Subsequent to the above case, the Labour Relations Act was amended to take into account these difficulties.[42]

Various South African revenue statutes also ensure that they are made applicable to offshore mining activities. Thus the Income Tax Act 58 of 1962 deems any amount generated from any services rendered, or work or labour done beneath or above the continental shelf as defined, to be from a South African source if it is generated 'in the course of operations carried on . . . under any prospecting or mining lease granted under the Mining Rights Act . . . or under any sublease granted under any such lease wheresoever payment for such services or work or labour is or is to be made'.[43]

Similarly, the Value-Added-Tax Act 89 of 1991 ensures that activities taking place beyond the territorial waters do not escape the tax net. This Act defines 'Republic' as including the territorial waters, the fishing zone and the continental shelf.[44]

16.9.4 Common-law principles

The underlying South African common-law rule is expressed in the Roman law maxim: cuius est solum eius est usque ad caelum ut usque ad inferos, meaning that he who is owner of the land also owns the space above and the material below its surface. It was endorsed in *Union Government v Marais*.[45] Modern-day needs have, however, resulted in many statutory provisions departing from, and amending, this rule. For example, sectional title legislation permits the ownership of space above the surface, without ownership of the land below. Mineral law generally, outlined in chapter 15, has also departed from this rule to allow for the separation of the ownership of the land's

[40] Rogers 'Seismic-bathymetric and photographic evidence of widespread erosion and a manganese-nodule pavement along the continental rise of the Southeast Cape Basin' 1987 (78) *Marine Geology* 57–76.
[41] 1988 (9) *ILJ* 846.
[42] Section 2(1) as amended by s 2*(a)* of Act 9 of 1991.
[43] Section 9(1)*(f*A*)*.
[44] Section 1(xlv).
[45] 1920 AD 240.

surface from the minerals below. The separation of ownership of surface rights from ownership of mining title is fundamental to contemporary mining law.

The juristic nature of mineral rights is also found in common law. It is accepted that mineral rights are real rights as opposed to personal rights, but the nature of these real rights is not entirely clear. One school of thought holds that they are personal servitudes but inclines to the view that they are quasi-servitudes because they differ in some respects from personal servitudes. This appears to be the attitude of the courts.[46] Another school, favoured by academics, regards mineral rights as real rights sui generis.[47]

Fundamental to the applicable legal regime in all mining law is the nature of the land in which minerals are found. In general, three categories of land are referred to in mining law: unalienated state land (also referred to simply as state land), where the land and mineral rights are owned by the State; alienated state land, where the land is not owned by the State but where the State has reserved the mineral rights in it, and, thirdly, private land, where ownership of the land and mineral rights vests in persons other than the State.

Minerals found seaward of the high-water mark would fall into the first-mentioned category, because, although the Sea-Shore Act vests ownership of the area below high-water mark up to 12 nautical miles in the State President, this Act and the Territorial Waters Act regard the area up to the 200 m isobath to be state land for purposes of any mining law. The land beyond 12 nautical miles does not fit neatly into any of the above three categories, but nevertheless is deemed to be part of the South African continental shelf, as has been explained. The ensuing discussion on legislation accordingly focuses on the first category of land mentioned.

Whatever the nature of the land and mineral rights, the State controls exploitation of minerals as elaborated on below.

16.9.5 Statute Law

16.9.5.1 *Introduction*

The common-law regime applicable to mineral exploitation has been fundamentally altered by legislation. A general feature regarding offshore minerals is that the control of their exploitation is not dealt with by a specific statute applicable to offshore minerals but rather by the statutory regime applicable to mining generally. This section, although focusing on offshore minerals, must accordingly be read in conjunction with chapter 15 above, which deals with terrestrial mining activities. Some particular statutory provisions refer to the marine environment specifically and these are referred to where appropriate below.

Before the newly enacted Minerals Act 50 of 1991, the chief relevant statutes were: the Mining Rights Act 20 of 1967, which dealt with 'base minerals', 'natural oil' and 'precious metals';[48] the Precious Stones Act 73 of 1964, which controlled the exploitation of precious stones, including diamonds;[49] the Mining Title Registration Act 16 of 1967 (not repealed), which establishes a mining titles registration office and is concerned with the registration of mining title; and the Mines and Works Act 27 of 1956, which provided for occupational safety on mines, the environmental effects of mining activity and related matters.

The Minerals Act came into force on 1 January 1992 and repeals and replaces the

---

[46] For example, *Rocher v Registrar of Deeds* 1911 TPD 311; *Webb v Beaver Investments (Pty) Ltd* 1954 (1) SA 13 (T).

[47] See, generally, Franklin & Kaplan *The mining and mineral laws of South Africa* (1982).

[48] As defined in s 1.

[49] Section 1 defines 'precious stones' as diamonds, rubies, sapphires and any other substances which the State President may by proclamation in the *Gazette* declare to be precious stones.

above-mentioned statutes (except the Mining Titles Registration Act) as well as a number of other mining laws. Its coming into force effectively singals a move towards the codification of South Africa's mining law. The effects of the new Act are described in chapter 15. In view of the fact that prospecting and mining leases concluded before 1992 are governed by the previous legislation[50] and that existing regulations continue to be applicable,[51] the legal regime prevailing before the Minerals Act is described here and reference is made to the new Act where applicable.

The statutory regime controlling mining of unalienated state land (which, as seen above, is mainly the case as far as offshore minerals are concerned) generally makes a distinction between three phases: prospecting, mining and post-mining activities such as marketing and environmental rehabilitation. The Mining Rights Act and the Precious Stones Act dealt with the first two phases with respect to minerals falling under their respective regimes, while environmental rehabilitation is dealt with generally in terms of regulations made under the Mines and Works Act, which regulations continue to apply. See chapter 15.

The statutory regime is dealt with here under the following specific headings: oil and gas, diamonds (the chief minerals found offshore), and 'other minerals', which outlines the regime applicable to minerals found in unalienated state land immediately landward of high-water mark such as in the dune sands. Where private land is concerned, reference should be made to chapter 15. Since the sea is in principle not subject to private ownership, offshore mining concerns state land.

16.9.5.2 *Oil and gas*

Under the Mining Rights Act, rights to prospect and mine as well as to dispose of 'natural oil' vested in the State.[52] The Act did not refer to oil and gas but controlled the exploration for and exploitation of 'natural oil.'[53]

As regards prospecting for natural oil, provision was made for the Minister of Mineral and Energy Affairs to grant prospecting leases with or without calling for tenders.[54] In granting such a lease, the Minister had to satisfy himself that the scheme according to which the prospector intends to carry out operations is satisfactory and that he has adequate financial resources for doing so.[55] Before granting or refusing a prospecting lease, the Minister was required to submit the application to the Mining Leases Board for a report.[56]

A prospecting lease might have been granted for a period considered appropriate by the Minister after consulting the Mining Leases Board[57] and should have contained certain provisions stipulated in the Act. For example: the prospecting lease had to stipulate the scale and manner in which prospecting operations should have been carried on.[58] The Minister had to be supplied with certain technical information concerning the site and depth of boreholes and the formations penetrated;[59] the keeping of records of prospecting operations and for their inspection as well as the inspection of

[50] Cf, generally, ch VII of the Minerals Act.

[51] Section 68(2) of the Minerals Act.

[52] Section 2. See also s 30.

[53] Defined in s 1 as any liquid or solid hydrocarbon or combustible gas existing in a natural condition in the earth's crust but does not include coal or bituminous shales or other stratified deposits from which oil can be obtained by destructive distillation, or gas arising from marsh or other surface deposits.

[54] Section 14(1)*(a)* and *(b)*.

[55] Section 14(1)*(a)*(i) and (ii).

[56] Section 14(2).

[57] Section 14(4).

[58] Section 14(3)*(a)*.

[59] Section 14(3)*(b)*.

the lease area and substances brought to the surface;[60] the payment by the holder of the lease of compensation where the surface rights holder might suffer damage to his crops or improvements on his land.[61] In addition, the Minister may have included any terms and conditions in the lease which may be agreed to after consultation with other Ministers regarding matters falling under the purview of their respective departments.[62] No specific provision was made for environmental considerations to be incorporated into the prospecting lease, but these were sometimes included. Under the Minerals Act, environmental provisions have to be taken cognizance of in certain situations.[63] See chapter 15.

The prospecting lease may also have embodied any, or all, the terms and conditions which the prospector may have been subject to should prospecting operations be successful and application be made for a mining lease.[64] This raises an interesting administrative-law question as to the extent to which the Minister of Mineral and Energy Affairs can bind the State contractually to a mining lease which may be entered into sometime in the future.[65]

The Minerals Act maintains the distinction between prospecting and mining by providing for the granting of a prospecting permit[66] and the issue of mining authorization.[67] See chapter 15.

In accordance with these provisions, a prospecting lease was entered into with Soekor (Pty) Ltd in 1967 to prospect in the whole offshore area comprising the territorial waters and continental shelf of South Africa, excluding certain stipulated areas.[68] By implication, the offshore area off the Ciskei and Transkei coasts is excluded. An interesting aspect of the lease is that it includes all the terms and conditions of the mining lease which may be granted under it in the future.[69] The prospecting lease contains a number of provisions including prohibitions on Soekor from carrying out operations which 'may interfere unjustifiably with navigation or fishing or with the conservation of the living resources of the sea'.[70]

Soekor was subsequenty granted a mining lease in 1991 in terms of the Mining Rights Act.[71] This has been assigned to Mossgas and applies to the F-A and E-M areas where production drilling has already commenced.

The Mines and Works Act 27 of 1956 regulated the operations on mines and machinery used in connection with them. Extensive regulations concerning various aspects of mining have been passed in terms of the Act[72] and now apply in terms of the Minerals Act.[73] These control a wide variety of mining activities, conditions on mines and environmental aspects. In 1990 these regulations were supplemented by the addition of a specific chapter[74] to deal with offshore installations. The definition of 'offshore installation' makes it clear that it is applicable only to offshore operations

---

[60] Section 14(3)*(c)* and *(d)*.
[61] Section 14(3)*(e)*.
[62] Section 14(3).
[63] For example, ss 9(3)*(c)* and 38, read with ss 14(1) and 41.
[64] Section 14(3) of the Mining Rights Act.
[65] See Rabie 'The applicability of legislation through contract: Soekor and the Mossel Bay offshore gas development project' 1988 *THRHR* 28.
[66] Section 6.
[67] Section 9.
[68] See, generally, Schippers *The extent of rights under the Soekor leases* Special publication 9 (1989) Institute of Marine Law, University of Cape Town.
[69] See Rabie above n 65.
[70] Clause 10 of the prospecting lease.
[71] Section 25(1)*(a)*.
[72] GN R992 of 26 June 1970.
[73] Section 68(2).
[74] Chapter 31, added by GN 1644 of 13 July 1990.

involving natural oil and not other forms of offshore mineral exploitation.

In terms of these regulations, an owner of an offshore installation is required to apply to the Government Mining Engineer for a permit to use such an installation in the sea.[75] Every application for such a permit must be accompanied by a certificate of fitness granted by a certifying authority and must contain certain stipulated details.[76] The regulations contain further clauses, including provisions to ensure that the installation is capable of withstanding oceanic conditions,[77] conditions of accommodation (if any)[78] and other details concerning safety and conditions on such installations.[79]

16.9.5.3 *Diamonds*

The chief statute which governed the prospecting and mining for diamonds (whether offshore or inland) was the Precious Stones Act 73 of 1964, while marketing and related aspects were controlled by the Diamonds Act 56 of 1986. The latter remains in place even after the coming into operation of the new Minerals Act, while prospecting and mining for diamonds is controlled by the general regime laid down by the Minerals Act for all minerals as from January 1992.

Prospecting operations were governed by the Precious Stones Act. Provision was made for the Minister of Mineral and Energy Affairs to grant prospecting leases in respect of diamonds occurring on state land with or without calling for tenders.[80] It has been seen that in terms of the Territorial Waters Act, the area seaward of the high-water mark is deemed to be state land for the purposes of South Africa's mining laws. In granting prospecting leases, the Minister had to have been satisfied that the scheme was satisfactory, that the aspirant prospector's financial resources were adequate or that satisfactory arrangements for the obtaining of capital had been made.[81]

Furthermore, in issuing prospecting leases, the Minister could have imposed any conditions he might have deemed fit.[82] In addition, certain specific conditions providing for, inter alia, the scale and manner in which prospecting operations are conducted, the furnishing of statements concerning the nature of prospecting operations, the keeping and examination of records, the payment of compensation to surface owners who may suffer surface damage or damage to crops and the payment of rent to the State, had to have been contained in the lease.[83] In addition to rental, the prospector may have been obliged to pay a share of the proceeds of any precious stone found by him to the State.[84] Significantly, this section did not stipulate any particular clauses relating to environmental protection.

16.9.5.4 *Concession areas*

Acting in accordance with the above provisions, the Minister published two notices in the *Government Gazette* in 1981 and 1985, inviting tenders for prospecting leases in respect of precious stones occurring in certain designated areas in the offshore area between Cape Columbine (Olifants River mouth) in the south and the Orange River mouth in the north.[85] Prospecting leases have been granted since 1970, when a number of prospecting areas were designated by the Department of Mineral and Energy Affairs

---

[75] Regulation 31.2.
[76] Regulation 31.3.
[77] Regulation 31.12.
[78] Regulation 31.22.
[79] See generally regs 31.12–31.
[80] Section 4(1).
[81] Section 4(1)*(a)*.
[82] Section 4(2).
[83] Section 4(2)*(a)*(i)–(vi).
[84] Section 4(2)*(b)*.
[85] GN 593 of 24 July 1981; GN 528 of 30 August 1985.

for the offshore area. A rough rectangular block has been created the boundaries of which can generally be described as follows: the northern and southern boundaries of the block are imaginary lines running seawards from the Orange and Olifants River mouths respectively, while the western and eastern sides of the block are the outer edge of South Africa's continental shelf and the shoreline respectively. The exact demarcation of these prospecting and concession area boundaries is elaborated on below.

Within this 'block' a number of concession areas have been created by dividing it by 21 horizontal lines and three vertical lines, as elaborated on below. The three vertical 'strips' created in this way have been designated 'a', 'b' and 'c', being 'shallow water', 'midwater' and 'deep water' areas respectively. The horizontal strips are simply numerically designated. The concession areas created by the resultant grid are easily referred to as a result—for example, 3(c) would be a deep-water area in area 3. The 1981 notice included an accompanying map which is depicted in Figure 16.4.

16.9.5.5 *Boundary demarcation*

The exact location of the northernmost line, that is the maritime boundary between South Africa and Namibia, is not certain. Under general international-law principles, this line would be an equidistant line out to sea commencing from the middle of the river mouth, but the position is complicated in this case because the river boundary between the two countries is the northern bank of the Orange River.[86] This boundary is currently the subject of negotiation between the governments of South Africa and of Namibia.

The latitudinal or horizontal lines are specified in the diagram accompanying the 1981 notice simply by reference to lines of latitude (Figure 16.4). These lines present no problem in theory but, being difficult to locate 'on the ground', could result in demarcation disputes between adjoining concession holders.

(a) Seaward boundary of deep-water area. The seaward extent of the deep-water area (and thus the whole concession area) is described as the '200 m isobath edge of the continental shelf'. (Figure 16.1). In practice, this isobath varies in distance from the coast from between 40 and 140 km.[87]

These lines have clearly been chosen to conform with the 1958 Geneva Convention on the Continental Shelf to which South Africa is a party. However, the convention has an open-ended 'exploitability' criterion in establishing the outer edge of the continental shelf. In this light and in the light of the more recent definition of the continental shelf in the 1982 LOSC, the question arises whether the South African legislature should not reconsider the location of this line.

(b) Boundary between deep-water and midwater areas. The boundary between the 'c' and 'b' areas is a straight line demarcated in Figure 16.4 in terms of geographical coordinates indicating where this line intersects with the latitudinal areas referred to above. In practice, this line is about 5 km out to sea, where the average depth is about 100 m.[88]

(c) Boundary between midwater and shallow-water areas. Figure 16.4 describes this boundary as '1 000 m from the nearest high-water mark on the coast at any location'.

---

[86] It is also not certain whether it is the high- or low-water line of the Orange River. See Hamman *River boundaries between South Africa and Namibia* (unpublished LLD thesis, University of Cape Town, 1991) and Erasmus & Hamman 'Where is the Orange River mouth? The demarcation of the South African–Namibian maritime boundary' 1987–88 *SAYIL* 49.

[87] Kidd 'Legal and technical problems of offshore concession boundary determination' *Proceedings of a symposium on the surveying of offshore mining concessions in South African waters* Department of Surveying, University of Cape Town (1984).

[88] Ibid.

It is thus a curvilinear line whose location has to be determined by reference to another line whose exact location is not fixed or certain.

(d) Boundary between shallow-water areas and land concessions. The shallow-water area (area 'a'), also known as the 'surf zone', is a most sought-after concession area, being easier to exploit and yielding good product. The landward boundary is not specified in Figure 16.4, but is presumed to coincide with the seaward boundary of land concessions. This line has traditionally been described as 'a line 31,49 metres (100 Cape feet) seawards from the low-water mark and parallel thereto'.[89]

From the above it will be evident that the offshore concessions lie seaward of the 100 Cape feet line. Between this line and the high-water mark is another concession area often incorrectly referred to as the Admiralty Strip.[90] This has historically been held by De Beers.

In anticipation of difficulties in physically locating these boundaries, the Department of Mineral and Energy Affairs included a condition in both tender notices, referred to above, obliging concession-holders to come to mutually acceptable arrangements or agreements with adjoining concession-holders regarding the location of their respective boundaries.[91]

Despite this condition, it became apparent that there were nevertheless practical difficulties in trying to establish the exact physical location of these various boundaries. The Department of Mineral and Energy Affairs accordingly entered into a collaborative effort with the various concession-holders to come to a more satisfactory arrangement regarding their location. It has been agreed to use specific coordinates under the National Trigonometric Survey System (the National L0 system). This is an ongoing process and thus far concession areas 1 to 15 have been demarcated under this system. These are now registered with the Mining Commissioner based in Springbok.

16.9.5.6 *Mining leases*

Normally, the holder of a prospecting lease applies for and receives a mining lease if he finds minerals in payable quantities in his prospecting area. The Precious Stones Act made specific provision for the grant of mining leases in respect of portions of the sea.[92]

A number of the above-mentioned prospecting leases have been replaced by the granting of mining leases under this provision and further applications are being considered by the department. An important legal consequence of converting a prospecting lease into a mining lease is that the latter fell under the rehabilitation provisions enacted under the Mines and Works Act while prospecting leases did not.

According to the Minerals Act, new prospecting leases and mining leases will be replaced by prospecting permits and mining authorizations respectively.[93] Existing rights remain unaffected, however. Chapter 2 of the Act, which deals with Administration, anticipates offshore mining in that it provides for the division of South Africa, including its territorial sea and continental shelf, into regions.[94]

16.9.5.7 *The marketing of diamonds*

The marketing of diamonds, whether mined offshore or not, is regulated by the Diamonds Act 56 of 1986, which has not been repealed by the Minerals Act. It establishes a South African Diamond Board which has as one of its objects 'to ensure

[89] Ibid.

[90] The term 'admiralty strip' is strictly incorrect in this sense, because the admiralty strip is landward of the high-water mark. See chapter 26.

[91] Regulation 9 of both notices referred to in n 85.

[92] Section 21(1).

[93] Sections 6 and 9 respectively.

[94] Section 3.

that the diamond resources of the Republic are exploited and developed in the best interest of the country'.[95] In practice the board ensures the control of production quantities and that the price paid to producers is reasonable.

The physical purchasing and marketing of diamonds is conducted by the central selling organization, based in London, which controls trade in the bulk of the world's production of gem diamonds.

16.9.6 Minerals found landward of high-water mark

The legal regime applicable to minerals landward of high-water mark is essentially that governing minerals generally. See chapter 15. It must therefore be emphasized that, while certain coastal-zone mining proposals—for example, to mine heavy mineral sands in the vicinity of St Lucia in Natal, or kaolin in Noordhoek in the western Cape—have elicited public controversy and resistance, there are no particular laws governing these proposals over and above the generally prevailing legal position.

In the case of both of the above-mentioned proposals, however, environmental impact assessments have been undertaken. It must be emphasized, though, that these are done on a voluntary basis and not because they are legally compulsory. See chapters 7 and 30. If and when the Minister of Environment Affairs exercises his discretionary power under the Environment Conservation Act 73 of 1989 and identifies mining as an activity which may have a substantial detrimental effect on the environment,[96] the situation will be different. The rehabilitation provisions contained in regulations passed under the Mines and Works Act and now applicable in terms of the Minerals Act, are potentially very important in mitigation of the environmental impact of mining activities in this sensitive area. These have been described in chapter 15.

16.10 Conclusion

Offshore mining activity is confronted with very different physical conditions to its terrestrial counterpart and makes use of different technology. The legal regime governing offshore mining, however, is fundamentally the same as that which governs the terrestrial industry. There is no separate Act governing offshore operations, but a few specific provisions complementing the general regulatory regime deal with offshore prospecting and mining operations. It is submitted that this is satisfactory and that it would not be practical to pass a separate Coastal Zone Mining Act.

As regards the exploitation of offshore diamonds, the potential for boundary disputes has to some extent been eliminated by the reliance on the scientific determination of co-ordinates to demarcate concession areas.

While the general legal regime applicable to Soekor's offshore operations is in compliance with international norms and standards, the question can be raised whether the law is sufficiently developed to cover liability for environmental damage should an accident occur. The Prevention and Combating of Pollution of the Sea by Oil Act 6 of 1981 governs liability for loss, damage or costs caused by discharge of oil. See chapter 18. While the definition of 'discharge' includes discharges from offshore installations, it applies only within the 'prohibited area' which in turn is defined to be the 'zone of 50 nautical miles from the low-water mark'. As Soekor's operations occur beyond this distance, it appears that they are not covered by the relevant provisions of this Act. The situation ought to be rectified.

It should, however, be noted that the F-A and E-M fields will not produce oil—only gas and condensate. Any major spillage of condensate is unlikely to cause an environmental problem. The area is 85 km from shore and the marine currents protect the shore. Each prospecting and mining lease constitutes a contract and the State may

---

[95] Section 4(1).
[96] Section 21.

claim damages from Soekor or Mossgas should the prevention of oil pollution clauses be breached. Overseas circumstances (e g distance from the mainland) differ greatly from those pertaining to Soekor/Mossgas.

In common with the international-law doctrine of the freedom of the high seas, South African municipal law has traditionally regarded the area immediately seaward of high-water mark as deserving special status. Thus in Roman law, the sea and sea-shore were regarded as res omnium communes, that is, free to be enjoyed by all but incapable of private ownership. This rule has been modified to a large degree but nevertheless remains the underlying philosophy of the Sea-Shore Act, which vests ownership of the area in the State President. In *Consolidated Diamond Mines of SWA Ltd v Administrator of SWA*[97] a terrestrial mining concession was granted 'to the coastline' and the question arose whether this meant to the high- or low-water mark. In the course of its judgment the Court held:

> 'the public have certain simple rights to the foreshore such as to go onto it, to bathe, to fish, to dry nets and to draw up boats . . . [and] any substantial interference with those rights would be a wrongful act. . . .'

In addition, the public has an interest in ensuring that the offshore environment is not irreversibly degraded by mining activity. The legal system has accordingly to seek a satisfactory balance between allowing mining activity and ensuring that the offshore environment does not suffer long-term environmental damage.

[97] 1958 (4) SA 572 (A) at 621H.

CHAPTER 17

AIR POLLUTION

J G PETRIE
Y M BURNS
W BRAY

17.1 INTRODUCTION

The technical part of this chapter addresses only the significance of air pollution derived from stationary fossil fuel processes. Though this may at first sight appear to be unduly restrictive, it should be appreciated that, with the exception of pollution generated by motorized transport, stationary fossil fuel processes produce the bulk of air pollution in this country. This study does not address air pollution from coal combustion in domestic stoves or fireplaces, though, where relevant, comparisons are made between domestic and industrial pollution levels.

The days of considering air as an infinitely renewable and resilient resource are over. No longer can it be assumed that the atmosphere in which we live will resist the indiscriminate discharge of wastes in the hope that dilution and dispersion will accommodate our inability (or reluctance) to treat wastes at source, or indeed to minimize their production. South Africa has demonstrated a commitment to the use of coal to meet its primary energy needs well into the 21st century. Air pollution problems which we experience are, in large measure, a manifestation of this pattern of energy production. Other forms of pollution, such as land damage from mining activity and water contamination from coal beneficiation practice, arise naturally from this coal-based energy economy.

There are several ways of classifying air pollutants. For the most part classification differences arise from the different bases used to legislate the control of pollution. Air pollutants are described by either the physical or chemical composition of the emission, or by the origin of the emission. For the purposes of this chapter, air pollution is defined simply as the anthropogenic discharge of matter (gas, liquid or solid) to the atmosphere at levels which have undesirable effects on the human, natural and physical environment.

In South Africa, five activities which generate air pollution are recognized:

- *Fuel combustion and gasification from stationary sources*. Examples of processes which fall into this category include the combustion of coal or oil for electrical power generation, steam generation and industrial energy requirements, coal gasification for the production of metallurgical coke and 'syn-gas' (a mix of hydrogen and carbon monoxide used in the production of synthetic fuels and ammonia), and domestic coal combustion for space heating.
- *Fuel combustion in mobile sources*. The transport sector dominates this category. Pollutants are combustion products, unburned fuel, and volatile lead species. The spectrum of pollutants is a function of fuel type.
- *Industrial and chemical processes*. This category is reserved for pollution generated by processes other than combustion or gasification. Here one considers such pollutants as alkali metals and fluorides from the ferro-alloy industries, nitrogen and phosphorus compounds from fertilizer production, and organic vapours from chemical production.
- *Solid waste disposal*. Incineration of industrial, residential and hospital wastes

contributes significantly to air pollution. In addition to normal products of combustion, incinerators produce a wide spectrum of heavy metals as well as a host of toxic chlorinated organics and alkali chlorides.

- *Land surface disturbances*. These include mining and construction activities, waste dumps, agricultural practices and veld fires. Particulate matter is the primary pollutant.

In all the above thermal processes, carbon dioxide is produced. Though not historically labelled a pollutant, the contribution which this gas makes to a global change in climate warrants its identification as such.

Pollutants are further distinguished according to the time scale of their evolution. Primary pollutants, of which the most important are sulphur and nitrogen oxides (SO_x and NO_x), particulate matter (PM), carbon monoxide (CO), and volatile organic compounds (VOC), are discharged directly to the atmosphere. Chemical transformation of these primary discharges, in the presence of sunlight or other primary sources (such as VOCs or NO_x), may result in the formation of secondary pollutants such as ozone and peroxyacylnitrates.

17.1.1 Areas of environmental concern in air pollution

In discussing the environmental effects of air pollution, it is important to identify major concerns as expressed by both an informed public and supported by a weight of scientific evidence. The impact of air pollutants on the biosphere can be ascribed to their contribution to ambient air quality through: acidic deposition, hazardous air pollutants, smog formation and visibility reduction, ozone depletion, and changes in global climate. Each of these is discussed briefly below.

17.1.1.1 *Acidic deposition*

Sulphur and nitrogen compounds, present in the atmosphere as either gases or particles, are transported to ground either directly by an expanded pollution plume layer (so-called 'dry deposition') or by being washed out by rain ('wet deposition') or by being captured by impaction on aerosols which are subsequently deposited on vegetation ('occult deposition'). All three ways are collectively termed *acid deposition* and the latter two are principally responsible for the phenomenon known as 'acid rain'. This phenomenon occurs when these pollutants combine with other compounds such as ammonia, certain hydrocarbons, chlorides, ozone and trace metals in complex oxidative transformations to produce sulphate and nitrate aerosols which are subsequently 'washed out' of the atmosphere during rainfall.

Documented environmental damage attributed to acid deposition includes the acidification of freshwater ecosystems (groundwater, rivers and lakes and their fish and bird populations), denudation of forests and agricultural crops, corrosion of metallic surfaces and destruction of masonry structures. Impact on human health is generally inferred from the ability of acids to dissolve lead and other heavy metals from water catchment areas and plumbing systems.

17.1.1.2 *Smog formation and visibility reduction*

Particulates emitted during solid fuel combustion are principally responsible for visibility reduction. Photochemical smog (brown haze) results from the presence of secondary pollutants such as ozone and peroxyacetylnitrate (PAN).

17.1.1.3 *Hazardous air pollutants*

Hazardous air pollutants include volatile lead, volatile organics such as benzene, polycyclic aromatics such as furans and dioxins, and heavy metals such as mercury and arsenic. Environmental damage attributed to these species is measured directly in terms of their effect on human health.

17.1.1.4 *Stratospheric ozone depletion*

The stratospheric ozone layer is being continuously depleted by chlorofluorocarbons (CFCs), halons and nitrous oxide which are released into the atmosphere by a variety of natural and industrial processes. CFCs are by far the most important contributor to ozone depletion, which in turn is responsible for increased levels of harmful ultraviolet radiation reaching the earth's surface.

17.1.1.5 *Global climate change—Greenhouse effect*

Gases which contribute to the so-called 'greenhouse effect' are known to include carbon dioxide (CO_2), methane, water vapour, nitrous oxide, CFCs, halons, and PAN. All of these gases are transparent to the short-wave radiation incident upon the earth's surface, but trap outwardly radiated long-wave radiation. It is predicted that this action will lead to a global warming of the earth's lower atmosphere with major changes in global and regional climates, the necessity to revise and adapt agricultural growing patterns, rising sea levels, and extended desertification.

Energy activity plays a major role in the production of greenhouse gases. It has been reported that fossil fuel burning accounts for about 75 per cent of anthropogenic CO_2 release and 65–75 per cent of nitrous oxide.[1]

17.1.2 Relationship between Energy and Environment

A useful indication of the significance of energy-related activities in the generation of air pollutants can be found in Table 17.1, which reflects global averages.

TABLE 17.1
Energy-related pollution.

Pollutant	Anthropogenic as % of total	Energy activities as % of total*	Source as % of energy release**	
SO_2	45	40	Coal usage	80
			Oil comb.	20
NO_x	75	64	Transport	51
			Stationary sources	49
Particulates	11,4	4,5	Transport	17
			Electricity	5
			Wood comb.	12
CO	50	15–25	Transport	75
			Stationary sources	25
CO_2	4	2,3–3,2	Solid fuels	40
			Oil	45
			Natural gas	15

* Global estimates.
** Estimates for OECD countries.
Source: *Energy and environment—policy overview* Organization for Economic Cooperation and Development/International Energy Agency (1989).

[1] *Energy and environment—policy overview* Organization for Economic Cooperation and Development/International Energy Agency (1989).

Two features of this table are striking. Firstly, note the extremely high contribution to global anthropogenic emissions derived from energy-related activities. This is most apparent for sulphur dioxide and nitrogen dioxide emissions, which represent, respectively, 90 per cent and 85 per cent of this total. In both cases, fossil fuel combustion is a major contributor. Secondly, note the anomaly with respect to particulate emissions. The contributions of various energy activities to energy-related emissions do not total 100 per cent. The discrepancy can be found in the less readily measurable, diffuse particulate emissions associated with mining activity.

Though the figures in this table reflect global emission patterns, it is predicted that, if anything, the pattern in South Africa would show an even greater contribution from fossil fuel combustion processes. These are the focus of this chapter.

17.2 FOSSIL FUELS IN SOUTH AFRICA

Fossil fuel utilization in South Africa (up to 1991) is divided between coal and oil. The contribution from off-shore natural gas, ie the Mossgas project, to come on line in 1993 and small by comparison, is discounted from this analysis. This section will attempt to identify, as far as possible, the tonnages of each fuel used and the nature of the pollution associated with its use.

17.2.1 Coal

The contribution of coal to South Africa's primary energy demand has recently been calculated as follows:

Energy form	*Percentage*
Coal	82,3
Oil	10,4
Biomass	6,1
Nuclear	1,0
Hydro	0,2

South Africa has extensive coal reserves, which have been estimated at 58 400 million economically recoverable tons.[2] This figure, which accounts for about 10 per cent of the global total, includes the vast Waterberg coal field in the north of the country. Though Iscor is currently mining coal from this field, there is some debate whether this operation is truly economical with today's technology, and it can be argued that the Waterberg fields should be discounted from the above total.

South African coals are generally lower in sulphur (less than 1 per cent) than their European or North American counterparts. Coal sales in 1988 totalled 168 million tons, of which 46 million tons were exported (more recent figures are not available). These figures do not include the vast quantities of discard material produced as a result of beneficiation practice to increase coal quality (ie reduce mineral matter or incombustible content). The energy value of this discard stock is exceedingly variable, ranging in calorific value from 4,0–24,0 MJ kg^{-1}. In terms of their pollution-generating potential, the most striking feature of coal discards is their high sulphur and mineral matter content. Sulphur values range from 1,0–7,8 per cent, and mineral matter (or ash) values from 24,0–63,4 per cent. These figures account for the contribution to acidic precipitation made by burning coal dumps in the eastern Transvaal. There is little call

[2] De Jager *An evaluation of the coal reserves of the Republic of South Africa* Department of Mineral and Energy Affairs (1982).

for this discard product within the local coal market, and stockpiles are increasing at a rate of 40–50 million tons per annum.[3]

Further coal residues include 4–5 million tons per annum of anthracitic and brown coal fines which, although high in energy value (21,8–30,8 MJ kg^{-1}), find little use in local industry. The sulphur and ash content of this material is in line with locally consumed coal.

Of the domestically consumed coal, about 94 per cent is used by three industries alone—Eskom (electricity), Iscor (steel), and Sasol (synthetic fuels). The balance of coal consumption includes industrial applications (steam raising and gas production), non-Eskom power production (local municipalities), and domestic heating in areas not served by the electrical network. Only the metallurgical grade coal used by Iscor requires beneficiation. Neither Eskom nor Sasol pretreats run-of-mine coals, and pollutant quantities generated by these industries are in direct proportion to coal composition.

Eskom has for many years been the largest domestic consumer of coal: in 1989, 67,5 million tons of coal were consumed in 18 power stations, resulting in a net electrical output of 28 233 MW. This figure constituted over 85 per cent of Eskom's total generating capacity, which, in turn, represents 85 per cent of the total electricity generated in southern Africa and roughly 50 per cent of the total generated in Africa.[4] Though Eskom had an excess capacity of 4 363 MW in 1989, it is committed to a major expansion programme which will result in an additional coal-generated capacity of some 12 700 MW coming into service by the year 2001.

More than 60 per cent of current coal consumption is associated with 8 power stations located in the eastern Transvaal Highveld. Consequently, concern over the environmental impact of Eskom's activities has focused on pollutant monitoring in this region. Measurement levels of major air pollutants from this region are discussed in section 17.4.

Sasol has accounted for the main growth in domestic coal consumption over the last decade, largely as a result of the Secunda synfuels plant's coming on stream. In 1989, Sasol coal consumption exceeded 40 million tons, up from 22,4 million tons in 1982.[5] However, future growth of this magnitude is not anticipated. With the relatively low price of crude oil (in real terms) and the anticipated synfuel contribution from Mossgas, further expansion in Sasol coal consumption is likely to come from a diversification into fine chemical production, with its own attendant pollution problems.

Iscor's coal consumption is directly related to steel production, which has declined since 1980. In addition, the coal requirement has decreased due to the implementation of new and more efficient steel production technologies. It is expected that Iscor's coal demand will remain static for the foreseeable future at around 6 million tons per annum.[6]

17.2.2 Oil

Because of its strategic nature, information on crude consumption, refinery capacities, and product split at South African oil refineries is protected by government legislation (the Petroleum Products Act 120 of 1977). This makes an analysis of air pollution from crude oil refining processes exceedingly difficult.

This point notwithstanding, it is possible to give an indication of the fate of some potential pollutants present in the crude feed stock. An example is sulphur, the primary

---

[3] Grobbelaar *South African discard and duff coal—a national inventory* Department of Mineral and Energy Affairs (1986).

[4] *Statistical yearbook* Eskom (1989).

[5] Bright 'Total utilization of coal resources—a macro view' in *Total utilization of coal reserves* South African Institute of Mining and Metallurgical Engineers (1989).

[6] Ibid.

pollutant. Crude oil processed in South Africa is relatively low in sulphur content 1,8 per cent—a figure which obviously varies with crude source. During the refining process, this sulphur is converted to hydrogen sulphide, from which elemental sulphur is recovered. The efficiency of this process is approximately 98 per cent,[7] with the balance of sulphur being exhausted to the atmosphere as sulphur dioxide.

However, only about 15 per cent of the sulphur content of the crude feed stock is recovered by this route. Roughly 40 per cent is retained in the refined products of gasoline, diesel and kerosene, and a further 40 per cent is retained in fuel oil storage. An additional small amount remains in bitumen products. The balance of feed sulphur shows up as sulphur dioxide in refinery energy requirements, which are met by a combination of fuel oil and gas (produced in situ) typically to a level of about 5 per cent of crude intake. The exact split between gas and fuel oil is refinery specific.

It is this energy requirement—for boilers, furnaces, incinerators and catalytic cracking units etc—which is principally responsible for sulphur emissions from oil-refining operations. The exact level of SO_2 emissions is determined by the sulphur content of the energy source and not directly from the sulphur content of the raw crude. Whilst the sulphur content of gas is effectively zero, that of fuel oil is in the region of 3 per cent, and this enters the atmosphere as sulphur dioxide along with other combustion products.

It has been estimated for refineries in France that total sulphur release into the atmosphere is in the range of 3–9 per cent of that entering in the feed.[8] Exact figures for South Africa are not available, though these are reliably thought to be more in the region of 4–5 per cent of feed sulphur. For a nominal crude throughput nationally of 400 000 barrels per day, sulphur dioxide emission would be approximately 80 tons per day. To put this figure in context, it is worthwhile to compare refinery SO_2 emission with that derived from local coal processing. It is important to realize that, as there is no statutory requirement for desulphurization technology in coal processing, all coal-based sulphur will enter the atmosphere as SO_2. In 1988, domestic coal consumption totalled 122 million tons. If an average coal sulphur content of 0,8 per cent is assumed (which for some of Eskom's new generation power stations is conservative), coal-based SO_2 emissions total 5 350 tons per day. Thus the total contribution from oil refining to complete SO_2 emission amounts to only 1,5 per cent of that from coal. Even if total refinery throughput was grossly overestimated at twice the figure above (ie 800 000 barrels per day), SO_2 emission from refinery operations would double to only 3 per cent of that derived from coal. By comparison, emissions of SO_2 from oil-refining operations in Western Europe have recently been calculated to account for 6 per cent of the total anthropogenic emission.[9] The discrepancy between the two totals is attributed to the much larger contribution which coal makes to South African energy usage.

Other air pollutants associated with oil-refining operations include particulates, oxides of nitrogen and volatile organic compounds. Particulates derive from such sources as catalytic cracking units (fine spent catalyst powder) and as aerosols from furnaces and boilers.

NO_x emissions derive principally from fuel-bound nitrogen in furnace and boiler installations and flare headers. If the operating temperatures of these units is high enough (>1 250 °C), generation of NO_x from nitrogen in the air stream becomes

---

[7] Meehan 'Environmental impact assessment of an oil refinery in Ireland' in *Environmental impact assessment: five training case studies* Department of Town and Country Planning, University of Manchester (1987).

[8] Marvillet *Environment and oil refining* First IUAPPA regional conference on air pollution, National Association for Clean Air, Pretoria (1990).

[9] Ibid.

significant. A further contribution to NO_x emissions comes from catalytic cracking units. NO_x emissions from refining operations are in the region of 300–400 ppm, compared to a range of 600–1000 ppm for coal combustion.

Hydrocarbons, in the form of volatile organics, are emitted as fugitive emissions from storage tanks and as a result of poor combustion efficiencies at flare headers. Fugitive emissions are reduced by the use of floating roof tanks.

The above figures indicate that, when we consider emissions from stationary sources, air pollution from oil refining operations is slight compared to pollution generated by coal processing. This is borne out by a 1986 study of air pollution in the UK,[10] which claimed that whereas the electricity supply industry accounted for 82 per cent of all emissions from stationary sources, only 6 per cent could be attributed to refining operations. The remaining 12 per cent came from other plant in the process industries. However, this picture does not tell the complete story. The bulk of sulphur present in crude oil is retained by petroleum products, whose combustion within the transport sector will result in significant, though diffuse, emissions of SO_2, along with other pollutants such as NO_x, carbon monoxide, unburned hydrocarbons, lead and other oxidants.

17.3 ATMOSPHERIC POLLUTANT FORMATION AND DISPERSION MECHANISMS

17.3.1 Atmospheric dispersion

The ability of the atmosphere to absorb pollutant discharges from fossil fuel point sources is dictated largely by the mechanisms of pollutant transport, dilution and dispersion. These three mechanisms in turn are affected by a number of variables including pollutant nature, emission point characteristics, meteorological conditions and surface terrain. The principal air pollutants have already been identified. They are typically discharged to atmosphere in the form of a plume from a tall stack, from which point they are advected away by wind.

17.3.1.1 *Atmospheric stability*

If the vertical temperature structure of the atmosphere resists vertical air motion by turbulence, the air is termed *stable*: this will always occur if temperatures increase with height—the so called *inversion* condition. If temperatures fall with height at a rate greater than that which occurs due to an air volume expanding adiabatically as it rises, the atmosphere is termed *unstable*, and mechanical turbulence is enhanced. This will always occur if the rate of temperature decrease with height exceeds 1 °C per 100 m.

Under stable atmospheric conditions, and particularly under inversion conditions, pollution accumulates in the stable air layers. Such inversion layers act as an effective lid to restrict vertical dilution of pollutants and are responsible for the high early morning levels of air pollution over many South African towns, especially those situated in valleys.

17.3.1.2 *Plume rise and effective stack height*

On emission from a stack, pollutants rise vertically upwards as a consequence of effluent gas stream inertia and buoyancy. At some point downwind of the stack, the plume bends and levels off horizontally due to wind motion. A useful parameter in

[10] Irwin 'Desulphurisation—not simply a CEGB concern' 1989 (70) *Process Engineering* 55.

determining the extent of pollutant mixing with the ambient air stream is the 'effective stack height', the sum of the physical stack height and the additional plume rise obtained before 'level off'. The greater this height, the greater the overall dilution of the pollutant stream before dispersion towards the ground. There is an inverse square relationship between effective stack height and ground-level pollutant concentration.

Dilution is also affected by plume shape (of which six types are recorded). Plume shape is in turn dictated by atmospheric stability. However, stack height and plume rise together say little about the accumulation of pollutants in highly stable atmospheres, a point which is often overlooked in monitoring exercises. This is addressed specifically with reference to the eastern Transvaal Highveld in section 17.4.

17.3.1.3 *Wind speed and direction*

A plume of pollutants will move across local terrain in line with the wind direction. The extent to which the contaminated gas plume is dispersed, by mixing with the surrounding air stream, is principally a function of wind speed. An increase in wind speed increases the rate of dilution of the effluent plume with distance from the emission source. However, this effect is tempered by the fact that an increase in wind speed will decrease plume rise, leading to increased ground level concentrations. The net result of this interaction is to influence the exact downstream location of maximum ground level pollutant concentration. It should be borne in mind that, in addition to this dilution process, the mixing process results also in the formation of secondary pollutants such as aerosol sulphates and sulphuric and nitric acids.

17.3.2 Consideration of meteorological factors: case study—the meteorology of the eastern Transvaal Highveld (ETH).

The ETH, covering an area of 30 000 km^2, has been identified as a region of major environmental concern for South Africa because it is both a major agricultural and forestry area, yet is home to 10 of Eskom's coal-fired power stations, including five which rank among the world's largest. Other pollutant generators include coal mines (with their smouldering coal dumps), Sasol petrochemical plants II and III, as well as a number of metallurgical industries, paper and pulp plants, brick works and other industrial activities. Together with the Vaal Triangle the ETH forms the country's industrial powerhouse.

Because of this industrial density, pollutant generation and dispersion in the ETH are subjects of great interest. Several recent studies have tried to unravel the complexities of these phenomena. The most definitive study in recent years was undertaken by Tyson, Kruger & Louw[11] in 1987 under the auspices of the National Programme for Weather, Climate and Atmosphere Research of the Council for Scientific and Industrial Research (CSIR). The findings of this study can be summarized thus:

'The ETH is characterised by climatic conditions which are highly adverse for the dispersion of atmospheric pollutants, namely high atmospheric stability, clear skies and low wind speeds, generally associated with a high pressure system prevailing over the region. Moist unstable conditions and rainfall are confined almost exclusively to the summer period. The dry stable winter period is obviously of greatest significance for accumulation of atmospheric pollution. During winter, inversions of temperatures occur almost every night at the surface, to a depth of between 150 and 300 m, while elevated inversions occur with high frequency, on average at a height of about 1 200 to 1 400 m above ground. This elevated subsidence inversion is steep enough to preclude vertical dispersion of pollutants above this level on most days throughout the year.'

---

[11] *Atmospheric pollution and its implications in the eastern Transvaal Highveld* FRD, CSIR (1988).

17.4 AIR QUALITY MEASUREMENTS IN SOUTH AFRICA

17.4.1 Total national pollutant quantities

For reasons already mentioned, atmospheric emissions in the ETH are well documented.[12] This data bank provides a useful yardstick by which the full extent of fossil-fuel generated air pollution in South Africa can be measured. Table 17.2 (due to Els[13]) shows the contribution to emissions from Eskom activities in this geographical area. Since Eskom coal consumption and quality figures are well documented, it is proposed that a conservative estimate of national emission levels can be derived by scaling the Eskom contribution. The underlying assumptions to this treatment are that

- total air pollution is in proportion to coal combustion, as per the OECD estimates in Table 17.1.
- pollution controls in the ETH will, if anything, be more efficient than the national average.

About 64 per cent of Eskom's total generating capacity is concentrated in the ETH, resulting in a coal consumption of 50,4 million tons per annum.[14] Total annual coal consumption nationally is in the region of 120 million tons. These figures, too, are reflected in Table 17.2. These emissions are in reasonable agreement with those reported by Lawrence,[15] in which total annual SO_2 and NO_x emissions for the country are listed as 2,9 and 1,25 million tons per annum respectively. It is interesting also to note that more than 90 per cent of each of the SO_2, NO_x, and CO_2 emissions in the ETH derive from coal combustion at Eskom power stations.

TABLE 17.2

Atmosheric pollution—eastern Transvaal Highveld and national figures.

Source	Emissions (tons y^{-1}) 1987*			
	Particulates	SO_2	NO_x	CO
Power stations	355 843	1 110 585	371 791	43 538
Total in ETH	427 264	1 217 728	407 011	371 888
Total nationally	1 059 000	3 305 000	1 106 500	

* Els *Strategies for dealing with eastern Tranvaal Highveld acidic deposition situation* First IUPPA regional conference on air pollution, National Association for Clean Air, Pretoria (1990).

Missing from such an analysis is air pollution caused by the stockpile of burning coal dumps in the ETH. Combustion of these coal discards is a subject of great concern, as much from the point of environmental awareness as from that of inventory control. Monitoring of emissions from smouldering discard stockpiles is in its infancy. From a knowledge of temperature profiles within dumps it is possible to predict which are likely to combust spontaneously. However, the rate and extent of combustion are less readily predictable. Understanding the pattern of emissions from these dumps is complicated

[12] Tyson, Kruger & Louw above n 11; Els *Emission inventory—identification of sources, quantification of emission factors in eastern Transvaal Highveld* Report C/85/13 (1987); Turner *A five year study of air quality in the highveld region* Eskom Engineering Investigations Report no S 90/002 (1990).

[13] Above n 12.

[14] *Statistical yearbook* above n 4.

[15] 'Impact of fossil power plants on air quality' in *Charting a course for the 90s* National Association for Clean Air Conference, Cape Town (1989).

by the fact that coal discards have a high but variable sulphur content. Els[16] predicted that burning coal dumps contributed roughly 5 per cent to total SO_2 emissions in the ETH, but this figure has not been substantiated. Particulate emissions are unknown.

The value of these absolute pollutant *amounts* in assessing environmental risk is questionable. It is far more important to relate energy activity to atmospheric pollutant *concentrations* across local, regional and national boundaries. The relationship between environmental degradation (current or anticipated) and air pollution can thus be more readily quantified, taking into consideration the dilution and dispersion mechanisms of pollutant transport which have already been identified. Specific attention is given to particulate and acidic deposition.

17.4.2 Pollutant concentrations in the ETH

Measurements of pollutant concentrations are typically recorded by monitoring sites installed at ground level. The question of how such measurements are related to point source emissions from tall stacks must be addressed. Data collection comes from three main sources—Eskom itself, the Climatology Research Group at the University of the Witwatersrand, and the Atmospheric Sciences Division of the CSIR.

Data from all sources are in general agreement. However, differences arise in interpretative style, and sampling and analytical procedures vary. No group has duplicated fully the measurements of any other. Eskom particularly has chosen to place much store in ground level measurements of sulphur dioxide as primary pollution indicators and, to a large extent, has formulated its environmental management policy accordingly.

17.4.2.1 *Ambient sulphur dioxide concentration*

Annual mean sulphur dioxide concentrations in the ETH vary from 8,8–41,3 $\mu g\ m^{-3}$, though daily mean values as high as 194 $\mu g\ m^{-3}$ have been reported.[17] Corresponding annual figures for areas of Soweto[18] are given as 52–78 $\mu g\ m^{-3}$. Diurnal variations show maximum ground-level pollution episodes during the midday period, with lowest values at night. Maximum levels occur during the winter period, which is a consequence of poorer mixing in the boundary layer, a greater demand for electricity, increased domestic coal consumption and a greater incidence of veld fires during this period. Spatial variation in SO_2 levels is slight, the highest values being recorded at the Komati monitoring site near the Komati power station, which has a relatively short stack. The new generation of Eskom power plant, namely Matla, Duvha, Lethabo, Kendal, Matimba, Tutuka and Majuba (to be built), all have stacks which discharge above the surface inversion layer. It is argued that pollutants from these stations are (or will be) adequately dispersed in the mixing layer.[19] The direct contribution from power stations to *local* ground level SO_2 emissions is thereby minimized.

17.4.2.2 *Ambient nitrogen oxides concentration*

Nitrogen oxides have been shown to be co-sourced with sulphur dioxide in the ETH, ie coal combustion dominates over emissions from the transport sector. Annual mean concentration figures are in the region of 34 $\mu g\ m^{-3}$, though, as for SO_2 emissions,

[16] Above n 12.
[17] Turner above n 12.
[18] Turner, Annegarn et al *Air pollution monitoring in Soweto* Sixth international conference on air pollution, CSIR, Pretoria (1984).
[19] Tosen & Turner 'The effect of stack height on observed ground level concentrations of sulphur dioxide on the Highveld' in *Charting a course for the 90s* above n 15.

daily mean values may greatly exceed this figure.[20] Dispersion and dilution of NO_x follow the same pattern as that for SO_2.

17.4.2.3 *Aerosol measurements*

Aerosols are formed by the oxidation of sulphur and nitrogen oxides to sulphates and nitrates by photochemical reaction in the presence of oxidizing agents such as ozone. Other aerosol particles include chlorides formed from hydrogen chloride vapour. Oxidation of acid gas species proceeds faster in summer months due to increased solar radiation. This is balanced, however, by improved pollutant dispersion during this period. Aerosol concentrations at ground level in the ETH[21] are in the range of 1–50 $\mu g\ m^{-3}$, with average values about 4 $\mu g\ m^{-3}$. Aerosol concentrations at high-level sites in the ETH are considerably greater, resulting in increased acidic deposition, 'due either to washout during rain, or to banking of this elevated pollution layer against forested mountain regions'.[22] There is good agreement between total emission of SO_2 from power stations in the ETH and sulphate aerosol levels.

17.4.2.4 *Visibility*

Poor visibility results from the scattering of light by fly ash particulates and aerosol particles (mainly sulphates) in the size range 0,1–1,0 μm. Coincidentally, this size of particulates is least readily captured by control devices installed in flue gas ducting at power stations (see section 17.5.1). Eskom's newest power stations operate to particulate emission targets in the range 94–170 mg Nm^{-3}, whereas older power stations report particulate emission levels as high as 868 mg Nm^{-3}.[23]

Recent qualitative observations of visibility decrease in the ETH confirm that haze formation is a real problem. Lawrence[24] has reported severe localized haze formation on 70 per cent of days between 1989–90.

There is no correlation between SO_2 ground level concentration and visibility decrease. Sulphate and nitrate pollutant concentrations, humidity levels, smoke density and dust concentrations, as well as nitrogen dioxide concentrations, more realistically indicate a propensity for haze formation and visibility decrease.

17.4.2.5 *Acidic deposition*

Normal rainfall is mildly acidic, with a pH of 5,6 due to the carbon dioxide equilibrium. Direct measurements of rainfall acidity in the ETH obtained by Eskom are in the range pH 3,9 to pH 4,6 (the lower value reflecting highest acidity).[25] Rainfall acidity readings are prone to inaccuracies. A more reliable estimate of acidic deposition can be construed from bulk sulphate and nitrate measurements at surface (combining figures for both wet and dry deposition). In this way it is possible to relate bulk precipitation to pollutant aerosol concentrations. Bulk sulphate loadings as high as

---

[20] Turner above n 12.

[21] Wells, Snyman, Held & Dos Santos *Air pollution in the eastern Transvaal Highveld* CSIR Atmospheric Sciences Division (1987).

[22] Tyson, Kruger & Louw above n 11.

[23] Albertyn *Baghouse versus ESP—an evaluation of the performance of the baghouse installation at Rooiwal Power Station* First IUPPA regional conference on air pollution, National Association for Clean Air (1990); Gore *Eskom's philosophy and strategy on air quality management and how it is implemented* First IUPPA regional conference on air pollution, National Association for Clean Air (1990).

[24] *Perceptions on the impact of particulate and gaseous emissions from fossil-fueled power plants in South Africa* First IUPPA regional conference on air pollution, National Association for Clean Air (1990).

[25] Bosman *The impact of atmospheric sulphate deposition on surface water quality in the eastern Transvaal highveld* First IUPPA regional conference on air pollution, National Association for Clean Air (1990).

76 kg ha^{-1} y^{-1} have been reported in the ETH.[26] Mean values were considerably lower (28–35 kg ha^{-1} y^{-1}). The dry deposition contribution is between 20 and 30 per cent of the total sulphate load. Mean bulk nitrate levels are in the range 9–17 kg ha^{-1} y^{-1}. Together, these bulk precipitation values yield some monthly groundwater acidity values of pH below 3,5.

17.4.2.6 *Pollution above surface inversion layer*

It has been reported that, between the subsidence inversion and the top of the mixing layer, pollutants emitted by tall stacks are trapped and accumulate, leading to a regional pollution hazard.[27] This is graphically demonstrated by measurements at two sites roughly 300 m above the general terrain. Sulphate levels in excess of 50 $\mu g\ m^{-3}$ were recorded. It was observed also that nitrate and chloride aerosols were present in much higher levels relative to sulphate at these higher altitude sample sites. This is consistent with a hypothesis proposed by Tyson, Kruger & Louw[28] in which regional air recirculation above the surface inversion is thought to result in frequent and widespread episodes of high pollutant concentration in the ETH.

These findings would seem to indicate that Eskom's tall stack policy, though effective in keeping ground level gaseous pollutant levels within current health guidelines serves to concentrate pollutants at higher elevations, resulting in increased acidic deposition.

17.4.3 Comparison with emissions elsewhere

Dust removal efficiencies reported by Eskom[29] range from 96 per cent for the Arnot power station to 99,88 per cent for the Lethabo power station. Emission levels are controlled by electrostatic precipitators, whose operation is discussed in section 17.5.1. Similar scale power plant in Europe, Japan and the USA are forced to conform to legislated limits of 50 mg m^{-3}, which is almost half of the best recorded emissions from Eskom stations. It should be appreciated that the Eskom dust control programme is the most rigorous in this country. Dust emissions from other industrial processes which burn coal (petrochemicals, steel-making, brick works, and paper and pulp processes) are likely to be at considerably higher concentrations than the Eskom figures.

Acidic pollutant concentrations in the ETH, expressed in terms of bulk sulphate and nitrate deposition, are easily referred to levels in other countries. The highest wet sulphate levels in the ETH are nearly double those reported in Pennsylvania, USA, where there is an equivalent energy generation density. Dry sulphate levels world-wide range from less than 1 kg ha^{-1} y^{-1} in Norway to 20 kg ha^{-1} y^{-1} in Florida, USA. South African figures are roughly half of the Florida value.[30] Wet and dry nitrate values in the ETH are generally lower than industrial sites elsewhere in the world because of a generally low contribution from the transport sector.

Ambient air quality emission standards for sulphate aerosols are not common. California guidelines are set at 25 $\mu g\ m^{-3}$ over a 24-hour period; detected emissions near ground level in the ETH generally meet this constraint.

It is worthwhile to compare the point source emission levels from Eskom power stations with legislated levels which apply to large new coal combustion facilities in other countries. This is because it is possible to size pollution control equipment in order to meet any given desired reduction in pollutant discharge. This comparison is made in Table 17.3.

---

[26] Bosman *Summarising world atmospheric sulphate deposition load with special reference to the South African eastern Transvaal Highveld* Department of Water Affairs (1987).

[27] Wells, Snyman, Held & Dos Santos above n 21.

[28] Above n 11.

[29] Gore above n 23.

[30] Bosman above n 26.

With the exception of Australia, South Africa lags far behind the other countries on this list. Most of the countries in the European Economic Community (EEC) have adopted the same limits as Germany, and the UK has recently embarked on a programme to retro-fit control technologies to existing power plant.

TABLE 17.3

Comparison of emission targets for new power plant and current Eskom emission levels.

	SO_2 (mg Nm^{-3})	NO_x (mg Nm^{-3})
Australia	2 000	500
Germany	400	200
Japan	223	411
UK	Best practicable means	
USA	1 240	475–620
Eskom (existing emissions)	2 000–2 500	600–700

17.4.4 Comparison with emissions in residential areas in South Africa

Discounting air pollution generated by industries located close to residential areas, the bulk of residential pollution in South Africa is a consequence of domestic coal consumption for cooking and space heating. The energy efficiency of domestic coal or wood stoves is very low, and atmospheric emissions comprise unburned char particles, fly-ash particles, coal volatiles (hydrocarbon species), carbon monoxide, sulphur and nitrogen oxides as well as carbon dioxide. These diffuse ground level emissions result in excessive smog formation (typically during the winter months).

Ambient SO_2 emissions in towns such as Soweto have already been identified as being in excess of ground level SO_2 emissions in the ETH. However, the value of this pollution indicator in predicting environmental degradation is questionable.

The level of smoke (suspended fine particulates) in the atmosphere above residential areas is the most graphic indicator of coal-generated pollution. Visibility readings at various sites in Soweto during the winter months attest to this fact. EPA guidelines for total suspended solids are regularly significantly exceeded.[31] The more lenient environmental guidelines recommended by South Africa's Department of National Health and Population Development, ie 250 μg Nm^{-3} over a 24-hour period, are exceeded less often.

It is difficult to relate residentially generated air pollution to particulate emissions over the ETH. Atmospheric dust levels over the ETH are much lower than those monitored in urban areas such as Soweto. However, smoke from coal fires is localized, close to the ground, and generally contains particles outside the respirable range. Fly-ash emissions from power stations are concentrated in the respirable range, heavily loaded with toxic species, and, because of their dispersion in the atmosphere, act as nucleation sites for acid aerosols which are subsequently 'washed out', consequently affecting surface acidity.

Residential pollution is a result of existing energy consumption practices, and environmental degradation will continue until such time as alternatives to solid fuel combustion are implemented. A comprehensive urban electrification programme would

[31] Rorich 'Soweto air pollution July to August 1984' *Residential air pollution* National Association for Clean Air (1988); Kemeny, Ellerbeck & Briggs 'An assessment of smoke pollution in Soweto' in *Residential air pollution* National Association for Clean Air (1988).

assist in this regard. However, such an increased demand for electricity will place an additional load on the power distribution network, leading to increased pollutant generation from coal-fired power stations.

17.4.5 Regional and national significance

The pollution data reported above serve to highlight several important facts about pollutant monitoring and control in South Africa.

First, from the pollutant information to hand it can be concluded that the ETH ranks with major industrial regions in the world in terms of atmospheric environmental degradation. As long as this country pursues a coal-based energy policy and continues to locate power plant in this region, the problem will not only persist but be aggravated.

Secondly, there is evidence to suggest that pollution generated in the ETH is exported to neighbouring regions such as Natal and the Orange Free State.

Thirdly, sulphate and nitrate deposition falls in the Vaal Triangle catchment area, the country's most important water source. Water quality, for drinking, agriculture and industry, is compromised.

Fourthly, it would appear that the Department of National Health & Population Development guidelines based on ground level SO_2 concentrations do little to stem the accumulation of upper level sulphate to concentrations which could result in massive sulphate deposition.

Finally, the ETH region is unique in South Africa. The density of coal-combustion operations, geography and climatology all combine to produce a polluted atmosphere which needs to be monitored very closely. The development of a comprehensive air management policy for the whole of South Africa will depend on what, and when, actions are taken to alleviate the environmental pressure in this region.

17.5 AIR POLLUTION CONTROL TECHNOLOGIES

It is important to identify clearly those technologies which are suited to the selective removal of pollutants, their capital and running costs, operating efficiencies and waste-disposal practices. Only in this manner can rational decisions be taken about their implementation. In South Africa especially, where pollution control legislation is couched in the language of 'best practicable means', the emission of air pollutants is often unrestrained on the grounds that to incorporate pollution control equipment into a particular process would render that process uneconomical and non-viable.

A case in point is the statement that 'the costs of flue gas desulphurization are so great that the introduction of this technology in South Africa is not economically justified.' This statement has been made often enough and with sufficient force that it has become generally accepted. But is it in fact true? Has its acceptance removed the incentive to look for alternatives? What other technologies are available for reducing emissions of SO_2 from combustion plant, and at what cost?

This section will identify technologies suited to the control of particulates, sulphur dioxide, nitrogen oxides and carbon dioxide in flue gases, as these have been identified as primary air pollutants. Technology choices will be referred to coal combustion plant, since emissions from such operations far outweigh those derived from crude oil refining processes. The electricity supply industry will be used as a case study and emphasis is placed on the following aspects of technology choice: efficiency and cost of technologies for environmental control; the impact on electricity generating costs and user tariffs; scope for advanced energy technologies; scope for mitigating the costs of environmental controls.

17.5.1 Particulate removal equipment

Fly-ash particles in combustion flue gases are removed typically by a combination of inertial and electrostatic separators (ESPs). Efficiencies for these devices range from

70 per cent for inertial separators such as course-cut primary cyclones to over 99 per cent for ESPs. Eskom has not achieved such high efficiencies with its ESP installations. It has recently undertaken to improve the performance of its older ESPs by flue-gas conditioning using sulphur trioxide, and the first installation at Kriel power station in the ETH has demonstrated a reduction in dust emission of 90 per cent.[32] However, both the capital and the operating costs for flue-gas conditioning plant are considerable.

Environmental emission limits for particulates are becoming more stringent. In Western Europe, Japan and the USA, there is a widely held belief that the current emission target for large-scale power plant will be reduced to a figure of 15–20 mg Nm^{-3} in the foreseeable future. There is concern that current-generation ESPs are incapable of meeting such a low target and this has prompted major research initiatives in the matter of barrier filtration, where dust removal is effectively total. Though South Africa is guided by developments elsewhere, particulate emission limits here are not as severe, as reflected by emission levels presented earlier.

The environmental performance of electrostatic precipitators is confounded by evidence which suggests that trace elements such as arsenic, cadmium, gallium, molybdenum, lead, thallium and zinc are concentrated within the precipitator, sometimes doubling in concentration before being discharged in the smaller size fractions which escape capture by the ESP.[33] The mechanism for such concentration entails condensation and surface adsorption from the gas phase. Other trace elements such as beryllium, bismuth, cobalt, copper, germanium, antimony, tin, nickel, vanadium, uranium and thorium are also found in fly-ash emissions downstream of ESPs.[34]

17.5.2 Sulphur dioxide controls

There are two approaches to the problem of SO_2 emissions from coal processing.

The first option is to reduce the sulphur content of coal sufficiently, prior to combustion, so that subsequent SO_2 emission levels are reduced to acceptable levels. The feasibility of this exercise in South Africa merits some discussion. South African run-of-mine coals are low sulphur coals. The three constituents which make up their total sulphur content are a pyrites fraction (inorganic sulphides), an organic fraction (mercaptans etc) and certain sulphates. The pyrites fraction, which can be as high as 50–60 per cent, is amenable to removal by physical washing and dense medium separation—established beneficiation practices employed on export coals to reduce their mineral-matter content. Some success has also been achieved in recent years in desulphurization of both pyritic and organic sulphur fractions by microbial action. While neither of these practices has yet been employed in this country, it is estimated that a combination of conventional coal cleaning and chemical and biological techniques has the potential to reduce total sulphur content by up to 90 per cent of that in the coal feed.

If no coal desulphurization is attempted prior to combustion, the second option—combustion gas treatment—is a possibility. This has been the topic of considerable research and commercial development in recent years. The technologies employed can be divided into a number of categories, depending on the following features: in-situ or post-combustion treatment; wet or dry process; sulphur or other by-product recovery; retrofit capability.

---

[32] Lawrence above n 24.

[33] Dale & Paulson *Characterization of electrostatic precipitator ashes from pulverized fuel combustion* Third CSIRO Conference on Gas Cleaning, Medlow Bath, NSW, Australia (1988); Kornelius 'The recovery of chemicals from gas filtration dust' in *Charting a course for the 90s* above n 15.

[34] Willis *Elemental characterisation of South African coal and fly ash* Department of Geochemistry, University of Cape Town (1980).

With the exception of the Koeberg nuclear facility, all of Eskom's large-scale plant employ pulverized coal combustion. Control of SO_2 emissions from such plant is most commonly effected by flue-gas scrubbing equipment, installed after particulate removal and just prior to the exhaust stack. Flue-gas desulphurization (FGD) systems use a sorbent (typically limestone or one of its derivatives) to absorb sulphur directly from the flue gas, producing a solid product. A large number of different systems exist for this process.

The most common variety is the wet scrubbing system, where an aqueous slurry of lime or limestone is brought into contact with the flue gas in a spray tower. A gypsum or calcium sulphite/sulphate product results. These systems are typically non-regenerable, i e deactivated sorbent is discarded. SO_2 reductions of above 90 per cent are common with this technique, but at significant capital and operating costs, including an energy penalty of 1–4 per cent.[35] Where a saleable product is recovered, e g if the slurry is dewatered and gypsum recovered, this is achieved at the expense of a much larger capital cost. It should be appreciated that gypsum recovery is not of significant interest in South Africa—any one of Eskom's new generation of 'six-pack' pulverized coal power stations alone releases enough SO_2 into the atmosphere, which, if recovered as gypsum, would saturate the local market! Wet FGD processes installed in South Africa would consequently result in an accumulation of huge quantities of slurry waste, the containment and final disposal of which would pose environmental problems not dissimilar to those associated with mining tailings and slimes dams and consequent groundwater contamination.

Another variant of the FGD process is the spray-drying option. Here, semi-dry lime is injected in atomized form into the absorber vessel. A dry product results which can be recovered by conventional particulate removal equipment. SO_2 reductions of 70–80 per cent are readily achievable by this process. It has the advantage over wet processes that both capital and operating costs, as well as energy consumption figures, are much lower. A lack of ready markets for the solids recovered in this way has inhibited its wide introduction.

FGD plant has demonstrated its success in many countries, both as new installations and as retrofits at existing electrical utilities. Research is being undertaken into the direct injection of suitable sorbents into the furnace chamber. This process has the advantage of improved kinetics owing to higher operating temperatures, and does not suffer energy penalties through the need for absorber columns operating at low temperatures, and the subsequent reheating of flue gases before discharge to atmosphere. The dry product which results can be readily recovered by conventional particulate removal equipment. SO_2 removal efficiencies in the region of 30–50 per cent have been reported for this method. Though still largely at the demonstration stage, this technology has shown a surprising capacity for retrofitting to existing pulverized coal furnaces and it is anticipated that the relatively low capture efficiencies recorded to date will be improved in the future by the careful control of combustion conditions and careful sorbent selection.

17.5.3 Nitrogen oxides control

Three different technologies are available for control of nitrogen oxides. In all processes, nitrogen oxide and nitrogen dioxide are reduced to nitrogen before discharge into the atmosphere.

The most straightforward control method applicable to pulverized coal furnaces is so-called 'combustion control' using 'low-NO_x' burners. This technology produces a fuel-rich zone within the combustion chamber where unburned coal volatiles and

[35] *Emission controls in electricity generation and industry* Organization for Economic Cooperation and Development/International Energy Agency (1988).

carbon char act as reducing agents. The balance of combustion air necessary for complete combustion is added at a suitable point within the combustion chamber, remote from the flame, where most of the NO_x conversion occurs. A reduction in NO_x levels of between 30 and 50 per cent is achievable by this method.

The next level of sophistication of removal equipment is termed Selective Non-Catalytic Reduction (SNCR) and entails the injection of ammonia into the combustion chamber at a point where the flue-gas temperature is in the region of 1 000 °C. Ammonia reacts with nitrogen oxides, producing nitrogen and water vapour which are subsequently discharged into the atmosphere. A reduction efficiency of about 50 per cent is possible by this method. Major drawbacks include the high operating cost of ammonia injection, ammonia bypass from the system, and the formation of ammonium sulphate by reaction with SO_2.

Selective Catalytic Reduction (SCR) processes employ catalysts to effect NO_x reduction in the presence of ammonia, at much lower temperatures (250–400 °C) than the non-catalytic option. Reduction efficiencies of about 90 per cent are attainable. Operating experience with this technology is growing rapidly and research and development work in the area of low-cost, robust catalysts will obviously lead to a significant reduction in capital costs. The attraction of SCR technology is its flexibility—it is possible to retrofit pulverized coal combustion plant by installing the SCR hardware in flue-gas ducting downstream of particulate capture equipment and (possibly) FGD equipment.

17.5.4 Advanced energy technologies

It is not the aim to describe in any detail developments in clean coal technologies such as pressurized, fluidized combustion (PFBC) and integrated gasification/combined cycle (IGCC) processes. These technology options, already proven at demonstration scale and expected to make significant gains in world-wide utility plant sales this decade, operate with increased thermal efficiency over existing pulverized fuel plant. Fuel consumption is reduced, and all gaseous and particulate emissions are correspondingly lessened. More significant, though, is their ability to reduce both sulphur and nitrogen oxide emissions by simple in-situ processes. As attractive as these options appear, their introduction locally is not envisaged within the next 15 years. This is due in part to a lack of local confidence. More important, however, is Eskom's commitment to a long-term expansion programme in which 'six pack' pulverized coal combustion plant plays a dominant role.

17.5.5 Costs of control technologies

Environmental policy decisions cannot be divorced from the financial implications of pollution clean-up. The local debate over the introduction of control technologies for sulphur and nitrogen oxides draws heavily on the projected costs of these technologies. Trade-offs are inevitable. A case in point is Eskom's mission statement of 'electricity for all', in which it is argued that social upliftment derived from increased urban electrification far outweighs the positive environmental benefit of an equivalent investment in power station pollution controls.[36]

Comparisons of this nature have questionable merit. Electricity is a resource which should be accessible to all, and Eskom is correct in pursuing this objective. But a healthy environment is also a resource to be treasured, and it is unwise to pit one objective against the other. It is important to clarify exactly how much these technologies cost, both in terms of capital and electricity generating costs, and their implications for user tariffs.

---

[36] McRae 1989 (9) *Engineering News* 18.

A number of cost estimates for pollution control technologies associated with pulverized coal combustion have recently been released. The Electric Power Research Institute in the USA lists pollution control costs as 40 per cent of the capital outlay of a new plant and 35 per cent of the operational costs. This estimate includes figures for SO_2, NO_x and particulate controls, effluents, noise, waste and other controls, but no individual component costs are available. In Germany, the Technical Association of Large Power Plant Operators (VGB) showed that the entire pollution control system for coal-fired power plant represented a 47 per cent increase in capital costs over the basic plant (without environmental controls). Controls for SO_2 accounted for 19 per cent of the cost, NO_x controls 9 per cent, and particulate controls 6 per cent. The most authoritative economic survey of pollution controls was conducted by the Organization for Economic Cooperation and Development (OECD) and published by the International Energy Agency (IEA).[37] This survey collated cost data from most of the developed countries in the Western World, including some, such as Australia, which display similar dependencies on coal combustion to South Africa's. A wide range of control technologies was reviewed. On average, SO_2 controls (in the form of flue-gas desulphurization equipment) are shown to account for a 15 per cent increase over base capital cost, whilst NO_x controls (selective catalytic reduction) add an additional 6 per cent to this figure. Furthermore, the levelized annual cost (LAC) for FGD technology (base load station operation, 5 per cent discount rate) amounts to only 9 per cent of electricity generation costs. Similarly, the predicted LAC for SCR de-NO_x technology represented a further 9 per cent increase in generation costs. FGD and SCR technologies are therefore together expected to account for roughly an 18 per cent increase in generation costs. SCR costs are dominated by catalyst replacement costs, which amount to 65 per cent of total cost. The incentive to develop more active and robust catalysts is obvious.

These cost figures differ markedly from those cited by Eskom:

'It can be shown in round terms that the cost of desulphurisation [alone] would add some 20 to 30 per cent to *the overall cost of generating electricity* over the lifetime of a station'.[38]

The IEA figures pertain to new utility plant. South Africa has a large investment in recently commissioned pulverized coal plant, and the costs of pollution control must give due consideration to retrofitting these existing installations. The costs of a retrofit for SO_2 and NO_x based on FGD and SCR technologies are respectively 30 per cent and 50 per cent greater than the capital cost of new plant. However, European and American development work has shown that there is considerable potential in retrofit technologies other than FGD and SCR. Though these alternatives (such as furnace sorbent injection and combustion burner modifications) are limited to operating efficiencies in the region of 60 per cent, their capital and operating costs are two to three times lower than those associated with either FGD or SCR. It is expected that their impact on electricity generation costs would be in direct proportion to these figures.

The attraction of new clean-coal technologies is further emphasized by the following cost data. Sulphur dioxide removal by repowering existing pulverized coal utility plant with clean coal technologies such as IGCC and PFBC is reliably estimated to cost, respectively, only 36 per cent and 47 per cent of the equivalent cost of retrofitting with FGD.[39]

The cost figures above pertain to pollution abatement. It has already been proposed that SO_2 emissions can be controlled by reducing coal-sulphur levels through a combination of physical washing and biological separations. Accurate cost data for

---

[37] Above n 35.

[38] Turner *Eskom's air quality impacts* Eskom Engineering Investigations Report no 590/054 (1990).

[39] *Emission controls in electricity generation and industry* above n 34; *Prospects for the use of advanced coal based power generation plant in the United Kingdom* Energy Paper no 56 (1988).

these processes are not available for South African coals—it should be appreciated that coal structure and quality play major roles in these processes.

Even if these additional costs of pollution abatement were passed on to consumers by way of increased tariffs, the above figures cast some doubt on the validity of Eskom's current position with regard to air pollution controls. At the very least, there is an urgent need to produce a detailed cost estimate for a reasonable reduction in both SO_2 and NO_x levels under local conditions. Given the long lead time to the operation of electric utility plant, attention should be given to the incorporation of clean-coal technologies in Eskom's scenario planning. In any such exercise it would be imperative to balance energy security against environmental protection objectives.

17.6 ANALYSIS OF AIR POLLUTION IN SOUTH AFRICA

The data presented in the preceding text highlight the severity of air pollution in the eastern Transvaal highveld. A comparison was made between industrial generation (principally from coal-fired power stations) and diffuse pollution from domestic coal combustion in residential areas. Electricity generation is seen as both saviour and villain—relieving urban pollution during the winter months, yet being responsible for severe acidic deposition in a region which is a major agricultural, forestry and water resource region in addition to being the power house of South Africa.

An analysis of South Africa's air pollution problems must take into consideration the major role played by fossil fuel combustion. Only the transport sector makes a further significant contribution to the degradation of air quality, and there principally through the production of nitrogen oxides which play a role in photochemical smog production.

Pollution controls are warranted in the ETH. The possibilities for mitigating the costs of environmental controls must be examined, both in terms of regulatory measures imposed and technologies installed. The legislative framework should actively encourage flexibility within industries in meeting environmental goals. Technological prescriptions are often shortsighted. Perhaps in this way the country can move towards renewable energy technologies which are less damaging to the environment.

The nature of South Africa's economy will, to a large extent, dictate the rate at which environmental control structures are put in place. Energy security and environmental protection are both fundamentally important to the concept of sustainable development. The value of one should not be understated in order to serve the other. The legal mechanisms operating in South Africa to regulate air quality will now be reviewed.

17.7 AIR POLLUTION CONTROL LEGISLATION

17.7.1 Introduction

The last two decades have shown that air pollution is no longer a national issue but a universal one which has transcended national or state boundaries and become a global concern.[40] The international community has recognized that air pollution can be successfully curtailed only with the co-operation of all nations. Global co-operation has several advantages: it ensures multi-disciplinary research that is conducted on a grand scale; less advanced countries derive the benefit of modern techniques applied by developed countries and financial costs may be shared between states. The occurrence of acid rain, ozone layer depletion and climatic changes has led to several relevant conventions. See chapter 9.

South African legislation, although providing for a limited degree of control since 1919, has comprehensively addressed the problem of air pollution only since the mid-sixties. The Public Health Act 36 of 1919 classified air pollution as a statutory nuisance to be regulated by local authorities and enforced by way of notice of

[40] Louw & Odendaal 'Ons atmosfeer en die kwesbaarheid daarvan' 1989 (7) *Clean Air Journal*. See, too, Weidner *Air pollution control strategies and policies in the Federal Republic of Germany* (1986) 14.

abatement and criminal sanction. Enforcement proved difficult, since the pinpointing of a particular industry or chimney as the culprit, and proof of injury or danger to health, was difficult to achieve. As research on air pollution progressed, however, it became apparent that legislation dealing with air pollution control in its entirety was essential.

A bill for air pollution control was first introduced in 1958. Although it was first read in parliament in 1961, it was not accepted before it had undergone a number of modifications—the result of material received from organizations and bodies and reports published by a parliamentary select committee.[41] The Atmospheric Pollution Prevention Act 45 of 1965 was finally promulgated in April 1965.

This Act is based on the British Alkali etc Works Regulation Act of 1906 (the control of noxious or offensive gases—basically industrial pollution) and the British Clean Air Act of 1956 (the control of smoke). The Act, which is administered by the Department of National Health and Population Development, provides for the control of four different types of air pollution, i e noxious or offensive gases, smoke, dust, and vehicle emissions. A distinction is drawn between control aimed at regulating the source of air pollution and control aimed at regulating the emission itself.

At a press conference held during September 1990, the department indicated that the levels of air pollution in some places in South Africa have dropped over the past 25 years. Smoke in areas where no electricity is available, together with power stations have been identified as two of the most important causes of air pollution. Furthermore, the department has stated that the following areas will receive priority in the future:

- residential areas without electricity;
- power station emissions;
- dust from mine dumps;
- the paper industry
- the petrochemical industry;
- the metallurgical industry;
- wood processing plants;
- lead in petrol;
- smoke from smaller industries; and
- motor vehicle emissions.

The need for public education regarding air pollution control, and research into its effects and prevention should be encouraged. Important issues are national and international liaison; international communication; the development of a uniform policy and its enforcement in southern Africa. A few areas such as the PWV area, the ETH, the greater Durban area and the western Cape have been singled out as requiring the most attention.[42]

The Atmospheric Pollution Prevention Act provides for the uniform and comprehensive treatment of almost all air pollution. The only other legislation which deals with limited aspects of air pollution control are the Health Act 63 of 1977, regulations in terms of the Mines and Works Act 27 of 1956 (now applicable in terms of the Minerals Act 50 of 1991) and the Road Traffic Act 29 of 1989.

During September 1990 the Department of National Health and Population Development outlined its national control strategy. The procedure adopted for the prevention and control of air pollution is that of the 'best practicable means'. This procedure is based on practical principles, including:

---

[41] At its meeting in October 1955 the following bodies were represented: the Council for Scientific and Industrial Research (CSIR) , the Department of Commerce and Industries, the United Municipal Executives, the Federated Chamber of Industries and SEIFSA.

[42] Press release, Department of National Health and Population Development, 17 September 1990.

- the need for a safe and healthy environment;
- the fact that South Africa is a developing country;
- the maintenance of a delicate balance between what is essential for a safe and healthy environment and what can be afforded; and
- the determination of realistic emission levels for the normal operation of plants.[43]

17.7.2 Establishment of committee, boards and officials

The Atmospheric Pollution Prevention Act provides for the establishment of a National Air Pollution Advisory Committee (NAPAC), an appeal board and the appointment of officers and their functions.

NAPAC consists of a minimum of seven and a maximum of 11 members appointed by the Minister of National Health and Population Development. It is a fairly representative body with membership drawn from commerce and industry, the scientific and academic professions and the public and private sectors. The main functions of the committee are to advise the Minister on matters relating to the control, abatement and prevention of air pollution, to monitor measures taken outside the Republic for the control of air pollution, and to stimulate interest in the problem of air pollution. This committee, which has established an overall policy for the control of air pollution, is at present concentrating on specific air pollution problems, such as air pollution in black townships and squatter camps and photochemical smog.[44]

The fact that NAPAC convenes infrequently on a part-time basis and that its membership is not fixed is a disadvantage when viewed from the perspective of continuity and the undertaking of in-depth studies on various aspects of air pollution.

The appeal board hears and determines appeals from decisions of the chief air pollution control officer (chief officer) relating to a scheduled process (section 17.7.3.2) and appeals relating to a notice served in terms of the provisions dealing with dust control or relating to notices served on the owner of a vehicle.

Provision is, furthermore, made for the establishment of regional appeal boards to hear and determine appeals from the decisions of local authorities regarding the nuisance caused by smoke or other products of combustion, and appeals stemming from the implementation of smoke control regulations. There have thus far been no appeals to regional boards.

The Act also provides for the appointment of the chief officer and as many inspectors as the Minister may consider it necessary to appoint.[45] The Minister may, after consultation with the Minister of Mineral and Energy Affairs, authorize the government mining engineer to exercise and perform the powers, duties and functions of the chief officer, with reference to mines and works; and may also appoint the chief inspector of explosives with reference to explosives factories.[46]

The chief officer and inspectors must be persons technically qualified to exercise control over atmospheric pollution by virtue of their academic training in the natural sciences or engineering and practical experience in industry, as well as their knowledge of atmospheric pollution.[47] Extensive powers have been conferred upon the chief officer and inspectors, including the right to enter a scheduled process at any time and the right to examine any process in which noxious or offensive gas is used or produced, as well as the apparatus for condensing gas or preventing the discharge of gas into the atmosphere. These officers may at any time require the production of a registration or provisional registration certificate where a scheduled process is carried on. They may

---

[43] Ibid.
[44] NAPAC Agenda 23 September 1990.
[45] Section 6(1).
[46] Section 6(2).
[47] Section 6(3).

also apply tests, take samples, and make enquiries and undertake investigations as they deem necessary.[48] Industrial air pollution can be satisfactorily controlled only where frequent inspection—preferably on a daily basis—of polluting premises, industries or other areas is carried out by technically qualified persons. This would of necessity entail the appointment of a large number of skilled and trained persons to implement the legislative directives and to ensure compliance with the standards laid down.

17.7.3 Control of noxious or offensive gases[49]

17.7.3.1 *Objectives and policy*

The department has indicated that its objectives with regard to industrial pollution are: the effective control of industries; the limiting of sulphur dioxide and nitrogen oxide levels in the ETH to acceptable levels; the limiting of volatile hydrocarbon levels to acceptable levels; the elimination of visible particle emissions from industries; the limitation of specific noxious emissions from specialized industries; the monitoring of all sources of emissions as far as possible and the monitoring of environmental pollution levels by industries as part of the national monitoring programme.

The department has also listed several key elements in the application of its air pollution control policy. These include:

- Sound physical planning practices for the siting of new industries;
- The installation of advanced air-cleaning equipment in all new plants;
- The regular reviewing of emission standards;
- A programme for the upgrading of existing equipment; and
- Regular inspections of all industries.[50]

17.7.3.2 *Scheduled processes*

The whole of South Africa has since 1968 been declared a controlled area.[51] A specification standard applies to the production of noxious or offensive gases. This means that pollution control equipment used in operating the process must conform to certain design criteria. At present, the Second Schedule to the Act has 69 scheduled processes listed which are generally regarded as the cause of industrial air pollution in South Africa.

No person may carry on a scheduled process in or on any premises[52] unless he is the holder of a current registration certificate.[53] The granting of a permit is subject to

---

[48] Section 7.

[49] 'Noxious or offensive gas' means any of the following groups of compounds when in the form of gas: hydrocarbons; alcohols; aldehydes; ketones; ethers; esters; phenols; organic acids and their derivatives; halogens; organic nitrogen, sulphur and halogen compounds; cyanides; cyanogens; ammonia and its compounds; inorganic acids; fumes containing antimony, arsenic, beryllium, chromium, cobalt, copper, lead, manganese, mercury, vanadium or zinc in their derivatives; gases and fumes arising from cement works; fumes and odours from purification plants, glue factories, cement works and meat-, fish- or whale-processing factories; and any other gas, fumes or particulate matter which the Minister may by notice in the *Government Gazette* declare to be noxious or offensive gas. It also includes dust from asbestos treatment or mining in any controlled area which has not been declared a dust control area in terms of s 27 of the Act.

[50] Press release above n 42.

[51] GN R1776 of 4 October 1968.

[52] 'Premises' is defined as any buildings or other structure together with the land on which it is situated and any adjoining land occupied or used in connection with any activities carried on in such building or structure, and includes any land without any buildings or other structures and any locomotive, ship, boat or other vessel which operates or is present within the area of a local authority or the precincts of any harbour: s 1(1).

[53] Section 9(1)*(a)*(i). Where a person was carrying on a process on any premises prior to the declaration of the area as a controlled area, he must apply for a registration certificate within three months: s 9(1)*(a)*(ii). A registration certificate must also be obtained by the State.

compliance with certain minimum standard specifications. The erection, alteration or extension to existing buildings or plants, intended to be used for the carrying on of any scheduled process, is also prohibited in the absence of the grant of a provisional certificate authorizing the erection, alteration or extension.[54] The alteration or extension of an existing building or plant in respect of which a current registration certificate has been issued is similarly prohibited unless application has been made to the chief officer for provisional registration of the proposed alteration or extension. A provisional registration certificate is not required where the alteration or extension will not affect the escape into the atmosphere of noxious or offensive gases.[55]

17.7.3.3 *'Best practicable means'*

All applications for registration certificates are lodged with the chief officer, who, after consideration of the application, must issue a registration (or provisional registration) certificate, if satisfied that the 'best practicable means' are being adopted to prevent or reduce to a minimum the escape of noxious or offensive gases into the atmosphere.[56] If not satisfied, the chief officer must notify the applicant to take the necessary steps to prevent or reduce air pollution.[57] Once these steps have been taken, the applicant is entitled to be issued with a certificate.[58]

'Best practicable means' is defined in the Act.[59] In summary, the definition relates to the adoption of measures which are technically feasible and economically possible, bearing in mind the well-being of the people in the area of the plant.

The chief officer has interpreted 'best practicable means' as the assessment of 'the problems of air cleaning associated with each type of process, of which there may be many examples in the country, and to decide what degree of air cleaning can be achieved, bearing in mind the different techniques available, the costs associated with their installation and operation and the effects which these costs will have on the ability of the firms concerned to operate without financial loss'.[60]

The department contrasts the 'best practicable means' with the 'best practical environmental option' as follows: the latter is the result of systematic consultation and procedures that stress the protection and preservation of the environment as a whole—ie air, land and water. This option results in the greatest benefit for, or least damage to, the environment at an acceptable cost in both the long and the short term.

The monitoring of the 'best practicable means', after a current or provisional certificate has been issued is problematic. In order to operate effectively, frequent inspections should be carried out. A further problem which arises is whether the process is closed down immediately upon expiry of the certificate where the best practicable means are not adhered to. Flowing from this, the question which crops up is what criteria the chief officer uses in determining the period of validity of a provisional certificate. Ideally, all applications for certificates and disputes arising from the chief

---

[54] Section 9(1)*(b)*.

[55] Section 9(1)*(c)*.

[56] Section 10(1) and (2)(i). Although there is no legal obligation on local authorities to control air pollution emanating from industries, or to notify the department of such pollution within its area, it appears that local authorities and the department have a good working arrangement in this respect.

[57] Section 10(1)(ii).

[58] Section 10(3).

[59] 'Best practicable means', when used with reference to the prevention of the escape of noxious or offensive gases or the dispersal or suspension of dust in the atmosphere or the emission of fumes by vehicles, includes the provision and maintenance of the necessary appliances to that end, the effective care and operation of such appliances, and the adoption of any other methods which, having regard to local conditions and circumstances, the prevailing extent of technical knowledge and the cost likely to be involved, may be reasonably practicable and necessary for the protection of any section of the public against the emission of poisonous or noxious gases, dust or any such fumes: s 1.

[60] Boegman 1972 (1) *Clean Air Journal* 2, 9.

officer's actions should be publicized via official channels and the media to focus attention on industrial development and associated problems of pollution.

The requirement of 'best practicable means' which involves a subjective evaluation on the part of the chief officer, is flexible and is interpreted in collaboration with the industries concerned. It is an adaptable concept which can accommodate changing and improved air pollution control measures. No overall standards of air cleanliness are set and the degree of industrial air pollution tolerated will depend almost entirely upon the discretion of the chief officer.

In theory the discretionary powers of the chief officer (and other officials) are subject to judicial control in that the courts may be approached to test the validity of the power exercised. In practice this means that the courts will determine whether officials have complied with specific statutory and common-law requirements, in short whether their actions were valid. Nevertheless, such judicial control of discretionary power is deficient, since the courts will not alter policy decisions or substitute their opinion for that of the official. This means that the matter will usually be referred back to the chief officer for reconsideration.

Although the legal system makes provision for the control of discretionary powers—albeit of a very limited nature—the question is who will bring the matter before the Court, since a person must have locus standi to do so. In order to test the validity of the exercise of administrative power, a concerned person or victim of pollution must show a direct, personal interest in the matter, usually by way of prejudice or harm suffered.[61] See chapter 8.

17.7.3.4 *Registration certificates*

With regard to the issue of a provisional registration certificate, the chief officer must be satisfied that the scheduled process in question may reasonably be permitted to be carried on in the area concerned, having regard to the nature of the process, the character of the locality in question, the purposes for which the premises are used and any other relevant considerations. Furthermore, he must be satisfied that the operation of the process on the premises will not conflict with any town-planning scheme in operation or about to be put into operation.[62]

A provisional registration certificate is valid for a period determined by the chief officer, who may extend the period of validity. The provisional certificate must contain information specifying the situation and extent of the proposed building or plant, the nature of the process to be carried out, the raw materials to be used, appliances to be installed, and the measures proposed for the purification of the discharged effluents.[63]

A registration certificate has no restricted period of validity. It is issued subject to the condition that all plant and apparatus used in the scheduled process and all appliances used for preventing or reducing to a minimum the escape into the atmosphere of noxious or offensive gases, shall be properly operated and maintained, and that the holder of the certificate must take all other necessary measures to prevent the escape of noxious or offensive gases.[64]

Moreover, the chief officer has the power to notify the holder of any certificate to take steps to ensure the more effective operation of the appliances mentioned in the

[61] *Society for the Prevention of Cruelty to Animals v De Swardt* 1969 (1) SA 655 (O); *Von Moltke v Coasta Areosa (Pty) Ltd* 1975 (1) SA 255 (C); *Bamford v Minister of Community Development and State Auxiliary Services* 1981 (3) SA 1054 (C).

[62] Section 10(4). Aspects which are considered are the topography, town-planning schemes and meteorological factors.

[63] Section 11(1)–(2).

[64] Section 12(1).

certificate.[65] He may similarly instruct the holder to utilize some other improved process or equipment as specified by notice, to prevent the escape of noxious or offensive gases.[66]

A certificate usually reflects the following:

- the certificate number, process and the period of validity of the certificate (where a provisional certificate is issued, the period may be 18 months);
- the situation and extent of the plant;
- the nature of the process;
- raw materials and products; and
- appliances and measures to prevent air pollution such as specifications for emissions, monitoring and recorder systems to be installed, specifications on handling and storage of raw and waste material to prevent secondary dust nuisance, regular reports to the chief officer, the immediate notification of any irregularities or non-compliance with the process specifications and the disposal of effluent from purification equipment.

Guidelines for each individual process are laid down by the department and are incorporated into the specific registration certificates. Once these guidelines form part of a certificate, they become legally binding on the industry concerned. At present there are approximately 2 000 certificates in operation for approximately 1 200 industries in the six regions.[67]

It is an offence to carry on a scheduled process in the absence of a registration certificate or to erect or alter buildings intended to be operated as a scheduled process in the absence of a provincial registration certificate.[68] The certificate may be cancelled or suspended if the holder fails to comply with its conditions, or if he fails to take the steps laid down by the chief officer to ensure the more effective operation of the appliances provided in the registration certificate, or to ensure the more effective prevention of air pollution.[69]

17.7.3.5 *Penalty*

Industrial pollution is very often the result of the maximization of profits through the minimization of the costs of waste disposal. The case for the use of the criminal sanction in such instances rests squarely on deterrence. If the criminal penalty is to be effective as a deterrent, the probability of detection must be high and the sanction must be stringent enough to overcome the motive of economic gain. If this is not the case, the fine will merely be regarded as part of the cost of doing business—a kind of tax, as it were. The maximum penalty involved for a contravention of the Act is a rather mild fine of R500 or imprisonment for a period of six months for a first offence or a fine of R2 000 or imprisonment for a period of one year in the event of a further conviction.

---

[65] Section 12(2).

[66] Section 12(3). The holder is allowed a reasonable time within which to take the specified steps: s 12(3)*(b)*.

[67] Departmental guidelines relating, for instance, to chromium processes (process 50) include:

— a description of the process;

— basic information on the chemical compounds;

— guidelines on specifications required for the process, for example, in the case of soluble chromium compounds the chrome salts must be removed by scrubbing and emissions must be less than 50 mg m^{-3}. In the case of ferro-alloys, ore dust and dust emissions must be less than 120 mg m^{-3}, enclosed furnaces with wet scrubbers are preferred, cyclones upstream of pressure-type bag filters are prescribed, motors and fans must be freely interchangeable and spare units must be available, monitors and recorders to determine the availability of air-cleaning equipment must be at least 96 per cent of the time per month at required efficiency.

[68] Section 9(2).

[69] Section 12(4).

17.7.4 Smoke control

17.7.4.1 *Applicability*

Part III of the Act regulates the emission of smoke from industry and from residential and rural areas, but only within areas in respect of which this part has been declared to be applicable.[70] In 1966 the first local authority had the Act declared applicable to its area. One year later there were 14 such authorities; in 1975 there were some 90; by 1980 there were 120 and in 1991 220. The provisions of the Act relating to the control of smoke do not apply to the State.[71]

17.7.4.2 *Objectives*

Departmental objectives include inter alia that all residential areas, excluding squatter areas, be declared smoke control zones; that smoke levels in residential areas be reduced to acceptable levels; that smoke from all non-scheduled industries be limited and that all local authorities be required to participate in a national monitoring programme.[72]

17.7.4.3 *Smoke control levels*

There are different levels of smoke control:[73]

Level 1 relates to the enforcement of provisions of the Act[74] which include the installation of fuel-burning appliances, the siting of new equipment and the control of smoke or other products of combustion causing a nuisance. This level applies to smaller authorities in country regions where industrialization is not as highly developed.

Level 2 regulates smoke problems of a more serious nature and includes exercising control over pollution emanating from boilers and space heating appliances in flats, office buildings, light industries (for example, bakeries and dry cleaners) and the burning of waste.[75] Dwelling houses are excluded.

Level 3 applies mainly to residential areas in which smoke control zones are established.[76] In these areas no one may permit the emission of smoke of a density or content which obscures light to an extent greater than 20 per cent.

17.7.4.4 *Control authorities*

The concurrence of the local authority concerned is required before the Minister can declare the provisions of the Act relating to smoke control to be applicable to the area of jurisdiction of the local authority.[77] The control of air pollution from the combustion of fuels lies in the main in the hands of local authorities. Nevertheless, the Minister may, after consultation with the Minister of Finance and the local authority in question, direct that the powers of the local authority be transferred to the chief officer.[78] Where the smoke control zone does not fall within the jurisdiction of a local authority, the Minister may appoint either the chief officer or an adjoining local authority to exercise the necessary powers.[79]

Where the Minister, after consideration of a report submitted by NAPAC, is satisfied that smoke is causing a nuisance, two courses of action are open to him. Where the smoke falls within a smoke control zone and the area of jurisdiction of the local

---

[70] Section 14(1).
[71] Section 47.
[72] Press release above n 42.
[73] *Air pollution in South Africa* Department of National Health and Population Development (2 ed 1989).
[74] Sections 15, 16, 17 and 23.
[75] Section 18.
[76] Sections 20, 21, 22, 23, 24 and 25.
[77] Section 14(2).
[78] Section 14(3). The local authority may also request the Minister to do so: s 14(4).
[79] Section 14(5).

authority, he may order that the powers be exercised by the chief officer if he believes that the local authority has not taken reasonable steps to prevent the continuation of the nuisance. Where the smoke does not emanate from a smoke control zone, he may declare the smoke control provisions of the Act applicable in the area to the extent necessary to prevent the continuation of the nuisance.[80] In that event he may authorize the chief officer to regulate smoke control in that area.[81] This provision specifically applies to smoke emanating from premises.[82]

17.7.4.5 *Regulations*

A local authority may make regulations prohibiting the emission of dark smoke (the colour and density is specified in the regulation); the installation, alteration or extension of fuel-burning appliances; the removal of such appliances; the use or sale for use of solid fuel for a fuel-burning appliance; the regulation of records relating to fuel-burning appliances; the inspection of fuel-burning appliances, and generally for the effective control of the emission or emanation of smoke from any premises.[83] The permissible density or colour of smoke is defined by reference to the chart set out in the First Schedule to the Act.[84]

In the event of the contravention of these regulations, the local authority can serve a notice upon the owner or occupier of the premises to bring about a cessation of smoke within a specified period. In determining the period the authority must consider the nature and magnitude of the measures to be taken. Where the smoke emanates from a scheduled process, the chief officer must be consulted before a notice is served on the polluter. Failure to comply with a notice constitutes an offence.[85] In the event of a polluter not taking adequate steps to comply with the notice within a period of one month of his conviction, the local authority may take the necessary steps to bring about the cessation of smoke, and recover the costs of doing so from the polluter.[86]

After confirmation by the Minister and consultation with NAPAC, the local authority may declare a smoke control zone and prohibit the emanation of dark smoke in that area.[87]

The local authority must give notice in local newspapers of the general effect of its order, the area within which the order is to apply, and the fact that objections may be lodged. It may delegate its powers of smoke control, except the power to issue regulations and to establish smoke control zones and may authorize any person to enter certain premises for inspection.[88]

The diverse number of authorities responsible for smoke control and the possibility of delegation, make it difficult to determine which specific authority is in fact controlling a specific pollution problem.

---

[80] Section 14(6).

[81] Ibid.

[82] 'Premises' is defined in s 1(1). Cf above n 52.

[83] Section 18.

[84] Section 18(2). The chief officer has indicated that the determination of colour or density of smoke appears to be based on outdated methods of assessment.

[85] Section 19(1)–(5).

[86] Section 19(6).

[87] Section 20. For examples on smoke control zone orders, see Municipality of Pretoria (GN R1026 of 15 June 1973); Municipality of Johannesburg (GN R489 of 14 March 1975 and GN R490 of 14 March 1975); Municipality of Germiston (GN R368 of 27 February 1987); and Municipality of Vereeniging (GN R369 of 27 February 1987).

[88] Sections 20(4) and 22.

17.7.4.6 *Manufacture and importation of fuel-burning appliances*

The Act criminally prohibits the manufacture or importation of any fuel-burning appliance (or any part of it) for use in a dwelling house unless written permission is received from the chief officer.[89]

17.7.4.7 *Installation of fuel-burning appliances*

The installation in or on any premises of fuel-burning appliances is prohibited, unless the appliance complies as far as is reasonably practicable to certain standards (the colour of the smoke is prescribed by regulation). Certain concessions are made for the unavoidable emission of dark smoke during the starting up, breakdown or disturbance of the appliance, or for any fuel-burning appliance designed to burn pulverized solid fuel, for example.[90]

No person may install a fuel-burning device in the absence of prior written notice to the local authority or chief officer.[91] The prohibition does not apply to the installation of a fuel-burning appliance in a dwelling house, nor to the situation where the installation was commenced or the agreement for its acquisition was entered into prior to a fixed date.[92]

17.7.4.8 *Siting of fuel-burning appliances and construction of chimneys*

A local authority may not approve of a plan providing for the construction of a chimney or other opening for carrying smoke, gases, vapours, fumes, grit, dust or other final escape from any building, or for the installation of any fuel-burning appliance, unless it is satisfied (in the case of a chimney or other opening) that the height is as far as practicable sufficient to prevent smoke or any other product of combustion from becoming prejudicial to health or a nuisance to occupiers of premises in the surrounding areas or, in the case of a fuel-burning appliance, that it is suitably sited in relation to other premises in the surrounding areas.[93]

17.7.4.9 *Smoke constituting a nuisance*

At common law the term 'nuisance', which derives from English law, is concerned with repeated unreasonable use of land by one neighbour at the expense of another.

---

[89] Section 14A. A 'fuel-burning appliance' is defined as any furnace, boiler or other appliance designed to burn or capable of burning liquid fuel or gaseous fuel or wood, coal, anthracite or other solid fuel, or used to dispose of any material by burning or to subject solid fuel to any process involving the application of heat: s 1(1).

[90] Section 15(1)*(a)*–*(b)*. In terms of ss 15(4), 16 and 18, 'appliance' also means any one mechanical stoker or any one burner on which there may be more than one stoker, but does not include a single chimney through which the products of several burners or furnaces may be discharged; 'stoker' means any mechanism or other means intended for feeding fuel into any place for the purpose of burning it in such place; and 'burner' means any furnace, combustion chamber, grate or other place to which fuel is fed by one or more stokers or manually for the purpose of burning such fuel in such furnace, combustion chamber, grate or other place: s 15(4).

[91] Section 15(2).

[92] Section 15(3). For example, the smoke control regulations in terms of s 18(5) of the Act (GN R1221 of 27 June 1975) applicable to the Municipality of Pretoria provides in reg 3(1) that no person shall install, alter or extend a fuel-burning appliance in or on any premises, other than in a dwelling-house, unless complete specifications in respect of such installation, alteration or extension have been approved by the control officer (air pollution) and unless such installation, alteration or extension is carried out in accordance with such approved plans and specifications. In other regulations issued in terms of s 18(5) the regulations do not apply to smoke emitted from any dwelling or to the installation, alteration or extension of any fuel-burning appliance in a dwelling: Provided that where a dwelling is subject to an order as contemplated in s 20 of the Act, the regulations shall apply (GN R2031 of 2 November 1973). Similar provisions appear in GN R121 of 7 June 1985; GN R1007 of 8 May 1987; and GN R2552 of 20 November 1987. See also GN R1448 of 13 July 1984.

[93] Section 16(1) read with s 16(2).

This term has been expanded by the courts to include, for example, nuisance created by air pollution and odours.[94] The Act does not define the word 'nuisance'.

The interpretation of the term 'nuisance', be it by the chief officer, the local authority or the courts, is fraught with difficulties, and although an objective evaluation must be sought, a measure of subjectivity will inevitably be present. Where a local authority is satisfied that smoke or any other product of combustion emanating from premises constitutes a nuisance to the occupier of the affected premises, the Act requires it to serve a notice on the polluter to abate the nuisance within a specific period and to take steps to prevent its recurrence.[95]

Smoke which is prejudicial to health or which adversely affects the reasonable comfort of occupiers of adjoining or nearby premises, or which affects the use of premises, is deemed to be a nuisance. Where the nuisance arises from a defect in the building the owner is responsible, and in any other instance the occupier of the premises is responsible for the nuisance.[96]

The Court may order a person who has failed to comply with an abatement notice to take such steps as may be necessary to prevent a recurrence of the nuisance. Failure to take the prescribed steps within the specified time, empowers the local authority to abate the nuisance, and to recover costs.[97]

In terms of the Health Act 63 of 1977 certain forms of air pollution emanating from factories and industrial or business premises may amount to a nuisance.[98] The Minister of National Health and Population Development may make regulations to regulate, control, restrict or prohibit any activity, condition or thing that constitutes a nuisance.[99] The abatement notice procedure is prescribed for instances in which the local authority is of the opinion that a condition has arisen which is offensive or would endanger health unless immediately remedied, and to which the provisions of the Atmospheric Pollution Prevention Act do not apply.[100]

17.7.4.10 *Offences*

The installation of fuel-burning appliances contrary to the provisions of the Act; failure to comply with an abatement notice; the contravention of smoke control regulations; failure to comply with an order relating to a smoke control zone, and the failure to supply required information to a local authority, or knowingly furnishing false or misleading information, amount to offences under part III of the Act.

17.7.4.11 *Appeals*

The recipient of a notice from the local authority regarding the causation of a nuisance through smoke may, subject to certain procedures, appeal to the regional appeal board. The regional appeal board's decision is subject to a right of appeal to the air pollution appeal board.[101]

---

[94] See, for example, *Herrington v Johannesburg Municipality* 1909 TH 179 and *Wynberg Municipality v Dreyer* 1920 AD 439.
[95] Section 17(1).
[96] Section 17(2).
[97] Section 17.
[98] Section 1(xxvii)*(f)* and *(g)*. See also s 39(2). In terms of s 1*(f)* and *(g)* of the Act, a nuisance is caused when a factory, industry or business premises is not kept clean and free from offensive smells. Any factory or industry or business premises causing or giving rise to smells or effluvia which are offensive or injurious and dangerous to health also constitutes a nuisance.
[99] Section 39(1).
[100] Section 27.
[101] Section 25(1).

17.7.4.12 *State not bound*

Although the Act specifically provides that the State is not bound by this part of the Act,[102] the chief officer has intimated that parastatals (semi-state organizations) such as Eskom and Sasol are bound.[103]

The State is required to give notice of the construction of a chimney or the installation of a fuel-burning appliance which falls under its control to the local authority in whose area the premises are situated.[104]

17.7.5 Dust control

17.7.5.1 *Sources of dust*

Part IV of the Act provides for the abatement of dust at two main sources, namely dust arising from waste mine-dumps and dust emanating from industrial processes not covered by part II of the Act. Examples of industrial processes which fall under part IV are sandblasting operations, dry powder spray-painting, woodworking and carpentry shops, and the handling of various chemicals in dry powder form. The abatement of dust thus centres on control at the source of the nuisance.

The mining areas of South Africa are characterized by a large number of waste rock dumps, slimes dams and waste coal dumps. This accumulation of waste has constituted a major source of wind-borne dust on the dry Transvaal Highveld. A number of methods have been adopted in the past to obviate dust nuisance—for example, spraying the surfaces with molasses.

17.7.5.2 *Control provisions*

Departmental objectives are aimed at limiting dust from mine-dumps to a minimum; eliminating health hazards from asbestos mine-dumps; and limiting dust from non-scheduled processes to acceptable levels.[105] For example, dust emanating from gold mine areas in the Witwatersrand which are not listed as scheduled processes falls within the dust control area of the local authority. In these cases the chief officer will appoint the Government Mining Engineer to control dust pollution.

The provisions relating to dust control find application in designated dust control areas.[106] Control is exercised via specific instructions issued by the chief officer, or the application of the best practicable means, or by way of regulations issued by the Minister. For example, the Minister may regulate the inspection of premises in a dust control area.[107]

---

[102] Section 47.

[103] Schools and hospitals which fall under a Provincial Administration are also excluded from this part of the Act. In practice smoke pollution emanating from schools and hospitals is resolved by way of negotiation—either between local authorities or the chief officer and the polluter concerned. Transnet Ltd (previously the South African Transport Services) is not bound by the smoke control provisions and complaints received regarding smoke emissions caused by Transnet Ltd must be laid before Parliament by the Minister for Economic Coordination and Public Enterprises. This procedure amounts to parliamentary control of smoke, as opposed to direct control exercised in terms of the Act.

[104] Section 47(2).

[105] *An approach to a national environmental policy and strategy for South Africa* Council for the Environment (1988).

[106] For example, the Minister has in terms of s 27 of the Act declared certain areas as dust control areas: the erstwhile Divisional Council of the Cape and the municipalities of Cape Town, Alberton, Bellville, Johannesburg, Kempton Park, Pietermaritzburg and Witbank; (GN R542 of 23 March 1984); Town Council of Parow and magisterial districts of Barberton, Carolina, Kuruman, Pietersburg, Prieska and Vryheid (GN R997 of 3 May 1985); the erstwhile Divisional Council of Stellenbosch (GN R2232 of 4 October 1985); and local authority of Midrand (GN R25 of 2 January 1987).

[107] Section 33. In terms of the regulations, the chief officer or an inspector may enter premises to determine whether a nuisance exists or whether the provisions of a notice have been complied with; he may also question persons during such investigation; he may require the owner, occupier or a person in

Any person in a dust control area who carries on an industrial process which creates dust and causes or is liable to cause a nuisance to residents in the vicinity must take the prescribed steps or, where no steps have been prescribed, must adopt the 'best practicable means' to abate the nuisance.

Where dust emanates from the deposition of matter in excess of 20 000 m^3 in volume (or in certain other cases where it does not exceed this limit), the owners or occupiers of land must carry out the directions of the chief officer with regard to the abatement of the dust nuisance.[108]

Dust pollution caused by owners or occupiers of land and constituting a nuisance is regulated by way of notice of abatement based on the 'best practicable means'.[109]

In certain circumstances, where the person required to take dust abatement measures is deceased or where the corporate body has ceased to exist, the Minister may ensure that steps are taken to alleviate the problem, and that the cost involved is carried by the State (payable out of the Dust Control Levy Account[110]), the local authority and the owner in proportions determined by the Minister.

Where the Government Mining Engineer is of the opinion that a mine will cease operations within a period of five years, he must notify the Minister of Mineral and Energy Affairs and the owner of the mine and advise the Minister of National Health and Population Development accordingly.[111] Notwithstanding the provisions of the Mines and Works Act 27 of 1956, now the Minerals Act 50 of 1991, the disposal of assets by mines in the absence of a certificate by the chief officer to the effect that the necessary steps have been taken or that adequate provision has been made to prevent the pollution of the atmosphere by dust emanating from the mine, is prohibited.[112] Should the owner of the mine dispose of any mine assets before he has received a certificate from the chief officer, he is guilty of an offence.[113] In effect, therefore, a mining operation which is due to cease operations cannot dispose of its assets unless the chief officer agrees to it.

Pollution by dust may also be controlled by the Minister of National Health and Population Development. He may, after consideration of a report by NAPAC, issue regulations inter alia prescribing steps to be taken to prevent the creation or continuation of a nuisance, or to minimize the nuisance; provide for the inspection of premises within a dust control area by the chief officer or an inspector; and prohibit the damage to any means adopted to prevent the dispersion in the atmosphere of matter

---

charge to assist him in such investigation and draw up programmes or make recommendations aimed at reducing or eliminating such dust nuisance: GN R1922 of 30 August 1985. See also GN R1599 of 19 August 1977.

[108] Section 28(1). The chief officer requires compliance with specific instructions or the adoption of the best practicable means for preventing dust from becoming dispersed or causing a nuisance.

[109] Section 29. For the purposes of s 28(1), 'best practicable means' includes in any particular case any steps within the meaning of that expression as defined in s 1 which may be determined by the chief officer and specified in a notice signed by him and delivered or transmitted by registered post to the person who is in terms of s 28(1) required to adopt such means: s 28(2).

[110] Section 30. In terms of s 31 the Minister may, after consultation with other Ministers, establish a Dust Control Levy Account for the more effective prevention of air pollution by dust. Contributions may be paid into this account in terms of ss 28 and 30. Contributions are made in single or periodic payments as the Minister may decide, and certain persons may be exempted from liability to contribute. All contributions are paid to the chief officer, who transmits the amount to the Director-General: National Health and Population Development, who also administers the account. Certain expenditures approved by the Minister are paid out of the account and moneys not required for immediate use are invested with the public debt commissioners.

[111] Section 32(1).

[112] Section 32(2).

[113] Ibid.

which may cause a nuisance.[114] The Minister is also authorized to transfer powers and duties of the chief officer to the Government Mining Engineer.[115]

17.7.5.3 *Appeals*

Any person aggrieved by a notice served on him in respect of dust control may appeal to the Air Pollution Appeal Board within 30 days after service of the notice. The board has the power to confirm, modify or set aside the notice, and the decision of the board is final.[116] Thus far no appeals have been lodged.

17.7.5.4 *Penalties*

Whether the penalties imposed, which are similar to those relating to the emission of noxious or offensive gases, are in proportion to the pollution caused—in other words, whether they effectively deter future dust polluters, is debatable. The same argument applies to the prohibition regarding the disposal of assets by mines where a failure to comply with the instruction is an offence carrying a similar fine. The procedure laid down with regard to the disposal of assets by mines is, in principle, sound, although regular inspection for possible pollution is essential, since the possibility of a mine's economic base changing detrimentally cannot be excluded.

17.7.6 Control of vehicle emissions

17.7.6.1 *Applicable areas and authorities*

Part V of the Act deals with pollution emanating from vehicles and is applicable to areas specifically designated by ministerial order. Control of vehicle emissions will apply only in an area under the jurisdiction of a local authority (after consultation with the NAPAC and the Administrator concerned).[117]

If, after consideration of a report, the Minister is of the opinion that the local authority has not exercised its powers satisfactorily, he may, after consultation with the Minister of Finance and the local authority concerned, direct that the powers be exercised by the chief officer. The costs incurred by the chief officer in that instance may be recovered from the local authority in question.[118]

17.7.6.2 *Objectives*

The department has stated its objectives to be:

- minimizing visible smoke from vehicles;
- gradually removing lead from petrol;
- limiting hydrocarbon emissions; and
- employing advanced technology to limit noxious emissions and implementing an efficient monitoring network.[119]

17.7.6.3 *Control procedure*

A person authorized by a local authority may require the driver of a vehicle on a public road to stop and may carry out a prescribed examination of the vehicle. Alternatively, he may serve a notice on the registered owner of the vehicle to make it

---

[114] Section 33(1).

[115] Section 6(2).

[116] Section 35.

[117] Section 36. The following regulations issued in terms of s 36 have been made applicable to Part V: local authorities of Alberton, Bloemfontein, Edenvale, Johannesburg, Pietermaritzburg, Pinetown, Pretoria, Roodepoort, Springs, Cape Town (GN R1652 of 20 September 1974); Municipality of Richards Bay (GN R2512 of 18 November 1983); Village Council of Bedfordview (GN R2427 of 9 November 1984).

[118] Section 36(4). This power may be delegated in terms of s 40.

[119] Press Release above n 42.

available for the prescribed examination. If, after examination of the vehicle, the authorized person is satisfied that the vehicle is emitting noxious or offensive gases contrary to the regulations, he shall notify the owner of the vehicle to take the necessary steps to prevent the emission and to make the vehicle available for re-examination. Any person who fails to stop; fails to co-operate; or interferes with or obstructs an authorized person is guilty of an offence.[120]

17.7.6.4 *Appeals*

Any person aggrieved by a notice served on him may appeal to the Air Pollution Appeal Board within fourteen days after receipt of a notice. The board may confirm, modify or set aside the notice, and its decision is final.[121]

Efficient vehicle emission control depends on the vigilance of the local authority and the carrying out of regular inspections. The current legal measures enacted require the support of good technical knowledge, and control must be extended to include petrol-driven vehicles.

Following upon an inspection and the prescription of certain methods of control, the problem is to ensure that the prescribed methods are implemented. Problems which immediately come to mind are the mobility of vehicles and the possibility of a car being unregistered or stolen, thereby obstructing the tracing of the vehicle.

17.7.6.5 *Regulations*

The Minister may regulate the use on a public road of vehicle emitting specific noxious or offensive gases, or gases which are of a darker colour or greater density or specific content and he may prescribe the steps to be taken to prevent the emission of noxious or offensive gases and the methods to be applied to determine whether noxious or offensive gases are being emitted.[122]

17.7.6.6 *Road traffic legislation*

The provincial traffic ordinances have been consolidated in the Road Traffic Act 29 of 1989. In terms of the Act it is an offence for any person driving or having a vehicle on a public road to cause or allow the engine thereof to run in such a manner that it emits smoke or fumes which would not be emitted if the engine were in good condition or ran in an efficient manner.[123]

The Minister may, after consultation with the Administrator, issue regulations regarding the emission of exhaust gas, smoke, fuel, oil, visible vapours, sparks, ash or grit from any vehicle operated on a public road.[124] Specifications for the examination of any vehicle may be laid down.[125] No scientific tests have been developed for petrol-driven vehicles and no regulations have as yet been issued under this Act. The implementation of measures to control the percentage of lead in petrol casts a financial burden on vehicle owners, since the estimated cost of installing a device to control the lead content is approximately R2 000 per vehicle.

---

[120] Section 37. In terms of s 40, the local authority may authorize any person to detain or inspect any vehicle on any public road within its jurisdictional area.

[121] Section 37(2).

[122] Section 39. The Minister has made regulations on vehicle emissions applicable to certain local authorities (GN R1651 of 20 September 1974; GN R1816 of 26 August 1983). See also GN R517 of 2 April 1974.

[123] Section 101(1)*(k)*.

[124] Section 132(1)*(e)*.

[125] Section 132(1)*(r)*.

17.7.7 Emissions in mines and workplaces

Persons in mines are protected against air pollution in terms of regulations[126] issued under the Mines and Works Act 27 of 1956, now applicable by virtue of the transitional clause of the Minerals Act 50 of 1991.[127] These regulations are extensive[128] and provide that no person may enter or remain in any place in a mine if the air contains harmful smoke, gas, fumes or dust, unless he is wearing effective apparatus to prevent the inhalation of such pollution.[129] Furthermore, no dust, fumes or smoke from any dust or fume extraction system may be discharged into the atmosphere unless adequate provision has been made or steps taken to ensure that such discharge is harmless and inoffensive.[130]

Specific air quality standards are prescribed with regard to the workings of mines[131] and special provisions apply to the use of internal combustion engines underground.[132] The regulations also provide that every mine-dump must be covered with sludge or soil, or otherwise treated, so as to prevent dust or sand being blown from the dump.[133] See also chapter 15.

The Machinery and Occupational Safety Act 6 of 1983 deals with the safety of persons in their workplace during the course of their employment, particularly when using machines. The Minister of Manpower is authorized to regulate any matter permitted under the Act. For example, regulations issued under the Act provide for control over the ventilation within these places of work and the natural and mechanical methods adopted for ventilation.[134]

17.7.8 Secrecy

The disclosure of information relating to manufacturing processes or trade secrets is prohibited in terms of the Atmospheric Pollution Prevention Act.[135]

17.7.9 Administrative Structure

The Minister of National Health and Population Development heads up the administrative structure, and he appoints the following officials and bodies to assist him in the execution of his functions:

- NAPAC to advise him on all matters relating to the control, abatement and prevention of air pollution. He may also appoint subcommittees.
- An Air Pollution Appeal Board to hear appeals relating to decisions by the chief officer; decisions relating to dust control; decisions relating to vehicle emissions, and decisions of regional appeal boards relating to smoke control.
- Regional appeal boards to determine appeals from decisions of local authorities.
- The chief officer and inspectors who are appointed by the Minister and who act under his direction. These persons must have the necessary technical qualifications, academic training and practical experience.

Local authorities also constitute part of the administrative structure. These authorities are particularly relevant to the control of smoke and vehicle emissions. They

[126] GN R992 of 26 June 1970.
[127] Section 68(2).
[128] See, generally, ch 10 of the regulations.
[129] Regulations 10.1.1 and 10.6.4.
[130] Regulation 10.4.
[131] Regulation 10.6.6. et seq.
[132] Regulation 10.25.1 et seq.
[133] Regulation 5.10.
[134] Section 35(1)*(b)*(iv) and (vi) and reg 5 GN R2281 of 16 October 1987.
[135] Section 41 (a blanket secrecy provision) provides that no disclosure of information may be made unless it is with the consent of the person carrying on the undertaking; or in connection with the performance of functions under the Act; or for the purpose of legal proceedings arising out of the Act.

originally derived their powers from the provincial councils, but since the abolition of those councils, they now fall within the structure of the provincial administration. At present the provincial administration consists of the Administrator and an Executive Committee who deal with own and general provincial affairs.

Finally, the Government Mining Engineer is involved both in the control of dust from mine-dumps and in air pollution control in mines.

17.7.10 Enforcement of legislation

17.7.10.1 *Fragmented administration*

Although the Atmospheric Pollution Prevention Act provides for both administrative and judicial control measures, in practice, air pollution control is administered by the chief officer, local authorities (which employ municipal pollution control officers) and the Government Mining Engineer.

The chief officer controls pollution of scheduled processes via the application of the 'best practicable means' concept. Local authorities regulate smoke emissions through the creation of smokeless zones. They exercise control over the type of fuel-burning appliances installed in their areas of jurisdiction, as well as emissions from diesel vehicles. The Government Mining Engineer is responsible for dust control at mine-dumps, as well as air pollution control in mines. Provincial government has limited powers relating to the control of smoke in theatres, on municipal buses, and in other public places, besides administrating the provisions of the Road Traffic Act in respect of vehicle emissions.

Reference has been made to the fact that, although the Act specifically binds the State in terms of pollution by noxious or offensive gases, dust and vehicle emissions, it is not bound by the provisions relating to smoke pollution.[136]

The legislative framework created by the Act has in reality fragmented air pollution control rather than provided a consolidated administrative structure to deal with all its aspects. For example, the air pollution officers appointed by local authorities are often responsible to central government, that is, the Medical Officer of the Department of National Health and Population Development. Monitoring of pollution levels is undertaken by city chemists and planning by city planners. In metropolitan areas it is not uncommon to have several air pollution control officials and town-planners, each of whom operate within their own municipal boundaries, despite the fact that air pollution moves freely between these municipal boundaries. The end result is that South Africa's air pollution control personnel do not form a coherent and recognizable body. It would have been preferable had all forms of air pollution control been enforced by the same group of officials.

17.7.10.2 *Monitoring stations*

Approximately 200 stations throughout the country monitor the levels of sulphur dioxide and particulate matter in the air; 150 monitor smoke while 114 monitor sulphur dioxide. About 41 local authorities are involved, and the department also sets up ad hoc stations to monitor pollution in problem areas. Moreover, industries such as AECI, Sasol and Eskom have their own monitoring stations. A central data bank of information compiled over the last two years is now available. Equipment is installed at the cost of the industry to monitor noxious and offensive emissions, the principle being that the polluter pays. In reality, however, the consumer and not the producer ends up paying for pollution control.

A monthly report must be submitted to the department on control and levels of emissions at the plant. The department requires 90 per cent compliance with the

---

[136] Research and monitoring are undertaken by the CSIR with the financial support of the Department of National Health and Population Development.

prescribed standard by industry. Non-compliance is difficult to conceal, since the report is compiled by the operators who present it to management, and the fact that local authorities also monitor air pollution further deters concealment. In practice, compliance with the prescribed levels of pollution is effected by way of negotiation and discussion. Written notice is given to the industry in the event of acceptable levels being exceeded and non-compliance results in a threat of cancellation of the certificate.

In the past the threat of the cancellation of a registration certificate has been very effective, proof of which lies in the fact that to date only 20 certificates have been cancelled. The success of the process of negotiation is reflected in the lack of appeals to the regional boards and the fact that only one appeal has gone before the Air Pollution Appeal Board since its inception.

17.7.10.3 *Smoke and dust*

Smoke and dust pollution is controlled by way of notice of abatement. In practice, a negotiation procedure is followed. Failure to comply with the abatement notice constitutes an offence, and the local authority or chief officer issuing the notice may take certain action to prevent pollution and recover the costs from the polluter. The offence does not relate to the causing of pollution but to the failure to comply with the notice. To date only a limited number of abatement notices have been issued.

17.7.10.4 *Vehicle emissions*

Roadside checks by local authorities monitoring pollution are infrequent and are conducted at random. Local officials are not in a position to impose spot fines for transgressions of the Act; rather, a polluter is given notice to repair the vehicle and make it available for inspection at a specified time. Good co-operation is usually received from the public, but in the event of failure to comply with the notice, legal action is instituted. The scarcity of manpower and the difficulty involved in testing the vehicle has meant that few prosecutions have been instituted under this part of the Act. For example, approximately five people have been prosecuted in the Pretoria municipal area during the last five years.

In the municipal area of Pretoria, for instance, inspections for diesel-driven vehicle emissions are held from approximately 09h00 to 12h00 once a week on weekdays, on a different main arterial route to the city. Records indicate the following number of incidents of excessive emissions:

1987—134 vehicles
1988—114 vehicles
1989—153 vehicles

17.7.11 Appeals

Any person aggrieved by a decision of the chief officer to grant, refuse, cancel or suspend a registration certificate, in respect of a scheduled process, may appeal to the Air Pollution Appeal Board, which may make any order it deems equitable. Its decision is final. See also chapter 8.

The Iscor case provides a good example of such an appeal. In May 1973 Iscor applied for a provisional certificate in order to go ahead with its plans to modernize the existing steel foundry by moving it to a new site at Kwaggasrand, Pretoria. Iscor alleged that the move would bring about a reduction in air pollution, but the application was refused, whereupon Iscor appealed to the board.

The board found that the appeal constituted an appeal in the wide sense in that it differs from both an ordinary appeal and from review. As such it amounted to a de novo consideration of the matter.[137] The board examined the nature of the functions exercised by the chief officer and the board itself. It found that the chief officer exercises a purely administrative function, while the board exercises a function of a judicial nature.[138] After considering the evidence, including expert evidence, the board dismissed the appeal, holding that Kwaggasrand is not a suitable place for an industry which causes air pollution. The alleged economic disability which the appellant would suffer by a refusal was also considered, but it was found that this would merely be a temporary setback.

17.8 CONCLUDING REMARKS

The preceding commentary on legislative aspects of air pollution control is constrained largely to a description of the Atmospheric Pollution Prevention Act, and to structural mechanisms put in place to enforce the provisions of the Act. It does not identify the gaps in existing legislation which stem from the fractured and piecemeal way in which such legislation evolved, nor complications at the interface between enforcement and compliance which arise from implementation of the Act. This concluding section will attempt to address some of these issues.

Two recent reports by the CSIR for the Department of Environment Affairs[139] give attention principally to the identification of waste types, quantities and sources. It is clear that waste and pollution are being generated, as a consequence of normal industrial activity, at levels hitherto unrecognized, and disproportionate to those arising from similar practices in other countries. Air pollution is no exception to this trend. The President's Council *Report on a national environmental management system*[140] proposes, amongst its other major findings, significant changes to the structure of governmental agencies responsible for pollution control. See chapter 5. The extent to which recommendations made in this last report will, if implemented, improve air quality by more effective pollution control, is discussed below.

In a move designed to overcome the present fragmented control of pollution by a myriad of government departments, it is proposed that a Pollution Control Branch be created within the Department of Environment Affairs. This body will be responsible for laying down policy and monitoring all aspects of its application. This shift is prompted by the desire to promote an holistic and interdisciplinary approach to pollution prevention and control. Formulation of such a policy is vitally important. It advocates the centralization of skills at central government level, whilst confirming and strengthening regional structures. In this way, line management will become more clearly defined. Ambiguities and uncertainties which arise when two or more government departments share responsibility for a common cause, will be removed, and resource management will be greatly improved. Whether such centralization should occur within the Department of Environment Affairs, or whether some extra-

---

[137] The board considered new facts and other evidence and conducted a new hearing of the case. It was, therefore, not confined as is a judicial review, only to a consideration of the validity of the chief officer's decision but could go much further in examining its correctness on the merits. This appeal differs from an ordinary appeal in that it is not confined to the record of the proceedings. It differs from both appeal and review in the sense that the board may make any decision which it considers reasonable. An appeal to the board is thus an appeal in the wide sense of the word. See Rabie 'Appèl deur Yskor ingevolge die Wet op Voorkoming van Lugbesoedeling' 1974 *THRHR* 186.

[138] If it is accepted that the board acted in a judicial capacity, the question of res iudicata is relevant. The position is that once an administrative judicial body has arrived at its decision, it is functus officio and the decision may be altered only at a higher level of control.

[139] *First report on the situation of waste management and pollution control in South Africa* CPE 1/1991; a draft report on hazardous waste, consisting of five volumes, has been released for comment and is to be published during the second half of 1992.

[140] PC 1/1991.

parliamentary structure should be given this overall responsibility is not well addressed in the report.

In whichever form this recommendation is implemented, control of air pollution will be wrested from the Department of National Health and Population Development, where sole discretionary power resides with the chief officer. The current structure relies heavily on the subjective evaluation of pollution sources by the chief officer, in consultation with industries concerned. Registration certificates (establishing, in effect, the right to pollute under certain constraints) are issued subsequent to this evaluation. Judicial control over actions and decisions of the chief officer is minimal. Such decisions, accordingly, are seldom contested. A workable system of 'checks and balances' does not exist. The President's Council report emphasizes the need for information on all forms of pollution and pollution sources to be freely in the public domain. In this way industrial compliance with existing legislation will be held up to scrutiny.

The existing pollution inspectorate is hampered in its attempts to monitor compliance with guidelines identified in each certificate. The number of pollution inspectors employed by the Department of National Health and Population Development is pathetically inadequate, and training methods do not keep abreast of industrial process development. Access to sophisticated equipment with which to measure different forms of atmospheric pollution is often difficult. These factors, coupled to the observation that penalties imposed on repeat offenders are trivial, means that motivation is poor. It is relatively easy for any industrial concern to deviate from the conditions of its registration certificate with impunity, simply because the existing system of inspection cannot cope. Any of the following reasons suffice for such deviation:

- process upset conditions never rectified
- installed technology not meeting design specifications
- economic constraints impinging on company viability.

The structural changes proposed by the President's Council report will not, of themselves, overcome any of these problems. However, unifying the various existing pollution inspectorates under one body, and assigning adequate resources to the proposed Pollution Control Branch, are steps in the right direction.

The report further recommends that the concept of 'best practicable environmental option' (BPEO)[141] be used to define the appropriateness of any activity which results in pollution. This concept differs from that of 'best practicable means' (BPM) which is embodied within the terms of the existing Act as discussed previously. The shift towards BPEO is seen to be consistent with the holistic approach to environmental management as perceived by the President's Council. The primary distinction between the two approaches rests in the flexibility afforded BPEO strategists. Whereas BPM focuses on 'end-of-pipe' technological fixes for pollution control, BPEO will first and foremost address the potential for waste elimination from a given process.

The previous technical discussion of air pollution control within South Africa has raised some issues regarding the cost of such technologies and their appropriateness in a developing economy. What needs to be emphasized is that as the country's chemical and industrial base is enlarged to meet development needs, environmental degradation will worsen unless due regard is given to waste generation and its abatement. 'Quick fix' solutions will not suffice. The BPEO option addresses this fact. The adoption of such a strategy within South Africa will lead to improved design and operation of industrial processes, minimizing waste generation through the application of 'clean technologies'.

---

[141] *Best practicable environmental option* Royal commission on environmental pollution, London (1988).

In addition, administrative duties of officials involved in monitoring compliance with BPEO directives will be reduced accordingly.

Though the legal framework that will ultimately give substance to the BPEO concept and other proposals (or any which arise out of the debate on the President's Council report) is not yet known, it is clear that the existing Act is deficient in several respects, and needs an overhaul. However, legislative changes alone will not lead to an improvement in air quality. Air pollution is rectifiable, but not without industrial commitment, correct political will, and involvement of the general population in any decision-making process.

CHAPTER 18

WATER POLLUTION

J A LUSHER
H T RAMSDEN

18.1 THE NATURE AND EXTENT OF THE WATER POLLUTION PROBLEM

18.1.1 Introduction

Water pollution control has two complementary aspects: control of the first use of water and control of the discharge of waste products. The one is as important as the other.

Multiple use of rivers and other water resources is inevitable and conflicts of interests unavoidable. The Department of Water Affairs and Forestry (DWA) is the instrument of government which regulates the uses made of water and attempts to reconcile conflicting interests. It strives to maintain a climate of understanding in which each user group can be persuaded to accommodate the needs of others. The holistic approach to the evaluation of user needs now pursued by the DWA requires the inclusion of less direct and less quantifiable demands, such as those of ecological systems, and determination of the types of assurances of supply the various demands may require. Demands for water range from those made to support life and health to those that support man's material needs through agricultural and industrial production and to those that provide psychological or spiritual fulfilment by conserving and beautifying the environment and supporting recreation.[1]

Neither science nor jurisprudence[2] has as yet supplied a satisfactory objective yardstick to evaluate one user demand against another. The DWA is developing allocation criteria to serve what is termed 'the best interests of the population'. As matters stand the department is the sole arbiter of what in fact is in the best interests of the population.[3]

With respect to the discharge of waste products, the DWA has, in the light of the steady deterioration of water quality in rivers, had to review its control and certain principles that are of general application within the Republic of South Africa have been devised.

On account of the fact that the skills, technologies, specified policies and strategies required to implement these principles have to be developed over a period of time, the DWA continues to apply and enforce the general and special standards for effluents alongside the new principles which are being gradually implemented.

18.1.2 Public attitudes to water

These are governed by quality, availability and price. The popular perception within the Republic is that there is an assured supply of good quality water at a price that is not

---

[1] *Management of the water resources of the Republic of South Africa* Department of Water Affairs (1986) para 2.25.

[2] Ramsden *Legal principles and wetland legislation in South Africa* Paper delivered at a national symposium on the technology and conservation of wetlands in South Africa October 1987, 1–2.

[3] Some indication of what might objectively be considered as the 'best interests of the population' could emerge out of the litigation between the Rand Water Board and the Far West Rand Dolomitic Water Association, in which the board contends that as a result of an exclusive use allocation conferred by the Department of Water Affairs on the Randfontein Estates Gold Mining Co Ltd, the board's consumers have suffered measurable financial loss.

a strain on the public pocket. However, on examination, it becomes apparent that there is a steady deterioration of the water quality in rivers, availability is far more apparent than real and the price, countrywide, is set as low as possible but could become unaffordable to some sectors of the population within the foreseeable future, and in its natural state is so polluted as not to be available for use in a Third World context. As this chapter is wholly devoted to water quality, this element will therefore not be addressed further here.

18.1.2.1 *Availability of water*

Contrary to belief, water is not readily available at the turn of a tap. Water derives from a supply and the supply is stochastically determined by rainfall. It follows that there is a finite probability of water supply in this country. Because of the scarcity of water and what has been referred to as 'the geographical mismatching of demand and supply',[4] the State has been obliged to construct interbasin transfer schemes such as the Orange–Fish, Tugela–Vaal, Riviersonderend–Berg River and Usutu–Vaal projects. These projects have involved large, expensive and sophisticated engineering works and the costs have been borne by the urban consumers.

It also follows that if natural replenishment is uncertain (only 8–9 per cent of precipitation reaches our rivers), the alternatives of recycling used water or desalination of seawater need to be considered. The present freshwater sources available for the areas supplied by the Rand Water Board have a firm yield of 1 776 million m^3 per annum supplemented by an indirectly reclaimed return flow of 290 million m^3 per annum.[5]

Changing land-uses have an effect both on the quantity and the quality of water. The DWA is using satellite imagery, computerized analytic techniques and monitoring equipment and is developing more sophisticated catchment management models to optimize quantity and minimize the deleterious impact on quality.[6] But the legal regimes already instituted to control land-uses fall to a large extent outside the control of the DWA and also outside the sphere of the Department of Environment Affairs.[7]

18.1.2.2 *Price of water*

When water is available, it is sold as a quasi-public good. The price is not market-determined in the same way as motorcars, for example. It is not a public good or service (such as police protection or public education) that is funded out of taxation that may not be proportional to the use or benefit derived. Water is sold as a quasi-public good because the waterworks that meet the demand in a particular area are financed and operated on commercial principles that require the full costs of the services to be recovered from the users. This lends to the sale of water the private part of its character. However, since a uniform tariff is established for a particular area, a good deal of cross-subsidizing of water prices results and prices may not be proportional to the economic benefit derived by a particular user. This lends to the sale of water the

[4] *Management of water resources* above n 1, para 1.11.

[5] For an overview of this topic readers are referred to the *Proceedings of the symposium on unconventional sources of water* SA Institute of Civil Engineers (Cape Town, October 1980).

[6] *Management of water resources* above n 1, ch 4.

[7] Many departments are authorized to play sometimes mutually conflicting roles in the conservation and use of water; for example, Agriculture through the Conservation of Agricultural Resources Act 43 of 1983; Mineral and Energy Affairs through the Minerals Act 50 of 1991 and the Nuclear Energy Act 92 of 1982; Transport through the National Roads Act 54 of 1971; National Health and Population Development through the Health Act 63 of 1977 (which provides for the delegation of powers to provincial administrations and local authorities) and the various authorities concerned with administering protected areas.

public part of its character.[8] Some factors that impact on the water price are now discussed.

The need for interbasin transfer schemes underlines the fact that water is an essential commodity that is becoming scarcer and more valuable through increasing competition between users. The DWA is increasingly applying the principle that each identifiable beneficiary pays the cost of providing him with an acceptable assurance and quality of supply. In the case of interbasin transfers these costs are not insubstantial.

Where freshwater sources have to be supplemented by return flow indirectly reclaimed from heavy industries, heavy metal pollution, salination, sediment blanket pollution and many water quality problems associated with eutrophication will be encountered. In these instances the water price reflects at least in part increased costs associated with cleaning water that has become contaminated in this way.

The most important water-demand region in the Republic of South Africa is the Pretoria–Witwatersrand–Vereeniging (PWV) area. It is probably the only large industrial urban area in the world that is not located on a river or near the coast and most of the water supplied has to be pumped to a high elevation and transported over long distances. This also adds to the cost of water.

Thus the congregation of large numbers of industries, businesses and people in the PWV area for economic reasons has necessitated interbasin transfers, the provision of storage, the acceptance as return flow of indirectly reclaimed water and the pumping of water to a high elevation and over long distances. It would therefore be wrong to suppose that the economic factors that have made this area the Republic's most important water demand region exercise no influence on the price of water.

Although a natural monopoly in the provision of water exists in the State and its satellites, this was not always the case. Water supply started in the hands of private water companies which exploited not only the resources but also the consumer. At the instance of those consumers the water supply passed into the hands of the public utility corporation in which the consumers had almost exclusive representation. This in time led to the frustration of development in other regions in the interest of local affairs. As a result, representation on the governing body of the public corporation was changed so as to include a broader spectrum of business people whose interests were not so parochial.[9] The dynamism of such a corporation depends upon the number of members of the governing body who have a vital interest as users of the services provided by the corporation, or whose supplies or manufacturing processes depend on it. Therefore the devolution of functions from the DWA to water boards, irrigation boards, regional services councils and, in the case of the most important water demand region in the Republic of South Africa, to a public corporation, recognizes that the self-interest of members of the governing bodies of these institutions will operate to establish between the State and the consumer a fair and reasonable price for water. It is submitted that as more functions are devolved upon these satellites and greater freedom conferred, their accountability to their constituents will lead to more effective management and control of the quality, quantity and price of water at local and regional level.

In the predecessor of this volume, *Environmental concerns in South Africa*, the authors considered that the established price of water was too low and that the real value of water needed to be expressed in supplementary charges. Since that view was expressed, several black local authorities within the PWV area have concluded that on account of the fact that their towns do not have industries and businesses to subsidize rate income, services supplied to black local authorities are unaffordable and charges that are below cost have been established. The Transvaal Provincial Administration has

---

[8] *Management of water resources* above n 1, xx.

[9] Cf Ramsden *The status, powers and duties of the Rand Water Board: a legal history and analysis* (unpublished PhD thesis, University of the Witwatersrand, 1986).

accepted the necessity of a subsidy to replace that which would ordinarily be forthcoming from the rateable value of industrial and business properties.

There is undoubtedly a need to balance First and Third World expectations, needs and pricing, and this matter is recognized by the DWA.[10]

18.1.3 Ineffective or plural legislation

A discussion of the relevant legislation and some of its defects follows later. The success of water management and pollution control is dependent to a very large degree on adequate legislation and its effective administration.[11]

18.1.4 Inconsistencies in secondary and tertiary government structure

In *Environmental concerns in South Africa*, the authors referred to the active pursuit of the decentralization of responsibilities. In 1987–88 a reorganization of departmental structures took place throughout the different directorates. Regional development advisory committees were established to co-ordinate the work done by the different directorates. Work done by the DWA is, however, intimately tied to river drainage regions or basin systems. These boundaries conflict with the geographical boundaries as laid down in the National Physical Development Plan. The DWA established six regions, whose reporting line is to the water utilization branch, as the best compromise that was possible. The objective of the water utilization branch and its two directorates is set out in Figure 18.1.

Not all of the functions have devolved upon the regions thus constituted. Matters of broad policy, strategic planning, project planning and design and construction, together with many other functions related to the national administration of the department, continue to be attended to from Pretoria. The responsibility for giving effect to policy rests with the local regional management.

As the different state directorates, each with their different objectives, co-ordinate development within the geographical boundaries as laid down in the National Physical Development Plan, it is clear that in some way or other one objective will give way in some measure to accommodate another. At the regional and local authority levels in particular, parochial needs and wants dominate discussions. It therefore becomes essential in the new interrelationship of departments that clear and immutable guidelines be formulated at the earliest opportunity to protect and conserve the water resources of the Republic from the continuing pressures exerted by the other role-players.

It will be observed from Figure 18.2 that the regions instituted by the DWA embrace the principle of river basin management, which principle, it is submitted, is the only workable basis on which to control river pollution.[12] Other state departments select smaller units as relevant.

At third-tier government level the unit is a town or at best a metropolitan area. Regions are the areas within which a regional services council operates and beyond these regions one encounters planning divisions such as that for the PWV complex—the so-called 'H Region'. In planning terms, therefore, 'region' may have two meanings. It may mean the area for which a regional services council has been established, or, in the context of the new Physical Planning Act 125 of 1991, it means a specified development region.

---

[10] *Management of water resources* above n 1, xix.

[11] For an overview of this topic readers are referred to the *Proceedings of a workshop to formulate a national policy and strategy for the fresh water systems of South Africa*, Wilderness April 1990 (in particular, see Ramsden 'Southern African and international approaches to legislation for fresh water systems'). Cf also Rabie 'The conservation of rivers in South African law' 1989 *SA Public Law* 1, 186.

[12] Ramsden above n 11, 9–10.

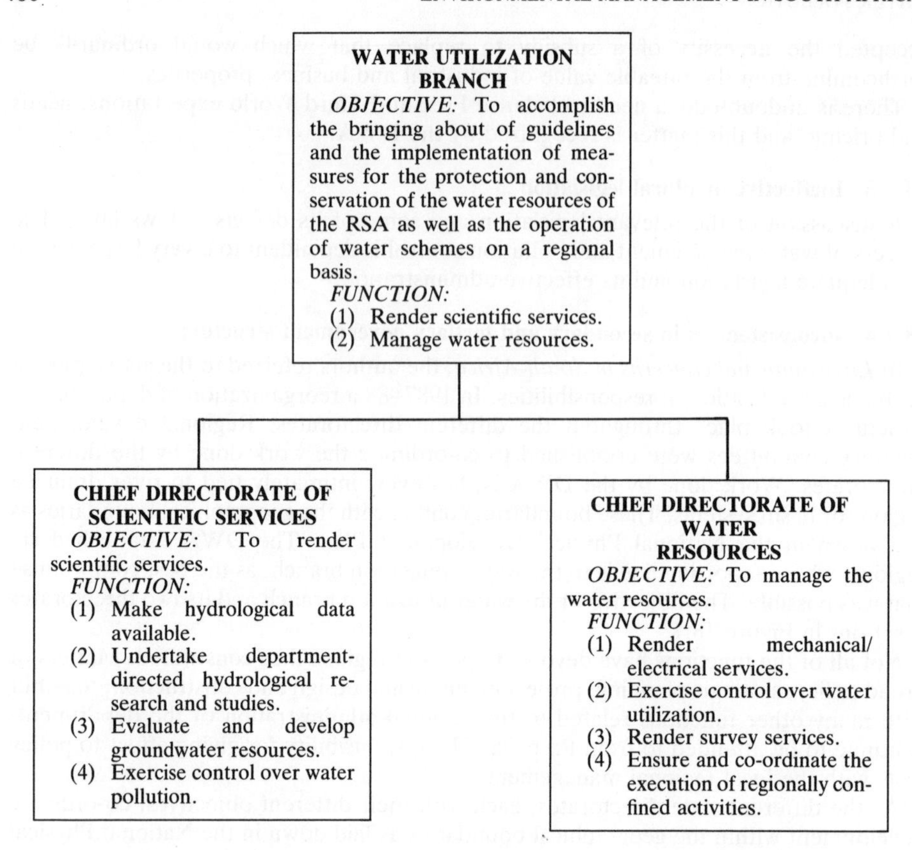

Figure 18.1 Schematic structure of the Water Utilization Branch of the Department of Water Affairs.

Source: *Department of Water Affairs: annual report* 1988–89, 11.

The Physical Planning Act provides for a hierarchy of policy plans in which guidelines are laid down for the future physical development of areas referred to in a specified plan. For a detailed discussion of these and other relevant provisions, see chapter 28.

An issue of great importance is the establishment of a satisfactory and binding policy in respect of the management of water resources. Environmental concerns have taken second place to even recreational factors in the past and it will require a strong presence by the DWA in all of the planning hierarchies to ensure that the objectives of its water utilization branch are realized, particularly in view of the disparity that is likely to arise between river drainage regions and development regions specified in terms of the physical planning legislation and urban planning. The only legislative provision for the declaration of such policy is contained in the Environment Conservation Act 73 of 1989. See chapter 7. It is therefore appropriate to consider the policies that the department will pursue in terms of its new approach to water pollution control.

18.2 POLICY REGARDING FRESHWATER POLLUTION

The DWA is responsible for protecting the water quality of the country's water resources. The proper management of water quality requires that comprehensive water quality and quantity plans are developed and implemented for each drainage basin in

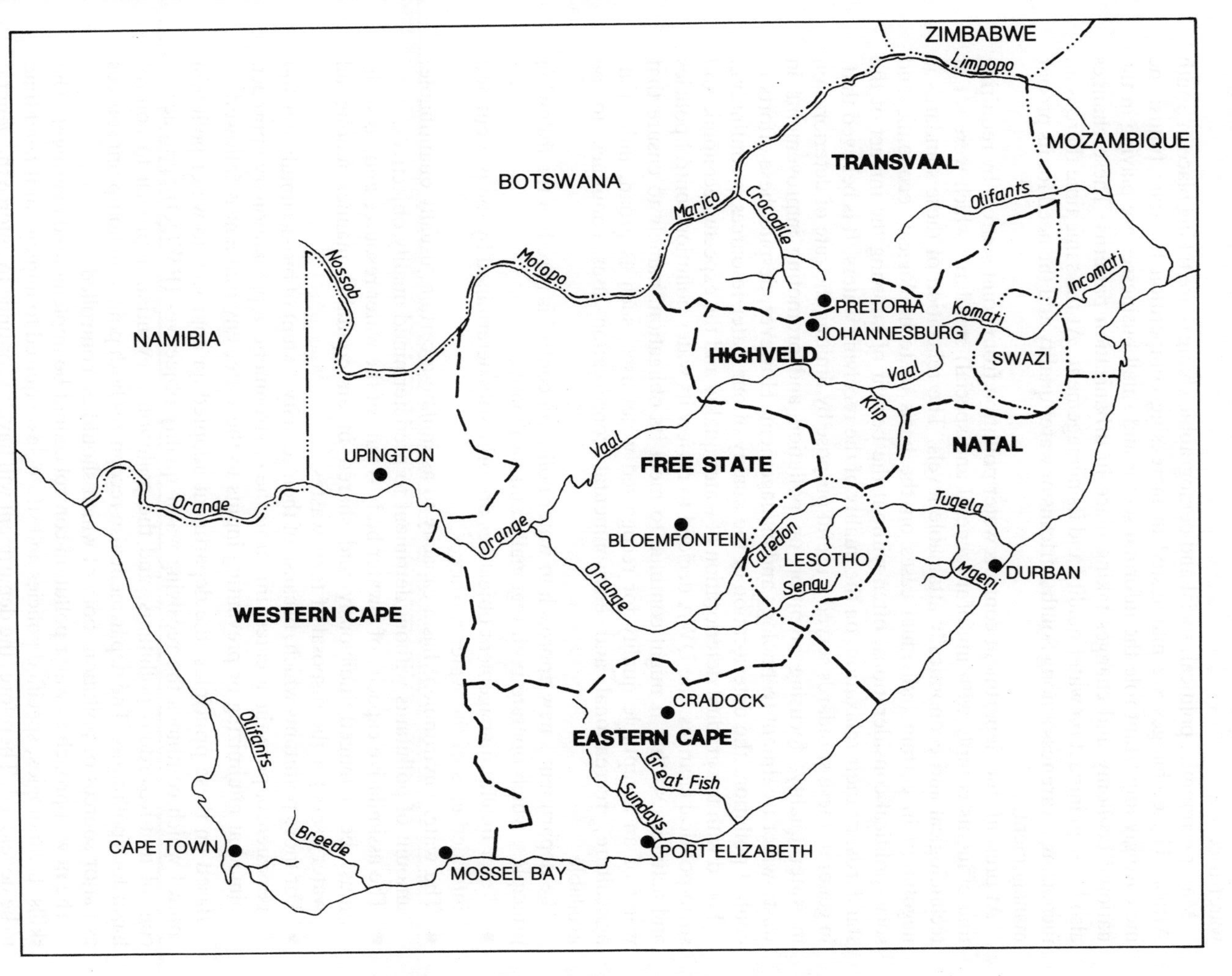

Figure 18.2 South African water management regions.

the Republic. For the development of such water resource management plans, pollution control must be integrated with the department's other water quality and quantity management activities and must be aimed at achieving quality objectives relating to water-use.

Major economic, political, social and demographic changes are taking place in South Africa. These changes are manifested in increasing competition for state funds; the increasingly important role the informal sector and small businesses are playing in the national economy and changes taking place in urbanization patterns. These changes also have an impact on water quality and its management. At the same time there is an increasing awareness among South Africans of water quality and the need for its proper management.

At present, the department controls water pollution from point sources by requiring that effluents comply with uniform (general and special) standards which were set at technological and economically attainable levels. The relaxation of these standards is negotiated in certain individual cases on the basis of technological, economic and socio-political considerations, often without the benefit of knowing the impact of the standards, or their relaxation, on the quality of the receiving waters. It is believed that, in general, these standards served a useful purpose by limiting the rate of deterioration in water quality, focusing attention on pollution and promoting improvements in waste-water treatment technology and management. However, despite these efforts to control pollution, the deterioration of the quality of our water resources is continuing.

Faced with the gradual deterioration of water quality and the expected economic and socio-political changes, the DWA decided to review its water pollution control policies and activities so that it might continue to meet its obligation, namely to ensure that water of an acceptable quality for recognized water-uses, such as urban, industrial, agriculture, recreational and environmental conservation uses continues to be available.

The department's new approach to water pollution control is based on the following principles, which operate both regionally and nationally:

- Water quality management objectives are primarily determined by the present and intended uses of the water resources.
- The water environment has a capacity to assimilate a certain, usually quantifiable, amount of pollutants without detriment to predetermined quality objectives.
- The assimilative capacity of a water body is part of the water resource and, as such, must be managed judiciously and shared in an equitable manner among all water-users for the disposal of their wastes.
- For those pollutants which, because of their toxicity, extent of bio-accumulation and persistence, pose the greatest threat to the environment, a precautionary approach aimed at minimizing or preventing inputs to the water environment is followed.

Based on these principles, the department adopted an approach to water pollution control which combines the receiving water quality objectives (RWQO) approach to control non-hazardous pollutants, and the pollution prevention approach to control hazardous pollutants. The department also recognizes both point and non-point sources as major sources of pollution, both of which should be controlled.

The new approach to water pollution control cannot be implemented overnight. The skills, technologies, specified policies and strategies required to implement it need time to be developed. Therefore, the department will have to continue to enforce the general and special standards for effluents discharged to the water environment as it did in the past while the new approach is being gradually implemented.

18.3 POLICY REGARDING MARINE DISCHARGES

The marine environment has a certain quantifiable capacity to assimilate pollutants without having any detrimental effect on the marine environment or a health risk being created. The necessary skills also exist in South Africa to evaluate and design marine outfalls to comply with these requirements. Recent experience has, however, shown that public opinion in some cases is seriously opposed to marine outfalls. Public opinion should always be taken into account before final approval is granted. The location of existing marine outfalls and their approximate capacity is given in the department's 1988–89 *Annual report*.

The objective of marine pollution control is to maintain the quality of the marine environment such that its beneficial uses are protected: the place of discharge and the quality of the effluent discharged to the marine environment are controlled. In terms of the Water Act, as will be shown below, disposal to the sea of effluent arising from sources of water other than the sea is prohibited unless an exemption to do so is granted by the Minister. However, from health-risk, land-use and economic points of view, the disposal of effluent at sea in coastal regions may be the most desirable option. For example, it might be advantageous to sound water quality management if industries which produce large volumes of saline effluent were situated at the coast so that they could discharge their effluent into the sea rather than into the country's limited freshwater resources.

Marine pollution control is also based on the RWQO approach. The desired sea water quality management objectives (SWQMO) are determined by laying down criteria for each of the beneficial uses of the marine environment. These beneficial uses include bathing, fishing, shellfish gathering, industrial use and conservation of the marine environment. In laying down these sea water quality criteria, special attention is given to the human health risk and to protecting the marine environment. Before an exemption to discharge effluent into the sea is given, the department needs to be assured that the design of the outfall is such that SWQMO will be met. In this process it will consult with many interested parties. In 1990 there were 61 sea outfall pipelines discharging daily about 700 000 m^3 of effluent into the sea surrounding South Africa. Comprehensive monitoring of the marine environment in the vicinity of marine outfalls takes place. To date, this monitoring has shown few or no detrimental ecological impacts resulting from these discharges off the South African coastline.

Although point source discharges to the marine environment are currently stringently controlled, problems still occur as a result of stormwater discharged from urban developments along the coast. Investigations are currently being conducted to develop guidelines for remedial and preventive measures to control this source of pollution of the marine environment. The claim that discharges to the marine environment are at present adequately controlled has been tested by Fijen,[13] who, in addition, draws a useful distinction in the size of the discharges. So far as the 12 major offshore pipelines (accounting for 86 per cent of the total effluent discharged) are concerned, Fijen found that they operate satisfactorily.

18.4 APPROACHES TO WATER POLLUTION CONTROL

18.4.1 Uniform effluent standards approach

Uniform effluent standards (UES) are usually set to limit pollutant concentrations in an effluent, using the 'best available technology not entailing excessive costs' to treat effluent. For example, cost-effective technology is available to treat sewage effluent to meet the general standard.

18.4.1.1 *Advantages of the UES approach*

It is simple, comprehensible and straightforward to apply.

---

[13] *A review of marine disposal in South Africa* Water Research Commission Report no 213/1/1988. For a useful general summary of water quality management in the coastal zone, see 'Water quality management in the coastal zone' 1989 (9) *Water, Sewage and Effluent* 21–3.

If standards are frequently revised to reflect the ability of the best pollution abatement technology, it should have the effect of reducing pollution from point sources.

18.4.1.2 *Drawbacks of the UES approach*

It is focused on effluent and largely ignores the impacts of effluent discharges on water quality in receiving waters.

In cases where there are multiple point sources of a particular pollutant, or where there are high background levels arising from diffuse sources, the UES approach may fail to protect the quality of water resources.

The UES approach is not necessarily cost-effective, because it requires all effluent to comply with the same standards irrespective of variations in the assimilative capacity of the receiving water or in the cost involved.

It also provides no incentive for industry to locate at the most advantageous environmental location and it provides no framework for the control of diffuse sources.

18.4.2 Receiving water quality objectives approach

The RWQO approach to water pollution control involves the specification of water quality requirements in receiving waters and the control of pollution to ensure that the quality requirements are met. It is based on acceptance of the principle that receiving waters have a capacity to assimilate pollution without detriment to accepted uses for the waters concerned. The application of this approach consists of three major activities:

- Defining the uses for which a water body is suitable.
- Specifying, on the basis of these uses, the concentrations of monitoring variables in the water body which must not be exceeded. These concentrations can also be based on the result of a waste load allocation. Monitoring variables are defined as the set of all variables which may have an effect on the determination of water quality.
- Controlling pollution from point sources by setting site-specific effluent standards which take into account the contribution of diffuse sources and the RWQO.

18.4.2.1 *Advantages of the RWQO approach*

The RWQO approach, because it is focused on managing the quality of receiving waters in such a way that there is a minimum interference with legitimate uses of those waters, has to consider both point and diffuse sources of pollution. This approach is cost-effective because, by considering the assimilative capacity of receiving waters for particular pollutants, it minimizes the level of control required for adequate protection of water-uses. It also provides an incentive for industry to locate where receiving waters are less sensitive to pollution.

18.4.2.2 *Drawbacks of the RWQO approach*

From a regulatory point of view, the RWQO approach is technologically much more demanding because it requires a thorough investigation and understanding of the fate of pollutants in the water environment and their impacts on water-uses. Because the RWQO approach leads to site-specific effluent standards being specified, it is also not as straightforward to apply as a uniform effluent standard. Problems will arise because RWQO will vary with different flow regimes and also because of a lack of manpower to implement the policy.

18.4.3 Pollution prevention approach

Some pollutants are regarded as hazardous or dangerous because they represent a major threat to the water environment as a result of their toxicity, persistence and/or capacity for bio-accumulation. The RWQO approach to managing such pollutants is considered to be inappropriate. An approach based on minimizing or preventing the input to the water environment, because of their toxicity, bio-accumulation and persistence must be followed to control the presence of hazardous or dangerous substances in the water environment. Agg & Zabel[14] discuss the creation of a 'red list' in Britain, which South Africa would do well to emulate.

18.5 COMPLIANCE MONITORING

The goal of compliance monitoring is to ensure that all permit or exemption holders comply with water quality standards which have been specified as well as with other accompanying conditions of discharge. The monitoring of effluent and receiving water is done to ensure that effluent producers meet the water quality or effluent standards which were set to meet the RWQO. The DWA's compliance monitoring programme consists of two different monitoring activities, namely, monitoring by the user and independent monitoring by the department.

The results of the permit or exemption holder's monitoring programme are used to determine compliance with standards. The monitoring programme is used to determine whether the results submitted by the permit or exemption holder are trustworthy. This is often termed 'auditing'.

18.5.1 Statistical methodology and hypothesis

The measurement of water quality variables in an effluent can be influenced by sources such as the hydrological cycle, variation in sampling and analysis of the effluent, and random fluctuations. As a result, measurements vary; the measured value can be within a certain range. A single monitoring variable complies if, at the end of a pre-determined continuous time period at least 95 per cent of the observations, of which there must be a minimum of 12, meet the standard with a type 1 risk less than or equal to 5 per cent. The type 1 risk is the risk of finding that someone has violated the standards when, in fact, this is not so. This is equivalent to a court finding someone guilty when the person is innocent. Our legal system, in which the principle applies that someone is innocent until guilt is proved beyond reasonable doubt, requires the type 1 risk to be small—hence that it should be 5 per cent or less. The lower the type 1 risk, the lower the reasonable doubt. This results in a percentage value: 95 per cent or more of 'confidence' in the conclusion. The above definition has been expanded to provide legally acceptable definitions of the department's interpretation of a standard and what constitutes its violation. Thus, a monitored variable complies with the standard (ie is legally identical with it) if the upper confidence limit of the 95th percentile is less than the standard. A monitored variable violates the standard (ie is in excess of it) if the lower confidence limit of the 95th percentile is greater than the standard. The status is unresolved if the standard lies within the 95 per cent confidence interval. The CSIR, working in close conjunction with the DWA, has developed a computer programme to do the necessary calculations.

18.5.2 Sampling techniques

Recent experience in the courts has emphasized the importance of having technically unassailable sampling techniques. Grab samples are always stipulated and their storage, the type of container used, the time elapsed between sampling and analysis, and whether preservatives are used must be recorded unequivocally. The South African Bureau of Standards continues to develop both sampling and analytical methods for these purposes.

---

[14] 'Red-list substances: selection and monitoring' 1990 *J Institute of Water & Environmental Management* 44–50.

18.5.3 Network design

Network design addresses the location of monitoring points, the selection of water quality variables and the determination of the sampling frequencies.

Experience gained during court cases has shown that there is considerable difference in opinion on exactly where monitoring for compliance with effluent standards should be done. This situation has probably arisen because neither the Water Act nor the regulations published in terms of the Act (ie the general, special and special phosphate standards) specifically state where effluent should be monitored. This has led to the development of many different practices for the selection of compliance monitoring points.

The situation is complex but, in general, compliance monitoring should be done at a point where there is no doubt that what is being monitored is only the effluent in question. No other streams, natural or effluent, must join the effluent in question before the compliance monitoring point. The location of compliance monitoring points must resolve issues related to accessibility, volume measurements and the possibility of further improvement in effluent quality taking place between the point of the effluent leaving the treatment plant and entering the receiving water body.

18.5.4 Sampling frequencies

This is a highly complex matter. It is important to realize that, although a minimum of 12 consecutive samples is to be used to determine compliance, this in no way overrules the use of established statistical methods of determining the number of samples required, given the population variance and the risk that an estimate of a population parameter deviates by a stated amount.

18.6 THE NATIONAL WATER QUALITY MONITORING SYSTEM (NWQMS)

18.6.1 A South African water quality index

Extensive use is made of water quality indices in Europe and North America: the subject has a long history but has only recently been addressed in this country. According to Harris & Moore,[15] a water quality index can be used to: determine priorities for resource allocation; determine the suitability of water for specific uses; analyse trends, and to provide information in easy and palatable form.

The first steps have been taken to construct a South African national water quality index, based on the well-known British Solway index and using the Delphi technique to obtain informed South African opinion as to which variables and what weightings should be used. The components of the South African water quality index as at mid-1990 are shown in Table 18.1

TABLE 18.1

Components and weightings of the South African Water Quality Index.

Variable	*Weight*
Total dissolved solids	0,27
E coli	0,21
Dissolved oxygen	0,16
Chlorophyll—alpha	0,13
pH	0,12
Turbidity	0,11
	1,00

[15] *Reporting water quality information with an index* Unpublished CSIR information paper for the Department of Water Affairs (1989).

18.6.2 Objectives and information reporting

In rough outline the proposed NWQMS will operate as in Figure 18.3. The difference between the functions of the Water Pollution Control Directorate and other bodies in the department, principally the Hydrological Research Institute, should be noted.

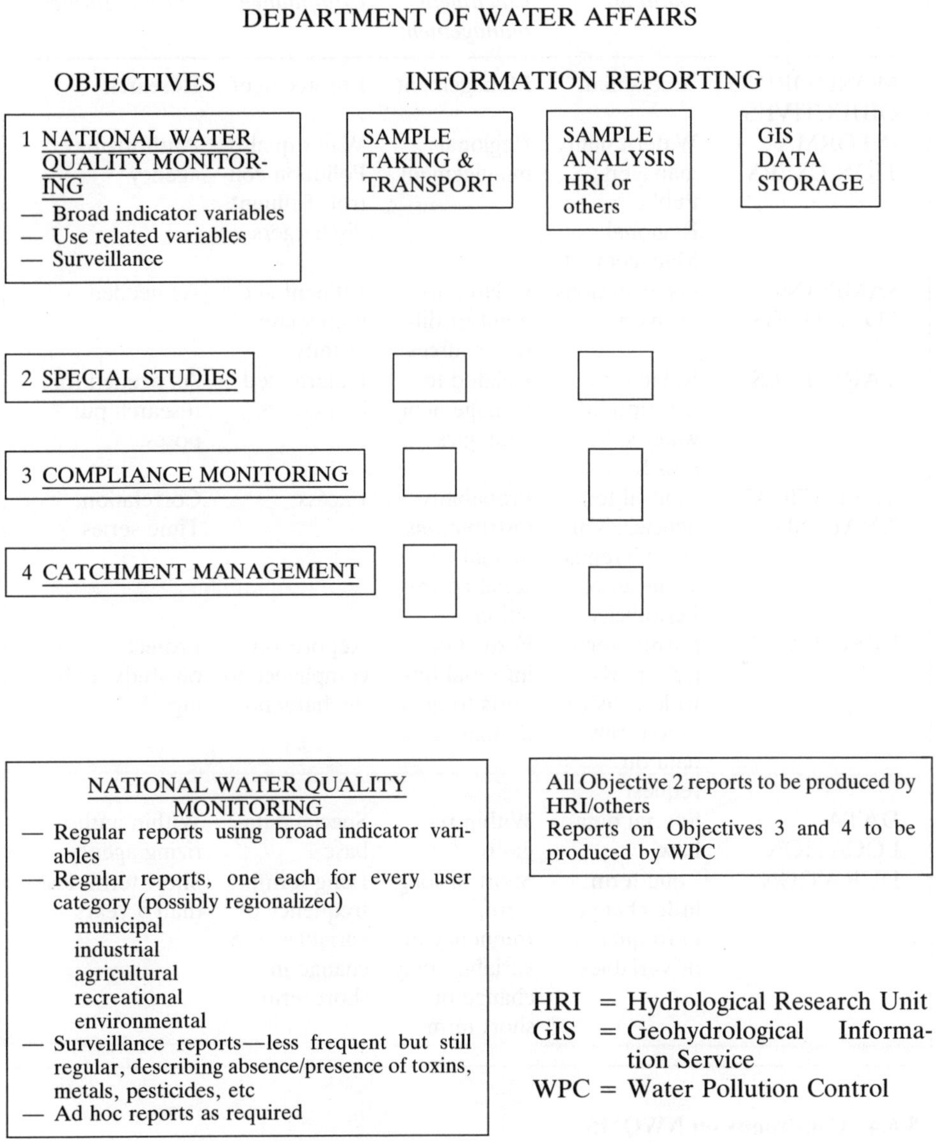

DEPARTMENT OF WATER AFFAIRS

OBJECTIVES	INFORMATION REPORTING		
1 NATIONAL WATER QUALITY MONITORING — Broad indicator variables — Use related variables — Surveillance	SAMPLE TAKING & TRANSPORT	SAMPLE ANALYSIS HRI or others	GIS DATA STORAGE
2 SPECIAL STUDIES			
3 COMPLIANCE MONITORING			
4 CATCHMENT MANAGEMENT			

NATIONAL WATER QUALITY MONITORING

- Regular reports using broad indicator variables
- Regular reports, one each for every user category (possibly regionalized)
  - municipal
  - industrial
  - agricultural
  - recreational
  - environmental
- Surveillance reports—less frequent but still regular, describing absence/presence of toxins, metals, pesticides, etc
- Ad hoc reports as required

All Objective 2 reports to be produced by HRI/others
Reports on Objectives 3 and 4 to be produced by WPC

HRI = Hydrological Research Unit
GIS = Geohydrological Information Service
WPC = Water Pollution Control

Figure 18.3 National water quality monitoring system.

18.6.3 The monitoring system

The perceived relation between all monitoring objectives and all operational parameters is given in Table 18.2. Again it should be remembered that this will operate on a national as well as a regional level.

TABLE 18.2

Relationship between monitoring objectives and operational parameters for the NWQMS.

	National	*Catchment management*	*Compliance*	*Special Studies*
MONITORING OBJECTIVES	Assessment	Management	Enforcement	Research
INFORMATION USERS	Water quality managers; Public; Regional Management	Regional management	Water quality; Pollution control; Effluent dischargers	Authorizing agency
SAMPLING LOCATIONS	Fixed stations in rivers	Related to point or diffuse sources	Effluent and immediate vicinity	As needed
VARIABLES	Related to description of water's 'fitness for use'	Related to management strategies	Determined by permits	As needed for research purposes
STATISTICAL ANALYSIS	Central tendencies; Variance; Trends; Time series; Periodicity	Probability distributions; Spatial or serial correlation	Excess	Correlation; Time series
REPORTING	Formal regular reports, widely distributed; raw data on request	Formal or informal bxports to quality managers	Reports on compliance to dischargers	Project report on study findings
DATA LOCATION	Special database	Within regions	Special database	Within authorizing agency
DURATION	Long term; little change in frequency or variables	Short or long term; frequency of variables may change in short term	Long term; frequency of variables may change in short term	Short term, less than 5 years

18.6.4 Constraints on NWQMS

There are many obstacles to be cleared before the NWQMS can be fully implemented.

18.6.4.1 *The Act as an 'administration generator'*

There are two aspects to consider, both of which are simple statements of fact:

(a) until the necessary regulations required to execute the NWQMS have been drawn up and promulgated in terms of the Water Act, the entire system is merely a statement of intent. There is, at the time of writing, no sign of such regulations.

The absence of any regulations save those concerning mining operations is a serious impediment.

(b) The Water Act, in general, is an administration generator. It was drawn up at a time when one-third of all white South Africans would, at some stage in their lives, be employed by the Public Service. It bristles with requirements for permits which are merely accountancy devices, or certificates of registration of some sort, being largely unenforceable because of the cost required to run the necessary inspectorate. They are therefore tokens with little relevance to planning needs or permissions and serve no particular control purpose.

18.6.4.2 *Public Service employment conditions*

The dissatisfaction within the Public Service concerning current conditions of employment is a matter of public record. Conditions are actually worse than what has been publically stated and have to do, not only with poor salaries but with unfair salary structures and a lack of perquisites, which are jealously guarded in the private sector. The result is that there is very little chance of attracting recruits with the extremely wide backgrounds and tertiary qualifications required to implement South Africa's evolving water management policy.

18.6.4.3 *Training*

From the inception of the Water Act in 1956 to 1988, no formal technical training courses were given to those entrusted with implementation of the sections of the Water Act devoted to pollution control. Experience was gained on the 'do as I do; say as I say' principle. In 1988, a 5-day course in water quality management was attended by some senior members of the department (as well as other practitioners in the field). Steps are under way to develop a central training programme.

18.6.4.4 *Divided Interests*

It is unfortunate (and it greatly detracts from the effectiveness of water quality management) that the interests in water quality of the Departments of Environment Affairs and of National Health and Population Development which directly impinge on those of the DWA continue to be administered separately, necessitating a complex and expensive system of referrals and commentaries in every case of discharge. The *Report of the President's Council on a national environmental management system*[16] favours the transfer of the Directorate of Pollution Control of the DWA to the Department of Environment Affairs. See chapter 5.

18.7 THE WAY AHEAD

The Republic's evolving system of water quality management is far more than the application of legal requirements through a changing politico-economic system subject to most of the constraints applicable to the Third World. Water quality is amenable to mathematical treatment which describes its depletion and replenishment: this treatment extends to regulatory public policy through the concept of management input matched to exploitative effort.

The underlying principles assumed to operate in any model of water quality management are: first, that all water is a common-property resource, that is, equally accessible under rights of common law. All persons therefore may share in an apportionment of water and since the (chemically) defined quality of the water is an inseparable aspect of its physical existence, it follows that water quality is also a common-property resource. Secondly, it follows from this that an instantaneous stock of quality may be visualized, to be preserved as a national asset. Thus 'quality' as a good

---

[16] PC 1/1991, para 6.4.4.

is exploitable in the market and the exploiter is subject to the requirements of the water law applicable. In their activities, exploiters assume as an invariant of their activity that quality is replaced, at least, at the rate at which it is consumed. Quality in natural aquatic systems is replaced at measurable rates by: appropriately conservative management by the regulator; compulsory purification of discharges by the exploiter and natural causes (dilution and replenishment). 'Conservative management', of course, implies legal control. The input of an exploiter in using quality to market advantage must be matched by an equal and opposite input by the regulator to maintain the natural stock (resource) of quality. Further, if there is an optimum path to maximize benefit for the exploiter, there is an equally optimum path for the regulator to manage the exploitation and maximize conservation of the resource. It is therefore fundamental that quantification of public policy, in acceptable terms, must mirror the market advantage conferred on the exploiter. It is therefore clear that all sorts of research possibilities are awakened by the department's long-term commitment to preserving and enhancing our national water quality.

18.8 WATER POLLUTION CONTROL LEGISLATION

18.8.1 Introduction

Until shortly before World War II and with the exception of the mining industry in certain regions agriculture was the only significant user of water, with urban use also accounting for a small percentage. Irrigation was generally by direct abstraction and diversion from rivers on the basis of the riparian system of water rights which had been adopted in South Africa by means of court decisions, particularly of the Cape Supreme Court, during the second half of the 19th century. Initially the State, enabled by the Irrigation and Conservation of Waters Act 8 of 1912, constructed large impoundments only to serve agricultural users.

Partly as a result of and certainly coincident with the exploitation of diamonds in Kimberley (from 1868) and later gold on the Witwatersrand (from 1886) the population moved in droves from rural areas to the cities and rapid urban development and industrialization took place, particularly after World War II. The existing legislation, being mainly agriculturally oriented, was incompatible with the needs of the rapidly growing requirements of the relatively new urban and industrial users. This problem was initially dealt with by means of ad hoc legislation in respect of particular water schemes for metropolitan areas such as the Durban Waterworks Consolidation (Private) Act 24 of 1921 and the Pretoria Waterworks (Private) Act 15 of 1929. More ambitious was the Rand Water Board Incorporation Ordinance of 1903 which resulted in the Rand Water Board growing into the biggest regional supplier of water for urban and industrial use in the country.

Although the Water Act 54 of 1956, administered by the Minister of Water Affairs and Forestry, is by far the most important statute relating to the control of water resources in South Africa, there are a number of provisions in other legislation, administered by a variety of bodies, which are also relevant to the control over the pollution of fresh water and marine pollution, the latter receiving increased attention of late. The relevant legislation can conveniently, be grouped together in three categories: legislation primarily affecting the source of pollution or dealing with activities that produce pollution; legislation primarily dealing with the effect of pollution; and legislation relating primarily to a geographical area.

18.8.2 Legislation primarily affecting the source of pollution or dealing with activities which cause pollution

18.8.2.1 *Pollution resulting from the use of water for industrial purposes*

The use of water for industrial purposes, including sea water brought ashore, is governed by the Water Act. Because industrial effluent, when disposed of by discharge to a water source, disadvantages other users, the authority to grant rights to the use of public water[17] for industrial purposes[18] has—with some important exceptions—been conferred on a water court.[19] No one may use public water for industrial purposes without the permission of a water court, except in the case of any person being supplied by a local authority or similar body that has the right to control or supply water, any person to whom water is supplied by the Minister from a government waterworks, any person using public water for industrial purposes in pursuance of ministerial permission resulting from the sufficiency of public water in a government water control area, and any person not exceeding the quantity of water lawfully used by him prior to the commencement of the Act.[20] A further exception is made in the case of a person who has a right to use public water for agricultural purposes. He may obtain a permit from the Minister to use water for the development of power or the winning or washing of sand, gravel or stone, which are both defined in the Act as uses for industrial purposes.[21]

In addition to the right obtained from a water court to use public water for industrial purposes, if the use of public water is to exceed 150 m^3 on any one day,[22] a permit from the Minister is required.

South Africa is relatively poorly endowed with water resources and cannot afford the loss from circulation of all water abstracted from its resources and used for urban and industrial purposes. For this reason, certain obligations are imposed on the users of water for industrial purposes. It is to be noted that although all three the main use categories recognized in the Act viz use for agricultural, urban and industrial purposes do give rise to water pollution, control measures are directed primarily at industrial use. The reason for this is that industrial use through the production of effluents as defined in the Act, to a large extent causes pollution through point sources which are more susceptible to control than diffuse sources of pollution.

By imposing certain obligations on users of water for industrial purposes, the Act strives to attain a balance between demand for water and deterioration in quality.

Certain duties and exceptions must be noted:

(a) Duty to purify effluent. Where any water, including sea water, is used for industrial purposes, the person so using the water must purify any resultant effluent so

---

17 'Public water' means any water flowing or found in or derived from the bed of a public stream, whether visible or not: s 1.

18 'Use of water for industrial purposes' means use of water (including effluent supplied by a person other than the user) for or in connection with—
(a) the manufacture, alterations, processing, treatment, repair, decoration, painting, spraypainting, electroplating, corrosion prevention, cooling, dyeing, washing, polishing, cleaning, finishing or breaking up of any article or part thereof, whether that article or part is a solid, liquid, vapour or gas or a combination of these states;
(b) the generation of power;
(c) railway purposes;
(d) mining or the winning or washing of sand, gravel or stone;
(e) an intensive animal feeding system or the breeding of fish or any mollusc;
(f) the slaughtering of livestock;
(g) any sewerage system or work or any watercare work;
(h) the conveyance of any substance;
(i) printing or photographic work; or
(j) any civil, mechanical or electrical engineering construction work, and includes use for domestic purposes or for the watering of stock or of streets and gardens in so far as such use may be incidental to use for industrial purposes: s 1.

19 Section 11(1). See also ss 11(2), (3), (4), (5) (6) and (7) and 12(6).

20 Section 11(1). .

21 Section 11(1A).

22 Section 12. The provisions of the section apply in respect of any water, including private water and underground water and also sea water brought ashore whether or not any portion of such water is, in the case of water abstracted from a public stream, subsequently returned to that stream: s 12(5).

as to conform to such requirements as the Minister may, after consultation with the South African Bureau of Standards, (SABS), prescribe by notice in the *Government Gazette*.[23] These requirements provide a large degree of flexibility in that they may be prescribed either—

(i) generally, or
(ii) in relation to water used for any particular industrial purpose, or
(iii) in relation to water or effluent to be disposed of by discharging it into any particular stream, or into the sea
(iv) or in relation to water or effluent to be disposed of in any particular area.

Standards at present comprise a general standard applied universally, a special standard for specified streams and a special standard for phosphate applicable to certain sensitive catchments. These effluent standards as well as the methods of testing waste water or effluents have been promulgated.[24]

Although effluent standards are at present based only on chemical and physical parameters, the results obtained from monitoring the waters into which the discharges are made may indicate that biological parameters should also be included.

(b) Duty to return water and effluent to origin. Purified or treated water that has been used for industrial purposes, including water recovered from any effluent, if derived from a public stream, must be discharged at the place where it was taken from the stream or at such other place where the Minister may indicate. If the water was sea water, it must be returned into the sea at the place where it was taken from the sea or at such other place as the Minister may indicate.[25] In addition, the person making the discharge into the stream or sea must furnish the Director-General with the written particulars of such use and disposal as may be prescribed by regulation.[26]

(c) Exemptions. Provision is made for exemptions from the duty to purify effluent or to return used water to its origin.[27] Unless the Minister directs otherwise, the discharge of industrial effluent into a sewer of a local authority is not subject to the above provision.[28] Since a local authority that uses water for the purification or disposal of sewage, effluent or waste is deemed to use such water for industrial purposes,[29] it must comply with the two duties discussed above. In short, this means that the local authority can take over the duties of the industries, or partly so, depending on its own water-supply and waste-acceptance policy.

After consultation with the SABS the Minister may grant exemption from compliance with the standards and from the requirement to return purified water to the stream of origin.[30] Anyone prejudiced by the exemption granted may appeal against the decision to a water court.[31] The Minister may himself withdraw any exemption or amend, withdraw or impose any condition in connection with such exemption.[32]

The granting of exemptions will always be unsatisfactory from a pollution control point of view. The Water Act does, however, contain provisions designed to ensure that

---

[23] Section 21(1)*(a)*.
[24] GN 991 of 18 May 1984, which lays down a special standard, a special standard for phosphates, a general standard and methods of testing. Schedule 1 is a list of catchments in which effluent must be purified to the special standard; schedule 2 is a list of catchments in which the special phosphate standard applies.
[25] Section 21(1)*(b)*.
[26] Section 21(1) read together with s 26.
[27] Section 21(4)*(a)*.
[28] Section 21(2).
[29] Section 21(3).
[30] Section 21(4)*(a)* and *(b)*.
[31] Section 21(4)*(c)* and *(d)*.
[32] Section 21(4)*(e)*.

exemptions are not granted freely. Conditions can be inserted in the exemption in terms of which the danger of pollution can be reduced.

(d) Administrative action. The Director-General may authorize any person to inspect land on which water is used for industrial purposes or on which certain substances[33] are used or are present. If the Director-General is of the opinion, based on the findings of the inspection, that under the particular circumstances the requirements to prevent water pollution are inadequate or insufficient, he may direct the person responsible to take such additional steps as he deems to be necessary. Moreover the Minister may, by notice in the *Government Gazette*, prohibit or restrict the manufacture, marketing or use of any substance which he believes may cause water pollution, or impose on such marketing, manufacture or use such conditions as he may deem fit. The use of phosphates in detergents could, for example, be controlled or prohibited if necessary.[34]

(e) Offences. Failure to comply with certain provisions of the Act or a condition of an exemption amounts to a criminal offence.[35]

18.8.2.2 *Pollution associated with mining operations*

This subject is addressed in chapter 15.

18.8.2.3 *General pollution*

The provisions discussed under industrial pollution apply only when water was used for industrial purposes and so rendered an effluent. Water pollution which does not result from the direct use of water for industrial purposes cannot be controlled in terms of those provisions, but it should be noted that for purposes of control by means of these measures, some activities which are foreign to what is normally seen as industrial, have been included in the definition of 'use for industrial purposes.' This also applies to industries that produce solid wastes or liquids without using water, e g the petroleum industry. A general provision is accordingly contained in the Water Act covering the above-mentioned instances of pollution and which, in fact, relates to any water pollution. It is an offence for any person wilfully or negligently[36] to commit any act that could pollute any public or private water, including underground water, or sea water in such a way as to render it less fit—

(a) for the purposes for which it is or could be ordinarily used by other persons (including the government, Transnet Ltd and any provincial administration); or
(b) for the propagation of fish or other aquatic life; or
(c) for recreational or other legitimate purposes.[37]

No definition or standard of pollution is provided, the criterion to determine whether water has been polluted being whether the water has been rendered less fit for the purposes for which it is or could be used. Contrary to the prevalent view that such proof is very difficult, several successful prosecutions have recently been brought.

18.8.2.4 *Pollution associated with waterborne transportation*

Persons using waterborne transportation are responsible for any resultant pollution of both inland waters and the sea. Although there are some provisions relating to the

[33] A substance capable of causing water pollution, whether such substance is a solid, liquid, vapour or gas, or a combination of those states: s 22.
[34] Section 23.
[35] Criminal liability is stipulated in numerous individual provisions of the Act and, generally, in s 170.
[36] Intention or negligence is presumed: s 23(1)*(b)* of the Water Act.
[37] Section 23(1)*(a)* of the Water Act.

control of pollution from boats on inland water,[38] most provisions refer to the pollution of harbour waters and to the sea generally. This legislation is discussed in the ensuing paragraphs.

18.8.2.5 *Pollution caused by wrecks*

When a ship, ie any kind of vessel used or designed to be used in navigation,[39] is wrecked, stranded or in distress within the territorial waters[40] of the Republic of South Africa, the Minister of Transport is authorized in terms of the Merchant Shipping Act 57 of 1951 to take a variety of actions regarding such ship or wreck.[41] A wreck includes flotsam, jetsam, lagan and derelict found in or on the shores of the sea or of any tidal waters of the Republic; any portion of a ship or aircraft lost, abandoned, stranded or in distress; any portion of the cargo, stores or equipment of such ship or aircraft and any portion of the personal property on board such ship or aircraft when it was lost, abandoned, stranded or in distress and belonged to any person who was on board that ship or aircraft at that time.[42] The provisions of the Merchant Shipping Act are supplemented by certain provisions of the Marine Traffic Act 2 of 1981.[43]

18.8.2.6 *Pollution through dumping of substances at sea*

The dumping of substances in the sea is controlled in terms of the Dumping at Sea Control Act 73 of 1980, which is administered by the Minister and Department of Environment Affairs. However, in relation to any matter affecting Transnet Ltd, the Minister may act only with the concurrence of the Minister of Transport.[44] This Act is the outcome of the Convention on the Prevention of Marine Pollution by Dumping of Wastes and other Matter (London, 1972), as has been discussed in chapter 9. The international convention relating to a discharge from a ship of harmful as well as ordinary substances has been enacted by the South African Government in the International Convention for the Prevention of Pollution from Ships Act 2 of the 1986,[45] which places certain reciprocal obligations on contracting parties to detect violations and to report them and requires enforcement of legal prohibitions and sanctions in accordance with the laws of the State under whose authority the ship is operating.

The Dumping at Sea Control Act applies to South African territorial waters and also in respect of the Prince Edward Islands.[46] Certain provisions even apply in respect of South African vessels,[47] aircraft[48] or citizens on the high seas, including the fishing zone.[49]

The Act relates to the dumping at sea of various types of substances:

---

[38] Cf eg art 30 of the schedule to the International Health Regulations Act 28 of 1974, read with s 2 of the Act.

[39] Section 2(1) of the Merchant Shipping Act.

[40] See s 2 of the Territorial Waters Act 87 of 1963.

[41] Section 304A.

[42] Section 2(1).

[43] Cf s 6(1).

[44] Section 1(2).

[45] Articles 6 and 8 of the Convention and Protocol I.

[46] Section 11.

[47] 'South African vessel' means any vessel registered in the Republic in terms of the Merchant Shipping Act, or deemed to be so registered: s 2(8) of the Dumping at Sea Control Act.

[48] 'South African aircraft' means any aircraft in the Republic: s 2(8) of the Dumping at Sea Control Act.

[49] Section 2(6). Cf also s 2(7).

(a) Substances mentioned in sch 1,[50] ie prohibited substances;
(b) Substances mentioned in sch 2,[51] ie restricted substances;
(c) Any other substance.[52]

It deals, moreover, with the loading of substances mentioned under *(b)*[53] and *(c)*[54] onto any vessel,[55] aircraft,[56] platform or other man-made structure[57] for dumping. It also deals with the disposal of any vessel at sea.[58]

Certain activities amount to an offence in terms of the Act:

(a) Dumping. 'Dump', in relation to any substance, means deliberately to dispose of at sea from any vessel, aircraft, platform or other man-made structure, by incinerating or depositing in the sea. It does not, however, include the disposal at sea of any substance incidental to or derived from normal operations. Nor does it include the lawful depositing at sea of any substance for a purpose other than its mere disposal.[59]

It is an offence to dump any substance mentioned in sch 1 into the sea[60] and no permit may be granted to authorize the dumping of such substance. It is also an offence to dump any substance mentioned in sch 2;[61] however, a special permit may be obtained to legalize such dumping.[62] It is also an offence to dump any other substance not mentioned in sch 1 or 2;[63] however, a general permit may be obtained to legalize such dumping.[64]

---

[50] Section 2(1)*(a)*. The prohibited substances included in this schedule are: organohalogen compounds; mercury and it compounds; cadmium and its compounds; persistent plastics and other persistent synthetic materials; high-level radioactive waste or other high-level radioactive matter prescribed by regulation with the concurrence of the Minister of Mineral and Energy Affairs, and substances in whatever form produced for biological and chemical warfare.

[51] Section 2(1)*(b)*(i). The restricted substances included in this schedule are: arsenic and its compounds; lead and its compounds; copper and its compounds; zinc and its compounds; organosilicon compounds; cyanides; fluorides; pesticides and their by-products not included in sch 1; beryllium and its compounds; chromium and its compounds; nickel and its compounds; vanadium and its compounds; containers, scrap metal and any substances or articles that by reason of their bulk may interfere with fishing or navigation; radioactive waste or other radioactive matter not included in sch 1, and ammunition. The Minister may by notice in the *Government Gazette* amend any schedule to the Act: s 9.

[52] Section 2(1)*(c)*(i).

[53] Section 2(1)*(b)*(ii).

[54] Section 2(1)*(c)*(ii).

[55] 'Vessel' means waterborne craft of any type whatsoever, whether self-propelled or not: s 1(1).

[56] 'Aircraft' means airborne craft of any type whatsoever, whether self-propelled or not: s 1(1).

[57] 'Platform' and 'other man-made structure' are not defined.

[58] Section 2(1)*(b)*(iii).

[59] Section 1(1).

[60] Section 2(1)*(a)*. On conviction, the responsible person is liable to a fine not exceeding R250 000 or to imprisonment for a period not exceeding five years, or both: s 6(1)*(a)*. Moreover, if the offence was committed over a period of more than one day, the penalty is a fine not exceeding R5 000 or imprisonment for a period not exceeding six months in respect of every day during which the offence continued: s 6(1)*(a)*.

[61] Section 2(1)*(b)*(i). On conviction, the responsible person is liable to a fine not exceeding R100 000 or to imprisonment for a period not exceeding two years, or both: s 6(1)*(b)*. Moreover, if the offence was committed over a period of more than one day, the penalty is a fine not exceeding R2 000 or imprisonment for a period not exceeding two months in respect of every day during which the offence continued: s 6(1)*(b)*.

[62] Section 3(1)*(a)*(i).

[63] Section 2(1)*(c)*(i). On conviction, the responsible person is liable to a fine not exceeding R5 000 or to imprisonment for a period not exceeding six months, or both: 6(1)*(c)*. Moreover, if the offence was committed over a period of more than one day, the penalty, is a fine not exceeding R500 or imprisonment for a period not exceeding 18 days in respect of every day during which the offence continued: s 6(1)*(c)*.

[64] Section 3(1)*(b)*.

(b) Loading for dumping. It is an offence to load any substance mentioned in sch 2 onto any vessel, aircraft, platform or other man-made structure at sea for dumping.[65] As has been mentioned, a special permit may be obtained to legalize such dumping. It is also an offence to load any substance other than those mentioned in sch 1 or 2.[66] But, as has been mentioned, a general permit may be obtained which would legalize such dumping.

(c) Disposal. The deliberate disposal[67] at sea of any vessel,[68] aircraft,[69] platform or other man-made structure is an offence;[70] however, a special permit may be obtained which would legalize such disposal.[71]

(d) Exemptions. In addition to the actions specifically excluded from the definition of 'dump',[72] there are two other instances which would exempt an accused from liability for the above-mentioned prohibited activities:

The accused may prove[73] that the substance in question was dumped for the purpose of saving human life or for securing the safety of the vessel, and that such dumping was necessary for such purpose or was a reasonable step to take in the circumstances. The other exemption relates to the granting of special or general permits by the Minister, who may authorize the dumping or disposal of certain substances.[74]

The Act imposes certain duties in respect of reporting and the furnishing of information.[75]

18.8.2.7 *Marine oil pollution*

Annex 1 of the schedule to the International Convention for the Prevention of Pollution from Ships of 1973 deals with the discharge of oil at sea. See chapter 9. This convention has been adopted in South African legislation by the International Convention for the Prevention of Pollution from Ships Act 2 of 1986. Another relevant instance where a South African statute is modelled on a convention is the International Convention Relating to Intervention on the High Seas in Cases of Oil Pollution Casualties Act 64 of 1987.[76] Both Acts are administered by the Minister of Transport.

Finally, the International Convention on Civil Liability for Oil Pollution Damage of 1969 served as the model for the introduction of South African legislation, although, unlike in the above-mentioned instances, it was not adopted by reference. Its philosophy and principles, nevertheless, were incorporated in the Prevention and Combating of Pollution of the Sea by Oil Act 6 of 1981. Moreover, some of the provisions of the International Convention for the Prevention of Pollution from Ships are enforceable under this Act, which, accordingly, overlaps to some extent with the International Convention for the Prevention of Pollution from Ships Act. It would have been more satisfactory if the preventive issues (the concern of the latter Act) and

---

[65] Section 2(1)*(b)*(ii). The penalty is the same as that which applies in respect of the dumping of substances mentioned in sch 2: s 6(1)*(b)*.

[66] Section 2(1)*(c)*(ii). The penalty is the same as that which applies in respect of the dumping of substances other than those mentioned in sch 1 or 2: s 6(1)*(c)*.

[67] 'Dispose' is not defined, but 'dump' is with respect to 'dispose'.

[68] Defined in s 1(1), above.

[69] Defined in s 1(1), above.

[70] Section 2(1)*(b)*(iii). The penalty is the same as that pertaining to the dumping of substances mentioned in sch 2.

[71] Section 3(1)*(a)*(ii).

[72] Section 1(1), above.

[73] Section 2(1).

[74] Section 3. Cf also s 8(1)*(a)* and *(b)* as regards regulations.

[75] Sections 2(5) and 4*(a)* and *(b)*.

[76] Criticism has been expressed regarding the implementation of the convention in question. See Devine 'Towards an effective implementation of the Intervention Convention in South Africa' 1988 (8) *Sea Changes* 56.

liability issues (the former Act's main concern) were dealt with in two entirely distinct and non-overlapping Acts. The Prevention and Combating of Pollution of the Sea by Oil Act provides for the prevention and combating of pollution by oil, discharged from ships, tankers or off-shore installations into South Africa's territorial waters and that portion of the fishing zone, situated within a distance of 50 nautical miles from the low-water mark, and includes the sea between the high- and low-water marks as well as any tidal lagoon or tidal river and internal waters. The principal features of the Act are that it makes provision for the criminal and civil liability of the master and/or owner of a ship, tanker or offshore installation, besides placing certain duties on these persons and empowering the Minister of Transport to undertake a wide range of actions with a view to preventing oil pollution. The key defined phrases of the Act concern the 'discharge' of 'oil' from a 'ship', tanker', or 'offshore installation' into the 'prohibited area' and the liability of the 'owner' and 'master'.[77] Since 1986 the Minister of Environment Affairs has also been involved in the administration of the Act. The practical dividing line between the respective jurisdictions of the two ministries is that Transport is responsible for control over oil while it is still on board, whereas Environment Affairs' jurisdiction arises only once oil is spilled into the sea or reaches the coastline.[78] Where oil pollution results or may result from a ship which is wrecked or in distress within the territorial waters of or on or near the coast of the Republic, the Minister of Transport may also act in terms of the Merchant Shipping Act in dealing with the problem.[79]

18.8.2.8 *Pollution from certain farming operations*

If the Minister of Water Affairs is of the opinion that the concentration of any livestock or any substance, or the carrying on of any farming operations on any land is causing, or is likely to cause, pollution of public or private water, including underground water, he may require the owner of such land, or the person carrying on such operations, to take such steps (at his own expense and within the determined period) as the Minister may deem necessary for the prevention of such pollution.[80] Should the landowner or other person fail to comply with this direction, the Minister may cause the required steps to be taken and may recover the costs from the owner or other person.[81] Failure to comply with the direction is an offence.[82] Provision is sometimes made for controlling the pollution of water used for irrigation purposes.[83]

18.8.3 Legislation dealing primarily with the effects of pollution

18.8.3.1 *Pollution detrimental to the marine habitat and its resources*

---

[77] For a detailed discussion of the Act's provisions, see Fuggle & Rabie (eds) *Environmental concerns in South Africa* (1983) 320–1.

[78] See, generally, the *First report on the situation of waste management and pollution control in South Africa* Report to the Department of Environment Affairs by the CSIR Programme for the Environment CPE 1/91 (1991) para 3.7.9.3.

[79] Section 304A.

[80] Section 23A(1) of the Water Act. This section is specifically directed at feedlots. This provision has been repealed by s 2(1) of Act 73 of 1978 from a date to be fixed by the State President by proclamation in the *Government Gazette*, apparently in order to allow the Department of National Health and Population Development to take over this control. (Cf reg 20 of the proposed general Health Regulations published in terms of the Health Act 63 of 1977, for general information—GN 85 of 27 January 1978). However, s 2(1) has not yet been put into operation: cf s 2(2).

[81] Ibid.

[82] Section 23A(3) read with s 170(2) of the Water Act.

[83] Cf e g s 17(1)*(q)* Kopjes Irrigation Settlement Act 38 of 1935; s 11*(b)* of the Buffelspoort Irrigation Scheme Act 31 of 1948; s 12(1)*(b)* of the Mooi River District Adjustment Act 37 of 1954; and s 13*(b)* of the Mapochsgronde Irrigation Scheme Act 42 of 1954.

Adequate conservation of the marine habitat and its resources is dependent to a considerable degree upon international co-operation. A number of conventions accordingly deal with this matter. See chapter 9. But national legislation is also important. Some of the relevant Acts have been discussed: the Water Act,[84] and, in particular, the Prevention and Combating of Pollution of the Sea by Oil Act, both provide for the conservation of the marine habitat and its resources.

Furthermore, the Sea Fishery Act 12 of 1988 renders it an offence for anyone to dump, or to allow to enter or to permit to be dumped or discharged into the sea,[85] anything that is or may be injurious to fish,[86] fish food or aquatic plants, or which may disturb or change the ecological balance in any area of the sea, or which may detrimentally affect the marketability of fish or of seaweed, or which may hinder the catching of fish.[87] It is no defence for an accused in a prosecution for this offence to aver that he had no knowledge of a certain fact or that he did not act wilfully.[88] If in any prosecution for the above-mentioned offence it is proved that in any area in the sea, within a distance of 8 km from any factory, any fish or fish food has been or is being injured or has died or is dying or its marketability or that of seaweed has been or is being adversely affected, or the ecological balance has been or is being disturbed or changed, it shall be presumed, until the contrary is proved, that it has been or is being caused by something discharged from that factory into the sea.[89]

The Cape and Natal Nature Conservation Ordinances also contain provisions aimed at preventing the pollution of the sea. It is an offence in terms of the Nature and Environmental Conservation Ordinance 19 of 1974 (Cape) to deposit or cause to be deposited in any inland waters or in any place from where it is likely to percolate into or in any other manner enter any inland waters, anything, whether solid, liquid or gaseous, which is or is likely to be injurious to any fish or fish food or which, if it were so deposited in large quantities or numbers, would be so injurious.[90] Although 'inland waters' refers basically to all waters which do not permanently or at any time during the year form part of the sea, it does include tidal rivers.[91] 'Tidal river' is not defined in the

[84] Sections 12(1), 21(5)*(a)*(i) and (ii), 21(6)*(a)* and 23(1), all of which have been discussed above.

[85] 'Sea' means the water and the bed of the sea, including the sea-shore and the water and the beds of tidal rivers and tidal lagoons: 'sea-shore' means the water and the land between the low-water mark and the high-water mark: s 1.

[86] 'Fish' means every species of sea animal, whether vertebrate or invertebrate, and includes the spawn or larvae of any such sea animal, but does not include any seal or sea bird: s 1.

[87] Section 47*(k)*. The penalty for the above-mentioned offence is a fine not exceeding R50 000 or imprisonment for a period not exceeding six years, or both: s 47(1). Moreover, in addition to such punishment, the Court must summarily enquire into and determine the monetary value of any advantage which the convicted person may have gained in consequence of the offence in question, and impose a fine equal to three times the amount so determined and, in default of payment thereof, imprisonment for a period not exceeding one year: s 47(2)*(a)*. Furthermore, the Court convicting any person of the above-mentioned offence may, in addition to the above-mentioned penalties which it may impose,

(a) in the case of a first conviction, declare any fish, seaweed, salt, shells or implement in respect of which the offence was committed or which was used in connection with the commission thereof, or any rights of the convicted person thereto, to be forfeited to the State; and

(b) in the case of a second or subsequent conviction, also declare any fishing boat or other vessel or vehicle so used, or any rights of the convicted person thereto, to be forfeited to the State, and cancel or suspend for such period as the Court may think fit, any registration done in respect of the convicted person or any licence or permit issued or granted to him in terms of the Act: s 48(1). Cf also s 48(2) and (3).

[88] Section 50(5).

[89] Section 50(4). Cf also s 50(2) and (3) for other presumptions.

[90] Section 48 read with s 85*(a)* of the Cape ordinance.

[91] Section 23.

Cape Ordinance,[92] but according to the Sea-Shore Act 21 of 1935[93] and the Sea Fishery Act[94] the water and the bed of any tidal river form part of the sea. The above-mentioned offence, although dealing principally with inland waters, accordingly also applies to the sea.

The Nature Conservation Ordinance 15 of 1974 (Natal) (chapter on coastal fishing), prohibits anyone from depositing or discharging or allowing to enter or percolate into any waters any substance, matter or thing, whether solid, liquid or gaseous, that is injurious or is liable to become injurious to fish[95] or fish food.[96] 'Waters', in respect of coastal fishing, is defined as the Indian Ocean and includes any semi-enclosed bay, estuary and that portion of any tidal river which lies downstream or seaward of a point of demarcation fixed in terms of regulations.[97]

18.8.3.2 *Pollution detrimental to other aquatic environments*

The provisions dealing with water pollution control that have been discussed all lead to the conservation of aquatic habitats and their resources. Certain provisions, however, deal with water pollution control with the explicit aim of conserving aquatic resources. Thus the provincial nature conservation ordinances of the Transvaal, Natal and the Cape make it an offence for anyone to pollute water[98] with substances that are injurious, or are likely or liable to become injurious, to fish or fish food.[99]

18.8.3.3 *Pollution detrimental to public health*

Almost all water pollution control is aimed at protecting the health of people. But certain provisions relate specifically to the protection of public health. Among the functions entrusted to the Department of National Health and Population Development by the Health Act 63 of 1977 is the promotion of a safe and healthy environment.[100] As is the case with most of the other functions referred to in the Act,[101] the Minister may delegate this function to a provincial administration, subject to such regulations and conditions as may be imposed. The Minister refunds the provincial administration for the expenses incurred in performing this function.[102] If, on the other hand, the Minister is satisfied after consultation with the local authority that such local authority is able to perform this function and/or the other functions that the Minister may delegate, or if the local authority requests delegation of the functions, these can be delegated to the local authority and the Minister refunds to the local authority its expenses incurred.[103] More particularly, every local authority[104] must adopt all lawful, necessary and reasonably practicable measures to prevent the occurrence within its district of any nuisance, unhygienic condition, offensive condition, or other condition

---

[92] However, 'tidal waters' is defined in terms of s 2(1) of Proc 357 of 28 September 1972 (Cape) as that part of any inland waters which, owing to the influence of the sea, becomes saline at any time or the level of which rises at any time owing to the influence of the sea. Cf also the definition of tidal river and of tidal lagoon in s 1 of the Sea-Shore Act 21 of 1935.

[93] See the definition of 'sea' in s 1 of the Sea-Shore Act.

[94] See the definition of 'sea' in s 1 of the Sea Fishery Act.

[95] 'Fish' is defined in s 1.

[96] Sections 183 and 185(1)*(a)* of the Natal Ordinance.

[97] Section 1 of the Natal Ordinance.

[98] For the definition of 'waters' see s 1(lx) of the Transvaal Nature Conservation Ordinance 12 of 1983; s 1 of the Natal Nature Conservation Ordinance; and s 2(lxxi) of the Cape Nature and Environmental Conservation Ordinance.

[99] Section 84 of the Transvaal Ordinance; s 152 read with s 208(1)*(b)* of the Natal Ordinance; and s 48 read with s 86(1)*(d)* of the Cape Ordinance.

[100] Section 14(1)*(c)*.

[101] Section 14.

[102] Section 14(2).

[103] Section 20(2), (3) and (4).

[104] Defined in s 1.

which will or could be harmful or dangerous to the health of any person within its district or the district of any other local authority, or, where a nuisance or condition has occurred, to abate, or cause to be abated, such nuisance, or remedy, or cause to be remedied, such condition, as the case may be.[105] A local authority must also prevent the pollution of any water intended for the use of the inhabitants of its district, irrespective of whether such water is obtained from sources within or outside its district, or purify water which has become so polluted.[106] An abatement notice procedure has been prescribed in cases where in the opinion of a local authority a condition has arisen in its district which is of such a nature as to be offensive or a danger to health unless immediately remedied.[107] Finally, the Minister of National Health and Population Development has wide powers to make regulations for the control of water pollution.[108]

The Sea-Shore Act 21 of 1935 makes specific provision for the protection of human health against pollution of the sea-shore or the sea. Notwithstanding the provisions of the Health Act, it empowers the Minister of National Health and Population Development by notice in the *Government Gazette* to declare that any local authority may exercise, in respect of the sea-shore and the sea situated within or adjoining its area of jurisdiction, any of the powers that are conferred by the Health Act on a local authority.[109]

Moreover, the Minister of Environment Affairs (whose powers in this respect may be delegated to the executive committee of a province)[110] may make regulations or by notice in the *Government Gazette* authorize a local authority to make regulations for the prevention or regulation of deposit or discharge upon the sea-shore or in the sea of offal, rubbish, or anything liable to be a nuisance or danger to health.[111] See chapter 26.

The International Health Regulations Act 28 of 1974, which will be discussed below, also contains a number of provisions pertaining specifically to the protection of human health against water pollution. Furthermore, water can, as a 'foodstuff',[112] be controlled in terms of the Foodstuffs, Cosmetics and Disinfectants Act 54 of 1972. The Minister of National Health and Population Development may make regulations prescribing the nature and composition of a 'foodstuff' or standards for the consumption, purity or quality of it.[113] He may also prescribe any 'foodstuff' to be deemed harmful or injurious to human health.[114] Finally, reference can also be made to the control over the dumping (and other forms of disposal) of certain hazardous substances, and of radioactive waste in terms of the Hazardous Substances Act 15 of 1973 and the Nuclear Energy Act 92 of 1982, as set out in chapters 19 and 21.

18.8.4 Legislation relating primarily to pollution in geographical reas

18.8.4.1 *Pollution of harbours*

Regulations issued in terms of the repealed South African Transport Services Act 65 of 1981,[115] now applicable by virtue of the Legal Succession to the South African

---

[105] Section 20(1)*(b)*.
[106] Section 20(1)*(c)*.
[107] Section 27.
[108] Sections 34, 36A, 37, 38 and 39.
[109] Section 7(1) of the Sea-Shore Act. Cf also s 7(2) in respect of the delegation of functions or duties regarding the sea-shore and the sea.
[110] Section 11(2).
[111] Section 10(1)*(d)*.
[112] 'Foodstuff', for purposes of the Foodstuffs, Cosmetics and Disinfectants Act 54 of 1972, means any article or substance ordinarily eaten or drunk by man: s 1.
[113] Section 15(1)*(a)* read with ss 15(5) and 18.
[114] Section 15(1)*(e)* read with ss 15(5) and 18.
[115] Section 73 of the Act.

Transport Services Act 9 of 1989[116] provide for control over waste, including oil, in the water of harbours.[117] It is an offence for anyone to throw or deposit into any harbour stones, gravel, ballast, carcasses, cargo, dirt, ashes, bottles, baskets, rubbish, objectionable or malodorous matter or any other article or substance of whatsoever nature, or to spill paint in any harbour or cause or allow oily or waxy effluent or oil of any description, whether or not such oil be of a mineral, animal or vegetable origin, to be discharged or to escape into a harbour.[118]

If oil of any description or flammable liquid, effluent or water from an uncleaned oil tank, fish-oil tank, bilge or hold which has contained oil, flammable liquid or cargo of any kind, is discharged or allowed to escape into a harbour from a ship, the master of such ship shall be deemed to have committed a breach of this regulation and shall be personally liable to punishment for the breach and, in addition, shall be liable for any costs that may be incurred by Transnet Ltd.[119]

If any act that constitutes a contravention of this regulation results in the obstruction of any berth in the harbour, the owner or master of the ship responsible for the obstruction must forthwith cause the obstruction to be removed at his expense, failing which Transnet Ltd may remove the obstruction at the expense of the owner or master, and should any other ship sustain damage as a result of the obstruction, the said owner or master will be liable for such damage.[120]

The master of every ship that is berthed alongside a quay or jetty must cause all the discharge outlets of his ship facing the quay or jetty to be closed or provided with adequate covers to prevent any inadvertent discharge of water or effluent onto the quay or jetty surface, bollards, moorings, telephone cables, fenders or hose connections.[121]

The International Health Regulations Act provides that every seaport or inland port must be provided with an effective system for the removal and safe disposal of excrement, refuse, waste water, condemned food, and other matter dangerous to health.[122] Moreover, a health authority is empowered to adopt all practicable measures to control the discharge from any ship of sewage and refuse which might contaminate the waters of a port, river or canal.[123] It is an offence for the master of a ship or person in charge of any other means of transport to cause or permit any ballast, or refuse of any kind, to be ejected from the ship or other means of transport and a duty is cast upon such persons to cause all such matters to be removed to a place set apart for that purpose, or otherwise to dispose of as the port health officer may direct.[124] Moreover, when a cattle ship is in a filthy condition, it must be cleaned in an area designated by the health officer.[125] The port health officer, after consultation with the port captain, may require the master of the ship to keep all water-closets and latrines on the ship closed while in port.[126] Contravention of any of these provisions is an offence.[127]

Pollution of fishing harbours is controlled in terms of regulations issued under the Sea Fishery Act.[128]

[116] Section 21(2).
[117] Regulation 38 GN R562 of 26 March 1982.
[118] Ibid.
[119] Ibid.
[120] Ibid.
[121] Ibid.
[122] Article 14(3) of the schedule to the Act.
[123] Article 30 of the schedule to the Act.
[124] Regulation 28(1) of the supplementary regulations under the International Health Regulations Act GN R2001 of 24 October 1975.
[125] Regulation 28(2).
[126] Regulation 28(3).
[127] Regulation 34(1). Cf also reg 34(2) for the personal liability of the master of the ship.
[128] Section 45(1)(i). For the regulations, cf GN R1805 of 27 July 1990 parts III and IV.

It may, finally, be remarked that the Prevention and Combating of Pollution of the Sea by Oil Act applies to any harbour under the jurisdiction of Transnet Ltd and to any fishing harbour.[129]

18.8.4.2 *Pollution of protected water areas*

The Lake Areas Development Act 39 of 1975 provides for the establishment of lake areas, now transformed into national parks, under the control of the National Parks Board. It should be noted that the water and the bed of any tidal river and of any tidal lagoon are included in the definition of the sea in terms of the Act.[130] The Minister of Environment Affairs may make regulations to regulate the use of the sea-shore and the sea within the area concerned[131] or to provide for the control, generally, of the sea-shore, of the sea and of any lake or river within the protected area.[132] Such regulations have been published with respect to the Wilderness National Park.[133] See, generally, in respect of protected areas, chapter 27.

18.9 AN ANALYSIS OF EXISTING WATER POLLUTION LEGISLATION AND ITS ADMINISTRATION

In attempting to analyse to what degree existing enactments meet present requirements, we must clarify several points: what should in general constitute water management; whether this is covered by legislation; the detailed nature of defects; and finally, likely remedies. We shall deal with each of these points in turn.

18.9.1 Water management

18.9.1.1 *Surface water*

The ideal goal of management is to achieve a quality that ensures the maintenance of aquatic life and recreational use, with the implicit assumption that such water will be a suitable source for potable supply and agricultural and industrial use. The DWA has as its major goal to ensure the ongoing equitable provision of adequate quantities and qualities of water to all competing users at acceptable degrees of risk and cost under changing conditions.[134] These uses (direct and indirect demand and including ecological use) and their respective percentages as they were in 1980, are the following:[135]

Municipal and domestic	9,3
Industrial	6,3
Mining	2,9
Power generation	1,7
Irrigation	52,2
Stock-watering	1,6
Nature conservation	1,1
Forestry	7,9
Estuaries and lakes	17,0

The department views the aim of water pollution control as the 'preservation of the water environment so that water of a quality acceptable for industrial, urban, agricultural and recreational use and for the propagation of the fish and wildlife species

---

[129] Cf the definition of 'prohibited area' in s 1(1) of the Act, read with the definition of 'internal waters' in s 1 of the Marine Traffic Act.

[130] Section 1 of the Lake Areas Development Act. Cf s 1 of the Sea-Shore Act.

[131] Section 23(1)*(c)*.

[132] Section 23(1)*(d)*.

[133] GN R311 of 22 February 1980.

[134] *Management of water resources* above n 1, xvii.

[135] *Management of water resources* above n 1, ch 2.

that could reasonably be expected in a particular environment continues to be available. The protection of human health is of particular importance.'[136] Where the stated goals were not being achieved, those cases should be isolated and the degradation reversed. The department envisages 'closer monitoring of receiving waters as a prerequisite for the effective evaluation and adaptation of pollution control strategies and policies'.

The many legal, technical, economic and management problems associated with increasing re-use are complex and dynamic, policies directed at the management of recycled water may change with time and different policies may be appropriate for different regions of the country.[137] The principle applied is that discharges must be controlled at their sources. This presupposes a careful examination of effluent requirements, the eradication of harmful substances (assuming it is known what they are) and the establishment of the degree of dilution which can, by dispersion, nullify the harmful effects of substandard and even standard discharges. So far as the quality of surface waters is concerned, it is vital that equity be achieved: the available supply must be fairly shared. This requires a quality–quantity relationship throughout the catchment area, controlled abstractions, conservation of resources and intelligent inter-basin transfers.

Notwithstanding the lapse of several years since the goals were identified, the water quality of South African rivers continues to deteriorate further. This fact, together with the prospect of the doubling of the Republic's population within a comparatively short space of time, demands that more vigorous action be taken.

18.9.1.2 *Subterranean water*

In theory, much the same can be said of subterranean water. What is aimed at is to protect quality for the greatest number of beneficial uses, of which abstraction for human and agricultural use is predominant. However, much greater emphasis has to be laid on subterranean water, because, if contamination occurs, this can be well-nigh permanent. Equity in the supply of subterranean water is tempered by three considerations: the possibilities of subsidence on over-abstraction, the rate at which foreign water replenishes the aquifer (as well as its quality) and the economic advantage of emptying a compartment so that mining can be conducted in dry conditions.

In South Africa all subterranean water west of a line drawn from Bredasdorp northwards through Laingsburg, Williston and Kuruman and terminating at Mafikeng is of very poor quality, having dissolved solids in the range 2 000 to over 4 000 parts per million. Subterranean water in a hemispherical area extending from East London to Middelburg (Cape), Kimberley, Pretoria, Warmbaths, Vryheid and terminating at Empangeni is of good quality (0–499 parts per million). All other areas are either of intermediate quality (average to poor) or worse.[138] This is why emphasis is laid on the preservation of dolomitic waters on the Witwatersrand at the expense of, say, pumping out and purifying subterranean water for the northern or western Cape. Consequently, subterranean water management in South Africa has not, to date, been accorded the emphasis it receives in the Northern Hemisphere. This attitude is rapidly changing as we approach the end of our reserves, roughly coinciding with the turn of the century. Plans are far advanced to supplement local aquifers in the Cape with purified effluent. Recent amendments to the Water Act, though preserving the private nature of subterranean water, increase the degree of control exercised by the department and subterranean water boards over subterranean water.

---

[136] *Management of water resources* above n1, para 4.3.
[137] Ibid.
[138] See, generally, Bond *Geological survey memoir* no 41 Department of Mines (1945).

18.9.1.3 *Marine matters*

So far as marine matters are concerned, it is sufficient to say that the maintenance of fish stocks and unhindered coastal recreation are of importance, with the implicit understanding that concern also extends to the marine environment in general, taking into account man's necessary exploitation of it.

18.9.1.4 *Research*

It seems appropriate at this point to introduce very briefly the functions of research in water management. The Water Research Act 34 of 1971 created the Water Research Commission, the objects of which are to co-ordinate, promote, encourage or cause to be undertaken research in respect of: *(a)* the occurrence, preservation, conservation, utilization, control, supply, distribution, purification, pollution or reclamation of water supplies and water; and *(b)* the use of water for agricultural, industrial or urban purposes.

The Water Research Act makes specific provision for collaboration with the CSIR, state departments and universities. Needless to say, ties with the DWA are close. A particular function of the commission is to accumulate and disseminate knowledge and the Minister is entitled to levy a rate per cubic metre on all water supplied in this country plus a rate per hectare of land irrigated, to derive income.

Pollution research which the commission has initiated includes countrywide surveys of the pollution problems of the fishing industry, the fruit and vegetable canning industry, and the textile industry. The list may be expanded into a very large and broadly based field covering most aspects of water care in our country.

Fundamental research—which the commission does not undertake—is done by the National Institute for Water Research of the CSIR as well as by a number of university departments. South African expertise derived in this manner is held in high regard.

18.9.1.5 *Conclusion*

In summary, it may be said that we have been dealing with environmental standards in respect of emissions to inland water and the sea. Excellent comment—which applies to South Africa—can be found in descriptions of British practice[139] which can be paraphrased in the following way:

Water provides a wide range of biological pathways for pollutants to reach man, and because of slow dispersion biochemical accumulation risks are high. On the other hand, water has, for most pollutants, a self-regenerative capacity and the toxic pathways are fairly predictable. Damage, once it is recognized, can usually be put right by controls. For this to be done efficiently, the uses to which natural water is put must be recognized by constructing quality objectives which define acceptable contamination. The sea has some similarities but its assimilative capacity is far greater: but so is its sensitivity to a wider range of pollutants which can act on natural food chains, terminating in mankind. The disposal of substances at sea, whether by pipeline or from ships is practised on a global scale, largely because there is no economic alternative, and also because, in a surprisingly high number of cases, nothing but superficial damage results.

[139] *Environmental standards: a description of United Kingdom practice* Pollution Paper 11 HMSO London (1977).

18.9.2 Legislation

We must now examine critically the Water Act, the intentions behind it and its shortcomings.[140]

18.9.2.1 *The control of consumption*

Reference has been made to the provisions of the Water Act concerning the control of the consumption of public water for industrial purposes, and to the requirement for a permit. This permit gives in detail the purpose for which the water is to be used and the amount and mode of reporting-back by the consumer to the department. The intention of the provision in question is to enlist the co-operation of the industrialist, assumed to be the major user, in what is essentially a bookkeeping exercise. The provision as it is now applied suffers from a serious defect: it does not apply to the use of water by local authorities.

The consumer, on the other hand, can experience severe disadvantages in the application of the provision of the Water Act which requires the permission of a water court for the industrial use of water unless such water emanates from a local authority.[141] Since the court has to be in possession of a permit issued to the applicant before reaching its decision, the consumer is at a time disadvantage, since all these matters are of necessity protracted. Indeed, the expense and time-consuming nature of applications to the water court were recognized by Parliament when the relevant provision of the Water Act was recently changed to facilitate the grants of permits for agricultural uses and, in particular, feedlots.[142] Fortunately, industrialists requiring water court permission constitute a small minority as most industrial undertakings are served by local authorities or other water suppliers.

18.9.2.2 *The discharge of effluents*

The provisions of the Water Act dealing with industrial water pollution[143] are explicit in their requirements, the most important of which are: effluent purification is a concomitant of industrial use; persons using water for industrial purposes must purify effluent to a predetermined standard before discharge; the Minister may lay down standards in respect of any area. Several difficulties arise, however.

A very important and significant aspect of South African water pollution control is the concept of a standard quality of purity, as has been pointed out. It may seem ideal to prescribe fixed maximum permissible concentrations for every toxic substance. Unfortunately, though, in view of the fact that a great number of toxic substances are known to exist, and the fact that approximately 400 new chemical compounds appear annually on the South African market, this is well-nigh impossible. A small number of such substances are controlled in such a way,[144] but the omnibus effluent standard for dissolved solids provides that the total dissolved solids content of the waste water or effluent may not be increased by more than 15 per cent (in the case of the special standard), or by more than 75 milli- Siemens m (determined at 25 °C) (in the case of the general standard), above that of the intake water.[145] A problem with this standard is that the unavoidable increase in the use of water for industrial purposes will steadily

---

[140] For a comprehensive analysis, see Wiseman & Glazewski *South African Law pertaining to the causes and effects of pollution affecting water resources* CSIR Report CPEI 5/91 (1991). See also the *Report of the President's Council on a national environmental management system* above n 16, paras 5.5.4–5.5.6.7.

[141] Section 11.

[142] Section 3 of the Water Amendment Act 68 of 1990. And see *House of Assembly debates* 28 to 30 May 1990, 105 94, 105 97ff.

[143] Section 21.

[144] See tables of constituents of the effluent standards in GN 991 of 18 May 1984.

[145] See para 1.8.1 and 3.8.1 of the effluent standards.

lead to an increased pollution load. As long as the effluent standard is related to the per unit quantity of water used, increased pollution and an unnecessary increase in the use of water will result.[146] But whether or not toxic substances are diluted does not make a difference to the quantity of the resultant pollution, although the dilution of pollutants does normally reduce their toxicity to living organisms. Moreover, many of the toxic substances mentioned above never reach the water. It is also very difficult to determine their toxic levels and how this is affected by treatment processes. Some industries use water only for cooling purposes and it might seem unfair to expect them to purify the water of possible toxic substances. But the use of water for cooling purposes often entails the addition of toxic chemicals, usually chlorine, to prevent or destroy organic growth in the cooling system. Finally, it must be remembered that we are here dealing with an effluent standard and not with a standard for drinking water.

One difficult problem is that enforcement of these effluent standards is dependent, inter alia, on an adequate number of inspectors who should constantly monitor the effluents from industries. There are simply not sufficient inspectors available to perform this task thoroughly, but the problem is to some extent being solved technologically by the use of automatic monitoring devices. Although such devices are successfully being used to accumulate data on river quality, the necessary analyses for, say, compliance of effluents with the general standard could never be achieved by these means. Another difficulty with an effluent standard is that it becomes a basis of argument for claiming permission to cause pollution up to that level; it does not offer an incentive to reduce pollution. Furthermore, reliance on effluent standards, with deviations from them sanctioned by exemption, has several other side-effects.

Standards simplify very greatly the administration of the law by a relatively small country such as South Africa with limited skilled personnel, since a standard is either met or it is not; and effluent standards, where they exist, conform to what could reasonably be attained by a properly designed and correctly operated industry. On the other hand, it could be held that they confer unique privileges and responsibilities on the originating authority, which is not primarily concerned with water technology or research, and the imposition of countrywide water standards can lead to unfairness in that they must be able to cope with the worst case to be encountered, and may well be too stringent for the best. In addition, a single effluent standard will not necessarily bear any relation to the overall health of a river if effluent is introduced at several places, for it fails to take into account the total load per volume of receiving water. These objections are overcome by a system of relaxations from the standard, set by the South African Bureau of Standards (SABS), approved by it and embodied in exemptions approved by the Minister and issued to each discharger.

Opinions differ markedly as to the usefulness of the system of standards.[147] In any event, it is apparent that effluent exemptions regulate not only discharges but also water utilization and ultimately water resources. Consequently, water pollution control is a part of the framework of the general regulation of water resources and their use and is not a legal singularity.

A fundamental objection against reliance upon an effluent standard only is that a standard for the concentration of a specific toxic substance is not enough to ensure a relatively clean effluent. This is only the beginning. What is definitely required is a study of the whole waterway into which the effluent is discharged. Individual effluents conforming to a general standard do not present the real problems; it is the cumulative effect of several effluents into a waterway, together with the relevant natural flow,

---

[146] See Van Duuren & Funke *Optimization of water use by means of water quality and volume requirements* Water Year Convention, Pretoria, (1970).

[147] Zunckel 'Current trends in South Africa regarding effluent discharges and legislation' 1981 (7) *Water, Sewage and Effluent* 9–12.

which must be taken into account in order to determine the standard for that specific volume of water. An altogether different approach to industrial water pollution, which is followed in Germany, would be to rely on a system of discharge or emission fees. Although the system of discharge fees offers promising solutions, there are a number of problems that still have to be ironed out in its operation.[148] A most important consequence of this approach would be that pollution costs would become internalized. See chapter 3. In South Africa the costs that water pollution bring about to persons other than the producer of the pollution are not adequately reflected in industries' production costs. Water is, in the economic sense, still very much regarded as a free resource; this applies particularly where exemptions are allowed. It must, however, be pointed out that effluent standards in general conform to what a properly designed and correctly operated industry could be expected to attain, and that emission or discharge fees are accordingly often applied only where effluents do not conform to those that a well-designed industry could attain. This would be unsatisfactory because it would mean that pollution costs would still not be fully internalized. If emission fees are used, they should apply to any degree of pollution.

There are a number of other minor flaws in the South African provisions dealing with industrial water pollution. For example, because local authorities are defined in the Act, institutions such as hotels, caravan parks, marinas, prisons and private hospitals are excluded from the provisions of the section. Again, 'effluent' is defined as residual water or any other liquid produced by or resulting from the use of water for industrial purposes, including any substance dissolved or suspended therein, but excluding any liquid produced for commercial purposes. From this definition it is clear that stormwater, for example, containing high organic loads and lead, is not an effluent.

18.9.2.3 *General pollution*

The apparent intention with the provisions dealing with general pollution was to reconcile two irreconcilable views: to provide safeguards for state policy regarding water pollution, without actually saying what such pollution was; and to preserve the maximum amount of civil liberty for the person discharging effluents. Presumably, the view was held that the criminal offences defined in the provision dealing with industrial pollution were in themselves overriding deterrents: consequently, in early versions of the provision dealing with general pollution, the onus was placed on the State to prove any allegations made, particularly that pollution did occur. As has been pointed out, matters were changed in amendments made in 1972 and 1975 but the fact remains today that magistrates tend to consider pollution as a diffuse term and unless damage or loss of enjoyment can be clearly established, the Court will favour the defendant and consequently impose only meagre penalties, if any. The Courts fail to recognize that they are not only dealing with damage or loss of enjoyment but with much more serious long-term social and national issues. Moreover, it is known from experience that as much harm can come from pollution arising from the omission of an act as from commission: the law as it stands is not concerned with these questions. The increased public awareness of the importance of environmental conservation could, however, result in these attitudes becoming more positive.

Three other points arise. A high degree of technical proof is required for a successful prosecution. It is customary for the department to rely on sworn affidavits from the SABS, but in complex cases the State may incur very considerable costs. Secondly, the concept of 'rendering water less fit than' clearly presupposes knowledge of the quality of the water before it was polluted. The effort that has to be made is indeed great but in recent prosecutions where the department exerted itself to present a good case, the

[148] See also Rabie 'Legal remedies for environmental protection' 1972 *CILSA* 252–4.

result was positive and the effect of the wide publicity given to convictions has proved to be an even stronger deterrent than the actual penalty imposed. Finally, the acute shortage of public prosecutors in the Department of Justice, and particularly those with experience in handling highly technical matters, has greatly hindered successful prosecutions in the past, although increased environmental awareness on the part of the public in general has also resulted in progress on this score.

18.9.2.4 *Definition of 'pollution'*

It is often stated that a serious shortcoming in the Water Act is that nowhere is 'pollution' adequately defined. Consequently, the Courts have to abide by the statements made in the section dealing with general pollution as practical guidelines—and these are far from satisfactory—and subsequently consider damage, or loss of enjoyment, as the overriding factors in coming to a legal decision. This again is unsatisfactory since more subtle social (public) losses must perforce be excluded from consideration and it is unfortunately these that often count most. Definitions of pollution are not lacking in foreign legislation; the following one is from Canada:[149]

'"pollution" means a *detrimental alteration or variation* of the physical, chemical, biological or aesthetic properties of the *environment* which results in or may result from an act or omission over which the legislature has jurisdiction and "pollute" has the same meaning.'

The italicized words and phrases are also defined. It is comforting to note that South Africa is not alone in the difficulty of formulating an equitable public policy on water pollution legislation. In Britain, formal legal power to control pollution was vested in water authorities only by the Water Act of 1973, reinforced by the Control of Pollution Act of 1974, and matters are currently complicated in the extreme by the conflicting (or impossible) requirements of a host of EEC directives. In the United States, the implementation of the famous PL 96-500 has become a source of confusion between federal, state, local and private authorities. It could well be that attempts to define pollution will in essence prove to be self-defeating by virtue of the fact that the phenomenon to be defined is so wide in concept that any exact definition is doomed to be incomplete. In practice, the present wording of the provision dealing with general pollution may well prove to be adequate provided the social norms of the public against the background of which court decisions are rendered are such as to result in convictions, also under circumstances where pecuniary losses did not occur.

18.9.2.5 *Some marine pollution problems*

The Dumping at Sea Control Act applies basically to South African territorial waters. It is not an offence in terms of this Act to dump outside the territorial limit, say at 13 nautical miles, although the effect on marine life may be just as profound. Nor does the Act apply to the territorial waters of Transkei. In addition, it is by no means clear whether the Act applies to internal waters as defined in the Marine Traffic Act, which includes False Bay, Saldanha Bay, Hout Bay, Knysna lagoon and others. Where legal doubt exists, the possibility of pollution increases. Apart from the fact that the London Dumping Convention prompted the promulgation of the above-mentioned Act, it also has implications for the cities of Cape Town, East London and Durban, all of which discharge raw sewage into the sea. Therefore the question arises, to what extent should the normal departmental safeguards on such discharges—embodied in exemptions approved in terms of the provisions of the Water Act dealing with industrial pollution—be related to international requirements? This question is perhaps not always taken into account in local planning.

But these are domestic matters. The parties to the above-mentioned London

[149] Environmental Protection Act of 1973, ch 6, Nova Scotia.

Convention meet in London every two years to consider what are essentially international politically controlled questions of marine pollution. These usually include scientific reports, reviews of annexures to the convention, relations with other bodies, the status of observers, technical assistance and so on. Each country has its own views. South Africa has full status (the Department of Environment Affairs sends a delegation) but it is often found expedient to adopt 'low profile' attitudes and to exercise considerable tact in the approach to the problems of others.

Another serious problem affecting water pollution control generally, and marine pollution in particular, is the difficulty of effective enforcement of the legislation in question. This is particularly evident as far as the administration of the Dumping at Sea Control Act and the Prevention and Combating of Pollution of the Sea by Oil Act is concerned.

18.9.3 Divided administrative control

A striking fact as far as water pollution control legislation is concerned is the wide variety of such legislation and the many government departments at national, provincial and local level, as well as other statutory bodies, that are involved in implementing the legislation. The legislature, at least in bygone days, appeared to pay little attention to existing legislation when framing provisions in new legislation.[150] This suggests the need for some body to co-ordinate the actions of the above-mentioned bodies, if not for efforts to consolidate the relevant legislation, and to provide for more centralized control.

As far as the administration of water pollution control is concerned, the following government departments are involved:

The Department of Agriculture administers the Conservation of Agricultural Resources Act and its supporting Sub-Division of Agricultural Land Act. The department is concerned with the use of water for agricultural purposes and the control of landfills of waterlogged agricultural land. It also possesses specified knowledge of the relationship between water quality and its use in irrigation.

The Department of Environment Affairs administers the Environment Conservation Act, the Sea Fishery Act, the Sea-Shore Act and the Dumping at Sea Control Act.

The Department of Mineral and Energy Affairs administers the Minerals Act, while the Nuclear Energy Corporation is the most important government body as regards the implementation of the Nuclear Energy Act.

The Department of National Health and Population Development administers the Health Act, the International Health Regulations Act, the Hazardous Substances Act and the Foodstuffs, Cosmetics and Disinfectants Act.

The Department of Transport administers the Prevention and Combating of Pollution of the Sea by Oil Act (together with the Department of Environment Affairs), the Merchant Shipping Act, the Marine Traffic Act, the International Convention for the Prevention of Pollution from Ships Act and the International Convention Relating to Intervention of the High Seas in Cases of Oil Pollution Casualties Act.

The Department of Water Affairs administers the Water Act, which is the most important legislation controlling pollution.

18.9.4 Future trends

Although the DWA has recognized 'a strong motivation for integrated catchment management at regional level by co-ordination of the activities of local bodies such as

---

[150] For example s 23 of the Water Act confers on the department general powers to combat water pollution, and penalties are provided in s 170 for contravention. Section 139 of the Rand Water Board Statutes (Private) Act 17 of 1950 also confers similar powers and sanctions on the Rand Water Board but in respect of its area of interest only.

irrigation boards, water boards, agricultural unions, regional development advisory committees and conservation committees under the auspices of the department',[151] there nevertheless appears to be a much greater need to accomplish river management at national level. See chapters 13 and 25.

It is suggested that until the DWA is able to persuade its neighbouring departments to join with it in the planning, leadership, organization and control of strategies for river management at national, regional and local levels, pollution of our inland and coastal waters will be exacerbated.

Taking criticism voiced against the Water Act, together with improvements suggested in *Environmental concerns in South Africa*[152] and subsequent amendments to the Water Act[153] as a baseline, it is possible, with hindsight, to compare the recommended improvements with the amendments that were in fact made. By so doing one should be in a better position to forecast trends for the future.

18.9.4.1 *Suggested improvements to the Water Act*

The following improvements to the Water Act were suggested:

(a) 'Effluent' should be defined and the definition of 'pollution' improved.
(b) The mechanisms applied to uses for industrial purposes should also be available in relation to other uses such as agricultural uses and, in particular, feedlots.
(c) More control is required over the use of private water to ensure that it is not used contrary to the public good.
(d) The powers of water courts over use for industrial purposes ought to be curtailed.
(e) The consumption of water by local authorities ought to be regarded as use for industrial purposes and controlled by permit so as to impose on such use the duties to purify the water so used and effluent to a required standard on penalty of criminal sanctions.
(f) Quantitative effluent standards should be set for each locality.
(g) The general standard for pollution requires revision and the penalties provided in the Act need to be increased considerably.

18.9.4.2 *Subsequent legislative amendments*

The following legislative amendments have been effected since 1983:

(a) A definition of 'effluent' was introduced into the Act.[154] The description of water pollution in the Act[155] was expanded.[156]
(b) Pollution of water occurring through farming operations is dealt with by the Water Act;[157] and the Act[158] was amended[159] to make it clear that the Minister may issue a permit in respect of feedlots without the necessity for a water court application. Intensive animal feeding systems have been included in the use of water for industrial purposes and now falls within the ambit of measures relating to industrial water pollution.
(c) The use of private water for industrial purposes has been made subject to the same provisions of the Act as apply to the use of public water for industrial purposes.[160] In certain circumstances a local authority is given the same authority and discretion

[151] *Management of water resources* above n 1, 6.67.
[152] Above n 77, 333–4.
[153] The Water Amendment Acts 96 of 1984, 110 of 1986, 68 of 1987, 37 of 1988 and 68 of 1990.
[154] By s 1 of Act 96 of 1984.
[155] Section 23.
[156] Section 13 of Act 96 of 1984.
[157] Section 23A.
[158] Section 11.
[159] By s 3 of Act 68 of 1990.
[160] Section 2 of Act 96 of 1984.

to control the use of private water by permit as is conferred on the Minister.[161] In this way local authorities can ensure that private water is used for the best public good.

(d) The authority of the water court is now not required in the case of the use for industrial purposes during any month of a quantity that does not exceed a quantity used by him during any month within the 12 months immediately preceding the commencement of Act 96 of 1984.[162] Nor is the permission of the water court required where the Minister is for the reasons stated or for any other reason convinced that there is sufficient public water available in a government water control area. In such circumstances he may grant permission for a quantity of water to be used within or outside that area for industrial purposes.[163]

(e) The Water Act now makes the requirements of purifying water to a standard and the penalties in connection with those requirements applicable to local authorities in the purification of effluent sent to them for processing.[164] The definition of 'use for industrial purposes' was extended to include 'any sewage system or work or any water care work'.[165] Therefore a local authority is obliged to clean the water entering its sewage works, whether produced by industrial or urban use, to the required standard and is subject to the sanctions imposed.

(f) The department's dynamic approach to quantitative effluent standards has already been dealt with.

(g) The Water Amendment Act 68 of 1987 introduced certain improvements aimed at regulating water pollution,[166] and increased the penalties for pollution.

The question remains whether these improvements have brought about better conservation of the Republic's water resources. It has been shown that the water quality in rivers deteriorates principally for two reasons.[167] The development of sewage treatment works does not always keep pace with population growth, giving rise to effluents high in plant nutrients (phosphates and nitrates). River systems, such as the Vaal, are subjected in industrial areas to heavy metal pollution, salination and sediment blanket pollution in addition to the many water-quality problems associated with eutrophication. In the case of the Vaal River both of these problems continue to increase notwithstanding regulations in terms of the special standard and the special standard for phosphate as a result of the continual recycling of return flows. The inter-basin transfers between the Assegai and Vaal rivers and the Tugela and Vaal rivers may alleviate pollution from heavy metals and salinization but could aggravate the eutrophication problem.

18.9.5 Conclusion

Where do we go from here? We should recall why water pollution control was first attempted and what was done. Water pollution control was not attempted because of the diminution in water quality by pollutive emissions, despite the fact that riparian rights derived from English common law were historically anterior to all other considerations. Pollution control was forced by considerations firstly of convenience

---

[161] In terms of s 5(2) of the Water Act: s 5 of Act 68 of 1987.

[162] Section 6 of Act 96 of 1984.

[163] Section 20 of Act 96 of 1984.

[164] Section 21(3) of the Water Act as substituted by s 11 of Act 96 of 1984.

[165] Section 1*(e)* of Act 96 of 1984.

[166] Section 1 broadened the definition of 'use for industrial purposes'; ss 4, 8, 9, 12, 14, 15 and 16 amended and improved respectively ss 5, 11, 12, 13, 22, 24 and 26 of the Water Act, while s 35 increased the penalties prescribed in s 170 of the Water Act.

[167] Heeg, Appleton, Davies, Joubert & Walmsley 'Uses of, and human impact on rivers' in O'Keeffe (ed) *The conservation of South African rivers* South African National Scientific Programmes Report no 131 (1986) 24, 28.

(the reduction of stench and the removal of waste matter by conveniently flowing rivers) and, secondly and overwhelmingly, by health considerations as the link between sanitation and public health gradually came to be recognized. It is true that in England in the 14th and 16th centuries there were royal embargoes on the discharge of contents to rivers but what sewers there were in the larger towns were expressly for the transport of surface waters and not ordure. This was changed in London in 1847 with disastrous results, such as widespread aquifer pollution and, finally, the great cholera epidemic of 1854. This epidemic forged the link of recognition between disease and water supply, referred to above, and matters were not brought under control until 1870 with regulation of abstraction and trunk sewer construction. Even as late as 1906 there were between 650 and 700 typhoid cases per 100 000 of population in Philadelphia, Pennsylvania.

The immediate improvement in cities in the incidence of waterborne disease tended to overshadow the fact that downstream river users received the full disadvantages of untreated sewage. From this outcry sprang the science of sewage purification and riverine management. The absolute baseline, then, below which no civilized country should sink, is the prevention of waterborne diseases such as cholera, dysentery and typhoid. Considerations such as aesthetics and convenience are some way above this line, and should in Third World countries, or in South Africa with its limited supply of skilled professional manpower, play little part in planning for emergencies.

It would be futile to ignore the fact that water pollution control as we know it now is a dispensable luxury in times of armed conflict. Key personnel are absent, central government is preoccupied and regional authorities concerned with directives and state priorities. Under such circumstances, water pollution control reverts, in a semi-automatic mode, to the health aspect of civil defence and must be subject to its needs. The prime need is the avoidance of infection and the preservation of water for abstraction for drinking purposes: this need not be 'pure' but it must be treatable. For this reason, the regionalization of services is a welcome step forward, as is their division into essential (hard) and ethnically based (soft) components. In times of national emergency and with very restricted civil manpower, the ability of water services to 'run themselves' must not be questioned and this can be achieved more easily by the metropolitan control advocated, as well as by much reduced state requirements for standards. The future of water pollution control is, therefore, like much else in a South African context, linked to future socio-political developments and it needs strong and unequivocal legislation to determine it.

CHAPTER 19

SOLID WASTE

R LOMBARD
L BOTHA
M A RABIE

19.1 INTRODUCTION

Southern Africa is experiencing a burgeoning population growth and rapid urbanization. This, together with the need for economic growth to accommodate aspirations for an improved standard of living, tends to lead to a disproportionate escalation in the rate of waste generation. In South Africa, where unprecedented demands are being placed on available resources and the environment, a responsible waste management strategy must be implemented without delay.[1]

Waste management has become one of the more rapid developing multi-disciplinary applied sciences and offers practical, effective and often innovative solutions to many modern waste problems. Historically, the lack of a clear waste management strategy in many public and private sector organizations in the Republic has resulted in the belated discovery of the devastating effects of poor waste management on the environment.

Despite the existence of a considerable number of statutes that allude to some form of control over the production and disposal of wastes that was in line with that in the countries of the developed world, it was realized in the early eighties that more specific legislation was needed to control the waste management industry in the RSA.[2]

Although the statutory provisions for waste disposal operations have been in place for more than two years, in terms of the Environment Conservation Act 73 of 1989,[3] the necessary regulations have still to be promulgated and effectively implemented. The legislative control, together with the principles of integrated environmental management (IEM) as recommended by the Council for the Environment, should assist in preventing the expensive consequences of bad environmental planning in the waste industry. See chapters 30 and 31.

This chapter is designed to fulfil the role of a first reference and deals briefly with the principles underlying the development of waste management strategies and the practical aspects of good waste management planning and practice before dealing at greater length with urban solid waste. The management of waste is a multi-disciplinary exercise and requires the input of a team with a wide field of expertise in order to deal comprehensively with the many facets of the waste management problem.

19.2 WASTE MANAGEMENT STRATEGY FOR SOUTH AFRICA

The process of waste management may be divided into six functional components as illustrated in Figure 19.1.

---

[1] Lombard 'Rotating the cube. Environmental strategies for the 1990s' 1990 (April) *IPSA Issue Focus:* The rape of the land—society's waste stream 73–6.

[2] Lord, Ahrens, Tworeck & Rabie 'Solid waste' in Fuggle & Rabie (eds) *Environmental concerns in South Africa* (1983) 388.

[3] Sections 20 and 24.

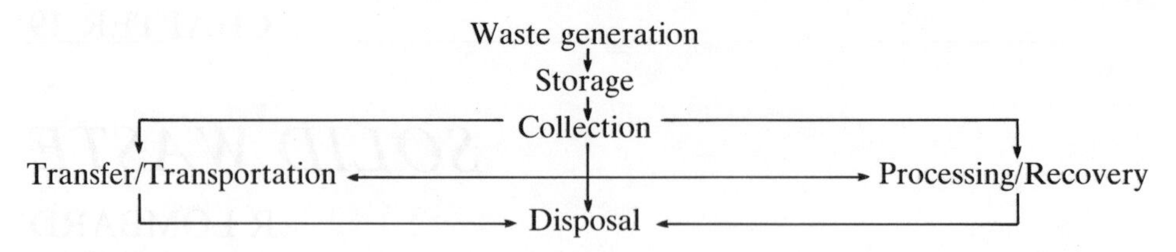

Figure 19.1 The Tchobanoglous[4] model of the waste management process.

The waste management process takes place within a complex milieu of ever-changing economic, social, political and biotic factors, all of which have to be taken into account in the development of any waste management strategy. The term *waste management strategy* implies a holistic approach to waste management where waste is dealt with in an environmentally responsible way from its generation to its ultimate disposal. The formulation of a waste management strategy should not be based on crisis management, although allowance must be made for this. It should be the implementation of a logical and systematic discipline which has considered all appropriate alternatives and in which all sectors co-operate in an informed and responsible way to arrive at the best practicable environmentally acceptable option for the disposal of any given waste.

Non-waste technology provides the point of departure in the development of any waste management strategy where the fundamental principle is waste avoidance or waste minimization wherever possible. Every activity has its associated wastes, but in every economically possible way the volume of the waste stream must be minimized, be it by recycling, resource recovery, incineration, biological pretreatment, or compaction on a landfill site.

Public relations is an important but often neglected element in the effective implementation of any waste management strategy. This must be ongoing and aimed at every level of government and all sectors of the population. The more informed people are, the greater the opportunity for co-operation and tolerance among the various sectors of society.

Logistics is associated with the diversity of options with respect to containers, vehicles and machines available today for the collection and transport of wastes. There are systems suitable for services run by the smallest operator through to those handling urban solid wastes for metropolitan regions. A waste management strategy should specify the most appropriate collection and transport system for any given situation.

Landfill is invariably the method of disposal for virtually all wastes and the strategy must specify requirements to be met in the selection of landfill sites, the licensing requirements and operating standards for landfill sites and a code of ethics to ensure minimal adverse environmental impacts. Provision should also be made for the enforcement of acceptable standards, the introduction of incentives (for instance, reduced transport rates for recycled materials) as well as education at all levels as to the significance of the strategy.

Training of personnel involved in managing and handling wastes must take place so that these persons are kept up to date with developments in the industry.

Applied research and development and appropriate technology transfer must be encouraged to enable the waste management industry in South Africa to keep abreast of developments in other countries.

Informal urbanization contributes to the degradation of the environment around major conurbations. Informal settlements in areas such as the Cape Flats, the Durban Functional Region and the PWV will have an increasingly negative impact on the

[4] *Solid wastes engineering principles and management issues* (1977).

environment as the population densities increase. Particular attention must be paid to the management of wastes in informal settlements.

Strategy implementation must be managed: the question of who is to formulate, implement and enforce the strategy arises. Waste management budgets are neglected in most organizations, hence the available funds are seldom adequate. There is a shortage of skilled workers in the industry and waste managers with an overall grasp of the subject are rare. The Institute of Waste Management (Southern Africa) has the expertise and representation to play an important role, but ultimately any progress will depend on the availability of funds and manpower to implement the strategy.

Obsolescence of strategies is a reality. An up to date database is needed to identify trends, so that incipient problems may be identified and proactively managed.

The *challenge* to the waste manager and legislator alike is effectively to implement the best practical environmentally acceptable option (BPEO) or the best available techniques not entailing excessive costs (BATNEEC).[5]

19.3 WASTE GENERATION AND CLASSIFICATION

A database is fundamental to the development of any waste management strategy. The Foundation for Research Development and the CSIR, briefed by the Department of Environment Affairs, are making a concerted effort to establish a waste database. This work will provide accurate figures on quantities and types of wastes generated by the various sectors of South African society.

All waste producers and waste management organizations should contribute to this national waste database and should accurately monitor the types and quantities of wastes produced and handled. This data must be made available to the authorities on request.

The extent of waste generation in any given area may be deduced by evaluating the industries present. A waste stream investigation is facilitated by the use of a questionnaire or an interview-type survey which evaluates the following: raw materials, processes, products, by-products, contaminants in the waste stream, quantities, and other occasional wastes.

The process of evaluating waste requires its classification. In some cases the wastes produced are highly specific to the industries concerned and the presence of these materials in effluent can be diagnostic. It is necessary to evaluate the following aspects: storage, collection, pretreatment, transportation, treatment, and disposal.

The classification of waste is a complex subject and there are many different classification systems in use internationally. In the text below only urban solid wastes (USW) is discussed. Nuclear wastes, mining wastes and power generation wastes have not been included as these have been specifically excluded from the jurisdiction of the Environment Conservation Act.

USW is classified in broad terms as follows:

- Inert wastes: builders' rubble, tyres, cover and spoil. These wastes are not regarded as exerting a negative impact on the environment unless they are disposed of in unacceptable disposal sites.
- General wastes: household, commercial, and garden refuse as well as inert industrial wastes. These wastes can exert a negative impact when the products of their breakdown, including leachate, pollute the environment.
- Special wastes: that group of wastes which, because of quantity, concentration or physical, chemical or infectious characteristics may cause ill-health or increased mortality or may adversely affect the environment. They may also pose an immediate or potential threat when improperly treated, stored, transported,

[5] Rossi House of Commons (UK) session *Environment committee's second report on toxic waste* (1989).

disposed of or otherwise managed, and exhibit the characteristics of corrosivity, toxicity, inflammability, volatility, explosivity or radioactivity.

It is clear that considerable care must be exercised in the management of special wastes and the emphasis in the definition is placed firmly on management (or mismanagement).

The RSA Code is based on a modification of the International Maritime Dangerous Goods Code (IMDG). The IMDG Code was developed to control the international transportation of pure hazardous substances and is based on the chemical attributes and toxicity of the substances. It proved to be a good starting point for the development of the RSA Code, which is illustrated in Table 19.1.[6] The notable modifications to the IMDG classification system which have led to the RSA Code for special or notifiable wastes are the inclusion of ecotoxicity, environmental fate, and the provision that has been made for mixtures of wastes (because all wastes are mixtures of substances in various proportions).

TABLE 19.1

The basic RSA Code for special or notifiable wastes.

CLASS 1	Explosives
CLASS 2	Gases compressed or under pressure
CLASS 3	Flammable liquids
CLASS 4	Flammable solids or substances
CLASS 5	Oxidizing substances
CLASS 6	Poisonous (toxic) and infectious substances
CLASS 7	Radioactive substances
CLASS 8	Corrosives
CLASS 9	Miscellaneous dangerous substances
CLASS 10	Ecologically hazardous substances
CLASS 11	Reactive mixes

The classes of dangerous substances are further divided into hazard groups and are allocated subsidiary risk characteristics, aquatic toxicity ratings, threshold limit values, biodegradability ratings, and disposal criteria such as pretreatment and incineration.

The mass or volume of the dangerous substance in the waste stream is also evaluated in this system where, for instance, an accidental spillage above a certain specified limit must be reported to the relevant authorities.

All materials that have a mutagenic, carcinogenic, teratogenic or toxic effect on human beings or any other life form are also assessed separately.

19.4 WASTE STORAGE

Waste-handling systems are often the most poorly planned feature of any development, whether it be a factory, an office block or an apartment building.

On-site handling refers to activities associated with the management of solid wastes until they are placed in the storage containers used for collection. Factors to consider when designing on-site waste storage and processing systems are: type of collection system; the economic radius of operation, and the on-site processing method to recover material, reduce volume and treat the waste.

[6] Bredenhann & Malan 'The adaptation of waste disposal criteria to the International Maritime Dangerous Goods Code in order to harmonise control measures relating to dangerous substances' *Proceedings of the Institute of Waste Management (SA) Transvaal Branch seminar on waste management in South Africa* (27–28 September 1989).

Most on-site handling is unfortunately not planned and usually evolves to meet the crises that arise from time to time in the processes that they are designed to serve.

19.5 WASTE COLLECTION

The planning of domestic waste collection has evolved along with the development of modern infrastructure and includes the consideration of: collection vehicle systems; manpower; collection routes; public health by-laws and regulations, and aesthetics.

Industrial waste collection and storage has been highly mechanized because of the bulk materials handling problems created by industrial wastes. Factors that must be considered in the choice and siting of an industrial waste collection system include: the type of container and size; the transport and collection vehicle system; manpower; space constraints and internal logistics peculiar to the premises producing the waste; public health by-laws and regulations, and aesthetics.

As Table 19.2 illustrates, containerized waste storage relates strongly to the collection system selected, which, in turn, relates to the characteristics of the waste to be handled, its classification, compactability, density and quantity.

TABLE 19.2
Storage and collection systems.

Waste	*Storage*	*Transport*
Bulk, moderate volume liquids and pumpable sludges not acceptable to sewer	Tanks and sumps	Tanker, Roll-on, roll-off (RORO) tanker (10 m^3) Super Sucker (7 m^3)
Small volumes of more viscous liquids and sludges	210 ℓ drums and sludge containers (6,5 m^3)	Skiploader
High density and low bulk	From 6,5 m^3 to 10 m^3 skip containers	Skiploader
High bulk, compactable and low volume	240 ℓ to 7 m^3 containers	Rear-end loader (RL); Side loader (SL); Front-end loader (FEL)
High bulk, not compactable and high volume	30 m^3 open containers	RORO
High bulk, compactable and high volume	Static compaction for industrial wastes (11–27 m^3 containers) Transfer stations for domestic waste	RORO
Domestic waste	From 90 ℓ bin to 240 ℓ polycart	REL, SL, FEL, tip pack or other

19.6 WASTE TRANSFER/TRANSPORTATION

There are various types of transfer stations. The capacity requirements, materials handling system, vehicles, containers and the nature of the waste are important in the design of a transfer station. The transport modes, ie rail, road, pneumatic, water, and the location of the transfer station must also be considered.

In the transportation and transfer of waste, regionalization (at local-government as well as national level) must be considered. The situation is made more complex through the influence of other logistic constraints on the selection of an appropriate waste management strategy. Taking economic operating radius as an example:

- Tractor/trailer operations are cost effective only over an operating radius of 5 km.
- Tip pack units with little compaction and hence sub-optimal payloads are cost effective only over a radius of up to 15 km.
- The rear end loader mobile compaction vehicle, depending on body size (viz 10 to 19 m^3), gives excellent compaction to the extent that special dispensation has been sought because these vehicles are always overloaded in relation to the bridge formula. The main reason for this state of affairs is the considerable overhang of the tailgate mechanism beyond the load-bearing axles. The newer Rotopress type machines are not overloaded because they have a much better mass distribution. These vehicles operate efficiently within a 30 km radius.
- The side loader mobile compaction vehicle is somewhat less efficient as a compactor than the rear end loader, but usually has a larger body which is lighter in relation to the payload carried and is legal in terms of roads ordinances. The maximum operating radius is 30 km.
- The front end loader mobile compaction vehicle is much the same as the side loader, but this machine is used almost exclusively for industrial waste in developed countries, where its excellent productivity makes it highly competitive. These vehicles do not violate axle-loading constraints when correctly loaded and it is possible for a good driver to operate this vehicle on his own, which results in labour savings. Its operating radius is 30 km.
- Roll-on roll-off rigid vehicle and transfer trailer and truck tractor haulage vehicles operate efficiently up to a radius of 90 km and beyond.

The transfer and transportation of hazardous wastes is a separate and highly specialized subject where the Hazchem signs and handling procedures apply.

19.7 REDUCTION POTENTIAL AND DISPOSAL OPTIONS

19.7.1 Goals

On-site processing and the sorting of waste at source have the following goals: recovery of usable material; volume reduction; treatment of the waste in order to transform it so as to facilitate cheaper transport and disposal (e g processing and recovery—chemical, biological); isolation (fixation, encapsulation); destruction (incineration), and landfill.

Once a waste database has been established, a number of disposal options are available. The ultimate choice or combination of choices must meet BPEO criteria. The application of the IEM method will result in similar choices to those resulting from the application of BPEO criteria.

19.7.2 Waste disposal options

These include any or all of the following:

19.7.2.1 *Thermal treatment*

This consists of various methods of heat treatment of wastes and includes the following:

Incineration, the thermal destruction of waste.

Low-technology incineration is based on the controlled open burning of small daily inputs (5–10 tons or 40 m^3 per day) at small waste-disposal sites. Trench and fill operations are generally adequate provided that the burned residues are well covered.

Volume reduction is achieved by the burning of the waste and the manual compaction of the residue. The burning of putrescible waste helps to control odours and pests on a small scale. This option, though still widely practised, is becoming increasingly unacceptable to the general public.

High-technology incineration may use purpose-built equipment such as double-chamber incinerators, rotary kilns, fluidized bed combustors, plasma arc furnaces or even mobile incinerators, and in some cases cement kilns are also used.

The benefits of high-technology incineration are the reduction of waste volumes (which conserves landfill airspace), the reduction in transport costs, and the destruction of intractible wastes. The disadvantages include the high cost of the incinerator and of sophisticated gas cleaning and monitoring equipment.[7] The record of municipal solid waste incinerators as producers of dioxin, heavy metal fallout, sulphur and nitrogen oxides as well as chlorine-containing pollutants in the 1970s precipitated considerable research into the control of gaseous emissions, and pollution associated with incinerator ash, fly ash and the scrubbing liquors. Strictly controlled and monitored high-technology incineration may be environmentally safe but there is always the risk that a point source of pollution may be converted into a general source of pollution through stack fallout.[8]

Incineration has a place in waste management strategies for the treatment of organic chemical wastes (e g DDT) and infectious wastes from hospitals, clinics and doctors' rooms where the high costs associated with the process and its control are justified.[9] Relatively few incinerators currently operate in South Africa.

Pyrolysis of wastes[10] is the heating of waste material in an oxygen deficient atmosphere in order to convert the waste, by processes of thermal cracking and condensation, into gaseous, liquid, and solid fractions which may be used as energy sources. This is not yet proven technology.

Refuse-derived fuel (RDF) and waste-derived fuel (WDF) are based on the recovery of thermal energy from the incineration of USW. WDF is unprocessed USW which is burned as a fuel, whereas RDF is the result of processing USW to extract the combustible fraction which is pelletized, briquetted or incinerated as a finely divided fluidized fuel. Gaseous emissions and ash residues can pose a problem when certain household hazardous wastes find their way into the domestic waste stream. These processes are used in Europe where district heating schemes are viable.[11]

19.7.2.2 *Isolation from the environment*

The definition of the process is largely self-explanatory and includes a number of methods of dealing with intractible wastes that are not amenable to thermal treatment or physico-chemical methods. These include the following:

---

[7] Du Plessis & Nero 'Can privatisation work?' 1991 (1) *Resource J of Waste Management.*

[8] *Waste management and research* (1987).

[9] Lubie 'Bio-hazardous waste management' *Proceedings of the international conference on waste management in the nineties* 10th Congress of the Institute of Waste Management (SA) (1990) 121–43.

[10] Perry, Green & Maloney *Perry's chemical engineers' handbook* (50 ed, 1984).

[11] Stronach 'Refuse-to-energy. A proposed Department of Energy Assessment of novel combustion technology' 1989 (79) *J of the Institute of Wastes Management* 276–7.

Encapsulation involves the sealing of selected wastes in 30 MPa reinforced concrete. This method is currently used in South Africa to deal with wastes which cannot be safely landfilled, e g PCBs. The method was specified by the Pollution Control Division of the Department of Water Affairs in co-operation with Waste-Tech (Pty) Ltd. Encapsulation offers an alternative to incineration but is also relatively costly.

Stabilization, solidification and chemical fixation of wastes involve the blending of selected wastes with fly ash or other pozzolanic material, or vitrification under high voltage. The residue or encapsulated waste which has become unreactive and therefore isolated from the environment is then landfilled in a Class I waste-disposal facility. Chemical fixation is successfully employed by one contractor in the Republic using locally developed technology.[12]

19.7.2.3 *Recycling/resource recovery*

This traditionally involves the recovery of plastics, glass, paper, cardboard, metal and rubber from the waste stream. However, the recovery of chemicals should also be part of any waste management strategy. The recovery of these materials will achieve significant volume reduction (on average up to 30–40 per cent of domestic refuse), but should be economically viable and produce marketable goods.[13]

19.7.2.4 *Physico-chemical treatment*

The processes represented here include polymerization, reduction, oxidation, neutralization, adsorption and precipitation reactions which are all employed in processes that are designed to render wastes compatible for co-disposal in a landfill-based method of waste disposal.

19.7.2.5 *Biological treatment/Bioremediation*

A rapidly growing field of research is bioremediation technology, initiated in the late eighties. Many well-established waste-treatment methods already exploit the adaptability of microbial populations to a wide variety of organic substrates, as well as their ability to multiply under favourable conditions.[14] These include: composting (an aerobic process); sewage and waste-water treatment, activated sludge, rotary biological contactors (aerobic and anaerobic); landfarming (aerobic), e g petroleum wastes; clean-ups (aerobic and anaerobic), e g oil spills, and contaminated groundwater; and landfill—effectively, a very large anaerobic bioreactor.

19.7.2.6 *Landfill and disposal*

Most of the options discussed above result in residues or discards which will require ultimate disposal. Landfill-based disposal is currently the most cost-effective method and still appears to be the most forgiving of all the established disposal methods.[15]

A landfill which is well designed and managed can operate with minimal adverse environmental impacts and, as a bioreactor, can produce utilizable landfill gas. Thus it is inherently the most appropriate method for a developing economy such as that of the Republic. However, as suitable sites for landfill operations become scarcer and

[12] Lombard 'Hazardous waste' *Proceedings of the business programme, pollution and the quality of life workshop* Durban (1–4 June 1990).

[13] *World action for recycling materials and energy from rubbish* (Warmer) bulletin (several issues).

[14] Lawson & Alston *UK Department of Energy landfill microbiology R & D workshop* (November 1989).

[15] Knox 'The Pitsea experience' *Proceedings of the international conference of the Institute of Waste Management (SA)* 9th Congress (1988).

therefore more costly, the more expensive disposal options will become relatively more attractive.

A sanitary landfill is not a dump site. It is a scientifically selected, designed, engineered and managed refuse-disposal operation where the daily input of waste is spread, compacted and covered with soil to a pre-planned development programme. The development programme specifies the types of wastes that are acceptable and those that are unacceptable to the site and also the way in which the site will be managed.

19.8 LANDFILL SITE CLASSIFICATION, SELECTION AND DESIGN

19.8.1 Site classification

Waste disposal sites are classified according to the permeability of the underlying strata, whether naturally occurring or engineered, and the types of wastes which they may safely receive.

All landfill-based disposal technology employs varying degrees of co-disposal whether this is planned or inadvertent. Co-disposal is generally defined as the controlled disposal of special wastes with general wastes.

19.8.1.1 *Class I sites*

These are containment sites which accept special wastes requiring containment because they cannot be safely disposed to Class II landfill sites; other special wastes which may be safely bioremediated when co-disposed with general USW; and residues from pre-treatment processes that have rendered special wastes compatible with the other wastes already disposed of in the site.

The basic strategy underlying these containment facilities is the isolation of waste and its degradation products from the environment. These facilities rely on the underlying low-permeability soils and weathered rock strata, in addition to engineered impervious barriers such as geomembrane or soil/bentonite liners. The underlying unsaturated zone should have permeabilities in the range of $k \leq 10^{-6}$ to 10^{-8} cms^{-1} and an appropriate thickness.

Where natural materials are used, considerable care must be taken in the evaluation of the suitability of the strata. The macro-permeability and the micro-permeability must be evaluated. The materials that are selected must be compatible with the waste that will be disposed of in the site. An engineered soil/bentonite liner may be preferable to a geomembrane liner, depending on the nature of the waste that must be contained.

Where synthetic materials are used, e g low-permeability geomembrane liners, these will have a thickness of at least 2 000 microns and a permeability of $k \leq 10^{-28}$ cms^{-1}. Selection of the lining material is important as some waste materials or their degradation products will attack many of the lining materials that are commonly available. The associated damage will severely curtail the life of the liner and compromise the environmental safety of the site.

The experience of landfill engineers in the United States and elsewhere suggests that there is no real substitute for suitable geology and hydrogeology, hence landfill sites should be established in areas where these site attributes are suitable. In practice, a combination of liner and low-permeability strata effectively contains both the waste and the leachate in the site.

Two types of Class I site are distinguished, namely:

- Containment lagoons—for the storage of liquid and sludge monotypic pre-treated chemical wastes, which are typical of chemical industry applications.
- Containment landfills—where dry intractible wastes, sludges and limited volumes of liquids are co-disposed with general USW.

Containment landfills are easier to rehabilitate physically and aesthetically than containment lagoons because of the properties of the landfilled solid waste. Class I sites must always be isolated from the environment even after operations have ceased and care should be taken to ensure that this is noted on title deeds. The Love Creek Canal disaster in the United States was largely attributed to the construction of houses and a school on top of a containment site that had been closed some years previously.

19.8.1.2 *Class II sites*

These waste disposal facilities are licensed and designed to accept domestic, trade and general industrial wastes. The unsaturated attenuation zone below the site must have a permeability of $k \leq 10^{-5}$ cms^{-1} and be deep enough effectively to contain the degradation products of the wastes. Many of the principles applied to containment sites also apply in the case of Class II sites.

Two types of Class II site are distinguished, namely:

- Class II co-disposal sanitary landfill sites—in which municipal solid waste is co-disposed with certain industrial wastes of specified chemical nature.
- Class II domestic sanitary landfill sites—which accept domestic waste, garden refuse and commercial wastes. Industrial wastes requiring special treatment or handling may not be accepted at these sites.

19.8.1.3 *Class III & Class IV sites*

These are sites where the waste is in contact with surface water or groundwater.

Class III sites are those where the waste comes into contact with the natural water table during the wet-season elevation of the water table. During the dry season the water table is lowered but a characteristic pulsed groundwater pollution plume becomes established downstream of such a site. These sites are typically found in vleis, pans and other seasonal wetlands.

Class IV sites are those where the waste is continuously in contact with the water table and well-developed continuous groundwater pollution plumes become established downstream of such sites. These sites are typically found in estuaries, permanent wetlands and some quarries.

Class III and IV sites are being used as disposal sites in South Africa, but this practice is environmentally unacceptable and such sites should be avoided for landfill. They should be closed and rehabilitated as soon as practically possible.

19.8.2 Site selection

The selection of waste disposal sites is a complex process in which many factors must be considered before a final selection can be made. Many potential sites may be eliminated through the early identification of unavoidable shortcomings.

19.8.2.1 *Legal requirements*

The legal requirements in respect of waste disposal facilities must be clearly understood prior to embarking on the complex investigation needed to identify the most suitable sites. The main points that require attention are the following:

- Alienation of land-use—Department of Regional and Land Affairs
- Conservation of agricultural resources—Department of Agriculture
- Public health impacts and air pollution—Department of National Health and Population Development
- Environmental conservation—Department of Environment Affairs
  - Water pollution—Department of Water Affairs and Forestry

- Regional and local authority controls—regional services councils and joint services boards, tribal authorities, cities, towns etc.

19.8.2.2 *Environmental impact assessment*

The Environment Conservation Act may require the completion of an environmental impact control report (EICR) to ensure that *all* the environmental impacts associated with the development of the site are investigated in order to ensure that environmental degradation is averted. See chapters 7, 30 and 31.

The large private waste disposal contractors and most of the larger local authorities are demonstrating corporate social responsibility by pro-actively adopting and voluntarily enforcing these regulations in order to ensure that the transition to the final application of the Environment Conservation Act is as smooth as possible and that the local environments and communities are adequately protected.

The EICR forms the basis of application of the IEM philosophy in waste management and is designed to be used as an iterative document subject to frequent updating. The updating takes place by means of a feedback loop that identifies deficiencies in the original plans and improvements are driven by the implementation of the findings of periodic environmental impact audits of site operations. The selection of a waste disposal site depends very much on the outcome of the investigation under the following headings:[16]

19.8.2.3 *Site selection criteria*

(a) Description of the proposed site

Locality
Access
Present land-use of the site and surrounding areas
Rare, vulnerable and endangered flora and fauna or ecosystem/habitat
Historical or archaeological significance.

(b) Need for development

Overview of existing and projected USW disposal
The Regional significance of the site
Alternatives
Cost implications.

(c) Description of site conditions

General topography
Ecological processes
Visibility
Social context
Legal constraints
Geology
Geohydrology and hydrology
Rainfall and wind
Infrastructure.

(d) Site development proposals

Types of wastes and volumes, ie the waste database
Phasing and duration of the project
Screening and landscaping requirements.

---

[16] Beaumont 'Environmental study and its relevance to the planning, approval and management of waste-disposal sites' *Proceedings of the international conference of the Institute of Waste Management (SA)* 9th Congress (1988).

(e) *Impact of development proposals and mitigating measures*

Nature of impacts
Operational controls and procedures
—Leachate control
—Odour control
—Aesthetics
—Traffic
—Noise
—Dust
—Pests
Public involvement
—Proximity to residential areas
—Attitudes and perceptions
—Public relations
—Planned use after project completion
Management proposals
—Staff
—Equipment
—Landfill operations
—Monitoring requirements
Data limitations and constraints.

19.8.2.4 *Site design*

Detailed site design guidelines are beyond the scope of this chapter and it is recommended that consultants competent in the field of waste management be employed to carry out this work.[17]

The consultants will develop the design through a thorough understanding of site attributes (geology, hydrogeology, and topography, including drainage axes and water courses, etc); site planning (boundaries of the property, location of site facilities, site infrastructure, site preparation, including lining systems designed to be compatible with the wastes to be handled in the site, stormwater control, and leachate management); implications of site closure, and final rehabilitation plans.

19.8.2.5 *Operational guidelines*

These form the basis of the day-to-day operation and should accompany the permit application and design documentation. Site management and operation are, in many ways, as critical to the success of a project as site design and must be incorporated into the conditions for the operation of the site.

The operational guidelines relate very strongly to the concerns discussed in the text above and will include the following:

- Waste specifications in respect of wastes that are site specific. Acceptable wastes and unacceptable wastes will be specified. Whether or not the following wastes will be accepted, and how they will be treated, needs to be specified: aqueous inorganics; acids/alkalis; heavy metal cations; cyanides; redox compounds; oil/aqueous separation and recycling of solvents and oils, and toxic organics.
- Leachate management and the water balance. Despite good design, engineering and operational strategy, waste disposal sites will leach after heavy rainfall, as Table 19.3 indicates.

[17] Blight 'Draft guidelines: the design of sanitary landfills for domestic waste to minimize groundwater pollution' *Proceedings of the first methane from landfill summer school* Chemistry Department, Rhodes University (1990).

TABLE 19.3

Groundwater monitoring data in a water-surplus region of southern Africa following heavy rain (mg ℓ^{-1}).

Constituent	August 1981 (before rain)	October 1981 (after rain)
pH	7,0	6,9
COD	100,0	1 400,0
Chlorine	284,0	2 769,0
Nitrogen	0,9	75,0
Cadmium	—	$\leq$ 1,0
Total Chrome	—	—
Copper	—	0,7
Total Iron	—	15,5

The August result meets the accepted revised general standard, whereas the October result (after 120 mm of rain) shows clear evidence of a developing leachate profile in the order of magnitude increase in most of the parameters. If leaching is allowed to continue unabated because of poor landfill management, the situation will eventually reach that reflected in Table 19.4.

TABLE 19.4

A comparison of landfill leachate and raw sewage typical of southern Africa (mg ℓ^{-1}).

Constituent	Leachate	Raw Sewage
pH	4,9–8,4	6,8–7,5
COD	246,0–75 000,0	72,0–1 500,0
Chlorine	116,0–2 096,0	30,0–79,0
Nitrogen	0,2–1 106,0	1,6–33,0
Cadmium	0,003–17,0	0,004–0,016
Total Chrome	0,03–0,18	0,05–0,13
Copper	0,03–0,75	0,03–0,11
Total Iron	2,0–1 000,0	0,35–5,6

Note that leachate is more polluting than raw sewage with respect to chemical oxygen demand (COD) and heavy metals.

- Good site design, engineering, construction supervised by a civil engineer and quality assurance are the primary factors in environmentally sound landfills. They ensure that leachate is contained, captured and not allowed to disperse freely into the environment.
- Good landfill management is the second major factor associated with environmentally sound landfills. It is necessary to manage the landfill process in order to minimize the negative impacts. A shortage of manpower trained and experienced in waste management exists in the Republic.

Leachate pollution of surface water and groundwater is one of the most serious problems facing landfill-based technology. The control of the formation of leachate is critical to the management of the problem. Such control is carried out through the application of water balance[18] calculations and ongoing rehabilitation systems of landfill as llustrated in Figure 19.2.

The ongoing rehabilitation system of landfill minimizes the areas of uncovered waste that are exposed to rainfall through the systematic covering of landfilled waste.

If the leachate control system should fail or the site lining become impaired, a number of attenuation mechanisms form the last line of defence in reducing the impact of the leachate on the water regime. Attenuation was at one stage, in the history of the development of landfill design, the only basis for site design when all sites were managed on the dilute and disperse philosophy.[19] Although this design philosophy has largely been discredited in favour of the containment philosophy, recent research into biodegradation in waste has confirmed the existence of the following attenuation mechanisms:

In the strata beneath the base of the site—

Physical —filtration
—dilution/dispersion
Biological —biodegradation
—cell synthesis
Geochemical —complexation
—acid/base reaction
—redox
—precipitation
—ion exchange
—adsorption/absorption.

In the waste itself—
Physical —as above
Biological —aerobic biodegradation
—anaerobic biodegradation
Chemical —as for Geochemical above.

Attenuation mechanisms taking place in the waste itself are regarded as being more important in the bioremediation of the wastes and so-called biorector landfill sites are currently being designed to enhance the biodegradation of wastes in the landfill site and generate landfill gas (45–65 per cent methane) for use as a low-grade fuel in the provision of thermal and electrical energy.[20]

- Leachate disposal may be effected in a number of ways. In very small sites slow migration is promoted through specially designed drainage systems. In larger sites leachate is best impounded and discharged to sewer. In those cases where the sewer is not conveniently located or unable to accept the leachate, recirculation is practised. However, it should be noted that the recirculation of an anaerobic liquor such as leachate will result in the propagation of unacceptable odours if residences are in close proximity to the site.[21]
- Security is a neglected but important subject, because a good security service keeps unauthorized people off the site. Injury to or death of members of the general public is always a serious consideration to contractors and local authorities. The security service should monitor vehicle movements and control waste inputs.

[18] *Waste management* Paper no 26 Department of the Environment UK (1989).

[19] Sumner *Final report of the policy review committee of the co-operative programme of research on the behaviour of hazardous wastes in landfill sites* (UK) (1978).

[20] *Waste management* Paper no 27 Department of the Environment (UK) (1990).

[21] 'The treatment of leachate from landfill sites' 1984 (4) *County Surveyor's Society Report.*

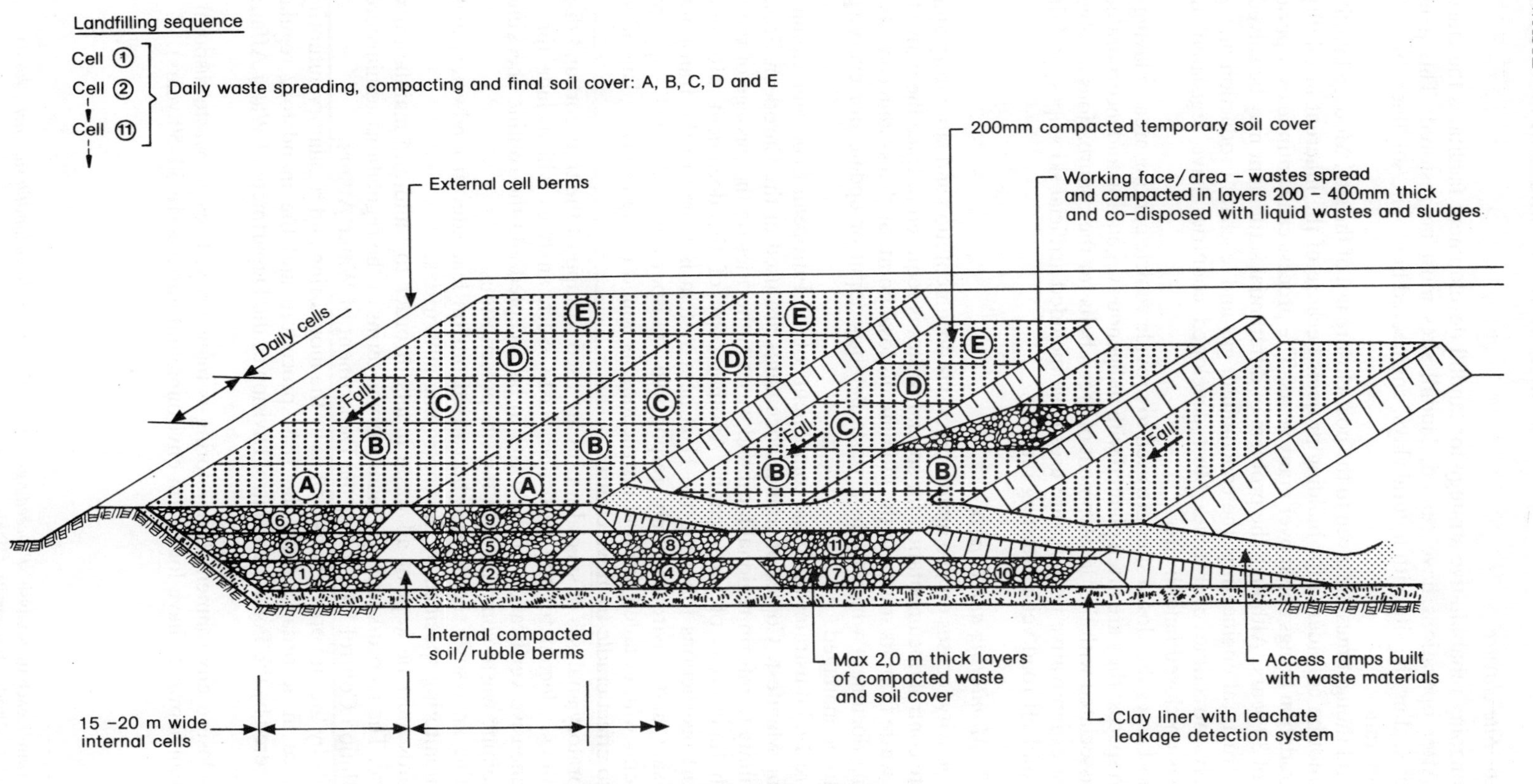

Figure 19.2 Ongoing rehabilitative landfill.

19.8.2.6 *Site closure*

An ongoing rehabilitative strategy for landfill development facilitates the closure of sites. After operations have ceased, landfill sites must be restored. This generally involves sealing the site with natural clays, engineered bentonite/soil liners or synthetic geomembranes.

Careful thought must be given to the post-closure use of the site. Modern landfill sites should not be considered for building projects because of the inherent instability that biodegradation brings about over many years. The process can continue over periods in excess of 30 years. Although the problem of differential settlement may be solved with sound structural engineering, the concomitant gas and leachate production may prove relatively intractible over time. Most developed countries have legislated against buildings on closed landfill sites.

In most cases the closed sites are used to provide vehicle parking areas, playing fields or open spaces; they are often planted with indigenous vegetation and incorporated into parks associated with the development of green belts for the conurbations involved. In some cases innovative post-closure uses have included artificial ski slopes, golf driving ranges and off-road vehicle-testing ranges.

19.8.2.7 *Monitoring and control*

This activity focuses on two major topics, viz documentation and laboratory analysis.

Waste control documentation for special wastes is required to trace the path of each special waste from its source to the ultimate disposal point. Such a system consists of an initiating document which forms a waste database input or update, for every special waste to be managed.

Figure 19.3 illustrates the basic components of the European Economic Community Shipping Manifest. Copies of similar documents are used in the European Economic Community to inform regional/local and waste authorities on the passage of the waste through their areas of jurisdiction. Another copy of the document with detailed transport instructions following the HazChem system is issued to the transporter to effect safe and environmentally responsible transportation. A final copy of the document, with detailed disposal instructions, is issued to the receiving landfill site in order to effect cradle-to-grave control.

Laboratory analyses of special wastes are used to support the transport and disposal precautions selected for the particular waste. Such analyses will include the initial comprehensive verification of the waste to be accepted and the routine checking that the incoming waste complies with the site prescriptions.

Routine analyses[22] should also be carried out on leachate, groundwater, and any other monitoring specified by the controlling authorities.

Records must be kept of all waste inputs in order to build and maintain a waste database. The record-keeping is mandatory in terms of the regulations administered by the Pollution Control Division of the Department of Water Affairs.

Audits by the site operator as well as by the monitoring and regulatory authority will take place in accordance with the IEM procedure and the mandatory regulations administered by the Pollution Control Division of the Department of Water Affairs and Forestry.

Post-closure environmental monitoring is mandatory, because waste disposal sites have been shown to have long-term environmental impacts (ie 30–50 years).

[22] Baldwin 'Leachate analysis' *Proceedings of the first methane from landfill summer school* Chemistry Department, Rhodes University (1990).

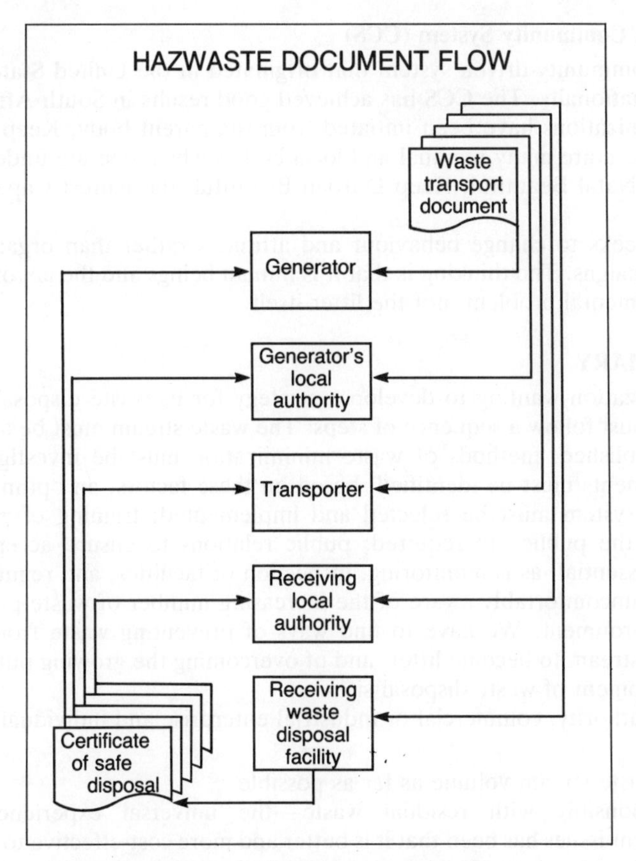

Figure 19.3 The EEC Shipping Manifest

19.9 FORMAL AND INFORMAL WASTE STREAMS

19.9.1 The problem of litter

Litter is waste that has been misplaced. It must be recovered and brought into the formal waste stream, where it can be managed with the resources that are available for the task. Local authorities have found that it costs up to three times as much to collect and dispose of litter and illegally tipped waste as it does to handle waste that is placed in the formal waste stream.

19.9.2 Informal urbanization

The litter problem is exacerbated by the rapid informal urbanization that is taking place in the environs of most of the country's development nodes.[23] It has been shown recently in South Africa that up to 5 000 people can establish themselves in an area within a fortnight.

These developments are so rapid that the provision of services, including water, sewerage and waste management, is compromised because construction cannot keep up with the demand. Funding is not available and formal planning seems to be too slow a process to keep up with the rate of urbanization.[24]

---

[23] Reilly & Van der Merwe 'Refuse collection in black urban areas' *Proceedings of the international conference on waste management in the nineties* 10th Congress of the Institute of Waste Management (SA) (1990) 284–97.

[24] *The urban edge* Issues and innovation series, World Bank (1989–90).

19.9.3 Clean Community System (CCS)

This is a community-driven system that originated in the United States and is now applied internationally. The CCS has achieved good results in South Africa and many regional organizations have been initiated from the parent body, Keep South Africa Beautiful. There are many regional and local bodies which operate under names such as Keep KwaNatal Beautiful, Keep Durban Beautiful, the Fairest Cape Association, etc.

The CCS seeks to change behaviour and attitudes rather than organizing one-off clean-up campaigns. The thinking is that it is human beings and the act of littering that are the fundamental problem, not the litter itself.

19.10 SUMMARY

Any organization wanting to develop a strategy for its waste disposal or cleansing department must follow a sequence of steps: The waste stream must be analysed and a database established; methods of waste minimization must be investigated; specific local requirements must be identified; based on these factors, an optimum collection and disposal system must be selected and implemented; training of personnel and education of the public are required; public relations to ensure acceptance of the proposals is essential, as is monitoring, inspection of facilities, and regular audits.

We are all uncomfortably aware of the increasing number of waste products in our everyday environment. We have to find ways of preventing waste from leaving the formal waste stream to become litter, and of overcoming the growing public resistance to the development of waste disposal sites.

Every local authority, commercial or industrial enterprise and individual should strive to:

- Reduce waste stream volume as far as possible.
- Deal responsibly with residual waste—the universal experience in waste-management issues has been that it is better and more cost-effective to spend money sooner rather than later. If the costs of waste disposal are built into production and development costs at the design stage of any project, the situation where millions of rands are required for clean-ups and rehabilitation can be avoided. The old adage 'prevention is better than cure' holds true.
- Be pro-active rather than reactive as regards the development and implementation of a waste management strategy. The Environment Conservation Act has already made the licensing of any waste disposal facility mandatory and the promulgation of the associated regulations governing waste disposal is imminent.
- Inform and train at all levels. The vehicles to achieve this already exist, ie the Clean Community System organizations and the Institute of Waste Management (SA).

If all local authorities, commercial and industrial enterprises and individuals were to do everything in their power to optimize their individual waste management strategies and co-operate with one another in order to find regional solutions where feasible, our environment would benefit substantially and so would our children.

19.11 WASTE CONTROL LEGISLATION

19.11.1 Introduction

For the purposes of this section, discussion is confined to solid waste on land, although it is acknowledged that water and air are also polluted by solid waste. For the latter instances of solid waste pollution reference is made to chapters 17 and 18. The subject of solid waste on land is referred to in some European countries as soil pollution, whereas it is customarily identified as solid waste management in South Africa. The parameters of the subject are somewhat diffuse on account of the overlap with air pollution and especially with freshwater and marine pollution.

Solid waste has been controlled in terms of South African legislation in a haphazard and unco-ordinated manner. A variety of Acts, ordinances, by-laws and regulations deal with certain aspects of solid waste, there being no comprehensive treatment of the subject-matter. In fact, the comprehensive report on *The situation of waste management and pollution control in South Africa*, prepared by the CSIR Programme for the Environment, for the Department of Environment Affairs during 1991 revealed that an assortment of provisions dealing with waste on land is to be found scattered among at least 37 Acts of Parliament, 16 provincial ordinances and numerous local by-laws. This legislation, which is administered by a variety of public bodies, encompasses a diversity of activities which generate waste and many different types of waste that are produced.

In the past, solid waste legislation has dealt mainly with the prohibition of littering and with refuse removal, and has been administered mainly at local government level. It has become apparent that litter and refuse form only a relatively small—albeit conspicuous—part of the problem, and that the active involvement of the provincial and central governments is necessary if the problem is to be combated in a co-ordinated and effective manner. As a result of a resolution at an Administrators' Conference during 1971, the Second Schedule to the Financial Relations Consolidation and Amendment Act 38 of 1945 was amended 'in order to confer more powers on the provinces for the passing of effective legislation against littering and other forms of environmental pollution'.[25] This was accomplished in 1973 with the addition of a paragraph to the Second Schedule.[26] Although provision was made for the transfer of legislative powers in respect of environmental pollution generally, it is clear from the abovementioned resolution that litter control was the priority.[27]

The provision enabling erstwhile provincial councils to legislate for the control of environmental pollution and defacement was contained in the Second Schedule to the Financial Relations Act 65 of 1976.[28] The national government also followed suit and during 1977 published for general information a draft bill on the disposal of containers.[29] This bill would have empowered the then Minister of Planning and the Environment to issue regulations in order to prevent environmental pollution by means of empty containers. The bill was subsequently referred to a select committee of the House of Assembly, which was then transformed into a commission of inquiry into the control of pollution by empty containers and, in fact, of littering in its wider context. This commission submitted its report during 1978[30] and, while recommending that the above-mentioned bill should not be proceeded with, it submitted its own bill on the disposal of solid waste and the combating of litter. This bill covered a much wider field than the previous bill, since it encompassed solid waste disposal and littering generally and was not confined to the disposal of containers. In terms of this bill, control would have been effected by a national council on solid waste and littering, and through regulations issued by the then Minister of Planning and the Environment.

This new bill suffered the same fate as its predecessor, however. Although the government did in principle accept the recommendation of the above-mentioned commission of inquiry,[31] it did not proceed with the recommended bill. Instead, during 1980 it published a *White Paper on a national policy regarding environmental conservation*[32] in which an Environment Conservation Act was envisaged. In the eventually promulgated Environment Conservation Act 100 of 1982, provision was

[25] *Pollution 1971* 166.
[26] Para 25.
[27] *Pollution 1971* 166–7.
[28] Paragraph 24.
[29] GN 175 of 18 March 1977.
[30] RP 121 of 1978.
[31] *White Paper on a national policy regarding environmental conservation* WPO–1980 para 4.8.
[32] WPO–1980.

made for issuing regulations in respect of solid waste control, and this provision has been carried further in the Environment Conservation Act 73 of 1989.

No attempt is made in this section to compile a comprehensive list of all the legal provisions dealing with solid waste (even if confined only to solid waste on land), although reference will be made to the most important relevant legislation. As has been pointed out, waste control legislation is not characterized by homogeneity or by comprehensive regulation of the subject-matter. Moreover, practically every local authority has promulgated legislation pertaining to waste control, if only in relation to the protection of public health.

It does seem, nevertheless, that a new direction, aimed at achieving a more comprehensive legislative treatment of solid waste control, is developing in the Environment Conservation Act of 1989. The Act, as will be shown, provides for control over waste disposal sites and for extensive waste management regulations. However, its provisions do not supersede the numerous existing provisions in other legislation.

19.11.2 Definition of waste

Perusal of the legislation identified as pertaining to urban solid waste[33] reveals that 'waste' has been described in such legislation by the use of numerous nouns. Among them are the following: 'by-product', 'carcass', 'cuttings', 'debris', 'dung', 'excrement', 'filth', 'garbage', 'litter', 'manure', 'nightsoil', 'offal', 'refuse', 'residue', 'rubbish', 'rubble', 'scrap', 'sewage', 'tailings', 'trimmings', 'waste' and 'waste products'. These nouns, however, have seldom been defined, although some of them have been subsumed under the concept of 'nuisance', which normally has been defined in general terms, encompassing many varieties of waste.[34]

The Environment Conservation Act 73 of 1989, nevertheless, now defines both the concepts of 'litter' and of 'waste'. 'Litter', the more restricted concept and, in fact, a component of the broader concept of 'waste', is defined as any object or matter discarded by the person in whose possession or control it was.[35] 'Waste' means any matter, whether gaseous, liquid or solid or any combination of these states, originating from any residential, commercial or industrial area or agricultural area identified by the Minister of Environment Affairs as an undesirable or superfluous by-product, emission, residue or remainder of any process or activity.[36] In pursuance of this power the Minister has identified[37] as an undesirable or superfluous by-product, emission, residue or remainder of any process or activity, any matter, gaseous, liquid or solid or any combination thereof, originating from any residential, commercial or industrial area, which

(a) is discarded by any person; or
(b) is accumulated and stored by any person with the purpose of eventually discarding it, with or without prior treatment connected with the discarding thereof, or
(c) is stored by any person with the purpose of recycling, re-using or extracting a usable product from such matter, excluding
  (i) water used for industrial purposes or any effluent produced by or resulting from such use which is discharged in compliance with the provisions of the Water Act 54 of 1956[38] or on the authority of an exemption granted under the

[33] See Botha *South African urban solid waste legislation and its application: proposals towards reform* (Unpublished MA thesis, University of Cape Town, 1988).
[34] For instance, see the definition of 'nuisance' in s 1, read with s 20(1)*(b)* of the Health Act 63 of 1977.
[35] Section 1(xiv).
[36] Section 1(xxii).
[37] GN 1986 of 24 August 1990.
[38] Section 21(1).

Act;[39]

(ii) any matter discharged into a septic tank or french drain sewerage system and any water or effluent contemplated by the Water Act;

(iii) building rubble used for filling or levelling purposes;

(iv) any radioactive substance discarded in compliance with the provisions of the Nuclear Energy Act 92 of 1982;

(v) any minerals, tailings, waste-rock or slimes produced by or resulting from the activities at a mine or works as defined in the Mines and Works Act 27 of 1956 (now the Minerals Act 50 of 1991); and

(vi) ash produced by or resulting from activities at an undertaking for the generation of electricity under the provisions of the Electricity Act 41 of 1987.

It is not clear

- why the Minister has not identified any matter originating from an agricultural area as undesirable or superfluous, and thus as 'waste';
- why the Minister has excluded the matter set out in subparagraphs (i) to (vi) of paragraph *(c)*;
- whether the exclusions apply to the matter which is referred to in paragraph *(c)* only or whether it is intended that they should apply to the matter referred to in paragraphs *(a)* and *(b)* also.

Further, whilst the matter referred to in subparagraphs (i), (ii), (iv) , (v) and (vi) of paragraph *(c)* may well be controlled in terms of the legislation referred to therein—and thus not require additional measures—no control appears to be in place for 'building rubble used for filling and leveling purposes' (subparagraph (iii)). The reason for the exclusion of building rubble from the provisions of the Environment Conservation Act is thus not clear.

It is submitted that the definition of 'waste' in the Environment Conservation Act, read with the notice by the Minister, requires clarification.

It should be borne in mind that what is waste to one person is a resource to another. The concept of waste is thus a subjective one. It is significant, therefore, that the CSIR in its study of waste and pollution control saw fit to formulate its own working definition of waste. The CSIR assumed it to be any substance having no perceived use for the organism or system that produces it.[40] This definition takes care of the subjective aspect and would appear to be more appropriate. Its .adoption in the Environment Conservation Act would compliment the definition of 'litter' in the Act.

19.11.3 National waste management policy

There is no national policy on waste management and pollution control. The closest the central government has come to declaring such a policy is contained in the *White Paper on a national policy regarding environmental conservation*.[41] This clearly states[42] that, in order to place the disposal of solid waste and the combating of littering on a sound basis, it will be necessary to

- co-ordinate the activities of organizations concerned with the control of solid waste and littering and the stimulation of anti-littering and anti-pollution campaigns:
- adopt measures and apply incentives to promote the re-use, recycling and reclamation of re-usable packaging material (containers), prevent the depletion of raw materials and combat the pollution of the environment;

---

[39] Section 21(4).

[40] *The situation of waste management and pollution control in South Africa* Report to the Department of Environment Affairs by the CSIR Programme for the Environment CPE 1/91 (1991).

[41] Above n 32.

[42] Para 4.8.

- apply measures and processes to regulate the production, decrease, utilization and disposal of solid waste;
- create procedures for the profitable use or re-use of urban solid waste, including its use for the generation of energy;
- establish installations, facilities and machinery to make the recovery, recycling and re-use of urban solid waste possible;
- develop methods and measures to be applied to make the sorting of urban solid waste at source possible and enforceable; and
- lay down guidelines for the evaluation of packaging material and containers.

Despite the provisions of the *White Paper*, there has to date been limited co-operation, consolidation or comprehensive planning at central or provincial government level in respect of solid waste management and legislation pertaining to it. Until recently, solid waste management in South Africa has been considered to be the function of local government. A feature of South African solid waste by-laws is that they relate primarily to the protection of public health and the prevention or combating of nuisances, as opposed to facilitating the management of solid waste.

Legislative provision for the determination of a national waste management policy seems to have been made in the Environment Conservation Act. The Act authorizes the Minister of Environment Affairs to determine the general policy to be applied with a view, inter alia, to the protection of the environment against disturbance, deterioration, defacement, poisoning or destruction as a result of man-made structures, installations, processes or products or human activities.[43] See, generally, chapter 7. No such policy has yet been determined.

19.11.4 National Legislation

19.11.4.1 *Wastes on roads*

Both the Advertising on Roads and Ribbon Development Act 21 of 1940 and the National Roads Act 54 of 1971 prohibit the leaving of any disused vehicle or machine or any rubbish or other refuse on certain roads, or within a certain distance of such roads.[44] In addition to the criminal sanction, a procedure is created to deal with the removal of discarded objects. The authority in question may remove such objects or may order that they be removed, and may recover the costs of removal from the person who deposited or left them on the road in question.[45] No time limits or formalities are prescribed in relation to the removal and disposal of the disused vehicles or machines. 'Disused vehicle or machine', 'rubbish' and 'refuse' are not defined.

The Road Traffic Act 29 of 1989 prohibits the depositing of offensive matter or other refuse from a vehicle upon a public road,[46] or the abandonment or leaving of objects on public roads which may constitute a danger.[47] It is, however, administered at provincial level and also provides for the relevant authorities to remove abandoned vehicles left on public roads.[48] At least three statutes therefore deal with abandoned vehicles on roads. The transportation of hazardous wastes, on the other hand, is discussed below.

---

[43] Section 2(1)*(c)*.
[44] Section 8(1) of Act 21 of 1940 and s 16(1) of Act 54 of 1971.
[45] Section 8(3) of Act 21 of 1940, and s 16(2) and (3) of Act 54 of 1971.
[46] Section 101(1)*(m)*.
[47] Section 113(2).
[48] Section 114.

19.11.4.2 *Wastes in protected areas*

It is an offence to dispose of solid waste in any national park,[49] state or private forest[50] or along the national hiking way system.[51] See chapter 27.

19.11.4.3 *Mine waste*

Solid waste associated with mining is controlled in terms of regulations, issued by virtue of the Mines and Works Act 27 of 1956, and now applicable in terms of the Minerals Act 50 of 1991. See chapter 15.

19.11.4.4 *Health-related wastes*

Most solid waste provisions are directly or indirectly related to the protection of public health. Among the more specific legislation is the Health Act 63 of 1977, which provides for the control of nuisances[52] and the making of regulations.[53] Moreover, the International Health Regulations Act 28 of 1974 provides that every port and airport must be provided with an effective system for the removal and safe disposal of refuse.[54]

Regulations in terms of the Animal Slaughter, Meat and Animal Products Hygiene Act 87 of 1967 deal with the methods of disposal from an abattoir.[55] The Sea-Shore Act 21 of 1935 makes provision for the regulation of deposition or discharge upon the sea-shore, or in the sea, of offal, rubbish or anything liable to be a nuisance or danger to health.[56] Finally, the Medicines and Related Substances Control Act 101 of 1965 regulates the disposal of medicines and related substances.[57]

19.11.4.5 *Littering*

The Environment Conservation Act renders it an offence to discard, dump or to leave any litter[58] on any land or water surface, street, road or site in or on any place to which the public has access, except in a container or at a place which has been specially indicated, provided or set apart for such purpose.[59] Control of littering is also regulated through local by-laws, as is explained below.

19.11.4.6 *Waste-disposal sites*

It is an offence in terms of the Environment Conservation Act to establish, provide or operate any waste disposal site[60] without a permit issued by the Minister of Water Affairs and subject to its conditions.[61] An environmental impact report may be required, but only if the Minister of Environment Affairs should declare waste disposal

---

[49] Regulation 43*(c)* GN R2006 of 6 October 1978, issued by virtue of the National Parks Act 57 of 1976. Cf also regulations 6(1)*(h)* and (34) GN R311 of 22 February 1980, issued in terms of the Lake Areas Development Act 39 of 1975.

[50] Section 75(3)*(a)*(vii) of the Forest Act 122 of 1984.

[51] Section 75(9)*(i)* of the Forest Act.

[52] Section 1 read with s 20(1)*(b)* of the Health Act 63 of 1977.

[53] Cf ch V of the Health Act.

[54] Article 14(3) of the schedule to the Act, read with s 2 of the Act.

[55] Section 38(1)*(n)*. Actually, very little waste results from abattoirs, since virtually all parts of the slaughtered animals are used.

[56] Section 10(1)*(d)*. Cf GN R2513 of 5 December 1980.

[57] Sections 23 and 35(1) (xxvA), (xxvi) and (xxviA).

[58] 'Litter' means any object or matter discarded by the person in whose possession or control it was: s 1(xiv).

[59] Section 19(1) read with s 29(3). A duty is imposed upon persons in control of places to which the public has access to ensure the availability of containers at such places: s 19(2).

[60] 'Disposal site' is defined as a site used for the accumulation of waste with the purpose of disposal or treatment of such waste: s 1(vii).

[61] Section 20(1) read with s 29(4).

as an identified activity.[62] See chapters 7 and 31. The Minister of Water Affairs may by notice in the *Government Gazette* issue directions with regard to the control and management of disposal sites.[63] Subject to the provisions of any other law, no person may discard waste or dispose of it in any other manner, except at a disposal site for which the required permit has been issued or in a manner or by means of a facility or method and subject to such conditions as the Minister of Environment Affairs may prescribe.[64]

19.11.4.7 *Waste management regulations*

The Minister of Environment Affairs may, by virtue of the Environment Conservation Act, make regulations with regard to waste management concerning a variety of aspects, inter alia the classification of different types of waste and the handling, storage, transport and disposal of such waste, the reduction of waste by modifications in the design and marketing of products, modifications to manufacturing processes and the use of alternative products, the utilization of waste by way of the recovery, re-use or processing of waste and control over the management of sites, installations and equipment used for waste disposal.[65] Such regulations have yet to be made. Nevertheless, two sets of draft regulations dealing with waste disposal were issued in terms of the Act's predecessor, the Environment Conservation Act 100 of 1982,[66] while after the expiry of two years since the promulgation of the 1989 Act, yet another set of draft regulations (dealing specifically with waste disposal site permits) was issued in terms of the latter Act.[67] One of the difficulties in providing meaningful control through the regulations proposed in the Act is that there are already many existing provisions dealing with the very aspects in respect of which regulations may be made.

19.11.4.8 *Hazardous waste*

Control over the dumping[68] and other forms of disposal of certain hazardous substances[69] may be effected through regulations made in terms of the Hazardous Substances Act 15 of 1973,[70] and administered by the Minister of National Health and Population Development. Such regulations have been issued[71] in respect of the disposal of empty containers[72] of any Group I hazardous substance.[73] Returnable containers of certain hazardous substances[74] must, before being returned, be securely closed.[75] After

[62] Section 21(2)*(i)* read with s 22(1) and (2).

[63] Section 20(5).

[64] Section 20(6). Cf GN R1481 of 28 June 1991, which contains the draft regulations relating to waste disposal site permits.

[65] Section 24.

[66] Cf GN 1549 of 12 July 1985 and GN 591 of 26 August 1988.

[67] GN R1481 of 28 June 1991.

[68] 'Dump' means deposit, discharge, spill, release or cause or permit to be deposited, discharged, spilled or released (whether or not the substance in question is enclosed in a container), in such a place, under such circumstances or for such a period that the person depositing, discharging, spilling or releasing or causing or permitting this action, may reasonably be assumed to have abandoned it: s 1 of the Hazardous Substances Act 15 of 1973.

[69] ie of any grouped hazardous substance. Cf s 2 of the Hazardous Substances Act.

[70] Section 29(1)*(a)*(vi).

[71] GN 453 of 25 March 1977 (Cf also GN R2778 of 21 December 1984 and GN R72 of 11 January 1985).

[72] 'Container' means the receptacle or package in which a product is offered for sale, but does not include any outer wrapping or box that is not customarily displayed: reg 1(1)*(a)*.

[73] Cf GN R452 of 25 March 1977 (Cf also GN R2777 of 21 December 1984 and GN R72 of 11 January 1985).

[74] ie a Group I hazardous substance.

[75] Regulation 10(1).

being cleaned, such a container may be used as a container only for the hazardous substance that it originally contained.[76] Every empty hazardous substance container, the label of which does not specify that it should be returned to the supplier, must be perforated and flattened and then buried in the ground, or disposed of in an alternative safe manner.[77] There are also provisions relating to containers of hazardous substances being used as containers for foodstuffs and vice versa.[78] Contravention of any of these provisions amounts to an offence.[79]

Regulations issued in terms of the Hazardous Substances Act[80] govern the transportation of grouped hazardous substances (which may include hazardous wastes) by means of a road tanker. The regulations are, however, restricted in that they apply to some 300 chemicals only, involve only certain defined road tankers with a total capacity of not less than 500 ℓ and require no special roadworthiness requirements. See also chapter 9 in respect of international regulation of the transportation of hazardous waste.

Hazardous waste has not been comprehensively and adequately addressed by legislation to date. During 1990 the Department of Environment Affairs commissioned the CSIR to undertake a comprehensive study of hazardous waste and the legislation pertaining to it. The aim of the investigation was to establish a strategy and action plan for the disposal of this type of waste in an environmentally responsible manner, in order also to give effect to the provisions of the Basel Convention on the Control of Transboundary Movements of Hazardous Wastes and their Disposal (1989), once South Africa becomes party to it. A draft report (in five volumes) has been compiled and is to be released in June 1992, encompassing the following aspects:

- a situation analysis, including the quantities of waste generated and its hazard rating;
- an assessment of available technologies for hazardous waste treatment and disposal;
- a proposed strategy, policy and regulatory system for hazardous waste management in South Africa;
- legislative options for hazardous waste regulation in South Africa;
- an impact assessment to compare different policy options for the regulation of hazardous waste in South Africa.

19.11.4.9 *Pesticides*

The Minister of Agriculture may in terms of the Fertilizers, Farm Feeds, Agricultural Remedies and Stock Remedies Act 36 of 1947 by notice in the *Government Gazette* prohibit the disposal of agricultural remedies or stock remedies.[81] See chapter 20.

19.11.4.10 *Radioactive waste*

Although the disposal of radioactive waste could be controlled in terms of the Hazardous Substances Act,[82] it is in fact controlled by regulations issued in terms of the Atomic Energy Act 90 of 1967,[83] and applicable now in terms of the Nuclear Energy Act 92 of 1982.[84] The position in respect of radioactive waste is set out in chapter 21.

---

[76] Regulation 10(2).
[77] Regulation 10(3).
[78] Regulation 10(4) and (5).
[79] Regulation 11 read with s 29(8) of the Hazardous Substances Act.
[80] GN R73 of 11 January 1985.
[81] Sections 7*bis* and 18(1)*(c)bis*. Cf GN R928 of 1 May 1981.
[82] Section 29(1)*(r)*.
[83] Section 8. GN R2410 of 28 November 1980.
[84] Sections 50(1) and 83(9) of the Nuclear Energy Act.

19.11.4.11 *Tax deductions for recycling plant*

One of the few provisions which take account of economic factors is encountered in the Income Tax Act 58 of 1962. Tax deductions are allowed on new or unused machinery or plant which is brought into use by a taxpayer for the purposes of his trade (other than mining or farming), and is used by him directly in a process of manufacture or any other process which in the opinion of the Commissioner for Inland Revenue is of a similar nature.[85] It has thus been held that a processor of scrap metal who brought a new machine into use to process scrap metal qualified for this deduction.[86]

19.11.5 Provincial Legislation

At the level of provincial regulation the range of topics is not as wide as it is at national level. Nevertheless, two ordinances are aimed at dealing with specific environmental issues raised by the question of waste.

Reference was made to the extension of the powers of erstwhile provincial councils to enable them to legislate for the control of environmental pollution, particularly of littering.[87] Utilizing this authority, the Orange Free State was the first province to exercise the above-mentioned powers. In that province the dumping of rubbish is controlled in terms of the Prohibition of the Dumping of Rubbish Ordinance 8 of 1976: No person may without authority throw, dump or leave any rubbish[88] on public land or water, except in a container or at a place specially adapted and set apart for such purpose;[89] or on private property in a defined area[90] in such manner that it is visible from a public road or place, unless such act is performed in connection with farming activities or for the purpose of immediately burying or destroying such rubbish.[91] Contravention of this prohibition is an offence.[92] Moreover, where an accumulation of rubbish exists, or rubbish lies scattered in sight of a public road or place, an authorized officer[93] may order[94] the owner or occupier of the land to clean up or remove such rubbish within a certain period.[95] Failure to comply with this order constitutes an offence[96] and entitles the officer to clean up or remove the rubbish at the expense of the owner or occupier.[97]

The Natal Prevention of Environmental Pollution Ordinance 21 of 1981 renders it an offence for any person in any manner whatsoever and whether wilfully or negligently to perform any act of littering or pollution on, in or into any land, whether public or private or the sea or inland waters.[98] Provision is made for several exceptions.[99] The

---

[85] Section 12(1)*(a)*. Cf also s 12(1)*(b)*.
[86] *Secretary for Inland Revenue v Hersamar (Pty) Ltd* 1967 (3) SA 177 (A).
[87] Cf para 24 of the Second Schedule to the Financial Relations Act 65 of 1976.
[88] 'Rubbish' means refuse, garbage, rubble or discarded article, fluid, matter, substance or thing: s 1.
[89] Section 2(1)*(a)*.
[90] 'Defined area' means—
(a) the road reserve of a public road and the land situated within 150 m from the boundaries of such reserve in so far as such reserve or land is not situated within the area of jurisdiction of a local authority;
(b) land which is in the possession or under the control of the provincial administration; and
(c) an area which has been declared a defined area by the Administrator by notice in the *Gazette*: s 1.
[91] Section 2(1)*(b)*.
[92] Section 4(1)*(a)* read with s 4(1)(i). When in a prosecution in terms of the ordinance it is alleged that rubbish has been thrown out or dumped from a vehicle, there is a rebuttable presumption that such rubbish was dumped by the owner or driver of the vehicle: s 4(2).
[93] Cf s 3.
[94] ie by written notice.
[95] Section 2(2).
[96] Section 4(1)*(b)* read with s 4(1)(ii).
[97] Section 2(2).
[98] Section 2(1) and (2), read with s 6.
[99] Section 2(1)*(a)*–*(f)*.

ordinance also provides for the appointment of inspectors[100] and the making of regulations.[101] The provisions of the ordinance apply in addition to and not in substitution for the provisions of any other ordinance, by-law or regulation.[102]

The control of solid waste at provincial level has in the past been exercised mainly in respect of solid waste pollution along roads. The various Roads Ordinances prohibit anyone from depositing or leaving waste[103] on roads,[104] while the Road Traffic Act—which is administered at provincial level—prohibits anyone driving or having a vehicle on a public road from negligently or wilfully depositing or causing or permitting to be deposited any offensive matter or other refuse from such vehicle upon or alongside such road.[105] These provisions are enforced through a criminal sanction.[106] The Road Traffic Act which is administered at provincial level, as has been mentioned, also creates a procedure to deal with abandoned vehicles on public roads.[107]

The various nature conservation ordinances regulate litter and waste in protected areas under provincial control.[108]

The powers of the Minister of Environment Affairs to make solid waste control regulations in terms of the Sea-Shore Act,[109] as has been set out above, have been delegated in terms of the Act[110] to the executive committees of the Cape[111] and of Natal.[112]

Finally, it should be noted that, according to the Environment Conservation Act, it is envisaged that the regulations that may be issued in terms of the Act in respect of waste management[113] may assign functions to a provincial administration.[114]

19.11.6 Local legislation

The most common control of solid waste by local authorities is exercised by virtue of the empowering provincial local government ordinances over the littering of public places, streets, private premises, streams, dams etc. 'Refuse' or 'rubbish' is usually not

---

[100] Section 3.
[101] Section 4.
[102] Section 5.
[103] Section 34(1)*(b)* of the Roads Ordinance 22 of 1957 (Transvaal) refers to any obstructions which may be dangerous to the traffic, or any rubbish, debris, ash-heaps, earthenware, glass, tins, nails, pieces of metal, timber, tree stumps, boulders or stones or any other material; s 21(1)*(b)* of the Roads Ordinance 4 of 1968 (OFS), refers to rubbish, stones, boulders, ash-heaps, glass, wire, tins, nails, pieces of metal, timber, tree stumps or any other waste material or abandoned property; s 23*(e)* of the Roads Ordinance 10 of 1968 (Natal) refers to refuse or rubbish; while s 64(1)*(d)* and *(e)* of the Roads Ordinance 19 of 1976 (Cape) refers to anything of whatsoever nature which is or is likely to be offensive, dangerous, harmful or injurious to traffic.
[104] Section 34(1)*(b)* of the Transvaal ordinance, s 21(1)*(b)* of the OFS ordinance; s 23*(e)* of the Natal ordinance and s 64(1)*(d)* and *(e)* of the Cape ordinance.
[105] Section 101(1)*(m)*.
[106] Section 34(2) of the Transvaal ordinance; s 54*(a)* of the OFS ordinance; s 73 of the Natal ordinance and s 149 of the Road Traffic Act.
[107] Section 114.
[108] Cf, eg, reg 15(1) AN 276 of 12 December 1969, issued in terms of the OFS Nature Conservation Ordinance 8 of 1969.
[109] Section 10.
[110] Section 11(2).
[111] Initially on 10 February 1977 and replaced by a delegation of 1 June 1988.
[112] On 21 January 1980. Cf, however, the assignment of powers on 18 November 1986 by the State President to the Administrators of the Cape and Natal, which excluded the making of regulations. Cf Rabie 'Mechanical roars on our shores: control over off-road vehicles on the sea-shore' 1991 *SA Public Law* 189.
[113] Section 24.
[114] Section 28*(a)*.

defined, although a number of items are usually enumerated.[115] The provisions are generally enforced through a criminal sanction. Another common method of refuse control is through the abatement notice procedure prescribed for dealing with nuisances. In terms of this procedure, a notice is served on the author of the nuisance calling upon him to remove or abate it within a specified time. Failure to comply with the notice is an offence and entitles the local authority concerned to remove or abate the nuisance itself, and to recover the costs incurred from the author of the nuisance.[116]

Control of solid waste by local authorities is also exercised through prescriptions relating to the keeping of animals,[117] the disposal of dead animals[118] and the regulation of offensive trades.[119]

The main functions of local authorities in connection with solid waste are their obligations in the course of providing sanitary services for the collection and disposal of refuse.[120] Some local authorities have subdivided refuse into a number of different categories such as 'house refuse', 'garden refuse', 'builder's refuse', 'business refuse' etc. The purpose of this subdivision is to differentiate between different kinds of refuse as far as charges and procedures relating to the collection, removal, storage and disposal of these wastes are concerned. An exemplary set of such by-laws has been promulgated for the Johannesburg municipality.[121]

Reference should again be made to the Sea-Shore Act, which empowers the Minister of Environment Affairs, and the executive committees of the Cape and Natal to whom this power has been delegated, to authorize local authorities, with his approval, to make regulations for the prevention or the regulation of the depositing or the discharging upon the sea-shore (or in the sea) of offal, rubbish or anything liable to be a nuisance or danger to health.[122] Many local authorities have accordingly had such regulations promulgated.[123]

Reference should, finally, also be made to the provisions of the Environment Conservation Act, according to which regulations may be issued in respect of waste management[124] and functions may be assigned to a local authority.[125] However, regulations which may affect the activities of a local authority may be promulgated only with the concurrence of such local authority.[126] Furthermore, if in the opinion of the Administrator of a province any local authority within the province in question fails to perform any function assigned to it, the Administrator may, after affording the local authority an opportunity of making representations to him, by written notice direct such local authority to perform such function within a specified period and, if the local

[115] The position in the Transvaal is taken as an example. Cf, for example, s 79(2)*(a)* and s 80(4)*(a)*, *(b)*, *(c)* and (6) of the Local Government Ordinance 17 of 1939 (T); ss 5, 6*(a)* and 7 of the Uniform Public Health By-laws and Regulations (AN 148 of 21 February 1951); and ss 24 and 25 of the Refuse (Solid Waste) By-laws of Johannesburg (AN 1037 of 18 June 1975). In terms of the last-mentioned Johannesburg provisions, two different offences are distinguished, i e 'littering' and 'dumping', the latter being the more serious one. Underlying this distinction seems to be the fact that while littering is generally a casual and unpremeditated act, dumping is a deliberate act to pollute.

[116] Section 27 of the Health Act 63 of 1977.

[117] Section 80(7) Transvaal Local Government Ordinance and AN 2208 of 9 October 1985.

[118] Cf eg s 47 of the Uniform Public Health By-laws.

[119] Section 80(15) and (18) of the Transvaal Local Government Ordinance; and, eg, ch 3 of the Uniform Public Health By-laws.

[120] Cf s 20 of the Health Act 63 of 1977 and ss 79(2)*(a)* and 80(3) of the Transvaal Local Government Ordinance; and see, for example, Refuse Removal By-laws (Sandton) (AN 1866 of 21 November 1973) and the Refuse (Solid Wastes) By-laws (Johannesburg) (AN 1037 of 18 June 1975).

[121] Refuse (Solid Wastes) By-laws (AN 1037 of 18 June 1975).

[122] Section 10(1)*(d)*.

[123] Cf also the uniform sea-shore regulations applicable in Natal: GN R168 of 2 February 1962.

[124] Section 24.

[125] Section 28*(a)*.

[126] Section 28*(i)*(iii).

authority fails to comply with the direction, the Administrator may perform the function as if he were the local authority and may authorize any person to take all steps required for that purpose.[127] He may, in addition, recover the expenditure involved from the local authority concerned.[128] As a final back-up, the Minister of Environment Affairs is granted the same powers as those which the Administrator enjoys, if the latter has not acted in terms of the abovementioned provision.[129]

19.11.7 Shortcomings in solid waste legislation and its application

The major objectives of waste management, according to the President's Council,[130] should include

- the avoidance of waste production as far as possible;
- greater use of degradable packaging material;
- the sorting of household waste at source to facilitate disposal and recycling;
- the recycling and utilization of waste;
- the disposal of all residual waste in an environmentally acceptable manner.

These objectives should be backed up by a national waste management policy.

Solid waste legislation fails to contribute adequately to the achievement of the above objectives. As has been mentioned, there is no national policy on waste management. There is, moreover, no adequate provision for incentives aimed at the reduction of waste, nor for the gathering of data on solid waste produced. Furthermore, provisions for the encouragement of the optimum use of solid waste are lacking, as are comprehensive national provisions for the encouragement of the proper disposal of residual waste. In particular, waste legislation is not aimed at avoidance, source separation, or at stimulating re-use or recycling. The fundamental problem probably is that insufficient account has been taken in legislation of the underlying economic factors involved in waste generation, its reduction, its re-use and recycling and its disposal. See chapter 3.

Solid waste legislation is fragmented and diffuse. A variety of government departments administer different aspects of waste control, while provincial and local authorities as well as the private sector are also involved. No single government department has taken the lead for overall control. Although the Environment Conservation Act would seem to be gradually shifting this responsibility to the Minister of Environment Affairs, the important function in terms of the Act of controlling waste disposal sites is left to the Minister of Water Affairs.

Further, the important subject of control over hazardous wastes is regulated by a number of diverse statutes, which are administered by different bodies, thus frustrating a uniform approach.

At the level of local government, where most of the control of waste seems to lie, there is no uniform set of by-laws for waste management.

The penalties which are provided in the legislation for transgressions are often not appropriate or stringent enough. They are also not uniformly applied. Further, interest among and support from justice officials in the enforcement of the provisions of the legislation is poor.

19.11.8 Towards comprehensive waste management legislation

It is submitted that a single comprehensive Waste Control Act should be promulgated which should regulate all aspects of waste management, including those for solid waste.

---

[127] Section 31(1).
[128] Section 31(2).
[129] Section 31(3).
[130] *Report of the three committees of the President's Council on a national environmental management system* PC 1/1991 para 2.6.3.2.

The Act should supplement and co-ordinate (and, as far as possible, consolidate) all relevant legislation which exists and which is contemplated at all levels of government. The Act, which should be administered by the Minister of Environment Affairs, should at least

- Contain the statement of a national policy for the reduction of waste, focusing on the avoidance, re-use and recycling of waste, as well as the proper disposal of residual waste. The policy should
  — have the control of pollution and conservation of natural resources as its basis; and
  — take cognizance of and make allowance for the unique South African context within which the relevant waste legislation has been, and will be, formulated and applied.
- Be comprehensive in that it should deal with all facets of waste. The legislation should deal with the generation of waste, its avoidance, re-use and recycling, through its collection to, finally, its disposal.
- Contain separate sections for at least solid, liquid and gaseous wastes, and possibly one for hazardous wastes.
- Confer powers on regional and local authorities to regulate aspects that require a particular regional or local approach.
- Be the vehicle for the publication of a model set of regulations relating to waste management.
- Standardize waste terminology.
- Standardize approaches to the various aspects of waste management.
- Provide for the education of the public with regard to environmental issues affected by the management of waste from generation to disposal.
- Provide for the acquisition of data in respect of waste.
- Incorporate effective incentives and sanctions. Specific emphasis should be placed on the provision of appropriate economic instruments to stimulate the reduction of waste streams and the re-use and recycling of waste. See chapter 3.

* Since going to press the Environment Conservation Amendment Act 79 of 1992 has been promulgated. It introduces some amendments relevant to solid waste control, inter alia relating to the definition of waste, a duty on those in control of places to which the public has access, to remove litter and an authorization to make regulations regarding litter.

CHAPTER 20

PESTICIDES

J H GILIOMEE
P D GLAVOVIC

20.1 DEFINITION

Pesticides are chemicals used by human beings to kill organisms that threaten their health and well-being, pets and livestock or cause damage to crops. Antibiotics in the medical sense are excluded, but included are insecticides, herbicides, fungicides, acaricides, nematicides and rodenticides. Of these, insecticides and herbicides are used in the biggest quantities and have the most severe impact on the environment.

20.2 HISTORICAL BACKGROUND

Since pesticides are by definition toxic to living organisms, there is great public concern over the effect of these chemicals, not only on human beings, but also on non-target organisms in the environment. People fear that they themselves may be poisoned by the indiscernible residues on the food that they eat and that birds, fish and other valued forms of wildlife are being adversely affected as a result of the application of pesticides against harmful organisms. This fear was expressed in an articulate yet emotional book by Rachel Carson[1] which gave impetus to the quest for the safer use of pesticides in particular and to the environmental movement in general.

The insecticidal activity of some naturally occurring compounds such as nicotine and pyrethrum, derived respectively from the tobacco plant and certain chrysanthemum species, has been known for centuries. They have since early times been supplemented by inorganic compounds such as the arsenicals for insect control and the sulphur and copper-based compounds for fungus control.

In the years between 1939 and 1953 tremendous advances were made in insect control as a result of the discovery of the insecticidal activity of a number of synthetic organic compounds, such as organochlorines like DDT, BHC (already synthesised as chemicals in the previous century), dieldrin and toxaphene; the organophosphates (parathion and others) and the carbamates (such as carbaryl). Only much later, in 1978, did a powerful new group, the synthetic pyrethroids with their characteristics of low acute mammalian toxicity and broad spectrum effectivity, appear on the market.

These new organic compounds kill insects not only when ingested like the inorganic compounds, but also after absorption through the skin, i e on contact, when organisms are hit by a droplet of spray or when they walk across a sprayed surface. DDT proved to be extremely successful in the control of insect vectors of disease, such as lice, during World War II and it seemed that their total elimination was at hand. Also, tremendous increases in agricultural production were foreseen through the elimination of insect damage to crops and livestock. However, the enthusiasm over the benefits brought about by these chemicals was soon dampened by the appearance of DDT-resistance in houseflies in 1946 and recognition of the ecological problems that might be caused by the widespread use of DDT and other persistent insecticides.

The immediate post-war years also saw the discovery of the phenoxy herbicides, primarily 2,4D. The selective action of this chemical enabled farmers to control

[1] *Silent spring* (1962).

broad-leaved weeds among their cereal crops. Subsequently, a great variety of herbicides with a wide range of chemical structures and with many different characteristics, most of them with a relatively low toxicity to humans, has been developed and the quantities used equal or surpass those of insecticides in many countries. However, the detection of their residues in soil and water, evidence of potential health hazards caused by some of them (such as the impurity dioxin in 2,4,5-T, now withdrawn) and their possible effect on rare plants have raised public concern in recent years.

Fungicides are a third major group of agricultural pesticides, though the quantities used are less than the insecticides and herbicides. Some of them, like sulphur and copper sulphate, have been in use for more than two centuries and are still on the market, but many new compounds have been developed since the 1950s. Their acute toxicity to humans and wildlife is generally very low and as a result there was less concern about their use than that of insecticides. However, recent discoveries about the carcinogenic properties of many of the commonly used fungicides have caused concern.

20.3 ENVIRONMENTAL IMPACT

The formulations, toxicity and application of biocides have been described by Genis & Rabie.[2] More recently, in 1991, a comprehensive review of the use and environmental impact of pesticides in South Africa has been published.[3] Many recommendations in this review on ways of reducing the risk of pollution by pesticides deserve careful consideration. Rather than repeating the information and comments in these publications, an attempt will be made to approach the subject from a more ecological perspective. The aim is to explain the impact of pesticides on the different levels of organisation which ecologists recognise as giving structure to the great diversity found in nature. These levels include the individual, the population, the community and the ecosystem.

20.3.1 Impact on the individual level

Two types of effect on the individual can be distinguished, i e an acute and a chronic effect.

The acute effect is the effect within seconds or hours after intake, i e the immediate effect on the organism, usually manifested after exposure to a single large dose. The acute oral and dermal toxicity of all pesticides for mammals, usually laboratory rats or rabbits, are established before their registration and release onto the market. They can be found in the lists of registered pesticides published annually by the Department of Agriculture.[4]

The toxicity is expressed as an LD_{50} (lethal dosage) value, which refers to the dosage in milligrams of pesticide per kilogram of body weight of the test animal that is lethal to 50 per cent of the test population. This value ranges from less than 1 for extremely toxic pesticides to more than 5 000. The value gives only a general indication of the toxicity of a pesticide for it may vary with the species, sex and age group. It bears no relation to the toxicity of the chemical against insects. In general, the ideal for pesticide companies is to find chemicals that are toxic to noxious organisms, but that have little or no effect on other organisms, particularly beneficial ones and humans beings.

Pesticides kill in many different ways. The most commonly used insecticides are

---

[2] 'Biocides' in Fuggle & Rabie (eds) *Environmental concerns in South Africa* (1983) 412.

[3] Barlin-Brinck *Pesticides in southern Africa—an assessment of their use and environmental impact* (1991).

[4] Vermeulen & Rankin *A guide to the use of herbicides* (12 ed, 1990); Vermeulen, Sweet, Krause, Hollings & Nel *A guide to the use of pesticides and fungicides in the Republic of South Africa* (34 ed, 1990).

nerve poisons, i e they interfere with the transmission of nerve impulses from one nerve ending to another or to innervated tissues. Thus the organophosphate and carbamate insecticides combine with, and so inhibit the action of acetylcholinesterase, the enzyme responsible for the breakdown of acetylcholine. The latter is a neurotransmitter which is liberated at the synapses of neurons in response to an impulse and accumulates when the action of acetylcholinesterase is blocked. When the transmission of nerve impulses in the brain of higher animals is impaired, respiration is depressed and death from suffocation results. Symptoms of poisoning and treatment procedures have been described.[5]

The poisoning of human beings by pesticides must be notified in terms of the Health Act 63 of 1977. According to figures supplied by the Department of National Health and Population Development, a total of 1 261 cases, with an average of 78,8 per annum have been notified for the years 1971–1986 in South Africa, including the TBVC countries. The number of deaths for the same period was 129, an average of 8,06 per year.[6] This figure includes cases of suicide.

The acute effect of pesticides causes the death of many non-target organisms, be they mammals, birds, fish or insects. Vultures are often killed when poison is placed by farmers in sheep in an attempt to poison troublesome carnivores like the black-backed jackal. Guinea-fowl and blue cranes can be killed when wheat or maize lands are sprayed or seeds treated with insecticides.

The chronic effect, i e the cumulative effect of the continuous exposure to low levels of pesticides, is less well known than the acute effects and is often discovered only after the product had been in use for many years. Many earlier studies,[7] have indicated that some of the organochlorine compounds, particularly DDT and dieldrin, affected the reproduction of birds by reducing the number of eggs laid, the thickness of the eggshell, the hatching percentage and the viability of the progeny. These compounds were also found to be stored in body fats (in direct proportion to the level of intake) and to be concentrated as they moved up the food chain from plants to herbivores and carnivores, rendering the latter particularly vulnerable.

Many cases have been reported in world literature where pesticide residues, particularly of the organochlorine insecticides, had been found in human beings and other mammals, birds and fish—also in South Africa. The mean concentration of total DDT-derived material stored in human adipose tissue collected during 1969 was found to be 6,38 ppm for the general population of South Africa.[8] In birds 13,62 mg kg^{-1} dry weight DDT was found in a raptor egg from Ermelo,[9] and 1,429 mg kg^{-1} DDT in the fat and 0,025 mg kg^{-1} (wet mass) dieldrin in the heart of an open-billed stork in the Hluhluwe Game Reserve.[10] Fish-eagle eggs from the Kruger National Park contained up to 6,36 mg kg^{-1} DDE, a breakdown product of DDT.[11] This chemical was also found at levels as high as 28,80 and 44,30 mg kg^{-1} in fish and francolin respectively in the Transvaal, together with BHC, endosulfan, dieldrin and DDT.[12] The fat of one

[5] Fourie *Poisoning by chemicals in agriculture and public health* (1984).

[6] Barlin-Brinck above n 3, 96.

[7] Grier 'Ban of DDT and subsequent recovery of reproduction in bald eagles' 1982 (218) *Science* 1232.

[8] M Wasserman, D Wasserman, Lazarovici, Coetzee & Tomatis 'Present state of the storage of the organochlorine insecticides in the general population of South Africa' 1970 (44) *South African Medical Journal* 646, 647.

[9] Peakall & Kemp 'Organochlorine residue levels in herons and raptors in the Transvaal' 1976 (47) *Ostrich* 139, 140.

[10] Macdonald, Brooks & Gardner 'Environmental pollutants as possible factors in the survival of the openbilled stork in southern Africa' 1985 (56) *Ostrich* 280.

[11] De Kock & Lord *Chlorinated hydrocarbon residues in African fish eagle (Haliaectus vocifer) eggs* Institute for Coastal Research Report no 10 (Port Elizabeth) (1986) 8.

[12] Pick, De Beer & Van Dyk 'Organochlorine insecticide residues in birds and fish from the Transvaal, South Africa' 1981 (10) *Chemosphere* 1243.

guinea-fowl contained 29,32 mg kg^{-1} dieldrin. In a later study of the lower Vaal River, minute quantities of DDT, DDT-metabolites and dieldrin (up to 48 μg kg^{-1} wet weight) were found in most of the fish sampled.[13] All the birds and fish sampled in the Wilderness Lakes System during 1983 had DDE residues in their tissue, also at very low levels.[14] As regards marine organisms, low levels of dieldrin was found in mussels and mullet along the coast near Durban,[15] while traces of DDT and its metabolites were detected in the blubber of all the sperm whales and most of the minke and fin whales sampled off Durban during 1974.[16]

While the decline in numbers of certain birds of prey can be attributed to chronic poisoning by organochlorine compounds, there is little evidence on detrimental effects to humans by the intake of low levels of these chemicals. However, cancer, reproductive toxicity and liver effects are given as potential hazards.[17] In view of their stability, their ability to spread to remote areas, their effect on wildlife and the potential harm they could cause to humans, the use of most of these pesticides, e g DDT, BHC (except the gamma isomer lindane), dieldrin, aldrin, endrin and chlordane has been restricted or banned in First World countries, including South Africa.[18] In 1985, however, South African Government officials used large quantities of stockpiled BHC against locusts, while materials such as DDT and dieldrin are still used occasionally by farmers who (illegally) own or procure supplies; high levels of dieldrin were detected in melons as late as 1991.[19] As a special case, the use of DDT on the inside walls of huts in Natal and Transvaal for the control of mosquitoes (transmitters of malaria) is still permitted, despite concern that the chemicals may pollute soil and water through negligence during use or when huts are demolished. Recent studies conducted in KwaZulu reveal that levels of DDT in human serum[20] and breast milk[21] in areas where DDT is used for mosquito control are significantly higher than in non-control areas. The levels found in milk are considered a possible health risk to infants.[22] In certain areas fish also showed increased levels of DDT, particularly those higher up in the food web.[23] This does not seem to pose a health hazard to the local population, but possible deleterious effects to species in higher trophic levels seem possible.[24]

The fear that pesticides may be carcinogenic or at least oncogenic (inducing either benign or malignant tumours) has increased considerably in recent years as many herbicides, insecticides and fungicides have been tested positively on rodents in the USA. As a result of investigations, the Environmental Protection Agency (EPA)

---

[13] Bruwer, Van Vliet, Sartory & Kempster *An assessment of water related problems of the Vaal River between Barrage and Douglas Weir* Technical Report TR121, Department of Water Affairs (1985) 109.

[14] De Kock & Boshoff *PCB's and chlorinated hydrocarbon insecticide residues in birds and fish from the Wilderness lakes system, South Africa* Marine Pollution Bulletin 18 (1987) 413, 414.

[15] Sibbald, Connell, Butler, Naidoo & Dunn 'A limited collaborative investigation of the occurrence of dieldrin in selected biota in the Durban area' 1986 (82) *S Afr J Sci* 319.

[16] Henry & Best *Organochlorine residues in whales landed at Durban, South Africa* Marine Pollution Bulletin 14 (1983) 223.

[17] Mott & Snyder *Pesticide alert—a guide to pesticides in fruit and vegetables* (1987) 18.

[18] 'Gebruik van verskeie insekmiddels ingetrek of ingekort' 1970 (674) *Agricultural News* 1.

[19] *Die Burger* 19 February 1991.

[20] Bouwman *DDT levels in serum, breast-milk and infants in various populations in malaria and non-malaria controlled areas of KwaZulu* Medical Research Council (1991); Bouwman, Cooppan, Becker & Ngxongo 'Malaria control and levels of DDT in serum of two populations in KwaZulu' 1991 (33) *J of Toxicology and Environmental Health* 141.

[21] Bouwman above n 20; Bouwman, Reinecke, Cooppan & Becker 'Factors affecting levels of DDT and metabolites in human breast-milk from KwaZulu' 1990 (31) *J of Toxicology and Environmental Health* 93.

[22] Ibid.

[23] Bouwman, Coetzee & Schutte 'Environmental and health implications of DDT-contaminated fish from the Pongolo Flood Plain' 1990 (104) *J Afr Zool* 275.

[24] Ibid.

considered a substantial number of commonly used pesticides to be oncogenic (tumour producing) or potentially oncogenic in animal studies.[25] On the basis of kilograms of pesticides applied, 60 per cent of all herbicides fall in this category, and by volume 90 per cent of all fungicides and 30 per cent of all insecticides. About 90 per cent of the estimated dietary oncogenic risks from pesticides can be attributed to uses sanctioned by tolerances granted before 1978. As a result, many well-known pesticides will have to be re-evaluated and may lose their registration.

The potentially oncogenic pesticides identified by the EPA include many chemicals commonly used in South Africa today, e g the herbicides alachlor (Lasso) and paraquat (Grammoxone), the fungicides benomyl (Benlate) and mancozeb, (Dithane M45), and the insecticides azinphos-methyl (Gusathion), cypermethrin (Cymbush, Ripcord), dicofol (Kelthane), gamma-BHC (Lindane), parathion (Folidol) and permethrin (Ambush).

Certain toxicologists question the validity and value of rodent carcinogenicity studies for assessing the cancer risks to human beings posed by pesticides. It is contended that tests in which near-toxic doses are applied to rodents do not provide enough information to predict the excess numbers of human cancers that might occur at low-dose exposures. Moreover, the quantity of synthetic pesticide residues in a normal diet is minute compared to that of natural pesticides, i e chemicals that plants use to defend themselves against insects and pathogens; furthermore, there is no fundamental difference between these groups of chemicals.[26] Other workers found that carcinogenic effects were generally not limited to the top exposure level and were frequently observed at lower levels where there is no evidence of toxicity; in fact, increases in tumour rates are often present at lower doses.[27] A further consideration is that comparisons based strictly on the relative mass of synthetic and natural pesticides consumed are of little scientific value because the carcinogenic potency of the various chemicals is not taken into account. It should also be borne in mind that many people are exposed to more sources of pesticides than just residues in food, particularly farmers, occupationally exposed workers, pesticide applicators and weekend gardeners.[28]

Whatever the case may be, it is very important that the presence of pesticide residues in food be monitored on a regular basis. In view of the great range of pesticides, the variety of products in which they can occur and the many marketing outlets for foodstuffs, it is extremely difficult and expensive to do justice to the real requirements in this regard. Presently, routine analyses for certain pesticides are carried out on export fruits, but products on the local markets are mostly tested for residues only on an *ad hoc* basis, i e certain products are tested for certain pesticides when samples are submitted by health inspectors.[29] Since it is almost impossible to control the way in which farmers use pesticides, i e whether they spray a registered pesticide, at the registered dose and according to the prescribed safety period before marketing products, regular monitoring for residues on products that reach the market is the only way to ensure that consumers are not exposed to toxic chemicals. Some products do not pass through the big wholesale markets—where samples can easily be obtained—but are sold directly to supermarkets and cafés or along roads in farm stalls, where special

---

[25] *Regulating pesticides in food* National Research Council (1987) 20.

[26] Ames & Gold 'Natural plant pesticides pose greater risks than synthetic ones' 1991 (69) *Chemical and Engineering News* 48; Ames & Gold 'Cancer prevention strategies greatly exaggerate risks' 1991 (69) *Chemical and Engineering News* 28.

[27] Huff & Haseman 'Exposure to certain pesticides may pose real carcinogenic risk' 1991 (69) *Chemical and Engineering News* 33.

[28] Haseman & Huff 'Arguments that discredit animal studies lack scientific support' 1991 (69) *Chemical and Engineering News* 49.

[29] Barlin-Brinck above n 3, 71.

attempts should be made to determine whether farmers have used pesticides responsibly. Particular attention should be given to those products that may have required sprays during the extended periods over which the crop is harvested, such as strawberries and tomatoes.

20.3.2 Impact on the population level

Members of the same species that constitute a population have many inherent genetic differences, also regarding their response to a stress factor like a pesticide application. In a large population of weeds, pathogens or insects, there may be some individuals that can survive a generally effective dosage at the registered rate of application. Some individual insects may have superior qualities in metabolising the insecticide, in others the rate of penetration and transport of the chemical to the site of action may be reduced, while yet others may succeed in detecting and avoiding (or are repelled by) insecticide treated surfaces. Some are merely less sensitive. Those that survive spray applications because of genetic characteristics will transmit these traits to the next generation. Through repeated selective action by subsequent sprays a resistant population can eventually develop.

More than 500 species of arthropods worldwide are now resistant to one or more insecticides.[30] In South Africa the problem is particularly severe in the cases of red spider mite and citrus red scale. Lack of effective acaricides and insecticides has stimulated investigations into using biological control agents against these two pests, with remarkable success. In view of the ability of organisms to adapt to new compounds—in some cases very quickly—and the high cost of developing new pesticides, it is realized that we may sooner or later run out of replacements for the chemicals on which we rely heavily today. New strategies in managing pest numbers and in delaying the development of resistance have therefore become a high priority.

20.3.3 Impact on the community level

The different populations that constitute a community are affected differentially according to the general inherent susceptibility of the species to the dosage applied. Species of insects that have been exposed to a wider range of chemicals in their evolutionary history, such as those with a wide range of host plants, are better equipped to detoxify pesticides than the monophagous species.[31] One would also expect the carnivores (predators and parasitoids), which have not been exposed to the vast array of toxic chemicals in plants, to be generally less efficient in detoxifying chemicals than the herbivores. The implication of this is that the natural enemies (carnivores) of our pest organisms (mostly herbivores) are killed more easily than the pests themselves. Not only the direct mortality caused by the pesticides is important, but also the effect of sublethal doses which may interfere with normal behaviour patterns (e g host recognition, sexual communication) or the physiological processes of the natural enemies.[32] Where natural enemies have been important in depressing populations of pests or potential pests, this impact of pesticides can result in the resurgence of pest numbers soon after a spray application or the emergence of new pests from the community.

In addition to their effect on natural enemies, pesticides may also kill other beneficial insects such as the pollinators on which most plants, including those of many

[30] Georghiou 'Overview of insecticide resistance' in Green, Lebaron & Momberg (eds) *Managing resistance to agrochemicals: from fundamental research to practical strategies* ACS Symposium Series 421 (1990) 421.

[31] Wilkinson 'Role of mixed function oxidases in insecticide resistance to pesticides' in Georghiou & Saito (eds) *Pest resistance to pesticides* (1983) 175, 191.

[32] Elzen 'Sublethal effects of pesticides on beneficial parasitoids' in Jepson (ed) *Pesticides and non-target invertebrates* (1989) 129.

commercial crops, depend. They also kill numerous susceptible non-pest species, which may, in turn, affect the species on the next trophic level (such as insectivorous birds) for which they have served as food.

Herbicides, like other pesticides, simplify communities through their selective action on populations—the so-called weeds and other susceptible species are removed and with them the many insect species that feed on them. They therefore not only remove plants that provide shelter to animals but also a source of food for the herbivores and indirectly also for the carnivores.

20.3.4 Impact on the ecosystem level

Ecosystems are communities of interacting plants and animals together with their physico-chemical environment. Pesticides are not only found in the living component of ecosystems (as described above) but can also remain for some time in the air, water and soil.

Aerosol cans containing insecticides to control 'flying insects' are specifically designed so that small toxic droplets remain in the air for as long as possible. The insecticide therefore becomes part of the air that higher animals inhale. When crops are sprayed with pesticides, only minute quantities reach the target organisms—the rest contaminate the air, the soil and water in the ground, rivers, dams, lakes and the ocean. Depending on the type of pesticide, shorter or longer periods may elapse before it is degraded through physical, chemical and biological processes.

Most pesticides are insoluble in water, but since water is the most commonly used diluent and carrier from the sprayer to the target, they are formulated in such a way that they form suspensions or emulsions when mixed with water. This facilitates their dispersal in soil, groundwater and streams. They are also carried with the organic and clay particles to which they adsorb, while some of them can move as organic vapour through the unsaturated zone of the soil. Detailed descriptions of the processes involved are given by Yaron.[33] The result is that these toxic substances are eventually found far beyond the area where they were applied. Recent studies have shown that pesticides can move through the soil much faster and to greater depths than previously expected.[34] Information on the behaviour of pesticides in soil is summarized by Saltzman & Yaron.[35]

The presence of pesticides in groundwater is causing concern in the USA and in Europe, where it has recently been shown that pesticides are leaching through the soil in many more areas and much more commonly than preconceptions of a decade ago would have predicted.[36] This applies to the post-DDT chemicals, which were thought to be safer because they would degrade relatively rapidly in the topsoil, would be adsorbed to soil particles long enough to degrade and whose bioaccumulation and toxicity were thought to be less than they actually are.[37] Pesticides commonly found were the herbicides alachlor and atrazine, the insecticides aldicarb and carbofuran (also used against nematodes) and the nematicides DBCP and EDB. Typical concentrations ranged from 0,1 to 20 $\mu g\ \ell^{-1}$. Some of these pesticides have also been found in groundwater in Europe, where the Council of the European Communities established a maximum admissible concentration of 0,1 $\mu g\ \ell^{-1}$ for any pesticide in drinking

---

[33] Yaron 'General principles of pesticide movement to groundwater' 1989 (26) *Agriculture, Ecosystems and Environment* 275.

[34] Hallberg 'Pesticide pollution of groundwater in the humid United States agriculture' 1989 (26) *Agriculture, Ecosystems and Environment* 299, 348.

[35] Saltzman & Yaron *Pesticides in soil* (1986).

[36] Hallberg above n 34, 357.

[37] Hallberg above n 34, 300.

water.[38] This value represents a detection limit in chemical analysis: the idea is that there should be no pesticide residues in drinking water. In the Netherlands, the use of certain pesticides is not allowed in proclaimed groundwater protection areas.[39]

In South Africa, a project undertaken by the Groundwater Programme of the CSIR during the 1989–90 irrigation season investigated the impact of pesticides in current use in the Hex River Valley on the shallow aquifer present in the area. All the pesticides in use were assessed in terms of their potential impact on groundwater, their toxicity and the quantity used. Of these, the eleven pesticides most likely to contaminate groundwater were selected for analysis. Nine shallow wells and three tile-drains were sampled three times during the year. Analysis by the SABS showed that none of the pesticides was present in any of the water samples in quantities above the detection limits. In all the water samples collected, nitrate and potassium fertilizers were detected, indicating that leaching did take place, but that pesticides either did not leach to the water-table or that they degraded before they reached the water-table.[40]

In a survey conducted during 1984 and 1985 of surface water in the Orange Free State, high levels (up to 80 $\mu g\ \ell^{-1}$) of the herbicide atrazine, the most commonly used chlorinated pesticide in the region, were found. Other chlorinated pesticides occurred at low concentration levels, usually below 0,3 $\mu g\ \ell^{-1}$.[41] Atrazine was also detected during a survey of the water system of the Vaalharts Irrigation Scheme during the period 1987–89 by the Department of Water Affairs.[42] The highest concentrations (up to 1,61 $\mu g\ \ell^{-1}$) were found during January and February in the Harts River. The groundwater was free of the pesticides monitored.

20.4 REDUCING IMPACTS THROUGH PEST MANAGEMENT

Concern over the widespread occurrence of resistance, as well as health and environmental hazards associated with the use of pesticides, have prompted scientists to develop pest control strategies that rely less heavily on pesticides. In insect control the aim is to move away from routine or calendar spraying, where applications are made at regular intervals or at fixed periods in the development of the crop, regardless of infestation levels. Instead, pesticides are applied only when the numbers of pest insects exceed predetermined thresholds which may result in economic damage. At the same time, conditions are created that are unfavourable for the pest in an effort to keep its numbers below the threshold. Thus resistant crop plants are bred and used as far and for as long as possible; the effect of the pests' natural enemies is enhanced by introducing new species, using selective sprays that are 'soft' on them and augmenting their numbers by rearing and releasing; sanitary measures are applied to destroy infested plant residues or fruit; sticky materials are used to trap or exclude insects and sex pheromones are released which interfere with the communication between sexes.

This approach is called Integrated Pest Management (IPM). It requires, of course, that pest numbers are monitored regularly and that decisions are made on the appropriate action to be taken. It is also dependent on the availability of reliable information on the damage potential of pests, their rate of development and the potential of natural enemies to suppress them. Successful IPM therefore depends on sophisticated biological research and management inputs.

In South Africa, the greatest progress with IPM has been made in the cases of citrus

---

[38] Leistra & Boesten 'Pesticide contamination of groundwater in Western Europe' 1989 (26) *Agriculture, Ecosystems and Environment* 369, 370.

[39] Leistra & Boesten above n 38, 369.

[40] J M C Weaver CSIR Division of Water Technology pers comm.

[41] Hasset, Viljoen & Liebenberg 'An assessment of chlorinated pesticides in the major surface water resources of the Orange Free State during the period September 1984 to September 1985' 1987 (13) *Water SA* 133, 136.

[42] J C White unpublished report.

and cotton, and the number of pesticide sprays applied has been reduced considerably.[43] For many other major pest species such as codling moth and spider mites on deciduous fruit, the maize stalk borer and the Russian wheat aphid, thresholds have been determined that have to be reached by pest numbers before spraying is considered necessary. In many cases, however, these levels are regularly reached because no effective biological or other non-chemical control measures are available. Also many crops have a range of pests and diseases attacking them and when sprays have to be applied for one pest (e g citrus thrips) the biological control of others on the same trees (e g red scale) may be upset.

This illustrates the dynamic nature of pest problems and the need for continued research to produce the information on which management decisions can be based. Many farmers are reluctant to follow IPM because they lack the management expertise and are not prepared to take the risk of producing lower-quality fruit as a result of incorrect monitoring of pest numbers or wrong decisions on the actions they should take. Other restraints are the possibility of bad weather or insufficient equipment if spraying is delayed until threshold levels are reached.[44]

Towards the end of the 1980s a movement was started in Europe to sell deciduous fruit under a special label if produced with environmentally friendly methods.[45] Strict guidelines were set up by government agencies or farmers' co-operatives on various aspects of fruit production, including the use of chemicals such as fertilizers or pesticides, and adherence to these guidelines was supervised. It is to be hoped that this fruit will fill a market niche and find individual buyers or supermarkets that are prepared to give preference to and even pay more for such fruit, thus rewarding growers for their efforts in protecting the environment and consumer health. In a fruit-exporting country such as ours, growers will have to take note of these developments[46] and produce their own guidelines for what is now called Integrated Fruit Production. Perhaps market forces will succeed where ecologists failed in reducing or eliminating the use of harmful chemicals.

The pesticide industry in South Africa is acutely aware of its obligation in promoting the responsible use of pesticides and generally subscribes to the IPM approach. Nearly all the companies active in the field belong to the Agricultural and Veterinary Chemicals Association of South Africa (AVCASA) and their employees are not allowed to advise farmers or to sell chemicals before they have passed the examinations of AVCASA. The Association also issues certificates to crop-spraying pilots who have passed an examination and, in conjunction with the Boskop Training Centre of the South African Agricultural Union, is training farm labourers in the responsible handling and application of pesticides.

20.5 CONTROL LEGISLATION

20.5.1 Private-law controls

In South African common law an individual who suffers injury to his person or property as a result of the application of pesticides—for example, loss of crops by drifting chemicals—may have a proprietary or a delictual claim for an interdict or for damages. However, in practice, a claimant is often faced with many obstacles. Although the Appellate Division of the Supreme Court has examined and ruled on the

---

[43] Annecke & Moran *Insects and mites of cultivated plants in South Africa* (1982) 35, 254.

[44] Giliomee 'Integrated pest management in apple orchards: where do we stand?' 1989 (85) *S Afr J Sci* 361.

[45] Oberhofer 'Integrated apple production in western Europe' *Cape Pomological Association Symposium Proceedings* (1990) 17.

[46] Giliomee 'A green perspective on fruit production' Cape *Pomological Association Symposium Proceedings* (1990) 49.

rights of a property owner who has suffered harm in consequence of his neighbour's polluting activities, there is still considerable uncertainty as to his rights in our property law.[47] In applications or actions based on delict, not only may negligence be difficult to prove, but causation and computation of damages could pose insuperable problems.[48] This would be so even if strict or absolute liability were imposed. Private-law remedies do not afford adequate protection to individuals suffering harm from pesticide pollution. There is therefore a need for appropriate legislation to regulate the use of these chemicals.

20.5.2 Fertilizers, Farm Feeds, Agricultural Remedies and Stock Remedies Act

20.5.2.1 *Legislative history*

The first national legislation in South Africa to deal with pesticides was the Fertilizers, Farm Foods, Seeds and Pest Remedies Act 21 of 1917. The preamble to the Act indicated its purpose as being 'to regulate the sale of fertilizers, farm foods, seeds and pest remedies'. It was therefore intended purely as a regulatory enactment and its general intent seems clearly to have been the protection of consumers. Thus, the Act provided that 'no person shall supply any fertilizer, farm food, seed or pest remedy which is not of the nature, composition or quality as described when sold to the purchaser.[49] This provision really amounted to no more than a fairly simple confirmation and extension of the individual purchaser's common-law rights. However, the Act then proceeded to provide that the Governor-General may make regulations in regard to labelling, registration, the furnishment of guarantees to purchasers with regard to composition, and the regulation of the importation of products which contain 'injurious or deleterious substances'.[50] The regulations could prescribe penalties not exceeding the sum of ten pounds (twenty rand).[51] Apart from these regulatory provisions, the Act specifically provided that any imported products may be detained for analysis or examination and may be re-exported if not labelled or if found to be otherwise than required by the Act.[52] There was no reference in the Act to a more general public interest, public safety, health or environmental harm.

The 1917 Act was repealed and replaced in 1947 by the Fertilizers, Farm Feeds, Agricultural Remedies and Stock Remedies Act 36 of 1947, which, after several amendments, is still the current legislation. This Act represents a significant advance over its predecessor. It provides for the appointment by the Minister of Agriculture of a Registrar of Fertilizers, Farm Feeds, Agricultural Remedies and Stock Remedies. Registration of such products is required and provision is made for the cancellation of such registration. Moreover, the Act regulates the importation, sale, acquisition, disposal and use of those products. There was little indication in the Act, in its original formulation, that the legislature was motivated by any considerations other than

---

[47] See *Regal v African Superslate (Pty) Ltd* 1963 (1) SA 102 (A). It is interesting that in the United States litigants have generally opted to proceed on the basis of delict rather than nuisance. Litigation for the most part is confined to seeking compensation for injury to crops, persons, or other living things (typically honeybees) caused by drifting pesticides. Usually plaintiffs shun a nuisance theory, which is better suited to governing a continuing relationship between the parties, in favour of a theory more readily associated with an isolated tortious event—negligence, trespass, and strict liability.

[48] The scientific mechanisms involved are often complicated, and there may also be a long delay before the injury becomes manifest. Not surprisingly, having regard to the difficulties confronting a would-be claimant, a considerable body of relevant case law has not been 'spawned' in South Africa. See *Natal Fresh Produce Growers' Assoc v Agroserve (Pty) Ltd* 1990 (4) SA 749 (N) (the '*Tala Valley* case') for a recent illustration of some of the difficulties facing a litigant.

[49] Section 6.

[50] Section 7.

[51] Section 7(2).

[52] Section 8.

agricultural efficiency and protection of the consumer.[53] After several amendments, however, the Act now reflects a concern for the protection of the general public and for the environment.

20.5.2.2 *Comparative perspectives*

The Federal regulation of pesticides in the United States of America followed a similar pattern to that which evolved in South Africa, and for this reason it is useful briefly to consider developments in that country. The emphasis was initially on the protection of the consumer and this shifted in time to protection of the general public and of the environment. The 1910 Insecticide Act was primarily concerned with protecting consumers from ineffective products and deceptive labelling. After World War II the agricultural chemical industry blossomed and in 1947 the Federal Insecticide, Fungicide and Rodenticide Act (FIFRA) was passed, requiring that pesticides distributed in interstate commerce be registered with the Department of Agriculture, and contain labelling provisions. This Act, like its predecessor, was more concerned with product efficacy than with safety, but the statute did declare pesticides 'misbranded' if they were harmful to man, animals or vegetation (except weeds) even when properly used.[54] The late 1960s witnessed the growth of the environmental movement in the United States. In 1970 the Environmental Protection Agency (EPA) was established. In 1972 the conditions which had to be met for registration of a pesticide were amended to include the requirement that 'it will perform its intended function without unreasonable adverse effects on the environment'. The phrase 'unreasonable adverse effects on the environment' is defined in FIFRA as meaning 'any unreasonable risk to man or the environment, taking into account the economic, social and environmental costs and benefits of the use of the pesticide.[55] The use of a registered pesticide for a purpose other than in accordance with its registration or regulations is prohibited.[56] The penalties for violation are stiff and include fines of up to $25 000 and imprisonment for up to one year.[57] FIFRA also makes provision for cancellation and suspension procedures. Cancellation is used where a substance may pose a 'substantial question of safety' relative to man or the environment. Pending determination of the proceedings the product may be freely manufactured and distributed. A suspension order is issued when a substance is an 'imminent hazard' to man or the environment, and has the effect of an immediate ban on the production and distribution of the product. The procedures required by FIFRA are complicated, but the clear intention is protection of man and the environment against pesticide pollution as far as it is possible for the law to do so. However, implicit in its provisions is the notion that social benefit must be weighed against environmental risk.[58] Unfortunately,

[53] The sort of situation which appears to have been aimed at by the Act in its original form is perhaps exemplified by a civil claim which came before the Court in 1963 (*Marais v Perks* 1963 (4) SA 802 (EC)). An agent had sold two drums represented to contain tick oil, the one being labelled and the other not. The unlabelled drum contained sheep dip, which was used in an undiluted form on cattle by means of hand-dressing as was prescribed for the use of the tick oil on the label of the other drum. The result of this application was that the complainant lost 81 head of cattle. The Court stated (at 808) that it was his view that it was 'reasonably clear from the Act as a whole that its dominant purpose is the control of the trade. . . . The whole emphasis is on control to the extent of the maintenance of prescribed standards.' A breach of the Act did not ground an action for damages, so that in this case even the consumer was not adequately protected.

[54] See Arbuckle, Frick, Hall, Miller, Sullivan & Vanderver *Environmental law handbook* (7 ed, 1983) 273–4.

[55] Section 2*(bb)*.

[56] Section 12*(a)*(2)(F).

[57] Section 14.

[58] For a brief discussion of the FIFRA cancellation and suspension provisions, see Arbuckle et al above n 54, 279–85.

the tight controls of FIFRA do not apply to exports from the United States.[59] Two reasons have been suggested for the apparently irresponsible decision to permit exports. First, the agricultural chemical producers were faced with a dwindling market for some of their products within the United States and thus loss of profits. They maintained that they should be entitled to continue to compete with foreign producers who were not restricted by FIFRA. Secondly, decisions made in the United States would be based on a risk-benefit analysis which was irrelevant in importing countries in which malaria and tsetse fly, for example, which are not problems in the United States, interfere with development.[60] However, this sort of economic reasoning clearly does not take into sufficient account the health impacts and ecological side-effects in the countries importing such chemicals.[61]

The historical pattern that emerges from developments in the United States represents a gradual shift of emphasis from promotion of agricultural efficacy to considerations of general public safety and environmental impact. Initially the primary concern of legislation and the administration was protection of the farmers and promotion of marketing efficiency and adequate labelling. One of the changes brought about in the United States as a result of growing public concern about the environment in the 1960s was the transfer in 1970 of administrative authority over pesticides from the Department of Agriculture to the newly created EPA.[62] It was thought that the transfer of authority to the EPA would ensure a more thorough consideration of the ecological and health risks involved in the use of pesticides.[63]

Not only in the United States but in other countries too, the problem of pesticide pollution is perceived as being so vital as to warrant specific and exclusive pesticide control legislation. Examples are the 1978 Pesticides Act of New South Wales in Australia, and the 1979 Pesticides Act of New Zealand. The New South Wales statute adopts the threefold approaches of protection (protection of the health of the users of pesticides, of public health, and of the environment) and methodology (prohibition, registration and permit). The sale and use of unregistered pesticides is prohibited, provision is made for a system of registration of pesticides, and authority is required for their sale and use.[64] In New Zealand a Pesticides Board, established for the purposes of administration of the New Zealand Pesticides Act of 1979, comprises twelve members representative of the ministries of Agriculture, Science, Health and the

[59] Section 17*(c)* specifically excludes exports from the operation of the Act other than for record-keeping purposes. American manufacturers of pesticides that are 'cancelled or unapproved' for use in the United States are therefore free to export them. In 1982–83, large quantities of some 40 such pesticides were exported to more than 50 other countries. See Talbot *A World Resources Institute working paper: helping developing countries help themselves: toward a congressional agenda for improved resource and environmental management in the Third World* (1985) 58.

[60] Arbuckle et al above n 54, 299.

[61] The United Nations has estimated that 1,5 to 2 million people in developing countries suffer acute pesticide poisoning annually and that pesticide-related deaths total some 10 000 a year. Ironically, the export of pesticides has also produced health threats to American citizens when used on cash crops that are then shipped back to the United States. About half of the imported green coffee beans tested by the American Food and Drug Administration in 1978 contained measurable levels of pesticides that had been 'cancelled' for most uses internally. Freshly cut flowers imported from Colombia caused poisoning of American florists and overuse of pesticides in Central America not only resulted in a resurgence of malaria locally, which endangered American visitors as well as locals, but also led to high levels of pesticide residues in produce and beef destined for the United States. See Talbot above n 59, 58–9.

[62] Earlier in 1970 the department's activities in the area of pesticide safety had been criticized as 'scandalously derelict'. See Rodgers 'The persistent problem of persistent pesticides: A lesson in environmental law' 1970 (70) *Columbia Law Review* 567, 571.

[63] Spector 'Regulation of pesticides by the Environmental Protection Agency' 1975–76 *Ecology Law Quartely* 234, for example, writes: 'With its presidential mandate to "ensure the protection ... and enhancement of the total environment", EPA was likely to be more concerned than was its predecessor about the long-term risks associated with pesticide use.'

[64] See Fisher *Environmental law in Australia* (1980) 163.

Environment, and of the agricultural and horticultural industries. Its functions are to promote the prudent, effective and safe use of pesticides in New Zealand and to consider and determine applications under the Act for the registration of pesticides, and the grant of licences. In the exercise of its powers and functions the board must at all times have regard to the environmental effects of use of pesticides.[65]

20.5.2.3 *The concepts 'agricultural remedy' and 'stock remedy'*

Although the South African Act deals also with fertilizers and farm feeds, only agricultural remedies and stock remedies are important in the context of pesticides. 'Agricultural remedy' is defined as any chemical substance or biological remedy, or any mixture or combination of any substance or remedy intended or offered to be used—

(a) for the destruction, control, repelling, attraction or prevention of any undesired microbe, alga, nematode, fungus, insect, plant, vertebrate, invertebrate, or any product thereof, but excluding any chemical substance, biological remedy or other remedy in so far as it is controlled under the Medicines and Related Substances Control Act 101 of 1965 or the Hazardous Substances Act 15 of 1973 or

(b) as plantgrowth regulator, defoliant, desiccant or legume inoculant,

and anything else which the Minister has by notice in the *Government Gazette* declared an agricultural remedy for the purposes of the Act.[66] 'Stock remedy' means any substance intended or offered to be used in connection with domestic animals, livestock, poultry, fish or wild animals (including wild birds), for the diagnosis, prevention, treatment or cure of any disease, infection or other unhealthy condition, or for the maintenance or improvement of health, growth, production or working capacity, but excluding any substance in so far as it is controlled under the Medicines and Related Substances Control Act.[67] The phrase 'agricultural remedy' may be preferable in the context of bio-ethics and respect for non-human species, in that it is less pejorative than 'pesticide'. However, in the discussion which follows, the better known[68] and more convenient generic term 'pesticides' will be employed in reference to substances which are used to control those organisms that are regarded as noxious or inimical to human interests.

20.5.2.4 *Administration*

Perhaps because the primary purpose of the Act is the protection of farmers, the Department of Agriculture is charged with its administration. The Department of Agriculture also administers the Agricultural Products Export Act 51 of 1971, which will be referred to below. The other relevant legislation which will be discussed, i e the Health Act 63 of 1977, the Foodstuffs, Cosmetics and Disinfectants Act 54 of 1972 and the Hazardous Substances Act 15 of 1973, are administered by the Department of National Health and Population Development, the relevant provisions of which are aimed at the protection of public health against pesticides. Virtually all legislative control over the use of pesticides is thus administered at national level, although there is some limited control at municipal level by virtue of by-laws.[69]

20.5.2.5 *Registration*

As has been mentioned, the Act provides for the designation by the Minister of an officer in the Department of Agriculture as the Registrar of Fertilizers, Farm Feeds,

[65] See Williams *Environmental law in New Zealand* (1980) 214–15.

[66] Section 1.

[67] Section 1 of the Fertilizers, Farm Feeds, Agricultural Remedies and Stock Remedies Act.

[68] The relevant legislation in other English-speaking countries—for example, the United States, New Zealand and New South Wales—uses the term 'pesticides'.

[69] For an overview and discussion of administrative responsibility for and control of pesticides, and their manufacture, formulation and distribution in South Africa, see Barlin-Brinck above n 3, 7–22.

Agricultural Remedies and Stock Remedies. Subject to any instructions issued by the Minister, the registrar exercises the powers and performs the functions and carries out the duties set out in the Act.[70] These powers are extensive, including inter alia, the right of entry upon and examination of places, premises or vehicles in respect of which he has reason to believe relevant substances are being manufactured, processed, and treated; the examination of books and documents, operations or processes; seizure of relevant substances, and the taking of samples.[71] The Minister may from time to time also designate persons as technical advisers, and analysts to analyse samples of agricultural or stock remedies referred to them by the registrar.[72]

Application for the registration of agricultural and stock remedies, and of pest control operators,[73] must be made to the registrar in the prescribed manner, accompanied by the prescribed application fee, and the applicant must make available to the registrar any samples and particulars that the latter may require.[74]

The registrar may make such investigation and inquiry as he deems necessary in consideration of an application for registration, and must be satisfied that the remedy is suitable and sufficiently effective for the purposes for which it is intended, and complies with any requirements that may be prescribed. He must also be satisfied that registration will not be contrary to the public interest, and that the establishment where the remedy is manufactured is suitable.[75] The requirement of public interest is significant, and this was inserted in 1970.[76] The provision for cancellation of registration also contains reference to public interest—the registrar may cancel registration if he is satisfied that it is contrary to the public interest that the product should remain registered.[77] Similarly, in respect of an application for registration of a pest control operator, the registrar must be satisfied that he has the prescribed qualifications and is sufficiently skilled in the use of agricultural remedies, and that it will not be contrary to the public interest that he be registered as a pest control operator.[78] Any such registration is subject to any prescribed and additional conditions as may be determined by the registrar, and will be valid only for such period as may be prescribed.[79] When the period for which a certificate of registration has been issued has lapsed, application may be made for its renewal. The same provisions applicable to applications for registration apply to applications for renewal.[80] Extensive regulations have been promulgated in respect of the registration and duties of pest control operators.[81]

20.5.2.6 *Cancellation of registration*

The registrar may cancel the registration of any agricultural or stock remedy at any time if he is satisfied:

- that a person has in connection with the registration concerned contravened or failed to comply with the provisions of the Act;
- that a person has contravened or failed to comply with a condition to which the registration concerned is subject;

[70] Section 2(1).
[71] Section 15(1).
[72] Section 14.
[73] 'Pest control operator' is defined in s 1 as a person who administers agricultural remedies, in the course of his trade or occupation, for the purposes for which they are intended.
[74] Section 3(1).
[75] Section 3(2)*(a)*.
[76] By s 3 of Act 60 of 1970.
[77] Section 4(1)*(e)*.
[78] Section 3(2)*(c)*.
[79] Section 3(3).
[80] Section 3(4).
[81] GN R1449 of 1 July 1983.

- that the remedy is not of the composition and efficacy specified in the application for registration, does not possess the chemical, physical and other properties so specified, or does not comply with any requirements that may be prescribed;
- that the practices followed and facilities available at or in respect of the establishment or the operation of the undertaking at such establishment are not suitable for the manufacture of the remedy concerned;
- that the person managing such undertaking does not have sufficient knowledge of the relevant provisions of the Act or of the practices to be followed in the operation of such undertaking;
- that it is contrary to the public interest that the remedy shall remain registered; or
- that any incorrect or misleading advertisement is used in connection with the remedy.[82]

The registrar may order pest control operators to discontinue the use of any equipment if he is of the opinion that it is so unsuited for the administration of a particular remedy that the purpose for which the remedy is being administered may be defeated.[83] If the operator fails to comply with such an order, the registrar may cancel his registration. He may also cancel the registration of any pest control operator at any time if he is satisfied that the operator has contravened or failed to comply with a provision of the Act or a condition of his registration, or that it is contrary to the public interest that he should remain registered.[84]

20.5.2.7 *Appeals against decisions of the registrar*

The registrar is required to furnish written reasons for refusing an application for registration, for determining conditions subject to which any registration is granted, or for cancelling any registration, if requested to do so by an applicant.[85] The Act makes provision for appeals to the Minister against such decisions by any person who feels aggrieved by the decision. The Minister is required to refer the appeal for consideration and decision by a board of which the members are appointed by him, consisting of one person designated as chairman on account on his legal knowledge, and two persons who, in the opinion of the Minister, command sufficient knowledge regarding the matter which will probably be an issue when the appeal is considered.[86]

20.5.2.8 *Manufacture and related actions*

Control is exercised over the manufacture of agricultural and stock remedies in that, in considering an application for registration of such remedies, the registrar must be satisfied that the establishment where these remedies are manufactured is suitable for such manufacture.[87] Moreover, as has been pointed out, the registrar may cancel the registration of any remedy if he is satisfied that the practices followed and facilities available at or in respect of the establishment or the operation of the undertaking at such establishment are not suitable for the manufacture of the remedy concerned[88] or that the person managing such undertaking does not have sufficient knowledge of the relevant provisions of the Act or of the practices to be followed in the operation of such undertaking.[89] The registration of the above-mentioned remedies may also lapse if the

---

[82] Section 4(1).
[83] Section 6A.
[84] Section 4(3).
[85] Section 5.
[86] Section 6.
[87] Section 3(2)*(a)*. The provision is applied in a rather general manner.
[88] Section 4(1)*(c)*.
[89] Section 4(1)*(d)*. 'Sufficient knowledge' is a rather vague term leaving almost everything to the discretion of the registrar.

establishment in question is no longer used for the manufacture of the remedies concerned.[90]

Extensive control is exercised over establishments where agricultural remedies are manufactured, controlled, packed, marked or labelled for the purpose of sale, through the prescription of requirements for such establishments,[91] the maintenance and care of facilities and equipment,[92] the practices to be followed[93] and the keeping of records at such establishments.[94]

20.5.2.9 *Importation*

No person may import any agricultural or stock remedy into the Republic unless it has been registered in terms of the Act, is of the composition and efficacy specified in the application for registration, possesses all chemical, physical and other properties so specified, and complies with the prescribed requirements and is packed in a sealed container which is marked or labelled in the manner and with the particulars prescribed.[95] However, the registrar may, in his discretion and upon such conditions as he may determine, in writing permit the import of a consignment of a remedy which does not comply with these requirements.[96]

Agricultural and stock remedies may be imported only through a prescribed port or place, and if the registrar directs that a sample be taken, it may not be removed from such port or place without his written authority. If a sample has been taken, the remedy may not be sold in the Republic except on his written authority and subject to conditions which he may specify.[97] If imported contrary to the provisions of the Act, the remedy shall, at the option of the importer and at his expense, be removed by him from the Republic within a period determined by the registrar, or be forfeited to the State and either be destroyed or otherwise disposed of as the registrar may direct. If the importer fails to do so, it shall be forfeited to the State and be destroyed or otherwise disposed of, and any costs incurred by the State may be recovered from him.[98]

20.5.2.10 *Sale, disposal or use*

No person may sell[99] any agricultural or stock remedy unless:

- it is registered in terms of the Act under the name and mark under which it sold;
- it is packed in such manner and mass or volume as may be prescribed;
- the container in which it is sold complies with the prescribed requirements and is sealed and labelled or marked in such manner as may be prescribed or, if it is not sold in a container, it is accompanied by an appropriate invoice; and
- it is of the composition and efficacy specified in the application for registration, possesses all chemical, physical and other properties so specified, and complies with the prescribed requirements.[100]

---

[90] Section 4A(2)*(b)*.

[91] Regulation 8 GN R2561 of 27 November 1981.

[92] Regulation 9 GN R2561.

[93] Regulation 7 GN R2561.

[94] Regulation 10 GN R2561. Contravention of any of these regulations is an offence: reg 20*(a)*, *(b)* and *(d)*.

[95] Section 16(1).

[96] Section 16(2).

[97] Section 16(3).

[98] Section 16(6).

[99] 'Sell' includes agree to sell, or to offer, advertise, keep, expose, transmit, convey, deliver or manufacture for sale or to exchange or to dispose of to any person in any manner for any consideration whatever, or to transmit, convey or deliver in pursuance of a sale, exchange or disposal: s 1.

[100] Section 7(1). Section 9 requires any person who sells a remedy not in a container to give the purchaser an invoice setting forth prescribed particulars.

Advertisements relating to agricultural remedies must comply with certain prescriptions.[101]

In addition to prescribed specifications as to the nature of containers in which remedies may be sold and as to the labelling and marketing of containers,[102] the Act also provides that no person may for reward or in the course of business use, or recommend the use of, any remedy for a purpose or in a manner other than that specified on the label or container.[103] The Minister may also, by notice in the *Government Gazette*, prohibit the sale, acquisition, disposal or use of remedies, either totally or subject to such conditions as he may specify in the notice or in a permit. Any such prohibition may apply throughout the Republic, or in one or more specified areas, or to persons belonging to, or not belonging to, a specified class or group, or in respect of all or one or more classes or kinds of remedies.[104]

Any person who, at the request of the owner or the person in control of a thing, administers any remedy for reward must, before such administration, notify the owner or person concerned of the purpose of such administration, the registered name and number of the remedy to be administered, the precautions to be taken before, during and after such administration, and the number of his certificate of registration if he is a registered pest control operator.[105]

20.5.2.11 *Offences and penalties*

The Act provides a detailed list of offences,[106] including the following:

- obstruction or hindering the registrar, technical adviser or analyst in the exercise of their powers or performance of their duties under the Act;
- failure to make any statement or give any explanation when requested by the registrar in the exercise of his powers;
- unauthorized acquisition, disposal, sale or use of agricultural or stock remedies;
- tampering with any sample taken or anything seized in terms of the Act;
- making any false or misleading statement in connection with any such remedy in an application for its registration, or in the course of any advertisement or sale thereof;
- selling any such remedy upon the container of which is a false or misleading statement in connection with its contents;
- the sale of any such remedy which is not of the kind, nature, composition, strength, potency or quality described or represented when sold.

The Court convicting any person of an offence under the Act may declare any such remedy in respect of which the offence has been committed, as well as all other remedies of a similar nature to that in respect of which the accused has been convicted, and of which he is the owner or possessor, to be forfeited to the State.[107]

20.5.3 Other relevant legislation

The Fertilizers, Farm Feeds, Agricultural Remedies and Stock Remedies Act does not make any specific reference to the exportation of pesticides. However, some control

---

[101] Regulation 17 GN R2561 of 27 November 1981.

[102] Section 7(1)*(c)* and regs 14 and 15 GN R2561 of 27 November 1981.

[103] Section 7(2)*(a)*.

[104] Section 7*bis*(2)*(c)*. In terms of GN R928 of 1 May 1981 a total prohibition in respect of the whole of the Republic was imposed on the acquisition, disposal or sale of remedies which contain the following prohibited substances: a mixture of different isomers of BHC, excluding gamma-BHC with a purity grade of at least 99 per cent (Lindane); Dichlor-diphenyl-trichloroethane (DDT); and Dieldrin or Aldrin, with the exception of Aldrin for use underneath buildings for the control of wood destroying termites.

[105] Section 10(1).

[106] Section 18(1). The penalties on conviction range from R500 or imprisonment not exceeding 12 months, or both, to R1 000 or imprisonment for a period not exceeding two years, or both.

[107] Section 18(2).

can be exercised over pesticide residues in agricultural products destined for export by virtue of the provisions of the Agricultural Produce Export Act 51 of 1971. The export of a product is prohibited unless it has been approved for export by an inspector in terms of this Act,[108] and the Minister may make regulations as to the amount of foreign matter that may be permissible in such products.[109] 'Product' is defined as a commodity specified or declared as such by the Minister by notice in the *Government Gazette* or listed in Part 1 of schedule 1 to the Act.[110] Those specified are what are generally regarded as agricultural produce—for example, maize, fruit, tobacco, meat, eggs and butter. This does not, however, cover the exporting of pesticides themselves.

Pesticides may also be controlled under the Hazardous Substances Act 15 of 1973, in terms of which any substance or mixture of substances which, in the course of customary or reasonable handling or use, including ingestion, might by reason of its toxic nature cause injury, ill-health or death to human beings, may be declared by the Minister of National Health and Population Development to be a Group I or Group II hazardous substance.[111] Declared Group I substances may not be sold except under licence and subject to conditions.[112] The Minister may make regulations relating to the manufacture, importation, storage or dumping and other disposal of any group hazardous substance.[113]

Regulations in respect of Group I hazardous substances have been promulgated in terms of the Hazardous Substances Act.[114] These regulations regulate the process of licensing,[115] the conditions of sale or supply,[116] the records to be kept by licensees,[117] the labelling[118] and disposal of empty containers[119] and the duties of inspectors and analysts.[120]

Both the Fertilizers, Farm Feeds, Agricultural Remedies and Stock Remedies Act and the Hazardous Substances Act accordingly make provision for the control of related aspects as far as pesticides are concerned. The former Act, which is aimed principally at the protection of agriculture, seeks to ensure that only approved pesticides reach the consumer and that only approved pesticides are used, while through the latter Act, which is aimed at the protection of public health, an attempt is made to ensure that only approved persons deal in highly toxic pesticides, and then only in a prescribed manner. Both Acts have regulations dealing with pesticide containers. The necessary co-ordination between the administration of these Acts is sought to be achieved through the inter-departmental advisory committee for the protection of man against poisons, which consists of representatives from the departments of National Health and Population Development and of Agriculture. The appointment of this committee, which transpired in 1969, was recommended by the committee of inquiry into safeguarding man against poisons in its 1967 report.

The Foodstuffs, Cosmetics and Disinfectants Act 54 of 1972 contains provisions aimed at the prohibition of the sale,[121] manufacture[122] or importation[123] of any

[108] Section 2(1).
[109] Section 4(1)*(o)*.
[110] Section 1.
[111] Section 2(1)*(a)*.
[112] Section 3(1)*(a)*.
[113] Section 29(1)*(a)*.
[114] GN R2778 of 21 December 1984. Cf also GN R73 of 11 January 1985 governing the conveyance of hazardous substances by road tanker.
[115] Regulations 2 and 3.
[116] Regulation 4.
[117] Regulations 5 and 6.
[118] Regulation 8.
[119] Regulation 10.
[120] Regulation 9.
[121] Cf s 1 for the definition of 'sell'.

foodstuffs[124] which contain or have been treated[125] with a prohibited substance,[126] or which contain a particular substance in a greater measure than that permitted by regulation, or have been treated with a substance containing a particular substance in greater measure than that permitted by regulation.[127] Contravention of these provisions is an offence.[128] The Minister of National Health and Population Development may make regulations prescribing any foreign substance, or the nature of foreign substances, that may be considered as unavoidably present in any foodstuffs or cosmetic as a result of the process of its collection, manufacture or treatment, or the greatest measure in which any such substance or substances of such nature may be present in any foodstuffs or cosmetic.[129] Utilizing this power, the Minister has promulgated regulations concerning the sale of various products on the domestic market.[130]

In terms of the Health Act 63 of 1977, poisoning from any agricultural or stock remedy registered in terms of the Fertilizers, Farm Feeds, Agricultural Remedies and Stock Remedies Act is a notifiable medical condition.[131]

20.6 CONCLUSION

20.6.1 Public interest

At present the registrar, in considering registration of pesticides and cancellation of registration, is required to take 'public interest' into account.[132] It may be argued that because public interest is not defined, it follows that he is given a wide discretion. To avoid any doubt, public interest should be legislatively defined so as to include reference to any unreasonable risk to human health or the environment (including risk to fish and wildlife), whether in the short or long term, having regard to the economic, social and environmental costs and benefits of the use of the pesticide.

20.6.2 International implications

Because pesticide pollution does not respect national boundaries, not only must there be liaison between neighbouring states in order to control trans-border effects, there should be stricter control of the manufacture, handling and use of pesticides for exportation purposes. An export licence should be required and the onus should be on the applicant for such a licence to prove that the proposed use of the pesticide will not be contrary to the public interest in both South Africa and the importing country.

20.6.3 Criminal sanction

The penalties at present prescribed for contravention of the provisions of the Act are inadequate, having regard to the potential impact of pesticides on human health and the environment, and should be substantially increased so as to be an effective deterrent, not only to individuals but also to manufacturing industrialists.

---

[122] Cf s 1 for the definition of 'manufacture'.
[123] Cf s 1 for the definition of 'import'.
[124] Cf s 1 for the definition of 'foodstuffs'.
[125] Cf s 1 for the definition of 'treated'.
[126] Section 2(1)*(a)*(i).
[127] Section 2(1)*(a)*(ii).
[128] Section 2(1) read with s 18.
[129] Section 15(1)*(d)*. Contravention of the regulation may be an offence: s 15(5).
[130] GN R1267 of 26 July 1974, GN R24 of 2 January 1981, GN R1386 of 3 July 1981, GN R2227 of 23 October 1981 and GN R556 of 18 March 1983.
[131] Section 45 and GN R1802 of 24 August 1979.
[132] Sections 3(2)*(b)* and 4(1)*(e)*.

20.6.4 Health risk to end-users

The inadequacy of existing controls in respect of the 'end-users' of pesticides has been highlighted.[133] The misuse of pesticides in agriculture would be reduced if farmers applying large quantities of pesticides were required to register as pest control operators.[134] The re-use of empty pesticide containers for domestic purposes—for example, for the storage of drinking water in rural areas—is also clearly a potential risk to health because of the residues that may remain in them. There should be stricter control over the collection and disposal of empty containers and excess chemicals.

20.6.5 State liability

The Environment Conservation Act 73 of 1989 provides that the State, including any provincial administration, is bound by that Act, apart from its criminal provisions.[135] There is no equivalent provision in Act 36 of 1947, which stipulates that, except where it is expressly otherwise provided for in the Act, no compensation shall be payable by the State, the Minister or the registrar in respect of any act done in good faith under the Act.[136] Even if the State is unwilling to accept liability for the consequences of its use of pesticides or for allowing their use by others, surely state departments and officials should at least be bound by the controls relating to the use of pesticides.

20.6.6 Law reform

The mounting evidence of contamination of human health and the environment has stimulated public awareness of the potential risks associated with the use of pesticides and has produced a favourable climate for law reform. A complete ban on the use of the substances concerned is clearly neither practical nor desirable, and pesticides will continue to play an important role in the production of food and the protection of health, especially in developing countries. But the price paid for these benefits must not be too high. Strict control is essential, and it is vital that the law fulfil its regulatory role in this context. To what extent is the following statement made in the United States some 20 years ago relevant in South Africa today?

> 'The story of DDT is a story of uncontrolled experimentation with the world's population and environment. The vehicle for protecting us from ourselves—the law—was tried and found wanting. . . . Whether that vehicle will be repaired for the voyage ahead is currently being debated. Certainly no goal surpasses in importance the need to prevent man from harming, abusing or destroying himself and his environment. No one is immune from the challenge nor secure from the consequences of failure.'[137]

The Fertilizers, Farm Feeds, Agricultural Remedies and Stock Remedies Act deals substantively in one statute with such diverse matters as pesticides, food for domestic animals and livestock, substances for improving the growth of plants and the productivity of the soil, and remedies intended for the maintenance or improvement of the health of domestic animals, livestock, poultry, fish or wild animals (including wild birds). There is no doubt that all of these matters are of sufficient importance to warrant legislative control and regulation; but such wide-ranging treatment and mixture of topics is unnecessarily complex. The health and environmental implications of pesticide use are of sufficient importance to justify the enactment of a specific Pesticides Control Act, in which provision is made for a Pesticides Board to administer the Act (not the Department of Agriculture, the primary function of which is to promote agricultural development), in the same way as has been done in New Zealand, having public and

---

[133] Genis & Rabie above n 2, 424, 430–1.
[134] Barlin-Brinck above n 3, vii, 33–4.
[135] Section 40.
[136] Section 23A.
[137] Rodgers above n 62, 611.

private sector representation and comprising persons appointed from the relevant State departments, non-government organizations, and the agricultural and horticultural industries.[138] Consideration should, moreover, be given to consolidating all pesticide legislation in the proposed Pesticides Control Act.

20.6.7 Final considerations

It is clear that, when pesticides are applied against pest organisms, they are in fact impinging on highly complex ecosystems, affecting individuals, populations and communities in many different ways. In so far as they reduce the numbers of harmful organisms in crop and animal production, as well as disease vectors, they are of great benefit to humankind. However, their use and persistence in the environment should continuously be monitored so that the effects of the ecological disturbance and possible hazards they cause could become known and be prevented where possible. Although the pesticide levels so far determined for groundwater, surface water and the tissues of wildlife specimens in South Africa are relatively low compared to levels in many other countries, this work should continue, especially in areas of intensive agriculture or where specific pesticides are used in large quantities. Of particular concern is the potential danger of pesticide residues in food such as fruit and vegetables where the chemical is applied directly to the edible part of the plant. Since there is and can be no effective direct control over the way farmers use pesticides, this should be done indirectly by extensive monitoring of their products—not only those reaching the big markets but also those that are sold in supermarkets and smaller outlets such as farm stalls. At the same time, consumers should be made more aware of the need to wash fruit and vegetables thoroughly before consumption, although this would not remove all residues because of the insolubility and systemic nature of some pesticides. These precautions are particularly relevant in view of the recent discoveries in the USA about the oncogenic potential of low levels of pesticides.

At present there are a number of alarming shortcomings in the system of pesticide use. Amongst these are the lack of control over the end user of pesticides so that ignorant, negligent or reckless farmers cannot be exposed and penalized; the lack of knowledge about the extent of pesticide levels in fruit and vegetables sold on the formal and informal markets; the problem of identifying some of the pesticides by routine laboratory methods, and the uncertainty concerning the safety of pesticide levels (tolerances) officially allowed in food.

A report by the EPA ranks pesticides as one of the most serious health and environmental problems in the USA.[139] The South African authorities should take note of the concern expressed there, extend the work in determining base levels of pesticides in our general environment and in food in particular, and act speedily when pesticides are misused or the normal use causes unacceptable risks and environmental damage.

---

[138] For a further discussion of the role of law in protecting man and his environment against the adverse effects of pesticide pollution, see Glavovic 'Persistent pesticides: elixirs of death or boon to mankind'? 1985 *SALJ* 674.

[139] Mott & Snyder above n 17, 18.

CHAPTER 21

RADIATION

P R LE ROUX
D VAN AS
Y M BURNS
G P DE BEER
M G VAN DER MERWE

21.1 INTRODUCTION

Radiation from both natural and man-made sources spans a frequency range of 20 orders of magnitude and includes the electromagnetic spectrum, illustrated in Figure 21.1 and the acoustic spectrum. The latter spectrum is conveniently subdivided into infrasound (ie frequencies less than 20 Hz) , sound (those frequencies lying between 20 Hz and 20 kHz which are audible to the human ear) and ultrasound (ie frequencies greater than 20 kHz). Ultrasound is illustrated further in Figure 21.2, while acoustic radiation, or noise, is dealt with in chapter 22.

The energy of the radiation is proportional to the frequency and covers an energy range from 10^{-11} electronvolt for long radiowaves to 10^{10} electronvolt for the most energetic X-rays. When any radiation falls onto matter—including living tissue—its energy is absorbed by and dissipated in the atoms and molecules. Certain frequencies are detected by the human senses as light, heat and sound.

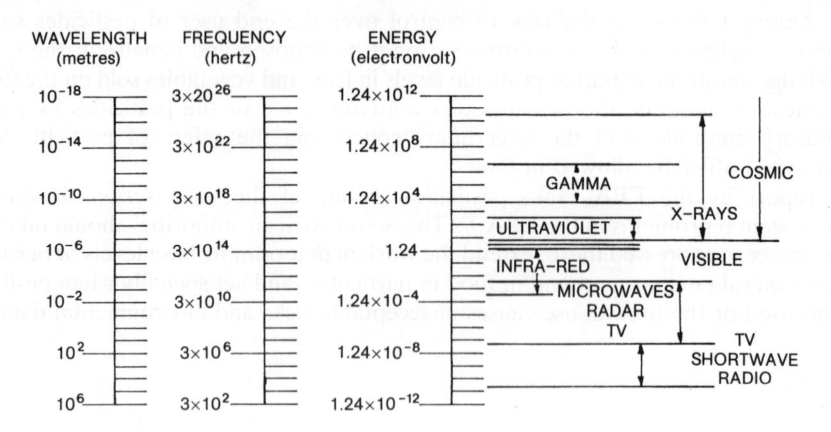

Type of radiation	*Wavelength range** (metres)	*Frequency range* (hertz)	*Energy range* (eV)
Radio waves	$3 \times 10^{4} - 3 \times 10^{-4}$	$\times 10^{4} - \times 10^{12}$	$4,1 \times 10^{-11} - 4,1 \times 10^{-3}$
Infra-red	$3 \times 10^{-3} - 7,6 \times 10^{-7}$	$\times 10^{11} - \times 10^{14}$	$4,1 \times 10^{-4} - 1,6$
Visible	$7,6 \times 10^{-7} - 3,8 \times 10^{-7}$	$4 \times 10^{14} - 7,9 \times 10^{14}$	$1,6 - 3,3$
Ultraviolet	$3,8 \times 10^{-7} - 3 \times 10^{-9}$	$7,9 \times 10^{14} - \times 10^{17}$	$3,3 - 410$
X-rays	$1,2 \times 10^{-7} - 4,1 \times 10^{-17}$	$2,5 \times 10^{15} - 7,3 \times 10^{24}$	$10 - \times 10^{10}$
Gamma rays	$1,5 \times 10^{-10} - 1,2 \times 10^{-13}$	$2 \times 10^{18} - 2,5 \times 10^{21}$	$8 \times 10^{3} - 10^{7}$
Cosmic rays	$1,2 \times 10^{-7}$ – ——	$2,5 \times 10^{15}$ – ——	10 – ——

Figure 21.1 The electromagnetic spectrum.

Radiation in the high-frequency range (10^{15} Hz) with energy in excess of 10 eV transfers sufficient energy to knock an electron from the outer shells of atoms with which it interacts, resulting in a positively charged ion and a negatively charged electron. This process, known as ionization, can result in biological effects but is not detected by human senses. It can best be observed at very low intensities by instruments such as ionization chambers, Geiger–Muller detectors or scintillation detectors. Familiar forms of ionizing radiation are Roentgen (or X-rays) and gamma rays.

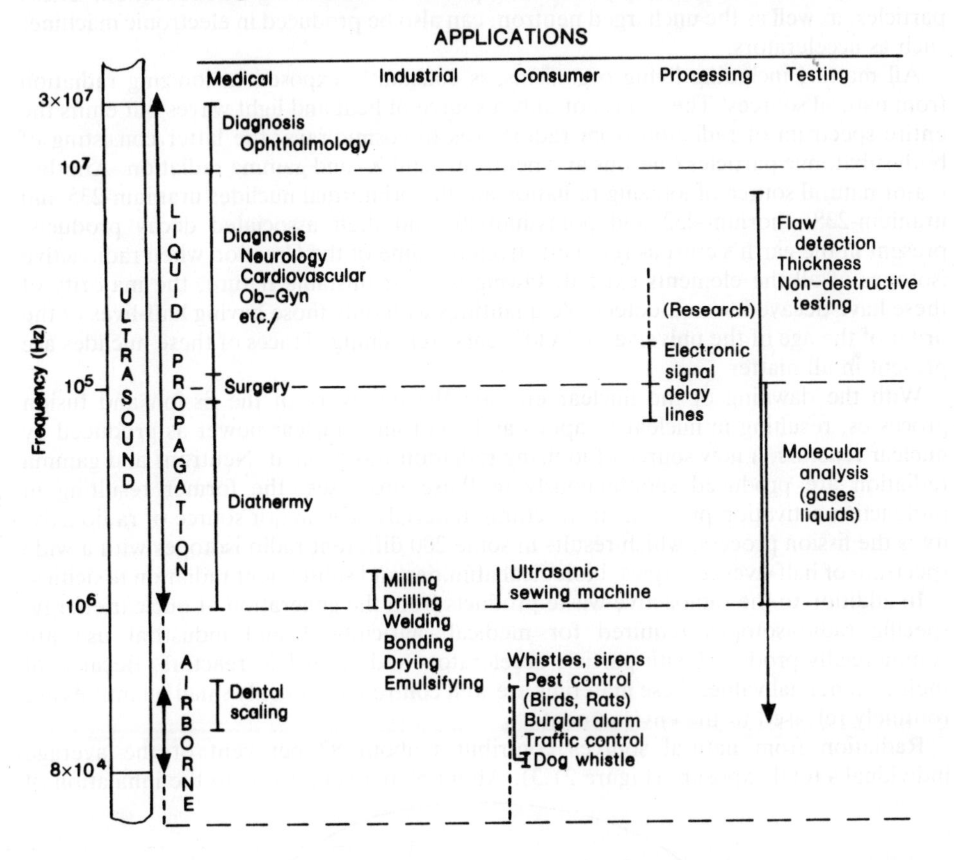

Figure 21.2 The ultrasound spectrum. Applications of ultrasound in medicine, industry, consumer products, signal processing and testing are shown in relation to ultrasound frequency in megahertz.

Other forms of radiation such as ultraviolet, visible and infra-red light waves, lasers, microwaves, short, medium and long radiowaves do not dissipate enough energy to cause ionization but can result in other biological effects which require distinctive norms and standards of control.

21.2 IONIZING RADIATION

21.2.1 Sources of ionizing radiation

Ionizing radiation consists essentially of two components, namely electromagnetic waves and subatomic particles. The electromagnetic component, i e X- and gamma rays, are emitted spontaneously by radioactive isotopes. The X-rays originate from the outer electron bands of the atom, while the gamma rays are produced in the nucleus of the atom itself. Both these rays can also be produced in electronic machines: X-ray machines or accelerators. In these cases the bombardment of different target materials with electrons or other atomic projectiles produces high fluxes of X- or gamma radiation.

The subatomic component of ionizing radiation consists of charged nuclear particles, e g alpha particles and beta particles or electrons which move at very high speeds. These particles are spontaneously emitted by radio-isotopes, but, because of their particulate nature, do not have the same penetrating power as electromagnetic radiation. These particles, as well as the uncharged neutron, can also be produced in electronic machines such as accelerators.

All matter, including living organisms, is constantly exposed to ionizing radiation from natural sources. The sun is not only a source of heat and light waves but emits the entire spectrum of radiation from radiowaves to cosmic rays, the latter consisting of both subatomic particles (mesons and neutrons) and X- and gamma radiation. Another major natural source of ionizing radiation are the primordial nuclides uranium-235 and uranium-238, thorium-232 and potassium-40, and their associated decay products, present in the earth's crust as remnants from the time of the Creation when radioactive isotopes of all the elements existed. Owing to their unstable nature, the majority of these have decayed to non-detectable quantities with only those having half-lives of the order of the age of the universe ($4,5 \times 10^9$ years) remaining. Traces of these nuclides are present in all matter.

With the dawning of the nuclear era and the discovery of the fission and fusion processes, resulting in nuclear weapons and controlled nuclear power as produced by nuclear reactors, a new source of ionizing radiation was created. Neutrons and gamma radiation are produced spontaneously in these processes, the former resulting in radioactive activation products in structural materials. The major source of radioactivity is the fission process, which results in some 200 different radio-isotopes with a wide spectrum of half-lives, energies, biological affinities and subsequent radiation toxicities.

In addition to the radioactive waste products from the generation of nuclear energy, specific radio-isotopes required for medical, agricultural and industrial use are commercially produced with particle accelerators and in nuclear reactors. Because of their commercial value, these materials are well controlled and only small quantities are routinely released to the environment.

Radiation from natural sources contributes about 87 per cent of the average individual's total exposure (Figure 21.3). About 50 per cent is due to the inhalation of

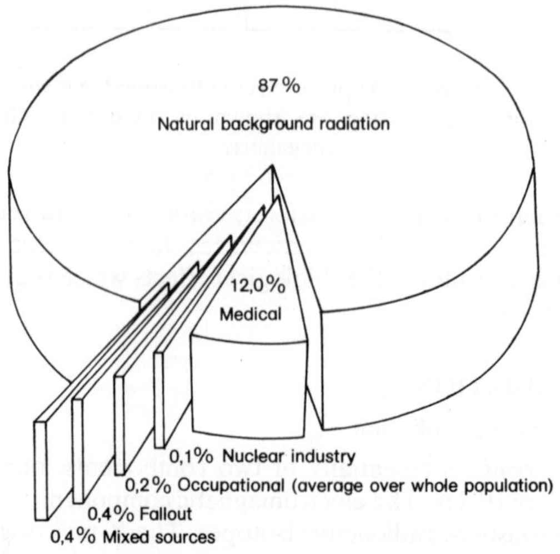

Figure 21.3 Contribution of various sources to the average total annual effective dose to the UK population (UKEA, 1989).

radon daughter products. Radon is a natural radioactive gas which emanates from any material containing uranium, thorium and their radium decay products. Depending on the soil type, radium content and building structure, varying concentrations of radon and its subsequent decay products will accumulate indoors. In poorly ventilated spaces this can result in unsafe conditions for the inhabitants. The remaining contribution from natural sources is mainly due to the exposure from potassium-40, other uranium and thorium decay products and cosmic radiation.

The next most important source of radiation to the average individual (about 12 per cent) derives from radiography for medical diagnosis (X-rays). Other man-made radiation sources such as nuclear tests and nuclear power contribute only about 1 per cent of the average individual's total radiation exposure.

21.2.2 Radiation effects

The ionizing radiations from X-ray machines and radioactive materials have been recognized as detrimental to human beings since the closing years of the 19th century. Radiologists were the first to become aware of the hazards of ionizing radiation, and at the second international congress of radiology in 1928 (held in Stockholm) it was decided to establish an International X-ray and Radium Protection Commission. It assumed the present name of International Commission on Radiological Protection (ICRP) in 1950 in order to cover more effectively the rapidly expanding field of radiation protection. Furthermore, the need for internationally accepted units of radiation dosage had already led to the establishment of an International Commission on Radiological Units and Measurements at the first international congress of radiology in 1925. Since that time—and especially in the post-war era of nuclear science—a great deal has been learnt about the biological effects of radiation and radioactive materials.

These materials may be ingested or inhaled and, depending on a material's physical and chemical properties, it can be metabolized and concentrated in particular body organs, where it can cause high localized irradiation, especially from particulate emissions. The hazards of ionizing radiation lie in the chemical and biological effects produced when tissue material is irradiated. The energy of the ionizing radiation is transferred to electrons, which are stripped from atoms in the tissue. These energetic electrons cause further stripping of other atoms, thus forming many ions which have high chemical reactivity and which disrupt the normal function of cells in the body.

If cellular damage is not adequately repaired, the cell may not survive or reproduce. Through a second mechanism the cell may be modified with profoundly different implications.

As most organs and tissues are unaffected by the loss of even a substantial number of cells, the first mechanism above will cause observable (deterministic) effects only when such organs are irradiated above a specific threshold dosage. Above the threshold the severity of the effect increases with dosage. The second mechanism may result in a clone of modified cells which may be triggered in future to become cancerous. This may happen even at low irradiation with a proportionality equal to the dose and is termed a stochastic (statistical) effect. Although no stochastic effects have been noted at very low doses, a linear relationship between dose and effect is assumed. Stochastic effects may also occur in germ cells, in which case the effect is hereditary and will be manifested as disorders in descendants.

The biological effects of ionizing radiation have been extensively studied for many years. It is probably true to say that more is known about the effects of radiation than those of any other pollutant and that through the efforts of international bodies such as the ICRP, the International Atomic Energy Agency (IAEA), the World Health Organization (WHO) and the United Nations Scientific Committee on the Effects of

Atomic Radiation (UNSCEAR) as well as various national bodies, more is done to protect human beings and their environment from ionizing radiation than from any other form of pollution.

21.2.3 Principles of radiation protection

The approach adopted by the ICRP in preparing its recommendations is to assist regulatory and advisory agencies at regional, national and international levels mainly by providing guidance on the fundamental principles for an appropriate radiological protection system.

A slightly different approach is adopted for activities which increase existing radiation levels (called practices) and activities which decrease existing radiation levels (called interventions). A distinction is also made between real and potential exposures. In the first case some dosage constraints are recommended, whereas risk constraints are recommended in the second case.

For practices the following basic principles regarding a radiation protection system are recommended:

(a) Any practice should be *justified* and not adopted unless it produces sufficient benefit to the individuals or to society to offset the radiation detriment it causes.

(b) The radiation impact of the practice to people should be *optimized* to be kept as low as reasonably achievable (the so-called ALARA principle), economic and social factors being taken into account.

(c) The exposure of individuals from all relevant practices should be subject to *dose limits* for real exposures or *risk limits* for potential exposures.

In the case of interventions, no dosage or risk limits are recommended, but

(a) the proposed intervention should be *justified* in terms of producing a reduction of dose which outweighs the cost of the intervention; and

(b) the intervention should be *optimized* to maximize its net benefit.

Very similar techniques may be applied for the justification and optimization procedures and various qualitative as well as quantitative techniques are proposed. Optimization is achieved by reducing the collective dose of those individuals exposed to such a value that the cost of further reduction is not justified by the additional protection obtained.

Dose limits proposed would ensure that prolonged exposure at or near this level will not result in an unacceptable increase in risk to individuals compared with the risk from natural hazards or other acceptable practices.

Radioactivity is measured in units of becquerel (Bq) (formerly curie (Ci)) with 1 Bq = 1 disintegration per second (= $2,7 \times 10^{-11}$ Ci).

Each disintegration is associated with the emission of one or more particles or rays. When these particles or rays are absorbed in matter, their energy is transferred and a radiation dose is delivered to the absorbing medium. The absorbed radiation dose is measured in gray (Gy) with 1 Gy = 1 joule per kilogram of absorbing medium.

Because of the different properties of the various particles (alpha, beta, neutron) and energies of the rays (X, gamma) the biological effect of the absorbed radiation doses from the various particles or rays is different. The absorbed dose is hence corrected by radiation weighting factors w^R to account for this. Averaged over a specific organ, this new quantity is called the equivalent dose $H^T = Gy \times w^R$ for organ T and is expressed in sievert (Sv).

The radiation weighting factor is a constant for each particle type and, in the case of neutrons, energy dependent. The value of the radiation weighting factor varies between about 0,3 and 20. A further sophistication is introduced by the quantity effective dose E, which makes provision for the fact that different body organs have different sensitivities for the same equivalent dose. The effective dose is also expressed in sievert and is the equivalent dose normalized for the sensitivity of the particular organs and summed over all organs through multiplication with an organ or tissue weighting factor wr and summed over all organs exposed.

Epidemiological data from major events of radiation exposure ie the exposure of early radiologists, thoracrast patients, radium dial painters and victims from Hiroshima and Nagasaki, made possible the determination of a quantitative relationship between radiation and risk. A reassessment in 1986 of doses received by the Hiroshima and Nagasaki survivors has resulted in increased lifetime risk estimates of radiogenic cancer by the ICRP from the previous 1,25 per cent per sievert to a value of 5 per cent per sievert. No drastic increase in the risk of hereditary effects (estimated at 0,6 per cent) has been observed.

The annual risk of death due to radiation among workers increases with age, reaching a maximum near an age of about 75 years. A risk of 0,1 per cent per annum at a retirement age of 65 years is considered as acceptable and, based on this, the ICRP recommends a dose limit of 0,02 Sv per year to workers. For the general public a dose limit of 0,001 Sv per year is recommended based on a maximum annual risk of 0,01 per cent.

21.2.4 Environmental control

Standards for the release of radioactivity to the environment were initially based on dose limits which were defined as levels of exposure not expected to result in any significant increase in harm. These dose limits related both to individuals and the population as a whole; in practice, however, the criteria for releases were set almost entirely in terms of the individual most exposed. Because of the greater sensitivity of the higher organisms to radiation, it is considered that, if human beings are protected, all other organisms are protected too.

The environmental media of air and water were considered to be the major carriers of the pollutants from source to man; from the assumed average daily volume of air inhaled and water consumed, as well as from knowledge of the metabolic behaviour of particular elements, annual limits on intake (ALI) which would not result in the specific dose limits being exceeded were calculated for each individual nuclide. Release limits are calculated by taking into account normal dilution and dispersion that will not lead to the annual limits on intake in air or water being exceeded at any point where the public may be exposed. This procedure, although a vast improvement on previous procedures, did not, if effluent rates were high, prevent substantial amounts of radioactive material from reaching the environment, nor did it take ecological concentration processes into account.

As a further development of the process of setting emission standards, the principle of the critical pathway by means of which the released material could return to man had to be investigated. Those resulting in the highest exposure were termed the critical pathways. A concentration limit was then derived for the critical food product which, if consumed at the rate determined by a habits survey, would result in a dose limit to the critical group. By applying data on environmental dispersion and transfer, a permissible release-rate limit could be determined. These limits were never to be exceeded and encouragement was given to keep the release rate as low as reasonably achievable (ALARA).

Further sophistication, to ensure that individual doses will not be exceeded and that optimization of protection is ensured, was brought about by the recommendation that national authorities lay down a source-related dose upper limit. This will ensure that the contributions from all potential sources of exposure to the individual, present and future, are taken into account when setting limits for the release of radio-nuclides into the environment from a particular source. Although the current exposure of individual members of the public to regional or global releases is a very small fraction of the internationally accepted dose limits and of the natural radiation background, the application of this principle should ensure that with the further development of nuclear power throughout the world the population will be protected not only from present sources but from all future sources.

Normal releases from the nuclear industry to the environment result in radiation doses that cannot be detected above the natural variation in radiation dose. The doses can best be calculated from the measured release rates using mathematical models of environmental behaviour. In addition, environmental monitoring is used to verify the assumptions of the model and to ensure that all pathways are accounted for.

Accidental exposure to radiation may occur (eg the Chernobyl accident; the loss of a therapeutic caesium-137 source in Brazil, etc). The probability of the occurrence of such exposures must be kept to acceptable levels by the introduction of multiple barriers to prevent releases and strict control measures and the employment of highly skilled operators in accordance with accepted international nuclear safety regulations.

21.3 NON-IONIZING RADIATION

21.3.1 Introduction

Non-ionizing radiation (NIR) is the term generally used to characterize all those forms of electromagnetic and mechanical radiation whose primary mode of interaction with matter is other than by ionization. Therefore, as generally defined, NIR refers to electromagnetic radiation with photon energy equal to or less than 10 eV which encompasses the electromagnetic spectrum below the ultraviolet (UV), as well as mechanical radiation or acoustic pressure waves. In the latter, only ultrasonic frequencies above approximately 20 kHz are usually considered as NIR. Sound intensities—that is, energy flow per unit area—of approximately 1 W cm^{-2} may cause appreciable internal heating and/or cavitation. Audible sound, in the range from 20 Hz to 20 kHz, and infrasound at frequencies below 20 Hz are excluded, because their effects are usually related to sound pressure rather than to sound intensity.

The significance of exposure to NIR varies considerably according to the type of NIR involved, the exposure conditions and the persons at risk. The rapidly expanding scientific, medical, industrial and home use of devices, designed specifically to emit NIR, have led to a steady increase in the amount of NIR in the environment. This may be a cause for concern because of the potential health hazards to workers and the general public through uncontrolled or excessive exposure to these radiations.

Considering these rapidly expanding uses of NIR-producing devices, it is important to assess realistically the potential hazards of exposure to NIR and to establish exposure limits so that workers or the general public will be adequately protected without unduly restricting the beneficial applications of these energies.

Devices utilizing NIR are conveniently grouped into one of the following three categories: electro-optical devices, radio-frequency and microwave devices, and ultrasound devices (not electromagnetic radiation but rather acoustic pressure waves).

21.3.2 Sources of non-ionizing radiation

21.3.2.1 *Electro-optical devices*

Optical radiation covers the ultraviolet, visible and infra-red portions of the electromagnetic spectrum. While visible light is generally safe, hazards can arise from certain high-intensity sources such as projector bulbs, spotlights and floodlights.

Occupational health hazards resulting from exposure to conventional infra-red (IR) and UV radiation have been known for many years and occur in a number of situations such as working near high-temperature sources (IR and UV), the use of electrical arcs in metal welding and cutting (UV), the fabrication, control and occupational use of fluorescent and mercury vapour lamps (UV), and UV sterilization. An important source of occupational exposure to UV is the exposure to natural UV of all people working out of doors. Exposure of the general population to this range of NIR results mainly from the expanded use of IR heating apparatus and the widespread leisure activity of sunbathing (natural UV) and tanning by voluntary exposure to UV from UV lamps and tanning booths.

The rate of development and use of laser devices since their appearance some 20 years ago has been truly phenomenal. The term 'laser device' refers to a device emitting a coherent, monochromatic, narrow and intense beam of electromagnetic radiation with a wavelength depending on the active medium used and ranging from the far UV region to the microwave (MW) range. Occupational hazards associated with lasers are found mainly in high-power scientific and industrial applications such as the microwelding and microfinishing of metals, drilling, telemetry, applied optics (holography), telecommunications, guidance systems and illuminating techniques in the entertainment field (laser light shows). Laser devices are a useful scientific research tool in the fields of nuclear fusion, isotope separation and spectroscopy. In the medical field lasers were first used in ophthalmology for photocoagulation and are now recognized as an excellent tool for microsurgery of the eye. Surgical lasers can be used as the primary tool to create a surgical incision in heavily vascularized areas; to excise or necrose tissues after incision; to excise or necrose endoscopically accessible tissue; and to vapourize surface anomalies (e g warts). Lasers are also currently promoted for use in pain relief by direct irradiation of nerves or acupuncture points, and also in non-invasive cosmetic surgery, where its advocates suggest that the laser can smooth out wrinkles and improve skin tone.

21.3.2.2 *Radio-frequency and microwave devices*

The number of devices which, by design, emit electromagnetic waves into the atmosphere is growing rapidly and their power is increasing. Occupational exposure remains the main source of chronic and acute exposure to MW and radio-frequency (RF) radiation, particularly with respect to the following activities: broadcasting, telecommunications, air- and shipborne radar navigation, air traffic control, satellite communication, food processing, sterilization techniques and using RF dielectric heaters.

Members of the public may be exposed to MW and RF because they live in the vicinity of high-power sources such as radar installations, broadcasting stations and television transmitters or because of the increasing domestic use of microwave ovens.

Medical exposure is chiefly due to shortwave and microwave diathermy applications.

21.3.2.3 *Ultrasound devices*

First used in submarine echo sounding, ultrasound has found a wide range of practical applications in recent times. Major industrial applications of ultrasound are found in industrial cleaning, machining, plastic welding, emulsifying, flaw detection and sonar detection of submerged objects. The general public may be exposed through the use of various consumer-oriented products such as devices sold for bird and rodent control, burglar alarms, traffic control and also dog whistles.

Medical uses, however, seem to be the most rapidly increasing source of exposure, with ultrasound devices being used for diagnostic, surgical, dental and therapeutic purposes, where ultrasound therapy is a common procedure in physical therapy. Diagnostic applications are associated with many medical specialities but particularly with obstetrics, where they include foetal cephalometry, placental localization, detection of intra-uterine life and diagnosis of multiple pregnancy. Surgical applications employ high-intensity ultrasound to destroy tissue purposely. At present the most important surgical applications are: neurosurgery and ophthalmic surgery. In dentistry ultrasound instruments are used for the removal of calculus, and other deposits from teeth.

21.3.3 Biological effects of non-ionizing radiation

It is important to distinguish between an effect per se and a phenomenon that constitutes a health hazard. It is also important to realize that most information on bioeffects is derived from animal experimentation, model studies and epidemiological research on the health status of persons occupationally exposed to NIR.

The analysis of bioeffects requires consideration of a chain of events that starts with the primary interaction between the NIR and the biosystem, the physiological responses, immediate local or generalized effects and the late or delayed effects.

21.3.3.1 *Ultraviolet radiation*

The effects of UV radiation on man are normally restricted to the skin, eyes and, under special circumstances, to the oral cavity.

(a) Skin. In the skin, four types of immediate changes occur: a darkening of pigment, probably due to an oxidation of existing pre-melanin granules; an onset of erythema (reddening of the skin) which at higher levels of exposure can be complicated by vascular permeability, giving rise to oedema and blistering; an increase in pigmentation which manifests itself as the well-known suntan and is in fact initially a spreading of existing pigment granules into neighbouring cells throughout the exposed skin. Production of new pigment granules commences slightly later; and an interference with the growth of cells in the skin, seen as a decrease in thymidine labelling of single cells in the basal layer.

Delayed effects of prolonged exposure to UV include degeneration of the elastic fibres and other histological changes in the dermal tissue, resulting in a decrease in the skin's elasticity and other symptoms of premature ageing.

Cancer of the skin is another well-recognized effect of UV irradiation over an extended period. Three types of cancer are most frequent: basal cell carcinoma, spindle cell carcinoma and melanoma.

(b) Eye. Ultraviolet radiation is largely absorbed in the cornea and surrounding sclera and conjunctiva, while radiation of slightly longer wavelengths is able to penetrate the anterior chamber and, to some degree, the lens. The clinical effect of UV radiation is photokeratitis, which appears up to 24 hours after irradiation with acute hyperaemia and photophobia.

(c) Mouth. Plastic materials used in dentistry that have to be hardened with UV treatment have introduced a certain risk to the mucous membrane of the mouth. As far as is known, the only effect has been severe erythema of the skin around the mouth.

21.3.3.2 *Lasers*

Turning to the biological effects of laser radiation, it should be noted that, while technical achievements usually move in advance of the understanding of the associated hazards, it has been encouraging to see the attention given to the effects of laser radiation on biological systems since its inception.

(a) Eye. There has never been any dispute about the fact that the most critical organ, in terms of vulnerability to laser radiation, is the eye. The cornea, lens and ocular medium are largely transparent in the visible region with most radiation being focused on and absorbed by the melanin granules in the retinal pigment epithelium and choroid which underlie the rods and cones. There is general agreement that the physical destruction of biological tissue can be attributed to thermal, thermo-acoustic or photochemical phenomena.

(b) Skin. The biological consequences of irradiating the skin with lasers are considered to be less than those caused by the exposure of the eye to lasers with the same power, since skin damage is often repairable or reversible. However, exposure of

the skin to high-intensity laser radiation can cause depigmentation, severe burns and possible damage to underlying organs.

21.3.3.3 *Radio-frequency and microwave devices*

Exposure of biological systems to RF energy leads to temperature elevation if the rate of energy absorption exceeds the rate of energy dissipation. At frequencies above 10 MHz tissue heating is certainly the established mechanism for producing most reported biological effects. At frequencies below 10 MHz the theory of electrical stimulation of excitable tissues, such as nerves and muscles, is also well established. This latter mechanism of interaction becomes more dominant than heating at frequencies below 100 kHz.

There is some reassurance in the fact that for about 10 years no additional subtle adverse health effects other than behavioural disruption have been found.

The knowledge that has thus far been gained from in-vitro experiments has provided only limited insights for in-vivo studies. Studies on experimental animals have revealed a variety of responses which always appear to be related to heating when the incident RF radiation has a frequency greater than 10 MHz. The animal data (particularly primate) suggest that acute effects may occur in mammals in response to a heat load which causes the body temperature to rise by 1 °C or more.

Epidemiological studies of human populations which are exposed to RF fields predominantly in the work environment are limited in scope and quality. All epidemiological studies on this topic suffer from some design and methodological shortcomings. None of the studies shows evidence of a strong association between RF exposure and any particular health effect. Where associations have been found they have been, at most, very weak. The RF fields in these studies have generally been at the relatively high levels that are typically encountered in the work environment. The best conducted studies suggest that prolonged low-level RF exposure does not increase morbidity or mortality. However, the lack of dosimetric information which precludes determination or even estimation of the level of RF exposure, reduces even further the value of these studies.

(a) Behavioural effects. Disrupted behavioural performance appears to be the most sensitive biological response to RF radiation. Protecting against these effects will protect against most other thermal responses. The RF energy input required for behavioural changes can sometimes be less than half the resting metabolic rate of the animal. Behavioural changes have also been observed at RF levels that are far below those which cause any other measurable biological changes. Whether these disruptions of behaviour are truly an indicator of adverse health effects, however, is open to question. In itself, evidence of behavioural changes is not a defined hazard—it is, however, assumed that chronic exposure under such conditions may be a health hazard. The fact that behavioural effects occur as a result of temperature increases makes direct extrapolation from animal to man a conservative assumption, given the demonstrated superb thermoregulation of human beings compared to that of the reference species (i e rats, monkeys).

(b) Ocular effects. The lens of the eye is potentially very sensitive to RF exposure, because it lacks a blood supply and therefore has a reduced ability to dissipate heat. In addition, the fibres which make up the bulk of the lens have a limited capacity for repair and tend to accumulate the effects of minor insults. Most studies have used the rabbit as the experimental animal model, because its eye dimensions approach those of the human eye. The threshold RF power density necessary to produce a cataract was found to be approximately 150 mW cm^{-2} when applied exclusively to the eye for at least 1 hour. The RF field intensity associated with this kind of acute induction of cataracts in the rabbit would have been lethal had it been applied to the whole animal. Chronic

whole body exposures at lower levels of power density did not produce any lens opacities.

(c) Genetic effects. Most studies seem to indicate that exposure to RF radiation is not mutagenic, i e RF radiation of low-to-moderate intensity does not cause mutations in biological systems in which the temperature is adequately controlled. This implies that hereditary effects are unlikely. The only exposures that are potentially mutagenic are those where very high RF power densities are involved, i e exposures that result in substantial thermal loading or extremely high electric field forces at sensitive sites.

(d) Cardiovascular effects. The responses of the intact cardiovascular system to RF exposure are consistent with those associated with conventional heating.

(e) Cancer. The majority of epidemiological studies have concentrated on investigating the association between elevated cancer incidence and exposure to RF radiation. A number of these studies have suggested that there may indeed be such an association. This means that animal studies have become very important in determining the existence of any laboratory support for these epidemiological results. A number of laboratory studies reviewed in a preliminary draft report by the Environmental Protection Agency (EPA) on the potential carcinogenicity of electromagnetic fields suggest that the findings of carcinogenicity in human beings are biologically plausible. It is not understood which biological processes are involved nor how these processes relate causally to each other and to the induction of malignant tumours.

Also, most of the observed effects have been at field strengths that are many times higher than the ambient fields which are supposedly related to the increased incidence of certain childhood cancers in residential situations.

While some of the epidemiological studies mentioned in the EPA report suggest an elevated risk for cancer as a result of exposure to RF radiation, others do not. All these studies, however, suffer from design and methodological problems which preclude any definitive statement regarding the carcinogenicity of RF radiation.

21.3.3.4 *Ultrasound*

Ultrasound is known to produce biological effects in-vitro and in-vivo by at least three primary mechanisms, namely, heat, stress and a process known as cavitation in which gas cavities in a liquid can be created, enlarged and imploded in response to the ultrasound waves. The implosion of the gas cavities can in turn lead to the formation of shock waves as well as localized 'hot spots' in the vicinity of the implosion.

As with other forms of radiation, extensive studies have been done on the effect of ultrasound on non-human biological material. Such examples include increased incidence of foetal abnormalities in mice, induction of mutations in Drosophila, lysosomal damage and blood stasis in the blood of chicken embryos, and many more. From the point of view of questions considering hazards to human beings, it would be of great value to have clear evidence of effects, or the absense of them, in human beings. However, the small amount of information of this type needs to be supplemented by the evidence related to other mammals and lower animals.

It can therefore be seen that biological research and human population studies form a confusing picture of the potential risk associated with exposure to ultrasound. That a risk exists, however, is undeniable, and users of ultrasound, for whatever purpose, are urged to use this modern tool conservatively and prudently.

At present, diagnostic ultrasound is considered to be potentially safer than diagnostic X-rays. However, the long-term effects of ultrasound have yet to be fully investigated and established. The absence of reported adverse effects of the clinical use of ultrasound is accepted by man as the single most compelling argument for its safety, but this is a simplistic view, since subtle and delayed effects may still manifest themselves.

The American Institute of Ultrasound in Medicine (AIUM) issued the following statement in 1987 on 'mammalian in-vivo ultrasonic biological effects':

'In the low megahertz frequency range there have been no independently confirmed significant biological effects in mammalian tissues exposed to intensities below 100 mW cm^{-2}. Furthermore, for ultrasound exposure times less than 500 seconds and greater than 1 second, such effects have not been demonstrated even at higher intensities, when the product of intensity and exposure time is less than 50 J cm^{-2}.'

Considering the use of ultrasound in therapy, various international safety standards, including the International Electrotechnical Commission's (IEC) safety standard for ultrasonic therapy equipment, recommend that the effective intensity of therapy devices should not exceed the level of 3 W cm^{-2}, since it has been shown that intensity levels above this limit may retard bone growth.

21.4 RADIATION CONTROL LEGISLATION

21.4.1 Ionizing radiation

21.4.1.1 *Introduction*

Legislative control of ionizing radiation was introduced in 1948 via the Atomic Energy Act 35 of 1948. This Act was repealed by the Atomic Energy Act 90 of 1967, which was in turn repealed by the current Act—the Nuclear Energy Act 92 of 1982.

The Nuclear Installations (Licensing and Security) Act 43 of 1963 provided for control over nuclear installations and regulated the liability of licensees for nuclear damage. At that stage the Atomic Energy Board was the body responsible for controlling ionizing radiation, although a certain amount of control—of electronic products—was exercised by the Department of Health and by the Government Mining Engineer in respect of uranium and thorium mining operations. This Act has also been repealed by the Nuclear Energy Act. The Nuclear Energy Act, which is administered by the Minister of Mineral and Energy Affairs, provides for the establishment of the Atomic Energy Corporation and a Council for Nuclear Safety. The objects of the corporation include the undertaking of research in the field of nuclear or atomic energy; the production of nuclear or atomic energy and the development and promotion of nuclear technology and expertise.

The functions of the council are to safeguard the public against the risk of nuclear damage. In order to ensure that the risk of nuclear damage is consistent with the requirements of health and safety, the construction of nuclear installations as well as the use, possession and production of nuclear-hazard material capable of causing nuclear damage—ie all aspects of the nuclear industry from mining of nuclear ores to the ultimate disposal of nuclear waste, are regulated and controlled.

Control over hazardous substances is exercised by the Minister of National Health and Population Development in terms of the Hazardous Substances Act 15 of 1973. The sections of the Act relevant to radiation control are those dealing with the declaration of electronic products as Group III hazardous substances and radioactive material as Group IV hazardous substances and related matters. The Minister has to date not utilized the provision of the Act relating to the declaration of radioactive material as a Group IV hazardous substance.

The responsibility for the control (ie of the production, acquisition, disposal and importation) of radioactive nuclides vests in the corporation in terms of the Nuclear Energy Act. The State President is, however, empowered to assign this power, in so far as it relates to radioactive nuclides outside a nuclear installation, to any Minister. This power, as will be shown, has indeed been transferred to the Minister of National Health and Population Development.

Although the Nuclear Energy Act and the Hazardous Substances Act are the only two Acts controlling ionizing radiation, reference may be found in other legislation to radioactive material—for example, the Minerals Act 50 of 1991, the Dumping at Sea

Control Act 73 of 1980, the Foodstuffs, Cosmetics and Disinfectants Act 54 of 1972 and the Health Act 63 of 1977.

The Minerals Act provides for the protection of the health and safety of persons employed in mines who are exposed to radiation emanating from mining operations. The Dumping at Sea Control Act prohibits the loading or dumping at sea of certain prohibited substances such as high-level radioactive waste or other high-level matter prescribed by regulation. The regulations promulgated under the Foodstuffs, Cosmetics and Disinfectants Act[1] prohibit the sale of irradiated foodstuffs in the absence of ministerial approval.[2] The Health Act[3] empowers the Minister of National Health and Population Development to regulate, restrict or prohibit any trade or occupation entailing a special danger to health and to determine the measures to be taken to prevent or restrict the danger. Since the Nuclear Energy Act and the Hazardous Substances Act are the most important statutes regulating radiation, they will be discussed in greater detail.

21.4.1.2 *Nuclear Energy Act*

(a) Introduction. The main objects of the Act are to provide for the establishment of the Atomic Energy Corporation of South Africa Limited and the Council for Nuclear Safety, and to define their powers and functions; to regulate the licensing and security of nuclear activity; to provide for the control of source material, special nuclear material, restricted material, and radioactive nuclides, and to provide for the control of certain patents for inventions relating to nuclear or atomic energy.

(b) Atomic Energy Corporation. The Act makes provision for the establishment of a juristic person known as the Atomic Energy Corporation of South Africa Limited, whose affairs are managed and controlled by a board of directors.[4]

The corporation is vested with the sole right to produce nuclear or atomic energy on behalf of the State,[5] and no person other than the corporation or a subsidiary company[6] may produce or otherwise acquire or dispose of, import or export, possess, use or convey any radioactive nuclide, in the absence of a nuclear licence granted by the corporation under the Act.[7]

Although the power to grant the authority and to determine conditions vests in the corporation, the State President may by proclamation assign this power to any Minister in so far as it relates to radioactive nuclides which are outside a nuclear installation.[8] On 16 May 1986 this power was assigned to the Minister of National Health and Population Development.[9]

---

[1] Section 15(1).

[2] GN R1600 of 22 July 1983.

[3] Section 34.

[4] Section 2. The board consists of a chairman; the chief executive officer; an official in the Department of Mineral and Energy Affairs; an official in the Department of Foreign Affairs and not more than six other directors, of whom two shall be involved in the mining and extraction of source material and one shall be appointed to represent Eskom: s 5.

[5] Section 19.

[6] 'Subsidiary company' means a company in which all the issued shares are held by the corporation or its nominees or a company of which all the issued shares are held by a subsidiary company (or by the subsidiary company and its nominees) or by its nominees: s 1(1).

[7] Section 50(1). Conditions for the acquisition, possession, disposal, importation, exportation, use and conveyance of radioactive nuclides were promulgated by the President of the then Atomic Energy Board: GN R2410 of 28 November 1980. Although these conditions were promulgated under the repealed Atomic Energy Act, the regulations are deemed to have been promulgated under the Nuclear Energy Act: s 83(9).

[8] Section 50(2).

[9] Proclamation 85 of 16 May 1986.

The control and regulation of the discarding of radioactive waste vests in the corporation.[10]

The objects of the corporation are:

— to undertake research in the field of nuclear or atomic energy and to produce nuclear or atomic energy;
— to develop, promote and make nuclear technology and related expertise available;
— to enrich[11] source material[12] and special nuclear material;[13]
— to process[14] source material, special nuclear material and restricted material;[15]
— to reprocess[16] source material and special nuclear material, and
— to exercise control over certain nuclear activities in the Republic.[17]

The corporation has certain additional powers and functions, the most important being the conclusion of agreements relating to the production of source material; the undertaking of prospecting for and the mining of source material; the processing of source material, restricted material and special nuclear material; the importation and exportation of source material, special nuclear material, restricted material and radioactive nuclides; the acquisition, disposal and holding of any source material, special nuclear material, restricted material and radioactive nuclides, the production of nuclear or atomic energy and of radioactive nuclides, and the establishment and control of facilities for the collection and dissemination of scientific and technical information relating to nuclear and atomic energy.

The corporation also has certain powers of entry and inspection, and the power to obtain information regarding source material or restricted material, radioactive nuclide or special nuclear material.[18] Under certain circumstances, the corporation may acquire rights to patents from patentholders.[19] No person may disclose information regarding reserves of ores containing source material, the extent of the output of source materials and the price paid for source materials, in the absence of written consent by the corporation.[20]

(c) Council for Nuclear Safety. The council, which was established as an

---

[10] Section 51. See Barrie 'Radioactive disposal: an international law perspective' 1989 *TSAR* 177.

[11] 'Enrich' means to increase the ratio of an isotopic constituent of an element to the remaining isotopic constituents of that element relative to the naturally occurring ratio: s 1(1).

[12] 'Source material' means uranium and thorium and any other substance which the Minister declares to be source material: s 1(1).

[13] 'Special nuclear material' means
(a) uranium-233;
(b) uranium enriched in its uranium-235 isotope;
(c) transuranium elements; or
(d) any compound of the materials referred to in *(a)*, *(b)* and *(c)*, or of anything so referred to and any other substance which the Minister has declared to be a special nuclear material: s 1(1). The State President has declared any compound of uranium-233 and uranium enriched in its uranium-235 isotope and transuranium elements derived from source material, which contains a mass of the said isotopes or elements above 0,49 g, regardless of their concentration, to be special nuclear material: GN R51 of 15 April 1983.

[14] 'Process' in relation to source material, special nuclear material and restricted material means to recover, extract, concentrate, refine or convert it, but does not include enriching: s 1(1).

[15] 'Restricted material' means beryllium and zirconium and any other substance which has been declared restricted material by the Minister: s 1(1).

[16] 'Reprocess' in relation to source material or special nuclear material means to extract or separate constituents occurring in source material or special nuclear material that has been subjected to irradiation capable of causing transmutation of that material: s 1(1).

[17] Section 3.

[18] Sections 4 and 52.

[19] Section 57.

[20] Section 68. The corporation may also prohibit the disclosure of information regarding certain past activity in connection with the production, importation, exportation, refinement, possession, ownership and sale of source materials.

independent body in 1982, initally performed a consultative role in the process of the issue of nuclear licences by the Atomic Energy Corporation. When the Act was amended in 1988, the Council for Nuclear Safety was granted the status of a juristic person, assuming powers of regulation over nuclear installations and activities involving nuclear-hazard material, which previously vested in the corporation.

In terms of the Act[21] the council shall consist of not more than 14 members appointed by the Minister, who may not be licensees (or employees of licensees), and of whom at least four must be officers of state departments who have knowledge of physical planning and development, environmental health matters, transport and environmental conservation.[22] The Amendment Act has altered the status of the council from a body with certain veto powers to that of an independent regulatory authority. The responsibility of safeguarding the public against nuclear damage by exercising control over the construction and use of nuclear installations, and other activities involving nuclear hazard-material which is capable of causing nuclear damage, now vests in the council. Although the council is an independent body, it must be remembered that the members are appointed by the Minister of Mineral and Energy Affairs. Thus, although the council does not fall directly within the hierarchy of the Department of Mineral and Energy Affairs, the Minister exercises indirect control by way of appointment of its members.

The council has certain additional powers and functions such as the establishment and control of facilities for the collection and dissemination of scientific and technical information relating to nuclear and atomic energy, insurance against loss, damage, risk or liability, and advising the Minister on matters relating to activities or conditions which are capable of causing nuclear damage.

(d) Nuclear licenses: nuclear installations, nuclear-hazard material and vessels. The council is responsible for the issuing of licences relating to the pursuance of activities relating to nuclear installations,[23] sites, nuclear-hazard material[24] and vessels propelled by nuclear or atomic energy.

In its *1988–89 Annual report* the Council for Nuclear Safety has stated that the licensing process entails assessing the risk of nuclear damage associated with the operation of nuclear installations and activities involving nuclear-hazard material in

---

[21] Section 24C.

[22] At present the council consists of a chairman, vice-chairman and 11 members drawn from departments associated with national health, road transport administration, development planning, and environmental affairs as well as various institutes.

[23] 'Nuclear installation' means any installation, plant or structure designed or adapted for or which may involve the production, use, processing, reprocessing, storage or disposal of nuclear-hazard material; or the carrying out of any process involving nuclear-hazard material and which is capable of causing nuclear damage; or the production of nuclear or atomic energy. The term does not include any installation, plant or structure which is situated at any mine or works as defined in s 1 of the Mines and Works Act 27 of 1956, which is used in connection with operations at, and pertaining to the mine or works, whereby source material is produced: s 1(1). The Mines and Works Act has been replaced by the Minerals Act 50 of 1991.

[24] 'Nuclear-hazard material' is defined as any material which consists of or contains isotopes of uranium, thorium or special nuclear material, or any radioactive daughter product, or radioactive waste, which has been declared to be nuclear-hazard material, or any radioactive nuclides produced in the generation of nuclear or atomic energy, or any other radioactive nuclides, but does not include fabricated radio-isotopes which are outside a nuclear installation and which are used or intended to be used for medical, scientific, agricultural, commercial or industrial uses: s 1(1).

The Minister may by notice in the *Government Gazette* declare any material which consists of or contains isotopes of uranium, thorium or special nuclear material, or any radioactive daughter product or any radioactive waste, above concentration and mass limits specified in the notice, to be nuclear-hazard material: s 1(2).

order to ensure that persons employed within such activities as well as members of the public are not faced with a level of risk that is unacceptable.[25]

A licence is required for the construction or use of a nuclear installation, the use of any site for the purposes of a nuclear installation, or the use, possession, production, storage, processing, reprocessing, conveyance or disposal of nuclear-hazard material, or the carrying out of any other activity involving nuclear-hazard material which is capable of causing nuclear damage.[26]

A licence is not required (in cases other than an application to produce nuclear or atomic energy) where the council has declared in writing that, in its opinion:

> 'the risk of nuclear damage associated with the activity can under no circumstances exceed the limits consistent with health and safety; or
>
> the objects of the Act (relating to the control over activity carried out in respect of any nuclear installation, site or nuclear-hazard material) are effectively achieved by the provisions of other applicable legislation.'[27]

The council may at any time withdraw such declaration and must notify the relevant persons of the withdrawal.

The council may grant one nuclear licence where, in its opinion, two or more installations are situated sufficently close to one another as to be regarded as one installation or site.

A nuclear licence may not be granted to any person other than a body corporate and is not transferable.[28] Nuclear licences granted in respect of nuclear installations, sites and nuclear-hazard material may be issued subject to prescribed conditions and such conditions relating to health or safety as the council may impose.[29] A licence has, for example, been issued subject to the condition that a safety assessment be conducted of the operations and activities involving nuclear-hazard material at the site; that an inventory control system approved by the council be established to record the amount and location of nuclear-hazard material on the mine site; that the radiation dose to members of the public, employees and visitors comply with the system of dose limitation laid down; and that radiological hazards and effluents discharged from the site, and radioactive waste be controlled in accordance with the council's requirements.

Vessels propelled by nuclear or atomic energy, or which have any nuclear installation or nuclear-hazard material on board, may not enter the territorial waters of the Republic, or anchor or otherwise sojourn in such waters, without the authority of a nuclear licence granted by the council.[30] A nuclear licence granted in respect of a vessel is subject to certain conditions regulating the liability for nuclear damage, the provision of security for damage, and such conditions as the council may deem necessary or desirable in the interest of health and safety. In the case where a vessel is registered outside the Republic, the licence is also subject to the appropriate terms of any

---

[25] Page 13 of the report. The risk of nuclear damage consists of two elements: the chance of exposure to radiation and the possibility of consequent nuclear damage. The establishment of a level of risk is undertaken by determining the risk that society as a whole, and groups within society (eg a workforce), would accept. From these studies fundamental standards are laid down—for normal operation of nuclear installations and for possible accidents.

[26] Section 30(1)*(a)*.

[27] Section 30(1)*(b)*.

[28] Section 33.

[29] Section 34(1)*(a)*. These conditions may specifically include provisions relating to the maintenance of an efficient system for detecting and recording the presence and intensity of ionizing radiations emitted from nuclear installations or sites; the design, siting, construction, installation, operation, modification and maintenance of nuclear installations to be constructed or used; preparations for dealing with nuclear accidents or other emergencies; the production, storage, processing, reprocessing, handling, treatment, conveyance or disposal of nuclear-hazard material and radioactive waste: s 34(2).

[30] Section 32.

agreement between the government of the Republic and the government of the country in which the vessel is registered.[31]

Any person aggrieved by the refusal to grant a nuclear licence, the withdrawal of a declaration, the conditions imposed or the revocation of a licence granted by the council may appeal to the Minister within 60 days.[32]

A licence may at any time be revoked by the council or surrendered by a licensee.[33] The council may, on the revocation or surrender of a licence and, where a licence has been granted for a nuclear installation, site and nuclear-hazard material, during the period of responsibility[34] give the licensee any other directions as it may deem fit for preventing the causing of nuclear damage at or in the nuclear installation or on the site, or for giving warning of any risk.[35]

(e) Liability for nuclear damage. The council may not grant a nuclear licence to any person unless security has been given to the satisfaction of the Minister for the fulfilment of obligations relating to the liability for nuclear damage.[36]

The licensee of a nuclear installation, site and nuclear-hazard material is liable for any nuclear damage caused during his period of responsibility as follows:

In the case of a licence for a nuclear installation or site by anything being present or being done at or in the nuclear installation or on the site, or by any radioactive waste which is conveyed, discharged or released from the nuclear installation or site; or by any nuclear-hazard material in the course of conveyance to or from the nuclear installation or site to any place in the Republic, including the territorial waters of the Republic;

in the case of a nuclear licence (not relating to a particular nuclear installation or site), by or as a result of the performance or carrying out of any activity in connection with nuclear-hazard material in the possession or under the control of the licensee.[37]

No person other than the licensee is liable for nuclear damage.[38] This liability is subject to the following exceptions:

- The licensee is not liable for nuclear damage to any person where the damage is attributable to the presence of that person or his property at a licenced nuclear installation or near nuclear-hazard material, in the absence of permission.
- A licensee is also not liable to any person who deliberately caused or contributed to the damage.

(f) Duties when nuclear accidents occur. Certain duties are imposed upon the licensee[39] and council[40] and procedures are prescribed[41] in the case of nuclear

[31] Section 35.
[32] Section 45.
[33] Section 40(3).
[34] Period of responsibility in relation to a licence in respect of which a licence referred to in s 30(1)*(a)* has been granted, means the period beginning on the date of the grant of the relevant licence and ending on whichever of the following is the earlier, namely—
(a) the date on which the council gives notice in writing to the licensee that, in its opinion, there has ceased to be any risk of nuclear damage from anything on the site, or at or in the nuclear installation in question, or from any activity referred to in s 30(1) carried out in regard to the nuclear-hazard material, or from any act performed in regard to the nuclear installation or site in question, as the case may be; or
(b) the date on which a nuclear licence in respect of the nuclear installation, nuclear-hazard material or site in question is granted to some other person.
[35] Section 40(3).
[36] Section 39. In terms of a recent amendment the Minister may call for additional security, reduce or refund the security or discharge the licensee from providing security.
[37] Section 41.
[38] The licensee may not raise the defence of fault by another person: s 41(2).
[39] The licensee must report the accident to the council and any other prescribed persons: s 42(1).

accidents.[42] Provision is also made as to the liability of the corporation for injuries suffered by persons employed by the corporation and its subsidiary companies.[43]

(g) Control of source material, special nuclear material and restricted material. The Nuclear Energy Act prohibited the prospecting for or mining of source material or its recovery from tailings, slimes or other residues, in the absence of written ministerial permission or in accordance with the provisions of the Mining Rights Act 20 of 1967.[44] This provision, however, has been repealed by the Minerals Act 50 of 1991, which now controls all prospecting and mining.

The Minister is authorized to acquire, purchase, lease or expropriate any source material which has been mined or processed and any special nuclear material.[45] The ownership and control of all source material and special nuclear material thus acquired vests in the corporation on behalf of the State.

No person other than the corporation or a subsidiary company may perform any of the following activities in the absence of written ministerial permission:

- possess and dispose of source material;
- enrich or reprocess source material or special nuclear material;
- import or export source material;
- acquire, import, possess or dispose of restricted or special nuclear material;
- fabricate nuclear fuel; or
- produce nuclear or atomic energy.[46]

No person other than the corporation or a subsidiary company may, except under written authority of the corporation, manufacture or otherwise produce uranium hexafluoride (UF6).[47]

(h) Control of radioactive nuclides. The production, acquisition, disposal, importation into or exportation from the Republic, the possession, use or conveyance of any radioactive nuclide is similarly prohibited in the absence of written authority by the corporation, and in accordance with certain conditions.[48] The control of radioactive nuclides (outside a nuclear installation) is administered by the Department of National Health and Population Development.

The conditions to which an authority is subject include the following:[49]

(i) *Responsible person.* The applicant for authority to possess and use radioactive nuclides must nominate a person (the responsible person) and an alternate who are acceptable to the corporation to accept responsibility, on behalf of the holder of the authority, for compliance with the conditions to which the authority is subject.[50] The

---

[40] The council must direct an inspector to investigate and report upon the accident and upon receipt of the report it must define the period during which and the area within which health and safety limits are threatened by the risk of nuclear damage. The council must keep a record of the names of persons who were within the defined area: s 42(2) and (3).

[41] Section 42.

[42] 'Nuclear accident' means any occurrence or succession of occurrences having the same origin, which causes or is likely to cause nuclear damage: s 1(1).

[43] Section 73(1).

[44] Section 47.

[45] Section 48.

[46] Section 49(1).

[47] Section 49(5).

[48] Section 50.

[49] GN R2410 of 28 November 1980. Although these conditions were promulgated in terms of the Atomic Energy Act of 1967, they are now deemed to have been promulgated in terms of the Nuclear Energy Act: s 83(9).

[50] Chapter I, 3.

conditions relate mainly to the safe use, conveyance, handling, storage and disposal of radioactive material.[51]

(ii) *Radiation workers.* Extensive provision is made for the medical supervision of radiation workers.[52] For instance, before anyone can be employed as a radiation worker, he must be medically examined and during his employment he must be regularly examined and monitored. A health register of all radiation workers must be kept by the holder of the authority.

(iii) *Accidents and incidents.* Special conditions apply to the holder of the authority in the event of loss and spillage of radioactive material, contamination and over-exposure.[53]

(iv) *Unsealed and radioactive material and sealed sources.* Certain conditions relate specifically to the use and handling of unsealed radioactive material[54] and of sealed sources.[55]

(v) *Import and export of radioactive material.* Authority granted by the corporation is required to import or export radioactive material[56] and a number of obligations are imposed upon the authorized importer.

(vi) *Possession and use of radioactive material for medical purposes.* The possession and use of radioactive material for medical purposes is subject to a number of conditions.[57] Control over compliance is exercised by radiation inspectors.[58]

Consideration is at present being given to the possible repeal of the above provision of the Nuclear Energy Act regarding radioactive nuclides and its substitution through the declaration of such material as a Group IV hazardous substance by virtue of the Hazardous Substances Act.

(i) Exemptions. The Minister may, whenever he deems it in the interests of the security of the State, with the concurrence of the corporation, exempt any person or category of persons or any institute for a defined or undefined period, either conditionally or unconditionally, from any provision of the Nuclear Energy Act, excepting the provisions relating to liability for nuclear damage.[59] The exemption may at any time be amended or withdrawn.[60]

(j) Radioactive waste. The Nuclear Energy Act defines radioactive waste as radioactive material produced in, or any material made radioactive by exposure to the radiation incidental to the fabrication, utilization or reprocessing of nuclear fuel.[61] It could be argued that this definition is inadequate since it does not include radioactive

---

[51] Chapter I, 4; chs III, IV, V, VIII, IX, X and XI. 'Radioactive material' is defined as any substance which consists of or contains any radioactive nuclide whether natural or artificial, and whose specific authority exceeds 0,002 microcurie per gram (74 becquerel per gram) of chemical element and which has a total activity greater than 0,1 microcurie (3,7 kilobecquerel).

'Radioactive nuclide' is defined as an unstable atomic nucleus which spontaneously decays, with the accompanying emission of ionizing radiation.

At present South Africa's nuclear energy programme is directed towards the application of the by-product of nuclear energy—radio nuclides—which are used in medicine (for clinical diagnoses and therapy), in agriculture and in industry. See Barrie 'South Africa and nuclear energy—national and international legal aspects' 1978 *TSAR* 153, 157.

[52] Chapters V, VI and VII.

[53] Chapter VIII.

[54] Chapter IX.

[55] Chapters X, XII and XIII.

[56] Section 50(1) of the Act and chs XIV and XV.

[57] Chapter XVI.

[58] Chapter XVI.

[59] Section 78(1).

[60] Section 78(2).

[61] Section 1(1).

waste arising from the mining and minerals processing industry such as uraniferous material, nor does it include radioactive material produced in accelerators which are commonly used.

Radioactive waste may not be disposed of without permission,[62] and the recipient of the material or waste must be an authorized person. The control and regulation of radioactive waste vests in the corporation.[63] In terms of the Nuclear Energy Act, the council, which is the body responsible for licensing nuclear hazard material, must license waste disposal sites and facilities. The licensing process entails conducting a detailed safety assessment which identifies the limitations on material to be disposed of in a particular facility, together with operational controls and monitoring requirements. In addition, the council may, in granting a nuclear licence in respect of nuclear installations and activities involving nuclear hazard material, impose conditions relating to the disposal of radioactive waste arising from the operation of the facilities.[64]

In practice no authorization for the use of radioactive material is granted without a thorough examination of the proposed method of radioactive waste disposal. Meticulous care must be taken in the discarding process and records must be maintained.

The policy of the corporation is to ensure compliance with national regulatory requirements. The recommendations of the ICRP are also considered. Until such time as the dumping of radioactive material into the sea has been more closely studied, it is not considered a suitable or approved method of disposal.

The discarding of hazardous waste into the environment is a source of international concern and it has been estimated that in 1980 alone 57-m metric tons of hazardous waste were generated in the USA.[65] The problem is that medical scientists have been unable to prove empirically that specific environmental pollution is the direct cause of a particular health effect, and the fact that most hazardous waste-related diseases and cancers do not have a single cause.[66] In the American context, in order to prove a causal link between the agents released from the hazardous waste site and the injury at issue, the plaintiff must fulfil four essential conditions of the traditional approach to legal causation. First, he must substantiate the presence of significant amounts of the pollutant which is alleged to have caused the injury. Secondly, the plaintiff must reconstruct the manner in which the exposure occurred by tracing the path of contaminant migration from the waste site to the victim. Thirdly, he must identify the source of the contamination and show a breach of due care by the defendant. Fourthly, he must demonstrate the effect of the pollutant in question on the injured person.[67]

(k) International co-operation. The Energy Act 42 of 1987 provides that the government may, subject to certain provisions of the Nuclear Energy Act,[68] enter into an agreement with the government of another country with regard to the production, manufacture, marketing or distribution of raw material.

21.4.1.3 *Hazardous Substances Act*

(a) Grouped hazardous substances. The provisions of the Hazardous Substances Act 15 of 1973 apply to a substance once the Minister of National Health and Population Development has declared it a Group I, II, III or IV hazardous substance.

---

[62] Section 30.
[63] Section 51.
[64] Section 34(1).
[65] See in this regard Seltzer 'Personal injury hazardous waste litigation: a proposal for tort reform' 1982 (70) *Boston College Environmental Affairs Law Review* 797.
[66] Seltzer above n 65, 809-11.
[67] Seltzer above n 65, 822.
[68] ie ss 19, 48, 49, 51, 52, 53, 68 and 70.

Groups I and II are not relevant to this discussion, since they relate to substances of a toxic, corrosive, irritant, strongly sensitizing or flammable nature, whereas Groups III and IV relate to electronic products and radioactive material.

The Act empowers the Minister to declare any electronic product[69] to be a Group III hazardous substance and radioactive material to be a Group IV hazardous substance.[70]

The consequence of a declaration as a Group III hazardous substance is that no person may sell, let, use, operate or apply any such substance, or install (or keep installed) any such hazardous substance on any premises except under licence.[71] A licence may be withdrawn or suspended if any condition of the licence is not complied with.

In the event of a person having a Group III substance in his possession before its declaration as a hazardous substance, he may still sell, lease, use, operate, apply or install the substance within a period of 180 days from the date of declaration, provided that he applies for a licence authorizing his proposed activity before the expiry of the period mentioned.[72]

Provision is made for the issue of licences for Group III hazardous substances by the Director-General[73] and for the appointment of inspectors for Group III and Group IV hazardous substances.[74]

The Minister may regulate inter alia:

- the manufacture, modification, importation, storage, transportation, dumping and other disposal of any grouped hazardous substances; the application of a grouped hazardous substance for any specific purpose;
- the description of a particular grouped hazardous substance, the name under which it may be sold, or the manner of advertising;
- the safety precautions to be taken for the protection of certain persons (such as employees or persons likely to be exposed to grouped hazardous substances) from injury, ill health or death;
- the keeping of records and the submission of statistics and reports

pertaining to the manufacture, operation, application, modification, use or sale of grouped hazardous substances, the premises on which they are used, sold or installed or persons employed in connection with Group III hazardous substances;

- the notification of cases or suspected cases of poisoning, intoxication, illness or death of persons who have been exposed to grouped hazardous substances;
- the control over the dumping or disposal of radioactive waste.[75]

Extensive regulations control listed electronic products, as will be shown.[76]

---

[69] 'Electronic product' is defined in s 1 as any manufactured product which, when in operation, contains or acts as part of an electronic circuit; and emits (or in the absence of effective shielding or other controls would emit) electronic product radiation; or any manufactured article which is intended for use as a component, part of accessory of a product and which, when in operation, emits (or in the absence of effective shielding or other controls would emit) such radiation.

'Electronic product radiation' means:

(a) any ionizing or non-ionizing electromagnetic or particulate radiation; or

(b) any sonic, infrasonic or ultrasonic wave which is emitted from an electronic product as the result of the operation of an electric circuit in the product.

[70] Section 2*(b)* and *(c)*. Section 2*(c)* of the Act has not as yet been utilized. If the Minister intends declaring an electronic product or radioactive material to be hazardous substance, he must publish a notice of his intention in the *Government Gazette*, inviting interested persons to make comment and representations: s 2(2).

[71] Section 3(1).

[72] Section 3(2).

[73] Section 4.

[74] Section 8.

[75] Section 29.

[76] GN R1332 of 3 August 1973.

The following electronic products were declared Group III hazardous substances by regulation on 14 June 1991:[77]

- electronic products generating X-rays or other ionizing beams, electrons, neutrons or other particle radiation;[78]
- electronic products generating electromagnetic radiation in the ultraviolet region;[79]
- electronic products emitting coherent electromagnetic radiation produced by stimulated emission (laser products);[80]
- electronic products emitting electromagnetic radiation in the infra-red region;[81]
- electronic products emitting microwaves, radio or low frequency electromagnetic radiation;[82]
- electronic products emitting ultrasonic vibrations;[83]
- electronic products used for medical, dental or veterinary applications employing radioactive nuclides;[84]
- high risk electronic products used for medical, dental or veterinary applications,[85] and
- medium risk electronic products used for medical, dental or veterinary applications.[86]

Licensing regulations have been promulgated which control the sale of a listed electronic product, the manner of application for a licence, the records to be kept, the notification of defects and non-compliance with applicable standards, and the repair

---

[77] GN R1302 of 14 June 1991.

[78] This category includes diagnostic and therapeutic X-ray units, X-ray units used for industrial, research, educational, security or other purposes, electron and heavy particle accelerators, neutron generators and electron microscopes, visual display units and cold cathode gas discharge tubes.

[79] This category includes sunlamps designed for suntanning, therapeutic lamps, high-intensity mercury-vapour discharge lamps, intra-oral curing devices and ultraviolet A lamps, including 'black lights'.

[80] Laser products emitting radiation in excess of $0,8 \times 10^{-9}$ W in the wavelength region up to and including 400 nm or emitting radiation in excess of $0,39 \times 10^{-6}$ W in the wavelength region greater than 400 nm, are included in this category.

[81] In this region industrial heating and drying lamp installations exceeding 200 W and medical heating lamps exceeding 200 W are included.

[82] This category includes microwave ovens, microwave and shortwave diathermy units, electrosurgical units, medical magnetic and neuro-muscular stimulators, radio-frequency generating devices, systems or installations including radars, generating a radio-frequency output exceeding 200 W RMS, low power radio-frequency generating devices, systems or installations, including citizen band radios, land mobile transmitters, marine transmitters and two-way (walkie-talkie) radios, the normal operation of which entails close proximity to the operator or third parties, which generates a radio-frequency output exceeding 25 W RMS, microwave generating devices, systems or installations, including radars generating a microwave output exceeding 400 W RMS, radio-frequency sealers, magnetic resonance imaging devices and blood warmers.

[83] Ultrasonic vibrations include diagnostic, therapeutic and surgical ultrasound appliances, lithotripsy appliances and pest and rodent control appliances.

[84] This category includes gamma cameras, whole body counters, position emission tomographs, linear scanners, and single photon emission computerized tomographs (SPECTS).

[85] This category includes intra-aortic balloon pumps, electronically controlled ventilators, electronically controlled anaesthetic machines, cardiac pacemakers, intracardiac electrocardiographic and phonocardiographic monitors, electroconvulsive therapy units, photocoagulators, infusion and syringe pumps, infant incubators and infant transport incubators, hyperbaric chambers, haemodialysis devices, peritoneal dialysis machines, heart–lung bypass (perfusion) devices, shockwave lithotripsy, autotransfusion, high-pressure injection, and cryosurgical devices, and transcutaneous O_2/CO_2 monitors.

[86] Audiometers, ambulatory electrocardiographic recorders, electrocardiographs, electroencephalographs, electromyopgraphs, cardiac catheterisation laboratory systems, physiological monitors (ECG, pressure, respiration, temperature), phonocardiographs, non-invasive bloodpressure monitors, cardiac output computers, plethysmographs, evoked response devices, pulmonary function and bloodgas analysers, infusion controllers, interferential devices, capnographs, and diagnostic exercise devices, including treadmill and cycle ergometers.

and modification of a listed electronic product.[87] Other regulations govern the conveyance of hazardous substances by road tanker.[88]

Regulations were issued during 1973 to control the use or installation of electronic products capable of emitting radiation.[89]

(b) Regulations relating to the licensing of electronic products capable of emitting ionizing radiation and of the premises on which they are to be used. The regulations provide that before anyone can use, modify or dispose of any listed electronic product on any premises, such product, as well as the premises on which it is to be used, must be licensed. No person may use or dispose of a licensed electronic product or modify licensed premises, or the type of or layout of equipment (including the electronic product) in the absence of approval. A heavy burden is placed on the licensee, who is vicariously liable for any act of any other person unless he proves that he did not permit or connive at such act, that he took all reasonable measures to prevent the act in question, and that the act did not fall within the course of the work or the scope of the authority of the person concerned. The licensee is also liable for the entire scope of radiation protection with regard to a listed electronic product or premises for which he holds a licence. Extensive provisions exist to ensure that a licensee is a person with adequate knowledge and experience as regards radiation protection. Any licence may be suspended or cancelled if the licensee or any of his radiation workers contravenes any of the regulations or, in a case of emergency, where it is in the public interest to do so.

The sale of listed electronic products is controlled via a licensing system. Although a licence is issued in respect of the model and not the individual product, the licence covers each separate listed electronic product of the model in question. A licence which has been issued and not withdrawn or suspended is deemed to be in force in respect of each separate listed electronic product of that model. The issue of a licence, or the sale of a listed electronic product (in respect of which a licence has been issued), is subject to the conditions laid down by the Director-General (if any) and the conditions prescribed by regulation.

The application for a licence must be accompanied by a report which identifies the model and describes the electronic product radiation, its characteristics, the methods and procedures employed in testing electronic product safety and the durability and stability of the listed electronic product. Moreover, the report must state the standards or design specifications and furnish particulars of warning signs, labels and instructions for its installation, operation and use.

The identification particulars and the licence number must be affixed to each listed electronic product of the licensed model. Moreover, a dealer must keep a record of the sale and leasing of listed electronic products, including particulars such as the name and address of the purchaser, the brand and model name and serial number, the date of sale or lease and the quality control procedures relating to electronic product safety when so directed by the Director-General.

An approved dealer is obliged to notify the Director-General of any defect in a listed electronic product. The notification must stipulate the conditions upon which a product may be used, operated, modified or disposed. Furthermore, where the Director-General is of the opinion that a licensed model has a defect or flaw in that it no longer complies with an applicable standard, he must notify the approved dealer. The Director-General is also empowered to stop the manufacture or importation of a listed electronic product which he believes to be injurious to health.

---

[87] GN R690 of 14 April 1989.

[88] GN R73 of 11 January 1985. Chapter 2 prohibits the transport of unlabelled grouped substances by road and requires the display of certain particulars for the conveyance of single loads and multi-loads. Chapter 3 regulates the duties of the consignor, conveyor, operator and driver of a road tanker containing grouped hazardous substances, and those regulations have been amended on several occasions—see, for example, GN R1640 of 22 July 1983 and GN R1462 of 10 July 1987.

[89] GN R1332 of 3 August 1973.

The modification and marketing of a licensed listed electronic product is prohibited, unless a supplementary report is submitted to and approved by the Director-General. The repair of a licensed listed electronic product is similarly prohibited unless it carries a label or inscription.

(c) Regulations relating to the protection of radiation workers. With a view to protecting radiation workers, every licensee is obliged to keep a health register of all personnel employed by him as radiation workers and only registered workers may, with his approval, handle radiation sources under his control and be exposed to radiation while they are working with such sources. The licensee must satisfy himself that any person who is registered as a radiation worker is medically fit, has adequate knowledge and experience to handle, and is fully conversant with the health and safety measures and operating instructions applicable to the radiation equipment under his control. A copy of this register must be filed with the Department of National Health and Population Development in order that a central register of radiation workers can be compiled. The licensee must, moreover, arrange for registered radiation workers to be medically examined and to be monitored in accordance with the requirements of the regulations.

(d) Regulations relating to the protection of patients. A number of obligations are imposed upon a licensee in order to ensure that patients are protected against unnecessary radiation. He must ascertain that there has been no previous radiological examination that would make further examination unnecessary and he must keep a record of every patient exposed to radiation from an electronic product for which he is the licensee. Exposure of a person to a useful beam[90] for non-medical purposes is allowed only in exceptional circumstances.

(e) National Advisory Committee. Regulations provide for the institution of a National Advisory Committee on Electronic Products.[91]

21.4.2 Non-ionizing radiation control legislation

Initially, no control was exercised over non-ionizing radiation, with the exception of noise (acoustic radiation) which may be regarded as constituting such a form of radiation. The position as regards noise control is dealt with in chapter 22.

The position was that electronic products declared to be Group III hazardous substances were restricted to products causing ionizing radiation. The position was altered on 14 April 1989, when certain electronic products generating electromagnetic radiation in the ultraviolet region, products emitting electromagnetic radiation in the infra-red region, or emitting microwaves, radio or low-frequency electromagnetic radiation, products potentially susceptible to electromagnetic radiation interference and products emitting ultrasonic vibrations were declared Group III hazardous substances.[92] The list of electronic products declared to be Group III hazardous substances during 1989 was extended on 14 June 1991.[93] The new list includes diagnostic and therapeutic X-ray units, microwave ovens, blood warmers, linear scanners, electronically controlled anaesthetic machines and electrocardiographic recorders.

As described above, two further sets of regulations for Group III hazardous substances (electronic products) have been published in terms of the Act. One set regulates the end-user and the premises on which the source (electronic product) of the radiation will be used. The second set regulates the manufacture and sale of electronic products and thus provides an opportunity of making sure that all safety requirements have been attended to before the product becomes available for purchase by the end-user.

---

[90] 'A useful beam' is defined as any ionizing radiation from a listed electronic product that can be employed for the purpose for which such product is used.

[91] GN R326 of 23 February 1979.

[92] GN R689 of 14 April 1989.

[93] GN R1302 of 14 June 1991.

The mechanism of control is licensing. The dealer applies for a licence to be able to sell a product and the end-user applies for a licence to be able to use the product. The Directorate: Radiation Control, through its inspectorate in the various major centres, performs inspections to ensure that the licence conditions are adhered to.

In the case of electronic products such as television sets that are designed for domestic use, it is assumed that the end-user will have no special technical skills or measurement equipment regarding safety. All the necessary safety requirements must therefore be built into the design of the product and no end-user licence is required—only the dealer requires a licence to sell the product.

To the man in the street the most frequently encountered nuisance caused by non-ionizing radiation is likely to be interference with television or radio reception. But uncontrolled radiofrequency radiation may also interfere with telecommunications, with industrial, commercial and scientific communications, with navigation and with civil aviation. Control over such interference is vested in the Postmaster-General. The applicable regulations are to be found in the chapter on radio regulations in the *Post Office Guide*, which is published annually.

21.5 ADMINISTRATION OF LEGISLATION

At present the enforcement of legislation regulating radiation is divided between the Council for Nuclear Safety and the Department of National Health and Population Development.

The production of nuclear or atomic energy, research into the field of nuclear or atomic energy and the development of nuclear technology and expertise vests in the Atomic Energy Corporation, whilst the Council for Nuclear Safety has the task of safeguarding the public from the risk of nuclear damage. This task is achieved by licensing all aspects of the nuclear industry from the mining of nuclear ores to the ultimate disposal of nuclear waste. The control of radioactive nuclides outside a nuclear installation vests in the Department of National Health and Population Development.

The Nuclear Energy Act, which is a product of several repealed Acts, is in the process of being amended. A revised consolidation is indeed necessary, for although the Act is effective in regulating and controlling nuclear energy, it is a rather cumbersome legislative document.

The Hazardous Substances Act is also in the process of amendment. It is proposed that the legislature make provision in this Act for the control of radioactive nuclides outside a nuclear installation to be exercised by the Department of National Health and Population Development. The current position, whereby the State President has assigned this power to the Department in terms of the Nuclear Energy Act, unnecessarily complicates the issue.

In its *Report on a national environmental management system*[94] the President's Council has proposed radical changes with regard to the control and management of the environment. It has proposed that a Directorate of Pollution Prevention be established in the Department of Environment Affairs, including a subdirectorate for hazardous substances and has also proposed that the Council for Nuclear Safety resort under this Directorate of Pollution Prevention. This directorate, together with the Directorates of Water, Air, Sea and Noise Pollution, should form part of the Pollution Control Branch. See also chapter 5.

While it is conceded that a co-ordinating body should be established to control and regulate ionizing radiation and other environmental issues, the question is whether the sweeping changes at administrative level proposed by the council can be implemented at this delicate stage of constitutional negotiation, particularly in view of the world-wide trend towards the devolution of power rather than centralization.

---

[94] PC 1/1991 para 6.4.4.

CHAPTER 22

NOISE

C J JOHNSTON

22.1 INTRODUCTION

Noise is a particular category of sound. It may be defined as undesirable sound, the factors influencing the degree of undesirability being covered in section 22.1.2. In order to understand noise, so that it may be quantified, measured and controlled, it is necessary to know some basic concepts relating to sound.

22.1.1 *Sound*

22.1.1.1 *Amplitude and frequency*

Sound may be described loosely as that which we can hear. Our ears perceive rapid fluctuations in the static air pressure that surrounds us as audible sound if these fluctuations occur roughly between 20 and 16 000 times per second. The more rapidly the fluctuations occur, the higher will be the apparent pitch of the sound. The rate at which the fluctuations occur, in cycles per second, is known as the frequency of the sound, the unit for frequency being the hertz (Hz). Frequencies of 1 000 Hz or more are usually described in kilohertz (kHz), where 1 000 Hz is equal to 1 kHz.

The sensation of loudness is related to the amount by which the air pressure deviates from its static value while fluctuating within the range of audible frequencies. At any given frequency, the greater the pressure deviations, also known as the amplitude, the greater the loudness will be. The fundamental measuring unit for loudness is therefore the unit of pressure, i e the pascal (Pa), although it is seldom quoted in this context. As will be seen presently, other descriptors are commonly used for loudness.

22.1.1.2 *Sound propagation*

The air-pressure fluctuations causing the sensation of sound arrive at our ears through a mechanism known as wave propagation. An initial localized disturbance in the static air pressure spreads out through the surrounding air in a manner analogous to the spreading of concentric ripples on the surface of water. The depth of the ripples corresponds to the amplitude (loudness) of the sound and the rate at which successive peaks pass a stationary point corresponds to the frequency (pitch). The surface of the water is a 2-dimensional representation of what occurs 3-dimensionally in air, the concentric rings being analogous to concentric spheres. The speed at which sound spreads (propagates) is much higher than that of the water ripples, and at sea-level it is about 344 m s^{-1} (1 238 km h^{-1}). For completeness it should be stated that sound waves can propagate through media other than air, such as water and solid structures. The propagation can transfer from one medium to another, although only a small part of the wave energy is usually so transferred. The balance is reflected back towards the source. In buildings sound is frequently propagated through the structure.

The geometric simplicity of the water ripple analogy has encouraged widespread teaching of a physical law of sound propagation known as the inverse square law. This law states that as an observer moves away from a sound source, the amplitude of the sound wave decreases in such a way that if the distance from the source to the observer position doubles, then the amplitude of the sound wave is reduced to one quarter of its value at the initial observer position. Probably the most important aspect of the inverse square law is that it seldom describes a practical situation accurately. Throwing objects into ponds illustrates that the geometric simplicity (which forms the basis of the inverse square law) is destroyed by reflections of the wave from the pond boundaries as well as by reflections from, and bending of the wave around, certain (but not all) objects in the path of the wave. In air the situation is even more complex. The sound source is usually close to at least one major boundary (eg the ground) which is seldom flat. There are often objects (eg barriers) in the path of the sound wave and the wave may diffract (ie bend) around the edges of the barrier to varying degrees, depending on circumstances. The air itself is of varying density as a result of temperature gradients and wind shear. A sound wave passing through air layers of differing density is refracted (ie its direction of propagation changes). In enclosed spaces, multiple reflections from the boundaries create a confused situation known as reverberation. It is virtually impossible to describe this analytically, and statistical methods must be employed.

Thus, real sounds are propagated in complex and perplexing ways, the calculation and prediction of which is not a trivial exercise. It is reasonable to assume that, in general, the loudness of a sound reduces as the distance from the sound source increases, although the rate of reduction may be large or small, and may vary at different distances from the source. Exceptions to this assumption occur

(a) in heavily reverberant enclosed spaces, where, after an initial reduction the loudness tends not to reduce further with distance from the source,
(b) where a new observer position exposes a source previously behind a barrier, and
(c) outdoors, at large distances (say, 1 km or more) from a source, where certain atmospheric conditions (eg temperature inversion) can cause the loudness to increase with distance.

This does not mean that prediction of sound propagation say, for planning purposes, is impossible. In fact good models for this purpose exist, as will be shown,. It is important, however, that those engaging in such work should have a good knowledge of physics as well as considerable practical experience.

22.1.1.3 *Human perception of sound*

Human hearing is sensitive to a very wide range of frequencies and amplitudes. The ratio of the lowest to the highest audible frequency is about 800 times. To accommodate such a wide range, human perception of pitch is not proportional to the actual frequency of the sound, but rather to the ratios between frequencies. Thus the difference in pitch between frequencies of 100 Hz and 200 Hz is perceived to be the same as the difference in pitch between frequencies of 1 000 Hz and 2 000 Hz (ie one octave, corresponding to a frequency ratio of 2:1 in both cases). When sound is analysed and displayed graphically the frequency axis of the graph should correspond to the perception of pitch rather than to the physical frequency. For this reason the scale markings on the frequency axis of such graphs are usually unequally spaced according to a logarithmic function. This ensures that equal distances along the frequency axis correspond with equal frequency ratios, and hence with equal increments in perceived pitch.

The quietest sound that can be heard corresponds to an amplitude of about 20 millionths of a pascal, while the loudest sound that can be tolerated without pain corresponds to an amplitude of about 30 pascals. The ratio of the smallest to the largest of these amplitudes is 1 500 000 times. Again, to accommodate this huge range human perception of loudness is not proportional to the actual pressure levels, but to ratios of pressure levels. Because the numbers associated with actual pressures become unwieldy, the decibel (dB) is used as a measure of loudness. This is a logarithmic measure derived, in this case, from the amplitude (in pascals). A 2:1 change in the amplitude of a sound results in a change of 6 dB (actually 6,02 dB) regardless of whether the actual amplitudes are large or small, and the human ear perceives it as such (just as it perceives a 2:1 change in audible frequency as an octave, regardless of the actual frequencies involved). The decibel scale starts at 0 dB for sounds that can just be heard and reaches 130 dB at the onset of pain. A change in loudness of 3 dB is just perceptible, and a 10 dB increase is perceived roughly as a doubling in loudness.

22.1.2 *Noise*

As mentioned at the beginning of this chapter, noise may be defined as undesirable sound. The factors that may cause a sound to be undesirable are given below.

22.1.2.1 *Physical effects*

These occur at the most severe end of the scale. Really intense noise of a continuous nature, can cause severe trauma in human beings and can cause material fatigue effects in structures and components. Such intense noise levels, fortunately, only exist in the immediate vicinity of sources such as rockets and gas turbine engines where they are of concern only to the originating organization. Nevertheless, noise from such sources can propagate considerable distances, at lower levels, and give rise to other undesirable consequences, as dealt with in more detail below.

Intense noise of a transient nature, usually in the form of a shock wave, is rather more common and typically results from blasting operations or aircraft fly-pasts at supersonic speeds. These shock waves can remain intense for considerable distances (1 km or more) from the source and their propagation is very dependent on weather conditions. Physical damage to structures, particularly weak ones such as historical buildings, is possible but unlikely—damage is more likely to be caused by the ground vibration that accompanies many shock waves. In general, physical damage by intense noise is rare in South Africa, and the subject is not treated further here.

22.1.2.2 *Physiological effects*

These effects occur further down the severity scale. The most important is loss of hearing acuity caused by repeated exposure to high noise levels. Such exposure occurs primarily in the workplace. This subject is not normally considered to be an environmental concern. An exception to this is the high level of noise found in certain places of entertainment, such as discotheques, where regular patrons might run the risk of incurring hearing damage.

22.1.2.3 *Effects on communication and productivity*

The noise levels that can result in hearing damage are quite loud. Even at the limit below which labour legislation does not require hearing conservation measures, it is necessary to raise one's voice considerably in order to communicate with a person standing next to one. Clearly at these, and even much lower, noise levels there is significant interference with communication. At the one end of the scale conversation becomes impossible (e g on a busy street corner) and at the other it becomes difficult to communicate in a meeting, conference or classroom situation. In between these extremes the quality of telephone communication is impaired.

Such interference with communication leads to quantifiable productivity losses. While much of this problem lies within the control of the employer, there remains a significant portion that is not (e g noise from an adjacent construction site). Whenever such a problem is not under the employer's or occupier's control it becomes an environmental problem. It should be noted, however, that in cases where communication is of little or no consequence, the effect of noise on productivity has not been conclusively demonstrated.

22.1.2.4 *Psychological effects*

These occur towards the lower end of the severity scale and are by far the most significant from an environmental point of view. Noise causes annoyance which leads to negative community reaction. Because of the relatively low levels of sound that can result in annoyance, the offending sound may propagate over considerable distances and consequently affect a large population. For example a single noisy motorcycle may wake almost an entire suburb or more in the early hours of the morning. On the other hand, seemingly quiet sources may be the cause of isolated complaints, such as an automatic swimming pool cleaner operating close to a neighbour's bedroom window. It should be made clear that most annoyance effects occur at sound levels well below those of all the aforementioned effects, and apart from the as yet unproven allegations of stress and hypertension, there are no other consequences. It is simply a matter of the right of the individual to '. . . live, work and relax in a(n) . . . aesthetically and culturally acceptable environment.'[1]

The range of sources that can produce annoyance is too wide to catalogue. Nevertheless experience has shown that the chief offenders fall within the category of transportation noise (road, air and rail in descending order of importance). Commercial activities within or close to residential areas also form an important category that includes both noise from the activities themselves (eg music from a discotheque) and that of associated machinery (eg refrigeration compressors). Noise from industrial activities is problematic whenever there are independent residences nearby. The last important category includes noise from the community itself (eg lawn mowers, pets, radios and parties).

22.1.2.5 *Summary of environmental effects of noise*

From the above it may be deduced that the negative influences of noise are limited to human beings and the built environment; their activities are also the predominant causes. Control measures are hence confined to human-generated noise, and humans are the principal beneficiaries of these measures.

22.1.3 *Measurement of noise*

22.1.3.1 *Frequency Weighting*

The human ear is not equally sensitive to all audible frequencies. It is most sensitive at about 3–4 kHz, and its ability to hear low amplitude sounds decreases towards both ends of the audible frequency range. Thus the decibel as described in section 22.1.1.3 is not the ideal measure of noise. The sensitivity of the measuring instrument needs to be adapted at different frequencies so that it reacts in a similar fashion to the human ear. This adaptation is known as frequency weighting. In the past a number of different frequency weighting methods were proposed, some quite complex,[2] but by now only one, known as A-weighting, has found general use for this purpose. The terms commonly used to denote sound measurements employing A-weighting are dBA or dB(A), neither of which is strictly in accordance with international recommendations on units (which do not permit the abbreviation 'dB' to be suffixed, except to denote a reference value).[3] The (correct) alternatives are awkward and since the terms dBA or dB(A) are unambiguous they remain in use.

22.1.3.2 *Time weighting*

Most noises vary in loudness over time. It is therefore essential that the measuring instrument performs some averaging function. If an arithmetic average of the positive and negative pressure deviations (see section 22.1.1.1) is made the result will be zero which is unhelpful. The numerical values of the pressure deviations are therefore

---

[1] GN 798 of 30 October 1987: reg 2(1)*(a)*.

[2] Meij 'A critical, historic survey of methods of measurement and assessment of annoyance caused by noise' in *Transactions of the South African Institute of Electrical Engineers* (September 1971) 149–201.

[3] ISO 31/7–1978, IEC 27–3 (1989).

squared (ie multiplied by themselves) so that all negative values become positive values. The result is averaged and the square root taken. This process is known as root-mean-square. In a sound level meter the result will be displayed on a logarithmic scale indicating dBA. Depending on the averaging characteristic (known as the time weighting characteristic) selected, the response of the indicator to changes in noise level will be rapid or sluggish. Two time weighting characteristics are in common usage, known appropriately as Fast (F) and Slow (S). The Slow characteristic is the more suitable for general noise measurements because the eye is more able to keep track of the indicator fluctuations.

Another time weighting characteristic of note is the Impulse (I) characteristic. It responds even faster than the Fast characteristic to increasing noise levels, but is more sluggish than the Slow characteristic for reducing noise levels. In this way the eye is better able to keep track of short impulses of noise.

Table 22.1 shows noise levels that would be measured in some typical environments in dBA using the Slow time weighting characteristic.

TABLE 22.1

Noise levels to be expected in some typical environments

Noise Level, dBA	*Typical environment*	*Subjective description*
140	30 m from jet aircraft during take-off	
130	Pneumatic chipping and riveting (operator's position)	Unbearable
120	Large diesel power generator	
110	Metal workshop (grinding work), circular saw	
100	Printing press room	Very noisy
90	7 m from heavy truck, 5 m from large pneumatic drill	
80	Kerbside of busy street	
70	Blaring portable radio	Noisy
60	Supermarket	
50	Average home (day conditions)	Quiet
40	Average home (night conditions, urban environment)	
30	Average home (night conditions, rural areas)	
20	Background in professional recording studio	Very quiet
10	Good acoustic laboratory	
0	Threshold of normal hearing	

22.1.3.3 *Long-term noise descriptors*

Even when using the Slow time-weighting characteristic the indication on a sound level meter varies considerably. It is thus necessary to determine some sort of average or maximum value over a period of time between, say, 10 minutes and 24 hours. As with frequency weighting (see section 22.1.3.1) a number of methods have been proposed to obtain consistent and meaningful results.[4] Of these, only two have achieved any widespread current usage, viz. L_{eq} and L_{10}.

L_{eq} (or L_{Aeq}) can be thought of as a very long-term average over the entire measurement period. The individual dBA readings taken during the measurement period are scaled, antilogged, squared and summed. The result is then averaged, its

[4] Johnston *Assessment of annoyance due to varying noise levels* (unpublished PhD thesis, University of Natal 1979).

square root taken, logged and scaled again to produce a single dBA measurement in much the same way as the root-mean-square value is obtained (see section 22.1.3.2). This admittedly complex process maintains consistency in the fundamental measurement units which allows for great flexibility of application. For example, it is possible to calculate an overall L_{eq} value from a number of constituent L_{eq} values together with their durations. This facilitates the integration of measurement and predictive modelling. The instrument that measures L_{eq} is known as an integrating sound level meter. L_{10} (or L_{A10}), another long-term noise descriptor sometimes encountered, is defined as the A-weighted noise level exceeded for 10 per cent of the time over the period of measurement. Its continued use (mainly in the field of traffic noise) seems largely as a result of tradition since it is incompatible with, and has none of the advantages of, L_{eq}. When both L_{10} and L_{eq} have been included in subjective tests, it is the latter that has shown greater correlation with subjective response even with exclusively traffic noise (for which L_{10} was developed)[5] although the differences tend to be slight.

22.1.3.4 *Additional correction factors*

Although L_{eq} is used as the basis for most noise measurements there are two additional corrections that may need to be applied. It has long been known that noises containing tones such as squeaks, whistles, hums and even music are more annoying than noises of similar L_{eq} without such tones.[6] Up to now no practical instrument has been developed that reliably detects the presence of these tones in all types of noise. A subjective assessment is therefore necessary and a correction of + 5dBA is usually applied to the measured result where a pure tone is audible.

Noise of an impulsive nature (eg riveting, hammering or banging) is also more annoying than noises of similar L_{eq} without such impulses. Once again when a subjective assessment is made a correction of + 5dBA is applied to the measured result.[7] The impulsiveness of noise is, however, amenable to detection by an instrument and more appropriate corrections can be obtained by taking the mean difference between the sound level meter readings when set to the Impulse and Slow time weighting characteristics (see section 22.1.3.2). An even better way is to perform the L_{eq} operation (see section 22.1.3.3) on the output of a sound level meter set to the Impulse time weighted response. This gives a result that incorporates the impulse correction factor. An instrument that does this is known as an integrating impulse sound level meter.

22.1.4 Assessment of Noise

Noise is subjective. Different people respond differently to the same noise. This creates difficulties when attempting to assess the impact of a given noise and when setting limits. In practice the most appropriate criterion in a given situation is the level beyond which a significant number of reasonable people could be expected to start complaining. Setting noise limits is a problem similar to setting motoring speed limits based on the accident potential. In both cases accurate measurement is really only needed for law enforcement purposes.

The South African standard SABS 0103 relates probable community response to a rating level, L_r, which is the A-weighted L_{eq} with both tone and impulse corrections applied, where appropriate. A comparison is made between L_r and the residual sound

---

[5] Voigt *Physikalische Immissionsgrösse und subjektive Störung durch Strassenverkehrslärm* (PhD ETH Zürich 1974) 12; Andrew & May *A laboratory study of annoyance due to traffic noise and the choice of noise descriptors* (1977) Report no 77-AC-1 Acoustics Division, Ministry of Transportation and Communication, Ontaria, Canada.

[6] Kryter & Pearsons 'Judged noisiness of a band of random noise containing an audible pure tone' 1965 (38(1)) *J of the Acoustical Society of America* 106–12.

[7] ISO R1996 1971.

level, which is the A-weighted L_{eq} value at the same time and place in the absence of the noise that is alleged to be annoying. The scale of community response extends from 'no observed reaction', where there is no difference between L_r and the residual sound level, to 'vigorous community action' where the difference is 20 dB or more. Communities will accept differences of up to 5 dB fairly well, but by 10 dB widespread complaints may be expected. It is sometimes difficult to eliminate the alleged noise source when attempting to measure the residual sound level. For such cases SABS 0103 provides comparison criteria for different outdoor and indoor spaces that may be used instead. In non-residential indoor spaces these criteria remain fixed with time, whereas in residential spaces (both outdoor and indoor) the criteria vary with the time of day (and also over weekends). These comparison criteria are also very useful for planning purposes. SABS 0103, the first edition of which was issued in 1967, has been used widely in South Africa and enjoys a good reputation with academics and practitioners alike as the basis for all noise assessment work in this country.

22.2 NOISE CONTROL

22.2.1 Control at source

Because of the ease with which noise spreads, the most economic means of control is usually at the source, preferably incorporated during the planning and design stages. For this to occur there needs to exist:

- an awareness of potential problems,
- appropriate design criteria, and
- some incentive for the extra cost involved, or alternatively, a regulatory requirement.

Awareness about noise is achieved through the formal and informal education processes. It is necessary that environmental education programmes address noise with the same emphasis as is given to, say, littering or air pollution.

Appropriate design criteria, specifically developed or adapted for South African conditions, exist for many noise sources. Conditions affecting noise generation and propagation are significantly different in South Africa in comparison with other parts of the developed world. For example, the poorer thermal insulation performance of South African buildings in comparison with those in most developed countries, coupled with an open-window life-style, leads to lower inherent acoustic isolation. Noise levels acceptable at building facades overseas could be unacceptable here. Furthermore, motor vehicles used on South African roads differ significantly with respect to noise from those in North America and Europe, and the roads themselves are designed to different standards. Thus criteria developed overseas should not be used before being carefully validated as applicable to local conditions.

In the field of transportation, maximum noise levels for the different classes of motor vehicles are given in SABS 097 and SABS 0205. The criteria given in these standards are based on European Community requirements, and represent, as such, a compromise between the need for quieter road vehicles and the cost of achieving noise reduction. It makes sense for the South African motor vehicle industry to follow European noise standards because of close alignment in respect of other vehicle standards. Local vehicle models tend to have more extended production runs than in Europe, however, so when vehicle noise levels in Europe are reduced there is a time lag before a similar reduction can be achieved locally. SABS 0181 provides a simplified roadside measurement method, with compatible criteria, that is useful for law enforcement measures.

The road itself can also be considered to be a noise source. SABS 0210 gives a method of predicting the noise from roads given such information as traffic flow rate, speed, light/heavy traffic mix, topographical data, etc. This standard is based on work carried out by the National Institute for Transportation and Road Research (NITRR) of the Council for Scientific and Industrial Research (CSIR) under contract to the Department of Transport.[8] Although based on a Welsh source[9] this model has been adapted to South African conditions.[10] For example, the basic noise level prediction was adjusted to reflect local road and vehicle conditions, and the output of the model was changed from L_{10} to L_{eq}. This is the only officially issued road noise model that has been adapted for local conditions and validated locally.

Noise in the vicinity of airports can be predicted and evaluated using the method given in SABS 0117. This method was also developed locally at the CSIR[11] and produces total noisiness index (NI) contours which are basically L_{eq} values averaged over 24 hours. It requires specific noise information and other performance data to be supplied regarding the aircraft types using the airport. The performance data can be obtained from the aircraft manuals, while the noise data can either be measured (with the aircraft on the ground) in accordance with SABS 0115 or derived, in accordance with SABS 0116, from international noise certification data for the aircraft.

No methods have been developed for local use for predicting and evaluating noise from rail vehicles or from rail routes, although the need for such methods has been expressed.

Local design criteria exist for a few other noise sources viz. distribution transformers,[12] room air conditioners[13] and overhead projectors.[14] In other cases the principle of noise labelling has been adopted. For such products, including vacuum cleaners,[15] floor polishers,[16] compressors,[17] welding generators,[18] rotating electrical machinery,[19] and pneumatic equipment[20] it is recommended that the noise produced be indicated by means of a label or in the operating instructions. In this way the purchaser or user may determine the maximum acceptable noise output for his specific application by referring to a basic document (such as SABS 0103) and performing calculations to account for the modification of the noise levels by the path between the source and the receiver. A product may then be selected that just meets this noise criterion, thus avoiding unnecessary expense.

The only real incentive to incur the extra cost of noise control measures is the threat of an interdict, costly litigation and subsequent closure or limitation of the operation concerned. Absence of effective legislation and consequent reliance on private-law remedies have in the past rendered this threat innocuous in most instances. With the emergence of national regulations dealing with noise (see section 22.3.3.2) this threat will assume greater significance in the future.

Often the most appropriate noise abatement measure is to resite the noise source.

---

[8] Davinroy & Reeves *Interim procedure for calculating road traffic noise* (1983) Technical manual K65 CSIR.

[9] *Calculation of road traffic noise* Department of Environment, Welsh Office 1975.

[10] Reeves & Wixley *Predicting road traffic noise from traffic parameters* First South African Congress on Acoustics CSIR Pretoria (1985); Reeves & Wixley *Statistical analysis of the relationship between observed values of L_{eq} and L_{10} (1986)* Technical report RV/8 National Institute for Transport and Road Research CSIR; Reeves *The predictive accuracy of the interim noise prediction procedure* (1986) Technical report RV/9 National Institute for Transport and Road Research CSIR.

[11] Robertson *The South African aircraft noise prediction procedure* (1989) Annual Transportation Convention CSIR Pretoria.

[12] SABS 780–1979.

[13] SABS 1125–1977.

[14] SABS 1452–1988.

[15] SABS 1486: Part I–1989.

[16] SABS 1486: Part II–1989.

[17] SABS 1417: Part I–1988.

[18] SABS 1470: Part II–1988.

[19] SABS 1470: Part III–1990.

[20] SABS 1470: Part IV–1990.

This could be a major undertaking (eg resiting a planned road), or something quite trivial (eg moving a portable compressor to a different side of a building). The cost implications are least when noise abatement measures are introduced during the planning stage and the principles of Integrated Environmental Management (IEM) (see chapter 30) are particularly relevant to dealing with noise at its source during the planning phase of any project. It is important that noise always be considered as a possible factor during the screening procedure which is one of the early stages of all IEM activities.

Noise from existing sources is invariably a more complex problem and sometimes the only practical solution is to shut down the offending operation. Nevertheless, the majority of noise problems are amenable to some mitigation by engineering methods. Much time and money can be saved by employing expertise with practical experience in an applicable field of noise abatement.

22.2.2 Control in transmission path

Where the source cannot be sufficiently abated, the next most economic means is to deal with the transmission path. This can be done by enclosing the source, by the erection of suitable barriers, and by ensuring that buildings provide reasonable attenuation to noise generated externally as well as internally (eg in other rooms).

The design of suitable enclosures is a complex affair with conflicting demands of ventilation (to ensure cooling of machinery) and isolation (to prevent the noise from escaping). Forced ventilation through acoustic attenuators (or silencers) is often necessary, and this requires careful design to ensure an optimum cost/benefit ratio. Similarly, the design of acoustic barriers, for example along highways, is a highly specialised activity with many compromises to be made between material costs, acoustic effectiveness and aesthetics. SABS 0210 is not a roadside barrier design document (no locally developed document exists for this function), but it can (and should) be used to evaluate the results of a roadside barrier design. A common fallacy is the belief that trees or shrubbery will provide effective attenuation of noise, particularly from roads. In most cases the effect on the noise level will be negligible (unless the planted strip is very wide, say 100 m or more, and the vegetation very dense),[21] although the result may be visually more acceptable.

Distance is an attenuator of most noise (see section 22.1.1.2) and may be very effective near the source. While a vast tract of open land is not a very economic option, much can be done with the relative positioning of noise generating and noise sensitive activities in given spaces. Orientation of buildings away from noise sources can also help significantly, particularly if windows and doors facing the source can be minimised or eliminated. Buildings themselves can form very effective barriers to noise, especially if the structure is continuous, as in some commercial developments and terrace housing. Once again the value of proper planning becomes apparent, and noise should be a major criterion to be considered in all town planning activities. Particular attention should be paid to the siting of areas for hospitals, churches and schools away from noisy activities and busy roads. Noise contours around busy roads are seldom straight, being very dependent on topography. The prediction model in SABS 0210 thus provides a basis for the creative planning of residential, commercial and industrial areas without necessarily resorting to strip development. The Buchanan principle[22] can also be applied to the noise information obtained from SABS 0210. This town planning technique achieves noise abatement by utilizing a pattern of roads to divide a town into 'districts' and 'local areas'.

The acoustic isolation provided by buildings is an important element in noise control.

---

[21] Moore *Design for good acoustics and noise control* (1978) 91–2.

[22] Buchanan *Traffic in towns: Buchanan report* (1963).

Traditional brick and mortar building methods provide good inherent noise isolation, but this tends to be negated by ill-fitting doors and windows, the latter being open much of the time. In high density residential developments, the use of lightweight partitions with poor acoustic performance between different dwelling units leads to major problems. With the move towards less traditional building construction methods in South Africa, the danger exists that such problems will become widespread. SABS 0218: Part I provides appropriate design standards for the acoustical isolation properties of a wide variety of residential and non-residential buildings. Two grades of isolation (Higher Grade and Standard Grade) are provided for. Part II of SABS 0218 gives recommendations for the assessment of building plans and buildings to the performance standards of Part I and is useful to both property developers and local authorities. It is possible for the reasonableness of noise complaints to be challenged on the basis that the isolation of the complainant's building is inadequate when assessed against this standard.

22.2.3 Control at receiver

The least economic means of noise control, although frequently necessitated through lack of attention during the planning stages, is to isolate the recipients. In city centres where high levels of traffic noise are unavoidable, soundproofing of offices and shops is the only solution. Soundproofing of dwellings away from city centres, while viable in certain instances overseas, is much less successful in South Africa owing to the emphasis on outdoor and open-window living here. In the South African climate, soundproofing implies the need for air-conditioning, or at least forced ventilation, which in turn can be a source of noise both for the occupants and their neighbours. Increasing the acoustic absorption in a room by the introduction of soft furnishings, carpeting and drapes can help to some extent, but the maximum improvement is usually insufficient to solve a noise problem unless used in combination with other measures.

When all other attempts have failed, the only recourse is to move the recipients themselves. They may eventually do this out of desperation. Where the problem is widespread and permanent, significant reduction in property values can occur. In some instances the problem can be resolved satisfactorily by rezoning affected properties from 'residential' to 'commercial' or 'light industrial'. If there is a demand for such property in the area, such action will provide a financial incentive for the affected persons to move elsewhere.

22.3 LEGISLATION

22.3.1 National legislation

22.3.1.1 *Standards Act*

The Standards Act 30 of 1982 makes provision for the issue of compulsory specifications for commodities or their manufacture.[23] No person may sell a commodity for which a compulsory specification is in force unless that commodity complies with or has been manufactured in accordance with the compulsory specification.[24] The term 'sell' is given a wide definition in the Act and includes offering, displaying or possessing for trade purposes.[25] The Standards Act is administered by the South African Bureau of Standards.

[23] Section 16.
[24] Section 17.
[25] Section 1(xx).

Compulsory specifications issued in respect of certain motor vehicles place limitations on noise.[26] Most passenger and commercial vehicles are affected, the major exceptions being caravans and trailers (for which noise requirements are not relevant), and motorcycles (for which no compulsory specification exists). The noise requirements are those recommended in SABS 097. These will be updated to the recommendations of SABS 0205 (which is based on the most recent European legislation) as soon as an appropriate lead time has elapsed (see 22.2.1).

22.3.1.2 *Environment Conservation Act*

The Environment Conservation Act 73 of 1989[27] makes specific provision for the issue of regulations with regard to noise (also the related topics of vibration and shock). The first set of such regulations relates to the control of noise by local authorities.[28] An innovative aspect of these regulations is the fact that they apply only in the areas of jurisdiction of local authorities which request them. They thus form, in effect, a standardized set of noise by-laws but with the advantage that they are easier to issue, the powers that they are able to confer are greater and the penalties higher than would be the case with by-laws. Because these regulations were designed for application by local authorities, their details are discussed under that section (see section 22.3.3.2).

The other aspect of the Environment Conservation Act that may be used to advantage with respect to noise is the prohibition of certain activities,[29] identified by the Minister,[30] unless written authorization is issued on the basis of an impact study. See chapter 7. It is unlikely that any activities will be identified solely on the basis of noise. Where activities are identified for other reasons, however, the IEM process (see chapter 30) implied in the requirement to conduct an impact study should ensure that noise is covered if it is at all relevant.

22.3.1.3 *Road Traffic Act*

The Road Traffic Act 29 of 1989 replaced the four provincial ordinances relating to the use of motor vehicles on public roads. This Act came into operation on 1 June 1990[31] and provides[32] inter alia that no person shall operate or permit to be operated on a public road a vehicle causing noise

(a) in excess of the prescribed noise level; or
(b) resulting from the use of methods, accessories or appliances the use of which is prohibited by regulation.

The Act does not prescribe noise levels, but it does empower the Minister to issue regulations prescribing them.[33] The consolidated Road Traffic Regulations,[34] however, fail to prescribe any noise level nor do they prohibit the use of any relevant 'methods, accessories or appliances'. Until subsequent regulations are issued, therefore, these provisions of the Act cannot be applied.

The provision of the Act relating to the use of a hooter provides that no person shall on a public road use the sounding device or hooter of a vehicle except when such use is necessary in order to comply with the provisions of the Act or on the grounds of

[26] GN 957 of 14 May 1982; GN 786 of 15 April 1983; GN 1187 of 15 June 1984; and GN 1286 of 17 June 1986.
[27] Section 25.
[28] GN 896 of 27 April 1990.
[29] Section 22.
[30] Section 21.
[31] GN 73 of 27 April 1990.
[32] Section 103.
[33] Section 132(1)*(f)*.
[34] GN R910 of 26 April 1990.

safety.[35] The Act also empowers local authorities to promulgate by-laws relating to the use of hooters, bells or other warning devices and the conditions under which they may be used.[36]

As far as exhaust silencers are concerned, the regulations provide that no person shall operate on a public road any motor vehicle unless an efficient exhaust silencer or muffling device is affixed in such a manner that the exhaust gas from the engine is projected through the silencer or muffling device, which shall be so constructed as to reduce and muffle sound in an effective manner.[37] This is difficult to apply in practice because of the absence of legal definitions to determine what is 'efficient' and 'excessive'.

The Act outlaws the use on a public road of a vehicle that is not in a roadworthy condition.[38] A noisy vehicle may be regarded as unroadworthy in terms of the applicable part of SABS 047. The limits used are those given in SABS 0181. This standard describes a quick and simplified procedure of noise measurement suited to roadside and test ground use, and the limits are aligned with the vehicle design criteria given in SABS 097. When the anticipated introduction of routine roadworthy retesting (at least for heavy vehicles) becomes a reality, this provision will assume greater significance.

22.3.1.4 *Aviation Act*

The Aviation Act 74 of 1962 authorizes the Minister of Transport to make regulations relating to the prevention of nuisance arising out of air navigation or aircraft factories, airports or other aircraft establishments. This includes the prevention of nuisance due to noise or vibration from the operation of machinery in aircraft on or above airports, by the installation in aircraft, or on airports, of means for the prevention of such noise or vibration, or otherwise.[39] No such regulations have been issued.

22.3.1.5 *Occupational exposure*

Noise control can be exercised in terms of the Machinery and Occupational Safety Act 6 of 1983, which aims at providing for the safety of persons at a 'workplace' or in the course of their 'employment' or in connection with the use of 'machinery'. Apart from extensive provisions of the Act dealing with such safety, the Minister of Manpower is authorized to make regulations which, in his opinion, are necessary or desirable in the interest of the safety of persons in the above-mentioned circumstances.[40]

Provision is likewise made for the control of noise related to mining. The Minister of Mineral and Energy Affairs is authorized in terms of the Mines and Works Act 27 of 1956 to make regulations concerning the health and safety of persons employed in mines.[41] The regulations[42] now apply by virtue of the Minerals Act 50 of 1991[43] which replaced the Mines and Works Act.

Reference is again made to the observation that noise in the workplace is not normally considered to be an environmental problem. (See section 22.1.2.2.)

---

35 Section 104.
36 Section 133(1)*(j)*.
37 Section 344*(a)*.
38 Section 62(1).
39 Section 22(1)*(s)*.
40 Section 35(1)*(b)*. The regulations are contained in GN R2281 and R2282 of 16 October 1987.
41 Section 12(1)*(g)*.
42 GN R1130 of 2 June 1989.
43 Cf s 68(2).

22.3.2 Provincial legislation

Prior to the introduction of the Road Traffic Act (see section 22.3.1.3), motor-vehicle noise was controlled under the Road Traffic Ordinances of the four provinces. The implementation of the new Act, however, remains the responsibility of the provinces.

There are also provincial ordinances dealing with town-planning, but these are too vague with regard to noise to have any significant effect in practice, and are not dealt with further.

22.3.3 Local authority legislation

22.3.3.1 *By-laws*

Historically, local authorities have dealt with noise through so-called 'nuisance' by-laws which prohibit the creation of a nuisance. Noise is seldom specifically identified as a nuisance factor and these by-laws are generally regarded as ineffective.

In 1978 the first specific noise-control by-laws in the country were promulgated by the municipalities of Pretoria[44] and Johannesburg.[45] These were followed between 1979 and 1982 by by-laws promulgated by Sandton,[46] the Transvaal Board for the Development of Peri-Urban Areas,[47] Roodepoort,[48] Kempton Park,[49] Germiston,[50] Randburg,[51] Boksburg,[52] Secunda,[53] Brakpan,[54] Witbank[55] and Standerton.[56] Pietermaritzburg issued its noise control by-laws in 1984,[57]—the only local authority outside the Transvaal to do so. These by-laws are all almost identical and define 'disturbing noise' as a noise level which exceeds the ambient sound level by 7 dBA or more (this has resulted in these by-laws becoming known as the '7 dB law'). Both the noise level and the ambient sound level are objectively ascertained with reference to readings on an integrating sound-level meter (i e A-weighted L_{eq}) to which a subjective correction of 5 dBA is added if the sound is impulsive or contains a pure tone component. It is an offence to cause or permit to be made by any person, machine, animal or apparatus or any combination of these, a noise which is a disturbing noise. Moreover, if the Medical Officer of Health (or the appropriate equivalent officer), as a result of a complaint lodged with him, is satisfied that a noise emanating from any building, premises or street is a disturbing noise, he may issue an abatement notice to the person responsible for the noise, or the owner of the building or premises in question. Failure to comply with this notice is also an offence. In certain instances he may, subject to such conditions as he may deem fit, permit the noise to continue. The by-laws issued by nine of these local authorities contain an additional section entitled 'noise disturbance' listing specific activities which are prohibited if they 'disturb or hinder the comfort, convenience, peace or quiet of the public'. No measurement is involved in these cases but the right to serve an abatement notice is also lacking. Thus the onus is on the Medical Officer of Health (or equivalent officer) to show that a disturbance has

[44] AN 816 of 27 June 1978.
[45] AN 1784 of 29 November 1978.
[46] AN 955 of 29 August 1979.
[47] AN 1433 of 5 December 1979.
[48] AN 13 of 2 January 1980.
[49] AN 324 of 19 March 1980.
[50] AN 542 of 14 May 1980.
[51] AN 1277 of 10 September 1980.
[52] AN 1330 of 17 September 1980.
[53] AN 1153 of 16 September 1981.
[54] AN 1216 of 23 September 1981.
[55] AN 1355 of 7 October 1981.
[56] AN 708 of 16 June 1982.
[57] PN 514 of 4 October 1984.

occurred. A curious variation of these by-laws was issued by Bedfordview;[58] in it the field of application is limited to the noise from, and other matters pertaining to, amusement machines in places of amusement.

These by-laws represented a major advance for the local authorities that introduced them. They were, however, completely reactive in application and the maximum penalty specified (R300, plus R50 per day for continuing offences) was an inadequate deterrent. Legislation was needed that provided for a pro-active approach that aimed at preventing noise problems through proper planning. This did not appear feasible through the instrument of by-laws and the Environment Conservation Act provided a more appropriate alternative.

22.3.3.2 *Local authority implementation of national noise regulations*

(a) Implementation. The noise regulations issued under the Environment Conservation Act (see section 22.3.1.2) were developed by the Council for the Environment after extensive consultation with local authorities. They are far more comprehensive than the by-laws described in section 22.3.3.1 and provide the local authority with a multi-faceted instrument to control noise both pro-actively and reactively. By March 1992, these regulations had been promulgated in the area of jurisdiction of some 27 local authorities. Because of their significance, they are discussed in some detail, even though feedback on their practical implementation is lacking.

(b) Noise nuisance. These regulations[59] contain a whole range of prohibitions[60] of activities if such activities give rise to a 'noise nuisance', defined as 'any sound which disturbs or impairs or may disturb or impair the convenience or peace of any person'. These prohibitions are similar in principle to those contained in some of the by-laws (see section 22.3.3.1). Unlike the by-laws, however, the local authority has the right to issue an abatement notice[61] and it is an offence not to comply with such a notice.[62] The prohibitions cover noise from radios, music, shouting, ringing of bells, animals (including birds and poultry), noise from the building and repair of vehicles, vessels and aircraft, and noise from the use of explosives and firearms as well as from the use of recreational vehicles, the sounding of various types of alarms, loading and unloading operations and the operation of power tools and garden implements. An interesting prohibition under this regulation is the driving of a vehicle on a public road in such a manner that it may create a noise nuisance.[63] This applies even if the vehicle itself complies with all noise requirements, which means that the driver can commit an offence purely by his manner of driving. This provision is expected to be effective against antisocial elements such as late night motorcycle revellers, and also against the indiscriminate use of noisy engine brakes in heavy vehicles.

(c) Power tools. A higher level of prohibition applies to the use of power tools or power equipment for construction, earth drilling and demolition works in residential areas during evenings and on Sundays, certain holidays and other days determined by the local authority.[64] These activities are prohibited outright during the stated times, without the need to establish or suspect a disturbance or nuisance. The only circumstances in which these activities may take place during these times is under an exemption issued by the local authority and subject to the conditions imposed by it.[65]

---

[58] AN 2269 of 12 December 1984.
[59] GN R2544 of 2 November 1990.
[60] Regulation 5.
[61] Regulation 2*(c)*.
[62] Regulation 3*(f)*.
[63] Regulation 5*(j)*.
[64] Regulation 3*(i)*.
[65] Regulation 7.

Such conditions could include a requirement to use only labelled equipment (see section 22.2.1) with a specified maximum noise output.

(d) Noise levels. One aspect dealing with hearing conservation (see section 22.1.2.2) is the requirement in places of public entertainment, where the music level exceeds 95 dBA, for the display of signs warning of possible hearing damage.[66] The music level is termed 'noise level' in the regulations because of its undesirable health consequences.

The '7 dB law' (see section 22.3.3.1) has been retained in the regulations, despite criticism from some quarters that the 7 dB excess should be substantially reduced. This criticism has arisen mainly in those areas where the by-laws do not apply, and those local authorities using the '7 dB law' have generally found the limit to be practical. The subjective element involved in applying the impulse correction factor has been eliminated by specifying the use of an impulse-integrating sound-level meter[67] the reading of which incorporates the impulse correction (see section 22.1.3.4). The subjective tone correction of + 5 dBA, however, remains. A more valid criticism of the '7 dB law' is that it can, under certain circumstances, give rise to a 'creeping background' effect. This occurs when a series of new activities commence, the first producing a noise level just within the permissible limit. This defines an increased background noise level which the second activity may in turn exceed by up to 7 dBA, and so on. In practice this occurs less frequently than may be expected, owing to the usual reduction of noise with distance (see section 22.1.1.2) and the fact that different activities will normally be spaced some distance apart. Nevertheless, to deal with this the regulations have introduced the concept of noise zoning as an alternative to the '7 dB law'. This solves the creeping background effect at the expense of some extra work by the local authority. The regulations give the local authorities the power to declare 'zone sound levels' for different areas by means of notices in the relevant *Official Gazette*.[68] It takes considerable survey work to arrive at practicable zone sound levels, but these need be defined only in specific problem areas.

(e) Disturbing noise. 'Disturbing noise' is defined in the regulations as a noise level which exceeds the zone sound level or, if no zone sound level has been designated, a noise level which exceeds the ambient sound level at the same measuring point by 7 dBA or more. The ambient sound level is also measured using an impulse-integrating sound-level meter. In this way both the '7 dB law' and zoning are catered for. It is an offence to produce a disturbing noise or to permit it to be made.[69] As in the case of a 'noise nuisance' the local authority has the power to issue an abatement notice in respect of a 'disturbing noise'.

(f) Motor-vehicle noise. SABS 0181 is used as the control instrument for motor-vehicle noise. This simplified method (see section 22.2.1) ensures that local authorities will be able to conduct the measurements and control modifications to, and inadequate maintenance of, vehicle exhaust systems. It is an offence to drive a vehicle, or allow it to be driven, if the sound level measured in accordance with SABS 0181 exceeds stated values.[70] An amendment to SABS 0181 introduced during 1990 enables this code to be used to ensure that engine brakes fitted to certain heavy vehicles do not produce excessive noise.

(g) Land-use planning. The regulations contain a number of provisions intended to prevent noise problems through proper planning. The local authority may designate

---

[66] Regulation 3*(h)*.
[67] See the definition of 'noise level'.
[68] Regulation 2*(m)*.
[69] Regulation 4.
[70] Regulation 3*(j)*.

'controlled areas' where the noise level exceeds, or is predicted to exceed within 15 years, laid down criteria (effectively an 18-hour L_{eq} of 65 dBA for traffic and aircraft noise, and a 24-hour L_{eq} of 61 dBA for industrial noise).[71] Educational, residential, hospital, church or office buildings may not be erected within a controlled area unless appropriate acoustic screening measures have been provided to limit the inside noise level to 40 dBA.[72] Erven for these buildings may not be situated within controlled areas in a new township or in an area which has been rezoned, unless the local authority allows this on the basis of appropriate screening measures in the approved building plans.[73] The local authority may require noise impact assessments or tests to be conducted before changes are made to existing facilities or land use or before new buildings are erected.[74] No person may build a road, or change an existing road, or even alter the speed limit on a road such that an increase in noise levels may result, unless appropriate steps have been taken in consultation with the local authority to ensure that land in the vicinity of the road is not designated as a controlled area.[75] The Environment Conservation Act[76] binds the State, so these provisions should have the effect of forcing negotiation on aspects where there was previously none.

(h) Additional powers. Local authorities have a number of additional powers and may, for instance, require that the layout plan of a new township shall indicate existing and future (projected to 15 years) sources of noise, with concomitant dBA values.[77] A local authority may also require notification of the intention to install, replace or modify a plant with a total input power exceeding 10 kW[78] and may request the owner or person in control of the plant to furnish proof to its satisfaction that the plant shall not cause a disturbing noise.[79] Written consent from the local authority is also required to stage an organized open-air music festival or similar gathering.[80]

A local authority can issue an instruction to discontinue making a noise nuisance or a disturbing noise or to lower its level within a period stipulated in the instruction (exceptions to this are noise from rail vehicles and from (non-recreational) aircraft).[81] It can enforce the cessation of excavation, earth-moving, pumping, drilling, construction or demolition work, or similar activity, power-generation or music that causes a noise nuisance or disturbing noise, until such conditions as it deems necessary have been complied with.[82] It can impound animals where the person in charge of them has failed to heed an instruction[83] and it can attach a noisy vehicle if its measured sound level exceeds the relevant limit by more than 5 dBA.[84] It has the right of entry into a premises and the right to stop, test or refer for testing vehicles using any road in its area of jurisdiction (including private, provincial and national roads).[85]

(i) Exemptions. Provision is made for the local authority to issue exemptions upon written application.[86] The implementation of such an exemption is subject to a written

---

71 Regulation 2*(f)*.
72 Regulation 3*(b)*.
73 Regulation 3*(e)*.
74 Regulation 2*(c)*.
75 Regulation 3*(d)*
76 Section 40.
77 Regulation 3*(a)*.
78 Regulation 3*(k)*.
79 Regulation 2*(i)*.
80 Regulation 3*(g)*.
81 Regulation 2*(c)*.
82 Regulation 2*(e)*.
83 Regulation 2*(g)*.
84 Regulation 2*(h)*.
85 Regulation 2*(a)*.
86 Regulation 7.

undertaking by the applicant to comply with all conditions imposed.[87]

(j) Penalties. The maximum penalty for a contravention of any of these provisions is R20 000 (and/or two years' imprisonment) plus R250 (and/or 20 days' imprisonment) per day for each day that the contravention continues.[88] This is considerably higher than the maximum penalty prescribed under the by-laws and should lead to more effective control in those areas that choose to request the regulations.

(k) Noise control officers. In the preamble to the regulations it is stated that a local authority wishing to apply the regulations in their entirety should have the services of a noise control officer at its disposal (not necessarily in its full-time employ) whose qualifications are of a standard equal to a Senior Certificate plus four years' tertiary education in engineering or physical sciences. In the absence of such a noise control officer, a local authority may apply a reduced set of the regulations, with the planning aspects eliminated, provided that it has in its employ an inspector with a National Certificate in Noise Control issued by a Technikon. This National Certificate involves a relatively short course which can be studied by correspondence.

22.4 NOISE CONTROL IN DEVELOPING COMMUNITIES

The noise control measures and criteria used in South Africa are based on the experience of the developed world. In a changing society the needs of the developing sector should not be ignored. Will existing criteria continue to be relevant? Can (or should) they be applied in all areas? In seeking answers to these questions, it is necessary to recognize that in this respect South Africa's situation is not unique and there are many parallels in the developing world. In a study of the subject[89] it was concluded that a community will remain relatively insensitive to noise as long as its more basic needs, such as food, shelter, security and employment are not adequately served. This conclusion has important implications for noise control in a future South Africa. It indicates that time and money should not be spent on remedial actions against noise in underdeveloped communities: it would be better to apply those resources to serve the more basic needs.

It can be assumed, however, that the basic needs of developing communities will be satisfied ultimately, at which stage a more vigorous response to noise can be expected. In these communities noise control measures should at present be enforced only on developments of a more or less permanent nature, such as the routeing of roads or railways, the siting of industrial and residential areas and the siting of airports. Non-industrial buildings with an expected life of, say, 25 years or longer should also be subject to basic noise control considerations in the design stage. However, it probably matters little if these communities seem willing to tolerate 'excessive' noise from commercial and social activities in the short to medium term; that aspect can be dealt with later. The greater need at present is to promote the development of these communities with a minimum of constraints.

The national noise regulations (see section 22.3.3.2) make provision for such selective application. Indeed, the preamble to them makes it clear that they will be made applicable within a local authority only if that local authority requests them. The Environment Conservation Act (see section 22.3.1.2) entrenches this safeguard by providing that regulations which may affect the activities of any local authority shall be promulgated only with the concurrence of that local authority.[90]

---

[87] Regulation 7(4).

[88] Regulation 9.

[89] Johnston 'Noise control in a changing South Africa', Paper read at a symposium on acoustics today, University of Natal, Durban September 1989.

[90] Section 28*(i)*(iii).

It would be prudent for local authorities of developing communities to have those aspects of the noise regulations that cover planning made applicable in their areas of jurisdiction. In this way they would be in a position to control developments that may have a long-term influence on the noise environment. The drawback is the requirement that the local authority must have the services of a highly qualified noise control officer at its disposal (see section 22.3.3.2) and this may be beyond its financial capability. It seems, however, that this requirement could be met by using the services of a noise control officer from a neighbouring local authority or by employing the services of a consultant.

TABLE 22.2
National and international standards referred to by number

NOTE: All SABS standards are issued by the South African Bureau of Standards.

IEC 27–3 1989: 'Letter symbols to be used in electrical technology—Part 3: Logarithmic quantities and units', International Electrotechnical Commission, Geneva.

ISO 31/7 1978: 'Quantities and units of acoustics', incorporating amendment no 1 (1985) International Organization for Standardization, Geneva.

ISO R1996 1971: 'Assessment of noise with respect to community response', first edition, Table 1, International Organization for Standardization, Geneva.

SABS 047: 'Testing of motor vehicles for roadworthiness';

Part I–1972: 'Light vehicles', (incorporating Amendments 1:1974, 2:1975, 3:1977, 4:1978, 5:1984, 6:1988);

Part II–1978: 'Motor cycles (including motor tricycles)', (incorporating Amendment 1:1984);

Part III–1988: 'Heavy vehicles';

Part IV–1990: 'Buses';

Part V–1990: 'Minibuses'.

SABS 097–1975: 'The measurement of noise emitted by motor vehicles', 1st revision (incorporating Amendment 1:1983).

SABS 0103–1983: 'The measurement and rating of environmental noise with respect to annoyance and speech communication', second revision (incorporating amendment 1: 1986).

SABS 0115–1974: 'The measurement of noise and determination of disturbance from aeroplanes for certification purposes'.

SABS 0116–1974: 'The procedure for calculating basic noise parameters from ICAO aeroplane noise certification data'.

SABS 0117–1974: 'The determination and limitation of disturbance around an aerodrome due to noise from aeroplanes' (incorporating Amendment 1:1984).

SABS 0181–1981: 'The measurement of noise emitted by road vehicles when stationary' (incorporating Amendments 1:1990, 2:1990, 3:1991 and 4:1992).

SABS 0205–1986: 'The measurement of noise emitted by motor vehicles in motion'.

SABS 0210–1986: 'Calculating and predicting road traffic noise'.

SABS 0218: 'Acoustical properties of buildings',

Part I–1988: 'The grading of buildings according to their airborne-sound insulation properties';

Part II–1988: 'The assessment of building plans and buildings with respect to their acoustical properties'.

SABS 780–1979: 'Distribution transformers', first revision (incorporating Amendments 1:1981, 2:1983, 3:1984, 4:1987 and 5:1990).

SABS 1125–1977: 'Room air conditioners'.

SABS 1452–1988: 'Overhead projectors'.

SABS 1470: 'Sound power labelling';

Part I–1988: 'Compressors';

Part II–1988: 'Welding generators';

Part III–1990: 'Rotating electrical machinery';

Part IV–1990: 'Pneumatic equipment'.

SABS 1486: 'Domestic electric floor treatment machines';

Part I–1989: 'Vacuum cleaners'.

Part II–1989: 'Floor polishers'.

TABLE 22.3
Government and provincial notices

NOTE: 'AN' refers to Administrator's Notices published in the Transvaal Provincial Gazette, 'GN' refers to Government Notices published in the Government Gazette and 'PN' refers to Provincial Notices published in the Official Gazette of the Province of Natal.

AN 816 of 27 June 1978: 'Pretoria Municipality: Noise abatement by-laws.'

AN 1784 of 29 November 1978: 'Johannesburg Municipality: Noise control by-laws.'

AN 1433 of 5 December 1979: 'Transvaal Board for the Development of Peri-Urban Areas: Noise abatement by-laws.'

AN 13 of 2 January 1980: 'Roodepoort Municipality: Noise control by-laws.'

AN 324 of 19 March 1980: 'Kempton Park Municipality: Noise control by-laws.'

AN 542 of 14 May 1980: 'Germiston Municipality: Noise abatement by-laws.'

AN 1277 of 10 September 1980: 'Randburg Municipality: Noise abatement by-laws.'

AN 1330 of 17 September 1980: 'Boksburg Municipality: Noise control by-laws.'

AN 1216 of 23 September 1981: 'Brakpan Municipality: Noise control by-laws.'

AN 1153 of 16 September 1981: 'Secunda Health Committee: Noise abatement regulations.'

AN 1355 of 7 October 1981: 'Witbank Municipality: Noise abatement by-laws.'

AN 708 of 16 June 1982: 'Standerton Municipality: Noise control by-laws.'

AN 2269 of 12 December 1984: 'Bedfordview Municipality: By-laws relating to amusement machines'

GN 957 of 14 May 1982: 'Category M1 motor vehicles', as amended by GN 1494 of 5 July 1985, GN 53 of 10 January 1986, GN 1204 of 20 June 1986, and GN 309 of 15 May 1987.

GN 786 of 15 April 1983: 'Category N1 motor vehicles', as amended by GN 1495 of 5 July 1985 and GN 311 of 15 May 1987.

GN 1187 of 15 June 1984: 'Category M2 and M3 motor vehicles', as amended by GN 1492 of 5 July 1985 and GN 310 of 15 May 1987.

PN 514 of 4 October 1984: 'City of Pietermaritzburg: Noise abatement bylaws.'

GN 1286 of 17 June 1986: 'Category N2 and N3 motor vehicles', as amended by GN 1496 of 5 July 1985 and GN 312 of 15 May 1987.

GN R2281 of 16 October 1987: Machinery and Occupational Safety Act—Environmental Regulations for Workplaces.

GN R2282 of 16 October 1987: Machinery and Occupational Safety Act—Environmental Regulations for Workplaces—Incorporation of Safety Standards.

GN 798 of 30 October 1987: Bill on Environment Conservation

GN R1130 of 2 June 1989: Mines and Works Act—Amendment of Regulations.

GN R910 of 2ril 1990: Consolidated Road Traffic Regulations.

GN 73 of 27 April 1990: Road Traffic Act: Commencement of certain sections.

GN 896 of 27 April 1990: Regulations in terms of sections 25 and 28 of the Environment Conservation Act, promulgated with the concurrence of local authorities in respect of their respective areas of jurisdiction.

The regulations (A = in their entirety; B = with the exception of reg 3*(a)*, *(b)*, *(c)*, *(d)* and *(e)*) have been promulgated by the following local authorities:

TABLE 22.3 (contd)

No.	Local authority	Category
Published in GN R2544 of 2 November 1990.		
1	Municipality of Simon's Town	A
2	Town Council of Potchefstroom	B
3	City Council of Pietermaritzburg	B
4	Municipality of Daniëlskuil	A
5	Municipality of Bethlehem	A
6	Borough of Greytown	A
7	Municipality of Beacon Bay	A
8	City Council of Pretoria	A
9	Municipality of Koffiefontein	B
10	Town Council of Sandton	A
Published in GN R314 of 22 February 1991		
11	Municipality of Fish Hoek	A
12	Town Council of Ellisras	A
13	City Council of Akasia	A
Published in GN R638 of 28 March 1991		
14	Town council of Alberton	A
15	Town Council of Bedfordview	A
16	City Council of Port Elizabeth	B
17	Town Council of Springs	B
Published in GN R1193 of 24 May 1991		
18	Municipality of Virginia	A
19	Municipality of Vredendal	A
20	Municipality of Westville	A
Published in GN R156 of 10 January 1992		
21	Borough of Eshowe	A
Published in GN R157 of 10 January 1992		
22	Municipality of Stellenbosch	A
Published in GN R158 of 10 January 1992		
23	Town Council of Verwoerdburg	A
Published in GN R159 of 10 January 1992		
24	Everton Health Committee	A
Published in GN R499 of 14 February 1992		
25	Municipality of Pinetown	A
Published in GN R500 of 14 February 1992		
26	Town Council of Vereeniging	B
Published in GN R501 of 14 February 1992		
27	Town Council of Hartbeespoort	A

CHAPTER 23

ENVIRONMENTAL HEALTH

Y E R VON SCHIRNDING

23.1 INTRODUCTION

The discipline of environmental health emerged with prominence in the 1980s, with increasing recognition that efforts at environmental improvement and protection could have a positive effect on disease prevention.[1] Other than immunization programmes, few areas exist with similar opportunities for primary prevention. In order to implement preventive measures, it is necessary to appreciate the way in which the environment influences human health. As was stressed by the chairman of the World Commission on Environment and Development, Gro Harlem Brundtland, health and sustainable development are closely inter-linked.[2]

23.1.1 Scope of environmental health

23.1.1.1 *Definition*

According to the World Health Organization (WHO), health is more than the absence of disease and infirmity; it is 'a state of complete physical, mental and social well-being'.[3] In its broadest context, *environmental health* comprises those aspects of human health and disease that are determined by factors in the environment. WHO includes in this the study of both the direct pathological effects of chemical, physical and some biological agents, as well as the (often indirect) effects on health and well-being of the broad physical and social environment, which includes housing, urban development, land-use and transportation.[4]

Virtually every aspect of the environment may affect physical or mental health in some way, either positively or negatively. An approach to the discipline of environmental health which focuses on environmental hazards of human origin is useful in that it addresses potentially remediable problems (as opposed, for example, to 'natural' pollutants such as background radiation, pollens and climatic factors).[5]

23.1.1.2 *Environmental health concerns*

Typical environmental health concerns include health aspects of air and water pollution, water supply and sanitation, waste disposal, chemical and food safety, housing and settlements. Some problems may be of particular relevence at the micro level, whilst others may be important at the regional or global level. While occupational health may be considered within the ambit of environmental health concerns, the emphasis here is on the non-working environment. Nevertheless, issues in the working environment are on occasion alluded to as appropriate.

(a) Industrialized countries. In industrialized countries, typical environmental health issues include, for example, radon in homes and schools, lead in drinking water,

---

[1] Blumenthal 'A perspective on environmental health' in Blumenthal (ed) *Introduction to environmental health* (1985).

[2] Address to World Health Assembly (1988).

[3] 'Alma Ata reaffirmed at Riga—a statement of renewed and strengthened committment to health for all by the year 2000 and beyond' *Alma Ata to the year 2000* WHO, Geneva (1988).

[4] *Environment and health. The European charter and commentary* (WHO, Copenhagen 1990).

[5] Blumenthal above n 1.

non-ionizing electromagnetic radiation, asbestos in building materials, pesticide residues in food, and indoor air pollution.

(b) Developing countries. Environmental health problems in developing countries are frequently poverty-related and arise largely as a result of factors such as rapid and uncontrolled urbanization, and agricultural and land-use practices.

Urbanization. While Africa is the least urbanized continent, it also has the fastest rate of urbanization occurring anywhere in the world. With the abolition of influx control in South Africa, by some estimates an influx of around 20 million people can be expected into the urban areas by the year 2000. This represents a doubling of the proportion of Africans who will be 'urbanized' by then (ie 80 per cent of the African population).[6]

Health implications. Such rapid urbanization of an already poor and disadvantaged group will have profound implications for all aspects of development, the environment and health. Poverty and associated slum conditions may result in increased nutritional deficiencies, declines in child survival, increases in diseases associated with overcrowding such as TB and respiratory infections, as well as hazards associated with environmental pollution and inner-city decay.[7]

23.2 STATE OF KNOWLEDGE

23.2.1 Uncertain hazards

Despite well-documented cases of environmental disasters and chemical spills,[8] there is considerable uncertainty about the extent of both direct and indirect risks to human health which may be caused by agents present in the environment. Whilst in some instances one may be dealing with known, identified hazards, frequently one is not. For many substances, it is not known whether or not there are safety thresholds for an adverse effect and, if so, what those levels are.

It is likely that much environmentally related disease goes unrecognized. It has been estimated, for instance, that many of the cancers that result from asbestos exposure, arsenic, radon, cigarettes or other environmental agents are probably not attributed to their actual causes.[9] Other environmentally related diseases and disorders such as intelligence impairment caused by excessive exposure to lead during childhood may not be recognized as such.

Some have estimated, using a very broad definition, that between 80 and 90 per cent of cancers may be related to environmental influences. However, only a very small percentage of cancers have in fact been related to specific agents. The single most important factor isolated so far is tobacco smoke, which is related not only to lung cancer but also to cancer of the larynx, the buccal cavity, the pancreas and the bladder.[10]

Human beings may typically be exposed to complex mixtures of chemicals, which may not be well characterized. Of the millions of chemicals known, and the thousands in commercial use, relatively few (less than one percent) have been characterized toxicologically.[11] In particular, the effects of exposure to two or more chemicals, or to a chemical and other harmful agents, are not well understood.

---

[6] Van der Merwe 'A geographical profile of the South African population as a basis for epidemiological cancer research' 1988 (74) *S Afr Med J* 513–8.

[7] Von Schirnding & Aucamp 'Urbanisation and environmental health' 1991 (79) *S Afr Med J* 414–5.

[8] Lave & Upton *Toxic chemicals, health and the environment* (1987).

[9] Ibid.

[10] *Environmental health criteria 27: guidelines on studies in environmental epidemiology* (WHO, Geneva 1983).

[11] Lave & Upton above n 8.

23.2.2 Databases

There exist certain databases for established health effects of environmental contaminants. For example, there is the Environmental Health Criteria programme of WHO, which was initiated in 1973 and whose main objective is to assess the available information on the effect of environmental pollutants and other physical factors on human health in order to provide guidelines for exposure limits. This programme has now been incorporated into the International Programme on Chemical Safety (IPCS). So far over 50 criteria documents have been published.

There is also the International Register of Potentially Toxic Chemicals (IRPTC), which is part of the United Nations Environment Programme. Then there exists the International Agency for Research on Cancer (IARC), which was established in 1965 by the World Health Assembly and is based in Lyon, France. Over the past few decades IARC has published a series of monographs evaluating the possible carcinogenicity of chemical substances.[12]

WHO, together with the Food and Agricultural Organization (FAO), has also co-ordinated expert reviews on pesticides and food additives,[13] and WHO guidelines for drinking water quality[14] and air quality[15] have been developed.

23.2.3 The nature of ill-health effects

The ill-health effects of environmental exposures may be acute. For example, they may follow relatively shortly after an exposure (often a single major dose of a substance, such as may occur by accident or due to a chemical spill). More often, however, chronic disease occurs as a result of an individual cumulative exposure to complex mixes over long periods of time.

A long time may elapse between the initial exposure and the appearance of an adverse health effect. Examples include asbestos exposure and mesothelioma, and radiation exposure and malignancy. Dispersal of the population at risk over time and the long incubation period make it difficult to reconstruct exposures. Acute health effects are thus usually easier to detect than chronic health effects, which may be difficult to relate to specific hazards or sources.

Almost any chemical could cause harm if taken into the body in sufficiently large amounts.[16] However, one is often concerned in environmental health with those chemicals which in small doses may have adverse health effects.

A whole hierarchy of health effects may occur, ranging from minor temporary ailments through to acute illness to chronic disease, with relatively resistant and susceptible persons at either extreme of the distribution. Thus there may occur different exposure–effect relationships for different subsets in the population.[17]

Infants and young children may be at particular risk, as they take in more of a contaminant relative to their size than do adults, and they have immature and therefore particularly vulnerable physiologies. The unborn foetus is particularly susceptible to most toxic chemicals. Elderly people are also vulnerable from a physiological point of view, and may be more susceptible to lung infections than younger people.[18] The vulnerability of individuals (as opposed to groups) may vary, however, and a range of susceptibilities to hazardous substances may occur. A better understanding is needed of

[12] De Koning *Setting environmental standards* (WHO, Geneva 1987).
[13] Ibid.
[14] *Guidelines for drinking-water quality* vols I–III (WHO, Geneva 1984).
[15] *Air quality guidelines for Europe* WHO Regional publications, European series no 23 (1987).
[16] Lave & Upton above n 8.
[17] *Environmental health criteria* above n 10.
[18] Lave & Upton above n 8.

biological disposition to a particular health outcome and the way in which human activities and life styles put people at higher risk.

23.2.4 The nature of exposures

Most environmental diseases are multifactorial in so far as the causal factors are concerned, and it may be difficult to determine the effects of one exposure in the light of the possible existence of effects of simultaneous exposure to other factors.

When dealing with low-level chemical exposures in particular, one may often deal with factors which play a contributory rather than a primary role in the causation of an increased incidence of disease. The co-action of other factors may be needed for effects to occur. Exposures may be interactive, resulting in a reductive, an additive or a synergistic effect (where the combined effect is greater than the sum of the individual effects). Thus, for example, the incidence of lung cancer is very high in uranium miners and asbestos workers who are smokers, but may be less significantly elevated among workers with similar occupational exposures who are not smokers.[19]

Combined effects may often arise from the influence of nutritional, dietary and other life style factors such as smoking and alcohol intake. This is reflected in the 1986 Ottawa Charter for Health Promotion, which stresses the need to promote both a healthy life style and sustainable environmental conditions.[20]

Environmental monitoring. Exposure to chemical substances is normally mediated by complex environmental pathways, and more than one route may contribute to human uptake. People may be exposed through the air they breathe, the water and food that is ingested or by contact via the skin. Lead, for example, may be deposited in the air, dust, soil and water and intake may occur via direct inhalation or ingestion[21] (See Figure 23.1).

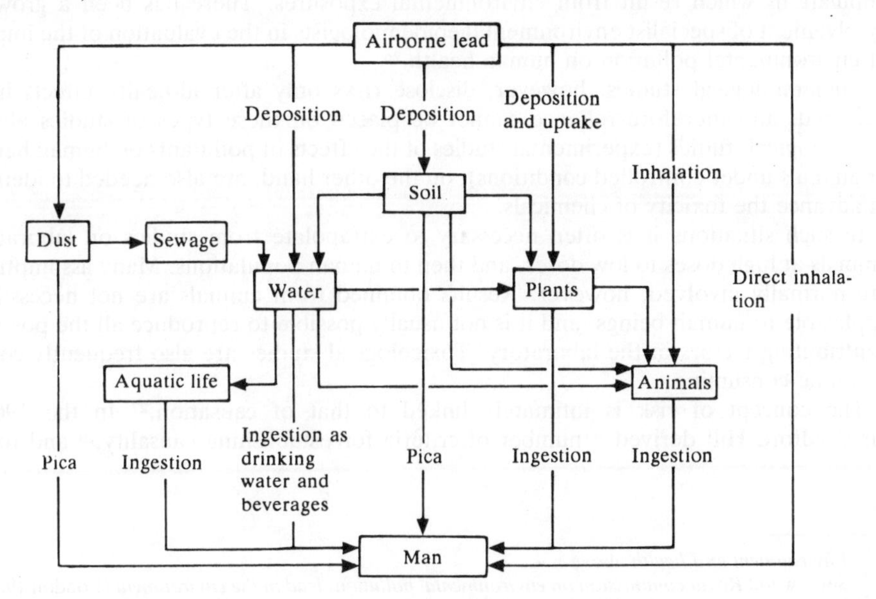

Figure 23.1 Contribution of airborne lead to total lead intake.
Source: WHO (1977).

---

[19] Lippmann & Schlesinger *Chemical contamination in the human environment* (New York, 1979).
[20] *Ottawa charter for health promotion* International conference on health promotion, Ottawa, Canada17–21 November, 1986.
[21] *Environmental health criteria 3: lead*. (WHO, Geneva 1977).

Adequate control measures can be applied only when the relative importance of the various routes of exposure have been established. Often, environmental data are collected with the aim of detecting peak levels in terms of assessing compliance with standards or guidelines which are normally at places of little relevance in terms of typical human exposures.

Many current environmental monitoring programmes do not have specific objectives and are not effectively co-ordinated, particularly as regards the various routes of human exposure. In most situations, the criteria and procedures for the monitoring and evaluation of effects on the environment and health are inadequate.[22] Frequently, only relatively few areas and substances are monitored. What is generally required, however, is detailed knowledge of temporal and spatial variability of concentrations of exposures. For many pollutants there is a sharp decrease in the concentration level as one moves away from the source. Air lead levels, for example, may decrease by over 50 per cent at a distance 50 m from a road.[23] Similarly, significant vertical variations may occur in the concentration level of a pollutant. Exposure in the occupational setting is often easier to characterize than in the environmental setting.[24]

There is growing interest and research being conducted into biological and biochemical markers of exposure (for example, DNA adducts), which should improve the effectiveness of exposure assessments in the future.

23.2.5 Health risk assessment

In assessing health risks arising from environmental exposures, reliance is frequently placed on epidemiology and toxicology. Epidemiology is concerned with health effects occurring in human populations and is a core science of public health and preventive medicine.[25] *Environmental epidemiology* is concerned with health effects in human populations which result from environmental exposures. There has been a growing involvement of specialist environmental epidemiologists in the evaluation of the impact of environmental pollution on human health.[26]

Epidemiological studies, however, disclose risks only after ill-health effects have occurred, and therefore reliance cannot be placed on these types of studies alone. Toxicological studies (experimental studies of the effects of pollutants on human beings or animals under controlled conditions), on the other hand, are also needed to identify in advance the toxicity of chemicals.

In such situations it is often necessary to extrapolate from studies on laboratory animals at high doses to low doses, and then to human populations. Many assumptions are normally involved, however. Results obtained from animals are not necessarily applicable to human beings, and it is not usually possible to reproduce all the possible contributing factors in the laboratory. Toxicological studies are also frequently costly and time-consuming.

The concept of risk is intimately linked to that of causation.[27] In the 1960s, Sir Bradford Hill derived a number of criteria for establishing causality,[28] and these

---

[22] *Environment and health* above n 4.

[23] Southwood *Royal commission on environmental pollution: lead in the environment* (London 1983).

[24] Meyers 'Occupational epidemiology' in *Introductory manual for epidemiology in southern Africa* (Medical Research Council 1991).

[25] Holland, Detels & Knox *Oxford textbook of public health* vol 1 (1986).

[26] Goldsmith 'Improving the prospects for environmental epidemiology' 1988 (43) *Arch Environ Health*.

[27] Gordis 'Estimating risk and inferring causality in epidemiology' in Gordis (ed) *Epidemiology and health risk assessment* (1988).

[28] Bradford Hill 'The environment and disease: association or causation?' 1965 (58) *Proceedings of the Royal Society of Medicine* 295.

have been helpful in assisting scientists to make reasoned judgements about often contradictory findings and uncertain evidence.

The Health Component of environmental impact analysis (EIA). In most developing countries, and even in many developed countries, little attention has been paid to the health impacts of planned developments. In line with the principle of sustainability, development should minimize negative health impacts and maximize health benefits. WHO has taken the lead in developing the health component of EIA, the purpose of which is 'the creation of an environment conducive to the achievement of physical, mental and social well-being'.[29]

In 1982, WHO recommended that environmental health impact analysis (EHIA) studies be carried out for all development projects (see Table 23.1). Assessments of

TABLE 23.1

World Health Organization suggested procedure for EHIA.

Step 1	Assessment of primary impacts on environmental parameters	regular EIA process
Step 2	Assessment of secondary or tertiary impacts on environmental parameters resulting from the primary ones	regular EIA process
Step 3	Screening of impacted environmental parameters of recognized health significance (EH factors)	epidemiological knowledge
Step 4	Assessment of impacts on the magnitude of exposed populations for each group of EH factors	census, land-use planning
Step 5	Assessment of impacts on the magnitude of risk-groups included in each group of exposed population	census
Step 6	Computation of health impacts in terms of morbidity and mortality	results from risk-assessment studies
Step 7	Definition of acceptable hazards (or of significant health impacts)	trade-off between human and economic requirements
Step 8	Identification of efficient mitigation measures to reduce significant health impacts	abatement of EH factors magnitude, reduction of exposure, reduction of exposed populations, protection of risk-groups

Source: Giroult, *The health component of environmental impact assessment* Paper presented at the International Seminar on Environmental Impact Assessment (University of Aberdeen 1984).

[29] *Environmental health impact assessment of urban development* (WHO, Copenhagen 1983).

health impacts need to be explicitly incorporated in such studies where appropriate, and environmental health professionals should form an integral part of the EIA team. They should be involved in 'scoping' activities to ensure that health and safety effects are considered at the outset, and that, should a development proceed, it should be followed by epidemiological monitoring and evaluation programmes.

The EHIA approach aims to identify and predict the impacts of the proposed development on environmental parameters that have a strong health significance.[30] Using information from epidemiological and toxicological studies, researchers attempt to identify, predict and evaluate possible changes in health which could occur as a result of the development under consideration. The major elements of risk assessment[31] are given in Figure 23.2.

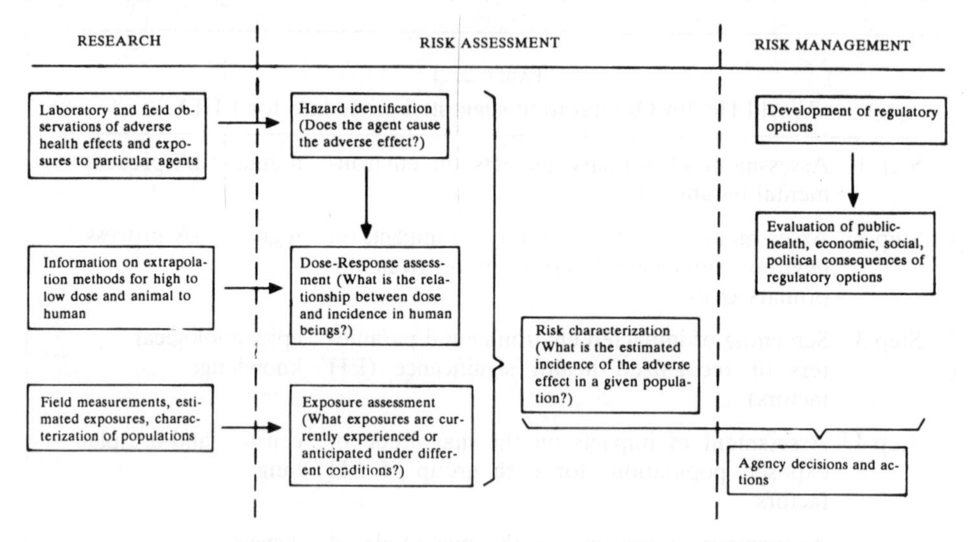

Figure 23.2 Major elements of risk assessment and risk management.
Source: Gordis (ed) *Epidemiology and health risk assessment* (1988).

23.3 HEALTH ASPECTS OF AIR POLLUTION

23.3.1 Introduction

Concern about the health effects of air pollution has been noted for centuries (at least since the 13th century), but increased significantly during and after the the Industrial Revolution,[32] when the problem assumed greater proportions. Despite various methodological problems associated with environmental epidemiological studies as discussed above, it is nevertheless well established that an association exists between exposure to air pollution and respiratory effects in human populations. Air pollution may cause both acute health effects (as, for example, in major air pollution episodes) and chronic effects associated with relatively low levels of pollution. In addition to adverse health effects, it may have a considerable nuisance value, causing irritation to the eyes and mucous membranes and objectionable odours.

---

[30] Giroult *The health component of environmental impact assessment* International seminar on environmental impact assessment, University of Aberdeen (1984).

[31] Upton 'Epidemiology and risk assessment'. in Gordis above n 27.

[32] Blumenthal & Greene 'Air pollution' in Blumenthal (ed) *Introduction to environmental health* (1985).

23.3.1.1 *Deposition of pollutants in respiratory tract*

Although air pollutants may affect the skin and gastro-intestinal tract,[33] pollutants in the form of gases or particulates affect primarily the respiratory tract. The fate of a contaminant in the respiratory tract depends on the form in which it exists—i e gaseous or particulate. Several mechanisms act to remove suspended particles in the respiratory tract. Particles of 10–20 microns or more are trapped in the nasal passages if breathed through the nose and, if breathed through the mouth, are retained in the mouth, pharynx and larynx.[34] Particles of 2–10 microns are trapped mainly in the nasal passages and/or bronchial tree, while those less than 2 microns in size penetrate to the bronchioles and alveoli. With respect to gases, the site and extent of inhalation are determined by their solubility in water. Highly soluble gases such as SO_2 are absorbed largely in the upper respiratory tract, while less soluble gases such as NO_2 and ozone may reach the lower airways.[35]

23.3.1.2 *Air pollution episodes*

Increased death rates have occurred in association with several acute air pollution episodes in some countries in the past. In many of these, adverse environmental conditions such as temperature inversions contributed to the accumulation of aerosol and gaseous pollutants such as SO_2 and particulates. Such episodes as occurred in the mid-20th century first led to the awareness of the magnitude of the health effects caused by air pollution. For example, in December 1930, an air pollution episode in the Meuse River Valley in Belgium was responsible for the deaths of 63 people (mainly the elderly and those suffering from heart or lung ailments) and ill-health effects were documented among thousands of individuals. A similar episode occurred in Donora, Pennsylvania in 1948 and the famous London smog episode in 1952 is thought to have been responsible for the deaths of nearly 4 000 people.[36] Many other acute air pollution episodes have since occurred in the United States and elsewhere.

23.3.1.3 *General nature of health effects*

It is not yet clear to what extent air pollution actually causes disease, as opposed to exacerbating pre-existing disease.

(a) Chronic obstructive pulmonary disease. Potential effects include chronic obstructive pulmonary disease (COPD) (e g emphysema and bronchitis), asthma, acute respiratory infections, cardiovascular diseases and cancer. Cigarette smoking and certain occupational exposures are well-known causes of lung cancer, but there is some evidence that ambient air pollution may play a role. It is known that, in general, the incidence of lung cancer is higher in urban areas than in rural areas[37] (controlling for smoking), but the contribution of air pollution is uncertain.

While asthma is most usually related to allergy, exposure to polluted air can precipitate acute attacks. For example, studies have shown a correlation between emergency room visits and low and high air pollution days.

(b) Acute respiratory tract infections. Air pollution is linked not only to chronic non-infectious disease but also to acute episodes of infectious respiratory disease. For example, lower respiratory tract infections such as pneumonia and bronchitis have been shown to be associated with increased levels of air pollution (such as NO_2, SO_2),

---

[33] Ibid.
[34] Lippmann & Schlesinger above n 19.
[35] Ibid.
[36] Blumenthal & Greene above n 32.
[37] Goldsmith 'Effects on human health' in *Air pollution* vol VI (1986); Lipmann & Schlesinger above n 19.

although the association with upper respiratory tract infections (colds and pharyngitis) is less clear.[38]

23.3.2 *Ambient air pollutants*

Although people are normally exposed to several air pollutants simultaneously (which may have synergistic effects), for purposes of clarity they are here considered separately.

23.3.2.1 *Ozone*

Ozone is a strong oxidizing agent and is the principal component of photochemical smog, which is formed by the action of sunlight on nitrogen dioxide. It is a respiratory irritant which can cause histological changes in the lung.[39] Respiratory symptoms and lung function may be affected in exercising individuals, and pulmonary oedema (a condition in which fluid enters the alveolae spaces) may occur as a result of intense exposure. Ozone may be responsible for aggravating asthma and chronic bronchitis[40] and may cause irritation to the eyes and mucous membranes as well as ear, nose and throat irritation and headaches. A continuum of health effects occurs over varying concentration levels, with some evidence for no threshold.[41] WHO has recommended a one-hour guideline in the range of 150–200 $\mu g\ m^{-3}$, and an eight-hour guideline of 100–120 $\mu g\ m^{-3}$.

23.3.2.2 *Carbon monoxide*

Carbon monoxide (CO) is the most common and widespread of air pollutants. Incomplete combustion processes are the largest sources of CO emissions,[42] but carbon monoxide exposure from active and passive cigarette smoking may be greater than that for community air pollution.[43] Inhaled carbon monoxide reacts with haemoglobin to form carboxyhaemoglobin (COHb), and in so doing reduces the oxygen-carrying capacity of the blood.

Exposure to CO may impair mental functions, reduce tolerance for exercise and aggravate cardiovascular disease. Exposure at high levels may lead to secondary effects such as decreases in blood pH and changes in fibrinolysis. Effects on birth weight and postnatal development have also been noted.[44] WHO guidelines are: 100 $\mu g\ m^{-3}$ (maximum) for periods not exceeding 15 minutes; 60 $\mu g\ m^{-3}$ for 30 minutes; 30 $\mu g\ m^{-3}$ for 1 hour, and 10 $\mu g\ m^{-3}$ for 8 hours.[45]

23.3.2.3 *Nitrogen dioxide*

Nitrogen dioxide (NO_2) is a strong oxidant and is also an acid anhydride. It is a product of fossil-fuel combustion in stationary sources and motor vehicles. Nitrogen dioxide may aggravate respiratory symptoms and illnesses (such as asthma), it may cause increased susceptibility to respiratory infections, and may affect pulmonary function. The WHO-recommended one-hour guideline is 400 $\mu g\ m^{-3}$ and the 24-hour guideline is 150 $\mu g\ m^{-3}$.[46]

23.3.2.4 *Sulphur dioxide and particulate matter*

Sulphur dioxide (SO_2) and suspended particulates derive mainly from the combustion of fossil fuels. Sulphuric acid is formed by the reaction of sulphur trioxide gas (SO_3)

---

[38] Blumenthal & Greene above n 32.
[39] Ibid.
[40] Goldsmith above n 37.
[41] *Air quality guidelines for Europe* above n 15.
[42] Ibid.
[43] Goldsmith above n 37.
[44] *Air quality guidelines for Europe* above n 15.
[45] Ibid.
[46] Ibid.

with water. Particulate matter is a mix of organic and inorganic substances and consists of both coarse particles (>2,5 μm) and fine particles (<2,5 μm). The acid component of particulate matter is normally found in the fine fraction.[47] SO_2 is soluble in aqueous media and absorption occurs in the mucous membranes of the nose and upper respiratory tract (very little reaches the lower respiratory tract).

SO_2 exposure (as well as acid aerosols) may aggravate respiratory diseases, including asthma and chronic bronchitis, and may affect lung function. Increased mortality, morbidity and lung-function deficits may occur as a result of increases in the SO_2/particulate complex, such as happened in the London smog episodes in the 1950s and 1960s. The WHO-recommended guideline for SO_2 is 500 $\mu g\ m^{-3}$ for a 10-minute period and 350 $\mu g\ m^{-3}$ for a one-hour period. Guideline values for combined exposure to SO_2 and particulate matter have also been derived.[48]

23.3.3 Other air pollutants

Other organic and inorganic substances emitted into the atmosphere which may have adverse effects on health (and for which standards or guidelines exist) include formaldehyde, vinyl chloride, arsenic, asbestos, mercury, cadmium, manganese, nickel, radon and others.

23.3.3.1 *Cigarette smoke*

Cigarette smoking remains the number one causative factor associated with lung diseases. Evidence exists that exposure to other people's cigarette smoke (so-called passive smoking) may cause an increase in respiratory effects (particularly in small children),[49] as well as a slight excess risk of cancer. It is also known that sidestream smoke contains larger amounts of carcinogens than mainstream smoke.[50]

23.3.3.2 *Indoor air pollution*

(a) Vulnerable groups. In recent years, a lot of attention has been given to indoor air quality, which may be an important problem, considering that people spend on average 80 per cent of their time indoors. Those most vulnerable to the effects of air pollution (the old, young and the sick) are mostly indoors.

(b) Household activities and furnishings. Normal household activities associated with cooking and cleaning may release hazardous substances into the air, and cigarette smoke, construction materials and methods, materials for furniture and fittings, coupled with more effective thermal insulation, have posed increased risks to health.

Studies have shown that the use of gas stoves may result in increased levels of NO_2 inside homes, and SO_2 levels may be elevated as a result of domestic coal combustion. Because indoor air is enclosed, substances emitted into it may be concentrated (depending on the ventilation systems in question). Concentrations of NO_2, CO and other indoor pollutants may exceed outdoor levels; however, there is considerable variability in entry rates, ventilation rates and reaction rates.[51]

The use of certain household cleaning products, stains, paint strippers and thinners, and other volatile organic substances can also lead to toxic concentrations of certain pollutants.[52]

(c) Building materials. Buildings may contain potentially hazardous materials such

---

[47] Ibid.
[48] Ibid.
[49] Goldsmith above n 37.
[50] *Air quality guidelines for Europe* above n 15.
[51] *Indoor air quality research* EURO reports and studies 103 (WHO, Copenhagen 1984).
[52] Ibid.

as asbestos, radioactive radon gas and urea foam insulation which contains formaldehyde and may cause eye and respiratory irritations.

Asbestos-cement products. Under normal circumstances asbestos-cement products used in housing should not produce a respiratory hazard; special circumstances such as dust produced from re-modelling or demolition[53] may, however, have harmful effects.

Radon. Some buildings may have significant levels of radon (which is drawn from the underlying soil by small differences in air pressures indoors and outdoors)[54] and certain building materials themselves (for example stone, brick and granite) may release radon. Radon follows tobacco smoking as a causal factor for lung cancer, and it has been estimated that at least five percent of lung cancers may be attributable to it.[55]

Infectious Agents. Infectious agents such as viruses and bacteria may also be more concentrated indoors than outdoors[56] and particularly in overcrowded homes transmission rates of disease may be higher. Morbidity and mortality rates from influenza and pneumonia are higher during the winter months, when people spend more time indoors. 'Natural' air pollutants such as mould spores, danders and dust may also be more concentrated indoors.[57]

(d) Sick building syndrome. The term 'sick building syndrome' has been applied to blocks of flats, offices, hospitals and schools constructed mainly in the last 20–30 years where sickness and discomfort have been experienced by occupants.[58] In many new energy-efficient buildings (especially those with large ventilation systems dependent on limited fresh air sources),[59] occupants may complain of vague symptoms such as fatigue, dizziness, headaches, or eye or respiratory tract irritation.[60] The sensation of dry mucous membranes is most noticeable in sick building syndrome.[61] Formaldehyde and other organic vapours are possible causes and in larger buildings central heating and air conditioning can spread biological and chemical contaminants.

23.3.3.3 *Global air pollution*

There are several consequences for health of air pollution which are of global concern. Depletion of the stratospheric ozone layer due to the use of chlorofluorocarbons (CFCs) may increase skin-cancer rates and cause cataracts. Although difficult to quantify, it has been suggested that for every one per cent decrease in stratospheric ozone concentrations there will be an eight per cent increase in skin cancers in fair-skinned people.[62] The greenhouse effect (associated with a possible rise in mean global temperatures of 1,5–4 °C within the next 50 years) may affect health by causing an increase in the prevalence of tropical diseases in some areas, affecting the toxicity of pollutants, causing flooding in certain coastal areas, and reducing freshwater supplies due to sea-water incursion.[63]

23.3.4 South African situation

In South Africa, smoke and SO_2 emissions from domestic and industrial coal combustion are probably largely responsible for the diminished air quality in parts of

---

[53] Goldsmith above n 37.
[54] Nero 'Controlling indoor air pollution' 1988 (258) *Scientific Am* 24–30.
[55] *Environment and health* above n 4.
[56] Blumenthal & Greene above n 32.
[57] Ibid.
[58] *Environment and health* above n 4.
[59] *Indoor air quality* above n 51.
[60] Goldsmith above n 37.
[61] Harris 'Lead encephalopathy' 1976 (50) *S Afr Med J* 1371–3.
[62] *Environment and health* above n 4.
[63] Ibid.

the country. Smoke and SO_2 emissions in South Africa have remained virtually constant over the period 1982–1986, in contrast to decreasing trends observed with respect to these pollutants over previous years.[64] Smoke levels exceed WHO safety limits in areas where heating by coal is prevalent or where conditions are unfavourable for the dispersal of pollutants.

23.3.4.1 *Domestic air pollution*

African children may be significantly exposed to indoor and outdoor air pollution. The African townships are among the most severely polluted environments in which South Africans live. The inefficient combustion of coal in domestic stoves (particularly in poor dispersion conditions) results in significant smoke and SO_2 emissions, which may have negative effects on the respiratory systems of susceptible groups. There is nevertheless a dearth of information on prevailing pollution levels and illness rates in the townships.

23.3.4.2 *Acute respiratory infections*

Worldwide, whilst millions of children die each year from acute respiratory infections (ARI), many more suffer acute and chronic morbidity. In many developing countries, ARI accounts for one-quarter to one-third of deaths in young children and is the main reason for utilizing the health services.[65] In South Africa, mortality rates for ARI among coloured infants are still around 10 times those of whites (980 per 100 000).[66] Although death rates from pneumonia in all population groups have shown an impressive decline over the past two decades, there is nevertheless an urgent need to prevent deaths from ARI.

It has been estimated that children living in urban areas have 5–8 episodes of respiratory illness annually during the first five years of life, compared with 1–3 episodes in the rural areas.[67] In some urban areas in South Africa there is evidence that deaths from ARI are now becoming more significant even than diarrhoea.[68]

There is preliminary evidence from a survey of the major metropolitan areas in South Africa that domestic fuel combustion (for example, coal) is associated with excessive respiratory illness in children.[69] There is a need for more information on the role of domestic air pollution in influencing respiratory infections in the South African population. Longitudinal epidemiological studies in Soweto are currently being conducted to address this issue.

23.3.4.3 *Industrial air pollution*

There is little epidemiological information regarding the impact of industrial pollution on the health of populations situated near emission sources. A study carried out in Sasolburg by Coetzee et al[70] provides some evidence of an adverse effect on lung function among schoolboys (but not girls) living in the area.

---

[64] Walker et al *Statistics on smoke and sulphur dioxide pollution in South Africa* (NPRL, CSIR, 1987).

[65] Pio, Leowski & Ten Dam 'The magnitude of the problem of acute respiratory infections' in Douglas & Kerby Eaton (eds) *Acute respiratory infections in childhood* (1984) 3–17.

[66] Von Schirnding, Yach & Klein 'Acute respiratory infections as an important cause of childhood deaths in South Africa' 1991 (80) *S Afr Med J* 79–82.

[67] Pio, Leowski & Ten Dam above n 65.

[68] Von Schirnding, Yach & Klein above n 66.

[69] Von Schirnding, Yach, Blignaut & Mathews 'Environmental determinants of acute respiratory symptoms and diarrhoea in young coloured children living in urban and peri-urban areas of South Africa' 1991 (79) *S Afr Med J* 457–61.

[70] Coetzee, Smith, Van der Merwe & Dreyer *Effects on health of air pollution in the Sasolburg area* 6th International Conference on Air Pollution, CSIR, Pretoria, 23–25 October 1984.

Another study was conducted by Zwi et al[71] in the eastern Transvaal highveld area, where 80 per cent of the country's electrical power requirements is generated by coal-fired stations. Particularly poor dispersion conditions exist where most of the coal mines and power stations are situated. Zwi's prevalence study was conducted among white schoolchildren in the eastern Transvaal highveld and in 'non-polluted' towns in the Transvaal. Cough, wheeze, asthma and chest illnesses were more frequently reported in children from polluted areas than those from non-polluted areas, taking into account parental smoking and home cooking fuel. Children in the polluted areas were found to be shorter, too. No significant differences in lung function were found, however.

Both Zwi[72] and Coetzee[73] focused on schoolchildren, thus minimizing the potential confounding effects of smoking and occupational exposure. Nevertheless, pollution measurements were lacking in many respects, particularly in the 'control' areas and were limited to mean smoke and SO_2 levels. Further studies are currently being conducted in the Vaal Triangle area, under the auspices of the Medical Research Council.

23.3.5 Environmental lead exposure

23.3.5.1 *Low-level health effects*

The epidemiology of lead exposure has been extensively studied in industrialized countries. Whilst in the past two decades the incidence of clinical lead poisoning in children (mainly as a result of ingestion of leaded paint chips) has substantially declined, there is mounting evidence linking lead at increasingly lower levels of exposure to a broad range of adverse health effects in young children, even below 25 $\mu g\ d\ell^{-1}$, the current USA 'safety' level for lead in blood[74] (likely to be lowered even further soon).

Exposure to lead during the early stages of a child's development has been linked to reduced gestational age, lowered birth weight and deficits in later neuro-behavioural development.[75] It has been estimated that a decrease in IQ of between 4 and 7 points may result in a threefold increase in the rate of severe deficit (IQ <80) in the population as a whole.[76]

Electrophysiological and haeme synthesis effects have been documented at correspondingly low blood-lead levels, as have impaired vitamin D metabolism and erythropoietic pyrimidine metabolism.[77] No socio-economic or ethnic group is exempt from risk, although poor inner-city children are at greatest risk of exposure. In adults, low levels of lead exposure have been found to contribute to the prediction of raised systolic and diastolic blood pressure in middle-aged men.[78]

23.3.5.2 *Multifactorial nature of exposure*

Unlike overt toxicity, low-level environmental lead exposure is multi-factorial, and many sources and pathways play a role.

---

[71] Zwi, Davies, Becklake, Goldman, Reinach & Kallenbach *Respiratory health status of children in the eastern Transvaal highveld* 1st IUAPPA Regional Conference on Air Pollution, CSIR, Pretoria, 24–26 October 1990.

[72] Ibid.

[73] Above n 70.

[74] *Preventing lead poisoning in young children: a statement by the centers for disease control.* (US Department of Health and Human Services, Washington DC, 1985).

[75] Davis & Svendsgaard 'Lead and child development' 1987 (329) *Nature* 297–300.

[76] Needleman, Leviton & Bellinger 'Lead-associated intellectual deficit' 1982 (306) *N Engl J Med* 367.

[77] *Air quality criteria for lead* vols I–IV (EPA-600/8–83/028 a–dF 1986).

[78] Harlan, Landis, Schmouder, Goldstein & Harlan I 'Blood lead and blood pressure' 1985 (253) *JAMA* 530–4; Pirkle, Schwartz, Landis & Harlan 'The relationship between blood lead levels and blood pressure and its cardiovascular risk implications' 1985 (121) *Am J Epidemiol* 246–58.

(a) Contribution of lead-in-petrol. Petrol-derived lead is the most widely distributed source in the environment. For children, the direct inhalation route of exposure is not the major one of importance—of greater significance is the lead deposited into the soil and dust which may be ingested via hand-to-mouth activities. The United States' Environmental Protection Agency (EPA) estimates that 25–50 per cent of the body burden is petrol-derived (taking into account both direct and indirect routes of exposure).[79] In the United States a 37 per cent decrease in national blood levels occurred between 1976 and 1980, which correlated closely with decreases in petrol-lead and air-lead,[80] even after controlling for numerous potentially confounding factors.

(b) Other sources of exposure. In the United States today, where paint is virtually lead-free, as is petrol, attention has focused on the contamination of drinking water by, inter alia, lead-soldered joints in water pipes (now banned). There are, in addition, still large reservoirs of lead in soil, dust and house paint, even in countries where the control of lead has been vigilant, and these sources will continue to contribute to the exposure of the population to lead in years to come.[81]

23.3.5.3 *Blood lead levels in South African children*

(a) Childhood lead poisoning. It is remarkable that so few cases of overt lead poisoning have been detected in South African children—there have been a few cases of lead poisoning in African children as a result of burning battery casings for fuel,[82] but there have been few documented cases of poisoning from the ingestion of paints, even though a nationwide survey by the Department of Health in 1979 revealed that many homes have highly leaded paints.[83] (Lead-based paints were in use until recently, and are still used, although to a much lesser degree.)

(b) Undue lead absorption. In South Africa, studies in the Cape Town area indicate that significant numbers of children are at risk of undue lead absorption.[84] Further, there is some evidence of biochemical and behavioural effects in lead-exposed South African children.[85] Studies of specifically urban children in Cape Town have shown that about 13 per cent of coloured preschoolers and first-grade children[86] (but no white children) have raised blood lead levels ($\geq$25 μg dℓ^{-1}).

Risk factors. Intra-urban variations in blood lead levels have been shown to occur, with children exposed at school to heavy traffic densities having significantly higher blood lead levels than other inner-city children, controlling for various other contributory factors.[87]

In addition, among high-risk children, factors such as the condition of the child's home (for example, the degree of accessible flaking leaded paint or lead-rich dust), the

---

[79] *Air quality criteria for lead* above n 77.

[80] Annest, Pirkle, Makuc, Neese, Bayse & Kovar 'Chronological trend in blood lead levels between 1976 and 1980' 1983 (308) *N Engl J Med* 1373–7.

[81] Von Schirnding 'Reducing environmental lead exposure—time to act' 1989 (76) *S Afr Med J* 293–4.

[82] Harris above n 61.

[83] *Lead poisoning in children* (Department of Health 1979).

[84] Von Schirnding above n 81.

[85] Von Schirnding & Fuggle 'A study of the relationship between low level lead exposure and classroom performance in South African children' 1984 (6) *Int J Biosoc Res* 97–106; Von Schirnding & Fuggle 'Zinc protoporphyrin levels and lead absorption in children attending schools in the Cape Peninsula, South Africa' 1986 (1) *S Afr J Epidemiol Infect* 11–15.

[86] Deveaux, Kibel, Dempster, Pocock & Formenti 'Blood lead levels in preschool children in Cape Town' 1986 (69) *S Afr Med J* 421–4; Von Schirnding *Environmental lead exposure among inner city Cape Town children: a study of associated risk factors* (unpublished PhD thesis, University of Cape Town, 1989); Von Schirnding, Bradshaw, Fuggle & Stokol 'Blood lead levels in inner-city South African children' 1991 (94) *Environ Health Perspect* 125–30.

[87] Von Schirnding, Bradshaw, Fuggle & Stokol above n 86.

quality of parental supervision and behavioural patterns such as excessive hand-to-mouth activity, are important in determining a child's risk profile.[88] Children from socially disadvantaged homes are at greatest risk.

23.3.6 Exposure to environmental asbestos from mine dumps

Mining activities such as those associated with asbestos are a potential source of environmental exposure among populations living in the vicinity of the mines. South Africa produces only a fraction of the world's asbestos, but most of the world's crocidolite (blue asbestos), which carries a higher risk of mesothelioma (cancer of the lining of the lung) than other types of asbestos.

23.3.6.1 *Mortality rates*

In a study of death rates among people living in crocidolite-mining areas and control areas in South Africa, increased death rates from asbestosis/mesothelioma and cancer of the lung and stomach were found among people with low employment rates (such as in younger age groups and women).[89] Exposure could occur through workers exposing family members to asbestos dust carried home from the mines, through living in the vicinity of asbestos mines and works, or through exposure to asbestos dust from mine dumps.

23.3.6.2 *Morbidity rates*

A survey to assess the prevalence of asbestos-related lung disease in Mafefe, the most densely populated region of the Pietersburg asbestos fields, was carried out recently.[90] Although mining in this area ceased 15 years ago, asbestos is still an environmental hazard, due to the existence of uncovered asbestos tailings dumps and the erosion of the dumps. Asbestos tailings were also used as building and surfacing materials.

A prevalence rate of 34 per cent (excluding people with occupational exposure) was found for pleural changes (for example, pleural plaques and diffuse pleural thickening), which suggests that the community has had sufficient exposure to asbestos to increase significantly the risk of developing mesothelioma. Ongoing reclamation programmes, education programmes and health service provision are needed.

23.4 HEALTH ASPECTS OF WATER

23.4.1 Introduction

Historically, the majority of water-related health problems have related to infectious waterborne diseases rather than to chemical contamination. John Snow, in his classic investigations of the cholera epidemic in London in 1853, was among the first to make the association between water pollution and disease.[91] At that time, water pollution was causing concern in England, mainly for aesthetic reasons.

Today, while in developed countries such as the United States outbreaks of waterborne disease are relatively rare, in other parts of the world diseases due to microbial contamination (viral, bacterial or parasitic diseases) still prevail. Waterborne diseases such as typhoid, cholera, polio, hepatitis A and gastro-enteritis may occur as a result of pathogenic micro-organisms in water. Diarrhoeal diseases are the most important of the water-and-excreta-related diseases.

---

[88] Von Schirnding, Fuggle & Bradshaw 'Factors associated with elevated blood lead levels in inner-city children' 1991 (79) *S Afr Med J* 454–6.

[89] Botha et al 'Excess mortality from stomach cancer, lung cancer and asbestosis and/or mesothelioma in crocidolite mining districts in South Africa' 1986 (123) *Am J Epidemiol* 30–40.

[90] Felix, Mabiletja, Roodt, Carlin & Steinberg *Aftermath of asbestos mining—health effects of fibres in the environment* 1st IUAPPA Regional Conference on Air Pollution, CSIR Pretoria 24–26 October 1990.

[91] Lippmann & Schlesinger above n 19.

23.4.2 Water and sanitation

23.4.2.1 *Access to basic facilities*

The provision of a safe, sufficient and accessible water supply and the hygienic disposal of wastes are fundamental factors in disease prevention. This was recognized by the United Nations in pronouncing the 1980s the 'international drinking water supply and sanitation decade'. At the international conference on primary health care held in Alma Ata (USSR) in 1978, it was concluded that safe water and basic sanitation are an important component for achieving primary health care, which is the basis of the international strategy of 'health for all by the year 2000'.

In some developing countries around three-fifths of the population may have poor access to a safe and adequate drinking water supply,[92] and an even lower proportion to basic sanitation. Particular attention needs to be paid to the provision of sanitary facilities in dense urban areas (particularly in informal settlement areas), where a higher level of services is often required than in rural areas.[93]

23.4.2.2 *Water-related diseases*

Diseases related to water (and sanitation) may be grouped as follows:

- waterborne diseases, which are spread by drinking contaminated water or washing hands, food or utensils in it.
- water-washed diseases, which are spread by personal hygiene, insufficient water for washing and a lack of adequate facilities for waste disposal.
- water-based diseases, which are transmitted by a vector which spends a part of its life-cycle in water.
- diseases with water-related vectors, which are contracted through infection-carrying insects that breed in water.
- faecal disposal diseases, which are caused by organisms that breed in excreta when sanitation is defective.

Water-related diseases are a major cause of morbidity and mortality in developing countries, still today. It has been estimated that access to adequate water and sanitation could reduce infant mortality by as much as 50 per cent worldwide.[94] Excreta-related diseases account for 10–25 per cent of childhood illnesses that reach the health-care services.[95]

Gastro-intestinal infections. Gastro-intestinal infections, in particular, are the leading cause of death in young children in many developing countries. These infections may reduce absorption of nutrients and affect the body's general defence mechanisms. This in turn can lead to susceptibility to diseases such as measles and pneumonia, which are responsible for around one-quarter of deaths in young children in developing countries.[96]

23.4.2.3 *South African situation*

(a) Mortality from diarrhoea. In South Africa, diarrhoea accounts for over 10 000 deaths annually. Of these deaths, in 1984, 8 984 occurred in children under the age of five years. In that age group, diarrhoeal deaths accounted for 27,7 per cent of all deaths

---

[92] Van Damme 'The essential role of drinking water and sanitation in primary health care' in *Tropical and geographical medicine* (1990) 21–32.

[93] Jones *Water supply and waste disposal* (The World Bank, Washington 1983).

[94] Van Damme above n 92.

[95] Feacham, Bradley, Garelick & Mara *Sanitation and disease—health aspects of excreta and waste management* (1983).

[96] Pio, Leowski & Ten Dam above n 65.

in South Africa.[97] The vast majority are undetected. Rates are generally lowest in the settled urban areas, followed by the peri-urban areas, with the rural areas still experiencing the highest mortality rates.

(b) Access to basic facilities. Inadequate water supply and sanitation facilities in the rural and peri-urban areas are critical problems in South Africa. Associated with rapid urbanization, there is an ever-increasing need for adequate housing and basic environmental health services. The results of a survey of a representative national sample of the urban coloured population of South Africa[98] revealed that 18 per cent of households do not have access to reticulated water, whilst 25 per cent of the population do not have flush toilets. These aspects were found to be risk factors for diarrhoea in young children.

Overall it has been estimated that roughly 33 per cent of the urban population of South Africa has minimal access to sanitation and 18 per cent minimal access to water[99] (these are probably considerable underestimates, due to sampling problems encountered in informal settlement areas and areas with backyard shacks).

23.4.3 Tropical diseases

Tropical diseases such as malaria, schistosomiasis, trypanosomiasis, filiarasis and yellow fever are related to water, and in some areas vector-borne diseases such as malaria and schistosomiasis may be increasing.

23.4.3.1 *Malaria*

(a) Geographical distribution and transmission. Malaria is a disease that is widespread throughout Africa (it is on the increase in cities), particularly in tropical Africa where it is most common. In South Africa, it is present mainly in the northern and eastern parts of the country. It is transmitted primarily by the anopheles mosquito, which carries the malaria parasite, the most geographically widespread one being *Plasmodium vivax*. Other malaria parasites such as *Plasmodium ovale* and *Plasmodium falciparum* (which causes often fatal cerebral malaria) occur in tropical Africa, but *Plasmodium vivax* does not occur in large areas of tropical Africa.

(b) Mortality and morbidity. Reliable data on the prevalence of the disease in Africa are scarce, as case-finding and reporting are inadequate. It has been estimated, however, that 56 per cent of the world's population lives in areas where malaria continues to be a public health problem,[100] of which sub-Saharan Africa has a high incidence. Deficiencies in death registration systems and unreliable diagnoses of causes of death in Africa make it difficult to estimate the number of deaths due to malaria. It is an important cause of child mortality in Africa, however, and in the 1970s was estimated to have caused about one million deaths in sub-Saharan Africa—today the figure is thought to be below this.[101]

It also exacerbates or triggers other diseases, such as respiratory infections and diarrhoea in early childhood. Children born to women with malaria may have a lower birth weight and therefore a poorer chance of survival in early childhood. Chronic or repeated infection causes impaired growth in children and a loss of productivity in adults—it is thus a debilitating disease which has been a retarding factor in African development.

---

[97] Yach, Strebel & Joubert 'The impact of diarrhoeal disease on childhood deaths in the RSA, 1968–1985' 1989 (76) *S Afr Med J* 472–5.

[98] Von Schirding, Yach, Blignaut & Mathews above n 69.

[99] 'Water and sanitation 2000 working group' *Workshop report: strategies for water supply and sanitation provision* (1991).

[100] *Tropical disease research: a global partnership* (WHO, Geneva 1987).

[101] Ibid.

(c) Control Measures. The increasing efforts to control the disease have been hampered by the emergence of mosquitos resistant to the more readily available insecticides. Other control measures include biological controls as well as environmental measures such as eliminating mosquito breeding sites. Clearance of marshland however, is often ecologically unacceptable. Other obstacles to control include the fact that parasites are becoming resistant to many anti-malarial drugs, for example chloroquine. Other preventive measures include the use of mosquito repellants, impregnated bed nets, door and window screening and protective clothing.[102] Effective application of any of these methods, however, is hampered by inadequate local malaria epidemiology—in other words, studies of the distribution patterns of the disease are patchy.

23.4.3.2 *Schistosomiasis (bilharzia)*

(a) Geographical distribution and transmission. Schistosomiasis is the most prevalent waterborne disease, and is caused by flatworms or 'flukes' of the genus *Schistosoma*, with the species *Schistosoma haematobium* and *Schistosoma mansoni* occurring in Africa. *Schistosoma haematobium* is endemic over practically all of Africa and is associated with a urinary form of the disease, whilst the distribution of *Schistosoma mansoni* is more restricted, and it is associated with an intestinal form of the disease. In South Africa, the geographic distribution of schistosomiasis is confined mainly to the north-eastern part of the country.

The snail acts as an intermediate host for the parasites, the larvae of which undergo several weeks of development in the snail and then re-enter the water and penetrate the human skin. The disease is thus common in settlements located near rivers or lagoons and is endemic in areas of important irrigation schemes. Highest rates of the disease are found in countries such as Ghana, Sudan and Egypt[103] and near large bodies of freshwater, where the entire population may be infected.

(b) Mortality and morbidity. It is largely a chronic disease and is not associated with high mortality rates. Nevertheless, the disease is becoming more prevalent in Africa and globally—this is due to movements of people into endemic areas and development projects that create large bodies of water. In South Africa, an estimated two million people are infected with schistosomes.[104] Of these, it is estimated that less than 10 per cent experience morbidity and mortality from the infection.[105]

(c) Control measures. Control methods include chemotherapy, the use of chemical molluscicides (as well as biological control agents (competitor snails)) aimed at reducing the host snail populations, and preventive measures such as improved sanitation, water supply and health education.

23.4.3.3. *Polio*

The incidence of polio has declined substantially in recent years in South Africa.[106] Only four cases were reported in 1990, and South Africa is now on target to move towards the eradication of poliomyelitis by the end of this century.

23.4.3.4 *Hepatitis A*

Hepatitis A is a sensitive indicator of faecal-oral transmission. A large proportion of the African and coloured population are immune to it, which explains why the majority of notified cases are among whites.

---

[102] Isaacson 'Malaria' in Kibel & Wagstaff (eds) *Child health for all: a manual for southern Africa* (1991).

[103] *Tropical disease research* above n 100.

[104] Schutte 'Combating parasitic diseases of man in South Africa' 1985(81) *S Afr J Sci* 451–2.

[105] Coopen, Schutte, Mayet et al. 'Morbidity from urinary schistosomiasis in relation to intensity of infection in the Natal province of South Africa' 1986 (35) *Am J Trop Med NY* 765–76.

[106] 'The eradication of poliomyelitis from South Africa' 1990 (17) *Epidemiological Comments* 3–9.

23.4.3.5 *Cholera*

The last major cholera outbreak in South Africa was reported in 1987, when there were in excess of 20 000 cases. Since 1989, there has been an increase in the case rates reported in Mozambique, Malawi, Swaziland and Zambia. Even in the presence of a good water supply, outbreaks of cholera can be expected due to the poor state of sanitation.

23.4.3.6 *Typhoid*

Typhoid remains one of the major notifiable diseases in South Africa. Around half the cases occur between five and 14 years of age, the vast majority among Africans in the rural areas.

23.4.4 Chemical contamination of water

Little is known of the health effects of the proliferation and variety of unidentified and potentially toxic chemicals that enter the water supply from sources such as sewage and industrial effluents, which are not effectively removed at water treatment plants.[107] Where freshwater resources are limited (as in South Africa), a greater supply of water may be drawn from rivers and groundwater that may be polluted from a range of toxic substances from domestic, industrial and agricultural sources.[108]

Increases in nitrate concentrations and potentially harmful pesticides in drinking water may result from agricultural practices. Trihalomethanes may result from chlorination of water with a high organic content. The occurrence of 'natural' pollutants such as arsenic and fluoride may pose health problems, and the degree of softness of water may be a factor in cardiovascular disease.[109] Old lead plumbing systems may also contaminate water.

23.4.4.1 *Drinking water standards*

The 1984 WHO guidelines for drinking-water quality[110] (currently being revised) give guideline levels for microbiological and biological quality, aesthetic quality, radioactivity and inorganic and organic chemicals (see Table 23.2). Whilst around 800 organic and inorganic chemicals have been identified in drinking water, sufficient information on the health effects is available for only nine inorganic and 18 organic constituents to warrant guideline levels, according to WHO.[111] For the majority of chemicals for which guideline levels are recommended, the toxic effects predicted are based on toxicological data.

Different countries will have different priorities for control, however. Microbiological and biological aspects may be more important in developing countries than chemical quality, which may be a priority in industrialized countries.

South African specifications. In South Africa, there are no legally enforceable drinking-water standards[112] and the quality of drinking-water has been guided by specifications established by the SABS (for example, SABS Specification No 241 of 1984). The Department of National Health and Population Development is responsible for setting health-related water-quality guidelines, which are currently under consideration, with three criteria levels having been proposed, namely a 'recommended

[107] Lippmann & Schlesinger above n 19.
[108] *Environment and health* above n 4.
[109] Ibid.
[110] Above n 14.
[111] Ibid.
[112] Pieterse 'Drinking-water quality criteria with special reference to the South African experience' 1989 (15) *Water SA* 169–78.

TABLE 23.2
Summary of WHO Guidelines (Sayre, 1988).

Substance	WHO guideline
Inorganics	**mg ℓ$^{-1}$**
Arsenic	0,05
Barium	NS
Cadmium	0,005
Chromium	0,05
Fluoride	1,5
Lead	0,05
Mercury	0,001
Nitrate	10,0 (N)
Selenium	0,01
Silver	NS
Organics	**μg ℓ$^{-1}$**
2,4-D	1
Endrin	NS
Lindane	NS
Methoxychlor	1
Pesticides (total)	NS
Toxaphene	NS
2,4,5-TP silvex	NS
Trihalomethanes	30 ($CHCl_3$ only)
Volatile organic chemicals	**μg ℓ$^{-1}$**
Benzene	10
Carbon tetrachloride	3
1,1-Dichloroethylene	3
1,2-Dichloroethane	10
para-Dichlorobenzene	NS
1,1,1-Trichloroethane	NS
Trichloroethylene	30
Vinylchloride	NS
Microbials	
Coliforms—organisms/100 ml	0
Turbidity—NTU	<1
Radionuclides	
Beta particle and photon activity	1,0 Bq ℓ$^{-1}$
Gross alpha particle activity	0,1 Bq ℓ$^{-1}$
Radium-226 + radium-228	NS
Chloride	240 mg ℓ$^{-1}$
Colour	15 CU
Copper	1,0 mg ℓ$^{-1}$
Corrosivity	
Fluoride	1,5 mg ℓ$^{-1}$
Foaming agents	NS
Iron	0,3 mg ℓ$^{-1}$
Manganese	0,1 mg ℓ$^{-1}$
Odour	
pH	6,5–8,5
Sulphate	400 mg ℓ$^{-1}$
Total dissolved solids	1 000 mg ℓ$^{-1}$
Zinc	5,0 mg ℓ$^{-1}$

Key
CU = Colour units
NS = Not specified
NTU = Nephelometric turbidity units

(working) limit', a 'maximum permissible limit' and a 'crisis limit'.[113] In general, the development of drinking-water criteria is an ongoing process, with better information needed in particular on the impact of carcinogenic chemicals at low doses.

23.4.5 Recreational water quality

The contamination of rivers, lakes and coastal waters can also cause problems when they are used for recreation. It has been well documented that a wide variety of micro-organisms may be transmitted via polluted recreational water, and potentially contractable diseases include gastro-enteritis, respiratory, ear, eye and skin infections, hepatitis A, cholera and typhoid. Studies from different parts of the world have shown that increased rates of infection are associated with direct-contact recreation (for example, bathing, diving, surfing) and indirect exposure (seafood consumption).[114]

23.4.5.1 *Bathing-related health aspects*

Epidemiological studies now provide firm evidence that bathing in sewage-polluted seawater can cause a significant excess of gastro-intestinal disease, in some cases associated with relatively low concentrations of enterococci and E coli in the water.[115] Differences in disease rates at equivalent enterococcal densities have been documented among various population groups, which are thought to reflect differing levels of immunity. For instance, in one study it was found that disease rates were lower in Egypt (where enteric diseases are endemic) compared to New York, at similar pollution levels.[116]

23.4.5.2 *South African situation*

Marine pollution. In South Africa, little is known about the implications for health of the disposal of sewage to sea. Pollution in the coastal zone is of concern due to the rapid population growth and massive urbanization taking place along the coast (which is accompanied by increased disposal of waste water into the sea), which is occurring simultaneously with rapid growth in the seaside holiday and tourist industry.

Urban run-off. In addition to the conventional sources of waste-water discharges into the marine environment in South Africa, diffuse sources such as urban (storm) water runoff may be a significant source of pathogens, particularly runoff from sites with inadequate water and sanitation. Sites along the South African coast have been identified where contamination of seawater and shellfish pose a potential threat to health.[117] Small fishing communities may be at particular risk.

Inadequate health-related monitoring. In South Africa, however, the available monitoring data is not sufficient to quantify the likely impact on health of current water quality—either the suite of indicator organisms being measured are not particularly sensitive indicators of human faecal pollution or monitoring is not carried out frequently enough.[118]

Need for epidemiologically derived guidelines. Because of the increased use of recreational resources in South Africa, there is an urgent need for epidemiologically

---

[113] Ibid.

[114] Cabelli *Health effects criteria for marine recreational waters* (EPA-600/1-80-031 1983) 1–97; Shuval 'Thalassogenic diseases' 1986 (79) *UNEP Regional Seas Reports and Studies* 1–44.

[115] Shuval above n 114.

[116] Cabelli above n 114.

[117] Grabow, Idema, Coubrough & Bateman 'Selection of indicator systems for human viruses in polluted seawater and shellfish' 1989 (21) *Water Sci Tech* 111–7.

[118] Cabelli & Von Schirnding *Report of consultation on the applicability of microbiological monitoring procedures in South Africa towards estimating the health risks associated with swimming in sewage polluted water* (1988).

derived water-quality guidelines and standards[119] (the present water-quality guidelines are based on faecal coliform densities and are not derived from epidemiological studies).[120] With the exception of a preliminary study carried out early in 1990 by the Medical Research Council[121] in collaboration with the Council for Scientific and Industrial Research (CSIR), no epidemiological studies have been carried out to assess the likely health risk associated with deteriorating water quality in this country.

The pilot study carried out in the Cape Town area found some evidence of a potential risk of gastro-intestinal, respiratory and skin infections among swimmers relative to non-swimmers at a clean and moderately polluted beach. Of particular interest in South Africa is the use of tidal pools as marine 'bathing beaches'.

23.5 HEALTH ASPECTS OF HAZARDOUS WASTE

23.5.1 Introduction

Hazardous wastes are widely dispersed in the environment and have accumulated over many decades. In the United States, for example, it is estimated that there are between 30 000 to 50 000 waste disposal sites,[122] many being illegal or abandoned. It is thought that the number of potentially hazardous materials produced is rising by approximately 5–10 per cent annually.[123] At greatest risk to hazardous waste exposure are industrial workers and residents of communities living in the vicinity of toxic waste dumps.

Workers may become exposed during the routine handling and disposal of waste, during which they may be splashed with acid or exposed to solvents and pesticide fumes, sludges and other substances. They may be at particular risk when decontaminating abandoned dump sites or undertaking emergency clean-ups, during which wastes may burn or explode and toxic combustion products formed during fires.[124] In rural areas in particular, workers may be inadequately prepared to deal with emergency fires.

23.5.1.1 *Pathways of environmental exposure*

In contrast to occupational exposures, community exposures are more likely to produce chronic rather than acute effects. Substances can be routinely released from hazardous waste sites to the atmosphere by volatilization, by evaporation or aerosol formation, or to surface and groundwater, by overflow, drainage, seepage, percolation or leaching.[125] Thus, for example, pesticide intermediates have been detected in groundwater near a waste dump in Tennessee (USA) and trichloroethylene has been found in drinking wells.[126] Exposure of the community at large can occur from the consumption of contaminated drinking water, by the inhalation of vapours, particulates, combustion products or by skin contact.

---

[119] Von Schirnding 'Sewage to sea: what are the health implications?' 1989 (76) *S Afr Med J* 642–3.

[120] Lusher 'Water quality criteria for the South African coastal zone' 1984 (94) *S Afr Nat Sci Prog Rep* 1–25.

[121] Von Schirnding *A preliminary epidemiological study of morbidity among bathers exposed to polluted seawater* Report submitted to Foundation for Research Development and Cape Town City Council (1991).

[122] Roht, Vernon, Weir, Pier, Sullivan & Reed 'Community exposure to hazardous waste disposal sites: assessing reporting bias' 1985 (122) *Am J Epidemiol* 418–33.

[123] Ibid.

[124] Landrigan & Gross 'Chemical wastes—illegal hazards and legal remedies' 1981 (71) *Am J Public Health* 985–7.

[125] Roht et al above n 122.

[126] Langdrigan & Gross above n 124.

23.5.2 Epidemiological studies

Though large-scale epidemiological studies have been carried out in the vicinity of toxic waste sites, as well as detailed studies of cancer clusters (for example, childhood leukemias), findings have not been conclusive.[127] Normally, studies are carried out in situations of uncertain exposures (due to the unknown nature of the substances dumped) and there are few objectively measurable health effects.

23.5.2.1 *Self-reported symptoms: Recall bias*

In many situations self-reports of symptoms are often used as health outcomes. Over-reporting of symptoms has been documented to be a potential problem in communities that are worried about toxic waste site exposures.[128] In the United States, for example, the public perceives hazardous waste sites (both current and abandoned) as being associated with a very high risk.[129] At this stage it is difficult to quantify the extent to which over-reporting of symptoms is due to pervasive environmental worry as opposed to physical effects on health.

23.5.2.2 *Documented ill-health effects*

Some studies have found that residential proximity to hazardous waste sites is associated with factors such as low birth weight,[130] certain reproductive outcomes, increased rates of certain cancers,[131] growth defects,[132] and a range of vague and non-specific symptoms associated with a general deterioration of health and well-being. According to some, an exacerbation of pre-existing conditions such as bronchitis or emphysema is likely to be associated with increased exposure to toxic waste sites, rather than the appearance of overt clinical disease.[133]

Love Canal. One of the most extensively studied toxic waste sites is that of Love Canal in the United States, which was used as a burial site for organic solvents, chlorinated hydrocarbons, acids and other hazardous wastes during the 1940s.[134] When the canal was filled in 1953, schools and homes were built on it. By the mid-1970s chemicals had been detected in creeks, sewers, the soil and even in the indoor air of homes (over 250 chemicals were identified). It was subsequently established that there was an excess of miscarriages in the local community and in 1980 the evacuation of more than 800 families occurred.

No evidence for a higher cancer rate has been found among those living near Love Canal;[135] however, there was an increase in the incidence of low birth weight babies

---

[127] Philips & Silbergeld 'Health effects studies of exposure from hazardous waste sites—where are we today?' 1985 (8) *Am J Ind Med* 1–7; Upton, Kneip & Toniolo 'Public health aspects of toxic chemical disposal sites' 1989 (10) *Ann Rev Public Health* 1–25.

[128] Mendell *Interpretation of self-reported symptom data in settings with likely over-reporting due to environmental worry* 2nd Annual Meeting of the International Society for Environmental Epidemiology California, 13–15 August 1990; Shustermann, Lipscomb, Neutra & Satin *Symptom prevalence and odour-worry interaction near hazardous waste sites* 2nd Annual Meeting of the International Society for Environmental Epidemiology California, 13-15 August 1990; Roht et al above n 122.

[129] *Unfinished business: a comparative assessment of environmental problems.* (EPA 230/2-87-025A 1987).

[130] Vianna & Polan 'Incidence of low birth weight among Love Canal residents' 1984 (226) *Science* 1217–19.

[131] Dunne, Burnett, Lawton & Raphael 'The health effects of chemical waste in an urban community' 1990 (152) *Med J Aust* 592–7.

[132] Paigen, Goldman, Magnant, Highland & Steegmann jr. 'Growth of children living near the hazardous waste site, Love Canal' 1987 (59) *Human Biol* 489–508.

[133] Philips & Silbergeld above n 127.

[134] Paigen et al above n 132.

[135] Janerich, Burnett, Feck, Hoff, Nasca, Polednak, Greenwald & Vianna 'Cancer incidence in the Love Canal area' 1981 (212) *Science* 1404–7.

during the period 1940–78,[136] and children living there have been found to be of significantly shorter stature for age than control children.[137] It would appear that the growth of children may be particularly sensitive to environmental hazards, with males being more sensitive than females.

23.5.3 Need for epidemiological surveillance and monitoring

In general, there is a need for improved epidemiological surveillance around toxic waste sites, which in the first phase might be concerned with the monitoring of routinely collected vital statistics and routes of community exposure, and in the second phase might involve carrying out more detailed epidemiological studies using the available exposure data.[138]

Comprehensive exposure assessments are required, including environmental and biological monitoring in the vicinity of waste sites and detailed inventories of wastes disposed of. In South Africa, for example, there is a lack of information on the location and composition of current and old waste dumps, and housing and other developments may unknowingly be allowed on such sites.

There is also a need for more sensitive and specific indicators to identify early manifestations of disease and to develop measures which are sensitive to reporting bias in epidemiological studies.

Policy-makers should be aware of the limitations of studies which have been carried out, and of the adequate environmental monitoring and epidemiological surveillance systems implemented in the vicinity of toxic waste sites. Comprehensive legislative, administrative, technical and educational measures need to be developed for the safe handling, transport and disposal of wastes in this country.

23.6 HEALTH ASPECTS OF PESTICIDES

23.6.1 Introduction

Pesticides, being inherently toxic to living organisms, are more likely to impact on human health than other agricultural chemicals.[139] By far the largest proportion of pesticide use is in agriculture, with public health programmes (for example the control of vectors associated with bilharzia, schistosomiasis, trypanosomiasis, onchocerciasis) accounting for around 10 per cent of pesticides used in developing countries. Although the percentage of pesticide use in Africa is relatively small, it is also the fastest-growing market.[140]

People can become intentionally exposed (for example, through suicides and homicides) or unintentionally exposed through the skin and eyes or through ingestion and inhalation in various settings, both occupational and non-occupational (ie water, air, food, accidents).

23.6.2 Ill-health effects

More is known about the acute effects associated with high, short-term levels of exposure than about the effect of chronic, low-level exposure to pesticides which accumulate in the body. Even for pesticides such as DDT (for which there exists quite

---

[136] Vianna & Polan above n 130.

[137] Paigen et al above n 132.

[138] Hardy, Schroder, Cooper, Buffler, Prichard & Crane 'A surveillance system for assessing health effects from hazardous exposures' 1990 (132) *Am J Epidemiol* S32–S42.

[139] *Public health impact of pesticides used in agriculture* (WHO, Geneva 1990).

[140] Ibid.

good evidence for its occurrence in breast milk,[141]) there have been few studies into the long-term effects. In particular, effects resulting from pesticide residues in food are difficult to quantify.

The health status of the individual may alter the sensitivity to pesticides. For example, people who are malnourished and dehydrated may be more susceptible to poisoning. Potential health outcomes include effects on the skin (for example, contact dermatitis and allergic reactions), allergies, neurotoxic and behavioural effects, reproductive effects (for example, infertility in males), effects on the immune system and potential carcinogenicity.[142]

23.6.2.1 *Accidental exposures*

With respect to non-occupational exposures, accidents from unsafe packaging and leakage during storage or transport may occur, as happened, for example, in Iraq in the early 1970s, when thousands of people were poisoned from bread prepared from cereals treated with a methylmercury fungicide.[143] Other cases of poisonings have been reported when insecticides have been inappropriately used against other pests such as bedbugs and body lice. Poisonings have also resulted from people using pesticide containers for carrying water or storing food.

23.6.2.2 *Airborne exposure*

Aerial spraying, if properly conducted under conditions in which the necessary precautions are taken, should not result in hazardous exposure. There seems to be little evidence currently of significant health effects of exposure to airborne pesticides, except where inappropriately used (for example, in enclosed and unventilated spaces).[144]

23.6.2.3 *Uptake by crops*

In general, amounts taken up by crops are small, although cases of contamination have been reported—for example contaminated watermelons led to an outbreak of poisoning.[145] In developing countries (where there is often little control over the timing of applications), pesticides are frequently applied only shortly before harvesting, which may lead to increased human exposures if crops are consumed directly after the harvest.[146]

23.6.2.4 *Drinking water contamination*

Incidents of contaminated drinking water have been reported, although relatively rarely. WHO drinking water guideline levels (for organochlorine pesticides) were found to be exceeded in rivers in five countries and in lakes in three countries, in the UNEP/WHO Global Environmental Monitoring System.[147]

23.6.2.5 *Mortality and morbidity statistics*

Crude estimates are that the annual incidence of unintentional acute poisoning is probably above one million cases, whilst mass poisoning by food has accounted for

---

[141] Bouwman, Cooppan, Reinecke & Becker 'Levels of DDT and metabolites in breast milk from KwaZulu mothers after DDT application for malaria control' 1990 (86) *Bulletin of the World Health Organization* 761–8.

[142] *Public health impact of pesticides* above n 139.

[143] Conference on intoxication due to alkyl mercury-treated seed, Baghdad, 9–13 September 1974 1976 (53 Suppl) *Bulletin of the World Health Organization*.

[144] *Public health impact of pesticides* above n 139.

[145] Green et al, 'An outbreak of watermelon-borne pesticide toxicity' 1987 (77) *Am J Public Health* 1431–4.

[146] *Public health impact of pesticides* above n 139.

[147] *GEMS water data summary* Center for Inland Waters, Burlington, Canada (1983).

around 15 000 cases.[148] Reasonable estimates of the incidence of chronic health effects are difficult to derive.

Attention needs to be given to educating people about the hazards associated with pesticides and on their correct use. In hot climates, in particular, protective clothing may seldom be used because of excessive heat. Pesticides are likely to become an increasingly important problem in southern Africa, where a high proportion of the population is dependent on agriculture, even though the overall use is as yet relatively low.

23.7 MICROBIOLOGICAL AND CHEMICAL SAFETY OF FOOD

Most food-borne infections and poisonings result from poor food safety and sanitary measures. Reporting of food-borne infections is for the most part inadequate, however—only around five percent of acute episodes are notified in most countries.[149] In Germany and Spain, the deaths of over 500 people, and effects on health of another 2 000 people, resulted from toxic oil contamination.[150] Efforts are continuing to control potentially harmful food additives.

23.8 HEALTH IMPLICATIONS OF NOISE

Noise essentially is unwanted or harmful sound. Many factors affect people's perception of sound, among them the time of day at which noise is experienced and whether the sound is continuous or intermittent. Effects at high levels (around 85 decibels and above) and prolonged duration range from loss of hearing at certain frequencies to total deafness. Physiological effects include changes in heartbeat and respiration rate, eye and skin responses, and exacerbation of certain stress-related disorders such as hypertension. At lower levels, sound may have psychological effects, including sleep disturbance, annoyance and irritation.[151] In Europe, it is estimated that 10–20 per cent of the population is exposed to sound above acceptable levels.[152] This figure is likely to increase in the future.

23.9 ACCIDENTS

23.9.1 Common cause of death

Accidents are the third most common cause of death in Europe, of which motor vehicles account for 40 per cent.[153] For every death in a road accident, it is estimated that 15 people are severely injured and 30 people slightly injured.[154]

Among children over the age of one year living in industrialized countries, accidental injuries are the leading cause of death. In developing countries, the number of accidental deaths and injuries is rising as a consequence of increasing industrialization. In South Africa, injuries are the leading cause of death among people aged between five and 34 years.[155]

23.9.2 Work-related accidents

Mortality and morbidity from work-related accidents vary, but in South Africa this is a serious problem (see section 23.10).

[148] *Public health impact of pesticides* above n 139.
[149] *Environment and health* above n 4.
[150] *Toxic oil syndrome* (WHO, Copenhagen 1983).
[151] *Environmental health impact assessment* above n 29.
[152] *Environment and health* above n 4.
[153] Ibid.
[154] Ibid.
[155] Bradshaw, Botha, Joubert, Pretorius, Van Wyk & Yach *Review of South African mortality (1984)* Medical Research Council Technical Report 1987.

23.9.3 Accidents in and around the home

Accidents in the home affect, in particular, the young and the elderly. In homes where open fires and paraffin burners are used, accidental poisonings and burns occur frequently, particularly in overcrowded living conditions. The mortality rate from burns among coloured children under five years of age is seven times greater than that for white children.[156]

Temporal variations occur in the incidence of poisonings. For example, accidental ingestion of paraffin occurs mainly in the summer months, when thirsty children may mistake paraffin for water. Similarly, poisonings by insecticides correlate with their use in agricultural seasons.[157]

Socio-economic factors play an important role in influencing the pattern of injuries and accidental deaths in South Africa. Swimming pool drownings are more common among white children from affluent homes, for example, whereas among children from lower socio-economic groups drownings in dams, rivers or buckets occur more frequently.[158]

23.9.4 Industrial accidents

Large-scale industrial accidents such as those that occurred in Chernobyl and Bhopal, while of devastating impact, are, in general, associated with a much lower risk than accidents in the home, at work or on the roads. Improved design and construction of roads, vehicles and buildings, and proper planning of human settlements in relation to these is important, as is the need for careful contingency planning and emergency response units to mitigate the adverse effects of disasters.

23.10 OCCUPATIONAL HEALTH

In South Africa, relatively more is known about the extent of occupational diseases than about environmental diseases. Nevertheless, routinely available data on mortality and morbidity is limited. While the incidence of diseases such as pneumoconiosis and poisonings by metals are thought to be relatively high in industry,[159] little is known about the incidence of cancer or about neurological and muscular-skeletal conditions resulting from exposure to chemicals, solvents and radiation. Most epidemiological surveys have centred on dust-induced occupational diseases,[160] and most of the available information relates to the white workforce. More data is available on accidents in the workplace: in 1986, 1 954 employees were killed in South Africa in work-related accidents.[161] A high prevalence of accident-related mortality and morbidity occurs in the mines.

23.10.1 *Health services*

With respect to occupational health services, apart from the mining industry, provision is poor. A survey carried out in the Greater Cape Town area found that only 13 per cent of workplaces had a health service, with a similar percentage found in the heavily industrialized area of Germiston.[162] There have been various state-initiated

---

[156] Kibel, Joubert & Bradshaw 'Injury-related mortality in South African children 1981-1985' *S Afr Med J* (in press).

[157] Hay 'Childhood poisoning' in Kibel & Wagstaff (eds) *Child health for all: a manual for southern Africa* (1991).

[158] Kibel, Joubert & Bradshaw above n 156.

[159] Myers & Macun 'The sociologic context of occupational health in South Africa' 1989 (79) *Am J Public Health*.

[160] Ibid.

[161] Statistics available from the office of the Workmen's Compensation Commissioner.

[162] Sitas *Report on occupational health services in the Germiston magisterial district* National Centre for Occupational Health Report no 16 (1986).

investigations into occupational health conditions in South Africa, of which the Erasmus Commission of Enquiry in 1975 drew attention to the lack of health services outside of the mining industry.[163] Other researchers have addressed the issue more recently.[164]

Workers may be particularly susceptible to occupational diseases as their general health status is poor, due to deficiencies in diet, poor domestic conditions such as fuel burning, damp and overcrowding, high rates of stress and of alcohol and tobacco use.

23.11 GENERAL MANAGEMENT CONSIDERATIONS

23.11.1 Acceptable risk

It would obviously be virtually impossible to reduce all environmental exposures to a level where the risk to health of the human population was virtually zero. Therefore one needs to set an acceptable level of risk of morbidity and mortality in managing environmental health hazards. This is particularly relevant, for example, when dealing with the regulation of certain carcinogens, where there may be no safety threshold.

A prudent policy on acceptable exposure levels (for example, for chemicals and radiation) is important. Policies should always be revised and updated with new scientific knowledge, however. In some cases this may lead to more stringent standards being introduced (as, for example, in the case of lead); in other cases standards may be shown to have been unnecessarily restrictive (in the case of waste water used for irrigation, for example).[165]

23.11.1.1 *Public perception of risk*

The public perception of risks may often differ from that of scientists and regulators. Risks which are familiar to people may be less threatening than risks which are unfamiliar, and people are normally more willing to accept a risk which they believe is under their own individual control (and when they may derive a direct benefit from taking the risk) than otherwise.

Many people may reject situations which pose a small risk—for example, living near nuclear power plants or toxic waste dumps—but may nevertheless accept situations that have demonstrably larger risks—for example, road travel or occupational exposure to toxic chemicals.[166] In general, substances which are unfamiliar to the public, that are out of the individual's control and that provide no direct benefit are likely to cause more anxiety.

23.11.1.2 *Ready access to information*

It is becoming increasingly important that the public have ready access to accurate information on environmental health hazards and that this data is conveyed in a readily comprehensible way, but with due regard given to the complexities and uncertainties inherent in the data. The media have an important role to play in enhancing public awareness in this respect.

---

[163] *Report of the commission of enquiry on occupational health* RP 55/1976.

[164] Cornell 'Workplace health services and employment in the manufacturing industry in greater Cape Town' 1986 (6) *Indus Rel J S Afr* 41–53; Sitas, Davies, Kielkowski & Becklake 'Occupational health services in South African manufacturing industries: a pilot survey' 1988 (14) *Am J Indus Med* 545–57; Lowe, Barron, Steyn, Malakela, Steinberg & Reid 'Occupational health services in Johannesburg and Randburg' 1990 (77) *S Afr Med J* 581–4.

[165] Mara & Cairncross *Guidelines for the safe use of wastewater and excreta in agriculture and aquaculture* (WHO/UNEP, Geneva 1989).

[166] *Environment and health* above n 4.

23.11.2 Training needs

Environmental health professionals have as their main duties and responsibilities the identification, assessment, management, communication and remediation of health risks resulting from environmental factors.[167]

23.11.2.1 *Shortage of environmental health professionals*

In the light of the considerable rise in environmental health activities which are likely to occur in the future, it is possible that the shortage of appropriately trained environmental health professionals will become critical unless immediate steps are taken to rectify this. Owing to the lack of people trained in environmental health, people with little knowledge of epidemiology, biostatistics, toxicology and risk assessment fill key positions, as is the case in the United States, for example.[168] South Africa, with as yet no school of public health, has fewer opportunities for training environmental health professionals than the United States, although even there most are trained in accredited environmental health programmes outside schools of public health.

23.11.2.2 *Multi-disciplinary approach*

There is a need in South Africa for well-trained specialists as well as generalists in the broad tradition of public health. Environmental health officers will need basic grounding in the general principles of public health and environmental science as well as familiarity with risk assessment and risk management procedures.[169] A multi-media and multi-disciplinary approach will be required, as many monitoring problems are not limited to a single medium such as the air, water or soil. An increased emphasis will therefore be placed on the ability to function as part of a multi-disciplinary team.[170]

23.11.2.3 *Technikon courses*

At present, the basic academic qualification required for a health inspector is the National Diploma in Public Health (recently changed to Environmental Health), which is a three-year course at various technikons. In 1982, a national higher diploma qualification was introduced for the attainment of specialized skills in environmental hygiene, industrial hygiene and food hygiene. It has been recommended that a period of practical experience (six months to one year) after training (before students qualify as health inspectors) may be beneficial.[171]

23.11.2.4 *University courses*

Training at undergraduate level as well as advanced training at Masters and Doctoral level is needed in addition to the more practically oriented diploma courses offered at technikons.

A course in environmental health at Honours level is offered to environmental science students at the University of Cape Town and post-graduate diploma courses in occupational health are offered at various medical schools around the country. The University of Stellenbosch and, as of 1991, the University of Cape Town, offer an Honours degree in epidemiology. Various medical schools around the country provide training in community health at post-graduate level to medical doctors, although the

---

[167] Sexton & Perlin 'The federal environmental health workforce in the USA' 1990 (80) *Am J Public Health* 913.

[168] Gordon 'Who will manage the environment?' 1990 (80) *Am J Public Health* 904.

[169] Sexton & Perlin above n 167.

[170] Ibid.

[171] Van Rooyen 'The health inspector in a changing South Africa' 1991(2) *J Comprehensive Health* 111.

environmental health component is generally weak. There is a clear need in the country for a school of public health to provide interdisciplinary and multi-disciplinary training in environmental health.

There is also a need to train medical doctors to recognize and treat environmentally induced disease (such as chemical sensitivity). There will also be a demand for environmental health experts who can communicate the risks of environmental exposures and their uncertainties, particularly to non-scientists.[172]

23.11.3 Research

Both the research organizations and the health services need to give priority to environmental research. Environmental health research and management both require multi-disciplinary approaches. Because of the multi-disciplinary nature of the subject, it may be difficult to persuade any organization to take full responsibility for funding or managing it.[173]

23.11.3.1 *Medical Research Council*

The Medical Research Council recently established the Research Institute for Environmental Diseases, which addresses environmental health problems in South Africa. The institute has branches in Pretoria and Cape Town. Other institutes within the council which conduct some environmentally related research include the Research Institute for Diseases in a Tropical Environment, the Research Institute for Nutritional Diseases, and the Centre for Epidemiological Research in Southern Africa.

23.11.3.2 *Other related research activities*

Both the CSIR and the Human Science Research Council (HSRC) also conduct health-related environmental research and, to a limited extent, so does the private sector, industry, some universities and various health authorities.

In respect of occupational health, the National Centre for Occupational Health (NCOH) and the Medical Bureau for Occupational Diseases conduct research, and industrial health research groups are situated in Departments of Sociology at the Universities of Cape Town and Durban.

Not only in the research bodies and administrative bodies is expertise needed but so too in the private sector, including industry, is there a need for environmental health research. Environmental epidemiologists and toxicologists will be in increasing demand in this respect.

23.11.4 Environmental health legislation

23.11.4.1 *Introduction*

It is not the intention here to discuss details of legislation relating to environmental health matters, as this is covered in other chapters. Some aspects of the legislation of particular relevance from the health point of view, however, are mentioned below. It should be stressed that, as important as appropriate legislation is, the provision of adequately staffed systems of regulation, inspection and enforcement is vital. Environmental auditing will no doubt become of increasing importance in South Africa.

23.11.4.2 *Health Act*

The Health Act 63 of 1977 makes provision for the rendering of health services, defines the duties of health authorities and co-ordinates health services, provides for the establishment of a National Health Policy Council and a Health Matters Advisory Council. It repealed the Public Health Act 36 of 1919 which made provision for the

[172] Sexton & Perlin above n 167.
[173] *Environment and health* above n 4.

prevention and control of, inter alia, infectious diseases, epidemics, nuisances and other related public health matters, the protection of public water supplies and food, sanitation and hygiene. The Minister of National Health and Population Development is empowered by this Act to make regulations relating to various environmental health matters.

23.11.4.3 *Atmospheric Pollution Prevention Act*

Related relevant legislation includes the Atmospheric Pollution Prevention Act 45 of 1965. See chapter 17.

23.11.4.4 *Hazardous Substances Act*

The Hazardous Substances Act 15 of 1973 provides for control of substances which may cause injury, ill-health or death by reason of their toxic, corrosive, irritant, sensitizing or flammable nature. See chapters 20 and 21.

23.11.4.5 *Other relevant legislation*

This includes the following:

- Housing Act 4 of 1966
- Development and Housing Act (House of Assembly) 103 of 1985
- Housing Act (House of Representatives) 2 of 1987
- Slums Act 76 of 1979
- Prevention of Illegal Squatting Act 52 of 1951
- National Building Regulations and Building Standards Act 103 of 1977.
- Foodstuffs, Cosmetics and Disinfectants Act 54 of 1972
- Water Act 54 of 1956
- Sea-Shore Act 21 of 1935
- Sea Fishery Act 12 of 1988
- Environment Conservation Act 73 of 1989
- Nuclear Energy Act 92 of 1982
- Basic Conditions of Employment Act 3 of 1983
- Minerals Act 50 of 1991
- Workmen's Compensation Act 30 of 1941
- Occupational Diseases in Mines and Works Act 78 of 1973.

23.11.4.6 *Regulation in the workplace*

Legislation with respect to regulation in the workplace has been reviewed by several authors.[174] The Machinery and Occupational Safety Act 6 of 1983 is the principal statute regulating occupational health and safety in South Africa. It is based on the principle of self-regulation. There exists an Advisory Council for Occupational Safety, and the Act provides also for a safety inspectorate, safety representatives and safety committees. (The Minerals Act has similar provisions.) Regulations that have been promulgated in terms of the Act relate inter alia to noise, asbestos, lead, environmental safety, temperature and lighting in the workplace.

23.11.5 Environmental health administration

It is well established that an ever-increasing number of conditions have come to be recognized as environmental health problems, including air and water pollution, noise

---

[174] Benatar, Mets & Elmes 'Occupational health and safety in South Africa' 1983 (63) *S Afr Med J* 952–4; Mets & Benatar 'Occupational health legislation—progress since 1983' 1987 (72) *S Afr Med J* 451–2; Erasmus 'Occupational health and hygiene' 1987 (72) *S Afr Med J* 279–82.

pollution, solid and hazardous waste. Not all of these, however, may be housed administratively in traditional public health agencies.[175]

23.11.5.1 *Intersectoral responsibility*

As has been discussed, potential hazards to health may originate via many agents from a wide variety of sources, which can reach human beings by complex routes and exposure pathways. Thus hazards with which one sector must cope, such as the water supply and food industry, may originate in the practices of another, such as agriculture.[176] Therefore the co-operation of all sectors is necessary: environmental health is both a multi-sectoral and an intersectoral responsibility. The defence of sectoral interests is a major obstacle to achieving intersectoral co-operation. Public participation is also necessary—a good example of how this can work at the municipal level is the WHO 'Healthy Cities' project.[177]

23.11.5.2 *Rationalization of environmental health services*

Despite the increasing recognition of the magnitude of environmental health problems, it can be anticipated that diminishing resources will in future be available for environmental health control. There is probably no optimal organizational arrangement in terms of rationalization of environmental health services, as these are determined by factors such as the structure, staffing, resources and political support of an agency.[178] Many different arrangements can effectively deliver environmental health services, some of which might involve the private sector.

The question arises as to what the respective responsibilities of central, provincial and local government should be. Some environmental health problems are best tackled at the local level, whilst others may be regional or international in scope. Whatever approach is adopted, the responsibilities at different levels of government should be clearly specified and intersectoral links established.[179]

(a) State-level involvement. In terms of setting and enforcing uniform environmental standards, there will be a continual demand for state-level involvement. Among the functions of the Department of National Health and Population Development are to take steps for the promotion of a safe and healthy environment. Environmental health administration within the department is at three levels: the non-personal (which deals, for example, with drinking water, waste disposal, sanitation, food, radiation, medical and toxic wastes, foodstuffs, cosmetics, and dangerous substances), the personal level (for example environmental hygiene at primary health care level), and at secondary and tertiary care level (for example, occupational health). The department plays an important co-ordinating role.

(b) Role of local authorities. In South Africa the primary responsibility for environmental health services rests with the local authorities, with overall control resting with the Department of National Health and Population Development.[180]

(i) *Local health authority functions.* The first of the local health authorities' duties are listed as being to take all lawful, necessary and reasonably practical measures to maintain its district at all times in a hygienic and clean condition.

In particular, local health authorities are required to prevent occurrences of any nuisance, unhygienic condition, offensive condition, or any other condition harmful to

[175] Treser 'Redefining our mission: environmental health personnel seen as agents of change' 1990 *J Environ Health*.
[176] *Environment and health* above n 4.
[177] *City networks for health* (WHO, Geneva 1991).
[178] Treser above n 175.
[179] *Environment and health* above n 4.
[180] Sections 14(1)*(c)* and 20 of the Health Act.

health, as well as to prevent pollution of water, or to purify water and render services for the prevention of communicable diseases and the promotion of health.[181] In addition to national legislation applicable to local authorities' areas of jurisdiction, local authorities are empowered to promulgate by-laws relating to environmental health.

(ii) *Specialist environmental health functions.* Specialist environmental health functions relating to the provision of purified water supplies, drainage, sewerage, solid waste disposal, housing and public amenities such as beaches and swimming pools, are normally the responsibility of departments such as the City Engineer, Housing and others. This applies in some cases to scientific services for air and water monitoring also.

23.11.5.3 *Health inspectorate*

Environmental health control and the provision of environmental health services in the local authorities is the main responsibility of the health inspectorate, who are law-enforcement officers. The term 'health inspector' however is no longer reflective of the true nature of their duties, which go well beyond hygienic food handling and law enforcement.[182] The Health Officers Association of South Africa has consequently recommended that their name be changed to that of Environmental Health Officer, to reflect the changing nature of their responsibilities.

(a) Role in primary health care. Today, the health inspector has a particularly important role to play in terms of primary health care. The control of food premises and other business premises, while important, can no longer be considered as the number one priority in terms of the health inspector's main function. In contrast, the education of food handlers and street vendors, for example, is probably of greater priority.[183]

In so far as the basic elements of primary health care are concerned, the provision of safe drinking water, adequate sanitation and the promotion of food hygiene and nutrition, as well as health education, are areas in which the health inspectorate has a critical role to play.

(b) Health education. A particularly important duty is in terms of educating and training people on how to better utilize or upgrade existing facilities. Not only do health inspectors in rural areas have an important role to play in this respect but increasingly, with rapid urbanization and the growth of informal settlement areas, also in urban areas, particularly peri-urban fringes.

There is a need for environmental health officers at all levels to focus on identifying environmental health problems, to characterize and evaluate the various factors involved and to determine intervention strategies for preventing and controlling adverse health impacts. Environmental health officers are agents of change, ie to inform, motivate, and, if necessary, legally enforce people to adopt behaviours, practices and processes which are environmentally sound and which will result in the enhancement of community health.[184] With increasing deregulation of health legislation likely, the role of the health inspector as educationalist will become increasingly important.

23.11.5.4 *Need for national environmental health objectives*

Of fundamental importance is the need for national environmental health objectives and indicators to measure success or failure.[185] WHO (Europe) have developed a number of targets to enable the objectives of 'Health for All' to be achieved. The

---

[181] Section 20(1)*(b)*(iv) of the Health Act.
[182] Van Rooyen above n 171.
[183] Ibid.
[184] Treser above n 175.
[185] Van Rooyen above n 171.

Directorate of Public Hygiene of the Department of National Health and Population Development has formulated such objectives and indicators for the environmental health elements of primary health-care. Work is being done to determine the availability of basic environmental amenities in the rural and urban areas of South Africa, about which some information is already available.[186] A national environmental health task group has been set up to facilitate further work in this area.

[186] Von Schirnding, Yach, Blignaut & Mathews above n 69.

CHAPTER 24

MOUNTAINS

M A RABIE
P E BLIGNAUT
L P FATTI

24.1 DEFINITION OF MOUNTAIN

A mountain is usually defined in dictionaries as a natural elevation of the earth's surface, rising notably above the surrounding level or as any part of a land mass which projects conspicuously above its surroundings. This definition may equally be applicable to the concept of hill. Indeed, the latter formerly included the concept of mountain, but has now been restricted to projections of lesser elevation. Two features have been suggested whereby mountains may be identified:[1]

24.1.1 Topographical features

To qualify as a mountain the land projection above the surrounding area must at least achieve a certain elevation; it must be notable or conspicuous. Such elevation obviously cannot be expressed in altitude, ie in height above sea-level, since many plains or plateaus reach elevations far in excess of mountains closer to sea-level. A more satisfactory criterion would be that of local relief, ie the elevational distance between the highest and lowest points in a given area. The exact or even approximate elevational distance (or height) required for a land projection to qualify as a mountain—in contradistinction to a hill or koppie—is the subject of uncertainty and arbitrariness, with figures ranging between 300 m and 900 m. Much also depends upon the elevation relative to the surrounding landscape: a range below the qualifying figure may thus be regarded as a mountain in a relatively flat area. A further uncertain factor is the horizontal distance between the point of vantage and the top of the land projection, especially where a gradual slope over an extended area of several kilometres is concerned. Moreover, local relief, taken by itself, is an incomplete measure of mountains. For instance, a canyon may satisfy the requirement of local relief, but, even when looking up from the canyon floor, the phenomenon is not perceived as a mountain. Furthermore, a mountain is envisaged as containing a dissected landscape.

24.1.2 Ecological features

In addition to topographical features mountains normally also display distinct altitudinal zonation, mainly through their climatic and vegetational variation. A basic difference between mountains and the surrounding level area is that mountains have significantly different climates at successive elevational levels, which are, in turn, usually reflected in the vegetation. In short, mountains mostly display a substantial environmental contrast within a relatively short distance.

24.1.3 Mountain catchments

Probably the most important property of South African mountains is their function as natural drainage areas. Their capacity for rainfall and mist interception and eventual

---

[1] See generally Price *Mountains and man* (1981) 1–4. This chapter is based upon Rabie 'The conservation of mountains in South African law' 1989 *SA Public Law* 213–31, 1990 *SA Public Law* 66–79.

release of water into rivers is of the greatest importance to a relatively arid country like South Africa. South African mountain catchments, which comprise only 10 per cent of the total area of the RSA, yield over 50 per cent of our water sources. Mountains in South Africa, accordingly, have been viewed by the legislature mainly in the context of their capacity of serving as water catchments.

The only legal definition in South Africa related to 'mountain' is that of 'mountain catchment area' in the Mountain Catchment Areas Act 63 of 1970; such an area is defined simply as any area defined and declared by the Minister of Environment Affairs by notice in the *Gazette* to be a mountain catchment area.[2] This definition, satisfactory though it may be from a legal point of view, fails to describe the characteristics of such an area. Such characteristics have been described as including the main mass of a mountain or range, together with any spurs or connected outliers, above the general level of the surrounding plains; it therefore comprises the crest or watershed, plateaus, slopes, foothills and connecting valleys. Disconnected outliers are regarded and dealt with either as separate catchments or as sub-catchments.[3] Another substantive definition of a mountain catchment is that it consists of an area of mountainous or elevated, usually broken terrain of insignificant agricultural potential, where natural precipitation is sufficient to produce surface or subsurface water yields that contribute significantly to national, regional or local water supplies.[4]

24.2 THE EXTENT AND OWNERSHIP OF MOUNTAINS IN SOUTH AFRICA

In the 1950s the interdepartmental committee on the conservation of mountain catchments in South Africa set out to identify the principal mountain catchments of South Africa. Some 109 such catchments were listed, although it was pointed out by the committee that this number is largely arbitrary, since many catchments are of a compound nature, comprising several distinct sub-catchments, while others, which have been treated as single units, feed more than one river system and could equally well have been subdivided into smaller units.[5] These catchments have been identified on account of their national importance as sources of water supply. Their importance was related to the long term, according to the potential use of the water, assessed according to the criteria of quantity and exploitability.[6]

It should be noted that the Republic of South Africa is to a material extent dependent on the water resources of mountain catchments in neighbouring states, particularly Lesotho. Although this fact is recognized, it is not taken into account for the purposes of the present study, which deals only with the Republic of South Africa.

During the 1930s it became government policy to purchase or expropriate mountain land where this was deemed necessary for the conservation of water sources. This aim was supported in the *Report of the commission of enquiry concerning the water laws of the Union* of 1952[7] and the *Report of the interdepartmental committee on the conservation of mountain catchments in South Africa* of 1961.[8]

However, by 1961 it was calculated that state land comprised only 10 per cent of the major catchments (with black areas making up another 10 per cent).[9] It may be noted, nevertheless, that in some instances, almost an entire catchment had in this process become subject to state ownership. A prominent example is the Natal Drakensberg

---

[2] Section 1.

[3] *Report of the interdepartmental committee on the conservation of mountain catchments in South Africa* (1961) para 9.

[4] Bands Management of fynbos mountain catchments in *Forestry handbook* (1987) 509–10.

[5] *Report of the interdepartmental committee* above n 3, para 10.

[6] *Report of the interdepartmental committee* above n 3, paras 23–7.

[7] UG 11/1952 par 114.

[8] Above n 3, para 150(4).

[9] *Report of the interdepartmental committee* above n 3, para 94.

catchment area of which only 6 per cent remains in private ownership and even this is to be purchased by the State. Examples in the western Cape include the catchments of the Voëlvlei and Theewaterskloof dams.

Today the area of mountain catchments on state land amounts to 1,7 million ha. This still represents only about 15 per cent of the total area of major catchments.

Private land which has been declared as mountain catchment areas in terms of the Mountain Catchment Areas Act amounts to 616 811 ha or about 5,5 per cent of the entire area regarded as constituting catchments. The interdepartmental committee on the conservation of mountain catchments in South Africa established in 1961 that land held in private ownership accounted for some 80 per cent of the total area of South Africa's catchments.[10] The figure today amounts to approximately 9 700 000 ha of major mountain catchments. This means that only about 6,4 per cent of this area has been declared as mountain catchment areas, leaving some 9 100 000 ha, or 93,6 per cent, undeclared. The undeclared area, although not subject to the Mountain Catchment Areas Act, is, as will be shown, nevertheless subject to other legislation partly aimed at conservation.

Nearly all of South Africa's major, medium, small and 'dry' mountain catchments are included in the report of the interdepartmental committee, only isolated mountains having been excluded. Together, these mountains account for approximately 12,4 million ha, or 10 per cent of South Africa's land. If mountains and distinctive hills are taken as having a minimum local relief of 450 m, so as to include mountain ranges such as the Magaliesberge and the Cape Peninsula mountain chain, then the above report, the 1 : 2 500 000 scale *Terrain morphological map of southern Africa*[11] and the relevant 1 : 50 000 scale topographical maps reveal that 10 per cent of South Africa is covered by mountains, while 15 per cent is covered by distinctive hilly terrain, coastal escarpments and canyons.

24.3 THE VALUE OF MOUNTAINS AND THE NEED FOR THEIR CONSERVATION

Owing to their ruggedness and inaccessibility, mountains have generally remained as bastions of the natural environment, while agriculture, urban and industrial development have swallowed up most of the lowlands. Whereas the extent of plant types such as fynbos has been much reduced in the lowlands, extensive areas of natural communities are still present in the mountains. About 200 000 ha or two thirds of South Africa's indigenous forest occur in mountainous areas. In fact, the relative inaccessibility of mountains has contributed to the survival of several endangered plant species. Mountains may to some extent be regarded as the final retreat or Noah's arks of natural plant communities and of certain endangered species; they are invaluable reservoirs of genetic material.

The majestic splendour and beauty of mountains, coupled with their wilderness atmosphere and rich habitat diversity, have provided unmatched opportunities for recreation. In addition to their relatively well-preserved, unique ecosystems and their aesthetic appeal, mountains contain a number of natural resources. First and foremost among these—and probably the single most important practical reason for their conservation—is the capacity of mountains to serve as water reservoirs. Mountains tend to receive higher levels of precipitation, fog and mist interception than the surrounding lowlands. It has been stated that our major mountain catchments, which

---

[10] Ibid.

[11] Kruger, Soil and Irrigation Research Institute, Department of Agriculture (1983).

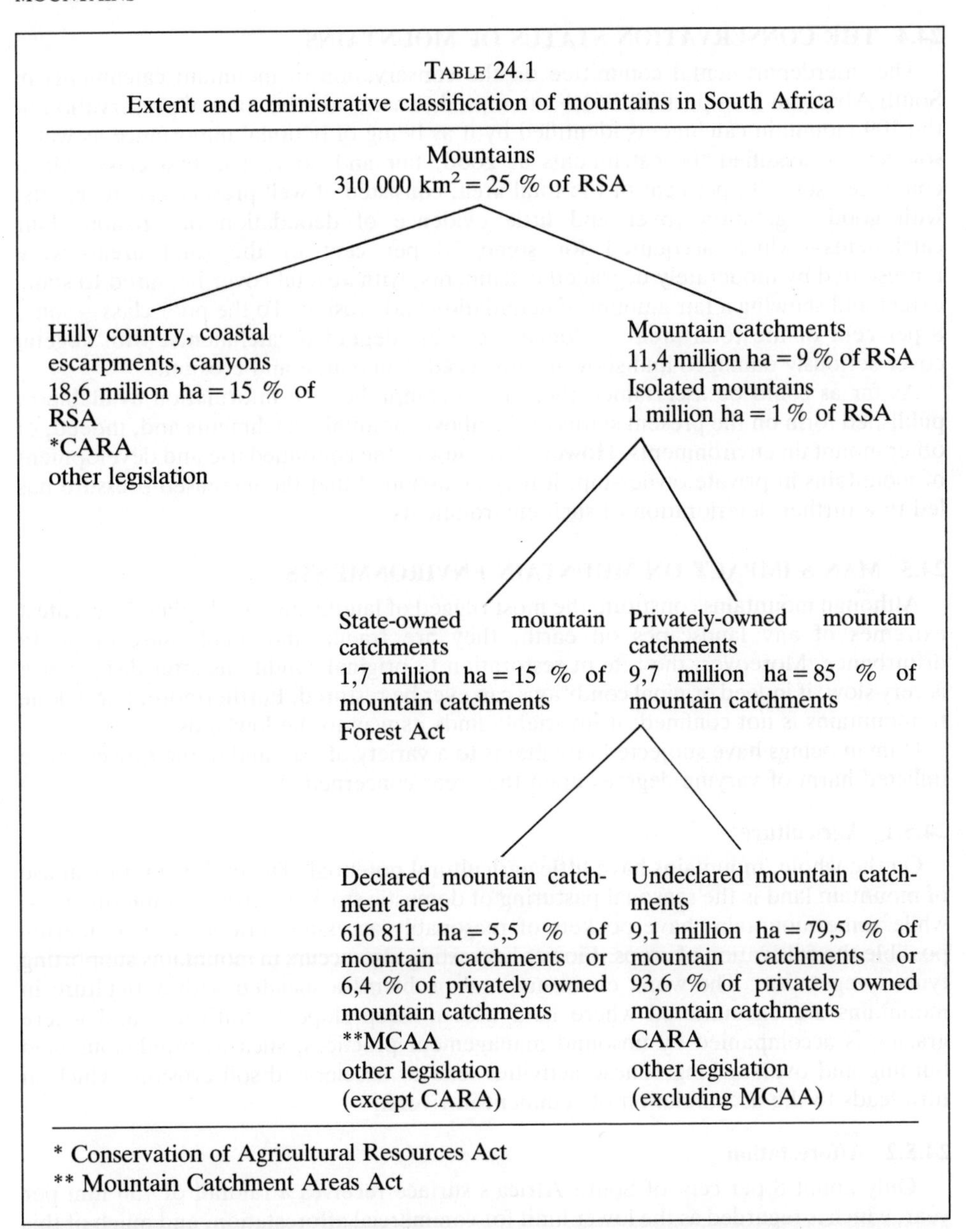

TABLE 24.1
Extent and administrative classification of mountains in South Africa

cover some 10 per cent of South Africa's land surface, provide almost 50 per cent of the combined average annual runoff (ie water that reaches our rivers). Moreover, given the fact that mountain catchments are generally in a more healthy state of conservation than other catchments, the quality of the runoff is superior to runoff from other areas.

If South Africa's natural resources must be ranked in order of priority, water would certainly qualify among the first. Abundant motivation therefore exists for mountain catchments to be maximally conserved in order to provide optimum sustained yields of water of an acceptable quality. In view of their overall importance as sources of water, all other uses of mountains should be subordinate to, and compatible with their use as catchments.

24.4 THE CONSERVATION STATUS OF MOUNTAINS

The interdepartmental committee on the conservation of mountain catchments in South Africa, in its report of 1961,[12] attempted to ascertain the state of preservation of the 109 mountain catchments identified by it as being of national importance as water sources. It classified the catchments as good, fair and poor. The first class, which comprised some 14 per cent of the total area, consisted of well-preserved catchments, with good vegetation cover and little evidence of denudation or erosion. Fair catchments—which accounted for some 78 per cent of the total area—were represented by moderately degraded catchments, with vegetal cover impaired to some extent and showing a fair amount of denudation and erosion. To the poor class—some 8 per cent of the total area—belonged severely degraded catchments, with vegetal cover seriously damaged and showing advanced denudation and erosion.

As far as could be ascertained there is no comprehensive information available in published form on the present status of the above mountain catchments and, indeed, of other mountain environments. However, in view of the continued use and development of mountains in private ownership, it may be assumed that the increased pressure has led to a further deterioration of such environments.

24.5 MAN'S IMPACT ON MOUNTAIN ENVIRONMENTS

Although mountains constitute the most rugged of landforms and display the greatest extremes of any landscapes on earth, they are fragile and highly susceptible to disturbance. Moreover, the rate of restoration to original conditions after disturbance is very slow, if indeed original conditions can ever be restored. Furthermore, harm done to mountains is not confined: it invariably finds its way to the lowlands.

Human beings have subjected mountains to a variety of uses and in the process have inflicted harm of varying degrees upon the areas concerned.[13]

24.5.1 Agriculture

On the whole, mountains have little agricultural potential. The major traditional use of mountain land is the seasonal pasturing of domestic stock in certain mountain areas, while some mountains have pockets of reasonably accessible arable land, rendering possible the cultivation of crops. Flower harvesting also occurs in mountains supporting fynbos vegetation. The worst environmental problems associated with agriculture in mountains are encountered where land with a steep slope is cultivated and where grazing is accompanied by unsound management practices, such as injudicious veld burning and overstocking. These activities lead to accelerated soil erosion, which in turn leads to the accumulation of sediment in rivers.

24.5.2 Afforestation

Only about 8 per cent of South Africa's surface receives a rainfall of 750 mm per year, which is regarded as the lower limit for commercial afforestation, and much of this area consists of highly productive agricultural land. The tendency accordingly has been to afforest only ground that is too steep or too rocky to plough. Forestry thus has been limited mainly to hills and mountains.

Some major negative impacts of the afforestation of mountains are that it reduces run-off and streamflow to a greater degree than natural plant cover, and that certain timber species such as *Pinus pinaster* have tended naturally to spread into the

---

[12] Above n 3, para 31 and table III.

[13] See generally Price above n 1, ch 12; Bands *The influence of mountain catchment area control measures on land management in the Groot-Winterhoek area of the western Cape: ecological, economic and social implications* (unpublished MSc thesis, University of Stellenbosch 1985) ch 4; *Report of the interdepartmental committee* above n 3, ch 4.

neighbouring mountain regions where their control has been very difficult and costly. Moreover, extremely wide firebreaks (up to 4 km) are sometimes required to protect plantations from fires occuring in neighbouring mountains. Such activities, as well as the building of roads and clear-cutting of plantations may contribute to soil erosion and sedimentation in streams and rivers. A serious consequence of afforestation is that natural ecosystems are severely affected. Finally, exotic timber plantations constitute an aesthetic infringement in natural mountain landscapes.

24.5.3 Infrastructure services

The adequate supply of electricity and of post and telecommunication services is of vital importance to South Africa. However, the provision of these services has potentially detrimental consequences for mountain environments. Open-conductor power transmission towers as well as microwave and other towers can constitute serious aesthetic infringements in mountain areas. Moreover, these structures necessitate some disturbance of the fragile plant cover of mountains and are attended by the building of access roads which may lead to soil erosion. Road and railway building generally constitute a potential threat to mountain environments, besides having a negative visual impact.

Narrow, deep mountain valleys, which can relatively easily be spanned by dams, provide attractive sites for the generation of hydro-electric power. Added to this attraction are the considerations that mountain areas are usually sparsely populated, undeveloped, and therefore relatively inexpensive or already in state ownership. Moreover, such dams, apart from being used for the generation of electricity, also provide water storage capacity, flood protection and recreational opportunities. Furthermore, industrial development tends to occur in the vicinity of such low-cost energy. All this may eventually lead to the creation of a node of intensive development, with all its attendant potential for environmental damage in sensitive mountain areas. The dams themselves have irreversible consequences for the permanently inundated valleys in that their terrestrial ecosystems are lost forever.

24.5.4 Mining

A variety of minerals and other materials suitable for mining, such as silica (eg Magaliesberg), iron (eg Thabazimbi), coal (eg Vryheid), zinc (eg Springbok-Pofadder area), copper (eg Okiep), granite (eg Bitterfontein–Garies), gravel (eg Tygerberg) lime (eg Langvlei and Hankey) and kaolin (eg Fish Hoek and Grahamstown), are found in mountain areas. Although the great importance of mining to the South African economy—contributing some 13,5 per cent of the GNP—is acknowledged, it should also be recognized that the processes of prospecting, extracting, concentrating, refining and transporting minerals have great potential for disrupting mountain environments. The abandonment of worked-out mines constitutes a further problem and has particularly detrimental consequences in mountain areas which are more prone to soil erosion and seepage and where the visual blight would be persistent and often visible from long distances.

24.5.5 Recreation

Although mountains have long been used for outdoor recreation, their attraction for this purpose has grown considerably. Their vastness and wilderness atmosphere stand in marked contrast to the stress of urbanization, and has led to an influx of tourists and an increased pressure upon the mountain environments concerned. Among the recreational activities are mountaineering in all its forms, picknicking, camping, fresh water fishing and swimming in mountain streams, horse riding, sight-seeing, hang gliding, off-road vehicle and rally driving and skiing. The establishment of holiday cottages, mountain resorts and hotels has also become more popular. Most of the above activities and development have some impact on the environment, depending upon the sensitivity of the area, the type of activity and the numbers of people involved. Soil erosion, water pollution, noise, disturbance of fauna and flora, as well as visual disturbance, constitute some of the problems.

24.6 SOUTH AFRICAN LEGISLATION: GENERAL REMARKS

On the whole, South African law does not deal with mountains as a geomorphological phenomenon, comparable, for instance, to rivers or the sea-shore, which are regulated extensively through legislation. Although an assortment of various legislative provisions may also relate to mountains, the only statute dealing exclusively with mountains and their conservation is the Mountain Catchment Areas Act 63 of 1970 (MCAA).

A precedent for mountain-related conservation legislation, nevertheless, had been set more than 300 years ago. Within 30 years of white settlement at the Cape, legislation had been introduced to protect some of Table Mountain's resources through prohibitions against the felling of trees[14] and against grazing.[15]

The need for action at central government level to conserve South Africa's water resources, particularly those provided by mountain catchments, has long been recognized and implemented to some extent through legislation aimed at controlling water, forestry and soil erosion. In other words, to the extent that mountains have been conserved, this, traditionally, has been due to their importance as water sources, not because of any inherent merit.

The first extensive Forest Act, i e the Cape Forest Act 28 of 1888, did not however, relate specifically to mountains or mountain catchments, nor did its post-union successor, the Forest Act 16 of 1913. The Forest and Veld Conservation Act 13 of 1941 and the Forest Act 72 of 1968 provided for the setting aside of state forests as nature reserves and protection forests, but it was only with the amendment of the latter Act during 1971 that provision was made for formal conservation status to be conferred on relatively large mountainous areas through the establishment of wilderness areas. This provision is retained in the present Forest Act 122 of 1984. It should be noted, nevertheless, that state forests which, in a sense, may also be viewed as conservation areas, have often included mountain land which has been conserved by the Department of Forestry as mountain catchments. In fact, government policy, framed during the early 1930s, led to the State's mountainous forestry estate gradually being extended through the purchase or expropriation of private land, in order to realise the above conservation goal.

Soil conservation legislation since the promulgation of the first Soil Conservation Act of 1946 has always been potentially applicable to mountains. Since, as will be shown, the overwhelming majority of mountains belong to private individuals and qualify as agricultural land, it is obvious that the effective enforcement of this legislation is of decisive importance to the conservation of mountains. The current Act is the Conservation of Agricultural Resources Act 43 of 1983 (CARA).

Water law, on the other hand, has never had any great significance as far as the conservation of mountain catchments is concerned. Although some provisions of the Water Act 54 of 1956 are potentially applicable to mountain catchments, they have hardly been used in this regard.

The MCAA was promulgated during 1970. Its purpose is to provide for the conservation, use, management and control of land situated in declared mountain

---

[14] Placaaten of 1/4 July 1671 and of 10 July 1676.

[15] Placaat of 23 February 1683.

catchment areas.[16] The underlying reason for the Act is the national importance of co-ordinated action at central government level to conserve South Africa's mountain catchment water sources, while recognition is also given to other compatible uses.[17] Reference has been made to other legislation that could have been used to the same effect, but the relevant legislation was applied by a number of different government departments and this was not conducive to uniformity of approach or to concerted and effective action;[18] neither did it lead to good relations with landowners who sometimes had to comply with conflicting directions issued by different administrative bodies. On account of its extensive experience with the management of mountain catchments on state land, in terms of the Forest Act, the Department of Forestry was eventually singled out as the government department to be responsible also for the conservation of mountain catchment areas in private ownership. During 1987 the administration of the Act devolved upon the nature conservation authorities of the various provincial administrations.

The conservation of mountains is furthered also by nature conservation legislation in so far as such legislation is applied to mountains.

In addition to the above legislation, which is conservation-orientated, a wide variety of other legislation may be applicable to land use in mountains. In the following sections an attempt is made to systematize and to set out the relevant legal provisions on the basis of the resources, activities or areas involved.

24.7 INDIVIDUAL CONTROL PROVISIONS

24.7.1 Conservation of soil, vegetation and water

The conservation of soil and of vegetation—with the ultimate purpose of conserving water sources—may be effected within declared mountain catchment areas by virtue of the MCAA. The nature conservation authorities of the various provincial administrations may have directions declared applicable, relating to the conservation, use, management and control of such land and to the prevention of soil erosion and the protection and treatment of the natural vegetation.[19] This power may be delegated.[20] Such direction, which must be made known in the *Government Gazette* or communicated by written notice to the owner and occupier of the land in question,[21] is binding upon such owner and occupier as well as their successors in title.[22] Refusal or failure to comply with a direction constitutes a criminal offence.[23]

Moreover, the administrative authority concerned may on its own perform or cause to be performed on the above land any act which has been ordered in terms of any direction or generally any act which it deems necessary in order to achieve any object of the Act.[24] Provision is made for the establishment of advisory committees to assist with the above matters.[25]

Outside declared mountain catchment areas, black areas and urban areas,[26] the principal applicable legislation is the CARA. For a detailed discussion of the Act, see chapter 10. This Act is aimed at the conservation of South Africa's natural agricultural

---

16 Long title of the Act.
17 *House of Assembly debates* 9 September 1970 para 3762 (Afrikaans text).
18 Ibid.
19 Section 3(1)(i)*(aa)* and *(bb)*.
20 Section 17.
21 Section 3(2)*(a)*.
22 Section 3(2)*(c)*.
23 Section 14*(b)*.
24 Section 12.
25 Section 6.
26 Cf s 2.

resources (ie the soil, natural vegetation and water sources[27]) by the maintenance of the production potential of the land, by the combating and prevention of erosion and weakening or destruction of the water sources and by the protection of natural vegetation.[28]

The CARA's provisions correspond with those of the MCAA in that the Minister of Agriculture may, likewise, prescribe control measures which must be complied with by land users[29] to whom they apply.[30] This power may not be delegated.[31] Such measures may relate to, inter alia, the cultivation of virgin soil, the utilization and protection of water sponges, water courses and water sources, the utilization and protection of vegetation, the grazing capacity of veld and, generally, any matter which the Minister may deem necessary or expedient in order to achieve the objects of the Act.[32] Control measures have, in fact, been prescribed through regulations.[33] Such measures, relate to, inter alia, the cultivation of land with a slope,[34] the protection of cultivated land against erosion,[35] the utilization and protection of water sponges and water courses,[36] the utilization and protection of veld,[37] the grazing capacity of veld[38] and the number of animals that may be kept on veld.[39] Failure to comply with a control measure constitutes an offence.[40] Unlike the MCAA, the CARA contains yet a further provision empowering the executive officer,[41] who may delegate his functions,[42] by means of a direction to order a land user to comply with an applicable control measure.[43] Such direction, as in the case of the MCAA, is binding upon land users and their successors in title[44] and must be published by notice in the *Gazette* or be contained in a written notice and served upon the land user concerned.[45] Refusal to receive a direction or refusal or failure to comply therewith constitutes yet a further offence.[46]

In similar fashion to the MCAA, the CARA empowers the Minister to perform or cause to be performed on any land any act which may have been the subject of a control measure.[47] Likewise, provision is made for the establishment of an advisory body, the conservation advisory board.[48]

24.7.2 Control of afforestation

Control of afforestation in mountains can be exercised in terms of various Acts. If the area in question is a declared mountain catchment area such control may be effected through the MCAA which provides for the relevant provincial nature conservation authorities to declare directions applicable with respect to the conservation use,

---

[27] Section 1 (xviii).
[28] Section 3.
[29] Cf s 1(xiv) for the definition of 'land user'.
[30] Section 6(1).
[31] Section 26.
[32] Section 6(2).
[33] GN R1048 of 25 May 1984.
[34] Regulation 3.
[35] Regulation 4 and 5.
[36] Regulation 7.
[37] Regulation 9.
[38] Regulation 10.
[39] Regulation 11.
[40] Sections 6(5) and 23(1)*(a)*.
[41] Cf s 4(1).
[42] Section 4(3)*(a)*.
[43] Section 7(1).
[44] Section 7(4)*(a)*.
[45] Section 7(3)*(a)* and *(b)*.
[46] Sections 7(6) and 23(1)*(a)*.
[47] Section 11(1).
[48] Section 17.

management and control of such land.[49] This provision seems wide enough to encompass control of afforestation.

The CARA could likewise possibly be applied to achieve the above purpose. The Minister of Agriculture is empowered to impose obligatory control measures upon land users, relating to the regulation of the flow pattern of run-off water, the utilization and protection of the vegetation and generally any matter which the Minister may deem necessary or expedient in order that the objects of the Act (which include the weakening of water resources), may be achieved.[50]

The principal form of control in practice over the use of land for purposes of afforestation is effected through the Forest Act. Such land use is subject to the approval of the Director-General: Environment Affairs.[51] Moverover, the Minister of Environment Affairs may in respect of land which in terms of the Act is being or may be used for the planting of trees to produce timber, prohibit the afforestation or the reafforestation of the land concerned or may prohibit any other act or direct the landowner to take any other steps which may be necessary for the protection of any natural water source.[52]

24.7.3 Control of invader plants

The principal legislation aimed at the control of invader plants (weeds or pest plants) is the CARA. Intruding vegetation may also be dealt with by virtue of the MCAA, while a very limited form of control over invader plants is also provided by some provincial nature conservation ordinances. This issue is dealt with in chapter 11.

24.7.4 Fire control

Fire control in a declared mountain catchment area is effected in terms of the MCAA. Provision is made for the declaration of a fire protection plan to be applicable to land situated in such an area.[53] This plan, which may be amended,[54] must provide for the regulation or prohibition of veld burning and the prevention, control and extinguishing of veld and forest fires.[55] A fire protection committee may be appointed,[56] in which case its functions in relation to the execution of the fire protection plan must also be included in that plan.[57] A fire protection plan must be published by notice in the *Gazette*[58] and a copy may be served on individual owners or occupiers of land.[59] It is binding upon every owner and occupier of land to which it applies, as well as upon their successors in title.[60] Contravention or failure to comply with any provision of a fire protection plan constitutes an offence.[61]

Fire control on agricultural land outside mountain catchment areas is provided for in the CARA. Control measures relating to the prevention and control of veld fires, which the Minister is empowered to prescribe,[62] have been established through regulations.[63]

---

[49] Section 3(1)*(a)*(i)*(aa)*.
[50] Section 6(2)*(f)*, *(q)* and *(p)*.
[51] Section 7(1).
[52] Section 8(1). Cf also s 8(2).
[53] Section 8(1).
[54] Section 9.
[55] Section 8(2)*(a)* and *(b)*.
[56] Section 7.
[57] Section 8(2)*(c)*.
[58] Section 8(3)*(a)*.
[59] Section 8(3)*(b)*.
[60] Section 8(4).
[61] Section 14*(e)*.
[62] Section 6(2)*(j)*.
[63] Regulation 12 GN R1048 of 25 May 1984.

Extensive provision for fire control is made also in the Forest Act.[64] The Minister of Environment Affairs may declare any area to be a fire control area or any two or more such areas to be a fire control region.[65] Fire control committees and regional fire control committees, which must prepare fire protection schemes,[66] may be established by the Minister.[67] The Minister may approve, or amend and approve, a fire protection scheme and must direct that it applies in the area in question,[68] whereafter it must be made available for inspection,[69] and a copy thereof may be served on any owner of land to which it applies.[70] An approved fire protection scheme binds every owner of land to which it applies as well as his successors in title.[71] Failure to comply with a provision of such scheme amounts to an offence.[72] Further provisions relating to fire control include those which apply to the making of fire belts within as well as outside fire control areas,[73] and to extraordinary precautions in times of fire hazard.[74] Finally, a number of specific provisions deal with actions related to the causing of fire.[75]

Three different administrative bodies thus administer three different Acts providing for fire control. However, fires do not respect these different jurisdictions, and mountains should not be artificially subdivided for the purpose of fire control. The decisive issue would seem to be the policy underlying the relevant fire protection plan (MCCA), fire protection scheme (Forest Act) or control measure (CARA). However, the various purposes for which fire protection is effected may vary according to the different requirements of the respective bodies involved, leading to different fire protection policies; this may not be conducive to the effective conservation of mountains. Moreover, the spreading of resources available for fire control among different bodies may be counter-productive in that it may lead to duplication of services, equipment and personnel. A good case, accordingly, can be made out for the rationalization or co-ordination of fire control, at least as far as mountains—where special circumstances apply—are concerned.

Finally, reference may be made to the respective provisions of the above Acts dealing with the limitation of liability. These provisions purport to absolve the State, its officials and other persons from liability for anything done in good faith in the exercise of their functions in terms of the legislation in question.[76] Fire control usually involves controlled burning, an activity which is potentially dangerous and which has, in fact, often caused damage to landowners. The issue which would presumably feature prominently where such damage was caused would be that of negligence. Limitation clauses should be interpreted restrictively since they involve an interference with individual rights. It would accordingly seem that they would not cover negligent acts.[77] This means that in addition to the direct costs of fire control, which in state mountain catchments and declared mountain catchment areas amounts to well over R1 million annually, the State should also reckon with potential claims for damages—a factor which might serve to inhibit fire control.

---

[64] Part VI.
[65] Section 18(1).
[66] Section 20(1).
[67] Section 19(1).
[68] Section 20(3).
[69] Section 20(4)*(a)*.
[70] Section 20(4)*(b)*.
[71] Section 20(5).
[72] Section 75(7)*(b)*.
[73] Sections 22 and 24. Cf s 75(8) for offences.
[74] Section 25.
[75] Section 75(2).
[76] Section 18 of the MCAA, s 87 of the Forest Act and s 28 of the CARA.
[77] Cf *Mjuqu v Johannesburg City Council* 1973 (3) SA 421 (A) 441E–H; *Kenly Farms (Pty) Ltd v Minister of Agriculture* 1984 (1) SA 406 (C) 410D–G.

24.7.5 Control of flower harvesting

Whereas the various provincial nature conservation ordinances generally regulate the picking, purchase and sale of indigenous plants, the Cape Nature and Environmental Conservation Ordinance 19 of 1974 makes special provision for the registration and licensing of persons as flora growers and flora sellers, authorizing them to sell protected plants on the premises to which the certificate of registration relates.[78]

24.7.6 Mountains in protected areas

Comprehensive conservation management is practised in respect of mountains which are situated within protected areas such as national parks (National Parks Act 57 of 1976), provincial and local nature reserves (provincial nature conservation ordinances 8 of 1969 (OFS), 15 of 1974 (Natal), 19 of 1974 (Cape) and 12 of 1983 (Transvaal)), and forest nature reserves and wilderness areas (Forest Act). In fact, wilderness areas have been declared almost exclusively in respect of state mountain catchments. Mountain catchment areas also fall within the category of protected areas. All the above protected areas are declared almost exclusively in respect of state land, which greatly facilitates their management and control.

Three further protected areas, which may also include mountains, should be mentioned. However, these areas comprise mainly or exclusively private land and conservation management is not practised on the same scale as in those areas in the first category. They are private nature reserves (provincial nature conservation ordinances), protected natural environments (declared in terms of the Environment Conservation Act 73 of 1989) and national monuments (National Monuments Act 28 of 1969). Two of the three existing protected natural environments, i e the Magaliesberg (101 000 ha) and the Cape Peninsula (29 000 ha) as well as at least one national monument, i e Table Mountain (5 520 ha) have been established mainly or exclusively for the conservation of mountains. See, generally, chapter 27.

24.7.7 Mountains in defence areas

The management and control of mountains in defence areas—which comprise approximately 443 000 ha of land—are provided for by the Defence Act 44 of 1957. Wide powers are conferred upon the Minister of Defence to control land which is subject to military control.[79] Moreover, policy directives stipulate that nature conservation is a secondary objective in respect of such land and that management plans regarding this objective must be submitted annually.

24.7.8 Control of recreation

Apart from general control of the recreational use of conservation areas, formal legislative recognition has been given to control through the National Hiking Way System over hiking ways which have been constructed mainly on state forest land in mountain catchments.[80]

Control over the availability of state mountain land for recreational purposes, depends generally upon the policy of the relevant administrative authority, mainly that of the provincial directorates of nature conservation. Access to such areas and the undertaking there of any recreational activities, depend upon the permission of the public body involved.[81]

Control over recreational activities on private land could, as far as mountains are concerned, be exercised indirectly in terms of the general provisions of the MCAA and

---

[78] Sections 65 and 66 and part V of the regulations PN 955 of 29 August 1975.
[79] Sections 76 and 87.
[80] Part VII of the Forest Act.
[81] Cf s 73(1)*(a)*(xi) of the Forest Act.

the CARA concerned with land use and the conservation of soil, vegetation and water.

The establishment of holiday townships, also in mountains, for which no separate provision is made, is regulated mainly by the various provincial ordinances concerned with town and land-use planning,[82] while the erection of buildings is generally controlled in terms of provincial legislation relavant to local government.[83] It would seem that such control can also be exercised, in a somewhat indirect fashion, through the MCAA where declared mountain catchment areas are concerned, and in terms of the CARA as regards agricultural land.

Finally, the provisions of the Physical Planning Act 125 of 1991 could be made applicable to mountain regions. See chapter 28.

24.7.9 Control of mining

The protection of the environment in which prospecting or mining occurs, is provided for through regulations issued by virtue of the Mines and Works Act 27 of 1956[84] and now applicable by virtue of the Minerals Act 50 of 1991. See chapter 15 for a full discussion of these and other relevant provisions.

24.7.10 Control over the provision of infrastructure services

See, generally, chapter 28.

24.8 ADMINISTRATIVE FUNCTIONS RELATED TO CONSERVATION MANAGEMENT

In order to assess their potential effectiveness, it may be useful to analyse the different types of administrative functions exercised by the various government departments and other administrative bodies concerned with the conservation of mountains. These functions should not be viewed in isolation, since they are frequently exercised in combination with one another.

24.8.1 State conservation management

24.8.1.1 *State-owned mountains*

The most comprehensive powers conferred upon administrative bodies usually relate to those instances in which the body in question performs its functions in respect of mountains held in state ownership. In these instances the bodies themselves regulate, extensively and professionally, and in the public interest, the use of the mountain area concerned. The Forest Act thus empowers the Ministers of Environment Affairs and of Water Affairs and the relevant provincial bodies concerned with forestry to control and manage state forests, which include some 1,7 million ha of mountain catchments.

Where mountains are included in other state land enjoying a conservation status, the relevant authority also has extensive control over the mountains concerned, e g mountains included in national parks and provincial and local nature reserves.

The power of direct performance is a most comprehensive one and enables the administrative body concerned to pursue the public interest in the conservation of mountains to the utmost. Given a sound management policy and adequate resources to implement that policy effectively, few problems over which humans have control should arise.

---

[82] Cf generally Meyer 'Townships and town planning' in Joubert (ed) *The law of South Africa* vol 28 (1987).

[83] Cf generally Meyer *Local government law* Vol 2 Part 4 (1983)

[84] Section 12(1). The standing regulations are contained in GN R992 of 26 June 1970, while the relevant regulations were added by GN R537 of 21 March 1980.

24.8.1.2 *Private mountains*

Even where the State does not own the mountain area concerned, administrative bodies are sometimes empowered to perform the necessary actions in respect of land held in private ownership. Both the MCAA[85] and the CARA[86] empower the respective administrative bodies themselves, out of money appropriated by Parliament for that purpose, to perform any action in respect of private land, which action may have been the subject of a direction or control measure imposed upon individual landowners.

24.8.2 State control of management by individuals

Where private mountains are concerned the administrative body in question mostly does not itself perform the conservation action required, but sees to it that that action is performed by the individual to whom the legislative provision is made applicable. Both the MCAA[87] and the CARA[88] thus empower the respective Ministers to issue directions or control measures with which the individuals concerned are obliged to comply. These obligations can be of either a positive or negative nature, ie the individual concerned is compelled either to do something or to refrain from undertaking a certain action. The administration of the relevant legislation thus usually means that the administrative body sees to it that the individuals who are subject to the legislation are familiar with their obligations and that they comply with the relevant provisions. Considerable effort is normally expended in assisting persons to comply with their obligations. Failure to comply with the relevant directions or control measures amounts to an offence,[89] which means that although the administrative body concerned may assist in gathering and supplying information against the transgressor, the primary role in bringing the offender to justice is played by the bodies responsible for the administration of the criminal law.

When it is borne in mind that some 9 700 000 ha (or 85 per cent of the total area of our major mountain catchments) are held in private ownership, compared to the 1,7 million ha of state mountain catchments, the importance of the above measures becomes obvious. In other words, for the legislation to succeed there must be a determined effort by the administrative body in question to enforce its legislation. This means that where the relevant legislation empowers it to bring private land within the purview of the legislative disposition by declaring the Act applicable—such as is the case with the declaration of mountain catchment areas—this power should be exercised. Moreover, it should impose the required obligations upon the individuals concerned and vigorously monitor their compliance.

However, the powers conferred by the MCAA—the principal statute aimed at the conservation of mountain catchments—have not been used extensively. Only 6,4 per cent of all the major mountain catchments on private land have after some 20 years been declared in terms of the Act which means that the Act presently does not apply to some 9,1 million ha.

A further indication that the Act is not being implemented is that its provisions have hardly ever been used in respect of those areas that have been declared. It comes as a considerable surprise to learn that not one single direction has yet been issued in terms of the Act during its entire 20 years of existence. In practice the Minister (now the chief directorates of nature conservation of the various provinces), relying upon the advice furnished by advisory committees (which are appointed by virtue of the Act[90]),

---

[85] Section 12.
[86] Section 11(1).
[87] Section 3.
[88] Section 6.
[89] Section 14*(b)* of the MCAA and ss 6(5), 7(6) and 23(1) of the CARA.
[90] Section 6.

communicates land-use instructions to landowners in the form of guidelines. These guidelines, however, have no binding legal force, which means that reliance has thus far been placed upon voluntary compliance by landowners.

24.8.3 Formulation of policy

The formulation of policy is of the greatest importance as far as the conservation of mountain catchments is concerned. Although the interdepartmental committee on the conservation of mountain catchments in its report of 1961 recognized an existing policy on the conservation of mountain catchments, its own formulation of a national policy was the first comprehensive policy in this regard. The only legislation which provides for environmental policy is the Environment Conservation Act 73 of 1989 according to which the Minister of Environment Affairs is empowered to determine the general policy to be applied with regard to, inter alia, the protection of natural systems and the promotion of ecosystems as well as the effective application of natural resources.[91] This authorization would seem to make allowance for the determination of policy regarding mountains. The relevant provisions are discussed in chapter 7.

24.8.4 Mountain zoning

Human beings require that the natural environment should remain in good order to assure their survival. At the same time they need to exploit that environment for their survival. Zoning may serve as a mediator and synthesizer between the often conflicting needs of humans and the environment.

Mountain zoning, which may serve as a powerful planning tool, requires an initial thorough analysis of the available environmental resources, their nature, extent and scarcity, followed by an appraisal of their significance to humans and the formulation of management objectives to strive for sustainable utilization and conservation of the resources.

Mountain zoning may be perceived as the allocation of resources in such a manner as to obtain maximum efficiency, while paying heed to the nature and needs of the natural environment and the welfare of the community, thereby ensuring the greatest benefit to all.

There exist significant character and user differences between mountain land and other areas such as deserts, the bushveld and the coast. Mountains are more complex, variable and dynamic than other land areas due to their physiographic and geological diversity, the altitudinal and climatic variations and the effect of gravity and steepness on the rate of erosion. Mountains require special zoning and specialized management to cater for their special and in some case unique needs and uses.

24.8.4.1 *Zoning as a holistic concept*

A surge of interrelatedness-awareness seems currently to be sweeping the world—a realization that everything is connected to everything else, although not equally strongly. This is evidenced in changing social, economic, political and environmental attitudes. This shift is also affecting planning concepts: the rigorous observance of pre-ordained zoning schemes is being replaced by more flexible viable policies which place emphasis on integration, diversity, multiple use, public participation and review zoning.

Zoning is a form of distribution of land between competing uses and may therefore be perceived as analytical, compartmentalized and reductionist, but if an integrated management approach is applied, then zoning may be perceived as a holistic concept. Regional planning has in the past tended to be more holistic in its thinking than urban

[91] Section 2.

planning as it concerns itself with the spatially oriented macro-environment. This holism is dependent on the roles of the parts (differing zones) being analysed, understood and synthesized in a creative way with the overall objectives of the whole (the mountain range and the impacted area). The zones are therefore managed for their specific needs as well as the needs of the entire mountain range and beyond, and the management of the mountain range should synthesize with the objectives of the zones. In this way the functions of the zones are influenced by the overall functions of the mountain range, and the functions of the mountain range are influenced by those of the zones. Systems can malfunction if the balance between subsystem welfare and total system welfare is disturbed. The objectives for the subsystem should not be allowed to subvert the objectives of the total system. Conversely, too much central control at the expense of subsystems will create problems. Mountain management should not be directed at preserving individual species and organisms but should rather attempt wisely to manage the complex web of relationships within and between the zones. Provided the management is creative, reappraisive and alive to changes, and brought about by physical observation, scientific research, and environmental, economic and social needs, then a management synthesis should develop between the zones and the whole mountain range. This is a reiterative process which should gradually and consistently evolve towards the most effective management, taking into account all the factors concerned with the conservation and utilization of mountain resources. The reductionist zoning tool is therefore holistically employed and executed.

24.8.4.2 *Some uses and advantages of zoning over natural resource lands*

- Zoning can be used to establish and protect large regional land units, such as wilderness areas and national parks (a traditional use).
- Extensive mountain areas may be divided into differing management zones, such as those requiring sustained-yield policies, total conservation zones, water-catchment zones, intensive use zones and wildlife-management zones.
- Resource allocation maps can be prepared which spatially define the natural resources of the mountains. These may be used in evaluations for zoning and management objectives.
- Geographical information systems, remote sensing and computer mapping are technologies which are very suitable for facilitating the preparation of zoning maps. They can be used in subtle ways, such as determining carrying capacities and watershed quality.
- Zoning means more than securing management objectives. It can provide security for resource users, minimize land-use conflicts and prevent uncontrolled development and ad hoc decision-making.
- Zoning represents a flexible process through the incorporation of the latest scientific and social data in order to review and adapt management techniques. This will ensure that the management of mountains will be prospective and not reactive.
- Zoning allows management roles to be clearly defined and can facilitate their proper execution. Zoning is the result of an analysis of the resources and the allocation of roles and management objectives to mountains, specifying the degree and type of utilization to be permitted and the degree and type of protection that is required.
- Zoning has the advantage of bringing the specific needs and the question of where they are required to the attention of mountain managers.
- Without zoning a general management malaise can exist, with little attention being given to specific needs of the natural resources of the mountains and no one being held responsible for inappropriate management and utilization decisions.
- Once a binding zoning plan exists, it can form the legal basis for actions by landowners, developers, farmers and the authorities.

TABLE 24.2
Mountain zoning synopsis

category	selection criteria	management objectives
mountain conservation zone	endangered species, special habitats vulnerable to human interference.	optimum protection.
mountain feature zone	distinctive natural or anthropogenic features of special interest.	to protect feature. to provide and control public access.
mountain wilderness zone	pristine, unmodified mountain or canyon land containing major ecosystems or important water catchments.	conservation for sustained clear, unpolluted water supply. to protect genetic resources. to provide recreation, scientific research.
recreation zone	reasonably benign, interesting mountain land suitable for hiking. provision of facilities.	to provide for outdoor recreation. conservation of water sources and natural environment. to promote environmental awareness.
social development zone	base of mountain at pool or river. vehicular access needed. picnic area, holiday resort, mountain village.	managed for intensive recreational use. to provide social and recreational enjoyment. to control water pollution. to promote environmental awareness.
mountain sport zone	mountain terrain suitable for specific sport types (skiing, fishing, mountaineering, cycling, orienteering).	to safeguard the utilization of the land for sport. to prevent user conflict. conservation of natural environment and water sources.
multiple-use catchment zone	sites and corridors for infrastructural services, afforestation etc. appropriate, less environmentally sensitive land.	comprehensive management needed to achieve minimum degradation of natural resources.
transitional management zone (buffers)	a strip of land adjacent to zones. width dependent upon the objectives of the zones.	to promote the flexible transition of objectives between zones, or used as a buffer.
indigenous settlement zone	mountain catchment land either settled on or used by indigenous peoples.	through education and example to promote sustainable land-use practices. to prevent erosion and conserve water sources.
mountain national park (a combination of appropriate categories)	selection of appropriate land containing outstanding landscapes. suitable for multiple uses: intensive use, hiking, wilderness.	zoned and managed in accordance with the zoning scheme. to conserve sources and natural systems. to promote tourism through recreation, inspiration and education.
national monument	not specific to mountains. a natural or artificial feature of major significance to the nation.	protected for posterity.
biosphere reserve	important natural resources not confined to mountains. the scale of human involvement, exploitation and utilization of mountains and surroundings justifies forming a biosphere reserve.	integration of mountain zones and surrounding lands with widely differing management objectives. bound together by a common policy of sustainable use. all users brought together to resolve conflicts. management objectives of each zone to apply.
world heritage site	an area of outstanding universal value. habitats where rare or endangered species or communities of plants or animals survive in a pristine environment.	managed to conserve the natural resources for mankind. responsibility to the international community.

24.8.4.3 *Proposed categories of zoning for South African mountains*

Zoning involves an analysis of resources, an assessment of their present and future importance to man, establishment of the goals to be achieved and the development of management strategies to achieve the objectives. Appropriate categories of zoning can be selected to meet the required management objectives for a particular mountain area. Table 24.2 describes the zoning categories:

24.9 MOUNTAIN CLUB OF SOUTH AFRICA AND OTHER VOLUNTARY CONSERVATION ORGANIZATIONS

Mountaineers and hikers are the prime recreational users of mountains. While the first recorded ascent of Table Mountain dates back to the early 16th century,[92] it was only towards the end of the 19th century that mountains started to be used to any great extent for recreational climbing and hiking. Since then the number of people using the mountains has increased steadily, so that today climbers and hikers will be found on Table Mountain on all but the worst weather days. Nevertheless, because of South Africa's rich endowment of mountain regions, it is possible, even today, for a party to spend several days in some of the more remote mountain areas without seeing any other people.

This recreational use of mountains has naturally led to concern among mountaineers for their preservation in pristine form, and even to a resentment against other types of users (such as those using mountain bicycles, or trail bikes). Thus mountaineers have from the early days, often for selfish reasons, been active in campaigning for the conservation of mountains and for their protection from unwanted (often interpreted as any form of) development.

The Mountain Club of South Africa (MCSA), founded in 1891, is the oldest amateur body in South Africa with an interest in conservation. What started off with a gathering of enthusiasts in a Cape Town cafe has grown into a national body with 13 sections representing more than 4 000 mountaineers and climbers throughout South Africa and Namibia. While its prime function has been to promote mountaineering in South Africa, its members have always been involved in conserving our mountains and in protecting them from the ravages of fellow human beings.

The club's conservation activities over the past 100 years have ranged from firefighting and combating alien vegetation, to proposing legislation and acting as a pressure group for mountain conservation. The club campaigned for the declaration of the Cape Peninsula and Magaliesberg nature areas (now transformed into protected natural environments) and its members serve on the management committees of both. They also serve as honorary forest wardens and advise on the conservation of the Drakensberg.

A number of other voluntary organizations are also actively concerned with the conservation of South Africa's mountains. The Habitat Council was, together with the MCSA, instrumental in the establishment of the Magaliesberg Protection Association in 1975, and organized a conference on mountain environments in May of the following year. The conservation of the Drakensberg has been a focus of attention of both the Habitat Council and the Wildlife Society. For example, they were involved with the Natal Parks Board and the KwaZulu and QuaQua authorities in resolving the question of the management of the escarpment area of the Drakensberg in the Mont-Aux-Sources region.

A key conference on the Magaliesberg, organized by the Roodepoort and Krugersdorp Centres of the Wildlife Society, in conjunction with the Magaliesberg Protection Association, at Hunters Rest on 17 and 18 April 1980, shaped the future

[92] See generally Burman *A peak to climb* (1966).

management policy for this range and led to the establishment of the Magaliesberg Management Committee by the Administrator of the Transvaal. The Wildlife Society is also involved in a project for establishing a conservation management structure for the Blouberg in the northern Transvaal.

The voluntary organizations serve as the eyes and ears for conservation, particularly in mountain areas where their remoteness and inaccessibility make it very difficult for the authorities to detect problems and abuses. From time to time the MCSA is involved in purchasing key pieces of mountain land in order to conserve them and to ensure access by its members. These pieces of land are managed as wilderness areas by the club, including the imposition and enforcement of limitations on the numbers and behaviour of visitors. Other conservation organizations, notably the South African Nature Foundation, have also been involved in purchasing mountain land, but have usually entrusted its management to the appropriate authorities.

24.10 CONCLUSION: TOWARDS UNIFORM ADMINISTRATION OF MOUNTAIN CATCHMENTS

While there seems to be no reasonable prospect of all mountains being uniformly controlled, it does seem advisable that at least all major mountain catchments should be subject to uniform and comprehensive management by a single administrative authority.

24.10.1 The interrelationship between the MCAA and the CARA

Most mountain catchments are presently conserved and administered by different administrative bodies in terms of three different Acts, i e the MCAA, the Forest Act and the CARA.

The first two Acts, or parts relevant to mountain catchments, are in practice administered by the various provincial bodies entrusted with nature conservation, in terms of a devolution of functions. The Forest Act applies to mountain catchments situated on state forest land, while the MCAA is relevant to mountain catchment areas on private land which have been declared in terms of the Act. Although, as has been pointed out, in practice different powers of management apply depending upon whether state or private land is involved, all the abovementioned mountain catchments are administered according to more or less homogeneous management plans by a single authority. A difficulty, however, is the principle applicable in the case of the devolution of powers, i e that the central government department is supposed to establish the policy in terms of which the relevant provincial authorities are to administer the legislation in question. This may lead to a further diversion of functions and funds and may prove to be difficult, if not impossible, to apply in practice. Moreover, the management of mountain catchments on private land cannot be of the same intensity as that of mountain catchments on state land. As far as private land is concerned, the State's role is, in practice, restricted to the conservation of water sources, while the private landowner in most instances carries on with his existing land use such as agriculture, albeit subject to potential control in terms of the Act. As far as state-owned mountain catchments are concerned, the overriding management objective is water-source conservation with which all other uses must be in harmony. In practice all state-owned mountain catchments, unlike private land, constitute protected areas in the strict sense.

The other major statute relevant to the conservation of mountain catchments is the CARA, which is administered by the Minister of Agriculture through the Directorate of Resource Conservation. This Act applies to almost all mountain catchments, other than those mentioned above. In particular it governs the 9,1 million ha of major mountain catchments on private land that have not been declared in terms of the MCAA as well as almost all minor mountain catchments.

Both the MCAA[93] and the CARA[94] contain provisions aimed at the prevention of overlap between the application of the similar precepts of the respective statutes: Provisions of the latter Act do not apply to land situated within a declared mountain catchment area.

24.10.2 Revocation of the MCAA not desirable

The provisions of these two Acts are, in fact, of a similar nature and either one may, in principle, be applied to achieve the same purpose. Suggestions have accordingly been made to revoke the MCAA and to use only provisions of the CARA to achieve the aims of mountain catchment conservation.[95] Moreover, while less than 7 per cent of our major mountain catchments have been subjected to the MCAA, more than 90 per cent of such catchments are regulated in terms of the CARA. To be sure, uniform management of all mountain catchments by a single administrative body certainly seems to be a desirable goal. Management of different mountain catchments by different administrative bodies applying different legal provisions is not conducive to effective control. Also, the dispensation applicable to financial relief available to private landowners obliged to comply with the relevant restrictive legislation, is different, depending upon which Act is applicable. While the MCAA provides for grants as well as for compensation and tax exemption,[96] the CARA provides only for subsidies and certain other forms of practical assistance.[97]

It is submitted, nevertheless, that the repeal of the MCAA would not be in the interest of mountain conservation. Should the MCAA be repealed, South Africa would in principle revert to the situation that existed before 1970. At that stage there was no specific mountain-related conservation legislation in existence. To be sure, the Soil Conservation Acts of 1946 and 1969—which were superseded by the CARA—could have been used to conserve mountain catchments. In fact, the interdepartmental committee on the conservation of mountain catchments in its 1961 report[98] was of the opinion that the then existing laws were adequate and that there was no need for further legislation, although there was room for improvement as far as the application of existing legislation was concerned. A further factor to be borne in mind is that the CARA considerably improved the Soil Conservation Act of 1969. However, during the second-reading debate on the Mountain Catchment Areas Bill (1970) the responsible Minister indicated that it was considered essential that mountain catchments should be conserved in a co-ordinated fashion at central government level by the Department of Forestry.[99] Parliament judged that this aim could best be achieved by the introduction of new legislation.

If there are shortcomings in the MCAA and its practical application, the logical approach seems to be that they should be remedied by amendments to the Act and by the provision of adequate funds, personnel, etc, rather than by the abolition of the Act. In any case, both the MCAA and the CARA, as has been shown, are implemented through similar administrative procedures. Nevertheless, the MCAA may be more expensive to administer than the CARA in view of the former's provision for compensation for the State's curtailment of land use by the owner or occupier.

The Department of Forestry, and, after the devolution of powers, especially the various provincial administrations' directorates of nature conservation, qualify as true

---

[93] Section 20.

[94] Section 2(1)*(c)*.

[95] Jordaan *Multiple-use management in fynbos mountain catchment areas* Paper delivered at a symposium on research in mountain catchments, Jonkershoek 11–12 November 1987 58–9.

[96] Sections 4, 5 and 10.

[97] Sections 8, 10 and 11.

[98] Para 137.

[99] *House of Assembly debates* 9 September 1970 para 3762 (Afrikaans text).

conservation agencies. Extensive experience and expertise have been gained in the management of mountain catchments, spanning some 60 years as regards state land and some 20 years for private land. Moreover, considerable success has been achieved in respect of the combined management of mountain catchments which encompass both state and private land. If the MCAA should be repealed it would mean that such combined management by a single conservation body would no longer be possible, since, although state land would continue to be managed by the various provincial nature conservation directorates, all private land, including that surrounding or adjoining state mountain catchments, would then be administered by the Department of Agriculture in terms of the CARA.

It is true that the CARA is aimed at the conservation of our natural agricultural resources (the soil, water sources and vegetation[100]) through the maintenance of the production potential of land, the combating and prevention of erosion and weakening or destruction of water sources and the protection of vegetation and combating of weeds and invader plants.[101] However, the Act presupposes the use of land for agricultural purposes and this necessarily brings about a greater or lesser degree of deterioration of the land. Although the stimulation of land use and the conservation of land may possibly be reconciled theoretically, this is very difficult to realize in practice, especially where it concerns mountain catchments which have a relatively low agricultural potential and are extremely vulnerable to disturbance. The point is that the Department of Agriculture cannot be regarded as a conservation agency in the strict sense of the word since it has a dual assignment: on the one hand it is supposed to conserve our natural agricultural resources, but at the same time it is required to stimulate the use or exploitation of those resources.

Moreover, the natural agricultural resources are not of importance only to agriculture. It has been shown that mountain catchments are conserved mainly as water sources. This relatively scarce resource has become of vital importance for development in South Africa. With the expansion of industry (including mining) and urbanization, water as a resource is assuming increasing importance. The allocation of water to agriculture, in fact, has decreased proportionally over the last 25 years from some 83 per cent to about 67 per cent of the total water consumption. Mountain catchments as our primary water sources accordingly, should not be viewed as an exclusively agricultural resource, but should indeed be managed in the broad national interest by a body whose primary concern is conservation-orientated. In other words, the status quo, in terms of which mountain catchments are administered by the provincial directorates of nature conservation, by virtue of a statute directed exclusively at the conservation of mountain catchments, should be maintained.

24.10.3 Extended implementation of the MCAA

It is submitted that ample justification exists for subjecting at least all the major mountain catchments on private land to the provisions of the MCAA to enable the responsible authority to apply the Act's provisions to the relevant landowners. The promulgation of this Act during 1970 signalled a new approach to mountain catchments in that it attempted to provide a legislative framework for the uniform management of such areas by making private land subject to control by the Department of Forestry (now the various provincial administrations), which, had more than half a century before, been chosen by the government to manage mountain catchments. It is therefore submitted that the MCAA be fully implemented. This means that the area subject to the Act should be extended drastically so as to include all significant mountain catchments on private land, as has been recommended by the President's Council in its

[100] Section 1(xviii).
[101] Section 3.

Report on a national environmental management system.[102] Moreover, the provisions of the Act should be used to oblige land users to act responsibly as far as the conservation of their land is concerned. Finally, the responsible authority should act vigorously to secure compliance with its directions.

24.10.4 Continued role of the CARA

However, even if the MCAA's implementation is extended substantially, it seems unlikely that the Act would be used to control all mountain catchments in South Africa. Many mountains do not constitute nationally significant catchments. This applies particularly to the more arid regions. If the conservation of mountains remains linked to the safeguarding of national water resources, the MCAA probably should continue to be restrictively applied. As has been suggested, however, it should encompass at least all significant mountain catchments held in private ownership.

Almost all minor mountain catchments, indeed most remaining mountains, as agricultural land, would accordingly remain under the jurisdiction of the Department of Agriculture. The CARA should therefore continue to be implemented in respect of such mountains. This means that the existing dichotomy would persist, but that the MCAA should assume far greater importance than it does at present and that our major mountain catchments would be managed uniformly.

24.10.5 Integrated catchment management

Reference has already been made to the fact that mountain catchments are managed primarily for the conservation of water resources, an eminently rational approach, since mountains almost invariably constitute our principal sources of fresh water. If the intention then is to conserve water resources by conserving catchment areas, the logical approach would seem to be to manage the entire catchment of a given river or rivers as a whole. It does not make sense to isolate one part of a river's catchment—even the most important part—and to subject that area to extensive control, while other parts of the catchment area are not also comprehensively and uniformly managed by the same administrative authority.

According to this approach, it may be argued that the Department of Water Affairs and Forestry is, in theory, the ideal body to manage such integrated catchments. Indeed, the Department of Water Affairs has attempted to co-ordinate the activities of bodies concerned with catchment management. At central government level some degree of consultation takes place in the processing of applications for various permits and exemptions. At regional and local level co-ordination is limited to the activities of voluntary bodies such as conservation committees established in terms of the CARA and catchment associations, which are voluntary non-statutory bodies, representing users of soil and water in the relevant catchment area.[103] The task of co-ordinating the activities of all government and other administrative bodies as well as those of all voluntary bodies, which are related to the management of an entire catchment area, would seem to be awesome indeed. Firstly, co-ordination, in essence, must rely upon the voluntary co-operation of all the parties involved. Futhermore, it may prove to be difficult in practice to identify entire catchments and manage them effectively, bearing in mind that one is often dealing with an area subject to intense and varied land-use patterns established over a long period.

Mountain catchments are at least more readily identifiable and generally have not been subjected to development on nearly the same scale as most other catchment areas. In other words, for practical reasons we may have to be content with management

---

[102] PC 1/1991 para 5.7.6.

[103] *Management of the water resources of the Republic of South Africa* Department of Water Affairs (1986) para 6.17.

of mountain catchments in relative isolation. On catchment control generally, see chapter 13.

24.10.6 Final remarks

The past three decades have each witnessed a major event which underscored the importance of mountain conservation in South Africa. The pioneering event was the investigation and the 1961 report of the interdepartmental committee on the conservation of mountain catchments in South Africa, followed by the promulgation of the MCAA in 1970. Next followed a conference on mountain environments, organized by the Habitat Council and held in Johannesburg during 13 and 14 May 1976. More recently, during 6 to 8 March 1989, the Council for the Environment convened a workshop in Franschhoek on a national policy and strategy for the conservation and utilization of mountain areas in South Africa. This workshop served to emphasize the urgent need for the formulation by the government of a national policy, followed by the implementation of a strategy for the conservation of our mountain environments. Mountains have remained among our least altered landscapes and thus constitute bastions of relatively natural environments. They are our chief sources of water supply and offer unsurpassable opportunities for escape from the almost totally modified environments in which most people today must work and live.

CHAPTER 25

RIVERS

M A RABIE
J A DAY

25.1 WATER AVAILABILITY IN SOUTH AFRICA

Although South Africa is richly endowed with many natural resources, water, one of our most strategic resources, is unfortunately in short supply. The average annual rainfall for the country as a whole is only some 497 mm, compared to a world average of 860 mm. Rainfall is unevenly distributed, with 65 per cent of the country receiving less than 500 mm of rain annually and 21 per cent receiving less than 200 mm. Another factor is rainfall variability; the lower the annual precipitation, the greater the variability. Moreover, the average annual potential evaporation, which ranges between 1 100 mm to more than 3 000 mm, is well in excess of the annual rainfall.[1]

Water sources may for management purposes be classified into five types: surface runoff from rainfall (ie rivers), ground water, unconventional water sources (eg desalination and rainfall augmentation), re-use of effluent returned to public streams and water imported from other countries.[2] The first and, to a lesser extent, the second, constitute the most important sources of water.

South Africa has one of the lowest conversions of rainfall to runoff. The total average annual runoff (ie the average annual quantity of water that reaches our rivers, which on average represents only some 10 per cent of the total rainfall), is estimated to be 53 500 million m^3. As this source is highly variable from year to year (up to 10 consecutive years of less-than-average flow may occur) and is unsuitably distributed relative to the demand at growth points, and because not all runoff can be diverted for use, it has been calculated that at present it is economically practicable to exploit only some 60 per cent of the total, or approximately 33 000 million m^3 annually.[3] Roughly 20 000 million m^3 of water was used in 1990 and it was estimated in 1986 that 22 438 million m^3 will be required annually in 2000.

Our groundwater resources are contained in a multitude of mostly secondary aquifers or aquifer systems with limited quantities of extractable ground water. Although dolomitic primary aquifers contain substantial quantities of exploitable ground water, their size and distribution in South Africa are very limited.[4] The potential groundwater yield is estimated at 12 000 million m^3y^{-1}, of which only some 5 400 million m^3y^{-1} may be practically utilized.[5]

From these figures it is evident that rivers constitute our most vital water resource. Not only do they contain and convey surface runoff, but ground water and surface waters are intimately interrelated in that ground water may eventually reach rivers on the surface or even flow in underground rivers.

---

[1] See, generally, on the influence of climate and topography on water availability in South Africa, *Management of the water resources of the Republic of South Africa* Department of Water Affairs (1986) para 1.1. This chapter is based upon Rabie 'The conservation of rivers in South African law' 1989 *SA Public Law* 1–18, 186–204.

[2] *Management of water resources* above n 1, para 10.3.

[3] *Management of water resources* above n 1, paras 1.3, 3.3 and 10.3.

[4] Marker 'Karst' in Moon & Dardish (eds) *The geomorphology of southern Africa* (1988) 175.

[5] *Management of water resources* above n 1, paras 1.3 and 3.4.

25.2 SOME ASPECTS OF SOUTH AFRICAN RIVERS

25.2.1 Freshwater systems

From the previous section it appears that rivers constitute our only substantial sources of fresh water. More than 50 per cent of the mean annual runoff is channelled through the many relatively short rivers of the eastern seaboard, while the southern and western coastal regions receive less than 20 per cent, most of which flows through a few rather short rivers such as the Berg and the Breede. The extensive central plateau, representing more than 50 per cent of South Africa's surface area, receives only some 27 per cent of the total runoff, most of which through the huge catchment of the Orange–Vaal system.

Rivers, however, are not the only aquatic ecosystems in South Africa. Although the country is poorly served with natural lakes, there are numerous smaller endorheic pans and freshwater lakes,[6] as well as coastal and estuarine lakes,[7] estuaries and estuarine lagoons,[8] wetlands,[9] vleis and floodplains.[10] Since rivers are by far the most important freshwater systems, this study is directed at them. The many demands for water, and the erratic flow of most South African rivers, have led to the creation on all of our major rivers of artificial lakes, ie impoundments, in order to stabilize flow and therefore guarantee supply.[11] The total capacity of state impoundments amounts to more than 50 per cent of South Africa's total average annual river runoff.[12] Impoundments, like other freshwater systems, constitute an ecosystem type.

Wetlands, often but not always associated with river channels, form a valuable yet threatened resource. Wetlands include shallow vleis, bogs, marshes, pans and reedbeds associated with rivers along water courses. Wetlands perform a number of important functions such as the removal of silt, water purification (artificial wetlands are increasingly being constructed for sewage purification), water storage and flood attenuation. Because these systems are often considered, quite erroneously, to be 'wasteland', they are frequently drained or filled in, resulting in increased flooding and decreased water quality.

25.2.2 Classification of rivers

South African rivers have been classified according to their type, region, zonation, geological features, water quality and biotic features.[13] Yet a further classification has been undertaken, based upon their conservation status.[14]

25.2.3 River zones

A river usually, although not invariably, consists of various major zones, ie the headwaters, the middle reaches, the mature lower reaches and the estuary.[15]

[6] Noble & Hemens *Inland water ecosystems in South Africa—a review of research needs*. South African National Scientific Programmes Report no 34 (1978) 21–8.

[7] Noble & Hemens above n 6, 37–47.

[8] Noble & Hemens above n 6, 47–58.

[9] See generally Walmsley & Botten (eds) *Symposium: ecology and conservation of wetlands in South Africa* 15–16 October 1987 Occasional report no 28.

[10] Noble & Hemens above n 6, 15–20.

[11] Noble & Hemens above n 6, 28–37.

[12] Cf Noble & Hemens above n 6, 28–9.

[13] Noble & Hemens above n 6, 14; Alanson, Hart, O'Keeffe & Roberts *Inland waters of southern Africa: an ecological perspective* (1990) para 5.2; King, De Moor & Chutter 'Alternative ways of classifying rivers in southern Africa' in Boon, Petts & Calow (eds) *River classification and management* (in press).

[14] Para 25.2.6 below.

[15] O'Keeffe (ed) *The conservation of South African rivers* South African National Scientific Programmes Report no 131 (1986) 1–6; Noble & Hemens above n 6, 12; Davies & Day *The biology and conservation of South Africa's vanishing waters* (1986) 34–50.

25.2.4 Constituent parts of rivers

Roman law identified three constituent parts of rivers ie the water or stream (flumen), the bed (alveus) and the banks (ripae). The legal relevance of this distinction is that, although ownership of the water vested only in the State, the other parts could be subject to individual ownership.

25.2.5 The need for river conservation

Rivers are of value not only as sources of and channels for water but also, by virtue of their biotas, as a means of purifying water and therefore improving water quality. Further, they support a diverse array of plants, animals and micro-organisms that contribute to the biodiversity of the country. Thus these systems should be managed and utilized conservatively. This necessarily implies the optimal conservation of rivers and of their catchments in order to ensure that their essential features are not destroyed or degraded.

25.2.6 The conservation status of South African rivers

A map depicting the conservation status of South African rivers (ie the extent to which a river has been modified from its natural state) has been compiled.[16] Apart from the many rivers, or stretches of rivers, for which insufficient information is available for assessment, four categories have been distinguished: pristine rivers in which the channel and catchments have not been significantly modified; rivers in which significant changes can be detected; rivers in which substantial, and in many cases practically irreversible, changes are apparent; and rivers in which all natural aspects of the channel and catchments are badly degraded. The great majority of rivers for which sufficient information is available fall into the two middle categories. Rivers belonging to the first category are restricted mainly to high mountains and protected areas.[17]

25.3 HUMAN USE OF AND IMPACT ON RIVERS

The multiple uses to which rivers have been put has had a severe impact upon them.[18] Such use in general relates to consumptive use, which removes water from the system, and non-consumptive use, which often produces effluent. Moreover, practices not directly related to the use of water may nevertheless have a detrimental impact upon rivers in that a river's condition is always a reflection of all activities within the river as well as in its catchment areas. The intensity of impacts upon rivers has been varied, but the following uses and their respective impacts may be identified.

25.3.1 Agriculture

Agriculture—the great importance of which is indisputable—has always enjoyed the lion's share of our water sources. By 1965 consumption for irrigation and stockwatering had reached more than 83 per cent of the total water consumption. In spite of a growth in water use for irrigation, such use has now decreased proportionally to about 67 per cent of direct water use.

25.3.1.1 *Excessive abstraction*

A river cannot withstand unlimited abstraction of water without losing its viability as a functioning ecosystem. Irrigation is particularly consumptive and the intensity of such

---

[16] O'Keeffe above n 15, 111–12. Cf O'Keeffe *The conservation status of South African rivers,* Scale 1:2 500 000.

[17] See, generally, O'Keeffe, Davies, King & Skelton 'Conservation status of southern African rivers' in Huntley (ed) *Biotic diversity in southern Africa* (1989) 226–89.

[18] Cf, generally, O'Keeffe above n 15, ch 3; *Management of water resources* above n 1, ch 2; Fuggle & Rabie (eds) *Environmental concerns in South Africa* (1983) 241–7; Davies & Day above n 15 passim.

use has been aided by the highly subsidized water tariffs on government water schemes and on many irrigation board schemes. Each new scheme is to be subjected to cost-benefit studies in order to ensure that the socio-economic benefits render it truly productive in the national interest.

25.3.1.2 *Destruction of riparian vegetation*

The stabilization of river banks to withstand floods or even normal flow may be detrimentally affected by the destruction of riparian vegetation. This leads to soil erosion and a consequent increase in the silt load in the river. Sediment carried by rivers is also responsible for the reduction in the storage capacity of dams to the extent of some 0,5 per cent annually because the sediment is trapped by the dam walls. Moreover, river wetlands that serve as important wildlife refuges may be destroyed, while the riverine fauna is deprived of its primary energy source.

25.3.1.3 *Weed infestation*

The infestation of river banks by several species of exotic plants has served to supplant indigenous riparian vegetation. This has also affected riverine fauna dependent upon such vegetation. Moreover, certain exotic water plants such as water hyacinth and black wattle have detrimentally affected the flow and quality of several rivers.

25.3.1.4 *Catchment mismanagement*

Injudicious management of catchments can severely affect the conservation status of the rivers involved. Cultivation of wetlands, veld-burning and overgrazing constitute some such malpractices which lead to a deterioration of the vegetal cover of catchments. (Such cover combats soil erosion, delays storm runoff and encourages infiltration.) The resultant soil erosion has caused many rivers to carry considerably increased loads of sediment.

Because plants reduce streamflow by increasing evaporation, excessive plant growth in catchments, such as that brought about by deliberate afforestation, may severely reduce natural runoff, thus detrimentally affecting the river in question. On the other hand, there is a temptation to increase river flow through manipulation of catchments. Purely from a perspective of maximizing water yield, it may seem an attractive option to manage a catchment by reducing dense vegetation, which tends to diminish water flow. Such action may have detrimental consequences for the affected river.

25.3.1.5 *Deterioration in water quality*

This has occurred through sediment caused by soil erosion, as has been mentioned, but also through the use of fertilizers and biocides which eventually reach rivers, and by dumping, often illegally, of toxic pollutants and effluents, while the spread of waterborne diseases such as cholera, typhoid and bilharzia has been aided by the spillage of stock and human wastes into rivers. The natural dilution effect of rivers has largely been lost through decreased river flow brought about by excessive abstraction and impoundments and the natural cleansing effects are reduced when the biota is disturbed by excessive pollution of the water.

25.3.1.6 *Impoundments*

The downstream availability and flow of water in rivers have been severely affected by impoundments, constructed both by the State and by private landowners. A list of dams, compiled by the Department of Water Affairs, reveals that there are over 500 government dams on rivers in South Africa,[19] besides literally thousands of smaller farm dams. The extent of waterworks on private property has in fact increased considerably and a particular cause for concern is that, by means of such works, private water such as stormwater is intercepted before it reaches a public stream.

25.3.1.7 *Salinization*

Irrigation in arid and semi-arid areas leads to increased salt loads in rivers because, although some of the irrigated water evaporates, the small quantities of salt in the water cannot do so. The salt accumulates in the soil, is washed into the groundwater and ultimately seeps into rivers. Several rivers in the south and south-east are seriously polluted in this way.

25.3.1.8 *Indirect demands*

Certain agricultural practices such as dryland farming and afforestation, although not requiring direct abstraction of water from rivers, nevertheless make an indirect demand upon such water through the reduction of runoff. Reduction in runoff from afforested areas thus amounts to almost 8 per cent of the total water use.

25.3.2 Urbanization

Although representing only some 16 per cent of South Africa's direct water use, municipal and domestic water consumption has a considerable impact on rivers, mainly because the effects are concentrated into relatively small areas.

25.3.2.1 *Impoundments*

Although impoundments are mostly associated with agricultural needs, urban complexes also require water-storage facilities and this is usually effected through impoundments. The negative effects of impoundments have been dealt with above.

25.3.2.2 *Sewage effluent*

Urban complexes generate large amounts of sewage, which, even if treated, may yet give rise to effluents that are high in salts and in phosphates and nitrates (nutrients). When effluents containing high levels of nutrients reach rivers, they stimulate plant growth, leading to accelerated eutrophication, increased biochemical oxygen demand and a reduction in faunal diversity.

25.3.2.3 *Urban refuse*

Seepage from urban refuse-disposal sites, frequently containing a variety of pollutants, often finds its way into rivers, thereby contributing to water pollution.

25.3.2.4 *Stormwater drainage*

Urbanization leads to increased runoff from surfaces that are often polluted, thus eventually leading to the pollution of rivers.

25.3.2.5 *Interbasin transfers*

The scarcity of water at certain urban growth points has stimulated the construction of interbasin transfer schemes such as the Tugela–Vaal and Riviersonderend–Berg schemes. In this way the impact of a growth point is extended to other catchments, with detrimental effects for the rivers concerned. Detrimental consequences include loss of biogeographical isolation, loss of endemic biotas, introduction of invasive alien plants

[19] *Management of water resources* above n 1, Appendix 2.

and animals, change in water quality, alteration of hydrological regimes and the spread of disease vectors.[20]

25.3.3 Human population concentrations in rural areas

Since water is a basic requirement for human existence, there is a tendency towards population concentrations near watercourses. Unlike the situation in organized urban complexes, however, water abstraction, use and return to source in many rural areas and squatter communities are often not adequately controlled, while sewage and effluent are untreated. Moreover, the impact of such communities usually extends to the vegetation in the catchment.

25.3.4 Industrial use of water

Although industry, including mining and power generation, accounts for only some 16 per cent of South Africa's direct water use, its impact is disproportionately high because effluents often contain toxic and other pollutants.

25.3.4.1 *Mining*

In view of this sector's great importance to the national economy, mining demands a high assurance of water supply, using almost 3 per cent of all water used. However, it may have severe impacts upon rivers. Mining effluents, produced through the use of water as a medium for mineral abstraction, often contain highly toxic chemical compounds. Moreover, seepage from coal mines especially may lead to a drastic increase in the acidity of nearby rivers.

25.3.4.2 *Manufacturing industries*

Industries other than mines account for over 7 per cent of the total water use. Many manufacturing industries generate a variety of effluents that eventually find their way to rivers.

25.3.4.3 *Power generation*

It has been estimated that power generation uses over 2 per cent of the total water use, although the use of water is much reduced in more modern plants. Power plants require water, abstracted from rivers, for cooling purposes. The return, after use, of the water to the river raises the temperature of the river water, thereby detrimentally affecting the river biota. Riverine biotas are also affected by hydro-electric power plants, which bring about fluctuations in downstream flow that are quite unlike the natural seasonal fluctuations to which the biotas are adapted.

25.3.5 Aquaculture

Aquaculture consists of the commercial cultivation and harvesting of aquatic organisms. The products include a wide range of commodities such as food, fodder, hides and fish. Fish harvesting in state and private dams is probably the best-known form of aquaculture that is practised. The use of water by aquaculture has certain negative effects. It is partly consumptive in that water is lost by evaporation or seepage. In so far as it is non-consumptive, it may lead to pollution since the quality of the water which is returned to the stream in question is usually degraded.

Probably the most severe impact of a type of aquaculture, although not usually practised primarily for commercial gain, has been the introduction of exotic predatory fish into certain rivers. This has seriously threatened certain indigenous fish species.

---

[20] Petitjean & Davies 'Ecological impacts of inter-basin water transfers: some case studies, research, requirements and assessment procedures in southern Africa' 1988 (84) *S Afr J Sci* 819–28.

25.3.6 Road-building

The construction of roads along rivers, bridges (also for railway purposes) and causeways may have a negative impact upon river banks and river-beds, as well as on streamflow. Such activities have often been responsible for the degradation of estuaries.

25.3.7 Recreation

Recreational activities are often practised in, on and along inland waters such as rivers and dams. Such activities include swimming, angling, canoeing, power boating, sailing and hiking. A considerable recreational industry has been established to support these activities, besides the development of the required infrastructure, camping facilities and holiday townships. On the whole, recreation may act as a stimulant to conservation because it is mostly dependent upon high standards of water quality. There are nevertheless also negative effects associated with recreation, such as the destabilization of river banks, the destruction of riparian vegetation, littering and other forms of pollution and generally the artificial development of the riverine environment.

25.3.8 Environmental conservation

A competing water demand that has only relatively recently been recognized is that for the environmental management of estuaries, lakes, wetlands, riverine habitats and conserved areas.[21] Such management—contrary to the other use categories referred to above—of course should have no negative impact upon rivers since its very aim is conservation. The estimated water allocation need of this somewhat diffuse use category—sometimes referred to simply as 'the needs of the environment'—has been variously estimated as amounting to between 10 per cent (or 2 160 million $m^3\ y^{-1}$) and 13 per cent (or 2 947 million $m^3\ y^{-1}$) of the total water demand.[22] This is more than 10 times the allocation for nature conservation (in which category was included only Lake St Lucia and the Kruger National Park) estimated by the Commission of Enquiry into Water Matters in 1970.

25.4 SOUTH AFRICAN WATER LAW

South African water law is the product of rules derived from some four different legal systems. It was built, initially, upon Roman law and Roman-Dutch law, after which the Cape Supreme Court on its own superimposed principles of English and even American law upon the prevailing system governing water law. The latter process commenced in 1856, with obiter dicta in *Retief v Louw*,[23] after which the principles contained in these dicta were confirmed in several other decisions.

Among the most important 'amendments' brought about in this manner were the granting of exclusive water rights to riparian landowners and the concomitant loss by the State of its original position of dominus fluminis. Water law took on a distinctly private-law orientation, with the emphasis on the rights of respective riparian landowners. This served to underscore the traditional conception of landownership as a so-called absolute or plenary right. This private-law dispensation was eventually to prevail for a full century.

Until the first part of the 20th century agriculture was the only significant user of water, with urban development accounting for no more than a small percentage. Irrigation was generally by direct abstraction and diversion from rivers, the water rights of riparian landowners having been secured by decisions of the old Cape Supreme

[21] *Management of water resources* above n 1, para 2.9.

[22] Cf Jezewski & Roberts *Estuarine and lake freshwater requirements* Department of Water Affairs Technical Report no TR 129 (1986) 2, 19; O'Keeffe above n 15, 16, 60–1; *Management of water resources* above n 1, para 2.9.

[23] Decided in 1856, but reported in 1874 Buch 165.

Court. In order to facilitate irrigation, the State constructed large impoundments. This was the purport of the Irrigation and Conservation of Waters Act 8 of 1912.

This dispensation was clearly incompatible with the water requirements of a rapidly developing and industrialized country. It was, however, only with the introduction of the Water Act in 1956 that water law in South Africa again took on a predominantly public-law guise. This was essential to ensure the equitable distribution of water for the various competing users and to serve the public interest in our water sources. The promulgation of the Water Act was a symptom of changes in water use experienced in South Africa after the Second World War. The rapid growth of mining, industrial and urban development served to underscore the limitations of our available water resources and the inordinate share that agriculture had hitherto enjoyed. Extensive provision was now made for control over the abstraction, use, supply, distribution and pollution of water.

Although the Water Act is by far the most important legislation relating to the control of our water resources, and therefore also of rivers, there are a number of provisions in other legislation which are also relevant to the conservation of rivers.

25.5 LEGAL CATEGORIES OF RIVERS

25.5.1 Public and private rivers

A distinction according to size was drawn in Roman law between a rivus (streamlet or brook) and a flumen (river).[24] Roman law further distinguished between a flumen publicum and a flumen privatum. This distinction was also drawn in Roman-Dutch law. A public river was characterized by its perennial flow, not its navigability.[25] The fact that a river, although normally perennial, sometimes ceased to flow, did not affect its public status.[26] It would seem, however, that the flow should have been strong enough to sustain common use by the respective riparian landowners.[27] Most rivers accordingly were classified as public rivers.[28] If the river in question was not public, it was private and was treated like any other private property.[29]

Since water in the Netherlands was often regarded as a nuisance, the Roman-Dutch text writers did not contribute much to the concept of a public river, at least as far as consumptive use of its water was concerned. However, in Roman-Dutch law more emphasis was placed upon the navigability of public rivers, although it does not seem to have become a condition which has to be satisfied before a river qualifies as a public river.[30]

The Cape Supreme Court which, as has been noted, played an important role during the second half of the 19th century in pronouncing its own water-law principles for the country, designated as public streams all perennial rivers, whether navigable or not, and all streams which, though not large enough to be considered rivers, are yet perennial and are capable of being applied to the common use of riparian landowners.[31]

The first post-Union statutory definition of 'public river' was contained in the Irrigation and Conservation of Waters Act 8 of 1912, which relied to some extent upon the judicial pronouncements of the Cape Supreme Court. This Act defined a 'public stream' as a natural stream of water which, when it flows, flows in a known and defined channel (whether or not the channel is dry during any period) if the water thereof is

---

[24] D 43.12.1.1.
[25] D 43.12.1.2 and 3; D 43.13.1.2.
[26] D 43.12.1.2 and 3.
[27] Cf Van der Merwe *Sakereg* (2 ed, 1989) 34.
[28] D 1.8.4.1.
[29] D 43.12.1.4.
[30] Nunes 'Sources of public streams in modern South African law' 1975 *Acta Juridica* 298.
[31] *Van Heerden v Weise* 1880 Buch AC 5, 7.

capable of being applied to the common use of the riparian owners for purposes of irrigation.[32]

This description formed the basis for the Water Act which now defines a 'public stream' as a natural stream of water which flows in a known and defined channel, whether or not such channel is dry during any period of the year and whether or not its conformation has been changed by artificial means, if the water therein is capable of common use for irrigation on two or more pieces of land riparian thereto which are the subject of separate original grants or on one such piece of land and also on riparian state land. A stream which fulfils these conditions in part only of its course is deemed to be a public stream as regards that part only.[33]

The concept of public stream is more extensive than the public river of our common law, in that it discards the requirement of perennial flow. The substitution of 'stream' for 'river' is therefore misleading. Rivers which flow for a short period, even if there are long intervals between periods of flow, qualify as public streams, given compliance with the other requirements set in the definition of public stream. The water of such a river, for instance, may by flood-storage or flood-diversion works be applied to the common use of riparian landowners for purposes of irrigation.

The definition of public stream now expressly requires that the water should be capable of common use on two or more pieces of certain riparian land, but limits this use to irrigation. The Act gives no indication as to the extent of such irrigation or the value of the crops concerned. Should the river have sufficient water, but should its quality render it unsuitable for irrigation, e g on account of its being brackish, the river would not qualify as a public stream, unless, of course, it is only the normal flow which is brackish, while the surplus flow in the form of floodwater may well be utilized for irrigation.[34]

A further condition that was not expressly set in our common law is that a river will qualify as a public stream only when it has a known and defined channel. This means that if at a certain point the water of a public stream flows into a wetland such as a vlei or flood-plain comprising an extensive level area through which no defined channel is visible, the stream from that point ceases to qualify as a public stream, even if the water should eventually again find its way into a public stream.[35] Water flowing underground could qualify as a public stream only if it flows in a defined channel.

In order to qualify as a public stream the river must extend over at least two pieces of riparian land which are the subject of separate original grants (or one such piece of land and state land). Should the entire course of the river be contained on one piece of land, such river will be a private river, even if the land is subsequently subdivided. Conversely, a river remains a public stream even if the pieces of land which were the subject of separate original grants are subsequently consolidated.[36]

The proviso seems to have the effect that estuaries and tidal rivers, even if they did not form part of the sea, as indeed they do, in any case would not qualify as public streams in so far as irrigation cannot be practised along such parts of the river. Conversely, however, it has been argued that the headwaters of a public stream which occur on one piece of land already qualify as part of the public stream even before the water reaches further riparian land upon which it is utilized for irrigation.[37]

---

[32] Section 2.
[33] Section 1.
[34] De Wet *Opuscula miscellanea. Regsgeleerde lesings en adviese* edited by Gauntlett (1979) 28.
[35] *Hall on water rights in South Africa* (4 ed, 1974) by Hall & Burger 19.
[36] De Wet above n 34, 26.
[37] De Wet above n 34, 29.

Moreover, it has been held—confirming a rule already laid down in *Van Heerden v Weise*[38]—that if a river conforms to the requirements of a public stream, such public character adheres also to the river's sources even though a particular source does not conform to the attributes of a public stream. In other words, although a source may be private in its own right, it is regarded as public on account of its connection to the public stream.[39] The view that the headwaters and even the sources of a public stream should also be classified as part of that stream seems entirely satisfactory. Should this not be the case, such headwaters and sources would otherwise presumably have to be regarded as private water, which would imply that the landowner concerned may exhaust or severely diminish or pollute the water supply to the detriment of the entire river.[40]

On the other hand, the operation of the proviso to the definition of public stream makes allowance for certain lower parts of a river which do not conform to the definition, to be excluded from the public nature of that river. A wetland, which is not contained within a known and defined channel or which does not form the source of a public stream, would contain private water, with the consequence that the landowner(s) in question would in principle have the exclusive ownership of that water, implying that he may even destroy the wetland, eg by filling it in. Barring other legislation which might possibly control such an action,[41] the only limitation upon a landowner in his use of such private water is the private-law principle that he may not thereby unreasonably affect neighbouring landowners.[42] Burning, grazing or ploughing of wetlands will almost inevitably affect downstream landowners. There seems to be an inconsistency in regarding the sources of a public stream—which sources do not themselves comply with the definition of public stream—as being endowed with a public character, but in refusing to do so in respect of lower parts of the same river which likewise do not satisfy the definition. Ideally a river, being a longitudinal ecosystem, should be managed as an entity, and this can be done satisfactorily only if it has the same status or nature along its entire course. Should a river over that part of its course which does not satisfy the definition of a public stream be regarded as private, while the rest constitutes a public stream, it would constitute serious managerial difficulties, since the State has very little control over private water. It is difficult to understand what the legislature wishes to achieve through the proviso to the definition of public stream. Its deletion should be considered.

The fact that, as has been noted, estuaries and tidal rivers would normally fail to comply with the requirements of a public stream may to some extent be compensated thereby that the water in question is not regarded as private water but as forming part of the sea. However, this also gives rise to managerial problems since different bodies manage the sea, while a tidal river and estuary in fact form an integral part of the river which flows into them.

The Water Act does not define a private river or private stream. It may therefore be assumed that a river which lacks the essentials of a public stream would qualify as a private stream. However, this is not invariably the case, as has just been seen with regard to tidal rivers and tidal lagoons which, although not complying with the definition of public stream, nevertheless do not amount to private streams. Finally, it

---

[38] Above n 31.

[39] Cf Nunes above n 30, 310–31; Hall above n 35, 21–2; Vos *Principles of South African water law* (2 ed, 1978) 8–9; Rabie 'Sources of public rivers—status and control' 1991 *THRHR* 75,79–83. A contrary view was held obiter in *Le Roux v Kruger* 1986 (1) SA 327 (C).

[40] The proviso to s 5(1) of the Water Act, based on the 'ancient custom' rule, does not severely limit the landowner's rights. See, generally, Rabie above n 39, 84.

[41] Cf s 5(2) of the Water Act, which controls the disposal and conveyance of private water.

[42] Cf Ramsden *Legal principles and wetland legislation* Paper delivered at a national symposium on the ecology and conservation of wetlands in South Africa, October 1987.

should be noted that the water court is empowered to investigate, determine and record whether any particular stream is a public or a private stream.[43]

25.5.2 Tidal rivers and tidal lagoons

A 'tidal river' is defined in the Sea-Shore Act 21 of 1935 as that part of any river in which a rise and fall of the water-level takes place as a result of tidal action.[44] The water and the bed of any tidal river and of any tidal lagoon are included in the definition of 'sea' in the Sea-Shore Act and accordingly form part of the sea,[45] of which the State President formally is the owner.[46] This means that tidal rivers and tidal lagoons are subject to a different dispensation from that pertaining to public rivers of which they form an integral part and are thus managed on a different basis.

The definitions of 'tidal river' and of 'tidal lagoon' both relate to water bodies in which a tidal rise and fall of the water-level is discernible. Some uncertainty as to its status may arise in respect of an estuary which undergoes a stage during which its mouth to the sea is closed, at times of low river flow.[47] Do the river and lagoon during such a stage, which may last for a considerable period of time, qualify as a 'tidal river' or 'tidal lagoon' or should they be regarded as a public river, in accordance with the definition of 'public stream', if their water is suitable for common irrigation?

25.6 PUBLIC RIVERS AS RES PUBLICAE

Although there is some authority to the effect that running water (aqua profluens), along with the sea and the air, was classified in Roman law as common things (res omnium communes),[48] it would seem that public rivers, including the water flowing in them, were in fact regarded as public things (res publicae).[49] This position prevailed also in Roman-Dutch law[50] and in the Cape for at least two centuries. Both res omnium communes and res publicae were destined for the use and enjoyment of the general public. However, unlike the former, which belonged to the community as a whole, res publicae belonged to the State in ownership. This probably explains why the State more readily placed restrictions upon the use of res publicae.[51]

During the second part of the 19th century, after the decisions of *Retief v Louw*[52] and *Hough v Van der Merwe*,[53] nevertheless, the Cape Supreme Court, relying partly upon principles of Anglo-American law, introduced an entirely new dispensation. It held that the water of a public river (public or running stream) was subject to the common use of the owners of land riparian to such a river and that no one else had any claim to the water in a public river.[54] These decisions, which by the end of the 19th century had been generally followed in South Africa, in effect emasculated the concept of public river to such an extent that it became a misnomer. A public river containing only water destined for private use is, after all, a contradiction in terms. See, generally, chapter 13.

Riparian landowners proved to constitute such a powerful pressure group that even

---

[43] Section 40*(d)* of the Water Act.
[44] Section 1.
[45] Ibid.
[46] Section 2(1).
[47] Cf Noble & Hemens above n 6, 50.
[48] I 2.1.1; D 1.8.2.1.
[49] I 2.1.2; D 1.8.4.1; D 43.12.1.2–3. Cf De Wet 'Water' 1956 *THRHR* 28; 'Hundred years of water law' 1959 *Acta Juridica* 31; *Opuscula miscellanea* above n 34, 7.
[50] De Wet 1959 *Acta Juridica* above n 49, 31–2; *Opuscula miscellanea* above n 34, 7.
[51] Voet 1.8.1. Cf Van der Merwe 'Things' in Joubert (ed) *The law of South Africa* vol 27 (1987) para 24. In *Butgereit v Transvaal Canoe Union* 1988 (1) SA 759 (A) 767D–F, nevertheless, it was stated that public rivers, as res publicae, belonged to the whole community.
[52] Above n 23.
[53] 1874 Buch 148.
[54] See generally De Wet above n 34, 11–19.

legislatures were reticent in introducing amending legislation. It was only with the promulgation of the Water Act during 1956—a full century after *Retief v Louw*—that provision was made for other users of the water in public rivers.

25.7 NAVIGABILITY OF PUBLIC RIVERS

It has been shown that navigability is not a requirement for the public nature of a river.[55] Navigability, however, continues to play a role since the rules of Roman law and of Roman-Dutch law are still applicable that non-navigability is a requirement for alluvion and for ownership of islands in rivers.[56]

The common-law concept of navigability seems to have a commercial connotation and it is probably in this sense that our courts have proceeded from the supposition that both of our two principal rivers, the Vaal River[57] and the Orange River[58] are non-navigable. It would therefore seem that, with the possible exception of the Buffalo River at East London, there are no navigable rivers (in the common-law sense) in South Africa. However, there seems to be no good reason why the concept of navigability could not be modified to local conditions, detached from a commercial perspective, which has almost always been inapplicable to South African rivers.[59] In any case, it has been held that commercial navigability is not a requirement for the public's rights to use public rivers for the purposes of sport, recreation, boating, fishing and swimming.[60]

25.8 OWNERSHIP OF PUBLIC RIVERS

Unlike common things, which belong to the community as a whole, public things belong to the State in ownership. Although it is generally acknowledged that public rivers, as res publicae, belong to the State, such ownership does not extend to all the constituent parts of a public river. There is even some doubt whether ownership of public water in a public river vests in the State. The Water Act[61] provides that there shall be no ownership ('right of property') in public water. A literal interpretation of this provision would imply that the State thereby forfeits its right of ownership, derived from the status of public rivers as res publicae. Moreover, this provision would rule out public water's taking on the nature of res nullius, since the latter category of things implies that such things are at least capable of being owned. The only remaining category of things which the above provision would seem to allow for public water is that of res extra commercium, i e things that are not susceptible of ownership. However, it seems more likely that the purport of the provision is that public water is not susceptible of *individual* ownership and that the State remains owner of public water, but that it is authorized to control its use. (The water and the bed of tidal rivers and tidal lagoons—which do not constitute public streams—belong in ownership to the State President.)

The river banks are subject to the ownership of the respective riparian landowners, although in Roman law the use of river banks was considered as a right which the public could have exercised.[62] Ownership of the river-bed depends upon how the boundary of the land adjacent to the river is described in the deed concerned: if the boundary is described as the river (ager non limitatus), then it is deemed to be the middle of the river, implying that the riparian landowner in question owns also the river-bed ad medium filum fluminis. Should the boundary be described not as the river itself but as

---

[55] Cf also *Butgereit v Transvaal Canoe Union* above n 51, 767A–B.
[56] Van der Merwe above n 51, paras 137 and 139.
[57] *Van Niekerk & Union Government (Minister of Lands) v Carter* 1917 AD 359, 373.
[58] *Lange v Minister of Lands* 1957 (1) SA 297 (A) 299G–H.
[59] Cf *Transvaal Canoe Union v Butgereit* 1986 (4) SA 207 (T) 212F–213E.
[60] *Butgereit v Transvaal Canoe Union* above n 51, 769J–770C.
[61] Section 6(1).
[62] I 2.1.4. Cf Van der Merwe above n 51, para 24.

the bank thereof (ager limitatus), the river-bed is owned by the State.[63] Although the mid-river boundary rule—which was introduced into our law from English law—is cast in the form of a rebuttable presumption, it seems to have developed into a more or less fixed rule.

It is submitted that private ownership of public river-beds is undesirable. It implies that should a member of the public in the exercise of any of his rights in respect of public rivers, such as swimming or canoeing, at some or other stage be in physical contact with the river-bed, he would be trespassing. Moreover, should the river temporarily cease to flow, as often happens in South Africa, very little, if anything, would remain of the river's public nature and the public would have little or no access to the river. It is conceivable that rivers which have dried up, either wholly or partly, may yet be susceptible of recreational activities such as hiking or canoeing, even if involving considerable portage along the river-bed. Furthermore, islands that may arise in public rivers would belong to the respective riparian landowners where the mid-river boundary rule applies.[64] Such islands constitute strategic conservation sites, especially for birds, and should preferably be under the full control of the State.

River banks, which, as has been mentioned, are privately owned, are even more important from a conservation perspective. The stabilization of river banks and control of their soil erosion are of crucial importance in water management, while the riverine vegetation constitutes an important ecological zone which harbours a variety of wildlife. Although, as will be shown, a variety of conservation legislation is indeed applicable to river banks and does theoretically restrict riparian landowners, this legislation has proved difficult to administer effectively, especially in view of the fact that damage to river banks and their vegetation may often prove to be practically almost irreparable.

Private ownership of river banks has a further detrimental consequence in that it inhibits access to rivers. This applies particularly to members of the public who wish to exercise their rights in respect of public rivers, but it also has implications for the State's role in water management. River banks may, in a sense, be compared to the sea-shore, which belongs to the State and is destined for the use and enjoyment of the public. Even if river banks are to remain subject to the ownership of riparian landowners, a revival of the Roman-law principle that their use is available to the public would pave the way for more ready access to public rivers and would, moreover, allow for the establishment of river hiking trails. Perhaps this may be accomplished through the expropriation of a public servitude.

25.9 STATE CONTROL OF PUBLIC RIVERS

25.9.1 The principle

In Roman law the principle was accepted that the use of water flowing in public rivers was subject to State control. This function of the State as dominus fluminis was continued and even intensified in Roman-Dutch law and prevailed in South Africa until the middle of the 19th century.

It has already been shown that the Cape Supreme Court was instrumental in the 'depublicization' of public rivers. This had the effect not only of depriving the public by judicial fiat of their rights to the use of public rivers; for all practical purposes, it also brought about the loss by the State of its authority as dominus fluminis to control public rivers in the public interest.

The Water Act and its subsequent amendments to some extent restored the public status of public rivers and the State has partly regained its original position as dominus

[63] Cf Van der Merwe above n 27, 234; Van der Merwe above n 51, para 137; Badenhorst 'The use of public rivers by the public' 1987 *TSAR* 108, 109, 112. *Van Niekerk and Union Government (Minister of Lands) v Carter* above n 57, 378; *Lange v Minister of Lands* above n 58, 301E–303G.

[64] Van der Merwe above n 51, para 139.

fluminis.[65] It is submitted that the conservation of rivers in the public interest can be satisfactorily effected only if full control is vested in the State.

25.9.2 Administrative bodies involved

A striking facet of state control of public water, and therefore also, if sometimes indirectly, of public rivers, is the large number of administrative bodies which are entrusted with such control.[66] These bodies are elaborated upon in chapter 13.

25.10 LEGAL CATEGORIES OF WATER

The different categories into which water is classified legally are discussed in chapter 13.

25.11 RIGHTS IN RESPECT OF WATER IN RIVERS

25.11.1 Private water

Although no extensive survey has been undertaken, it would appear that there are relatively few rivers that fail to qualify as public streams and that may be regarded in their entirety as private streams. Nevertheless, it has been pointed out that, owing to the proviso of the definition of 'public stream', certain integral parts of public streams may yet be regarded as private streams. Private landowners' rights in respect of the water in such parts of public streams may detrimentally affect the ideal of conservation, since the ownership of private water vests in the owner of the land on which such water is found.[67]

It should be noted, however, as has been shown, that much of the water in catchment areas of public streams, as well as certain underground sources, which may otherwise have been classified as private water, nevertheless is public water if it constitutes a source of a public stream.

25.11.2 Public water

25.11.2.1 *Rights of riparian owners*

The bulk of water law deals with rights to the use of public water. As a user group, riparian land owners enjoy by far the most extensive rights to the water in public rivers. These rights are not of common-law origin, but were in effect granted by the judiciary during the second half of the 19th century, as has been explained. Although the exclusive and comprehensive nature of these rights has been modified by the Water Act, particularly in government water control areas and certain other declared areas, they remain the most important rights to the use of public water.[68] See chapter 13.

25.11.2.2 *Other individual rights granted in terms of the Water Act*

Our water law has traditionally been aimed at securing and apportioning the rights of riparian landowners to the use of public water, mainly for irrigation purposes. It was only after the promulgation of the Water Act that some recognition was given to the rights of non-riparian landowners, mainly for industrial purposes, including mining. Powers are thus conferred upon the water court to authorize certain uses of water by non-riparians.[69] The Minister of Water Affairs, likewise, may confer certain water rights upon non-riparian landowners, both within and outside of declared water areas.[70]

---

[65] Cf Hall 'Water law at the crossroads' 1970 *SALJ* 356.
[66] Cf Rabie above n 1, 16–18.
[67] Section 5(1).
[68] Cf generally ss 4, 9 and 10.
[69] Cf ss 11(1) and (2) and 14.
[70] Cf ss 11(1A), 12, 12A, 12B and 13.

A difficulty as far as the distribution of public water is concerned, is, as Findlay[71] points out, that the Water Act itself—unlike its predecessor, the Irrigation and Conservation of Waters Act of 1912, which distinguished primary, secondary and tertiary uses—provides no criteria as to how the water is to be apportioned among claimants within divergent use-categories. The discretion of the Minister or other responsible authority concerned would seem to be decisive. The Minister himself may well establish guidelines to structure the exercise of his discretion, but even such guidelines remain in his discretion.

25.11.2.3 *Public rights*

The rights of the public in respect of public rivers are of a very limited nature, especially when viewed against the extensive rights of riparian landowners.

(a) Common-law rights. A member of the public who has legal access to a public river may in principle fish or bathe in it or boat on it.[72] The right of canoeists to paddle along public rivers, even where the river-bed in question is privately owned, was recently confirmed by the Appellate Division.[73]

These rights of the public, limited though they are, have been further modified by legislation dealing with water management, nature conservation, pollution control and public health.

(b) Statutory rights. The Water Act empowers any person, while he is lawfully at any place where he has access to a public stream, to take and use water from such stream for the immediate purpose of watering stock or drinking, washing or cooking, or use in a vehicle at that place.[74]

Bodies responsible for road construction are likewise empowered to take and use water from public streams.[75]

25.12 STATUTORY CONTROL MEASURES

A variety of statutory measures, authorized mainly by the Water Act, regulate aspects related to the conservation of rivers. The classification which follows is merely one of convenience and in no way represents watertight categories.

25.12.1 Declared water-related areas

The Water Act makes provision for the declaration by the Minister of Water Affairs of a whole variety of water areas, if in his opinion certain circumstances or conditions prevail. Different considerations apply for the establishment of the various areas, but the result of such a declaration is that governmental control over the water resources and related matters in the area concerned is established or intensified. These areas are set out in chapter 13. Moreover, in addition to the Water Act, other legislation also provides for the declaration of yet further areas related to water and to rivers. Such areas, likewise, are discussed in chapter 13. Special note should be taken of the establishment of river conservancy districts in terms of the Natal Nature Conservation Ordinance 15 of 1974.[76] Furthermore, South African legislation makes provision for the establishment of a variety of protected areas.[77] See chapter 27. Depending upon the type of area involved, rivers within the area in question enjoy a greater or lesser degree

---

[71] 'A proper basis for water rights' 1969 *THRHR* 338.
[72] *Butgereit v Transvaal Canoe Union* above n 51, 769I–770C.
[73] *Butgereit v Transvaal Canoe Union* above n 51.
[74] Section 7*(a)*.
[75] Section 7*(b)*.
[76] Section 136.
[77] Cf Rabie 'South African law relating to conservation areas' 1985 *CILSA* 51–89.

of protection. Reference has already been made to the fact that most of South Africa's partly pristine rivers are situated within formal protected areas.

25.12.2 Control of water use

The Water Act provides for several forms of control over the use of water. Such controls are explained in chapter 13.

25.12.3 Control of water quality

In a semi-arid country such as South Africa, water pollution control assumes special significance. See chapter 18.

25.12.4 Control of course and flow of rivers

25.12.4.1 *Alteration in the course of rivers*

It is an offence in terms of the Water Act for any person to alter the course of a public stream, except under the authority of a permit issued by the Minister of Water Affairs and in accordance with conditions subject to which such permit was issued.[78] There are, however, a number of exceptions to this provision.[79] Moreover, the Minister may grant exemptions from this provision.[80]

A number of provisions safeguarding existing rights apply where an alteration in the course of a public stream has occurred[81] and, where this was due to natural causes, the holders of the relevant water rights who are cut off from the stream or are impeded in the exercise of their rights may apply to the water court for an order authorizing them to construct such works which, in the opinion of the Court, are necessary to revert the stream to its previous course.[82]

The need for the regulation or control over the flow of a public stream by altering the course of its channel may lead to the Minister's declaration of a particular area as a catchment control area.[83]

25.12.4.2 *Interference with river flow*

The Water Act makes extensive provision for the lawful interference with the flow of water in rivers, for instance through the abstraction of water or the construction of impoundments. It nevertheless is a specific offence for any person unlawfully to construct or enlarge a waterwork[84] or to interfere with or to alter the flow of the water of a public stream.[85]

25.12.5 Conservation of aquatic fauna and flora in rivers

The respective provincial nature conservation ordinances generally regulate the conservation of fauna and flora. See chapters 11 and 12. In addition, there are provisions in other legislation which are aimed at the conservation of fauna and flora in declared protected areas. See chapter 27.

As far as aquatic flora are concerned, the above legislation relating to the conservation of flora would generally be applicable, although no separate treatment is provided for aquatic flora, except for provisions relating to the control of water pollution which may be injurious to fish food (which includes forms of aquatic flora), and of noxious aquatic growths. See chapters 11, 13 and 18. Aquatic plants and fish in

---

78 Section 20(1)*(a)* read with ss 20(11) and 170(2).
79 Section 20(1)*(b)*.
80 Section 20(10)*(a)*.
81 Section 20(8).
82 Section 20(9).
83 Section 59(2).
84 Section 170(1)*(a)*.
85 Section 170(1)*(b)*.

tidal rivers and tidal lagoons—which form part of the sea—are protected to some extent by virtue of the Sea Fishery Act 12 of 1988. See chapter 14.

Freshwater fish and aquatic fauna generally (except mammals and birds) are separately conserved by virtue of the above-mentioned nature conservation ordinances, which all contain extensive provisions for this purpose. There are also provisions dealing with species of fish that are considered to be harmful or injurious to other fish. See chapter 13.

25.12.6 Control of land use

25.12.6.1 *Land-use planning*

It is obvious that land-use planning which is sympathetic to the environment, particularly to rivers, can contribute substantially to the satisfactory management and conservation of South African rivers. See chapter 28.

25.12.6.2 *Expropriation of land or rights*

In certain instances it has been deemed necessary for the State to expropriate land or rights in order effectively to conserve a particular natural resource such as water. This would be the case where mere control of the actions of an individual landowner would not suffice to achieve the desired goal and where the State's use of the land would be so extensive that it would require all or some of the rights of ownership in order to serve the public interest effectively.

Expropriation is governed basically by the Expropriation Act 63 of 1975. In addition to this Act, and relying upon its provisions, the Water Act also authorizes the Minister of Water Affairs to expropriate or use temporarily land for purposes related to a government waterworks or to a catchment control area.[86] Irrigation boards[87] and water boards[88] are also vested with powers of expropriation. Moreover, both the Conservation of Agricultural Resources Act 43 of 1983[89] and the Forest Act 122 of 1984[90] make provision for the expropriation of land with a view, at least indirectly, to conserving water resources.

25.12.6.3 *Conservation of soil and vegetation in river catchments*

There is an intimate relationship between the state of a river's catchment and the quality and flow of its water. In its turn the state of the catchment is decisively influenced by the state of the soil, which, again, is directly related to the prevailing vegetative cover.

The soil and vegetation of catchments situated within protected areas, especially mountain catchment areas,[91] potentially enjoy comprehensive protection in terms of the relevant legislation. A similar result can be achieved in catchment control areas declared in terms of the Water Act.

Apart from the Water Act, the principal legislation aimed at the integrated conservation of the soil, water resources and vegetation is the Conservation of Agricultural Resources Act and the Forest Act. The Conservation of Agricultural Resources Act accordingly stipulates that the Minister of Agriculture may prescribe obligatory control measures in respect of land-users, which measures may relate, inter alia, to the cultivation of virgin soil, the use and protection of land which is cultivated,

---

[86] Section 60(1).
[87] Section 94(1).
[88] Section 112(1).
[89] Section 14(1). Cf the definition of 'natural agricultural resources' in s 1 which include water sources.
[90] Section 14(2).
[91] Established by virtue of the Mountain Catchment Areas Act 63 of 1970.

the irrigation of land, the use and protection of vleis, marshes, water sponges, watercourses and water sources, the regulation of the flow pattern of runoff water, the use and protection of vegetation, the grazing capacity of veld, the prevention and control of veld fires, the control of weeds and invader plants, the restoration or reclamation of eroded land and the protection of water sources against pollution on account of farming practices.[92] Extensive control measures have been prescribed.[93] See chapter 10.

The Forest Act provides for extensive protection of state forests,[94] while the establishment of forest nature reserves is aimed particularly at conservation and wilderness areas at the preservation of an ecosystem.[95] Moreover, trees on private land may be protected for the conservation and development of natural resources, which, obviously, would include water resources.[96] The Act also regulates the prevention and combating of veld, forest and mountain fires, mainly through the declaration of fire control areas and fire control regions and the establishment of fire control committees and regional fire control committees.[97]

Finally, species of indigenous plants, as has been pointed out, are conserved in terms of the various provincial nature conservation ordinances.

25.12.6.4 *Control of afforestation in river catchments*

Afforestation in catchments has a tendency to reduce natural runoff, thereby detrimentally affecting the river in question. Apart from control in declared mountain catchment areas in accordance with the Mountain Catchment Areas Act 63 of 1970, the Forest Act also provides for control over the use of land for purposes of afforestation. Such land-use is subject to the approval of the Director-General: Environment Affairs.[98] Moreover, the Minister of Environment Affairs may in respect of land which in terms of the Act is being or may be used for the planting of trees, prohibit the afforestation or the reafforestation of the land concerned or may prohibit any other act or direct the landowner to take any other steps which may be necessary for the protection of any natural water source.[99]

25.12.7 Control over the impoundment of water

A number of provisions of the Water Act regulate the construction, alteration or enlargement of waterworks such as dams. See chapter 13.

25.12.8 Assessment of potential environmental impact of proposed water projects

The undertaking of water projects, particularly the construction of dams by both the government and private individuals, is justified on account of their obvious benefit to society. However, they do also impose a cost upon society in that they usually have a detrimental impact upon the riverine environment involved. Unfortunately, this latter aspect traditionally has not been taken into account satisfactorily when waterworks have been planned, constructed and operated. During the past two decades it has gradually come to be recognized that the potential environmental impact of such projects should be revealed and evaluated before the relevant decisions are taken. See chapters 7 and 31 on environmental impact assessment generally and chapter 13 with regard to such assessment in respect of proposed water projects.

---

[92] Section 6(1).
[93] GN R1048 of 25 May 1984.
[94] Part III.
[95] Section 15(1)(a).
[96] Section 13.
[97] Part VI.
[98] Section 7(1).
[99] Section 8(1). Cf also s 8(2).

25.13 CONCLUSION

South African water law contains many and varied legal provisions that may be employed with a view directly or indirectly to effect river conservation. Although a number of shortcomings have been identified, it would appear that these provisions have the potential adequately to conserve our rivers. The decisive factor seems to be the policy which determines the application of the relevant legal provisions and this depends upon the administration's approach to water management and the value which it attaches to river conservation.

25.13.1 Uniform and comprehensive management of water sources

The conservation of rivers should not be considered in isolation. Since the condition of a river is to a large extent a reflection of the catchment and its condition, it is obvious that river conservation should include control over catchments. Moreover, since rivers form part of a hydrological cycle, attention to the conservation status of other components of the cycle is essential if the ideal of river conservation is to be realized. In other words, what is required is a holistic approach.

Our water law should be more comprehensive in the sense that all available water should be subjected to the same fundamental rules. No artificial classification should require different rules to be applied to the same water as it moves from one phase to another in the hydrological cycle.[100] This applies particularly to the distinction between ground water and surface water, as has been pointed out in chapter 13. In fact, the same body of water, ie a river, may even be subject to a different legal dispensation, where it may in part be classified as public and in part as private, while tidal rivers and tidal lagoons qualify as neither but are regarded as part of the sea.

Also, the concept of private water being a private commodity would appear to be an anachronism. Many of the important components of hydrological cycles, such as most wetlands[101] and ground water not flowing in a defined channel, qualify as private water and as such are subject to private ownership and largely beyond the reach of the Water Act. It is submitted that the overriding public interest in our water resources, including rivers, requires comprehensive control over all water sources. Either the category of private water must disappear or private water should be regulated in the public interest, along with public water.

Furthermore, the entrenchment of existing riparian water rights outside government water control areas should be reviewed. The State should superimpose control over the exercise of such rights, should the public interest demand this. The recognition of existing rights is a general principle of law, but if this is found to be in conflict with the public interest in the management of a vital and strategic natural resource, it should be done away with or the same standards and conditions, safeguarding the public interest, should at least apply to all water-users within a given category, whether or not they were prior in tempore.

Finally, another factor which tends to impede the uniform and comprehensive management of the water resources of southern Africa is the fact that these resources, which respect no political boundaries, are nevertheless subject to administration by different governments. In addition to the neighbouring states of Lesotho, Swaziland, Botswana, Mozambique and Zimbabwe, the government's policy has led to the emergence of a number of independent states and self-governing regions in the territory which was formerly part of the Republic of South Africa. The result is that situations of joint interest in common water resources pertain in most major river basins of southern

---

[100] The President's Council in its *Report on a national environmental management system* (PC 1/1991 para 5.4.19) also holds this view.

[101] Ramsden above n 42 has pointed out that the majority of wetlands would qualify as private water.

Africa. International law, therefore, is of considerable interest to the conservation of rivers. See chapter 9.

25.13.2 Water management strategy and river conservation

The point of departure for river conservation would seem to be the Department of Water Affairs' mission, as embodied in the Water Act and in the recommendations of the commission of enquiry into water matters (1970), which were then accepted as government policy. This mission is expressed in the form of a flexible national water management strategy related to supply, demand and quality.[102] The strategy entails the ongoing, equitable provision of adequate quantities and qualities of water to all competing users at acceptable cost and assurance of supply under continuously changing conditions. In order to realize this strategy, different user-categories have been identified and quantities of water allocated to each category and to individual users within the category, mostly subject to the existing rights of riparian owners. Water demand for the environmental management of estuaries, lakes, wetlands, riverine habitat and protected areas has been recognized as a competing need only since the seventies and its importance relative to other competing demands is in fact still being assessed.[103] Reference has been made to suggestions that environmental demands require between 10 and 13 per cent of South Africa's total water demand.

The national water-management strategy clearly indicates that water is regarded as a scarce national resource which must be shared by the different user-categories which have been identified by the Department of Water Affairs, in accordance with the allocations determined by that department. For management purposes, rivers are thus seen primarily as sources of water for use by people.

Viewed from an ecological perspective, however, rivers should not be regarded merely as water sources, but as highly complicated dynamic longitudinal ecosystems;[104] they should accordingly be managed as such. In view of the predominance of many other water demands, the ideal of river conservation management may in practice nevertheless amount merely to an exercise in mitigation. There seems to be an inevitable conflict between the need to develop a river system as a water source and the need for conservation of the river as an ecosystem. Moreover, the long-term benefits of the ecological maintenance of rivers are often less obvious and less capable of being quantified than the relatively short-term and obvious economic benefits with which the former are mostly in conflict. This is a fundamental problem of river conservation.

The vital importance of water to South Africa, which has already been demonstrated, renders it imperative that this scarce but renewable resource should be wisely managed. This necessarily implies the optimal conservation of rivers and of their catchments and, in fact, of the entire hydrological cycle. In other words, a water-management strategy should be environmentally sound. Water resources should be developed and administered in harmony with ecological constraints. The fact should be recognized that our water resources and their capacity for renewal are not unlimited and that there is a point in the development of water resources when water can no longer be matched to the economy, but the economy must be matched to the available water. In short, a water-management strategy should contain, as one of its basic principles, the formulation of a policy for the management of river systems so as to ensure their optimum use and conservation.

Reference has been made to the 'needs of the environment' constituting a separate water demand. It may be that all water use, including that for purely environmental conservation purposes, can be justified only if it is to serve human beings, according to

[102] *Management of water resources* above n 1, xvii and para 6.1.
[103] *Management of water resources* above n 1, paras 2.9 and 10.5.
[104] O'Keeffe above n 15, ch 1.

the Roman adage cum igitur hominum causa omne ius constitutum sit.[105] It should nevertheless be remembered that rivers, as well as riverine fauna and flora, have intrinsic scientific, aesthetic and educational values which cannot readily be assessed in monetary terms, but that definitely serve human beings, especially as urbanization and the hectic pace of modern living rapidly increase.

Finally, the fact that environmental needs now seem to be acknowledged as constituting a separate and legitimate competing water demand may lead to the misconception that environmental factors have thereby been satisfied. However, an environmentally sound management strategy—as has been set out above—transcends all water demands and is fundamental to all water use. River conservation can therefore be justified on both counts.

25.13.3 River conservation options

25.13.3.1 *Total conservation of rivers*

(a) River reserves. From a conservation perspective it would seem appropriate to protect certain pristine rivers in their entirety as formal reserves, comparable to the conservation of fauna and flora within national parks and other nature reserves. However, this ideal is usually not feasible, owing to the longitudinal nature of rivers—which means that they flow through different properties under the control of different landowners and management authorities.[106] Moreover, for a river conservation area to succeed it will have to include control over the entire catchment. In any case, unfortunately, very few pristine rivers or parts of rivers have been identified in South Africa.

The closest that we have come to the establishment of river reserves is the concept of river conservancy districts in Natal, as explained in chapter 13. The other declared water-related areas for which our law provides, some of which overlap, do not accommodate the conservation of entire rivers, although they may include parts of rivers.

(b) Rivers flowing through protected areas. The only instances where parts of rivers are totally protected are those stretches of rivers which are included in protected areas such as national parks and provincial nature reserves. However, with the possible exception of the Blyde River reserve, none of these areas has been declared primarily for the sake of the river. Moreover, the conservation of a certain stretch of river is detrimentally affected by the upstream status of the river in question, if mismanagement has occurred in the latter area. On the other hand, many headwater streams enjoy a relatively secure conservation status on account of their being included in declared mountain catchment areas.

25.13.3.2 *The conservation of rivers as a compromise with development*

It appears that the total conservation of rivers or even of stretches of rivers is something that can be practically achieved only in exceptional instances. In most instances the goal of river conservation—if it is at all strived for—must be achieved as a compromise with development. The premise of our water law and water management is in fact that water is a resource subject to the demands of multiple use-categories. At best a river can be put to various uses, but subject to a management plan drawn up according to conservation principles. At worst it can be allowed to degenerate into a paved stormwater canal or even into an open sewer.

---

[105] D 1.5.2.

[106] O'Keeffe above n 15, 39.

25.13.4 River conservation authority

While the principle of state control over public rivers is generally acknowledged, the problem is that there is no single authority which is responsible for an entire river and its catchment. In fact, there are a number of administrative bodies that exercise various forms of control in respect of the same river. Control is further complicated where parts of a river fail to satisfy the definition of a public stream, implying that individual landowners may deal with the water as their private property. It is submitted that a suitable body—perhaps a newly created river conservation authority—should be established to co-ordinate efforts to conserve an entire river and its catchment. A single authority per river system may be required as regards major rivers, while a regional authority may operate in respect of several minor rivers. A complicating factor is that in many instances co-operation between the various states of southern Africa will be required if such an authority should have any chance of successfully conserving rivers flowing through more than one state. The conservation management of a river should be undertaken in accordance with a management plan which reflects an understanding and implementation of the principle that a river constitutes an ecological unit and forms part of a hydrological cycle. The degree of conservation management would depend upon the river's present conservation status, its potential for rehabilitation and its importance as a water resource.

CHAPTER 26

THE COASTAL ZONE

A E F HEYDORN
J I GLAZEWSKI
B C GLAVOVIC

26.1 INTRODUCTION

South Africa has a coastline some 3 000 km long, extending from the desert coast of Namibia to tropical Mozambique. The character of this coast is determined by a number of factors, including: the geomorphology of coastal regions; the influence of three major marine water bodies off the southern African continent—the Indian, Atlantic and Southern oceans; the air–sea interaction generated by these water bodies, which has a decisive influence upon the climate of southern Africa; the land–sea interaction, which shapes beaches, dunes and estuaries; and the impact of a multitude of human activities which have transformed large areas of the coast through development and the exploitation of resources.[1]

The South African coastline can be divided into three broad coastal regions: the subtropical east coast, the warm temperate south coast and the cold temperate west coast.[2]

The east coast, which stretches southwards from the Mozambique border to about Port Elizabeth, is subtropical in character due to the warm southward-flowing Agulhas Current. In the northern parts off Maputaland, sandy and rocky shores extend seawards and the submarine reefs support prolific coral growth. Large estuaries and lakes occur in this coastal region, including the Kosi estuarine system, Lake Sibayi, St Lucia and Richards Bay, and Umgazana in Transkei.

The subtropical influence along this coast gives rise to humid, warm temperatures, lush vegetation and a diversity of sea-life. Durban has an average temperature of 20,5 °C and an annual rainfall of about 1 000 mm. These conditions have been conducive to human settlement. It is estimated that the Durban metropolitan area, the second largest such area in South Africa, will have a population of some 4,4 million by the year 2000, and some 6 million by the year 2010. About half of this population lives in informal settlements.[3]

The south coast extends roughly from Port Elizabeth to Cape Town and is a zone of transition between subtropical and cold temperate conditions. Between Port Elizabeth and Cape Agulhas, the rock-dominated coastline is incised by deep river gorges, for example that of the Storms River, or by meandering rivers which enter the sea at places such as Knysna, Cape Infanta and Still Bay. Seawards the continental shelf broadens into the Agulhas Bank, which is a major mixing area of subtropical water carried southwards by the Agulhas Current, water of Antarctic origin which upwells sporadically and Atlantic surface water. Bottom trawling on the Agulhas Bank contributes substantially to South Africa's fishing industry and the recently developed

---

[1] Branch & Branch *The living shores of southern Africa* (1981); Payne & Crawford (eds) *Oceans of life off southern Africa* (1989).

[2] Branch & Branch above n 1, 14.

[3] *Urban debate 2010: policies for a new urban future—population trends* vol 1 Urban Foundation (undated) 26, 30.

offshore gas and oil industry may become a major generator of revenue and employment. Cape Town is a major industrial and urban centre with a population expected to reach 3,3 million people by the year 2000, rising to some 4 million by the year 2010.[4]

The west coast extends northwards from Cape Town to the Orange River. This coastal region becomes progressively more arid northwards, despite frequent coastal fog. Air passing from the cold Benguela system onto hot land gives rise to the frequent occurrence of fog but does not yield much rain. Nutrient-rich water of Antarctic origin upwells sporadically along the west coast, making the area one of the richest fishing grounds in the world. Large colonies of sea birds and seals are also found in this region.

Conditions along the west coast are generally not conducive to human settlement. Port Nolloth, for example, has a mean temperature of 14,1 °C and an average rainfall of 61 mm annually. With the exception of scattered diamond-mining towns and fishing villages, and the more urbanised town of Saldanha, the west coast stretches for about 600 km virtually uninhabited. The main human activities along the Namaqualand coast are diamond mining, marginal agriculture and fishing. Along the southern west coast agricultural activities are more viable, but are concentrated inland of the coast. The fishing industry is concentrated around St Helena Bay and is an important source of employment on the west coast. Other than at Saldanha, there has been relatively little development of secondary or tertiary industry on the west coast. In recent years there has, however, been considerable growth in nature-oriented tourism and recreation. The Langebaan lagoon, now part of the West Coast National Park, and the spring flowers of Namaqualand have been major attractions to visitors.

The need to manage the coast as a distinct component of the broader environment has been recognized by people in developed and developing countries around the world.[5]

The following issues highlight the need for a dedicated coastal zone management effort in South Africa:

- The coastal zone has particularly important strategic and economic value. The total wholesale value of the products of the South African fishing industry (excluding Walvis Bay) alone was about R1,155 billion in 1989.[6] The industry currently employs some 27 000 people.[7] In addition, there are at least 530 000 recreational fishermen who spend more than R150 million on their sport annually.[8] Given its diversity of resources and development opportunities, the coastal zone supports a growing population and a variety of often competing human activities. These include recreation, residential and industrial development, mining (on land and offshore), power stations, infrastructure (roads, rail, harbours, airports), military installations, agriculture, forestry, nature reserves and national parks, solid waste disposal sites, sewage and effluent disposal via marine pipelines, cooling water intake systems for industry, exploitation of living marine resources by commercial and recreational fishing, and a host of other activities. In future, our rapidly increasing population, with its growing demands, will intensify pressures on the coastal zone, which is a limited area with finite resources.
- Many features of the coastal zone are sensitive to human-induced perturbations.

---

[4] *Urban debate* above n 3, 30.

[5] Sorensen & Brandani 'An overview of coastal zone management efforts in Latin America' 1987 (15(1)) *Coastal Management* 1–25; Degong 'Coastal zone development, utilization, legislation and management in China' 1989 (17(1)) *Coastal Management* 55–62; Cullen 'Coastal zone management in Australia' 1982 (10(3)) *Coastal Zone Management J* 183–212.

[6] Unpublished official statistics of the Chief Directorate: Sea Fisheries, Department of Environment Affairs.

[7] Ibid.

[8] Van Der Elst in Payne & Crawford above n 1, 164–76.

Examples include the over-exploitation of fishery resources, the erection of fixed structures in the dynamic sediment-dominated zone of the coast, and the degradation of wetlands and estuaries. Such activities can lead to the collapse of natural systems, reduced biological productivity, declining economic returns, high maintenance costs and the loss of irreplaceable assets, and generate negative aesthetic impacts.

The sea is the ultimate sink for virtually all human waste[9] and the coastal zone is prone to pollution from all three environmental media: air, land and water. Environmentally sensitive coastal waters such as estuaries and bays have been subject to ever-increasing pollution problems.[10] Although spectacular bulk carrier oil tanker spills attract much media attention, over three-quarters of marine pollution emanates from land-based sources.[11] Currently 800 million litres of effluent is discharged daily into the sea through over sixty pipelines located at various points around South Africa's coastline, necessitating extensive monitoring.[12]

Recent times have also seen a drastic escalation of plastic pollution, both of the sea and the sea-shore. A scientific study has identified the Agulhas Current as a major transporter of pollution of the sea off the south-western coast.[13]

While the coastal zone has always attracted a substantial portion of the country's population and industry, resulting in pollution problems, the recent past has seen a dramatic influx of people into South Africa's coastal cities and towns, exacerbating the problem. The proliferating informal settlements surrounding coastal cities lack basic services, including waste and sewage disposal facilities. Storm-water drains from squatter areas near Cape Town into False Bay; the Swartkops River near Port Elizabeth and rivers around Durban have all been found to contain inordinately high levels of pathogenic bacteria.[14] In the South African context it has been said:

> 'The single most influential effect in the coastal zone over the next ten years will arise from the points of run-off and discharge arising from rapid urbanisation and deregulated industry'.[15]

The Department of Water Affairs has identified four main water quality problems in South Africa generally: eutrophication, salinization, trace metals and micropollutants.[16] To some extent, these problems are concentrated in the coastal zone. Clearly, a major challenge for the authorities lies ahead.

- Coastal zone management is fraught with difficulty because of the inherent complexity of land–sea interactions. In addition to the vexing socio-environmental issues, there are complex global trends that could dramatically impact on the South African coastal zone in the future. Scientists report that there may be climatic changes related to the accumulation of 'greenhouse' gases, and a rise in sea-level of approximately 20 cm within the next 35 years. This could be followed by as much as a 1,5 m rise by the end of the next century. Although there is uncertainty about the precise nature and magnitude of these predictions, even a small rise in sea-level and

---

[9] Brown 'Marine pollution and health in South Africa' 1987 *SAMJ* 244–8.

[10] For example, see Molden & Ridder (eds) *Marine pollution—a 1988 perspective* South African National Scientific Programmes Report no 161 (1989).

[11] Kwiatkowska 'Land based pollution' 1984 (14(3)) *ODIL*.

[12] Lord, Anderson & Basson (eds) *Pipeline discharges of effluents to sea* South African National Scientific Programmes Report no 90 (1984).

[13] Ryan 'The characteristics and distribution of plastic particles at the sea-surface off the southwestern Cape Province, South Africa' 1988 (25(4)) *Marine Environmental Research* 249–73.

[14] Glazewski & Manuel 'The oceans—our common heritage' in Cock & Koch (eds) *Going green* (1991).

[15] Lord *South African coastal waters—assimilation or pollution?* Maritime Conference, Cape Town, May 1989.

[16] *Management of the water resources of the Republic of South Africa* Department of Water Affairs (1986).

a marginal shift in climatic patterns will have dire consequences for human activities in the coastal zone. These could include increased coastal erosion, flooding and inundation, increased salt-water intrusion and raised groundwater tables, increased vulnerability to extreme storm events, changes in rainfall patterns and shifts in the distribution of fish stocks and productive agricultural land.[17]

Given the need for a dedicated coastal zone management (CZM) effort, the Council for the Environment (CE) undertook to draft a policy for CZM for the Republic of South Africa in co-operation with the Department of Environment Affairs. The policy is designed to be published in the following three parts: Principles and objectives for CZM (Part 1), Guidelines for coastal land-use (Part 2), and Integrated coastal management (Part 3). Part 1 was published in 1989,[18] while Part 2 was published in 1991.[19]

26.2 COASTAL ZONE MANAGEMENT IN SOUTH AFRICA

26.2.1 Definition of Coastal Zone

An initial question is: 'what constitutes the coastal zone and what are its boundaries?'

The coastal zone is a complex region incorporating components such as coastal uplands, floodplains and wetlands (which may be characterised by fresh water or salt water depending on the degree of tidal penetration), estuaries, dunes and beaches, rocky shores and headlands and the continental shelf, which extends seawards from the low-water mark. Depending on the bottom topography, the continental slope may then drop off to abyssal depths of thousands of metres. In some cases, such as off the south and west coasts of South Africa and off the coast of Namibia, offshore islands occur close enough to the mainland to be regarded as part of the coastal zone. This can obviously not be the case with oceanic islands such as Marion, Prince Edward or Gough, because these islands have their own coasts. As a general rule, however, the laws pertaining to CZM of the country to which such islands belong are also applicable to the island environments.

While components of the coastal zone such as those mentioned above may be readily identified, the coastal zone itself is not easily definable. It is readily acceptable that the intertidal area between high- and low-water marks is part of the coastal zone as well as certain components such as estuaries. However, there is no clearly ascertainable seaward or landward boundary. Both an ecological and an administrative approach can be considered in defining the coastal zone for legal purposes.

An ecological approach is discerned in the 1972 Coastal Zone Management Act of the USA, which defines the 'coastal zone' as:

'the coastal waters (including the land therein and thereunder) and the adjacent shorelines (including the waters therein and thereunder) strongly influenced by each other and in proximity to the shorelines of the several coastal states and includes islands, transitional and intertidal areas, salt marshes, wetlands and beaches. The zone extends seawards to the outer limit of the US

---

[17] Titus 'Greenhouse effect, sea level rise and coastal zone management' 1986 (14(3)) *Coastal Zone Management Journal* 147–71. See, generally, conference on geosphere–biosphere change in southern Africa 1990 (86) *S Afr J Sci* 278–472; Sowman, Glazewski, Fuggle & Barbour 'Planning and legal responses to sea-level rise in South Africa' 1990 (86) *S Afr J Sci* 294; Hughes & Brundrit 'The vulnerability of the False Bay coastline to the projected rise in sea level' 1991 (47) *Transactions of the Royal Society of South Africa* parts IV and V 519–34; Hughes, Brundrit, & Shillington 'South African sea level measurements in the global context of sea level rise' *S Afr J Sci* (in press); Hughes & Brundrit 'The development of an index to assess South Africa's vulnerability to sea level rise' *S Afr J Sci* (in press); Hughes & Brundrit 'Planning for our mistakes: how to cope with rising sea levels' 1991 *Town and Regional Planning* (in press).

[18] *A policy for coastal zone management in the Republic of South Africa, Part 1—Principles and objectives* Council for the Environment (1989).

[19] *A policy for coastal zone management in the Republic of South Africa, Part 2—Guidelines for coastal land-use* Council for the Environment (1991).

territorial sea. The zone extends inland from the shorelines only to the extent necessary to control shorelines, the uses of which have a direct and significant impact on the coastal waters. . . .'

Coastal waters are in turn defined as:

'Those waters, adjacent to the shorelines, which contain a measurable quantity or percentage of seawater including but not limited to, sounds, bays, lagoons, bayous, ponds and estuaries.'

However desirable such a definition may be from an ecological perspective, it is too open-ended and thus not practical from an administrative or legal point of view. The US Coastal Zone Management Act recognizes this and requires each coastal state to define the coastal zone more specifically if that particular state wishes to participate in certain federally funded CZM programmes.

In response, South Carolina adopted an ecological approach by defining the coastal zone inland to include all land and water of the eight coastal counties. It also defines critical areas—for example, coastal waters, tide lands, beaches and primary ocean front dunes. Oregon also uses an ecological approach by drawing its landward boundary along the crest of its coastal mountain range. By contrast, California adopted an administrative approach, by defining an arbitrary line of 5 miles landward of, and parallel to, the high-water mark. Connecticut adopted a similar approach by also using a line, but only of 500 feet above the high-water mark. Alabama follows an administrative approach, but in a different manner by adopting a contour line of 10 feet above mean sea-level.[20]

As regards the seaward boundary of the coastal zone, a 3 nautical mile (5,5 km) seaward boundary is used by many countries and can be accepted as a general guideline. There may, however, be special cases (for example, marine reserves or areas with offshore gas or oil deposits) that require further extension into the sea and the concept of incorporating the internationally accepted 200 nautical mile economic zone out to sea therefore warrants serious attention if coastal and marine resources are to be properly managed. This approach would certainly be applicable in South Africa with its pelagic and benthic fish resources and its offshore gas and oil deposits.

It is against this background that the CE adopted an ecological approach by defining the coastal zone as:

'A system with open boundaries which may include estuaries, onshore areas and offshore areas, wherever they form an integral part of the coastal system'.[21]

Such an open-ended definition provides for interactions between land and sea in the widest sense and it recognizes the need for protection of the natural processes which govern such interactions. The concept also recognizes constituent components of the coastal zone as ranging from watersheds to deep oceans.

While this definition is acceptable from a scientific point of view, experience in many parts of the world has shown that CZM is most successful in those countries where it is confined to a relatively narrow coastal strip which encompasses the actual coastal features such as lakes, estuaries, lagoons, dunes, beaches, rocky shores and, in appropriate cases, offshore islands. It should furthermore be noted that there is no definition of the 'coastal zone' in current South African legislation. The South African legislature has, however, defined the 'sea-shore' in the Sea-Shore Act 21 of 1935 as the area between high- and low-water marks. Clearly, the coastal zone encompasses more than the sea-shore, and a broader definition and regulatory framework are required.[22]

---

[20] Meagher & Pembroke 'Aspects of the legal regime in the United States pertaining to coastal zones' 1982 (49(293)) *Ekistics* 156.

[21] *A policy for coastal zone management* above n 18.

[22] This aspect is elaborated on in para 26.3.2 below.

26.2.2 Objectives of CZM

The overall aim of CZM is to promote development in the coastal zone, a common heritage of the nation, in such a way as to benefit the greatest number of people possible, while at the same time safeguarding the intrinsic environmental features and ecological processes of the coast. This aim promotes wise use of the coast and its resources and encompasses the concepts of optimal utilization and protection of the coastal environment.

Objectives for CZM in South Africa have been defined by the CE as:

- integration of conservation principles into planning processes for development;
- promotion of necessary and desirable development in keeping with the intrinsic environmental features and ecological processes within specific coastal regions;
- restriction of ecologically harmful developments and ensuring that major developments are concentrated as far as possible at focal growth points;
- discouragement or strict control of development in as yet undeveloped areas so as to retain the coast's natural character as far as possible;
- protection of ecologically sensitive coastal features such as coastal lakes, lagoons, estuaries, dunes, beaches, rocky shores and offshore islands, together with the natural processes governing their functioning;
- promotion of environmental education to solicit general support and voluntary collaboration in the implementation of CZM procedures.

In addition to the aforegoing objectives, there is a need to promote opportunities for all South Africans to gain access to the coast, to use coastal resources and to benefit from coastal development opportunities. Particular attention needs to be given, however, to formulating principles for undertaking activities in high-risk areas of the coastal zone.

26.2.3 Principles for undertaking activities in high-risk areas of the coastal zone

The CE identifies two types of high-risk areas in the coastal environment which need to be taken into account:

(1) High-risk areas caused by natural processes, including:
   - naturally dynamic beach-dune areas;
   - tidal regions of estuaries and/or river mouths;
   - floodplains adjacent to rivers;
   - steep slopes subject to slumping or rockfalls.

(2) High-risk areas caused by human activity. Such areas frequently coincide with those mentioned under (1) above, but vulnerability to damage is often enhanced by human activity, e g where the vegetation binding river banks or steep slopes is destroyed, where the dynamic equilibrium of river mouths, estuaries or dunes is disturbed, or where the emergence of a high-water table during wet, high-precipitation periods has been ignored.

There is a need to protect the environment against unnecessary damage, and the developer and investor against losses. Planning of development should therefore not be based on average conditions but on extreme conditions which may occur only once every 50 or 100 years. The massive damage to private property and infrastructure, including major road bridges, during the Natal floods of 1987 provides graphic examples.[23]

The principles developed by the CE and accepted by both the Department of Environment Affairs and the Cape and Natal Provincial Administrations entail the following:

---

[23] Perry *The impact of the September 1987 floods on the estuaries of Natal/KwaZulu; a hydro-photographic perspective* CSIR Research Report no 640 (1989).

- In areas of high risk as a result of natural processes development should be discouraged, for example, through official refusal to grant permits and withdrawal of insurance privileges and/or the right to claim compensation in the event of a catastrophe.
- In areas where the natural equilibrium is easily disrupted development should be planned in such a way that it does not cause unnecessary disruption of the equilibrium of natural systems. Specific attention must be given to preventing undesirable disturbance of sediment pathways in the nearshore zone or on land or of driving forces such as river flow, tides and waves. The role of plant communities on floodplains, swamps and dunes is of special importance in this context.

In both high-risk areas and areas in which the equilibrium is easily disturbed, developers should be encouraged to participate in decision-making processes aimed at avoiding unnecessary environmental disruption or hardship to present or potential users, or loss of options in future use of the environment. Hence the requirement that they themselves should provide risk assessments of the possible consequences of their developments on vulnerable components of the environment. They should also indicate what alternatives have been considered. This would require adhering to the comprehensive integrated environmental management (IEM) procedure developed by the CE.[24]

The following additional measures should also be implemented:

- The responsible governmental authority should call for a properly conducted environmental impact assessment by competent specialists if the risk of environmental consequences revealed in the IEM process is unacceptable. The costs of such an assessment should be borne by the developer.
- Sound planning of developments in the coastal zone requires contributions from a wide spectrum of specialists. Such planning and its implementation therefore needs to be performed on a multi-disciplinary basis.
- The above principles should apply to new developments and extensions to existing developments by both the private and public sectors.
- If a governmental authority is the developer, it should be subjected to the same principles as a private developer.

The aforegoing principles and objectives for CZM have been logically developed on the basis of the features and variability which characterize the South African coastline, and have been accepted by the responsible authorities. In order to ensure effective implementation, there is an urgent need to explain these principles and objectives to local communities, political groups and the business sector. These groups may identify additional concerns which should be addressed. Once the principles and objectives have been modified accordingly, and have the backing of the various coastal resource user groups and controlling authorities, attention can be given to formulating a policy for CZM in South Africa. This leads to the question whether the legal regime in the country can ensure that the accepted policy can be implemented.

26.3 THE LEGAL REGIME

26.3.1 Juridical nature of the sea, sea-shore and marine resources

26.3.1.1 *The sea and sea-shore*

In Roman law the sea and sea-shore were classified as res omnium communes, i e the area fell into the category of objects which were enjoyed by everybody but was incapable of ownership. This classification was modified in Roman-Dutch law, which classified the sea and sea-shore as a res publicae. This vested ownership of the area in

[24] *Integrated environmental management in South Africa* Council for the Environment (1989).

the authorities, but they owned it in a custodianship capacity, i e for the benefit of the public and not in a private capacity.

This common-law position was further modified by the Sea-Shore Act 21 of 1935, which is the prevailing statutory instrument governing the status of the sea and sea-shore. It vests ownership of the sea and sea-shore in the State President.[25] Alienation thereof is prohibited, but any alienation which took place prior to the passing of the Act is respected.[26] The Minister of Environment Affairs enjoys a number of powers and is responsible for the administration of the Act; certain executive responsibilities and functions have to a large extent been assigned to the provincial authorities.[27]

The Act authorizes the Minister to let portions of the area for designated purposes such as the erection of bathing boxes, tea-rooms, beach shelters and the construction of public facilities such as wharves, jetties, piers, drainage and sewerage systems and so on.[28] Before any such lease is entered into, certain procedural requirements, such as advertising details of the proposed lease, have to be complied with.[29] The area may, however, be used for government purposes under authority of the Minister.[30]

The Act also provides that any alienation, letting or other permission not specifically authorized by the Act may take place only by special resolution of the House of Assembly.[31] It also preserves the rights of any member of the public to use the sea-shore or the sea except in so far as such rights may be inconsistent with any rights granted under the Act.[32]

It is thus clear that the Roman law philosophy, that the sea and sea-shore constitute an area which is subject to the enjoyment of all, still prevails in current South African law, although the Act has departed from it to some extent. Thus the Appellate Division has held:

'. . . the public have certain simple rights to the foreshore such as to go on to it, to bathe, to fish, to dry nets, to draw up boats . . . [and] any substantial interference with those rights would be a wrongful act. . . .'[33]

While this philosophy is inherent in the Act, it unfortunately is not clear about the extent of public rights. This has resulted in inroads being made into the public's rights, for example, legislation relating to separate amenities.[34] Nevertheless, the provisions of the Sea-Shore Act have probably also served to inhibit certain controversial development. For example, it is likely that the controversial proposal to construct a marina at Robberg in the vicinity of Plettenberg Bay was not approved because it militated against both the spirit and the letter of the Act.

The nature and extent of the public's right to the sea and the sea-shore should be considered afresh in the light of the government's relatively recent policy of privatization. It is conceivable that certain portions of the sea-shore in particular could be privatized. However, the advantages and disadvantages of doing so should be subject to public debate and approval before any legislative changes are made.

---

[25] Section 2.

[26] Section 2(2).

[27] State President's Minute no 1109 of 18 November 1986. See Rabie 'Mechanical roars on our shores: control over off road vehicles on the sea-shore' 1991 *SA Public Law* 189.

[28] Section 3(1)*(a)*.

[29] Section 3(4) and (5).

[30] Section 5.

[31] Section 6(1).

[32] Section 13*(c)*.

[33] *Consolidated Diamond Mines of SWA Ltd v Administrator SWA* 1958 (4) SA 572 (A) 621.

[34] See, for example, *R v Carelse* 1943 CPD 242. See also Van der Vyver 'The étatisation of public property' in Visser (ed) *Essays on the history of law* (1989) 261.

26.3.1.2 *Marine resources*

In Roman law wild animals, which included living marine resources such as fish, were categorized as res nullius. This classification referred to objects which are not owned but are capable of individual private ownership. Ownership is obtained by occupatio, which entails taking physical control of the object together with having the intention of becoming the owner.[35]

While this common-law position still prevails in South Africa, it has been significantly modified by statute. The currently applicable legislation is the Sea Fishery Act 12 of 1988, which imposes various forms of control on all fishing activities. The law governing living marine resources is elaborated on in chapter 14.

For a long time it was not clear whether a person who captured a wild animal, including fish, illegally, could be the owner of it.[36] In *S v Frost; S v Noah*[37] F and N, employees of a company, were prosecuted for capturing 5 000 kg of snoek in the closed season. The court considered the question of ownership and decided that, although the fish had been captured illegally, the company was nevertheless the owner.[38]

26.3.2 Definition of coastal zone and coastal zone regulations

As noted above, there is no definition of the 'coastal zone' in current South African legislation, although the 'sea-shore' is defined in the Sea-Shore Act as the area between high- and low-water marks.[39] However, the coastal zone encompasses more than the sea-shore.

The promulgation of regulations under the repealed Environment Conservation Act 100 of 1982, the so-called coastal zone regulations, was an important step towards recognizing the coastal zone as a distinct area requiring particular legislative attention.[40] These regulations demarcated the strip of land between the high-water mark and an imaginary parallel line 1 000 m from and landward of the high-water mark to be an area, known as the limited area. Any proposed development in this strip would require particular environmental scrutiny. The regulations stipulated that notice had to be given of a proposed activity (as defined) in the area. The authorities had to consider certain principles before approving the development and could require an environmental impact assessment to be undertaken before the proposed activity was approved. The authorities had the power to refuse, grant approval or approve the proposal subject to conditions.

From the point of view of a definition of the coastal zone, these regulations were welcome because they recognized that, ecologically, the area landward of the high-water mark is part of the coastal system. Any definition of the coastal zone should seek a sensible and practical balance between taking into account ecological factors which are a true reflection of natural processes influencing the coastal zone and administrative needs such as the desirability of having a readily identifiable area.

The regulations were also a welcome step towards more effective CZM, their purpose being to close loopholes in planning legislation that permitted environmentally undesirable developments in the coastal zone. Unfortunately, soon after their promulgation, the Cape Provincial Administration used an exemption power in the

[35] See, generally, Van der Merwe *Sakereg* (2 ed, 1989) 218.

[36] See Van der Merwe & Rabie 'Eiendom van wilde diere' 1974 *THRHR* 38; Rabie & Van der Merwe 'Wildboerdery in regsperspektief—enkele knelpunte' 1990 *Stell LR* 112; *Dunn v Bowyer* 1926 NPD 516.

[37] 1974 (3) SA 466 (C).

[38] In *Dunn v Bowyer* above n 36, a case concerning the illegal capture of a hippopotamus, the opposite view was adopted.

[39] Section 1 defines 'sea-shore' as the water and the land between the low-water mark and the high-water mark. High- and low-water marks are also defined in s 1.

[40] GN R2587 of 12 December 1986. Interestingly, the preceding draft regulations included the sea-shore but extended landwards only 500 m: GN 2806 of 20 December 1985.

regulations to exclude their application for any activity proposed in the area falling within the jurisdiction of a local authority.[41] In Natal, the authorities demarcated particularly ecologically sensitive areas within the limited area for application of the regulations.

The coastal zone regulations were probably ultra vires, both on account of their vague contents and of not being authorized by the Act,[42] and in any case seem to have been repealed by the Environment Conservation Act 73 of 1989.[43] Indeed, the chief state law advisor informed the Department of Environment Affairs that these regulations were ultra vires. Given this advice, the authorities ceased applying the coastal regulations. It was, however, obvious that the coastal zone regulations had been an important and necessary tool to control environmentally undesirable coastal development. Consequently, an interdepartmental working group, comprising representatives from central, provincial and local government, was established to formulate an effective replacement mechanism. It emerged that limited development areas[44] offer the most suitable replacement mechanism that does not duplicate existing legislation and which will be binding on all developers, including the State. See chapter 7.

Proclaiming all environmentally sensitive areas along the South African coast as limited development areas, has, regrettably, been delayed by the need to introduce several essential amendments to the Environment Conservation Act of 1989. See chapter 7. Urgent attention has, in the meantime, been given to identifying specific priority areas.[45] Declaration of such areas, consistent with the principles of IEM, is under way.

26.3.3 Admiralty reserve

In certain areas of the coastline, particularly in Natal, there is an admiralty reserve. This reserve comprises narrow strips of land, seldom more than 200 feet (61 m) wide, immediately adjoining and landward of the high-water mark. The admiralty reserve has its origins in the first grants of land made by the government during the 19th century. A typical clause in an original grant, and which has survived to the present day, reads: 'A strip of land two hundred feet in width above high-water mark is reserved by the government.'[46]

While the historical purpose and current potential of the admiralty reserve is not entirely clear, it has been argued that a general survey of the admiralty reserve along the South African coastline could serve as a potential conservation tool, particularly in so far as dunelands are concerned.[47]

26.3.4 Territorial extent of South African law

The territorial extent of application of South African law is not a straightforward matter. Typical questions which arise include: Is there a particular line out at sea where South African law simply stops applying? Are South African nationals subject to South African law however far out to sea they may be? To what extent are foreigners or

---

[41] PN 267 of 5 June 1987.

[42] See Rabie 'Towards a new legislative and administrative dispensation for coastal zone management' 1987 *THRHR* 195 and Glazewski & Sowman 'An assessment of the new coastal zone regulations' 1987 (5) *Sea Changes* 145.

[43] Rabie 'A new deal for environmental conservation: aspects of the Environment Conservation Act 73 of 1989' 1990 *THRHR* 2, 19–20.

[44] Section 23 grants the Minister power to declare limited development areas.

[45] For instance, the Department of Environment Affairs has indicated that it is looking at Blombos on the Cape coast for possible declaration.

[46] See, generally, Glazewski 'The Admiralty Reserve—an historical anachronism or a bonus for conservation in the coastal zone?' 1986 *Acta Juridica* 193.

[47] Ibid.

foreign vessels plying South African waters, subject to South African law? These questions have important practical consequences and some of the relevant legal principles are elaborated on here.

Two general international-law principles relating to jurisdiction are pertinent: territoriality and personality. By virtue of the first-mentioned principle, South African law may claim a territorial sea of 12 nautical miles (22 km), subject to the right of innocent passage of foreign vessels; this has been done.[48] South African law may also apply beyond the territorial waters in respect of certain activities. Thus, as regards the exploitation of both living and non-living marine resources, international law grants coastal states jurisdiction over such resources up to the extent of its Exclusive Economic Zone, usually 200 nautical miles (370 km) and in the case of non-living marine resources, sometimes even beyond 200 nautical miles.[49] This territoriality principle is the basis for the presumption against the extra-territorial applicability of domestic statutes in South African law.[50]

It follows that all South African law is applicable up to the extent of South Africa's territorial sea of 12 nautical miles and, beyond that, where international law allows and where South African legislation has specifically claimed such jurisdiction. Thus, the Territorial Waters Act 87 of 1963 claims a 200 nautical mile exclusive fishing zone[51] and also claims jurisdiction over non-living resources beyond the territorial waters by virtue of the continental shelf doctrine.[52]

It further follows that South African fishery legislation, in particular the Sea Fishery Act and regulations made under it applies up to the extent of the 200 nautical mile fishing zone, and beyond that in respect of South African vessels and persons.[53] See chapter 14.

Similarly, South African mining legislation applies up to the extent of the continental shelf, the Territorial Waters Act providing that any South African law relating to mining shall also apply to the continental shelf adjoining the Republic.[54] See chapter 16.

Practical problems have arisen in this regard—for example, in *Chemical and Industrial Workers' Union v Sopelog CC*[55] a preliminary question considered by the Industrial Court in a labour dispute was whether the Labour Relations Act 28 of 1956 applied to drilling crews working on oil rigs beyond South African territorial waters. The Court, relying on the presumption against the extra-territorial applicability of domestic statues, held that in the absence of any provision in the Labour Relations Act or other legislation giving the Labour Relations Act extra-territorial operation, the Labour Relations Act does not enjoy such extra-territorial operation.

The question of the extent of South African courts' jurisdiction over foreign vessels within South African territorial waters was considered in *Yorigami Maritime Construction Co Ltd v Nissho-Iwai Co Ltd*.[56]

Two Japanese parties, Y and N, entered into an agreement in Japan whereby Y chartered a tug to N for purposes of towing two of N's motor tankers from Greece to Formosa. The towline snapped in the vicinity of Table Bay, beyond 3 nautical miles

---

[48] Section 2 of the Territorial Waters Act 87 of 1963.

[49] See the discussion on the doctrine of continental shelf in chapter 14.

[50] Cockram *The interpretation of statutes* (3 ed, 1987) 134 et seq.

[51] Sections 3 and 4. South Africa has not claimed a 200 nautical mile exclusive economic zone, but an exclusive fishing zone of 200 nautical miles.

[52] Section 7.

[53] In terms of s 3 of the Territorial Waters Act, South Africa exercises the same rights in its fishing zone as it does in its territorial sea. Section 52 of the Sea Fishery Act regulates foreign vessels operating in South Africa's exclusive fishing zone.

[54] Section 7.

[55] 1988 (9) *ILJ* 846.

[56] 1977 (4) SA 682 (C) and 1978 (2) SA 391 (C).

(5,5 km) but within 6 nautical miles (the extent of South Africa's territorial sea at the time). The two tankers drifted ashore and were wrecked. A dispute developed between the parties and N applied for an order of attachment in the Cape Supreme Court. The question before the Court was whether the Cape Supreme Court has jurisdiction over an alleged delict which occurred in South African territorial waters but which concerned two foreigners and an agreement entered into abroad. The broader issue was whether South African law extends over its territorial waters.

Both courts (the single and the full bench) were of the view that the South African Court did have jurisdiction over the dispute notwithstanding the fact that historically the Cape Colony may only have extended to the low-water mark. The full bench held that, whatever may have been the position with regard to the Cape Colony, after South Africa became a sovereign state, it enjoyed full legislative and judicial power over its territorial sea. The Court therefore had jurisdiction to hear the dispute.[57]

26.3.5 Moving or ambulatory boundaries

In demarcating property boundaries it is often convenient to use natural features such as the high-water mark, dunes or rivers to indicate their physical borders. Because the coastline is a dynamic natural system, it is particularly prone to these physical boundaries moving—rivers meander, the high-water mark fluctuates and may shift over time.[58]

The legal principles applicable to locating the legal boundary are first described below. Thereafter, a related problem—that of physical accretion or decretion of land—is considered. A permanent rise in the tide level may cause a physical loss of land, while a receding of the tideline may result in a physical gain of land. Similarly, on-going sediment transport may result in the hardening of river mouths or banks, resulting in physical gains or losses of land for riparian property owners. These natural physical processes are often affected by human intervention, for example, a dune stabilization programme may result in the cutting-off of sediment transport, resulting in physical accretion or decretion in adjoining properties. The legal rules governing the gains and losses of land as a result of the physical boundary moving are accordingly considered below.

As regards the problem of boundary location, the position of the high-water mark at a particular point in time is pertinent. The Sea-Shore Act defines this line as:

'The highest line reached by the waters of the sea during ordinary storms or storms occurring during the most stormy period of the year, excluding exceptional or abnormal floods.'[59]

This definition had its origins in *Pharo v Stephan*[60] concerning a dispute between a landowner whose land adjoined Paternoster Bay and an alleged trespasser. The Court had to consider the landward extent of the sea-shore and, after considering various options, adopted the above line, which subsequently was adopted in the Sea-Shore Act.

In practice it may be impractical to wait for the 'most stormy period of the year'. A professional land surveyor will nevertheless be able to ascertain the location of the high-water mark by examining the terrain, vegetation and the debris line and canvassing the views of local inhabitants and fishermen.

There has also been statutory intervention to alleviate doubt in particular cases. Thus the Sea-Shore Act makes provision for the surveyor-general to replace a boundary

---

[57] Booysen argues that the Court was wrong. See 'Jurisdiction of the South African Courts over the South African territorial waters' 1977 *SAYIL* 184. This article was written after the decision of the single bench, but his argument still applies after the full-bench decision. See Botha 'Municipal jurisdiction over territorial waters' 1978 *SAYIL* 177.

[58] See, generally, Simpson & Sweeney *The land surveyor and the law* (1973).

[59] Section 1.

[60] 1917 AD 1.

extending to, or a stated distance from, the high-water mark by another boundary where this is in the public interest or where mineral rights are concerned and certain formalities are complied with.[61] Similarly, the Land Survey Act 9 of 1927 makes provision for alleviating uncertainty and ambiguity in certain situations.[62]

Apart from physical problems concerning the location of the boundary, certain legal aspects also have to be borne in mind. An initial step in determining the seaward boundary of land is to consult the title deed and accompanying diagram. This will establish whether the boundary is indeed the high-water mark or some other line.[63]

In a number of cases it has been held that descriptions of property boundaries in title deeds such as 'the coastline', 'bounded by the sea' or 'extending to the ocean' mean extending to the high-water mark.[64] However, such phrases have acquired a secondary meaning at least in Natal, where there is an admiralty reserve, so that a property boundary would extend up to the admiralty reserve and not to the high-water mark.[65]

Thus the general rule is that landward property extends up to the high-water mark or to the admiralty reserve where there is one. However, in *Consolidated Diamond Mines of SWA v Administrator, SWA*,[66] a case concerning the extent of mining rather than property title in the Sperrgebiet in what was then South West Africa, a different view was taken. The question before the Court was whether the mining lease granted 'to the Atlantic Ocean', extended to the high- or the low-water mark. After reviewing the Roman Law and the pertinent law of Germany (South West Africa having been a German colony for some time), the Court concluded that the lease extended to the low-water mark. It was held that 'under special circumstances and subject to special safeguards res publicae which form portion of the regalia may become the subject of private ownership'.[67]

A further related problem particularly relevant to natural boundaries in the coastal zone is the possibility of a conflict between the title deed and an accompanying diagram. Such a conflict arose, for example, in *Surveyor General (Cape) v Estate De Villiers*,[68] a case concerning the physical extent of property boundaries adjoining Fish Hoek Bay in the Cape.[69] The general rule is that the title deed prevails over the diagram.[70] Where a river rather than the high-water mark constitutes the property boundary, the general rules have to take cognizance of the ad medium flumen presumption, namely that there is a rebuttable presumption that the boundary of a property abutting a river is the middle of the river.[71]

The second problem concerning natural features, referred to above, namely the gains or losses which may occur as a result of the accretion or decretion of land, is not

---

[61] Section 9.

[62] Section 31*bis*.

[63] See, generally, Simpson & Sweeny above n 58.

[64] For example, *Union Government v Lovemore* 1930 AD 13 and, more recently, *S v Msomi* 1988 (1) SA 612 (N).

[65] Oosthuizen *The application of the Sea-Shore Act and related legislation along the Natal coast* Natal Town and Regional Planning Commission (1985) 7. See also *Karim v Union Government* 1933 NLR 167, where it was stated that the 'expressions "bounded by the bay" and "bounded by the ocean" . . . had in 1854 acquired secondary meaning "bounded by a reserve of 150 ft"'.

[66] Above n 33.

[67] At 620G–H.

[68] 1923 AD 588.

[69] See also *Horne v Struben* 1902 (19) SC 317; *Durban City Council v Minister of Agriculture* 1982 (2) SA 361 (D & C).

[70] See *Durban City Council v Minister of Agriculture* n 69 above, 367 and *Union Government v Lovemore* above n 64. For a case where the contrary was held, see *Milnerton Estates v Colonial Government* 1899 (16) SC 177.

[71] *Van Niekerk and Union Government (Minister of Lands) v Carter* 1917 AD 359; *Lange v Minister of Lands* 1957 (1) SA 297 (A); *Durban City Council v Minister of Agriculture* n 69 above; *Transvaal Canoe Club v Butgereit* 1986 (4) SA 207 (T) and 1988 (1) SA 759 (A).

confined to the coastal zone. For example, the high-water mark may change and rivers shift their course. The question arises whether the legal boundary moves with such gains or losses.

The legal rules governing these phenomena have their origins in the Roman law of accessio (accession). More specifically, there are rules governing three types of natural accession: alluvio, where the accession is gradual and imperceptible; avulsio, where the accession is a result of a sudden and violent event, for example a storm; and insula nata, where an island is formed in a river.

As regards alluvio, the doctrine of alluvion applies: where there is a gradual and imperceptible increase, through the natural action of water or other natural forces, in the extent of property bounded by a river or the sea, the resultant accession causes the boundary to move with the river or the variable high-water mark. In Roman law this rule applied to land which was ager non limitatus, ie land bounded by a natural boundary. However, in South African law, this rule has been qualified to the effect that even if the boundary is natural, it is ager limitatus if it was land granted by exact measurements.[72] Where land is ager limitatus, it is not entitled to natural accretion. These rules can be further complicated by the ad medium flumen presumption referred to above.[73] Where the process is not natural but brought about by artificial means, such as the building of dykes or stabilizing dunes, the landowner is not entitled to the alluvion.[74] These rules are also subject to certain statutory provisions.[75]

Where the gain in land is brought about by avulsio, ie through the annexure of land disannexed elsewhere by violent natural causes, there is no change in the original boundary. The rules regarding islands appearing in the sea or rivers are similarly governed by the basic rules of accession.[76]

26.3.6 Planning and development control

Spatial development, in the form of the laying out of new townships, housing estates, recreational amenities and industrial areas, is continuing apace in the coastal zone. Apart from the coastal zone regulations referred to above, there are no laws specifically governing planning and development in the coastal zone. However, the country's general planning laws are applicable and are reviewed here in broad outline. See chapter 28 for a more detailed discussion of land-use planning legislation.

A feature of planning law is that most of the pertinent legislation is found at provincial authority rather than national government level. Thus the key ordinances governing planning in the two coastal provinces are the Town Planning Ordinance 27 of 1949 applicable in Natal and the Land Use Planning Ordinance 15 of 1985 applicable in the Cape Province.

The chief administrative body concerned with planning in Natal is the Directorate: Physical Planning, while in the Cape these functions are carried out by the Chief Directorate: Land Development Co-ordination.

National statutes, for example the Physical Planning Act 125 of 1991, are also relevant to controlling development in the coastal zone. The Department of Regional and Land Affairs is the central authority administering this Act.

The chief development controls imposed by the ordinances are control of sub-division and zoning. The sub-division of land is prohibited unless it takes place in conformity with certain laid down requirements and procedures. The concept of zoning, in terms of which land may be used only for certain designated uses, is manifested in the

---

[72] *Van Niekerk and Union Government (Minster of Lands) v Carter* n 71 above.
[73] See *Durban City Council v Minister of Agriculture* above n 69.
[74] *Colonial Government v Town Council of Cape Town* 1902 (19) SC 87.
[75] Cf s 20 of the Water Act 54 of 1956.
[76] See Van der Merwe above n 35; Miller *The acquisition and protection of ownership* (1986).

preparation of town-planning schemes by local authorities. The purpose of a town-planning scheme in Natal has been stipulated as the co-ordinated and harmonious development of the local authority area in such a way as will most effectively tend to promote health, safety, order, convenience and general welfare, as well as efficiency and economy in the process of development and the improvement of communications.[77]

The Cape Ordinance has supplemented its regime by an attempt to regulate future spatial development by means of structure plans.[78] The general purpose of a structure plan is to lay down guidelines for the future spatial development by the area to which it relates in such a way as will most effectively promote the order of the area as well as the general welfare of the community concerned.[79] A structure plan does not confer or take away any rights in respect of land.[80] Structure plans are complementary to guide plans drawn up under the previous Physical Planning Act.[81] The Cape authorities have also drawn up a set of sub-regional structure plans for the coastal zone.

Planning law as applied in the coastal zone raises some difficult policy questions relating to balancing the public interest with private rights in property. For example, the question whether to compensate landowners whose rights are restricted in favour of the public interest is not addressed directly in the legislation. See chapter 28.

26.3.7 Natural resources

The most important natural resources related to the coastal zone are living marine resources, which are discussed in chapter 14, and minerals, which are discussed in chapters 15 and 16.

26.3.8 Protected areas

A variety of terrestrial and marine reserves encompass the coastal zone. Reference is made to these in chapter 27 which deals generally with protected areas.

26.3.9 Pollution control laws

There are no all embracing laws dealing with pollution control in the coastal zone specifically. Air pollution, water pollution, solid waste and radiation are dealt with by the general regulatory regime applicable to the country as a whole. These are outlined in chapters 17, 18, 19 and 21 respectively.

26.4 CURRENT PROBLEMS WITH THE IMPLEMENTATION OF CZM

The comprehensive scientific information base about South Africa's coastal and marine environments and the living and non-living resources they contain forms a sound foundation for effective CZM. In addition, the Minister of Environment Affairs has accepted a set of principles and objectives for CZM which have been developed through the initiative of the CE. Guidelines for regional planning and for the use of individual components of the coastal zone (dunes, beaches, intertidal and subtidal zones, estuaries, islands, etc) have been developed in a collaborative effort by the CE and the Department of Environment Affairs. The CE is now also working collaboratively with the department on developing strategies for implementing the principles, objectives and guidelines. Through its Coastal Management Advisory Programme, the department aims to increase the environmental awareness of controlling authorities, the public and major coastal resource user groups. Particular attention has been focused on local

---

[77] Section 59 of Ord 27 of 1949 (N) and s 23 of Ord 15 of 1985 (C).
[78] Ch 1 of Ord 15 of 1985 (C).
[79] Section 5(1).
[80] Section 5(2).
[81] A number of such guide plans have been drawn up for areas in the coastal zone, for example the Plettenberg Bay zone and the Wilderness–Knysna guide plan.

authorities, for it is at this level that much of the control over the utilisation and manipulation of the coast is exercised.

It has also been shown that a considerable body of legislation exists in South Africa, furthering directly or indirectly effective CZM and control over the exploitation of the living and non-living resources of the coastal zone and the adjacent marine environment. This legislation encompasses the shoreline and land and sea areas associated with it, boundary definition, resource exploitation, pollution and planning, and development control.

Despite these measures there are shortcomings in the effective implementation of CZM in South Africa. This is seen in a very serious light because of the escalating human pressure on the country's irreplaceable and finite coastal resources.

It is therefore necessary to highlight current legal and administrative problems and to rectify them as far as possible and as a matter of urgency.

26.4.1 Current legal and administrative problems

The following hinder the effective implementation of CZM efforts:

26.4.1.1 *Plethora of legislation and fragmented, unco-ordinated administration*

There are three levels of government authority in South Africa—central, provincial and local. In addition, there are autonomous governments in the independent states and homelands. Within these various levels of government there are numerous departments which exercise authority over diverse activities in the coastal zone. These include Agriculture, Defence, Environment Affairs, Foreign Affairs, Mineral and Energy Affairs, National Health and Population Development, Regional and Land Affairs, Transport, and Water Affairs and Forestry. There are, furthermore, three Own Affairs administrations which exercise authority in the coastal zone, especially in matters of land-use planning and development control. Provincial Administrations in the Cape and Natal comprise a number of departments which also have executive responsibility for certain activities in the coastal zone, including nature conservation, land-use planning and development control, public works and roads. Local government authorities, including Regional Services Councils in the Cape and numerous municipalities in both coastal provinces, are being given increasing responsibilities in CZM, in terms of the present constitutional policy of devolution of the executive function. Other state bodies, including the National Parks Board, National Botanical Institute and the National Monuments Council have responsibility for certain CZM activities. Semi-state and private organizations, including Eskom and Transnet, also exercise control over certain activities in the coastal zone.

The multiplicity of authorities involved in various aspects of CZM, with responsibility for specific aspects of legislation, obviously frustrates an integrated approach to CZM and inhibits effective monitoring of actions impinging on the coastal zone. Furthermore, CZM is hampered by the fact that administrative boundaries do not correspond to ecological boundaries. Responsibility for managing a single natural ecological system may therefore be divided between different authorities, with inevitable co-ordination problems. The fact that rivers rather than watersheds frequently represent administrative or geographical boundaries exacerbates this problem.

26.4.1.2 *Staff shortages and limited environmental expertise*

Effective and cohesive CZM is not possible unless there is a strong central authority which defines policy and ensures its implementation by continuous liaison with all other authorities carrying responsibility in the coastal zone. In terms of the Environment Conservation Act, this responsibility rests with the Department of Environment Affairs and, more specifically, its Environment Conservation Chief Directorate. However, at the time of writing, the Chief Directorate was severely hampered by chronic manpower and financial constraints and cannot fulfil the role it should in CZM.

The devolution of executive functions to lower tiers of government means inter alia that the assessment of the consequences of many forms of coastal development, and control over the exploitation of living resources, are now primarily the responsibility of the provincial administrations. In certain circumstances, responsibility for assessing the environmental consequences of coastal development also rests with Own Affairs departments, and in some cases, with local authorities. There has been uncertainty about the precise boundaries of responsibility for CZM between these various authorities. This uncertainty is magnified by a widespread, acute shortage of appropriately trained staff in the agencies responsible for CZM at all levels of government. The shortages of staff and skills have had a marked impact on the implementation of effective CZM measures. The problems experienced with the implementation of the coastal regulations provide a good example of the ineffectiveness of this situation.

26.4.1.3 *Inadequate control over administrative actions*

In terms of the South African constitutional dispensation, one minister or department cannot prescribe to another minister or department on the same level of government unless, in exceptional circumstances, legal provisions empower such prescription. Discretionary powers exercised by administrative bodies are by and large not subject to independent review, even if such actions result in substantial environmental impacts. Environmentally undesirable activities or decisions by government bodies can therefore be controlled only by voluntary co-operation. See chapters 5 and 8.

The Department of Environment Affairs therefore cannot interfere in the activities of other central government authorities, unless empowered by statute to do so. The Environment Conservation Act does not give such powers to the department, although it stipulates that the Minister of Environment Affairs and the Administrators of the provinces can perform any function assigned to a local authority in terms of the Act but which it has failed to do.[82] Also, expenses thus incurred can be recovered from the local authority. However, this right has, as far as can be ascertained, never been invoked by either the Minister or the Administrators.

The Environment Conservation Act provides the opportunity for any person whose interests are affected by a decision of an administrative body under the Act, to obtain written reasons for the decision.[83] Opportunity is provided by the Environment Conservation Act for review of the decision by the Supreme Court. The Minister may also appoint a Board of Investigation to assist him in the evaluation of any matter or any appeal under that Act.[84] Apart from these provisions which have severe limitations, there is little control over administrative actions likely to cause environmental harm. See chapters 7 and 8.

26.4.1.4 *Legislation not specifically aimed at promoting effective CZM*

The majority of laws affecting the use of coastal resources are not aimed specifically at promoting effective CZM. Consequently, poor environmental practices may be carried out without effective control, despite the abundance of legislation. For example, in the Cape Land Use Planning Ordinance and Natal Town Planning Ordinance, the control of development does not include control over the clearing of vegetation and the reclamation of wetlands. Considerable environmental damage can thus be done by such activities in the course of development without effective legislative control.

---

[82] Section 31.
[83] Section 36.
[84] Section 15.

The variance between legal and ecological definitions of natural features or processes also highlights this shortcoming. For example, the Sea-Shore Act provides for control over certain activities between the high-water mark and the low-water mark, but neither above nor below, despite the fact that the beach–dune area above the high-water mark and the shallow water area below the low-water mark may be part of the same ecological system. Furthermore, authority granted in terms of the respective nature conservation ordinances of the Cape and Natal extends only up to the high-water mark. Certain controls can thus be extended up to this administrative boundary, but not beyond, because of currently applicable legal boundaries.

26.4.1.5 *Limitations of criminal sanctions*

Apart from the difficulty of apprehending offenders and of obtaining adequate proof of the offence, there are serious limitations to the use of criminal sanctions which could further the objectives of CZM. Pollution and environmental degradation may not be seen to be a 'criminal offence' by the general public, particularly by groups whose livelihood may depend on the exploitation of certain coastal resources. The criminal process is effective only if it serves as a deterrent. The fines imposed on those who pollute or degrade the coastal environment are, however, frequently ridiculously low (particularly in relation to the returns from illegally exploited resources) and usually do not require rehabilitation of the damaged environment. See chapter 8. The introduction of provisions relating to reparations for environmental damage under the Environment Conservation Act[85] is a positive step in this regard. See chapter 7.

26.4.1.6 *Dominance of private rights over public interest*

Effective CZM is sometimes thwarted by the fact that Roman-Dutch law strongly upholds private rights even though at times this may not be in the interests of society. Ownership encompasses extensive rights to use property. Poor farming practices resulting in soil erosion or industrial activities leading to the degradation and pollution of estuaries, provide graphic examples. However, legislation increasingly provides for the limitation of landowners' rights in favour of the public interest in environmental conservation.[86]

26.4.1.7 *Narrow definition of locus standi*

Strict application of the locus standi requirement prevents public-minded individuals or groups of people from participating in public-law litigation on environmental issues. See chapter 8. A consequence has been the appropriation of some coastal areas which have public heritage value, for private financial gain.

26.4.1.8 *Alienation of state land in the coastal zone*

The cabinet decision to deregulate and privatize certain state activities has important consequences for the future use and management of the coastal zone. Some areas of the sea-shore have traditionally been held in trust by the State for the benefit of the public (in terms of the Sea-Shore Act and in terms of land designated as admiralty reserve). The privatization of the South African Transport Services (now Transnet) has raised the issue of the future utilization of substantial areas of coastal land under its jurisdiction (harbours, waterfronts, etc) and the possible alienation of 'public property' for exclusive private development and use. While recognizing the necessity of promoting opportunities for development and private initiative, the limited area of coastal land

---

[85] Section 29(7).

[86] Cf Rabie 'The impact of environmental conservation on land ownership' 1985 *Acta Juridica* 289; Rabie 'The influence of environmental conservation on private landownership' in Van der Walt (ed) *Land reform and the future of landownership in South Africa* (1991) 81.

and the common property nature of many coastal resources, nevertheless, mean that every effort should be made to retain state land as far as possible for the enjoyment of the general public.

26.4.2 Limitations inherent in the Environment Conservation Act

The Environment Conservation Act was drawn up for the purposes of effective protection and controlled utilization of the environment, but not specifically for protecting the coastal zone. Nevertheless, some of the shortcomings in the Act are particularly evident in the coastal zone as elaborated on below. For a full analysis of the Act, see chapter 7.

26.4.2.1 *No legally entrenched national environmental policy, including a CZM policy*

The Environment Conservation Act itself does not outline a national policy on environmental conservation. The Minister of Environment Affairs, nevertheless, has discretionary powers to determine a general policy,[87] but he is required to obtain the concurrence of other Ministers who could be affected by such a policy. To date no such policy has been declared.

The *White Paper on a national policy regarding environmental conservation*[88] has no legal standing. Without a legally entrenched national environmental policy, there is no guiding basis for the multiplicity of controlling authorities to apply accepted forms of CZM. The principles and objectives for CZM, developed by the Council for the Environment, have been disseminated to a wide variety of coastal zone users and all controlling authorities. However, these principles are not legally enforceable. Consequently, vitally important principles for CZM will not necessarily be integrated into planning and decision-making processes, nor are they applied consistently by the various authorities responsible for addressing environmental concerns in land-use planning.

In the absence of a legally enforceable CZM policy, there is no effective basis for the execution of the monitoring function assigned to the Department of Environment Affairs by the Environment Conservation Act. Nothing can be done other than by persuasion and the invoking of goodwill to rectify unsound practices in the coastal zone which may come to the attention of the department or the provincial authorities.

26.4.2.2 *Compensation for loss of development opportunity*

The Act provides for compensation to be paid to landowners who may suffer loss as a result of limitations imposed in terms of the Act.[89] At present, the government does not dispose over sufficient funds to pay such compensation. Therefore there is no effective way of protecting the public interest against individuals exercising private development rights. Expropriation subject to the payment of compensation based on the true nature of the land, that is on the basis of public open space value and not the 'loss of opportunity' value, is therefore a matter which requires serious attention.

26.4.2.3 *No legal requirement for the application of environmental impact assessment procedures*

Although some provision is made in the Cape Land Use Planning Ordinance for addressing environmental concerns, there is no statutory requirement for administrative bodies or private individuals to undertake environmental impact assessments before implementing development proposals. Short-term financial considerations thus

---

[87] Section 2.
[88] WPO–1980.
[89] Section 34.

invariably predominate over the longer-term environmental implications of a development proposal.

The provisions of the Environment Conservation Act relating to environmental impact reports presuppose the identification of activities and the declaration of limited development areas. These provisions, however, seem to be utilized only in exceptional cases—for example, if a proposed development or activity has triggered a public controversy. Proposed mining for heavy minerals on the eastern shores of St Lucia is a case in point.

There is accordingly no legal requirement for the application of the IEM procedures, which have been developed by the CE and which have received wide acclaim in governmental and private-sector circles. As with the principles and objectives for CZM, their implementation is at present totally dependent on voluntary action and goodwill.

26.5 THE CHALLENGE FOR CZM

South Africa has a varied and beautiful coastline. Because of the wide range of geomorphological features and the influence of three oceans upon the coast, its living resources are equally rich and varied. Wise management of the coast will therefore pay handsome dividends to the nation.

But the problems inherent in managing this coast and its resources are as manifold as the benefits which it bestows upon us. The reasons have been outlined—immense and increasing human pressure with associated socio-political problems, and a cumbersome bureaucratic system which is hamstrung by a plethora of unco-ordinated legislation and by severe and growing financial constraints.

The *Report of the three committees of the Presidents' Council on a national environmental management system*[90] highlights some of the problems regarding the coastal zone described here.[91] It recommends a new Coastal Zone Management Act to replace the Sea-Shore Act and other related legislation.[92] It also recommends a specific directorate for coastal zone management within the Marine Resources Branch of a consolidated Department of Environment Affairs.[93] It is submitted that, if these recommendations are implemented, the objectives of coastal zone management will be greatly furthered.

The difficulties which have arisen over the past five years due to a wave of urbanization and informal settlement in many coastal areas which may have inherently sensitive ecological characteristics, have to be faced. Moreover, it is hoped that in meeting the need for a complete revision of South Africa's constitutional dispensation, environmental considerations will have high priority.

Effective CZM will be possible in the developing 'New South Africa' only if it addresses the real and genuine needs of all sectors of the population. This means that a fine balance will have to be struck between development needs such as:

- the creation of job opportunities;
- low-cost housing in and around urban growth points;
- the provision of water, electricity, health services and other infrastructure at these growth points;
- the provision of recreational outlets for both the existing and the new urban populations; and
- the need to protect the aesthetic and resource-based attributes of the coastal environment.

While the focus of CZM in South Africa needs to be people-oriented, prudent

[90] PC 1/1991.
[91] See paras 2.5.7.5 to 2.5.7.7.
[92] Para 5.7.1.
[93] Para 6.4.6.

management of the coastal environment and its resources remains of paramount importance. Without this, human well-being and, indeed, long-term survival are simply not possible. The current value of food harvested from the seas surrounding our coast is well over R1 000 million per annum. This is a protein supply and a source of revenue which we cannot afford to neglect or degrade, however compelling socio-political or other pressures may be. By the same token tourism, which depends to a large extent on coastal regions, is rapidly becoming South Africa's top foreign-exchange earner. Sound management and effective protection of our coast and all it holds and offers is therefore of inestimable importance.

Thus the challenge is clear. First, to meet the needs and aspirations of all coastal-dwelling South Africans, particularly those who are destitute and struggling to survive, while simultaneously preventing degradation of the coast. Secondly, and concomitantly, to protect vitally important coastal features and processes, thus ensuring that the benefits of the coastal zone can be enjoyed by present and future generations. A drastic and innovative new legislative and administrative approach is required to meet this challenge. Merely to address the present shortcomings of the Environment Conservation Act will not suffice.

Coastal management principles should outline a comprehensive national policy for CZM that will guide the activities of the State and private developers. While it would not be practical to consolidate the existing plethora of laws pertaining to the coastal zone in a single Act, consideration should be given to rectifying anomalies in existing legislation. A possible approach would be to repeal the existing Sea-Shore Act and replace it with a comprehensive Coastal Zone Management Act.[94] Such an Act would incorporate the principles of CZM discussed above and a wider geographic area than the existing Act, which is in general inapplicable above the high-water mark. Such an Act could also include a means for re-instituting effective control over environmentally undesirable development in the coastal zone.

Consideration could also be given to appointing an environmental ombudsman with wide powers, including the power to investigate coastal zone matters that are of public concern. See chapter 8.

Perhaps the most effective way of implementing sound CZM policy would be the establishment of an independent environmental agency that could serve the needs of the country as a whole. This has been suggested by the CE to the President's Council, but the latter body, in its *Report on a national environmental management system* declined to follow this suggestion.[95] A dedicated CZM unit could be established within this agency, the staff of which would need to include recognized experts in the field of CZM. The unit should have an advisory and 'watchdog' role on CZM matters. As an independent body with CZM expertise, it could offer impartial advice to government agencies. The agencies it advises must, however, have the 'teeth' to ensure that advice is adhered to and that sound principles of CZM are effectively implemented. Particular attention should also be given to building the environmental proficiency of regional and local government agencies with executive responsibilities for implementing and monitoring CZM measures.

CZM in South Africa faces great challenges. It has to take into account fundamental changes in socio-political structures and aspirations, urbanization, including the squatter phenomenon, and develop innovative legal and planning procedures to deal with this dynamic situation. The satisfactory future utilization and protection of this fundamental resource will ultimately depend on an effective and adequate system of CZM.

---

[94] See, for instance, Rabie above n 42, 200.

[95] Cf para 6.2.

CHAPTER 27

PROTECTED AREAS

J HANKS
P D GLAVOVIC

27.1 MODERN INTERNATIONAL CONCEPTS OF PROTECTED AREAS

27.1.1 Introduction

During the past three decades, conservation philosophy has undergone a remarkable change, moving from being a rather obscure concern of a handful of enthusiasts who were worried about threatened species to becoming an integral part of our everyday lives. Conservation has evolved from being anti-people and anti-development to the point where even the designated protected areas are now recognized as offering major sustainable benefits to society on the condition that human intervention is conducted in harmony with the retention of biological diversity.[1] This modern concept of conservation was encapsulated in the *World conservation strategy*[2], which had as its primary goal the wise maintenance and use of the world's natural resources. The establishment and management of protected areas is one of the most important ways of ensuring that the biological diversity of the world is conserved so that a wide range of species and ecosystems can better meet the material and cultural needs of mankind now and in the future.[3] Since the first national park was established at Yellowstone in the United States in 1872, the concept of protected areas has grown in scope and the number of such areas increased to the point where today there are more than 2 600 protected areas covering nearly 4-million km^2 in 124 countries throughout the world.

During the 1970s, the number of these areas increased by 46 per cent and the total area protected increased by over 80 per cent.[4]

27.1.2 Primary conservation objectives for protected areas

The International Union for the Conservation of Nature (IUCN) has identified the following primary conservation objectives for protected areas:[5]

- Maintain essential ecological processes and life-support systems.
- Preserve genetic and biological diversity.
- Protect aesthetic values and natural ecosystems.
- Conserve watersheds and their production.
- Control erosion, sedimentation and soil depletion.
- Maintain air quality.
- Protect the habitat of representative as well as rare and endangered species.
- Provide opportunities for ecotourism and recreation.
- Provide opportunities for research, education and monitoring.
- Contribute to sustainable use and ecodevelopment.

---

[1] Eidsvik *A framework for the classification of terrestrial and marine protected areas* IUCN (1990).

[2] IUCN (1980).

[3] MacKinnon, Child & Thorsell *Managing protected areas in the tropics* IUCN/UNEP (1986).

[4] Harrison, Miller & McNeely 'The world coverage of protected areas: development goals and environmental needs' in McNeely & Miller (eds) *National parks, conservation and development: the role of protected areas in sustaining society* IUCN (1984).

[5] Eidsvik above n 1.

- Protect the natural and cultural heritage.
- Retain future options.

In keeping with the evolution of conservation thinking, an essential element of the protected area network is the conservation of cultural heritage, including, where appropriate, the accommodation of the needs and lifestyles of local native communities.

These primary conservation objectives go far beyond the traditional concept of 'preservation' commonly associated with a national park, and today many countries recognize several different types of protected areas, each with distinct conservation and management objectives. The obvious advantage of this system is that at a national level, each country can design a system of protected areas which corresponds to its own resources and needs, but which still has, as a unifying theme, varying degrees of protection from unrestricted use of its resources. The great advantage of this range of protected area options is that it can provide enhanced protection to the more strictly protected categories by taking away human pressure and directing it to those places where heavier sustained use is permissible.[6]

27.1.3 IUCN's revised criteria for classifying protected areas

The classification of the world's protected areas into a limited number of categories with different management objectives will obviously result in a more co-ordinated approach to many aspects of management. For example, an accepted system of classification will facilitate legislating for protected areas, planning management strategies, making appropriate management decisions, controlling both the type and intensity of use, and justifying the benefits claimed for the protected areas policy.

Furthermore, a set of acknowledged categories enables IUCN and the international conservation community to work more effectively with national conservation departments. Having several categories of protected areas has the additional advantage of permitting more flexibility in management in that the responsibility for certain categories can be delegated away from a single national protected area management authority to a provincial authority or to non-government organizations or even private landowners.[7]

With this in mind, IUCN initially proposed and published a system of ten management categories,[8] but at the 1990 IUCN General Assembly held in Perth, Australia, a revised list of five categories was accepted.[9] These primary categories, together with their South African counterparts, are given in Table 27.1.

27.1.3.1 *IUCN Category I: Scientific reserves and wilderness areas*

(a) Introduction

Scientific reserves and wilderness areas are largely free from human intervention. They are available primarily for scientific research, environmental monitoring and non-mechanized, non-disruptive forms of ecotourism.

(b) Objectives for the management of scientific reserves

To maintain essential ecological processes and to preserve biological diversity in an undisturbed state, in order to have representative examples of the natural environment available for scientific study, environmental monitoring, education, and for the maintenance of genetic resources in a dynamic and evolutionary state. Research activities need to be planned and undertaken carefully to minimize disturbance.

---

[6] MacKinnon, Child & Thorsell above n 3.

[7] Ibid.

[8] *Categories, objectives and criteria for protected areas* IUCN (1978); 'Categories, objectives and criteria for protected areas' in McNeely & Miller (eds) above n 4.

[9] Eidsvik above n 1.

TABLE 27.1
South African classification of terrestrial and marine protected areas

PRIMARY CATEGORIES: SOUTH AFRICAN SCHEDULE		
Category I	Scientific Reserves Wilderness areas	Special nature reserves Wilderness areas
Category II	National parks and equivalent reserves	National parks Provincial or regional parks Nature reserves (either regional or provincial)
Category III	Natural/cultural monument	National monuments Botanic gardens Zoological gardens Natural heritage sites Sites of conservation significance
Category IV	Habitat and wildlife management areas	Private nature reserves Indigenous state forest
Category V	Protected land-/seascapes	Protected natural environments Natural resource areas Scenic landscapes Urban landscapes

Areas recognized/designated under international instruments or agreements

(i) World heritage sites
(ii) Ramsar sites
(iii) Biosphere reserves
(iv) Transfrontier protected areas or peace parks

Source: *The South African classification of terrestrial and marine protected areas* Council for the Environment (1991).

(c) Objectives for the management of wilderness areas

Wilderness areas incorporate all the objectives for scientific reserves. Wilderness is an enduring natural area protected by legislation and of sufficient size to protect the pristine natural environment which serves physical and spiritual well-being. Wilderness is an area where little or no persistent evidence of human intrusion is permitted, so that natural processes will take place largely unaffected by human intervention.

Wilderness area stress non-mechanized access. As pristine natural areas, they should be established to ensure that future generations will have an opportunity to seek understanding in largely undisturbed areas.

(d) Criteria for selection and management

These areas possess some outstanding and representative ecosystems, features or species of flora and fauna of scientific importance. Research areas are generally closed to public access, and wilderness areas do not provide for mechanized forms of recreation and tourism. They often contain fragile ecosystems or life forms or areas of important biological or geological diversity, or are of particular importance to the conservation of genetic resources. Size is determined by the area required to ensure the integrity of the ecosystems and to accomplish the management objective which provides for its protection.

Control and ownership should, in most cases, be by governments, foundations, universities or institutions which have a research or conservation function. Exceptions may be made where adequate safeguards and controls relating to long-term protection are ensured.

27.1.3.2 *IUCN Category II: national parks and equivalent reserves*

(a) Introduction

Spiritual, scientific, recreational or economic reasons have led nations to identify outstanding natural features or areas as warranting exceptional consideration with respect to their protection and management. National parks, as large conservation areas, generally contain a range of functions, from scientific reserves and wilderness to recreation/tourism facilities. Generally, these are delineated in management plans by zoning systems. Over a period of more than 2 000 years, such areas have been identified as sanctuaries, shrines and nature reserves, and the concept of identifying and establishing some of a nation's most treasured natural areas as national parks continues to evolve.

A national park is defined as a relatively large, outstanding natural area managed by a nationally recognized authority to protect the ecological integrity of one or more ecosystems for this and future generations, to eliminate any exploitation or intensive occupation of the area and to provide a foundation for spiritual, scientific, educational and tourism opportunities.

Equivalent reserves (state parks, provincial parks, tribal council parks, trusts) are defined as outstanding natural areas managed by a state or provincial government, a tribal council, a foundation or other legal body which has dedicated the area to long-term conservation. In all other respects, these areas meet the criteria established for Category II.

(b) Objectives for management

To protect natural and scenic areas of national or international significance for spiritual, scientific, educational, recreational and tourism purposes. The area should perpetuate, in a natural state, representative samples of physiographic regions, biotic communities and species, in order to provide ecological stability and diversity.

National parks and equivalent reserves, as relatively undisturbed natural areas, contribute to sustaining society by: maintaining essential ecological processes and life-support systems, including large ecosystems and watersheds; preserving genetic and biological diversity; taking into account social and economic considerations, as well as ecological integrity, and providing spiritual, intellectual, social and economic opportunities through tourism.

(c) Criteria for selection and management

National parks and equivalent reserves are relatively large areas which contain representative samples of major natural regions, features or scenery, and where plant and animal species, geomorphological sites and habitats are of special spiritual, scientific, educational and recreational interest. They contain one or several entire ecosystems that are not materially altered by human exploitation and occupation. The highest competent authority of the people having jurisdiction over the area has taken steps to prevent or eliminate, as soon as possible, exploitation or occupation in the area and to enforce effectively the respect of ecological, geomorphological or aesthetic features which have led to its establishment.

The ecosystems are managed so as to sustain tourism and educational activities on a controlled basis. The area is managed in a natural or near-natural state. Visitors enter under special conditions for inspirational, educational, cultural or recreational purposes; sport hunting is not a compatible use, but culling species for management purposes is an accepted practice.

27.1.3.3 *IUCN Category III: natural monuments*

(a) Introduction

Most countries possess outstanding natural and cultural features of particular scientific and educational interest; often, however, the features receive no special national recognition. Natural features might include spectacular waterfalls, caves, craters, volcanoes, unique or representative species of flora and fauna, and sand dunes. Cultural features may include archaeological sites and native heritage areas.

All such sites are of such scenic, scientific, educational or inspirational importance that they merit special designation. Because of their uniqueness, these areas deserve protection for scientific purposes and public enjoyment.

A natural monument is defined as a natural, or natural–cultural feature which is an area of outstanding or unique value because of its inherent attributes.

(b) Objectives for management

To protect and preserve outstanding natural features because of their special interest, unique or representative characteristics and, to the extent consistent with this, provide opportunities for interpretation, education, research and public appreciation.

(c) Criteria for selection and management

This category normally contains one or more features of outstanding significance which, because of their uniqueness, rarity or representativeness, should be protected. These features are not of the proportions of a national park, nor do they contain a diversity of features which would justify their inclusion as one. Size is not such a significant factor, because the area needs to be only large enough to protect the integrity of the site.

These sites may be owned and managed by either central or other government agencies, non-profit trusts or corporations as long as there is the assurance that they will be managed to protect their inherent features for the long term.

27.1.3.4 *IUCN Category IV: habitat and wildlife management areas*

(a) Introduction

All categories of management play important roles in protecting the habitat for flora and fauna. Generally, management intervention in protected areas is limited. It is essential, however, that some areas be established where manipulative management techniques can be applied to guarantee the stability or survival of certain plant and animal species (through protection of breeding populations, and feeding and breeding grounds), and critical habitats for the protection of rare and endangered flora and fauna species.

Habitat and wildlife management areas are subject to human intervention, based on research into the requirements of specific sites for nesting, feeding and survival. Maintaining sustainable populations as well as protecting rare and threatened species are integral functions of these areas.

(b) Objectives for management

To assure the natural conditions necessary to protecting significant species, groups of species, biotic communities or physical features of the environment where these may require specific human manipulation for their perpetuation. Scientific research, environmental monitoring and educational use are the primary activities associated with sustainable resource management of this category.

(c) Criteria for selection and management

A Category IV area is desirable when protection of specific habitats is essential to the continued well-being of resident or migratory fauna. Although a variety of areas fall within this category, each would have as its primary purpose the protection of nature and the survival of species; the production of harvestable, renewable resources may play a role in management.

The size of an area is dependent upon the habitat requirements of the species to be protected; these areas may be relatively small, but should incorporate nesting areas, marshes, lakes, estuaries, forest or grassland habitats, fish spawning areas or seascapes incorporating feeding beds for marine mammals. On the other hand, some bird sanctuaries may be very extensive.

The area may require habitat manipulation in order to provide optimum conditions for the species, vegetative community or feature, according to individual circumstances. For example, a particular grassland or heath community may be protected and perpetuated through grazing; a marsh for wintering waterfowl may require continual removal of excess reeds and supplementary planting of waterfowl food; or a reserve for an endangered animal may need protection against its predators. Limited areas may be developed for public education and appreciation of the work of wildlife management.

Ownership may be by the central government or, with adequate safeguards and controls, by other levels of government, non-profit trusts, corporations, private individuals or groups.

27.1.3.5 *IUCN Category V: protected land-/seascapes (ecosystem conservation areas)*

(a) Introduction

This is the most complex of the conservation categories. These areas are frequently very extensive, often incorporating sophisticated planning techniques in multizoning and ecodevelopment areas. They may, therefore, incorporate characteristics of national parks (strictu sensu), scientific reserves, natural and cultural monuments and wildlife management areas. Each of these categories may appear as a zone within these outstanding natural areas where human use is harmoniously integrated.

In general, the areas incorporate rural agriculture, villages, towns and other communities as well as selective forestry and wildlife management projects. Recreation and tourism are significant elements in their management.

Protected land-/seascapes are defined as areas which are a product of the harmonious interaction of people and nature. They may demonstrate cultural manifestations such as customs, beliefs, social organizations or material traits as reflected in use patterns. These areas are often scenically attractive or aesthetically unique patterns of human settlement. Traditional practices associated with agriculture, grazing or fishing are evident.

(b) Objectives for management

The objectives of this category are to maintain significant areas which are characteristic of the harmonious interaction of nature and culture, while providing opportunities for public enjoyment through recreation and tourism, and supporting the normal life style and economic activity of these areas. The category also has as its main objectives the maintenance of biological and cultural diversity and use for scientific and educational purposes.

(c) Criteria for selection and management

The scope and character of areas falling within this category are necessarily broad because of the wide variety of natural, cultural or scenic areas that occur within each nation.

These areas may demonstrate certain cultural manifestations such as customs, beliefs, social organization, or material traits as reflected in use patterns. They are characterized by either scenically attractive or aesthetically unique patterns of human settlement. Traditional practices associated with agriculture, grazing and fishing dominate. The size of the area would be large enough to ensure the integrity of the use pattern.

Natural or scenic areas found along coastlines and lake shores, or in hilly or mountainous terrain, or along the shores of rivers, or inland adjacent to important tourist highways or population centres, offering scenic views, are often included. Many will have the physical qualities and potential to be developed for a variety of outdoor recreational uses.

In some cases an area would be privately held and the use of either central or delegated planning control would likely be necessary to assist in the perpetuation of both the use and life style. Subsidization or other government assistance might be required. Efforts would be made to maintain the quality of the landscape through appropriate management practices. In other instances the areas are established and managed under public ownership in perpetuity.[10]

27.1.4 Transfrontier protected areas

Over the past five years, there has been a significant increase in international recognition for the concept of transfrontier protected areas, also known as border parks, transfrontier parks or international peace parks. By definition, these are protected areas of two or more countries which meet at international borders.

Transfrontier protected areas have an unrealized potential for reducing international tensions and for creating conditions which make peace more likely. Such areas can also result in improved management of resources and ecosystems, and enhance and preserve cultural values of local communities of people, particularly where natural areas and migration routes do not respect the artificial boundaries of man.[11]

Within South Africa, the Kalahari Gemsbok National Park is an obvious candidate for a peace park. It has international boundaries with both Namibia and Botswana, but at the latter there is common boundary with the Gemsbok National Park in Botswana, separated only by the ancient bed of the Nossob River.

In 1990, negotiations started between government and conservation authorities of South Africa and Mozambique to explore two other options for transfrontier protected areas, namely the Kruger National Park/Banhine National Park linkage, and an equally ambitious concept involving the linkage of Maputo Elephant Reserve in Mozambique with the Tembe Elephant Park and Ndumu Game Reserve in Maputaland, South Africa. In both cases, natural movements of wildlife have been curtailed by fences. In the case of the Kruger National Park, elephant, eland and wild dog were involved in long-distance movements across the frontier before a game-proof fence was erected along the border in 1974. If a national park or equivalent protected area could be proclaimed in Mozambique which would link the Kruger National Park to Banhine National Park by means of a corridor across the Limpopo River, a major wildlife system in southern Africa could be rehabilitated. Similarly, elephants from the Maputo Elephant Reserve in Mozambique used to migrate southwards to Lake Sibayi in South

[10] Ibid.

[11] Thorsell & Harrison 'Parks that promote peace: a global inventory of transfrontier nature reserves' in Thorsell (ed) *Parks on the borderline: experience in transfrontier conservation* IUCN (1990).

Africa before the international boundary fence cut off these traditional movements.

The first phase of the preparation of a land-use plan for the Kruger/Banhine linkage started in 1991.

27.2 PROTECTED AREAS RECOGNIZED UNDER INTERNATIONAL INSTRUMENTS

27.2.1 Introduction

In any of the five categories recognized by IUCN, particular sites may be given special recognition or distinction under an international legal instrument.

Protected areas are of importance to all people of the world and these international legal instruments ensure that important sites are given appropriate recognition and support in the retention of their integrity.[12]

27.2.2 World heritage sites

World heritage sites are designated by the World Heritage Commission, which has a secretariat located in Unesco. These sites can be either cultural or natural, and in exceptional circumstances they may embrace both values. IUCN is the technical adviser to the World Heritage Commission with respect to natural sites and the International Commission on Monuments and Sites (ICOMOS) has a similar role with respect to cultural sites. All sites must have strict legal protection and, although recreation and interpretation facilities will usually be developed, some sites may be of such significance as a heritage for the world that public use will be either prohibited or very strictly controlled.

27.2.3 Biosphere reserves

Biosphere reserves are internationally designated protected areas which are managed to demonstrate the value of conservation. The management objectives of these sites are to conserve for present and future use the diversity and integrity of biotic communities, plants and animals within natural ecosystems, and to safeguard the genetic diversity of species on which their continuing evolution depends. Emphasis at these sites is given to the integration of functions such as monitoring, research, resource management, training and education in order to help solve problems locally, nationally and internationally. Each biosphere reserve must be approved by Unesco's Man and the Biosphere International Coordinating Council before it is officially designated.

27.2.4 Ramsar sites

Ramsar sites (wetland areas) are wetlands of particular significance which have been designated under the Convention of Wetlands of International Importance. The Ramsar Convention was adopted in 1971 in Ramsar, Iran, and entered into force in 1975 following the accession of the seventh party, Greece. (See chapter 9.) It now has contracting parties from all regions of the world. Wetlands are defined as 'areas of marsh, fen, peatland or water, whether natural or artificial, permanent or temporary, with water that is static or flowing, fresh, brackish or salt, including areas of marine water, the depth of which at low tide does not exceed six metres'. In addition, the convention provides that wetlands 'may incorporate riparian and coastal zones adjacent to the wetlands, and islands or bodies of marine water deeper than six metres at low tide lying within the wetlands'. The secretariat for the convention is maintained by IUCN in

---

[12] Eidsvik above n 1.

Switzerland and activities include the drafting of site descriptions and the maintenance of official lists and files of the sites listed under the convention.[13]

27.3 PROTECTED AREAS: LEGISLATION[14]

27.3.1 Introduction: historical background

The roots of modern South African nature conservation legislation were struck soon after the first Dutch settlers arrived at the Cape. In setting up a victualling station, the Dutch East India Company required fresh fruit and vegetables, meat and timber. This necessitated the introduction of laws to protect the natural resources on which such a station depended. Wild animals provided meat, and the company introduced restrictions on the right of free burghers to hunt. In 1658 a ban was imposed on the cutting of trees. Official woodcutters were appointed from whom timber and firewood had to be purchased.[15] These controls represented the genesis in South Africa of the principle of state responsibility for and control over the nation's natural resources.

The first formal conservation areas in South Africa were the forest reserves demarcated in terms of the Cape Forest Act of 1888. A forestry officer was appointed in Natal in 1891, and by 1903 there were forest services also in the Orange Free State and the Transvaal, and control was extended to include the forests of Transkei and Pondoland. Both flora and fauna were protected in these forest reserves. Other areas were established primarily for the protection of wild animals: the Pongola Game Reserve in 1894 and the Sabie Game Reserve in 1898 in the Transvaal, the Hluhluwe, Umfolozi and Mkuzi Game Reserves in Zululand in 1897, and Giant's Castle in the Drakensberg in 1903.[16] After Union in 1910 the central government assumed conservation responsibility for forestry (which included the management of coastal driftsand areas, indigenous forests and mountain catchments), inland waters, islands, and the sea-shore between the high and low water marks. In addition to these large tracts of natural areas, its responsibility also extended to management of crown lands.[17]

27.3.2 National Parks Act

27.3.2.1 *National parks*

The first National Parks Act was promulgated in 1926 as a direct result of representations made to the central government for the permanent protection of the Sabie Game Reserve for the whole nation. This reserve had been proclaimed as a game reserve in 1898 by the South African Republic, and it was feared that the area was inadequately protected against agricultural and mining development. The 1926 Act reproclaimed the Sabie Game Reserve as part of the Kruger National Park. The current legislation is the National Parks Act 57 of 1976.

(a) Object of a park. The purpose for which national parks are established in South Africa is stated in the 1976 Act as follows:

'The object of the constitution of a park is the establishment, preservation and study therein of wild animals, marine and plant life and objects of geological, archaeological, historical,

---

[13] A comprehensive database on the protected areas of the world, including Ramsar sites, is maintained by the Protected Areas Data Unit (PADU), World Conservation Monitoring Centre, 219c Huntingdon Rd, Cambridge CB3 0DL, England. Further information is available from the Commission on National Parks and Protected Areas (CNPPA) IUCN, 1196 Gland, Switzerland.

[14] See generally on protected areas Lampaert *De wetgeving betreffende de natuurgebieden in Zuid Afrika* (unpublished LLM thesis, University of Port Elizabeth 1982) and Rabie 'South African law relating to conservation areas' 1985 *CILSA* 51.

[15] See *Report of the Planning Committee of the President's Council on nature conservation in South Africa* PC 2/1984 22.

[16] *President's Council Report* above n 15, 23–4.

[17] *President's Council Report* above n 15, 23.

ethnological, oceanographic, educational and other scientific interest and objects relating to the said life or the first-mentioned objects or to events in or the history of the park, in such a manner that the area which constitutes the park shall, as far as may be and for the benefit and enjoyment of visitors, be retained in its natural state.'[18]

(b) Scheduled parks. Existing parks are enumerated and their areas defined in schedule 1 of the Act. The Minister of Environment Affairs is authorized to declare by notice in the *Government Gazette* any other area to be a national park under a name to be assigned to it in such notice, and to amend schedule 1 by the addition of the name and definition of the area of the park so established. He may also include any land or, subject to parliamentary approval, exclude any land from any park and amend schedule 1 accordingly.[19] The high degree of inviolability of scheduled parks is illustrated by the fact that the Act provides specifically that no land included in a park described in sch 1 may be alienated or excluded or detached from the park, except under the authority of a resolution of Parliament.[20]

(c) Establishment of parks on state land. The Minister of Environment Affairs may, by notice in the *Government Gazette*, with the concurrence of the Minister of Mineral and Energy Affairs, declare state land 'in respect of which no right in connection with prospecting or mining has been granted in terms of any law' to be a park, and amend schedule 1 accordingly. Notwithstanding the provisions of the Lake Areas Development Act 39 of 1975, he may also declare state land situated in a declared lake area to be a scheduled park or part of it.[21]

(d) Acquisition of land for purposes of a scheduled park. The Minister of Regional and Land Affairs may, with the concurrence of the Minister of Mineral and Energy Affairs, by purchase or otherwise, including the exchange for state land situated outside a park or, failing agreement with the owner, by expropriation, acquire land or a mineral right to land for the purposes of a park.[22] Land so acquired which is not already included in a park, must forthwith be included by the Minister of Environment Affairs in a park by notice in the *Government Gazette*.[23]

(e) Registered parks. In addition to parks which are listed in schedule 1, thereby enjoying the parliamentary protection referred to above, the Act makes provision for land to be declared to be a park or part of a park. Registered parks are established by the Minister of Environment Affairs by notice in the *Government Gazette*, with the concurrence of and subject to conditions determined by the Minister of Mineral and Energy Affairs and the Minister of Regional and Land Affairs, and after consultation with any other Minister who has an interest by virtue of the functions of his department. If the land is privately owned, the Minister must consult with the Minister of Mineral and Energy Affairs and his declaration of the park is subject to any agreement entered into between the National Parks Board and the Minister and any other minister having such an interest, as well as the owner of the land.[24]

(f) National Parks Board. The National Parks Board is charged with the control, management and maintenance of parks,[25] and its constitution and functions are defined in the Act.[26] The board may also, with the approval of the Minister of Environment Affairs, make regulations consistent with the Act with regard to a variety of matters,

---

[18] Section 4.
[19] Section 2A.
[20] Section 2(3).
[21] Section 2A.
[22] Section 3(1).
[23] Section 3(3).
[24] Section 2B.
[25] Section 5(1).
[26] Sections 5–12.

including the exclusion of members of the public from certain areas within a park, the killing, capturing or impounding of any animals, the burning of grass, the cutting of trees, reeds and grass, the admission of motor cars or other vehicles, the maintenance, protection and preservation of a park and the animals, plant life and property therein, and generally for the efficient control and management of a park.[27] No action lies against the board for the recovery of any damage caused to any person by any animal in a park.[28]

(g) Funding. The Act makes provision for the establishment of a fund to be known as the National Parks Land Acquisition Fund, consisting of all monies received by the board by way of subscriptions, donations and bequests, in addition to monies appropriated by Parliament for the purposes of the fund.[29]

(h) Prohibited activities. No prospecting or mining of any nature may be undertaken on land included in a scheduled park.[30] No one may enter a park without the permission of the board, and the Act specifically prohibits various other activities within a park, including the following: being in possession of any weapon, explosive, trap or poison; hunting or otherwise wilfully or negligently killing or injuring any animal; disturbing any animal; damaging or destroying any egg or nest of any bird, or taking honey from a beehive; wilfully or negligently causing a veld fire, or any damage to any object of geological, archaeological, historical, ethnological, oceanographic, educational or other scientific interest; removing any animal, whether alive or dead, or any part of an animal; cutting, damaging, removing or destroying any tree or other plant (including any marine plant); removing seed from any tree or other plant without permission; and feeding any animal.[31] Contravention of any of these provisions constitutes a criminal offence.[32]

27.3.3 Mountain Catchment Areas Act

27.3.3.1 *Mountain catchment areas*

Mountain catchment areas are established in terms of the Mountain Catchment Areas Act 63 of 1970. The Act is discussed in chapter 24.

27.3.4 Lake Areas Development Act

27.3.4.1 *Lake areas*

(a) Definition and establishment. The Lake Areas Development Act 39 of 1975 does not specifically indicate the purpose of the establishment of lake areas; nor does it define them. They are established by the Minister of Environment Affairs by notice in the *Government Gazette*.[33] He may declare any land comprising or adjoining a tidal lagoon, a tidal river or any part thereof, or any other land comprising or adjoining a natural lake or a river or any part thereof, which is within the immediate vicinity of a tidal lagoon or a tidal river, to be a lake area.[34] All existing lake areas have been transformed into national parks or parts thereof. No land which is under the control of

---

[27] Section 29(1).
[28] Section 28(1).
[29] Section 12A. Cf s 16 with regard to revenue for operating expenses.
[30] Section 20.
[31] Section 21(1).
[32] Section 24.
[33] Section 2.
[34] Section 2(1). Before 1986, lake areas were proclaimed by the State President. His powers and duties were transferred to the Minister by the Transfer of Powers and Duties of the State President Act 97 of 1986.

a Provincial Administration shall be declared a lake area or part of a lake area except after consultation by the Minister with the Administrator concerned.[35]

(b) Administration. The Act establishes the Lake Areas Development Board.[36] Its objects are to control, manage and develop any state land situated within a lake area.[37] However, with effect from 1983, the powers of the Lake Areas Development Board were transferred to the National Parks Board.[38] In controlling, managing and developing any state land within a lake area, the board has extensive powers.[39]

(c) Regulations. The Minister may make regulations providing, inter alia, for the regulation and control of state land within a lake area, the construction, maintenance and control over buildings and other improvements, the use and control generally of the sea-shore and of the sea, and of any lake or river, within any lake area, and the use of amenities provided for visitors.[40]

(d) Private land. Provision is made for the acquisition of private land within a lake area. The Minister may, by exchange of state land situated either within or outside any lake area, acquire private land in a lake area for the purposes of the Act. If he is unable to acquire the land by purchase, he may expropriate the land, but subject to the provisions of the Expropriation Act 63 of 1975. Any land so acquired must be transferred to the State.[41]

27.3.5 Environment Conservation Act

27.3.5.1 *Protected natural environments*

An Administrator may in terms of the Environment Conservation Act 73 of 1989 by notice in the *Official Gazette* concerned declare any area defined by him to be a protected natural environment, and he may allocate a name to such area; provided that he may issue such declaration only if in his opinion there are adequate grounds to presume that the declaration will substantially promote the preservation of specific ecological processes, natural systems, natural beauty or species of indigenous wildlife or the preservation of biotic diversity in general. He must also consult with the owners of, and the holders of real rights in, land situated within the defined area, and invite them to lodge any complaints against the intended declaration.[42]

In order to achieve the general policy and object of the Act, the Administrator may issue directions relating to any land or water in a protected natural environment. However, he is required to furnish owners and holders of real rights in the land with a copy of the directions, which may be issued only with the concurrence of each Minister charged with the administration of any law which in the opinion of the Administrator relates to a matter affecting the environment in that area.[43] Owners and holders of real rights, and their successors in title, are subject to the provisions of such directions.[44] The Administrator is required to direct the relevant Registrar of Deeds to make appropriate entries of the directions in his registers and to endorse the office copy of the title deeds of affected properties accordingly.[45] With the concurrence of the Minister of Finance and subject to such conditions as he may determine, the Administrator may

---

[35] Section 2(2).
[36] Section 3.
[37] Section 11.
[38] Section 30B of the National Parks Act.
[39] Section 11.
[40] Section 23. Cf GN R311 of 22 February 1980.
[41] Section 16.
[42] Section 16(1).
[43] Section 16(2).
[44] Section 16(3).
[45] Section 16(4).

render financial aid by way of grants or otherwise to such owners or holders of real rights in respect of expenses incurred in compliance with any such directions.[46] The Administrator may, with its concurrence, assign the control and management of a protected natural environment to a local authority or 'government institution',[47] or he may withdraw such control and management.[48]

The Administrator may also establish management advisory committees to advise him on the control and management of protected natural environments in order to advance the objects for which they are established.[49] The membership of management advisory committees is determined by the Administrator.[50] He is, however, required to appoint members from relevant government agencies and owners, holders of real rights, and users of the affected land. Where control and management has been assigned to a local authority or government institution, the appointment of members must be made with its concurrence.[51] The Act also makes provision for administrative support for the performance of the functions of the committee.[52]

The Physical Planning Act 88 of 1967—which has been repealed by the Physical Planning Act 125 of 1991—introduced the legislative category of 'nature area', defined in the Act as any area which could be utilized in the interests of and for the benefit and enjoyment of the public in general, and for the reproduction, protection or preservation of wild animal life, wildlife, wild vegetation or objects of geological, ethnological, historical or other scientific interest.[53] Nature areas were managed in terms of the Environment Conservation Act 100 of 1982 (which was repealed and substituted by the Environment Conservation Act 73 of 1989) by the Minister of Environment Affairs, advised by a management committee which he was authorized to appoint for such areas.[54] The Environment Conservation Act of 1989 deleted the provisions relating to nature areas in the Physical Planning Act, but deemed any land reserved as a nature area under the latter to be declared a 'protected natural environment'.[55]

27.3.5.2 *Special nature reserves*

The Minister of Environment Affairs may by notice in the *Government Gazette* declare any area defined by him in the RSA, including the territorial waters,[56] to be a special nature reserve.[57] The purpose for which he may make such a declaration is the protection of the environment in the area.[58] He may make such a declaration only in respect of land or water of which the State is the owner, or which is under the exclusive control of the State,[59] and he may do so only with the concurrence of the Committee for Environmental Management.[60] The declaration of a special nature reserve may not be

---

[46] Section 16(5).

[47] Defined in s 1(xii) of the Act as 'any body, company or close corporation established by or under any law or any other institution or body recognized by the Minister by notice in the *Government Gazette*'.

[48] Section 16(6).

[49] Section 17(1).

[50] Section 17(2).

[51] Section 17(2), (3) and (4).

[52] Section 17(7) and (8).

[53] Section 4(1)*(b)*.

[54] Section 9. See generally Gordon *The management of nature areas declared in terms of section 4(1)*(b) *of the Physical Planning Act 88 of 1967* (unpublished LLM thesis, University of the Witwatersrand 1987) and Visser 'Nature area legislation in South Africa' 1988 *SALJ* 249.

[55] Sections 43 and 44.

[56] ie the sea within a distance of 12 nautical miles from low-water mark: s 2 of the Territorial Waters Act 87 of 1963.

[57] Section 18.

[58] Section 18(2)*(a)*.

[59] Section 18(2)*(b)*.

[60] Section 18(2)*(c)*.

withdrawn or its boundaries altered except by resolution of Parliament.[61] With its concurrence and subject to a management plan being drawn up in consultation with it, the Minister may assign the control of a special nature reserve to any local authority or government institution.[62] Entry into a special nature reserve is strictly controlled. No person may gain admittance, nor perform any activity in or on such an area, except upon written exemption granted by the controlling local authority or government institution, after consultation with the Minister, granted only to a scientist occupied with a specific project, or an officer charged with specific official duties.[63] In respect of such admission and activity, the air space to a level of 500 m above the ground level of the reserve is treated as included in the reserve.[64]

27.3.5.3 *Limited development areas*

A third category of protected area introduced by the Environment Conservation Act 73 of 1989 is a limited development area. The Minister may by notice in the *Government Gazette* declare any area defined by him as a limited development area, and no person may then undertake any development or activity prohibited by the Minister by notice in the *Government Gazette*, or cause such development or activity to be undertaken, unless he has on application been authorized to do so by the Minister or a local authority designated by the Minister in the notice, and then only subject to the conditions contained in any such authorization.[65] In considering any application for such authorization, the Minister or the designated local authority may request the applicant to submit a report as prescribed concerning the influence of the proposed activity on the environment in the limited development area, in effect an environmental impact assessment.[66] See generally chapter 7.

27.3.5.4 *Protected areas recognized under international instruments*

The Minister may make regulations relating to the application of the provisions of any international convention, treaty or agreement relating to the protection of the environment which has been entered into by or has been ratified on behalf of the Government of the RSA.[67] Such regulations may relate, for example, to wetland areas or world heritage sites. The State President may also by proclamation in the *Government Gazette* add to the Environment Conservation Act any schedule containing the provisions of an international convention, treaty or agreement relating to the protection of the environment which has been entered into or ratified by the Government of the Republic.[68] See chapter 9.

27.3.5.5 *Penalty*

When the Administrator has issued directions in respect of a protected natural environment, any person who contravenes any provision of such directions, or fails to comply therewith, is guilty of an offence.[69] In relation to special nature reserves, any person who has gained admittance or performed an activity without exemption, or who contravenes a condition of exemption, shall be guilty of an offence. The Environment Conservation Act is discussed in chapter 7.

---

[61] Section 18(3).
[62] Section 18(4).
[63] Section 18(6) and (7).
[64] Section 18(8).
[65] Section 23(1) and (2).
[66] Section 23(3).
[67] Section 28*(c)*.
[68] Section 38(1) and (2).
[69] Section 29(2)*(a)*.

27.3.6 Forest Act

Before Union in 1910 each colony had its own laws for the preservation of trees and veld. The various laws relating to forests, grass, grass-burning and veld conservation were consolidated by the Forest Act 13 of 1941 which, in turn, was repealed and substituted by the Forest Act 72 of 1968, while the applicable legislation today is the Forest Act 122 of 1984.

27.3.6.1 *State forests*

'State forest' is widely defined so as to include not only state plantations and land controlled and managed by the Department of Water Affairs and Forestry for research purposes or for the establishment of a commercial timber plantation, but also areas which have been set aside for the conservation of fauna and flora, for the management of a water catchment area, for the prevention of soil erosion or sand drift, or for the protection of indigenous forests.[70]

If the Minister is of the opinion that it is necessary for the better achievement of the objects of the Act that an undemarcated forest or a part thereof be entrenched against alienation by being converted into demarcated forest he may, after following a procedure aimed at accommodating objections, declare the undemarcated forest or part of a forest to be demarcated.[71] The consequence of such a declaration is that the affected area may not be withdrawn from demarcation except with the approval, by resolution, of Parliament.[72]

No servitudes or any other rights of whatever nature may be acquired by prescription in respect of a state forest or any part thereof. However, the Minister may grant such rights with the approval, by resolution, of Parliament on such conditions as Parliament may determine.[73] On the other hand, and somewhat inconsistently, the Director-General may in the prescribed manner grant any right, whether of a permanent or temporary nature, to various government agencies, as well as temporary rights to any person for a wide variety of purposes, such as trading, grazing, cultivation of land, drilling, and the erection of factories, residences or camping facilities, or for utilization of any part of a state forest for any other purpose whatsoever; provided that the exercise of such rights will not be detrimental to the forest or any forest produce occurring in it.[74] Prospecting and mining for precious metals, base minerals, precious stones, natural oil and source material within forests are permitted, save that no forest produce may be cut, damaged, taken or removed by the holder of such rights except on the authority of a licence or permit of the Director-General.[75] Servitudes, rights to forest produce, rights of grazing, cultivation, residence or camping, rights to water, or any other rights in respect of state forests which existed at the commencement of the Act, remain in force, but may be exercised only in the prescribed manner. The Director-General is required to keep a register in which all such servitudes and rights are noted.[76] In his discretion, the Director-General may at any time temporarily or permanently close any road in a state forest, or prohibit access to it.[77]

27.3.6.2 *Nature reserves and wilderness areas*

The Act provides for the establishment of nature reserves and wilderness areas within state forests. No clear definition of either category is offered, although the purposes for

[70] Section 1.
[71] Section 10(1).
[72] Section 10(2).
[73] Section 11(1).
[74] Section 11(2)*(a)*.
[75] Section 11(2)*(b)*.
[76] Section 11(3) and (4).
[77] Section 12(1).

which they may be established indicate their respective natures. The Act simply states that a nature reserve is a state forest or part thereof which has been set aside as such, and a wilderness area, similarly, is a state forest or a part thereof set aside as such.[78] The title 'forest nature reserve' may have been more appropriate in the Act because such reserves may be established only within state forests, and secondly because of the possiblity of confusion with provincial nature reserves.

The Minister may by notice in the *Government Gazette* set aside any state forest or any defined part thereof as a nature reserve for the preservation of a particular natural forest or particular plants or animals or for some other conservation purpose mentioned in the notice and, on the recommendation of the Council for the Environment, as a wilderness area for the preservation of an ecosystem or the scenic beauty. The control and management of such areas vest in the Director-General.[79] No land set aside as a nature reserve or a wilderness area or any part thereof may be withdrawn from such setting aside except with the approval, by resolution, of Parliament, and the Minister must by notice in the *Government Gazette* give notice of such withdrawal.[80]

No person may in any such area cut, disturb, damage, take, collect, destroy or remove any forest produce.[81] Forest produce is widely defined so as to include anything which grows in a forest or is produced by any vertebrate or invertebrate member of the animal kingdom or any member of the plant kingdom in a forest, timber plantation or state forest.[82] However, the Director-General may perform acts which are not inconsistent with the objects for which the nature reserve or wilderness area was set aside.[83] Some of such acts which are identified in the Act as being those which the Director-General may take are the restoration of ecologically disturbed habitats, the prevention and combating of soil erosion and fires, the maintenance of the natural genetic and species diversity, the exercise of control over undesirable plants and animals, the removal and marketing of any forest produce, research and education. These are all activities which may be undertaken in both nature reserves and wilderness areas, although it should be noted that the removal and marketing of forest produce from a wilderness area is inconsistent with the concept of wilderness as an area subject to minimal interference from man. The making available to the public of open-air recreation facilities is permitted within nature reserves, but not within wilderness areas.[84]

Servitudes and other rights may be granted by the Minister in respect of any nature reserve or wilderness area or part thereof only with the approval, by resolution, of Parliament and on such conditions as Parliament may determine.[85] However, if the Minister is satisfied that the national security necessitates it, he may grant a servitude or other right of a temporary nature to any person, subject to such parliamentary approval as soon as practicable thereafter and subject to such conditions as Parliament may then determine.[86] Servitudes and other rights existing at the date of setting aside remain in force, and the Director-General may renew temporary rights if he is satisfied that their continuance will not materially prejudice the objects for which the area was set aside.[87]

---

[78] Section 1.
[79] Section 15(1).
[80] Section 15(2).
[81] Section 15(3)*(a)*(i).
[82] Section 1.
[83] Section 15(3)*(a)*(ii).
[84] Section 15(3)*(b)*.
[85] Section 15(4)*(a)*.
[86] Section 15(4)*(b)*.
[87] Section 15(5) and (6).

Penalties are provided for contraventions of the provisions of the Act.[88] It is often difficult to enforce protective laws and to apprehend offenders, particularly in remote areas. The Act accordingly authorizes a court to award a sum not exceeding one-fourth of the fine recovered to an informant upon whose information the offender is convicted or who assisted materially in bringing him to justice.[89]

27.3.6.3 *National botanic gardens*

Existing national botanic gardens are listed in the first schedule[90] to the Act. The Minister may by notice in the *Government Gazette* declare procured or reserved state land, or any land made available by the owner by agreement with the Minister of Regional and Land Affairs, for the purposes of a national botanic garden for such period and on such conditions as the Minister of Environment Affairs, after consultation with the National Botanical Institute may approve, to be a national botanic garden.[91] State land which forms part of a national botanic garden may not be alienated or employed for any other purpose except with the approval, by resolution, of Parliament.[92] The institute may, with the concurrence of the Minister, make by-laws relating, inter alia, to public access, the protection or conservation of any animal, plant or property, and any other matter which in the opinion of the institute is necessary for the control and management of a national botanic garden.

27.3.7 National Monuments Act

The National Monuments Act 28 of 1969 provides for the preservation of certain property, both immovable and movable, as national monuments,[93] and establishes a National Monuments Council.[94]

27.3.7.1 *National monuments*

The National Monuments Council has the power, inter alia, by notice in the *Government Gazette*, to declare any immovable property in respect of which it is investigating the desirabilty of recommending as a national monument, provisionally to be a national monument.[95] However it may not do so in respect of any property belonging to the State, unless the Minister of National Education consents, or any property belonging to any other person, without the consent of such person, unless the council has at least a month before the date of such notice served upon the owner of such property a written notice advising him of the proposed declaration and calling upon him to lodge objections within one month of the date of service of such notice.[96]

Whenever the Minister considers it to be in the national interest that any immovable or movable property of aesthetic, historical or scientific interest be preserved, protected and maintained, he may on the recommendation of the council by notice in the *Government Gazette* declare such property to be a national monument.[97] However, he may not do so in relation to any property belonging to a person other than the State or the council, without the consent of such person, unless the Minister is satisfied that the council has at least one month before making its recommendation, served upon the owner a written notice advising him of the proposed recommendation and calling upon

[88] Section 75.
[89] Section 82.
[90] Schedule 1.
[91] Section 66(2)*(a)*.
[92] Section 66(3).
[93] Section 10(1).
[94] Section 2.
[95] Section 5(1)*(c)*.
[96] Section 5(5).
[97] Section 10(1).

him to lodge objections with the council within one month of such service. The council has to submit to the Minister all objections lodged with it by the owner.[98]

Any person who sells, exchanges, or otherwise alienates, or pledges or lets any monument shall forthwith inform the council of the name and address of the person to whom it has been alienated, pledged or let.[99] No person may destroy, damage, excavate or alter any monument except under the authority of and in accordance with a permit issued by the council subject to the directions of the Minister.[100] Whenever the council refuses an application for such a permit, or has granted the application subject to any terms, conditions, restrictions or directions, the applicant for the permit may appeal against the decision of the council to the Minister, who may confirm such decision or direct the council to grant the application subject to such terms, conditions, restrictions or directions as he may determine.[101] Failure to comply with these provisions constitutes an offence. Upon conviction of such offence, the council may, in writing, direct the offender to put right the result of the act of which he was found guilty and, upon failure to comply, the council may put right or cause to put right the result of the act constituting the offence, and recover the cost of doing so from such person.[102]

Whenever any area of land has been declared or provisionally declared to be, or has been recommended to be declared or has been included in, a national monument, or whenever the council is investigating the desirability of having any area of land so declared or included, the council must furnish the relevant registrar of deeds with a copy of the relevant notice and particulars of any survey and diagram, and the registrar is required to endorse upon the title deeds of the land in question reference to such notice and particulars.[103]

Penalties are prescribed for the offence of failing to comply with the above provisions.[104] Moreover, the Minister may make regulations, inter alia, in relation to all matters which he considers to be necessary or expedient for achieving the objects of the Act.[105]

27.3.7.2 *Conservation areas*

The council is empowered to compile and maintain a register of immovable property which it regards as worthy of conservation on the ground of its historic, cultural or aesthetic interest and to supplement, amend or delete any entry in the register from time to time by notice in the *Government Gazette*; provided that an entry shall not be made until such time as it has consulted with the local authority in whose area of jurisdiction such immovable property is situated.[106] The council may also, after consultation with the relevant authority, by notice in the *Government Gazette*, designate any area of land to be a conservation area on the ground of its historic, aesthetic or scientific interest; provided that in the absence of any agreement the relevant authority may appeal to the Minister who may, after consultation with the council, revoke such designation by notice in the *Government Gazette*.[107] Any planning authority and the owner of immovable property appearing in such register, or of a

---

[98] Section 10(3).
[99] Section 12(1).
[100] Section 12*(a)* and (4).
[101] Section 12(5).
[102] Section 12(6).
[103] Section 13.
[104] Section 16.
[105] Section 17.
[106] Section 5(1)*(cC)*.
[107] Section 5(9).

conservation area, are required to consult with the council in respect of planning which affects such immovable property or such a conservation area.[108]

The council may, with the approval of the Minister, make by-laws regulating, inter alia, admission of members of the public to monuments under its control; the safe-guarding of monuments and conservation areas from damage, disfigurement, alteration, destruction, or defilement; and the conditions of use by any person of any area of land which has been declared to be a monument and which is under the control of the council, as well as of conservation areas.[109] Similarly, any local authority may with the approval of the Minister and of the council make such by-laws in respect of monuments under its control, as well as conservation areas.[110] Such by-laws made by the council or a local authority may prescribe fines for any contravention.[111]

27.3.8 Defence Act

27.3.8.1 *Defence areas*

Extensive powers are conferred by the Defence Act 44 of 1957 upon the Minister of Defence to do or cause to be done all things which in his opinion are necessary for the efficient defence and protection of the country.[112] He may prohibit or restrict access to land which is subject to military control.[113] These controlled areas are used primarily for training and testing purposes. However, it is declared policy that the areas be managed scientifically with a view to nature conservation as a secondary objective.

27.3.9 Sea Fishery Act

27.3.9.1 *Marine reserves*

The Sea Fishery Act 12 of 1988 empowers the Minister of Environment Affairs by notice in the *Government Gazette* to set aside an area as a marine reserve for the protection within such reserve, of fish in general or of fish belonging to a particular species or any aquatic plant.[114]The protection of fish[115] and marine organisms is accomplished through prohibitions against their catching, disturbance or possession.[116]

Since the Tsitsikamma Forest and Coastal National Park extends 0,8 km to seaward of the low-water mark, the extensive provisions of the National Parks Act regarding the conservation of all animals relate also to marine animals. Provincial nature reserves that border on the sea, however, do not extend to seaward of the high-water mark, although control over the sea-shore has been devolved upon the provincial administrations of the Cape and Natal, thus allowing for some control of marine life.

27.3.10 Sea-Shore Act

27.3.10.1 *Sea-shore*

The sea-shore, ie the water and the land between the low-water mark and the high-water mark, may to some extent, and broadly speaking, be regarded as constituting a protected area. The sea-shore is regulated in terms of the Sea-Shore Act 21 of 1935. See chapter 26.

---

[108] Section 12(1A).
[109] Section 18(1).
[110] Section 18(2).
[111] Section 18(3).
[112] Section 76.
[113] Section 89.
[114] Section 34(1)*(a)*.
[115] Defined in s 1 as every species of sea animal, whether vertebrate or invertebrate, including the spawn or larvae of such sea animal, excluding any seal or seabird which are conserved separately by virtue of the Sea Birds and Seals Protection Act 46 of 1973.
[116] Regulations 3, 4 and 5 of the schedule to GN R1810 of 27 July 1990.

27.3.11 Sea Birds and Seals Protection Act

Most islands around the South African coast in effect constitute protected areas. Some 46 such islands[117] are controlled in terms of the Sea Birds and Seals Protection Act 46 of 1973. The Minister of Environment Affairs is empowered, by notice in the *Government Gazette* to insert into or delete from the schedule the name or description of any island.[118]

These islands are controlled as sanctuaries and breeding stations for sea birds, while commercial exploitation of guano is simultaneously undertaken on some of the islands. Control is effected in that it is a crime for anyone to set foot on or remain upon an island or there to disturb, capture or kill any sea bird or seal, or to damage the eggs of any sea bird or to collect or remove any such eggs or feathers or guano, except in the performance of duties under the Act or under the authority and subject to the conditions of an exemption or a permit.[119] Further control can be exercised through regulations.[120]

27.3.12 Provincial Nature Conservation Ordinances

The conservation of flora and fauna is the responsibility of the provincial administrations.[121] In discharging that responsibility, the provinces either extended the system of reserves that were extant at the time of Union, or started new reserves. Protected areas are established in terms of the Nature Conservation Ordinance 8 of 1969 (Orange Free State); the Nature and Environmental Conservation Ordinance 19 of 1974 (Cape); the Nature Conservation Ordinance 15 of 1974 (Natal), and the Nature Conservation Ordinance 12 of 1983 (Transvaal). See, generally, chapters 11 and 12.

27.3.12.1 *Cape Province*

The Cape Ordinance makes provision for the establishment of three classes of nature reserves: provincial, local and private.

The Administrator may by proclamation establish provincial nature reserves on any land under his control or management and, after consultation and conclusion of an agreement with any state department, on land which is under the control or management of such state department. He may by agreement or expropriation acquire any land which he considers necessary and suitable for the purpose of establishing a provincial nature reserve, and is given wide-ranging powers to make regulations relating to such reserves.[122]

Any local authority may, with the approval of the Administrator and subject to such conditions as he may specify, establish a local nature reserve on land vested in it or under its control or management, and it may, for that purpose, acquire land by agreement or expropriation.[123] If the Administrator is of the opinion that any action taken or proposed by a local authority in the course of management, control or development of a local nature reserve established by it will be detrimental to the reserve or the purposes for which it was established, he may, after consultation with the local authority by order in writing prohibit such action or the continuance thereof, or allow it to continue subject to conditions. If adequate steps to comply have not been taken by

---

117 Cf the first schedule to the Sea Birds and Seals Protection Act and schedule 2 of the Sea Fishery Act.

118 Section 14.

119 Section 3.

120 Section 11.

121 Pursuant to s 11(1)*(a)* read with schedule 2 paras 2 and 2A of the Financial Relations Act 65 of 1976.

122 Section 6.

123 Section 7(1).

the local authority, the Administrator is authorized to abolish the local nature reserve concerned.[124]

Subject to the approval of the Administrator and any conditions he may specify, any owner of land may establish a private nature reserve on his land. With the approval of the Administrator, he may alter the boundaries of the reserve, or abolish it. Any alteration or abolition must be notified in the *Provincial Gazette*.[125] Subject to any conditions imposed by the Administrator, any person who has established a private nature reserve must manage, control and develop it with a view to the propagation, protection and preservation of fauna and flora.

27.3.12.2 *Natal*

The Natal Ordinance defines no fewer than seven different types of protected area: commercial game-reserve, game park, game reserve, national park, nature reserve, private nature reserve and private wildlife reserve.[126]

National parks, game reserves and nature reserves are established by the Administrator by proclamation in the *Official Gazette*. He may also, by subsequent proclamation, increase or decrease the area of any such place or alter the boundaries thereof; provided that the area of any game reserve or nature reserve established on state land may not be increased or its boundaries altered except with the prior approval of the Minister of Agriculture.[127] The ordinance contains detailed provisions relating to restriction of entry into such areas, and the prohibition of certain acts therein. For example, it is unlawful to enter such an area without the permission of the Natal Parks Board, or to kill, injure or disturb any animal, or cause a veld fire or injure a tree, or be in possession of a snare within such an area.[128]

The Administrator may also, upon the recommendation of the board and after application by an owner of land wishing to have any area of his land proclaimed a private nature reserve or a private wildlife reserve, by proclamation in the *Official Gazette* establish such areas.[129] The gathering of indigenous plants and the hunting of wild birds within such private reserves without permit issued by the board are prohibited.[130] A limiting provision relating to private nature reserves requires that no area may be declared as such unless or until it is, in the opinion of the board, effectively enclosed within a fence kept in good repair or otherwise suitably demarcated. The fence must conform to minimum prescribed standards.[131] There are areas of land in private or local authority ownership which are eminently suitable for proclamation as private nature reserves, but the cost of fencing is prohibitive. Any area proposed as a private wildlife reserve must be effectively enclosed with the fence kept in good repair and conforming to minimum prescribed standards.[132] The owner is also obliged to undertake, in writing, that he will properly and adequately maintain the reserve and the fencing.[133]

27.3.12.3 *Orange Free State*

The Orange Free State Ordinance makes provision for the establishment of two classes of nature reserves: provincial nature reserves and private nature reserves.

The Administrator may establish, maintain and manage a nature reserve and may for

[124] Section 10.
[125] Section 12.
[126] Section 1.
[127] Section 2.
[128] Section 15(1).
[129] Section 59.
[130] Section 60.
[131] Section 62.
[132] Section 64.
[133] Section 67*(a)*(i).

this purpose also establish a transport service and provide accommodation and camping and other facilities for visitors to such reserve. He may, by notice in the *Official Gazette*, declare a nature reserve established by him to be a provincial nature reserve. No person may hunt a wild animal or pick an indigenous plant in a provincial nature reserve without his permission.[134]

The Administrator may also, on the application of the owner of land and on such conditions as may be prescribed, declare such land or any portion thereof, by notice in the *Official Gazette*, to be a private nature reserve. He may, by similar notice, amend or withdraw such a declaration. No person may hunt a wild animal or pick an indigenous plant in a private nature reserve except with the permission of the owner.[135]

27.3.12.4 *Transvaal*

The Transvaal Ordinance makes provision for the declaration of nature reserves. The Administrator may, by notice in the *Official Gazette*, declare an area defined in the notice to be a nature reserve and he may at any time by like notice amend the definition of such an area or withdraw the declaration of such an area to be a nature reserve.[136]

No person may hunt game in a nature reserve, provided that upon written application by the owner of land within such reserve, a permit may be issued to him or to any other person indicated by him in the application, authorizing the holder to hunt the species, number and sex of game referred to in the permit on the land of the owner.[137]

Where the Administrator is of the opinion that land is fenced in such a way that game cannot readily gain access to it or escape from it, he may, on written application from the owner of the land, exempt the owner or any other person indicated by the owner in his application, from all or any of the provisions of the ordinance applicable to hunting, catching or sale of game on such land.[138]A system of private nature reserves has been applied extensively in the Transvaal. Private nature reserves are in effect exempt from hunting restrictions, as indicated above, and this may be the reason for the number of such reserves in this province.

No person may establish or operate a game park, zoological garden, bird sanctuary, reptile park, snake park or similar institution, unless he is the holder of a permit which authorizes him to do so.[139]

27.3.13 Other protected areas

27.3.13.1 *Conservancies*

The conservancy system was developed in Natal and has also spread to the Transvaal and the Orange Free State. The Natal Parks Board defines a conservancy as a group of farms whose owners have combined resources for the improved conservation and well-being of wildlife inhabiting the area. The term wildlife in this instance encompasses mammals, birds, fish, natural vegetation and all desirable natural life forms. The board assists landowners in a conservancy by the training of staff, provision of animals at reasonable prices for re-stocking, and technical advice on management planning. The conservancies are, however, run and financed entirely by the farmers themselves. Conservancies do not have any legal nature conservation status.

27.3.13.2 *Biosphere reserves*

The concept of biosphere reserves has been introduced in Natal, while the Cape Province is also considering the establishment of such a reserve. Biosphere reserves are

[134] Section 35.
[135] Section 36.
[136] Section 14.
[137] Section 19(1)*(a)*.
[138] Section 47(1).
[139] Section 50(1).

founded on the co-operative management of natural resources by an authority, e g the Natal Parks Board, and the neighbours of a reserve. Humans are regarded as an integral part of the process, and the importance of the concept is the notion of consolidating established protected areas with local community involvement. Although the concept of biosphere reserve as applied in Natal is not quite the same as the Unesco Man and the Biosphere Programme in that the areas do not enjoy full legal protection and, because of South Africa's past isolation from the international community, the local programme has not been incorporated in the international programme, the local initiative holds great conservation potential and should be encouraged, developed and introduced in the other provinces.

27.3.13.3 *Natural heritage sites*

The South African Natural Heritage Programme was launched in 1984 under the auspices of the Department of Environment Affairs. The programme aims to encourage the protection of important natural sites, large or small, in private and public ownership. It is a voluntary programme, participation being at the discretion of the landowner. On registration, each site owner receives management advice, but retains full rights over the property and may withdraw from the programme. The status of natural heritage sites, like that of conservancies, is based upon agreement and not upon legislation.

27.3.13.4 *Public resorts*

Although many public resorts are sufficiently large to give protection to flora and fauna, they cannot strictly be regarded as protected areas because their primary purpose is the provision of recreational and entertainment facilities to the public. Such resorts are established, in the case of three provinces, in terms of provincial ordinances, namely the Transvaal Public Resorts Ordinance 18 of 1969, the Cape Public Resorts Ordinance 20 of 1971, the Natal Recreational Facilities Ordinance 24 of 1972, and the Natal Nature Conservation Ordinance 15 of 1974. In the Orange Free State public resorts are established by virtue of the provisions of the Financial Relations Act 65 of 1976.[140] They may also be established in terms of municipal by-laws.

A summarized list of the controlling authorities, number and total area of protected areas is provided in table 27.2.

27.3.14 The need for national policy and for uniform legislation

Environmentally detrimental land-use decisions are being made continually and unless a co-ordinated strategy is developed in terms of a uniform national policy in respect of the establishment, status and management of protected areas, the retrograde tide may not be stemmed and potential areas may be lost, possibly forever, while a considerable degree of uncertainty will continue to prevail with regard to the jurisdiction and management of existing areas. The formulation of a national policy to serve as a guide for the establishment of future protected areas and for the rationalization of the many different types of protected areas currently in existence, is consequently of the utmost importance. Provision for the determination of environmental policy is made in the Environment Conservation Act, as has been explained in chapter 7.

Moreover, it is submitted that the time is ripe for a reconsideration of all legislation dealing with protected areas, with a view to rationalizing the situation by establishing an Act dealing comprehensively with all such areas. It is not contended that the variety of protected areas should be dissolved, nor that they should all be established and

[140] Schedule 2 para 23.

TABLE 27.2
South African protected areas: Summary

Agency	Number of sites	Area (ha)
1. *State land*		
National Parks Board	22	3 177 904
National Botanical Institute	9	1 341
Department of Water Affairs and Forestry	138	612 954
Cape Provinical Administration	143	1 324 118
Natal Provincial Administration	76	581 390
OFS Provincial Administration	14	164 443
Transvaal Provincial Administration	65	302 892
SA Defence Force	31	550 294
Bophuthatswana	3	59 880
Ciskei	8	27 818
Gazankulu	5	81 244
Kangwane	3	58 300
KwaZulu	16	88 743
Kwandebele	2	4 852
Lebowa	11	22 417
Transkei	10	35 240
Venda	2	18 200
Total:	558	7 112 030
2. *Private land*		
Department of Environment Affairs	177	233 067
Cape Provincial Administration	180	751 651
Natal Provincial Administration	100	703 100
OFS Provincial Administration	26	350 375
Transvaal Provincial Administration	54	1 360 327
Total:	360	3 398 520
Total Table 2:	918	10 510 550

Main source: Wahl & Cohen *National register of protected areas in South Africa* Department of Environment Affairs (1992).

Note: The above figures are subject to continuous adaptation as new areas are established and existing areas are enlarged or reduced. Moreover, they are controversial because uncertainty exists as to the exact requirements which an area should satisfy in order to qualify as a protected area. The above total area is more extensive than previous estimates, mainly because protected areas which have no legislative status have been included in the list and because a few areas enjoying simultaneous protection in terms of different statutes may be reflected in more than one entry. Also, the division between protected areas on state and on private land does not represent exclusive categories, since certain areas include both state and private land.

administered by the same authority. What is necessary, however, is a systematic anduniform treatment of the subject-matter in accordance with a national policy, in order to avoid the currently prevailing ad hoc, fragmented and often complex provisions for the establishment, status, designation, management and control of protected areas.[141] It is submitted that this will be facilitated by the enactment of a comprehensive statute on protected areas. This is also the recommendation of the President's Council.[142]

[141] Cf Rabie above n 14, 89.

[142] *Report of the three committees of the President's Council on a national environmental management system* PC 1/1991 para 5.4.8.

CHAPTER 28

LAND-USE PLANNING

P E CLAASSEN
J R L MILTON

28.1 INTRODUCTION

Planning is derived from the noun plan, which can be defined as 'a formulated or organized method according to which something is to be done; a scheme of action'.[1] In the case of town and regional planning the 'something to be done', that is, the goal to be achieved by the planning, is to improve the quality of life and the general welfare of the community concerned. This embraces the creation of better living environments, which is achieved through both development and conservation. Indeed, the best way to promote conservation and environmental awareness in developing countries is through socio-economic development. 'Once the present seems relatively secure, people can focus on the future', that is, on the long-term impacts of development on the environment.[2]

Land-use planning is one of the means applied to achieving this goal. Town and regional planning, however, comprises more than land-use and physical planning. It provides a system through which communities can address their development problems. The system is also the first line of action for addressing many local and regional environmental problems. When properly undertaken it incorporates environmental impact analyses and integrated environmental management.

Town and regional planning can be divided into two interdependent functions. One deals with the ideal arrangement of land-uses, based on theories derived from empirical and scientific analysis, to create cities and regions pleasant to live in and functioning optimally. However, because of the changing nature of cities, the subjective nature of what is desirable, and especially because of the conflicting expectations of people and groups, it is not possible to achieve such an ideal pattern of land-uses. This leads to the second function of town and regional planning, that is to provide a fair, just and efficient process for arbitrating between conflicting land uses. This control aspect, which will generally be referred to as the town and regional planning system, is an integral part of government.

The purpose of this chapter is to give a short description of the town and regional planning system as it functions in South Africa today. The fields of environmental conservation that can best be addressed by means of this system will be highlighted, as well as ways in which such conservation should be undertaken.[3] Finally, land-use planning legislation will be discussed.

28.2 THE SCOPE OF TOWN AND REGIONAL PLANNING

28.2.1 Origins of modern town and regional planning

In the course of recorded history human beings have attempted to adapt the

---

[1] *The Oxford English dictionary*, (2 ed, 1989).

[2] Reilly 'Economic growth and environmental gain.' 1991 (3) *Dialogue* 20.

[3] A thorough, though perhaps idealistic, description of the evolution of thought on town and regional planning, its organization and relevant legislation in South Africa (up to 1983) has been provided in Fuggle & Rabie (eds) *Environmental concerns in South Africa* (1983) ch 20.

environment to their needs.[4] The origin of modern town planning is often ascribed to British efforts to cope with unhealthy living conditions in cities, created by the Industrial Revolution. These conditions inspired philanthropists such as Robert Owen and Ebenezer Howard to plan and create new environments that would ensure good living conditions, enhance social interaction and preserve the countryside. This growing concern with the plight of humankind, together with the growth of socialism, led to increasing control of development, culminating in the Green Belt of London and the creation of New Towns in an attempt to syphon off excess population from London and other urban conurbations. These ideas, as well as the concomitant legislation and control measures developed in Britain, had a great influence on town planning in South Africa. Our thinking on this matter was also influenced by developments in the United States, from where we inherited our strong emphasis on land-use zoning, based on the Euclidean model.[5]

Regional planning in South Africa was inspired by grand regional development schemes such as the Tennessee Valley Authority in the USA. That scheme was created during the depression of the 1930s under President Roosevelt's New Deal policy to alleviate poverty by more effectively utilizing natural resources. The rise of socialism and of increased government control and intervention also influenced regional and national planning in South Africa.

28.2.2 Nature of town and regional planning in South Africa

Planning action is constantly evolving in order better to address the problems of society. In South Africa, town planning developed as a control-oriented physical planning system. Although much lip service was paid to its idealistic aims 'to improve the quality of life and the general welfare of the community', the actual impact of planning action was much more mundane. That is due partly to the legal mechanisms of town planning being bent mainly on control. It soon became clear that zoning land for a specific use, by itself, would not initiate development. The intentions of the owner of the land, and especially market forces, carry much more weight than the allocated zoning on the town-planning scheme.

Although this weakness in the town-planning system has long been felt, it is only recently, with the large numbers of impoverished people streaming to cities, that serious efforts are being made to make planning more development-oriented and less control-oriented, more pro-active and less reactive, more process-oriented and less blueprint-oriented.[6] Although the legislation for town and regional planning defines the purpose of planning as 'orderly physical (or spatial) development',[7] many feel that this quest for order is a Western concept that is less important than socio-economic development; in fact, it can be an obstruction to development. The drive towards the promotion of development is not specifically legislated for, but is, to a large degree, taking place through the structures created by town and regional planning, local

[4] Fuggle & Rabie, above n 3, 465.

[5] Krueckeberg (ed) *Introduction to planning history in the United States* (1983) 96. In the 1926 case of *City of Euclid v Ambler Realty*, the Supreme Court of the USA ruled with a 5 to 4 majority that a local government has the right to control the use of land. That ruling formed the basis for all subsequent land-use zoning in the United States.

[6] The term 'pro-active planning' indicates that the planning process should lead the development process. This is in contrast to 'reactive planning', which is more intent on control and which reacts to problems that occur rather than anticipating and preventing such problems.

The term 'blueprint-planning' refers to a process where plans are prepared by experts and then presented to the people concerned. Process planning is more people-oriented. That is, through a process of negotiation people affected by it participate in the development process, from initial formulation of concepts to implementation.

[7] For instance, s 5 of the Physical Planning Act 125 of 1991, and s 5 of the Land Use Planning Ordinance 15 of 1985 of the Cape Province.

government and other legislation. Yet, in the last instance, socio-economic development, especially where poor people are concerned, still depends to a large degree on actual state-funded physical development.

Parallel with these developments, another line of thought developed, namely that of conservationists, which became particularly strong in the late sixties and early seventies; it was partially inspired by a world movement towards greater environmental awareness. To achieve their aims of limiting pollution and conserving the natural and cultural heritage, conservationists demand greater state control over development. In the conflict of demands for both development and conservation, the concept of 'sustainable development' was born, indicating the general acceptance that the promotion of both development and conservation is imperative 'to improve the quality of life and the general welfare of the community'.

Town and regional planning today is trying to shake off its technocratic, bureaucratic, social-engineering image, and is striving to become a people-oriented system to be utilized by the whole community and to which a wide range of professions contributes. It is not the domain of one particular profession.[8] Ideally, town and regional planning should create a negotiation forum for communities to examine their problems, to contemplate the various alternative solutions, to compromise on political differences, and then to decide on a course of action.

Town and regional planning operates at three levels: local, regional and national. The systems and functions at these levels are distinctly different. Whereas local planning is well developed, no ideal systems for regional or national planning have as yet been developed. Consequently, these systems are constantly being adapted as new ideas replace the old. The accent at the local level is very much on physical planning and control, although measures for long-range policy formulation, in the form of structure plans, have recently been strengthened. At the national level the accent is on socio-economic development policy. Regional planning mostly has a co-ordinating function, although land-use control and the promotion of development are also present.

The town and regional planning process is provided for at the local level by the various town-planning ordinances[9] and at regional and national level by the Physical Planning Act 125 of 1991. Many other ordinances and Acts are, however, also used in this negotiation–arbitration process, as will be shown. Systems have also been developed outside the legal framework—for example, process planning and strategic planning.

28.3 SCALE AND NATURE OF ENVIRONMENTAL PROBLEMS

Environmental problems cover a wide range of types and occur at various scales.[10] Many of these problems fall clearly outside the legal and organizational framework of town and regional planning. There are, however, a group of environmental aspects which can and should be addressed through the mechanisms created by town and regional planning legislation, and associated non-statutory organizations. It is essential to understand the scope, area of jurisdiction and power of control of each town and

[8] The changing image of town and regional planning is reflected in more appropriate designations such as 'development planning' (stressing the need to improve the welfare of society) and 'environmental planning' (stressing the importance of an acceptable physical and socio-economic environment).

[9] Cape Province: Land Use Planning Ordinance 15 of 1985; Natal: Town Planning Ordinance 27 of 1949; Transvaal: Town Planning and Townships Ordinance 15 of 1986; Orange Free State: Townships Ordinance 9 of 1969. On 16 May 1991 the State President announced that the government intends replacing the town-planning ordinances with one Act of Parliament. Dr C J van Tonder of the then Department of Planning, Provincial Affairs and National Housing was appointed to co-ordinate the writing of the new Town-planning Act.

[10] Claassen has designed a matrix for classifying environmental problems according to type and scale ('Stads- en streekbeplanning binne die konteks van 'n nasionale beleid vir omgewingsbestuur' 1990 (29) *Town and Regional Planning* 11).

regional planning system, so that it may be clear which environmental problems can be addressed by the system and what level is appropriate.

Norms for controlling development and for conservation are often based on highly subjective perceptions, strongly influenced by the income level and culture of the beholder, and particularly on how any specific action will affect him or her financially. Examples of such subjective issues are: the development of agricultural land or coastal areas for urban purposes; mining in sensitive areas; the replacement of historic buildings by new development, and even architectural aesthetic control. These types of environmental threats can be referred to as threats on cultural norms.[11]

In the case of control on cultural norms it is essential that the system by which decisions are taken is fair and democratic so that the will of the majority will prevail rather than that of pressure groups. It will be shown that the town-planning system, particularly at the local level, goes a long way towards providing such a system. It is, however, primarily a problem-solving arbitration system and it seldom provides absolute control. For control of a more absolute nature other legislation needs to be invoked.[12] Through the planning system the necessity of protective action can often be identified and brought to the attention of the relevant government body.

However, it is often necessary for central government to intervene at the local level because of local incompetence, indifference or a lack of legal and financial means. An example is coastal development affecting a national asset which sometimes falls under the jurisdiction of a small municipality or regional services council.

28.4 THE TOWN-PLANNING SYSTEM IN SOUTH AFRICA

Modern town planning consists of separate yet interrelated elements. The most important functions at the local or municipal level of planning are:

- development control through land-use zoning;
- policy formulation and long-term planning through structure plans;
- implementation of planning proposals through development plans;[13]
- promotion of socio-economic development through strategic planning.

28.4.1 Development control mechanisms

Ever since Van Riebeeck landed in the Cape, there has been some form of official control over development, especially over the establishment of new towns and the subdivision of land. However, control of what can be done on land, that is, land-use zoning, developed only late in the first half of this century. Subsequently, especially since the fifties, various other control mechanisms at the local level have also been created.[14]

Land-use control provided for in the various town-planning ordinances is a well-established system which communities exercise control over land-uses within the legal framework created by these ordinances. It aims to provide a fair and pragmatic

[11] Claassen above n 10, 6.

[12] Examples are the Water Act 54 of 1956 for controlling water pollution, the Atmospheric Pollution Prevention Act 45 of 1965 for controlling air pollution, and the Environment Conservation Act 73 of 1989 for proclaiming 'protected natural environments'.

[13] Development planning, as the term is used here, is a system of budgeting and scheduling of works in order to ensure that structure plan proposals are implemented. Although specifically provided for in the Cape Province (s 5) and Natal (s 40) town-planning ordinances, it does not, bar one or two exceptions, seem to function in South Africa and will therefore not be discussed further.

[14] Examples of Acts controlling development at the local level are the National Monuments Act 28 of 1969, Urban Transport Act 78 of 1977, Environment Conservation Act 73 of 1989 and the Physical Planning Act 125 of 1991. Gasson ('Some environmental concerns in city development' 1987 (spec ed) *Town and Regional Planning* 38) gives a breakdown of legislation related to environmental conservation.

system which communities can participate in decisions on land-use, and in this way it allows for 'informed decision-making, and accountability for decisions taken'.[15]

Control of development in the form of zoning is based on the principle that a landowner voluntarily subjects himself to control because he wants his neighbours to be controlled also. Or, put differently, the will of the individual is subject to what is good for the community.[16]

The various town-planning ordinances provide for town-planning schemes (zoning schemes in the Cape Province[17]) to be drawn up by local authorities. These schemes indicate the legal use for which land can be utilized as well as the degree of development that is permitted, such as the number of floors, bulk, building lines, and parking requirements. Particular areas where special controls are in force can also be demarcated on a town-planning scheme. This mechanism is mostly used to protect historic areas, but it can also be used to protect other sensitive areas.

Whenever a landowner or a local government wants to change the zoning of land, the rezoning process must be followed.[18] This process requires advertising the intention to rezone. The exact form of such advertisements differs from province to province, but usually includes notices in the press and written notices to landowners in close proximity to, or clearly affected by, the intended new land-use. The process allows all interested and affected parties the opportunity to comment and object. An advertisement usually specifies a time period for objections. The applicant is given the opportunity to react on any objections received and then the town or city council must decide on the application.

The internal administrative processing of such an application is also of importance. The principle of 'scoping'[19] is important at this stage—that is, determining what information is necessary to ensure an informed decision. The process is usually managed by the town-planning department of a local authority and consists of the compilation of the relevant data (including the collection of additional data and/or the gauging of expert opinions) and the writing of a report. A town-planning committee of the town or city council makes a recommendation to council, which takes the final decision.[20]

The town-planning ordinances also allow for appeals to the Administrator or appropriate 'own affairs' Minister.[21] The Administrator or Minister, whose decision is

---

[15] Fuggle, Preston, Sowman, Hill, Short & Robins *Integrated environmental management* (1991) 1.

[16] The socialistic view that the individual is subject to what is best for the community is not well developed in South Africa (in contrast with Europe). In fact, this notion is declining in popularity, and making way for a more capitalistic laissez-fare approach. This has important implications for the conservation of land held in private ownership.

[17] With the promulgation of the Land Use Planning Ordinance 15 of 1985 in the Cape Province, all land that did not fall under a town-planning scheme then, was deemed to be zoned for the use that was legally in force at that time (s 14(1)). All land in the Cape Province therefore has an assigned or implied zoning, namely that use for which it is legally applied. Every change of use will require a rezoning, except for rights allocated under the previous ordinance, but not yet utilized. These rights will lapse in the year 2001.

In the other provinces, zonings indicated on the town-planning scheme exist in perpetuity, irrespective of whether the land is applied for that use or not. See note 26 below.

[18] In some cases a simpler process is prescribed, for instance, where a deviation from physical restrictions is requested. Where the land-use applied for is listed in the zoning regulations as a 'consent use', that is a use which is compatible with the zoning, it can be ratified by the local authority without prior advertisement.

[19] Fuggle et al above n 15, 3.

[20] In complex cases this process can involve a large degree of liaison between the applicant, the local government, and even other interested parties before a final decision is taken.

[21] Town planning is regarded as an 'own affair' under the present Constitution. The fact that appeals go to different higher authorities, depending on the 'group area' where the property in question is situated, was a highly unsatisfactory innovation that came into force with the new Constitution in 1983. With the 1991 suspension of group areas but not yet of 'own affairs', the situation became even more anomalous.

final, can approve or deny an appeal, or approve it with specified conditions. It is not required of the Administrator to give reasons for, or to motivate, a specific decision.

The provinces have different appeal systems. In the Cape Province the Administrator or appropriate Minister may decide on the matter or refer it to the Planning Advisory Board for advice. In the Transvaal and Orange Free State a Townships Board must first consider the matter and advise the Administrator or Minister. In Natal, the Town and Regional Planning Commission processes appeals.

Provincial rezoning systems can certainly be improved, but, if measured against acceptable norms of good administration, they fare quite well.[22] Similar systems are in operation in most Western countries, which is an indication that our present systems are basically sound.

Any arbitration system must find a balance between the time needed to process an application and accessibility to the public, for instance by providing ample opportunity for affected persons and groups to state their case and for general public participation. Ideally, most rezonings should be processed within one month. Also of importance is the cost of the process to the parties concerned and to the local government.

Land-use control and the rezoning process are of particular importance for certain types of environmental conservation. Most developments must be preceded by rezoning, which means that all groups concerned can petition the relevant authority (in the first instance the local authority) and then the Administrator or Minister who handles the appeal. The system also allows for special measures to be taken to ensure that adequate information is available. For instance, before an application for rezoning is considered, the local authority can insist on an environmental impact assessment. It can also prescribe conditions for the ratification of a rezoning decision, for instance, that the process of integrated environmental management be applied in the construction of the project.

Development control invariably affects the welfare of the people involved. Furthermore, opinions as to what is right and what is wrong are often subjective, depending on the income group, culture and political affiliation of the beholder, and the effect of a decision on him or her. It is therefore essential that all decisions be taken on a democratic basis. That is, final decisions must be taken by a democratically elected person or body, which is responsible to the public.

28.4.2 Subdivision of land and establishment of towns

The subdivision of land and the establishment of towns are controlled in very much the same way as rezonings and will not be discussed in detail here. The system offers the same opportunities for environmental conservation.[23]

For coping with the housing problem, new process-oriented methods are being developed, giving expression to the maxim 'planning by the people'. This is particularly appropriate in South Africa today, as most of the unhoused people are not yet represented on governmental bodies.

The Less Formal Township Establishment Act 113 of 1991 provides for a shorter process, aimed at the establishment of towns primarily for low-income groups, in special cases where speed is of the essence.

---

[22] Van Tonder *An evaluation of physical planning administration in terms of provincial legislation in the Cape Province and preliminary proposals for the improvement thereof* (unpublished MAdmin thesis, University of Cape Town 1981) 98.

[23] The Land Use Planning Ordinance of the Cape Province stipulates that one of the conditions on which a local government can interfere with the particulars of a design is 'the preservation of the natural and developed environment': s 36(2).

28.4.3 Development policy and long-range planning[24]

When the first town-planning ordinances were drafted in the early thirties, the intention was that both development control and long-range planning would be achieved through town-planning schemes; in fact, there is no indication that they were regarded as separate issues by early South African planners.[25] In reality town-planning schemes have primarily become development control mechanisms rather than policy documents for future development.[26] To rectify this shortcoming, structure plans were introduced in the Cape Province with the adoption of the Land Use Planning Ordinance 15 of 1985. Natal also introduced structure plans at that time. In the Transvaal and the Orange Free State structure plans are used in practice as a means of long-range planning, although the ordinances of these two provinces do not make specific provision for this. The Physical Planning Act of 1991 also allows for structure plans at the local and regional level.

The purpose of a structure plan is to lay down guidelines (formulate policy) for future development. Structure planning now allows local governments to stipulate aims and objectives for development. Ideally, all development aspects, physical (transportation and land-use), environmental and socio-economic, should be addressed and policies should be formulated in order to improve the welfare and living environment of the people concerned. In practice, however, it seems as if structure plans, in their proposals, mostly concentrate on physical aspects.[27]

An important difference between the structure plans of the Cape Province and those of the Physical Planning Act is the degree to which proposals of a structure plan are enforceable. In the Cape Province a structure plan is regarded as providing broad guidelines for development, that is, it is not a zoning document defining land-use rights. A potential rezoning which conflicts with a structure plan can be passed without first changing the structure plan, although such a rezoning must undergo a stricter process to ensure that the deviation is justified. The basic theory behind the system followed by the Cape Province is that one layer of control—the zoning scheme—is sufficient. According to the Physical Planning Act, however, any lower-order plan must at all times conform to a higher-order structure plan.[28]

Structure planning creates a powerful tool for environmental conservation, because it allows a local (or regional) government to demarcate environmentally sensitive areas and to stipulate appropriate action if development in such areas is contemplated. For example, the level of environmental impact assessment which will be appropriate can be stipulated, as well as the desired integrated environmental management process. It is at this level that the potential conflict between development and the environment can, to a large degree, be reconciled, by clearly stating the policy on development and

---

[24] In South Africa long-range planning is sometimes referred to as 'forward planning'. Here the international terminology will be employed.

[25] This in contrast to the United States, where there has always been a clear distinction between development control, referred to as 'zoning', and long-range planning, referred to as 'planning'.

[26] According to the Financial Relations Act 32 of 1961, (Sch 2, s 14) all indications of land-use on an official plan adopted by a local government body confer permanent rights, which inhibits local governments from adopting long-range plans. To rectify this problem, the Cape Land Use Planning Ordinance (s 5, and the Physical Planning Act (s 29) state specifically that structure plans do not confer rights.

[27] This is in conformity with the purpose of a structure plan as defined in the Physical Planning Act: 'to promote . . . orderly physical development' (s 5). In their comments on the Bill, the Institute of Town and Regional Planners strongly objected to this narrow interpretation of the purpose of a structure plan.

[28] The Act provides for four layers of plans, from a 'national development plan' to regional development plans, regional structure plans and urban structure plans. See Claassen (ed) for a description of the functions of each type of plan. ('New Physical Planning Bill' June 1991 SAITRP Newsletter 3.) See also para 28.5.1 below.

conservation for sensitive areas. It must, however, be clearly understood that a structure plan does not in itself protect the environment. It prescribes policy, procedures and intended action for conservation. A structure plan must also be carefully assessed to ensure that the plan itself will not lead to a loss of environmental quality in the area to which it relates.

28.4.4 Strategic planning

Strategic planning is a non-statutory process defined as 'a systematic way to manage change and create the best possible future—a creative process for identifying and accomplishing the most important actions in view of strengths and weaknesses, threats and opportunities'.[29] In short, it is a method by means of which a community can analyse its problems and create a mechanism for addressing these problems. In many ways it is similar to the normal structure-planning process, but it was born out of frustration with the inability of the statutory town-planning process to deal with the real problems of a community.

The normal town and regional planning process has become very much oriented towards control and physical planning. Also, it tends to be intermittent in nature rather than continuous. There is a strongly felt need to make planning more development-oriented, rather than control-oriented, and to address all the problems of a community rather than physical aspects only. This need is particularly important in South Africa, where strong central control and compartmentalization at central and municipal level hinder a local authority's ability to address the real problems of a community.[30]

Strategic planning is usually initiated by the local authority, but it mobilizes a wide section of a community to participate in analysing problems, to formulate policy and to suggest action to alleviate these problems. Ideally, the organization for strategic planning will consist of a main co-ordinating committee and a series of subsidiary committees, one each for every problem area, for instance, housing, health care, employment, adult education, parks, the natural environment and historical areas.

Strategic planning offers a powerful tool for constantly monitoring the state of the environment in a community and for influencing town and city councils to take appropriate action timeously. It is, however, a new field, and it can be expected that only towns and cities with dynamic councils and personnel will embark on it.

28.5 REGIONAL PLANNING

Regional planning grew from the notion that a country is too big for government to plan as a whole, and therefore the country must be divided into smaller regions for which realistic plans can be devised. Two types of region are distinguishable for planning purposes, that is, metropolitan and rural. The planning systems for these two types are distinctly different.

28.5.1 Metropolitan regions

Metropolitan regions are areas where two or more towns have grown into one urban conglomeration. Certain development problems are therefore the concern of all the towns in the region and can best be addressed through co-ordinated effort. Various types of metropolitan governments have developed since the Second World War, but no particular model seems to be ideal in all circumstances. Models vary from complete

---

[29] Sorkin, Ferris & Hudak *Strategies for cities and counties: a strategic planning guide* (1983) 2.

[30] In the United States the broad approach to planning has been addressed through comprehensive planning, which in its best form consists of a series of plans or reports which address different aspects—among others, transportation, parks, employment and land-use.

metropolitan government controlling the full range of urban functions to purely advisory bodies, concentrating mostly on physical planning.[31]

In South Africa there are several bodies, with overlapping duties, concerned with metropolitan planning. The most important of these are: joint municipal planning committees; metropolitan transportation boards; guide plan committees (now 'planning committees') and regional services councils.

Joint municipal planning committees, instituted under the town-planning ordinances, represent the oldest efforts at metropolitan planning. An example of this type of organization was Metplan, established in 1940, the planning body for the Cape Town metropolitan area. It has now been absorbed into the Western Cape Regional Services Council. These committees were purely advisory bodies and helped to co-ordinate planning and development.

The metropolitan transport advisory boards, instituted under the Urban Transport Act 78 of 1977, are similar co-ordinating bodies. The Act also provides for the 'core city' to plan and construct transportation-related projects, and it gives the provincial roads engineers control over rezonings which increase the floor area of traffic-generating land-uses.

The only function of guide plan committees, instituted under the old Physical Planning Act 88 of 1967, was to draw up guide plans for metropolitan regions and other areas. Guide plans are binding statutory plans and no rezoning can be ratified unless it conforms with the guide plan. In cases of conflict, the guide plan must be changed first. In principle the system is retained in the new Physical Planning Act 125 of 1991. Guide plans have been replaced by regional structure plans, to be drawn up by a 'planning committee' appointed by the Administrator. However, the Act also provides for 'urban structure plans' to be drawn up by a 'regional authority', which at present means a regional services council. It is not clear which of these two tiers of regional plan will be the preferred level for metropolitan planning.

With the introduction of regional services councils in 1985, new possibilities have been created for metropolitan planning. The Regional Services Council Act 109 of 1985 provides for the Administrator to allocate functions to a council and, although metropolitan planning is not specifically listed, a number of functions which can be regarded as such are so listed. The way in which regional services councils function is substantially different in the Cape Province, where the old divisional councils have been incorporated, from that of the rest of the country. In Natal, 'joint services boards' created under the Natal/KwaZulu Joint Services Act 84 of 1990 fulfil a similar function.[32]

Regional services councils have a number of important features that render them potentially important bodies for regional planning and thus for environmental conservation.[33] They can draw up structure plans under the Physical Planning Act (or under the Land Use Planning Ordinance in the Cape Province). They have their own sources of income and they are responsible to the public through indirect representation, that is, they are closest to a democratic system of any governmental body at present functioning in South Africa.

There are pressures on the government to simplify the present overlapping metropolitan planning systems. It is suggested that this can best be done by concentrating the various overlapping functions in regional services councils.

---

[31] Claassen 'Regional services councils as metropolitan planning institutions' 1988 (23) *SAIPA* 75ff.

[32] The basic difference with regional services councils is that, instead of being directly responsible to the Administrator, the joint services boards are responsible to the Joint Executive Authority of Natal/KwaZulu, which consists of five members of the KwaZulu cabinet and five members of the provincial executive committee of Natal.

[33] Claassen above n 31, 86.

28.5.2 Rural regions

There are at present two regional planning systems with the potential to influence development and environmental conservation on a regional scale, namely the regional development hierarchy created by the Good Hope Plan,[34] and regional services councils.

The Van Eck Commission[35] in its 1944 report strongly recommended regional planning as a means to promote development and thus stability. In the sixties and seventies regional planning was embraced by the government to implement its 'homeland' policies, and its policies of decentralization and deconcentration, policies that are generally rejected today. A high-water mark in regional planning was reached in 1975 with the announcement of the National Physical Development Plan, which was in reality a plan for socio-economic development.[36] Since that time, regional development policy and the systems of regional organization have changed several times.

The system of regional planning, created in 1975 and later amended, consists of a hierarchy of three tiers, namely regional development associations, regional development advisory committees, and the National Regional Development Advisory Council, which is an advisory body to the government.[37] The Department for Regional and Land Affairs provides a secretariat for the National Regional Development Advisory Council. The committees and associations are, however, independent, non-statutory organizations without permanent sources of income and with no executive powers.

Representation on regional development associations is voluntary and consists mainly of municipalities and interest groups such as chambers of commerce, agricultural societies and publicity associations.

Representatives on regional development advisory committees are appointed by the Minister of Regional and Land Affairs from nominations made by institutions invited by him to make nominations. These institutions include the constituent regional development associations, special interest groups, self-governing territories, provincial administrations and representatives from relevant government departments. Municipalities are specifically forbidden to make nominations.[38] The purpose of the regional development advisory committees is to advise the government on all regional development matters.[39]

The chairmen of the regional development advisory committees in turn form part of the National Regional Development Advisory Council together with other members appointed by the Minister. The purpose of the council is to co-ordinate and evaluate development objectives and regional projects formulated by the committees.[40]

Because of its voluntary nature, attention to environmental conservation by regional development organizations will be directly proportional to the interest that environmental pressure groups take in the proceedings of regional development associations. Such groups can also petition the Minister for representation on regional development advisory committees.

It is essential that problems of local communities be constantly brought to the attention of the central government, so that funds can be channelled to problem areas,

---

[34] *The Good Hope Plan for southern Africa* Department of Foreign Affairs (1981) 70.

[35] *Regional and town planning* Social and Economic Planning Council (1944) 3.

[36] *National Physical Development Plan* Department of Planning and the Environment (1975).

[37] There are 38 planning regions (also called socio-economic planning regions) each with a regional development association, which are grouped into eight 'national development regions' lettered from A to H, each with a regional development advisory committee.

[38] *Regional development* Department of Constitutional Development and Planning (1988) 12.

[39] *Regional development* above n 38, 11.

[40] *Regional development* above n 38, 8.

especially in the present centrally controlled government system of South Africa.[41] In this respect the regional development hierarchy plays an important role and it certainly has positive aspects. On paper it has some points of similarity with strategic planning. It is, however, a cumbersome structure. Its contribution to real development is often queried.[42]

Regional services councils, as in the case of metropolitan regions, have the potential to play an important role in regional development, and therefore conservation of the environment on a regional scale.[43] The great advantage of regional services councils over regional development associations is that they are, at least potentially, fully representative of the people, and that they have independent sources of income. They also have a direct link with municipalities, which are, in spite of limited powers and income, important development organizations in rural regions.

28.6 NATIONAL PLANNING

'National planning' does not connote a single action by one department, but rather the combined efforts of the government as a whole. Most government departments, through a variety of legislation, have an influence on planning and development, and therefore also on environmental conservation at local, regional and national level.

The Department of Regional and Land Affairs and its predecessors have traditionally been in charge of national development planning.[44] This department manages the Regional Industrial Development Programme announced in 1991, which provides financial incentives for new industries outside of core metropolitan areas such as the central Witwatersrand. It is also in charge of the Physical Planning Act and therefore the planning committees to be appointed to prepare the national development plan and regional development plans.[45] These plans, if they are drawn up, will most probably concentrate on socio-economic policy in spite of the definition in the Act that they shall 'promote the orderly physical development of the area'.[46] However, these plans will also be important documents for the demarcation of environmentally sensitive areas and for formulating policy on environmental conservation.

28.7 SUMMARY

The town and regional planning system created by the provincial planning ordinances and the Physical Planning Act provides a system where the various sectors of society can negotiate about the type of environment that they would like to create, especially at the local and regional levels. It further provides a means to demarcate environmentally sensitive areas and to formulate policy on environmental conservation. It can prescribe analytical methods, such as environmental impact analyses, to ensure adequate knowledge for informed decisions. Finally, it provides a mechanism for initiating integrated environmental management for specific projects. It is, however, primarily a system for managing change. For more absolute control over conservation other measures must be invoked. Even with the many environmental problems falling outside the jurisdiction of local and regional governments, which must be handled by

[41] At present 94 per cent of all taxes are levied by the central government and only 5 per cent by local authorities. (Croeser in Swilling, Humpries & Shubane (eds) *Apartheid city in transition* (1991) 141.)

[42] Davies 'Institutions in search of direction' 1991 (2) *Urban Forum* 7; Claassen 'The contribution of urban and regional planning towards regional development in southern Africa' 1985 (2) *Development Southern Africa* 243.

[43] Van der Bank *An evaluation of the organizational framework for rural regional planning in South Africa* (unpublished M (URP) thesis, University of Stellenbosch 1991) 86.

[44] Fuggle & Rabie above n 3, 450–5.

[45] Sections 4 and 7.

[46] Section 5.

departments of the central government, the planning system can play a role in identifying problems and petitioning the relevant state departments.

In the final count, it is certain that control of development and enforcement of conservation are justified only if performed by democratically elected bodies after adequate opportunity for consultation with all affected persons and groups. The town and regional planning system goes a long way towards providing that.

28.8 LAND-USE PLANNING LEGISLATION

28.8.1 The objects of land-use planning legislation

28.8.1.1 *Introduction*

Legal regulation of the manner in which owners or occupiers use, develop or exploit land has a variety of different but related objects. It may be said, in broad terms, that the use of land is controlled (1) for cadastral reasons (in order to ensure that land units are of a proper size and location in order to achieve proper usage for residential and other purposes); (2) in the interest of promoting the health, welfare and amenities offered to people living together in urbanized society (achieved through the zoning of land-uses in town-planning schemes); (3) to prevent nuisance (4) to promote the proper and efficient exploitation of land as an agricultural and industrial resource (achieved through national and regional planning); (5) in order to protect and conserve the natural environment. In South Africa, for many years there existed a sixth rationale for land-use control: the promotion of racial segregation. The abolition of the apartheid system has removed this as one of the bases of land-use control in South Africa.

28.1.1.2 *Cadastral controls*

A fundamental form of land-use regulation in South Africa is the regulation of the division and subdivision of land.

The Subdivision of Agricultural Land Act 70 of 1970 regulates the subdivision of agricultural land.[47] The purpose of this legislation is simply to prevent the subdivision of agricultural land into units that are not economically viable.

More pervasive is subdivision control in terms of town-planning ordinances.[48] Under this legislation, any subdivision of land as a prelude to the residential, commercial or industrial development of the land must be approved by an appointed body. As a general rule, subdivision will be permitted by the authorities only if the developer submits a comprehensive plan indicating the size of land parcels, the layout of streets, public services and facilities. Since the subdivision of land for residential, commercial and industrial development cannot be undertaken without permission, the existence of subdivision regulations provides a method of controlling the urbanization process.

Displaced and homeless persons who establish squatter ('informal') communities make use of land in a way that presents social and sanitary problems. The control of the use of land by squatter communities as residential settlements is now regulated under the Less Formal Township Establishment Act 113 of 1991, which provides for shortened procedures for the establishment of townships in squatter settlements. When an application is made to establish a township in terms of this Act, certain uses of land (notably by building on it) are prohibited.[49] In addition, the Upgrading of Land Tenure Rights Act 112 of 1991 provides procedures for the recognition of informal settlements

---

[47] Section 3.

[48] eg s 23 of the Cape Land Use Planning Ordinance 15 of 1985; s 16(1)*(h)* Natal Town Planning Ordinance 27 of 1949, s 92 Transvaal Town-Planning and Townships Ordinance 15 of 1986 (and see also the Division of Land Ordinance 20 of 1986); s 20 of the OFS Townships Ordinance 9 of 1969.

[49] Section 13.

as 'formalized' townships.[50] The Administrator may by notice impose conditions for the regulation of the use of erven or other pieces of land in such formalized townships.[51]

28.8.1.3 *Zoning*

Most town-planning schemes delimit the town into a variety of regulated and co-ordinated 'zones'.

Typically, a scheme will zone land as residential (subclassified as general or special), industrial (general or special), commercial (general or special), educational, institutional, agricultural or open. The plan will specify the purposes for which the land in each zone may or may not be used. This specification is elaborated by an additional provision indicating the purposes for which the land may be used at the discretion of the local authority (so-called consent uses). A manual is provided containing 'clauses' and tables elaborating or explicating the scheme of zones. In addition, the clauses will set out additional planning specifications touching matters such as building regulations (eg floor area ratios (bulk), coverage and height, building lines, appearance), road traffic, streets, parking and the various other aspects of a proper scheme of town planning. The clauses (which have the force of law) implement these provisions by prohibiting land-uses in a zone that are not in conformity with the scheme and, likewise, proscribe 'consent' uses for which the requisite permission has not been obtained.

28.8.1.4 *Nuisance*

The common-law concept of nuisance involves a form of land-use control.[52] The nuisance concept evolved to cope with the disputes arising between neigbours practising mutually discordant land-uses. Relying on the concept of locality, the common law was able to identify and terminate certain land-uses which conflicted with the broad interests of the neighbourhood. The effect of the application of the nuisance doctrine was to create localities in which only particular land-uses were lawful and to prohibit in these localities harmful uses of land. Under the doctrine, what was a nuisance in one locality would not necessarily be a nuisance in another, thereby creating a system of land-use zones that allowed the pursuit of residential, commercial, agricultural and industrial land-uses in some sort of harmony.

The emergence of town-planning schemes, whose zoning provisions emulate more efficiently the common-law device, has rendered the common-law nuisance device obsolete. However, the notion of preventing discordant land-uses in neighbourhoods and localities survives in the zoning provisions of town-planning schemes and the provisions of the Abolition of Racially Based Land Measures Act 108 of 1991.

Under this Act a majority of all the owners of residential premises in any neighbourhood may by agreement lodge draft by-laws in relation to any such neighbourhood with the local authority concerned regarding—*(a)* the election and establishment by the owners of residential premises in any such neighbourhood of a neighbourhood committee; *(b)* overcrowding of residential premises, including norms or standards for the determination of overcrowding, and the prohibition, prevention, combating and termination of any overcrowding inconsistent with such norms or standards; *(c)* the use for habitation of premises which are unfit for that purpose, including norms or standards for the determination of such fitness, and the prohibition, prevention, combating and termination of any such use that is inconsistent with such norms or standards; *(d)* the maintenance of residential premises in a clean and hygienic condition; *(e)* the repair, cleaning up or removal of nuisances on premises by the owner;

[50] Section 15.
[51] Section 12.
[52] See, generally, on nuisance in South African law Milton 'Nuisance' in Joubert (ed) *The law of South Africa* vol 19 (1983) para 179ff.

(f) the repair and maintenance of buildings, structures, machinery, accessories, fences and open spaces on or in any residential premises; and *(g)* the orderly use of amenities established and maintained for the residents of the neighbourhood concerned, the determination of norms or standards in respect of any such use and the combating and prohibition of any offensive, indecent, unhygienic or dangerous conduct in the use of such amenities.[53]

Upon receipt of such draft by-laws the local authority concerned shall, if it is of the opinion that such draft by-laws comply with the provisions of the Act, promulgate them in respect of the neighbourhood.[54] Any by-law which discriminates on the ground of race, colour or religion or is grossly unfair shall be of no force and effect.[55] Any person who contravenes or fails to comply with any provision of any by-law commits an offence.[56]

28.8.1.5 *Agricultural and industrial development*

(a) Planning legislation. Land-use controls of a different order are required when planning is conducted at the regional or national level. In this connection, the development in South Africa of an appropriate legal framework for planning has, up until the present, proceeded in a rather spasmodic and haphazard fashion.[57]

• *Natural Resources Development Act.* The first attempts at some sort of legislative framework for macrocosmic planning was the Natural Resources Development Act 51 of 1947, which provided for the establishment of a Natural Resources Development Council whose broad objective was to plan and promote the better and more effective co-ordinated exploitation, development and use of the natural resources of South Africa.[58] For the purpose of attaining its object, the council could advise the Minister of Economic Development, inter alia, as to the establishment of so-called controlled areas.[59] Controlled areas were established with a view to achieving an orderly and systematic development of a given area.

The council was empowered to investigate the manner in which natural resources could best be exploited, developed or used in such areas, including the use to which any land could best be allocated.[60] Schemes for the exploitation, development or use of such resources in these areas could be prepared by the council.[61] The council could also stimulate the teaching and study of town and regional planning and advise bodies in regard to the establishment of townships and town planning.[62]

The Act was important because for the first time it was officially recognized that land-use planning was more than a local affair, that it was in fact of national importance, and had to be controlled and co-ordinated at the highest level if effective and orderly planning were to result.

• *Physical Planning and Utilization of Resources Act.* The Natural Resources Development Act was amended in 1955[63] and, after the establishment of the Department of Planning in 1964 and the Resources and Planning Advisory Council in 1965, eventually repealed and substituted by the Physical Planning and Utilization of

[53] Section 98(1).
[54] Section 98(2).
[55] Section 99(1).
[56] Section 98(3)*(a)*.
[57] See Van Wyk 'Into the 21st century with the reform of planning law' in Van der Walt (ed) *Land reform and the future of landownership in South Africa* (1991) 81ff.
[58] Section 3.
[59] Section 4*(a)*. See also s 14.
[60] Section 4*(b)*.
[61] Section 4*(c)*.
[62] Section 4*(f)* and *(g)*.
[63] By Act 30 of 1955.

Resources Act 88 of 1967. The Planning Advisory Council, a non-statutory body, gave advice regarding the promotion and effective utilization of natural resources on a national and regional basis and the manner in which overall physical planning could be achieved on a co-ordinated basis. The Act retained the principles pertaining to resource utilization[64] and the provisions concerned with controlled areas.[65] In addition, it contained provisions dealing with zoning and the subdivision of land for industrial purposes,[66] which were aimed at the decentralization of industries, and a prohibition against the establishment or extension of a factory without the permission of the Minister of Planning.

• *Environment Planning Act.* In 1975 the Act was substantially amended and renamed the Environment Planning Act. The most significant provisions were those pertaining to the drafting, approval and effect of guide plans[67] and the restriction of the use of land for brickworks, potteries, quarries and other processing of minerals.[68] The Act was thus an instrument for overall physical planning at central government level, which was done by means of guide planning. It was also an instrument for the control of land-uses by way of industrial zoning, the reservation of certain natural resources. Owing mainly to the rationalization of the civil service, the Environment Planning Act was amended in 1981 and renamed the Physical Planning Act 88 of 1967.

• *Physical Planning Act of 1991.* A different dispensation was introduced in 1991 when the Physical Planning Act of 1967 was replaced by the Physical Planning Act 125 of 1991.

The enactment of the 1991 Act represents something of a culmination in the process of providing the necessary legislative basis for a system of national and regional land-use planning. The Act emanates from a directive by the government in the *White Paper on urbanization* of 1986. This directive was to the effect that adjustments to the Physical Planning Act of 1967 should be considered in order to set out clearly the physical-planning responsibilities of the various governmental institutions. Further attention was to be given to the establishment of a hierarchy of plans in relation to the various levels of government. These recommendations are given effect by the Physical Planning Act of 1991, which contains no direct land-use control measures. Rather, the purpose of the Act is solely to establish a planning instrument to ensure orderly physical planning in the Republic at all levels of government.[69]

(i) Objectives: The main objectives of the Act are, first, to establish the responsibility for physical planning at the various levels of government in order to remove uncertainty regarding the responsibility for regional planning. It also establishes that provincial administrators have the authority to carry out town planning.

Secondly, the Act provides for a hierarchy of plans in which guidelines are laid down for the future physical development of areas referred to in a specific plan. The ostensible intention is that the three higher-order plans—the national development plan, the regional development plan and the regional structure plan—should concentrate on broad policy issues. The details of planned land-use are to be set out in the lowest-order plan, the urban structure plan. The Act does not dictate any contents of the respective plans.

Thirdly, the Act provides for proper co-ordination between the different levels of government in the preparation and implementation of the various plans.

---

[64] Section 4.
[65] Sections 5 and 6.
[66] Section 2.
[67] Section 6A.
[68] Section 6B.
[69] The actual legislative regulation of land-use is to be carried out by the provincial administrations in terms of existing provincial or other legislation (such as the Minerals Act 50 of 1991).

Fourthly and fifthly, the Act promotes public participation in the preparation of plans and requires that in the preparation of plans proper consideration be given to the potential for economic development, the socio-economic and development needs of the population, the existing transport planning and future transport needs, the physical factors which may influence orderly development in general and urbanization in particular, and the possible influence of future development upon the natural environment.

(ii) Policy plans: The Act—which is administered by the Minister of Regional and Land Affairs—provides for the division of the Republic into two or more development regions, which may be subdivided into planning regions.[70] In relation to these areas the Minister may cause 'policy' plans to be prepared.[71] The object of a policy plan is to promote the orderly physical development of the area to which the plan relates to the benefit of all its inhabitants.[72] A policy plan consists of broad guidelines for the future physical development of the area to which the plan relates.[73] The plan may provide that land shall be used only for a particular purpose.[74]

The Act envisages the following sorts of policy plans:[75] a *national development plan* (prepared for the Republic),[76] a *regional development plan* (prepared for a development region),[77] and a *regional structure plan* (prepared for a planning region).[78] Within a planning region an *urban structure plan*[79] may be prepared (for the area of jurisdiction of one or more local authorities, or for the region of a regional authority). An urban structure plan consists of guidelines for the future physical development of the area to which the plan relates.[80] Presumably, the system of urban structure plans will largely retain the present town-planning ordinances in the respective provinces, and the planning process will proceed as before under the provisions of these ordinances.[81] A plan may provide that land shall be used only for a particular purpose.[82]

A policy plan consists of broad guidelines for the future physical development of the area to which that policy plan relates.[83] It may provide that land shall be used only for a particular purpose or, with the consent of the Minister, an Administrator or any other authority specified in the policy plan, also for the other purposes for which provision is made in the policy plan.[84]

(iii) Preparation of policy plans: In order to cause a policy plan to be prepared, the planning authority[85] concerned may establish a planning committee[86] to prepare a draft of that policy plan for the area concerned. The planning authority is required to invite

---

[70] Section 3.
[71] Section 4(1)*(b)*.
[72] Section 5.
[73] Section 6(1).
[74] Section 6(2).
[75] Section 1, s v 'policy plan'.
[76] See s 4(1)*(a)*.
[77] Section 4(1)*(b)*.
[78] Section 4(2).
[79] Section 22.
[80] Section 24(1).
[81] It is unfortunately so that the ordinances display divergent approaches to the planning process. Thus the nature and manner of town planning is not the same for each province. Whether the Physical Planning Act of 1991 will bring about some uniformity in this regard is not clear.
[82] Section 24(2).
[83] Section 6(1).
[84] Section 6(2).
[85] In regard to a national development plan or a regional development plan, the planning authority is the Minister of Planning, Provincial Affairs and National Housing. In relation to regional structure plans, the planning authority is the Administrator of the province: s 1, s v 'planning authority'.
[86] The composition of the planning committee is prescribed by s 8(1).

interested persons to submit to the committee proposals in writing for inclusion in the draft plan.[87]

Before a planning committee prepares a draft plan, it must consider any proposals submitted to it.[88] It may make such investigation in connection with a draft plan, including the area to which the draft plan relates, as it may deem necessary, and for the purposes of such investigation it may in its discretion consult any department of state, provincial administration, regional or local authority or any person.[89]

The draft plan, when prepared, is submitted to the departmental head,[90] who must make copies of the plan available for inspection at the prescribed places; and publish[91] a notice stating that such plan is available for inspection at the places specified in the notice and inviting interested persons to submit to him in writing within a specified period[92] any representations that they may wish to make in connection with the said plan.[93]

The departmental head must submit the draft plan, any comments or representations received by him in connection with it, the recommendations of the investigating committee[94] and his own comments on such plan to the planning authority concerned.[95] After having considered the draft plan and any comments, representations or recommendations submitted to it, the planning authority may in its discretion approve such plan, with such amendments as it may deem necessary, as a policy plan.[96] The planning authority must make known that a policy plan has been approved by it in respect of the area described in the notice and that copies of it are available for inspection.[97]

An Administrator of a province may cause to be prepared an urban structure plan for the area of jurisdiction of one or more local authorities, or for the region of a regional authority, within the province in question.[98] An urban structure plan consists of guidelines for the future physical development of the area to which that urban structure plan relates.[99] The plan may provide that land shall be used only for a particular purpose or, with the consent of the Minister, an Administrator or any other authority specified in the urban structure plan, also for the other purposes for which provision is made in the urban structure plan.[100]

The Act contains provisions for the removal of conflicts, ambiguities or administrative difficulties regarding plans,[101] and for the amendment,[102] review[103] or withdrawal[104] of plans.

---

[87] Section 9.

[88] Section 10(1).

[89] Section 10(2).

[90] Section 10(3). The departmental head is the Director-General of the Department of Regional and Land Affairs (national or regional development plans) or a Director-General of a provincial administration (regional structure plans): s 1.

[91] Twice in an Afrikaans and in an English newspaper circulating in the area to which the draft plan relates: s 11(2).

[92] Which period shall be not less than 21 days from the date of the last publication of the notice: s 11(1)*(b)*.

[93] Section 11.

[94] Which may be appointed (in terms of s 12) by the planning authority if the departmental head so requests. The composition of an investigating committee is prescribed by s 13.

[95] Section 15(1).

[96] Section 15(2)*(a)*.

[97] Section 15(3).

[98] Section 22.

[99] Section 24(1).

[100] Section 24(2).

[101] Section 17.

[102] Sections 18–19.

[103] Section 20.

[104] Section 21.

(iv) Effect of policy plans: The legal effect of a regional structure plan or an urban structure plan is[105] the following. First, no town-planning scheme which is binding on the date of commencement may be amended in such a way that, and no new town-planning scheme may be introduced in which, provision is made for the zoning of land for a purpose which is not consistent with the regional structure plan or the urban structure plan. Secondly, no person may use any land in the area to which the regional structure plan or the urban structure plan, as the case may be, applies for a purpose other than the purpose for which it was being used immediately before that date or the purpose for which it is zoned in terms of a town-planning scheme which is or may become binding in that area. Thirdly, no permission, approval or authorization shall in terms of any law or in terms of any town-planning scheme be given for the subdivision or use of land in the area to which the regional structure plan or the urban structure plan, as the case may be, applies for a purpose which is not consistent with the relevant plan. Fourthly, all land in the area to which the plan applies,[106] and which in terms of the relevant plan may be used for agricultural purposes only, shall be excluded from the provisions of the Subdivision of Agricultural Land Act 70 of 1970.[107]

A regional development plan, regional structure plan or urban structure plan and an urban structure plan are valid so long and in so far only as it is not repugnant to or inconsistent with any national development plan, regional development plan or regional structure plan.[108]

(b) Land-use control legislation

• *Agriculture.* The control of land used for agriculture is effected mainly through the Conservation of Agricultural Resources Act 43 of 1983. In order to achieve the objects of the Act,[109] the Minister of Agriculture may prescribe control measures which must be complied with by land-users to whom they apply.[110] Land-users may be 'directed' to comply with particular control measures.[111] For a detailed discussion of these and other relevant provisions of the Act, see chapter 10.

A more general control of land-use is effected through the provisions of the Environment Conservation Act 73 of 1989. In terms of this Act, the Minister of Environment Affairs may identify activities which in his opinion may have a substantial detrimental effect on the environment, whether in general or in respect of certain areas.[112] The undertaking of any activity so identified can be prohibited, although exemptions may made by the Minister or a local authority.[113] The provisions of the Act are discussed in chapter 7.

• *Mining.* The exploitation of land by way of mining the minerals in or upon it is regulated by the Minerals Act 50 of 1991. For a full discussion of the provisions of the Act, see chapter 15.

---

[105] Section 27(1).

[106] Other than land which is agricultural land as defined in s 1 of the Subdivision of Agricultural Land Act 70 of 1970.

[107] Provided that without the prior written approval of the Minister of Agriculture, or an officer designated by him, no permission shall be granted in terms of any law for the subdivision of land which in terms of the relevant plan may be used for agricultural purposes as well as any other purpose: s 27(1)*(d)*.

[108] Section 28.

[109] Cf s 3.

[110] Section 6.

[111] Section 7.

[112] Section 21(1).

[113] Section 22.

•*Nuclear installations.* The Nuclear Energy Act 92 of 1982 requires a nuclear licence to be issued before anyone may construct or use a nuclear installation or use a site for any purpose connected with a nuclear installation.[114] See chapter 21.

28.8.1.6 *Environmental protection*

The prevention of environmental pollution and the conservation of natural resources has in recent years emerged as a major purpose of land-use regulation legislation.[115] Before this, wildlife, plants and natural features were considered by many to be the subjects of private property rights and liable to use, exploitation and destruction at the will of the owner. The idea that elements of the natural environment ought to be conserved was thus in direct confrontation with the institution of private property. The only truly effective manner to achieve environmental conservation has been through the enactment of legislation which overrides private property rights or creates legal protection for the natural environment.

Environmental land-use planning and control legislation regulates land-use principally by setting aside areas exclusively for a specific form of land-use. Provision is usually also made for a specialized authority to administer the area in question in order to achieve the desired land-use goals or to prevent certain undesired consequences.

(a) Protected areas. The establishment of various types of protected areas is provided for by a number of Acts and ordinances. See chapter 27.

(b) Water control areas. A variety of control areas may be established in terms of the Water Act 54 of 1956. Extensive provisions apply with regard to the use of land and water in such areas. See chapter 13.

(c) Air pollution control areas. The Atmospheric Pollution Prevention Act 45 of 1965 makes provision for the declaration of several types of control areas. Extensive provisions apply in respect of land-use in these areas with a view to preventing and combating air pollution. See chapter 17.

28.8.2 Land-use control mechanisms of planning law

28.8.2.1 *Introduction*

The different statutes noted above have one common feature: they all involve or imply a limitation[116] upon the right and powers of landowners. These limitations constitute a matter of some significance in a social order in which freedom of property is a constitutionally recognized civil right. Before discussing the implications of this, it is useful first to examine the forms that these limitations upon ownership may take.

28.8.2.2 *Expropriation*

Expropriation of ownership or other rights in land is a method of land-use control. It is resorted to when mere control of the actions of the individual landowner concerned would not suffice to achieve the desired goal, and where the State's use of the land would be so extensive that it would require all the rights of ownership in order to serve the public interest effectively.

Expropriation is governed by the Expropriation Act 63 of 1975. This Act provides generally for the process of expropriation and the principles upon which compensation is to be paid to the person deprived of property. 'Property' means both movable and

---

[114] Section 30(1).

[115] See, generally, Rabie 'The impact of environmental conservation on land ownership' 1985 *Acta Juridica* 289; Van der Walt 'The effect of environmental conservation measures on the concept of landownership' 1987 *SALJ* 469; Rabie 'The influence of environmental legislation on private landownership' in Van der Walt (ed) *Land reform and the future of landownership in South Africa* (1991) 81ff.

[116] Cf Rabie 'The influence of environmental legislation on private landownership' above n 115, 83.

immovable property,[117] while 'immovable property' includes a real right in or over immovable property.[118] The Act also establishes the principle that property may be expropriated only for public purposes.[119]

The power of authorities to expropriate is derived from a great number of Acts and ordinances, e g the Water Act,[120] the Electricity Act 41 of 1987,[121] the Conservation of Agricultural Resources Act,[122] the National Roads Act 54 of 1971,[123] the National Parks Act 51 of 1976,[124] the Minerals Act,[125] and various provincial road[126] and local authority[127] ordinances.

Although expropriation is a simple and effective means of gaining control of the way in which land is used, the obligation to pay compensation renders it an expensive mechanism. For this reason, and because of the public antipathy towards expropriation, it is not commonly resorted to.

28.8.2.3 *Prohibitions and restrictions*[128]

A statute may simply prohibit landowners from using land in a particular manner.[129]

A related mechanism is that of the restriction of land-uses to those specified in the legislation. A sophisticated form of this mechanism is found in the zoning provisions of town and regional planning schemes. Land-use planning implies in the first instance the identification of the social goals of the planning exercise and the devising of a plan that will achieve the goals. The plan, in turn, sets out the mechanism by which the goal will be realized. Plans seek to achieve the goals by regulating the manner in which the land in the planning area is used. The regulation is either negative or positive: that is, the plan either prohibits land-uses (because the usage is inimical to the objects of the plan) or requires uses (because the usage advances the objects of the plan). In essence, therefore, a land-use plan is a series of prohibitions upon certain land-uses and an accompanying encouragement of those uses not prohibited.

This form of planning relies upon the mechanism of zoning of land-uses, particular uses being prohibited or permitted according to the nature of the zone in which they occur.

28.8.2.4 *Licensing of land-use practices*

One of the most popular methods of subjecting land-use to control is to make the legitimate undertaking of certain actions relative to land-use dependent upon obtaining a licence or permit, or at least the approval of the administrative authority in question.[130] Such licensing is frequently employed in combination with the restriction of land-use purposes discussed above.

---

[117] Section 1.
[118] Ibid.
[119] Section 2(1).
[120] Section 60.
[121] Section 19.
[122] Section 14.
[123] Section 8(1) and (2).
[124] Section 3(1) and (2).
[125] Section 24.
[126] See, for these, Gildenhuys & Grobler 'Expropriation' in Joubert (ed) *The law of South Africa* vol 10 (1980) para 53ff.
[127] Gildenhuys & Grobler above n 126, para 57ff.
[128] Cf Rabie 'The influence of environmental legislation on private landownership' above n 115, 89.
[129] For example, the Forest Act empowers the responsible Minister to prohibit the planting of trees on certain land. See chapter 11.
[130] For example, under the Nuclear Energy Act. See chapter 21 and cf Rabie 'The influence of environmental legislation on private landownership' above n 115, 89.

28.8.2.5 *Purchase and sale of land*

Reliance does not invariably have to be placed upon expropriation if the State wishes to obtain landownership in order to control its use. The Lake Areas Development Act 39 of 1975 empowers the acquisition through exchange of private land situated in a lake area (now a national park),[131] while the National Parks Act allows the acquisition of land for a national park through purchase or exchange.[132] State land may likewise be disposed of, through sale, exchange, donation or lease, in terms of the State Land Disposal Act 48 of 1961.[133]

As in the case of expropriation, this is an expensive method of obtaining control of the use of land and is thus not commonly resorted to.

28.8.2.6 *Administrative directives*

A number of Acts make provision for the administrative authority concerned to issue environmentally relevant directives relating to the use of land to the owner or occupier of the land in question. Thus the Conservation of Agricultural Resources Act empowers the serving of a notice on the occupier or owner of land, calling upon him to eradicate weeds which grow on the land in question.[134] This Act also provides for the issuance of directives prescribing to owners or occupiers of land certain agricultural practices aimed at conservation farming.[135] The Mountain Catchment Areas Act 63 of 1970 provides for the issue of directives to owners and occupiers of land with respect to the conservation, use and management of such land situated in mountain catchment areas.[136]

Such directives are binding on owners or occupiers as well as upon their successors in title.[137] Failure to comply with a directive constitutes an offence.[138] Moreover, the administrative authority in question may, either upon its own initiative or after failure by the owner or occupier, itself perform any act relating to the directives,[139] and may even recover the costs involved from the landowners in question.[140] See, generally, chapters 10 and 24.

28.8.3 Land-use limitations and private property

The notion of land-use control implies a restriction upon freedom. The freedom concerned is the power traditionally said to be vested in the owner of private property to use, exploit and dispose of the object of the rights of ownership according to his own personal and individual discretion and wishes. In other words, the legal paradigm of ownership of private property is that there are no external controls upon the owner in the exercise of ownership. The concept of a land-use control thus stands in contradiction of this paradigm, postulating as it does an externally imposed constraint upon the owner of land in the exercise of his power of using and exploiting his land.

The question which arises is whether landowners are or ought to be entitled to some sort of redress for the effect upon their legal rights of land-use controls. The issue is

---

[131] Section 16(1). Cf s 16(2) in respect of purchase.

[132] Section 3(1).

[133] Section 2(1). Cf also the Sea-Shore Act 21 of 1935 in respect of letting of the sea-shore (ss 3 and 4) and disposal to a local authority (s 4).

[134] Section 5(2).

[135] Section 7 read with s 6.

[136] Section 3(1).

[137] Section 7(4) of the Conservation of Agricultural Resources Act, s 3(2)*(c)* of the Mountain Catchment Areas Act and s 10(2) of the Environment Conservation Act.

[138] Sections 5(6) and 7(6) of the Conservation of Agricultural Resources Act, s 14*(b)* of the Mountain Catchment Areas Act.

[139] Section 5(2)*(c)* of the Conservation of Agricultural Resources Act and s 12 of the Mountain Catchment Areas Act.

[140] Sections 5(2)*(d)* and 11(2) of the Conservation of Agricultural Resources Act contains such a provision.

important since the scope of intensity of land-use planning and control might be inhibited by the manner in or extent to which landowners may invoke such remedial measures as the law might allow them.

28.8.3.1 *Compensation*[141]

(a) Expropriation. There is no question but that owners are entitled to redress where they are entirely deprived of their rights in land by way of expropriation. Although South African law recognizes no constitutional right to compensation for expropriation, and compensation is payable only if provision for it has been made in the legislation in question,[142] the Expropriation Act and the other Acts referred to above, as a matter of course, provide that compensation should be paid in cases of expropriation.[143]

(b) Injurious affectation. The provincial townships ordinances provide generally for compensation to landowners whose land is 'injuriously affected' by the implementation of a town-planning scheme.[144] However, many of the more prevalent forms of injurious affectation brought about by town-planning provisions are expressly excluded from the compensation provision.[145] Further, the compensation, when payable, is payable only in respect of an *approved* scheme. Since the provincial authorities as a matter of course never seek final approval of schemes,[146] this form of compensation is virtually never paid.

(c) Patrimonial loss. The Mountain Catchment Areas Act provides that if in terms of a directive limitations are placed on the purposes for which land may be used, the owner or occupier of such land must be paid compensation in respect of actual patrimonial loss[147] suffered by him.[148] A similar instance is provided by the Environment Conservation Act.[149] (See chapter 7.) The Forest Act 122 of 1984 also entitles the owner of land in respect of which trees or forests have been declared by the Minister of Environment Affairs to be protected to recover damages for patrimonial loss resulting from a refusal to consent to cutting or from the imposition of onerous restrictions.[150]

(d) Grants in aid. The Mountain Catchment Areas Act[151] and the Environment Conservation Act determine that financial aid by way of grants or otherwise may, in the discretion of the Minister of Environment Affairs, be rendered to the owner or occupier of land who has to comply with ministerial directions relating to the land in question.[152] The Conservation of Agricultural Resources Act grants the Minister of Agriculture a discretion to render financial assistance to owners or occupiers of land in connection with the eradication of weeds, and generally to make grants to any person in order to

---

[141] Cf Rabie 'The influence of environmental conservation on private landownership' above n 115, 95ff.

[142] Gildenhuys *Onteieningsreg* (1976) 16.

[143] Cf ss 2(1) and 11–14 of the Expropriation Act.

[144] See Milton 'Planning and property' 1985 *Acta Juridica* 267, 273.

[145] Ibid.

[146] See *McCulloch v Munster Health Committee* 1979 (4) SA 723 (N).

[147] Cf on the term 'actual financial loss' in s 12(1)*(a)*(ii) of the Expropriation Act, Jacobs *The Law of Expropriation in South Africa* (1982) 73–87.

[148] Section 4(1). The amount of such compensation is determined by agreement between the relevant authority and the owner or occupier (s 4(1)) and in the absence of such agreement by a compensation court in terms of the Expropriation Act 63 of 1975 (s 4(2) of the Mountain Catchment Areas Act and s 14 of the Expropriation Act).

[149] Section 34(1).

[150] Section 14. Cf also s 59(4)*(c)* of the Water Act 54 of 1956.

[151] Section 10*(b)*.

[152] Section 16(5).

enable such person to perform an act for the achievement of an object of the Act,[153] and to pay subsidies to any person for costs incurred by such person in connection with the construction of any soil conservation works.[154]

(e) Tax relief. Some measure of tax relief is also granted by the Mountain Catchment Areas Act. The Act exempts any land situated within a mountain catchment area upon which in terms of any directive no farming may be carried on from all taxes imposed by a local authority on the value of immovable property.[155]

28.8.3.2 *Uncompensated limitations upon land-use*

Where restrictions short of expropriation are placed upon the ownership of land, there is no all-embracing principle or legislative provision that the person prejudiced is generally entitled to compensation.[156] Restrictions upon the powers of landowners derived from zoning, planning, legislative or administrative directives generally do not give rise to any right to compensation.[157]

The reason for this is the following. Land-use controls—though not always identified as such—have been long recognized, condoned and applied in most legal systems. The oldest and most pervasive example is the body of common-law doctrines and principles regulating the relationships between adjoining parcels of land, and known as 'neighbour' or 'nuisance' law.

Nuisance law evolved as a consequence of the fact that the propinquity of adjoining units of land creates a relationship of cause and effect which impinges upon and affects the individual interests of the respective landowners in the use and enjoyment of their land. Disadvantageous effects are designated as 'nuisances' and the dispute between competing landowners is resolved in law by a process of limitation and adjustment of the 'property rights' of the parties according to judicially evolved 'criteria of reasonableness' derived from the homely common-sense doctrine of 'give and take, live and let live'. The adjustments so achieved usually involve a prohibition of particular use activities upon one or other of the parcels of land, the decision to prohibit reflecting in some measure a judgment as to the social or economic utility of the preferred activity in relation to the activity which is suppressed.

This form of regulation of land-uses enjoys general acceptance and approval, it being understood as a necessary consequence of the neighbourhood of land units and as applied in the interests of the individual landowners concerned.[158]

The nuisance idea that land-use controls were merely a beneficial regulation of land-use was later on borrowed by legislators who invoked it to justify legislatively imposed restrictions upon land-uses. Although the prohibition of public nuisances, the imposition of regulatory provisions for the advancement of the public health and town-planning legislation all restricted the powers and freedoms of landowners, the invasion of property rights involved was not perceived as a major or unacceptable interference with private property.

The distinction between the taking and the regulation of property rights is of central significance in the evaluation of the impact of land-use controls upon the concept of ownership. In constitutional theory regulation of property rights is contrasted with the taking of property rights. Taking or expropriation is a violation of a civil right, to be condoned only where performed against the payment of compensation. The regulation

---

153 Section 8.

154 Section 13.

155 Section 5(1). Cf also s 15 of the National Monuments Act 28 of 1969.

156 *Feun v Pretoria City Council* 1949 (1) SA 331 (T) 342; *Cape Town Municipality v Abdulla* 1976 (2) SA 370 (C) 375D, 376A.

157 *Cape Town Municipality v Abdulla* above n 156, 375D, 376A. Cf Milton above n 144, 273ff.

158 Milton above n 144, 274.

of property rights, on the other hand, is conceived as a necessary and proper incident of government carried out in the public interest and for the public benefit. As such it is not considered to involve any taking of property and does not give rise to an entitlement to compensation. For a further discussion of this principle, see chapter 7.

The extensive regulation of land-use activities inherent in modern land-use controls derives its justification from the recognition of the advantage to the general welfare of communities involved in the proper planning of land-use activities. Implicit in all this is the acceptance of the dogma that the rights of ownership in land are not purely egotistical but involve an altruistic element of social obligation.[159] This in turn suggests a revision of the concept of ownership[160] that would conceive this fundamental institution as involving not only rights and powers but also social duties whose performance are obligatory and a natural incident of the enjoyment of ownership. From such a concept would arise a social and legal regime in which land would be used in a manner that recognized and advanced the various social, economic and human values and interests that are the rationale for modern land-use controls. The President's Council has concluded that no pattern seems discernible in our legislation as to when compensation will be payable and when not, and that legislative guidance is required to bring clarity to this matter.[161]

---

[159] Cf Van der Walt above n 115; Rabie 'The influence of environmental conservation on private landownership' above n 115.

[160] Cf Lewis 'The modern concept of ownership of land' 1985 *Acta Juridica* 241, 258ff.

[161] *Report of the three committees of the President's Council on a national environmental management system* (PC 1/1991) para 5.6.2.

CHAPTER 29

AGRICULTURE

J H GILIOMEE

29.1 INTRODUCTION

Agriculture can be defined as a human activity which changes natural ecosystems in such a way that the yield of plant and animal products desired is increased. Where hunting and gathering once produced enough food to feed the human population, we depend today on highly artificial and simplified agro-ecosystems. The level of agricultural development varies from place to place, depending on the quality of the physical resource base (soil, water, terrain, climate), socio-economic conditions and the skills available. As a result, agro-ecosystems vary in the extent to which they differ from natural ecosystems. At the one end of the spectrum one finds game or stock farming and shifting agriculture where little else but human labour is added to the system; at the other end there is, for example, vegetable production, where high inputs of fertilizers, crop-protection chemicals, energy (for cultivation, irrigation, pesticide application, etc) and labour are made.[1].

In South Africa agriculture has drastically altered the landscape over the three-and-a-half centuries since Van Riebeeck arrived here, a brief period which represents no more than a few grains of sand in the hourglass of time. In order to increase farming profits by producing food for the growing human population at home and abroad, more and more land has been brought under cultivation and agricultural activities intensified on the land already cultivated. Some farmers have achieved great wealth despite the fact that the conditions in South Africa generally are not favourable for agriculture: the soils are generally shallow and erosion-prone, water is scarce and the climate highly variable. The agricultural practices followed often had, and are still having, a negative impact on the environment, constituting a cost seldom included in economic calculations. See chapter 3.

In this chapter the main characteristics of agro-ecosystems will be described and the various impacts on the environment examined. Then the agribusiness paradigm is contrasted with the agro-ecological paradigm.

29.2 CHARACTERISTICS AND ENVIRONMENTAL IMPACTS OF MODERN AGRO-ECOSYSTEMS

29.2.1 Diversity changed to uniformity

The most prominent characteristic of agro-ecosystems is their high degree of biotic simplification or lack of biodiversity, i e the dominance of a small number of plant and animal species. The natural vegetation is removed and large tracts of land are covered by monocultures of maize, wheat, sugarcane, cotton, vineyards, fruit trees, etc. Other plants competing with these crops for nutrients, water and light are considered as weeds and are removed manually, mechanically or chemically. Animals such as nematodes, insects, birds or rodents feeding on these plants are poisoned or otherwise excluded. At

[1] Tivy *Agricultural ecology* (1990).

present, about 49 per cent of the Transvaal highveld and between 12 and 13 per cent of South Africa as a whole is under cultivation.[2]

Likewise, livestock farmers have by and large eliminated competition from other herbivores and predation from carnivores on their land. The result is that the large herbivores such as elephant, giraffe, rhinoceros and hippo, the magnificent herds of antelopes, wildebeest and zebra, as well as their associated predators—once common over most of South Africa—are today represented only in small enclaves, designated as nature reserves or game farms. They have been replaced by flocks of sheep and herds of cattle, fenced off into camps where water and feed additives are provided.

Impacts

The major impact is the loss of plant and animal species. Most endemic plant species disappear as a result of cultivation and are replaced by crop plants, and the few species that can adapt to the changed conditions, mostly exotic weeds. Even in the absence of cultivation, stockfarming can reduce plant diversity through selective overgrazing. Favoured species may be eliminated directly when sheep or cattle are fenced in for too long or in too large numbers on the same land, or indirectly when plants lose their competitive ability as a result of feeding damage. This may allow undesirable, unpalatable species to increase and become dominant, as is the case with black thorn (*Acacia mellifera*) and sickle bush (*Dichrostachys cinerea*) in the arid savanna of Namibia, karoo thorn (*Acacia karoo*) in the semi-arid grasslands of the western Transvaal, central Orange Free State and eastern Cape, wire grass (*Aristida junciformis*) in the Ngongoni veld of Natal and karoo bushes over extensive areas of the south-western Orange Free State and north-eastern Cape previously covered by grass. In severe cases this results in accelerated soil erosion and eventually desertification,[3] while the denudation of the grass cover in river catchment areas can lead to the formation of devastating floods, as is regularly experienced in South Africa. Since 87 per cent of the land used for agriculture in South Africa consists of natural grazing,[4] the impact of the livestock industry on vegetation and the soil is considerable.

The expansion of agriculture together with urbanization, the spread of invasive exotic plants and changes in fire regimes has indeed resulted in the survival of many plant species being threatened. It is estimated that of the approximately 17 500 vascular plant species in southern Africa, 1 915 are regarded to be either extinct (39), or variously threatened.[5] The loss of species is not only a moral dilemma, but in the process potentially valuable genes are lost—genes that might have been used in breeding programmes to increase the pest, disease and drought resistance of crop plants, or to introduce other valuable characteristics. Plants are also a source of medicines and other pharmaceutical products, as well as other potentially useful substances which may disappear when species become extinct. Finally, the diversity of plant and animal life is a source of enjoyment to many people, from laymen to scientists, and this is continuously being diminished as species disappear and the natural veld is converted to agricultural land.[6]

---

[2] Schoeman & Scotney 'Agricultural potential as determined by soil, terrain and climate' 1987 (83) *S Afr J Sci* 260.

[3] Novellie 'The Karoo region' in McDonald & Crawford (eds) *Long-term data series relating to southern Africa's renewable natural resources* South African National Scientific Programmes Report no 157 (1988) 280, 283.

[4] Scotney 'The agricultural areas of southern Africa' in McDonald & Crawford (eds) above n 3, 316.

[5] Hall, De Winter, De Winter & Van Oosterhout *Threatened plants of southern Africa* South African National Scientific Programmes Report no 45 (1980).

[6] Many aspects of biotic diversity in southern Africa are discussed in Huntley (ed) *Biotic diversity in southern Africa* (1989).

29.2.2 High nutrient inputs

In the case of most crops grown today, high yields can be obtained only if inorganic fertilizers containing nitrogen, phosphorus and potassium (N, P and K) are applied. This is because the soils are either inherently deficient in these elements or, more likely, because they have been depleted by the removal of harvested products. In natural ecosystems the nutrients present in plant and animal material are constantly being returned to the soil, but in agro-ecosystems the object is to produce large quantities of these materials for export to centres of urbanization. With vegetable crops such as carrots, onions and peas the entire plant is removed and the replenishment of nutrients removed from the system is imperative. This is mostly done by way of inorganic fertilizers which are more readily available in large quantities than manure or compost. During the 1980s about 100 000, 200 000 and 400 000 tons of potassium, phosphatic and nitrogenous fertilizers respectively were applied annually to South African soils.[7]

Impacts

N, P and K fertilizers are produced by depleting a limited non-renewable resource, natural gas or coal in the case of N, phosphate and potassium rock deposits in the case of P and K. In addition, the production of N from the air is energy-intensive, requiring high temperatures and pressures to combine nitrogen and hydrogen for the synthesis of ammonia, the basis of N fertilizers.

Nutrients, particularly nitrates, are leached from the soil to contaminate groundwater and streams. The increased nutrient levels in aquatic systems can stimulate organic growth, such as algae, and may eventually lead to eutrophication when oxygen is depleted during decomposition. This in turn can affect the structure of the faunal and floral communities in the water by eliminating many species and possibly favouring some.

The repeated application of certain fertilizers may lead to the build-up of some elements to levels toxic to plants. This has been found at Vaalharts, where high levels of phosphorus are causing crop reductions.[8] A serious consequence of the application of ammonium-containing fertilizers is acidification of the soil. This is caused by the hydrogen ions that are released during the nitrification of ammonium to nitrates. As the acidity of the soil increases (lower pH), aluminium in the soil becomes more freely available for plants to absorb, causing problems with root development and the uptake of other nutrients. Application of these fertilizers is usually considered necessary for achieving high yields, but experimental evidence shows that excessive amounts are used. Some experts regard increased acidity as one of the biggest problems of soil uitlization in South Africa.[9] It is estimated that of the approximately 4 million ha of land used for maize production, more than 0,5 million have serious acidity problems.

Nitrates themselves are not considered hazardous to human beings, but their secondary products, namely nitrites and nitroamines, can cause serious illnesses in both human beings and livestock. Nitrites cause the conversion of haemoglobin, the carrier of oxygen in the blood, to methaemoglobin, which cannot transport oxygen. This blood disorder is known as methaemoglobinaemia or blue baby disease and affects infants under the age of six months. The nitroamines are carcinogens and have been suspected of inducing gastro-intestinal cancers.[10] Most health authorities consider water with a

---

[7] Scotney above n 4, 321.

[8] Laker 'Die invloed van landbouwanpraktyke op grondagteruitgang en omgewingsbestuur' 1990 (2(3)) *Plantvoedsel* 4.

[9] Du Plessis 'Grondagteruitgang' 1986 (5) *SA Tydskrif vir Natuurwetenskap en Tegnologie* 126, 132.

[10] Adam 'Health aspects of nitrate in drinking-water and possible means of denitrification' 1980 (6) *Water SA* 79; Terblanche 'Health hazards of nitrate in drinking water' 1991 (17) *Water SA* 77.

nitrate concentration of up to 10 mg dm^{-3} N (equivalent to 45 mg dm^{-3} NO_3) as safe for domestic use.

Little is known about the health effects of nitrates in South African drinking water, but in an extensive study conducted on infants in Namibia a strong correlation was found between nitrate intake and levels of methaemoglobinaemia.[11] High concentrations of nitrates (above 45 mg ℓ^{-1}) were present in groundwater immediately after the planting of maize in the north-western Free State.[12]

It must be realized that fertilizers are not the only source of nitrates in groundwater, they also originate from N-fixing legumes, geological formations, animal wastes, cultivation and rain, the latter washing out nitrates and ammonia from the atmosphere.

29.2.3 The addition of water through irrigation

In South African agro-ecosystems water is often a limiting factor which affects both the type of crop that can be produced and its yield. Most fruit crops, such as citrus, apples and peaches, cannot be grown commercially without irrigation, while the yield of crops such as maize, wheat and grapes, which are usually satisfactory under natural conditions, can be more than doubled when irrigated.

Irrigation schemes often take water to dry areas where low precipitation levels have left the soils rich in nutrients and therefore potentially very productive. Examples are the irrigation schemes along the Orange, Olifants and Breede rivers. It is estimated that agriculture uses 67 per cent of the total amount of water consumed in South Africa.

Impacts

Usually irrigation is possible only after the damming of natural watercourses, thus drastically interfering with the normal streamflow. In the case of some rivers, such as the Olifants River in the Cape Province and the Letaba, Crocodile and Levubu rivers in the Transvaal lowveld, so much water is removed for agriculture that these formerly perennial streams stop flowing during dry periods. This can have a devastating effect on the fish and other animal life dependent on the water, as well as on the riparian vegetation. On the other hand, constant high volume flows as a result of the building of dams, weirs and irrigation canals favour the development of blood-sucking black flies (Simuliidae). These now cause problems to human beings and livestock along the Vaal River from the Hendrik Verwoerd Dam to Oranjemund and along the Great Fish River.[13]

Many rivers require flash floods to clean them from accumulated debris and silt. To the extent that damming reduces peak flows, this process is impeded. Damming and water extraction may also cause a reduction in the downstream water quality when solutes derived from agricultural, urban, industrial and natural sources are concentrated. This may render water unsuitable for domestic consumption and irrigation purposes. Reduced downstreamflow may also result in increased salinity levels in estuaries to the extent that aquatic life is affected in these important nursery areas for fish. Even in upstream sections of rivers the salinity levels may increase substantially when salts dissolved in drainage reach rivers. Severe salinization could result in a loss

---

[11] Super, De Heese, MacKenzie, Dempster, Du Plessis & Ferreira 'An epidemiological study of well water nitrates in a group of South West African/Namibian infants' 1981 (25), *Water Research* 1265.

[12] Henning & Stoffberg 'Nitraatkonsentrasies in grondwater van die noordwestelike Oranje-Vrystaat' *Handelinge van die 16de kongres van die grondkundevereniging van Suid-Afrika* (1990) 708.

[13] Nevill 'The creation of permanent blackfly problems by the construction of dams' in McDonald & Crawford (eds) above n 3, 353.

of plant and animal species normally associated with the river and as a result reduce its self-cleansing ability.[14]

In certain areas soils can become saline and less productive as a result of irrigation. This may be due to the use of low-quality (e g saline) water, but more particularly it is the result of certain properties of the soil that is irrigated. Thus when soils are poorly drained the levels of solutes can become so high that water uptake by plant roots is slowed down and the physiological processes of the plant disturbed.

29.2.4 Regular cultivation

Before the seeds or seedlings of annual crops are planted, soil is tilled, usually with heavy mechanical equipment, to remove weeds and to create soil conditions conducive to germination and growth. In perennial crops the soil is also regularly ploughed, though less these days than before, to remove weeds and to loosen the soil. It is estimated that 12 915 600 ha (12,26 per cent) of the 105 373 400 ha owned by whites in South Africa is currently under cultivation, mostly for maize and wheat. This represents 90,5 per cent of the area considered to be suitable for rain-fed crop production.[15]

Impacts

While tilling creates loose, absorbent soil conditions that are temporarily favourable for plant growth, it can have very destructive long-term effects.

Regular ploughing changes the structure of the soil, mainly because the decay of organic material is enhanced. As a result, the soil loses its natural crumb or granular structure and consequently its inherent porosity. This results in soil compaction, characterized by slower water infiltration, increased runoff and a higher risk of erosion. In such soils more fuel and heavier equipment are needed to work the soil. The heavy equipment can also compact the soil, especially fine sandy to sandy loam soils, which in turn is detrimental to root penetration and water infiltration. A compact layer, called a plough pan, is often formed in heavy soils which are regularly ploughed to the same depth, affecting root and water penetration to the deeper layers of the soil.

One consequence of intensive cultivation is a rapid decline in the amount of organic matter in the soil as a result of enhanced microbial activity causing increased decomposition rates. One of the decomposition products is nitrates, which may leach into the groundwater and become hazardous, as has been explained. This happens mainly when soils with a high organic content are newly cultivated. Cultivation of the black turf soils of the Springbok Flats was found to be the main cause of the high nitrate levels found in the groundwater of the region.[16]

Intensive cultivation and loss of organic material, together with overhead irrigation, all contribute to crust formation, which has in recent years became a widespread form of soil deterioration in South Africa.[17]

Ultimately the most serious impact of cultivation is that it increases the erosion potential of the soil. Where the vegetation is removed and the soil turned over, the soil particles are exposed to the full force of moving water and wind which dislodges them and sweeps them away. The impact of falling raindrops can scatter the particles in all directions, from where they are transported by moving water to lower levels and eventually into streams, dams and the ocean. It is estimated that South Africa is currently losing 300 million tons of soil annually. This is the equivalent of about 150 000

---

[14] Day, Davies & King 'Riverine ecosystems' in O'Keeffe (ed) *The conservation of South African rivers* South African National Scientific Programmes Report no 131 (1986) 1.

[15] Scotney above n 4, 318.

[16] Heaton 'Isotopic and chemical aspects of nitrate in the groundwater of the Springbok Flats' 1985 (11) *Water SA* 199.

[17] Laker above n 8, 6.

ha 150 mm deep.[18] One of the consequences is that heavy loads of silt are deposited in our streams, rivers and estuaries. This habitat change may seriously affect all aquatic organisms, and fish may disappear when their feeding, breeding and refuge areas are destroyed by sediments.

The loss of the topsoil also reduces the fertility of the soil, which has to be replenished by fertilizers, adding to the cost of production.

29.2.5 Application of chemicals for pest control

Modern agriculture relies heavily on highly effective chemicals for the control of organisms such as insects, mites, fungi and bacteria that cause damage to or disease in crops, while weeds that compete with crop plants for nutrients and water are killed with herbicides. However, despite a tenfold increase in insecticides used in the USA since the 1940s, crop losses due to pests have nearly doubled.[19]

Impacts

The impacts of pesticides are discussed in chapter 20. The major concern is their toxicity to non-target organisms, including human beings. Even when used carefully they may kill honey bees, birds and fish, and endanger human health. They kill the insects and mites that are natural enemies of plant-feeders, causing pest numbers to resurge after spraying or new pests to arise. They also act selectively on populations, with the result that the latter eventually lose their susceptibility to the pesticides used against them.

29.3 TOWARDS SUSTAINABLE AGRICULTURE

29.3.1 Past Failure

From the above it is evident that modern agriculture is responsible for the degradation of ecosystems in causing, amongst other things, species to disappear, the soil to erode and lose its natural fertility, and the general environment to be contaminated by dangerous chemical substances and other pollutants. It relies heavily on external sources of energy (fuel and electricity), chemicals (fertilizers and pesticides), large machines and capital. As the soil, water and biological resources have deteriorated and the cost of inputs has risen, without a concomitant rise in the prices of agricultural products, the financial position of many farmers has deteriorated. Their position is exacerbated by the susceptibility of their monocultures of narrowly selected crop plants and overgrazed natural pastures to pests and adverse climatic conditions. Exceptions are the highly profitable, export-based deciduous and citrus fruit farms, but even here progressive farmers are trying to reduce their impact on the environment by practising what is known as integrated fruit production.

Not only the natural but also the social environment has been adversely affected. Larger farm units, mechanization and the decline in profitability of farming have contributed, through direct and multiplier effects, to the depopulation of many rural areas and increased rural poverty.

Conditions in tribal areas, where mostly subsistence farming is practised, are even worse than on commercial farms. Years of overcrowding by financially poor people and livestock on too little land have resulted in a deterioration of soil quality, a frightening degree of soil erosion and ever-expanding areas where all the trees have been cut down for fuel.[20] Ironically, the agricultural policy in these areas promotes the methods and

---

[18] Ibid.

[19] Pimentel 'Agroecology and economics' in Kogan (ed) *Ecological theory and integrated pest management* (1986) 308.

[20] Cooper *Working the land* (1988) 94.

technology which have caused so many problems in commercial agriculture.[21] The restoration of the former productivity of these lands would require a very carefully considered blend of First and Third World technologies, appropriate to rural conditions.

It is clear that agriculture, as practised today in many places in South Africa and elsewhere, is not sustainable in the long term.

29.3.2 The challenge: Agro-ecology

The challenge for agriculture is seen as the 'necessity to produce an economically viable crop while preserving the short- and long-term integrity of the local regional and global environment'.[22] The question is whether this can be achieved within the present agribusiness paradigm where increasing use is made of the energy derived from fossil fuels, where the research emphasis is on biotechnological improvement of crop plants, finding new pesticides and the replacement of manual labour by machines, while the protection of natural processes such as soil formation, water infiltration, nutrient recycling and predation is ignored or even impeded. Also included is a value system in which conservation takes a minor position, as is evident from the attitudes and practices of farmers, society in general and the government. The lack of governmental concern is evident from the fact that only 14 inspectors have been appointed to apply the Conservation of Agricultural Resources Act 43 of 1983 countrywide.[23] See, generally, chapter 10.

Instead, it is proposed that we need a new scientific discipline called agro-ecology that will define, classify and study agricultural systems from an ecological and socio-economic perspective.[24] It should provide a methodology to diagnose the 'health' of agricultural systems and delineate the ecological principles necessary to develop sustainable production systems.

In the agro-ecological paradigm the farmer is a steward with a deep commitment to the land and its well-being. Managerial decisions are based on the constraints of conservation rather than the tantalizing prospects of exploitation. The farmer understands and works with natural processes, and minimizes impact on the environment by reducing energy requirements based on fossil fuels and avoiding the use of synthetic fertilizers, pesticides, livestock feed additives, etc. The farmer strives to maximize sustainable net yields rather than gross yields achieved at high environmental and social costs. Finally, the agriculturalist is the kind of entrepreneur who finds fulfilment in restoring and maintaining soil fertility by using as much compost, manure and legume crops as possible, in succeeding to control pests by biological and cultural means, and in experiencing a diversity of plant and animal life on his farm.

Noteworthy progress towards sustainable agriculture has been made by the livestock farmers of Natal and the Orange Free State with the establishment of conservancies over some 650 000 and 340 000 ha of farm land respectively. Adjoining landowners co-operatively employ trained conservancy guards who not only patrol the land to stop poaching of game and indigenous plants but also convey environmental education to the farm labourers and other rural people. As a result, wildlife has increased in conservancies as well as the conditions for stock farming.[25] Also, the resources on these farms are utilized for conservation-oriented, revenue-generating activities. Hiking

---

[21] Cooper above n 20, 102.

[22] Paul & Robertson 'Ecology and the agricultural sciences: a false dichotomy?' 1989 (70) *Ecology* 1594, 1595.

[23] Vosloo 'Gebreke in landboubeleid en wetgewing' in *Red ons grond* Veldtrust konferensie oor bewaringstatus van landbouhulpbronne in die RSA (1990).

[24] Altieri 'Agroecology: a new research and development paradigm for world agriculture' 1989 (27) *Agriculture, Ecosystems and Environment* 37, 38.

[25] Earle 'The story of the Orange Free State conservancy concept' 1991 (45) *African Wildlife* 141, 142.

trails have been established, old farmhouses restored for overnight accommodation and hunts organized. See chapter 27.

For subsistence farmers in the tribal areas it has been suggested that the 'downward spiral of ecological destruction' can be halted only with a shift from individually based family plots to collectively organized village production.[26] This would allow for a diversified form of agriculture where the best arable land is cultivated intensively and the marginal land used for grazing. In these areas low-cost, low-input, labour-intensive techniques would be particularly appropriate.

29.3.3 Future prospects

Commercial agriculture in South Africa today faces enormous problems. Economically the farming community is massively in debt by some R17 billion (despite state aid of R10 billion since 1980),[27] politically there is the prospect of reduced power and demands for the redistribution of land, and environmentally there is the degraded resource base on which they operate together with the real possibility of impending climatic changes as a result of global warming. The prospects for the subsistence farmers are not much better, except that they might expect more support and possibly more land from future governments.

What will the future impact of agriculture on the environment be? Based on the expectation that a future government may be financially less favourably disposed towards the commercial farmer[28] by keeping prices of farm products low, terminating cheap loans and other subsidies (such as those for soil conservation measures and stock reduction), imposing a land tax, and privatizing agricultural research and extension work, two scenarios seem possible. On the one hand, the weaker financial position of commercial farmers may prevent them from following conservation measures such as contouring sloping lands, restoring erosion gullies, rotating annual row crops with cover crops, draining water logged soils, combating invasive plants and preserving natural areas. This will have severe implications for the environment. On the other hand, their financial position may force them to abandon high-tech, high-cost strategies and to switch to LISA (Low Input Sustainable Agriculture), using less energy derived from fossil fuels and less pesticide, fertilizer and cultivation. This will obviously reduce the impact of agriculture on the environment.

Whatever the future holds, this country will always need farmers who can manipulate the environment in order to feed the nation. May they have the dedication, commitment and knowledge to do this with minimum-impact, sustainable agriculture.

29.4 LEGAL ASPECTS

Legal provisions relating to agriculture are encountered in many statutes and regulations.[29] Environmentally relevant provisions are discussed mainly in chapters 10, 11, 20 and 24.

29.5 CONCLUSION

Many of the agricultural practices followed today by crop and stock farmers are harmful to the environment and are causing a steady decline in the quality of the resource base. Thus soils are eroded, nutrients depleted, rivers pumped dry or polluted by chemicals and many valuable plant and animal species eliminated or replaced by weeds. We need a shift in emphasis from maximizing short-term gains through the use

---

[26] Cooper above n 20, 129.

[27] Kassier 'Agriculture in the new South Africa: an outlook' 1991 (1) *J of the Fertilizer Society of South Africa* 3.

[28] Kassier above n 27, 4.

[29] See Gering 'Agriculture' in Joubert (ed) *The law of South Africa* vol 1 (1976).

of exploitative practices to approaches that would lead to sustainable productivity over the long term—ie a paradigm shift from agribusiness to agro-ecology. This will be achieved only if education changes the attitudes and norms of the farmers. Research should provide alternatives to harmful practices and economic measures be used to reward those farmers who follow ecologically sound practices and penalize those who fail to do so. Not only the biophysical but also the sociological environment should be considered. Ultimately, sustainable agriculture should be a solid building block that supports and interfaces with the social, economic and political structures of a region.

CHAPTER 30

INTEGRATED ENVIRONMENTAL MANAGEMENT

G R PRESTON
N ROBINS
R F FUGGLE

30.1 INTRODUCTION

30.1.1 The emergence of environmental impact assessment

The 1960s heralded a growing awareness of the adverse and often complex impacts of development, and of the need to understand and deal with these impacts if serious problems were to be avoided. See chapter 2. The procedure adopted was environmental impact assessment and, by the end of the decade, the basic principles of impact assessment had been formulated. In 1969, the National Environmental Policy Act (NEPA) of the United States introduced environmental evaluations into the realm of public policy. Many countries followed this lead and environmental evaluation procedures became widely institutionalized, predominantly in Western industrialized countries.

30.1.2 Environmental evaluation requirements in South Africa

As South Africa is a less developed country, policy-makers need to reflect carefully on the conditions at home before simply imitating the policies of industrialized countries. South Africa is in a position to learn from the two decades of research and experience with environmental evaluations in other countries.[1] This experience led to the realization that, unless carefully structured and regulated, environmental assessments could become reactive, excessively negative, and the cause of great expense and delay to the development process.[2]

The integration of environmental concerns into public policy depends on an open system of government, a wide disclosure of information and an informed citizenry. South Africa has historically lacked these elements of government. Additional problems are likely to include the lack of scientific data, inadequate administrative structures and the lack of trained personnel.

Furthermore, environmental assessment directs considerable attention at long-term or inter-generational ecological criteria, aesthetic considerations and scientific/educational interests. In most less-developed countries, including South Africa, scientific, educational or aesthetic requirements are regarded by many to be a luxury, while concern for the future is seldom as pressing as present needs for food, shelter and security. As a result, environmental concerns do not carry a strong electoral basis in many of these countries, leading to a lack of political will to introduce environmental assessments.[3]

---

[1] Schweizer *Working document for the development of a national policy on environmental impact assessment in South Africa* Council for the Environment (unpublished, 1985).

[2] Council on Environmental Quality *Ninth annual report* (1978).

[3] Hill & Fuggle 'Integrated environmental management of development in South Africa', *Proceedings of the eighth quinquennial convention of the SAICE*, South African Institute of Civil Engineers, Pretoria 1988.

These factors exist in a context in which economic growth and development are necessarily national goals. Clearly, an approach to environmental evaluations in South Africa is needed which is reflective of these conditions, taking account of both the limitations and requirements of this country. Of utmost importance is that the choice in environmental evaluation should differ from the stop/go approach in industrialized countries. Rather, an approach should encourage decision-makers to formulate an appropriate compromise, with the emphasis on identifying options and facilitating a choice between options, rather than only detailing the negative impacts of a development.[4]

In 1984, the Council for the Environment established a committee to recommend a national strategy to ensure the integration of environmental concerns into developmental actions. After an extensive period of research and consultation, a constructive process of guiding and documenting development decisions was recommended. This process was called integrated environmental management (IEM).[5]

30.2 RATIONALE FOR IEM

30.2.1 Purpose

IEM is a procedure designed to ensure that the environmental consequences of developments are understood and adequately considered in the planning process. It is intended to guide, rather than impede, the development process by providing a positive, interactive approach to gathering and analysing useful data and presenting findings in a form that can easily be understood by non-specialists. It thus serves to refine and improve proposed policies, programmes and projects through a series of procedures which are linked to the development process. These procedures aim to:

- stimulate creative thinking in the planning and initial design stage;
- provide a systematic approach to the evaluation of proposals;
- formalize the approval process in the decision-making stage, and
- ensure that monitoring and desirable modifications take place in the implementation stage.

30.2.2 Principles of IEM

The basic principles which underpin IEM are:

- a broad understanding of the term 'environment';
- informed decision-making;
- accountability for decisions and for the information on which they are based;
- an open, participatory approach in the planning of proposals, and
- pro-active and positive planning.

Consequently, the term 'environment' is taken to include physical, biological, social, economic, cultural, historical and political components. Informed decision-making is achieved by integrating contributions from professionals involved in all disciplines relevant to the planning of a particular proposal. Due consideration is given to alternative options for the development, including, where appropriate, the no-go option.

A record of a decision and the rationale behind it is required for each decision taken, and should be available to the public on request. This will facilitate accountability for decisions taken.

Participation is encouraged through an opportunity for public input in the

[4] Fuggle *Integrated environmental management: an appropriate approach to environmental concerns*, Paper delivered to International Association for Impact Assessment conference, Brisbane, Australia 5–9 July 1988.

[5] *Integrated environmental management in South Africa* Council for the Environment (1989).

decision-making process. This may involve consultation with interested and affected parties during scoping or more active participation of affected groups during the planning stage.

Finally, a positive and pro-active approach is encouraged through the enhancement of positive impacts as well as the mitigation of negative impacts. IEM attempts to ensure that the social costs of development (those borne by society) are outweighed by the social benefits (the benefits to the society as a result of the development).

30.3 THE IEM PROCEDURE

A flow diagram indicating the major steps in the IEM procedure is given in Figure 30.1. IEM recognizes three stages in the development of any proposal: first, develop and assess the proposal; secondly, the decision; and thirdly, implementation. All proposed actions with potentially significant environmental consequences should be formally investigated in some way; however, not all will require a full impact assessment. In many cases, a brief investigation will convince the decision-taker that the proposed action will have no significant impacts, or that effective mitigatory measures may easily be implemented.

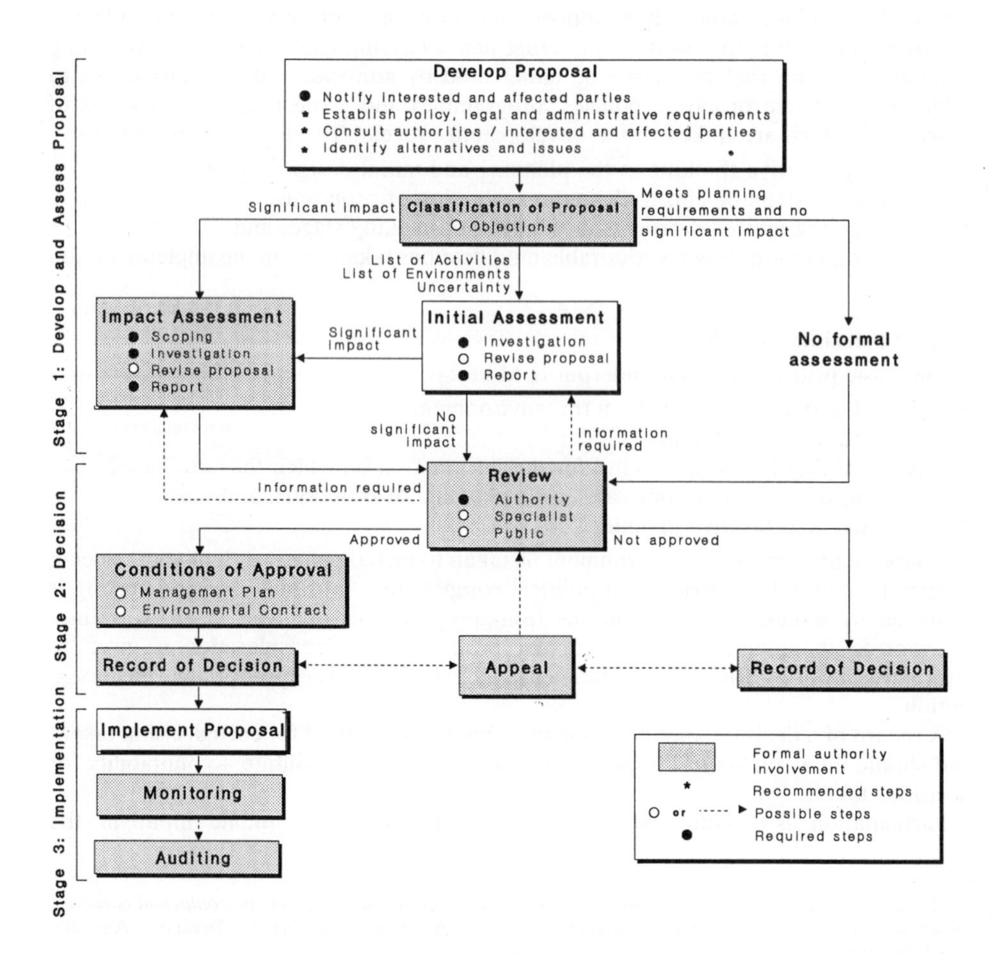

Figure 30.1 Major steps in IEM procedure

This section outlines the three stages that should be followed by a proposal. Thereafter, the IEM requirements are set out for each possible route in the assessment of a proposal.

30.3.1 Stage 1: Develop and Assess Proposal

30.3.1.1 *Develop proposal*

A key concept in IEM is that its underlying principles should be incorporated into the planning of proposals, rather than being considerations to be addressed after the proposal has been planned. IEM suggests a number of steps when developing the proposal, which, if incorporated during planning, are likely to result in better planning and a streamlined decision-making process. The recommended steps include:

- Establishing the policy, legal and administrative requirements applicable to the proposal.
- Notifying interested and affected parties of the proposed development.
- Discussing the development with authorities and interested and affected parties.
- Identifying and considering environmental issues and possible alternatives.
- Considering appropriate mitigatory options.

International experience indicates that, by undertaking these steps at the inception of the development of a proposal, the proponent will integrate the planning and assessment of the proposal, and so streamline the process and facilitate informed decision-making.

30.3.1.2 *Classification of proposal*

Classification of proposal (or screening, as it is known in some countries) determines whether the proposal follows the *impact assessment, initial assessment* or *no formal assessment* route. This classification is done by the proponent (or his/her consultant) in consultation with the relevant authority. The IEM procedure is structured to channel proposals down one of three routes:

(a) for an impact assessment, when it has become clear that the proposal will result in significant adverse impacts;

(b) for an initial assessment, where the proposal is a listed activity, or is in a listed environment, or there is uncertainty as to whether the proposal may result in significant impacts, or

(c) for no formal assessment, if the proposal meets planning requirements, and indications are that the proposal will not result in significant adverse impacts. (The *Checklist of environmental characteristics*, available from the Department of Environment Affairs, provides a checklist of the environmental factors which need to be considered before concluding that a proposal will require no formal assessment. The proposal which follows this route is submitted directly for authority review.)

30.3.2 Stage 2: Decision

30.3.2.1 *Authority review*

At this stage, a decision as to the acceptability of the proposal is taken. The authority responsible for approving the development should be satisfied:

- that sufficient information is provided in order to make a decision;
- that sufficient consultation with interested and affected parties has taken place, and
- that the proposal complies with requirements.

The authority will usually find it necessary to set conditions of approval. This occurs when approval is given subject to certain mitigating measures or other conditions, which should be clearly specified. For example, the proponents may be required to prepare and submit an environmental management plan describing how the proposal will be implemented, as well as controls over its implementation (see section 30.3.3.2). The conditions of approval might also specify how environmental restoration will be carried out, or provide for final rehabilitation of the environment on termination or decommissioning of the project.

30.3.2.2 *Record of decision*

Whether or not a proposal is approved, there should be a record of decision. This provides an opportunity for an explanation to be given of how environmental considerations were taken into account and weighed against other considerations. The record of decision is crucial for more open and accountable decision-making and should be made available on request to any interested party. The record of decision must also reflect the conditions of approval.

30.3.2.3 *Appeal*

An administrative procedure should make allowance for appeals against decisions taken. This might involve an appeal by the proponent against the conditions of approval of the development or an appeal by an affected party (such as a neighbour) against the approval of the development.

IEM provides for opportunity for appeal to a higher authority (eg, higher tier authority, review panel, court of law). As appeals can be a costly and delaying exercise, time limits are generally set on the filing of and ruling on an appeal.

30.3.3 Stage 3: Implementation

30.3.3.1 *Implementation of proposal*

Once approval has been obtained, the proposal is likely to be implemented. In certain instances there may be conditions of approval, a management plan and/or an environmental contract.

30.3.3.2 *Environmental management plan*

The purpose of a management plan is to describe how the proposal will be implemented and the control over the implementation. It should detail how negative environmental impacts will be managed and monitored; how positive impacts will be maximized, and how the affected areas will be rehabilitated. The various mitigation measures are organized and co-ordinated into a structured and well-formulated plan, which guides the construction, operation and eventually the decommissioning of the development.

A management plan might simply be required to detail the mitigation of one variable during the construction phase (such as drainage), or it might be required to provide a comprehensive overview of the management and monitoring requirements for the duration of the project. It should therefore be viewed as a dynamic document, which may require updating or revision during the life of the development.

30.3.3.3 *Environmental contract*

An environmental contract may be required as a condition of approval. It is a contractual control over development where the penalties for not complying with the stated conditions are stipulated. The contract lists certain mitigatory requirements (such as revegetation) and associated penalties which will have been negotiated with the proponent (such as financial compensation).

The establishment of a contract may also improve relations between conflicting parties, as it provides a guarantee that the developer will make a sincere effort to minimize environmental damage.

30.3.3.4 *Monitoring*

A monitoring programme should be required for all approved proposals, irrespective of whether there are conditions of approval and/or a management plan. Monitoring ensures that the project is progressing as intended and that it is in compliance with any conditions of approval which might have been imposed. It also provides invaluable information regarding the accuracy of predictions and the suitability of proposed mitigating measures.

Monitoring may include:

- a check that actions are in accord with conditions of approval;
- a check that mitigation measures are being implemented during the construction phase;
- a check on the efficacy of these measures;
- emissions monitoring, and
- monitoring of selected environmental variables.

30.3.3.5 *Audits*

Auditing is a reassment of the project or policy proposal in the light of developments during the implementation. Periodic audits of the positive and negative aspects of the development should be undertaken. These provide feedback on the adequacy of planning at the *develop proposal* stage; the accuracy of investigations during the *initial assessment* and/or *impact assessment* stages; the wisdom of the decisions at the *authority review* stage, and the effectiveness of the conditions of approval (and the management plan) at the *implementation* stage.

30.4 REQUIREMENTS OF THE ASSESSMENT ROUTES

The essence of the IEM procedure is that an impact assessment is either undertaken or is not necessary. Provision is made for an initial assessment to establish whether or not an impact assessment is required, when appropriate. The intention is that careful planning, incorporating the necessary assessment, will expedite the process and allow for informed decision-making in both the planning and the authority review of the proposal. Requirements of the three possible assessment routes are presented below.

30.4.1 No formal assessment

If classified as requiring no formal assessment, the proposal is referred directly for authority review. The authority nevertheless may require an initial assessment, should it feel that further information is required in order to make an informed decision.

30.4.2 The initial assessment

If the proposal is a listed activity or is located in a listed environment and no significant impacts are identified during the develop proposal stage, then an initial assessment must be undertaken. It will also be undertaken if there is uncertainty as to whether a project will result in significant impacts.

In a technical sense, the purpose of an initial assessment is to present just enough information to determine whether a proposal will result in a significant adverse impact or not. In other words, it should indicate whether a proposal should proceed to *review*, or whether a full impact assessment should be undertaken. In practice, however, the initial assessment will also fulfil an important function through providing input into project planning.

It may be possible at this stage to identify mitigation measures which could reduce the potential impacts to insignificant levels, thus avoiding the need for an impact assessment. These measures may be drawn up into a management plan, adherence to which could form part of the conditions of approval of the development.

A further possible step may be the revision of the proposal itself, in order to achieve an insignificant level of impact, or to optimize potential benefits. If the initial assessment report indicates that a development will result in a significant negative impact, the report will provide important input to the impact assessment.

The nature of initial assessment reports will therefore vary, depending on the extent to which they are envisaged by the developer as planning documents. An initial assessment may need to present information in order to justify a finding of no significant impact. This may take the form of separate specialist reports on specific areas of concern (such as pollution) or environmental features (such as groundwater).

30.4.3 The impact assessment

If it is clear that significant impacts will result from a proposal, an impact assessment is conducted. There are three principal components of an impact assessment:

- *Scoping*. This determines the extent of and approach to the investigation. The proponent, in consultation with the relevant authorities and the interested and affected parties, determines which alternatives and issues should be investigated; the procedure that should be followed, and particular report requirements. An opportunity is provided for objections to the scoping procedure undertaken. The *Scoping guidelines* of the Department of Environment Affairs provide detailed information on scoping procedures.
- *Investigation*. The investigation is guided by the scoping decisions, and is intended to provide the authorities with enough information on the positive and negative aspects of the proposal, and feasible alternatives, with which to make a decision.
- *Report*. This should be based on the *Guidelines for report requirements* of the Department of Environment Affairs. Particular requirements for the report may be established by the parties during the scoping stage.

The scope of the impact assessment investigation will vary from a relatively brief assessment by a competent party to a very detailed assessment by a team of professionals.

It should be reiterated that, if the proponent undertakes detailed environmental investigations at the develop proposal stage, the scoping stage could then find that the necessary investigations have been done and that the proposal includes the necessary report findings. No further environmental investigations would then be required.

30.5 IMPLEMENTING IEM

As part of the development of the IEM procedure, guidelines on scoping, report requirements and review were developed by the Department of Environment Affairs in order to help proponents, consultants and authorities to carry out the requirements of IEM. In addition, various tools have been developed in order to facilitate the classification of proposals and to help in the identification of potential impacts of a development.

30.5.1 Listed environments, listed activities and checklist of environmental characteristics

The listed environments indicate particularly sensitive areas which alert the authority or developer to the need for an initial assessment. Likewise, the listed activities indicate development actions which, based on past experience, are likely to result in significant environmental impacts.

The checklist of environmental characteristics identifies environmental factors which may potentially be affected by development actions or which might place significant constraints on a proposed development. Although it includes the major attributes and linkages which should be considered by the developer, his or her consultant(s) and authorities, the list is not exhaustive. The assistance of experts may be required to assess certain potential impacts and to identify unlisted attributes which nevertheless may be important in specific cases. Cumulative impacts (see section 30.6.4) should always be borne in mind.

The above checklists can be used by both proponents and reviewers as an aid to ensuring the completeness of assessments and proposals, and their accuracy.

30.5.2 Scoping

Scoping is a procedure for determining the extent of and approach to an impact assessment. The main purpose of scoping is to focus the EIA to ensure that only the significant issues and reasonable alternatives are examined. It involves the following tasks:

- involvement of the relevant authorities, and interested and affected parties;
- identification and selection of alternatives;
- identification of significant issues to be investigated, and
- determination of specific guidelines or terms of reference for the impact assessment (e g whether a draft report should be prepared).

Scoping is an ongoing, open and iterative process which may continue throughout the planning and assessment stages, depending on whether additional issues or alternatives are introduced or eliminated as a result of new information.

It provides an opportunity for the proponent(s), consultant(s), authorities, and interested and affected parties to exchange information and express their views and concerns regarding a proposal before an impact assessment is undertaken. It thus aims to facilitate an efficient assessment process that saves time and resources, and reduces costly delays which could arise were consultation not to take place. It also avoids costly additional work that often arises at a later stage when planning is not well done.

The proponent and his or her consultant(s) have the final responsibility for scoping. In certain instances, they may wish to appoint a multi-disciplinary team, advisory group, or facilitator to guide the scoping process.

30.5.2.1 *Identification and notification of interested and affected parties*

One of the most important aspects of scoping is the identification and notification of parties who would be interested in, or affected by, the proposed development.

Established lists and the process of networking are probably the most effective methods of making direct contact with interested and affected parties. However, for certain proposals, there is no clearly definable public—especially for projects or plans which may have regional or national implications. In these instances, notifying the public through advertisements in the press or other media may be the most appropriate approach.

Other techniques include: telephonic contact; exhibits/displays; written information; surveys; interviews and questionnaires; open house; workshops, and advisory groups.[6]

The method of notifying disadvantaged communities of proposals and opportunities to participate in public involvement programmes needs special consideration.

30.5.2.2 *Participation of disadvantaged communities*

In the South African context, disadvantaged communities are those communities which have historically been denied access to resources and adequate opportunities for educational, social and economic development, as well as those excluded from the political process. Possible ways of notifying these communities include:

- employing established methods of community participation, where they exist and are acceptable to the community (consultants/researchers should work with community leaders and representative groups within the community);

---

[6] These techniques are discussed at length in the Department of Environment Affairs' *Scoping guidelines*.

- appointing a locally based organization or credible service organization familiar with, and acceptable to, the community, to inform them of the proposal and to conduct meetings, workshops or interviews to ascertain the most appropriate form of community involvement;
- displaying a simple and well-illustrated fact sheet of the proposal in prominent places (e g a noticeboard in a community centre) and inviting interested persons to meet with the proponent at a fixed time to discuss what form community involvement should take, and
- identifying key players, social groups or committees within the communities through informal discussions and inviting them to participate in the process.

Other factors which need to be considered when exploring appropriate methods of notifying disadvantaged communities include literacy levels, language medium, level of organizational structure within the community, social biases (e g absent migrant workers), cultural biases (e g male dominance), and social hierarchy.

30.5.2.3 *Identification and selection of alternatives*

The identification and examination of alternatives provide a basis for choice among options available to the decision-maker, and is therefore a fundamental component of an impact assessment.

In evaluating alternatives, it is necessary to consider the social context in which a development will take place. An example which illustrates this is technology, which in South Africa ranges from traditional to high-tech. The initial choice of technology will influence the operational, personnel and maintenance requirements of a development. It should therefore be matched to the level of skills of local people.[7]

The following questions must be addressed when considering the identification and selection of alternatives:

- How should alternatives be identified?
- What is the reasonable range of alternatives that should be considered?
- What level of investigation should be applied to each alternative?

The following general categories of alternatives should be considered at the initial concept-planning stage:

- **Demand alternatives:** For example, tourism and residential development are common demand alternatives for coastal areas on a high-quality recreational beach.
- **Activity alternatives:** Impoundments, river channelization, levees and flood-plain zoning are examples of activity alternatives for reducing the hazards of river floods.
- **Location alternatives:** This is the consideration of alternative sites where the proposal could occur.
- **Process alternatives:** For example, many industrial or service facilities have a number of alternative design configurations, each of which may have different input, output and pollution dimensions. Construction alternatives could also be considered, e g the use of a labour-intensive approach.
- **Temporal alternatives:** This is the consideration of alternative timing of development activities. For example, it may be more appropriate to transport materials during the evenings when there will be less impact on existing traffic flows.

For certain proposals, the consideration of the no-go alternative should be examined in the impact assessment, but discretion needs to be applied before automatically including this option.

[7] Fuggle 'The need for environmental management procedures in third world countries', Paper presented at the symposium on institutional transition in the changing societies, fourth Sino-South African conference, Taipei, 19–21 January 1989.

30.5.3 Report requirements

In response to the costly and voluminous reports produced in the initial years of EIA, comprehensive guidelines on report requirements have been developed to help those submitting reports to present just what is necessary for an authority to reach a decision. The fundamental requirements of environmental reports are:

- integrated and accurate information;
- concise writing, and
- accessibility to non-specialists.

The Department of Environment Affairs' *Guidelines on report requirements* give guidance on the format of reports as well as the elements which should be included in an impact assessment. The document consists of an extended and annotated list of requirements and is intended to assist those developers and their consultants who have had little experience in the production of environmental reports.

A balance needs to be struck between an easily administered and uniform set of requirements and a more flexible accommodation of the diversity of proposals and the creativity of consultants. The *Guidelines on report requirements* will consequently be subject to ongoing revision as the procedure becomes widely adopted in the country.

The level of detail and extent of a report will generally be established during scoping discussions. The size and nature of the proposal, its location and its potential for generating controversy are important factors guiding these decisions. While guidelines are an aid in this respect, it will remain the responsibility of the proponent and his or her consultant(s) to present sufficient information in such a form as to indicate clearly the potential impacts and the overall suitability of the development.

The extent to which these report requirements are adhered to will be at the discretion of the relevant authorities. A review of international experience strongly suggests that the elements contained in the guidelines are necessary for an authority to make an informed decision regarding a development.

A summary of report requirements for an impact assessment is presented in Table 30.1.

It should be noted that the guidelines are not exhaustive. Additional and more detailed sections may well be necessary, depending on the specific proposal under consideration.

30.5.4 Review

The purpose of review is to provide an evaluation of the strengths and weaknesses of the proposal and of the environmental reports submitted. Reviewers assess the content and adequacy of reports as a decision-making tool as well as the organizational and presentational qualities of reports.

After having determined that the report is an acceptable document on which to base a decision, the authority may also be responsible for approving (or not approving) the development. This is an interactive process—the degree of concern about potential impacts of a development should determine the level of detail for the review. All proposals and reports are reviewed by the relevant authorities, but IEM also makes provision for review by the public and specialists.

30.5.4.1 *Department of Environment Affairs' review guidelines*

It is important that the review process is systematic and that the role of subjective judgement is decreased as far as possible. The *Review guidelines* were prepared to establish consistency in review and to clarify the role of reviewers throughout the process.

TABLE 30.1
Summary of report requirements as determined by the Department of Environment Affairs.

1. Cover page
2. Executive summary
3. Contents page
4. Introduction
5. Terms of reference
6. Approach to the study
7. Assumptions and limitations
8. Administrative, legal and policy requirements

9. Alternatives
   For each alternative identified:
   9.1 Proposed actions
   9.2 The affected environment
   9.3 Assessment of impacts

10. Evaluation of the proposed development
11. Incomplete or unavailable information
12. Conclusions and recommendations
13. Definitions of technical terms
14. List of preparers
15. References
16. Personal communications
17. Appendices

Assessments may vary widely in terms of type, scope and complexity, and it is therefore difficult to generalize about what constitutes an adequate report. Basic questions that reviewers will consider include:

- Have the principles underpinning IEM been applied?
- Is the procedure followed in the planning and assessment process adequate for the proposal concerned?
- Has there been sufficient consultation with interested and affected parties?
- Is it clear where accountability for the information lies?
- Has a broad understanding of the term 'environment' been adopted in the planning and assessment?
- Does the initial assessment report or impact assessment report provide the necessary information in terms of the *Guidelines for report requirements*?
- Is the information in the report accurate, unbiased and credible?
- Is adequate attention given to the reasonable alternatives identified during the scoping stage?
- Does the report consider the possibility of cumulative impacts?
- Is the information synthesized and integrated, indicating the main issues to be evaluated?
- Are the judgements made around the issue of significance valid? Is it clear how they were made?
- Is the information in the report communicated clearly?
- Is further information required in order to make a decision?

If a document does not contain sufficient information for a decision-maker to assess the impact of a development, or if a reviewer has identified new reasonable alternatives which could reduce the negative impact of the development, the document will be returned to the proponent with a request for further information.

30.5.4.2 *Common inadequacies in assessment*

Inadequate assessment documents are a problem. Apart from hindering the decision-making process, some assessments may be seen by interested parties as public relations documents or 'sweetheart' reports. This will be discouraged if all parties involved in an assessment carry out a systematic review of the quality of the report. This might include public review, specialist or peer review, and authority review. This process is likely to highlight deficiencies and allow them to be rectified at the earliest opportunity.

A second problem area concerns inadequacies in the composition of assessment teams. Experience has shown that teams consisting of only one or two disciplines are unlikely to address all aspects of an evaluation adequately. Although projects vary widely in scope, experience indicates that successful teams will incorporate at least biological, geophysical, sociological and project management disciplines.[8]

Thirdly, the adequacy of review should also be considered. In the same way that auditors review the work of accountants, so a responsible independent environmental professional should review assessments undertaken by consultants. Such review is best built into the assessment process of large developments from the outset. When the proponent of a development is also the decision-making authority, the IEM process recommends that compulsory specialist review of the impact assessment or initial assessment reports be carried out. Likewise, should a consultant stand to obtain further work as a result of the findings of the assessment, there should be compulsory specialist review of the reports.

30.6 PROBLEM AREAS

30.6.1 Defining 'significance'[9]

The word 'significant' is not easy to define. To say that an impact will be significant is to suggest that it will have, or is likely to have, considerable influence or effect on some aspect of human well-being. But this is bound to be a subjective judgement: there are no objective measures which can be used to judge significance. Judgements as to what constitutes a significant impact require consideration of both context and intensity.

Context has both a spatial and a time dimension. An action may not be significant on a national level, but it may be regarded as quite significant on a regional or local level. Similarly, an action may not seem particularly significant in the short term, but the long term implications may be regarded as significant. For example, the loss of a local resource may not significantly affect the present national interest or level of welfare, but local residents or future generations may be profoundly affected by this loss.

Intensity refers to the severity of the impact resulting from an action, as judged either by some knowledgeable authority or by the people affected by the impacts. If reputable persons with special knowledge or experience believe the impact will be significant, then it should be regarded as such. Similarly, if those who bear the impact genuinely believe that it will significantly affect their well-being, or if the action is highly controversial, then the action should be regarded as a significant one.

Considerations of intensity would include, among other things:

- the degree to which the proposed action affects public health and safety;

---

[8] Fuggle *Environmental management in South Africa: practical challenges* Paper presented at the sixth Sino-South African conference, Human Sciences Research Council, Pretoria 1990.

[9] This section is based on *Integrated environmental management in South Africa* Council for the Environment (1989).

- the degree to which the possible effects on the human environment are highly uncertain or involve unique or unknown risks;
- the degree to which the action or impact is irreversible;
- the degree to which the action affects the availability or functioning of life support systems, natural amenities, cultural resources and other environmental goods, services and conditions which are considered to be of a special or unique character, in limited supply, or essentially irreplaceable;
- the degree to which the action violates the spirit or the letter of any law or statute;
- the degree to which the action may establish a precedent for future actions with significant effects or represents a decision in principle about an issue with significant implications;
- the degree to which the action is related to other actions or proposed actions which individually may have insignificant impacts but which cumulatively could result in significant impacts, and
- the degree to which social costs have been absorbed as private costs (eg that scrubbers are installed by a factory to ensure that its air pollution does not detrimentally impact on the livelihood of others).

Reviewers should ensure that the reasons for assigning significance are clearly indicated and justified in the reports so that an assessment of their validity can be made.

30.6.2 Cumulative impacts

Cumulative impacts can occur when:

- impacts on the environment take place so frequently in time or so densely in space that the effects cannot be assimilated by the environment, or
- impacts from one activity combine with those of another to produce a greater impact or a different impact (referred to as a synergistic effect).

Such effects can be local, regional or global in scale and typically across jurisdictional boundaries. As such, dealing with cumulative impacts usually requires co-ordinated institutional arrangements, which are sometimes difficult to achieve.

Most approaches to impact assessment are not well adapted to cope with these problems, as assessments tend to be carried out on specific developments. IEM does require the assessment of developments in terms of their regional context. However, the identification of cumulative impacts is a difficult task, often requiring much foresight on the part of consultants.

An additional problem is that cumulative impacts are often a result of broader social and economic policies which cannot be assessed at the project level. IEM recognizes the need to assess the impacts of policies and programmes as well as projects. However, a number of established policies are likely to remain of concern. The recommendation that IEM be integrated into the broader planning context in South Africa provides a framework within which the consideration of cumulative impacts may be encouraged.

30.6.3 Bias

The notion of biased or 'sweetheart' reports has been mentioned in section 30.5.4.2. The need to avoid bias should be borne in mind from the inception of the scoping process to the final production of reports. Clients may attempt to bias an assessment by placing restrictions on the scope of the study when formulating the terms of reference for the assessment. A common problem is the tendency for clients (and, at times, consultants) to omit an assessment of the social implications of a development.

A further concern is the reluctance to involve interested and affected parties, often due to doubt on behalf of professionals of the general public's ability meaningfully to contribute to project planning. Fuggle[10] notes:

'In no instance in our experience has a refusal to consider the views of affected parties helped the environmental evaluation process and led to quicker approval of the project under consideration. The exact opposite has usually resulted.'

30.6.4 Confidentiality

In South Africa there is a tendency for both private and public proponents to keep developments confidential. In the private sector, reasons given for secrecy include competitive advantage and concern that ideas may be stolen. The public sector proponent may be concerned about speculative actions in property or resources affected by prior knowledge of the project, which might not be in the public interest. The result is that as few people as possible are drawn into initial project planning, and often the authorities and environmental consultants are excluded.

This process leads inevitably to delays in approval and construction, as the authority is not in a position to provide adequate review or significant impacts may not have been identified. A further consequence is the loss of trust between the proponent and both the authority and the general public. While every effort should be made to ensure that proposals will be treated with confidence, the notification, public scoping and review stages are crucial elements of IEM.

At the same time, it should be recognized that the involvement of interested and affected parties in development planning requires an element of trust between all parties. Public access to information and draft reports is provided in good faith, and should not be used by organizations or individuals to manipulate public opinion or to serve hidden agendas. Special procedures may need to be established for the handling of particularly sensitive or controversial issues and proponents should have recourse to the courts if confidentiality is abused.

30.6.5 Legal status[11]

Although the Environment Conservation Act 73 of 1989 makes provision for the legal enforcement of IEM procedures, the required statement of policy, identification of activities, definition of limited development areas, as well as the necessary regulations have not yet materialized. See chapter 7. IEM procedures are thus being undertaken in South Africa on a voluntary basis rather than because of a legal framework. Nevertheless, both public-sector and private-sector project proponents have been following the Council for the Environment's IEM procedures, with very few exceptions. The reasons for this are varied, but include: policy directives requiring most state departments to comply with IEM procedures; social responsibility considerations by major corporations; advice to comply with IEM requirements by planning professionals; requirements of institutions providing finance for new developments.

The strong support professed for the IEM process by the President's Council, in its *Report on a national environmental management system*,[12] as well as the Department of the Environment's active preparation of IEM guideline documents, suggest that the Council for the Environment's recommendation that IEM should be legally enforceable is likely to find expression in the near future.

---

[10] Above n 8, 6.

[11] See, in respect of the legal implementation of aspects of IEM, Rabie 'Disclosure and evaluation of potential environmental impact of proposed governmental administrative action' 1976 *THRHR* 40; 'Strategies for the implementation of environmental impact assessment in South Africa' 1986 *SA Public Law* 18; Barnard 'Regsmaatstawwe by die beoordeling van projekte wat die omgewing kan benadeel' 1992 *THRHR* 35.

[12] PC 1/1991.

CHAPTER 31

ENVIRONMENTAL EVALUATION

R F FUGGLE

Environmental evaluations have become an established part of good development planning throughout the world. They were first formalized in the United States of America through the National Environmental Policy Act of 1969. This Act required the preparation of a formal statement documenting the consequences of any major Federal action on the environment. It also required that this environmental impact statement had to accompany all other documents through any decision-making process so as to ensure that the environmental consequences of projects, plans or programmes were considered together with economic and technical considerations. Such administrative reform legislation was subsequently emulated by most of the world's leading nations.

In South Africa an initiative by the Council for the Environment led to the formulation of the integrated environmental management (IEM) policy which is the subject of the preceding chapter. This chapter will explore the methods and techniques that may be used in the assessment stage of the IEM procedure.

31.1 ENVIRONMENTAL EVALUATIONS: PURPOSE AND DEFINITIONS

31.1.1 Purpose

The primary purposes of environmental evaluations are:

(1) to aid decision-making by providing objective information on the environmental consequences of actions, plans and projects.
(2) to provide sound, comprehensive data to inform and direct development planning.
(3) to analyse plans objectively so as to ensure that benefits are maximized and that negative effects are mitigated to the greatest extent possible.
(4) to propose solutions to problems that may arise through interactions between the environment and project actions.
(5) to communicate information as to the positive and negative effects of development proposals to both decision-makers and interested parties.

Several consequences flow from these purposes. First, the information needs of the decision-maker must be met by both the methods used and the report produced. Decision-making consists of formulating alternatives and selecting that which has the greatest net benefit to those affected. It follows that an environmental evaluation must be relative rather than absolute and that comparative analyses of equitable and reasonable alternatives should form the basis for the analysis. This point often goes unrecognized and environmental evaluations which are undertaken without explicit alternatives having been formulated are forced into comparing the proposed action with either the 'as is' situation or with a hypothetical alternative. This is seldom satisfactory. Evaluations which do not address alternatives within the purview of decision-makers are not serving their primary purpose and lead to the charge that environmental evaluations are superfluous or unhelpful. Similarly, the methods used in the evaluation must be capable of addressing alternatives. If assumptions, or the nature of variables, must be changed in order to accommodate analysis of different alternatives, the validity of later comparisons will be doubtful. Finally, the evaluation report must address the decision-maker's need for objective comparative information adequate for the judgement required. Compendia of technical material are not helpful.

A second consequence of the premise that environmental evaluations should be objective aids to decision-makers is that environmental evaluations must be free of sectional or personal bias (as far as this is humanly possible). This does not mean that only quantitative data can be used in environmental evaluations or that non-quantified analyses are suspect as many, if not most, important decisions in everyday social and business life are made without an analysis of numbers. But objectivity does imply balanced investigation and reporting of alternatives, and the use of methods and techniques that professional peers would consider valid. Various methods are usually used in different parts of an overall evaluation. For instance, laboratory tests may be appropriate for establishing chemical water quality while public opinion surveys may be appropriate for establishing the quality of a water body for recreational purposes. No method should be considered inherently superior to another because it is associated with a particular discipline.

In environmental evaluations it is usual to have methods and techniques from many disciplines occurring together. Each method must allow the subject specialist to assess the accuracy and credibility of a particular conclusion but should also be such as to allow laymen to judge the significance of the results. In essence this means that two components enter into each detailed assessment of a particular action on a specific element of the environment: there is a technical component and a social component. Sometimes the technical component is referred to as assessing the magnitude of the impact, ie assessment in material terms such as small or large. The social component, also referred to as assessment of significance, reflects an informed value-judgement as to the importance of a particular impact to society as a whole using criteria that most people will accept as reasonable. This judgement must reflect the values of the society affected and not those of the analyst if it is to be objective in the sense of being free from personal bias. In practice, subject specialists often attribute greater social significance to their subject than other people do. It is therefore advantageous to have multi-disciplinary teams working together on environmental evaluations, not only to cover individual subject specialties but to provide cross-disciplinary insights and assessments of the social significance of particular impacts. Civic leaders and opinion-formers should be brought into evaluations of the social significance of particular impacts.

In this section it has been indicated that environmental evaluations are not the same thing as technical reports or scientific papers. Environmental evaluations are aids to decision-making and planning and must contribute to judgements between alternative courses of action being made on the basis of both technical and social criteria. Environmental evaluations are not research projects to discover new knowledge; their aim is rather to assemble and evaluate existing information and provide sufficient supporting argument in an intelligible format to show how technical analyses and social judgements lead to a conclusion about the overall significance of choosing one alternative over another. The evaluation should ensure that the proposal is optimized so as to bring greatest benefit to those affected while at the same time minimizing undesirable consequences. It should also try to provide solutions to problems that are identified and not become merely a negative critical exercise aimed at preventing or delaying development proposals.

31.1.2 Definitions

31.1.2.1 *Environmental impact assessment and related terms*

A broad but useful definition of environmental evaluation has been given by Munn[1] as an activity designed to identify and predict the impact on mankind's health and

---

[1] Munn (ed) *Environmental impact assessment: principles and procedures* (2 ed, 1979).

well-being of legislative proposals, policies, programmes, projects and operational procedures, and to interpret and communicate information about the impacts.

As the term 'environmental evaluation' has such broad connotations, it has been redefined and other related terms have been introduced. *Environmental impact assessment* should be understood as the administrative or regulatory process by which the environmental impact of a project is determined. In South Africa the process is termed *integrated environmental management* (IEM). See chapter 30. Environmental assessment procedures, approaches, or methodologies are the conditions pertaining to the activity of conducting an environmental impact investigation (ie the conditions and terms of reference by which the impacts of a project are investigated, presented, incorporated into planning and, finally, considered by decision-makers). The nature of the process is normally defined by social values, administrative constraints and legal provisions. Details of the process vary considerably from country to country, but the underlying principles have much in common.

Environmental impact analysis is a process contained in environmental impact assessment (EIA) by which the environmental effects of a project are analysed. A method of environmental analysis describes a complete activity for analysing impacts within an environmental assessment and within the South African IEM process. Clark et al[2] reserve the term 'technique' for specialized procedures within environmental analysis which evaluate (rather than identify) impacts. Generally, techniques are procedures that prescribe to some portion only of an environmental analysis.

In the United States the documentary reports resulting from a particular environmental analysis or assessment are termed the *environmental impact statement*. This component of the environmental assessment projects the process into the decision-making arena. In other countries the formal documentation of an environmental investigation are known by different names. In South Africa the IEM process requires the preparation and presentation of *initial assessment reports* or *impact assessment reports* as the outcome of environmental evaluations.

31.1.2.2 *Types of impacts*

Environmental analysis has been defined as a process aimed at the recognition of causes and effects, a cause being any action of the proposed project which has an effect upon the environment. These effects are the consequences of the action. Any effect in the bio-physical and socio-economic environments that arises from a cause directly related to the project is termed a *first-order or primary impact*.

Secondary impacts are those effects on the bio-physical and socio-economic environments which arise from an action but which are not initiated directly by that action. Their nature is determined by pre-existing linkages or interdependencies which exist in the system.

Figure 31.1 symbolically traces the secondary impacts which could arise from the dredging and filling of an estuarine mudflat (supposing that the proposed project was the construction of a marina). The top row of rectangles shows a set of environmental components linked by various dependencies (the second row of boxes). The way in which the primary impact of dredging and filling the mudflats affects all the components is shown as a progression of causes and effects (in rows three and four). Note that the commercial facilities component of the socio-economic system has a fourth-order dependency on salt-marsh plants. Similarly, the action of dredging and filling the mudflats has a fifth-order impact upon commercial facilities.

While secondary impacts are propagated by existing linkages in a system, *induced secondary impacts* occur when a project introduces new linkages, allowing a

[2] *Assessment of major industrial applications: a manual* (1976).

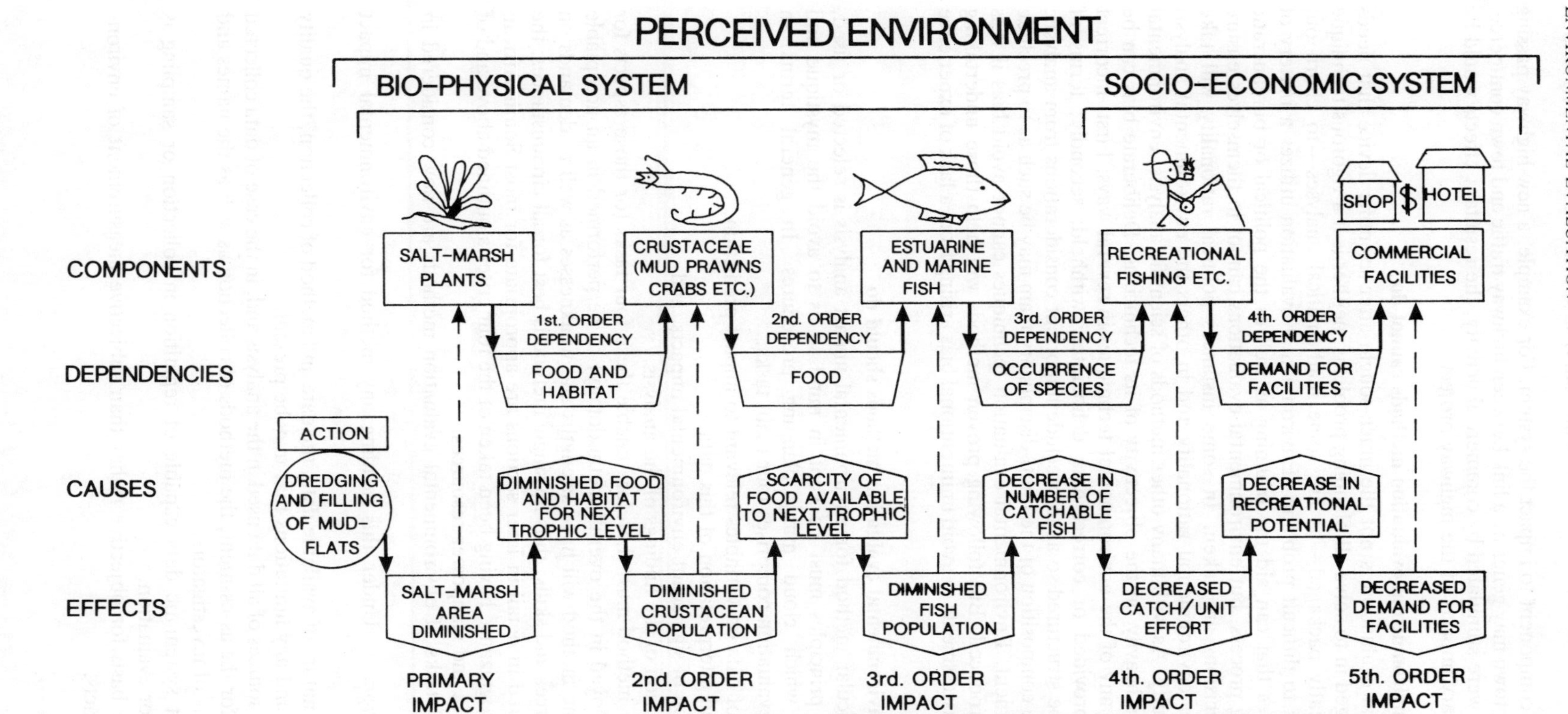

Figure 31.1 Symbolic representation of the secondary impacts which could arise from the dredging and filling of an estuarine mudflat. The relationships between environmental components, their interdependencies, and the causes and effects of secondary impacts are illustrated.

now-connected component to impact the system. For example, a new highway passing near an existing town may generate a link between highway traffic and town commerce. If town growth were stimulated by commercial activity, the resultant effects would be induced secondary impacts of the highway project.

31.1.3 What environmental evaluation methods cannot do

Environmental evaluation is not the much-sought-after scientific device that needs only to be plugged in to solve all planning problems; neither is it a rigorous technique that can be neatly packaged—as are some mathematical analyses—to churn out specific answers to difficult problems. Environmental evaluation utilizes a battery of useful techniques that can aid the planning as well as the political or bureaucratic decision-making process, but environmental evaluations cannot in themselves ensure that correct decisions are taken. In some instances political rationality will take precedence over environmental rationality and in others the environmental analysis itself may be faulty. As with many other methods of scientific analysis, environmental evaluation relies heavily on the objectivity of its technicians. Deliberate bias can be introduced into any of the environmental techniques in several ways. First, incorrect data may be provided or correct data deliberately withheld; secondly, terms of reference may be structured so as to preclude important considerations from analysis; and, thirdly, the composition of the multi-disciplinary team may be such as to preclude balanced judgement. Environmental evaluation techniques cannot avoid bias if it is deliberately introduced. But following proven methods will help those undertaking environmental assessments to avoid unintentional bias arising from a lack of experience or carelessness.

31.1.4 What environmental evaluation methods should do

When a particular method for environmental impact analysis is selected or used, certain general principles must be kept in mind so as to avoid the mystique and pseudo-science which cloud many planning procedures. In general terms an environmental evaluation comprises four main tasks:

(a) Collection of data on variables relevant to impact prediction;
(b) Analysis and interpretation of this data;
(c) Identification of significant environmental impacts, and
(d) Communication of the findings of the analysis.

A satisfactory method must therefore enable these four tasks (or those aspects for which it is employed in the overall methodology) to be performed in an acceptable manner. Any one method will have strengths and weaknesses as well as demands on particular resources and skills; thus no single method is best for all circumstances: the methods presented in detail in later sections are appropriate for most South African situations, due cognizance having been taken of the four criteria outlined above and of the country's data and manpower resources.

These general tasks of environmental evaluation methods are now considered in greater detail.

(a) Data collection. Under this heading any method for environmental impact analysis should:

(i) Outline the nature of available data, the date and method of collection, the quality of the data and any limitations that may be present.
(ii) Identify the sources of all data used in the analysis and, in the case of data collected specifically for the assessment, the methods of collection as well as the names and qualifications of investigators.
(iii) Ensure that systematic data capable of repetition in collection or sampling is employed for evaluation.
(iv) Provide the basis for objective rather than subjective measurement of environmental impacts.

(b) Analysis and interpretation. Analysis and interpretation should:

(i) Assess the significance of measured or postulated impacts.
(ii) State explicitly the criteria and assumptions employed to determine impact significance.
(iii) Indicate the degree of confidence or amount of uncertainty inherent in any impact project.
(iv) Identify areas of potential risk or hazard, i e impacts of low probability but high deleterious effect should they occur.
(v) Allow for the comparison of alternatives, including the no-project alternative.
(vi) Indicate clearly and unambiguously any weighting systems that may be used to aggregate impacts or to place them in rank order.
(vii) Allow for the involvement of interested parties and the public in a responsible manner.

(c) Impact identification. Any method used in environmental evaluation should be:

(i) *Comprehensive:* the method must encourage a review of the full range of environmental impacts associated with a given project or plan (and relevant alternatives), including secondary or induced impacts. Lateral thinking must be encouraged and tunnel vision prevented.
(ii) *Precise:* particular actions (e g blasting) and specific environmental elements (e g rock outcrops) must be identified and used for assessment. General categories of action (e g road construction) or environment (e g farmland) should be avoided.
(iii) *Project-specific:* the method must separate project or plan impacts—primary or secondary—from environmental changes due to other factors.
(iv) *Accurate:* location, time and duration of impacts must be identified. *Time* relates to the phase of the project or plan which will cause the impacts—site preparation, infrastructure, construction operation or shut-down, and *duration* refers to the time period over which the impacts will occur.
(v) *Consistent*: the method must be free from analyst bias so that broadly the same assessment of a project or plan will be made by different analysts using the same method.
(vi) *Adaptable:* the method must be capable of identifying impacts from a variety of projects in different types of environment.

(d) Communication. It is important that any environmental evaluation method should:

(i) Provide a format for highlighting key issues and impacts identified in the analysis.
(ii) Identify affected parties and indicate the extent of gains and losses.
(iii) Provide details of the project's setting (geographic areas, sites of special scientific, historic or scenic interest, current land-uses, communities or social groups affected) to aid readers, reviewers and decision-makers.
(iv) Outline the reason for the development. This should not be a superficial statement but should indicate underlying social, economic or land-use goals.
(v) Enable the main arguments and findings of the study to be communicated intelligibly to the general public and elected representatives, whilst also providing the additional technical content necessary for competent specialists to formulate informed views on the analysis.
(vi) Indicate the extent to which remedial measures to minimize or offset negative impacts are possible and are planned.

31.2 A SHORT SURVEY OF METHODS OF EVALUATION

31.2.1 Checklist and matrix methods

Checklists and matrices are the most frequently used tools of environmental evaluation. Both methods are designed to stimulate thought about possible consequences of specific actions and so ensuring comprehensiveness as well as precision in analysis. The methods are simple to use and do not require extensive material or manpower resources.

31.2.1.1 *Checklists*

These are comprehensive lists of structured questions related to environmental parameters and specific human actions. They help to order thinking, aid data collection and presentation and alert against the omission of possible impacts. Despite their usefulness as an *aide-mémoire*, the more comprehensive and precise, and consequently lengthy, they become, the less useful they are in other respects, viz project specificity, adaptability, and the ability to highlight key issues.

Checklists contain a set of environmental elements and actions. Since these are determined prior to a study of the area, these questions provide a static picture of possible relations between a development and its environmental setting. The structure of most checklists suggests that a project or plan has only direct effects, though this drawback can be overcome by extending the questionnaire to cover secondary effects. A major drawback of checklists is their lack of help in highlighting the structure of linkages between environmental parameters and between specific actions and environmental elements.

By providing predetermined lists, checklists omit an important preliminary step—the task of environmental description. By identifying the important relations in, say, an ecosystem, impact investigation can relate specific development actions to these important relationships and use information on the ecosystem to follow the ramifications of changes in these relationships throughout the system. In this manner high-order impacts can be recognized. The same argument applies to the description of social, economic or cultural systems.

Predetermined lists also have the propensity to lead investigators through an analysis in a set manner, thus possibly influencing their perception of problems. Items not on the list may also be ignored. Similarly, they do not provide a means for identifying impacts considered important by the public or interested parties. Checklists are also deficient in that they cannot readily provide information on the timing and duration of impacts or on aspects of risk or uncertainty.

As a vehicle for communication checklists are poor. The text of questions and answers is the sole means of information transfer and no separation of material for general and technical assessment occurs. Finally, checklists provide no guidance for the interpretation of impacts and there is no indication to reviewers of the analyst's reasons for arriving at specific answers.

Checklists alone therefore have severe limitations. Their most useful features are as *aides-mémoire* and as bases for constructing cause–effect matrices.

31.2.1.2 *The Leopold matrix*[3]

This approach to impact analysis was developed by Dr Luna Leopold and others of the United States Geological Survey in 1971. Although derived from a checklist approach, the simple expedient of dividing the checklist into *two data sets* (one related to environmental elements and the other to human actions) and arranging the two sets at right angles so as to form a cross-tabulation, or matrix, greatly expanded the scope and usefulness of checklists.

The original Leopold system listed 100 project actions along the horizontal axis and 88 environmental elements on the vertical axis, thus identifying 8 800 possible interactions between actions and environment on a single sheet of paper. The method

---

[3] Leopold et al *US Geological Survey circular* no 645 (1971).

is thus exceptionally comprehensive and precise and incorporates fundamental information on first-order cause–effect relationships. The format is also useful for highlighting areas of particular concern, of high risk or where further investigations are required. The method is also highly adaptable to various projects and environments.

The matrix is used by considering each action involved in the project against each environmental characteristic of the area. All cells which represent a possible impact are marked with a diagonal line and evaluated individually. Each marked cell is then scored twice, once from a technical perspective of the scale or magnitude of the impact, and in the second instance in terms of the social importance (significance) of the impact. A high score represents the greatest impact and a low score the least. Plus signs are used to identify beneficial impacts and minus signs negative impacts. Leopold's original scheme is not explicit on how the matrix should be used beyond this point. It is nevertheless evident that the matrix format lends itself to displaying, through numbers, symbols or shadings, cells with above-average impact, importance, risk or uncertainty. One matrix with numerous entries or several matrices with single characteristics can be used. Similarly, the timing, duration and probability of particular actions on specific environmental elements can be readily displayed.

Despite these considerable advantages, the method does fail to fulfil several of the features desirable in an impact assessment methodology (see section 31.1.4). Criticisms have centred on the apparent complexity and unfamiliar format, the focus on first-order interactions and on the numerical scoring system. Other omissions to note are: the failure to address aspects of data collection—the nature, sources and reliability of data must be discussed in an accompanying text; the lack of explicitly stated assumptions; the inability to involve the public; and no consideration of reasons for development or affected parties except as considered in a supplementary text. Separate matrices must also be prepared for each alternative project and also for each time horizon evaluated; evaluation of alternatives is therefore difficult because of the large number of matrices involved. The method is also incapable of indicating the spatial characteristics of likely impacts. Finally, the consistency of matrix evaluations can be questioned, because the scoring system requires subjective estimates of magnitude and significance without the aid of specific guidelines or standardized weightings. No objective total score for each matrix can be derived, making comparison between matrices a subjective matter even if based on the number of cells marked and on their numerical value.

31.2.2 Overlays and mapping methods

The use of maps in land-use planning is a sine qua non, and the superimposition of maps showing different characteristics of an area, in order to see spatial coincidence and variations is a very old technique. In 1968 Ian McHarg formalized the method when advocating its use for highway route selection; this was reinforced in his influential book *Design with nature* (1969), in which he outlines the method as follows:

'[The method] consists, in essence, of identifying both social and natural processes as social values. We will agree that land and building values do reflect a price value system, we can also agree that for institutions that have no market value there is still a hierarchy of values . . . so too with natural processes. It is not difficult to agree that different rocks have a variety of compressive strengths and thus offer both values and penalties for building; that some areas are subject to inundation during hurricanes and others are immune; that certain soils are more susceptible to erosion than others. Additionally, there are comparative measures of water quantity and quality, and soil drainage characteristics. It is possible to rank forest or marsh quality in terms of species, numbers, age and health in order of value. Wildlife habitats, scenic quality, the importance of historic buildings, recreational facilities can all be ranked.

. . . For instance, let us map physiographic factors so that the darker the tone, the greater the cost. Let us similarly map social values so that the darker the tone, the higher the value. Let us make the maps transparent. When these are superimposed, the least social-cost areas are revealed by the lightest tone.'

The approach has been elaborated and modified by many users so that the basic technique may now find expression through computer simulation, multi-coloured printed maps or in map transparencies. The basic tasks of parameter selection, internal ranking, and between parameter weighting nevertheless remain consistent. Computer manipulation merely permits greater data manipulation and flexibility, while cartographic technique influences locational accuracy and subjective assessments of the final maps. The rapidly evolving technology associated with geographical information systems (GIS) has provided a sophisticated computer-based way of generating and superimposing mapped data for present-day users of the technique.

When viewed against the ideal criteria for environmental impact analyses, overlay methods are weak in many respects, but strong in others. Their two main strengths are the explicit prediction of spatial patterns, and the direct, familiar presentation of summarized data in a form that can be interpreted without difficulty. Other positive features are the ease with which project alternatives can be considered whenever spatial relationships are important, and the method's effectiveness in communicating the number, types and location of affected parties. On the negative side the method's main drawbacks are its lack of comprehensiveness and precision and its inability to consider non-spatial variables or second- or third-order interactions. Uncertainties in data or impact predictions cannot be accommodated and the implicit assumptions underpinning rankings and weightings are well hidden from the uninitiated: though methods which include coded keys indicating parameter values on which particular map shadings are based partially overcome the latter problem.

The difficulties of this method hinge on impact identification, prediction and weighting procedures. These are precisely the major problems when EIAs are required. It is for these reasons that overlays are best suited to initial pre-planning studies of possible routes and locations when no attempt is made to investigate the detailed impacts of each route or site on the surrounding area. The method may also be useful after a detailed impact analysis has been completed to aid in the resolution of problems highlighted by other methods. The method's greatest strength lies in its ability to provide a summarized visual impression of the suitability of an area for a particular type of development.

31.2.3 Panel evaluation techniques[4]

The Delphi technique was pioneered by Olaf Helmer at the Rand Corporation and is designed to encourage consensus from a panel of evaluators on issues or questions which cannot be evaluated in a classical quantitative sense. The opinions of these experts are usually subjective, albeit guided by some objective background; they can best be described as informed judgements. A number of approaches could be used to obtain expert opinion. One extreme is using a single expert, the other is the use of a committee—which is based on the premise that many opinions are better than one. Committees have many drawbacks, vocal minorities or dominant individuals have undue influence, individuals are unwilling publicly to change their minds or to contradict persons in higher positions, and, where opinions differ strongly, polarization of views rather than consensus is usual.

By the use of panel evaluation methods direct exchanges of views amongst experts

[4] See, for example, Hart & Cullen *Search* (1976); Mathews *Environmental conservation* (1975); Dee et al 'An environmental evaluation system for water resource planning' 1973 (9) *Water Resources Research* 523; Golden et al *Environmental impact data book* (1979); Stauth 'A methodology for determining the socially optimum uses of estuarine resources' Research Report 32, School of Environmental Studies, University of Cape Town (1982).

are avoided and a strong iterative feedback system is used to keep team members informed on a group's thinking. This procedure ensures anonymity of opinions and thus eliminates the risks of dominant personalities, desires for conformity and peer acceptance. The result is a convergence of expert opinion without individual bias. In an environmental context a panel may be asked to assign weightings to environmental parameters. Participants are asked to give their best informed judgement in answering and the reasons for their opinions. These are submitted in writing to a co-ordinator, edited and fed back to the panellists together with some indication of the spread of responses. The panellists are then required to repeat the procedure. Successive iterations narrow the spread of responses and approach consensus. Sometimes weighted voting schemes are introduced as an aid in assessing panel response, but this is not essential.

The best known system for impact analysis based on this approach is the *Environmental Evaluation System*, designed by the Battelle, Columbus Laboratories in the United States. This is one of the most complex and detailed quantitative methods devised for EIA purposes. In principle it is adaptable to a wide variety of projects and environments, but in practice the fact that new weighting schemes must be devised for different environments and different applications limit its use.

The method is based on two weighting systems obtained by Delphi procedures. First, all environmental parameters are weighted according to their relative importance, a checklist of environmental parameters together with associated importance units results. Secondly, value functions are derived for each parameter in order to convert appropriate measured values into environmental quality units on a 0 to 1 scale, (eg a dissolved oxygen concentration of 6 mg/ℓ transforms into an environmental quality score of 0,7). Thus, starting from an objective measured value, environmental quality units are determined and multiplied by the associated parameter importance units to yield Environmental Impact Units. Since all parameters can be converted into these units, the values obtained can be summed to provide a total score for all impacts. Alternative projects can thus be directly compared while individual problem areas are highlighted. The latter is achieved by marking potential problem areas in a final summary table with 'red flags'. When a red flag is assigned, the problem area must be investigated in detail.

As the method starts from a checklist all the difficulties of comprehensiveness and precision that relate to checklists apply. Also, as the method uses discrete parameters in isolation, interactions and chains of relations between parameters are not considered. The method also ignores uncertainty, risks and remedial measures, and no account is taken of affected parties or public opinion. The method does not overcome problems of timing, duration and spatial location of impact, nor is it particularly useful for communication with those unfamiliar with the method's output tables.

The strengths of the procedure lie in its high degree of objectivity as value-functions are standardized and are public knowledge, as are the weights assigned to particular environmental parameters. The numerical weighting system is explicit, permitting the calculation of a project impact for each alternative. Although any weighting system will be controversial, this one is developed from systematic studies and its rationale is documented; furthermore, small changes in weightings do not cause wide fluctuations in final scores. The method has much to recommend it, but its lack of adaptability and heavy demands on resources will limit widespread applications particularly for preliminary studies.

31.3 METHODS SUITABLE FOR USE IN SOUTH AFRICA

31.3.1 Introduction

These methods outlined below are intended to assist persons in both the planning and conservation professions who wish, or are required, to undertake a preliminary study of possible environmental effects which may be associated with a particular development project. The object of such studies is to ensure that all benefits and problems associated with a project are exposed and considered. The methods advocated are not a panacea for those wishing to avoid the necessity of making political, social or moral choices: they will only ensure that better informed planning is undertaken and that decisions are made with knowledge of possible environmental impacts. Similarly, the methods proposed do not provide explicit solutions to the problems they identify; they rather identify problem areas, thereby facilitating the search for solutions by appropriate technical experts.

It must also be stressed that the methods are not intended for use by individuals attempting to solve problems on their own. The methods anticipate analysis by a small multi-disciplinary team co-ordinated by a team leader. The methods will promote co-ordinated and disciplined thinking on complex issues and should promote both professional and public confidence in decisions which utilize them. The methods must not be regarded as tests of the acceptability of proposals but should be introduced early in the planning and formulation stages of a project so that adequate attention can be given to problems which they identify. Used in this way the methods should reduce delays in projects approval and will minimize controversial issues detrimental to the image of the project and its promoters.

31.3.2 The Cross-tabulation or matrix approach

This section describes more fully an approach to preliminary assessment of potential environmental impacts which should be easily applicable in South Africa. (Section 31.2.1.2 should be read as an introduction to this section.)

31.3.2.1 *General features and formats*

The cross-tabulation of specific environmental characteristics and specific human actions provides an easy way of focusing thinking on to particular issues which may cause concern in a development project. The format also provides a useful means for displaying and summarizing a lot of information that will be required by those assessing the project at a later stage. The method will not provide final solutions to environmental problems, but it will identify problem areas in a precise way, allowing effort to be applied constructively in overcoming specific rather than nebulous problems.

The essential feature of the physical format is two lists (one of environmental characteristics and one of human actions) arranged at right angles to one another along two edges of a simple ruled grid. The grid cells may be square if the lists are of approximately equal length, or rectangular if one list is longer than the other, this being immaterial. An example of a matrix format which has been used in South Africa appears in Figure 31.2.

For any particular project each list will probably contain between 30 and 50 items relevant to local environmental characteristics and to actions associated with the project. In highly diverse environments with a variety of features 50 environmental characteristics may be inadequate, but in a simple uniform landscape 20 elements may be sufficient. Similarly, a small-scale single-phased project may be adequately described by 20 or so activities, while a large, complex multi-stage project might best be handled by compiling activity lists separately for each phase—site preparation and infrastructure, construction, operation—with 20 or so elements in each list rather than using one list of 70 or 80 elements.

In practice it has been found desirable to work with grid cells at least 1 cm square, or 2 cm wide and 0,5 cm high. Smaller cells make data entry difficult and confuse the eye.

Sheets of standard A3 size accommodate a 30 × 50 matrix with ease and if the matrix is compiled to this format, reproduction of copies of the matrix is straightforward. Larger sizes make handling as well as reproduction more difficult.

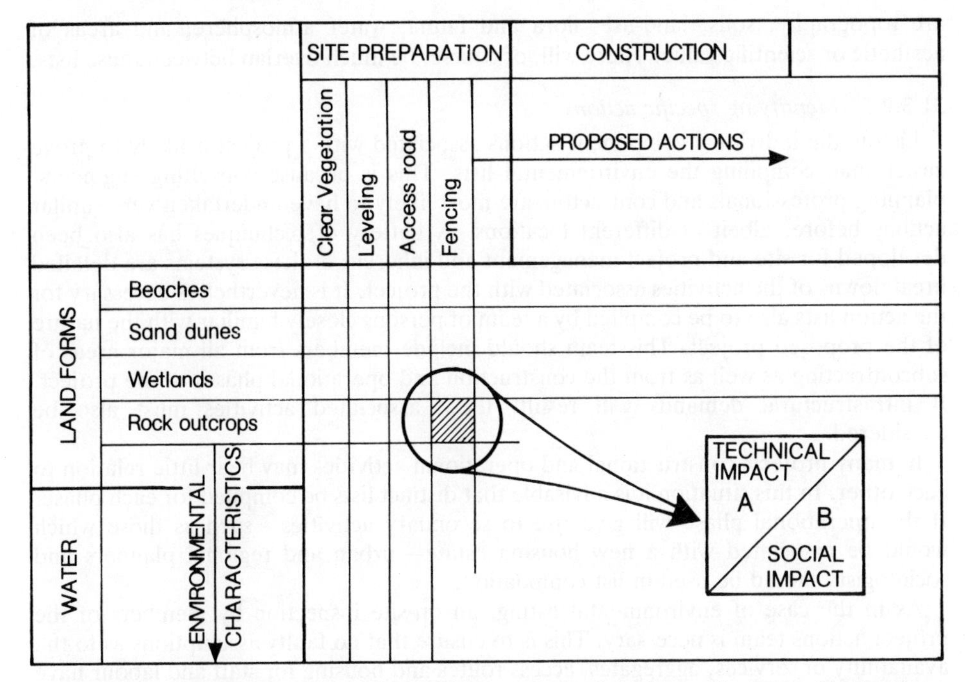

Figure 31.2 A simplified matrix format with an example of the Leopold system of evaluation.

31.3.2.2 *Identifying environmental elements*

Identification of environmental characteristics cannot be undertaken in an abstract way by someone merely extracting items from a checklist without first-hand knowledge. Checklists may, however, prove helpful in jogging the memory following on-site inspections by a small group of persons with an 'eye for country' from different professional backgrounds. This feeling for the intricacies of the environment may stem from formal training or from extensive practical experience. The listing of environmental elements should thus be undertaken by a small interdisciplinary team of persons with appropriate backgrounds after they have made on-the-spot inspections of the site and surrounding areas.

The study leader or co-ordinator will usually have sufficient knowledge of the site and of any particularly sensitive issues to make an initial choice of the types of backgrounds required. This initial team must then be told specifically to recommend the addition of any other fields of expertise which they view as important and in which they lack competence. The final team is unlikely to exceed four or five individuals except in very complex environments.

Before the first site inspection by the environmental team a thorough objective briefing on the nature of the project should be given. No attempt should be made to focus on expected problems, nor to exclude these from review. An analysis of project actions detail by detail will follow later, but it is imperative that those selecting the environmental elements have knowledge of the scale and types of activity contemplated so as to adopt the appropriate scale and frame of reference when viewing the area likely to be affected. No attempt should be made, at this stage, to delimit the area thought to be of concern nor to bias the environmental listings by deliberately excluding any topics from consideration. It should be recognized that in urban areas environmental considerations will include such items as services, safety, health, psychological well-being, community structure and organization, historic and cultural sites, and visual quality. In rural areas the features of the environment that are likely to be paramount are topography, soils, land-use, flora and fauna, water atmosphere, and areas of aesthetic or scientific value. There will, of course, be much overlap between these lists.

31.3.2.3 *Identifying specific actions*

Listing the individual component actions associated with a project is likely to prove easier than compiling the environmental lists. This is because consulting engineers, planning professionals and contractors are most likely to have undertaken very similar actions before, albeit at different locations. A battery of techniques has also been developed for site and project management and inherent in these systems are detailed breakdowns of the activities associated with the project. It is nevertheless necessary for the action lists also to be compiled by a team of persons closely familiar with the nature of the proposed project. This team should include members from all major areas of subcontracting as well as from the construction and operational phases of the project. If infrastructural demands will result, these associated activities must also be considered.

In many projects constructional and operational activities may bear little relation to each other. In this situation it is advisable that distinct lists be compiled for each phase. If the operational phase will give rise to secondary activities—such as those which would be associated with a new housing estate—urban and regional planners and sociologists should be used in list compilation.

As in the case of environmental listing, an on-site inspection by members of the project actions team is necessary. This is to ensure that no faulty assumptions as to the availability of services, aggregates, access routes and housing for staff and labour have been made and that all essential supporting activities will be appropriately listed. It should be remembered that it is not unusual for environmental damage to be caused more by poorly planned supporting activities (e g roads and quarries) than by the main project. All associated activities should therefore appear on the list of actions compiled by the planning professionals.

31.3.2.4 *Assessment*

After the lists of environmental characteristics and project actions have been brought together to form the final matrix, the assessment of the impact of each action on each element of the environment can proceed. If the final matrix is, say, 30 × 30, 900 cells will have to be considered. In practice about one-third of these will represent the valid interaction of environment and activity and will need evaluation. Allowing an average of, say, 2 minutes per cell, some 10 hours will be required for this preliminary evaluation. Adequate time must be allowed for this procedure or the entire exercise may lose validity.

It is highly desirable that the majority, if not all, of the members of the teams that compiled the component lists, should participate in the assessment procedure. On no account should anyone not intimately familiar with the project and its setting attempt to do so. A co-ordinator will be required to lead the assessment panel through its deliberations and to record group decisions and disagreements.

31.3.2.5 *Entries in matrix cells*

For each matrix cell the potential impacts can be assessed in terms of importance, probability, time of occurrence, duration, benefit, effect of remedial measures, and risk. This information can be entered in each cell by means of appropriate symbols, letters or numbers. In a rectangular cell a string of digits in a fixed order is used, while digits in fixed locations are employed in square cells.

(a) Importance. The subjective judgement of the evaluation team as to the significance that a particular action on a specific environmental characteristic has for the environment as a whole. A numerical scale from 1 (minor importance) to 5 (major

importance) is used. In the event of inadequate information on which to form judgement, or in the event of no consensus being reached, a ? is used. Importance should be assessed, assuming planned remedial measures—if any—to be operative.

(b) Probability. An assessment of the degree of certainty underlying the potential impact. A letter is used to denote the degree of confidence: C - certain occurrence; P - probable occurrence; U - unlikely occurrence; ? - unable to assess.

(c) Time of occurrence. An indication of when the impact will be felt. A letter is used to indicate timing: I - immediate effect; D - delayed effect; L - long-term effect. The time horizons associated with each of these divisions must be defined in the accompanying text.

(d) Duration. An indication of whether the effect will be transient (T), of short or temporary duration (S), or final (permanent) (F). These terms must be precisely defined in the accompanying text.

(e) Benefit. An assessment or whether the effect will be beneficial (+), detrimental (-) or undeterminable (?).

(f) Remedial measures. An indication of whether remedial measures have been planned; Y - Yes; N - No. (Importance should be assessed assuming remedial measures to be operative.)

(g) Risk. An assessment of high risk associated with an impact of low probability of occurrence. Denoted by the symbol (!).

Other symbols can be employed, if desired, to indicate that a particular primary impact will give rise to significant secondary impacts (*), or to indicate that the impact in a particular cell is a second-order or induced impact rather than the direct effect of an action on an environmental element (″).

31.3.2.6 *Review of completed matrix*

A completed matrix is no more than a detailed record of an evaluation team's judgements on a wide range of issues relevant to the environmental implications of a project. Unfortunately no objective quantitative index can be formulated to indicate the degree of acceptability of the project. Review of the completed matrix will nevertheless reveal precise areas of concern. This concern might be occasioned by a number of reasons: identification of major impacts (scores of 4 or 5); inability to reach decisions or inadequate data (occurrence of question marks); areas of risk (!); or because no remedial measures are planned for certain impacts. Attention can therefore be focused on each specific problem area in turn to resolve difficulties. Matters shown to be non-contentious or insignificant need no longer be of concern.

Apart from the consideration of individual cells, a matrix review must also look at the total effects of specific actions, and total effects on particular environmental characteristics. This is done by considering each row and column of the matrix as an entity. Environmental elements subject to numerous small impacts which could cumulatively be of significance might consequently be seen; or, similarly, an action of no particular significance might be seen to have a widespread low-key effect. Actions or environmental characteristics subject to several elements of risk may also be identified.

31.3.2.7 *Presentation*

A completed matrix contains so much information that it will confound almost everyone if presented unaccompanied by summary formats, preferably in both written and matrix form.

Presentation of a *summary matrix* is strongly recommended. The same matrix as is used for scoring is employed, but only those cells giving rise to significant concern are completed, preferably by coloured shading. Problem areas (cells), may thus be coloured red, cells for which inadequate data are available could be shaded orange, asterisks or hazards yellow. The attention of the user is thus focused immediately on problems which have been identified and he is made aware of the cause of concern in general terms. It is also recommended that *summary sheets* or paragraphs be prepared for each cell shaded on a summary matrix. Summary sheets provide means of drawing together all available technical information on the particular topic. These sheets should present all relevant information in concise writing understandable to all interested parties. They should contain objective statements of facts, as accurately as they can be determined, followed by a concise statement of the reasons for particular concern.

While it is possible that a fully completed matrix, a summary matrix, and summary sheets are all that may be required for internal preliminary assessments of potential environmental impact, it is nevertheless highly desirable that these items be contained in a report containing additional information. This is to ensure that the environmental impact analysis is seen in proper context by others who may gain access to the evaluation, as well as to preserve a record of all factors which influenced the evaluation. It is recommended that a *report* should contain the following components:[5]

(a) An outline of the reasons for the development project.
(b) A description of the nature of the development project.
(c) A description of the environmental setting of the development, including maps.
(d) A statement of the nature, sources and quality of data used.
(e) The identification of all persons involved in the evaluation, with details of their experience and qualifications.
(f) An explicit statement of all assumptions employed in the evaluation.
(g) A fully completed matrix (or matrices).
(h) A summary matrix (or matrices).
(i) Summary sheets.
(j) A review of the problems revealed by the analysis.
(k) A conclusion.

31.3.3 The environmental mapping or overlay approach

This section outlines an approach to environmental impact analysis particularly useful for the selection of routes or sites for development. (Section 31.3.2 should be read as an introduction to this section.)

31.3.3.1 *General feature*

The overlay or environmental mapping approach is, as the name suggests, based on maps, and the ultimate locational accuracy and impact of the technique are largely determined by technical cartographic skills and resources. The use of modern computer-based geographical information systems may, however, make for easy manipulation of mapped data on different scales and in different formats, thus leading to a renewal of interest in the method.

Various environmental characteristics relevant to the selection of a physical location for a project are first classified according to suitability for the project, a value scale ranging from highly favourable to highly unfavourable is employed. A map is then compiled for a particular characteristic, say soil type, and the areas falling into each category are identified and coloured or shaded. A separate map is drawn for each environmental characteristic evaluated. Finally, all maps are overlayed one on another, physically if transparent bases are used, or a composite map can be generated in a computer, and a project suitability map derived from a study of the suitability of the combined components.

---

[5] See also section 30.5.3.

31.3.3.2 *Selecting data for mapping*

The overlay method of site evaluation is extremely sensitive to what components of the environment are selected for mapping. The method becomes increasingly unwieldy as the numbers of controlling factors mount, and 10 or 12 factors can be considered the maximum number of components practically feasible. Most overlay evaluations use fewer maps than this. It is therefore essential that those components which are mapped represent the key issues amongst which site evaluation must be resolved. This cannot be achieved by selecting components for mapping from a standard checklist, nor can it be done by reference to the criteria mapped in different studies of a similar nature. First-hand on-site knowledge of the terrain must be acquired by a small team of competent observers from different backgrounds in relevant disciplines. These backgrounds will differ depending on the nature of the environment to be studied, but at least one person should be present from each of the geological, ecological and sociological sciences, with experts from agriculture and architecture being drawn in as required.

After the initial site inspection by the environmental team, it is imperative that the team be asked to identify any areas in which they feel ill-equipped to advise, and assistance from appropriate additional experts must be sought. Without an initial site appraisal from a wide range of possible viewpoints, a highly biased study may ultimately emerge due to particular important issues being ignored at the start of the study.

Following on-site inspections and team agreement that all relevant aspects are appreciated, team selection of controlling factors is undertaken. This is essentially a subjective decision and no fixed guideline exists on how this should be done, though Delphi-type is recommended (see section 31.2.3). A suggested procedure is that each of the team independently list the 10 factors that they personally consider critical to that particular site selection. These lists are co-ordinated by someone assisting the team—with five team members, 15 to 20 different factors are likely to appear. This co-ordinated list should now be referred back to the team with the instruction that each member study the list and rank the 10 criteria they consider to be most important in descending order. After this is done, the co-ordinator allocates points to each item on each list—top-ranked criteria scoring 10 points, down to 1 point for the last criterion appearing on each list. The number of points voted for each controlling factor is then added up, and a ranked listing of factors selected by the panel results. A subjective decision must now be taken as to the cut-off point below which factors will not be mapped: the consolidated votes cast for each factor as well as a consideration of balance and completeness should enable this decision to be made without undue difficulty.

31.3.3.3 *Evaluation*

Once the most important controlling factors have been identified, the *first stage of evaluation* is to decide on the criteria to be employed to map each factor in terms of its suitability for development. In some circumstances objective physical measurements (angle of slope, depth to bedrock) can be used as a basis from which to obtain measures of suitability. Thus slopes of 0–2° may be considered 'highly favourable', 2,1–5° 'favourable', 5,1– 7,5° 'unfavourable' and over 7,5° 'highly unfavourable'. Similarly, price, rateable value, or some other numerical economic indicator could be used to rank land values. Land selling at R5 000 per hectare, therefore, may be considered too expensive and thus 'highly unfavourable' for development, while a price of below R500 might be considered 'highly favourable'. It is essential to realize that in these instances it is the validity of the criteria used to convert the quantitative data to rank orders that is important and not the fact that the rank orders are derived from numerical data. If the conversion values, which are subjective, are wrong or incorrectly used, the resulting maps also lose their validity. For other controlling factors no simple numerical measure is available from which to derive ranked values. Scenic quality, historic importance or ecological value may therefore not easily reduce to 'highly favourable', 'favourable' or 'unfavourable' for a particular type of development, but provided the criteria used to make such value judgements are valid, the resulting maps will be just as valid as maps derived from quantitative data.

There is no standard or generally accepted way to evaluate controlling factors in terms of suitability for development. In certain fields professional experience is the best guide and collective opinions will be worthless (eg relating geological data to foundation stability, or diversity indices to ecological value), but in other fields collective public opinion will be all important—as, for example, in assessing amenity values of recreational areas, or the scenic quality of particular vistas. Here professional help from those with expertise in sociological survey techniques may be required. The precise formulation of the criteria to be used to evaluate each controlling factor in terms of suitability for development must therefore be carried out by the appropriate members of the study team with outside professional advice being sought when necessary. These criteria must be recorded, as the validity of this method depends heavily on the correctness of these value judgements.

The *second stage of evaluation* is the production of suitability maps for each of the controlling factors which have been selected. Data from aerial photographs, field surveys, opinion polls and published sources must be collated and represented on a base map in terms of suitability for the proposed development. The scale of the maps and the accuracy with which boundaries between rankings need be placed will be determined largely by the size of the area being studied and on the nature of the development project. Map scales are in general unlikely to be smaller than 1:50 000 and the accuracy of boundaries will in most instances be poor, especially for such values as scenic quality where the true situation is one of gradual change rather than abrupt transition at a line on a map.

The *third stage of evaluation* is the synthesis of the component maps into a project suitability map. This may be done in two ways, both of which are outlined below.

If each ranked value on a factor map is given a grey tone or numerical value corresponding to its value category (eg light to dark, or one to n for most to least favoured situations), it is possible to combine the tones, or add the number values by overlaying all component maps. Light areas or low numbers will represent favourable locations and dark areas (high numbers) favourable locations for the development. This simple method assumes implicitly that all controlling factors have equal weight in the final assessment. (The addition of ordinal values—which is of dubious mathematical validity—is also implicitly accepted.) A major drawback of this simple system lies in the fact that it is extremely difficult to explain in words exactly why certain areas have been found favourable and others unfavourable. Critical review of the final synthesized map is therefore difficult, although the map will convey the location of most suitable areas to interested parties more readily than any other method.

A second system for evaluating component factors uses letters to denote rating or value; thus 'A' may indicate 'highly favourable', with B, C and D denoting 'favourable', 'unfavourable' and 'highly unfavourable'. The final map is then drawn to indicate areas having particular combinations of characteristics, and hence letters. An area described by the sequence of letters DBACD would thus indicate that the first and fifth factors assessed were 'highly favourable', the second 'unfavourable', the third 'highly unfavourable' and the fourth 'favourable'. With four values and six component maps, the possible combinations amount to 65 536: considerable patience and cartographic skills are thus required to map all this information. Once all combinations of factor values have been mapped and letter-coded, it is then tedious but straightforward to produce a composite suitability map.

The presence of an 'A' in the sequence of letters indicates that one of the controlling factors poses major problems to development. The specific area to which that sequence of letters refers is thus considered 'highly unsuitable' and coloured dark red to indicate this status. If the worst letter-rating in the sequence of letters had been a 'B' the area would be considered 'suitable with limitations' and shaded light red; if a 'C', the area would be 'suitable' and coloured light green; and if all letters were 'D', the area would be 'highly suitable' and shaded dark green to denote this.

This method is preferable to the additive method outlined before, for two reasons. First, it does not presume that all factors have equal weight or that they are additive. Secondly, it provides a means by which the precise reasons for an area being suitable or unsuitable for development can be understood.

31.3.3.4 *Presentation*

The major advantage of the overlay or mapping system of evaluation is that the final maps which are produced present a composite picture of the evaluation in a form readily acceptable to decision-makers and other interested parties. If carefully executed, the maps have an intrinsic appeal, especially if produced in colour. If areas unfavourable for development are shaded red and suitable areas shaded green, an immediate impression of the spatial arrangement of development controls is presented.

The final presentation should consist of a *portfolio of maps* accompanied by an explanatory text. Maps should be presented for each of the controlling factors as well as for the final composite syntheses. *Summary sheets* should also be prepared for each controlling factor. On these sheets a concise factual account of the following points should be given:

(a) The relevance of the factor to site selection.
(b) The criteria used to evaluate the controlling factor in terms of suitability for development.
(c) A brief review of the limitations for development revealed by this controlling factor.

Although the maps and summary sheets may be adequate for internal purposes in professional planning offices, it is recommended that a *report* on the assessment should also be compiled to provide a full and lasting record of the evaluation. It is recommended that the report contain the following sections:[6]

(a) An outline of the reasons for the development project.
(b) A description of the nature of the project.
(c) A brief description of the environmental setting of the project.
(d) A statement on the nature, sources and quality of data used in the study.
(e) Details of the persons involved in the study, their names, qualifications, affiliations and experience.
(f) A summary of the procedure used for the selection of the controlling factors that were mapped.
(g) A portfolio of maps of controlling factors.
(h) A composite map synthesizing the data from controlling factors.
(i) Summary sheets for each controlling factor.
(j) A review of the locational problems shown by the analysis.
(k) A conclusion.

31.4 CONCLUSION

Through training and experience, an environmental professional will have acquired an array of methods that can be used to address environmental evaluations. This chapter has sought to provide an overview of some commonly used methods that many have found to be helpful. Individuals attempting environmental evaluation for the first

---

[6] See also section 30.5.3.

time are advised first to understand the principles of IEM (set out in chapter 30). Thereafter, application of a matrix analysis, followed by a map-overlay analysis, and a summary report, will provide a sound basis through which to meet South African requirements for environmental evaluations.

INDEX TO LEGAL MATERIALS

	Page
1 Cases	781
1.1 South African	781
1.2 Other jurisdictions	782
1.3 International	783
2 Other legal materials	783
2.1 South African legislation	783
2.1.1 Pre-Union	783
2.1.2 Post-Union	784
2.2 Foreign legislation	800
2.3 International legal materials	800

1 CASES

1.1 SOUTH AFRICAN

Admadiyya Anjuman Ihaati-Islam Lahore (South Africa) v Muslim Judicial Council (Cape) 1983 (4) SA 855 (C) 136
Adminstrator, Cape v Associated Buildings Ltd 1957 (2) SA 317 (A) 110
Aucamp v Nel NO 1991 (1) SA 220 (O) 133, 134
Bagnall v The Colonial Government 1907 (24) SC 470 .... 132, 133, 134
Bamford v Minister of Community Development and State Auxiliary Services 1981 (3) SA 1054 (C) 132, 133, 135, 440
Brauer v Cape Liquor Licensing Board 1953 (3) SA 752 (C) 135
Butgereit v Transvaal Canoe Union 1988 (1) SA 759 (A) 297, 310, 657, 658, 661, 681
Cabinet for the Transitional Government for the Territory of South West Africa v Eins 1988 (3) SA 369 (A) 132
Cape Town Municipality v Abdulla 1976 (2) SA 370 (C) 737
Chemical and Industrial Workers' Union v Sopelog CC 1988 (9) ILJ 846 .... 408, 679
Christian League of Southern Africa v Rall 1981 (2) SA 821 (O) 136
Colonial Government v Town Council of Cape Town (19) SC 87 682
Consolidated Diamond Mines of SWA Ltd v Administrator of SWA 1958 (4) SA 572 (A) 416, 676, 681
Dalrymple v The Colonial Treasurer 1910 TS 372 .... 132, 133, 134, 135
Deary NO v Acting President, Rhodesia 1979 (4) SA 43 (R) 136
Dell v Town Council of Cape Town 1879 (9) Buch 2 134
Director of Education, Transvaal v McCagie 1918 AD 616 .... 132, 133, 134, 135
Dunn v Bowyer 1926 NPD 516 677
Durban City Council v Minister of Agriculture 1982 (2) SA 361 (D) 681, 682
Elektrisiteitsvoorsieningskommissie v Fourie 1988 (2) SA 627 (T) 365
Feun v Pretoria City Council 1949 (1) SA 331 (T) 737
Foentjies v Beukes 1977 (4) SA 964 (C) 365
Great Fish River Irrigation Board v Southey 1928 Hall's Rep 237 305
Gluckman v Solomon 1921 TPD 335 367
Government v Marais 1920 AD 240 367
Herrington v Johannesburg Municipality 1909 TH 179 445
Hiscock v De Wet 1880 (1) Buch SC 58 304
Hough v Van der Merwe 1874 (4) Buch 148 .... 297, 657
Horne v Struben 1902 (19) SC 317 681
Hudson v Mann 1950 (4) SA 485 (T) 363
Johannesburg Consolidated Investment v Johannesburg Town Council 1903 TS 111 115
Karim v Union Government 1933 NLR 167 681
Kenly Farms (Pty) Ltd v Minister of Agriculture 1984 (1) SA 406 (C) 634
Lange v Minister of Lands 1957 (1) SA 297 (A) 296, 658, 659, 681
Le Roux v Kruger 1986 (1) SA 327 (C) 656
Marais v Perks 1963 (4) SA 802 (E) 533
Madrassa Anjuman Islamia v Johannesburg Municipality 1917 AD 718 134
McCulloch v Munster Health Committee 1979 (4) SA 723 (N) 736
Milani v South African Medical and Dental Council 1990 (1) SA 899 (T) 132, 135
Milnerton Estates v Colonial Government 1899 (16) SC 177 681
Minister of the Interior v Bechler 1948 (3) SA 409 (A) 302

Page
Mjuqu v Johannesburg City Council 1973 (3) SA 421 (A) 634
Motolegi v President of Bophuthatswana 1989 (3) SA 119 (B) 136
Municipality od Beaufort West v Wernich 1882 (2) SC 36 296
Nasopie (Edms) Bpk v Minister van Justisie (2) 1979 (4) SA 438 (NC).... 142
Natal Bottle Store-Keeping and Off-Sales Licensees Association, Ex parte 1962 (4) SA 273 (D) 136
Natal Fresh Produce Growers' Association v Agroserve (Pty) Ltd 1990 (4) SA 749 (N) .. 132, 136, 532
National Education Crisis Committee v State President of the Republic of South Africa (WLD case no 16736/86, unreported) 136
Parents Committee of Namibia v Nujoma 1990 (1) SA 873 (A) 136
Patz v Greene & Co 1907 TS 427.... 132, 133, 134
P E Bosman Transport Works Committee v Piet Bosman Transport (Pty) Ltd 1980 (4) SA 801 (T) 135, 136
Pharo v Stephan 1917 AD 1 680
Publications Control Board v William Heineman Ltd 1965 (4) SA 137 (A) 138
R v Carelse 1943 CPD 242 676
R v Carter 1954 (2) SA 317 (E) 262
Regal v African Superslate (Pty) Ltd 1963 (1) SA 102 (A).... 532
Retief v Louw 1874 (4) Buch 165 .... 297, 653, 657, 658
Roberts v Chairman, Local Road Transportation Board, Cape Town 1979 (4) SA 604 (C) 133
Rocher v Registrar of Deeds 1911 TPD 311 409
Roets v Secundior Sand BK 1989 (1) SA 902 (T).... 367
Roodepoort-Maraisburg Town Council v Eastern Properties (Prop) Ltd 1933 AD 87... 132, 133, 134
S v Anglo American Prospecting Services (Nelspruit Magistrate's Court case no SH 438/91, unreported).... 150
S v Frost; S v Noah 1974 (3) SA 466 (C) 677
S v Nyele (Mtubatuba Magistrate's Court case no 2288/89, unreported).... 150, 151
S v Msomi 1988 (1) SA 612 (N).... 681
Secretary for Inland Revenue v Hersamar (Pty) Ltd 1967 (3) SA 177 (A) 518
Shifidi v Administrator-General for South West Africa 1989 (4) SA 631 (SWA) 132, 133, 134
Society for the Prevention of Cruelty to Animals v The University of the Witwatersrand (WLD case no 23288/87, unreported) 137
Society for the Prevention of Cruelty to Animals, Standerton v Nel 1988 (4) SA 42 (W) 137
Society for the Prevention of Cruelty to Animals v De Swardt 1969 (1) SA 655 (O).... 440
South African Optometric Association v Frames Distributors (Pty) Ltd 1985 (3) SA 100 (O) ... 136
Southey v Schombie 1881 (1) EDC 286 304
Southey v Southey 1905 (22) SC 650 304
Struben v Colonial Government 17 SC 249 296
Surveyor General (Cape) v Estate De Villiers 123 AD 588 681
Transvaal Canoe Union v Butgereit 1986 (4) SA 207 (T) 136, 658, 681
Transvaal Indian Congress v Land Tenure Advisory Board 1955 (1) SA 85 (W)
Union Government v Lovemore 1930 AD 13 681
Union Government v Marais 1920 AD 240 408
United Watch and Diamond Co (Pty) Ltd v Disa Hotels Ltd 1972 (4) SA 409 (C).... 135
Van der Merwe v McGregor 1913 CPD 497 305
Van der Westhuizen v Rabie 1915 Krummeck's Rep 58 305
Van Heerden v Weise 1880 (1) Buch AC 5 .... 297, 654, 656
Van Niekerk & Union Government v Carter 1917 AD 359.... 296, 658, 659, 681, 682
Von Moltke v Costa Areosa (Pty) Ltd 1975 (1) SA 255 (C).... 133, 134, 440
Waks v Jacobs 1990 (1) SA 913 (T) 132, 134
Webb v Beaver Investments (Pty) Ltd 1954 (1) SA 13 (T).... 409
West Witwatersrand Areas Ltd v Roos 1936 AD 62 363
Wood v Ondangwa Tribal Authority 1975 (2) SA 294 (A) 132, 136, 137
Wynberg Municipality v Dreyer 1920 AD 439.... 445
Yorigami Maritime Construction Co Ltd v Nissho-Iwai Co Ltd 1977 (4) SA 682 (C); 1978 (2) SA 391 (C) 679

1.2 OTHER JURISDICTIONS

United Kingdom
Paton v British Pregancy Advisory Service Trustees (1979) 1 QB 276, (1978) 2 All ER 987.... 135

United States of America
City of Euclid v Amber Realty.... 716
Citizens to Preserve Overton Park, Inc v Volpe 401 US 402 (1971) 148

Page
Hanly v Mitchell (I) 460 F 2d 640, 2 ELR 20216 (2d Cir 1972) ... 85
Kennecott Copper v EPA 462 F 2d 846 (DC Cir 1972) ... 148
United States v Students Challenging Regulatory Agency Procedures 412 US 699 (1973) ... 133

1.3 INTERNATIONAL
Corfu Channel case (United Kingdom v Albania 1949) ... 162
Lac Lanoux arbitration (France v Spain 1957) ... 162
nuclear tests cases (Australia v France; New Zealand v France 1974) ... 162–3
Trail Smelter arbitration (United States v Canada 1941) ... 160, 161, 170

2 OTHER LEGAL MATERIALS

Page
2.1 SOUTH AFRICAN LEGISLATION
2.1.1 Pre-Union
2.1.1.1 *Cape*
Placaaten
14 October 1652 ... 13, 193
21 December 1653 ... 13, 193
22 August 1654 ... 13
10/12 April 1655 ... 13, 14
26 August 1656 ... 14
1 January 1657 ... 14, 260
17 July 1657 ... 193
20 July 1657 ... 13
2/3 October 1658 ... 193
12/13 October 1658 ... 193
19 November 1658 ... 13, 193
1 October 1659 ... 13
26 September 1660 ... 13
6 February 1661 ... 14
16 December 1661 ... 13, 14, 193
23 July 1665 ... 14
3 October 1667 ... 14
25 October 1667 ... 14
3/11 September 1668 ... 14
3/6 December 1670 ... 13
1/4 July 1671 ... 13, 193, 630
10 July 1676 ... 13, 630
22 December 1676 ... 14
5 January 1677 ... 14
8 April/11 June 1680 ... 13
8/9 April 1680 ... 14, 260
13 May 1681 ... 193
31 August 1682 ... 14
17 February 1683 ... 13
23 February 1683 ... 680
10/11 February 1687 ... 14
19/20 February 1687 ... 13, 193
20 January 1688 ... 14
20 July/23 August 1690 ... 14
18 October/17 November 1692 ... 193
20 October 1709 ... 14
27 April 1751 ... 14
3/9 September 1771 ... 14
18 September/1 October 1792 ... 14
29 September/ 1 October 1792 ... 14

Laws
20 October 1795 ... 14
26 January 1801 ... 14
5 of 1836 ... 15
28 of 1846 ... 15
18 of 1859 ... 15
28 of 1888 ... 15

Page
20 of 1902 ... 15
20 of 1908 ... 15
Acts
18 of 1859 ... 193, 251
27 of 1864 ... 14
10 of 1867 ... 14
7 of 1883 ... 14
36 of 1886, 38 of 1891, 33 of 1899, 11 of 1908 14
22 of 1888 ... 251
28 of 1888 ... 15, 72, 193, 630, 698
29 of 1890 ... 14
43 of 1899 ... 14
20 of 1902 ... 193
22 of 1905 ... 14
20 of 1908 ... 193
11 of 1909 ... 14
Ordinances
5 of 1836 ... 193
28 of 1846 ... 193, 251

2.1.1.2 *Natal*
Acts
20 of 1861 ... 14
38 of 1874 ... 14
24 of 1894 ... 14
4 of 1904 ... 14
8 of 1906 ... 14
18 of 1910 ... 14

Laws
21 of 1865 ... 15, 193
8 of 1866 ... 14
10 of 1866 ... 14
8 of 1868 ... 14
13 of 1880 ... 14
21 of 1884 ... 14
23 of 1884 ... 14
24 of 1885 ... 14
28 of 1890 ... 14
16 of 1891 ... 14
31 of 1895 ... 15, 193
18 of 1902 ... 15, 193

2.1.1.3 *Orange Free State*
Acts
32 of 1908 ... 15, 193
7 of 1909 ... 14
23 of 1909 ... 14

Law Book
1891 ... 15
1891 Chapter 126 ... 14
1891 Chapter 125 ... 193

Page

Ordinances
2 of 1874 ... 14
10 of 1880 ... 14
11 of 1895 ... 14

2.1.1.4 *Transvaal*
Acts
4 of 1897 ... 14
Laws
2 of 1870 ... 15, 193
2 of 1872 ... 366
8 of 1870 ... 15, 193
15 of 1880 ... 15, 193
1 of 1883 ... 366

2.1.2 Post-Union
2.1.2.1 *National legislation*
Abolition of Racially Based Land Measures Act 108 of 1991 ... 198, 208, 209, 210, 229, 727, 728
s 2 ... 198
s 13 ... 209
s 41 ... 198
s 11(2) ... 210
s 28*(b)* ... 208
s 43 ... 229
s 98(1)–(2) ... 728
s 98(3)*(a)* ... 728
Advertising on Roads and Ribbon Development Act 21 of 1940 ... 16, 210, 514
s 12 ... 210
s 8(1) ... 514
s 8(3) ... 514
Advocate-General Act 118 of 1979 ... 141
Advocate-General Amendment Act 104 of 1991 ... 141
s 4(1)*(a*A*)* ... 141
Agricultural Products Export Act 51 of 1971 ... 535, 540
s 1 ... 540
s 2(1) ... 540
s 4(1)*(o)* ... 540
Agricultural Pests Act 36 of 1983 ... 237–8, 243
s 1 ... 237, 238
s 2*(a)* ... 238
s 3 ... 237
s 3(1)*(a)* ... 237
s 3(1)*(b)* ... 238
s 3(2)*(c)* ... 238
s 6(1) ... 238
s 6(2)*(a)*–*(b)* ... 238
s 6(2)*(d)* ... 238
s 6(2)*(f)*–*(g)* ... 238
s 6(3)*(b)* ... 238
s 6(4) ... 238
s 7(1) ... 238
s 7(5) ... 238
s 8(1)*(b)* ... 238
s 9 ... 238
s 10(1) ... 238
ss 13–15 ... 238
s 16(1) ... 238
Animals Protection Act 71 of 1962 ... 137
s 8 ... 137

Page

Animal Slaughter, Meat and Animal Products Hygiene Act 87 of 1967 ... 515
s 38(1)*(n)* ... 515
Atmospheric Pollution Prevention Act 45 of 1965 ... 17, 93, 113, 122, 123, 124, 125, 126,127, 130, 139, 205, 338, 354, 375, 376, 436, 437–49, 451, 620, 718, 733
s 1 ... 439
s 1(1) ... 438, 443, 444
s 2(1) ... 125
s 5 ... 125
s 6 ... 375
s 6(1) ... 125, 437
s 6(2) ... 437, 448
s 6(3) ... 437
s 7 ... 438
s 8 ... 123
s 9(1)*(a)* ... 123
s 9(1)*(a)*(i)–(ii) ... 438
s 9(1)*(b)*–*(c)* ... 439
s 9(2) ... 441
s 10(1) ... 439
s 10(1)(ii) ... 439
s 10(2)(i) ... 439
s 10(3) ... 439
s 10(4) ... 440
s 11(1)–(2) ... 440
s 12(1) ... 440
s 12(2)–(3) ... 441
s 12(3)*(b)* ... 441
s 12(4) ... 127, 441
s 13 ... 125, 139
s 13(2) ... 139
s 14 ... 123
s 14(1)–(5) ... 442
s 14(6) ... 443
s 14A ... 444
s 15 ... 442
s 15(1) ... 122
s 15(1)*(a)*–*(b)* ... 444
s 15(2)–(4) ... 444
s 16 ... 442, 444
s 16(1)–(2) ... 444
s 17 ... 126, 442, 445
s 17(1)–(2) ... 445
s 18 ... 122, 442, 443, 444
s 18(2) ... 443
s 18(5) ... 444
s 19 ... 122, 126
s 19(1)–(6) ... 443
s 20 ... 442, 443, 444
s 20(4) ... 443
s 21 ... 442
s 22 ... 442, 443
ss 23–24 ... 442
s 25 ... 125, 139, 442
s 25(1) ... 139, 445
s 27 ... 123, 438, 446
s 28 ... 375, 447
s 28(1)–(2) ... 447
s 29 ... 447
ss 30–31 ... 375, 447
s 32(1)–(2) ... 447
s 33 ... 375, 446

Page
s 33(1) 448
s 35 ..... 125, 139, 448
s 35(1) 139
s 36 ..... 123, 448
s 36(4) 448
s 37 ..... 122, 449
s 37(2) 449
s 38 ..... 125, 139
s 38(1) 139
s 39 ..... 122, 449
s 40 ..... 448, 449
s 41 450
s 45A*(a)* 124
s 47 ..... 442, 446
s 47(2) 446
Atomic Energy Act 35 of 1948 ..... 18, 555
Atomic Energy Act 90 of 1967
18, 517, 555, 556, 561
s 8 517
Aviation Act 74 of 1962 580
s 22(1)*(s)* 580
Basic Conditions of Employment Act 3 of 1983 620
Black Administration Act 38 of 1927 229
s 25(1) 229
Black Land Act 27 of 1913 210
Buffelspoort Irrigation Scheme Act 31 of 1948 477
s 11*(b)* 477
Cannon Island Settlement Management Act 15 of 1939 208
s 16*(a)*, *(e)*, *(l)* 208
Children's Status Act 82 of 1987 94
Coal Act 32 of 1983 23
Coal Resources Act 60 of 1985 23
Commisions Act 8 of 1947 245
Common Pasture Management Act 82 of 1977 208
s 1 208
s 2(1)*(a)*–*(c)* 208
s 3(1)*(a)* 208
s 3(1)*(c)* 208
s 4(1)–(2) 208
s 5(1)*(e)* 208
Conservation of Agricultural Resources Act 43 of 1983 ..... 21, 93, 121, 122, 124, 125, 127, 130, 197–206, 208, 225, 234–7, 240, 243, 245, 248, 303, 306–7, 312, 314, 457, 489, 627, 630–7, 642–5, 663–4, 732, 734, 735, 736–7, 745
s 1 ..... 199, 202, 235, 236, 248, 663
s 1(xiv) 632
s 1(xviii) 632, 644
s 2(1)*(b)* 248
s 2(3) 200, 236
s 3 ..... 198, 234, 632, 644, 732
s 4 201
s 4*(a)* 236
s 4(1) 632
s 4(3) 201
s 4(3)*(a)* 632
s 4(5) 201
s 5 312
s 5(1) 236
s 5(1)*(d)* 208
s 5(2) 735
s 5(2)*(a)* 237
s 5(2)*(c)*–*(d)* 735
s 5(3)*(a)* 237
s 5(6) 735
s 6 ..... 200, 236, 312, 637, 732, 735
s 6(1) 122, 198, 235, 632, 664
s 6(2) 199, 632
s 6(2)*(f)* 633
s 6(2)*(g)*–*(h)* 235
s 6(2)*(j)* 633
s 6(2)*(l)* 236
s 6(2)*(o)* 235
s 6(2)*(p)*–*(q)* 633
s 6(3) 199
s 6(4) 198
s 6(5) 199, 235, 236, 632, 637
s 7 ..... 201, 312, 732, 735
s 7(1) 202, 235, 236, 632
s 7(2) 235
s 7(3) 202, 235
s 7(3)*(a)*–*(b)* 632
s 7(4) 202, 235, 735
s 7(4)*(a)* 632
s 7(5) 202
s 7(6) 202, 235, 236, 632, 637, 735
s 8 ..... 199, 200, 643, 737
s 8(1) 124, 199, 235
s 8(1)*(a)*(ii) 235
s 8(1)*(a)*(v) 235
s 8(1)*(a)*(vi) 236
s 9 200
s 9(2) 200
s 10 ..... 201, 643
s 10(1)–(2) 202
s 10(6) 202
s 11 643
s 11(1) 121, 200, 236, 632, 637
s 11(2) 200, 735
s 11(2)*(a)* 236
s 11(3) 200
s 11(2)*(a)*–*(b)* 121
s 11(4) 200
s 11(4)*(b)* 200
s 11(5)–(6) 200
s 12(1)—(2) 202
s 12(2)*(b)* 202
s 12(4)–(5) 203
s 13 737
s 13(1)–(2) 203
s 14 ..... 200, 235, 734
s 14(1) 125, 663
s 15(1) 201, 248
s 15(2)–(3) 201
s 15(3)*(f)* 201
s 15(4)–(11) 201
s 16(1) 200
s 16(2)–(3) 201
s 16(3)*(b)*–*(c)* 201
s 16(3)*(e)*–16(9) 201
s 17 ..... 200, 632
s 17(3)–(6) 200
s 18 ..... 127, 202

Page

s 18(2)–(5) 202
s 19(2)–(3) 203
s 20 .... 127, 202
s 20(2)–(5) 202
s 21 .... 200, 203
s 21*(c)* 643
s 22 203
s 23 .... 198, 235
s 23(1) 637
s 23(1)*(a)* 632
ss 24–25 203
s 26 .... 200, 632
s 27 203
s 28 .... 203, 634
s 29 200

Customs and Excise Act 91 of 1964 94

Deep Level Mining Research Institute Act 27 of 1946 366

Defence Act 44 of 1957 .... 635, 708
s 76 .... 635, 708
s 87 635
s 89 708

Dental Technicians Act 19 of 1979 94

Development and Housing Act (House of Assembly) 103 of 1985 620

Development Trust and Land Act 18 of 1936 210, 229
s 2(1) 229
s 21(1) 229

Diamonds Act 56 of 1986 .... 23, 412, 414, 415
s 4(1) 415

Dumping at Sea Control Act 73 of 1980 21, 93, 474–6, 488, 489, 556
s 1(1) 475, 476
s 1(2) 474
s 2(1) 476
s 2(1)*(a)* 475
s 2(1)*(b)*(i) 475
s 2(1)*(b)*(ii) 475, 476
s 2(1)*(b)*(iii) 475, 476
s 2(1)*(c)* 476
s 2(1)*(c)*(i) 475
s 2(1)*(c)*(ii) 475, 476
s 2(5) 476
s 2(6)–(8) 474
s 3 476
s 3(1)*(a)*(i) 475
s 3(1)*(a)*(ii) 476
s 3(1)*(b)* 475
s 4*(a)–(b)* 476
s 6(1)*(a)* 475
s 6(1)*(b)* 475, 476
s 6(1)*(c)* 475
s 8(1)*(a)–(b)* 476
s 9 475
s 11 474

Durban Waterworks Consolidation (Private) Act 24 of 1921 470

Electricity Act 41 of 1987 .... 303, 513, 734
s 19 734

Energy Act 42 of 1987 .... 23, 563

Environment Conservation Act 100 of 1982 .... 20, 21, 22, 23, 74, 84, 99, 107, 112, 117, 312, 511, 516, 677, 702

Page

s 9 702
s 10(5)*(a)–(c)* 117
s 10(6) 117
s 12(2)*(a)–(e)* 112

Environment Conservation Act 73 of 1989 .. 21, 22, 23, 75, 84, 85, 86, 93, 99–119, 122, 123, 125, 127, 128, 130, 131, 135, 138, 139, 147, 225, 231, 240, 243, 244, 245, 249, 312–13, 314, 373, 415, 460, 489, 493, 495, 503, 510, 512–16, 519, 520–1, 542, 579, 582–5, 620, 635, 638, 678, 685, 686, 687, 688, 701–3, 712, 718, 732, 735, 736, 761
s 1 512
s 1(vii) 515
s 1(viii) 103
s 1(ix) 103
s 1(x) 85
s 1(xii) 106, 113, 702
s 1(xiv) 515
s 2 .... 313, 314, 638, 687
s 2(1) 103, 123
s 2(1)*(a)* 86
s 2(1)*(c)* 514
s 2(2) 102, 104, 123
s 2(3) 103
s 3 .... 105, 106, 123, 313, 314
s 4 .... 107, 231
s 5(1)*(a)–(b)* 107
s 6(1) 108, 125
s 10(2) 735
s 12 107
s 13*(a)–(b)* 107
s 14(1) 108
s 15 .... 139, 685
s 15(1) 108, 114, 125
s 15(2) 125
s 16 .... 86, 112
s 16(1) 701
s 16(1)*(b)* 102
s 16(2) 313, 701
s 16(2)*(b)* 102
s 16(3)–(4) 701
s 16(5) 117, 702, 736
s 16(6) 702
s 17(1) 108, 702
s 17(2)–(4) 702
s 17(7)–(8) 702
s 18 .... 112, 702
s 18(1) 313
s 18(2)*(a)–(b)* 702
s 18(2)*(c)* 102, 702
s 18(3)–(4) 703
s 18(4)*(a)* 102
s 18(4)*(b)* 102, 313
s 18(6)–(8) 703
s 19 313
s 19(1) 112, 515
s 19(2) 515
s 20 493
s 20(1) 112, 123, 515
s 20(2)–(4) 112
s 20(5)–(6) 112, 516
s 21 .... 123, 313, 415, 579
s 21(1) 108, 732

Page
s 21(2) 108
s 21(2)(i) 516
s 21(3) 102, 108
s 22 .... 579, 732
s 22(1) 108, 516
s 22(2) 109, 123, 516
s 22(3)–(4) 109
s 23 678
s 23(1) 109, 123, 703
s 23(2) 109, 110, 703
s 23(3) 110, 123, 703
s 23(4)*(a)–(b)* 109
s 23(4)*(c)* 100, 109
s 23(4)*(d)* 102, 109
s 24 .... 112, 493, 516, 519, 520
s 25 .... 112, 122, 579
s 25*(a)* 113
s 26*(a)* 109
s 26 111
s 26*(a)*(ii)–(iii) 86
s 28*(a)* 519, 520
s 28*(c)* 703
s 28*(i)* 102
s 28*(i)*(i)–(ii) 113
s 28*(i)*(iii) 113, 520, 585
s 29 116
s 29(2)*(a)* 703
s 29(3) 112, 515
s 29(4) 108, 109, 110, 112, 116, 515
s 29(7) 116, 127, 131, 686
s 29(8) 116, 128, 131
s 29(9) 116
s 30 116
s 31 685
s 31(1)–(3) 521
s 32(1) 100
s 32(1)*(b)* 108, 109
s 32(2) 100, 109
s 33 114
s 34 687
s 34(1) 117, 736
s 34(2)–(3) 117
s 35 .... 114, 125, 138, 139
s 35(1)–(4) 114
s 36 .... 135, 685
s 36(1) 114
s 36(2) 115
s 38(1)–(2) 703
s 40 .... 105, 542, 584
ss 43–44 702
Environment Planning Act 88 of 1967 ... 19, 729
ss 6A–6B 729
Expropriation Act 63 of 1975
94, 197, 200, 231, 663, 701, 733–4, 735, 736
s 1 734
s 2(1) 734, 735
ss 11–12 736
s 12(1)*(a)*(ii) 736
ss 13–14 736
s 82 197
Factories, Machinery and Building Work Act 22 of 1941 21
Fertilisers, Farm Foods, Seeds and Pest Remedies Act 21 of 1917 .... 15, 532
ss 6–7 532
s 7(2) 532
s 8 532
Fertilizers, Farm Feeds, Agricultural Remedies and Stock Remedies Act 36 of 1947
18, 122, 123, 125, 127, 517, 532, 535–41, 542
s 1 .... 535, 536, 538
s 2(1) 536
s 3(1) 536
s 3(2)*(a)* 536, 537
s 3(2)*(b)* 541
s 3(2)*(c)* 536
s 3(3)–(4) 536
s 4 127
s 4(1) 537
s 4(1)*(c)–(d)* 537
s 4(1)*(e)* 536, 541
s 4(3) 537
s 4A(2)*(b)* 538
s 5 537
s 6 .... 125, 537
s 6(2) 125
s 6A 122, 537
s 7(1) 123, 538
s 7(1)*(c)* 539
s 7(2)*(a)* 539
s 7*bis* 517
s 7*bis*(2)*(c)* 539
s 9 538
s 10(1) 539
s 14 536
s 15 127
s 15(1) 536
s 16(1)–(3) 538
s 16(6) 538
s 18(1) 539
s 18(1)*(c)bis* 517
s 18(2) 539
s 23A 542
Financial Relations Act 10 of 1913 236
Financial Relations Act 65 of 1976
260, 511, 518, 709, 712, 721
s 11(1)*(a)* 260, 709
sch 2 paras 2 and 2A 260, 518, 709
sch 2 para 23 712
sch 2 s 14 721
Financial Relations Amendment Act 50 of 1935 236
s 4*(a)* 236
Financial Relations Consolidaton and Amendment Act 38 of 1945 511
Foodstuffs, Cosmetics and Disinfectants Act 54 of 1972 .... 94, 480, 489, 535, 540–1, 556, 620
s 1 .... 480, 540, 541
s 2(1) 541
s 2(1)*(a)*(i)–(ii) 541
s 15(1) 556
s 15(1)*(a)* 480
s 15(1)*(d)* 541
s 15(1)*(e)* 480
s 15(5) 480, 541
s 18 .... 480, 541
Forest Act 16 of 1913 .... 15, 193, 630

Page

Forest Act 13 of 1941 .... 230, 704
Forest Act 72 of 1968 .17, 20, 206, 207, 630, 704
Forest Act 122 of 1984 .... 20, 93, 121, 122, 124, 125, 197, 206–7, 224 , 225, 228–34, 243, 245, 246–7, 307, 310, 312, 377, 515, 630, 631, 6 33, 634, 635, 636, 642, 663, 664, 704–6, 734, 736
s 1 .... 206, 229, 310, 312, 704, 705
s 2(2) 229
s 3 229
s 4(1) 229
s 4(2) 229, 247
ss 5–6 229
s 7(1) 229, 633, 664
s 7(2) 229
s 7(4) 229
s 8 247
s 8(1) 122, 230, 307, 633, 664
s 8(2) 230, 633, 664
s 9 .... 230, 247
s 9A 230
s 10 230
s 10(1) 704
s 10(2) 230, 704
s 10(2)*(b)–(c)* 230
s 11(1) 230, 704
s 11(2) 230
s 11(2)*(a)* 230, 232, 704
s 11(2)*(a)*(i)–(ii) 230
s 11(2)*(b)* 230, 377, 704
s 11(3)–(4) 230, 704
s 12 230
s 12(1) 704
s 13 664
s 13(1) 230
s 13*(b)*(i) 206
s 13(2)*(a)–(c)* 230
s 13(4)*(a)*(i)–(ii) 231
s 13(5) 207
s 13(5)*(a)–(b)* 231
s 13(6) 207, 231
s 14 736
s 14(1) 231
s 14(2) 125, 231, 663
s 15 312
s 15(1) 705
s 15(1)*(a)* 664
s 15(1)*(a)*(i)–(ii) 206, 231
s 15(1)*(c)* 231
s 15(2) 231, 705
s 15(3) 121
s 15(3)*(a)*(i) 231, 705
s 15(3)*(a)*(ii) 705
s 15(3)*(b)* 705
s 15(3)*(b)*(i) 231
s 15(3)*(b)*(ii)–(iii) 206, 231
s 15(3)*(b)*(iv)–(ix) 231
s 15(4)*(a)* 124, 232, 705
s 15(4)*(b)* 232, 705
s 15(5)–(6) 232, 705
s 18 207
s 18(1) 232, 634
s 18(2) 232
s 19 .... 207, 232

Page

s 19(1) 634
s 20 207
s 20(1) 232, 634
s 20(2) 232
s 20(3) 232, 634
s 20(4) 232
s 20(4)*(a)–(b)* 634
s 20(5)–(7) 232
s 21 232
s 21(1)*(a)*(i) 310
s 21(2)*(b)* 310
s 22 .... 207, 247, 634
s 22(1)*(a)–(b)* 232
s 22(2) 232
s 22(4)–(7) 232
s 22(8) 232, 247
s 23 232
s 24 .... 207, 232, 634
s 24A 232
s 25 634
s 25(1) 232, 233
s 25(2)–(4) 233
s 26 233
s 26(1)–(3) 233
s 27 233
s 48 233
s 57 233
s 57(3) 229
s 58 233
s 61(1) 233
s 61(1)*(a)* 233
s 61(1)*(k)* 233
s 66(2)*(a)* 706
s 66(3) 706
s 73(1)*(a)* 233
s 73(1)*(a)*(v) 207
s 73(1)*(a)*(vi) 207
s 73(1)*(a)*(xi) 635
s 73(1)*(a)*(xiv)–(xv) 207
s 73(1)*(b)* 233
s 73(1)*(c)* 207, 233
s 73(1)*(e)–(g)* 233
s 73(1)*(i)* 233
s 75 .... 234, 706
s 75(2) 634
s 75(2)*(b)* 207
s 75(3)*(a)*(i) 207
s 75(3)*(a)*(vii) 515
s 75(7)*(b)* 634
s 75(8) 634
s 75(8)*(cA)* 232
s 75(9)(i) 515
ss 76–80 234
s 82 706
s 87 634
Forest and Veld Conservation Act 13 of 1941 16, 17, 194, 195, 205, 630
s 4 194
s 5 194
Game Theft Act 105 of 1991 259–60
s 1 259
s 2(1)*(a)–(b)* 260
s 2(2)*(a)–(b)* 260
s 3(1) 260

Page

General Education Affairs Act 76 of 1984 96
General Housing Matters Act 102 of 1984 96
Group Areas Act 36 of 1966 96
Hazardous Substances Act 15 of 1973 ... 22, 93, 95, 123, 130, 480, 489, 516–17, 535, 540, 555, 556, 562, 563–7, 568, 620
s 1 516, 564
s 2 123, 516
s 2*(b)–(c)* 564
s 2(1)*(a)* 540
s 2(2) 564
s 3(1) 564
s 3(1)*(a)* 540
s 3(2) 564
s 4 564
s 8 564
s 29 564
s 29(1)*(a)* 540
s 29(1)*(a)*(vi) 516
s 29(1)*(r)* 517
s 29(8) 517
Health Act 63 of 1977 ... 22, 93, 121, 436, 445, 457, 479–80, 489, 512, 515, 520, 525, 535, 541, 556, 619–20, 621
s 1 479, 515
s 1(xiv) 512
s 1(xxii) 512
s 1(xxvii)*(f)–(g)* 445
s 14 479
s 14(1)*(c)* 479, 621
s 14(2) 479
s 20 520, 621
s 20(1) 121
s 20(1)*(b)* 480, 512, 515
s 20(1)*(b)*(iv) 621
s 20(1)*(c)* 480
s 20(2)–(4) 479
s 27 445, 480, 520
s 34 480, 556
s 36A 480
ss 37–39 480
s 39(1)–(2) 445
s 45 541
Housing Act 4 of 1966 620
Housing Act (House of Representatives) 2 of 1987 620
Income Tax Act 58 of 1962 93, 94, 206, 408, 518
s 9(1)*(f*A*)* 408
s 12(1)*(a)–(b)* 518
s 17A 206
International Convention for the Prevention of Pollution from Ships Act 2 of 1986 93, 329, 474, 476, 489
International Convention Relating to Intervention on the High Seas in Cases of Oil Pollution Casualties Act 64 of 1987 93, 476
International Health Regulations Act 28 of 1974 474, 480, 481, 489, 515
s 2 515
Irrigation and Conservation of Waters Act 8 of 1912 ... 15, 17, 295, 374, 470, 654–5, 661
s 2 655

Page

s 25 374
s 26(3) 374
Jointed Cactus Eradication Act 52 of 1934 15, 236
Kopjes Irrigation Settlement Act 38 of 1935 477
s 17(1)*(q)* 477
Klipdrift Settlement Act 23 of 1947 208
s 6*(h)–(j)* 208
Labour Relations Act 28 of 1956 408, 679
s 2(1) 408
Labour Relations Amendment Act 9 of 1991 408
s 2*(a)* 408
Lake Areas Development Act 39 of 1975 .. 21, 93, 125, 225, 234, 307, 482, 515, 698, 700–1, 735
s 1 482
s 2 700
s 2(1) 700
s 2(2) 701
s 3 701
s 11 701
s 16 701
s 16(1) 735
s 16(2) 125, 735
s 23 234, 701
s 23(1)*(c)–(d)* 482
Land Survey Act 9 of 1927 681
s 31*bis* 681
Legal Succession to the South African Transport Services Act 9 of 1989 481
s 21(2) 481
Less Formal Township Establishment Act 113 of 1991 720, 726
s 13 726
Livestock Improvement Act 25 of 1977 237
Machinery and Occupational Safety Act 6 of 1983 21, 450, 580, 620
s 35(1)*(b)* 580
s 35(1)*(b)*(iv) 450
s 35(1)*(b)*(vi) 450
Mapochsgronden Irrigation Scheme Act 42 of 1954 477
s 13*(b)* 477
Mapochsgronden Water and Commonage Act 40 of 1916 208
s 5*(a)* 208
s 5*(d)–(e)* 208
s 5*(i)* 208
Marine Traffic Act 2 of 1981 327, 328, 474, 482, 488, 489
s 1 327, 482
ss 2–4 327
s 6(1) 474
s 7 327
Mediation in Certain Divorce Matters Act 24 of 1987 94
Medicines and Related Substances Control Act 101 of 1965 515, 535
s 23 515
s 35(1)(xxvA) 515
s 35(1)(xxvi) 515
s 35(1)(xxviA) 515
Merchant Shipping Act 57 of 1951 474, 477, 489

Page
s 2(1) 474
s 304A 474, 477
Mineral Laws Supplementary Act 10 of 1975 366
Minerals Act 50 of 1991 .... 23, 45, 127, 202, 210, 340, 366–77, 409, 410, 411, 412, 414, 415, 436, 450, 457, 489, 513, 515, 555, 556, 558, 561, 580, 620, 636, 729, 732, 734
s 1(xiii) 368
s 1(xiv) 367
s 1(xxviii) 368
s 1(xxix) 368
s 1(xxxv) 369
s 1(xxxviii) 367
s 3 .... 369, 414
s 4 369
s 5(2) 369, 372
s 6 .... 411, 414
s 6(1) 369
s 6(2) 373
s 6(2)*(b)* 369
s 7(1) 377
s 7(1)*(c)–(d)* 377
s 8(1) 369, 371, 372
s 9 .... 411, 414
s 9(3)*(b)* 369, 370
s 9(3)*(c)* 369, 370, 411
s 9(5) 373
s 9(5)*(e)* 370
s 14(1) 127, 369, 372, 411
s 24 734
s 24(1) 373
s 38 .... 202, 371, 372, 411
s 38*(b)* 369
s 39 .... 202, 369
s 39(1) 370, 372
s 39(2)–(3) 370
s 40 .... 202, 369, 371, 372
s 41 .... 202, 411
s 41(1) 373
s 42 202
s 42(1)*(a)* 373
s 42(2) 373
s 44 377
s 47 377
s 60*(a)* 372, 373
s 60*(a)*(i) 369
s 61(1)*(a)* 369
s 62(3) 369
s 63(1)*(c)–(d)* 372
s 63(1)*(p)* 372
s 63(5) 372, 373
s 68(2) 210, 369, 375, 376, 410, 411, 450, 580
Mines and Works Act 27 of 1956 .... 210, 366–77, 409, 410, 411, 414, 415, 436, 450, 513, 515, 558, 580, 636
s 1 558
s 1(x) 368
s 1(xi) 367
s 12(1) 374, 636
s 12(1)*(g)* 580
s 12(1)*(h*A*)* 366, 369
s 12(4) 373
Mines and Works Amendment Act 83 of 1973 .... 366, 369

Page
s 3*(b)* 366, 369
Mining Rights Act 20 of 1967 .... 18, 366, 367, 375, 376, 395, 408, 409, 410–11, 561
s 1 .... 409, 410
s 1(xviii) 367
s 2 410
s 14(1)*(a)* 410
s 14(1)*(a)*(i)–(ii) 410
s 14(1)*(b)* 410
s 14(2) 410
s 14(3) 411
s 14(3)*(a)–(b)* 410
s 14(3)*(c)–(e)* 411
s 14(4) 410
s 30 410
s 25(1)*(a)* 411
s 161 376
Mining Titles Registration Act 16 of 1967 18, 409, 410
Mooi River District Adjustment Act 73 of 1954 477
s 12(1)*(b)* 477
Mountain Catchment Areas Act 63 of 1970 .. 20, 93, 121, 122, 124, 207–8, 225, 234, 237 , 240, 243, 302–3, 307, 625, 627, 630–7, 642–6, 663, 664, 700, 735, 736, 737
s 1 .... 208, 625
s 2 .... 207, 302, 631
s 3 .... 207, 637
s 3(1) 122, 237, 735
s 3(1)*(a)*(i)*(aa)* 633
s 3(1)*(a)*(i)*(bb)* 234, 237
s 3(1)*(b)*(i) 207
s 3(1)*(b)*(ii) 207, 234, 237
s 3(1)(i)*(aa)–(bb)* 631
s 3(2)*(a)* 631
s 3(2)*(c)* 631, 735
s 3(3) 207
s 4 .... 207, 643
s 4(1)–(2) 736
s 4(2)*(c)* 234
s 5 643
s 5(1) 737
s 6 .... 631, 637
s 7 .... 208, 633
s 8 208
s 8(1) 633
s 8(2)*(a)–(c)* 633
s 8(3)*(a)–(b)* 633
s 8(4) 633
s 9 633
s 10 643
s 10*(b)* 124, 736
s 12 .... 121, 631, 637, 735
s 14*(b)* 234, 237, 631, 637, 735
s 14*(e)* 633
s 17 631
s 18 634
s 20 643
Natal/KwaZulu Joint Services Act 84 of 1990 723
National Building Regulations and Building Standards Act 103 of 1977 620
National Education Policy Act 39 of 1967 107
s 1B(1) 107

Page
National and Historical Monuments, Relics and Antiques Act 4 of 1934 15
National Monuments Act 28 of 1969 .... 17, 21, 91, 225, 234, 377, 635, 706–8, 718, 737
s 2 706
s 5(1)*(c)* 706
s 5(1)*(cC)* 707
s 5(5) 706
s 5(9) 707
s 10 234
s 10(1) 91, 706
s 10(3) 707
s 12*(a)* 707
s 12(1) 707
s 12(1A) 708
s 12(2) 377
s 12(2)*(a)* 234
s 12(4)–(6) 707
s 13 707
s 15 737
s 16 .... 234, 707
s 17 707
s 18(1)–(3) 708
National Parks Act 56 of 1926 ... 12, 15, 17, 698
National Parks Act 42 of 1962 .... 17, 20
National Parks Act 57 of 1976 .... 20, 93, 121, 123, 125, 224, 236, 261, 310, 312, 377, 515, 635, 698–700, 701, 734, 735
s 1 310
s 2(3) 699
s 2A 699
s 2B 699
s 3*(a)* 125
s 3(1) 125, 699, 734, 735
s 3(2) 734
s 3(3) 699
ss 4–5 699
s 5(1) 125, 699
ss 6–11 699
s 12 .... 121, 699
s 12A 700
s 16 700
s 20 .... 377, 700
s 21 312
s 21(1) 700
s 21(1)*(c)* 310
s 21(1)(i) 236
s 21(2)*(f)* 236
s 24 700
s 24(8) 377
s 28(1) 700
s 29(1) 700
s 30B 701
National Policy for General Education Affairs Act 76 of 1984 107
s 2(1) 107
National Policy for General Housing Matters Act 102 of 1984 107
s 6 107
National Policy for Health Act 116 of 1990 .... 96, 107
s 2(1) 107
National Roads Act 54 of 1971
93, 209–10, 457, 514, 734

Page
s 5(1)*(c)* 209
s 5(1)*(e)* 209
s 8 210
s 8(1)–(2) 734
s 16(1)–(3) 514
s 20(1)*(a)* 209
Natural Resources Development Act 51 of 1947 .... 18, 73, 91, 728
s 1 91
s 3 728
s 4*(a)*–*(c)* 728
s 4*(f)*–*(g)* 728
s 14 728
Natural Resources Development Amendment Act 30 of 1955 728
Nuclear Energy Act 92 of 1982 .... 22, 93, 123, 125, 127, 148, 366, 377, 457, 480, 489, 513, 517, 555, 556–63, 568, 620, 733, 734
s 1(1) 556, 557, 558, 561, 562
s 1(2) 558
s 2 556
ss 3–4 557
s 5 556
s 19 .... 556, 563
s 24(2) 125
s 24C 558
s 30 563
s 30(1) 123, 560, 733
s 30(1)*(a)* 559, 560
s 30(1)*(b)* 559
ss 32–33 559
s 34(1) 563
s 34(1)*(a)* 559
s 34(2) 559
s 35 560
s 39 560
s 40(1) 127
s 40(3) 560
s 41 .... 148, 560
s 41(2) 560
s 42 561
s 42(1) 560
s 42(2)–(3) 561
s 45 560
s 47 .... 366, 377, 561
s 48 .... 561, 563
s 49 563
s 49(1) 561
s 49(5) 561
s 50 561
s 50(1) 517, 556, 562
s 50(2) 556
ss 51–52 .... 557, 563
s 53 563
s 57 557
s 68 .... 557, 563
s 70 563
s 73(1) 561
s 78(1)–(2) 562
s 83(9) 517, 556, 561
Nuclear Installations (Licensing and Security) Act 43 of 1963 .... 18, 555
Ombudsman Act 118 of 1979 141

Page
Occupational Diseases in Mines and Works Act 78 of 1973 620
Patents Act 57 of 1978 94
Petroleum Products Act 120 of 1977 421
Physical Planning and Utilization of Resources Act 88 of 1967
18, 19, 21, 73, 112, 702, 723, 729
s 2 729
s 4 729
s 4(1)*(b)* 702
ss 5–6 729
s 9 702
Physical Planning Act 125 of 1991 .... 21, 94, 107, 459–60, 636, 682, 702, 716, 718, 721, 723, 725, 729–32
s 1 .... 730, 731
s 3 730
s 4 725
s 4(1)*(a)–(b)* 730
s 4(2) 730
s 5 .... 716, 725, 730
s 6(1)–(2) 730
s 7 725
s 8(1) 730
s 9 731
s 10(1)–(3) 731
s 11 731
s 11(1)*(b)* 731
s 11(2) 731
ss 12–13 731
s 15(1) 731
s 15(2)*(a)* 731
s 15(3) 731
ss 17–21 731
s 22 .... 730, 731
s 24(1)–(2) 730, 731
s 27(1) 732
s 27(1)*(d)* 732
s 28 732
s 29 721
Precious Stones Act 73 of 1964
18, 366, 367, 409, 410, 412, 414
s 1 409
s 4(1) 412
s 4(1)*(a)* 412
s 4(2) 412
s 4(2)*(a)*(i)–(vi) 412
s 4(2)*(b)* 412
s 21(1) 414
Precious Stones (Alluvial) Amendment Act 15 of 1919 366
Pretoria Waterworks (Private) Act 15 of 1929 470
Prevention and Combating of Pollution of the Sea by Oil Act 67 of 1971 21
Prevention and Combating of Pollution of the Sea by Oil Act 6 of 1981 .... 21, 93, 121, 122, 124, 127, 329, 415, 476–7, 478, 482, 489
s 1 329
s 1(1) 482
s 4(1) 122
s 4(2)*(a)* 127
s 5(1) 121

Page
s 5(2) 121
s 19 127
s 22(1) 127
s 25(1) 124
Prevention of Illegal Squatting Act 52 of 1951 .... 150, 620
Provincial Government Act 69 of 1986 74
Public Health Act 36 of 1919 .... 15, 22, 435, 619
Public Service Act 111 of 1984 105
ss 19–20 105
Rand Water Board Statutes (Private) Act 17 of 1950 .... 299, 489
s 139 489
Regional Services Council Act 109 of 1985 723
Road Traffic Act 29 of 1989
210, 270, 436, 449, 514, 519, 579–80, 581
s 62(1) 580
s 101(1)*(k)* 449
s 101(1)*(m)* 514, 519
s 103 579
s 104 580
s 113(2) 514
s 114 .... 514, 519
s 132(1)*(e)* 449
s 132(1)*(f)* 579
s 132(1)*(r)* 449
s 133(1)*(j)* 580
s 149 519
s 344*(a)* 580
Sea Birds and Seals Protection Act 46 of 1973 .... 21, 329, 708, 709
s 3 709
s 14 709
Sea Fisheries Act 10 of 1940 .... 16, 21, 329
Sea Fisheries Act 58 of 1973 .... 21, 329
Sea Fishery Act 12 of 1988 .... 21, 93, 107, 122, 124, 127, 131, 225, 235, 237, 239, 328, 329, 331–5, 478, 479, 481, 489, 620, 663, 677, 679, 708, 709
s 1 .... 235, 237, 332, 478, 479, 708
s 2 .... 107, 332
s 3 332
s 3*(a)–(c)* 332
s 5(x) 334
ss 7–12 333
s 20 127
s 25 .... 124, 334
s 23(1)*(b)* 239
s 25(3)*(c)* 127
s 30(1) 334
s 30(4)–(7) 334
s 31 334
s 33(1) 122, 333
s 34(1)*(a)* 335, 708
s 35(1) 122
s 35(1)*(a)* 333
s 36(1) 122
s 37(1) 122
s 38(1) 235
s 41(1) 124
s 45 235
s 45(1)*(c)* 335
s 45(1)(i) 481
s 47*(k)* 478
s 47(1) 478

Page
s 47(1)*(g)* 235
s 47(1)*(k)* 235
s 47(2)*(a)* 131, 478
s 48(1)–(3) 478
s 50(2)–(5) 478
s 52 328, 331, 679
s 52(4) 332
s 53 127
Sea-Shore Act 21 of 1935 15, 21, 93, 122, 332, 407, 409, 416, 479, 480, 482, 489, 515, 519, 520, 620, 657, 673, 676, 677, 680–1, 686, 689, 708, 735
s 1 479, 482, 657, 677, 680
s 2 676
s 2(1) 657
s 2(2) 676
s 3 735
s 3(1)*(a)* 676
s 3(4)–(5) 676
s 4 735
s 5 676
s 6(1) 676
s 7 407
s 7(1)–(2) 480
s 9 681
s 10 122, 519
s 10(1)*(d)* 480, 515, 520
s 11(2) 480, 519
s 13*(c)* 676
Settlement Committee and Management Act 21 of 1925 208
s 6*(a)* 208
s 6*(h)*–*(k)* 208
Skanskop Settlement Act 24 of 1947 208
s 6*(a)* 208
s 6*(e)* 208
s 6*(l)* 208
Slums Act 76 of 1979 620
Soil Conservation Act 45 of 1946 16, 194, 195, 196, 205, 630, 643
s 9 194
s 10 194
s 13*(a)* 194
s 13*(b)* 194
s 16 194
s 16(5) 194
s 19 194
Soil Conservation Act 76 of 1969 16, 21, 195–7, 198, 201, 202, 205, 206, 207, 208, 234, 643
s 2 234
s 3(1) 195, 196
s 3(1)*(a)*–*(n)* 196
s 3(2)–(3) 195
s 4(1) 196
s 4(2)*(a)*(i)–(ii) 196
s 4(2A) 196
s 4(4) 196
s 6*(a)*–*(b)* 196
s 9(1)–(2) 196
s 9(6) 196
ss 10–11 196
s 12(1)*(a)*–*(b)* 196
s 12(3)–(5) 196

Page
s 13 196
s 13(1) 196
ss 16–17 196
s 18(1)*(a)*–*(c)* 196
s 21(1)*(cA)* 196
s 23 195
s 29*(c)* 196
South African Transport Services Act 65 of 1981 480
s 73 480
State Land Disposal Act 48 of 1961 735
s 2(1) 735
Standards Act 30 of 1982 578–9
s 1(xx) 578
s 16 578
s 17 578
Strategic Mineral Resources Development Act 88 of 1964 366
Subdivision of Agricultural Land Act 70 of 1970 21, 94, 209, 489, 726, 732
s 1 209, 732
s 3 726
s 8 209
Territorial Waters Act 87 of 1963 326, 327, 328, 329, 330, 407, 408, 409, 412, 474, 679, 702
s 1 326
s 2 327, 474, 679, 702
s 3 328, 679
s 4 328, 679
s 7 329, 407, 679
Territorial Waters Amendment Act of 1977 328
Tiger's-Eye Control Act 77 of 1977 23, 366
Transfer of Powers and Duties of the State President Act 97 of 1986 700
Unbeneficial Occupation of Farms Act 29 of 1937 208–9
Upgrading of Land Tenure Rights Act 112 of 1991 726–7
s 12 727
s 15 727
Urban Transport Act 78 of 1977 718, 723
Value-Added-Tax Act 89 of 1991 408
s 1(xlv) 408
Water Act 54 of 1956 17, 22, 93, 121, 123, 124, 130, 131, 206, 207, 288, 293, 295–306, 308–11, 315, 374–5, 463, 468–9, 470–3, 477, 478, 483, 485, 488, 489–91, 512, 513, 620, 630, 654–64, 666, 682, 718, 733, 734, 735, 736
s 1 295, 304, 305, 309, 471, 655
s 2 121, 300
s 2(1)*(f)*–*(h)* 300
s 2(1)*(i)* 300
s 2(1)*(m)* 300
s 3 300
s 4 660
s 4(2) 299
s 5 295, 305, 491
s 5(1) 656, 660
s 5(2) 491, 656
s 6 295
s 6(1) 296, 658
s 7 297

Page
s 7*(a)*–*(b)* 661
s 7(1) 297
s 9 .... 296, 308, 660
s 9(1) 296
s 9(1)*(a)* 299
s 9A 299, 300
s 9B 299, 300, 308
s 9B(1)*(c)* 308
s 9C 299, 300, 308
s 10 .... 304, 660
s 11 .... 485, 490, 491
s 11(1) 297, 471, 660
s 11(1A) 471, 660
s 11(1A)*(a)* 300
s 11(2) 297, 471, 660
s 11(3)–(7) 471
s 12 .... 300, 306, 471, 491, 660
s 12(1) 124, 478
s 12(5)–(6) 471
s 12A 300, 660
s 12B 304, 374, 660
s 13 .... 301, 491, 660
s 14 660
s 19 .... 299, 308
s 20 .... 299, 300, 682
s 20(1)*(a)*–*(b)* 662
s 20(8)–(9) 299, 662
s 20(10)*(a)* 662
s 20(11) 662
s 21 .... 306, 485
s 21(1) 299, 472, 512
s 21(1)*(a)*–*(b)* 472
s 21(2) 472
s 21(3) 472, 491
s 21(4) 513
s 21(4)*(a)* 124, 472
s 21(4)*(b)*–*(e)* 472
s 21(5) 299
s 21(5)*(a)*(i)–(ii) 478
s 21(6)*(a)* 478
s 22 .... 306, 311, 473, 491
s 23 .... 306, 473, 489, 490
s 23(1) 299, 478
s 23(1)*(a)* 473
s 23(1)*(a)*(ii) 311
s 23(1)*(b)* 473
s 23A 490
s 23A(1) 477
s 23A(3) 477
s 24 .... 306, 491
s 24(2) 131
s 25 299
s 25(1)*(c)* 206
s 25(2) 206, 299
s 26 .... 374, 375, 472, 491
s 28 .... 298, 301
s 29 .... 299, 304
s 30 301
s 32B 301
s 32C 308
s 32F 301
s 33B 309
s 33D 300, 309
s 33F 300, 309

Page
s 34 299
s 40*(d)* 657
s 42*ter* 300
s 52 299
s 52(5) 206
s 56 .... 304, 308
s 56(3)–(4) 304, 308
s 56(5) 308
s 59 .... 300, 306
s 59(2) 298, 306, 662
s 59(2)*(a)* 206
s 59(4) 308
s 59(4)*(a)* 298
s 59(4)*(c)* 736
s 59(5) 298, 303
s 59(6) 303
s 60 .... 300, 308, 734
s 60(1) 663
s 61 .... 206, 300
s 61(1) 298
s 62 .... 298, 299, 300, 301
s 62A 298, 300, 301, 308
s 63 .... 298, 299, 300, 301
s 64 300
s 67 .... 300, 304
s 68 300
s 71 .... 298, 300
s 73 .... 298, 300
s 75 298
s 79 .... 298, 300
s 89 298
s 89(1)*(b)* 299
s 94(1) 663
s 95 301
s 95A 301
s 108 299
s 110 299
s 112(1) 663
s 138 300
s 157 300
s 164*bis* 298
s 164*bis*(2) 298
s 164*quat* 298
s 166 299
s 168A 300
s 170 .... 473, 489, 491
s 170(1) 299
s 170(1)*(a)* 662
s 170(1)*(b)* 299, 662
s 170(1)*(c)* 299
s 170(1)*(e)* 299
s 170(2) 298, 477, 662
s 170(3) 375
Water Amendment Act 45 of 1972 309
Water Amendment Act 42 of 1975 309
Water Amendment Act 96 of 1984 .... 490, 491
Water Amendment Act 110 of 1986 490
Water Amendment Act 68 of 1987 490
Water Amendment Act 37 of 1988 490
Water Amendment Act 68 of 1990 .... 485, 490
Water Research Act 34 of 1971 484
s 2 313
Wild Birds Export Prohibition Act 6 of 1925 15
Weeds Act 42 of 1937 .... 15, 21, 197, 236

Page
Weeds Amendment Act 32 of 1964 236
Workmen's Compensation Act 30 of 1941 620

2.1.2.2 *Provincial legislation*
2.1.2.2.1 Cape
Land Use Planning Ordinance 15 of 1985
94, 682, 683, 685, 686, 687, 716, 717, 718, 719, 720, 721, 723, 726
s 5 .... 716, 718, 721
s 5(1)–(2) 683
s 14(1) 719
s 23 .... 683, 726
s 36(2) 720
Nature Conservation Ordinance 26 of 1965 12
Nature and Environmental Conservation Ordinance 19 of 1974 ...... 84, 225–8, 235, 237, 239, 260, 310, 311, 478–9, 635, 709–10
s 1(xxiv) 226
s 1(xxxiv) 226
s 1(xlvii) 227
s 1(liv) 226
s 2(v) 239, 311
s 2(xi) 239
s 2(xxvii) 227
s 2(xxviii) 225
s 2(xxxii) 227
s 2(xxxiii) 225
s 2(xxxv) 239
s 2(xlv) 239
s 2(lxi) 228, 239
s 2(lxxi) 479
s 6 709
s 7(1) 709
s 10 710
s 12 710
s 13 311
s 16(1)*(c)*(iii) 237
s 17 227
s 19(1)–(2) 239, 311
s 23 478
s 41 228
s 43 228
s 48 .... 235, 478, 479
s 48*(a)* 311
s 49 .... 310, 311
s 50 .... 239, 311
s 51 311
s 52 310
ss 53–54 311
s 55(1)*(b)* 310
ss 56–57 311
s 59 311
s 60 .... 239, 311
s 62(1) 227, 228
s 62(2) 228
s 63(1)*(a)* 227
s 63(1)*(b)*(i)–(ii) 226, 227
s 63(1)*(c)* 226, 227
s 63(2)–(3) 227
s 64 .... 226, 228
s 65 .... 228, 635
s 66 .... 226, 228, 635
s 67 226
ss 68–72 .... 226, 228

Page
s 85 .... 227, 228
s 85*(a)* 227, 478
s 86(1)*(d)* 479
Public Resorts Ordinance 20 of 1971 712
Roads Ordinance 19 of 1976 519
s 64(1)*(d)*–*(e)* 519

2.1.2.2.2 Natal
Nature Conservation Ordinance 15 of 1974
12, 225, 226, 227, 228, 235, 260, 261–8, 303, 310, 311, 332, 479, 635, 661, 709, 710, 712
s 1 .... 225, 226, 227, 228, 261, 262, 265, 266, 268, 303, 310, 479, 710
s 2 710
s 4(1) 261
s 11 261
s 11(1)*(a)* 261
s 15 261
s 15(1) 710
s 15(1)*(c)* 310
ss 16–17 261
s 22(1) 261
s 24(1) 261
s 25 261
s 26(1)–(2) 262
s 27 262
s 29 261
s 31 262
s 33(1)*(a)*–*(b)* 262
s 33(2)–(3) 262
s 34(1)*(b)*–*(d)* 263
s 34(2)–(3) 263
s 35(1)–(2) 263
s 37 263
s 38(1)–(2) 263
s 39 266
s 40(1) 266
s 42(1) 262
s 42(2) 265
s 44 265
s 45(1) 265
ss 46–47 265
s 48(1) 265
s 48(3) 265
ss 49–50 265
s 51 266
s 55 266
s 57 266
s 58 263
s 59 .... 266, 710
s 60 710
s 62 710
s 64 710
s 67*(a)*(i) 710
ss 78–80 266
s 80(1) 267
s 81 266
ss 82–83 267
s 84 266
ss 85–86 267
ss 88–90 267
ss 93–96 267
s 100 267
ss 101–103 268

Page
s 104A ... 268
s 109 ... 268
s 109A ... 268
s 110 ... 268
s 112 ... 268
s 136 ... 661
s 136(1) ... 303
s 136(2) ... 303
s 142 ... 311
s 143(2)*(a)* ... 311
s 143(2)*(b)* ... 310
s 143(2)*(d)* ... 311
s 143(3) ... 311
s 145(1) ... 311
s 151(1)*(d)* ... 310, 311
s 151(1)*(e)* ... 311
s 151(2) ... 311
s 152 ... 235, 311, 479
s 183 ... 235, 479
s 185(1)*(a)* ... 479
s 194 ... 226, 228
s 195 ... 226
s 195(1)–(2) ... 228
s 196(1) ... 227, 228
s 197 ... 226
s 197(1) ... 228
s 198 ... 226
s 198(1)–(2) ... 228
s 199 ... 227
s 199(1)–(2) ... 228
s 200 ... 227
s 200(1)–(3) ... 227
s 202 ... 226
s 202(1)–(2) ... 227
s 203 ... 228
s 205 ... 226
s 208 ... 227, 228
s 208(1)*(a)*(i) ... 228
s 208(1)*(a)*(ii) ... 227
s 208(1)*(b)* ... 479
s 215B(1)*(c)* ... 268
s 215B(2) ... 268
Licences and Business Hours Ordinance 11 of 1973 ... 265
Prevention of Environmental Pollution Ordinance 21 of 1981 ... 22, 84, 93, 518–19
s 2(1)–(2) ... 518
s 2(1)*(a)*–*(f)* ... 518
s 3 ... 519
s 4 ... 519
s 5 ... 519
s 6 ... 518
Recreational Facilities Ordinance 24 of 1972 712
Roads Ordinance 10 of 1968 ... 519
s 23*(e)* ... 519
s 73 ... 519
Town Planning Ordinance 27 of 1949
682, 683, 685, 686, 717, 718, 726
s 16(1)*(h)* ... 726
s 40 ... 718
s 59 ... 683
Water Services Ordinance 27 of 1963 ... 299
s 7 ... 299

Page
2.1.2.2.3 Orange Free State
Nature Conservation Ordinance 8 of 1969
12, 225, 226, 227, 228, 237, 239, 260, 310, 311, 519, 635, 709, 710–11
s 1 ... 225, 227, 228, 310
s 23 ... 311
s 25(1) ... 310
s 25(2)*(a)* ... 311
s 25(2)*(b)* ... 311
s 26 ... 311
s 26(2)*(d)* ... 310
ss 27–28 ... 311
s 29 ... 239, 311
s 29(1) ... 239
s 30(2) ... 226
s 30(3) ... 226, 227
s 30(3)*(a)* ... 227
s 31 ... 226
s 31(1) ... 227
s 32 ... 226, 227
s 33(1) ... 226, 227, 228
s 33(1)*(a)*–*(b)* ... 228
s 33(2) ... 226, 227, 228
s 33(3) ... 228
s 34 ... 226
s 34*(a)*–*(d)* ... 228
s 35 ... 711
s 35(3) ... 310
s 36 ... 711
s 36(3) ... 310
s 38(1)*(h)* ... 237
s 38(1)*(o)* ... 237
s 40 ... 227, 228
s 40(1)*(b)* ... 228
s 40(1)*(c)* ... 239
s 40(1)*(d)* ... 227
Prohibition of the Dumping of Rubbish Ordinance 8 of 1976 ... 22, 93, 518
s 1 ... 518
s 2(1)*(a)*–*(b)* ... 518
s 2(2) ... 518
s 3 ... 518
s 4(1)*(a)*–*(b)* ... 518
s 4(1)(i)–(ii) ... 518
s 4(2) ... 518
Roads Ordinance 4 of 1968 ... 519
s 21(1)*(b)* ... 519
s 54*(a)* ... 519
Townships Ordinance 9 of 1969 ... 717, 726
s 20 ... 726

2.1.2.2.4 Transvaal
Division of Land Ordinance 20 of 1986 726
Local Government Ordinance 17 of 1939 .. 520
s 79(2)*(a)* ... 520
s 80(3) ... 520
s 80(4)*(a)*–*(c)* ... 520
s 80(6)–(7) ... 520
s 80(15) ... 520
s 80(18) ... 520
Nature Conservation Ordinance 17 of 1967 12
Nature Conservation Ordinance 12 of 1983
225, 226, 227, 228, 235, 239, 260, 310, 311, 479, 635, 709, 711

Page
s 1(iii) 228, 239
s 1(xxvi) 225
s 1(xxix) 227
s 1(xlv) 225
s 1(liv) 225, 226
s 1(lx) 239
s 1(lxii) 310
s 1*(k)* 479
s 7 310
s 14 711
s 19 310
s 19(1)*(a)* 711
s 47(1) 711
s 50(1) 711
ss 68–69 310
ss 71–76 311
ss 77–78 .... 310, 311
ss 79–82 311
s 84 .... 235, 311, 479
s 85 311
s 85(1)–(2) 239
s 86(2) 226

Page
s 87 .... 226, 227
s 87(1) 227
ss 89–90 .... 226, 227
s 91 .... 226, 228
s 91(1)*(a)–(b)* 228
ss 92–93 .... 226, 228
s 93(1)*(b)* 228
ss 94–95 228
s 96 .... 227, 228
s 96(1) 228
s 97 227
s 98 .... 227, 228
s 101*(g)*(ii) 237
s 101*(g)*(iii) 237, 239
s 101*(h)*(iii) 237, 311
Public Resorts Ordinance 18 of 1969 712
Roads Ordinance 22 of 1957 519
s 34(1)*(b)* 519
s 34(2) 519
Town Planning and Townships Ordinance 15 of 1986 .... 717, 726
s 92 726

2.1.2.3 *Subordinate legislation* Page
Atmospheric Pollution Prevention Act 45 of 1965
declaration of controlled areas
GN R1776 of 4 October 1968 438
dust control areas
erstwhile Divisional Council of the Cape and the municpalities of Alberton, Bellville, Cape Town, Johannesburg, Kempton Park, Pietermaritzburg and Witbank (GN R542 of 23 March 1984); Town Council of Parrow and magisterial districts of Barbeton, Carolina, Kuruman, Pietersburg, Prieska, and Vryheid (GN R997 of 3 May 1985) the erstwhil Divisional Council of Stellenbosch (GN R2232 of 4 October 1985) and the local authority of Midrand (GN R25 of 2 January 1987) 446
smoke control zone areas
Municipalities of: Pretoria (GN R1026 of 15 June 1973); Johannesburg (GN R489 of 14 March 1975 and GN R490 of 14 March 1975); Germiston (GN R368 of 27 February 1987); Vereeniging (GN R369 of 27 February 1987) 443
smoke control regulations in terms of s 18(5)
Municipality of Pretoria (GN R1221 of 27 June 1975) 444
vehicle emissions control regulations in terms of s 36
local authorities of Alberton, Bloemfontein, Cape Town, Edenvale, Johannesburg, Pietermaritzburg, Pinetown, Pretoria, Roodepoort, Springs (GN R1652 of 20 September 1974); municipality of Richards Bay (GN R2512 of 18 November 1983); Village Council of Bedfordview (GN R2427 of 9 November 1984) 448
see also GN R1651 of 20 September 1974; GN R1816 of 26 August 1983 and GN R517 of 2 April 1974 449

Atomic Energy Act 90 of 1967
disposal of radioactive waste
GN R2410 of 28 November 1980 517
(*see also* Nuclear Energy Act 92 of 1982)

Common Pasture Management Act 82 of 1977
conservation of vegetation and the prohibition of hunting
GN R1916 of 22 September 1978, regs 9 and 10 208
Conservation of Agricultural Resources Act 43 of 1983
control measures applying to land users or areas
GN R1048 of 25 May 1984 .... 199, 200, 236, 632, 633, 664
soil and weeds (regs 2–16); directives (regs 17–18); conservation committees (regs 19–26); beacons and marks (regs 27–28); appeals (regs 29–31); general matters (regs 32–33) 199, 200
conservation of wetlands
GN R1048 of 25 May 1984 306–7

Environment Conservation Act 100 of 1982
coastal zone regulations
GN 2587 of 12 December 1986 .... 21, 677

Page

solid waste control
GN 1549 of 12 July 1985 .... 22, 516
GN 591 of August 1988 .... 22, 516

Environment Conservation Act 73 of 1989
noise control regulations (see Tables 22.2 and 22.3 pp 587–9 for noise control standards and regulations)
GN R2544 of 2 November 1990 .... 22, 112, 582–5
control of noise by local authorities
GN 896 of 27 April 1990 579
solid waste control
GN R1481 of 28 June 1991 22
waste disposal sites (draft)
GN R1481 of 28 June 1991 516
identification of materials as 'waste'
GN 1986 of 24 August 1990 512

Fertilizers, Farm Feeds, Agricultural Remedies and Stock Remedies Act 36 of 1947
disposal of agricultural or stock remedies
GN R928 of 1 May 1981 517
manufacture, control etc of agricultural remedies
GN R2561 of 27 November 1981 .... 538, 539
prohibition on sale acquisition, disposal and use of remedies
GN R928 of 1 May 1981 539
registration and duties of pest control operators
GN R1449 of July 1983 536

Foodstuffs, Cosmetics and Disinfectants Act 54 of 1972
sale of foodstuffs treated with a prohibited substance
GN R1267 of 26 July 1974, GN R24 of 2 January 1981, GN R1386 of 3 July 1981, GN R2227 of 23 October 1981, GN R556 of 18 March 1983 541
GN R1600 of 22 July 1983 556

Forest Act 122 of 1984
claims for compensation
GN R602 of 27 March 1986 231

Hazardous Substances Act 15 of 1973
control of electronic products
GN R1332 of 3 August 1973 .... 564, 565
GN R1302 of 14 June 1991 565
disposal of hazardous substances
GN R452 of 25 March 1977 516
GN 453 of 25 March 1977 .... 516, 517
GN R2777 of 21 December 1984, GN R72 of 11 January 1985 516
GN R2778 of 21 December 1984 .... 516, 540
institution of national advisory committee on electronic products
GN R326 of 23 February 1979, GN R689 of 14 April 1989, GN R1302 of 14 June 1991 567
transportation of hazardous substances
GN R73 of 11 January 1985 .... 517, 540, 566
see also GN R1640 of 22 July 1983, GN R1462 of 10 July 1987, GN R690 of 14 April 1989 ... 566

Health Act 63 of 1977
poisoning from agricultural or stock remedy
GN R1802 of 24 August 1979 541

International Health Regulations Act 28 of 1974
supplementary regulations on waste in ports
GN R2001 of 24 October 1975 481

Lake Areas Development Act 39 of 1975
control of land in lake areas, use of river, lake, sea and sea-shore
GN R311 of 22 February 1980 .... 234, 515, 701
regulations for Wilderness National Park
GN R311 of 22 February 1980 482

Legal Succession to the South African Transport Services Act 9 of 1989
waste in harbour waters
GN R562 of 26 March 1982 481

Page

Machinery and Occupational Safety Act 6 of 1983
noise in the workplace (see Tables 22.2 and 22.3 pp 587–9 for noise control standards and regulations)
GN R2281 and R2282 of 16 October 1987 ... 580
ventilation of work areas
GN R2281 of 16 October 1987 reg 5 ... 450

Marine Traffic Act 2 of 1981
leaving and entering internal waters
GN R194 of 1 February 1985 ... 327

Mines and Works Act 27 of 1956 (regulations under this Act may still apply under the Minerals Act 50 of 1991 by virtue of s 68(2) of the latter Act)
noise control (see Tables 22.2 and 22.3 pp 587–9 for noise control standards and regulations)
GN R1130 of June 1989 ... 580
rehabilitation of mining surfaces
GN R537 of 21 March 1980 ... 210, 366, 369–75
mining and water pollution (*see also* regulations under the Water Act 54 of 1956)
GN R537 of 21 March 1980 ... 375
mining and air pollution
GN R992 26 June 1970 ... 376, 450
mining and waste
GN R537 of 21 March 1980 ... 376–7
mining and off-shore installations (addition of chapter 31 to regulations in GN R992 of 26 June 1970)
GN 1644 of 13 July 1990 ... 411, 412
standing regulations amended by GN R537 of 21 March 1980
GN R992 of 26 June 1970 ... 369, 411, 636
rehabilitation of mining surfaces (draft)
GN 275 of 22 March 1991 ... 369–73

National Parks Act 57 of 1976
solid waste in national parks
GN R2006 of 6 October 1978 ... 515

Nuclear Energy Act 92 of 1982
acquisition, possession, disposal, etc of radioactive nuclides
GN R2410 of 28 November 1980 ... 556, 561–2
special nuclear materials
GN R51 of 15 April 1983 ... 557

Road Traffic Act 29 of 1989
consolidated road traffic regulations
GN R910 of 26 April 1990 ... 579

Sea Fishery Act 12 of 1988
implements, mesh sizes, etc
GN R1804 of 27 July 1990 ... 322, 334
licensing requirements for fishing boats, factories and premises
GN R1804 of 27 July 1990 ... 334
marine reserves
GN R1819 of 27 July 1990 ... 335
protection of fish and marine organisms
GN R1810 of 27 July 1990 ... 708
control of pollution in fishing harbours
GN R1805 of 27 July 1990 ... 481
standing regulations
GN R1804 to R1811 of 27 July 1990 ... 329

Sea-Shore Act 21 of 1935
uniform sea-shore regulations
GN R168 of 2 February 1962 ... 520
deposit or discharge of substances on sea and sea-shore
GN R2513 of 5 December 1980 ... 515

Soil Conservation Act 76 of 1969
guidelines to land owners and occupiers
GN R494 of 26 March 1970 ... 196

Standards Act 30 of 1982 (see Tables 22.2 and 22.3 pp 587–9 for noise control standards and regulations)

Page
Water Act 54 of 1956
water pollution and mining
GN R287 of 20 February 1976 .... 22, 374, 375
effluent standards
GN 991 of 18 May 1984 .... 472, 485

2.2 FOREIGN LEGISLATION
Australia
Commonwealth Environment Protection (Impact of Proposals) Act of 1974 85
New South Wales
Pesticides Act of 1978 534
Queensland
State and Regional Planning and Development, Public Works Organization and Environmental Control Act of 1971 85
Tasmania
Environment Protection Act of 1973 88
Victoria
Environment Protection Act of 1970 88

Canada
Ontario Environmental Assessment Act 85
Nova Scotia Environmental Protection Act of 1973 488

Namibia
Constitution of 1990 .... 144, 145, 146

New Zealand
Pesticides Act of 1979 534

United Kingdom
Alkali etc Works Regulation Act of 1906 436
Control of Pollution Act of 1974 488
Clean Air Act of 1956 436
Water Act of 1973 488

United States of America
Administrative Procedure Act 147
Clean Air Act (s 304*(a)* 42 USC 7604*(a)* (1976 & Supp IV 1981)) 135
Clean Water Act (s 505, 33 USC 1365 (1982)) 135
Coastal Zone Management Act of 1972 672–3
Comprehensive Environment Response, Compensation and Liability Act 149
paras 122, 42 USC 9622*(b)* (3) (Supp IV 1986) 149
Federal Insecticide, Fungicide, and Rodenticide Act of 1947 533–4
Federal Insecticide, Fungicide, and Rodenticide Act of 1972 (PL92-516) 88
Insecticde Act of 1910 533
National Environmental Policy Act of 1970 .... 12, 18, 85, 106, 111, 147, 748, 762
Toxic Substances Control Act 15 USC 1601 88
15 USC 1601, s 3(5) 88
43 USC para 1131*(c)* 87
Michigan
Environmental Protection Act of 1970 (Mich comp Laws Ann 691.1201-1207 (Weas Supp 1984) 135

2.3 INTERNATIONAL LEGAL MATERIALS (see, generally, chapter 9 pp 155–80)
See Table 9.1 p 180 for international environmental conventions to which South Africa is a party.

2.3.1 Agreements
Agreement for Co-operation in Dealing with Pollution of the North Sea by Oil 1969 176
Nordic Agreement concerning Co-operation in Measures to deal with Pollution of the Sea by Oil 1971 .... 177, 178
Agreement concerning the Protection of the Sound from Pollution (Between Denmark and Sweden) 1974 177
Agreement Governing the Activities of States on the Moon and Other Celestial Bodies 1979 .... 172, 173
Agreement on Co-operation for the Protection and Improvement of the Border Area (Between the United States and Mexico) 1983 177
Agreement on an Action Plan for the Environmentally Sound Management of the Common Zambezi River System 1987 177
Agreement on Co-operation regarding International Transport of Urban Pollution 1989 177

Page
Agreement on Co-operation for the Protection and Improvement of the Environment in the Metropolitan Area of Mexico City (Between the United States and Mexico) 1989 177

2.3.2 Charters
Charter of the United Nations 157, 160, 161
Charter of Economic Rights and Duties of States (GA Res 3281 (XXIX)) 159
World Charter for Nature 1982 178

2.3.3 Conventions
Convention relative to the Preservation of Fauna and Flora in their Natural State 1933 180
Convention for the Regulation of the Meshes of Fishing Nets and the Size Limits of Fish 1946 173
International Convention for the Regulation of Whaling 1946 .... 173, 180
European Convention for the Protection of Human Rights and Fundamental Freedoms 1950 ... 144
International Plant Protection Convention 1951 180
International Convention for the Prevention from Pollution of the Sea by Oil 1954 .... 163, 164
Interim Convention on Conservation of North Pacific Fur Seals 1957 174
Convention on Fishing and Conservation of the Living Resources of the High Seas 1958 180
Convention on the Continental Shelf 1958 .... 167, 180, 326, 328, 329, 406, 407, 413
Conventions on the Law of the Sea 1958 .... 163, 326
Convention on the Territorial Sea and the Contiguous Zone 1958 .... 168, 180, 326
Convention on the High Seas 1958 .... 164, 166, 180, 326
North East Altantic Fisheries Convention 1959 177
Convention on the Liability of the Operators of Nuclear Ships 1962 164
Convention for the Prevention of Marine Pollution by Dumping from Ships and Aircraft 1962 .. 166
Fisheries Convention (Europe) 1964 177
International Convention for the Conservation of Atlantic Tunas 1966 180
Convention on the Law on Treaties 1969 155
Convention on the Conservation of the Living Resources of the Southeast Atlantic 1969 ... 177, 180
International Convention on Civil Liability for Oil Pollution Damage 1969 .... 166, 180, 476
International Convention Relating to Intervention on the High Seas in Cases of Oil Pollution Casualties 1969 .... 165, 166, 180
Convention on the Establishment of an International Fund for Compensation for Oil Pollution Damage 1971 167
Convention on Wetlands of International Importance Especially as Waterfowl Habitat 1971 175, 180, 697
Convention Concerning the Protection of the World's Cultural and Natural Heritage 1972 175
Convention on the Prohibition of the Development, Production and Stockpiling of Bacteriological and Toxic Weapons and their Destruction 1972 172
Convention on the Prevention of Marine Pollution by Dumping of Wastes and Other Matter 1972 166, 180
Convention for the Conservation of Antarctic Seals and Antarctic Fauna and Flora 1972 174, 175, 180
Convention on the Prevention of Marine Pollution by Dumping of Wastes and Other Matter 1972 180, 474, 488, 489
Convention for the Prevention of Pollution from Ships 1973 .... 165, 180, 329
Convention on International Trade in Endangered Species of Wild Fauna and Flora 1973 175, 180, 242
International Convention for the Prevention of Pollution from Ships 1973 .... 180, 476
Convention for the Prevention of Marine Pollution from Land-Based Sources 1974 167
Safety of Life at Sea Convention 1974 165
Nordic Convention on the Protection of the Environment 1974 176
Convention on the Protection of the Marine Environment of the Baltic Sea Area 1974 176
Convention for the Protection of the Mediterranean Sea against Pollution 1976 176
Convention of the Mediterrranean Sea against Pollution 1976 166
Convention on the Conservation of Migratory Species of Wild Animals 1979 175
Convention on Financing the Monitoring and Evaluation of Air Pollutants in Europe 1979 169
Convention on Long Range Transboundary Air Pollution 1979 .... 168, 180
Convention on the Conservation of Antarctic Marine Living Resources 1980 .... 175, 180
Convention for Co-operation in the Protection and Development of the Marine and Coastal Environment of the West and Central African Region 1981 176
Convention for the Conservation of Salmon in the North Atlantic Ocean 1982 177

Page

Law of the Sea Convention 1982
158, 164, 165, 166, 167, 168, 173, 175, 176, 180, 326, 327, 328, 407, 413
Regional Convention for the Conservation of the Red Sea and Gulf of Aden Environment 1982 176
Convention for the Protection and Development of the Marine Environment of the Wider Caribbean Region 1983 176
Convention for the Protection and Management of the Marine Environment in the East African Region 1985 176
Council of Europe Convention for the Protection of the Architectural Heritage of Europe 1985 177
Convention for the Protection of the Ozone Layer 1985 .... 169, 170, 180
Convention for the Protection of the Natural Resources of the South Pacific 1986 176
Convention on Assistance in case of Nuclear Accident or Radiological Emergency 1986.......... 171
Convention on the Early Notificationof a Nuclear Accident 1986 171
Convention on the Regulation of Antarctic Mineral Resource Activities 1988 .... 172, 175
Convention on the Control of Transboundary Movements of Hazardous Wastes and their Disposal 1989 .... 171, 172, 180, 517

2.3.4 Declarations

Stockholm Declaration on the Human Environment 1972 .... 160, 178
Nairobi Declaration 1982 178
Ottawa Declaration on Acid Rain 1984 169
Ministerial Declaration calling for a reduction of Pollution of the North Sea 1987 176
Amazon River Declaration 1989 177
Declaration of the Hague (air pollution) 1989 170
Helsinki Declaration on the Protection of the Ozone Layer 1989 169
Declaration and the Programme of Action on the Establishment of a New Economic Order (GA Res 3201(S-VI)) 159

2.3.5 Protocols

Protocol extending the Intervention Convention to Pollution by Substances other than Oil 1973 166
Protocol concerning Co-operation in Combating Pollution of the Mediterranean Sea by Oil and Other
Harmful Substances in Cases of Emergency 1976 177
Protocol for the Prevention of Pollution of the Mediterranean Sea by Dumping from Ships and Aircraft 1976 177
Protocol for the Protection of the Mediterranean Sea against Pollution from Land-Based Sources 1980 177
Protocol on Protection concerning Mediterranean Specially Protected Areas 1982 177
Protocol concerning Regional Co-operation in Combating Pollution of the Red Sea and Gulf of Aden by Oil and Other Harmful Substances in Cases of Emergency 1982 177
Protocol concerning Co-operation in Combating Oil Spills in the Wider Caribbean Region 1983 177
Protocol for the Prevention of Pollution of the South Pacific Region by Dumping 1986 177
Montreal Protocol on Substances that Deplete the Ozone Layer 1987 .... 169, 170, 180
Latin American Summit Declaration of Brazilia on the Environment 1990.......... 176
Protocol concerning Co-operation in Combating Pollution Emergencies in the South Pacific Region 176

2.3.6 Statutes

Statute of the International Court of Justice 155, 163

2.3.7 Treaties

Antarctic Treaty 1959 .... 158, 172, 180
Treaty Banning Nuclear Weapons Tests in the Atmosphere, in Outer Space and Under Water 1963
163, 171, 172, 180
Treaty on Principles Governing the Activities of States in the Exploration and Use of Outer Space, Including the Moon and Other Celestial Bodies 1967 172
Treaty on Non-Proliferation of Nuclear Weapons 1968 172
Treaty on the Prohibition of the Placement of Nuclear Weapons and other Weapons of Msss Destruction on the Sea-bed and the Ocean Floor and the Sub-soil Thereof 1971 172
Treaty of the South Pacific Fisheries 1987 177

SUBJECT INDEX

Abatement notice, 121, 126–7, 452, 520
Acid rain, 1, 50, 245, 418, 427, 435
Administration, defined, 64—*see also* Environmental administration
Administrative decision-making
  conditioning factors
    economic, 66
    political, 65–6
    social, 66
    technological, 66
  co-operative, 102
  state prerogative, 147
  see also Public participation
Administrative law, relevance for environmental law, 96—*see also* Appeal; Environmental tribunal; Judicial review; Standing
Administrative model, defined, 64
Administrative sanctions, 126–8
Administrative service—provision systems
  strategic options for
    collective services, 66–7
    constitutional placement, 69–70
    institutional diversity and diffusion, 79–80
    institutional types and arrangements, 68–9, 71
    macro-organizational aspects, 70, 71
    particular services, 67
    political approach, 68, 71
    sectoral placement, 66–7, 71, 79
Administrative system for environmental management
  dualistic assignments, 79
  historical perspective, 72–5
  problems, 78–9
Admiralty reserve—*see* Coastal zone
Advertisements—*see* Roads, advertisements along
Afforestation
  control of, 229–30
  demand on water, 651
  generally, 222, 229–30, 245, 246
  impact of, 246
  of catchments, 283–4, 628–9, 632–3, 650, 664
  permits, 249
  reduction of runoff, 283–4
  threat to indigenous plants, 222, 245
  threat to water sources, 307
  see also Forests; Indigenous plants; Mountains
African National Congress
  bill of rights, 144
  environmental policy of, 54
  specific environmental issues, 59
African National Soil Conservation Association, 24
African Wildlife Society, 24
Agricultural resources, conservation of—*see* Agriculture; Soil
Agriculture
  acid deposition, 418
  agro-ecology, 745–6, 747
  agro-ecosystems, 739, 741, 742
  biodiversity, lack of, 739–40
  characteristics, 739ff
  competition with wild animals, 275
  conservancies, 745–6
  conservation, purpose of, 248
  cultivation
    effect on plant resources, 220, 239, 740
    effect on soil, 743
  definition, 739
  development, level of, 739
  education of farmers, 747
  environmental cost, 739
  environmental impact, 740, 741, 742, 743, 744, 746
  fertility reduction, 1
  future prospects, 746
  genetic diversity, effect on, 1
  human health, impact on, 741–2
  impact on coastal zone, 670
  impact on indigenous plants, 220–1, 227, 243, 245
  importance of, 181
  irrigation, effect of, 742–3
  livestock farming
    effect on plants, 214, 218, 219, 221, 740
    effect on soil, 740
    effect on wild animals, 740
  mining surfaces rehabilitated, 341–2
  natural vegetation, removal of, 739
  noxious plants, 243, 739, 740, 743
  nutrient inputs, effect of, 741–2
  overgrazing, 740, 744
  pesticides, effect of, 744, 745
  pests, 237–8, 739, 744
  potential, 248
  problems, 746
  resources, conservation of, 235, 248, 630ff
  reversible impact, 5
  salinization, 742–3
  soil
    acidity, 741
    compaction, 743
    depletion, 741, 747, 744
    erosion, 1, 739, 743–4
  subdivision of land, 209
  subsistence farming, 744–5
  subsistence, 744–5, 746
  sustainable, 744–6, 747
  vegetable production, 739
  water pollution, 741, 744
  water sources, impact on, 649–51
  see also—Indigenous plants; Pesticides; Soil; Water
Agulhas Bank, 316, 317, 318, 320, 321, 324, 380, 398, 399, 669
Agulhas Current, 316, 317, 318, 319, 324, 380, 669, 671
Air pollution
  abatement notice, 126–7, 442, 446, 452
  Air Pollution Appeal Board, 139, 437, 445, 448, 450, 452–3
  air quality measurements, 425–30

Air pollution *(continued)*
appeals, 445, 448, 449, 452–3—*see also* Appeal
atmospheric dispersion, 423–4
best practicable environmental option, 454–5
best practicable means, 439–40
chief officer, 437–8, 439, 440, 441, 442, 446, 448, 450, 451, 454
classification of pollutants, 417
control technologies, 430–5
declared areas, 123, 438
Dust Control Levy Account, 375, 447
dust control, 375–6, 446–8, 452
eastern Transvaal Highveld, 424, 425, 426–8, 429, 430, 431, 435, 436, 438
enforcement of legislation, 451
environmental impact
acidic deposition, 418, 427–8
greenhouse effect, 419
hazardous pollutants, 418
ozone depletion, 418, 419
smog, 418
visibility, 418, 427
first national legislation, 17, 22
fossil fuels
coal, 420–1
oil, 421–3
generating activities, 417–18
international law, 161, 168–70
legislation, development of, 435–6
meteorological factors, 424
mines and workplaces, emissions in, 450
monitoring stations, 451–2
National Air Pollution Advisory Committee, 125, 437, 442, 443, 447, 448
national control strategy, 436–7
noxious or offensive gases
best practicable means, 439–40
control, 438–41
registration certificate, 123, 127, 440–1, 452
scheduled process, 123, 438–9
offences, 130, 441, 445, 448
policy, 438, 453
priority areas, 436
research, 124, 453
smoke
authorities, 442–3
control, 442–6, 452
fuel-burning appliances, 122, 444
levels, 442
nuisance, 444–5
regulations, 122, 443
vehicle emissions
control, 448–9, 452
regulations, 122, 449
see also Acid rain; Environmental health; Greenhouse effect; Ozone layer, depletion of; Terrestrial minerals
Alien animals, effect on freshwater resources, 292
see also Exotic animals
Alien plants—*see* Invasive plants, Noxious plants
Alternative dispute resolution
compared to litigation, 146
defined, 146
value of, 146, 152
see also Environmental dispute resolution
Amphibians
conservation status, 254–5
protection, 267–8
Animals—*see* Wild animals
Antarctica
krill, 174–5
mineral resources, 175
natural resources, 172
pollution of, 172
Anthropocentric ethic, 8, 99, 258
Apartheid
abolition of, 50, 143
effect on blacks, 25, 50
environmental management after, 62–3
protected areas, 233
tourism, 224
Appeal
as internal control, 114, 138–9
integrated environmental management, 752
judicial function, 125
to administrative tribunal, 105
to Board of Investigation, 114
to ministers and administrators, 113–14, 537
see also Air pollution; Environmental tribunal
Aquaculture, 292, 652
Atmospheric pollution—*see* Air pollution
Atomic Energy Board, 18, 22, 555—*see also* Nuclear Development Corporation of South Africa (Pty) Ltd
Atomic Energy Corporation, 22, 555, 556–7, 558
Audit—*see* Environmental audit
Authorization
cancellation of, 127, 131
of individual action, 123–4
suspension of, 127
Benguela Current, 317, 321, 324
Bible, relevance of for environmental conservation, 9
Bill of Rights
African National Congress, 144
environmental right, 143–5—*see also* International law
generally, 142
South African Law Commission, 143–5
see also Constitution, Constitutional law; Human rights
Biological impacts—*see* Irreversible biological and geophysical impacts; Reversible biological and geophysical impacts
Biosphere, 89
Biosphere reserve—*see* Protected areas
Birds
conservation status, 255
protection of, 268
see also Wild animals
Blacks
conservation, involvement in, 24–5
environment, attitudes towards, 25, 57
land distribution, views on, 57–8
land ownership, views on, 25
nature conservation legislation, 78
President's Council report, involvement, 54
rights, extension of, 257
Board of Investigation, 108, 114, 139, 685
Botanic gardens—*see* National botanic gardens
Botanical Society, 16, 24

Bubble policy, 44
Butterflies, conservation status, 252–3
Cabinet Committee on Environmental Conservation, 73
Caring for the earth, 2
Case law, role of, 13—*see also* Environmental litigation
Catchment
  biosystem management model, 303
  changes, 283–4
  conservation, 293–4
  control area, 298, 303, 306
  divided control, 315
  effect of, 277
  expropriation of land, 196
  integrated management, 293, 315, 489
  mismanagement, 650
  river, 663–4, 668
  see also Afforestation; Freshwater systems; Mountain catchment areas; Rivers
Central government
  development of concern, 73
  environmental management, 74, 76–8
  necessity, 80–1
  placement of service-provision, 69–70
Chamber of Mines, 338, 339, 342, 361, 362, 378
Charges—*see* Pollution charges
Chernobyl accident, 171
Chlorofluorocarbons, 89, 169–70
Christianity, relevance of for conservation, 8–10
Citizen suit clause, 135—*see also* Standing
Climate, modification of, 5–6, 170—*see also* Greenhouse effect
Coastal Zone
  admiralty reserve, 414, 678
  as limited development area, 111
  boundary, moving or ambulatory, 680–2
  coastal regions, 380
  coastline, 316, 669
  components, 672
  definition, 672–3, 677
  dunes, 674, 678, 682, 683
  east coast 317–18, 669
  ecological approach, 672–3, 677, 678
  erosion, 672
  floods, 672, 674
  high risk areas, 673, 674
  high-water mark, 413, 414, 415, 673, 677, 678, 680, 681, 682, 708
  intertidal area, 672, 683
  landward boundary, 414, 415, 673
  law
    generally, 675ff
    problems, 684–8
    state land, alienation, 686–7
    territorial extent of, 678–80
  legislation, 21, 675ff
  low-water mark, 414, 673, 677, 681, 708
  management
    generally, 672–5
    need for 670–2, 688–9
    new administration, 688
    objectives, 674
    policy, 689
    principles, 674–5, 683, 687
    problems, 683ff, 687
  people, influx of, 670, 671
  pollution, 670, 671
  regulations, 112, 677–8
  sea-level, rise in, 50, 671–2, 680
  seaward boundary, 673, 681
  separate Act, 118
  south coast, 609
  surf zone, 414
  tidal lagoon, 657, 658, 665, 673
  west coast, 316–17, 670
  see also Environmental impact assessment; Environmental impact report; Environmental ombudsman; Estuaries; Integrated environmental management; Offshore minerals; Sea-shore
Committee for Environmental Management, 23, 77, 107–8, 240, 243
Common law
  amendment of, 259, 653–4, 655, 657, 676, 677
  relevance of, 95, 137, 363–5, 408, 654, 661, 727
  see also Roman law; Roman-Dutch law
Common property resources
  abuse of, 36, 40
  access to, 36, 39
  air, 309
  exploitation of, 51, 294
  future task for policy-makers, 51
  valuation of, 36–7, 39
  water, 294, 303
Commons, tragedy of, 36
Community, responsibility for environmental care, 3
Compensation
  bond to provide, 45–6
  right to, 117, 118–19
  unsuitability of claims, 97
  see also Economic incentives
Concurrence/consent
  to determine policy, 104
  to identify activities, 108, 111
  undesirable, 113, 118
Conservancy, 711, 745–6
Conservation areas, 707–8—*see also* Protected areas
Constitutional law
  international law, incorporation of, 145–6
  parliamentary sovereignty, 142
  relevance of, 97, 143–6
  state, changing role of, 142, 143, 144
  treaty, effect of, 155–6
  see also Bill of rights; Constitution; Human rights
Constitutional negotiation
  confrontation, 54
  environmental administration, 55, 75
  environmental monitoring agency, 62
  policy, focus on, 61
Constitution
  bill of rights, 142
  courts, role of, 142
  environmental protection through, 142
  full judicial review, 142
  ombudsman, 145
  preamble to, 145
  principles of state policy, 145

Constitution *(continued)*
special status of, 142
supreme law, 142
see also Bill of rights; Constitutional law; Human rights
Consultation
to define limited development area, 109
to determine environmental policy, 104
to identify activities, 108, 111
Contiguous zone, 327–8
Continental shelf
basis for offshore mining, 406–7
coastal states, sovereignty, 328–9, 679
defined, 316
diamond mining, 386
extent of, 316
importance of, 316
international law, 163, 328–9
oil and gas exploration, 391, 393, 394, 395
pollution of, 167
Contingent valuation, 38
Co-ordination
implementation of, 101–2, 489, 729
lack of, 242–3, 245, 246
need of, 70, 249, 631, 668
plant protection, 242, 244
see also Fragmentation of functions
Cost-benefit
analysis, 35–6
concept of, 32–3
measuring rod, 33–5
unequal distribution, 48
see also Environmental costs
Council for Nuclear Safety, 22, 125, 555, 556, 557–60, 563
Council for Scientific and Industrial Research, 24, 426, 453, 465, 484, 530, 576, 611, 619
Council for the Environment
coastal zone management, 672, 673, 674, 683, 689
difference with Committee for Environmental Management, 107–8
differently constituted, 20
environmental policy, 104
establishment, 19, 73, 74, 83, 107, 125
integrated environmental management, 152, 749, 761, 762
members, 73
mountains, 646
noise, 22
protected areas, 240
publications, 24, 75
terms of reference, 19, 23, 74, 77, 243
wilderness area, 705
see also South African Committee on Environmental Conservation
Court order, enforcement of, 127–8
Criminal law
alternative remedies, 131–2
forfeiture, 131
limitations, 128–32, 686
order to repair damage, 116
penalties, 116, 130–1
primary application of, 128–9
prosecutions, 129–30, 150
prosecutors, 129
relevance for environmental law, 96
subsidiary application of, 128–9
Cultural resources
defined, 87, 90, 92
protection
commencement of, 15
international, 175–6, 177
Dams
capacity, 648
construction, 308, 654
control area, 308
ecosystem type, 648
favoured option, 282
government, 282, 307, 308, 648, 650–1
habitat, 307–8
impacts, 222, 284–5, 311, 312, 314, 650–1, 662, 742
irrigation needs, 742
private, 282–3, 307, 651
purpose, 648
urban complexes, 651
waterworks—*see* Water
see also Freshwater systems; Indigenous plants; Rivers; Water
Decision-making—*see* Administrative decision-making
Defence areas, 708
Delegation of authority, 70, 195, 200, 201, 229, 247, 479
Democracy, relevance of for environmental conservation, 12–13, 56–7, 68, 79, 80, 143
Department of Agriculture
crime investigation by, 129
jurisdiction, 77, 194ff
mining, 370
pesticides, 535
plant protection, 242, 243
potential conflict with conservation, 120, 244
Department of Environment Affairs
coastal zone management, 684–5
connection with Council for the Environment, 107
extension of jurisdiction, 19, 21, 77, 453, 469, 568
formation, 73–4
functions, 77, 120
integrated environmental management, 751, 754, 757, 758, 761
mountains, 636
origin, 19
overlap of jurisdiction, 101
pollution control branch, 77, 453, 568
President's Council recommendations, 75, 77, 78
publications, 24
sea-shore, 676
sub-directorate for built environment, 59
super department, 74
Department of Mineral and Energy Affairs
jurisdiction, 77–8
potential conflict with conservation, 120
radiation control, 555
Department of National Education
jurisdiction, 77

Department of National Health and Population Development
  air pollution control, 436, 437, 447, 450, 451, 453, 454
  crime investigation by, 129
  environmental health, 620, 621, 623
  jurisdiction, 77
  radiation control, 555, 561, 568
  water pollution control, 469
Department of Regional and Land Affairs
  jurisdiction, 77, 242, 724, 725, 730
Department of Transport
  jurisdiction, 77
Department of Water Affairs and Forestry
  aims, 302, 666
  conflict with conservation, 120
  devolution of functions, 458, 459
  environmental impact assessment, 308, 314
  forests, 229
  integrated catchment management, 293, 315
  jurisdiction, 77, 456, 469
  major publication, 24
  management options, 282
  mountains, 631, 636
  plant protection, 242, 244
  prosecutions, 130
  rainfall stimulation, 309
  reconciliation of conflicting interests, 456
  research, 312
  river management, 666
  uniform strategy, need for, 314
  water quality standards, 288
  water utilization branch, 459–60
Deposit—refund system, 45–6, 131—*see also* Economic incentives; Environmental bonds
Deregulation, 66, 79
Detention of objects, 127
Developed countries
  resource consumption, 55–6, 159
  waste production, 55–6
Developing countries
  attitudes to environment, 159
  environment, effect on, 159
Development, balance with conservation, 2, 3, 27–8, 51, 101, 104, 179, 244, 246—*see also* Sustainability
Development Bank of Southern Africa, 58
Devolution of functions
  certain protected areas, 74
  coastal zone, 676
  counterbalance, 81
  marine resources, 74
  mountains, 631
  plant protection, 244
  required, 80
  water management, 459
Direct controls, 39–40
Dispute resolution—*see* Alternative dispute resolution; Environmental dispute resolution
Drought, 16, 211
Dust—*see* Air pollution
Dutch East India Company, 13
Dynamic opportunity cost valuation, 38
Earth day, 18
Earthlife Africa, 153
Ecological impact assessment, 275—*see also* Environmental impact assessment
Ecology
  defined, 4
  use of term, 4
Economic development, 27
Economic growth
  defined, 27
  environment, effect on, 27
  rapid, 27
Economic ideology
  capitalism, 66, 67, 71
  socialism, 66, 67, 71
Economic incentives
  benefits, 46–7
  different types, 42–6, 131
  generally, 40–1, 131
Economic resources
  concept, 29
  role in international law, 158–9
Economists
  attitude to natural resources, 29
  environmental impact, consideration of, 29
Ecosystem
  conservation of, 2, 72, 231, 240, 260, 270–1, 705
  degradation of by agriculture, 744
  economic activity, effect of, 27–8
  see also Freshwater systems; Indigenous plants
Emissions trading programme, 44—*see also* Economic incentives; Marketable permits
Endangered species—*see* Indigenous plants; Wild animals
Energy, 151, 417, 419–20, 422—*see also* Air pollution; Offshore minerals; Eskom; Sasol
Environment
  anthropogenic, 91
  built, 84
  economic, 84
  definition, 4, 83–92, 118, 312
  exploitation of, 12, 26
  extensive approach to, 84–6
  individual components of, 83
  labour, 84
  limited approach to, 86–8
  natural, 84, 86–8, 89–90
  need for definition, 83–4
  political, 84
  semantic perspective, 84
  social, 84
  spatial, 84
  term, avoidance of, 88–9
  term, use of, 4, 64
  see also Cultural resources
Environmental administration
  co-ordination, 101–2
  contingency approach, 65
  international level, 76
  local level, 78
  multiple, 101
  national level, 76–8
  open-system approach, 65
  overlap, 101
  see also Administrative service—provision systems; Co-ordination; Fragmentation of functions

Environmental audit, 131
Environmental bonds, 44–5—*see also* Economic incentives
Environmental concern, rise of
  generally, 11–25
  history, 11–24, 72–5, 196–7
  indicators of, 13
Environmental costs
  external, 36–7, 40
  internalization of, 40–1, 487
  resource use, 29
  seriousness of, 28
  see also Cost-benefit
Environmental damage, reparation of, 116, 127–8
Environmental diseases—*see* Environmental health
Environmental dispute resolution
  primary areas of use, 147–53
  role of in US, 146–7, 148, 149, 151, 152, 153
  role of in South Africa, 147, 150–1, 152–3, 154
  see also Alternative dispute resolution
Environmental economics
  central concern of, 27–8
  defined, 27
  role of, 27
  underlying assumption of, 29
  see also Common property resources; Cost-benefit; Deposit-refund system; Economic growth; Economic ideology; Economic incentives; Economic resources; Economists; Emissions trading programme; Environmental bonds; Environmental costs
Environmental education
  change attitudes, 3
  solution to problems, 73
Environmental ethics, 2, 7–10, 55, 147, 250, 273–6, 294
Environmental evaluation
  alternatives, consideration of, 762
  analysis/interpretation, 767
  bias, 763, 766
  communication, 767
  data collection, 766–7
  defined, 763, 764
  environmental analysis, 764
  impact identification, 767
  impacts, types of, 764–6
  methods, 767–71
    checklists, 767–8, 771
    cross-tabulation approach, 772–6
    Delphi technique, 770, 771
    environmental evaluation system, 771
    Leopold matrix, 768–9
    mapping methods, 769–70, 776–9, 780
    matrix methods, 767–9, 772–6, 780
    overlays, 769–70, 776–9, 780
    panel evaluation techniques, 770–1
    suitability in South Africa, 771–9
  multi-disciplinary approach, 763
  objectivity, 763, 766
  origin, 762, 763
  purpose, 762, 766–7, 771–2
  social component, 763
  tasks, 766–7, 772
  technical component, 763
  unattainable goals, 766
  see also Environmental impact assessment; Environmental impact report; Integrated environmental management
Environmental health
  acceptable risk, 617
  accidents
  acute respiratory tract infections, 597–8, 601
  administration, 620–3
  agriculture, impact on health, 741–2
  air pollution
    ambient pollutants, 598–9
    emission levels, 600–1
    episodes, 597
    global, 600
    guidelines, 592
    health effects, 418, 596ff
    indoor, 599–600
    industrial, 601–2
  asbestos exposure, 592, 600, 604
  asthma, 597, 598, 602
  bilharzia, 607, 650
  bronchitis, 597
  buildings, 599–600
  cancer, 591, 597, 599, 604, 617
  carbon monoxide, 598
  cardiovascular diseases, 597
  chemical contamination, 608
  children, 592, 599, 601, 602, 603–4, 605, 606, 613
  cholera, 604, 608, 610, 650
  chronic obstructive pulmonary diseases, 597
  cigarette smoke, 591, 593, 597, 598, 599, 602
  concerns, 590–1
  data, 592, 594, 617
  description, 590
  diarrhoea, 604, 605–6
  education, 622
  emphysema, 597
  environmental epidemiology, 594
  environmental monitoring, 593–4
  epidemiological studies, 612–13
  epidemiological surveillance, need for, 613
  food-borne infections, 615
  gastro-entiritis, 604, 610
  hazardous waste, health effects, 611ff
  hepatitis A, 604, 607, 610
  ill-health effects, nature of, 592–3
  impact analysis, 595, 596
  information, access to, 617
  lead, exposure to, 418, 590, 591, 593, 594, 602–4
  legislation, 619–20
  malaria, 606–7
  marine pollution, 610–11
  national objectives, 622–3
  nitrogen dioxide, 598
  noise, health effects, 615
  occupational health, 616–17
  ozone, 598
  pesticides
    health effects, 541, 613ff
    review of, 592
    use of, 613
  pharyngitis, 598

Environmental health *(continued)*
pneumonia, 597
polio, 604, 607
professional staff, 618–19, 622
public perception of risk, 617
radiation, 592
research, 619
respiratory tract, deposition in, 597
risk assessment, 594–6
sanitation, 605–6
sick building syndrome, 600
sulphur dioxide, 598–9
sustainable development, link with, 590
training, 618–19
tropical diseases, 606–8
typhoid, 604, 608, 610, 650
unborn foetus, 592
uncertain hazards, 591
water
drinking water, 590, 592, 593, 603, 608–10, 614
health effects, 604ff
quality guidelines, 611
recreational water quality, 610–11
related diseases, 605, 650
Environmental impact assessment
as solution to problems, 73
assessment methodologies, 764
bias, 760–1
coastal zone, 687–8
confidentiality, 761
cumulative impacts, 760
defined, 764
emergence, 748
environmental impact analysis, 764
health component of, 595
impacts, types of, 764–6
mining, 373, 503
need for, 111, 748, 753
preconditions, 748–9
principal components, 754
problems, 748, 759–61, 770
public participation, 755, 760–1
scope, 754
significance of impact, 759–60
St Lucia mining controversy, 152–3
town/regional planning, 715
ultimate aim, 111
water projects, 308, 313, 314, 664
see also Environmental evaluation; Environmental impact report; Integrated environmental management
Environmental impact report
audi alteram partem, type of, 96
bias, 760–1
coastal zone, 688
contents, 754, 757, 758, 764, 726, 779
guidelines, 757–8
identified activity, 109, 111, 313
inadequacies, 759
innovation, 118
landfill sites, 503
limited development area, 110, 703
ministerial discretion, 123
obligation to submit, 111, 373
requirements, 757, 758
review, 757–9
see also Environmental evaluation; Environmental impact assessment; Environmental impact statement; Identified activity; Integrated environmental management; Limited development area
Environmental impact statement, 764—*see also* Environmental impact report
Environmental interpretation programme, 241
Environmental law
distinctive principles, 96–8, 118
identification, 95–6
implementation, 120–54
narrow sense, 96
nature, 96–8
scope, 83, 92–6
wide sense, 96
Environmental legislation
codification, 99
diffuse nature, 99
exploitive, 94, 95
gradations, 92–5
historical development, 13–23
indicator of concern, 13
spectrum, 92–5
Environmental litigation
discouragement of, 13
importance of, 146
international law, 161–3
scarcity, 13, 147
shortcomings, 146
see also Alternative dispute resolution; Case law
Environmental management
African context, 250–1
compass, 3
defined, 3
environmental law, object of, 92
low priority, 79
objective, 3
socio-political issues, 53–4, 60–2
see also Integrated environmental management
Environmental ombudsman
advocate-general, 141
coastal zone management, 689
constitution, 145
defined, 140
shortcomings, 141
South African position, 141
value of, 140–1
Environmental Planning Professions Interdisciplinary Committee, 19
Environmental policy
administratively determined, 103
compliance with, 105–6
contents, 104–5
determination, 104, 106–7, 123, 243–4, 244, 245
development, 75–6
enforcement, 105–6
freshwater systems, 312–13
judicial review, 105–6
lack of, 243, 245, 313, 314
legal basis, 96
legislature, determination by, 106–7, 244
mountains, 638
need for, 75, 102–3

Environmental policy *(continued)*
  non-governmental organizations, 54
  principles for, 104–5
  private sector compliance, 106
  scientific input, 80
  search for, 73
  waste, 514
  subordinate legislation, 103
  see also White Paper on a national policy regarding environmental conservation
Environmental problems
  classification of, 4–6
  reasons for, 6–7
Environmental right—*see* Bill of rights; Human rights; International law
Environmental tribunal
  ad hoc basis, 140
  different models, 140
  existing, 139
  issues relating to, 140
  need for, 139, 205
  shortcomings, 139–40
  standing, 140
  see also Air Pollution; Appeal; Board of Investigation
Eskom, 304, 421, 424, 425, 426, 427, 428, 433, 434, 451
Estuaries
  acquatic ecosystem, 648
  coastal zone, part of, 673, 683
  degradation of, 288, 671, 674, 686, 742, 744
  high-risk area, 674
  irrigation, effect of, 742
  not public streams, 655, 656
  siltation, 744
Ethics—*see* Environmental ethics
Eutrophication—*see* Freshwater systems
Exclusive economic zone, 167, 168, 173, 174, 329, 330, 336, 406–7, 673, 679
Exclusive fishing zone, 328
Executive supremacy, 119, 121, 147
Expropriation—*see* Land, acquisition
External control, 114, 138
Externalities, 40–1
Extinction
  animals, 5, 251, 252, 273, 275–6
  ecosystems, 5
  plants, 5
  resources, 5, 6
Financial aid, 117, 124—*see also* Compensation; Economic incentives; Subsidies
Fire—*see* Indigenous plants; Mountains; Mountain catchment areas; Soil
Fish—*see* Freshwater fish; Living marine resources; Wild animals
Fisheries—*see* Living marine resources
Food and Agricultural Organization, 592
Forests
  acid deposition, 418
  demarcated/undemarcated, 704
  fishing in, 310
  freshwater systems, relevance for, 277
  mining, 704
  mountains, 626, 628–9, 632–3
  nature reserves, 121, 231, 232, 247, 310, 312, 635, 664, 704–5
  produce, 312, 705
  protection of, 14, 15, 230–1, 704–6
  rights to, 704
  servitude, 704
  soil conservation, relevance for, 206–7; 704
  see also Afforestation; Indigenous plants; Mountains
Forestry Council, 233, 246
Forfeiture, 131
Fossil fuels—*see* Air pollution
Fragmentation of functions, 70, 78, 80, 242–3, 451, 453, 469, 489, 684, 714—*see also* Co-ordination
Free resources, 29
Freshwater fish
  conservation legislation, 309–12
  conservation status, 253–4
  exotic, 14
  fishing, 309–10
  forests, 310
  government control areas, 310
  habitat change by agriculture, 744
  impoundments, effect of, 312—*see also* Dams
  interference with stream course, effect of, 311
  invasive, 311
  migration, barriers to, 291
  national parks, 310
  provincial nature reserves, 310–11
  translocations, 284
Freshwater systems
  acidification, 418
  alien biotas, 291–3
  ecosystems, characteristics of, 297
  environmental allocation, 289–9, 293, 302, 653
  eutrophication, 286–8, 671, 741
  human population concentrations, 652—*see also* Urbanization
  interbasin transfers, 278, 282, 284, 458, 651–2
  invasive plants, effect of, 292–3
  lakes, 278, 648
  legislation, 295–314
  living resources
    fish—*see* Freshwater fish
    other, 312
  management, 277, 282, 294, 314
  minister, discretionary powers, 300–2, 310, 661
  natural vegetation, role of, 277, 279
  pollution, relevance of, 285–8, 294, 299, 311—*see also* Water
  problems, 283–93
  river regulation, 284–5—*see also* Rivers
  salinization, 285–6, 294, 651, 671, 742–3—*see also* Agriculture; Rivers; Soil
  see also Aquaculture; Catchment; Dams; Estuaries; Freshwater fish; Rainfall; Rivers; Water; Wetlands
Frogs, 254
Future generations, care for, 48, 50
Game farms, 20
Game reserve, 710—*see also* Protected areas
Geophysical impacts—*see* Irreversible biological and geophysical impacts; Reversible biological and geophysical impacts

Giant's castle, 15
Global warming—*see* Greenhouse effect
God
  concern for creation, 9–10
  creator of universe, 8, 9
Gough Island, 672
Government institution, defined, 106
Grass burning, control of, 13, 15—*see also* Indigenous plants
Greenhouse effect, 1, 50, 72, 170, 419, 600, 671
Habitat
  degradation, 291
  protection, 72, 240, 260, 261, 269, 270
  see also Protected areas
Habitat Council, 19, 20, 23, 641, 646
Hazardous substances—*see* Ionizing radiation; Pesticides; Waste
High seas, 157, 160, 163, 165
Hluhluwe Game Reserve, 11, 15
Human health—*see* Environmental health
Human population growth, 1, 7, 51, 55–7, 72, 159, 439
Human rights
  collective, 143
  first generation, 142, 144
  generally, 142
  individual, 143
  limitation clause, 144–5
  negative character, 142, 144
  opposition to, 145
  right to environment, 142, 143—*see also* International law
  second generation, 143
  state, involvement of, 143, 144
  third generation, 55, 143, 144
  see also Bill of rights; Constitution; Constitutional law
Hunting—*see* Wild animals
Identified activity
  area, 108
  concurrence, 108, 111
  conditions, 109, 111
  consultation, 108, 111
  effect, 108–9, 732
  environmental impact report, 109, 111, 313
  procedure, 108
  type of, 108, 313
  see also Environmental impact report
Impoundments—*see* Dams
Indian National Soil Conservation Association, 24
Indigenous plants
  afforestation, effect of, 220–1, 227, 243, 245
  agricultural pests, effect of, 237–8
  alien plants, effect of, 221–2
  aquatic, 235–6, 239, 662–3
  biodiversity, 212, 215–20
  biome
    desert, 219–20, 222, 223
    forest, 220, 222, 223, 228–9
    fynbos, 215–17, 222, 223, 224, 243
    grassland, 218, 222, 223
    Nama-karoo, 218–19, 222, 223
    savanna, 217–18, 222, 223
    succulent-karoo, 219, 222, 223, 224
  biotas, protection of, 230–2
  Cape Floristic Kingdom, 212, 215, 242, 247
  classification, 225–6
  climate, 213–14
  conservation, justification of, 223–4
  conveyance of, 228
  cultivation, effect on, 220–1
  definition, 225
  ecosystems, protection of, 230–2
  endangered, 175, 227, 241–2, 249
  environmental interpretation programme, 241
  exportation/importation, 228
  extinction, 5
  fire, 193, 196, 198, 199, 206, 207–8, 214–15, 218, 229, 231, 232–3, 244, 246, 247, 306, 664
  forest produce, 231
  grazing, effect of, 214, 218, 219, 221
  international protection, 175
  invasive plants, effect of, 237, 246, 248, 249, 740
  inventory data, lack of, 222–3
  legislation
    administration of, 242–9
    generally, 224–5
    sufficiency of, 239–49
  mining, effect of, 222, 245
  noxious plants, effect of, 236–9, 240, 241, 243, 248, 249, 292–3
  picking of, 227
  possession of, 228
  protected, 225–7
  protected areas, conservation
    inside, 222–3, 224, 225, 231, 240, 241
    outside, 223, 225–36, 240
  purchase/sale, 228
  riparian vegetation, destruction of, 650
  river impoundment, effect of, 222—*see also* Dams
  species density, 212
  state forests, 230, 244
  transportation networks, effect of, 222, 227
  trees
    prohibition of planting, 122
    protection of, 13, 15, 72, 206–7, 230–1, 233, 245, 246, 664
  urbanization, impact of, 221, 245
  weeds, effect of, 236–7, 249
  see also Afforestation; Agriculture; Invasive plants; Noxious plants; Protected areas
Inkatha Freedom Party
  conflict with UDF, 152
  environmental policy, 54
Input valuation, 37
Institute for Ecological Research, 754
Insurance law, 97
Integrated environmental management
  alternatives, identification and selection of, 756
  assessment inadequacies, 759
  assessment routes, 753–4
  checklist of environmental characteristics, 754–5
  coastal zone, 675, 688
  comprehensive perspective, 72
  confidentiality, 761
  disadvantaged communities, participation of, 755–6
  establishment, 749
  identification/notification of parties, 755, 760–1

Integrated environmental management (*continued*)
ignored, 246
impact assessment—*see* Environmental impact assessment
implementation, 754–9
initial assessment, 753–4
integration into broader planning, 760
legal enforceability, 245, 373, 761
listed activities, 754
listed environments, 754
noise, 577, 579
principles, 749–50
problems, 748, 759–61
procedure, 750–3
project proposal
appeal against decision, 752
approval, conditions, 751, 752
audits, 753
classification, 751
decision in respect of acceptability, 751–2
development, 751
environmental contract, 752
environmental management plan, 752
implementation, 752
monitoring programme, 753
record of decision, 752
screening, 751
purpose, 749
review, 757–9
scoping, 754, 755
town/regional planning, 715, 725
waste management, 493, 498, 503, 508
see also Environmental evaluation; Environmental impact assessment; Environmental impact report; Environmental management
Interbasin transfer—*see* Freshwater systems
Inter-departmental advisory committee for the protection of man against poisons, 540
Interdepartmental committee on the conservation of mountain catchments in South Africa—*see* Report of the interdepartmental committee on the conservation of mountain catchments in South Africa
Interdict, use by administrative body, 116, 128, 137—*see also* Private law
Internal control, 114, 138–9
Internal waters, 327
International Atomic Energy Agency, 171, 547
International Energy Agency, 434
International Commission on Radiological Protection, 547, 548
International law
binding nature, 156
court decisions, 161–3
customary law, 156, 160–3
economic factors, 158–9
good neighbourliness, 161
hazardous waste, 171
innocent passage, 162
living marine resources, 173–5, 330–1
marine environment, 325–9
marine pollution, 163–8
maritime zones, 326–9
municipal courts, application by, 145–6
Nairobi declaration, 178
nature of, 155
need for, 157
nuclear accidents, 171
nuclear weapon tests, 162–3, 171–2
outer space, 172–3
outstanding characteristic, 180
protected areas recognized by, 697–8
relevance of, 97
right to clean environment, 143
self-defence, 160–1
sources, 155–6
sovereignty, principle of, 160
state responsibility, prinicple of, 160
territoriality principle, 679
traditional law, limits of, 157
treaties/conventions
defined, 155, 158
effect of, 155–6
overview of, 163–79
World Charter for Nature, 178–9
see also Contiguous zone; Continental shelf; Exclusive economic zone; Exclusive fishing zone; High seas; Internal waters; Rivers; Territorial waters
International Maritime Organization, 164
International Union for the Conservation of Nature, 75, 690, 691, 697
International Whaling Commission, 173–4
Invasive plants
agriculture, effect on, 740
control of, 200, 234, 236, 248, 249
freshwater systems, effect on, 292–3, 311
indigenous plants, threat to, 246
mountain catchment area, 237, 240
soil degradation, 192–3
see also Agriculture; Indigenous plants; Noxious plants
Invertebrates
conservation status, 252–3
protection of, 267–8, 275
Ionizing radiation
Atomic Energy Corporation, 22, 555, 556–7, 558—*see also* Atomic Energy Board
Council for Nuclear Safety, 22, 125, 555, 556, 557–60, 563, 568
effects, 547–8
electronic product licenses, 566–7
electronic products, 564–7
environmental control, 549–50
hazardous substances, 123, 555, 563–7
international co-operation, 563
legislation
historical development of, 18, 22, 555–6
revision of, 568
mining, 555, 556, 561
nuclear accidents, 560–1, 562
nuclear damage, 555, 559, 560, 562, 568
Nuclear Development Corporation of South Africa (Pty) Ltd, 22
nuclear installations, 123, 556, 558–60, 568, 733
nuclear licences, 123, 127, 556, 558–60
nuclear-hazard material, 123, 558, 559, 560
protection principles, 548–9

Ionizing radiation *(continued)*
  radioactive material, 546, 547, 548, 555, 556, 557, 562, 564
  radioactive nuclides, 556, 557, 561, 568
  radioactive waste, 164, 166, 517, 559, 562–3, 564, 568
  range, 544–5
  source material, 557, 561
  sources, 545–7
  vessels, 558–60
  see also International law; Non-ionizing radiation; Waste
Irreversible biological and geophysical impacts, 5–6
Islands, 672, 709
Judeo-Christian ethic, 8–10
Judicial review
  court's power, 116
  environmental policy, 105–6
  giving of reasons, 114–16
  meaning of, 115–16
  shortcomings, 13, 138, 685
Kalahari Gemsbok National Park, 696
Keep South Africa Beautiful, 24
Krill, 174
Kruger National Park, 12, 15, 16, 253, 256, 294, 696, 697, 698
Lake area
  administration, 701
  definition, 700
  establishment, 700–1
  private land, 701
  protected area, 20–1, 700–1
  regulations, 701
  vegetation, 234
  water resources, 307
Land
  acquisition, 124–5, 196, 200, 205, 206, 663, 733–4, 735
  distribution, 57–8
  ethic, 30
  management, 58—*see also* Indigenous plants; Soil
  reform, 58
  subdivision, 209, 720, 726, 732
  see also Landowner; Land-use planning; Town/regional planning
Landowner
  compensation, 117, 687, 736, 737–8
  concept of landownership, revision of, 738
  financial aid, 117, 124, 736–7
  obligatory directives, 122, 201, 735
  rights, limitation of, 686, 729, 734, 735, 736, 737–8—*see also* Land-use, restrictions upon
  riparian owner—*see* Rivers; Water
  wetlands, rights in respect of, 306
  wild animals
    attitude to, 250
    rights to, 259, 269
  see also Land; Soil; Wild animals
Land-use planning
  cadastral controls, 726–7
  coastal zone, 682–3
  history of, 18
  justification, 738
  land, subdivision of, 209, 720, 726, 732
  macrocosmic, 728ff
  national development plan, 729, 730
  natural resources development, 728
  nuisance, 727–8
  overcrowding, 727
  physical planning, 728–32
  policy plans, 730–2
  property law, 96–7
  purpose, 726, 729
  regional development plan, 729, 730
  regional structure plan, 729, 730
  rivers, 663–4
  squatting, regulation of, 726–7
  structure plan, 683, 721–2
  urban structure plan, 730
  zoning, 638–41, 727, 729, 737
  see also Land; Landowner; Land-use; Town/regional planning
Land-use
  compensation, 117, 118–19, 736, 737–8
  environmental dispute resolution, 151, 152
  practices, 96–7, 734–5
  restrictions upon, 12, 117, 122, 195, 196, 201–2, 686, 729, 732, 734, 735, 736, 737–8
  see also Landowner; Land-use planning
Legislation—*see* Environmental legislation
Limited development area
  activity, 109, 703
  any area, 109
  coastal zone, 678
  conditions, 110, 111, 112, 703
  effect of, 109, 110
  environmental impact report, 110, 703
  procedure, 109
Litigation—*see* Environmental litigation
Living marine resources
  abalone fishery, 325
  bottom trawl fishery, 319–21
  categories, 319
  commissions of inquiry, 330, 334
  conservation, development of, 21
    history of, 14, 16, 73
  factories, licensing of, 334
  first protection of, 14, 16
  fish
    protection of, 122, 329–35
    status of, 329, 677
  fishing boats, licensing of, 334
  foreign fleets, role of, 331
  importance of, 318–19, 670
  international protection, 123–5, 177
  legislation
    geographic extent, 332, 679
    overview, 329–35
  line fishery, 324–5
  need for management, 332–3
  policy, 331–2, 335
  purse seine fishery
  quotas, 127, 333—*see also* total allowable catch
  rights, granting of, 124
  rock lobster fishery, 322–3
  sea, definition of, 332
  squid fishery, 323–4

Living marine resources *(continued)*
  total allowable catch, 320, 322, 333, 336
  total catch, 319
  see also—International law; Marine pollution; Whales
Local government
  coastal zone management, 683–4
  collapse of, effect on environment, 55
  environmental functions, 78, 442, 450–1, 452, 459, 579–80, 702
  environmental health, 621–2
  participation, 81
  placement of service-provision, 69–70
  suitability, 80
Locus standi—*see* Standing
Mammals
  protection, 266–7
  terrestrial, 256
  see also Wild animals
Management advisory committee—*see* Protected natural environment
Management agreement, 241
Marine pollution
  civil liability and compensation, 166–7
  classification, 335
  dumping at sea, 166, 177, 474–6, 484, 488–9
  from land-based sources, 167–8, 670, 671
  from sea-bed exploitation, 167
  habitat and resources, 477–9
  harbours, 480–2
  international law, 163–8
  noxious materials, 166, 167, 177
  oil, 121, 122, 127, 164–7, 176–7, 329, 476–7
  operational discharges from ships, 164–5
  public health, 480, 610–11
  regional protection, 176
  sea water quality management objectives, 463
  sea-shore, 480
  ship, detention of, 127
  wrecks, 474
  see also Environmental health; International law; Offshore minerals
Marine reserves, 16, 21, 240, 335, 673, 708
Marine resources—*see* Living marine resources; Offshore minerals
Marion island, 672
Marketable permits, 43–4, 131
  see also Economic incentives
Medical Research Council, 602, 611, 619
Minerals—*see* Offshore minerals; Terrestrial minerals
Mining—*see* Offshore minerals; Terrestrial minerals
Mossgas, 396, 416, 421
Mountain catchment areas
  administration, 636ff
  afforestation, 628–9, 632–3
  control of, 302–3, 630ff
  declaration, 20
  definition, 625
  fire, 633–4
  habitats, 240
  importance, 624–5
  integrated catchment management, 645–6
  legislation, 20, 630ff
  natural vegetation, 234, 244
  noxious plants, 237, 240
  relevance for freshwater, 302–3, 624–5, 625, 626–7, 631–2, 642, 645, 677
  report on conservation, 17, 20, 625, 626, 628, 638
  soil conservation, relevance for, 207–8
  total area, 626
  uniform administration, 642–5
  wetlands, 307
  see also Catchment; Mountains; Water
Mountain Club of South Africa, 641–2
Mountains
  conservation management, 636–8, 642–5
  conservation status, 628
  conservation, need for, 626–7
  definition, 624, 625
  ecological features, 624
  extent, 625–6
  legislation
    afforestation control, 632–3
    application of, 637, 642–5
    defence areas, 635
    fire control, 633–4
    flower harvesting, control of, 635
    generally, 630–1
    invader plants, control of, 633
    mining, 636
    protected areas, 635
    recreation, control of, 635–6
    soil, vegetation and water conservation, 631–2, 644
  man's impact, 628–30
    afforestation, 628–9
    agriculture, 628, 644
    infrastructure, 629, 636
    mining, 629
    recreation, 629–30
  mountain club, 641–2
  ownership of, 625–6
  policy, 638
  topographical features, 624
  value of, 626–7, 631
  zoning, 638–41
  see also Forests; Indigenous plants; Mountain catchment areas; Protected areas; Soil; Terrestrial minerals; Water; Wilderness area
Mozambique Current, 317
Namib-Naukluft Park, 222
Natal Parks Board, 261–2, 264, 710, 711
National Air Pollution Advisory Committee, 125, 437, 442, 443, 447, 448
National Advisory Committee on Electronic Products, 567
National botanic gardens, 229, 233, 241, 706
National Botanical Institute, 77, 233, 241, 243, 246, 706
National Committee for Nature Conservation, 107
National Committee on Air Pollution, 17
National Environmental Awareness Campaign, 24, 54, 57
National government—*see* Central government
National Institute for Water Research, 484

National Hiking Way Board, 77, 246
National hiking way system, 229
National Institute for Transportation and Road Research, 576
National monument, 21, 91–2, 234, 635, 692, 694, 706–7
National Monuments Council, 77, 243, 706–8
National Parks Board, 21, 24, 77, 242–3, 244, 699–700
National parks
 applicability of legislation, 123
 comprehensive powers, 121, 699–700
 definition, 693
 first legislation, 15, 17
 freshwater resources, 313
 funding, 700
 legislation, 698–700
 management, 693–4
 mountain, 635
 Natal, 710
 prohibited activities, 310, 700
 purpose, 698–9
 registered, 699
 river, 667
 scheduled, 699
 selection, 693–4
 state land, 699
 see also National Parks Board; Protected areas
National Regional Development Advisory Council, 724
National Veld Trust, 16
Natural heritage site, 252, 712—*see also* Protected areas
Natural Resources Development Council, 18, 73, 728
Nature area, 21, 112, 117, 702
Nature
 alienation from, 1
 defined, 86–7
Nature conservation
 growth of, 17, 20
 modern approach to, 260
Nature reserve
 forest, 121, 231, 232, 247, 310, 312, 635, 664, 704–5
 local, 709
 private, 20, 266, 635, 692, 709, 710, 711
 provincial, 17, 20, 667, 709, 710, 711
 special, 112, 313, 702–3
Noise
 airports, 576, 580
 assessment, 574–5
 buildings, 575, 577–8
 control officers, 585
 definition, 569, 571
 developing communities, 585–6
 environmental effects
  communication, 571
  physical, 571
  physiological, 571
  productivity, 571
  psychological, 571–2
 isolation of recipients, 578
 land use planning, 577, 583–4
 legislation
  by-laws, 581
  comprehensive, 113, 118
  disturbing noise, 583
  historical development, 17, 21–2
  local, 581
  national, 578–80
  nuisance, 582
  penalties, 585
  provincial, 581
  regulations, 112–13, 122, 579, 582–5
  selective application, 585
 measurement, 572–4
 occupational exposure, 580
 power tools, 576, 582–3
 private law remedies, 576
 resiting of source, 576–7
 roads, 575–6
 sound
  amplitude, 569
  frequency, 569
  human perception of, 570–1
  propagation, 569–70
 source control, 575–7
 transmission path control, 577–8
 transportation, 575, 579–80, 583
 see also Environmental health; Integrated environmental management
Non-government organizations, 15, 16, 53, 54, 61–2, 63
Non-ionizing radiation
 description, 550
 effects, 552–5
 electro-optical devices, 550–1
 lasers, 552–3
 legislation, 567–7
 microwave devices, 551, 553–4
 radio-frequency devices, 551, 553–4
 sources, 550–1
 ultrasound devices, 551, 554–5
 ultraviolet radiation, 550, 551, 552
 see also Ionizing radiation
Non-living marine resources, 175
Non-renewable resources, 3, 51, 18, 23—*see also* Offshore minerals; Terrestrial minerals
Noxious plants
 control of, 236–9, 243, 249
 early legislation, 14, 15
 freshwater systems, effect on, 249, 292–3
 indigenous plants, effect on, 248, 249
 mountain catchment areas, 241
 protected areas, 241
 river banks, 650
 river catchments, 664
 weeds, 198, 234, 236
 see also Agriculture; Freshwater systems; Indigenous plants; Invasive plants
Nuclear Development Corporation of South Africa (Pty) Ltd, 22
Nuclear installations—*see* Ionizing radiation
Nuclear licence—*see* Ionizing radiation
Nuclear weapon tests, 162–3, 171–2
Nuclear-hazard material—*see* Ionizing radiation
Nuisance, 15, 97, 727–8
Occupational health—*see* Environmental health
Offshore minerals, mining of
 coastal regions, 380, 670
 common law, 408–9
 deep sea-bed, 407–8

Offshore minerals, mining of *(continued)*
  diamonds
    exploitation, 383–90
    location/size of resource, 382–3
    nature of resource, 381–2
    value, 390
  environmental impact
    assessment, 415
    deep-sea areas, 404
    exploration of oil/gas, 405–6
    near-shore areas, 404
    production of oil/gas, 405
  geological surveys of coastal areas, 380
  glauconite
    exploitation, 400–1
    location/size of resource, 400
    nature of resource, 400
  heavy minerals
    exploration and exploitation, 397
    location/size of resource, 396–7
    nature of resource, 396
  international-law basis for, 406–8
  legislation, 409–15, 679
  manganese nodules
    exploitation, 402–4
    location/size of resource, 402
    nature of resource, 402
  off-shore, definition of, 406
  oil and gas
    exploitation technology, 396
    exploration and exploitation, 394–5, 396, 405–6, 673
    location/size of resource, 391–4
    mineral rights, 395–6
    nature of resource, 390–1
    production, 405
    value, 396
  phosphorite
    exploitation, 399–400
    location/size of resource, 398–9
    nature of resource, 397–8
  territorial extent of law, 408
  see also Continental shelf; Exclusive economic zone; International law
Oil pollution—*see* Marine pollution
Ombudsman—*see* Environmental ombudsman
Opencast mining—*see* Terrestrial minerals
Organization for Economic Co-operation and Development, 171, 179, 434
Outer space, 172
Output valuation, 38
Overpopulation—*see* Human population growth
Ozone layer, depletion of, 1, 27, 36, 50, 72, 89, 133, 169–70, 418, 419, 435
Pan Africanist Congress
  environmental policy of, 54
  view on land distribution, 57
Panel valuation, 38–9
Percy Fitzpatrick Institute for African Ornithology, 19
Pesticides
  agricultural products, 540, 543
  agricultural remedy, definition of, 535
  appeals, 537
  as hazardous substance, 540
  comparative law, 533–5
  concern over, development of, 523–4
  containers, 538, 539, 540, 542
  definition of, 523
  disposal of, control over, 539, 540
  environmental impact
    on communities, 528–9
    on ecosystems, 529–30
    on human beings, 525, 527, 543, 744
    on individual species, 524–8, 944
    on populations, 528
  foodstuff, 540–1, 543
  fungicides, 524
  herbicides, 523–4
  importation of, control over, 538, 540
  integrated pest management, 530–1
  international implications, 541
  legislation
    consolidation of, 542–3
    historical development of, 18, 532–3
    offences, 539, 541
    reform of, 542–3
  manufacture of, control over, 537–8, 540
  pest control operator, 122, 536, 537, 542
  private-law controls, 531–2
  public health, 541, 613–15
  registration, 127, 535–7, 541
  resistance to, 230, 523, 528, 744
  sale of, control over, 123, 538–9, 540
  state liability, 542
  stock remedy, definition of, 535
  use of, control over, 527, 539, 543
  see also Environmental health
Planning—*see* Land use planning
Planning Advisory Council, 19, 729
Plants—*see* Indigenous plants; Invasive plants; Noxious plants
Political transition, consequences for conservation, 54–5, 224
Polluter pays principle, 42, 159
Pollution charges, 42–3, 131—*see also* Economic incentives
Pongola Game Reserve, 11, 15
Population growth—*see* Human population growth
Poverty
  bearing costs of control, 46
  compensation, 47
  elimination of, importance, 50, 51, 58
  environment
    effect on, 159
    perspective on, 56
  increase of, 48
  over-exploitation, danger of, 27
Precipitation—*see* Rainfall
President's Council
  implementation of recommendations, 54
  land management, 57
  non-government organizations, 61, 62
  population increase, 55
  urban environments, 59–60
  see also the various Reports of the President's Council
Prince Edward Islands, 112, 255, 672
Private land
  public control over, 12, 117, 260

Private land *(continued)*
use of for conservation, 274
Private law
relevance for environmental law, 97, 259
remedies, 137–8
restricted role, 97, 137, 259
significance of, 137–8
wild animals, 259
Privatization, 66, 69, 79, 80, 204, 676
Problem animals, 14, 269
Property law, relevance for environmental law, 96–7
Property rights
immune to interference, 193
wild animals, 259
see also Common property resources; Land; Landowner
Prosecution—*see* Criminal law; Department of Agriculture; Department of National Health and Population Development; Department of Water Affairs and Forestry; Soil
Protected areas
biological diversity secured, 690
biosphere reserve, 697, 711–12
categories
international, 691ff
South African, 698ff
classification criteria, 691ff
conservation objectives, 690–1
establishment, 123, 241
extent, 690
growth, 15–6, 17, 20–1, 72, 690
indigenous plants, 222–3
international recognition, 697–8, 703
legislation
generally, 698ff
historical development, 698
rationalization, 712
uniform, need for 712–14
management objectives, 691, 692, 693, 694, 695
number, 221–3, 713
policy, need for, 712–14
proximate communities, access to, 58
public resort, 712
Ramsar site, 697–8
selection/management criteria, 692, 693, 694, 695, 696
size, 271–3, 693, 694, 695, 696, 713
strategy, lack of, 246
transfrontier, 696–7
world heritage site, 697
see also Conservancy; Game reserve; International law; Lake area; Limited development area; Mountains; National monument; National parks; Natural heritage site; Nature reserves; Protected natural environment; Wilderness area
Protected natural environment
category, 692
compensation, 117
declaration, 701
directions, 701
financial aid, 702
freshwater systems, 313
management advisory committee, 108, 702
management, 701–2
mountain, 635
nature area, substitution of, 112, 702
penalty, 703
see also Protected areas
Provincial administrations
air pollution control, 449
coastal zone, 684
forests, 28, 229, 243, 244, 247
land-use, 78
mountain catchment areas, 78, 240, 243
sea-shore, 78, 676
water management, 459
wild animals, 78, 260
see also Regional government
Public health, protection of, 15, 479–80—*see also* Environmental health
Public interest
balance with individual interest, 145
coastal zone, 686
furtherance by administration, 132
limitation clause, 144
litigation, 13
ministerial discretion, 300–2, 313–14
pesticide registration, 541
public rivers, 659, 665
remedies to assure compliance with, 132, 138
standing to litigate, 133, 686
state land, 121
Public participation
in administrative decision-making, 79, 80, 96, 147–8, 246, 308, 313, 455, 749–50, 755, 760–1
in parliamentary legislation, 99–100
lack of, 245
Public relations, 494
Public trust doctrine, application to wildlife law, 260
Quality of life
improvement of, 2, 56
reduction in, 1
role of law, 143
Radioactive material—*see* Ionizing radiation
Rainfall
acidic, 1
conversion to runoff, 647
exploitation, 647
mean annual, 213, 277, 280, 281, 647
modification of, 309
pattern, 281
runoff ratio, 277
summer, 213–14, 278
total runoff, 278, 647
variations, 278, 647
winter, 214, 278
see also Freshwater systems; Rivers; Water
Rand Water Board, 299, 457
Regional development advisory committee—*see* Town/regional planning
Regional development association—*see* Town/regional planning
Regional government
environmental functions, 78, 449, 459, 479
participation, 81
suitability, 80
see also Provincial administrations

Regional planning—*see* Town/regional planning
Regional Services Council—*see* Town/regional planning
Religion, role of in conservation, 8–10
Report of the commission of enquiry concerning the water laws of the Union, 17, 625
Report of the commission of inquiry into environmental legislation, 84
Report of the commission of inquiry into the allocation of quotas for the exploitation of living marine resources, 21, 23, 330, 334
Report of the commission of inquiry into the fishing industry, the utilization of fish and other living marine resources of South Africa and South West Africa, 21, 23, 330
Report of the commission of inquiry into certain aspects of the conservation and utilization of the living marine resources of the RSA, 21, 23, 330
Report of the committee of inquiry into safeguarding man against poisons, 540
Report of the drought investigation commission, 16
Report of the interdepartmental committee on the conservation of mountain catchments in South Africa, 17, 625, 626, 628, 638
Report of the Planning Committee of the President's Council on nature conservation, 20, 23, 74
Report of the Planning Committee of the President's Council on priorities between conservation and development, 20, 23, 74
Report of the scientific committee of enquiry into the exploitation of pelagic fish resources of South Africa and South West Africa, 21, 23, 330, 334
Report of the select committee on droughts, rainfall and soil erosion, 16
Report of the three committees of the President's Council on a national environmental management system
  air pollution, 453–4
  central government concern, 74
  coastal zone, 688
  compensation for landowners, 738
  delegation, 78
  environment, significance of, 53–4
  environmental ombudsman, 141
  environmental policy, 75, 77
  fragmented control rationalized, 77, 453, 469
  governmental concern manifested, 20, 23
  independent environmental agency, 689
  indigenous plants, 248
  integrated environmental management, 761
  mining, 355
  mountain catchment areas, 644–5
  nature conservation, 270
  policy differences with others, 54
  radiation, 568
  protected areas, 714
Reptiles
  conservation status, 254–5
  protection of, 267–8
Research Institute for Environmental Diseases, 619
Res nullius
  status of wild animals, 259
Resource management
  challenge of, 26–7
  criteria for, 32
  philosophy of, 27–32
  policy goal, 29, 31–2
  premises for, 31
  sustainability, 1, 2, 3, 31, 32, 33, 34, 35, 47, 49, 51, 744–6, 747
Resource policy, implementation method, 39
Resource use
  common property resources, 36–7
  cost and benefit, 32–3
  cost-benefit analysis, 35–7
  destruction, 25
  evaluation of, 32–9
  measuring rod, 33–5
  over-utilization, 6, 28, 39
  under-utilization, 28
Reversible biological and geophysical impacts, 5
Rivers
  abstraction of water, 649–50
  agricultural use, 649–51
  aquatic flora and fauna, 662–3
  banks, 658–9, 674, 680
  bed, 658–9
  boundary, 681, 682
  capital asset, 294
  classification, 648
  conservancy district, 303, 661, 667
  conservation authority, 315, 668
  conservation options, 667
  conservation status, 649
  conservation, need for, 649
  constituent parts, 649
  diversion of course, 162, 662, 682
  downstream users, costs to, 40–1
  environmental water allocation, 289–91, 293, 302, 653, 666–7
  flash floods, 742
  flow reduction, 288, 662, 742
  human impact on, 649–53
  industrial use, 652
  instream flow need, 290–1
  interbasin transfers, 278, 282, 284, 458, 651–2
  international law, 177, 665–6, 668
  islands, 659, 682
  law, development of, 653–4
  legal categories, 654
  legislative control measures, 661–4
  management, 177, 284–5, 294, 665–7
  navigability, 654, 658
  perennial, 654
  policy, 665
  pollution—*see* Water
  private river, 655, 656, 665
  private stream, 656–7
  protected area, 293–4
  public river, 654, 655, 657–60, 668
  recreation, effect of, 653, 659
  regulation, 284–5
  res publicae, 657–8
  reserve, 315

Rivers *(continued)*
riparian owner, 296–7, 308, 655, 656, 657, 658, 659, 660, 665
road-building, effect of, 653
salinization, 285, 294, 651, 742–3
sources, 656
state control, 659–60
tidal lagoon, 657, 658, 665, 673
tidal river, 655, 656, 657, 658, 665
urban use, 651–2
use of, 649–53
vital water resource, 647, 648, 668
water, rights in respect of, 660–1
zones, 648
see also Afforestation; Aquaculture; Catchment; Dams; Estuaries; Freshwater systems; Rainfall; Water
Roads
advertisements along, 16
building, impact of, 5
mountains, 629
noise, 575–6
rivers, 653
soil erosion, 209
Roman-Dutch law
international law, 326
rivers
classification, 654
navigability, 658
status, 296, 657
use, 310
sea-shore, status, 675–6
see also Common law
Roman law
air, status of, 309
fishing, 310
rivers
bank, 658
classification, 654, 658
common use, 297
navigability, 654
status, 296, 302, 657
sea-shore
status, 675, 676
Sabie Game Reserve, 11–12, 15, 698
Salinization—*see* Agriculture; Freshwater systems, Rivers; Soil; Urbanization
Sasol, 69, 421, 451
Sea Fisheries Advisory Council, 77, 333, 334
Sea Fisheries Research Institute, 330, 334, 336
Sea Fishery Advisory Committee, 333–4
Sea Fishery Fund, 331
Sea-level, rise in, 50, 671–2, 680
Seals, conservation of, 14, 174
Sea—*see* Coastal zone; International law; Living marine resources; Marine pollution; Sea-shore; Water
Sea-shore
alienation, 676, 686–7
definition, 673, 677
lease, 676
marina, 676
ownership, 676
protected area, 708
regulations, 122
rights to, 676
river bank, compared to, 659
status, 675–6
see also Coastal zone; Marine pollution
Seizure, power of, 127
Service-provision systems—*see* Administrative service-provision systems
Servitude, 230, 232, 241, 659
Shadow-pricing techniques, 37–9
Skeleton Coast Park, 222
Smoke—*see* Air pollution
Socio-political factors, 46, 53–63, 251, 273–6, 294, 492, 671, 730
Soekor, 394, 395, 396, 411, 415, 416
Soil
acidity, 189, 192, 741
alkalinity, 189–90
classification, 190
colour, 185–6
compaction, 191
components
gases, 183–4
liquids, 183–4
mineral fraction, 182
organic fraction, 183
particles, 183
soil pores, 183
conservation
advisory board, 200
committees, 194, 195, 196, 197, 198, 200–1, 204, 208
control measures, 198–9, 201
description of, 181
directives, 195, 196, 201–2, 732
executive officer, powers of, 201–2
expropriation, 196, 200, 205
fire protection, 193, 196, 198, 199, 206, 705—*see also* Indigenous plants
forests, 230, 231, 705
inspectors, 203–4
land user, duties, 202–3
legislation
black areas, 210
enforcement, 203–4
failure of, 195, 197
first, 16, 193
former, 194–7
overview, 193ff
new, reasons for, 197
objects, 197–8
related, 206–10
mining, relevance of, 210, 373–4
minister, powers of, 198–9, 200
mountain catchment areas, 207–8
nature conservation, relevance of, 209
official investigation, early, 16
pasture management, 199, 206, 208, 235
practical problems, 203–5
public attitude, 196–7
road and railway construction, 209–10
scheme, 194, 199, 200, 201
subdivision of land, 209
subsidies, 196, 199, 205–6
technicians, 203–4
unbeneficial occupation of land, 208–9

Soil, conservation *(continued)*
vegetation, role of, 194, 198, 206–7, 234–5, 283
water, relevance of, 194, 198, 206
works, 196, 199, 202, 203, 205, 208, 235
consistence, 188
crusting, 191
definition, 181–2
degradation
biological, 192–3
chemical, 192
physical, 191, 283
depth, 185
erosion
appeals, 205
battle against, 16
cultivation, cause of, 198, 206, 743–4
extent of, 191, 743–4
fertility loss, 192
land management, 283, 686
nature of, 191
prosecutions, 130, 195, 197, 198, 204–5
reduction by forests, 277
reports, early, 16
silt, 283, 744
state action, 121
subsistence farming, 744–5
susceptibility to, 191, 739
forests, 206–7, 704
formation of, 181
horizon, 184–5
lunar, 181
plant pathogens, 193
pollution, 192
profile, 184
properties, 185–90
river bank, 659
river catchment, 663–4
salinization, 189–90, 192, 198, 199
structure, 187
see also Agriculture; Terrestrial minerals
Solid waste—*see* Waste
South African Acoustics Institute, 22
South African Bureau of Standards, 17, 472, 486, 487, 530
South African Committee on Environmental Conservation, 19, 73, 107—*see also* Council for the Environment
South African Development Trust, 244, 248
South African Institute of Ecologists, 275
South African Law Commission, 143–5
South African National Council for the Deaf, 17
South African Ornithological Society, 15, 16
South African Tourism Board, 234
Southern African Nature Foundation, 17
Space, pollution of, 172–3
Spaceship mentality, 7
Squatting
impact on environment, 59, 150–1, 671
regulation, 726–7
St Lucia estuarine system
environmental dispute resolution, 153
threat to by mining, 152
St Lucia Game Reserve, 11, 15
Standing
adverse effects, types of, 133–4
citizen suit clause, 135
coastal zone, 686
environmental interest, 133
environmental tribunal, 140
generally, 132–7
group interests, 135–6
Strict liability, 148–9
Subordinate legislation
environmental policy, 103, 104
grounds for review, 104
principal control through, 112–13
Subsidies, 43, 131, 132, 205–6—*see also* Economic incentives; Financial aid
Sustainability, 1, 2, 3, 31, 32, 34, 35, 47, 49, 51, 590, 744–6, 747—*see also* Development, balance with conservation; Integrated environmental management
Tax
allowances, 131
deduction, 518
refund, 131
relief, 737
Terrestrial minerals, mining of
asbestos mining, 604
bord and pillar mining, 346–8
choice, 337
common law, 363–5
dredge mining, 343–4
dump reclamation, 344–5
environmental impact
aesthetic, 359
air pollution, 345, 346, 352, 354, 355, 357, 359, 375–6
assessment, 373
carcinogenic effects, 354
generally, 337, 338
industry guidelines, 338–40
ionizing radiation, 377
solid waste, 355, 376–7
surface subsidence, 346, 348, 350
water pollution, 342, 343, 345, 347, 349, 350–1, 352, 354, 355, 356–7, 374–5
water table, 344, 348, 350
environmental management programme, 339–40, 378–9
importance, 337, 362, 670
increased extraction method, 348–9
lateral and subsurface support, duty of, 365
law, sources of, 362–3
legislation, historical development, 366–7
liability for environmental degradation, 364–5
mine dewatering, 350–1
mine residue deposits
aesthetic effects, 359
air pollution, 357–9
rehabilitation, 360–1
water pollution, 356–7
mine, definition of, 367–8
mineral holder, rights of, 363–4
mineral policy, 362
mineral right, 367
mineral, definition of, 367
minerals, nature of
asbestos, 354, 604

Terrestrial minerals, mining of, minerals, nature of *(continued)*
chrome, 354
coal, 351–2
gold, 352–4
heavy minerals, 355
platinum, 354
mining authorization, 127, 369–70
mining methods, 340
surface mining, 340–5
underground mining, deep, 348–51
underground mining, shallow, 346–8
mountains, 629
open-pit mining, 342–3
opencast mining, 5, 341–2, 370, 371
philosophy, 338
process, definition of, 368
prospecting permit, 127, 369
prospecting, definition of, 368
protected areas, mining in, 377
research, 361–2
soil conservation, 210, 341, 373–4
St Lucia controversy, 152–3
state control, 363
strip mining, 5, 341–2, 370, 371
surface rehabilitation, 45, 338–9, 342, 343, 344, 347, 350, 360–1, 368–73
temporary nature, 337
see also Environmental health; Forests; Mountains; Soil
Territorial waters, 157, 163, 168, 327, 679
Tidal lagoon—*see* Coastal zone; Rivers
Threshold valuation, 38
Torrey Canyon disaster, 160, 165
Tourism, 224
Town/regional planning
development control mechanisms, 718–20
development policy, 721–2
environmental problems, 717–18
functions, 715
land, subdivision of, 209, 720, 726
levels, 717
metropolitan regions, 722–3
more than land-use planning, 715
national planning, 725
National Regional Development Advisory Council, 724
nature, 716–17
origins, 715–16
regional development advisory committees, 724
regional development associations, 724
regional industrial development programme, 725
regional planning, 722–5
regional services councils, 723
rural regions, 724–5
scope, 715–17
South African system, 718–22
strategic planning, 722, 725
structure plans, 683, 721–2
towns, establishment of, 720
see also Land-use planning
Transnet Ltd, 481, 486
Travel-cost valuation, 38
Tree Society, 17
Tribunal—*see* Environmental tribunal
Umfolozi Game Reserve, 11, 15
Umgeni Water Board, 293
United Nations Conference on Environment and Development, 53, 61
United Nations Conference on the Human Environment, 18, 178
United Nations Environment Programme, 75, 169, 170, 171, 178
Urbanization
environmental health, 591, 606
environmental problems, 59–60
mountains, contrast to, 629
plants, impact on, 221, 245, 740
rivers, impact on, 651–2
town/regional planning, 722–3
waste generation, 493, 494–5, 509
water salinity, 285
white paper, 729
Utilitarianism, 8, 257
Vehicle emissions—*see* Air pollution
Waste
avoidance, 521
best practical environmentally acceptable option, 495, 498
bioremediation, 500
classification, 495–6
clean community system, 510
collection, 497
database, 495, 521, 522
definition of, 512–13, 514, 518, 519–20
degradable, 5
disposal site, 123, 515—*see* landfill
disposal, 121, 166, 498–501, 517, 520, 521, 670
economic factors, 521
garbage, 165
hazardous/toxic, 121, 149, 151, 153, 164, 165, 166, 171, 514, 516–17, 521, 522—*see also* Environmental health
isolation from environment, 499–500
landfill, 494, 500–9
legislation
comprehensive, 118, 521–2
historical development, 22, 511–12
local, 519–21
national, 514–18
penalties, 521, 522
provincial, 518–19
regulations, 516
scope, 510–12, 521
shortcomings, 521
litter, 509, 515, 518, 519
management policy, 513–14, 521, 522
management strategy, 493–5
mining, 376–7, 515
persistent, 5, 6
protected areas, 515
public health, 515, 520
radioactive, 164, 166, 517, 559, 562–3, 564, 568
recycling, 44, 500, 518, 521, 522
reduction potential, 498–501, 521, 522
roads, 514, 519
rubbish, 518, 520
sewage, 165
sorting of, 521
storage, 496–7

Waste *(continued)*
tax deductions, 518
thermal treatment, 498–9
transportation, 497–8
vehicles, abandoned, 514, 519
see also Environmental health; Environmental impact assessment; Environmental impact report; Integrated environmental management; International law; Terrestrial minerals
Water Research Commission, 313, 361, 484
Water
abstraction, 288–91, 294
administration, 469, 489
advisory committee, 300, 315
apportionment, 661
aquatic plants, 235
availability, 278–83, 295, 296, 457, 647
board, 293, 299, 301
catchment control area, 663
compliance monitoring, 465–6
consumption, control of, 485
court, 296, 297, 299, 471, 490, 491, 657, 662
dam basin control area, 298
demand for, 293
effluent purification, duty, 471–2, 491
effluent standards, 287, 485–7, 490, 491
environmental impact assessment, 308
exemptions, 472–3
government drainage control area, 298
government water control area, 298, 310
ground water, 278, 279, 304, 314, 483, 647, 741, 743
in soil, 187–8
irrigation board, 300, 301
irrigation legislation, 15
ministerial discretion, 300–2, 310, 661
mountains, as sources of 625, 626–7, 631–2, 642, 645
natural water quality monitoring system, 466–9
offences, 130, 299, 473, 475, 476, 477, 478, 479
penalties, 130, 299
policy
freshwater pollution, 460–2
generally, 460
marine discharges, 462–3
pollution
aquatic environment, 479
definition of, 488
extent of, 285–8
farming operations, 477, 490, 650, 664, 741, 744
general pollution, 473, 487–8
industrial, 470–3, 485–7, 490, 652
legislation
historical development, 17, 22, 470
improvement of, 490–1
mining, 342, 343, 345, 347, 652
power generation, 652
protected areas, 482
public health, 479
threat to fish, 311
urbanization, 651
waterborne transportation, 473–4
pollution prevention approach, 464–5
precipitation, 309
price of, 457–9
private river, 655, 656, 665
private stream, 295–6, 656–7
private water, 295–6, 297, 301, 305, 306, 309, 314, 655, 656, 665
public attitudes, 456–7
public river, 654, 655, 657–60, 665
public stream, 295–6, 305, 664, 655–7, 668
public water, 295–6, 301, 304, 305, 306, 310, 314, 658, 661
receiving water quality objectives, 287–8, 462, 463, 464, 465
research, 484
return of purified water to origin, duty, 472
rights to, 296–7, 298, 302, 303–4, 306, 310, 314, 660–1
riparian owner, 296–7, 308, 655, 656, 657, 658, 659, 660, 665
running water, 295–304, 305
sea water quality management objectives, 463
shortage, 300
soil conservation, relationship with, 206
sources
classification, 647
quality, 285–8
state control of, 297–302
storage, 277
subterranean government control area, 297–8
subterranean water, management of, 483—*see also* ground water
supply of, 121
surface water, management of, 482–3
suspension of supply, 131
uniform effluent standards, 463–4
use for industrial purposes, 123–4, 470, 471
use, 278–83, 294, 295
water sport control area, 298
waterworks, 298, 301, 303, 308, 311–12, 314, 471, 662—*see also* Dams
see also Aquaculture; Catchment; Dams; Environmental health; Estuaries; Freshwater systems; Marine pollution; Mountain catchment areas; Rainfall; Rivers; Terrestrial minerals; Wetlands
Waterworks—*see* Dams; Freshwater systems; Water
Weather modification, 5–6, 50, 309
Weeds—*see* Noxious plants
Wetlands
benefits of, 305, 314, 648
cultivation of, 250, 306–7, 656
defined, 305
degradation, 671
drainage, 306–7, 648
high-risk area, 674
international recognition, 175, 697–8
legislation, 295, 305–7, 314, 664
policy, 305
private water, 655, 656, 665
rights of landowner, 306
threat to, 306, 648
vegetation, 306
see also Freshwater systems; Water
Whales
fish, included in definition, 329

Whales *(continued)*
  protection of, 14, 173–4
White Paper on a national policy regarding environmental conservation, 19, 23, 73, 75, 83, 84, 89, 90, 99, 102, 308, 511, 513, 514, 687
White Paper on agricultural policy, 16
White Paper on environmental education, 23
White Paper on the mineral policy of the Republic of South Africa, 362
White Paper on urbanization, 729
Wild animals
  amphibians, 254–5, 267–8
  anthropocentric perspective, 257–8
  attitude to, 250, 273–6
  biocentric perspective, 258
  birds, 255, 268
  butterflies, 252–3
  categories, 252
  conservation
    development of, 251
    status, 251–6
  crops, destruction of, 266
  decline, 256
  ecosystem-based conservation, 270
  endangered, 174, 252, 273
  extinction, 251, 252, 273, 275–6
  fish, 253–4—*see also* Freshwater fish; Living marine resources
  game
    capture, 262, 266
    categories, 262, 269
    defined, 262
    exportation, 265–6
    farming, 259
    purchase/sale, 265
    ranching, 259
    theft, 259–60
  hunter
    competence, 263–4, 267
    professional, 267
  hunting
    concern about, 14
    controlled area, 264
    defined, 262
    fees, 269
    licences, 262–3, 269
    restrictions, 262–5
  international law, 175, 258
  invertebrates, 252–3, 267–8
  law
    human orientation, 258
    primary purpose, 257
    reform, 268–70
  legal status, 259, 260
  legislation
    consolidation, 269–70
    first, 14, 72
    plethora of, 269
  local involvement, 258, 273
  mammals, terrestrial, 256
  national professional hunters committee, 264
  nature conservation officer, 261–2, 275
  private law, 259
  rare, 252, 271
  res nullius, 259, 677
  rights of, 257–8
  trophy, 265
  vertebrates, 253–6
  vulnerable, 252
  see also Protected areas
Wilderness area
  comprehensive powers, 121
  contrast to human development, 87, 705
  control, 247
  defined, 87
  deproclamation, 231
  establishment, 206, 231, 704–5
  legislation, 20, 206, 231
  management, 692–3, 705
  mountains, 630, 635
  penalties, 706
  purpose of, 312
  river catchment, 664
  servitudes in, 232
  soil conservation, 206
  see also Protected areas
Wildlife Society of Southern Africa, 15, 16, 24, 151, 641
World Bank, 60
World Health Organization, 55, 547, 590, 592, 595, 598, 599, 601, 608, 614, 622
World Meteorological Organization, 169, 170
World Wide Fund for Nature, 10, 17, 75
World Wildlife Fund—*see* World Wide Fund for Nature